The Book of

Bizarre
Truths

Publications International, Ltd.

When the Truth Is Stranger than Fiction

✳ ✳ ✳ ✳

WE CAN'T HELP OURSELVES. We humans are fascinated by the bizarre, drawn to it like moths to a freaky flame. The stranger something is, the more intrigued we are. Release a movie or publish a book about the horrific, heroic, spine-tingling, amazing, or out-of-this-world, and we'll turn it into a blockbuster. Give us all that and make it fact rather than fiction, and, well, we just can't get enough. (Don't believe us? Try sending a pet pig in a polyester pantsuit or a guy with a zebra-striped mohawk on a stroll through the typical shopping mall and just watch the wave of whiplash hit.)

Fortunately, *The Book of Bizarre Truths* is so jam-packed with unusual facts about people, places, animals, nature, history, sports, technology, and more, you'll be able to feed your appetite for the unusual for a long time to come. Read about:

✳ The man who's turning himself into a lizard

✳ The cat that trekked across 1,000 miles of Australian outback to rejoin his master

✳ The Polish mummy that killed ten researchers in the 1970s

✳ The most revolting foods in the world—and who eats them

✳ The guy who got hit by lightning seven times—and survived

✳ And much, much more!

It's a treasure trove of evidence that the truth really can be stranger than fiction. So dive on in and enjoy. And don't worry if you suddenly feel as if everyone is staring at you. They're probably just trying to get a closer look at the book.

Chapter One

Bizarre Truths About People

Tracing the First Tattoo

The story behind the person who got the first tattoo does not involve a bachelor party. Incredible, we know.

✳ ✳ ✳ ✳

The Iceman Cometh

THE FIRST TATTOO was probably an accident. Tattoos have been around for several thousand years and might have started when someone rubbed a wound with dirt, soot, or ash and noticed that the mark stayed after the injury had healed.

For the sake of providing definitive information, we turn to Iceman, who sports the oldest tats that modern eyes have ever seen on a body. (And with a name like that, he'd fit right in on MTV!) In 1991, the frozen and amazingly well-preserved remains of a Bronze Age man were found between Austria and Italy in the Tyrolean Alps. Iceman, as he was dubbed, is believed to be more than 5,000 years old, and he clearly has a series of lines tattooed on his lower back, ankles, knees, and foot. It is thought that the tattoos were applied for medicinal purposes, to reduce pain.

Over time, tattoos evolved into symbols and designs that have meaning. Mummified Egyptian women dating back to 2100 B.C.

Contents

✳ ✳ ✳ ✳

Highlights Include: Tall Tales About Napoleon ✦ The Curse of the Lottery Winners ✦ Celebrities' Real Names ✦ Psychic Detectives ✦ The People at the Ends of the Earth ✦ History's Most Famous Female Pirates ✦ In Search of Immortality ✦ Peculiar Presidential Facts ✦ How to Turn Yourself into a Witch ✦ Eight Famous People Who Died in the Bathroom ✦ Buried Alive! ✦ When One Wife Just Isn't Enough ✦ The Maligned Mrs. Lincoln ✦ The Bloodthirsty Countess ✦ Mass Murderers vs. Serial Killers

Highlights Include: Have You Had Your McAloo Tikki Break Today? ✦ Fact vs. Fiction: The Shelf Life of a Twinkie ✦ Delectable Dinners Throughout History ✦ The Real-Life Story of General Tso ✦ Tasty (but Troublesome) Foods ✦ A Feast for the Fearless: The World's Most Revolting Foods ✦ Food Science: How They Salt Peanuts in the Shell ✦ Calling Hannibal Lecter ✦ The World's Weirdest Cocktails ✦ It Should Be Stirred, Not Shaken ✦ *Grew-some* Gluttons ✦ The Green Fairy

Highlights Include: He Made His Mark ✦ A Snack of Convenience ✦ Six Pets that Traveled Long Distances to Get Home ✦ A Sewer Story ✦ The Restless Lives of Fish ✦ Alex Was No Birdbrain ✦ Your Pet Goldfish Just Might Save Your Life ✦ Hemingway's Cats ✦ Extreme Pet Pampering ✦ Why Did the Dog Pee on the Fire Hydrant? Because It Was There

Highlights Include: Vampires in the Real World ✦ America's Most Haunted Lighthouse ✦ Monsters Across America ✦ A Favorite Celebrity Haunt ✦ The Severed Ear of Vincent van Gogh ✦ A Superior Haunting: The *Edmund Fitzgerald* ✦ Seven Famous Curses ✦ Vlad the Impaler: The Original Dracula ✦ Who Wants to Be a Billionaire? ✦ Giant Frogman Spotted in Ohio! ✦ The Bell Witch of Tennessee ✦ Mythical Sea Monsters ✦ Fooled Ya!: Famous Hoaxes ✦ How to Kill the Undead

have patterns of lines and dots on their bodies that were applied, historians believe, to enhance fertility and provide protection. All tattoos in this period were thought of as ways of connecting the body to a higher power.

When did someone finally step it up and go with something more intricate than lines and dots? This question is impossible to answer conclusively, but a Nubian mummy, circa 400 B.C., has a tattoo of Bes, the Egyptian god of fertility and revelry, on her thigh. Several Egyptian paintings from the same period depict dancers and musicians who likewise have Bes tattoos on their thighs.

Style Issues

Tattoos have gone in and out of style. In early Rome, for instance, they were decidedly out of style and were even banned among the general populace because they were thought to taint the body's purity. Back then, body ink was reserved for criminals (as a form of punishment, like a scarlet letter) and slaves (so that they could be identified if they escaped). Eventually, attitudes changed—Roman soldiers began getting tattoos after fighting a rugged army of Britons who wore their body art like badges of honor.

Today, it's hard to find a professional basketball player or a rock musician who isn't sporting ink. There are even reality shows about the studios—don't say "parlors," because it isn't cool and you'll sound like a crusty old sailor—where tattoos are applied. A Harris Interactive poll in 2008 revealed that about half of Americans between ages 18 and 29 have at least one tattoo. No word on how much of that ink was still fresh the morning after a bachelor—or bachelorette—party.

The Extremely Wild Blue Yonder of Howard Hughes

Howard Hughes has been called many things: gifted, eccentric, reckless, crazy. The brilliant billionaire made his fortune in media and aviation, but his life was tempered by bizarre personal habits and activities.

✳ ✳ ✳ ✳

A Little Texan

BORN IN A Houston, Texas, suburb in 1905, Howard Robard Hughes Jr. was the son of an entrepreneurial oil baron father and a domineering mother. His father pioneered a revolutionary oil-drill bit and made a fortune with the Hughes Tool Company. His mother, fearing sickness for her son, rushed the boy to the doctor at the slightest hint of illness. If residents of the neighborhood suffered from bouts of colds or flu, she would bundle Howard off to a safe distance until the maladies passed. A fear of germs would plague Howard all of his life.

At age 14, Hughes took his first flying lessons, which triggered his lifelong love affair with the great blue yonder. He showed an interest and proficiency in math and engineering, briefly attending classes at Caltech in California and Rice University in Texas. His parents' unexpected deaths in the early 1920s left Howard rich and alone before his 20th birthday.

California, Here He Comes

As gifted as Hughes was with engineering, his true dream was to produce movies in Hollywood. He married a young woman named Ella Rice, and the newlyweds moved to Los Angeles.

But Hughes's wealth didn't necessarily guarantee success. His first film production, *Swell Hogan*, was so bad that it was never released, despite his investment of $60,000. His next two films, comedies called *Everybody's Acting* and *Two Arabian Knights*, were moderate successes that lead to his first epic production: *Hell's Angels* (1930). At nearly $4 million, it was by far the most expensive movie made up to that time, and it was loaded with Hughes's favorite subject—airplanes. Although he was pleased with the final product itself, the film had another cost—Rice divorced Hughes. She couldn't deal with his propensity to work up to 36 straight hours at a time and felt completely shut out of his life.

Thereafter, Hughes, ever the tall and handsome Texan, spent time with many Hollywood beauties. At one point or another, he was seen in the company of Katharine Hepburn, Bette Davis, Carole Lombard, Ava Gardner, Ginger Rogers, Terry Moore (an Oscar nominee for *Come Back, Little Sheba*), and Jean Peters (who appeared in *Viva Zapata!* and *Niagara*)—eventually marrying the last in 1957 (the couple divorced in 1971). While he was never romantically involved with Jane Russell, he did design a special bra to emphasize her already ample assets in the 1943 film *The Outlaw*.

Up, Up, and Away

Howard Hughes's only full-time companion was aviation. Despite being a self-educated pilot and engineer, he designed and built record-setting airplanes. His H-1 Racer cracked the airspeed barrier of 352 miles per hour in 1935 with Hughes, of course, at the controls. Within two years, he set the transcontinental speed record—flying from Los Angeles to New York City in just under seven-and-a-half hours. While evidence indicates that the Japanese Zero, German Focke-Wulf, and American Hellcat fighter planes were heavily influenced by the Racer's design, Hughes was unable to secure a military contract to build the plane.

Hughes did, however, design the XF-11 spy plane; the U.S. Army Air Forces ordered 100 of them, only to cancel the request when the war ended. On the very first test flight, Hughes crashed the prototype, destroying several homes in the Beverly Hills area and seriously injuring himself. A broken collarbone, numerous fractured ribs, a collapsed lung, and multiple third-degree burns kept him bedridden for five weeks. Not liking the hospital bed, he called his engineers at Hughes Aircraft and designed a special one over the phone.

Another proposed contribution to the Second World War effort was Hughes's Hercules H-4 cargo plane. With a wingspan of more than 300 feet and a height of nearly 80 feet, the eight-engine seaplane would be the largest ever built. Although nicknamed the "Spruce Goose," the H-4 was actually built from birch wood, as metal was extremely hard to come by during the war. Like the XF-11, the Hercules was canceled when the war ended, but Hughes did take it out for a test spin in November 1947. The enormous "flying boat" lifted off for nearly a mile, coasting at 135 miles per hour a mere 70 feet above the waters of Long Beach, California. It was the only time the Spruce Goose would fly.

A Restless Tenant

During his career, Hughes had owned Trans World Airlines (TWA), as well as RKO, a prominent movie studio. But as Hughes reached age 60, he began to shun his businesses and live in opulent and luxurious hotels in America, Central America, and the Caribbean. Locating himself in the top-floor penthouse, he would often buy the hotel that rested below his feet. In Las Vegas, Hughes lived in constant fear of radiation from nearby nuclear experiments—going so far as to offer one million dollars to President Lyndon Johnson in 1968 if he would stop the atomic tests.

By now, Hughes's germ phobia—along with a longtime addiction to codeine and other painkillers—had led to bizarre habits and rituals. Since the late 1950s, his diet had consisted mostly of fresh whole milk, chocolate bars with almonds, pecans, and bottled water. Unless he was traveling, Hughes spent his time stark naked in darkened rooms, declining to meet with anyone except his closest aides. He refused to touch anything unless he used a tissue as a barrier between his hands and the object. By 1970, his health had deteriorated so much that the 6'4" Hughes weighed less than 100 pounds. His hair and beard were long, shaggy, and gray, and the nails on his fingers and toes were inches long. He ordered his urine to be saved, stored in capped containers on shelves.

When Hughes died of kidney failure in April 1976, he was aboard a private plane en route to his hometown of Houston.

✳ **The base salary of the president of the United States— $400,000 in 2008—is less than the average salary of an NFL player, which is well over $1 million.**

✳ **The first newspaper advertisement, an announcement looking for a buyer for an estate in Oyster Bay, Long Island, was published in the *Boston News-Letter* in 1704.**

✳ **In 1898, the Royal Bank of Canada hauled a four-and-a-half-ton safe from Alaska to British Columbia to open a branch and cash in on the Klondike gold rush.**

✳ **Marlon Brando was originally slated to star in director David Lean's movie *Lawrence of Arabia*. When he turned it down, unknown Peter O'Toole snagged the role and began a stellar Hollywood career.**

✳ **It took a year to connect the first telephone line from New York to San Francisco. Approximately 14,000 miles of copper wire and 130,000 telephone poles were needed to link the country.**

✳ **The human head is a quarter of our total length at birth but only an eighth of our total length by the time we reach adulthood.**

✳ **Food typically travels from the mouth, through the esophagus, and into the stomach in seven seconds.**

✳ **A "Robin Hood" in archery is when two arrows are shot into a target, and the second arrow splits the first.**

Tall Tales About Napoleon

Napoleon Bonaparte, one of the most successful and brutal military leaders of all time, had a short fuse and was often shortsighted. But he was not, as is popularly believed, short in stature.

✳ ✳ ✳ ✳

Slighted by History

IT TURNS OUT that an error in arithmetic contributed to history's perception of Napoleon as a small man. The only known measurement of Bonaparte came from his autopsy, which reported a height of 5′2″. But it was not taken into account that this measurement was calculated in French units. Translating to slightly more than 168 centimeters, his height was actually 5′6″ by the English Imperial system. This was above average for a 19th-century Frenchman.

Another possible reason for this misconception is the fact that Napoleon kept himself surrounded by a group of relatively tall guardsmen. Napoleon was never seen in public without his "imperial guard." These soldiers averaged six feet in height and would have towered over Napoleon.

A Napoleon Complex

Napoleon wasn't short, but his temper was. Over time, the notion that the general's irascible, aggressive personality stemmed from his small size has been applied to any small-statured man who uses his temper to compensate for his height. This is referred to as a "Napoleon Complex," and it also proves to be a myth. In 2007, researchers at the University of Central Lancashire studied the effect of height on aggression in men. Using heart monitors to gauge reactions, scientists found that *taller* men were more likely to respond to provocation with aggressive behavior.

As Napoleon himself said, "History is the version of past events that people have decided to agree upon." It turns out that history cut Napoleon about four inches short.

A Human on Display

In the early 1900s, an African pygmy was put on exhibit at the Bronx Zoo, attracting huge crowds and creating all sorts of controversy.

✳ ✳ ✳ ✳

The Saga of Ota Benga

THE LONDON ZOO made a startling announcement on August 17, 2005: a "flock of *Homo sapiens*" would be on exhibit for four days that month, "cared for by our experienced keepers and . . . entertained through various forms of enrichment."

Of course, the zoo's temporary human exhibit, which featured a volunteer group of five women and three men, was conducted with tongue firmly planted in anthropological cheek. But 99 years earlier, a human exhibit at the Bronx Zoo triggered an uproar. On September 8, 1906, a sign appeared outside the zoo's monkey house: THE AFRICAN PYGMY, OTA BENGA. AGE 23 YEARS. HEIGHT 4′11″. WEIGHT 103 POUNDS.

Inside, visitors saw a slight young man dressed in white trousers and a khaki coat peering at them from behind the bars. His feet were bare, and his smile revealed teeth filed to points in the manner of his people, the Batwa tribe of the Belgian Congo. Sometimes, he played with an orangutan named Dohong. Other times, he shot arrows at straw targets. Occasionally, he was allowed out of the cage to buy soda from the snack bar with money he had earned by posing for photographers.

Over the next few days, thousands gathered at the monkey cage to watch Ota Benga. The crowds became nearly unmanageable, and clergymen registered their objections with *The New York Times*. "The person responsible for this exhibition degrades himself as much as he degrades the African," thundered the Reverend R. S. MacArthur of Harlem's Calvary Baptist Church.

A Tragic Ending

What did Ota Benga think of all this? He probably knew more about white people, or *muzungu* as he called them, than they knew about him. After all, he had been on display once before—at the 1904 St. Louis World's Fair, where he and several fellow pygmies recreated their native village as part of the fair's Living Exhibits program. But there, he had been among other human beings; at the Bronx Zoo, his presence in the monkey cage implied something quite different.

William Hornaday, the head of the zoo, defended the exhibit. He said Ota Benga was fed and treated well. Still, as one anonymous visitor put it, "There's something here I don't like."

Ota eventually was removed and taken by a sympathetic minister to live at the Howard Colored Orphan Asylum in Lynchburg, Virginia. After several years, he learned English and acquired a job in a tobacco factory. Despite his attempts to fit in, Ota Benga never quite adjusted to the ways of the *muzungu*. In March 1916, he went into a forest, performed a ceremonial dance around a fire, and shot himself in the heart with a borrowed gun.

✳ On his deathbed in 1640, Sultan Murad IV of the Ottoman Empire ordered the execution of his brother Ibrahim so that he would not succeed Murad. Years earlier, Murad had had other brothers killed. The order to kill Ibrahim was not carried out, and he became sultan against his brother's wishes.

✳ Red is the color of mourning in South Africa. In Egypt, it's yellow. Mourners wear purple in Thailand. White symbolizes death in much of the East.

✳ The year 1848 is known as the year of revolution in Europe because of the number of uprisings that came in the wake of an economic depression. These revolutions included rebellions in the Rhineland, Vienna, Berlin, Milan, and Venice.

✳ The first computer bug was an actual moth that got caught inside a Mark II Aiken Relay Calculator, a primitive computer at Harvard University.

Male Impersonators

A young girl nowadays has considerable freedom to choose what she wants to be when she grows up. It hasn't always been that way, but the women on this list didn't let that stop them: These fearless females did what they wanted to do, even if it meant masquerading as men for most of their lives.

✳   ✳   ✳   ✳

Charley Parkhurst

TIMES WERE ROUGH for ladies in the Wild West, so this crackerjack stagecoach driver decided to live most of her life as a man. Born in 1812, Parkhurst lived well into her sixties, though how she managed to do it is the stuff of miracles. She is remembered to have been a hard-drinking, tobacco-chewing, one-eyed brute with a taste for adventure. Parkhurst gave birth at one point, but the child died. She lived out the rest of her life pursuing her stagecoach career until she died in December 1879. It was then that her true identity was revealed, much to the surprise of her friends.

Dr. James Barry

The life of James Barry, M.D., is proof positive that truth is often stranger than fiction. A vegetarian, teetotaler, and gifted doctor with skills ahead of his time (he performed one of the first successful cesarean sections while serving as a military surgeon), Dr. Barry was also quite possibly a female. If you lived in 19th-century Britain and happened to be a girl, you could kiss your dreams of being a surgeon goodbye. Barry, whose real name may have been Miranda, allegedly assumed a male identity to become an army physician. Barry's voice was high and he reportedly challenged those who made fun of it to a duel on the spot. When Barry died in 1865, the woman who was preparing the body for burial was said to be the first to discover his secret.

Billy Tipton

Born in Oklahoma in 1914, Dorothy Lucille Tipton was a gifted musician from the start. Her love of the saxophone and the piano was bittersweet, as the school she was attending wouldn't let girls play in the band. After escaping high school, Tipton decided to do whatever it took to pursue her passion. She started going by "Billy," wore suits, and bound her chest with tape to create the illusion that she was one of the guys. It worked, and Tipton's musical career was on its way. Tipton performed with some of the era's jazz greats and even recorded an album with The Billy Tipton Trio. Tipton married a woman, adopted three sons, and was reportedly a good father. Tipton died in 1989, and it was then that Tipton's sons learned of their father's true identity.

Pope Joan

Long held up as a hero by feminists and anti-Catholics alike, Pope Joan's story is a debatable one. Even if the story is purely fictional, it's a good one nonetheless. "John Anglicus" was an Englishman in the 9th century who traveled to Rome, where his fame as a lecturer led to his becoming a cardinal in the church. According to the story, when Pope Leo IV died in A.D. 855, Anglicus was unanimously elected pope. Legend has it that during a citywide processional, this pope stopped by the side of the road complaining of a stomachache and suddenly gave birth to a child. The jig was up: Pope John was actually a woman. Was it true? The Catholic Church denies that any "John Anglicus" was ever pope—according to their documents, Benedict III succeeded Leo IV.

John Taylor

Mary Anne Talbot was a troublemaker, but she was also a brave soldier, a hard worker, and a true talent in the art of male impersonation. Born in Britain in 1778, Talbot was orphaned when her mother died during childbirth. She was the mistress of a naval officer and accompanied him on trips across the Atlantic by posing as his footboy. When the naval officer died in battle in 1793, she had no choice but to continue posing as a man—John Taylor. She was wounded in the leg in 1794 and suffered from complications from the injury for the rest of her life. During her life, Talbot was a prisoner of war in France, an officer aboard an American merchant vessel, a highway worker, a London pensioner, a jewelry maker, an actor, and a nurse.

William Cathay

Born in Missouri in the midst of slavery, Cathay Williams served as a house slave until Union soldiers freed her during the Civil War. The soldiers employed her after that, and she worked for them for a while before wanting to see more action firsthand. Since women weren't allowed in the army, Williams dressed as a man in order to enlist. Of the approximately 5,000 black infantrymen and cavalry who served in the frontier army, "William Cathay" was the only woman to serve as a Buffalo Soldier (the nickname, first given to members of the U.S. 10th Cavalry Regiment of the U.S. Army, is now often used to refer to soldiers in any of the six black regiments that served in the war). In 1868, Williams was examined by an army surgeon, who discovered her true identity. She was discharged and retired to New Mexico, where she passed away at age 82.

Joan of Arc

Born in France in 1412, 17-year-old Jeanne d'Arc disguised herself as a page when journeying through enemy territory so as to go unnoticed by soldiers. Before she was burned at the stake for being a heretic, Joan allegedly claimed that she was "doing a man's work" and therefore had to dress the part. The Catholic Church finally took back all the nasty things it said about Joan and recognized her as a saint in 1920.

✳ Cloud-to-cloud lightning can stretch over amazing distances. Radar has recorded at least one of these "crawlers" that was more than 75 miles long.

✳ In 1791, Vermont became the first state to be added to the United States since the original 13.

The Curse of the Lottery Winners

* At age 77, New Yorker Clarence Kinder won $50,000 in the state lottery on a Thursday night—and died from a heart attack the following night.

* Only a few hours after Carl Atwood won $57,000 on the televised lottery program *Hoosier Millionaire*, the 73-year-old was fatally hit by a pickup truck while walking to the store where he bought his winning ticket.

* Jeffrey Dampier won $20 million in the lottery and became a Tampa popcorn entrepreneur. Dampier's generosity to his sister-in-law, Victoria Jackson—gifts, apartment rent—evidently wasn't enough: Jackson and her boyfriend kidnapped and murdered Dampier for his fortune. They were sentenced to life in prison.

* After collecting the first of his annual $1.24 million checks, Billy Bob Harrell—a down-on-his-luck Texan who hit the state jackpot for $31 million—began spending like there was no tomorrow. He picked up a ranch, a fashionable home—and a never-ending line of family, friends, and even strangers with their palms outstretched, dogging him day and night. The spending spiraled out of control for 20 months, until Harrell, who had had quite enough, locked himself in his bedroom and let a shotgun solve his dilemma.

* William "Bud" Post won $16.2 million in the Pennsylvania lottery in 1988. When he died of respiratory failure on January 15, 2006, Post was living on a $450 monthly disability check and was estranged from his family. Not only was his fortune wiped out, but he ended up deeply in debt, and he served a jail term for threatening a bill collector with a shotgun. At one point, Post filed for bankruptcy, came out of it with a million dollars to his name, and spent it all in short order.

The Female Paul Revere

*Listen, my children, and you shall hear of the
midnight ride of… Sybil Ludington. Sybil who?*

* * * *

The Girl's Got Moxie

ALMOST EVERYONE HAS heard the story of Paul Revere, who
rode from Boston to Lexington on April 18, 1775, to
warn his fellow revolutionaries that the British were coming.
But how many people know that two years later, on April 26,
1777, 16-year-old Sybil Ludington of Fredericksburg (now
Kent) New York, mounted her favorite horse, Star, and set off
on a similar mission?

Earlier that night, an exhausted messenger had arrived from
Danbury, Connecticut, to tell Sybil's father that the town had
fallen into British hands. Located about 25 miles south of
Fredericksburg, Danbury served as a major supply depot for
Washington's Continental Army. The Redcoats had not only
seized the town, they had set fire to homes and storehouses.
The blaze could be seen for miles.

Henry Ludington, a colonel in the local militia, needed to rally
his troops immediately. But whom could he send to alert them?
Most of his men were at home on their farms tending to the
spring plowing. There was no way that he could rouse them himself; he had to stay put in order to organize the soldiers as they
assembled. And the messenger from Danbury was far too tired
to travel any farther.

Duty Calls

Henry's eldest daughter, Sybil, volunteered to carry the message to the scattered revolutionaries, and her father reluctantly
consented. Sybil was an accomplished rider, knew how to shoot,
and often watched her father drill the militia. She and her
sister Rebecca had guarded the family home while their father

was asleep or away. The previous year, Sybil had managed to outsmart a group of Tories (loyalists) who had surrounded the house in the hope of collecting a large bounty offered by the British for capturing or killing her father. Using muskets, a bunch of lit candles, and the support of her seven younger siblings, Sybil fooled the group of loyalists into believing that the house was protected by armed militia.

Now, Sybil was ready to do her patriotic duty again. Astride Star, she galloped over rain-sodden trails, through dark and dense forest, and over pitted, rock-studded roads during a thunderstorm. The terrain was dangerous in more ways than one: A young woman traveling alone was vulnerable to attack and other violence. "Muster at Ludington's!" she cried, stopping at the farmhouses of the men in her father's regiment. By dawn, Sybil had traveled more than 40 miles, and most of the 400 American soldiers under Henry's command were ready to march against the British forces.

The Legend Lives On

Sybil's bravery has not been forgotten. She was commemorated with a bicentennial stamp by the U.S. Post Office in 1976, the state of New York erected a monument to mark her route, and she is the subject of several children's books. There is even a poem about Sybil, which begins:

Listen, my children, and you shall hear
Of a lovely feminine Paul Revere

Who rode an equally famous ride
Through a different part of the countryside,

Where Sybil Ludington's name recalls
A ride as daring as that of Paul's.

Celebrities' Real Names

Many celebrities have catchy names that strike your interest and imagination. But you didn't think they were born with them, did you?

Anna Nicole Smith—Vickie Lynn Hogan

Whoopi Goldberg—Caryn Johnson

Twiggy—Lesley Hornby

Jack Palance—Volodymir Ivanovich Palahnuik

Winona Ryder—Winona Laura Horowitz

Carmen Electra—Tara Patrick

Vin Diesel—Mark Vincent

Brigitte Bardot—Camille Javal

Charlton Heston—John Charles Carter

Woody Allen—Allen Stewart Konigsberg

Rita Hayworth—Margarita Carmen Cansino

Gene Wilder—Jerome Silberman

Elle Macpherson—Eleanor Gow

Raquel Welch—Jo Raquel Tejada

Harry Houdini—Ehrich Weiss

Jennifer Aniston—Jennifer Anastassakis

John Cleese—John Cheese

Hulk Hogan—Terry Bollea

Natalie Portman—Natalie Hershlag

Nicolas Cage—Nicolas Coppola

Ralph Lauren—Ralph Lipschitz

Psychic Detectives

When the corpse just can't be found, the murderer remains unknown, and the weapon has been stashed in some secret corner, criminal investigations hit a stalemate and law enforcement agencies may tap their secret weapons—individuals who find things through some unconventional methods.

✳   ✳   ✳   ✳

"Reading" the Ripper: Robert James Lees

WHEN THE PSYCHOTIC murderer known as Jack the Ripper terrorized London in the 1880s, the detectives of Scotland Yard consulted a psychic named Robert James Lees, who said he had glimpsed the killer's face in several visions. Lees also claimed he had correctly forecasted at least three of the well-publicized murders of women. The Ripper wrote a sarcastic note to detectives stating that they would still never catch him. Indeed, the killer proved right in this prediction.

Feeling Their Vibes: Florence Sternfels

As a psychometrist—a psychic who gathers impressions by handling material objects—Florence Sternfels was successful enough to charge a dollar for readings in Edgewater, New Jersey, in the early 20th century. Born in 1891, Sternfels believed that her gift was a natural ability rather than a supernatural one, so she never billed police for her help in solving crimes. Some of her best "hits" included preventing a man from blowing up an army base with dynamite, finding two missing boys alive in Philadelphia, and leading police to the body of a murdered young woman. She worked with police as far away as Europe to solve tough cases but lived quietly in New Jersey until her death in 1965.

The Dutch Grocer's Gift: Gerard Croiset

Born in the Netherlands in 1909, Gerard Croiset nurtured a growing psychic ability from age six. In 1935, he joined a Spiritualist group, began to hone his talents, and within two years had set up shop as a psychic and healer. After a touring lecturer discovered his abilities in 1945, Croiset began assisting law enforcement agencies around the world, traveling as far as Japan and Australia. He specialized in finding missing children but also helped authorities locate lost papers and artifacts. At the same time, Croiset ran a popular clinic for psychic healing that treated both humans and animals. His son, Gerard Croiset Jr., was also a professional psychic and parapsychologist.

Accidental Psychic: Peter Hurkos

As one of the most famous psychic detectives of the 20th century, Peter Hurkos did his best work by picking up vibes from victims' clothing. Born in the Netherlands in 1911, Hurkos lived an ordinary life as a house painter until a fall required him to undergo brain surgery at age 30. The operation seemed to trigger his latent psychic powers, and he was almost immediately able to mentally retrieve information about people and "read" the history of objects by handling them.

Hurkos assisted in the Boston Strangler investigation in the early 1960s, and in 1969, he was brought in to help solve the grisly murders ordered by Charles Manson. He gave police many accurate details including the name Charlie, a description of Manson, and the fact that the murders were ritual slayings.

The TV-Screen Mind of Dorothy Allison

New Jersey housewife Dorothy Allison broke into the world of clairvoyant crime-solving when she dreamed about a missing local boy as if seeing it on television. In her dream, the five-year-old boy was stuck in some kind of pipe. When she called police, she also described the child's clothing, including the odd fact that he was wearing his shoes on the opposite feet. When Allison underwent hypnosis to learn more details, she added that the boy's surroundings involved a fenced school and a factory. She was proven correct on all accounts when the boy's body was found about two months after he went missing, floating close to a pipe in a pond near a school and a factory and wearing his little shoes still tied onto the wrong feet.

Allison, who began having psychic experiences as a child, considered her gift a blessing and never asked for pay. One of her more famous cases was that of missing heiress Patty Hearst in 1974. Although Allison was unable to find her, every prediction she made about the young woman came true, including the fact that she had dyed her hair red.

Like a Bolt Out of the Blue: John Catchings

While at a Texas barbeque on an overcast July 4, 1969, a bolt of lightning hit 22-year-old John Catchings. He survived but said the electric blast opened him to his life's calling as a psychic. He then followed in the footsteps of his mother, Bertie, who earned her living giving "readings."

Catchings often helped police solve puzzling cases but became famous after helping police find a missing 32-year-old Houston nurse named Gail Lorke. She vanished in late October 1982, after her husband, Steven, claimed she had stayed home from work because she was sick. Because Catchings worked by holding objects that belonged to victims, Lorke's sister, who was suspicious of Steven, went to Catchings with a photo of Gail and with Gail's belt. Allegedly, Catchings saw that Lorke had indeed been murdered by her husband and left under a heap of refuse that included parts of an old wooden fence. He also gave police several other key details. Detectives were able to use the information to get Steven Lorke to confess his crime.

Among many other successes, Catchings also helped police find the body of Mike Dickens in 1980 after telling them the young man would be found buried in a creek bed near a shoe and other rubbish, including old tires and boards. Police discovered the body there just as Catchings had described it.

Fame from Fortunes: Irene Hughes

In 2008, famed investigative psychic Irene Hughes claimed a career tally of more than 2,000 police cases on her Web site. Born around 1920 (sources vary) in rural Tennessee, Hughes shocked her church congregation at age four when she shouted out that the minister would soon leave them. She was right and kept on making predictions, advised by a Japanese "spirit guide" named Kaygee. After World War II, Hughes moved to Chicago to take a job as a newspaper reporter. She financed her trip by betting on a few horse races using her psychic abilities! She gained fame in 1967 when she correctly prophesied Chicago's terrible blizzard and that the Cardinals would win the World Series. By 1968, she was advising Howard Hughes and correctly predicted his death in 1976.

Hughes's more famous predictions included the death of North Vietnamese premiere Ho Chi Minh in 1969 (although she was off by a week), the circumstances of Ted Kennedy's Chappaquiddick fiasco, and that Jacqueline Kennedy would marry someone with the characteristics of her eventual second husband, Aristotle Onassis. Hughes operated out of a luxurious office on Chicago's Michigan Avenue and commanded as much as $500 an hour from her many eager clients. She hosted radio and TV shows, wrote three books, and in the 1980s and '90s, wrote a much-read column of New Year's predictions for the *National Enquirer*. Now in her eighties, she still works out of her home and writes a regular astrology column.

Massive Movement

Following a horrific car crash in July 2007, fire engulfed a vehicle near Augusta, Georgia. It had already claimed one life and was about to claim another. Luckily, a quick-thinking driver from a local plumbing firm saw the incident unfold and took action. He released 1,500 gallons of his liquid cargo onto the vehicle—a heroic move that extinguished the deadly flames and saved the passenger's life. It had been a stroke of luck that the plumber had just pumped a payload from a nearby client. But then, sucking raw sewage from septic tanks did comprise the bulk of his work.

The Wacky World of Female Druids

The ancient Celts—the culture that produced druids—
were far less gender-biased than their Greek and Roman
neighbors. Women could buy or inherit property, assume
leadership, wage war, divorce men, and, yes, become druids.

✳   ✳   ✳   ✳

DRUIDS WERE THE leaders—spiritually, intellectually, and sometimes politically—of Celtic societies. Because they did not use writing, we don't know exactly what druids (or their followers) believed or what they taught. From ancient stories, we've learned that they were well-educated and served as judges, scientists, teachers, priests, and doctors. Some even led their tribes.

At one time, Celtic tribes covered most of Europe, and their druids embodied wisdom and authority. In the ensuing centuries, however, druids have gotten a bad rap, due to lurid tales of human sacrifice that may or may not be true. (Most of the bad-mouthing came from enemies of the Celts, after all.)

Femme druids were described as priestesses, prophets, and oracles by Greek writers including Plutarch and Romans such as Tacitus. Several ancient authors mention holy women living on island sanctuaries, either alone or alongside male druids.

Irish tales are full of druids, some of them women. They helped win battles by transforming trees into warriors, they conjured up storms and diseases, and sometimes they hid children from murderous fathers. In the Irish epic *Cattle Raid of Cooley*, a beautiful young druid named Fidelma foretells victory for the hero Cúchulainn. Saint Patrick met female druids, and Saint Bridget, by some accounts the daughter of a druid, may have been a druid herself before converting to Christianity.

The ancient Celts knew what the rest of the world has slowly come to realize: Women can wield power as wisely—or as cruelly—as men.

Role Playing: The Non-Suspects in Police Lineups

Appropriately enough, these "fillers" (also known as "distractors") are mostly criminals or suspected criminals. Who better to act as possible perps?

✳   ✳   ✳   ✳

IN THE TRADITIONAL "live" police lineup, in which a witness tries to pick out the bad guy from behind a one-way mirror, the police typically present one actual suspect and four or five similar-looking inmates from the local jail. The lineup can be either simultaneous (with the suspect and fillers standing together) or sequential (with the possible perps—perpetrators—coming out one by one). When there aren't enough suitable inmates, police officers and other station staff may participate. Occasionally, the police will even recruit people with the right look off the street and pay them a small fee for their trouble.

Nevertheless, it can be difficult to come up with five people who closely match the description of a suspected perpetrator. Even when such fillers can be found, using people who bear similarities to the culprit can lead to false identifications—if one filler resembles the suspect much more closely than the other participants do, for instance, he stands a pretty good chance of being identified by the witness as the perp. Furthermore, if the police choose fillers who don't closely match the description of the suspect, a judge might later rule that the lineup was unfair.

For this reason, many police departments have switched from traditional lineups to photo arrays, or virtual lineups, in which the police select a series of mug shots that closely match the suspect's description. In the United States, the conventional virtual lineup includes two rows of three pictures (dubbed the "six pack"). As with the live lineup, some departments prefer a sequential virtual lineup (showing only one picture at a time).

The Men Behind the Beheadings

One of the great ironies in history is that Dr. Joseph-Ignace Guillotin was an opponent of capital punishment. But despite the fact that he was the guillotine's namesake, he did not invent the device.

✳   ✳   ✳   ✳

How the Guillotine Came to Be

THE INFAMOUS DEATH machine's true creators were Antoine Louis, the French doctor who drew up the initial design around 1792, and Tobias Schmidt, the German piano maker who executed it. (Pun intended.)

Joseph-Ignace Guillotin's contribution came a bit earlier. As a delegate to France's National Assembly of 1789, he proposed the novel idea that if executions could not be banned entirely, the condemned should at least be entitled to a swift and relatively merciful death. What's more, he argued that all criminals, regardless of whether they were rich or poor, should be executed by the same method.

This last point may seem obvious, but prior to the French Revolution, wealthy miscreants who were up to be offed could slip executioners a few coins to guarantee speedy dispatches. Poorer ones often went "coach class"—they got to be the coach while horses tied to their arms and legs pulled them in four different directions. What a way to go!

In April 1792, the Assembly used its new guillotine for the first time on a platform in Paris's Place de Grève. Two vertical wooden beams, standing about 15 feet high, served as runners for the slanted steel blade. At the bottom of the pair of beams, two boards with a round hole, called the *lunette*, locked the condemned person's head in place. The blade was hoisted to the top with pulleys and released with a lever. After a few grisly mishaps, executioners learned to grease the grooves on the beams with tallow in order to ensure that no one was left half dead, so to speak, after the blade came down.

The Reign of Terror

The first head to roll was that of Nicolas Jacques-Pelletier, a common thief. During the Reign of Terror, from January 1793 to July 1794, more than 10,000 people had an exit interview with "Madame Guillotine," including King Louis XVI and his wife, Marie Antoinette. The daily parade of victims drew crowds of gawkers. Journalists printed programs, vendors sold refreshments, and nearby merchants rented out seats with unobstructed views. This bloody period ended with the execution of Robespierre, one of the Revolution's leaders and an early advocate of the guillotine. France continued to use the guillotine in cases of capital punishment throughout the 19th and 20th centuries. The last official guillotine execution took place on September 10, 1977.

Because they were embarrassed by their association with this instrument of terror, the descendants of Joseph Guillotin petitioned the government of France to change the name of the machine. The government declined to comply, so the family changed its name instead and passed into obscurity. The same cannot be said for the guillotine itself: Though it is now relegated to museums, the device remains a grim symbol of power, punishment, and sudden death.

---

* Sweden has the greatest penetration of telephones. It has 229 phones for every 1,000 people.

* The longest phone cable is a submarine cable called Fiber-Optic Link Around the Globe (FLAG). It spans 16,800 miles from Japan to the United Kingdom and can carry 600,000 calls at a time.

* The telephone has been one of the most profitable inventions in the history of the United States.

The People at the Ends of the Earth

Who are these exotic folks? No one, really.
They're simply a figure of speech.

✳ ✳ ✳ ✳

THROUGHOUT HISTORY, PEOPLE from every culture and walk of life have conjured images of far-off, mythical places with exotic names like Xanadu, Shangri-La, and Milwaukee.

This universal desire to fantasize about unknown lands likely gave rise to such terms as "the four corners of the earth" and "the ends of the earth." These phrases suggest that somewhere on our plane of existence there lie identifiable, ultimate nether regions— locations farther away from us than any other. A search of the King James Bible turns up no fewer than 28 occurrences of the term "ends of the earth." Psalm 72:8, for example, reads, "He shall have dominion also from sea to sea, and from the river unto the ends of the earth." This is a translation of the Latin *Et dominabitur a mari usque ad mare, et a flumine usque ad terminos terrae.* At a time when guys in togas and sandals went around speaking to each other in Latin, most folks probably did believe that the earth was flat and really did have ends.

Today, most of us don't use the term so literally. It's relative and open to your imagination. The ends of the earth could mean the North Pole. If you live in Paris or Rome, perhaps it means the remote Amazon jungle. And if you live on a Himalayan peak, maybe it means Milwaukee.

✳ A 100-pound woman in high heels exerts more pressure per square inch (psi) when walking than a 6,000-pound elephant. The elephant clocks in at around 75 psi, but the woman can apply approximately 1,500 psi to the heel point of her shoe.

✳ Leo Tolstoy, author of *War and Peace,* left all of his possessions to the stump of a tree.

History's Most Famous Female Pirates

"Lady pirate" may not sound like a job description our great-great-grandmothers would have gone for, but according to historians, many women did indeed pursue lives of plunder on the high seas.

✳   ✳   ✳   ✳

The Roll Call

ONE OF THE earliest female pirates was Artemesia of Persia, whose fleet preyed upon the city-states of Greece during the 5th century B.C. The Athenians put a price of 10,000 drachmas on her head, but there's no record of anyone ever collecting it. Teuta of Illyria (circa 230 B.C.) was a pirate queen who led raids against Roman ships. Another notable female marauder was Alfhild (circa the 9th century A.D.), a Viking princess who reportedly kept a viper for a pet and whose all-female longboat crew ravaged the Scandinavian coast. Prince Alf of Denmark captured Alfhild, but her beauty so overwhelmed him that he proposed marriage instead of beheading her, and they ruled together happily ever after. At least that's one story; there's a little blarney in every pirate yarn.

Legend has it that Grania O'Malley (1530–1603), who was captain of a pirate fleet based in Ireland, gave birth to her son Toby while at sea. The next day, blunderbuss in hand, she led her men to victory over a Turkish warship.

Madame Ching (circa 1785–1844), perhaps the most notorious of all the pirate queens, ruled her league of 2,000 ships and 70,000 men with an iron hand—anyone who was caught stealing loot for private use was executed immediately. But she was relatively kind to some of her prisoners: For example, she ordered that captive women and children *not* be hung by their hair over the sides of her ships.

Anne Bonny and Mary Read

Closer to home, Anne Bonny (1698–1782) and Mary Read (circa 1690–1721) dressed as men and served aboard pirate ships that sailed the Caribbean. They met when Mary, disguised as one James Morris, joined a crew that was commanded by Anne and her husband, Calico Jack Rackham.

One night while the men were sleeping off a rum binge below deck, Anne and Mary were left to face down a British man-of-war alone. Despite their bravery, their ship was quickly captured and the pirates were hauled off to prison. After learning that Calico Jack had received a death sentence, Anne's last words to him were: "I am sorry... but had you had fought like a man, you need not have been hanged like a dog."

Anne and Mary escaped death by "pleading their bellies," meaning they both were conveniently pregnant. Mary died in childbirth a few months later; Anne dropped from historical view. She is said to have married again and become a respectable matron in the city of Charleston, South Carolina. But one rumor suggests that Mary only pretended to die and that she and Anne escaped to New Orleans—where they raised their kids and occasionally plied their former trade—remaining fast friends and pirates of the Caribbean to the very end.

---

* The annual revenue for the telephone industry is $210 billion, almost 8 times that of television and 23 times that of radio.

* Globally, about $1 trillion is spent annually on telecommunications products and services.

* One million threads of fiber-optic cable can fit in a tube one-half inch in diameter.

* The telephone is the most used piece of communication equipment in the world.

The Antichrist Is Everywhere

Who isn't the Antichrist? The Internet is full of raconteurs who accuse just about every celebrity and world leader— from David Hasselhoff to the Pope—of being the dark figure of biblical prophecy. But the Bible itself doesn't have much to say on the subject, at least not definitively.

✳   ✳   ✳   ✳

Biblical References

THE BIBLE CONTAINS only four mentions of the word "Antichrist," all of which appear in the letters of John, and they paint a murky picture. The passages say that the Antichrist comes at "the last hour" and denies the divinity of Jesus Christ. They also allude to multiple Antichrists who are said to have come already. (Some scholars believe that this refers to former followers of Christ who split with their congregation.)

Scriptural scholars have tried to get to the bottom of these ambiguous verses by connecting them with prophecies that are found elsewhere in the Bible. For example, there's a man known as "the little horn" in the Old Testament Book of Daniel; he is an evil figure who the prophet says will come to power over God's people and rule until God defeats him. Other Jewish texts mention a similar character called Beliar, an evil angel and agent of Satan who will be God's final adversary. Beliar also appears in the New Testament as a "man of lawlessness" who proclaims himself to be God and takes his seat in the temple in the final days. He also can be found in the Book of Revelation, as two beasts and a dragon that are defeated by Jesus in a climactic battle.

The Modern Interpretation

As with most religious matters, there's no definitive interpretation of the Antichrist. But the prevailing view among contemporary believers is that the Antichrist is the opponent of God and Jesus Christ described in these prophecies. He is seen as an agent of Satan, in a relationship analogous to the one between

Jesus and God. Many expect that the Antichrist will be a charismatic leader who will draw people away from Christianity in the time immediately before Jesus Christ returns to Earth. Then, in a final battle between good and evil, Jesus will defeat the Antichrist, ushering in the era of the Kingdom of God on Earth.

This concept evolved through centuries of biblical scholarship, involving a variety of theories about who or what the Antichrist is. Many prominent figures, beginning with the Roman emperor Nero, have been accused of being the Antichrist. Such condemnations continue today—just Google "Antichrist" for a roundup of the usual suspects. While it's impossible to rule anyone out definitively, we'll go out on a limb and say that David Hasselhoff is probably innocent of the charge.

---

* The busiest organization in the world is the Pentagon, which has 34,500 phone lines and receives 1 million calls a day. It received more than 1.5 million phone calls on the 50th anniversary of D-Day.

* The busiest telephone exchange was reportedly by BellSouth at the 1996 Olympic Games, during which 100 billion bits of information were transmitted per second.

* The "bones" in whalebone corsets were actually baleen—plates of "combs" in the jawbones of whales used to strain plankton from the water.

* Earth weighs approximately 5,940,000,000,000,000,000,000 metric tons.

* Geodesic domes have the highest enclosed volume-to-weight ratio of any known linear structure.

* In 1956, Johnny Mathis decided to record an album instead of answering an invitation to try out for the U.S. Olympic team as a high jumper. It turned out to be a fortuitous choice, especially for the singer and his future fans: Mathis became one of the top-selling artists of all time.

In Search of Immortality

Meet Gene Savoy, the "real Indiana Jones," who set off to discover cities and a whole lot more.

✳ ✳ ✳ ✳

BORN IN BELLINGHAM, WASHINGTON, on May 11, 1927, Douglas Eugene "Gene" Savoy had no formal training as an archaeologist. But that didn't stop him from heading deep into the jungles of Peru. Once dubbed "the real Indiana Jones" by *People* magazine, Savoy discovered more than 40 lost cities in his career, including Vilcabamba, the Incas' last refuge from the Spanish conquistadors.

Like movie-hero Indiana Jones, Savoy's expeditions weren't entirely driven by archaeology. Savoy had grander plans—including finding the legendary city of El Dorado, where it was rumored that one could delve into the "ancient roots of universal religion" and the fabled fountain of youth.

In 1969, Savoy left the jungle to search the sea. He captained a research ship and sailed around the world gathering information on sea routes used by ancient civilizations in order to prove that they could have been in contact with one another.

In 1984, Savoy returned to Peru, where he discovered Gran Vilaya, the largest pre-Columbian city in South America. On one of his last trips to Gran Vilaya, he unearthed a tablet that held inscriptions alluding to ships that were sent by King Solomon to the biblical land of Ophir to gather gold for the king's temple. This tablet sent Savoy on what was perhaps his most ambitious adventure: to find the exact location of Ophir, to find proof that the gold in Solomon's Jerusalem temple came from South America, and to learn the secret to immortality. Throughout his career, however, scholars scoffed at his theories and were skeptical of his findings.

But immortality alluded Savoy, and he died in 2007 in Reno, Nevada, where he was known as The Most Right Reverend Douglas Eugene Savoy, head of the International Community of Christ. Members of the church believed that staring at the sun would allow them to take in God's energy and become immortal (albeit damage their eyes)—a secret Savoy said was revealed to him in the jungles of Peru.

Say What?

Champions keep playing until they get it right.

—BILLIE JEAN KING

Religion is what keeps the poor from murdering the rich.

—NAPOLEON BONAPARTE

The best argument against democracy is a five-minute conversation with the average voter.

—WINSTON CHURCHILL

When the missionaries first came to Africa, they had the Bible and we had the land. They said, "Let us pray." We closed our eyes. When we opened them, we had the Bible and they had the land.

—DESMOND TUTU

Reality TV: The Saga of the Hatfields and McCoys

About a century after it began, America's most infamous feud spilled onto the boob tube.

✳ ✳ ✳ ✳

How It All Started

THINGS JUST AREN'T like they used to be. America has gone from a country of hardworking people to a consumer-based society that is driven by greed and empty entertainment. Even our family feuds have lost their integrity. Nowadays, people go on game shows to battle it out. Back in the good old days—back when America was America—folks just shot each other.

With apologies to Richard Dawson, the former host of the silly game show *Family Feud*, the most notorious family feud in American history is that of the Hatfields and the McCoys. In the mid-19th century, these two Appalachian clans settled on opposite sides of the quaintly named Tug Fork, a stream that forms part of the West Virginia–Kentucky border. On the West Virginia side lived the Hatfields, a logging family of 15 that was headed by "Devil Anse" Hatfield, a former Confederate officer who was none too happy that his state had joined the Union. The McCoys were equally large, with patriarch "Rand'l" McCoy siring 13 children, although some sources indicate that he fathered 16 children. For many years, the two families coexisted somewhat peacefully, working together and even intermarrying.

According to some historians, the trouble began when young Harmon McCoy joined the Union army and fought for the North during the Civil War, an offense for which, upon his return to Tug Fork, he was hunted down and killed by a group of Hatfields. Bad feelings simmered through the 1860s and 1870s. They flared up again when a dispute over ownership of a pig led to another murder, this one committed by the McCoys.

But things didn't really boil over until Roseanna McCoy fell in love with a Hatfield. This backwoods version of Romeo and Juliet eventually led to the murders of at least 20 members of the two families.

America Takes Notice

Though there was a great deal of family feuding in Appalachia during the late 19th and early 20th centuries, no squabble captured America's imagination quite like that of the Hatfields and McCoys. Countless folk songs, books, plays, and movies have been written about the two families, and their depiction as violent, poorly educated, incestuous hillbillies has been instrumental in creating the popular misperception of Appalachia. Some might say that the Hatfields and McCoys have done more to destroy Appalachia's image than anybody this side of Ned Beatty's "wooer" in *Deliverance*.

From Appalachia to *Family Feud*

But grudges can only last so long. In 1891, after the fighting got so bad that it was making national headlines, the families finally decided to call a truce. Over the next century, they lived in uneasy harmony. Then in 1979, the Hatfield and McCoy families emerged from their remote Appalachian homes to join the rest of the world—by appearing together on *Family Feud*.

---

* California boasts the oldest known living tree—a Bristlecone Pine named "Methuselah," which is estimated to be 4,767 years old.

* One ounce of pure gold can be made into a wire 50 miles long.

* The United States uses approximately 10 percent of the world's salt production each year just to salt roads.

* Though the Hope Diamond is more famous, the Cullinan is the largest diamond ever found. Unearthed in South Africa in 1905, this 3,100-carat monster was cut into several stones that are still part of the British Crown Jewels.

* There are 318,979,564,000 different ways to play the first four moves per side in a game of chess.

The Shocking Death of William Kemmler

William Kemmler was certainly no angel—after all, the guy admitted to bludgeoning his wife to death. Yet his shocking demise sparked death penalty protests and electrified a rivalry between powerhouse energy pioneers Thomas Edison and George Westinghouse.

✳ ✳ ✳ ✳

WILLIAM KEMMLER WAS an illiterate street peddler in Buffalo, New York, who possessed a jealous streak and a penchant for drinking—a dangerous combination. His common-law wife, Tillie Ziegler, suffered the consequences of these demons in March 1889, when a drunk Kemmler brutally killed her with a hatchet. He confessed to a neighbor, saying that he would willingly "take the rope" for his intentional actions. But instead of swinging for his sins, Kemmler went down in history as the first person ever to be executed by electrocution.

An Undercurrent of Rivalry

Given his admission of guilt, Kemmler's trial was swift. By May 13, he was sentenced to death by electrocution—a manner of capital punishment the New York legislature had recently deemed to be "less barbarous" than the noose.

Then a high-price lawyer mysteriously materialized in time to appeal Kemmler's death sentence on the grounds that electrocution was cruel and unusual punishment. When the appellate court upheld the electric chair as humane, another high-profile attorney argued Kemmler's case to the U.S. Supreme Court—again, unsuccessfully.

Although Kemmler's attorneys professed to be acting out of purely humanitarian interests, they were thought to be bank-rolled by George Westinghouse, a pioneer in the burgeoning electric industry. Westinghouse, who was a proponent of alternating current, was desperately trying to defend the merits of AC so that it would gain public favor as the preferred mode of electrical transmission. Thomas Edison, his direct-current rival, hoped to solidify DC's market share by vigorously publicizing the dangers of AC's high-voltage currents.

Sparks Fly

To secure the subliminal link between AC-generated electricity and death, Edison's allies made certain the electric chair would be powered with Westinghouse generators. This was no easy feat, since Westinghouse vigilantly attempted to block all generator sales suspected of being connected with Edison or the electric chair.

Electrician Harold Brown was commissioned to create the first deadly device. Rumored to be an Edison agent, Brown favored AC as a power source. He also cunningly sidestepped Westinghouse: By orchestrating the shipment of Westinghouse "dynamos" to Brazil, Brown rerouted the generators back to the United States for use in developing the electric chair.

Onlookers Shocked

Sober and reborn as a Christian, Kemmler calmly approached the electric chair on August 6, 1890. As the warden shakily attached electrodes to Kemmler's body, the prisoner advised him to take his time and keep calm. In fact, according to an eyewitness, Kemmler was the coolest person in the room.

Accounts of the day vary, but all agree that Kemmler's electrocution was badly bungled. The executioners seemed unclear on the amount of time the electricity was to be administered, volleying suggestions ranging from a few seconds to as many as 15 seconds. Finally, 10 seconds was agreed upon, and the switch was flipped. Kemmler's body convulsed and turned bright red, but to the horror of onlookers, he appeared to remain alive, groaning and gasping. Additional shocks were applied until at last he succumbed.

By some accounts, Kemmler died instantly—his latent reactions were compared to the phenomenon of a chicken running around after its head has been cut off. By other accounts, Kemmler suffered a slow, painful, and torturous death. Whatever the story, the Westinghouse and Edison camps placed their spin on the event, using Kemmler's death to further their own ambitions.

In the long run, neither side prevailed. Although alternating current became the standard, financial woes eventually caused Westinghouse to lose control of his company. Bankers later took over Edison's companies, which ultimately became General Electric.

✳ Tickling requires surprise. Since you can't surprise yourself, you can't tickle yourself, either.

✳ Comanche code-talkers, used in World War II by the Army Signal Corps to send encrypted messages that German troops could not break, referred to Adolf Hitler as *posah-tai-vo,* which means "crazy white man."

Peculiar Presidential Facts

* President William Taft had a new bathtub installed in the White House that could hold four grown men. Why? His 300-pound frame wouldn't fit in the original presidential tub.

* President John Quincy Adams started each summer day with an early-morning skinny-dip in the Potomac River.

* Grover Cleveland was the first and only president to marry in the White House itself. He wed Frances Folsom in 1886.

* With 15 children from 2 marriages, President John Tyler was the most prolific chief executive.

* President George Washington never shook hands with visitors, choosing to bow instead.

* The only president who never won a national election was Gerald Ford, who took office after Nixon resigned in 1974.

* President Jimmy Carter is said to be able to speed-read at the rate of 2,000 words per minute.

* Franklin Delano Roosevelt was related to 11 other presidents, either directly or through marriage.

* President James Garfield could write Latin with one hand and Greek with the other—at the same time.

* George W. Bush's brother Neil was scheduled to dine with John Hinckley's brother, Scott, the day after Hinckley tried to kill President Ronald Reagan.

* John Adams and Thomas Jefferson both died on July 4, 1826, 50 years to the day after the official signing of the Declaration of Independence.

* Edwin Booth, the brother of Abraham Lincoln's assassin, John Wilkes Booth, once saved the life of President Lincoln's son Robert. He kept the boy from falling off a train platform.

The Real Sherlock Holmes

The famous fictional sleuth is based on a 19th-century doctor from the University of Edinburgh who had a gift for piecing together tiny details.

✳ ✳ ✳ ✳

Paging Dr. Bell

SINCE BURSTING ONTO the scene in 1887, Sherlock Holmes has become quite the celebrity. The members of his fan club, sometimes dubbed the Baker Street Irregulars, number in the hundreds of thousands worldwide. In the 20th century, many readers were so convinced that Holmes was a real person that they sent mail to his address at 221b Baker Street in London. In the 21st century, he has his own page on Facebook.

Holmes is, of course, fictional. But is the detective based on fact? Author Sir Arthur Conan Doyle claimed that he modeled his famous detective on Dr. Joseph Bell (1837–1911) of the University of Edinburgh. Doyle had been Bell's assistant when Doyle was a medical student at the university from 1877 to 1881.

Like everyone else, Doyle was awed by Bell's ability to deduce all kinds of details regarding the geographical origins, life histories, and professions of his patients by his acute powers of observation. The doctor had what his students called "the look of eagles"; little escaped him. Reportedly, he could tell a working man's trade by the pattern of the calluses on his hands and what countries a sailor had visited by his tattoos.

In 1892, Doyle wrote an appreciative letter to his old mentor, saying, "It is most certainly to you that I owe Sherlock Holmes." The resemblance between Bell and Holmes was strong enough to impress Bell's fellow Scotsman Robert Louis Stevenson. After reading several Sherlock Holmes stories in a popular magazine, Stevenson sent a note to Doyle asking, "Can this be my old friend Joe Bell?"

When queried by journalists about the fictitious doppel-ganger, Bell modestly replied that "Dr. Conan Doyle has, by his imaginative genius, made a great deal out of very little, and his warm remembrance of one of his old teachers has coloured the picture." Nevertheless, Bell was pleased to write an introduction to the 1892 edition of *A Study in Scarlet*, the tale that had launched Holmes's career as a sleuth—and Doyle's as a writer. By the mid-1890s, Doyle had largely abandoned medicine for the life of a full-time writer.

A Crime-Fighting Legacy

Bell's association with Holmes wasn't his only claim to fame. He was a fellow of the Royal College of Surgeons of Edinburgh, the author of several medical textbooks, and one of the founders of modern forensic pathology. The University of Edinburgh honored his legacy by establishing the Joseph Bell Centre for Forensic Statistics and Legal Reasoning in March 2001.

One of the center's first initiatives was to develop a software program that could aid investigations into suspicious deaths. "It takes an overview of all the available evidence," said Jeroen Keppens, one of the program's developers, "and then speculates on what might have happened." Police detectives have praised the potential of the software, which is called, fittingly, Sherlock Holmes.

Say What?

A man in love is incomplete until he has married. Then he's finished.

—ZSA ZSA GABOR

You can't make up anything anymore. The world itself is a satire. All you're doing is recording it.

—ART BUCHWALD

The buck stops with the guy who signs the checks.

—RUPERT MURDOCH

How to Turn Yourself into a Witch

Let's get something straight: You can't become a witch by being mean, wearing black, or jumping off a roof with a broomstick between your legs. It just doesn't work that way.

✳   ✳   ✳   ✳

Myth vs. Fact

IF YOU'RE CONSIDERING becoming a witch because you want to learn how to cast a vengeful spell or get up close and personal with Satan, then you're barking up the wrong tree... and you're probably barking mad to boot. Please seek professional help immediately. Thanks.

Now that we've gotten that out of the way, there are a few things you should know about witchcraft, or Wicca, before you make the decision to devote yourself to this misunderstood religion. First, you need to put aside your preconceptions about being a witch (refer to first paragraph). Next, it is important to understand that being a witch means many different things; it involves creativity, empowerment, free thought, peacefulness, spirituality, and being connected to the earth.

Consider this: The word "witch" is a combination of two Old English terms: *wicce* ("wise one") and *Wicca* ("healer"). In ancient times, witches were admired and respected for their wisdom and ability to heal with herbs. It wasn't until the early 1300s that witchcraft was declared heresy by—guess who?—the Catholic Church. This resulted in a widespread fear of witches and led to the witch hunts that took place between the late 15th and 18th centuries.

Bewitching Reading

Once you've freed your mind of old myths, you might want to pick up a book or two—such as *Wicca for Beginners* by Thea Sabin—to learn more about modern, or eclectic, Wicca, the fastest-growing type of Wicca. It's preferred for its level of freedom from doctrines and the absence of traditional initiation practices. Many Wiccans are vegans, vegetarians, and/or environmentalists, but you don't have to change your diet or lifestyle to become a witch.

Wicca is about the mind, body, and spirit, along with a code of ethics and a few principles that some witches share. It's not about proselytizing, overuse of magic, exclusion, or controlling others, nor is it dualistic, satanic, or Goth. Respect the earth, live in harmony with the seasons, find your own purpose, and create your own path. *Poof!* You're a witch.

---

* Commercial deodorant became available in 1888. Roll-on deodorant was invented in the 1950s, using technology from standard ballpoint pens.

* Thanksgiving is celebrated on the fourth Thursday in November, by decree of President Franklin Roosevelt. Thus, the earliest date that Thanksgiving can fall is November 22.

* Diners Club was the first credit card that allowed a consumer to "buy now and pay later." The legendary piece of plastic was unleashed in 1950.

* The first great bank merger in U.S. history occurred in 1955 when Chase National Bank and the Bank of Manhattan amalgamated to form the Chase Manhattan Bank.

* America's modern interstate highway system was designed in the 1950s during the Eisenhower administration. Its primary purpose was not to enhance casual driving over long distances but to provide for the efficient movement of military vehicles if and when necessary.

* The average dollar bill lasts a little less than two years before it's worn out and pulled from circulation.

Eight Famous People Who Died in the Bathroom

When these people said they had to go, they weren't kidding! All of these people ended their time on Earth in the bathroom— some accidentally, others intentionally. One thing is certain— none of them got a chance to wash their hands before leaving!

✳   ✳   ✳   ✳

1. **Elvis Presley:** The King of Rock 'n' Roll was born in Tupelo, Mississippi, on January 8, 1935. He was discovered in Memphis by Sun Records founder Sam Phillips, who was looking for a white singer with an African-American sound and style. Elvis catapulted to fame following three appearances on *The Ed Sullivan Show* in 1956 and 1957. Although he was pushed off the charts by The Beatles and the rest of the British invasion in the early 1960s, he still sold more than a billion records in his lifetime, more than any other recording artist in history. His movie career kept him in the public eye until his comeback album in 1968, and in the 1970s, he sold out shows in Las Vegas as an overweight caricature of his former self. Elvis's addiction to prescription drugs was well known, and on August 16, 1977, he was found dead on the bathroom floor in his Graceland mansion. A vomit stain on the carpet showed that he had become sick while seated on the toilet and had stumbled to the spot where he died. A medical examiner listed the cause of death as cardiac arrhythmia caused by ingesting a large number of drugs.

2. **Lenny Bruce:** Controversial comedian Lenny Bruce was born Leonard Alfred Schneider in October 1925. Bruce

was famous in the 1950s and 1960s for his satirical routines about social themes of the day, including politics, religion, race, abortion, and drugs. His use of profanity—rarely done at that time—got him arrested numerous times. He was eventually convicted on obscenity charges but was freed on bail. On August 3, 1966, Bruce, a known drug addict, was found dead in the bathroom of his Hollywood Hills home with a syringe, a burned bottle cap, and other drug paraphernalia. The official cause of death was acute morphine poisoning caused by an accidental overdose.

3. **Elagabalus:** Scandalous 3rd-century Roman emperor Elagabalus married and divorced five women, including a Vestal Virgin (a holy priestess), who under Roman law should have been buried alive for losing her virginity. Elagabalus also may have been bisexual. Objecting to his sexual behavior and his habit of forcing others to follow his religious customs, his grandmother Julia Maesa and aunt Julia Avita Mamaea murdered Elagabalus and his mother (Julia Maesa's own daughter) in the emperor's latrine. Their bodies were dragged through the streets of Rome and thrown into the Tiber River.

4. **Robert Pastorelli:** Born in 1954, actor and former boxer Robert Pastorelli was best known as Candace Bergen's housepainter on the late '80s sitcom *Murphy Brown.* He had numerous minor roles on television and also appeared in *Dances with Wolves, Sister Act 2,* and *Michael,* as well as a number of made-for-TV movies. Pastorelli struggled with drug use and in 2004 was found dead of a suspected heroin overdose on the floor of his bathroom.

5. **Orville Redenbacher:** Orville Redenbacher, founder of the popcorn company that bears his name, was born in 1907, in Brazil, Indiana. Millions came to know him through his folksy television commercials for the specialty popcorn he invented. He sold the company to Hunt-Wesson Foods in

1976 but remained as spokesperson until September 20, 1995, when he was found dead in a whirlpool bathtub in his condominium, having drowned after suffering a heart attack.

6. **Claude François:** Claude François was a French pop singer in the 1960s who had a hit with an adaptation of Trini Lopez's folk song "If I Had a Hammer." On March 11, 1978, François's obsession with cleanliness did him in when he was electrocuted in the bathroom of his Paris apartment as he tried to fix a broken lightbulb while standing in a water-filled bathtub.

7. **Albert Dekker:** Actor Albert Dekker, who appeared in *Kiss Me Deadly*, *The Killers*, and *Suddenly, Last Summer*, was blacklisted in Hollywood for several years for criticizing anti-Communist Senator Joe McCarthy. Dekker later made a comeback, but in May 1968, he was found strangled to death in the bathroom of his Hollywood home. He was naked, bound hand and foot, with a hypodermic needle sticking out of each arm and obscenities written all over his body. The official cause of death was eventually ruled to be accidental asphyxiation.

8. **Jim Morrison:** Born on December 8, 1943, Jim Morrison was best known as the lead singer for The Doors, a top rock band in the late 1960s. His sultry looks, suggestive lyrics, and onstage antics brought him fame, but drug and alcohol abuse ended his brief life. On July 3, 1971, Morrison was found dead in his bathtub in Paris. He reportedly had dried blood around his mouth and nose and bruising on his chest, suggesting a massive hemorrhage brought on by tuberculosis. The official report listed the cause of death as heart failure, but no autopsy was performed because there was no sign of foul play.

Buried Alive!

Death is the most natural thing in the world, yet it inspires the most fear. And there are few things that horrify people more than the idea of being buried alive. Meet some people who, to paraphrase the poet Dylan Thomas, did not go gentle into that good night.

✳ ✳ ✳ ✳

Can't Keep a Good Person Down

THROUGHOUT HISTORY, URBAN legends have circulated about people being buried alive—whether voluntarily or not. The first recorded case of a burial gone wrong occurred during the 1st century, when a magician named Simon Magus buried himself alive, hoping that a miracle would save him. It didn't. When Thomas à Kempis, the 13th-century author of *The Imitation of Christ*, was dug up for reinterrment and potential canonization, they found the inner coffin lid striated with scratch marks and wood embedded underneath his fingernails. Unfortunately, since he did not willingly embrace his fate, he was denied sainthood.

In 1674, Marjorie Halcrow supposedly died and was purposely buried in a shallow grave by a church employee who planned to dig her up later to retrieve her jewelry. When the grave robber attempted to steal her ring by cutting off her finger, however, Halcrow scared him off when she reacted with a moan. After being rescued, she went on to raise two sons and outlive her husband by six years. And in 1996, a missionary named Reverend Schwartz reentered the land of the living when he heard his favorite hymn being played at his funeral. As mourners passed by his closed coffin, they could hear the good Reverend singing along with them.

Avoiding the Inevitable

Through the years, the alarming incidence of premature burials concerned some people so much that they took drastic steps to ensure that it didn't happen to them or their loved ones. "Waking the dead," the practice of sitting next to the deceased for several days until their burial, usually fell to friends and family, particularly in the 19th century. Many terminally ill patients have specified in their wills that after death, they be subjected to surgical incisions, scalded with boiling-hot water, stabbed through the heart, branded with red-hot irons, or even decapitated to ensure that they were genuinely departed before being interred. Others have requested that they be buried with guns, knives, or poison inside their coffins in the event that they needed to finish the job themselves.

If you think the problem of premature burial can be solved with embalming, consider the unfortunate demise of Cardinal Somaglia in 1837. After the Cardinal passed out and was pronounced dead, plans were made to immediately embalm his body. After the embalmer made the initial incision into his chest, he noticed that the Cardinal's heart was still beating. The Cardinal reached up and batted the scalpel away to prevent further damage but ultimately died from his wounds.

A newspaper article reported on an incident in 1984, in which a pathologist assigned to conduct a post-mortem examination was stunned when the corpse sat up and grabbed him by the throat. The victim continued to live a few more years but the pathologist died immediately from shock.

What's a Body to Do?

One surefire way to avoid being buried alive is to purchase a specially outfitted Italian coffin that's been available since 1995. The $5,000 casket comes equipped with a two-way microphone and speaker to enable the questionably deceased to communicate with their loved ones. A flashlight, small oxygen tank, heartbeat sensor, and cardiac stimulator are available at an additional charge.

Of course, for those who are really concerned about being buried alive, there are other solutions. According to a pamphlet published in 2003 by the Cremation Society of Australia, the number ten reason why you should consider their services: "Cremation eliminates all danger of being buried alive."

The Name Game: A Kentucky Fried Colonel

Chicken magnate Harland Sanders certainly dressed the part of a colonel—his famous white suit and black string tie were the sort of clothes a ranking Confederate might have worn on his day off. But he was born 25 years after the Civil War ended, and his U.S. Army record shows he never made it past private. What gives?

✳ ✳ ✳ ✳

Military Service Optional

IT TURNS OUT you can be a colonel without really being a colonel. The rank of colonel has a distinguished history dating to Roman times, though its precise meaning has varied. Generally, a colonel commands a regiment, which can include as many as 5,000 soldiers. Early Americans also adopted the British tradition of conferring colonelships on members of the upper class who didn't command soldiers directly but served as figureheads. In colonial and antebellum times, a wealthy landowner would earn the title of colonel by funding a regiment of a local militia. This honorific became linked to the figure of the "Southern gentleman" as a mark of his importance in the community.

Several states expanded this tradition by granting their governors the power to make ordinary citizens into honorary colonels in recognition of a special achievement or contribution. In 1935, Kentucky Governor Ruby Laffoon commissioned Harland Sanders as a Kentucky Colonel, and Governor Earle C. Clements did it again in 1949 (Sanders had lost the original proclamation paper). Sanders wasn't a celebrity at the time, but he operated a small, well-known restaurant—the Sanders Cafe—and was active in the community.

The Moniker that Sold Countless Chickens

Sanders liked how the title rolled off the tongue, and when he received his second commission, he embraced it whole-hog. He adopted the wardrobe, facial hair, and walking cane that evoked the image of an old-time Southern gentleman. The persona was certainly memorable, and it helped Sanders turn his restaurant into a thriving franchise operation. In February 1964, he sold Kentucky Fried Chicken for $2 million, and he appeared in ads for the company for years afterward.

Sanders is in good—if somewhat odd—company. Other honorary Kentucky Colonels include Muhammad Ali, Barry Manilow, Elvis Presley, Ronald Reagan, Bill Clinton, George H. W. Bush, Johnny Depp, and Pope John Paul II. While we're quite sure that John Paul II was deeply honored, he never went by Colonel Pope or sipped mint juleps on the veranda, at least as far as we know.

---

* Peep dueling is a popular "sport" that involves placing two Peep marshmallow confections in a microwave oven, facing each other. The duelists each insert a toothpick into the front of their Peep, and the microwave is turned on, causing the Peeps to expand. The first Peep to deflate the other with its toothpick wins!

* Bouvet Island in the South Atlantic is the most remote island on Earth. It lies almost a thousand miles from the nearest land (Queen Maude Land, Antarctica).

* The Torino Impact Hazard Scale is used to categorize the chances of an asteroid or comet hitting Earth. The scale goes from zero to ten, with zero being no risk and ten being a certain collision, with global catastrophe imminent.

* Asteroid 99942 Apophis was the first object to be categorized above level one on the Torino Scale—it was briefly rated as level four for a pass in 2029—but further observations have downgraded it again to level zero.

* Herman Melville's *Moby-Dick* was inspired by a real event perhaps more spellbinding than the book. In 1820, the Nantucket whale ship *Essex* was repeatedly rammed by a large sperm whale and sank in the Pacific Ocean, leaving the 20 crewmembers adrift in three small whaleboats for 95 days. Only eight men survived.

A Real Bag Lady

Brown paper bags are so ubiquitous that we take them for granted. It's time to give some props to the person who made them possible: a 19th-century inventor named Margaret Knight.

✳ ✳ ✳ ✳

A Can-Do Attitude

CONSIDER THE FAMILIAR, flat-bottom brown paper bag: It's useful and utterly simple. Now get a sheet of brown paper, a pair of scissors, and some glue, and try to make one yourself. Not so simple, huh?

In 1870, Margaret Knight of the Columbia Paper Bag Company in Springfield, Massachusetts, was doing the same kind of puzzling over paper bags. Back then, the only paper bags that were being manufactured by machine were the narrow, envelope kind, with a single seam at the bottom. Flimsy and easily broken, they were despised by merchants and shoppers alike. The paper bag business was not booming. So Maggie Knight set out to build a better bag.

Born in 1838, Knight had been tinkering with tools since childhood; while other girls played with dolls, she excelled at making sleds and kites. She was especially fascinated by heavy machinery. At the age of 12, Knight invented a stop-motion safety device for automatic looms after witnessing an accident in a textile mill that nearly cost a worker his finger. Though never patented, her invention was widely employed throughout the industry.

During her 20s and early 30s, Knight tried her hand at several occupations before finally landing at Columbia Paper Bag. Working alone at night in her boarding house, she designed a machine that could cut, fold, and glue sheets of paper into sturdy, flat-bottom bags. This time, she applied for a patent. On July 11, 1871, Patent No. 116842 was issued to Margaret E. Knight for a "Bag Machine." Her employer was eager to implement her design, but the male workers that were hired to build and install the new machines refused to take direction from a woman, until they were convinced that Maggie was indeed the "mother" of this particular invention.

Beyond Bags

Knight also had to fend off a challenge to her patent by a rival inventor, who had spied on the construction of Knight's first prototype. The court decided in Knight's favor, and she persisted in her career. After leaving Columbia, she cofounded the Eastern Paper Bag Company in Hartford, Connecticut, and supervised her own machine shop in Boston. Between 1871 and 1911, she received 26 patents in her own name and is thought to have contributed to more than 50 inventions patented by others; she also built scores of unpatented devices. Upon her death in 1914, the press lauded her as America's "female Edison."

Among her most successful inventions were an easy-to-install window frame, a number-stamping machine, and a mechanical roasting spit. The humble paper bag, however, remains her greatest contribution to civilization. Even today, bag manufacturers rely on her basic concept. So the next time you decide to brown-bag your lunch, stop and give thanks to Maggie Knight.

✳ The British royal family changed its name from "Saxe-Coburg and Gotha" to "Windsor" in 1917, during World War I, because its original name sounded too German. It would have been difficult to fit onto a business card, as well. The English royals are still known as the House of Windsor.

✳ Toys for Tots began its yearly donation drive during the 1947 Christmas season.

✳ The first charter for the United Nations was signed in San Francisco. Fifty countries signed the document, which was written in five languages.

The Cast of Characters at the O.K. Corral

The most notorious gunfight in the Wild West featured an array of people—from the good to the bad and the ugly—who were perfectly suited for a Hollywood movie.

✳ ✳ ✳ ✳

The Setting

FIRST, THE FAMOUS showdown in Tombstone, Arizona, didn't take place in the O.K. Corral—it happened in the city's vacant lot No. 2. Somehow, "The Shoot-out in Vacant Lot No. 2" doesn't have quite the same ring to it, so a savvy journalist or scriptwriter must have moved the action a few yards over.

Second, despite what the movies may suggest, it wasn't a simple tale of white hats versus black hats. The real story has as many twists and turns as a warren of prairie dog tunnels, with a roundup of suspects that includes carousing cowboys, contentious lawmen, corrupt politicians, card sharks, cattle rustlers, a dentist named Doc, and Doc's lady friend (the appropriately named Big Nose Kate).

The Characters

What do we know for sure? On October 26, 1881, at around 3:00 P.M., four men entered the lot behind the O.K. Corral: They were Wyatt Earp, his brothers Virgil and Morgan, and John Henry "Doc" Holliday. There, they encountered Ike Clanton, his brother Billy, Frank and Tom McLaury, and Billy Claiborne. Thirty seconds later, both of the McLaury brothers as well as Billy Clanton were dead. Virgil and Morgan Earp sustained serious wounds and Holliday suffered a minor injury while Wyatt walked out without a scratch.

What brought them there? Trouble had been brewing between the Earp and Clanton factions for quite some time. Doc Holliday, a Philadelphia-trained dentist, preferred playing cards to pulling teeth, and this habit often left him short of cash. Earlier in 1881, he had been accused of stagecoach robbery by his own girlfriend, Big Nose Kate. The Earp brothers suspected that Ike Clanton had put her up to it to deflect suspicion from Clanton's friends. When four of those friends turned up dead, Clanton accused the Earps, and the bad blood began to boil.

The Gunfight

Who fired first? Most historians agree that Holliday and Morgan Earp started it, one wounding Frank McLaury and the other Billy Clanton. With that, as the locals say, "the ball had begun." An estimated 30 shots were fired within half a minute. Wyatt claimed that 17 were his, though he is only thought to have killed one man, Tom McLaury.

The Earps and Holliday were ultimately acquitted of any wrongdoing. Several months later, Morgan Earp was shot to death by unknown assailants. Wyatt spent the next two years tracking down everyone he thought was connected with his brother's death. Was he "brave, courageous, and bold," as the song says? Or was he just a ruthless vigilante? The jury is still out. One thing is certain, though: Wyatt Earp was an American original, and his story will be told for generations to come.

✳ **The fastest wind ever recorded on Earth blew through the suburbs of Oklahoma City, Oklahoma, on May 3, 1999. The 318-mile-per-hour gusts were recorded during an F5 tornado that destroyed hundreds of homes.**

✳ **The most rain in a three-day period fell on the tiny island of La Reunion in the South Indian Ocean. In March 2007, close to 13 feet of rain fell as Tropical Cyclone Gamede passed within 120 miles of the French-owned island.**

When One Wife Just Isn't Enough

Who has had the most wives? After much detective work, we present several worthy candidates.

✳ ✳ ✳ ✳

The Front-Runners

IT'S NOT EASY to get to the bottom of this one, because some contexts are shrouded in mystery and lore. Take King Solomon—the biblical king was said to have had 700 wives and another 300 concubines. If you take the Bible literally, you can stop reading now because he's your winner.

But if you allow for a little creative license—or, perhaps, divinely inspired symbolism—in the King Solomon story, then Warren Jeffs is probably your champion. Jeffs, the former president of the Fundamentalist Church of Jesus Christ of Latter Day Saints (FLDS), was reported to have amassed approximately 80 wives (his followers refuse to provide an exact number) by the time he was arrested as an accomplice to rape in 2006. The FLDS is a fundamentalist Mormon sect that is not affiliated with the similarly named church based in Salt Lake City, Utah. Polygamy is codified in FLDS beliefs. In fact, when his father died in 2002, Jeffs married many of the widows, partly to consolidate his power within the sect.

Speaking of power, we should also consider Dinka tribal chief Majak Malok Akot, who was reported to have had 26 wives when *The New York Times* checked in on him in 2003. At the time, he had 65 sons and 86 daughters, and half of his wives were pregnant. "It is true that I have been turned down for marriage twelve times," the chief admitted. "But I built a very happy family, thanks to my knowledge of how to deal with wives."

The Curious Story of Glynn Wolfe

Then there's Glynn "Scotty" Wolfe, a California Baptist minister who had 29 wives over the last 70 years of his life. Wolfe, who died in 1997, also claimed to have had 19 children and 40 grandchildren, but one of his sons has said that he had never met any of his purported siblings and didn't even know his own mother. Anyhow, the number 29 isn't in doubt; in fact, his final wife, Linda Essex, holds the record for having the most husbands, with 23.

Essex married Wolfe as a publicity stunt, and they didn't share a home, but they wrote letters to each other and were said to be fond of one another. For Essex, that's something of an achievement, because she said that she couldn't remember the order in which she married her husbands and that one of her marriages lasted only 36 hours.

Say What?

There is nothing worse than a sharp image of a fuzzy concept.

—Ansel Adams

When the well's dry, we know the worth of the water.

—Benjamin Franklin

An intellectual snob is someone who can listen to the "William Tell Overture" and not think of The Lone Ranger.

—Dan Rather

A computer once beat me at chess, but it was no match for me at kickboxing.

—Emo Philips

I think men who have a pierced ear are better prepared for marriage. They've experienced pain and bought jewelry.

—Rita Rudner

All of the problems we face in the United States today can be traced to an unenlightened immigration policy on the part of the American Indian.

—Pat Paulsen

Mysterious Marilyn

Marilyn Monroe's life story has been exposed and analyzed countless times. The problem is that the many versions seem to contradict each other, making it difficult to sort out even the simplest details of her complicated life.

✳ ✳ ✳ ✳

THE ICONIC FILM star whose work includes classics such as *How to Marry a Millionaire* and *Some Like It Hot* continues to be the subject of intense scrutiny. Yet misconceptions about her life abound, including the following:

Myth: Marilyn was illegitimate.

Fact: According to Marilyn's birth certificate, her mother's estranged husband, Martin Edward Mortensen, was her father, but Marilyn never believed this. Her mother, Gladys, left Mortensen after several months of marriage and proceeded to have a series of affairs, most notably with Stanley Gifford, an employee at the film lab where she worked. Mortensen, who had never met Marilyn, always claimed he was her real father. After his death in 1981, a copy of Marilyn's birth certificate was found in his effects, and it is now widely believed that he was telling the truth.

Myth: Marilyn was born blonde.

Fact: Marilyn Monroe's natural hair color was brown. In 1946, she was offered a job modeling for a series of Lustre Cream shampoo ads on the condition that she trade her flowing brunette curls for a straightened blonde hairstyle. It is said that she strongly resisted coloring her hair but ultimately relented under pressure. She was 20 years old at the time and would remain a blonde for the rest of her life.

Myth: Marilyn personified the dumb blonde stereotype.

Fact: Marilyn Monroe rose to stardom playing the "dumb blonde" and was considered a master of this Hollywood archetype. But was she actually featherbrained? She definitely played up that image for the public, but her private pursuits were surprisingly intellectual. She wasn't interested in vapid romance novels; instead, she was often observed on her movie sets absorbed in classics such as Thomas Payne's *The Rights of Man*. Her library was filled with titles by Willa Cather, Dorothy Parker, and Carson McCullers, among other notable authors. In one famous photograph, she is sitting in front of her book collection reading a copy of *Poetry and Prose: Heinrich Heine*.

Marilyn also took her work as an actress very seriously and insisted that every take be perfect, which often resulted in her being perceived as difficult to work with. Her 1955 departure from Hollywood to study with Lee Strasberg at the Actors Studio in New York City was a bold attempt to take control of her career. She even went so far as to start her own production company, which enabled her to reject any director or script of which she did not approve.

Myth: Marilyn committed suicide.

Fact: On August 5, 1962, Marilyn was found dead in her home in Brentwood, California. The Los Angeles County coroner's office classified her death as "probable suicide," but many people, especially those closest to her, never believed it. During the summer of 1962, things were looking up for Marilyn. She had just achieved a publicity coup with a cover story in *Life* magazine. Her contract with 20th Century Fox studios had been successfully renegotiated, and several projects were in the works. She was busy planning renovations of her new house, the first she had ever purchased (albeit with the help of her ex-husband Joe DiMaggio). To those who knew her well, it did not make sense that she would take her own life, and there are even conspiracy theorists who claim that President John F. Kennedy had a hand in her death. But given the fact that her long-term addiction to sleeping pills had led to near-overdoses in the past, the most logical explanation is that her death was an accident.

Prince Edward: Nazi Sympathizer?

Romance in high places can lead to lofty regal fantasies—even some lifted by Nazi schemes.

✳ ✳ ✳ ✳

Absolute Ruler? Absolutely Not!

MEMBERS OF BRITAIN's royal family are taught from birth how to be regal, with the pomp, public works, privilege, and everything else it entails. If the family member is next in line to the throne, learning these skills is vital. So it was in the 1930s for Edward, eldest son of King George V.

Even before George's death in 1936, Edward's behavior was raising royal eyebrows. He was great on the pomp. His public works were passable, although critics said he sometimes lacked the proper enthusiasm. As for privilege, to him it meant that anything he might want, including the power to set policy for the country's governance, was his as a birthright. That simply could not work in a democratic country. Then there was the problem of his having fallen in love with Wallis Simpson, a divorced American socialite.

Whether Wallis truly loved him or loved the notion of becoming the Queen of England is moot. Edward VIII gave up the throne for her, and she left her second husband for him; their marriage was lauded as *the* romance of the 20th century. However, Edward still held on to the delusion that his subjects would eventually welcome him back to the throne.

Loose Lips

Nazi Germany was rearming, ostensibly to defend itself against Communist Russia. Edward believed Hitler had exactly the right aggressive anti-Communist plan. He also believed Britain should support Germany as an active ally. Moreover, Edward expounded his views to anyone within hearing, including Nazi officials, their spies, and collaborators.

Perhaps Edward felt vindictive; after all, he was distantly related to the Romanovs, who had been executed by the Communists. In Edward's opinion, one simply did not go about executing royalty. Edward must have asked himself where the Communist onslaught would end. He was related to most of the crowned heads of Europe, and his German ties ran particularly deep.

From his abdication in 1936 until 1940, when he accepted the governorship of the Bahamas, Edward and Wallis lived first in France (until its fall to Hitler) and then in pro-Nazi Spain. In 1937, the couple toured Germany, where they were lionized by Hitler, Goering, Goebbels, von Ribbentrop, and company. The Nazi leaders treated Edward and Wallis as royalty.

Close Ties

Among Edward's closest confidantes during this period was Charles Bedaux, a man suspected of being a high-ranking Nazi espionage operative. Edward and Wallis married in Bedaux's French chateau, and Bedaux was an almost daily visitor to Edward's household. But from there, things become a little murky. Circumstantial evidence suggests Bedaux was a go-between for Edward and Hitler. By accident or design, Edward provided Hitler valuable intelligence in the days leading up to the blitzkrieg through the Low Countries and France.

While in Spain and, briefly, in Lisbon, Edward was actively courted by the Nazis to become their quisling King of England. Edward may even have been the originator of the idea.

Shut Up, Cover Up

Needing to keep Edward out of Britain because of his outspoken appeasement policies, Prime Minister Winston Churchill coaxed Edward into shipping out to the Bahamas.

The most intriguing evidence of Edward's potentially traitorous relationahip with the Nazis is the lengths the royal family went to in the immediate postwar years to find and destroy any documents that defined that relationship.

The Maligned Mrs. Lincoln

Mary Todd Lincoln was a lot of things: first lady, extravagant spender, generous hostess. And though a Southerner by birth, she was not, as is widely suspected, a Confederate spy.

✳ ✳ ✳ ✳

Flawed First Lady

BEING THE PRESIDENT'S wife is a grueling job—the hours are long and the demands are wearisome. Most first ladies manage to get through it relatively well, but for Mary Todd Lincoln, wife of Abraham, it was an agonizing experience fraught with relentless criticism, borderline mental illness, and personal tragedy.

Mary deeply loved her husband, whom she married despite the disapproval of her family and social peers. She saw in Lincoln a good, honest, talented man and was delighted when he won the presidency in 1860. But because Mary was a native of Kentucky and thus a Southerner by birth, rumors swirled throughout the course of the Civil War that the first lady was, in fact, a Confederate spy.

Guilt by Relation

It's easy to see how such rumors got started. According to historians and biographers, Mary devotedly agreed with and supported her husband's political beliefs and, like him, wanted only that the nation become whole again.

But one of Mary's brothers, three half-brothers, and three brothers-in-law all served in the Confederate army during the Civil War. How then, people wondered, could she truly support the Union? Not surprisingly, certain individuals—including many of Lincoln's political enemies—started a whisper campaign that perhaps Mary wasn't the Unionist she said she was.

The entire issue, however, was just scandalous hearsay without a shred of proof. Even today, with nearly 150 years of hindsight, there is absolutely no evidence that Mary Todd Lincoln passed government secrets to the South or even had the opportunity to do so. Indeed, Mary's interests as first lady were generally more social than political.

Can't Win for Losing

The whispered allegation that Mary Lincoln was a Confederate spy was just one of many things that made her time in the White House miserable. The belles of Washington society considered her silly and uncouth and took every opportunity to denigrate her. For example, when she hosted a large party in the White House as the war raged, she was condemned for her extravagance. And because two of her sons were ill at the time, she was castigated as being unmotherly and cold.

All of this was made worse by Mary's many emotional and physical problems. She suffered from excruciating headaches that sometimes left her bedridden for days, and she also experienced violent mood swings that caused more than one White House aide to describe her as unpredictable and difficult to get along with.

Mary was also familiar with death. She lost three of her four sons to various ailments and, of course, witnessed the assassination of her beloved husband at the hands of John Wilkes Booth.

Mary Todd Lincoln was a flawed woman who did her best under dire circumstances. It's unfair and inaccurate for her character to be impugned by untrue rumors regarding her patriotism.

Varina Howell Davis

Varina Howell Davis, the young wife of Confederate president Jefferson Davis, suffered similar indignities over the course of the war. Though she was born in Mississippi, her father, a wealthy plantation owner, had deep Northern roots—his father was an eight-term governor of New Jersey. As a result, many within the Confederacy wrongly condemned Varina as a Union sympathizer.

Taking the Plunge

In 1886, Carlisle Graham became the first person to strap himself into a barrel at Niagara Falls. Since then, a head-scratching assortment of nut-jobs have followed suit.

✳ ✳ ✳ ✳

The Awesome Appeal of the Falls

NIAGARA FALLS, ONE of the natural wonders of the world, draws millions of visitors each year. It evokes a sense of awe, romance, and the desire to climb into a barrel and plunge more than 150 feet. Okay, it only evokes that emotion in wackos, but there have been a surprising number of them. Over the past 125 years, more than a dozen people have sealed themselves in barrels or mounted other devices and gone over the falls on the wildest ride possible.

Niagara Falls has always been attractive to aspiring daredevils. Long before barrels came into vogue, Niagara Falls was the domain of tightrope walkers. The most famous of these was The Great Blondin, who made multiple high-wire trips across the breach. Funambulists still talk about the stunt that he pulled at the Falls in 1859, when he carried a stove out to the middle of the gorge and cooked an omelet before continuing to the other side.

Enter Carlisle Graham

The odd marriage of barrels and Niagara Falls began in 1886, when British barrelmaker Carlisle Graham strapped himself into one of his barrels and did a little whitewater rafting in the whirlpools at the base of the Falls. Thus began a minor barrel-rafting fad that lasted until 1901, when a 63-year-old schoolteacher named Annie Edson Taylor—perhaps the least likely daredevil ever—kicked it up a notch. Taylor outfitted a barrel with some pillows and a mattress, climbed in, and then—to the astonishment of onlookers—proceeded to float over the edge of the Falls. Perhaps the only thing more astonishing than a sexagenarian schoolteacher coming up with this dumb idea was that she survived.

A Steady Stream of Daredevils

Since then, daredevils have attempted to mimic Taylor's stunt by going over the Falls in barrels made of wood, steel, rubber, and plastic, as well as by other means of conveyance, such as kayaks. Of course, several died. One man, Charles Stephens, thought it wise to tie an anvil to his feet as ballast; when he hit the water, the anvil crashed through the bottom of the barrel, dooming Stephens to a watery grave. Another, Robert Overacker, attempted the stunt using a JetSki and a parachute—the only problem was that he forgot to fasten the parachute to his back.

Then there's Bobby Leach, who became the first male to successfully go over the Falls in a barrel in 1911. A few years later, however, he met his maker. How? By slipping on an orange peel.

* The longest cells in the human body are the motor neurons. They can be up to four-and-a-half-feet long and run from the lower spinal cord to the big toe.

* The human eye blinks an average of 3.7 million times per year.

* The longest-living cells in the body are brain cells, which can live a human's entire lifetime.

* Fifteen million blood cells are produced and destroyed in the human body every second.

* The brain requires more than 25 percent of the oxygen used by the human body.

* If your mouth was completely dry, you would not be able to distinguish the taste of anything.

* The human body has enough fat to produce seven bars of soap.

The Bloodthirsty Countess

Born to George and Anna Bathory in August 1560, Countess Erzsebet (Elizabeth) Bathory came from one of the wealthiest families in Hungary. Of course, all families have their secrets, and Elizabeth's had more than its fair share. One uncle was allegedly a devil worshipper, and an aunt was believed to be a witch. So when Elizabeth herself started acting a bit odd and suffering from violent, uncontrolled fits of rage, no one really thought much about it.

✳ ✳ ✳ ✳

A Taste for Blood

AT AGE 15, with no sign of her fits subsiding, Elizabeth married Ferencz Nádasdy and moved into his castle. By most accounts, the castle's dungeon gave Bathory her first opportunities to experiment with torture. With her husband gone for long periods of time, she apparently began experimenting with black magic, often inviting people to the castle to take part in strange, sadistic rituals. Legend has it that, during this time, in a fit of rage, Bathory slapped a young servant girl across the face, drawing blood. Allegedly, Bathory looked down at her hand, which was covered in the young girl's blood, and thought the blood was causing her own skin to glow. This, according to the legend, is why Bathory believed that the blood of virginal girls would keep her young forever.

In 1604, Nádasdy died, leaving Bathory alone in the castle. For a while, she traveled abroad and, by all accounts, continued her quest to fulfill her insatiable thirst for blood. But she eventually returned and purchased her own castle. Shortly thereafter, servant girls and young girls from the neighboring villages began disappearing in the middle of the night, never to be heard from again.

Ungodly Horrors

During this time period, villagers knew better than to speak out against nobility. So when people started implying that the countess was kidnapping young girls and murdering them in her castle, the villagers kept their mouths shut. Even when Bathory's carriage would ride through town late at night with young girls in the back, villagers still kept their heads down and went about their business. Villagers were often awakened in the middle of the night 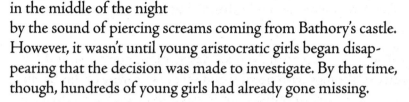 by the sound of piercing screams coming from Bathory's castle. However, it wasn't until young aristocratic girls began disappearing that the decision was made to investigate. By that time, though, hundreds of young girls had already gone missing.

In December 1610, King Matthias II of Hungary sent a group of men out to Bathory's castle to investigate claims that local girls were being held there against their will. Heading up the group was a man named Gyorgy Thurzo. It would be his subsequent testimony of what the group encountered that would bring the full weight of the court down on Bathory.

Thurzo later stated that when the group arrived at the castle, the things they found inside were so horrific and gruesome that he could not bring himself to write them down.

Thurzo said that inside the door they found a young girl, dead and apparently drained of blood. A short distance away, they found another girl, alive but near death. She also appeared to have lost a large amount of blood. Advancing down into the dungeon, the group encountered several young girls who were being held captive. The group released them and then began the search for Bathory herself. In the end, Bathory and four of her servants were taken into custody. The servants were taken into the village for questioning while Bathory herself was confined to her bedroom in the castle.

Unspeakable Acts

Twenty-one judges presided over the proceedings that began on January 2, 1611. Bathory remained in her castle while her four accomplices were questioned. The things these four individuals claimed took place in the castle were almost too horrific to describe. One of Bathory's employees, a dwarf named Ficzko, said that he personally knew of at least 37 girls the countess had killed. Bathory's childhood nurse, Ilona Joo, stated that she had personally helped Bathory kill somewhere in the neighborhood of 50 girls, using such horrific devices as cages filled with spikes, fire pokers, and oily sheets that were placed between victims' legs and set on fire.

As the proceedings went on, the descriptions got worse and worse: stabbings with needles and scissors, tearing off limbs, and even sewing girls' mouths shut. It was also made known that the countess enjoyed whipping and beating young girls until their bodies were swollen, at which point she would use a razor to draw blood from the swollen areas. There were even rumors that she bathed in the blood of the girls in an attempt to stay young.

In the end, the countess was found guilty of killing 80 girls. However, based on the number of bodies eventually recovered at the castle, the body count is probably as high as 650.

All four of Bathory's accomplices were put to death. But because the countess was a member of the nobility, she could not be executed for her crimes. Instead, she was moved to a series of small rooms in her castle and walled inside. All the doors and windows were sealed, with only a few small holes for air and one to allow food to pass though. The countess lived in her own private prison for three years before she died, still claiming she was innocent of all charges.

Mass Murderers vs. Serial Killers

Serial killers are made of sugar and spice and everything nice, and mass murderers are . . . wait, that's not right. The distinction between the two is actually very simple.

✳ ✳ ✳ ✳

The Mass Murderer

A MASS MURDERER KILLS four or more people during a short period of time, usually in one location. In most cases, the murderer has a sudden mental collapse and goes on a rampage, progressing from murder to murder without a break. About half the time, these outbreaks end in suicides or fatal standoffs with the police.

Various school shootings over the years have been instances of mass murder, as have been famous cases of postal workers, well, "going postal." A case in which someone murders his or her entire family is a mass murder. Terrorists are lumped into this category as well, but they also make up a group of their own.

The Serial Killer

A serial killer usually murders one person at a time (typically a stranger), with a "cooling off" period between each transgression. Unlike mass murderers, serial killers don't suddenly snap one day—they have an ongoing compulsion (usually with a sexual component) that drives them to kill, often in very specific ways.

Serial killers may even maintain jobs and normal relationships while going to great lengths to conceal their deadly habit. They may resist the urge to kill for long periods, but the compulsion ultimately grows too strong to subjugate. After the third victim, an aspiring killer graduates from plain ol' murderer to bona fide serial killer.

The Rest

In between these two groups, we have the spree killer and the serial spree killer. A spree killer commits murder in multiple locations over the course of a few days. This is often part of a general crime wave. For example, an escaped convict may kill multiple people, steal cars, jaywalk, and litter as he tries to escape the police. As with a mass murderer, a spree killer doesn't plan each murder individually.

The serial spree killer, on the other hand, plans and commits each murder separately, serial-killer style. But he or she doesn't take time off between murders or maintain a double life. It's all killing, all the time. One of the best-known examples is the Washington, D.C.-area beltway snipers who killed ten people within three weeks in October 2002.

Of course, if you see any of these types of killer in action, don't worry about remembering the right term when you call the police. They're all equally bad.

---

* Approximately 90 percent of crop circles in the world appear in England. The largest of these was found in Etchilhampton, Wiltshire, in 1996. The pattern formed an elongated group of circles 4,100 feet long. Another at nearby Milk Hill was made of 409 circles, the most in any one formation.

* The Romans worshipped some very specific gods. They had a goddess for Rome's sewer system (Cloacina) and another for thresholds and door hinges (Cardea). You just can't beat a divinely protected door hinge.

* There are 887 stone statues on Easter Island, though most never made it to their platforms.

* Galaxies often collide, and perhaps merge, with each other as they drift through the universe. Big galaxies tend to absorb smaller ones—the Milky Way Galaxy is currently merging with a tiny dwarf galaxy. Large galaxies interact, too. The Andromeda Galaxy, which is about the same size as our Milky Way, may collide with us in around 3 billion years, forming one huge elliptical galaxy.

* Investor, entrepreneur, and philanthropist Warren Buffett began his illustrious career by collecting and selling lost golf balls.

Chapter Two

Bizarre Truths About Cuisine

Chinese Food: Almost as American as Apple Pie

Sure, we call it "Chinese," but could the takeout Americans have grown so fond of actually be less East and more West? In that context, Chinese food is definitely a product of the United States.

✳ ✳ ✳ ✳

IN NEARLY EVERY case, so-called "American Chinese" foods were inspired by counterparts from China. Not surprisingly, however, the American versions of Chinese foods are more meat-centered and less dependent on vegetables than dishes that originate in the Far East. General Tso's chicken, sesame chicken, Chinese chicken salad, chop suey, chow mein, crab rangoon, fried rice, and Mongolian beef are among the many items at Chinese restaurants that are essentially American derivatives of staples from the motherland.

The origin of nearly every menu item at a typical American Chinese establishment is hotly contested. However, perhaps the most popular staple of these restaurants, the fortune cookie, is indisputably American—or more specifically, was created by a Chinese immigrant in the United States.

As with any great invention, several parties have been credited with thinking up the fortune cookie, including a Japanese landscape architect named Makota Hagiwara, who some say distributed the treat in San Francisco in the early 1900s. However, it is widely thought that Los Angeles baker and Chinese immigrant David Jung, later the founder of the Hong Kong Noodle Company, first handed out cookies containing encouraging words (the fortunes) to homeless Californians in 1918. Since Jung was a Presbyterian minister, the strips of paper he inserted in his cookies featured Bible scripture.

By the 1930s, several fortune-cookie factories were up and running. The paper-filled treats were folded by hand, and the fortunes were inserted using chopsticks until 1964. Today, fortune cookies are a hit everywhere. Even in . . . well, China. Fortune cookies first began surfacing in Asia simply because American tourists asked for them.

---

* Ermal Fraze invented the pop-top aluminum can in 1959. In 1963, he received U.S. patent number 3,349,949 for the design.

* Terminal velocity for a human is approximately 124 miles per hour. To reach this speed, you would have to fall from a height of at least 158 yards—about one and a half football fields.

* On September 13, 1859, California senator David Broderick established a record that is unlikely to ever be broken—or repeated, for that matter: He became the only sitting senator to be killed in a duel.

Have You Had Your McAloo Tikki Break Today?

The sun never sets on the McDonald's empire. Because the behemoth has restaurants on every continent except Antarctica and in more than 100 countries, it needs to adapt to local tastes and customs. Whether it's called "McDo," "Mackedonkan," or "de Mac," you'll find some menu items that are reassuringly familiar—and some, not so much.

✳ ✳ ✳ ✳

✳ **McAloo Tikki (India):** This vegetarian sandwich consists of a breaded, fried patty of spiced potatoes and peas topped with fresh tomato, onion, and vegan tomato mayonnaise on a toasted bun.

✳ **Twisty Pasta (Hong Kong):** Tired of pancakes for breakfast? Try this meal-in-a-bowl that contains chicken broth, pasta, tomatoes, cabbage, corn, greens, ham (or breakfast sausage), and a fried egg.

✳ **Rice Fantastic (Hong Kong):** Sometimes you feel like a bun; sometimes you don't. This sandwich is made from two flattened patties of sticky rice.

✳ **McOz (Australia):** This burger is made from Australian beef and "mouthwatering beetroot."

✳ **McShawarma (Israel):** In Israel, McDonald's offers kosher and nonkosher restaurants, but they all serve the McShawarma—a sandwich of shaved lamb wrapped in fluffy flatbread.

✳ **Tamago Double Mac (Japan):** This burger starts with the classic two all-beef patties, throws on some fairly typical bacon, but then finishes it with hot pepper sauce and a poached egg. Cheese is optional.

* **Seasoned Fries (Japan):** McDonald's famous french fries are shaken with powdered seasoning in a paper bag and are available in nori (seaweed), curry, BBQ, and Mexican flavors.

* **McKroket (Netherlands):** This breaded, deep-fried patty of beef and potato topped with Dijon mustard sauce is the McDonald's version of the traditional Dutch croquette.

* **Creamy Corn Ice Mix Sundae (Philippines):** When chocolate or caramel become too boring, consider corn. This sundae layers vanilla ice cream and sweet corn.

* **Spam Musubi (Hawaii):** Fancy some Spam in the morning? This breakfast dish consists of a slice of fried Spam on top of sticky rice, tied with a strip of seaweed.

* **McPoutine (Canada):** Poutine—the combination of french fries, gravy, and cheese curds—is practically the official dish of Quebec.

* **McCalabresa (Brazil):** This sandwich is the McDonald's take on a traditional Brazilian sandwich, consisting of a slab of pepperonilike sausage covered in vinaigrette.

* **Chicken McCurry Pan (India):** This dish is made of spicy bread filled with tomato curry, chicken, and peppers and topped with cheese.

* **McPalta (Chile):** This local favorite includes avocado paste smeared on pork or beef.

* **McChutney (Pakistan):** Ground meat and chutney are combined to make the patty for this sandwich.

* **McSpaghetti (Philippines):** This dish sounds like a small child's fantasy—a plate of spaghetti tossed with a sweet tomato sauce, chunks of hot dog, and powdered cheese.

Fact vs. Fiction:
The Shelf Life of a Twinkie

Can Hostess Twinkies really stay fresh for 50 years or more? If you were around during the Cold War in the 1950s and 1960s, when a nuclear attack from the Soviet Union seemed possible, you might believe they do.

✳   ✳   ✳   ✳

AT THE HEIGHT of the Cold War, Twinkies were staples of the survival foods people stocked in household bomb shelters. This helped spawn the notion that the spongy snacks could withstand not only a nuclear holocaust but also the ravages of time.

Truth is, a Twinkie's shelf life is about 25 days. If even that seems like a lot of stay-fresh time for a baked product, consider that Twinkies are a processed, packaged food and contain no dairy ingredients that can go bad in a hurry. Like many other commercially baked goods, they're tweaked with preservatives and stabilizing trans fats.

Check the label and you'll find such ingredients as vegetable and/or animal shortening and partially hydrogenated soybean, cottonseed, or canola oil. These artificially produced fats are more solid than clear liquid oils and are less likely to spoil. They help Twinkies stay soft and tasty, though not for years or decades.

The Cold War is history, but Twinkies are still plenty popular. Hostess bakers churn out 1,000 per minute, which puts the kibosh on another urban legend: Due to an error in market research, the company overproduced Twinkies two decades ago, hasn't made any since, and will not resume production until all the "vintage Twinkies" are eaten.

Delectable Dinners Throughout History

Throughout culinary history, people have eaten some mighty strange things. Although various odd foods probably seemed like good ideas at the time, believe it or not, they have fallen out of favor with most modern diners.

✳   ✳   ✳   ✳

Peacock

A POPULAR FOOD SERVED in ancient Greece, peacock also appeared at the court of Henry VIII. The whole roasted bird was often presented with a gold-leaf-gilded beak and adorned in an ornate cloak of its own feathers, which were removed and then replaced after cooking.

Roasted Locusts

John the Baptist ate this protein-rich insect in the desert, and the Book of Leviticus specifically mentions four species of locust that are permitted as food for Jews.

Grilled Beavers' Tails

Medieval Christians especially enjoyed beaver tails on the days when it was forbidden to eat meat. Because beavers live in water, they were conveniently classified as fish.

Sea Mammals

Seals and porpoises were eaten in England during the Middle Ages, along with boiled or roasted whale, a particularly economical choice because a single animal could feed hundreds of people. Plus, like beavers, the sea-dwelling animals were considered fish.

Swan

Swan consumption can be traced to the ancient Romans. Whole swans were also served by early English royalty for special occasions, often presented with a crown upon the roasted bird's head.

Raw Duck or Quail

Salted, without the heat of cooking, was a popular way for ancient Egyptians to enjoy duck and quail.

Cock Ale

Imbibers in 17th-century England could down a pint of this concoction made by boiling a whole rooster until it was jellified, then crushing it along with raisins and spices. The resulting fruity meat paste was then mixed with ale.

Ox Cheeks

Folks in merry ole England enjoyed ox in many forms. The cheeks were an especially popular and economical cut of meat and were served baked, boiled, or encased in a pie.

Dormouse

People from the days of ancient Rome through the Middle Ages enjoyed these rodents sauced, stuffed, or as a savory pastry or pie filling.

Rat, Dog, Elephant, et al.

While Paris was under siege by the Prussians between 1870 and 1871, folks pretty much ate anything that moved—including creatures from the Paris Zoo. Culinary delights of the time included rat, dog, cat, horse, feral sheep, and even elephant, all prepared with Parisian flair, of course.

There's Nothing Sweet About Them

A tip for those who rarely eat at trendy restaurants: If you see sweetbreads on the menu, don't start salivating at the thought of a warm muffin with butter dripping down the sides.

✳ ✳ ✳ ✳

Some Thymus Gland, Anyone?

WHEN YOU'RE THINKING sweetbreads, you should picture the thymus gland or pancreas of a young sheep, cow, or pig. And once you've conjured that unappetizing image, it might be best to exhale deeply and start focusing on taking a swig or two from your glass of wine.

Sweetbreads are a delicacy enjoyed throughout the world by people with adventurous palates, but the burger-and-fries types might not understand such culinary wanderlust. In fact, they might want to ask the question: What in the name of the Golden Arches is a thymus gland? The answer isn't pretty. A thymus gland contains two lobes—one in the throat and the other near the heart. The lobe near the heart—particularly from milk-fed young calves—is considered the best to eat because of its smooth texture and mild taste; as a result, it will cost you more at that trendy restaurant. Pancreas sweetbreads, or stomach sweetbreads, are much less common than their thymus counterparts.

Sweetbreads and other edible internal organs are often grouped together using the term "offal" (which, for those still ready to vomit, isn't a word for "awful" in some foreign language). It means the "off-fall," or the off-cuts, of a carcass.

Waste Not, Want Not

Since sweetbreads aren't sweet and aren't bread, how did they get their name? This is something of a mystery. The *historie of man*, published in 1578, sheds a splash of light on the matter:

"A certaine Glandulous part, called Thimus, which in Calues… is most pleasaunt to be eaten. I suppose we call it the sweete bread." Translation: They tasted good.

Back in those roughhewn days—before butcher shops and grocery stores—sweetbreads weren't considered a delicacy. Families butchered their own livestock and often ate every part, including the thymus gland and pancreas. Today, sweetbreads are prepared in many ways: You can poach, roast, sear, braise, or sauté them, and often season them with salt, pepper, onions, garlic, or thyme.

If you want to prepare sweetbreads, we have two pieces of advice. First, sweetbreads are extremely perishable, so be sure to cook them within 24 hours of your purchase. Second, they're probably not the ideal dish to serve on a first date.

---

* The halls of Congress are reputed to be haunted by a multitude of defunct politicians, among them John Quincy Adams and Daniel Webster. More surprising, perhaps, are the periodic sightings of a demonic cat.

* In the spring of 1930, the Senate almost voted to ban all dial telephones from the Senate wing of the Capitol, as the technophobic older senators found them too complicated to use.

* Morocco was the first country to recognize the United States as a sovereign nation, in 1777.

* The proud American motto "E pluribus unum"—out of many, one—was originally used by Virgil to describe salad dressing.

* Benjamin Franklin considered the bald eagle a "bird of bad moral character" and resented its being chosen to represent the United States of America.

* The founder of the Smithsonian, James Smithson, who in 1826 willed a then-staggering $508,318 to the United States "to found…an establishment for the increase and diffusion of knowledge," had never set foot in America.

The Real-Life Story of General Tso

For all of their military importance, generals have made many other notable contributions to civilization. Civil War general Ambrose Burnside, for example, had such an impressive pair of muttonchops that he inspired a new term: "sideburns." Then there's General Tso and his scrumptious chicken dish.

✳ ✳ ✳ ✳

General Tso's Incongruous Legacy

WHO WAS GENERAL TSO, anyway? And was he as good a general as he was a chef? As it turns out, General Tso (Zuo Zongtang) was a brilliant Chinese general who rose to fame during the Taiping Rebellion of 1850–64. By the time Tso helped crush the rebellion, his was a household name. Thus, it would seem likely that General Tso's chicken is a recipe that was invented for or named after him during his lifetime, in the same way that beef Wellington was named after the Duke of Wellington—right? Wrong.

Unfortunately, it appears that General Tso has about as much to do with the classic Chinese recipe that bears his name as General Eisenhower has to do with Mike and Ike's. According to most food historians, General Tso's chicken as we know it today wasn't even invented until the 1970s, when it was devised in New York City, far away from the southern provinces of China where Tso earned his glory.

Most accounts claim that General Tso's chicken—a sweet, spicy, crispy chicken dish—was introduced in 1973 by Peng Jia, a onetime chef to Chinese military and political leader Chiang Kai-shek and the proprietor of a Manhattan Chinese restaurant named Peng's. Peng claimed that he actually invented the dish while working for Chiang sometime in the 1950s, but that the original recipe was far different from the dish that so many Americans love today.

A Taste Sensation

It may be hard to believe now—every town has a "Best Hunan" languishing in a strip mall, after all—but when Peng opened his New York restaurant in 1973, Hunan cuisine was virtually unheard of in the United States. Instead, most Chinese restaurants in the United States featured Cantonese cuisine, which is far blander and sweeter than its Hunan counterpart.

Peng—concerned the American palate was unprepared for the fiery, sour taste of his original dish—sweetened the recipe. The dish was an instant hit and gained massive exposure when Henry Kissinger—whose every move was covered in the social columns and gossip rags of the day—made Peng's restaurant a regular hangout and General Tso's chicken his usual meal. Soon, General Tso's chicken could be found on Chinese menus from coast to coast.

Why the name General Tso's chicken? Peng never said. But considering that he invented the dish for Chiang Kai-shek, the name was probably one of several that the chef used to honor the military greats who had come before the Nationalist leader.

Rejected in the Homeland

Interestingly, Peng had less success with the dish in his native China. In 1990, he returned to Hunan province, where he opened a restaurant that featured the dish that had made Hunan ground zero for international Chinese cuisine. The establishment closed quickly.

The reason? General Tso's chicken, the symbol of Hunan cooking throughout the world, was too sweet for the Hunan people.

---

* The Bible contains 32 references to dogs, but none to cats.

* A mouse only takes 35 days to reach its adult sexual maturity.

* The average snail lives six years.

* Before Popeye, Olive Oyl's boyfriend was named Ham Gravy.

Tasty (but Troublesome) Foods

Some of the most common foods are among the worst offenders when it comes to causing indigestion. Learning what your body can and can't handle may therefore help you avoid those dreaded post-meal pains.

✳   ✳   ✳   ✳

SURE, TO SOME people, the foods below are among the top contenders on their list of all-time favorites. But some of these American classics may actually be behind many of the digestive system protests we experience. So do yourself a favor and start listening to what your body is telling you about these foods. Letting your body's digestive feedback guide your food choices may just put an end to some serious grumbling from your gut.

Chocolate

Unfortunately, this sweet treat tops the list of digestive downers. Chemicals in chocolate cause some of the digestive muscles to relax, allowing burning acid to creep back up out of the stomach, causing classic heartburn. It's not all negative, though: A small amount of chocolate shouldn't do much damage. Eating too much of it, nutritionists say, is when people start to see—or, more accurately, feel—problems.

Beans

It's no surprise that the so-called "magical fruit" doesn't sit well in the stomach. The reason? A specific enzyme must be present in order for beans to be broken down in the digestive tract, and most people don't have enough of it to properly digest these little gas producers.

Broccoli

It's the natural sulfur compounds in broccoli that can cause digestive discomfort for some folks. But the solution is definitely not to banish broccoli from your table—it's far too valuable a source of essential, health-preserving nutrients. Simply steam or otherwise cook the broccoli before eating it. Cooking helps break up the troublesome sulfur compounds and prevent the tummy tumbling act.

Chicken Nuggets

Doctors say the fried chicken nugget is just plain bad for your insides. The grease makes digesting it a chore for your system, especially if you are already prone to stomach problems. Bake the nuggets instead, and your belly will thank you.

Gum

Dieticians and dentists are at war on this one. Sugar-free gum, it turns out, is not always problem-free. Sorbitol, the sugar substitute used in many brands, can really get some guts grumbling. Gums that have ten grams or more of sorbitol seem to be the greatest offenders.

Ice Cream

If you aren't careful, this high-fat frozen treat can lead to bothersome bellyaches. The stomach needs more time to process both cold foods and foods high in fat compared to warm and/or fat-free foods. That slower transit time can leave you feeling full and bloated, especially if you overdo—and we all know how easy it is to do that with ice cream! Plus, ice cream contains the milk sugar lactose, and if you are among the many adults who do not have enough of the lactase enzyme needed to digest lactose, eating ice cream may leave your tummy rumbling and you fumbling for relief.

Mashed Potatoes

Dairy is also the potential troublemaker in this familiar food. The milk or cream mixed into most mashed creations can cause gastrointestinal upset in those who are short of the enzyme needed to digest lactose, the sugar found in milk-based foods. When eating at a restaurant, your best bet may be to order another type of spud (such as boiled potatoes) or a different side dish instead. At home, though, you can use lactose-free milk to make your mashed potatoes so they're easier on your digestive system.

Onions

Eating these tear-inducing vegetables raw isn't just bad for your breath—it can send your stomach into overdrive. Like broccoli, however, cooking the onions first can cut back their kick.

Orange Juice

Despite its status as a beloved morning beverage, OJ is probably not the first thing you should consume at the breakfast table. Its high level of acidity can cause irritation of the digestive tract, particularly when consumed on an empty stomach. So if you just can't face the day without your morning glass of orange juice, eat a bagel or some toast first.

Peppers

Sure, spice can be nice, just be aware it can come with a price. Some folks discover too late that the sweat- and tear-inducing heat of jalapeños and other hot peppers can linger, causing an unpleasant case of heartburn or indigestion. If you discover you're one of those sensitive sorts, there's not much you can do to prevent such unpleasant aftereffects other than skipping the spicy stuff to begin with.

---

* In 1843, the first commercial Christmas card was printed in England, using illustrations by John Calcott Horsley, a noted London artist of the time. The press run was 1,000 cards. Today, in the United States alone, two billion cards are sent every Christmas—something of a hallmark.

* Think you can go a long time without eating? Adult crocodiles can go an entire year without a bite.

* The word "nerd" comes from Dr. Seuss, who first used the term in his 1950 book *If I Ran the Zoo*.

The Bitter Truth About Toothpaste

If you've ever taken a sip of orange juice right after brushing your teeth, the taste probably almost made you gag. There's a simple reason why.

✳ ✳ ✳ ✳

WHAT EXACTLY MAKES good old orange juice taste downright disgusting right after you've brushed your teeth? The citric acid found in orange juice and an ingredient in toothpaste called sodium lauryl sulfate (SLS). Of course, your taste buds also play an important part.

Most toothpastes contain SLS, a foaming detergent that manufacturers add because they believe it makes users feel like the toothpaste is getting their teeth all sparkly and clean. Scientists, however, say that this agent doesn't actually do much of anything, except, well, make your orange juice taste putrid. The SLS affects the taste buds on the tongue by suppressing their sensitivity to sweet tastes and enhancing their sensitivity to bitter and sour tastes.

This means that all you can taste in that first swig of OJ are the bitter and sour of citric acid, which is found naturally in oranges. Many orange juice manufacturers actually add extra citric acid to their products, in which case that disgusting taste caused by SLS will be even more intense.

But fear not. Walk into any health-food store, and you'll find several natural toothpastes that don't contain SLS. You won't get much foam from them, but they will clean and whiten your teeth just as well as any SLS-laden brands. And, yes—orange juice will taste just as sweet as it's supposed to.

A Feast for the Fearless: The World's Most Revolting Foods

Turning our attention briefly to some of the most curious delicacies of the world, we present the following culinary adventures, from mouse-flavored liquor to garlic-seasoned spider.

❋   ❋   ❋   ❋

Baby Mice Wine

THOSE BRAVE MEN and women who enjoy eating the worm from the bottom of a tequila bottle and want to advance to spirit-soaked vertebrates might be interested in baby mice wine, which is made by preserving newborn mice in a bottle of rice wine. This traditional health tonic from Korea and China is said to aid the rejuvenation of one's vital organs. Anecdotal evidence, however, suggests that the sight of dead baby mice floating helplessly in liquor is more likely to break your heart than rejuvenate it.

Balut

Balut are eaten in the Philippines, Cambodia, Vietnam, and China. They are duck eggs that have been incubated for 15 to 20 days (a duckling takes 28 days to hatch) and then boiled. After boiling, the egg is consumed—both the runny yolk and the beaky, feathery, veiny duck fetus. Balut are usually sold on the streets for the equivalent of about 25 cents each; one can have them with coarse salt or vinegar or just plain. Folks who are trying balut for the first time are strongly advised to keep their eyes tightly closed.

Casu Marzu

The Sardinian delicacy *casu marzu* is a hard, sheep's milk cheese infested with *Piophila casei*, the "cheese fly." The larvae eat the cheese and release an enzyme that triggers a fermentation process, causing their abode to putrefy. The cheese is not considered true casu marzu until it becomes a caustic, viscous, gluey mass that burns your mouth and wriggles on your tongue when you eat it. *Nota bene:* The cheese fly is also called "the cheese skipper," because its larvae have the amazing ability to leap up to six inches in the air when disturbed. Since the larvae rightfully consider it disturbing to be eaten, it is suggested that consumers of casu marzu make use of protective eye gear during the repast.

Cobra Heart

This Vietnamese delicacy delivers precisely what it promises: a beating cobra heart, sometimes accompanied by a cobra kidney and chased by a swig of cobra blood. Preparations involve a large blade and a live cobra. If you find yourself in the uncomfortable situation in which the snake has already been served but you feel your courage failing, ask for a glass of rice wine and drop the heart into it. Bottoms up!

Escamoles

Escamoles are the eggs, or larvae, of the giant venomous black *Liometopum* ant. This savory Mexican chow, which supposedly has the consistency of cottage cheese and a surprisingly buttery and nutty flavor, can be found both in rural markets and in multistar restaurants in Mexico City. A popular way to eat escamoles is in a taco with a dollop of guacamole, but it is said that they are also quite delicious fried with black butter or with onions and garlic.

Hákarl

Hákarl, an Icelandic dish dating back to the Vikings, is putrefied shark meat. Traditionally, it has been prepared by burying a side of shark in gravel for three months or more; nowadays, it might be boiled in several changes of water or soaked in a large vat filled with brine and then cured in the open air for two months. This is done to purge the shark meat of urine and trimethylamine oxide. Sharks have an extra concentration of both to maintain essential body fluid levels, but the combination makes the meat toxic. Since rancid shark meat is not considered all that tasty, native wisdom prescribes washing it down with a hearty dose of liquor.

Lutefisk

If the idea of rotten shark meat does not appeal, consider *lutefisk*, or "lye fish"—possibly the furthest from rotten that food can get. This traditional Scandinavian dish is made by steeping pieces of cod in lye solution. The result is translucent and gelatinous, stinks to the high heavens, and corrodes metal kitchenware. Enjoy it covered with pork drippings, white sauce, or melted butter, with potatoes and Norwegian flatbread on the side. (As a side note: The annual lutefisk-eating contest in Madison, Minnesota, is scheduled right before an event called the Outhouse Race. This might not be entirely a coincidence.)

Pacha

This dish can be found everywhere sheep can be found, especially in the Middle East. To put it simply, *pacha*, which is the Iraqi name for it, is a sheep's head stewed, boiled, or otherwise slow-cooked together with the sheep's intestines, stomach, and feet for five to six hours. Other meats might also be added to the broth. Something to keep in mind: If you are served this dish in Turkmenistan, where it is called *kelle-bashayak*, this means two things—one, you're the guest of honor at the gathering, and two, you will be expected to help consume the head or else risk offending the hosts.

Spiders

Spiders are popular fare in parts of Cambodia, especially in the town of Skuon; however, they are not part of the traditional cuisine and were not widely eaten until the horror years of the bloody Khmer Rouge regime in the late 1970s, when food became scarce. After the country was rebuilt, the villagers' taste for spiders did not recede entirely. Today, tarantulas are sold on the streets for about ten cents per spider and are said to be very good fried with salt, pepper, and garlic.

What About the Other 56 Sauces?

The label on a bottle of Heinz ketchup says that the company makes 57 varieties of sauce. In fact, the famous slogan is merely a marketing ploy from way back when.

✳ ✳ ✳ ✳

In the Beginning...

IN OUR OPINION—ACTUALLY, in the opinion of most reasonable, intelligent humans—ketchup is a miracle sauce. It's a modern-day Balm of Gilead that not only heals all culinary wounds but turns everything it touches into something really, really delicious. We can't help but notice, though, that each time we take out a bottle of Heinz ketchup to douse our plate, the little label near the neck promises another 56 varieties of this magical substance. Could it be?

Sadly, no. In fact, there's only one type of ketchup—tomato. But ketchup isn't the only item that Heinz makes. Henry J. Heinz didn't even get his start in the condiment industry by selling ketchup. Born in 1844 in Pittsburgh, Heinz began his food-sales career as a preteen, hawking vegetables that he grew himself.

Later, in his spare time outside of his job managing the family brick-making business, Heinz began selling prepared horseradish door to door. He didn't get into the ketchup game until 1876, by which time he'd already built a relatively large condiments business selling horseradish, pickles, and sauerkraut (hey, he was in Pittsburgh).

The Origin of a Slogan

In 1896, Heinz struck upon his famous slogan. Unlike Heinz's delicious ketchup, the story behind the slogan's conception is rather bland. As Heinz was riding an elevated train in New

York City, he noticed an advertisement for a shoe store offering "21 styles" of shoes. For reasons unexplained, Heinz was captivated by this rather mundane advertisement and, soon after, decided upon the now-famous "57 varieties" motto.

There is no definitive explanation for why H. J. chose that number. At the time, he was not offering 57 sauce varieties, though he was peddling more than 60 kinds of food, including something called "euchred pickles." (We've played euchre while pickled, but we have no idea what euchred pickles are.) Despite the banality of the slogan, it seemed to resonate: By the early 1900s, the Heinz company was far and away the most popular purveyor of condiments and prepared sauces.

More than Just a Ketchup Company

Nowadays the Heinz company sells well more than a thousand products, ranging from baby food to barbecue sauce. Of course, only one of these products really matters—and all God-loving Americans know what it is.

This leads us to another pressing issue: What's the difference between catsup and ketchup? The answer: Nothing, really.

---

* A racehorse from the early 1900s named Lolly Pop provided the inspiration for the lollipop candy name.

* The average dog runs about 19 miles per hour.

* Prior to becoming a dictator, Fidel Castro spent some time in the ballpark: He played baseball for the University of Havana during the 1940s.

* On the first slot machines, the symbols on each reel were suits from playing cards. After slots were banned in 1902, the machines were changed to offer gum, candy, and drinks—and the card suits were covered over with images of gum and fruit. The cherries are still used, but the sticks of gum turned into the black bars seen on many slot machines today.

Food Science: How They Salt Peanuts in the Shell

No, bioengineers haven't created a super breed of plants that produce naturally salty peanuts (yet). The method for salting peanuts isn't nearly that complicated.

✳ ✳ ✳ ✳

To SALT PEANUTS while they're still in the shell, food manufacturers soak them in brine (salty water). In one typical approach, the first step is to treat the peanuts with a wetting agent—a chemical compound that reduces surface tension in water, making it penetrate the shell more readily. Next, the peanuts are placed into an enclosed metal basket and immersed in an airtight pressure vessel that is filled with brine. The pressure vessel is then depressurized to drive air out of the peanut shells and suck salt water into them.

Peanuts may go through several rounds of pressurization and depressurization. Once the peanuts are suitably salty, they are rinsed with clean water and spun on a centrifuge in order to get rid of the bulk of the water. Finally, they are popped into an oven so that the drying process can be completed.

Now, if they could just figure out how to cram some chocolate into those peanuts.

✳ Safe driving is a major concern for legislators: New York State has made it illegal for blind people to drive. Meanwhile, Tennessee took matters a country mile further when legislators prohibited driving while asleep.

✳ The McDonald brothers—founders of the "Billions Sold" fast food chain—sold their business to Ray Kroc for $2.7 million in 1961.

Calling Hannibal Lecter

As the villainous cannibal from The Silence of the Lambs *would confirm, there are some choice cuts of meat on the human body. What exactly are the tastiest parts? Read on to find out.*

✳ ✳ ✳ ✳

A Crash Course on Cannibalism

THIS TOPIC COMES up all the time. After all, what if the plane carrying your national rugby team crashes in the mountains, as happened to the Uruguayan team in 1972? Or your wagon train is trapped for the winter on a desolate mountain pass, like the infamous Donner Party? You may need to know just which cuts of human flesh are the tastiest in such situations.

Okay, we're kidding. This topic almost never comes up. And since *Bon Appétit* has yet to publish its "Cannibal" issue—the headline would be easy to write: EAT ME—we're forced to go to primary sources to determine which parts of the human body are the most succulent. Fortunately, there aren't many of them.

According to archaeological evidence, human cannibalism has a long history that dates back to the Neanderthals. Despite the stereotype that cannibals only live on remote islands or in the deepest jungles, evidence of cannibalism has been found in cultures on nearly every continent, including Europe and North America. However, most cannibalistic practices throughout history were of a ritual nature, and there were few food critics writing up snappy reviews of their human feasts. For that, we have to consult those individuals throughout history who dined on other humans for pleasure.

The current living expert on cannibalism—Armin Meiwes, the German cannibal who is serving a life sentence for devouring a willing victim—likened the taste of his "cannibalee" to pork. Meiwes prepared his meal in a green pepper sauce, with a side of croquettes and brussels sprouts. Science seems to agree with Meiwes. Some Japanese researchers manufactured "an electro-mechanical sommelier," a kind of gastronomist robot capable of sampling wines, cheeses, meats, and hors d'oeuvres and identifying what it has been fed. When one reporter stuck his hand in the robot's maw, the two-foot-tall robot immediately identified it as prosciutto. When the accompanying cameraman offered his hand, the mechanical gourmand declared, "Bacon."

And the Tastiest Part Is...

So, what is the tastiest part of the human body? That seems to be a matter of debate. Early-20th-century murderer and cannibal Albert Fish declared that the buttocks were the choicest cut, but latter-day cannibal Sagawa Issei disagrees, claiming that the thighs get that honor. In Fiji, where cannibalism was practiced until the late 1860s, men (women apparently were forbidden from partaking in this tasty treat) also favored the thighs (they also preferred the flesh of nonwhite women).

So there you have it: If you've been dying to know, the thighs and buttocks are the prime cuts of a human. Now just do us a favor: Lose our dinner invitation.

---

* Three presidents died on the Fourth of July: Thomas Jefferson, John Adams, and James Monroe.

* The most commonly used letter in the English language is "e." The most common consonant is "t," and the most common second letter in a word is "h." (No surprise, seeing as the most popular word in the English language is "the"!)

* There are pink dolphins in the Amazon River.

* The world's largest bagel weighed 868 pounds and was a full six feet in diameter. It was made at Bruegger's Bagels in Syracuse, New York.

A Curious Pairing: Asian Palm Civets and Coffee

That's right—Asian palm civets help to produce some of the most coveted coffee beans on the planet. But you'll never guess the role that the furry little animal plays.

✳ ✳ ✳ ✳

The Rumors Aren't (Entirely) True

So YOU'VE HEARD the stories, and you've sworn that you'd never drink coffee made from beans that have exited a weasel's backside. Luckily, you'll never get the opportunity. Those ultra-gourmet beans that sell for anywhere from $100 to $600 a pound didn't come out of a weasel. The animal in question is actually the Asian palm civet. Does that make you feel better?

No? Perhaps you're like columnist Dave Barry, who dismisses the stuff as "poopacino" and thinks the whole craze for exotic brews is nothing but a tempest in a coffee cup. But *kopi luwak*, as it is known in Indonesia, got a big thumbs-up from Oprah Winfrey in 2003 when representatives of the Coffee Critic—a Ukiah, California, coffee shop—offered her a taste. Winfrey gamely took a sip right on her show and declared the so-called "weasel coffee" eminently fit to drink. (Barry, for the record, opines that it "tastes like somebody washed a dead cat in it." Take your pick.)

Enter the Asian Palm Civet

What's the story here? The Asian palm civet, or luwak, is a cat-size nocturnal mammal that's native to Indonesia, southern India, East Africa, Southeast Asia, the Philippines, and the south coast of China. By all accounts, luwaks are particularly fond of ripe coffee fruit. They digest the flesh of the fruit and excrete the beans, which are then gathered by grateful coffee farmers. So what's the attraction? According to one theory, the acids in the luwak's stomach dissolve the proteins in the bean's coating that cause the bitter aftertaste that accompanies more traditional blends. When brewed, *kopi luwak* supposedly has a mellower and sweeter flavor than regular java.

This theory has been put to the test by researchers at Canada's University of Guelph. In 2004, food science professor Massimo Marcone concluded that enzymes in the luwak's digestive tract do indeed leach some of the proteins from the bean's outer shell. (It should be noted that most people in blind taste tests conducted by the same researchers could not tell the difference between *kopi luwak* and other coffees.) Marcone, who collected his own beans in Ethiopia and Indonesia, allayed fears of contamination by pointing out that coffee producers in Asia wash the luwak-derived beans extensively.

Exit the Asian Palm Civet

No one knows who first decided to clean and roast the luwak's droppings. *Kopi luwak* was cherished in Asia long before Western importers decided to capitalize on its rarity and unusual origin. And capitalize they do: A single cup in one of the few American bistros that serves it costs significantly more than normal joe. Who would have thought that a pile of poop could be transformed into a pot of gold?

✳ The cucumber is considered a fruit, not a vegetable.

✳ M&M's are named after the candy's two creators: Forrest Mars Sr. and Bruce Murrie.

✳ Armadillos are able to walk underwater.

✳ Couples married in the first three months of the year tend to have higher divorce rates than those married in the later months.

✳ The founder of Kodak, George Eastman, is said to have hated having his photo taken.

✳ Fish sometimes cough underwater.

✳ Over a lifetime, an average human spends about six months on the toilet.

The World's Weirdest Cocktails

In the good old days, those who bellied up to the bar had fairly limited choices—whisky, vodka, and maraschino cherries could only yield so many combinations. But these days, with advancements in liquor distilling, flavor infusing, and general food and beverage manipulation, bartenders seem to come up with funkier cocktails every day and late into the night.

✳ ✳ ✳ ✳

The Titanic

At Citarella: The Restaurant in the Big Apple, you can enjoy this concoction of mashed grapes, elderflower syrup, vodka, and scoops of champagne sorbet. But since this potent ship can take you down, you'll need to hail a cab after drinking one for sure.

The Mayoty Dog

Koji Nakamura owns the Mayonnaise Kitchen restaurant in suburban Tokyo. Here, mayo is featured in everything on the menu, including beverages like the Mayoty Dog—a version of the classic "Salty Dog" cocktail that has mayo instead of salt on the rim of the glass.

92 in the Shade

A combination of mango puree, tequila, and red habañero pepper syrup is what patrons at the Blue Water Grill in New York City get when they order this martini. What, no guacamole garnish?

The Hunter

At Kirkland, Washington's Jager Bar & Restaurant, order this martini made with horseradish-infused vodka, Grand Marnier, and a garnish of grilled beef tenderloin tip. We're guessing it comes well done.

The Amaretto Cheesecake

Who needs regular old cheesecake when you can have a cheese-cake cocktail? A consulting company called Drink Tank develops "Caketails" and "Pietinis." This particular offering contains cream cheese, amaretto, roasted almonds, and, of course, the traditional graham cracker crumbs.

Rhubarb & Vanilla

The manager of San Francisco's Aziza Restaurant wanted to increase bar traffic with some eye-catching cocktails, so he developed this one. With rhubarb-infused vodka, bourbon, vanilla bean, Stoli Vanil, lime juice, and black peppercorns, this cocktail is sweet, salty, *and* weird!

Brain Hemorrhage

This shot is ghoulishly good for Halloween, owing to its name and bizarre appearance. When Irish cream is poured into peach schnapps, the cream curdles instantly. With a dash of bright red grenadine, you've got a violent looking beverage with a sweet aftertaste. Mmm . . . hemorrhage.

The Man from Nantucket

This martini, served at the Biltmore Room in New York City, features Nantucket-made Triple 8 vodka and garlic-stuffed black olives. Pucker up!

History's Most Expensive Cocktail?

In 2007, a cocktail fetched £35,000 (nearly $70,000) at a nightclub in London. The beverage was made of Louis XII cognac, Cristal Rosé champagne, sugar, angostura bitters, and a few flakes of 24-carat edible gold leaf. There was an 11-carat white-diamond ring at the bottom of the glass, too. If anyone's up for another round, we're not buying.

It Should Be Stirred, Not Shaken

Contrary to what James Bond so famously declared, a martini should never, ever be shaken. And it should contain gin, not vodka.

✳ ✳ ✳ ✳

007 Shoots and Misses

Ah, the martini, that quintessential American symbol of class, elegance, and alcoholism. Journalist H. L. Mencken called it "the only American invention as perfect as a sonnet." Historian Bernard DeVoto opined that the martini is "the supreme American gift to world culture"—a sad testament to America's cultural legacy, if true (taking nothing away from the martini, of course). Winston Churchill and Franklin Roosevelt were known for sipping martinis as they went about defeating the Nazis and salvaging our civilization. But perhaps nobody did as much for the martini as fictional secret agent James Bond, who made the drink synonymous with debonair elegance. And we all know the recipe that Mr. Bond demanded from his bartenders: vodka, straight up, very cold, and—always, always—shaken, not stirred.

As it turns out, 007 might know a great deal about wearing tuxedos, using ingenious gadgets, and getting female foreign agents to bend to his will, but when it comes to the martini, he's a bit of a rube. According to tradition, a martini is made with gin and is always stirred.

Why Stirring Is the Way to Go

There are good reasons why a martini should only be stirred. Most mixologists agree that shaking should be reserved for cloudy drinks—cocktails made with fruit juice, dairy products, or eggs (yes, eggs)—and that clear drinks should usually be stirred. The ingredients in a cloudy drink require more thorough mixing; vigorous shaking does a better job of blending them than stirring. Meanwhile, clarity is an important part of a clear drink's presentation; shaking it causes air bubbles to form, which makes it less appealing to the eye.

But it's more than a matter of presentation. When a bartender mixes a drink, he's not just blending the ingredients—he's also chilling them with chunks of ice, which are typically strained out when the cocktail is poured. As the ice cools the drink during the mixing process, it begins to melt; this adds a small amount of water to the recipe.

This "watering down" is desirable as long as it's strictly controlled, because it helps to temper the bite of the liquor. Shaking a drink rather than stirring it results in a colder, more watery finished product. These qualities can sometimes enhance a cocktail, but in a drink like a martini—which is simply a precisely measured blend of gin and vermouth—a little extra water can be ruinous. It's obvious, based on this, that martinis need to be stirred.

---

* The game *Simon Says* was originally set to be called *Do This, Do That*.

* The spots on dice are called "pips."

* Chinese households used to set off firecrackers as a form of fire alarm.

* A typical American buys 17 yards of dental floss every year of his or her life.

* The world goes through about 1.75 billion candy canes every year.

* There was once a coffee-scented postage stamp in Brazil.

* Ever wonder why Chicago O'Hare Airport is abbreviated ORD? It used to be called Orchard Field, and the shorthand stuck.

* Talk about irony: The official motto of New Hampshire, printed on its license plates, is "Live Free or Die"—and those license plates are made at a state prison.

* The oldest university in America is Harvard.

* It cost nearly $41 million to build the Empire State Building. The New York City landmark has more than 10 million bricks.

The Gift that Keeps On Giving

We decided to find out how much beef jerky you can get out of a cow. Our results are certain to delight jerky lovers.

✳   ✳   ✳   ✳

The Wonders of Jerky

THERE'S A COMMON misconception that men would starve to death if they were left to their own devices. This is patently untrue—as long as there's a convenience store nearby that sells beef jerky. Indeed, a beer, a baseball game, and a bag of beef jerky might make for the perfect afternoon for the average male. A serious beef jerky habit can get pretty expensive, though—even the cheapo, gas-station variety costs a few dollars for just a couple of ounces of dried, peppery goodness. It makes you wonder whether it wouldn't be easier just to cut out the middleman and go straight to the cattle auction.

As it turns out, you can get quite a bit of beef jerky from a single cow, but determining just how much requires a little agricultural mathematics. A large "beef animal" can weigh over 1,200 pounds—this counts everything, including the guts, bones, and other inedible material. Before being turned into jerky, the cow needs to be butchered and trimmed into lean cuts (the best jerky is made from boneless steaks and roasts).

Pull Out Your Calculator

According to the agricultural school at South Dakota State University, the yield of an average cow that's butchered for lean beef is about 38 percent of its original weight—which means that a 1200-pound feeder will give you about 456 pounds of steaks, roasts, and ground beef with which to work. Next, the high-quality meat is cured and seasoned before being sliced into strips and dried. Meanwhile, the ground beef can be made into lower-quality jerky, which is labeled as "ground and formed" on the packaging. During the drying process, the meat loses up to three-quarters of its original weight; however, this still leaves us with a very generous portion of beef jerky from a single cow: roughly 115 pounds. Considering that an average bag of beef jerky weighs 1.8 ounces, we're talking more than 1,000 bags of beef jerky from a single cow.

Of course, this is only a hypothetical situation—in the real world, the fattier cuts of meat are almost never used for jerky, because they're more difficult to dry and are (in their jerky form) much more perishable. Besides, as delicious as jerky is, steakhouse patrons know that there are other, more satisfying uses for the loin, tenderloin, and rib-eye cuts.

At any rate, when you consider the massive amount of work that's involved in butchering, cleaning, curing, slicing, and dehydrating a cow, it's probably better to leave it to the professionals. Hey, we've got baseball to watch.

Say What?

The only place success comes before work is in the dictionary.

—Vince Lombardi

One of the definitions of sanity is the ability to tell real from unreal. Soon we'll need a new definition.

—Alvin Toffler

Carpe per diem—seize the check.

—Robin Williams

Death is no more than passing from one room into another. But there's a difference for me, you know. Because in that other room I shall be able to see.

—Helen Keller

There is more stupidity than hydrogen in the universe, and it has a longer shelf life.

—Frank Zappa

Grew-some Gluttons

When truly great eaters strap on the feedbag, their gastric achievements seem boundless. Here are a few grand masters who lived mostly to eat, and one amateur who ate solely to live.

✳ ✳ ✳ ✳

Diamond Jim Brady

RAILROAD MAGNATE Diamond Jim Brady could make quick work out of almost any meal placed before him. Cheekily described as "my best 25 customers" by the owner of Charles Rector's, a Manhattan bistro and favorite Brady haunt, the gilded-age gourmet devoured enormous quantities of food there. This included two to three dozen oysters, a half dozen crabs, a few servings of green turtle soup, two ducks, six to seven lobsters, a sirloin steak, two servings of terrapin, and assorted vegetables. Dessert consisted of a platter of pastries and a two-pound box of candy. After his death, the size of Diamond Jim's prodigious belly was discovered to be six times that of an average person!

Henry VIII

When England's King Henry VIII (1491–1547) sat to dine, it wasn't only the size of his meal that was so unusual but the outrageous items that he devoured, such as dolphin. For an appetizer, the King might nosh on pies stuffed with delectable songbirds. Since he loved to hunt, all manner of prey was considered fair game, and most would find their way down his gullet. Dessert? Perhaps a dish of gelatin made from deer antlers or stained with children's urine. Mmm, mmm, good!

King Farouk

The gastronomic prowess of Egypt's King Farouk (1920–1965) is typically not well known. Given to excess in most every aspect of his life, the rotund king also appreciated healthy portions at mealtime. Staples of his diet consisted of numerous tablespoons of caviar, slabs of roast lamb, dozens of oysters, beans, lobster thermador, pounds of chocolate, assorted cakes and fruit, and copious quantities of champagne and coffee. Not surprisingly, King Farouk, sporting some 300 pounds of well-earned heft, allegedly died from a heart attack at age 45.

Vitellius

Roman Emperor Aulus Vitellius (A.D. 15–69) was known for his prodigious appetite and "gags." In a gut-wrenching twist far less common in more modern tales of gluttony (but actually a fairly common practice in ancient Rome, at least among the elite), this iron-handed ruler swallowed agents to induce vomiting after each course, then bellied-up to the feeding trough for another round. He divided his feasts into four sessions including breakfast, brunch, lunch, and dinner, then capped them off with an evening drinking bout—always taken to excess. His cuisine typically included tongues of flamingos, brains of peacocks and pheasants, and the entrails of lampreys. One formal dinner for himself and his guests included 2,000 fish and 7,000 birds—bountiful victuals by even the most extreme standards. Vitellius's food obsession was best illustrated whenever he left his court. While roaming the countryside, the compulsive eater couldn't resist snatching bits of meat and pie from inns, including half-eaten portions left over from the previous day. Some might have gagged at the thought of eating such leftovers, but it likely aided Vitellius in his "process."

George Fordyce

As a noted 18th-century physician and chemist, Dr. George Fordyce (1736–1802) likely knew that gluttony was an unhealthy trait. Nevertheless, the good doctor regularly fed his compulsion by downing a super-size meal large enough to choke a horse. Arriving at his favorite restaurant around 4:00 P.M. each day, the doctor would first sip from a huge tankard of ale to prepare his palate. Next, he would down an entire bottle of port. Not quite juiced yet, Fordyce would then swallow a half-pint of brandy. When his main course arrived, it was generally a 1.5-pound steak accompanied by a broiled chicken, vegetables, and to top it all off, a tart. When Fordyce famously quipped, "One meal a day is enough for a lion, and it ought to be for a man," he was speaking from personal experience.

Nicholas Wood

Deemed the "Great Eater of Kent" in the early 1600s, England's Nicholas Wood was a veritable eating sensation. His consumptive exploits trump many of the world's most voracious gluttons, past and present, and feature a number of bizarre dishes. Items devoured in individual sittings reportedly included the following: 360 pigeons, 84 rabbits, 60 pounds of cherries, a whole hog, and an entire raw sheep. A celebrated breakfast consisted of a leg of mutton, 60 eggs, 3 large pies, and a bowl of pudding. After this waist-splitting meal (so excessive that it reportedly left the restaurant's cupboards bare), the glutton was reportedly still hungry. To remedy the situation, Wood's waiter fetched a large duck from a nearby pond and brought it to him. It is unclear if the bird arrived at his table alive or dead. With purposeful determination, the great masticator tore into it, leaving only its beak and feathers as proof of its earthly existence.

Donald Snyder

Though we often associate gluttony with eating oneself to death, we rarely, if ever, hear of times when it is used to accomplish the opposite. For Donald Snyder, gluttony represented sweet life. In the 1950s, Snyder was a 150-pound convicted murderer awaiting electrocution at New York's Sing Sing Prison. He reasoned that if he couldn't physically fit into "Old Sparky"—the whimsical name bestowed upon Sing Sing's electric chair—his would-be executioners would have one less convict to fry. How and where he secured his immense quantities of food is unclear, but nevertheless, he did manage to bulk up to more than 300 pounds. He was likely smiling when he took his final walk toward the chair. One can only imagine how quickly that smile faded when he discovered that "Old Sparky" fit him like a glove.

Beware of Poppy Seeds

The next time you enjoy a slice of poppy-seed cake with ice cream, you can say, "This will go straight to my hips ... and perhaps straight from my urine to a positive drug test in a lab."

✳   ✳   ✳   ✳

DEPENDING ON WHEN you take the test, simply eating one poppy-seed bagel can lead to a positive result. Such a finding is often referred to as a "false positive." This term, however, is false in itself: The test comes back "positive" because you do have morphine in your system. But the reason you test positive is what your employer or parole officer cares about: Were you chasing the dragon or chasing the complete breakfast?

Poppy seeds contain morphine, but after being gobbled up, they don't have any drug-related effect on the body. However, the morphine is detectable in your urine, and there's no way to tell from a basic urine test whether the morphine came from heroin or a muffin.

To address this curious problem, the legal threshold for a positive drug-test result was raised in 1998. The Mandatory Guidelines for Federal Workplace Drug Testing Programs adjusted the point at which a test is considered "positive" from 300 nanograms per milliliter to 2,000 nanograms per milliliter. This revised threshold does miss a few drug abusers, but it filters out most of the positive results that are caused by the munchies. Testing the subject's hair can help to clarify whether the morphine detected in the urine was the result of drug use.

The Green Fairy

Few alcoholic beverages have the mythic cachet of absinthe.
A notorious liqueur associated with Bohemian Paris during
the Belle Époque, it was blamed for making strong men sterile,
turning good girls bad, and leading nice people to murder.

✳ ✳ ✳ ✳

ABSINTHE IS AN aperitif made from alcohol and distilled herbs, particularly grand wormwood, green anise, petite wormwood, fennel, and hyssop. It's the wormwood that supposedly gives absinthe its narcotic and addictive properties, though some claim that the high alcohol content (at 140 to 160 proof) has something to do with it. Gentle heating of the herbs during the production process causes the telltale green color. The coloring combined with the liqueur's seductive intoxicating power give absinthe its nickname, the Green Fairy.

Because absinthe tastes bitter, the accepted way to consume it is to put a lump of sugar on a perforated flat spoon and rest it on the rim of a glass filled with a shot of absinthe. Ice water is then slowly poured over the sugar so it drips into the drink. The dispersing of the sugar water dilutes the alcohol (weakening the drink) and turns the drink a milky opaque color.

Dr. Pierre Ordinaire

Absinthe can be traced to the area near Couvet in Switzerland and to the Doubs region of France. Supposedly Dr. Pierre Ordinaire developed the drink as medicine around 1792, and his original formula ended up in the hands of the Henriod sisters. Major Henri Dubied purchased the formula from the sisters in the early 1800s so he could manufacture absinthe as an aperitif: a drink designed to stimulate the taste buds and stomach before a meal. But the origins of the story have been embellished over the years into an offbeat tale of an eccentric doctor and his peculiar elixir. Evidence indicates that an absinthelike drink was made in the Neuchâtel region during the 1750s, which means Ordinaire did not invent it. It is likely that the doctor simply picked up the method of making the drink and then sold it as a cure-all to make some extra money.

Production of the aperitif began in earnest in 1805 when the Pernod Fils distillery was established in Pontarlier in Doubs by the Major's son-in-law, Henri-Louis Pernod. By the time Pernod's grandsons were running the company, it was one of the largest and most successful businesses in France. The popularity of absinthe increased after the French troops used it to prevent fever while fighting in Algeria. By the time the soldiers returned home, they had developed a taste for the Green Fairy.

During the reign of Napoleon III (1852–1870), absinthe was the preferred drink of the bourgeoisie, who used it as an aperitif. When licensing laws were relaxed in the 1860s, thousands of bars and restaurants opened, launching a café culture that defined Paris for decades. Absinthe was so popular then that each café hosted a daily "l'Heure Verte," or Green Hour.

La Vie Bohème

The cafés of Montmartre attracted a highly creative and unconventional artistic crowd; they romanticized the Green Fairy in their poems, novels, and paintings. From Edgar Degas's painting *L'Absinthe* to Marcel Pagnol's poem "The Time of Secrets" to Pablo Picasso's *Woman Drinking Absinthe*, the liqueur became legendary as a symbol of la vie bohème ("the bohemian life").

Absinthe use peaked in Europe from 1880 to 1910, and it became popular in America in the 1890s. But a series of high-profile murders among the middle class in Europe were blamed on absinthe use, leading several countries to ban it. In 1905, Swiss family man Jean Lanfray drank two absinthes, then killed his pregnant wife and two kids. Three years later, a man named Saliaz binged on absinthe and then chopped his wife into bits. Absinthe was outlawed in Belgium, Switzerland, the United States, and finally, in 1915, in France. But no worries—many countries have lifted their bans. The Green Fairy dances again.

Chapter Three

Bizarre Truths About Dogs, Cats, and Other Pets

He Made His Mark

Indoor cats and their owners should give thanks to Ed Lowe, the inventor of Kitty Litter.

✳   ✳   ✳   ✳

Stumbling Upon Pay Dirt

Born in Minnesota in 1920, Ed Lowe grew up in Cassopolis, Michigan. After a stint in the U.S. Navy, he returned to Cassopolis to work in his family's business selling industrial-strength absorbent materials, including sawdust, sand, and a powdered clay called fuller's earth. Due to its high concentration of magnesium oxide, fuller's earth has an extraordinary ability to rapidly and completely absorb any liquid.

Back in those days, domestic kitties did their business in litter boxes filled with sand, wood shavings, or ashes. One fateful morning in 1947, a neighbor of Lowe's, Kaye Draper, complained to him about her cat tracking ashes all over the house. She asked if she could have a bag of sand from his company's warehouse.

Instead, Lowe gave her a sack of fuller's earth. Draper was so pleased with the results that she asked for more. After a while, her cat used only fuller's earth—it was the first Kitty Litter-using critter in the world.

Sensing that he was on to a good thing, Lowe filled ten brown bags with five pounds of fuller's earth each and wrote "Kitty Litter" on them. He never explained exactly how he came up with the name, but it was certainly an inspired choice.

The Idea Catches On in Catdom

Initially, convincing pet shop owners to carry Kitty Litter proved to be a challenge. Lowe's suggested price of 65 cents per bag was a lot of money at that time—the equivalent of about $5 today. Why would people pay so much for cat litter, the shop owners asked, when they could get sand for a few pennies? Lowe was so sure Kitty Litter would be a success that he told the merchants they could give it away for free until they built up a demand. Soon, satisfied customers insisted on nothing but Kitty Litter for their feline friends, and they were willing to pay for it.

Lowe piled bags of Kitty Litter into the back of his 1943 Chevy and spent the next few years traveling the country, visiting pet shops and peddling his product at cat shows. "Kitty Litter" became a byword among fastidious cat owners. The *Oxford English Dictionary* cites this advertisement from the February 9, 1949, issue of the Mansfield, Ohio, *Journal News* as the phrase's first appearance in print: "Kitty Litter 10 lbs $1.50. Your kitty will like it. Takes the place of sand or sawdust."

The Kitty Litter Kingdom

By 1990, Lowe's company was raking in almost $200 million annually from the sale of Kitty Litter and related products. He owned more than 20 homes, a stable of racehorses, a yacht, and a private railroad. He even bought up 2,500 acres of land outside of Cassopolis, where he established the Edward Lowe Foundation— a think tank dedicated to assisting small businesses and entrepreneurs. Lowe sold his business in 1990 and died in 1995. As far as anyone knows, he never owned a cat himself.

Up, Up, and Away

If your dog can fit into a purse, there's a chance that it can also fit into the talons of a bird of prey.

✳   ✳   ✳   ✳

HAWKS AND OWLS live in most parts of the United States and like to feast on small mammals such as rabbits and skunks. These prey are similar in size to many dogs recognized as "toy" breeds by the American Kennel Club.

Most hawks and owls aren't large enough to lift an animal that weighs more than five pounds. But the smaller the dog, the greater the risk. Small dogs are inviting targets for migrating birds, which are always on the lookout for a quick meal. On the bright side, some dogs that are picked up are dropped when the bird tires and is unable to carry the weight.

Tethering a dog outside or confining it in a closed area can keep it from wandering off, but it also makes it more susceptible to a hungry predator from above. The 2008 disappearance of a dog from the fenced-in yard of a Florida doggy day-care business was blamed on nearby hawks. The center responded by adding a mesh covering.

The best way to keep a small dog safe from flying predators is to accompany it outdoors or make certain it's in the company of larger animals. Nevertheless, these precautionary measures don't always do the trick.

Here's a somewhat disconcerting example: In 2006, an 11-year-old Boston boy took his dachshund, Dimi, outside on a leash and quickly found himself fighting off a red-tailed hawk that was attacking the puppy. "I felt a tug, and I look back and a hawk was on the back of my dog, trying to eat him," said the sixth-grader. But this story has a happy ending: He gave the bird several swift kicks and won the battle over little Dimi.

Dressed to the Nines

People dress up their pets for several reasons—some of which are practical, others psychological.

✳ ✳ ✳ ✳

WHY ON EARTH would people dress up their pets? On the practical side, certain breeds of dogs don't have enough meat on their bones or fur in their coats to keep themselves warm in cold weather, so you can buy little coats or wraps to help them stay warm.

Of course, you can also buy your dog a bathing suit, though there's no physiological need for it. Indeed, Web sites sell thousands of doggie Halloween costumes—from pirates to princesses, Superman to Darth Vader. And this brings us to the psychological part of the equation. Many people consider a pet to be a member of the family, which helps explain why Americans spend tens of billions of dollars per year on their animals.

What other reasons might we have for putting capes on our dogs or Santa Claus hats on our cats? One study suggests that it may be because we are lonely. In research conducted at the University of Chicago, 99 people were asked to describe their own pet or the pet of someone they knew. The lonelier the people were in their everyday lives, the more likely they were to use human traits to describe their pets, employing such words as "thoughtful" and "sympathetic."

The lesson? We are social creatures, and when our need to connect with other humans is not met, we seek out ways to fill the void. For some of us, Mr. Fluffy clad in a woolly sweater fits the bill.

Out of Sight, Out of Mind

If you think a cat isn't smart, consider that it's the only animal with enough sense to bury its waste.

✳   ✳   ✳   ✳

Don't Forget About Humans

Technically, cats aren't the only animals that bury their waste. We humans have been burying our bodily waste for thousands of years, and all signs point toward the continuance of this habit. It's a good thing, too, since our civilization would be overrun by stink if we didn't.

But in terms of "lower" animals, cats are indeed the only animals that have the courtesy to dispose of their droppings. The only other animal that possesses an inclination to do something special with its feces is the chimpanzee, which will sometimes chuck turds at rival chimps in fits of anger. Every other animal just lets the feces fall where it will.

Uncovering the Origins

The house cat's habit of covering its feces probably originated with its ancestors in the wild. In nature, cats sometimes bury their waste in an effort to hide it from predators and rival cats. In effect, it's the opposite of using urine to mark territory; in an effort to remain incognito, cats do their best to hide any trace of their presence.

By the same token, a dominant cat will leave its poop anywhere it pleases within its territory in order to scare off trespassing felines. A pile of fly-covered waste, not to mention the distinctive smell that wafts from that pile, functions like a BEWARE OF CAT sign. For another cat to ignore this warning would be to invite trouble in the form of teeth and claws.

Your house cat's tendency to bury its feces in a litter box may be a sign that it recognizes your dominance in the house. But if it uses the litter box but neglects to cover its leavings—as some cats do—it may be your tabby's way of acknowledging a kind of shared dominance over the abode.

You needn't worry about your place in the pecking order until you come home and find urine stains in the corners of the room and feces in the middle of the floor. At that point, you are trespassing on your cat's territory—sitting on *its* couch, watching *its* television, popping *its* popcorn—and you'd better start paying rent . . . or prepare to face the terrible wrath of the tabby cat.

Say What?

Opportunity is missed by most people because it is dressed in overalls and looks like work.

—THOMAS A. EDISON

Music should strike fire from the heart of man, and bring tears from the eyes of woman.

—LUDWIG VAN BEETHOVEN

Middle age is when you've met so many people that every new person you meet reminds you of someone else.

—OGDEN NASH

If slaughterhouses had glass walls, everyone would be a vegetarian.

—PAUL MCCARTNEY

I've done the calculation and your chances of winning the lottery are identical whether you play or not.

—FRAN LEBOWITZ

There is nothing so annoying as to have two people talking when you're busy interrupting.

—MARK TWAIN

True terror is to wake up one morning and discover that your high school class is running the country.

—KURT VONNEGUT JR.

A Snack of Convenience

Mice aren't really a cat's favorite food—
they just happen to be easy prey.

✳   ✳   ✳   ✳

THERE'S NO DENYING that cats have a thing for mice. It begins with the thrill of the chase, and if all goes as planned (for the cat), it ends with the satisfaction of downing a wiggling bundle of fur and bones, squeak and all.

It's feline instinct, but it's not entirely unlike the way you hit the couch, reach for the remote control, turn on the television, enjoy the thrill of a cop-show chase, and stuff your face with those special potato chips—the cheap, greasy ones that you'd never admit to loving. What's the similarity? For both the cat and you, it's the easiest thing that's available because it's right in front of you. It's low-hanging fruit, so to speak.

If a mouse is so brazen or so foolish as to wander into Tabby's territory, the cat is going to make entertainment and a snack out of it. If that television is just going to sit there and if those chips are simply going to take up cupboard space, your best option is to make entertainment and a snack out of them. You get the general idea, right?

A cat would rather dine on, say, a tuna, but there aren't any flopping around your family room. Mice, on the other hand, are plentiful. Remember, cats also dine on bugs—and you don't see bug-flavored cat food at your local pet store, do you?

Six Pets that Traveled Long Distances to Get Home

Salmon follow the smell of their home waters. Birds and bees appear to navigate by the sun, stars, and moon. We can't really explain how so many lost dogs and cats magically seem to find their way back to their owners over great distances, so we'll just tell you about them instead.

✳ ✳ ✳ ✳

1. **Emily the cat went across the pond:** Lesley and Donny McElhiney's home in Appleton, Wisconsin, wasn't the same after their one-year-old tabby Emily disappeared. But she didn't just disappear, she went on a 4,500-mile adventure! It seems Emily was on her evening prowl when she found herself on a truck to Chicago inside a container of paper bales. From there she was shipped to Belgium and then on to France, where employees at a laminating company found her thin and thirsty. Since she was wearing tags, it didn't take long for Emily to be reunited with her family, compliments of Continental Airlines.

2. **Howie the Persian traversed the Australian outback:** The Hicks family of Australia wanted their cat, Howie, to be lovingly cared for while they went on an extended vacation overseas. So, they took him to stay with relatives who lived more than 1,000 miles away. Months later, when they returned to retrieve Howie, they were told that he had run away. The Hicks were distraught, assuming that because Howie was an indoor cat, he wouldn't have the survival skills to make it on his own. A year later, as their daughter returned home from school one day, she saw a mangy, unkempt, and starving cat. Yep, it was Howie. It had taken him 12 months to cross 1,000 miles of Australian outback, but Howie had come home.

3. **Tony the mutt finds his family:** When the Doolen family of Aurora, Illinois, moved to East Lansing, Michigan, nearly 260 miles away, they gave away their mixed-breed dog Tony. Six weeks later, who came trotting down the street in East Lansing and made himself known to Mr. Doolen? That's right—Tony. Doolen recognized a notch he had cut into Tony's collar when they lived in Illinois.

4. **Madonna heads to the massage parlor:** Now here's a finicky cat! This seven-year-old tabby moved from Kitchener, Ontario, with her owner Nina, who was starting a new branch of the family massage parlor. Their new home base was Windsor, but within weeks, Madonna was nowhere to be found. She eventually showed up at her original massage parlor, where Nina's sister was the new proprietor. Total walking distance? About 150 miles.

5. **Troubles finds his way through ten miles of jungle:** Troubles, a scout dog, and his handler, William Richardson, were taken via helicopter deep into the war zone in South Vietnam in the late 1960s. When Richardson was wounded by enemy fire and taken to a hospital, Troubles was abandoned by the rest of the unit. Three weeks later, Troubles showed up at his home at the First Air Cavalry Division Headquarters in An Khe, South Vietnam. But he wouldn't let anyone near him—he was on a mission! Troubles searched the tents and eventually curled up for a nap after he found a pile of Richardson's clothes to use for a bed.

6. **Misele the farm cat goes to the hospital:** When 82-year-old Alfonse Mondry was taken to a hospital in France, his cat Misele missed him greatly. So she took off and walked across cattle fields, rock quarries, forests, and busy highways. She entered the hospital—where she had never been before—and found her owner's room. The nurses called the doctor right away when they found Mondry resting comfortably with his cat purring on his lap.

A Sewer Story

The moral of this tale? Don't flush unwanted pets down the toilet.

* * * *

THE URBAN LEGEND goes like this: In the early 20th century, some denizens of Gotham thought that baby alligators made great gifts for kids. Apparently, these knuckleheads couldn't foresee that cute baby alligators would become frightening, adult limb-manglers.

When the gators grew and became dangerous, these New Yorkers flushed the reptiles into the city's sewer system. There, it was said, the abandoned alligators formed a thriving colony beneath Manhattan's streets.

Fueling the legend was Robert Daley's 1959 book *The World Beneath the City*. According to the book, former sewer superintendent Teddy May claimed that in the 1930s he saw gators as long as two feet in the sewer tunnels. May said he issued orders that the reptiles be killed; it took a few months to complete the job.

Indeed, the 1930s were a golden age for news stories of alligator sightings in and around the city. Oddly, accounts involving the sewer system were rare. Most reports involved surface-level encounters, and the critters in question are believed to have been escaped pets. A February 1935 article in *The New York Times* told of a group of boys who discovered that the manhole into which they were shoveling snow contained an alligator. They used a clothesline to drag the reptile up to the street, then beat it to death with their shovels. Welcome to the Big Apple.

Curiously, no contemporary news coverage of May's alligator hunt can be found. Subsequent published reports painted May as a bit of a raconteur who quite possibly was having some fun at Daley's expense. We're not saying you won't encounter some sort of underground wildlife in NYC, but you're more likely to find it on the subway than in the sewers.

The Restless Lives of Fish

It's hard to tell whether fish are sleeping, because they don't have eyelids. That's why you'll never win a staring contest with your pet guppy—its eyes are always open.

✳ ✳ ✳ ✳

SINCE FISH CAN'T close their eyes, how do they get their beauty sleep? They don't, at least not in the way we humans do. Their body functions slow down and they get a bit dozy, but they're generally still alert enough to scatter when danger arises. You could say that they're having a relaxing daydream, but they never actually fall into a deep sleep.

Some fish simply float motionless in the water as they doze; others, such as grouper and rockfish, rest against rocks or plants. The craftier varieties, like bass and perch, hole up underneath rocks and logs or hide in crevices. Others stay on the move while in a daze, recharging without ever stopping.

In the 1930s, biologist David Graham watched a fish sleeping upright on its tail for an hour or so. Then Graham turned on the lights, and the fish jerked back into a swimming position and darted around. It was the aquatic equivalent of being caught napping in school.

When exactly do fish rest? It varies from species to species. Most fish rely on the weak light from the surface to see, and since that light pretty much disappears at night, it's thought that a lot of fish do their resting then. However, some fish rest during the day, while others do so randomly.

✳ The koala, which is not actually a bear but a primitive marsupial that has existed in its present form for more than a million years, gets almost all the liquid it needs from licking dew off tree leaves.

✳ When the male snowy owl wishes to arouse a female, he dances while swinging a dead lemming from his beak.

Alex Was No Birdbrain

Alex was an African Grey parrot who could talk, count, and follow orders from his trainers. Alex died in 2007, but the knowledge he lent to science about animal cognition ensures his legacy.

✳ ✳ ✳ ✳

The Avian Learning Experiment

Dr. Irene Pepperberg was not always interested in parrots. She had a parakeet as a child, but that was about it. In 1973, while working toward a Ph.D. in theoretical chemistry, she was inspired by a television documentary about animal communication and intelligence. Pepperberg continued working toward her doctorate while studying birds on the side, in an attempt to understand how animals think.

Pepperberg decided to test animal intelligence by working closely with a single animal from a young age. She picked an African Grey parrot because they live upward of 70 years, are known for their intelligence, and possess the anatomy required to imitate human sounds and syllables. Pepperberg went to a pet shop and chose a one-year-old parrot. She named him Alex, an acronym for her project, the Avian Learning Experiment.

A Nutty Way of Learning

The scientific community questioned whether animals learn through simple operant conditioning—in other words, simple input and output—or whether some are capable of more nuanced associative learning. Birds were taught how to say "hello" through repetition. But researchers had failed to teach parrots an extensive vocabulary with this kind of training.

Pepperberg suspected the problem was that researchers assumed birds are incapable of associative learning. In the wild, an associative learning scenario might go something like this: A parrot encounters a large variety of berries. Over time, the parrot learns that some berries are like or different than other berries and should be eaten at different times of the year and in different quantities. This leads to mental categorization. From this comes *representation*, or the ability to represent objects within these categories through social interaction. One bird pecking another bird's head might mean "macadamia nuts." This is linked to functionality, so that interaction might mean, "let's go find macadamia nuts." This implies the ability to have abstract thoughts about desire, intention, and future activities.

We may never know how birds think—the abstract thoughts and representations in avian brains may work in ways we can never fully conceive. But one path to understanding is to teach them *our* mode of representational communication: words. How parrots use these words might indicate whether they have abstract thought.

Alex's Abilities

Scientists believe that intelligence and learning are rooted in social interaction, so Pepperberg taught Alex in a social manner. He competed with his trainers for rewards and learned words in their social context. Alex soon knew over 150 words and could accurately label objects by color, shape, and material. He also answered questions about relative size and quantity. When he was tired of testing, he said, "I'm going to go away." If a trainer got annoyed, Alex replied, "I'm sorry."

Some argue that Alex was not capable of representational thought, that when he said, "I want nut," he might not know what the words "want" and "nut" mean. However, many instances suggested he understood what the words communicated. For example, Alex was once shown an apple, for which he did not have a word. But he did know the words "banana" and "cherry." Alex spontaneously said "banerry," which suggests he understood the words represented categories and items. Pepperberg's experiment was cut short by Alex's early death; another parrot, Griffin, is his successor.

Your Pet Goldfish Just Might Save Your Life

Research shows that gazing into a fish-filled aquarium can help to reduce a person's stress, at least temporarily. That's why there are fish tanks in the waiting rooms of many medical and dental offices.

✳ ✳ ✳ ✳

IN THE 1980S, researchers at the University of Pennsylvania found that watching fish in an aquarium is far more effective at reducing stress than watching an aquarium without fish. In 1999, Nancy Edwards, a professor of nursing at Purdue University, discovered that Alzheimer's patients who were exposed to fish-filled aquariums were more relaxed and alert and even began to eat a healthier diet. Another study showed that exposure to aquariums can contribute to decreased stress and hyperactivity among people who suffer from attention deficit hyperactivity disorder, or ADHD.

Nobody is sure exactly why fish are so calming. The Purdue University study theorized that the combination of movement, color, and sound in an aquarium has a relaxing effect.

But it's not just fish that help reduce stress. Having a pet of any kind leads to better health. A 2007 study at Queen's University in Belfast, Northern Ireland, showed that dog owners tended to have lower blood pressure and cholesterol than people who didn't own dogs. The study proposed that pet owners in general are healthier than the population on average and also suggested that having a dog is better for you than having a cat. However, the study didn't weigh in on how dogs and cats compare to fish.

✳ Most fish have voices that get deeper with age.
✳ A cockroach can regrow its wings, legs, and antennae and can live without a head for up to a week.

Hemingway's Cats

The great American author and proverbial "man's man" Ernest Hemingway was a big fan of bullfighting, boxing, hunting—and cats. Ever since he was given Snowball, a six-toed feline (known as a polydactyl) by a ship's captain in the 1930s, Hemingway allowed cats to multiply with abandon at his Key West, Florida, home.

✳ ✳ ✳ ✳

IN 2003, THE Hemingway Home and Museum, where the writer spent ten years living and working on novels including *To Have and Have Not* and short stories such as "The Snows of Kilimanjaro," became embroiled in a dispute over its nearly 60 resident felines. All of these cats are descendants of Snowball, and they all carry the gene for polydactylism; only half, however, have extra toes.

Just Trying to Help

The legal battle began after a neighbor complained to the museum and the local Society for the Prevention of Cruelty to Animals (SPCA), concerned about the excessive number of cats. She also contacted the USDA, citing animal welfare legislation requiring any business employing animals in acts or advertisements to have a special license. The Hemingway cats, many named after literary and entertainment celebrities (such as Audrey Hepburn, Emily Dickinson, Simone de Beauvoir, and Charlie Chaplin), are featured on the museum's Web site and are a huge tourist attraction, but they do not exactly perform, per se. The museum faced huge fines and confiscation of the cats by the Department of Agriculture if it didn't cage the furry creatures.

The hard-fought battle of the little six-toed guy against the big-bad government made its way through the courts, ending with a 2007 victory for the beleaguered and bewhiskered: The cats still freely roam the grounds, but a mesh fence has been installed to keep them from wandering beyond the compound.

Extreme Pet Pampering

When does pet pampering go too far? Some people are taking the idea of luxury for their furry friends to new extremes.

✳   ✳   ✳   ✳

THEY'RE MAN'S BEST friend, sure—but $12 million for a dog? Hotel heiress Leona Helmsley made her priorities clear when she left a large chunk of her family fortune to her pooch. A court ultimately intervened, reducing the canine's inheritance to a measly $2 million and redistributing the rest to Helmsley's charitable foundation. Still, a nearly $200,000 annual budget isn't bad for an animal. As it turns out, dogs living, well, *high on the dog* is not as unusual as one might think.

The Fashion

Plenty of pet owners are providing the high life for Fido. America's pet spending tops $40 billion a year—double what we're shelling out for children's toys. Some dogs are even amassing enormous accessory collections. Designer carriers made by companies such as Juicy Couture can go for nearly $300 a pop. Jewelers are marketing pricey dog-collar charms made of real sapphires and pearls. There are even perfume-scented leashes, fashionable doggy shoes, and specially designed dog sunglasses. But it doesn't stop at material possessions.

The Pampering

Animal spas all over the country offer services such as facials, massages, acupuncture, and even cosmetic surgeries for cats and dogs. Hotels such as Manhattan's Ritzy Canine Carriage House offer animal suites at $80 a night for large dogs. Throw in an hour-long massage for Sparky for $60. The hotel also offers grooming, training, a designer gift boutique, and room service. Other centers, such as the Inn's Naples Dog Center in Florida, provide special treatments that purportedly soothe an animal emotionally and spiritually. Some spas even have pet herbal rinses, mud baths, swimming sessions, and surfing lessons.

The Drinks

Tired of drinking alone? Now your four-legged friend can cozy up to the bar with you. Happy Tail Ale is a nonalcoholic brew made for dogs. It's noncarbonated and boasts all-natural beef drippings. Yum.

Perhaps your pet isn't bent on beer. How about fine wine? Bark Vineyards has built a business out of gourmet wine for cats and dogs. Also alcohol-free, the popular line includes such flavors as "Barkundy," "Sauvignon Bark," "Pino Leasheo," and "White Sniff 'N' Tail." Really.

The Food

What good are all the drinkable delights without some fancy food to accompany them? Companies such as Evanger's offer up organic meal creations that seem fit for a five-star restaurant. For an extra fee, your pet can opt for kosher meals instead.

Sounds pretty good, doesn't it? Well, don't be jealous: You can share your dog's dishes. Dick Van Patten's Natural Balance Dog Food is made for both dog and human consumption.

The Electronics

People aren't the only ones who can enjoy electronics. Gadgets such as the Talking Bone allow you to record messages for your pet that it can play when you aren't around. Meanwhile, the Pet Spa Grooming Machine gives them a spa treatment at home, complete with aromatherapy. You can also buy CDs to expose your animals to foreign languages. Perhaps best of all, though, Edible Greeting Cards offers animal-targeted holiday messages that your pet can eat. Creative and convenient!

One thing's for sure: The pet-pampering industry is a booming business, and many pet owners are more than willing to dish out the dough. Heck, if people are spending more on their Chihuahuas than they are on their children, maybe the hotel heiress wasn't as crazy as she seemed. Then again . . .

Why Did the Dog Pee on the Fire Hydrant? Because It Was There.

And because it provided a handy way for the canine to mark its territory.

✳ ✳ ✳ ✳

DOGS AND PEOPLE, animal-behavior specialists claim, are more similar than we might think. Indeed, humans share a number of characteristics with their pooches. They're both creatures of habit. They both enjoy being petted. And they both pee on everything in sight. Okay, maybe not the last one.

But even if humans don't urinate on fire hydrants, the urge that causes dogs to do so is rooted in a trait humans and canines do share: territoriality. In suburban neighborhoods across the land, picket and chain-link fences border our yards, signaling to our neighbors, "This is my turf." Dogs, however, can't build fences, so they use what they have available to them: a seemingly never-ending supply of urine. By spraying everything in the vicinity, dogs stake their claim in the neighborhood land grab.

Urinating also serves as a form of canine communication. When a dog raises its leg at a fire hydrant, it's announcing to other dogs in the area, "Fido was here"—much like the way humans spray graffiti or carve their initials into public property.

Why fire hydrants? Actually, fire hydrants are only one of many objects dogs enjoy peeing on. Fire hydrants, trees, mailbox posts—virtually anything with a wide enough surface to retain a scent is a potential victim. It's possible the cliché of the fire hydrant stems from the fact that in many areas, fire hydrants are common and accessible targets. The fact that dogs are the traditional mascot of firefighters may also play a role.

The next time one of your neighbors erects an enormous fence, don't get upset—be grateful. Consider the alternative.

Chapter Four

Bizarre Truths About Myths and Legends

Vampires in the Real World

According to organizations such as the New Jersey Association for Real Vampires, vampires are living among us! But please— put down your garlic wreaths and crucifixes. Modern-day vampires don't do it up Bram Stoker-style. Well, not entirely.

❋ ❋ ❋ ❋

The Vampire Legend

IN POPULAR LEGEND and lore, Dracula-like vampires are undead villains who live in coffins by day and turn into neck-biting, bloodsucking bats by night. They are pale-faced creatures with protruding incisor teeth who cast no shadows and produce no reflection in mirrors. Worst of all, these agitated souls can only be put to their final rest by driving stakes through their hearts.

This picture of the demonic vampire began with an old legend that is primarily Slavic and Hungarian in origin. By the mid-18th century, vampiric superstitions ran rampant all over Asia and Europe. People were accused of being vampires, and in some cases, corpses were dug up and staked in order to "kill" them. Through the 20th century and into the new millennium, the folk tradition of the immortal vampire has lived on through a whole slew of books, TV shows, and movies—from the classic *Dracula* film starring Béla Lugosi to the smash-hit *Twilight* books and movies.

The Real Ones Won't Suck Your Blood

Real vampires say pop culture is partly to blame for their bad rap. According to the Real Vampire Coalition, a group created to stop vampire hate, people know only what they see on TV and in the movies and read in books and magazines. Turns out real vampires aren't evil—they're just misunderstood.

Just what is a real vampire? Inanna Arthen, an expert in vampirology (and a trained psychic and initiated Pagan priestess), says, "A vampire is a person born with an extraordinary capacity to absorb, channel, transform, and manipulate 'pranic energy,' or life force."

Vampires can be classified into two general groups: psi/energy vampires (those who feed off psychic energy) and sanguinarian vampires (those who feed off blood energy). The sanguinarian vampires don't attack the necks of unwilling victims in the middle of the night. They typically get the blood they drink from uncooked meat and poultry or willing human donors—there are bona fide vampire-donor directories for this sort of thing. As for other characteristics, the portal Sanguinarius.org advises that real vampires may be more sensitive to sun and light—they may cover up with long sleeves, hats, and sunglasses in the daytime.

So you see, aside from an occasional craving for blood and perhaps an abnormally pale pallor, real vampires are just like the rest of us. Garlic and crosses do not repel them—though they will indeed die if they receive a stake through the heart. Hey, who wouldn't?

Truth is, real vampires aren't the contemptible characters we know from folklore and fiction. They're normal mortals who sleep in beds, wear suits and ties to work, and eat cereal for breakfast. Wonder if they prefer Count Chocula.

America's Most Haunted Lighthouse

Built in 1830, the historic Point Lookout Lighthouse is located in St. Mary's County, Maryland, where the Potomac River meets Chesapeake Bay. It is a beautiful setting for hiking, boating, fishing, camping—and ghost-hunting.

✳ ✳ ✳ ✳

The Most Ghosts

POINT LOOKOUT LIGHTHOUSE has been called America's most haunted lighthouse, perhaps because it was built on what later became the largest camp for Confederate prisoners of war.

Marshy surroundings, tent housing, and close quarters were a dangerous combination, and smallpox, scurvy, and dysentery ran rampant. The camp held more than 50,000 soldiers, and between 3,000 and 8,000 died there.

Park rangers and visitors to the lighthouse report hearing snoring and footsteps, having a sense of being watched, and feeling the floors shake and the air move as crowds of invisible beings pass by. A photograph of a former caretaker shows the misty figure of a young soldier leaning against the wall behind her, although no one noticed him during a séance at the lighthouse when the photo was taken. And a bedroom reportedly smelled like rotting flesh at night until the odor was publicly attributed to the spirits of the war prisoners.

The Lost Ghost

In December 1977, Ranger Gerald Sword was sitting in the lighthouse's kitchen on a stormy night when a man's face appeared at the back door. The man was young, with a floppy cap and a long coat, and peered into the bright room. Given the awful weather, Sword opened the door to let him in, but the young man floated backward until he vanished entirely. Later, after a bit of research, Sword realized he had been face-to-face with Joseph Haney, a young officer whose body had washed ashore after the steamboat he was on sank during a similar storm in 1878.

The Host Ghost

One of Point Lookout's most frequent visitors is the apparition of a woman dressed in a long blue skirt and a white blouse who appears at the top of the stairs. She is believed to be Ann Davis, the wife of the first lighthouse keeper. Although her husband died shortly after he took the post, Ann remained as the keeper for the next 30 years, and, according to inspection reports, was known for clean and well-kept grounds. Caretakers claim to hear her sighing heavily.

Who Said That?

Point Lookout's reputation drew Hans Holzer, Ph.D., a renowned parapsychologist, who tried to capture evidence of ghostly activity. Holzer and his team claimed to have recorded 24 different voices in all, both male and female, talking, laughing, and singing. Among their recordings, the group heard male voices saying "fire if they get too close," "going home," and more than a few obscenities.

Take Care, Caretaker

One former caretaker reported waking in the middle of the night to see a ring of lights dancing above her head. She smelled smoke and raced downstairs to find a space heater on fire. She believes that the lights were trying to protect her and the lighthouse from being consumed by flames.

A Full House

The lighthouse was decommissioned in 1966, after 135 years of service. In 2002, the state of Maryland purchased it, and it is now open for tours and paranormal investigations. The lighthouse continues to have a steady stream of visitors—perhaps including those who are no longer among the living.

I Know What It's Like to Be Dead: The "Paul Is Dead" Hoax

Four lads from Liverpool were the biggest thing in pop culture for much of the 1960s. But by the end of the decade, were the Beatles really a trio?

✳   ✳   ✳   ✳

THEY WERE BIGGER than Elvis ... bigger than Sinatra ... bigger than life. The Beatles had rewritten the book on stardom and fame, influencing not only the pop music world but also fashion, politics, and religion. Their slightest movements were reported by the media.

He Blew His Mind Out in a Car

In the fall of 1969, a Detroit radio DJ reported that Paul McCartney, "the cute Beatle," had been killed in a car crash three years earlier and replaced by a look-alike contest winner named William Campbell. The story, which had been floating around the rumor mill, was propelled by an Eastern Michigan University student writing a review of the Beatles' latest album, *Abbey Road*. The review claimed that many clues, collected from album covers and song lyrics, proved that McCartney was deceased (although the student admitted in a radio interview that most of his thesis was pure fabrication). Of course, the media had a field day. Radio and TV stations blared the "facts" nightly, and newspapers put their best investigative reporters on the story.

And, in the End

Life magazine devoted the cover story of a November 1969 issue to revealing the truth—McCartney was very much alive. Calling the whole story "bloody stupid," Paul hinted at something more serious—although he was still full of life, the Beatles were not—claiming "the Beatle thing is over." No one seemed to pick up on that clue—that the greatest band of the '60s would be DOA within six months.

Monsters Across America

Dracula, Frankenstein, the Wolf Man—these are the monsters who strike fear into the hearts of children. Of course, we adults know that such monsters don't really exist. But are we wrong?

* * * *

Dover Demon

FOR TWO DAYS in 1977, the town of Dover, Massachusetts, was under attack from a bizarre creature that seemed to be from another world. The first encounter with the beast, nicknamed the Dover Demon, occurred on the evening of April 21. Bill Bartlett was out for a drive with some friends when they saw something strange climbing on a stone wall. The creature appeared to be only about three feet tall but had a giant, oversize head with large, orange eyes. The rest of the body was tan and hairless with long, thin arms and legs.

Several hours later, the same creature was spotted by 15-year-old John Baxter, who watched it scurry up a hillside. The following day, a couple reported seeing the Demon, too. When authorities asked the couple for a description, it matched the ones given by the other witnesses except for one difference: The creature the couple encountered appeared to have glowing *green* eyes. Despite repeated attempts to locate it, the creature was never seen again.

Momo

In the early 1970s, reports came flooding in of a strange creature roaming the woods near the small town of Louisiana, Missouri. Standing nearly seven feet tall, Momo (short for Missouri Monster) was completely covered in black fur and had glowing orange eyes. The first major report came in July 1971 when Joan Mills and Mary Ryan claimed to have been harassed by a "half ape, half man" creature that made bizarre noises at them as they passed it on Highway 79. Even though the creature didn't make physical contact with them, both women believed it would have harmed them had it gotten the chance. That belief seemed to be confirmed the following year when, on July 11, 1972, brothers Terry and Wally Harrison spotted a giant, hairy beast carrying a dead dog. The boys screamed, alerting family members, who caught a glimpse of the creature before it disappeared into the woods. Sightings continued for a couple of weeks, but Momo hasn't been seen since.

Lawndale Thunderbird

If you're ever in Lawndale, Illinois, keep an eye out for giant birds lest they sneak up on you and whisk you away. That's what almost happened in 1977 when Lawndale residents noticed two large black birds with white-banded necks and 10- to 12-foot wingspans flying overhead. The birds, though enormous, seemed harmless enough. That is, until they swooped down and one of them reportedly tried to take off with 10-year-old Marlon Lowe while he played in his yard. The boy was not seriously injured, but the thunderbird did manage to lift the terrified boy several feet off the ground and carry him for nearly 40 feet before dropping him. Over the next few weeks, the birds were seen flying over various houses and fields in nearby towns, but, thankfully, they did not attack anyone else. And though they appear to have left Lawndale for good, reports of thunderbird sightings continue across the United States. The most recent one was on September 25, 2001, in South Greensburg, Pennsylvania.

Ohio Bridge Trolls

In May 1955, a man driving along the Miami River near Loveland, Ohio, came across a frightening sight. Huddled under a darkened bridge were several bald-headed creatures, each three to four feet tall. Spellbound, the man pulled over and watched the creatures, which he said had webbed hands and feet. Though they made no sound, the man said the creatures appeared to be communicating with each other and did not notice him watching them. However, when one of the creatures held up a wand or rod that began emitting showers of sparks, the man quickly left. He drove straight to the local police station, which dispatched a car to the bridge. A search of the area turned up nothing, and, to this day, there have been no more reported sightings of these strange creatures.

Maryland's Goatman

Think goats are cute and fuzzy little creatures? If so, a trip through Prince George's County in Maryland just might change your mind. Since the 1950s, people have reported horrifying encounters with a creature known only as the Goatman. From afar, many claim to have mistaken the Goatman for a human being. But as he draws nearer, his cloven feet become visible, as do the horns growing out of his head. If that's not enough to make you turn and run, reports as recent as 2006 state that the Goatman now carries an ax with him.

Gatormen

The swamplands of Florida are filled with alligators, but most of them don't have human faces. Since the 1700s, tales of strange half-man, half-alligator creatures have circulated throughout the area. Gatormen are described as having the face, neck, chest, and arms of a man and the midsection, back legs, and tail of an alligator. Unlike most other monsters and strange beasts, Gatormen reportedly prefer to travel and hunt in packs and even appear to have their own verbal language. What's more, recent sightings have them traveling outside the state of Florida and taking up residence in the swamplands of Louisiana and swimming around a remote Texas swamp.

Skunk Ape

Since the 1960s, a creature has been spotted in the Florida Everglades that many call Bigfoot's stinky cousin: the skunk ape. The beast is said to closely resemble Bigfoot except for one minor difference—it smells like rotten eggs. In late 2000, Sarasota police received an anonymous letter from a woman who complained that an escaped animal was roaming near her home at night. Included with the letter were two close-up photographs of the creature—a large beast that resembled an orangutan standing behind some palmetto leaves, baring its teeth.

Lizard Man

At around 2:00 A.M. on June 29, 1988, Christopher Davis got a flat tire on a back road near the Scape Ore Swamp in South Carolina. Just as the teen finished changing the tire, he was suddenly attacked by a seven-foot-tall creature with scaly green skin and glowing red eyes. Davis was able to get back into his car and drive away but not before the Lizard Man managed to climb onto the roof and claw at it, trying to get inside. As he drove, Davis could see the creature had three claws on each of its "hands." Eventually, the creature fell from the car and Davis was able to escape. A search of the scene later that day turned up nothing. Despite numerous subsequent sightings, the creature has yet to be apprehended.

Devil Monkeys

Far and away, some of the strangest creatures said to be roaming the countryside are the Devil Monkeys. Take an adult kangaroo, stick a monkey or baboon head on top, and you've got yourself a Devil Monkey. By most accounts, these creatures can cover hundreds of feet in just a few quick hops. They're nothing to tangle with, either. Although Devil Monkeys have traditionally stuck to attacking livestock and the occasional family pet, some reports have them attempting to claw their way into people's homes. Originally spotted in Virginia in the 1950s, Devil Monkeys have now been spotted all across the United States. On a related note, in May 2001, residents of New Delhi, India, were sent into a panic when a four-foot-tall half-monkey, half-human creature began attacking them as they slept.

Beware of Cries from the Bridge

Bridges provide us with a way to get from one place to another. But when that other place is the afterlife, a crybaby bridge is born. Located throughout the United States, crybaby bridges are said to mark locations where a baby died. And, according to legend, if you're brave enough to wait patiently on the bridge, you'll actually hear the baby cry. Here are some of the most popular crybaby bridges across the United States.

✳ ✳ ✳ ✳

Middletown, New Jersey

COOPER ROAD IS a lonely stretch of road that wanders through the backwoods of Middletown. Stay on this road long enough and you will eventually come to the crybaby bridge under which a baby is said to have drowned. If you want to hear the baby cry, just position your vehicle in the middle of the bridge and wait. But make sure you don't turn your car off, because you won't be able to start it again.

Monmouth, Illinois

It's a case of "the more the scarier" for this crybaby bridge in western Illinois. According to legend, an entire busload of small children drove off the bridge when the driver lost control. It is said that if you go to the bridge at night, turn off your car's engine, and put your vehicle in neutral, you'll hear cries from the dead children. Shortly thereafter, ghostly hands will push your car across the bridge and back onto the road, leaving tiny handprints on the back of your car.

Concord, North Carolina

Just outside of Concord is a bridge on Poplar Tent Road that locals refer to as Sally's Bridge. According to local lore, a young woman named Sally was driving home with her baby when she lost control of her car, skidded across the bridge, and crashed. The baby was ejected from the vehicle and fell into the water.

Panic-stricken, Sally dove into the water to try to save her child, but sadly both mother and child drowned.

Today, legend has it that Sally's ghost will bang on your car, desperately trying to find someone to help save her dying child.

Upper Marlboro, Maryland

The story associated with this crybaby bridge says that a young, single woman became pregnant. Embarrassed and afraid of being disowned, she somehow managed to conceal her pregnancy from her family and friends. When the baby was born, the woman waited until nightfall, walked to the bridge, and threw the baby from the bridge into the water below. Legend has it that if you go out to the bridge at night, you'll hear the baby crying.

Cable, Ohio

Far and away, Ohio harbors the most crybaby bridges, each with its own unique spin on the classic crybaby bridge story. For example, legend has it that on a cold November night in the tiny town of Cable, a deeply depressed woman bundled up her newborn baby and walked onto a bridge that crossed over some railroad tracks. She waited patiently until she heard the sound of a distant train whistle. With the baby still in her arms, the woman jumped in front of the oncoming train just as it reached the bridge. Both were killed instantly.

If you visit this bridge—especially when it's close to midnight—be forewarned. Unlucky travelers crossing the bridge at that time have reported that their cars suddenly stalled. When they tried to restart the engines, they heard the sound of a distant train whistle, which seemed to signal the start of a bizarre and ghostly flashback. As the whistle got closer, motorists reported hearing a baby crying. Then, just when it sounded as though the train was right next to the bridge, they heard a woman scream . . . and then everything went silent. Only then were they able to start their cars again.

A Favorite Celebrity Haunt

San Diego's grand Hotel del Coronado sparkles in the California sun. It's a popular seaside resort, a National Historic Landmark, and a very haunted hotel. Affectionately called "the Del," the hotel is proud of Kate Morgan, its resident ghost. Her story is just one of the hotel's many spine-tingling tales.

✳ ✳ ✳ ✳

The Mysterious Mrs. Morgan

ON NOVEMBER 24, 1892, Kate Morgan checked into the Hotel del Coronado under the name Lottie A. Bernard from Detroit. She looked pale and said she wasn't feeling well. She mentioned that she was planning to meet her brother, a doctor.

After a few days, the staff began to worry. The mysterious woman had checked in with no luggage. Her brother hadn't arrived, and she had barely left her room.

On Monday, November 28, the woman went into town and purchased a gun. Her body was found early the next morning on stairs that led from the hotel to the beach. From the gunshot wound to her head, it appeared she had committed suicide. When police investigated, they found few personal belongings in her hotel room.

Murder or Suicide?

After Kate's death, police determined that "Lottie A. Bernard" was an alias. They sent a sketch of her to newspapers, which described her as "the beautiful stranger." Further investigation uncovered that "Lottie" had been born Kate Farmer in Iowa and had married Tom Morgan in 1885.

Morgan was reputed to be a con artist as well as a gambler. He allegedly worked the rails and enlisted Kate's help in stealing money from train passengers. According to a witness, on a train somewhere between Los Angeles and San Diego, Kate and Morgan had an intense argument. Morgan got off the train before it reached San Diego; Kate stayed on the train until it arrived in San Diego and then checked into the Del.

Some people claim that the clues at the scene add up to murder rather than suicide. Attorney Alan May's 1990 book, *The Legend of Kate Morgan*, claims the bullet that killed Kate was a different caliber than the gun she'd purchased.

Haunting in Room 302

Whatever happened, Kate's ghost has lingered at the Del. She often manifests as eerie eyes and lips appearing in the mirror or reflected in the window of her room. Kate's spirit may be responsible for strange noises and unexplained breezes around her room as well. The curtains on closed windows billow for no reason, and lights and televisions turn themselves on and off. Kate also appears as a pale young woman in a black lace dress. A sweet fragrance lingers after her apparition disappears.

Kate stayed in Room 302. Later, during remodeling, the hotel changed the room number to 3327. The haunted room is so popular that people ask for it as "the Kate Morgan room." The hotel welcomes questions about the ghost, and everyone treats Kate as an honored guest.

The Mysterious Maid

Room 3519 at the Del is also haunted, perhaps even more intensely than Kate's room.

In 1983, a Secret Service agent stayed in Room 3519 while guarding then-Vice President George H. W. Bush. The special agent bolted from the room in the middle of the night claiming that he'd heard unearthly gurgling noises and that the entire room seemed to glow.

The Secret Service agent may have encountered a ghost related to the Kate Morgan mystery. According to one legend, while Kate was at the hotel, a maid stayed in what would later be Room 3519. In some versions of the story, the maid was traveling with Kate; in others, the maid had simply befriended her.

Whatever the connection between the two, the maid allegedly vanished the same morning Kate was found dead.

That's not the only ghost story connected with Room 3519. Another story goes that in 1888, the year the hotel was built, a wealthy man kept his mistress in that room. When the woman found out she was pregnant, she killed herself. Her body was removed from the Del, and nothing else is known about her, not even her name. Ghost hunters believe she is the one who causes the lights in the room to flicker and is responsible for the unexplained cold spot in front of the room's door.

The Blonde on the Beach

In recent years, some hotel guests have reported sightings of the ghost of Marilyn Monroe. She loved the Hotel del Coronado when she stayed there to film the movie *Some Like it Hot*. Monroe's ghost has appeared at several of her favorite places, including Hollywood's Roosevelt Hotel, where people see her in the lobby's mirror.

At the Del, Monroe is supposedly seen outdoors as a fleeting, translucent apparition near the door to the hotel or on the beach nearby. Those who see Monroe's ghost comment on her windswept blonde hair and her fringed shawl that flutters in the breeze. Others have allegedly heard her light giggle in the second and third floor hallways.

Whether they're from a rural farm or the silver screen, guests and ghosts alike love the Hotel del Coronado. If you choose to stay in one of its most haunted rooms, just remember that you're never alone.

1924 Murder Mystery

Who's at the heart of the cloaked-in-secrets demise of Thomas Ince? Who, of the loads of lovelies and gaggles of gents on the infamous Oneida *yacht that night, was the killer? Curious minds still demand to know.*

✳ ✳ ✳ ✳

THE NIGHT IS November 15, 1924. The setting is the *Oneida* yacht. The principal players are: Thomas H. Ince, Marion Davies, Charlie Chaplin, and William Randolph Hearst.

The Facts

✳ By 1924, William Randolph Hearst had built a huge newspaper empire; he dabbled in filmmaking and politics; he owned the *Oneida*. Thomas H. Ince was a prolific movie producer. Charlie Chaplin was a star comedian. Marion Davies was an actor. The web of connections went like this: Hearst and Davies were lovers; Davies and Chaplin were rumored to be lovers; Hearst and Ince were locked in tense business negotiations; Ince was celebrating a birthday.

✳ For Ince's birthday, Hearst planned a party on his yacht. It was a lavish one—champagne all around. In the era of Prohibition, this was not just extravagant, it was also illegal. But Hearst had ulterior motives: He'd heard rumors that his mistress, Davies, was secretly seeing Chaplin, and so he invited Chaplin to the party. The *Oneida* set sail from San Pedro, California, headed to San Diego on Saturday, November 15.

✳ There is no definitive version of events once everyone arrived onboard. It is known that Ince arrived at the party late, due to business, and that he did not depart the yacht under his own power. Whether he was sick or dead depends on which version you believe, but it's a fact that Ince left the yacht on a stretcher on Sunday, November 16. What happened? Various scenarios have been put forward over the years.

* Possibility 1: Hearst shoots Ince. Hearst invites Chaplin to the party to observe his behavior around Davies and to verify their affair. After catching the two in a compromising position, he flies off the handle, runs to his stateroom, grabs his gun, and comes back shooting. In this scenario, Ince tries to break up the trouble but gets shot by mistake.

* Possibility 2: Hearst shoots Ince. It's the same end result as in Possibility 1, but in this scenario, Davies and Ince are alone in the galley after Ince comes in to look for something to settle the queasiness caused by his notorious ulcers. Entering and seeing the two people together, Hearst assumes Chaplin—not Ince—is with Davies. He pulls his gun and shoots.

* Possibility 3: Chaplin shoots Ince. Chaplin, a week away from marrying a pregnant 16-year-old to avoid scandal and the law, is forlorn to the point that he considers suicide. While contemplating his gun, it accidentally goes off, and the bullet goes through the thin walls of the ship to hit Ince in the neighboring room.

* Possibility 4: An assassin shoots Ince. In this scenario, a hired assassin shoots Ince so Hearst can escape an unwanted business deal with the producer.

* Possibility 5: Ince dies of natural causes. Known for his shaky health, Ince succumbs to rabid indigestion and/or chronic heart problems. A development such as this would not surprise his friends and family.

Aftermath

Regardless of which of the various scenarios might actually be true, Ince was wheeled off Hearst's yacht. But what happened next?

That's not so clear, either. The facts of the aftermath of Ince's death are as hazy as the facts of the death itself. All reports agree that Ince did, in fact, die. There was no autopsy, and his body was cremated. After the cremation, Ince's wife, Nell, moved to Europe. But beyond those matters of record, there are simply conflicting stories.

The individuals involved had various reasons for wanting to protect themselves from whatever might have happened on the yacht. If an unlawful death did indeed take place, the motivation speaks for itself. But even if nothing untoward happened, Hearst was breaking the Prohibition laws. The damage an investigation could have caused was enough reason to make Hearst cover up any attention that could have come his way from Ince's death. As a result, he tried to hide all mention of any foul play. Although Hearst didn't own the *Los Angeles Times*, he was plenty powerful. Rumor has it that an early edition of the paper after Ince's death carried the screaming headline, "Movie Producer Shot on Hearst Yacht." By later in the day, the headline had disappeared.

For his part, Chaplin denied being on the *Oneida* in the first place. In his version of the story, he didn't attend the party for Ince at all. He did, however, claim to visit Ince—along with Hearst and Davies—later in the week. He also stated that Ince died two weeks after that visit. Most reports show that Ince was definitely dead within 48 hours of the yacht party.

Davies agreed that Chaplin was never aboard the *Oneida* that fateful night. In her version, Ince's wife called her the day after Ince left the yacht to inform her of Ince's death. Ince's doctor claimed that the producer didn't die until Tuesday, two days later.

So, what really happened? Who knows? Most of the people on the yacht never commented on their experience. Louella Parsons certainly didn't. The famed gossip columnist was reportedly aboard the *Oneida* that night (although she denied it as well). She had experienced some success writing for a Hearst newspaper, but shortly after this event, Hearst gave her a lifetime contract and wide syndication, allowing her to become a Hollywood power broker. Coincidence? No one can say for certain.

The Severed Ear of Vincent van Gogh

Vincent van Gogh is remembered as a brilliant, temperamental artist who sliced off his left ear in a fit of insanity. But like the ear itself, the veracity of this story is only partial.

✳ ✳ ✳ ✳

A Tortured Soul

THROUGHOUT HIS LIFE, the great Dutch artist was plagued by a wide range of physical and mental ailments, including epilepsy, lead poisoning, bipolar disorder, and depression. As a child, he was withdrawn and suffered from social paralysis, and his anxiety increased greatly after he was sent away to boarding school.

Van Gogh did indeed whack at his left ear, but he only severed part of the earlobe. He did this while spending time with his friend and fellow artist Paul Gauguin in Paris. Actually, the word *friend* may be imprecise here—van Gogh and Gauguin often drank heavily together and ended up in heated arguments. On the Parisian social and artistic scene, absinthe was a popular libation, and van Gogh had a particular fondness for it. At the time, it was thought that people who consumed too much of the powerful liquor were prone to violent behavior.

Fighting Dirty

During a spat with Gauguin on Christmas Eve in 1888, van Gogh attacked him with a razor. When he failed to cause Gauguin any harm, van Gogh filled the emotional void by razoring off a piece of his own earlobe. He gave the bloody chunk to his prostitute friend Rachel, advising her to keep it as something precious. (Laugh if you wish. What would it be worth today?)

The incident happened about two years before van Gogh shot himself to death. It's reasonable to assume that his suicide was connected to a general and final psychological collapse— another irrational, self-harming act.

A Superior Haunting: The *Edmund Fitzgerald*

Many ships have been lost to the dangers of the Great Lakes, but few incidents have fascinated the world like the sinking of the Edmund Fitzgerald off the shores of northern Michigan on November 10, 1975. The mysterious circumstances of the tragedy, which took 29 lives, and lingering tales of a haunting—all memorialized in a 1976 song by Gordon Lightfoot—have kept the horrific story fresh for more than three decades.

✳ ✳ ✳ ✳

Least Likely to Sink

Lake Superior is well known among sailors for its treachery, especially when the unusually strong autumn winds sailors call the "Witch of November" roil the waves. But the 729-foot-long *Edmund Fitzgerald* was considered as unsinkable as any steamer ever launched, and its cost of $8.4 million made it the most expensive freighter in history at the time.

At its christening in June 1958, it was the Great Lakes' largest freighter, built with state-of-the-art technology, comfortable crew quarters, and elegant staterooms for guests. Its name honored Edmund Fitzgerald, the son of a sea captain and the president of Northwestern Mutual Insurance Company, who had commissioned the boat.

During the christening, a few incidents occurred that some saw as bad omens from the get-go. As a crowd of more than 10,000 watched, it took Mrs. Fitzgerald three tries to shatter the bottle of champagne. Then, when the ship was released into the water, it hit the surface at the wrong angle, kicking up a wave that splattered the entire ceremonial area with lake water and knocking the ship into a nearby dock. If that weren't enough, one spectator died on the spot of a heart attack.

The Last Launch

The weather was unseasonably pleasant the morning of November 9, 1975, so much so that the crew of 28 men who set sail from Superior, Wisconsin, that day were unlikely to have been concerned about their routine trip to Zug Island on the Detroit River. But the captain, Ernest McSorley, the 29th man aboard the ship, knew a storm was in the forecast.

McSorley was a 44-year veteran of the lakes, had captained the *Fitzgerald* since 1972, and was thought to have been planning his retirement for the following year. He paid close attention to the gale warnings issued that afternoon, but no one suspected they would turn into what weather-watchers called a "once in a lifetime storm." However, when the weather report was upgraded to a full storm warning, McSorley changed course to follow a route safer than the normal shipping lanes, instead chugging closer to the Canadian shore.

Following the *Fitzgerald* in a sort of "buddy" system was another freighter, the *Arthur Anderson*. The two captains stayed in contact as they traveled together through winds measuring up to 50 knots (about 58 miles per hour) with waves splashing 12 feet or higher. Around 1:00 P.M., McSorley advised Captain Cooper of the *Anderson* that the *Fitzgerald* was "rolling." By about 2:45 P.M., as the *Anderson* moved to avoid a dangerous shoal near Caribou Island, a crewman sighted the *Fitzgerald* about 16 miles ahead, closer to the shoal than Cooper thought safe.

About 3:30 P.M., McSorley reported to Cooper that the *Fitzgerald* had sustained some minor damage and was beginning to list, or roll to one side. The ships were still 16 to 17 miles apart. At 4:10 P.M., with waves now lashing 18 feet high, McSorley radioed that his ship had lost radar capability. The two ships stayed in radio contact until about 7:00 P.M., when the *Fitzgerald* crew told the *Anderson* they were "holding [their] own." After that, radio contact was lost and the *Fitzgerald* dropped off the radar. Around 8:30 P.M., Cooper told the Coast Guard at Sault Ste. Marie that the *Fitzgerald* appeared to be missing. The search was on.

Evidently, the *Fitzgerald* sank sometime after 7:10 P.M. on November 10, just 17 miles from the shore of Whitefish Point, Michigan. Despite a massive search effort, it wasn't until November 14 that a navy flyer detected a magnetic anomaly that turned out to be the wreck of the *Fitzgerald*. The only other evidence of the disaster to surface was a handful of lifeboats, life jackets, and some oars, tools, and propane tanks. A robotic vehicle was used to thoroughly photograph the wreck in May 1976.

One Mysterious Body

One troubling aspect of the *Fitzgerald* tragedy was that no bodies were found. In most lakes or temperate waters, corpses rise to the surface as decomposition causes gases to form, which makes bodies float. But the Great Lakes are so cold that decomposition and the formation of these gases is inhibited, causing bodies to remain on the lake bottom. One explanation was that the crew had been contained in the ship's enclosed areas. The wildest speculation surmised that the ship was destroyed by a UFO and the men were abducted by aliens.

In 1994, a Michigan businessman named Frederick Shannon took a tugboat and a 16-foot submarine equipped with a full array of modern surveillance equipment to the site, hoping to produce a documentary about the ship. But his crew was surprised when they discovered a body near the bow of the wreck, which had settled into the lake bottom. The remains were covered by cork sections of a deteriorated canvas life vest and were photographed but not retrieved. However, there was nothing to conclusively prove that this body was associated with the *Fitzgerald*. Two French vessels were lost in the same region in 1918, and none of those bodies had been recovered either. A sailor lost from one of them could have been preserved by the lake's frigid water and heavy pressure.

Many have pondered whether the men of the *Edmund Fitzgerald* might have been saved had they had better disaster equipment, but survival time in such cold water is only minutes. Most of the life jackets later floated to the surface, indicating that the crewmen never put them on. The seas were much too rough to launch wooden lifeboats, and there was probably no time to find and inflate rubber life rafts.

What Sank the Mighty *Fitz*?

She went down fast, that much was evident. Three different organizations filed official reports on the ship's sinking without coming to any common conclusions. It was thought impossible for such a large, well-built, and relatively "young" ship, only in its 18th year, to break up and sink so quickly, particularly in this age of modern navigation and communication equipment.

One popular theory is that the *Fitzgerald* ventured too close to the dangerous Six-Fathom Shoal near Caribou Island and scraped over it, damaging the hull. Another is that the ship's hatch covers were either faulty or improperly clamped, which allowed water infiltration. Wave height may also have played its part, with the storm producing a series of gargantuan swells known as the "Three Sisters," a trio of lightning-fast waves that pound a vessel in quick succession—the first washing over the deck, the second hitting the deck again so fast that the first has not had time to clear itself, and the third quickly adding another heavy wash, piling thousands of gallons of water on the ship at once. Few ships have the ability to remain afloat under such an onslaught.

In addition, the ship was about 200 feet longer than the 530-foot-deep water where it floundered. If the waves pushed the ship bow first down into the water, it would have hit bottom and stuck (which is what appears to have happened), snapping the long midsection in two as a result of continuing wave action and exploding steam boilers. The ship's 26,000-pound cargo of iron ore pellets would have shifted as the ship twisted and sank, adding to the devastation.

Some fingers point to the ship's prior damages. In 1969, The *Fitzgerald* crunched ground near the locks at Sault Ste. Marie, Michigan, and less than a year later, in April 1970, it had a minor collision with the S.S. *Hochelaga*. In September 1970, the *Fitzgerald* slammed a lock wall—the third damaging hit in 12 months. It's possible that these impacts inflicted more structural damage than was realized or that it was not repaired properly.

Spirits of the Lake

Author Hugh E. Bishop says that sailors have claimed to see a ghostly ship in the vicinity of the sinking. The captain of the Coast Guard cutter the *Woodrush* was on duty in 1976, as his ship spent a night stuck in shifting ice masses directly over the *Fitzgerald* wreckage. All through the night, the captain's normally carefree black Labrador whined and cowered, avoiding certain spots on the ship as if some invisible presence existed.

Bishop also noted that on October 21, 1975, San Antonio psychic J. Nickie Jackson recorded in her diary a dream that foretold the *Fitzgerald's* doom. In her dream, she saw the freighter struggling to stay afloat in giant waves before it finally plunged straight down into the depths. The real-life event occurred just three weeks later. Jackson was familiar with the *Edmund Fitzgerald* because she had previously lived in Superior but was surprised to dream about it in her new life in Texas.

For Whom the Bell Tolls . . .

On July 4, 1995, a year after the lone body was documented, the bell of the *Edmund Fitzgerald* was retrieved from the wreckage and laid to rest in the Great Lakes Shipwreck Historical Museum in Whitefish Bay, Michigan. With the wreckage, the diving crew left a replica of the bell, which symbolizes the ship's "spirit." At a memorial service every year, the original, 200-pound bronze bell is rung 29 times—once for each man who perished on the *Edmund Fitzgerald*.

Grave Curiosities

Grave sites offer us a chance to make one final statement, one that will hopefully last for all eternity. Here are a few that certainly make walking through a cemetery a unique experience!

✳ ✳ ✳ ✳

Davis Memorial

JOHN DAVIS WAS a successful farmer in Hiawatha, Kansas. When his wife, Sarah, passed away in 1930, Davis spent the next seven years, and nearly all his money, building a memorial to honor his wife and their life together.

Created in stages, the memorial uses life-size granite and Italian marble statues to depict John and Sarah's life together. Beginning with statues of John and Sarah as a young couple, visitors follow the couple literally to their graves. The final "scene" involves miniature versions of John and an angellike Sarah kneeling over their own graves. The most touching, however, is the previous carving, which portrays John, sitting in an oversize chair and looking quite sad, shortly after Sarah's death. Next to him, where Sarah should be, is an empty chair marked "The Vacant Chair."

Yield to Oncoming Grave

When Nancy Barnett passed away on December 1, 1831, her family was determined to make sure her final resting place stayed just that—final. So, in the early 1900s, when it was announced that the proposed route for a new highway near Franklin, Indiana, was going to cut through the small cemetery where Nancy was buried, the family knew they had to act fast. When local workers showed up to exhume the bodies and relocate them to another cemetery, they found Barnett's grandson sitting on her grave, holding a shotgun. He made it clear that under no circumstances was he going to allow Nancy's body to be moved. The workers figured if they ignored him, he would eventually go away. But each day they returned, Nancy's grandson was there with his shotgun. Eventually, the authorities decided to leave Nancy where she was and build the road around her grave. Today, motorists traveling down County Road 400 just south of Franklin notice signs alerting them that there's a divided highway up ahead—divided because cars have to go around the grave in the middle of the road.

Victim of the Beast

With just four words and three numbers, a grave site in Salt Lake City Cemetery creeps people out. Lying quietly amongst the other tombstones is one belonging to Lilly E. Gray. Her stone is simple, containing only her name, birth and death dates, and the following statement: "Victim of the Beast 666." The first time people see the stone, they naturally assume that it's a hoax. It's not, but the meaning behind the cryptic statement is unclear. Theories range from "the Beast" being Lilly's husband, Elmer, to one that claims "666" is actually a reference to the local road, Route 666, and that Lilly might have had a bad accident there. If so, she survived the crash, because her death certificate lists no clues other than that she died at a local hospital from "natural causes."

Ray's Mercedes

Friends say that Raymond Tse Jr. always wanted to own a Mercedes-Benz. Sadly, those dreams all but died in 1981 when Ray passed away at just 15 years of age . . . or did they? In an effort to fulfill his brother's dream, David Tse had a life-size replica of a 1982 Mercedes-Benz 2400D limousine carved from a single block of granite. It took nearly two years and $250,000 to create, and when finished, it was "parked" behind the Tse mausoleum, complete with "RAY TSE" vanity plates.

Bill's Not Here

El Campo Santo is one of the oldest cemeteries in San Diego. When Bill Marshall met his untimely death in December 1851, he was buried in the far corner of the cemetery. However, as time went by, people stopped looking after El Campo Santo, and when a new streetcar line was being put in, the town took over much of the cemetery's property. When a new cemetery wall was erected in the 1930s, it was discovered that Bill Marshall's body, along with many others, was now outside the cemetery grounds. Today, visitors to El Campo Santo Cemetery will find a marker that reads "Bill Marshall is not here but on the other side of the wall" as well as a carved hand pointing toward the wall.

Midnight Mary's Grave

Just inside the entrance to Evergreen Cemetery in New Haven, Connecticut, is the gravestone of Mary Hart, aka Midnight Mary. At first glance, there seems to be nothing special about the stone—until you read the words carved on it:

> AT HIGH NOON
> JUST FROM, AND ABOUT TO RENEW
> HER DAILY WORK, IN HER FULL STRENGTH OF
> BODY AND MIND
> MARY E. HART HAVING FALLEN PROSTRATE:
> REMAINED UNCONSCIOUS UNTIL SHE DIED AT MID-
> NIGHT,
> OCTOBER 15, 1872
> BORN DECEMBER 16, 1824

Sure, the words are strange enough, but they don't hold a candle to the frightening words emblazoned in raised, black letters in an arch over the stone:

> THE PEOPLE SHALL BE TROUBLED AT
> MIDNIGHT AND PASS AWAY

No one knows for sure who Mary Hart was, but legend has it that she was a witch who used her tombstone to curse all those who persecuted her while she was alive. Another popular story claims that Mary was accidentally buried alive, but by the time the mistake was realized, she was already dead from suffocating in her coffin.

Seven Famous Curses

No one really knows for sure if there's any truth to these curses, but if you want to take James Dean's car for a spin, or dig up an ancient mummy, don't expect us to help!

* * * *

1. **James Dean and "Little Bastard":** On September 30, 1955, James Dean was killed when the silver Porsche 550 Spyder he called "Little Bastard" was struck by an oncoming vehicle. Within a year or so of Dean's crash, the car was involved in two more fatal accidents and caused injury to at least six other people. After Dean's accident, the car was purchased by hot-rod designer George Barris. While getting a tune-up,  Little Bastard fell on the mechanic's legs and crushed them. Barris later sold the engine and transmission to two doctors who raced cars. While racing against each other, one driver was killed, the other seriously injured. Someone else had purchased the tires, which blew simultaneously, sending the driver to the hospital. Little Bastard was set to appear in a car show, but a fire broke out in the building the night before the show, destroying every car except Little Bastard, which survived without so much as a smudge. The car was then loaded onto a truck to go back to Salinas, California. The driver lost control en route, was thrown from the cab, and was crushed by the car when it fell off the trailer. In 1960, after being exhibited by the California Highway Patrol, Little Bastard disappeared and hasn't been seen since.

2. **The Curse of Tutankhamun's Tomb:** In 1922, English explorer Howard Carter, leading an expedition funded by

George Herbert, Fifth Earl of Carnarvon, discovered the ancient Egyptian king's tomb and the riches inside. After opening the tomb, however, strange and unpleasant events began to take place in the lives of those involved in the expedition. Lord Carnarvon's story is the most bizarre. The adventurer apparently died from pneumonia and blood poisoning following complications from a mosquito bite. Allegedly, at the exact moment Carnarvon passed away in Cairo, all the lights in the city mysteriously went out. Carnarvon's dog dropped dead that morning, too. Some point to the foreboding inscription, "Death comes on wings to he who enters the tomb of a pharaoh," as proof that King Tut put a curse on anyone who disturbed his final resting place.

3. **"The Club":** If you're a rock star and you're about to turn 27, you might want to consider taking a year off to avoid membership in "The Club." Robert Johnson, an African-American musician who Eric Clapton called "the most important blues musician who ever lived," played the guitar so well that some said he must have made a deal with the devil. So when he died at 27, folks said it must have been time to pay up. Since Johnson's death, a host of other musical geniuses have gone to an early grave at age 27. Brian Jones, founding member of the Rolling Stones, died at age 27 in 1969. Then it was both Jimi Hendrix and Janis Joplin in 1970 and Jim Morrison the following year. Kurt Cobain joined "The Club" in 1994. All 27 years old. Coincidence? Or were these musical geniuses paying debts, too?

4. **"Da Billy Goat" Curse:** In 1945, William "Billy Goat" Sianis brought his pet goat, Murphy, to Wrigley Field to see the fourth game of the 1945 World Series between the Chicago Cubs and the Detroit Tigers. Sianis and his goat were later ejected from the game, and Sianis reportedly put a curse on the team that day. Ever since, the Cubs have had legendary bad luck. Over the years, Cubs fans have experienced agony in repeated late-season collapses when victory

seemed imminent. In 1969, 1984, 1989, and 2003, the Cubs were painfully close to advancing to the World Series but couldn't hold the lead. Even those who don't consider themselves Cubs fans blame the hex for the weird and almost comical losses year after year. The Cubs have not won a World Series since 1908—no other team in the history of the game has gone as long without a championship.

5. Rasputin and the Romanovs: Rasputin, the self-proclaimed magician and cult leader, wormed his way into the palace of the Romanovs, Russia's ruling family, around the turn of the last century. After getting a little too big for his britches, a few of the Romanovs allegedly decided to have him killed. But he was exceptionally resilient. Reportedly it took poison, falling down a staircase, and repeated gunshots to finally kill Rasputin. It's said that Rasputin mumbled a curse from his deathbed, assuring Russia's ruling monarchs that they would all be dead within a year. That did come to pass, as the Romanov family was brutally murdered in a mass execution less than a year later.

6. Tecumseh and the American Presidents: The curse of Tippecanoe, or "Tecumseh's Curse," is a widely held explanation of the fact that from 1840 to 1960, every U.S. president elected (or reelected) every 20th year has died in office. Popular belief is that Tecumseh administered the curse when William Henry Harrison's troops defeated the Native American leader and his forces at the Battle of Tippecanoe. Check it out:

✳ William Henry Harrison was elected president in 1840. He caught a cold during his inauguration, which quickly turned into pneumonia. He died April 4, 1841, after only one month in office.

✳ Abraham Lincoln was elected president in 1860 and reelected four years later. Lincoln was assassinated and died April 15, 1865.

* James Garfield was elected president in 1880. Charles Guiteau shot him in July 1881. Garfield died several months later from complications of the gunshot wound.

* William McKinley was elected president in 1896 and reelected in 1900. On September 6, 1901, McKinley was shot by Leon F. Czolgosz, who considered the president an "enemy of the people." McKinley died eight days later.

* Three years after Warren G. Harding was elected president in 1920, he died suddenly of either a heart attack or stroke while traveling in San Francisco.

* Franklin D. Roosevelt was elected president in 1932 and reelected in 1936, 1940, and 1944. His health wasn't great, but he died rather suddenly in 1945, of a cerebral hemorrhage or stroke.

* John F. Kennedy was elected president in 1960 and assassinated in Dallas three years later.

* Ronald Reagan was elected president in 1980 and survived an assassination attempt in 1981. This may have broken the curse, since George W. Bush, who was elected in 2000 and reelected in 2004, survived both of his terms.

7. **The Curse of the Kennedy Family:** Okay, so maybe if this family had stayed out of politics and off airplanes, their fate might have been different. Regardless, the number of Kennedy family tragedies has led some to believe there must be a curse on the whole bunch. You decide.

* JFK's brother Joseph Jr. and sister Kathleen died in plane crashes in 1944 and 1948, respectively.

* JFK's other sister, Rosemary, was institutionalized in a mental hospital for years.

* John F. Kennedy himself, America's 35th president, was assassinated in 1963 at age 46.

* Robert Kennedy, one of JFK's younger brothers, was assassinated in 1968.

* Senator Ted Kennedy, JFK's youngest brother, survived a plane crash in 1964. In 1969, he was driving a car that went off a bridge, causing the death of his companion, Mary Jo Kopechne. His presidential goals were pretty much squashed after that. He died in 2009 at age 77.

* In 1984, Robert Kennedy's son David died of a drug overdose. Another son, Michael, died in a skiing accident in 1997.

* In 1999, JFK Jr., his wife, and his sister-in-law perished when the small plane that he was piloting crashed into the Atlantic Ocean.

Say What?

I can accept failure, but I can't accept not trying.

—MICHAEL JORDAN

I think more people would be alive today if there were a death penalty.

—NANCY REAGAN

The execs don't care what color you are. They care about how much money you make. Hollywood is not really black or white. It's green.

—WILL SMITH

Every man has a right to a Saturday night bath.

—LYNDON B. JOHNSON

The best way to keep one's word is not to give it.

—NAPOLEON BONAPARTE

Start every day off with a smile and get it over with.

—W. C. FIELDS

Vlad the Impaler: The Original Dracula

Most people are aware of Bram Stoker's Dracula *and the many cultural reincarnations that the title character has gone through. But the fictional character of Dracula was based on a human being far more frightening than his fictional avatar.*

✳ ✳ ✳ ✳

Background

THE LATE 1300s and early 1400s were a dramatic time in the area now known as Romania. Three sovereign states—Transylvania, Moldavia, and Wallachia—held fast to their independence against the Ottoman Empire. Wallachia was an elective monarchy, with much political backstabbing between the royal family and the boyars, the land-owning nobles.

Vlad III, known after his death as Vlad the Impaler, was born in the latter half of 1431 in the citadel of Sighisoara, Transylvania. His family was living in exile when he was born, ousted from their native Wallachia by pro-Turkish boyars. He was the son of a military governor who himself was a knight in the Order of the Dragon, a fraternity established to uphold Christian beliefs and fight Muslim Turks. Vlad II was also known as Vlad Dracul—Dracul meaning devil in Romanian. The *a* at the end of Dracul means "son of."

The throne of Wallachia was tossed from person to person. In 1436, Vlad Dracul took over the throne of Wallachia, but two years after that, he formed an alliance with the dreaded Turks, betraying his oath to the Order of the Dragon. He was assassinated in 1447 for his treachery.

Unfortunately for Vlad the Impaler, while his father was negotiating deals with the sultan of the Ottoman Empire, he traded his sons as collateral for his loyalty. While in captivity, Vlad the Impaler was frequently beaten and tortured.

Battleground

Released by the Turks after his father was killed, Vlad the Impaler showed up in Wallachia and defeated the boyars who had taken over the throne. He ruled for a brief time during 1448, but Vlad was quickly kicked out when the man who assassinated his father appointed someone else to fill the kingly duties. Vlad the Impaler bided his time, and in 1456, he not only took back the throne of Wallachia but also killed his father's murderer. He ruled Wallachia until 1462, but he was not a happy monarch.

Vlad the Impaler had a habit of killing huge numbers of people—slaves who didn't work hard enough, weak people who he felt were wasting space in his kingdom, and of course, criminals. You really did not want to be a criminal in Vlad's kingdom. Mostly, as might be guessed from his nickname, Vlad liked impaling people and then perching them in circles around town, an example of what would happen if citizens stepped out of line. In addition, he was rumored to drink the blood of those he had killed. On the upside, however, the crime rate in Wallachia was impressively low.

Breakdown

In 1461, Vlad the Impaler took on the Turks but was run out of Wallachia the next year. He lost the throne to Sultan Mehmed II's army and eventually sought refuge in Transylvania. The sultan installed Vlad's brother Radu on the throne of Wallachia. Once again, Vlad the Impaler was not happy. In 1476, with help from his Transylvanian pals, he launched a campaign to take back the throne of Wallachia, and he succeeded, impaling up a storm along the way. The Turks retaliated, and even though Vlad tried to organize an army to fight them, he couldn't raise a battalion large enough to defeat the Turks permanently. In his final battle, Vlad was killed, though the manner of his death is unknown. Some say that he was mistakenly killed by his own army, while others say that he was killed and decapitated by the Turks. One thing is known, however: Unlike the hundreds of thousands he killed, Vlad the Impaler was never one of the impalees.

Curse of the (Polish) Mummy

In 1973, a group of research scientists entered the tomb of King Casimir IV, a member of the Jagiellon dynasty that once ruled throughout central Europe. Within weeks, only two of the scientists remained alive.

✳   ✳   ✳   ✳

The Jagiellon Curse

INDIANA JONES DIDN'T have it easy, but as work hazards in archaeology go, there are worse fates than snake pits and big rolling boulders. For example, there are strains of mold fungi that eat your body from the inside out. This was the inauspicious fate of several scientists who opened a tomb that had been shut for centuries, thereby unleashing a powerful and all too real mummy's curse—deadly microorganisms.

The tomb of King Casimir IV of Poland and his wife, Elizabeth of Habsburg, is located in the chapel of Wawel Castle in Krakow, Poland. Casimir served as king for more than 40 years in the 13th century. He left behind 13 children, many of whom went on to positions of great power. In 1973, the archbishop of Krakow, Cardinal Karol Wojtyla (who later went on to become Pope John Paul II), gave a group of scientists permission to open King Casimir's tomb and examine its contents. Within the tomb, the unlucky group found a heavily rotted wooden coffin—not so surprising, given the box had been in the tomb for nearly 500 years. However, within a few days, 4 of the 12 researchers were dead; 6 more died soon after.

Killer Fungi

While sensationalists blamed the tragedy on a mummy's curse, the scientific-minded questioned whether the sudden deaths were related to the icky molds and other parasites that would linger in a room that had been sealed off for centuries. This was precisely the suspicion of Dr. Boleslaw Smyk, one of the two surviving scientists. He set out to discover what exactly had killed his colleagues, and he came up with three species of mold fungi that had lingered in King Casimir's tomb: *Aspergillus flavus*, *Penicillim rubrum*, and *Penicillim rugulosum*.

Not a Mummy, but No Less Scary

These are not the kindest of specimens. *Aspergillus flavus* is toxic to the liver, while *Penicillim rubrum* causes, among a host of other afflictions, pulmonary emphysema. These toxins grow on decaying wood and lime mortar, both of which were in Casimir's tomb. The toxins remained in the tomb in the form of mold spores, which can survive for thousands of years in closed environments. It is likely the researchers breathed in the spores immediately upon entering the tomb, since the sudden influx of fresh air would have blown the spores about. Toxic spores that are inhaled in this fashion can lead to organ failure and death in a very short time.

It's therefore not surprising that whisperings of a "mummy's curse" abound. The more famous legend came from the 1922 Egyptian excavation of Pharaoh Tutankhamun's tomb. Lord Carnarvon, one of the main financiers of the King Tut excavation, died a few months after he entered Tut's tomb, which was laden with the same fungi spores that were identified in King Casimir's tomb. Stories of a mummy's curse followed, although it's unclear whether Carnarvon's death actually was related to his archaeological pursuits: Carnarvon had an insect bite on his cheek that became infected weeks after the excavation. He fell ill and eventually died of pneumonia and septicemia (blood poisoning).

Whether or not Carnarvon died of natural causes, rumors of the supernatural took on a life of their own. After news of his death spread, fantastical stories grew regarding the grisly deaths of anyone who had entered King Tut's tomb. Today, even modern archaeologists are warned of their potential exposure to the dreaded Mummy's Curse.

Who Wants to Be a Billionaire?

According to legend, more than $2 billion in gold may be hidden on Oak Island in Mahone Bay, about 45 minutes from Halifax, Nova Scotia. For more than 200 years, treasure hunters have scoured the island, looking for the bounty, but the pirates who buried the treasure hid it well … and left booby traps, too.

✳ ✳ ✳ ✳

Folklore Leads to Fact

SINCE 1720, PEOPLE have claimed that pirate treasure was buried on Oak Island. In 1795, young Daniel McGinnis went hunting on the island and found evidence that those stories might be true: An oak tree had been used with a hoist to lift something very heavy, and when McGinnis dug at that spot, he found loose sand indicating a pit about 12 feet in diameter.

He returned the next day with two friends, and after digging ten feet down, they encountered a wooden platform. Beneath it was more dirt. Ten feet further down, there was another wooden platform with more dirt beneath it. At that point, the boys gave up. They needed better tools and engineering expertise.

They didn't get the help they needed, but one thing was certain: Something important had been buried on Oak Island. Soon, more people visited the island hoping to strike it rich.

An Encouraging Message

In the early 1800s, a Nova Scotia company began excavating the pit. The slow process took many years, and every ten feet, they found another wooden platform and sometimes layers of charcoal, putty, or coconut fiber.

About 90 feet down, the treasure hunters found an oily stone about three feet wide. It bore a coded inscription that read, "Forty feet below, two million pounds lie buried." (Gold worth two million pounds in 1795 would be worth approximately $2 billion today.)

However, as they dug past that 90-foot level, water began rushing into the hole. A few days later, the pit was almost full of seawater. No matter how much the team bailed, the water maintained its new level, so the company dug a second shaft, parallel to the first and 110 feet deep. But when they dug across to the original tunnel, water quickly filled the new shaft as well. The team abandoned the project, but others were eager to try their luck.

More Digging, More Encouragement, More Water

Since then, several companies have excavated deeper in the original shaft. Most treasure hunters—including a team organized by Franklin D. Roosevelt—have found additional proof that something valuable is buried there. For example, at 126 feet—nearly "forty feet below" the 90-foot marker—engineers found oak and iron. Farther down, they also reached a large cement chamber, from which they brought up a tiny piece of parchment, which encouraged them to dig deeper.

A narrow shaft dug in 1971 allowed researchers to use special cameras to study the pit. The team thought they saw several chests, some tools, and a disembodied hand floating in the water, but the shaft collapsed before they could explore further.

Since then, flooding has continued to hamper research efforts. At least six people have been killed in their quests for buried treasure, but the digging continues. As of late 2007, the 1971 shaft had been redug to a depth of 181 feet. It offers the greatest promise for success. But just in case, investors and engineers plan to continue digging.

A Vacation Worth a Fortune?

Oak Island has become a unique vacation spot for people who like adventure and the chance to go home with a fortune. Canadian law says any treasure hunter can keep 90 percent of his or her findings. Some vacationers dig at nearby islands, believing that the Oak Island site may be an elaborate, 18th-century "red herring." Perhaps the treasure is actually buried on one of more than 100 other lovely islands in Mahone Bay.

It's Not What You Think: Famous Faked Photos

Some photographs are so iconic that it's nearly impossible to separate the image from the event: President John F. Kennedy's funeral, the Eagle *spacecraft landing on the moon, the raising of the flag at Iwo Jima. But seeing is not always believing.*

✳ ✳ ✳ ✳

A New Era

IN THE BRAVE new world of digital photography, photographers can manipulate images with ease while media mavens worry over the ethics of photographic alterations. But photographers were editing reality long before the computer: As early as the Civil War, photographers posed battlefield shots to get the best effect. Nineteenth-century photographers used double exposures and other darkroom sleight-of-hand to create photographs of spirits and the supernatural. In Stalinist Russia, discredited leaders were removed from the picture—in more ways than one. Check out these famous "faked" photographs from the days before Photoshop.

The Loch Ness Monster

In 1934, London surgeon Robert Kenneth Wilson sold a photograph, one he had taken while on a birding expedition, to the *London Daily Mail*. In the photo, the long slender neck of an unknown animal rises from the waters of Scotland's Loch Ness.

Wilson's story held for 60 years, until 1994, when a Loch Ness Monster believer named Alastair Boyd uncovered evidence that the photograph was a hoax. It turned out that in 1933, the *Daily Mail* had hired big-game hunter Marmaduke Wetherell to investigate reported sightings at Loch Ness and find the monster. Instead of Nessie, however, Wetherell found tracks that had been faked with a dried hippo foot. Working with his son and stepson, Wetherell staged the Loch Ness photograph in revenge for the faked tracks, attaching a head and neck crafted from plasticine to the conning tower of a toy submarine. A friend convinced Wilson to be the front man.

It was Wetherell's stepson who broke the story, admitting his part in the hoax to Boyd in 1994. However, Wetherell's son Ian had actually published his own version of the hoax in an obscure article in 1975.

Raising the Flag at Iwo Jima

Associated Press photographer Joe Rosenthal won a Pulitzer Prize for his photograph of American servicemen raising the flag at the Battle of Iwo Jima during World War II. He spent the rest of his life fighting charges that the picture had been posed.

The charges were based on a misunderstanding. Rosenthal was halfway up Mount Suribachi when he learned he had missed the flag-raising. Told the view was worth the climb, he continued up the mountain, where he found that the Marine commanders had decided to replace the original flag with a larger one.

He climbed on a pile of stones trying to get a better angle for a shot of the second flag raising and almost missed that one too. He saw the flag go up out of the corner of his eye and swung his camera and shot. Knowing a single exposure taken on the fly was a gamble and wanting to be sure he had something worth printing, Rosenthal took a picture of jubilant Marines under the flag, which he called the "gung-ho" shot. He sent his film to the military press center and left for his next assignment.

Rosenthal had no way of knowing his first, off-the-cuff shot had succeeded, and the congratulatory wire he received from the Associated Press didn't tell him which picture they were congratulating him for. When someone asked him a few days later if he had posed the picture, Rosenthal assumed they were talking about the "gung-ho" shot and said "Sure." A few days later, *Time* magazine's radio program reported the picture had been posed. *Time* retracted the story a few days later, but the misunderstanding haunted Rosenthal for the rest of his life.

Makeshift Propaganda

When Soviet war photographer Yevgeny Khaldei entered Nazi Berlin with the Red Army in 1945, he was looking for one thing: his own "Iwo Jima shot." When he didn't find one, he created it.

Khaldei chose the Reichstag building as the site for his photograph and then discovered he didn't have a Soviet flag to raise. He flew back to Moscow, took three red tablecloths his news agency used for official events, and spent the night sewing a Soviet flag to take back to Berlin.

But it took two days of fighting before the Red Army gained control of the roof. While the Germans surrendered the building, a team of soldiers chosen for their political significance stood on the roof and Khaldei posed his masterpiece of Soviet propaganda.

When official censors noticed one of the soldiers was wearing two watches, presumably acquired while looting, Khaldei was ordered to edit out the evidence. He also added smoke to heighten the drama.

Khaldei later justified posing his wartime photos by claiming that pictures should match the importance of the event.

Kisses Both Real and Fake

Alfred Eisenstaedt's photograph of a sailor kissing a nurse in Times Square on V-J Day, August 14, 1945, was real, snapped on the fly as the seaman kissed his way through the crowd.

French photographer Robert Doisneau, however, posed his seemingly spontaneous "Kiss by the Hotel De Ville" for a 1950 *Life* magazine photo spread on Parisian lovers. The photo found new life as an icon of romantic love when a poster company rediscovered it in the '80s.

The Pirate's Eye Patch: A Fictional Flourish

Nothing says "pirate" quite like a black eye patch. But the truth is, most of these villainous swashbucklers wore no such fashion accessory.

❋ ❋ ❋ ❋

Blackbeard and Company Went Patchless

READ THE BIOGRAPHIES of most of the famous pirates in history—Blackbeard, Bartholomew Roberts, Calico Jack, and others—and you will find that their portraits show them with two patch-free eyes. So the main reason that pirates wear eye patches is because the creators of fictional pirates like them that way. Patches have become an instantly recognizable part of pirate lore, largely because pirates are portrayed as wearing them in movies and books.

But that's not to say no pirate ever wore an eye patch. The primary reason anyone wears an eye patch—because he or she has a missing or injured eye—is a plausible explanation for why a pirate would wear one. Swashbuckling, after all, is an extremely dangerous activity.

Another, more fascinating theory involves a "trick of the trade" for all seamen, as well as for law-enforcement officers and armed forces. An eye patch (or simply closing one eye, which doesn't look nearly as cool) can help your eyesight when moving from a bright place into a dark one. For example, say you're a pirate and you've just boarded a ship at noon on a beautiful sunny day. If you're not wearing an eye patch and everyone you need to steal from is below deck, you could be compromised because your eyes have to become accustomed to the dark interior.

Not so with an eye patch! A patch gives you one eye that is already used to the dark. So when you get down below, you simply move the patch from one eye to the other. This allows for much more efficient pillaging.

You Can Be a Pirate, Too

In fact, you can use this trick the next time you go to see a pirate-themed movie: Close one eye while you're walking through the lobby, and then open it after you are in the theater. Call yourself a pirate, and find yourself a seat in the dark.

* About 75 percent of what we think we taste is actually coming from our sense of smell.

* Along with sweet, salty, sour, and bitter, there is a fifth taste, called umami, which describes the savory taste of foods such as meat, cheese, and soy sauce.

* Babies are born with taste buds on the insides of their cheeks—and, overall, they have more taste buds than adults—but they lose them as they grow older.

* Adults have, on average, around 10,000 taste buds, although an elderly person might have only 5,000.

* One in four people is a "supertaster" and has more taste buds than the average person—more than 1,000 per square centimeter.

* Twenty-five percent of humans are "nontasters" and have fewer taste buds than other people their age—only about 40 per square centimeter.

* A taste bud is 30 to 60 microns (slightly more than ¹⁄₁₀₀₀ inch) in diameter.

* Taste buds are not just for tongues—they also cover the back of the throat and the roof of the mouth.

* Cats' taste buds cannot detect sweetness.

* The "suction cups" on an octopus' tentacles are covered in taste buds.

* A butterfly's taste buds are on its feet and tongue.

* Attached to each human taste bud are microscopic hairs called microvilli.

Giant Frogman Spotted in Ohio!

For the most part, frogs are rather unintimidating—unless they happen to be more than four feet tall and standing along a dark road in the middle of the night.

✳ ✳ ✳ ✳

The First Encounter

ON MARCH 3, 1972, police officer Ray Shockey was driving his patrol car along Riverside Road toward the small town of Loveland, Ohio. At approximately 1:00 A.M., Shockey saw what he thought was a dog lying alongside the road, but as he got closer, the creature suddenly stood up on two feet. Amazed, Shockey stopped his car and watched the creature climb over a guardrail and scamper down the ditch toward the Little Miami River. Shockey drove back to the police station and described what he'd seen to fellow officer Mark Matthews. Shockey said the creature was approximately four feet tall and weighed between 50 and 75 pounds. It stood on two legs and had webbed feet, clawed hands, and the head of a frog.

After hearing his story, Matthews accompanied Shockey back to the site of the encounter. The pair could not locate the frogman, but they did find strange scratch marks along the section of guardrail the creature had climbed over.

Frogman Returns

On the night of March 17, Matthews was on the outskirts of town when he saw an animal lying in the middle of the road. Thinking that the animal had been hit by a car, Matthews stopped his squad car. But when the animal suddenly stood up on two legs, Matthews realized that it was the same creature that Shockey had encountered. Just as before, the creature walked to the side of the road and climbed over a guardrail. Matthews simply watched, although some reports say he shot at the animal. Either way, the creature moved down the embankment toward the river and vanished.

The Aftermath

When news spread of a second Frogman sighting, the town of Loveland was inundated with calls from reporters across the country. Obviously, reports of four-foot-tall froglike creatures are rarely considered newsworthy, but two witnesses had seen the creature on different nights, and both were police officers.

In the beginning, Shockey and Matthews stuck to their stories and even had sketches made of the creature they'd encountered. But over time, the public turned on the officers, accusing them of fabricating the whole thing. In recent years, the officers have claimed that what they encountered was merely an iguana. Most seem happy with that explanation. But it doesn't explain how an iguana stood up on two legs and walked across the road. Or why their sketches looked nothing like an iguana.

So Where Is the Frog Today?

A local farmer also claimed he saw the Frogman lumbering through his field one evening, but there have been no other sightings since the 1970s. Those who believe in the Loveland Frogman claim that after Matthews allegedly shot at it, it became frightened and moved to a more isolated area. Others think that Matthews's shot killed the creature. Of course, there are some who believe that the Loveland Frogman is still out there and has merely become more elusive. Just something to consider should you ever find yourself driving alongside the Little Miami River near Loveland on a dark night.

D. B. Cooper: Man of Mystery

D. B. Cooper is perhaps the most famous criminal alias since Jack the Ripper. Although the fate of the infamous hijacker remains a mystery, the origins of the nom de crime *"D. B. Cooper" is a matter that's easier to solve.*

✳ ✳ ✳ ✳

The Crime

AT PORTLAND (OREGON) International Airport the night before Thanksgiving in 1971, a man in a business suit, reportedly in his mid-40s, boarded Northwest Orient Airlines flight 305 bound for Seattle, Washington. He had booked his seat under the name Dan Cooper. Once the flight was airborne, Cooper informed a flight attendant that his briefcase contained an explosive device. In the days before thorough baggage inspection was standard procedure at airports, this was a viable threat. The flight attendant relayed the information to the pilots, who immediately put the plane into a holding pattern so that Cooper could communicate his demands to FBI agents on the ground.

When the Boeing 727 landed at Seattle-Tacoma Airport, the other passengers were released in exchange for $200,000 in unmarked $20 bills and two sets of parachutes. FBI agents photographed each bill before handing over the ransom. The FBI also scrambled a fighter plane to follow the passenger craft when Cooper demanded that it take off for Mexico City via Reno, Nevada. At 10,000 feet, Cooper lowered the aft stairs of the aircraft and, with the ransom money strapped to his chest, parachuted into the night, still dressed in his business suit. The pilot noted the area as being near the Lewis River, 25 miles north of Portland, somewhere over the Cascade Mountains.

The mysterious hijacker was never seen again. The FBI found a number of fingerprints on the plane that didn't match those of the other passengers or crew, but the only real clue Cooper left behind was his necktie. On February 10, 1980, an eight-year-old boy found $5,800 in decaying $20 bills along the Columbia River, just a few miles northwest of Vancouver, Washington. The serial numbers matched those of bills included in the ransom. Other than that, not a single note of the ransom money has turned up in circulation.

Who Was Dan Cooper?

Countless books, TV shows, and even a movie have attempted to answer this question. The FBI has investigated some 10,000 people, dozens of whom had at some point confessed to family or friends that they were the real D. B. Cooper. In October 2007, the FBI announced that it had finally obtained a partial DNA profile of Cooper with evidence lifted from the tie he left on the plane. This has helped rule out many of those suspected of (or who have confessed to) the hijacking.

The author of one book about the case, a retired FBI agent, offered a $100,000 reward for just one of the bills from the ransom money. He's never had to pay out. Officially, the FBI does not believe that Cooper survived the jump from the plane. However, no evidence of his body or the bright-yellow-and-red parachute he used to make the jump has ever been found. On December 31, 2007, more than 36 years after the man forever known as D. B. Cooper disappeared into the night sky, the FBI revived the case by publishing never-before-seen sketches of the hijacker and appealing for new witnesses.

Tree House Dream House

An 83-year-old man in eastern India has been living in a tree for more than 50 years after an argument with his wife. For years, Gayadhar Parida has turned down pleas from his wife and children to return home. "We quarreled over a tiny issue," his wife explained. Parida claims that his tree home has helped him grow spiritually and overcome tension. He spends days at a time in the tree, often going without food, and only coming down to get water from a nearby pond.

The Bell Witch of Tennessee

There is perhaps no haunting in America that resonates quite like the events that occurred on the farm of John Bell in rural Tennessee.

✳ ✳ ✳ ✳

THE STORY OF the Bell Witch stands unique in the annals of folklore as one of the rare cases in which a spirit not only injured the residents of a haunted house but also caused the death of one of them! For this reason, even though the haunting occurred in the early 1800s, it has yet to be forgotten.

The Bell Witch story will be forever linked to the small town of Adams (then known as Red River) in northwestern Tennessee. In 1804, John Bell, his wife, Lucy, and their six children came to the region from North Carolina. Bell purchased 1,000 acres of land on the Red River, and the family settled quite comfortably into the community. John Bell was well liked, and kind words were always expressed about Lucy, who often opened her home to travelers and hosted social gatherings.

Bumps in the Night

The Bell haunting began in 1817 after John Bell and his son Drew spotted odd creatures in the woods near their farm. When they shot at the strange beasts, they vanished.

Soon after, the Bells began to hear a series of weird knocking, scraping, and scratching sounds on the exterior of the house and then at the front door. In short order, the sounds moved inside and seemed to emanate from the bedroom belonging to the Bell sons. This continued for weeks, and before long, the irritating sounds were heard all over the house. They continued from room to room, stopping when everyone was awake and starting again when they all went back to bed.

The Bells also heard what sounded like a dog pawing at the wooden floor or chains being dragged through the house. They even heard thumps and thuds, as though furniture was being overturned. These sounds were frightening but not as terrifying as the noises that followed—the smacking of lips, gurgling, gulping, and choking—sounds seemingly made by a human. The nerves of the Bell family were starting to unravel as the sounds became a nightly occurrence.

The Coming of the Witch

The disembodied sounds were followed by unseen hands. Items in the house were broken, and blankets were yanked from the beds. The children's hair was pulled, and they were slapped and poked, causing them to cry in pain. The Bells' daughter Betsy was once slapped so hard that her cheeks stayed bright red for hours.

Whatever the source of this unseen force, most of its violent outbursts were directed at Betsy. She would often run screaming from her room in terror as the unseen hands prodded, pinched, and poked her. Strangely, the force became even crueler to her whenever she entertained her young suitor, Joshua Gardner, at the house. Desperately seeking answers, John Bell enlisted the help of some of his neighbors to investigate.

Even in the presence of these witnesses, the strange sounds continued, chairs overturned, and objects flew about the room. The neighbors formed an investigative committee, determined to find a cause for the terrifying events.

Regardless, the household was in chaos. Word began to spread of the strange happenings, and friends and strangers came to the farm to witness it for themselves. Dozens of people heard the banging and rapping sounds, and chunks of rock and wood were thrown at curious guests by unseen hands.

As the investigative committee searched for answers, they set up experiments, tried to communicate with the force, and kept a close eye on the events that took place. They set up overnight vigils, but the attacks only increased in intensity. Betsy was treated brutally and began to have sensations that the breath was being sucked out of her body. She was scratched, and her flesh bled as though she was being pierced with invisible pins and needles. She also suffered fainting spells and often blacked out for 30 to 40 minutes at a time.

Soon, a raspy whistling sound was audible, as if someone were trying to speak. It progressed until the force began to talk in a weak whisper. The voice of the force told them that it was a spirit whose rest had been disturbed, and it made many claims as to its origins, from being an ancient spirit to the ghost of a murdered peddler.

The excitement in the community grew as word spread that the spirit was communicating. People came from far and wide to hear the unexplained voice. Hundreds of people witnessed the activity caused by the witch. There were those who came to the Bell farm intent on either driving out the witch or proving that the entire affair was a hoax. But without fail, each of them left the farm confessing that the unusual events were beyond their understanding.

A Strange Affliction

John Bell began to complain of a curious numbness in his mouth that caused his tongue to swell so greatly that he was unable to eat or drink for days at a time. As the haunting progressed, he began to suffer other inexplicable symptoms, most notably bizarre facial tics that rendered him unable to talk or eat and often made him lose consciousness. These odd seizures lasted from a few hours to a week, and they increased in severity as time wore on.

No one knows why John Bell was targeted by the spirit, but from the beginning, the witch made it clear that it would torment him for the rest of his life. Bell was also physically abused by the witch, and many witnesses recalled him being slapped by unseen hands or crying out in pain as he was stabbed with invisible pins. Bell's doctor was helpless when it came to finding a cure for his ailments. The witch laughed at his efforts and declared that no medicine could cure Bell.

Some believe the reason for Bell's suffering was revealed one night when the spirit claimed to belong to Kate Batts, an eccentric neighbor who had disliked Bell because of some bad business dealings in the past. Whether the spirit was Batts is unknown, but people began calling the witch Kate.

The Death of John Bell

By 1820, John Bell's physical condition had worsened. His facial jerks and twitches continued, as did the swelling of his tongue and the seizures that left him nearly paralyzed for hours or days at a time. In late October, he suffered another fit and took to his bed. He would never leave the house again. As Bell writhed in pain, Kate remained nearby, laughing and cursing at the dying man.

On the morning of December 19, 1820, Lucy checked on her husband, who appeared to be sleeping soundly. An hour later, she returned to the bedroom and realized that he was in a stupor. When John Jr. went to get his father's medicine, he discovered that all of his father's prescriptions had vanished. In place of them was a small vial that contained a dark-colored liquid. No one knew what had happened to the medicines or what was in the vial.

Suddenly, Kate's voice took over the room. She claimed that she had poisoned Bell with the dark contents of the vial and that he would never rise from his bed again. The mysterious liquid was tested on a family cat, and the animal was dead in seconds.

John Bell never did recover. On December 20, he took one last shuddering breath and died. Laughter filled the house as the witch stated that she hoped John Bell would burn in hell.

Bell was laid to rest in a small cemetery a short distance from the family home. As mourners left the cemetery, the voice of Kate returned, echoing loudly in the cold morning air. She cheered the death of the man she hated so much.

This ended the most terrifying chapter of a haunting that left an indelible mark in the annals of supernatural history. But the Bell Witch was not finished—at least not yet.

The Broken Engagement

After the funeral, the activities of the witch seemed to subside, but she was not totally gone. Kate remained with the family throughout the winter and spring of 1821, but she was not quite as vicious as she had been, not even to Betsy, around whom her activities continued to be centered.

During the haunting, it was clear that Betsy would be punished as long as she allowed herself to be courted by Joshua Gardner. But Betsy and Joshua refused to give in to Kate's wishes. In fact, on Easter Sunday 1821, the couple became engaged, much to the delight of their family and friends.

But their joy would not last long, as the antics of the witch returned with horrific force. Realizing that the witch would never leave her alone as long as she stayed with Joshua, Betsy broke off the engagement and never saw him again.

The Return of the Witch

In the summer of 1821, the witch left the Bell family, promising to return in seven years. In 1828, she came back and announced her return in the same manner as when the original haunting first began—scratching and other eerie sounds inside and outside the house, objects moving, and blankets being pulled from the beds.

The Bells decided to ignore the activity. If spoken to by the spirit, they ignored that as well. In this way, they hoped the visitation might end quickly. And so it did—the witch left the house after a few weeks.

However, much of the activity during the witch's 1828 visit took place at the home of John Bell Jr., who had built a house on land that he had inherited from his father. The witch allegedly made several accurate predictions about the future, including the Civil War, the end of slavery, the rise of the United States as a world power, and the coming of the two world wars. She even predicted the end of the world, stating that the world would end with the temperature of the planet rising so high that it would become uninhabitable.

Kate stayed with John Bell Jr. for several months. Before she left, she promised to return again in 107 years (1935), and though there is no record that she ever did so, there are some that maintain that the Bell Witch has never left Adams, Tennessee. Strange events still occur where the old Bell farm stood. And old Kate is still talked about today. What really happened on the Bell farm in the early 1800s? No one knows for sure, but there's no question that it made an indelible mark on American history.

---

* Like plants, children grow faster during spring than any other season.

* In India, sunburns are typically treated with honey and boiled (and cooled) potato peels.

* The world's oldest still-existing amusement park is Bakken in Denmark, which opened in 1583.

* The best-selling fiction writer of all time is Agatha Christie, whose murder mysteries have sold more than two billion copies worldwide since 1920. Only the Bible and some playwright named William Shakespeare outsell her.

* Herbert Hoover, born in 1874, was the first U.S. president born west of the Mississippi River.

* Human taste buds are regrown every two weeks.

* Shaking hands spreads more germs than kissing does.

* A typical toilet flushes in the key of E flat.

* The human heart creates enough pressure while pumping to squirt blood 30 feet.

* The average adult body consists of approximately 71 pounds of potentially edible meat, not including organ tissue.

Mythical Sea Monsters

Seafarers of old were respectful and wary of the strange creatures that lurked below the surface. The reflection of sunlight upon water, overwhelming homesickness, or too much drink caused many sailors to see monsters.

✳ ✳ ✳ ✳

Kraken

THE KRAKEN WAS one of the most horrifying creatures that a sailor could encounter. It was believed to be a many-armed monster—described by one 14th-century writer as resembling an uprooted tree—that would wrap itself around a ship, pull down its masts, and drag it to the ocean floor. The creature was so large that it could be mistaken for a small island. Early whalers often saw tentacle and suction-cup marks on the bodies of sperm whales, which served to cement the kraken's terrifying reputation. Modern sailors recognize the kraken as a giant squid, which is an enormous, octopuslike mollusk. The giant squid has a long body shaped like a torpedo, even longer tentacles, and eyes that are more than 18 inches in diameter (larger than most hubcaps). They grow to lengths of 60 feet (sometimes more) and weigh nearly a ton. Although not often seen by humans, these deep-sea dwellers have been known to attack whales and tanker ships.

Sea Serpents

Some of the most famous sea monsters, such as Loch Ness's "Nessie" and Chesapeake Bay's "Chessie," are serpents. Whether in salt water or freshwater, a sea serpent looks similar to a snake or dragon and usually has several "humps." Although crypto-zoologists (those who study animals of legend) hold out hope that these creatures are some sort of surviving dinosaur, it's not likely. One theory is that freshwater sea serpents, such as Lake Champlain's "Champ," are actually snakes (perhaps giant anacondas) that escaped from passing boats. Naysayers point out that tropical anacondas wouldn't do well in upstate New York winters.

Ocean-dwelling sea serpents are easier to explain. For centuries, witnesses have mistaken basking sharks, rows of diving dolphins, clumps of sargassum seaweed, seals, and even undulating waves for the head and humps of a sea serpent. Perhaps the most common explanation, however, is the oarfish, which resembles an eel and grows to lengths of 25 to 60 feet (and possibly more).

Mermaids

Mermaids—aquatic creatures with a woman's head and torso and the lower body of a fish—have been spotted in oceans and lakes around the world since 1000 B.C. In the past few centuries, several supposedly authentic mermaid specimens have been displayed, but all of them have proved to be hoaxes. These include P. T. Barnum's famous "Feejee Mermaid"; taxidermic creations consisting of sewn parts of monkeys and fish; and "Jenny Hannivers," which are carcasses of rays, skates, or cuttlefish carved and varnished to resemble a winged sea monster with a hideous human head. (The name is likely an anglicization of *jeune d'Anvers*, or "girl of Antwerp," in reference to the Belgian port where 16th- and 17th-century sailors made and sold these popular souvenirs.)

Seals and sea otters, both known for their playful interaction with humans, have likely been mistaken for mermaids. The legendary selkie—a mythical seal that sheds its skin on land and resumes it while in the sea—derives from mermaid folklore. The dugong and manatee—both cowlike, sea-dwelling mammals that nurse their young above water—may also have prompted reports of mermaids. In fact, the word *manatee* comes from the Carib word for breasts, which could explain why mermaids are said to be naked from the waist up. Of course, it's also possible that mermaid sightings were simply the fertile imaginings of love-starved sailors and fishermen who had been at sea too long.

Fooled Ya!: Famous Hoaxes

Whether for fun, notoriety, or profit, hoaxers have moved amongst us since the beginning of humankind. Here are some of the boldest hoaxes of recent times.

❋ ❋ ❋ ❋

Milli Vanilli

MILLI VANILLI, a pop-singing duo from Germany that won the coveted Grammy Award for Best New Artist of 1989, ultimately proved too good to be true. The handsome, dreadlocked duo of Fab Morvan and Rob Pilatus sold more than 30 million singles and 14 million albums before their secret came out.

In July 1990, while performing their hit song "Girl You Know It's True," at a theme park in Connecticut, an obvious problem erupted when the first four words of the song repeated over and over again. Their obvious lip-syncing at the theme park wasn't a deal-breaker in itself, but it did cause critics to take notice.

By November, under intense scrutiny, it was learned that Morvan and Pilatus hadn't sung *any* of the tracks—at live performances or in the studio—for which they'd become famous. In reality, the songs were recorded by session musicians, and Morvan and Pilatus were simply chosen for their looks. To fans, it was an unforgivable transgression.

As a result, the artists were stripped of their Grammy and were treated as pariahs by their once-adoring fans. In a sad footnote, Pilatus died in April 1998 at age 32 when he overdosed on prescription drugs.

Sibuxiang Hoax

An unintentional hoax that mimicked America's famed "War of the Worlds" radio broadcast traumatized an entire city in northern China on September 19, 1994. In a scrolled message, television viewers in Taiyuan were repeatedly warned about the gruesome Sibuxiang Beast, a creature with a deadly bite. "It is said that the Sibuxiang is penetrating our area from Yanmenguan Pass and within days will enter thousands of homes," read the ominous type. "Everyone close your windows and doors and be on alert!"

Taiyuan residents panicked, some even barricading themselves inside their homes. Local officials were soon swamped with anxious telephone calls.

It was all a giant misunderstanding. The Sibuxiang Beast was real, but it wasn't an animal—it was a new brand of liquor. The townspeople had been watching a commercial!

The ad's creator was fined the equivalent of $600 for causing a public panic, but the incident turned Sibuxiang liquor into a household name virtually overnight. Three months after the incident, the owner reported that his client base had quadrupled.

Cardiff Giant

On October 16, 1869, a ten-foot-tall "petrified" man was discovered by workers digging a well in Cardiff, New York. Soon after, property owner William C. Newell began charging 50 cents to see the man up close, and thousands anted up for the privilege.

The "Cardiff Giant" was purchased by businessmen for $37,500 (a vast sum at the time) and shipped to Syracuse for display. There, he was more closely examined and the truth emerged. It had all been a hoax concocted by Newell and his friend George Hull. For $2,600, the devilish pair had created the statue out of gypsum and buried it on Newell's farm.

The giant proved even more popular after the truth came out, and people came from far and wide to see it. P. T. Barnum offered the new owners $60,000 for the giant. They declined, so Barnum constructed an exact plaster replica of the Cardiff Giant and placed it on display in his New York City museum. It drew even bigger crowds than the original, which is now on display at the Farmer's Museum in Cooperstown, New York. Barnum's replica can be seen at Marvin's Marvelous Mechanical Museum in Farmington Hills, Michigan.

Hitler's Diaries

In 1983, when German magazine *Stern* claimed to have discovered Adolf Hitler's diaries, more than a few folks took notice. They shouldn't have. After paying nine million German marks (at the time about five million U.S. dollars) to Gerd Heidemann, a German journalist who claimed to have discovered the diaries in an East German barn, the magazine realized that they'd been conned. But they were not alone.

Before the scam came to light, noted World War II historians Eberhard Jäckel, Gerhard Weinberg, and Hugh Trevor-Roper deemed the diaries authentic. Two weeks later, the diaries were revealed as fakes that had been produced on modern paper using modern ink. Notorious forger Konrad Kujau was found to be the grand architect of the scheme, and both he and Heidemann were sentenced to 42 months in prison.

I Buried Paul

In 1969, news broke that Beatle Paul McCartney had died in a car crash three years before. The story claimed that McCartney's bandmates, stricken with fear that their popularity might wane, used a body double named William Campbell in Paul's place.

To stir up interest, the mop-tops allegedly left clues, such as the words "I buried Paul," at the end of "Strawberry Fields Forever."

The story had publicity stunt written all over it, but many still believed Paul was dead. A report by NBC anchorman John Chancellor summed things up: "All we can report with certainty is that Paul McCartney is either dead or alive."

Then, *Life* magazine discovered a very much alive Paul McCartney and snapped some photos. Confronted with the damning evidence, the clearly annoyed Beatle grudgingly granted *Life* an interview, and the hoax was laid to rest.

The origin of the hoax remains unknown. Many believe the Beatles were directly involved, since the boys had a penchant for mischief and a good joke.

One Reptile to Rule Them All

Some people are ruled by their pets; others are ruled by their work. Conspiracy theorist David Icke believes that we're all being ruled by reptilian humanoids.

✳ ✳ ✳ ✳

Worldwide Domination

DAVID ICKE HAS worn many hats: journalist, news anchor for the BBC, spokesman for the British Green Party, and professional soccer player. But after a spiritual experience in Peru in 1991, he took on another role: famed conspiracy theorist.

Icke believes that a group called the Illuminati, or "global elite," controls the world, manipulating the economy and using mind control to make humanity submissive. Icke also believes the group is responsible for organizing such tragedies as the Holocaust and the Oklahoma City bombings.

Some powerful people in the world are members of the group, claims Icke, including ex-British Prime Minister Tony Blair and former U.S. President George H. W. Bush. However, not all members are human. According to Icke, those at the top of the Illuminati bloodlines are vehicles for a reptilian entity from the constellation Draco. They can change from human to reptile and back again, and they are essentially controlling humanity.

Is Icke Onto Something?

In the documentary *David Icke: Was He Right?*, Icke claims that many of his earlier predictions, including a hurricane in New Orleans and a "major attack on a large city" between the years 2000 and 2002, have come true. But are we really being ruled by reptilian humanoids, or is Icke's theory a bunch of snake oil? Icke was nearly laughed off the stage in a 1991 appearance on a BBC talk show. But with 16 published books, thousands attending his speaking engagements, and nearly 200,000 weekly hits to his Web site, perhaps it's Icke who's having the last laugh.

How to Kill the Undead

It's getting so you can barely drive to a remote wooded location or let a teeny-weeny little mutant virus loose without attracting the undead. Zombies and vampires are seemingly everywhere, from big cities to rural hamlets and from the frozen tundra to the blazing desert.

A person needs to be prepared—knowing how to kill the undead can prevent them from ruining your day.

✳   ✳   ✳   ✳

I Have Met the Enemy, and It Is Grandma

IN ORDER TO kill the undead, it's first important to know which type of creature you're facing. For example, there are numerous types of zombies. Imagine how you'd feel if you thought you were facing the slow, shambling zombies from *Shaun of the Dead* or a George A. Romero flick and figured you could easily outmaneuver them, and instead they turned out to be the fast-paced zombies of *28 Days Later*. Wouldn't your face be red! (Granted, as they ate your brain.)

Vampires are similar: Some vampires turn into crispy critters in the sunlight. However, Dracula himself walked around London in the daytime. A vampire's aversion to sunlight is strictly a 20th-century invention.

By the same token, you should realize that any former affiliations you may have had with the undead have no meaning anymore. If you see grandma lurching toward the house or floating outside your window—and she's been dead since last May—it's likely she's not back to offer you a plate of fresh-baked chocolate chip cookies. Common sense is key.

Killing Them Softly . . . Sort Of

Weapons for killing the undead abound. For zombies, the best weapon is a shotgun or any firearm that can dispatch the creature with a headshot from a distance. (As Romero put it: Kill the brain, kill the ghoul.) Of course, loading up with fresh ammunition is annoying, which is why a machete is a popular choice. A chainsaw also works well, but with the price of gasoline nowadays, you may not want to waste it on zombies. A baseball bat, crowbar, or other bludgeoning implement also gets the job done.

Setting a zombie on fire may look pretty, but until the flames melt the brain, all you've really done is create an animated torch. The same for explosives—since a zombie's dead already, it will simply shrug off the loss of a limb or the inconvenience of shrapnel wounds.

When battling zombies, always wear tight-fitting clothing. Zombies are like babies; they'll grab whatever they can and stick it in their mouths. Your clothes should be heavy, like leather, to provide bite protection. Taunting is also encouraged. Phrases like "Oh, you want some of this?" and "Hey, dead thing! Let's go!" can bolster your confidence.

Vampires: Old-School Slaughtering

Killing a vampire is more old-school, organic work. To kill a vampire, a stake—made of aspen, ash, hawthorn, or maple—through the heart usually does the trick. Decapitation also works; sometimes the head is placed under the arm or between the legs in the coffin to make it harder to rejoin the body. Some Slavic traditions specify that only a sexton's or gravedigger's shovel can be used for this purpose, so plan accordingly. Burning a vampire can be effective, but again it may take awhile.

Unlike zombies, vampires can be deterred. A simple smear of garlic often does the trick. According to legend, a vampire is compulsively neat, so throwing a handful of seeds, salt, or sand into its path will force it to pick up every grain before resuming its pursuit. Another legend says that a vampire will stop and read every word of a torn-up newspaper thrown in its way.

However, there is no word as to how well this works with an illiterate vampire.

Chapter Five

Bizarre Truths About Arts and Entertainment

Maybe Gilligan Was the Smart One

If the Professor on Gilligan's Island *could make a radio out of a coconut, why couldn't he fix a hole in a boat?*

※　※　※　※

The Backstory

THOSE OF YOU under the age of 25 might be staring blankly at this page and saying to yourself, "What the heck is *Gilligan's Island?*" Trust us—it was a television show, and a very popular one at that.

Gilligan's Island aired on CBS from 1964 to 1967 (and then ad infinitum on TBS, TNT, and Nick at Nite). It was based on a simple premise: A motley group of people on a "three-hour tour" are shipwrecked on a deserted island. One of these shipwrecked tourists was Roy "the Professor" Hinkley, a man with six college degrees and advanced knowledge of technology, science, and obscure island languages. Over the course of 98 episodes, the Professor was able to create radios, lie detectors, telescopes, sewing machines, and other gadgets out of little more than a few coconuts and some bamboo. In short, the Professor was the MacGyver of his era. (What? You don't know about the main characters on that show either? We are getting old. Okay, think of *Gilligan's Island* as a goofy precursor to *Lost*.)

The Confounded Boat Hole

With all of Hinkley's technological wizardry, the question must be asked: Why couldn't the Professor fix a simple boat? (Fortunately, most of the male viewers were too concerned with staring at Mary Ann and Ginger to think logically.) The answer, of course, was ratings. Though *Gilligan's Island* was never a smash hit, it was popular enough to last for several seasons. As anybody can tell you, if the Professor had been able to fix the boat, there would have been no show.

As it turns out, the Professor and his friends had to wait more than a decade to be rescued. Since CBS canceled the 1968 season of *Gilligan's Island* at the last minute, the final episode of the 1967 season found the crew still stranded on its island. In 1978, a special two-part made-for-TV movie, titled *Rescue from Gilligan's Island*, detailed the crew's long-awaited rescue.

It is only fitting that even after a decade, the Professor wasn't able to figure out simple boat repair. Instead, the castaways tied their huts together to make a raft, and they floated to freedom, where they presumably spent the rest of their lives watching reruns of themselves on cable television.

Say What?

If we worked on the assumption that what is accepted as true really is true, then there would be little hope for advance.

—WILBUR WRIGHT

It is an open question whether any behavior based on fear of eternal punishment can be regarded as ethical or should be regarded as merely cowardly.

—MARGARET MEAD

Uncovering the Truth About Superheroes

Ever wonder why guys like Superman prance around in a cape and tights? Early comic book illustrators were simply drawing inspiration from the real world.

✳ ✳ ✳ ✳

SURE, IT'S EMBARRASSING to prance around in your pajamas with your underpants on the outside and a silly cape flapping behind you. But if it compels criminals to laugh themselves to death, that's good, right?

Cartoonists borrowed the standard superhero outfit—colored tights, trunks, boots, and a cape—from circus strongmen and professional wrestlers of the early 20th century. The outfits certainly made sense at the time. Performers needed tight clothing for maximum flexibility and to give audiences a good look at their muscles. However, lycra and elastic had not been invented; with so much squatting and stretching, performers ran the risk of splitting their tights and exposing their...uh... little strongmen. So the thinking performer wore trunks over the tights to keep things family-friendly. And since this was show business, flashy colors were essential.

This ensemble also worked in early comic books. The illustrator had to show off the hero's muscles, but the character couldn't be running around shirtless—it wasn't proper. A skintight outfit delivered the goods without being offensive. And with some unique colors and a chest emblem, the hero was instantly recognizable.

For flying heroes such as Superman, a cape flapping in the wind, provided a perfect vehicle for illustrating both speed and direction. And, of course, capes were quite in fashion back in the day on the planet Krypton.

Art Work: When Guerilla Girls Attack

The art world is a wild and crazy place, full of mammoth sculptures, beautiful oil paintings, and thought-provoking installations. In most of the world's museums, the majority of the art on display is created by and about men—but not if the Guerilla Girls have anything to say about it.

✳ ✳ ✳ ✳

New York City in the '80s

MANHATTAN HAS LONG been regarded as one of the most dynamic areas on the planet. This was especially true in the 1980s—an era of Reaganomics, cheap rent, AIDS, punk rock and hip-hop, and a boundary-breaking art scene. Performance artists were blurring the lines between art and life, and solo performers as well as ensembles were causing quite a stir.

One such group, founded in 1985, called themselves the Guerilla Girls. The development of their all-female, politically charged posse was born out of the indignation they felt upon seeing an exhibit at the Metropolitan Museum of Art called *An International Survey of Painting and Sculpture*. Only 13 of the 169 artists represented at this important show were women, and all of the artists were white Europeans or white Americans. Many women were outraged at this clear display of discrimination, but the Guerilla Girls decided to do something about it. In the midst of the tumultuous '80s art scene, this group of anonymous females swore they would "reinvent the 'F' word: feminism."

Guerilla Warfare

The women who banded together to bring attention to the issue knew they'd have to be smart about it. Since the art world is rather small—and many of the Guerilla Girls were themselves artists—they decided to act anonymously. They figured that getting shunned for their activism wouldn't help get more female artists into galleries. Also, the group wanted the public to focus on their message, and not on whom they were as individuals.

The term "guerilla" was a reference to guerrilla warfare: Who were these women, and where would they strike next? They solved the anonymity problem by wearing big, hairy gorilla masks in public. And they were out in public a lot. Sometimes they wore fishnet stockings and high heels with their masks to humorously counter stereotypes of feminine sexuality.

The Guerilla Girls had arrived, and they had a lot to say. The group hung posters on city buses and in subway stations. The Guerilla Girl Web site tells the story behind one of their most famous posters: "One Sunday morning we conducted a 'weenie count' at the Metropolitan Museum of Art in New York, comparing the number of nude males to nude females in the artworks on display. The results were very 'revealing.'" The poster shows a classic sculpture of a nude woman but with a gorilla mask in place of her head. The headline reads: "Do women have to be naked to get into the Met Museum?" Underneath is this explanation: "Less than 5% of the artists in the Modern Art sections are women, but 85% of the nudes are female." Another poster, plastered around NYC's fashionable SoHo neighborhood, listed the names of 20 local art galleries under the headline: "These Galleries Show No More Than 10% Women Artists or None at All." Clearly, the Guerilla Girls were not afraid to call the art scene out.

Girl Power

Although heavy-handed, the Guerilla Girls' message was also a lot of fun, both for the women involved and for the public. By poking fun at the system that ignored or repressed them, they were able to take some of the power out of it. They also found that humor was a good way to get people involved.

Whether you loved them or hated them, it was almost impossible to ignore the Guerilla Girls. Today their message continues to spread, extending beyond the Manhattan art scene. Guerilla Girl posters can be found worldwide, there are Guerilla Girl books, and the group continues to give lectures at museums and schools—even in some of the places they previously targeted.

World's Most Unusual Museums

A list of every hyperspecific museum in the world could fill (and no doubt has filled) a book of its own, but perhaps this random sampling might fuel some interesting vacation ideas.

✳ ✳ ✳ ✳

Beatles for Sale

ANY PLACE WITH even the slightest Beatles connection has tried to cash in on the fame of the Fab Four, and although the most authentic sites are naturally in Liverpool, American fans need not despair. The Hard Day's Nite [sic] B&B & Beatles Mini-Museum in Benton, Illinois, is a house once owned by George Harrison's sister Louise and boasts a room used by George himself. Louise answered thousands of fan letters from here. Off the mainland, the Kauai Country Inn, the only Beatles museum in Hawaii, is also an organic farm with an "extensive 40-year collection...including a Mini Cooper 'S' car registered by [manager] Brian Epstein...and many other interesting items." It's also conveniently located near the Waialua River's "Fern Grotto," used as a location in Elvis Presley's *Blue Hawaii*.

Elvis Has Left the Building

Speaking of the King, aside from the obvious tour of Graceland and a visit to the Tupelo, Mississippi, shotgun shack (complete with gift shop and chapel) where he and his twin, Jesse Garon, were born, there's the "world's largest private collection of Elvis memorabilia" in Pigeon Forge, Tennessee. Where else can you see items such as Elvis's 1967 "Honeymoon" Cadillac, the headboard from his Hollywood bedroom, and artifacts from his last tour, including Prell shampoo and Crest toothpaste?

The Peanut Gallery

Elvis's favorite sandwich was fried peanut butter, bacon, and banana; and while we couldn't divine a shrine to pork, there is a First Peanut Museum (in Waverly, Virginia), with myriad peanut memorabilia. It competes against the Agrirama Peanut

Museum in Tifton, Georgia, which depicts "the dramatic transition from the horse and mule days to mechanized farming." Neither of these should be confused with the Charles M. Schulz Museum and Research Center in California's Santa Rosa, devoted to the man who created the comic strip *Peanuts*.

Gone Bananas

Top this off by visiting the International Banana Club Museum in Hesperia, California. *Guinness World Records* declared this the world's largest collection devoted to a single fruit. Established in 1976, it spent 32 years in Altadena, California, before moving to its present location. You'll find banana lamps, gold-plated bananas, banana body spray, and even a Banana Club golf putter.

There's No Such Thing as Too Much Cheese

Still peckish? Consider the Netherlands' Kaasmuseum (Cheese Museum), located in Alkmaar in a 14th-century chapel, which has an outdoor cheese market on Fridays. (Alkmaar also has its own Fab Four museum.) Then there is the chocolate museum in Barcelona (which features dioramas sculpted out of the sweet stuff) and one in Cologne (the Schokoladenmuseum has its own greenhouse to support cacao plants). But don't forget the Burlingame, California, Pez Museum, which has every dispenser ever made—including a rare counterfeit one of Adolf Hitler.

No Place(s) for the Squeamish

If that's not enough to kill an appetite, there's New York's Burns Archive, which houses photos of people with nightmarish medical conditions, and the Lizzie Borden B&B in Fall River, Massachusetts, site of two grisly ax murders, complete with gift shop. Or there's Philadelphia's Mütter Museum, which includes a full-body cast of original Siamese twins Chang and Eng, a soap woman (buried in chemicals that turned her to, yes, soap), body tissue from presidential assassin John Wilkes Booth, and a giant colon. And don't forget the Cockroach Hall of Fame in Plano, Texas, which features dead insects dressed as celebrities, such as Liberoache and Marilyn Monroach.

The True Story of the World's Favorite Rodent

Walt Disney long held that the inspiration for his most famous creation sprang from a cute little field mouse that visited him at his drawing board in his Kansas City studio. The real story is far more interesting.

✳ ✳ ✳ ✳

I N TRUTH, MICKEY MOUSE was born from a bad business deal. Walt Disney had originally pinned his cinematic success on an animated rabbit named Oswald, only to have the rights to the character stolen from him by New York film distributor Charles Mintz. Desperate for another moneymaking character, Disney brainstormed with his brother, Roy, and lead animator Ub Iwerks. Various animals were proposed and rejected until the trio finally settled on a mouse—basically because the only other cartoon mouse at the time was George Herriman's Ignatz, of "Krazy Kat" fame. Disney originally wanted to call his new creation Mortimer, but on the advice of his wife, Lilly, he changed it to Mickey.

Mickey's first cartoon was a silent effort titled "Plane Crazy," inspired by Charles Lindbergh's 1927 transatlantic flight. It was quickly followed by "The Gallopin' Gaucho," also a silent cartoon. Distributors were unenthusiastic, so Disney decided to make one more cartoon, this time with synchronized music and sound effects. It was a huge gamble—if the third cartoon failed, Disney would lose everything he had worked so hard to build.

"Steamboat Willie" premiered at New York's Colony Theater on November 18, 1928. It was an immediate hit and inspired Disney to add music and sound effects to "Plane Crazy" and "The Gallopin' Gaucho," so the three shorts could be sold to theaters as a package. More cartoons followed, and in just a few years, Disney headed one of Hollywood's most successful and groundbreaking movie studios—thanks to a mouse almost named Mortimer.

Gotta Dance

What do wild, maniacal dancing, a strange disease, and patron saints have in common with each other? If you guessed the medieval epidemic called "dancing mania," you'd be right!

✳ ✳ ✳ ✳

Taking the Fun Out of "Fungus"

"**D**ANCING MANIA" IS often associated with several diseases: St. Anthony's Fire, St. Vitus's Dance, and St. John's Dance. All three describe bizarre neurological diseases that hit Europe between the 13th and 18th centuries. The first outbreak of dancing mania affected the majority of the inhabitants of Aachen, Germany, in 1374, and it reached its pinnacle 100 years later in Strasbourg, France. While there are a number of plausible theories about how the disease took hold of nearly an entire population, the most widely accepted hypothesis involves the ingestion of *ergot*, a fungus that infects rye with toxic and psychoactive chemicals, including lysergic acid—the same acid that would ultimately be synthesized into LSD.

The symptoms of dancing mania were as peculiar as their origin. Those affected exhibited uncontrolled and painful seizures, diarrhea, paresthesias (a pins-and-needles feeling), itching, foaming at the mouth, maniacal laughter, erratic gyrations, jerking movements, nausea, hallucinations, headaches, and vomiting. But the most appalling symptoms were involuntary muscular contortions of the face and extremities that appeared to resemble dancing. That's where the bizarre treatments came in.

Take Two Tunes and Call Me in the Morning

Medicine had no plausible theories or cures for the diseases; the "science" relied on medieval witchcraft as much as the Catholic Church. Because the diseases affected thousands of people, physicians needed to come up with an effective treatment for the masses—and fast. After a number of unsuccessful treatments, the medical community finally agreed on a solution: music.

In the 14th century, music was considered a "magic bullet" for just about everything and was used extensively to drive demons from anyone with an inexplicable malady. So, the town's elders gathered the afflicted and marched them through the center of town to the accompaniment of upbeat music in hopes that it—coupled with copious amounts of sweat generated from the movement—would exorcise the demons. Being under the spell of the gyrating rhythms (and the ingredients of LSD), many of the afflicted ended up tearing off their clothes and dancing through the streets naked until they fell to the ground, exhausted. The few who weren't immediately cured were eventually hauled off to the nearest cathedral, where they offered themselves in prayer—that's where the saints come in.

The Saints Come Marching In

St. Vitus, the only son of a well-to-do Sicilian senator, went on to perform a number of documented miracles. The Sicilian administrator (think mayor) was fed up with Vitus's antics and sentenced him to martyrdom. Just before he literally lost his head, Vitus prayed to God that those afflicted by the dance mania be cured.

Dancing mania also came to be known as St. John's disease because one of the first major outbreaks arose in St. Johannestanz, Germany.

A continent away lived St. Anthony, who was an Egyptian monk (A.D. 251–356). Withdrawing into an abstemious life at an early age, he finally emerged from years of solitary confinement to establish one of the first monasteries. During his self-imposed confinement, it is said that he battled with the devil, who attacked him with wild beasts and temptations of exotic feasts and naked women. But Anthony's prayers and penitence prevailed over evil. During the 12th century, the Order of Hospitallers of St. Anthony in Grenoble, France, became the destination of those afflicted with dancing mania, which is also called St. Anthony's Fire.

Photographs that Steal Your Soul

Does life imitate art, or does art imitate life? This is one of those chicken-and-egg questions that resists an easy answer. But if you want proof that art exposes the otherwise concealed aspects of life, look no further than the photographs of Diane Arbus.

❋ ❋ ❋ ❋

Reality Bites

WHEN MODERN CULTURES first make contact with traditional cultures, it often isn't the guns or bombs or mysterious command of fire (in lighters) that most frightens the indigenous people. It's the photographs. Traditional cultures often believe that a person's soul is stolen by the camera and transposed into the photograph. Sounds strange, but what if there's something to it? One of the most controversial photographers in history, Diane Arbus, has often been accused of maliciously freezing her subjects in poses they never would have wanted the world to see. She reveals their innermost souls, which they would prefer to keep cloaked.

From High Society to Underworld

Diane (pronounced Dee-ann) Arbus was born in 1923 as Diane Nemerov, daughter of a wealthy Manhattan department store owner. Diane always felt self-conscious about her wealth and was more interested in black-and-white images than the silver spoon. After spending many years shooting commercial photographs for various New York City magazines, she became known in the 1960s for her meticulously crafted black-and-white portraits. She loved to capture individuals who were on the fringes of society: little people, giants, circus freaks, transvestites, the mentally insane, and the physically handicapped. In the last two years of her life, she photographed the inhabitants of New Jersey institutions for the mentally retarded.

Some charged Arbus with voyeurism, while others questioned whether her disabled subjects had the authority to allow her to take their picture. Arbus's photographs are undeniably eerie and powerful. They capture individuals in less-than-flattering poses. Susan Sontag accused Arbus of "suggesting a world in which everybody is alien, hopelessly isolated, immobilized in mechanical, crippled identities and relationships." In an artistic medium capable of capturing reality, some felt that Arbus unfairly and even immorally captured only its bleakest aspects.

One of Arbus's most famous photographs features seven-year-old identical twins dressed alike. There is something ghostly about the image, with one twin slightly frowning and the other smiling, just as slightly. Years later, the girls' father told the *Washington Post*, "We thought it was the worst likeness of the twins we'd ever seen." That comment goes to the heart of Arbus's art: She was not interested in immediate likenesses but in deeper, more universal truths.

Arbus also photographed middle-class families, journalists, artists, and movie stars. She revealed the ugliness and pain behind even the most illustrious of her subjects—undoubtedly why famous people tended to dislike her portraits of them. Arbus's husband Allan Arbus said that Mae West hated the photos his wife did of her "because they were truthful." Journalist and author Norman Mailer took one look at Arbus's picture of him and proclaimed that "giving a camera to Diane Arbus is like putting a live grenade in the hands of a child."

Arbus's critics lament her exploitation of the world's outcasts, but she never treated her subjects as outsiders or considered them repulsive. She spent hours getting to know them before beginning a shoot and preferred to photograph them in their own homes, among their own possessions. Of the "freaks" that she photographed, Arbus observed that "most people go through life dreading they'll have a traumatic experience. Freaks were born with their trauma... They're aristocrats." Arbus photographed what the world didn't want to see, and succeeded in capturing what is usually hidden. She committed suicide in 1971 at age 48.

The Dulcet Tones of David Hasselhoff

In addition to being a washed-up actor, 'Hoff is a singer. And believe it or not, there's a place where his music reigns supreme.

✳ ✳ ✳ ✳

From *Baywatch* to the Bandstand

FOR THE PAST three decades, David Hasselhoff has been a largely benign—if untalented—presence on the American entertainment landscape. Let's face it—nobody watched *Knight Rider* to see 'Hoff in a leather jacket; it was KITT, the talking car, that got viewers to tune in. And it hardly needs mentioning that people weren't dialing up *Baywatch* to take a gander at Hasselhoff's hairy chest.

It would seem obvious, then, that no one would even think about buying a David Hasselhoff album, even if it were in a dollar bin. Well, it might seem obvious to you, but there are several million people who apparently love the man's music. Over the past two decades, 'Hoff has churned out gold and platinum records at an astonishing rate.

There's No Accounting for Taste

Just who is buying these things? The Germans, that's who. And the Austrians and the Swiss. But mostly the Germans. Hasselhoff's popularity in Germany dates back to the late 1980s. At the time, Hasselhoff was in dire straits—*Knight Rider* had ended its brief run in 1986, and 'Hoff's stock couldn't have been any lower in Hollywood. He went to Europe in an attempt to reinvent himself as a soft-rock musician, in much the same way as marginal major-league baseball players go to Japan in desperate attempts to resurrect their careers.

Hasselhoff's reception as a musician was initially tepid, and his success was confined largely to Eastern Europe. Then came 1989—the year the Berlin Wall came tumbling down. The end of Soviet influence over East Germany was the most momentous historic event in Germany since World War II. That same year, Hasselhoff released a little album called *Looking for Freedom*. Never heard of it? You would have if you'd been in Berlin during those glorious days of reunification.

The title song, a cover of a 1970s German hit, had already achieved modest popularity in Eastern Europe in the days leading up to the fall of the Berlin Wall. But Hasselhoff's status in Germany as an iconic rocker was cemented when he performed "Looking for Freedom" from atop the crumbling wall during a concert on New Year's Eve in 1989. The song struck a chord with the euphoric Germans, and the album skyrocketed to number one on the country's charts. It stayed there for an incomprehensible eight weeks and eventually was certified triple platinum.

Hasselhoff's singing career has maintained its momentum in Germany—he's put out several albums that have gone at least gold in that country. But it is his performance of "Looking for Freedom" from atop the Berlin Wall that will always be remembered. Thus, one of the iconic moments in the history of their nation is symbolized for millions of Germans by a man who is best known in America for trotting around in red swim trunks.

✳ An accident on the north end of Boston on January 15, 1919, flooded the area with two-and-a-half million gallons of molasses in a wave as much as 15 feet tall. Twenty-one people were killed, and 150 more were injured.

✳ The shortest reign of a Portuguese king was 20 minutes. When the royal family was ambushed in February 1908, the king died immediately and his heir, Luis Filipe, died 20 minutes later.

✳ National Bathroom Reading Week is the second week in June.

✳ In about 200 B.C., the Carthaginian ruler, Hannibal, defeated an enemy's navy by stuffing poisonous snakes into earthen jugs and catapulting them onto the decks of his opponent's ships.

Tales from the Orchestra Pit

The baton—a seemingly innocuous piece of equipment used by conductors—has a strange and colorful history.

✳ ✳ ✳ ✳

The Tragedy of Jean-Baptiste Lully

A 17TH-CENTURY COMPOSER NAMED Jean-Baptiste Lully was conducting at a rehearsal, keeping time as usual with a huge wooden staff that he pounded on the floor. One fateful day, however, Lully missed the floor and drove the staff right into his foot.

No, this is not the moment the conductor's baton was conceived. Lully did not have an epiphany and say, "You know, I should use something smaller to direct my music." Nevertheless, the moment remains part of music history. An abscess developed on Lully's right foot that turned to gangrene. The composer did not have the foot amputated, causing the gangrene to spread and eventually leading to his death. There you have it—a conducting fatality!

The Birth of the Baton

So when did conductors trade in those clumsy, and potentially lethal, wooden staffs for the symbolically powerful batons? And do they really need them? Don't their hands have ten batons?

Some conductors today use their hands and fingers, but most have a baton that they move to the music. The theory is that the baton—usually 10 to 24 inches long and made of wood, fiberglass, or carbon—magnifies a conductor's patterns and gestures, making them clearer for the orchestra or ensemble.

Orchestras date to the late 16th century during the Baroque period, and conductors back then used the same type of staff that felled Lully. Sometimes there was no conductor at all. Instead, the leader was most often a keyboardist, who would guide the orchestra when his hands were free, or a violinist, who would set the tempo and give directions by beating the neck of his instrument or making other movements. At other times, the keyboardist or violinist simply played louder so the rest of the orchestra could follow his lead.

As written music grew more complex, orchestras needed more direction than a keyboardist or violinist could provide. Conductors started appearing in France in the 18th century and emerged in earnest early in the 19th century. Still, there was no baton—rolled up paper was the tool of choice.

German composer, violinist, and conductor Louis Spohr claimed to have introduced the formal baton to the music world in a performance in 1820, but he may simply have been boasting. It is widely thought that he only used a baton in rehearsals.

Felix Mendelssohn, the German composer, pianist, and conductor, may have been the first to use a real baton in a performance. According to *The Cambridge Companion to Conducting*, Mendelssohn used a baton in 1829 and again in 1832 with the Philharmonic Society of London. The next year, a baton was used regularly with the Philharmonic—and today, almost every conductor wields one.

Baton Wackiness

Even though the baton is a lot safer than the wooden staff, there have been some accidents. For example, German conductor Daniel Turk's motions became so animated during a performance in 1810 that he hit a chandelier above his head and was showered with glass. What is it with these guys?

There was more baton craziness in 2006 and 2007. First, the conductor of the Harvard University band set a record by using a baton that was 10½ or 12½ feet long, depending on whom you listen to. The next year, the University of Pennsylvania band claimed to have bested that record with its 15-foot, 9-inch baton. There were no reports of a Lully moment on either occasion.

Where *Is* That Confounded Mule?

It's worth noting that there isn't a donkey to be found in the legendary video game Donkey Kong.

✳ ✳ ✳ ✳

BEFORE ENTERING THE strange new world of video games in the late 1970s, Nintendo was a small but established Japanese toy company that specialized in producing playing cards. Early in its video game venture, the company found itself stuck with about two thousand arcade cabinets for an unpopular game called *Radar Scope*. Nintendo's president tapped a young staff artist named Shigeru Miyamoto to create a new game that enabled the company to reuse the cabinets.

Miyamato developed an action game in which the player was a little jumping construction worker (named Jumpman, naturally) who had to rescue his lady friend from a barrel-chucking ape. Thanks to the classic movie monster, nothing says "rampaging gorilla" like "Kong," in either English or Japanese, so that part of the name was a no-brainer.

Miyamoto also wanted to include a word that suggested "stubborn" in the title, so he turned to his Japanese-to-English dictionary, which listed "donkey" as a synonym. (English speakers at Nintendo did point out that "Donkey Kong" didn't mean what Miyamoto thought it did, but the name stuck anyway.)

Silly as the name was, things worked out quite well for everyone involved. *Donkey Kong* hit arcades in 1981 and became one of the most successful games in the world, defining Nintendo as a premier video game company in the process. Jumpman changed his name to Mario, became a plumber, and grew into the most famous video game character ever. Miyamoto established himself as the Steven Spielberg of game designers, racking up hit after hit.

Sadly, there has yet to be a hit game starring a donkey. Maybe someday Miyamoto will get around to designing one.

Crazy Entertainment Acts

From Vaudeville of old to today's Cirque du Soleil, wacky entertainers have always tried to rule the showman's roost. Here are a few acts that fall outside the traditional entertainment genre but astound, confound, and mesmerize just the same.

❋ ❋ ❋ ❋

David Blaine

AUDIENCE MEMBERS WILL grow old and gray before they see magician David Blaine pull a rabbit from a hat or saw an assistant in half. What they will see, however, perplexes as much as it entertains, and it often flirts with danger. One illusion called "Frozen in Time" saw Blaine encased between transparent blocks of ice. He remained a human ice cube for nearly 62 hours before being freed by chain saws. How he beat hypothermia is anyone's guess, but he was hospitalized for a week after the ordeal.

Not every stunt in Blaine's act is death defying. During street performances, Blaine sometimes levitates and hovers a foot or more above the ground for several seconds. Upon seeing this, amazed witnesses often believe they've seen something ethereal. And with David Blaine, they just might have.

Beautiful Jim Key

Starting in the late 1800s, Doc Key and his horse "Beautiful Jim Key" made a mighty strong case for the infinite power of kindness. From 1897 to 1906, the pair thrilled audiences with Jim's uncanny humanlike abilities. Billed as the "Marvel of the Twentieth Century" and "The Greatest Crowd Drawer in America," Jim could read, write, sort mail, tell time, use a cash register and a telephone, and perform a host of other human-like tasks. But it wasn't always so. In 1889, Jim Key was a sickly, near-lame colt that owner Doc Key half-expected to die. Nurtured by medicines of Doc Key's own concoction, as well as an abundance of love, the little misfit colt was eventually transformed into a gorgeous mahogany bay. People were so taken by Jim Key's abilities that they joined the Jim Key Band of Mercy to the tune of two million members. Their peaceful pledge? "I promise always to be kind to animals."

Growing Man

Billed as "the man who grows before your eyes," Clarence E. Willard could control his muscular and skeletal systems with such astounding ease that he could voluntarily lengthen and shorten his frame by some six inches. From the 1930s through the 1950s, Willard's ability confounded the scientific community as well as his audiences as he stretched from 5´10˝ to 6´4˝.

Signora Jo Girardelli

Known as the "incombustible lady," Signora Girardelli had a way with fire. Born in Italy around 1780, the fire-eater distinguished herself by performing daring feats above and beyond those of more pedestrian acts. She went to great lengths to prove that she was actually *eating*, or defying, fire. Her mediums consisted of nitric acid, molten metal, boiling oil, melted wax, and lit candles. In a performance designed to prove her mettle, Girardelli would fill a pan with boiling oil, drop the white of an egg into it so all could see it cook, fill her mouth with the burning liquid, swish it about for a few seconds for added effect, then spit it out into a brazier where it would instantly blaze up, proving that it was indeed hot oil.

Another favorite bit found Girardelli flaunting her prowess with hot metal. This feat involved heating a shovel until it was red hot and then setting wood ablaze with it. With this accomplished, the performer would stroke her arms, feet, and hair with the burning-hot shovel. No smoke or scorching of any kind was detectable by the audience. At this point, Girardelli was just getting warmed up (pun absolutely intended). The real showstopper arrived seconds later when she *licked* the shovel and an audible hiss was heard from her tongue.

Creepy, Catchy Murder Ballads

✳ ✳ ✳ ✳

"Mack the Knife"

Perhaps the most well-known murder ballad, "Mack the Knife" tells the tale of dashing, but murderous, highwayman Macheath as portrayed in the musical drama *The Threepenny Opera*. It was popularized by Bobby Darin in the late 1950s.

"Lizie Wan"

Taking an incestuous turn, this ballad tells the tale of poor Lizie, who is pregnant with her brother's child. He kills her, tries to pretend the blood is from an animal, but finally confesses before setting sail on a ship, never to return.

"Nebraska"

Before he cemented his place in musical history with "Born in the U.S.A.," Bruce Springsteen put a modern spin on the murder ballad with his 1982 song "Nebraska," based on the late 1950s killing spree of Charles Starkweather.

"Frankie & Johnny"

This song is based on an 1899 murder case in which a prostitute named Frankie kills her cheating teenage lover. Frankie was acquitted but died in a mental institution in the 1950s. The writer and origin of the song are debatable, but the tale led to a number of films, including a 1966 musical starring Elvis Presley.

"Banks of the Ohio"

Around since the 19th century, "Banks of the Ohio" tells the story of Willie, who proposes to his young love during a walk by the river. She turns him down, so he murders her. The song has been recorded by a variety of musicians, from Johnny Cash to Olivia Newton-John.

"Hey Joe"

Penned by Billy Roberts in the early 1960s, this song of love gone murderous was immensely popular among rock bands of the decade. One of the most popular versions was recorded by Jimi Hendrix and was played by the influential guitarist at the Woodstock Music Festival in 1969.

"Tom Dooley"

Based on the 1866 murder of Laura Foster, this tune tells the story of her boyfriend, Tom Dula, a former Confederate soldier from North Carolina. Dula was convicted and hanged for the girl's brutal stabbing death, but there is speculation that he had another lover named Ann Melton, who may have killed Foster in a fit of jealous rage. The story inspired a number one hit for the Kingston Trio in 1958 and a movie starring a young Michael Landon the following year.

"Lily, Rosemary and the Jack of Hearts"

Bob Dylan has performed numerous murder ballads in his career and has incorporated their musical style into his own songwriting. In 1975, he released his own take on the genre with this complex narrative song about a bank robber and the people of the town he has stumbled upon.

"Stagger Lee"

This song is based on the slaying of William Lyons by Lee Shelton, a black cab driver and pimp, on Christmas night 1895. The two men were friends, but after a night of drinking and gambling, things turned deadly. The tune became a staple of blues musicians, but the 1928 record by Mississippi John Hurt is considered the definitive version.

"Jellon Grame"

Drawing the story out over years, the song tells the tale of a man who kills his pregnant lover and removes the still living baby. He raises the child as his own, and, one day, when his son wants to know the truth about his mother, the man explains what happened and shows him the scene of the crime. The boy kills his father on the spot. The tale is intertwined with the history of the British Isles and has been retold for generations.

"Omie Wise"

This murder ballad is based on an 1807 murder case in which Naomi Wise, an orphaned servant and field hand, became pregnant by her boyfriend, Jonathan Lewis. He drowned her but was found not guilty of the crime. In 1820, Lewis confessed to the murder on his deathbed.

"The Twa Sisters"

Stepping away from the love triangle or murderous lover scenario, this song explores "sororicide"—sister killing sister. Dating back to at least 1656, "The Twa Sisters" is thought to be the inspiration for a number of other ballads. In a strange twist, the body of the dead sister is made into a musical instrument that sings of its own murder—in some versions at the wedding of the guilty sister.

"El Paso"

Written and performed by Marty Robbins, "El Paso" tells the fictional saga of love turned deadly in Mexico and was Robbins's best-known song. The ballad relates the story of a cowboy who falls in love with a cantina dancer and kills another man defending her honor. Originally, it was thought the song would be a flop because of its nearly five-minute running time, unheard of during the late 1950s. Incidentally, the song was covered by the Grateful Dead and became one of their most popular tunes, performed live more than 380 times.

"Jack the Stripper"

A foray into the modern murder ballad, "Jack the Stripper" was a serial killer who murdered prostitutes in London in the 1960s and dumped their naked bodies around the city. Modern heavy metal and hard rock bands have performed this song about his dirty deeds.

Band Names Only a Mother Could Love

Whether derived from pop culture references, or just a random pick from a book, a band's name is often as important as its music. But even a great sound can't save bands such as The Busiest Bankruptcy Lawyers in Minnesota. Here are the stories behind some interesting band names.

✳　✳　✳　✳

The Cranberries: The band was originally known as "The Cranberry Saw Us," a pun on "cranberry sauce." Members soon shortened the name for simplicity.

Lynyrd Skynyrd: The group is named after Leonard Skinner, an annoying gym coach some of the band members had in high school, who supposedly had them expelled for having long hair.

R.E.M.: The "rapid eye movement" period in the sleep cycle is the most intense and restful. But the members of R.E.M. didn't choose the name for its symbolic connection to their aesthetic. Instead, they found it while flipping through the dictionary.

Five for Fighting: The stage name for John Ondrasik came from his love of hockey. Players who fight in the National Hockey League get five minutes in the penalty box, or "five for fighting."

Three Dog Night: The name is derived from an Australian Aboriginal custom of sleeping with a dog for warmth during cold nights. The colder the night, the more dogs.

No Doubt: This funky, California-based "third wave" ska band was named after a favorite expression of its founder, John Spence, who ultimately committed suicide.

Toad the Wet Sprocket: Members of this alt-rock band drew their name from a monologue delivered by Eric Idle on a Monty Python album from 1980.

Frankenstein's Flattop

Pity poor Frankenstein's monster. Cursed with a head as flat as a tabletop, unable to find a hat or glasses that fit, he must wonder what happened. After all, the monster described in Mary Shelley's novel looked relatively normal (except for that whole reanimated-corpse thing). So why does the movie version have the flat head?

✳ ✳ ✳ ✳

Lugosi's Lament

IT WAS LATE spring of 1931 in Hollywood, and actor Bela Lugosi and Universal Studios had struck box office gold with *Dracula*. The film company, sensing a potential bonanza in horror films, immediately cast their new star in the upcoming *Frankenstein*—but, to Lugosi's dismay, he was to play the role of the monster rather than Dr. Frankenstein. Angrily, he wondered why a star of his caliber should play a grunting creature that "any half-wit extra could play."

More problems awaited Lugosi in the form of Universal's chief makeup artist Jack P. Pierce. Pierce and Lugosi had previously clashed on the set of *Dracula*, when the star refused to alter his appearance with pointed teeth and a beard (as author Bram Stoker had described the character).

For *Frankenstein*, Lugosi reluctantly agreed to apply blue-green greasepaint to his face (an effect that appeared gray when shot in black-and-white film), but that's as far as he would go. He and Pierce continued to clash over the monster's appearance, much to the displeasure of the makeup chief. "Lugosi thought his ideas were better than everybody's," Pierce reported with disdain.

When the film's director, Robert Florey, finally shot 20 minutes of *Frankenstein* test footage in June, costar Edward Van Sloan described Lugosi's appearance as "something out of *Babes in Toyland*," commenting that the broad wig made the star's head look four times its normal size, and that his skin was "polished and claylike."

Lugosi—who, during the shooting, had threatened to get a doctor's excuse so he wouldn't have to play the part—was through. "Enough is enough," said the Hungarian actor. "I was a star in my country and will not be a scarecrow over here!"

A Monster Makeover

After Universal executives screened the test footage, they banished both Lugosi and Florey to a lesser project and appointed Englishman James Whale as the new *Frankenstein* director. On Whale's recommendation, they selected an actor Whale had spotted in the Universal commissary—a fellow named Boris Karloff—to play the monster.

Over the next three weeks, Karloff and Pierce worked for three hours every night to develop the monster's signature appearance. The result, including the now-trademark flat head, was one of the most famous makeup jobs in Hollywood history. The unique noggin was no whim: Pierce had spent months researching surgery, anatomy, and other related fields. As he told *The New York Times*, "My anatomical studies taught me that there are six ways a surgeon can cut the skull in order to take out or put in a brain. I figured Frankenstein, who was a scientist but no practicing surgeon, would take the simplest surgical way. He would cut the top of the skull off straight across like a pot lid, hinge it, pop the brain in and then clamp it on tight. That is the reason I decided to make the Monster's head square and flat."

When released in December 1931, *Frankenstein* became an instant smash, and Karloff's rising star quickly eclipsed that of Lugosi. Throughout Karloff's career, he always knew who (or what) to thank for his golden opportunity: the infamous monster, flat head and all.

The Woman Behind the Beguiling Smile

It's been one of history's great mysteries: Who posed for Leonardo da Vinci when he painted art's most famous face, the Mona Lisa, in the early 1500s?

✳ ✳ ✳ ✳

The Possibilities

YOU WOULD THINK that the missing eyebrows would be a dead giveaway as to the identity of the woman who posed for the *Mona Lisa*. How many eyebrow-less ladies could have been wandering around Italy back then? As it turns out, quite a few—it was a popular look at the time. Those crazy Renaissance women.

The leading theory has always been that Lisa is Lisa Gherardini, the wife of wealthy Florentine silk merchant Francesco del Giocondo. Sixteenth-century historian Giorgio Vasari made this claim in *The Lives of the Artists*, noting that the untitled painting was often called "La Gioconda," which literally means "the happy woman" but can also be read as a play on the name Giocondo. (If you're wondering what the more popular title means, "Mona" is simply a contraction of *ma donna*, or "my lady," in Italian; the title is the equivalent of "Madam Lisa" in English.)

Vasari was infamous for trusting word of mouth, so there's a possibility that he got it wrong. Therefore, historians have proposed many alternative Lisas, including Leonardo da Vinci's mom, various Italian noblewomen, a fictitious ideal woman, and a prostitute. Some have believed that the painting is a disguised portrait of Leonardo himself, noting that his features in other self-portraits resemble Lisa's. Hey, maybe the guy wanted to see what he would look like as a woman—nothing wrong with that.

Lisa Gherardini

In 2005, Armin Schlecter, a manuscript expert at Heidelberg University Library in Germany, closed the case. While he was looking through one of the books in the library's collection—a very old copy of Cicero's letters—Schlecter discovered notes in the margin that were written in 1503 by Florentine city official Agostino Vespucci. Vespucci, who knew Leonardo, described some of the paintings on which the artist was working at the time. One of the notes mentions a portrait of Lisa del Giocondo, aka Lisa Gherardini, which proves fairly conclusively that Vasari had the right Lisa.

Historians know a bit about Lisa's life. She was Francesco's third wife; she married him when she was 16 and he was 30, a year after his second wife had died. They lived in a big house, but it was in the middle of the city's red-light district. She likely sat for the portrait soon after the birth of her third child, when she was about 24. She had five children altogether and died at age 63.

Now that this one seems to be solved, we can move on to other art mysteries, such as this: How did those dogs learn how to play poker?

✳ John D. Rockefeller's ambitions were to make $100,000 and live to be 100. He died 26 months shy of the century mark, but he left an estate worth $1.4 billion.

✳ On Christopher Columbus's fourth voyage to the new world, he saved the lives of his crew by convincing Jamaican natives that he made the moon disappear during a lunar eclipse in 1504.

✳ Prior to about the 1920s, underarm hair on women was generally no big deal. The invention of the safety razor and the acceptance of scantier clothing changed all that.

✳ Thanks to measurements provided by the satellite-based Global Positioning System, Mount Everest's peak has been discovered to be an additional seven feet higher than previously believed. It is now known to be 29,035 feet tall.

✳ During the "Malayan Emergency" in the 1950s—also known as the Malayan War for Independence—British forces relied on headhunters from Borneo to track guerrilla movements.

Enrico Caruso: The Superstitious Songster

One of the most famous tenors of all time, Italian opera singer Enrico Caruso played many unusual roles in his day, but none were as eccentric as Caruso himself.

✳ ✳ ✳ ✳

ETAILS OF CARUSO's birth in Naples on February 25, 1873, vary widely, but sources say he was the 18th of 21 children in a family that included 19 brothers and a lone sister; most of his siblings died in infancy. Because his mother was too ill, Enrico was nursed by Signora Rosa Baretti. He believed her milk caused him to be different from the rest of his family.

The Caruso family was quite poor—Enrico's father was a mechanic and he encouraged his son to become one as well. Instead, Enrico began singing in churches and cafés at age 16 to help support himself and his family. It may have been his impoverished youth or his need for order that led to his habit of obsessively recording even the most minor purchases in carefully tended books. And yet Caruso was extremely generous, dispensing handouts to almost everyone who asked.

Caruso moved to the United States after making a big splash at New York's Metropolitan Opera in *Rigoletto* in 1903. Later, while touring with the Met, he found himself smack in the middle of the 1906 San Francisco earthquake. Although he escaped unscathed, the experience compelled him to vow never to return. Upon his departure from the city, he is famously known to have shouted, "Give me Vesuvius!" (the explosive volcano of his native Italy that had erupted two weeks earlier).

The Weird Tenor's Tenets

Caruso regulated his life with a rigid set of curious and unexplained superstitions. In her account of Caruso's life, his wife, Dorothy Park Benjamin, revealed that he considered it bad luck to wear a new suit on a Friday, and he shunned the phrase, "Good luck!" for fear it would produce the opposite effect. For reasons unknown, he also refused to start any new undertakings on either a Tuesday or a Friday.

Like many artistic geniuses, he was deathly afraid of germs and bathed twice daily, often changing all of his clothes many times a day. As might be expected, some of Caruso's strongest and most peculiar beliefs were related to his magnificent voice. Before going on stage, he performed the following ritual:

1. Smoked a cigarette in a holder so as not to dirty his hands

2. Gargled with salt water to clean his throat

3. Sniffed a small amount of snuff

4. Sipped a cup of water

5. Ate precisely one quarter of an apple

6. Asked his deceased mother to help him sing

Caruso also believed he could enhance his vocal prowess by wearing anchovies around his neck and smoking two packs of cigarettes a day.

The Final Crazy Curtain

Enrico Caruso died in 1921 from complications of bronchial pneumonia. After his death, the Naples Museum in Italy claimed he had left them his throat for examination, and newspapers in Rome printed a diagram of what was supposedly the singer's internal sound system. According to *The New York Times*, doctors said Caruso had vocal cords twice as long as normal, a supersized epiglottis, and the lung power of a "superman." But the *Times* also printed his wife's denial that any organs had been removed from her husband.

Caruso left an almost superhuman legacy of music. With nearly 500 recordings, he remains one of the top-selling artists of record company RCA more than 80 years after his death.

The Great Piano Con

Lauded late in life as a great piano virtuoso, British pianist Joyce Hatto produced the largest collection of recorded piano pieces in the history of music production. But were they hers?

❋ ❋ ❋ ❋

JOYCE HATTO WAS known as an extraordinary pianist. Her recorded repertoire available in the UK grew to more than 100 CDs and included some of the most difficult piano pieces around. What was truly amazing is that she somehow managed to record this music while suffering the effects of cancer and dealing with the usual wear and tear of an aging body. How did she do it? Perhaps her penchant for plagiarism helped. As it turned out, the majority of her works were stolen from other artists' recordings and then reproduced as her own!

Having enjoyed a full, albeit rather insignificant, career as a concert pianist, Hatto abandoned her stage show in 1976 to focus on her advancing disease. On the cusp of 50, she had only a few recorded numbers under her belt. However, that soon changed, as she spent her remaining years prolifically, but as it turned out, falsely, adding to that collection.

The CD Deluge Begins

That Hatto's husband, William Barrington-Coupe, ran the Concert Artists Recordings label under which her recordings were released undoubtedly helped to assist in the harmonious heist. His music-business acumen provided both the technological savvy to engineer the pieces that had been previously released by other pianists and the means to unleash the forged works on an unsuspecting public.

Of course, the scam couldn't last forever. Internet rumors began surfacing in 2005, but *Gramophone*, a monthly music magazine in London, wasn't able to definitively break the news of the deception until February 2007, about eight months after

Hatto's death. In fact, her death at age 77 may have actually been an impetus for the discovery.

After Hatto's passing, her celebrity fire burned hotter than ever. Beloved by a small fan base during her life, Hatto-mania came out in full force upon her death. Some even deemed her one of the great pianists of modern times. But with that superstar status came a renewed flurry of suspicions surrounding the likelihood that a woman of her age and ailing health could produce such a copious collection. *Gramophone* issued a summons for anyone who knew of any fraudulence. Months passed with no evidence. Finally, a reader's computer discovered the deceit, and he contacted the magazine.

The Con Revealed

The reader told the magazine that when he was playing a CD of Hatto hits, his computer identified a particular piece as being performed by little-known pianist Lazlo Simon. *Gramophone* sent the recordings to a sound engineer, who compared sound waves from Hatto's ostensible recording of Liszt's 12 Transcendental Studies to Simon's version. An identical match was uncovered! After that, more and more of the pieces attributed to Hatto were found to belong to other musicians.

Hatto and husband had used music technology to recycle other artists' recordings, and that same technology uncovered the deception. How could they not foresee that music science would reveal them, even as they used its wizardry themselves? Barrington-Coupe has not yet produced a viable answer.

Barrington-Coupe eventually confessed to the fraud, insisting that Hatto knew nothing of the scheme and that he had made very little money on it. He claimed that the whole plot was inspired by nothing more than love for his ailing wife and his desire to make her feel appreciated by the music community during her final years. This assertion can neither be proved nor disproved, but *Gramophone* pointed out that Barrington-Coupe continued to sell the false CDs after she died.

Chapter Six

Bizarre Truths About the Sporting Life

When No Other Distance Will Do

To most of us, running a marathon is incomprehensible. Driving 26.2 miles is perhaps a possibility, though only if we stop at least once for snacks. Equally incomprehensible is the number itself, 26.2. Why isn't a marathon 26.4 miles? Or 25.9?

※ ※ ※ ※

The Answer Is Rooted in History

To FIND OUT why a marathon is 26.2 miles, we must examine the history of the marathon. Our current marathon is descended from a legend about the most famous runner in ancient Greece, a soldier named Philippides (his name was later corrupted in text to Pheidippides). For much of the fifth century B.C.,  the Greeks were at odds with the neighboring Persian Empire; in 490 B.C., the mighty Persians, led by Darius I, attacked the Greeks at the city of Marathon. Despite being badly outnumbered, the Greeks managed to fend off the Persian troops (and ended Darius's attempts at conquering Greece).

After the victory, the legend holds, Philippides ran in full armor from Marathon to Athens—about 25 miles—to announce the good news. After several hours of running through the rugged Greek countryside, he arrived at the gates of Athens crying, "Rejoice, we conquer!" as Athenians rejoiced. Philippides then fell over dead. Despite a great deal of debate about the accuracy of this story, the legend still held such sway in the Greek popular mind that when the modern Olympic Games were revived in Athens in 1896, a long-distance running event known as a "marathon" was instituted.

Homing In on 26.2

How did the official marathon distance get to be 26.2 miles if the journey of Philippides was about 25? In the first two Olympic Games, the "Philippides distance" was indeed used as the marathon distance. But things changed in 1908, when the Olympic Games were held in London. The British Olympic committee determined that the marathon route would start at Windsor Castle and end at the royal box in front of London's newly built Olympic Stadium, a distance that happened to measure 26 miles, 385 yards.

There was no good reason for the whims of British lords to become the standard, but 26.2 somehow got ingrained in the sporting psyche. By the 1924 Olympics in Paris, this arbitrary distance had become the standard for all marathons.

Today, winning a marathon—heck, even completing one—is considered a premier athletic accomplishment. In cities such as Boston, New York, and Chicago, thousands of professionals and amateurs turn out to participate. Of course, wiser people remember what happened to Philippides when he foolishly tried to run such a long distance.

✳ The first toothbrush—featuring bristles made from hog hair—was developed in China in 1498. Later toothbrushes had horse and badger hair. DuPont introduced nylon bristles in 1938.

Football Is Football—or Is It?

Football, no matter where it's played, is derived from an impromptu sport developed at Rugby School in England back in 1823 and credited to William Webb Ellis. Today, it's played in different countries under varying rules, most notably in Canada, Australia, and America. But it's not to be confused with what Americans call soccer, played as football throughout the world.

✳ ✳ ✳ ✳

Canadian Football Versus American Football

✳ The American field is 100 yards long and 53⅓ yards wide. The larger Canadian field is 110 yards long and 65 yards wide.

✳ Canadian football places the goalposts on the goal line. American football places them behind the end zone.

✳ American teams are allowed 11 players on the field at one time. Canadian teams can use 12.

✳ On kickoff, American receivers can call a fair catch, downing the ball when they catch it. Canada has no such rule, but the kicking team must give the player catching the ball a five-yard buffer zone.

✳ Canadian players have to move more quickly between plays, having only 20 seconds on the play clock from the end of one play to when the ball is snapped for the next. American players have a luxurious 40 seconds to run a new play after the ball was downed on the previous one; if the clock was stopped between plays, they have 25 seconds from when it is restarted.

✳ American teams get a two-minute warning before the end of a half. The Canadian warning is three minutes.

✳ When lining up for a play, all offensive players in the Canadian backfield (except the quarterback) are allowed to be in motion. In American football, not so much—only one player can be in motion.

* American teams at the line of scrimmage are separated by the length of the football. Canadian teams are a yard apart.

* If a Canadian team misses a field goal, the defensive team can run it out of the end zone; if the defense fails to do so, the kick is worth a point. When an American team muffs a field goal outside the 20-yard line, its opponent gets a first down at the same line of scrimmage.

Australian Football

* There is absolutely no similarity between Australian football (also known as Australian-rules football or footy) and American or Canadian football. These are just a few of the hundreds of differences in the Australian version:

* The football field (or pitch, as it's called) is an oval rather than a rectangle. It is 165 by 135 meters (roughly 180 by 148 yards) at its longest and widest points.

* There are 18 players from each team on the field at any given time. None wear any protective equipment—the uniform consists of shorts, a sleeveless shirt, and studded boots (cleated shoes).

* Players may either run with a ball or kick it, but they cannot pass it. If a player chooses to run with the ball, it must be bounced on the ground once every 15 meters (about 50 feet).

* A defender may not tackle a player below the waist or above the shoulders.

* There are two ways to score. A straight goal (six points) is scored when an attacking player kicks the ball over the goal line between the goalposts without touching a post or another player. If the ball strikes another player or post but still passes over the goal line, that's a "behind" goal worth one point.

* Any ballcarrier held firmly by a defender must get rid of the ball by kicking it or batting it with his hand. If that doesn't occur, the referee can award the defending team a free kick.

The Phantom Punch

When Sonny Liston hit the canvas less than two minutes into his second heavyweight-belt bout with Muhammad Ali, pundits immediately accused the former champ of taking a dive. Did the lumbering Liston really fake a fall?

✳ ✳ ✳ ✳

EVEN WITHOUT THE controversial conclusion to the widely publicized Sonny Liston-Muhammad Ali rematch on May 25, 1965, there was enough ink and intrigue to fill a John le Carré spy novel. The bout against Ali—who had just joined the Nation of Islam and changed his name from Cassius Clay—was held in a 6,000-seat arena in Lewiston, Maine, after numerous states refused to sanction the fight because of militant behavior associated with the Muslim movement.

Robert Goulet, the velvet-voiced crooner who had been entrusted with singing the national anthem, forgot the words to the song, and the third man in the ring, Jersey Joe Walcott, was a former heavyweight champion but a novice referee. One minute and 42 seconds into the fight, Ali threw a quick uppercut that seemed to connect with nothing but air. Liston tumbled to the canvas, though no one seemed sure whether it was the breeze from the blow or the blow itself that sent him there. Liston was ultimately counted out by the ringside timer, not by the in-ring referee.

Since it was a largely invisible swing (dubbed the "phantom punch" by sports scribes) that floored Liston, he was accused of cashing it in just to cash in. Evidence proves otherwise. Film footage of the bout shows Liston caught flush with a quick, pistonlike "anchor" punch that Ali claimed was designed to be a surprise. Liston actually got back up and was trading body blows with the Louisville Lip when the referee stepped in, stopped the fight, and informed Liston that his bid to become the first boxer to regain the heavyweight title was over.

The Skinny on Sumo Wrestling

*Contrary to what you may believe, you don't have
to be enormous to be a sumo wrestler. In some
instances, being (relatively) thin works just fine.*

✳ ✳ ✳ ✳

Supersize Them

HISTORICALLY, SUMO WRESTLERS *(rikishis)* have been
known to dent the scales from roughly 220 pounds, which
would comprise the sport's version of a 98-pound weakling, to
518 pounds. But in the world of professional sumo—with its
incessant hand-slapping, salt-tossing, foot-stomping, bull-
rushing, and chest-bashing—bigger isn't universally or undeniably better.

In the traditional ranks of
Japanese sumo, where kudos
to Shinto deities to ensure
healthy harvests once played as
large a role as the blubber-to-
blubber combat, the highest
order of achievers are given the honorable title *yokozuna*. (No,
yokozuna does not translate to "Is there any more cake?")

The Road to *Yokozuna*

To become a *yokozuna*, a wrestler must simultaneously satisfy
both subjective and objective criteria. He must dominate in the
dohyo, or ring, where two consecutive Grand Tournament wins
are considered a nifty way to attract the eye of Japan Sumo
Association judges. He also must demonstrate a combination
of skill, power, dignity, and grace. Fewer than 70 men in the
centuries-old sport of sumo have ascended to this lofty tier, and
most have been larger-than-life figures—literally.

The 27th *yokozuna*, known as Tochigiyama, was an exception.
A star of the sport between 1918 and 1925, Tochigiyama was

a comparative beanpole, at about 230 pounds. Yet he proved to be a crafty tactician, frequently moving mountains . . . of flesh. His won-loss record was 115–8.

At the opposite end of the spectrum loomed the mighty Musashimaru, the 67th *yokozuna*. He dominated the 18-square-foot *dohyo* while clad in his *mawashi* (not a diaper, though it looks like one) between 1999 and 2003. Musashimaru won about 75 percent of his 300 or so bouts, due in great measure to the fearsome nature of his physique. He tipped the scales at about 520 pounds, give or take a sack of bacon cheeseburgers.

Somewhere in the middle, we find perhaps the greatest of them all: Taiho, who reigned in the 1960s and became the 48th *yokozuna*. Taiho chalked up 32 tournament wins and weighed 337 pounds.

Bottom line? It isn't necessary to be a giant in order to make the grade as a sumo wrestler.

Say What?

Happiness is your dentist telling you it won't hurt and then having him catch his hand in the drill.

—JOHNNY CARSON

I think your whole life shows in your face, and you should be proud of that.

—LAUREN BACALL

Our greatest responsibility is to be good ancestors.

—DR. JONAS SALK

You can't wring your hands and roll up your sleeves at the same time.

—PAT SCHROEDER

Beefed Up

You're probably familiar with the terms "juiced," "roid-raged," "hyped," and "pumped"—all used to describe the effects of anabolic steroids. For better or for worse, steroids have invaded the worlds of professional and amateur sports, and even show business.

✳ ✳ ✳ ✳

Better Living Through Chemistry

ANABOLIC STEROIDS (ALSO called anabolic-androgenic steroids, or AAS) are a specific class of hormones that are related to the male hormone testosterone. Steroids have been used for thousands of years in traditional medicine to promote healing in diseases such as cancer and AIDS. French neurologist Charles-Édouard Brown-Séquard was one of the first physicians to report its healing properties after injecting himself with an extract of guinea pig testicles in 1889. In 1935, two German scientists applied for the first steroid-use patent and were offered the 1939 Nobel Prize for Chemistry, but the Nazi government forced them to decline the honor.

Interest in steroids continued during World War II. Third Reich scientists experimented on concentration camp inmates to treat symptoms of chronic wasting as well as to test its effects on heightened aggression in German soldiers. Even Adolf Hitler was injected with steroids to treat his endless list of maladies.

Giving Athletes a Helping Hand

The first reference to steroid use for performance enhancement in sports dates back to a 1938 *Strength and Health* magazine letter to the editor, inquiring how steroids could improve performance in weightlifting and bodybuilding. During the 1940s, the Soviet Union and a number of Eastern Bloc countries built aggressive steroid programs designed to improve the performance of Olympic and amateur weight lifters. The program was so successful that U.S. Olympic team physicians worked with American chemists to design Dianabol, which they administered to U.S. athletes.

Since their early development, steroids have gradually crept into the world of professional and amateur sports. The use of steroids has become commonplace in baseball, football, cycling, track—even golf and cricket. In the 2006 Monitor the Future survey, steroid use was measured in eighth-, tenth-, and twelfth-grade students; a little more than 2 percent of male high school seniors admitted to using steroids during the past year, largely because of their steroid-using role models in professional sports.

Bigger, Faster, Stronger—Kinda

Steroids have a number of performance enhancement perks for athletes such as promoting cell growth, protein synthesis from amino acids, increasing appetite, bone strengthening, and the stimulation of bone marrow and production of red blood cells. Of course, there are a few "minor" side effects to contend with as well: shrinking testicles, reduced sperm count, infertility, acne, high blood pressure, blood clotting, liver damage, headaches, aching joints, nausea, vomiting, diarrhea, loss of sleep, severe mood swings, paranoia, panic attacks, depression, male pattern baldness, the cessation of menstruation in women, and an increased risk of prostate cancer—small compromises in the name of athletic achievement, right?

While many countries have banned the sale of anabolic steroids for nonmedical applications, they are still legal in Mexico and Thailand. In the United States, steroids are classified as a Schedule III controlled substance, which makes their possession a federal crime, punishable by prison time. But that hasn't deterred athletes from looking for that extra edge. And there are thousands of black-market vendors willing to sell more than 50 different varieties of steroids. Largely produced in countries where they are legal, steroids are smuggled across international borders. Their existence has spawned a new industry for creating counterfeit drugs that are often diluted, cut with fillers, or made from vegetable oil or toxic substances. They are sold through the mail, over the Internet, in gyms, and at competitions. Many of these drugs are submedical- or veterinary-grade steroids.

Impact on Sports and Entertainment

Since invading the world of amateur and professional sports, steroid use has become a point of contention, gathering supporters both for and against their use. Arnold Schwarzenegger, the famous bodybuilder, actor, and politician, freely admits to using anabolic steroids while they were still legal. "Steroids were helpful to me in maintaining muscle size while on a strict diet in preparation for a contest," says Schwarzenegger, who held the Mr. Olympia bodybuilding title for seven years. "I did not use them for muscle growth but rather for muscle maintenance when cutting up."

Lyle Alzado, the colorful, record-setting defensive tackle for the Los Angeles Raiders, Cleveland Browns, and Denver Broncos, admitted to taking steroids to stay competitive but acknowledged their risks. "Ninety percent of the athletes I know are on the stuff. We're not born to be 300 lbs. or jump 30 ft. But all the time I was taking steroids, I knew they were making me play better," he said. "I became very violent on the field and off it. I did things only crazy people do. Now look at me. My hair's gone, I wobble when I walk and have to hold on to someone for support and I have trouble remembering things. My last wish? That no one else ever dies this way."

Recently, a few show business celebrities have come under scrutiny for their involvement with steroids and other banned substances. In 2008, 61-year-old *Rambo* star Sylvester Stallone paid $10,600 to settle a criminal drug possession charge for smuggling 48 vials of Human Growth Hormone (HGH) into the country. HGH is popularly used for its anti-aging benefits. "Everyone over 40 years old would be wise to investigate it (HGH and testosterone use) because it increases the quality of your life," says Stallone.

"If you're an actor in Hollywood and you're over 40, you are doing HGH. Period," said one Hollywood cosmetic surgeon. "Why wouldn't you? It makes your skin look better, your hair, your fingernails. Everything."

Extreme Sports: Playing on the Edge

The following activities exist well off sport's mainstream path. From 1,000 feet below ground to at least that high overhead, endorphin-hounds risk it all in pursuit of "epic" moments.

✳ ✳ ✳ ✳

"Swabbing" the Swabbie

WATER (OR SEA) jousting captures all the action of medieval jousting without that sport's messy mauling and death. Nevertheless, it features fearsome competitors such as the "Unrootable" Casimir Castaldo and Vincent Cianni, "the man of 100 victories."

The drill is simple: Two boats are rowed toward each other. When helm nears helm, competitors perched on protruding platforms draw their lances and get busy. The last one standing gets the girl, or at least a moment of glory. And the vanquished? That poor wet critter gets to joust another day.

The sport dates to at least 2780 B.C. (Egyptian bas-reliefs from that time depict nautical jousts that may have been a genuine form of warfare.) The most prestigious event is the Tournament de la Saint-Louis, held in Sète, France, every August. Since 1743 it has attracted hordes of enthusiastic fans who come to see their least favorite competitors "bumped off."

I Can't Believe I Ate the Whole Thing

Nathan's Famous is the name most often associated with eating contests, but there are many more out there. At the 2007 Coney Island event, a 230-pound Californian named Joey "Jaws" Chestnut rammed 66 hot dogs and buns down his gullet in 12 minutes to set a new world record.

Consider these impossible-sounding world marks: 22 slices of 16-inch-diameter pizza downed in ten minutes by 190-

pound Chicagoan Patrick Bertoletti in August 2007. Or how about 8.31 pounds of Armour Vienna sausage wolfed down in ten minutes? This eat feat was accomplished by petite Sonya Thomas in May 2005. At 105 pounds, Thomas proves that you don't have to be large to produce records.

Underwater Pursuits

Scuba diving is risky business, but cave diving ups the ante even more. Here practitioners do underwater what spelunkers do underground. The difference? If a spelunker gets lost, it's usually an inconvenience. To a cave diver equipped with limited oxygen, it can mean death.

Experts explore ever deeper and more distant passages, but even the greatest can have an off day. Sheck Exley of Jacksonville, Florida, was a pioneer in cave diving. The 45-year-old had captured numerous world records in the sport before he met with tragedy in 1994 at Zacatón, a forbiddingly deep sinkhole in Mexico. When his body was recovered a few days later, his depth gauge showed a maximum depth of 879 feet. To many, he was the absolute best; unfortunately, statistics show he probably won't be the last.

Peak Performance

Ordinary skiing features lifts that take people to the top of groomed trails, but heliskiing uses helicopters to deliver skiers to wild, often untouched terrain. Reaching a mountain's absolute peak opens up a brave new world of virgin powder and incomparable alpine views, as well as extreme avalanches and bone breaks. The latter two occur often enough that outfitters generally provide clients with GPS transponders to help locate them in the event of an accident or avalanche.

Heliskiing isn't cheap. On average, heliskiers can expect to pay between $500 and $1,000 for three to four full runs. But it's worth it, at least according to aficionados who are willing to pay the price and risk their lives for solitude on the slopes and the chance to ski thousands more feet per run.

The Ultimate (Ground) Rush

B.A.S.E. jumping—an acronym for Building, Antenna, Span, Earth—is the practice of skydiving from these four different, ground-anchored points. Popularized by endorphin junkies in the 1970s, the sport continues to grow despite inherent risks.

Though no single venue is typical, West Virginia's famed New River Gorge Bridge is revered as a glorious step-off spot. Once there, jumpers toss themselves into the 876-foot-high abyss. Freefall time before chutes open? About four seconds. Time from takeoff to "splat!" if they don't? Approximately eight seconds. Since 1981, more than 116 unlucky B.A.S.E. jumpers have been killed pursuing the sport.

Shredding the Tarmac

Developed by skateboarders in the 1970s, street luge (aka butt-boarding) is where speed freaks go when the melt is on. Without the benefit of snow, street luge relies solely on steep paved roadways of varying lengths for propulsion. As with winter luge, however, the first to reach the bottom wins.

Street lugers lay flat on their backs just as winter lugers do, but they ride an elongated version of a skateboard rather than the small snow sled after which the sport of luge is named. Steering is accomplished with leg pressure and by shifting body weight.

A modern "boarder" can hit speeds in excess of 70 miles per hour, with handling that boggles the mind. Even so, accidents happen, and when they do, they're generally spectacular.

Freestyle Walking

Despite its unimposing name, freestyle walking represents an all-new level of extreme sport. Using an urban landscape as their playground, practitioners outfitted with nothing more than their bodies fluidly jump from building to building, swing from fences, dive over benches and walls, and hop, skip, and jump over just about everything else. Unaware observers might think they're watching the filming of an action flick.

The extreme part of this sport kicks in when grip is lost, distances are misjudged, or Murphy's Law comes into play. Since the early 1990s, the sport of freestyle walking has attracted a youth culture that constantly raises the bar by attempting ever-more-dicey moves.

Wakeboarding Gets Gnarly

Occasionally, an expert in a given sport asks, "How can I make this less safe?" This seems to be the case with rail-sliding, a relatively new addition to the wakeboardist's bag of tricks.

Here's how it works: A wakeboarder is towed by a boat, as if waterskiing, toward a stationary rail in the water. The widths of these beams vary from a few inches to more than a foot, and some reach 90 feet in length. At the last second, the boarder bunny hops on top of this slicker-than-glass surface, landing his board in a standing position with feet straddling the rail.

If all goes well, he slides along to glory. If not, a host of really bad things can happen, including back-crushing "kickouts" (backward falls onto the rail), agonizing face plants (a kickout performed in reverse), and worse.

A Pick and a Prayer

Leave it to rock climbers to devise increasingly dangerous pastimes. Ice climbing raises the bar and offers a way to climb in the dreaded winter off-season.

With pickax in hand and crampons (metal spikes that attach to boots) strapped to feet, the climber advances . . . until he or she hears an ominous cracking sound. Though this scenario is infrequent, it does happen. When it doesn't, ice climbers enjoy the same rush as rock climbers.

With soft ice, falling ice, and avalanches posing additional risks, ice climbing is thought to be even more perilous than rock climbing. But that doesn't stop the adventurous from taking a swing at it—the swing of an ax, that is.

Down the Chute

Imagine whooshing down an icy luge track at breakneck speed, the course moving by in a blur. Now imagine lying headfirst on a sled and doing the same. Welcome to skeleton luge, where one false move produces one serious headache.

Competitors, or "sliders," must first run 100 feet while pushing their sleds. Then they jump aboard, navigate the course with their body movements, and hope all goes according to plan. The sled follows a steeply banked track, and there are no brakes. Fastest time wins the day. After hitting speeds of 80 miles per hour and pulling up to four Gs on a skeleton luge, the neighborhood toboggan hill will never look the same.

Getting Into It

Straight from New Zealand comes zorbing, an offbeat sport invented in the 1990s that's practiced inside a giant ball. Here's the drill: The zorbian (zorbing enthusiast) straps himself inside a fully inflated plastic ball. Then, with common sense jettisoned in favor of high adventure, an assistant sets the ball rolling down a steep hill. Happy shrieks can be heard as the zorbian attains speeds up to 25 miles per hour. If the ball veers off course or takes a bad bounce, shrieks of a far different sort can be heard.

Clearly on a roll, this sport has spread into Norway, Sweden, Switzerland, China, Japan, England, and the United States, among other countries.

✳ Of the 656 muscles in your body, it takes about 2.5 percent of them to smile.

✳ Actor Tom Cruise was a wrestler in high school.

Who Says Throwing Like a Girl Is Bad?

Girls have gotten a bum rap. In fact, throwing like a girl can sometimes be better than throwing like a guy.

❊　❊　❊　❊

FEMINISTS—AS WELL AS anyone who's being truly reasonable—will point out that the term "throwing like a girl" is condescending. And anyone who's watched a women's softball game knows the question is based on a faulty assumption, because women who've played a lot of ball throw every bit as well as men, though generally not as powerfully because they tend to be smaller and have less upper-body strength.

Atlantic Monthly belabored the point in its signature way several years ago, coming to this conclusion: "The crucial factor is not that males and females are put together differently but that they typically spend their early years in different ways. Little boys often learn to throw without noticing that they are throwing. Little girls are more rarely in environments that encourage them in the same way."

But *Atlantic Monthly* didn't consider why there's such opprobrium in throwing badly in the first place. It can't be just because baseball is so central to the American male psyche—baseball's big but not *that* big. We think it might have deeper anthropological roots, stretching back to a time when throwing deadly projectiles—spears, stones, etc.—was central to sustenance and protection. Someone who threw poorly would have been a liability to the clan.

This kind of formative reality is burned into our genes; it's possible that when we see someone throw awkwardly, we feel the primal fear of shared vulnerability. And that fear is as powerful today as it was in our knuckle-dragging days. Just ask anyone who ever watched Mitch "Wild Thing" Williams pitch.

The Strangest Baseball Injuries

Athletes are famous for sustaining injuries, but baseball players seem to have a knack for scoring some of the strangest afflictions of all.

✳ ✳ ✳ ✳

Lingerie Laceration

FORMER GIANTS MANAGER Roger Craig actually cut his hand while trying to undo a bra strap. No word on what kind of emotional damage was done to the lady.

Eating Exertion

First baseman Ryan Klesko pulled a muscle while with the Braves—by lifting his lunch tray.

Chili Power

Former second baseman Bret Barberie had to sit out during a Marlins game after accidentally rubbing some chili juice in his eye.

Butter Slip

Another dinner winner, former Rangers outfielder Oddibe McDowell ended up slicing his hand open while trying to butter a roll at a celebration luncheon.

Belly Achin'

A knife nearly caused then-Padres player Adam Eaton to pass out. Eaton was using a blade in an attempt to get a DVD out of its wrapper when he slipped and accidentally stabbed himself in the abdomen.

Food Force

Former Mets and Giants outfielder Kevin Mitchell may take the cake when it comes to food flaps. He once made the disabled list by straining his rib muscles while vomiting. Mitchell also missed the first four days of spring training after hurting himself while scarfing down a microwaved donut. He is also even rumored to have injured himself eating a cupcake at some point.

Given the Boot

Hall of Fame third baseman Wade Boggs got a little too excited putting on cowboy boots and was injured as a result. Boggs ended up missing seven games because of the back strain he incurred.

Toe Trouble

Not to be outdone, former Detroit Tigers catcher Mickey Tettleton tied his shoes so tightly that he gave himself a severe case of athlete's foot.

Protection Problems

Outfielder Ken Griffey Jr. found his protection to be his problem: Griffey had to miss a Mariners game after his protective cup apparently slipped and pinched the goods in a not-so-good way.

Virtual Spiders

One-time Blue Jay outfielder Glenallen Hill smashed a glass table while asleep. He dreamt that spiders were attacking him.

Not-So-Cool Move

Former Oriole pitcher Mark Smith hurt his hand when he reached into an air conditioning unit. He said he wanted to find out why it wasn't working.

Iron Man

Braves pitcher John Smoltz got a bit too hot below the collar when he tried to iron a shirt—while he was wearing it. Smoltz ended up burning his chest.

Operator Error

Former pitcher Steve Sparks wanted to show off his Brewers strength by tearing a phone book in half. Instead, he had a dislocated shoulder to show off.

Stressful Sneezes

Former outfielder Sammy Sosa suffered more than a stuffy nose when two sneezes struck him right before a Cubs game. The powerful projections caused Sosa to have back spasms, and he spent the rest of the afternoon getting treatment.

The Hidden History
of the Jockstrap

On November 28, 2005, the Bike Athletic Company celebrated the production of its 350 millionth jockstrap, which was promptly framed and flown to the company's headquarters. Lets take a closer look at some landmarks in the long history of this piece of men's protective underwear.

✳ ✳ ✳ ✳

The Birth of a Legend

THE STORY OF the jockstrap begins in 1874, thanks to Charles Bennett, who worked for the Chicago-based sporting goods company Sharp & Smith. Originally, Bennett designed his garment to be used by bicyclists in Boston. In 1897, Bennett and his newly formed BIKE Web Company (as Bike Athletic was known then) officially patented his invention.

At the time, a bicycle craze was sweeping the nation. These bikes weren't like today's average cruisers; instead, the bicycles of yore were high-wheeled and quite precarious. Folks raced these bikes around steeply banked velodrome tracks as well as through Boston's bumpy cobblestone streets. The daredevils on the velodromes were known as "bike jockeys," which led to Bennett naming his invention the "BIKE Jockey Strap," later shortened to "jockstrap." Two decades later, the U.S. Army issued jockstraps to World War I soldiers in order to reduce "scrotal fatigue." When the troops came home, the bicycle craze had been replaced by the rough and tumble sport of football; the jockstrap found a new home on the gridiron.

Manly Fact: There is some conjecture that the word "jock" is derived from a slang term for the penis.

Entering Manhood via the Locker Room

To most men of a certain age, the jockstrap is a right of passage that signals the arrival of puberty and a need to protect the male reproductive organs during vigorous exercise. To the uninitiated (or female), the jockstrap's construction might be a tad mysterious, but it really is rather simple. A jockstrap (or athletic supporter) consists of an elastic waistband and leg straps connected to a pouch that holds the testicles and penis close to the body, sometimes with the added plastic cup (ostensibly to avoid injury). The original design, with the addition of the cup, hasn't changed much since the early 1900s.

Manly Fact: Jockstrap size refers to waist size. In this case, bigger isn't necessarily better.

A Milestone Missed

In 1974, the jockstrap turned 100 years old, but the anniversary passed quietly—no national-magazine commemorative editions, no ticker-tape parade. Perhaps it was due to a national feeling of modesty. On the other hand, a mere 15 years later, as a journalist writing for the *Orlando Sentinel* remarked, a certain women's undergarment—the bra—received plenty of press for its centennial. In fact, when the bra turned 100, *LIFE* magazine issued six pages to celebrate, along with a pictorial and a headline shouting "Hurrah for the bra." Ten years later, as the jockstrap turned 125, a *Houston Chronicle* writer wondered why we'd forgotten about the forsaken jockstrap. Perhaps we'd been too distracted by Y2K in 1999, he wrote, or maybe "the jock just isn't in the same league [as the bra] ... A bra suggests female mystery; a jock suggests male vulnerability."

Manly Fact: In the early 1900s, the jockstrap influenced the invention of the Heidelberg Alternating Current Electric Belt, which claimed to cure nervous diseases in men and women.

The Decline of the Jock?

In the past few decades, there has been some encroachment on jockstrap territory by the likes of free-flowing boxer shorts, jockey shorts, and, for athletic types, "compression shorts." Still, after more than 130 years on the market, the jockstrap probably isn't going anywhere just yet.

The Shotgun Offense

Some college football coaches have armed state troopers with them on the sideline, a peculiar tradition that dates back more than 50 years.

✳ ✳ ✳ ✳

It Began with the "Bear"

A COUPLE OF STATE troopers are the ultimate accessories for a major-college football coach—especially in the pigskin-crazed South. No one is certain how the tradition started, but it's usually attributed to Paul "Bear" Bryant, who was a legendary coach at the University of Alabama. The story is that Bear got a trooper entourage for security in 1958 or 1959. Not to be outdone, Ralph "Shug" Jordan, coach at Auburn University, Alabama's bitter in-state rival, secured a larger posse of troopers soon after. Let the games begin.

The tradition is both ceremonial and practical. Ceremonially, the troopers represent state pride, whether at home or away. Troopers have no law enforcement authority in another state, but armed and dressed in their official garb, they can be an imposing presence on the sideline.

From a practical perspective, the troopers' chief responsibility is to provide protection. This rarely is an issue during the game, but the playing field can fill up quickly with excited and rambunctious fans once the final seconds have ticked away. It is the job of troopers to escort the coach through the chaos to midfield for the traditional handshake with the opposing coach (who also might be flanked by troopers) and then to the locker room.

The Price of Packing Heat

This sort of security doesn't come cheap. In 2008, for example, ten schools in Alabama each paid the state police more than $38,000 for "football detail." Some troopers in other states provide coach protection at no cost, as long as the college pays for meals and travel expenses.

The practice is nearly ubiquitous among NCAA Division I-A teams in the Southeastern Conference and has also caught on with some schools in the ACC, Big East, Big 12, and Big Ten conferences. Trooper detail hasn't taken root in the West, however—the Pacific-10 Conference is explicitly opposed to the practice. Teams that don't have trooper support generally rely on campus police for coach security.

For a trooper assigned to a coach, staying calm, cool, and collected might be the toughest part of the gig. Troopers typically are huge fans of their assigned teams, but they're expected to maintain stoic professionalism. And this is no small feat if they've just witnessed a game-winning touchdown.

---

* A person eating a big meal might swallow more than 200 times.

* The largest American corporation named for an owner's daughter is Sara Lee. Founder Charles Lubin first named a cheesecake for his daughter in 1949.

* American interstate highways going east and west have even numbers. North-and-south highways are given odd numbers.

* The Hunza, an ethnic group in northwest Kashmir, have not experienced cancer, coronary heart disease, or ulcers. Many of the men and women live to age 100.

* To conserve fuel during World War II, King George VI of England ordered that no more than five inches of lukewarm water could be used to take baths in Buckingham Palace.

* A normal person's bladder holds about 16 ounces of urine. They'll feel the need to "go" when it's about three-quarters full.

* Theodore Roosevelt was shot as he campaigned for the presidency in 1912. The bullet hit him in the chest but not before passing through his glasses' case and the speech he had folded in his pocket. Roosevelt received a superficial wound and finished his speech before going to the hospital for treatment 90 minutes later.

World War II Baseball and the One-Armed Outfielder

In January 1942, President Franklin D. Roosevelt responded to a letter from Baseball Commissioner Kenesaw Mountain Landis. FDR advised that baseball should continue during World War II because it was good for American morale. Perhaps he should have specified "good baseball."

✳ ✳ ✳ ✳

Service-able Baseball

WORLD WAR II-ERA baseball is known for many things: a one-legged pitcher, a 15-year-old pitcher, and a pennant win by a perennial doormat team, the St. Louis Browns. But there may have been nothing more memorable than a one-armed outfielder named Pete Gray.

Although baseball was allowed to continue during the war, many of its players went into the armed forces, including stars such as Bob Feller, Joe DiMaggio, and Ted Williams. So teams scrambled for replacements. The Boston Red Sox held open tryouts, while the Cleveland Indians found a fellow with feet so large— he wore size 17 shoes—the army rejected him. The Cincinnati Reds tried 15-year-old pitcher Joe Nuxhall, who proceeded to give up five runs in less than an inning for an Earned Run Average of 67.50. Bert Shepard, who had lost a leg in the war, fared better during his short stint with the Washington Senators: He held the opposition to one run in five innings.

By 1944, the quality of play in Major League Baseball had hit an all-time low. Fittingly, that year the St. Louis Browns, who usually finished last or awfully close to it, won the American League pennant for the first and only time in their history.

Not Quite Far Enough

In 1945, the Browns decided to give a one-armed outfielder by the name of Pete Gray a shot. He was born in 1915 as Pete Wyshner in Nanticoke, Pennsylvania. Right-handed, Gray lost his dominant arm as a young boy when it was amputated just above the elbow after an accident. At age 17, he hitchhiked to Chicago to watch the 1932 World Series between the Cubs and Yankees. From that point on, Gray was determined to play Major League Baseball.

Before joining the Browns, Gray had several successful minor-league seasons with teams that included the Brooklyn Bushwicks and the Trois Rivieres Renards of the Canadian-American League. On the field with the Browns, however, critics derailed him by saying he was a curiosity who was playing because of the dwindling talent pool. Gray had plenty of talent; he even devised a method of fielding that was so quick he had to demonstrate it in slow motion. However, Gray found that he could not hit major-league pitching because he had no second hand to temper his swing when pitchers threw him off-speed balls. And despite his quickness on the field, he could not stop runners from taking an extra base on him. Gray hit .218 in 1945, which was his only major-league season. Many of the balls he hit just didn't have enough force and died on the warning track just a few feet from the fence.

Back to Normal

In 1946, players returning from the service helped boost the quality of play—and none too soon. The 1945 World Series had been so miserable that it was dubbed "the fat men against the tall men at the office picnic." This made a prophet out of Chicago sportswriter Warren Brown. When asked before the series began to pick which team would eventually win, Brown remarked: "I don't think either of them can win it." As for Gray, he was dropped from the Browns in 1946 and went on to play in the minors until 1949. Still, he continues to serve as a source of inspiration.

How to Break a Concrete Block with Your Hand

It's an act that's synonymous with martial arts, and we reveal some of the tricks of the concrete-busting trade.

✻ ✻ ✻ ✻

Hand vs. Block

IN A FACE-OFF between hand and block, the hand has a surprising advantage: Bone is significantly stronger than concrete. In fact, bone can withstand about 40 times more stress than concrete before reaching its breaking point. What's more, the surrounding muscles and ligaments in your hands are good stress absorbers, making the hand and arm one tough weapon. So if you position your hand correctly, you're not going to break it by hitting concrete.

The trick to smashing a block is thrusting this sturdy mass into the concrete with enough force to bend the block beyond its breaking point. The force of any impact is determined by the momentum of the two objects in the collision. Momentum is a multiple of the mass and velocity of an object.

Velocity Is the Key

When striking an object, the speed of your blow is critical. You also have to hit the block with a relatively small area of your hand, so that the force of the impact is focused in one spot on the block—this concentrates the stress on the concrete. As in golf, the only way for a martial arts student to hit accurately with greater speed is practice, practice, practice.

But there is a basic mental trick involved: You have to overcome your natural instinct to slow your strike as your hand approaches the block. Martial arts masters concentrate on an impact spot beyond the block, so that the hand is still at maximum speed when it makes contact with the concrete.

Body Mass Counts, Too

You also need to put as much body mass as you can into the strike; this can be achieved by twisting your body and lowering your torso as you make contact. A black belt in karate can throw a chop at about 46 feet per second, which results in a force of about 2,800 newtons. (A newton is the unit of force needed to accelerate a mass.)

That's more than enough power to break the standard one-and-a-half-inch concrete slabs that are commonly used in demonstrations and typically can withstand only 1,900 newtons. Nonetheless, while hands are dandy in a block-breaking exhibition, you'll find that for sidewalk demolition and other large projects, jackhammers are really the way to go.

---

* The first Avon lady was Mrs. P.F.E. Albee of Winchester, New Hampshire, who went door-to-door selling Little Dot Perfume. An Albee Barbie doll was issued in 1997.

* The gluteus maximus, the muscle that makes up the buttocks, is the biggest muscle in the body.

* British geologist William Buckland was known for his ability to eat anything, including rodents and insects. When presented with the heart of French King Louis XIV, he gobbled it up without hesitation.

* In May 1861, a gold piece worth a dollar in the Union was worth $1.10 in Confederate currency. By war's end, that same piece of gold—still a Union dollar—was worth $60 in the Confederacy.

* Pianos come in 12 different sizes, ranging from the relatively tiny spinet (at about three feet in length) to the concert grand piano (nine feet long or more).

* While walking on the moon during the *Apollo 14* mission, astronaut Alan B. Shepard became the first galactic golfer, driving a pair of dimpled domes into space.

Managerial Musical Chairs

For Chicago Cubs fans in the early 1960s, the question wasn't "Who's on First?," but rather, "Who's in the dugout?" If ever there was an idea that deserved a failing grade, it would be Philip K. Wrigley's College of Coaches.

✳ ✳ ✳ ✳

Hibernation

THE CHICAGO CUBS were once one of baseball's elite teams. But that was many years ago; by 1961, the team hadn't had a winning record for over a decade. This was despite the presence of some good ballplayers on the roster, most notably Hall of Famers Ernie Banks and Billy Williams.

Cubs fans had put up with a lot as the team struggled for years under owner Philip K. Wrigley, the gum magnate who had inherited the team in 1932. Once, for example, Wrigley traded his team manager for another team's broadcaster.

But that was nothing compared to what Wrigley concocted in 1961. Scrambling for a new strategy, he unveiled not one new manager that season but eight. Instead of a single face in the dugout, Wrigley had devised a bizarre new system he called "The College of Coaches."

Coaching Carousel

Here's how it worked: From a pool of coaches, Wrigley would select one to be the head coach, or manager, for an unspecified period of time. Then, whenever he felt like it, Wrigley would pick a new head coach from the pool.

The concept behind the College of Coaches was that instead of firing the manager if the team played poorly, Wrigley could merely demote him and immediately choose a replacement from seven others rather than spend long hours searching for a new manager.

He also intended for the coaches, during the times they were not the head coach, to work with the players to instill a cohesive system and style. Therefore, whenever a new head coach was appointed, the players would already know the system.

The idea received a storm of ridicule. "The Cubs have been playing without players for years," said one critic. "Now, they're going to try it without a manager."

The Ship of Fools

Undeterred, Wrigley and the Cubs sailed into the 1961 season on the good ship College of Coaches—and promptly began listing to one side. The experiment violated a cardinal rule of successful sports teams: Consistency is vital. Under the College of Coaches, the players never knew who was going to be in charge, or for how long. The comfort and security a player felt under one manager might be yanked away the next day when a new man took over.

In addition, the other coaches weren't always inclined to help the existing head coach if things went bad, preferring to wait until they got their own shot at the top job. With each head coach set in his own way of doing things, chaos reigned in the Cubs dugout.

Report Card

In 1961, the first year of the College of Coaches, the team finished four games better than they had the previous year. But in 1962, the Cubs' ship really sank as the team went 59–103, finishing the season ahead of only the hapless New York Mets, who lost a record 120 games that year.

In 1963 and 1964, Wrigley kept up the pretense of rotating coaches, although he kept one man in charge all year. In November 1965, the system mercifully came to an end.

Although Wrigley Field was famous for its ivy-covered outfield walls, Wrigley's experimental "college" was anything but Ivy League. The College of Coaches had flunked out.

Fran's Father

It is said that the death of Fran Tarkenton's father was caused by officiating miscues in the 1975 playoff game between Minnesota and Dallas. But it's not true. Tarkenton's father did die during the game, but it was before the referees made their blunders.

* * * *

ONE MUST APPROACH such a macabre myth delicately, which is more than can be said for the perpetrators of this tall tale, who were probably the same lunatics who plunked an on-field official with a whiskey bottle during the tumultuous NFL contest that was played on December 28, 1975.

That year, the Minnesota Vikings had pillaged their way through the regular season, posting a 12–2 record. Bolstered by quarterback Fran Tarkenton, the Vikings were not expected to have any trouble subduing the Dallas Cowboys when they clashed in Minnesota on that solemn Sunday. Less than six minutes remained on the clock when the men in stripes began their football follies. The first questionable call came when Dallas receiver Drew Pearson appeared to step out of bounds before snagging a do-or-die pass on a fourth-and-sixteen play. The officials ruled that Pearson had kept both feet in play. With only a handful of ticks left in the game and Dallas still trailing 14–10, Roger Staubach pitched a prayer toward the end zone before disappearing under a mound of Minnesota muscle. Pearson caught the ball, but he appeared to push Viking defender Nate Wright to the ground before grabbing the toss. Once again, the on-field zebras ignored the malfeasance and signaled a touchdown. A shower of debris rained onto the field, including the well-flung bottle that bopped field judge Armen Terzian. After the contest, Tarkenton learned that his father had suffered a fatal heart attack during the third quarter of the game, long before the tables had turned.

Staubach's miracle missile was later described as a "Hail Mary," the first time that divine designation was applied to a flying football.

Nine Odd Sporting Events from Around the World

When it comes to sports, if it involves a ball or a club, men will play it, and if it's on TV, men will watch it. Here are some of the most unusual sports from around the world.

✳ ✳ ✳ ✳

1. **Cheese Rolling:** If you're a whiz at cheese rolling, you may want to head to Brockworth in Gloucestershire, England, where the annual Cooper's Hill Cheese Roll is held each May. The ancient festival dates back hundreds of years and involves pushing and shoving a large, mellow, seven- to eight-pound wheel of ripe Gloucestershire cheese downhill in a race to the bottom. With the wheels of cheese reaching up to 70 miles per hour, runners chase, tumble, and slide down the hill after their cheese but don't usually catch up until the end. The winner gets to take home his or her cheese, while the runners-up get cash prizes.

2. **Toe Wrestling:** This little piggy went to the World Toe Wrestling Championship held annually in July in Derbyshire, England. Contestants sit facing each other at a "toedium"—a stadium for toes—and try to push each other's bare foot off a small stand called a "toesrack." Three-time champion Paul Beech calls himself the "Toeminator." Toe wrestling began in the town of Wetton in 1970, and the international sport is governed by the World Toe Wrestling Organization, which once applied for Olympic status but was rejected.

3. **Tuna Throwing:** Popular in Australia, tuna throwing requires contestants to whirl a frozen tuna around their heads with a rope and then fling it like an Olympic hammer thrower. Since 1998, the record holder has been former Olympic hammer-thrower Sean Carlin, with a tuna toss of 122 feet. Paying out $7,000 in prize money overall, the event is part of Tunarama,

an annual festival held in late January in Port Lincoln, South Australia. Animal rights activists will be pleased to know that the tuna are spoiled fish that stores refused to sell.

4. Pooh Sticks: Christopher Robin knows that "pooh sticks" is not a hygiene problem but rather a game played with Winnie the Pooh. The game consists of finding a stick, dropping it into a river, and then seeing how long it takes to get to the finish line. There is even an annual World Pooh Sticks Championship held in mid-March in Oxfordshire, England. Individual event winners receive gold, silver, and bronze medals, and a team event has attracted competitors from Japan, Latvia, and the Czech Republic.

5. Man Versus Horse Marathon: The Man Versus Horse Marathon is an annual race between humans and horse-and-rider teams held in early June in the Welsh town of Llanwrtyd Wells. The event started in 1980 when a pub keeper overheard two men debating which was faster in a long race—man or horse. Slightly shorter than a traditional marathon, the 22-mile course is filled with many natural obstacles, and horses win nearly every year. But in 2004, Huw Lobb made history as the first runner to win the race (in 2 hours, 5 minutes, and 19 seconds), taking the £25,000 (about $47,500) prize, which was the accumulation of 25 yearly £1,000 prizes that had not been claimed. Apparently, the horse doesn't get to keep its winnings.

6. Bull Running: While bullfighting is popular in many countries, the sport of bull running—which should really be called bull outrunning—is pretty much owned by Pamplona, Spain. The event dates back to the 13th and 14th centuries as a combination of festivals honoring St. Fermin and bullfighting. Every morning for a week in July, the half-mile race is on between six bulls and hundreds of people. Most of the participants try to get as close to the bulls as possible, and many think it's good luck to touch one.

7. **Tomato Tossing:** Tomatoes aren't just for salads and sauce anymore. La Tomatina is a festival held in late August in the small town of Buñol, Spain, where approximately 30,000 people come from all over the world to pelt one another with nearly 140 tons of overripe tomatoes. The fruit fight dates back to the mid-1940s but was banned under Francisco Franco, then returned in the 1970s after his death. After two hours of tomato-tossing at La Tomatina, there are no winners or losers, only stains and sauce, and the cleanup begins.

8. **Human Tower Building:** If you enjoy watching cheerleaders form human pyramids, you'll love the *castellers*, people who compete to form giant human towers at festivals around Catalonia, Spain. Castellers form a solid foundation of packed bodies, linking arms and hands together in an intricate way that holds several tons and softens the fall in case the tower collapses, which is not uncommon. Up to eight more levels of people are built, each layer standing on the shoulders of the people below. The top levels are made up of children, and when complete, the castell resembles a human Leaning Tower of Pisa.

9. **Wife Carrying Championship:** During the Wife Carrying Championship, held annually in Sonkajärvi, Finland, contestants carry a woman—it needn't be their wife—over an 832-foot course with various obstacles en route. Dropping the woman incurs a 15-second penalty, and the first team to reach the finish line receives the grand prize—the weight of the "wife" in beer! This bizarre event traces its origins to the 19th century when a local gang of bandits commonly stole women from neighboring villages.

PETA Wouldn't Approve of This Sport

Imagine a game in which the "ball" is the carcass of a goat— decapitated, dehoofed, and soaked overnight in cold water to make it stiff. Such a game really exists, and it's called buzkashi.

✳ ✳ ✳ ✳

BUZKASHI IS THE national sport of Afghanistan. In addition to the interesting choice of a ball, the players in this rough-and-tumble game are mounted on horseback and wear traditional Uzbek garb: turbans, robes, and scarves around their waists. There's no complicated playbook, only a minimally regimented strategy that requires—encourages—no-holds-barred violence. The referees carry rifles in case things really get out of hand. The field has no set boundaries; spectators are in constant danger of being trampled. The objective is to gain possession of the goat and carry it to a designated goal. And the winning players cook and eat the carcass.

Buzkashi translates to "goat pulling" and likely evolved from ordinary herding. It originated with nomadic Turkic peoples who moved west from China and Mongolia from the 10th to 15th centuries. Today, it's played mainly in Afghanistan, but you can also find folks yanking the ol' carcass in northwestern China and in the Muslim republics north of Afghanistan.

The game has two basic forms: modern and traditional. The modern involves teams of 10 to 12 riders. In the traditional form, it's every man for himself. Both require a combination of strength and expert horsemanship.

The competitions often are sponsored by *khans* ("traditional elites"), who gain or lose status based on the success of the events. And in this case, success is defined by the level of mayhem that erupts. Biting, hair-pulling, grabbing another rider's reins, and using weapons are prohibited in buzkashi. Anything else goes.

※ **Chapter Seven**

Bizarre Truths About the Human Body

The Legal Ways to Dispose of a Body

Grandpa's gone, and for some people, the most pressing issue is whether to request a pillow in his coffin. For others, the question is not whether Gramps needs head support, but whether his earthly remains should be buried, cremated, frozen, or perhaps—in the not-too-distant future—liquefied.

※　※　※　※

Bring Out Your Dead

HUMANS ARE THE only creatures known to bury their dead in a systematic way. It's a practice that could date back 100,000 years or more, and today's most commonly legal method of burial involves a casket. In the United States, about 80 percent of the deceased are laid in a casket and buried. More than half are displayed in an open casket prior to burial; the rest bow out with the lid shut.

Cremation is the second-most popular method of disposal. Cremation reduces the average-size adult to eight pounds of ash and fragments. The remains typically are kept by loved ones in a small container, buried, or scattered in a location of special significance to the deceased. The ashes of *Star Trek* creator Gene Roddenberry, for example, were dispersed in outer space.

Cryonic suspension is another legal way to go, though it is far less common than burial or cremation. Also known as solid-state hypothermia, cryonic suspension involves freezing and maintaining a human body in the hope that scientific advances someday will make it possible to resuscitate the deceased. The corpse is frozen and stored at −321 degrees Fahrenheit, which is the boiling point of liquid nitrogen. Going the frozen route requires lots of cold cash: Cryopreservation can cost as much as $150,000, depending on the level of services one selects. Baseball great Ted Williams awaits his next turn at bat at a cryonic facility in Scottsdale, Arizona.

The volunteering of corpses for organ donation, or for medical or scientific research, is also gaining popularity. It's the only way that many people ever get into medical school.

Good to the Last Drop

Alkaline hydrolysis might be the future of legal body disposal. The process involves placing a body in a steel chamber, which contains lye that is heated to 300 degrees Fahrenheit and is pressurized to 60 pounds per square inch. Think of it as being boiled in acid. The remains are a liquid that can be poured down a drain. Alkaline hydrolysis is currently performed only in a couple of research hospitals in the United States, but there is growing support to make this environmentally friendly method of body disposal available through funeral homes.

As for illegal ways to get rid of a body, you need neither scientists nor undertakers. Guys with names like Big Nicky are the experts in this field; cross them or their cronies, and a body might end up "sleeping with the fishes."

Don't Blame Beer Alone for Your Beer Belly

You see them at the corner bar, and maybe even in the recliner in your TV room: gargantuan guts, worn by men who have devoted countless hours to quaffing and precious few to aerobic activity. But is it really the beer that's responsible for those whopping waistlines?

* * * *

THE CZECH REPUBLIC is the world champion in per capita beer consumption, and in 2007 a team of Czech researchers studied 2,000 male and female beer drinkers. They found no direct link between obesity and the amount of beer one consumes. That's not to say beer can't make you fat—it can. Each tasty glass of your favorite malt beverage contains plenty

 of gravity-enhancing calories. But beer on its own is apparently not the culprit.

Swiss physiologists in 1992 determined that alcohol in the bloodstream can slow the body's ability to burn fat by about 30 percent. That means high-fat foods become even more potent when combined with alcohol. And it doesn't take a scientific survey to determine that in a room full of beer drinkers, a plate of salad will go unmolested while bowls of potato chips and platters of cheeseburgers and bratwurst disappear faster than you can say "myocardial infarction."

Further, results of a recent study in Italy suggest that some men are genetically predisposed to develop a sizable midsection, regardless of what they choose to eat and drink. So beer can play an important role in the development and maintenance of a beer belly—but it's not required.

It's No Myth: A Human Voice Can Shatter Glass

You're not likely to do it accidentally, even if you do spend a lot of time yelling at your tableware, but it's definitely possible.

✳ ✳ ✳ ✳

Air, Space, and Sound

FIRST, A FEW words about air, space, and sound. The word "air" probably makes you think of nothingness—empty space. But the air we breathe is actually a fluid—a gas—in which we are immersed. And the sounds that we hear are actually vibrations that travel through this fluid like waves.

Your vocal cords are machines for creating these waves. When you speak, sing, freestyle beat-box, etc., air from your lungs rushes past your vocal cords, and those two taut membranes vibrate. First, the outrushing air makes your vocal cords flex outward, pushing out a wave of increased air pressure; then they rebound inward, creating a wave of decreasing air pressure.

When your vocal cords vibrate, they're moving in and out incredibly quickly to create waves of air pressure fluctuation, or sound. The sound's pitch is determined in part by how rapidly your vocal cords are vibrating—in other words, the *frequency* of the air pressure fluctuation. The sound's volume is determined by the force of each fluctuation, or the wave's amplitude.

Sound waves travel through the fluid air and vibrate against anything they encounter. For example, sound waves rapidly move your eardrums back and forth, which is how you hear. And if a sound is loud enough, its waves can have other effects. If you've ever been at a stop light behind a car with a booming audio system in the back, you may have noticed that the trunk looks like it's shuddering under the stress of those sound waves. But the auditory assault of even the loudest stereo isn't enough to break the car's windows, so how can the sound waves of a human voice shatter glass?

It has to do with frequency and resonance. The structure and composition of an object determine exactly how it will vibrate—this is known as its natural frequency. Think of a tuning fork that vibrates in just the right way to make a particular note, no matter how you hit it. You get an extra vibration boost—a resonant sound wave—when you produce a sound wave with a frequency that lines up with the object's natural vibration frequency. It's like pushing a kid on a swing—when he's moving away from you, you push him to add an extra boost. Every time you do this, the arc of the swing increases, and the kid goes higher and higher.

In the same way, just when an object is already vibrating to the left, the resonant sound wave pushes it to the left; just when it's vibrating to the right, the resonant sound wave pushes it to the right. The amplitude steadily increases, and the object vibrates more rapidly. A crystal glass has above-average natural resonance and is fragile, so the right tone can create enough vibration to shatter it.

Technique Is Everything

To break a glass with your voice, you have to do two things:

* Hit the note that has the strongest resonant frequency for the glass. This is called the fundamental frequency, or the natural frequency mentioned earlier.

* Produce a sound with enough amplitude to vibrate the glass violently. In other words, you have to be loud.

An untrained singer can accomplish this with an amplifier providing a boost. But you need a skilled singer with strong lungs to do it unassisted. Many have claimed success, but there wasn't conclusive proof until a 2005 *MythBusters* episode showed rock singer Jaime Vendera accomplishing the feat—after 20 attempts. Don't let that guy near your Waterford Crystal collection.

Body Talk: Anthropometrics and Human Engineering

Every day, anthropometry, and the related fields of ergonomics and biomechanics, directly affect your life. In fact, you'd be hard-pressed to name one modern, manufactured device that made it to market without first undergoing years of research on its size, shape, function, color, and marketability to its target consumers.

✳ ✳ ✳ ✳

The Measurement of Body Parts

ANTHROPOMETRY IS THE science of measuring human body parts, especially for comparison purposes. Today, it's typically done to supply data to the fields of architectural, industrial, and clothing design—in short, any field that can benefit from an understanding of the dimensions and proportions of the body and how they vary among individuals. Alphonse Bertillon, born in 1853, was one forerunner of the modern anthropometrist. His system, for measuring and cataloguing facial and bodily characteristics to help identify criminals, was in use by 1883. Eventually, his methods were replaced by modern fingerprinting. In the 1940s, William Sheldon took Bertillon's work one step further by identifying three *somatotypes*, or basic human body types: the ectomorph, mesomorph, and endomorph. According to Sheldon, every human fits into one of these basic body types.

In the early 20th century, anthropometry was being used to characterize the nuances between various human races in a misguided effort to identify those deemed "inferior." It played a similarly important but just as off-base role in so-called human intelligence testing, in which physical measurements such as height, width of the head, foot length, and width of the cheekbones were taken with crude devices and used to infer intelligence level.

Today, anthropometric measurements are taken using computerized 3-D scanners. General Dynamics Advanced Information Systems (GD-AIS) has used 3-D scanning to improve the design of clothing and other products. Using a scan of a human body, the system can show how the body fills a garment and how the garment moves with the wearer. GD-AIS also invented the "Faro Arm" to analyze how commercial and military pilots move within their cockpits and what happens to a pilot's concentration when their eyes wander from one instrument to another. This data can help designers determine the best place to put the controls.

Biomechanics: The Body Moving Through Space

Another area of study concerned with the physical characteristics of the human body is *biomechanics,* or how the body moves in the home, workplace, and everyday activities. Have you ever wondered how they came up with the cupholders that hold your drink while you're driving? How about the weight-training equipment at the gym? All of these were developed after years of painstaking research in biomechanics.

A number of new inventions that make our lives more comfortable are also based on biomechanical principles. Consider this example: The toothbrush existed for thousands of years as a series of fibers glued to a straight spine. It wasn't until recently that someone took a look at the design of the human mouth and determined through biomechanical and anthropometrical measurements that the back teeth could be cleaned more efficiently by tilting the end of the toothbrush.

Making Life Easier

If you've ever seen one of the new curved ergonomic computer keyboards used to eliminate long-term stress effects that result in carpal tunnel syndrome, you've seen an example of how science can work with medicine. *Ergonomics* is the science that determines how manufactured objects "fit" human beings. Ergonomists evaluate specific tasks in the home or workplace, study how they are performed, and determine the demands they put on the worker and on the equipment being used.

Ergonomists look at the safety, comfort, performance, and aesthetics of commonly used products. Their ratings have direct implications for how well the product will sell. For instance, the future looks bright for alarm clocks that use "contrast principles" rather than a stronger light (which could keep the owner awake at night) to improve readability in the dark. The same can't be said for the poorly designed electronics that spend their (numbered) days blinking "12:00" because their owners can't figure out how to set the time.

Say What?

Taxes are what we pay for civilized society.

—OLIVER WENDELL HOLMES, JR.

Those who have succeeded at anything and don't mention luck are kidding themselves.

—LARRY KING

Why does Sea World have a seafood restaurant? I'm halfway through my fishburger and I realize, oh my God, I could be eating a slow learner.

—LYNDA MONTGOMERY

If your ship doesn't come in, swim out to it.

—JONATHAN WINTERS

I have a theory that the truth is never told during the nine-to-five hours.

—HUNTER S. THOMPSON

Ninety-eight percent of the adults in this country are decent, hardworking, honest Americans. It's the other lousy two percent that get all the publicity. But then, we elected them.

—LILY TOMLIN

A Fiery Debate: Spontaneous Human Combustion

Proponents contend that the phenomenon—in which
a person suddenly bursts into flames—is very real.
Skeptics, however, are quick to explain it away.

✳ ✳ ✳ ✳

The Curious Case of Helen Conway

A PHOTO DOCUMENTS THE gruesome death of Helen Conway. Visible in the black-and-white image—taken in 1964 in Delaware County, Pennsylvania—is an oily smear that was her torso and, behind, an ashen specter of the upholstered bedroom chair she occupied. The picture's most haunting feature might be her legs, thin and ghostly pale, clearly intact, and seemingly unscathed by whatever consumed the rest of her.

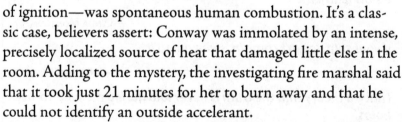

What consumed her—according to proponents of the theory that people can catch fire without an external source of ignition—was spontaneous human combustion. It's a classic case, believers assert: Conway was immolated by an intense, precisely localized source of heat that damaged little else in the room. Adding to the mystery, the investigating fire marshal said that it took just 21 minutes for her to burn away and that he could not identify an outside accelerant.

If Conway's body ignited from within and burned so quickly she had no time to rise and seek help, hers wouldn't be the first or last death to fit the supposed pattern of spontaneous human combustion.

The phenomenon was documented as early as 1763 by Frenchman Jonas Dupont in his collection of accounts, which

was published as *De Incendiis Corporis Humani Spontaneis.*
Charles Dickens's 1852 novel *Bleak House* sensationalized the
issue with the spontaneous-combustion death of a character
named Krook. That humans have been reduced to ashes with
little damage to their surroundings is not the stuff of fiction,
however. Many documented cases exist. The question is, did
these people combust spontaneously?

How It Happens

Theories advancing the concept abound. Early hypotheses held
that victims, such as Dickens's Krook, were likely alcoholics so
besotted that their very flesh became flammable. Later conjecture blamed geomagnetism. A 1996 book by John Heymer,
The Entrancing Flame, maintained emotional distress could lead
to explosions of defective mitochondria. These outbursts cause
cellular releases of hydrogen and oxygen and trigger crematory
reactions in the body. That same year, Larry E. Arnold—
publicity material calls him a parascientist—published *Ablaze!
The Mysterious Fires of Spontaneous Human Combustion.*
Arnold claimed sufferers were struck by a subatomic particle he
had discovered and named the "pyrotron."

Perhaps somewhat more credible reasoning came out of
Brooklyn, New York, where the eponymous founder of Robin
Beach Engineers Associated (described as a scientific detective
agency) linked the theory of spontaneous human combustion
with proven instances of individuals whose biology caused
them to retain intense concentrations of static electricity.

A Controversy Is Sparked

Skeptics are legion. They suspect that accounts are often
embellished or that important facts are ignored. That the
unfortunate Helen Conway was overweight and a heavy
smoker, for instance, likely played a key role in her demise.

Indeed, Conway's case is considered by some to be evidence
of the wick effect, which might be today's most forensically
respected explanation for spontaneous human combustion.

It holds that an external source, such as a dropped cigarette, ignites bedding, clothing, or furnishings. This material acts like an absorbing wick, while the body's fat takes on the fueling role of candle wax. The burning fat liquefies, saturating the bedding, clothing, or furnishings, and keeps the heat localized.

The result is a long, slow immolation that burns away fatty tissues, organs, and associated bone, leaving leaner areas, such as legs, untouched. Experiments on pig carcasses show it can take five or more hours, with the body's water boiling off ahead of the spreading fire.

Under the wick theory, victims are likely to already be unconscious when the fire starts. They're in closed spaces with little moving air, so the flames are allowed to smolder, doing their work without disrupting the surroundings or alerting passersby.

Nevertheless, even the wick-effect theory, like all other explanations of spontaneous human combustion, has scientific weaknesses. The fact remains, according to the mainstream science community, that evidence of spontaneous human combustion is entirely circumstantial and that not a single proven eyewitness account exists to substantiate anyone's claims of "Poof—the body just went up in flames!"

∗ The square most commonly landed on in the game of Monopoly is Illinois Avenue. (The Go space ranks second.)

∗ The Oklahoma State Penitentiary in McAlester hosts the world's only "behind-the-walls" prison rodeo each year. Convicts compete in events such as bull riding and steer wrestling.

∗ The original title of the Buddy Holly hit song "Peggy Sue" was "Cindy Lou."

∗ The city of Nome, Alaska, was inadvertently named when a British mapmaker—with really poor handwriting, apparently—circled the port and wrote "Name?" next to it.

∗ The first stolen car was reported in St. Louis, Missouri, in 1905.

When Stiffs Get Stiffed

A cadaver that is given to science is put to good use. But not all bodies are created equal—and not all make it through the rigorous donation process.

✳ ✳ ✳ ✳

Dissection 101

AFTER YOUR BODY is donated to science, you can be sure that it won't be taken out for wild, *Weekend at Bernie's*-style partying or propped up in a passenger seat just so that the driver can use the carpool lanes. Typically, donating your body to science means willing it to a medical school, where it will be dissected to teach medical students about anatomy.

Fresh cadavers aren't as critical to medical schools as they once were, thanks to detailed models, computer simulations, and our advanced ability to preserve corpses. But they're still an appreciated learning aid. If you have a rare deformity or disease, your corpse will be especially useful.

Whose Bodies Get In?

Medical schools aren't allowed to buy bodies, rob graves, or go door-to-door recruiting volunteers, so they rely on potential donors to initiate contact. If you want to donate your body, you'll need to find a medical school in your area that has a body donation program. Your state's anatomical board is typically a good place to start. Once you've found a program, you fill out some legal paperwork and perhaps get a body-donor identification card to carry in your wallet. Some schools will cover the cost of transporting your corpse to the school (within a certain distance), as well as cremation costs after they're done with you; others won't pay for transportation.

This is very different from organ donation, which you can arrange in many states by adding a note to your driver's license and sharing your wishes with your family. If you're an organ donor and die under the right circumstances (you're brain-dead but on a respirator), doctors may extract your heart, corneas, kidneys, lungs, liver, pancreas, and/or small intestine and whisk the pieces to recipients. But if you aren't on a respirator when you die, these internal organs won't be usable.

If you've already donated your organs, most medical schools won't accept what's left of your body. You're also out of luck if you died from a major trauma, had a contagious disease, or underwent major surgery within 30 days of your passing. And if you were obese or emaciated or your body has deteriorated? Again, you're out of luck.

Even when you're dead, it seems, getting into medical school is difficult.

Say What?

The best you can get is an even break.

—FRANKLIN P. ADAMS

I saw the angel in the marble and carved until I set him free.

—MICHELANGELO

The first time I see a jogger smiling, I'll consider it.

—JOAN RIVERS

He who joyfully marches to music in rank and file has already earned my contempt. He has been given a large brain by mistake, since for him the spinal cord would suffice.

—ALBERT EINSTEIN

When someone does something good, applaud! You will make two people happy.

—SAMUEL GOLDWYN

Diaper Dollars

How many diapers does a baby go through before becoming potty-trained? Budget-conscious parents-to-be won't like the answer.

✳ ✳ ✳ ✳

THE AVERAGE NEWBORN runs through (no pun intended) about 12 to 16 diapers per day, according to Diapering Decisions, a supplier of cloth diapers. If we define a newborn as being two weeks old or younger, a baby goes through 168 to 224 diapers in just the first 14 days of life.

Luckily, the pace slows a bit after that. Between three and six months of age, you'll change a baby 10 to 12 times a day; between six and nine months, ten times a day; from nine months to the end of the first year, eight times a day; and from 13 to 18 months, count on six to eight changes a day.

When will it end? That depends on your kid. It might be as early as two years; it might take as long as four. WebMD.com says that the average for boys is 38 months; for girls, who seem to do just about everything earlier than boys do, the average is 36 months.

In other words, you'll change little Georgie between 8,008 and 10,150 times before he's ready to tackle the potty. Little Susan will soil about 400 fewer diapers; you'll change her between 7,672 and 9,702 times.

If you start the potty-training process early and remain diligent, Georgie and Susan will beat those averages. Good thing, too. With disposable diapers averaging 20 cents apiece, your baby's bottom can drain you of $1.40 per day. So the sooner the little bugger does his or her business on the toilet, the better for your wallet.

The Body Farm

When will an employee not be reprimanded for laying down on the job? When that worker is a "Body Farm" recruit. Hundreds of rotting corpses get away with such shenanigans every day at the University of Tennessee's Body Farm, and they have yet to be written up for it. In fact, they are praised for their profound contributions to science.

✳ ✳ ✳ ✳

A Eureka Moment

FORENSIC ANTHROPOLOGIST William M. Bass had a dream. As an expert in the field of human decomposition, he couldn't fathom why a facility devoted to this under-studied process didn't exist. So, in 1972, working in conjunction with the University of Tennessee, he founded the University of Tennessee Forensic Anthropology Facility—otherwise known as the Body Farm.

Body Snatchers

If you're going to start a body farm, it doesn't take a forensic anthropologist to realize that there might be a problem in obtaining bodies. One way is to use bodies that have been donated for medical studies. Another focuses on cadavers that rot away each year at medical-examiners' offices, with nary a soul to claim them. Enter Bass and his associates. Like "pods" from *Invasion of the Body Snatchers*, these scientists grab every body they can lay their hands on.

A Creepy Joint

Just outside of Knoxville, the eerie three-acre wooded plot that Bass claimed for his scientific studies—which is surrounded by a razor wire fence (lest the dead bodies try to escape)—is where an unspecified number of cadavers in various states of decomposition are kept. While some hang out completely in the open, others spend their time in shallow graves or entombed in vaults. Others dip their toes and other body parts in ponds. And a few spend their days inside sealed car trunks.

Dying for the Cause

So why is this done? What can be learned from observing human flesh and bone decay in the hot Tennessee sun? Plenty, according to scientists and members of the media who have studied the Body Farm. "Nearly everything known about the science of human decomposition comes from one place—forensic anthropologist William Bass' Body Farm," declared CNN in high praise of the facility. The bodies are strewn in different positions and under varying circumstances for reasons far from happenstance. Each cadaver will display differing reactions to decomposition, insect and wildlife interference, and the elements. These invaluable indicators can help investigators zero-in on the cause and time of death in current and future criminal cases.

Stiff Legacy

Bass himself claims that knowledge gleaned from Body Farm studies has proven especially helpful to murder investigations. "People will have alibis for certain time periods, and if you can determine death happened at another time, it makes a difference in the court case," said Bass. Even the prestigious FBI uses the Body Farm as a real-world simulator to help train its agents. Every February, representatives visit the site to dig for bodies that farm hands have prepared as simulated crime scenes. "We have five of them down there for them," explains Bass. "They excavate the burials and look for evidence that we put there."

Such is life down on the Body Farm.

As Seen on TV

Keen on disproving a key point made in an episode of *CSI*, a 55-year-old South Dakota man was killed in 2007 after shooting himself in the stomach. The man was trying to prove that a woman featured in the episode could indeed shoot herself in the stomach, despite a script that showed otherwise. Sadly, he was absolutely correct.

Edging Closer to Immortality

No, scientists haven't yet unlocked the secret to eternal life, but they do say that we'll soon be living significantly longer than we are now.

* * * *

SOME SCIENTISTS BELIEVE that within 50 years, people in industrialized nations will routinely live 100 years or longer. When that time comes, you can bet that a few healthy, energetic individuals will be pushing 140, 145, 150, and beyond.

The average American these days is expected to live 78 years, and the average life expectancy worldwide has been increasing by about two years every decade since the 1840s. Back then, Sweden boasted the population with the most impressive longevity: Healthy folks lived to the ripe old age of 45.

The increasing life expectancy is attributed to a number of factors, such as vaccinations, antibiotics, improved sanitation, and stricter food regulations. Furthermore, improved safety regulations in the workplace and on the road have helped to prevent fatal injuries.

Experts such as James Vaupel, director of the laboratory of survival and longevity at the Max Planck Institute in Germany, believe that life expectancy will continue to climb as techniques improve for preventing, diagnosing, and treating age-related maladies such as heart disease and cancer.

Centennial birthday parties should be commonplace by early in the 22nd century. That's not such a long way off: Those centigenarians are being born now. The new baby that your sister-in-law just brought home may come close to reaching 140.

Without a crystal ball to forecast the medical advances we may achieve, it's impossible to say how long people eventually will be living. But as Daniel Perry, executive director of the Alliance for Aging Research, said, "There is no obvious barrier to living well beyond 100."

Don't Try This at Home: Body Modification Artists

Ever wish you looked different? Maybe you'd like to be a little taller or have a smaller nose. The following people wanted more than that. Read on to learn about a few of the more devoted individuals in the world of body modification.

✳   ✳   ✳   ✳

Dennis Avner, aka Stalking Cat

ONE OF THE more publicly known body modification artists these days, Stalking Cat has undergone numerous surgeries to transform himself into a tiger. Believing that resembling his totem animal is the destiny set forth by his Native American heritage, Avner began his lifelong project at age 23 with full-body cat-stripe tattoos. Since then, he's had his hairline altered and silicone injections added to his lips; he's gotten facial implants in order to thread whiskers through his cheeks, as well as implants to alter the shape of his brow and forehead; he's had his upper lip split and his ears surgically pointed; and his teeth are filed and capped to be pointy and fanglike. Stalking Cat is a computer programmer; however, he also makes appearances on television shows to show off his odd obsession.

Paul Lawrence, aka The Enigma

As a youth, Paul Lawrence studied piano, flute, and dance. But as a teenager, he decided swallowing swords was more fun, and thus began his career in the sideshow industry as The Enigma. Lawrence's entire body is covered with tattoos of interlocking puzzle pieces of a greenish-blue hue. He has had nubby horns implanted in his forehead and sports a long goatee. Some of his sideshow work includes music, some of it involves sword swallowing, but all of it is quite puzzling.

Isobel Varley, aka The Painted Lady

Proving you don't have to be young to be wild, in 2000, Isobel Varley was noted by *Guinness World Records* as being "The World's Most Tattooed Senior Woman." Varley didn't start getting inked until she was 49 years old, making her a media darling in the world of tattoo artists and aficionados. Varley makes special appearances at conventions, often appears in newspapers and magazines, and has been featured on television shows all over the world.

Eric Sprague, aka Lizardman

It's hard to say which aspect of Lizardman is most alarming: his split tongue; his green, scaly, tattooed face; or his bumpy brow and tattooed eyelids. Or maybe it's how well he articulates the reasons why he's done all this in the first place. Sprague began his transformation into Lizardman during college, after becoming interested in body-based performance art. He chose the lizard because he thought it would look good and age well. Lizardman (who has undergone more than 700 hours of tattooing) performs sideshow acts that involve suspension, drilling, sword-swallowing, and fire manipulation.

Your Name Here

If you have a really strong stomach, a lot of money, and a rather dark sense of humor, you too could join the body-modification subculture. People who aren't yet household names like the artists listed above are busy doing incredibly strange things to their bodies every day, such as ear-pointing and stretching, castration, tooth extraction, even amputations. Some claim it's a spiritual thing, some do it for sexual reasons, and some of them do it for reasons they'll never share. Whatever the case, extreme body modification is incredibly dangerous unless you have a qualified, trained professional helping out with sterile equipment and the proper tools. Don't try it at home—or anywhere—unless you're ready to make serious body alterations you can't reverse.

A Bigger Brain Doesn't Translate into a Smarter Person

*If you have an oversize noggin—and display it like a trophy—
we really hate to rain on your parade: You are not smarter
than the rest of us. Scientific studies continue to show that
size isn't everything where the human brain is concerned.*

✳ ✳ ✳ ✳

History Lessons

SURE, IT MIGHT be easy to assume that a colossal cranium is capable of holding more intelligence—just by sheer mass. History suggests otherwise. William H. Calvin, a theoretical neurophysiologist and affiliate professor emeritus at the University of Washington School of Medicine, points to notable periods in the historical timeline when the brain mass of ancient humans greatly increased, but toolmaking smarts did not.

Although *Homo sapiens* in Africa 200,000 years ago had developed a brain size comparable to that of contemporary people, they continued to use the same crude, round-edged rocks for some 150,000 years before graduating to points, needles, harpoons, and hooks. You can't exactly say those bigger-brained primates were the sharpest tools in the shed.

Modern Science Weighs In

As for modern people, advancements in magnetic-resonance-imaging (MRI)-based brain scans are giving researchers more pertinent data about the relationship between brain size and intelligence. (Before MRI, researchers had to measure the outside of a person's head to estimate brain size or wait until that person died to get an accurate measurement.) A 2004 study conducted by researchers at the University of California-Irvine and the University of New Mexico was one of the first to use MRI technology to demonstrate that it's not overall brain size that counts—it's brain organization.

How so? The researchers used MRI to get structural scans of the study participants' brains and then compared those scans to respective scores on standard IQ tests. What they discovered was that human intelligence is less about total girth and more about the volume and specific location of gray-matter tissue across the brain. It appears there are several "smart" areas of the brain related to IQ, and having more gray matter in those locations is one of the things that makes us, well, smarter.

Undoubtedly, the relationship between brain size and intelligence will continue to be studied and debated, but some in the medical field now believe that brain size is purely a function of genetics and doesn't result in a greater intellect. Researchers at Harvard Medical School have even been able to identify two of the genes (beta-catenin and ASPM) that regulate brain size.

So if you've got a big head, don't be so quick to get a big head. It turns out that Albert Einstein's brain weighed only 2.7 pounds. That's 10 percent smaller than average.

---

* The Library of Congress in Washington, D.C., is the largest library in the world, containing 28 million books and 532 miles of shelving.

* Oklahoma's nickname as the "Sooner State" refers to the first day that homesteading was allowed. On April 22, 1889, more than 50,000 people showed up to stake their claim, but some folks jumped the fence before the noon starting gun. They were called "sooners."

* The colors of the Campbell's soup label—carnelian (dark red) and white—were chosen from the colors of the Cornell University football team.

* Nike shoes got their distinct waffle-sole design in 1971, after track coach Bill Bowerman's wife served him breakfast. Inspired by the design, he put rubber in his wife's waffle maker and created what would become Nike's custom sole.

Getting a Charge Out of Life

It may seem odd to compare the human body to an electric power generator, but rare cases around the world have shown that some people are born with shocking abilities... literally. Jacqueline Priestman, a British woman, consistently produces ten times the static electricity of a normal human being.

❋ ❋ ❋ ❋

How to "Conduct" Oneself

PRIESTMAN, WHO IRONICALLY married an electrician before she knew about her strange ability, grew up with no more than the usual mild electromagnetic field that surrounds every human. But when she turned 22, sparks began to fly. Priestman noticed that her mere touch would cause ordinary household appliances to short out and fizzle, while others could use the same appliances with no problem. She could also change the channels on her TV by going near it.

Priestman has had to buy at least 30 new vacuum cleaners in her married life, plus five irons and several washing machines. Michael Shallis, a lecturer at Oxford University and a former astrophysicist, studied Priestman and told a British newspaper in 1985 that she was actually able to transmit tiny bolts of "lightning" that could affect any electrical system nearby. He had no explanation for the phenomenon but did say that most similar cases he had investigated involved women. For example, Pauline Shaw flooded her house every time she tried to do laundry because the washing machine fuses would blow when she touched the dials. The washer's door would then pop open and turn the machine into a fountain.

For more than four years, Shallis studied 600 people with Priestman's condition and, eventually, wrote a book about them called *The Electric Connection.*

SLI-ding Through Life

There is a name for those like Priestman and Shaw. Because people with abnormal amounts of static electricity often cause streetlights to flicker when they pass by, scientists call the strange disorder Street Light Interference, or SLI. People with the condition are called SLI-ders, or Sliders.

An older name for the phenomenon is High Voltage Syndrome, or HVS. Around 1930, one HVS patient, Count John Berenyi of Hungary, was reportedly able to make neon light tubes glow merely by holding them. And according to author Vincent Gaddis, the National Safety Council investigates what he calls "human spark plugs"—people who can start fires with the electrical abundance of their mere presence. One woman made a rather poor vocational choice in the early 1940s when she got a job gluing shoes together with rubber cement, a highly flammable substance. She allegedly started at least five fires in the factory and could ignite a pail of rubber cement merely by standing near it. She had to quit after suffering severe burns in one of the fires.

Even babies can act as superconductors. In 1869, a child born in France was so highly charged that anyone who approached him received a sharp electric shock. He even exhibited a faint glow around his hands. The infant died from undetermined causes when he was only nine months old, and, according to witnesses, his entire body radiated light at the time of his passing.

Radiant Blood

The strange baby was not the only human known to glow. Luminous people have been reported in many circumstances, and their abilities are often tied to medical conditions. Anna Monaro, an Italian woman, gained attention in 1934, when her breasts began to spontaneously emit blue phosphorescent light while she was sleeping. The weird condition lasted for weeks and drew many eminent doctors and scientists to study her firsthand. They were even able to capture the glow on film. Many theories were offered, from "electrical and magnetic organisms in the woman's body" to "radiant blood." Eventually, the bizarre condition went away and did not return.

Through No Fault of Her Own

Mary Jones, a Welsh woman and local preacher, set off a religious fervor in 1905 when glowing, exploding balls of lightning and electric-blue rectangles were seen hovering near her as she spoke. The light show appeared to emit from her body and lasted for several months and attracted hundreds of believers, along with a cadre of scientific observers. Various explanations were offered for the lights, from a misidentification of the planet Venus to fault lines under the chapel where Jones preached. Scientists speculated that movements of the earth had stressed the bedrock, issuing gases that resulted in geomagnetic anomalies in the air above.

Lightning Reactions

Not everyone with an electric attraction finds the sensation enjoyable. Grace Charlesworth, a woman from the United Kingdom, had lived in a house for almost 40 years when, in 1968, she began receiving unexplainable shocks both indoors and out. The weird voltage was strong enough to spin Charlesworth's body in a complete circle, and at times, it would even make her head shake uncontrollably. The voltage was sometimes visible as sparks, and she could escape only by leaving her house or yard, as she was never bothered elsewhere.

Charlesworth blamed her problem on the noise from a compressor in a nearby factory, but fixing the compressor did not stop the mysterious electricity. One possible contributing factor was that the house had been hit by lightning five times.

Some people become so sensitive to electrical currents that they cannot even live in homes with any sort of wiring or appliances. An Irish woman named Margaret Cousins had to move to a cabin with no utilities in 1996 because her condition had become so painful. But two years later she had to move again after two cell phone towers were installed nearby and caused her pain to return.

Here a Yawn, There a Yawn, Everywhere a Yawn

"Contagious yawning," as it is commonly known, is one of the strangest quirks of the human body. Stranger still are some of the theories about why a simple yawn can spread from person to person like wildfire.

✳ ✳ ✳ ✳

Why Do People Yawn, Anyway?

YOU MAY THINK we yawn because we're tired or bored or because oxygen levels in our lungs are low (that's the traditional medical explanation, after all). But did you know that babies yawn in utero? (They pick up the habit as early as 11 weeks after conception.) Fetuses don't take in oxygen through their lungs, and there's no way they are tired or bored—they sleep all day, and they certainly haven't viewed enough television to have problems with attention span.

Olympic athletes have been known to yawn right before competing in events. Yawning also has been connected to certain conditions, including multiple sclerosis and penile erection. Yes, it's all pretty weird.

And Why Do You Yawn When You See Me Yawn?

Scientists don't fully understand why we yawn. Does involuntarily opening one's mouth wide serve any useful or healthful purpose? It's something of a mystery. We do know, however, that 55 percent of people will yawn within five minutes of seeing someone else do it. It's a phenomenon called "contagious yawning." Sometimes just hearing, thinking, or reading about a yawn is enough to make you unconsciously follow suit. (Did it work?) Again, scientists don't know exactly why, though they have paid it enough mind to conjure a few theories.

Some researchers hypothesize that contagious yawning is more common among the empathetic crowd. In other words, those

of us who demonstrate a greater ability to understand and share other people's feelings are more likely to emulate their yawns. Makes sense.

Taking that theory one step further, Dr. Gordon Gallup and researchers at the University of Albany say that empathetic, or contagious, yawning evolved as a way to "maintain group vigilance." Gallup thinks yawning keeps our brains working at cool, efficient, and alert levels. So in the days of early man, contagious yawning helped raise the attentiveness and danger-detecting abilities of the whole group.

Even today, members of paratrooper regiments and airborne units report yawning together right before a jump. Could contagious yawning really be leftover hardwiring from the days of yore? Quite possibly. Other theories contend that contagious yawning may have been a more explicit form of early communication. The "herding theory" suggests humans might have used contagious yawning to coordinate their behavior. One member of the group would yawn to signal an event, as if to say, "Hey, let's go hunt for a sabertooth tiger." And the other members in the group would yawn back to reply, "Yeah, let's go."

Humans aren't the only creatures that yawn. Foxes, sea lions, hippos, dogs, and cats are among the animals that do it. Recent studies have even demonstrated that some animals, like dogs and chimpanzees, may suffer from contagious yawning.

✳ Male lions are able to mate 50 or more times in a single day. Tell your husband.

✳ A baby hippo weighs around 100 pounds.

✳ The first step on the moon by astronaut Neil Armstrong was with his left foot.

Tattoo You

When it comes to putting ink on your body, just about any spot is fair game. There are a couple places, however, where a tattoo artist can't venture.

✳ ✳ ✳ ✳

The Tattoo Culture

FASHION STYLES COME and go. Yet despite the ephemeral nature of fashion and style, every day hundreds of people—many, ironically, seeking a hip way to signal their individuality—file into tattoo shops to get the same Chinese characters permanently tattooed onto their upper arms.

Tattooing has been an important part of human culture for thousands of years. Evidence of tattoos has been found on skeletons dating back nearly ten millennia. And in many cultures, particularly those in the South Pacific, tattoos have played a major role in social and spiritual rituals.

In the United States, tattooing has traditionally been associated with rough-around-the-edges types—soldiers, sailors, rebels, and criminals—and for much of the 20th century, it was relegated to parlors located on the wrong side of the tracks. It is only in the past decade or so that tattoos have found acceptance in the mainstream (though some might argue that the original purpose for getting a tattoo has been lost in the popularization), leading to a mania that has made tattooing not only acceptable but almost *de rigueur*.

Pushing the Limits

In the face of this tattoo homogeneity, more and more people are seeking unusual places for body art. Recently, we have seen tongue tattoos, corneal tattoos, and even dental crowns adorned with inked designs.

There is, however, a limit to the human canvas. Because of the ephemeral nature of the hair, fingernails, and toenails, there is no way to apply a permanent tattoo to those body parts. Similarly, because of the enamel coating on the teeth, tattoos won't work there either. However, pretty much everywhere else is there for the inking, provided the tattoo artist will agree to do it and it's not prohibited by state laws. (Some states have laws against tattoos on the face, for example.)

Are tattoos here to stay as a staple of mainstream fashion? Perhaps, like pierced ears, they are. But a passing knowledge of fashion history would indicate that it's far more likely they are not. It's a testament to the changing times that in the past few years, the rise in tattooing has been matched by an increase in dermatological surgeries to have tattoos removed.

Unfortunately for all those college kids who are rushing to the local tattoo parlor, cleaning out the metaphorical closet is a very painful and expensive procedure indeed.

* The word "salary" comes from the word "salt," which ancient Roman soldiers received as part of their pay.

* The bikini swimsuit, which debuted in July 1946, was named after the American detonation of an atomic bomb at Bikini Atoll in the South Pacific on July 1. The bikini's designer, Louis Réard, hoped his swimsuit would make a similar explosion in the fashion world.

* Celery was once considered a trendy, high-fashion food. It was served in its own vase, which was placed in the middle of the table as a centerpiece.

* New York bookseller Harry Scherman started the first book-of-the-month club in 1926 to target people who lived in remote areas or were just too busy to keep up with new releases. The first selection was *Lolly Willowes, or the Loving Huntsman,* by Sylvia Townsend Warner, which was sent to 5,000 readers.

Old Age's Unwanted Growth Spurt

The older we get, the prettier we ain't. In addition to the sagging and the wrinkles, an ignominious side effect of aging is the dense thickets of hair that erupt from the ears, nose, and just about anywhere else you don't want them.

✳ ✳ ✳ ✳

WHILE YOU HAVE no choice but to accept the grim destiny of old age, you can at least know what cruel twist of anatomical fate produces the hair-growth-in-the-wrong-places phenomenon. Whether you are a man or woman, the culprit appears to be female hormones. And take notice of the word "appears." You should know up front that afflictions such as cancer and diabetes, not excessive nose hair, are what tend to get most of the medical attention and research funding. Consequently, the explanation that follows is mostly conjecture.

Both men and women produce female hormones such as estrogen. These hormones restrict the growth of body hair and counteract male-type hormones such as testosterone (also present in both men and women), which trigger the growth of body hair. When you're younger, the male and female hormones maintain the balance they should. As you get older, production of the female hormones slows down. In other words, the male-female hormonal balance gets out of whack, and you begin to look like a Yeti.

But it isn't all doom and gloom for old-timers: They get cheap movie tickets and can force people to sit through their long, rambling stories.

The First Plastic Surgeons

You might think that plastic surgery is a relatively new phenomenon, but the truth is that it's thousands of years old. No, cavewomen weren't getting tummy tucks, but the desire to improve one's looks seems to be about as old as the human race.

✳ ✳ ✳ ✳

Those Vain Egyptians

PHYSICAL APPEARANCE WAS obviously important to the ancient Egyptians—theirs was one of the first civilizations to use makeup. And if an Egyptian suffered an injury that no amount of makeup could conceal, reconstructive surgery was an option, provided that the person had a high enough social ranking. Papyrus records dating to 1600 B.C. detail procedures for treating a broken nose by packing the nasal cavity with foreign material and allowing it to heal—these were, in essence, primitive nose jobs. About 1,000 years later in India, a surgeon named Sushruta developed a relatively sophisticated form of rhinoplasty that eventually spread across the Arab world and into Europe.

During the 15th century, Sicilian doctors pioneered a method of suturing and closing wounds that left minimal scarring and disfigurement, and by the 16th century, early methods of skin grafting were being created. It wasn't until the 19th century, however, that this burgeoning medical field got its common name: "plastic surgery." For that, we can thank German surgeon Karl von Gräfe, a pioneer of reconstructive surgery.

A Jewel Eye, Anyone?

The types of procedures that we've described thus far were typically reserved for people who had suffered horrific damage to the face or body. Who, then, were the brave pioneers who gave plastic surgery a purely cosmetic bent? Well, the first silicone breast implants were developed in the 1960s by plastic surgeons Frank Gerow and Thomas Cronin; the first person to receive breast implants (not for medical reasons, such as after undergoing a mastectomy, but strictly to improve her appearance) was Timmie Jean Lindsey.

The industry seems to get a facelift every few years as new surgeries are developed. And some of them get pretty crazy. For example, the JewelEye—a procedure in which tiny platinum jewels are implanted into the eyes to create a glint—might soon be coming to an operating room near you. Makes the old Egyptian practice of stuffing junk into someone's nasal cavity seem pretty quaint, huh?

✳ Napoleon wore black silk handkerchiefs regularly as part of his wardrobe and steadily won battle after battle. But in 1815, he decided to vary his attire and donned a white handkerchief before heading into battle at Waterloo, France. He was defeated, and it led to the end of his rule as emperor.

✳ The shoe has historically been a symbol of fertility. In some Eskimo cultures, for example, women who can't have children wear shoes around their necks in the hope of changing their childbearing luck.

✳ In the Middle Ages, pointy-toed shoes were all the rage. The fad was so popular that King Edward III of England outlawed points that extended longer than two inches. The public didn't listen, and eventually the points were 18 inches long or more!

✳ Catherine de Medici popularized high-heel shoes for women when she wore them for her 1533 wedding to Henri II of France, who later became king. However, several sources say that men had been wearing heeled shoes long before that to keep their feet from slipping off stirrups while horseback riding. A century later, when King Louis XIV of France wore high heels to boost his short stature, the trend became popular with the nobility.

✳ When Joan of Arc was burned at the stake, she was condemned for two crimes: witchcraft and wearing men's clothing.

So You Want to Swallow Swords

With time, patience, and a tolerance for physical discomfort, you too can learn how to swallow a sword. But should you, just because you can? Here's a look at what goes into the art of sword swallowing.

✳ ✳ ✳ ✳

Gag Me with a Sword

BILLED AS THE most dangerous form of performance art, sword swallowing relies on mental and physical concentration. The act requires controlling more than 50 pairs of muscles. In fact, "sword sucking" is a more accurate description. Performers swallow a wide variety of potentially lethal objects, including neon tubes, umbrellas, and pool cues, but most stick to steel blades. The "industry standards" stipulate that swords must be nonretractable and noncollapsible, 15 to 24 inches long, and 1/2 to 1 inch wide.

First, the performer suppresses his or her gag reflex, relaxing the throat to allow the blade into the esophagus. It then passes the heart, lungs, and other organs, moving through the lower esophageal sphincter to the bottom of the stomach—a distance of about 16 inches from teeth to stomach. After a few seconds, the performer carefully slides the sword out.

Professional Hazards

In 2006, roughly 110 people worldwide could swallow a sword. These days, only a few dozen continue to perform the maneuver. The act itself is always physically unpleasant and dangerous. There are about four to eight serious injuries reported every year. Even when all goes well, nasty side effects include throat pain, sinus infections, esophageal or pharynx perforations, and a persistent metallic taste in the mouth.

If you still want to try sword swallowing, find a mentor; don't try to learn from books or online. It can take months to get control of your gag reflex; learning to swallow swords could take a decade. And don't forget: Each performance could be the last.

The Shocking Truth about Bad Hair Days

Researchers have actually studied the effects that ill-shaped locks can have on a person, and the results aren't pretty.

✳   ✳   ✳   ✳

A Horrific Way to Start the Day

S KY-HIGH FRIZZ, LITTLE sprigs of cowlick, the combover that won't comb over—no magic comb, curling iron, or straightening serum can fix this tress mess. It's only 8:00 A.M., but when your coif doesn't cooperate, a promising new day seems doomed. Oh, look: The cat just peed on your briefcase. What else can go wrong?

A whole lot, according to a Yale University "bad hair day" study. It seems that the effects of an unmanageable mane extend beyond what's in the mirror. The Yale research, headed by Dr. Marianne LaFrance in 2000, found a direct relationship between a bad hair day and psychological well-being.

"Interestingly, both women and men are negatively affected by the phenomenon of bad hair days," reported LaFrance. "Even more fascinating is our finding that individuals perceive their capabilities to be significantly lower than others when experiencing bad hair."

That's right—the study, commissioned by Procter & Gamble's Physique hair-care line, found that bad hair lowers performance self-esteem, increases social insecurity, and intensifies self-criticism. It turns out that a bad hair day can spiral into a self-loathing, self-destructive, mangy mess of a pity party. No wonder you missed the train, spilled coffee on your boss, and dropped your keys through a drainage grate.

What to Do When Good Hair Goes Bad

The positive news is, there's more than one way to lock down wayward locks. For starters, get the very best haircut you can afford. "It's the cut that determines how easy your hair will be to style," counsels Beverly Hills hairdresser Nick Chavez. "And a good one can go a long way in helping you avoid a bad hair day."

Next, use a shampoo and a conditioner that are designed to deal with your hair type. Got haystack hair? Go with a moisturizing formula. Your scalp is an oil slick? Get rid of the grease with an oil-controlling concoction. And there's a simple fix for staticky, flyaway, just-been-electrocuted hair: Rub it down with a dryer sheet. It'll keep hair from sticking together and make styling a lot easier.

But do you know what's even simpler? A fashionable hat.

---

* The king of diamonds in a standard card deck is designed after Julius Caesar. The king of spades is for King David; clubs for Alexander the Great; and hearts for Charlemagne.

* More Americans choke on toothpicks than on any other item. Ballpoint pens are blamed for a good amount of choking as well.

* Two dozen U.S. states consider impotence legal grounds for divorce.

* It took more than 1,700 years to build the Great Wall of China.

* The world's widest road is Brazil's Monumental Axis. It could hold 160 cars side by side.

* Ever wonder why there are always so many mirrors in lobbies? Designers say it's no mistake: The mirrors are there because visitors tend to be less bothered by slow elevators while they're absorbed in their own reflections.

* There are more than 600 rooms in England's Buckingham Palace.

* The complete name of Los Angeles is technically El Pueblo de Nuestra Señora la Reina de los Ángeles de Porciúncula. Try that, Mr. Hollywood!

* At any time, 0.7 percent of the world's population is drunk.

Frozen Stiff

People can learn a lot from a cadaver, especially if said corpse has a body temperature hovering around -100ºF and has single-handedly inspired an annual festival in its honor. Don't believe us? Check out Frozen Dead Guy Days, a festival guaranteed to ruin your taste for Popsicles.

✳   ✳   ✳   ✳

Dead Man Thawing

JUST AFTER BREDO MORSTOEL passed away in 1989, his doting grandson Trygve Bauge transported his body from Norway to Nederland, Colorado, with plans of putting him on deep ice for eternity. But Trygve's luck (and visa) ran out, and he was deported in a fairly cold manner. So his mother, Aud, stepped in to keep her deceased dad on the cryogenic rocks.

Unfortunately for Aud, her dead dad wasn't the only one with ice in his veins. In 1993, when local authorities learned she was living in a home with no electricity or plumbing, they kicked her to the curb, citing violations of local ordinances. Aud decided to go public, and soon, her neighbors heard of the plight of the cryogenically frozen man slowly thawing in a backyard shed.

The case brought about an ordinance forbidding residents from keeping human body parts in their homes. But Bredo was exempted through a "grandfather" clause, and someone in town even built him a climate-controlled shed for good measure.

Lucky Stiff

In 2002, a festival was held in Bredo's honor, and it has been repeated each March since then. One highlight is the Grandpa Look-Alike Contest, wherein homely humans try to emulate Bredo. Another popular event is the Polar Plunge. Participants jump into a frigid Colorado pond to simulate the cryogenic experience. There's also a coffin race and the Blues Masquerade Ball, where you can dance until your dead . . . on your feet.

The Human Lint Trap

It's called the belly button, and its primary duty seems to consist of gathering copious amounts of fuzz.

✻ ✻ ✻ ✻

The Experts Tackle BBL

IT'S AN AFFLICTION that embarrasses most people. Some call it "dirty" and "gross"; others simply find it mysterious. When it is discussed, it's usually late at night, behind closed doors. Yes, we're referring to belly button lint (BBL). But if there's one thing we've learned in our weekly BBL support group, it's that this accumulation of fuzz is natural. Still, each evening as we shamefully dislodge another tuft of blue-gray lint, we wonder just where it comes from.

Fortunately for humanity, not one but two scientists have taken on the Herculean task of identifying the source and nature of belly button lint. In 2001, Australian researcher Dr. Karl Kruszelnicki embarked upon a massive survey of nearly 5,000 people in order to identify the risk factors for attracting BBL. What did he learn? The typical BBL sufferer is male, middle-aged, and slightly paunchy, and he has a hairy stomach and an "innie" navel. Kruszelnicki suggested that BBL is merely minute fibers that are shed by the clothes we wear every day. These fibers are channeled by abdominal hair into the belly button, where they collect until they are extracted. Dr. K opines that the reason most BBL is a blue-gray color is that blue jeans rub the most against the body.

The Steinhauser Study

Dr. Kruszelnicki's research was a landmark study in BBL, but it wasn't quite detailed enough for some people. Enter Austrian chemist Dr. Georg Steinhauser, who decided that it was necessary to spend three years of his life chemically analyzing more than 500 samples of BBL, mostly of his own making. Along the way, Steinhauser discovered that BBL isn't merely fibers from clothes, as Kruszelnicki had believed, but also includes bits of dead skin, fat (perhaps from skin oils), dried sweat, and dust.

Steinhauser went even further, establishing a list of practices to discourage the development of BBL. Shaving the abdomen seems to be the most foolproof method, though this strategy is, of course, temporary. Wearing older clothes may also help, because they have fewer loose fibers than new duds. Additionally, a belly button ring appears to be of some help in preventing BBL.

But it's another Australian man (what is it with Aussies and belly button lint?) who has taken BBL research to a whole new level. Graham Barker has been collecting his own BBL—which he calls "navel fluff"—in jars since 1984, earning himself a spot in *Guinness World Records*. Thanks to Barker's courage, it is now safe for those afflicted with BBL to come out of the closet and show their lint-filled bellies to the world.

❋ In one day, a single cow discharges enough methane to fill 400 one-liter bottles.

❋ A *flink* is a group of 12 or more cows—perhaps cattle ranchers and dairy farmers should be called flinkers.

❋ Entomologists have learned that mosquitoes have 47 teeth—quite a mouthful for a bug on a liquid diet.

❋ The Haskell Free Library and Opera House is an official heritage site in both the state of Vermont and the province of Quebec—the international border runs right through the building. The books and the opera house stage are in Canada, but seating for the opera audience is in the United States.

❋ We know of boneheads, but as for muscleheads, caterpillars have the edge: The average caterpillar has 248 muscles in its head.

Optical Confusion

Do hair and nails continue to grow after your ticker has taken its final tock? It's not just your mortician who knows for sure!

✳ ✳ ✳ ✳

THE MACABRE MYTH that hair and nails continue to grow after we depart for our heavenly voyage is a tall tale fueled by an optical illusion. Even though it may look like the hair and nails have gotten longer since the time of death, this is one case in which seeing should not lead to believing.

After we die, all blood flow ceases, and slowly but surely the body begins to dehydrate. The skin surrounding the fingernails and toenails dries out and retracts, exposing more of the nail plate. So while the nail remains the same length it was when the soul took its final flight, skin shrinkage creates the illusion that the nail is still very much alive and growing.

The same notion applies to the hair on the head. It's not that the follicles around the forehead continue to flourish after death—instead, the scalp contracts, creating the impression that the hair has grown. We are so accustomed to the idea of nails and hair getting longer by growing that we fail to recognize the true cause of the apparent increase in length—the shrinking of the skin on the head, hands, and feet as a result of water loss.

Here's a similar illusion to illustrate the idea: Picture a tree growing in a swamp. When the water level drops, the tree dramatically—almost magically—appears to soar. But the tree hasn't grown; more of its trunk has simply been exposed.

So rest easy. There's no need to hire a barber and a manicurist to ensure that departed loved ones greet St. Peter at the golden gates in fine form and fettle.

Don't Try This at Your Next Backyard Barbecue

Walking barefoot on hot coals isn't quite as perilous as it may seem, although amateurs are still advised to steer clear of the embers.

✳ ✳ ✳ ✳

The Secrets Revealed

THERE WAS A time when the feat (pun most certainly intended) of walking on hot coals was the domain of mystical yogis who dedicated their lives to pushing the physical limits of the body by using the awesome power of the mind. Then along came reality television. Now on any given night, we can tune in to some pudgy actuary from Des Moines waltzing across a bed of glowing embers for the nation's amusement, seemingly unharmed. So what's the deal? Is walking on hot coals dangerous, or even difficult?

At the risk of prompting legions of idiots to inflict third-degree burns on themselves, the answer is no. Walking on hot coals is not as impressive as it seems—but please, please, read on before you try something stupid.

The secret to walking on hot coals has nothing to do with mental might and everything to do with the physical properties of what's involved. It comes down to how fast heat can move from one object to another. Some materials, like metal, conduct heat very well—they're good at transmitting thermal energy to whatever they touch. Think of your frying pan: You heat it up, slap a juicy steak down on it, and witness an instant sizzle—the metal easily passes its heat to an object of lower temperature. On the other hand, consider the bed of hot coals that's used for fire walks. It started out as chunks of wood—and wood is a terrible conductor of heat.

But don't go for a romp over hot coals just yet. It's also important that the hot coals are not, you know, on fire. If you've seen a fire-walking demonstration on TV, you may have noticed that there were no jumping flames, just smoldering embers—the coals probably had been burning for hours and had built up a layer of ash. And ash is another poor conductor of heat—sometimes it's used as insulation for this very reason.

Run, Don't Walk

All the ash in the world can't help you unless you keep one final thing in mind. Think about it: What sort of gait do you see when a person is traversing a bed of hot coals? A stroll? An amble? A saunter? No, no, and no—it's all about making a mad dash. As a result, the amount of time that any one foot is in contact with a coal might be less than a second. And the exposure is not continuous, as each foot gets a millisecond break from the heat with each step.

So if you take a poor heat conductor like wood, cover it with a layer of insulation, and have intermittent exposure to the heat, the likelihood of sustaining serious burns is low. Of course, we don't advise that you try this stunt at your next backyard get-together. What if you fall? Or even slip or stumble? You'll have a lot of explaining to do at your local ER.

❉ Not even acid can dissolve a diamond.

❉ An ant has five different noses, each for different scents.

❉ Honeybees can lay as many as 1,500 eggs in a single day.

❉ Congratulations: You have just practiced neology. (The study of new words.)

❉ A standard pencil could draw a 35-mile-long line before it runs out of lead.

❉ Hot water is lighter in weight than cold water.

❉ Finland is considered the country with the best water quality. Canada comes in second.

❉ An average penguin can run as fast as an average man.

Go Ahead—Try to Tickle Yourself

Your brain is expecting your attempts at self-tickling, so they won't work. When someone else tickles you, however, the contact is unexpected, and the shock contributes to the effect.

✳   ✳   ✳   ✳

WHEN THE NERVES of your skin register a touch, your brain responds differently depending on whether you're responsible for it. MRI scans show that three parts of the brain—the secondary somatosensory cortex, the anterior cingulated cortex, and the cerebellum—react strongly when the touch comes from an external source. Think of it like this: When you see a scary movie for the first time, you jump when the maniac suddenly appears and kills the high school kids as punishment for having teenage sex. The second time you see the movie, it isn't a surprise, so you don't jump. The same goes for tickling: It's the element of surprise that causes the giddy laughter of the ticklish.

Why do we laugh hysterically when other people tickle us? Scientists believe that it's an instinctual defense mechanism— an exaggerated version of the tingle that goes up your spine when an insect is crawling on you. This is your body's way of saying, "You may want to make sure whatever is touching you won't kill you." The laughter is a form of panic due to sensory overload.

If you're in desperate need of tickling but have no friends or family willing to help, you can invest in a tickling robot. People do respond to self-initiated remote-control tickling by a specialized robot that was developed by British scientists in 1998. There's a short delay between the command to tickle and the actual tickle, which is enough to make the contact seem like a surprise to the brain and induce fits of laughter.

The Jolt from a Lightning Bolt

Alas, of all the firsthand accounts of lightning strikes, nobody has reported gaining any new or exciting superpowers. Mostly, it's just a totally unpleasant experience, even if you survive without any major long-term effects.

✳ ✳ ✳ ✳

If It Isn't Your Lucky Day...

THE GOOD NEWS is, the chance of being struck by lightning is only one in 5,000, according to the National Weather Service. The bad news is, if you do get struck, it's going to do very harmful things to your body.

Lightning has several ways to get to your tender flesh. It can strike you directly; it can strike an object, such as a tree or another person, then leave it to pay you a visit; it can get you while you're touching something it's striking, like a car door; or it can travel along the ground and take a detour by rising up through your feet. What happens next varies from person to person and often depends upon the intensity of the strike.

Usually, the electrical current travels only over the surface of the skin, a phenomenon called a flashover. This can burn your clothes or, in some cases, shred them off completely and blow your shoes off as well, leaving you in pain and naked. Additionally, the metal you are wearing—zippers, belt buckles, jewelry—will become extremely hot, often causing serious burns.

The most immediately dangerous consequence of a lightning strike is cardiac and/or respiratory arrest, which cause most lightning-related fatalities. A strike can also cause seizures, deafness, confusion, amnesia, blindness, dizziness, ruptured eardrums, paralysis, and coma, among other things. Depending on the severity of the strike, some symptoms—such as blindness, deafness, and even paralysis—may disappear quickly.

At Least You Won't Turn to Ash

Contrary to urban legend, lightning does not reduce people to a pile of ash with a hat on top. Additionally, many people believe that lightning-strike victims remain "charged" and are dangers to others after being hit. This is not the case, and this idea too often leads bystanders to delay assistance that could save lives.

The most prevalent long-term effects from being struck by lightning are neurological. People can have trouble with short-term memory, distractibility, learning new information and accessing old information, irritability, and multitasking. Multitasking impairment can be especially frustrating.

Many times, tasks that had been easy before the strike suddenly take much longer because the person must focus on every component individually. Damage to the frontal lobe of the brain can cause personality changes, and some victims develop sleeping disorders, cataracts, and chronic pain due to nerve injury.

---

* Tiny shrews, sometimes only a few inches long, may be the fiercest of all mammals because they eat their own weight in food over the course of the day and can kill prey twice their size—everything from insects and snakes to mice and rats. They are able to do this partly because their saliva contains a paralyzing substance similar to cobra venom.

* The emperor penguin of the Antarctic has equality of the sexes down pat—the female lays the egg, but the male has the "brood pouch," a roll of skin and feathers between his legs that drops over the egg. He then must protect the egg and keep it still for two months until it hatches and the female returns to feed the chick.

* In a Mediterranean species of the cardinal fish, the male takes part in mouthbrooding—holding the fertilized eggs in his mouth until they are ready to hatch.

* The roadrunner takes a no-holds-barred approach to killing a rattlesnake. It jabs the snake with its sharp bill, shakes it, body-slams it, then administers a final peck in the head before devouring its prey headfirst.

A Real Head-Scratcher

The practice of cutting off an enemy's head and keeping it dates to at least the Stone Age, about 600,000 years ago. Which leads to a perfectly logical question: What did headhunters do with all those heads?

✳ ✳ ✳ ✳

Sacred Heads

AS BARBARIC AS headhunting might seem, the practitioners had good reasons for doing it. Aboriginal Australians and tribes such as the Dayak in Borneo believed that the head contained the victim's spirit or soul. Taking the head, they thought, took the essence of a person's soul as well as his strength. Chinese soldiers during the Qin Dynasty (221–206 B.C.) carried the heads of conquered enemies into battle to frighten their foes. The heads also served as proof of kills, which enabled soldiers to be paid.

Headhunting wasn't always associated with war. The ancient Celts, for example, incorporated it into fertility rites and other ritualistic practices.

Now What?

One problem for headhunters was that it doesn't take long for a severed head to begin to decompose. Some headhunters kept only the skull; they cleaned and boiled the head to remove all tissue and brain matter. Others cooked and ate parts of the head, literally consuming the essence of the conquered foe. Still others painstakingly preserved the heads, some of which are still with us.

In New Zealand, Maori headhunters removed the flesh from the skulls of their enemies, then smoked and dried it. This process preserved distinctive tribal tattoos, which meant that the deceased could be identified. Some of these heads were eventually sold to Europeans for private collections or museums, and Maori are today attempting to reclaim the dried heads of their ancestors. In New Guinea, tribes mummified the entire head and sometimes wore it as a mask.

Some of the best-preserved heads come from the Jivaro (or Shuar) tribe of South America. These are shrunken heads, known as *tsantsa*. They are unique among headhunting trophies because of the way the Jivaro preserved them.

After killing and decapitating an enemy, the Jivaro cut and peeled the skin from the skull in one piece and discarded the skull. Then they turned the skin inside out and scraped it to remove the tissue. The skin was then boiled for as long as two hours to shrink it to about one-third its original size. After sewing the eyes closed and skewering the mouth shut, the Jivaro filled the skin with hot rocks, being careful not to burn it, and molded the skin as it cooled so it retained its features. Finally, they removed the rocks, filled the skin with hot sand, and finished the process with a smoking technique. The resulting small, hard, dark mass was recognizable as a human head. Today, the Jivaro sell replicas of *tsantsa* to tourists.

There is evidence that some Allied soldiers took skulls as trophies and souvenirs during World War II, and there are indications of similar practices during the Vietnam War. As recently as 2001, the Borneo Dayaks practiced headhunting during conflicts with another ethnic group, the Madurese. Reports of headhunting still surface occasionally, so if you're visiting a remote locale, you are well advised to keep your head about you.

✳ The gag rule was instituted in the Senate in 1836 so the senators would not have to accept, debate, or vote on antislavery petitions.

✳ The average lifespan of a goldfish living in the wild is 25 years.

✳ Fingernails grow faster on your dominant hand.

Phrenology: Bumps in the Night

What if we told you that the bumps on your noggin could be mapped to reveal insight into your true character?

✳ ✳ ✳ ✳

PHRENOLOGY GOT ITS start in 1796 when Austrian physician Franz Joseph Gall proposed the notion that the brain controlled mental function, a science he initially called *cranioscopy*. This idea was groundbreaking, but it was not universally well-received, especially by the religious community. Suggesting that it was the brain—and not the soul—that controlled reason was the height of hypocrisy. Consequently, Austrian Emperor Francis I asked Gall to stop lecturing about his brain research in 1802.

This didn't stop Gall. In 1805, he published *On the Activities of the Brain*, which explained that various points within the brain are responsible for different functions. He also asserted that the shape of a person's skull allows a physician to study the internal workings of the brain. Gall believed that there were some 26 "organs" on the surface of the brain that affected the contour of the skull—and even pointed out a "murder organ."

By 1808, Gall had presented his most famous theory, that these bumps reveal one's true character, a theory that gave birth to modern phrenology. Phrenology blossomed during the Victorian era, as snake-oil peddlers and con men used the idea to profit from an unsuspecting public by opening phrenology parlors and using the practice for all kinds of things, from diagnosing illness to determining suitable marriage partners or appropriate careers. In 1931, Henry C. Lavery cut out the middleman by inventing an automated phrenology machine called the *psychograph*. The device was showcased at the 1933–34 World's Fair in Chicago.

Phrenology was ultimately rejected and relegated to the role of "pseudoscience." Today scientists can chemically and electronically detail the brain—no bumps needed.

The Mummy Still Lives

The ancient Egyptians would be happy to know that 5,000 years later, mummification is still around. The processes have changed over the centuries, but if you want your corpse preserved like King Tut's was, you definitely have options.

✳   ✳   ✳   ✳

How to Make a Mummy

MUMMIFICATION SIMPLY MEANS keeping some soft tissue—such as skin or muscle—around long after death. To create a mummy, you just need to keep the tissue from being eaten. Shooing vultures and cannibals away is simple enough, but keeping hungry bacteria at bay is no small feat. The trick is to make the body inhospitable to bacteria. Bacteria like it hot and wet, so mummification depends on keeping a body extremely cold and/or dry.

The ancient Egyptians removed the corpse's internal organs, filled the cavity with linen pads, sprinkled the body with a drying compound called natron, and then wrapped it in bandages. In 1994, Egyptology professor Bob Brier successfully replicated this process—but most other modern mummy-makers use other means.

When Vladimir Lenin died in 1924, the Russians decided to mummify him. Their secret process involved immersing the corpse in a chemical bath that replaces all the water in the body. The results are impressive—Lenin today looks like Lenin on his deathbed. In 1952, the Argentineans took a similar tack with Eva Peron, the wife of dictator Juan Peron. They replaced bodily fluids with wax, making a wax dummy corpse.

Since 1967, dozens of people have opted for cryonics, a form of mummification in which doctors replace the water in the body with chemicals and keep the deceased at a crisp −320 degrees Fahrenheit—at least until scientists figure out how to cure death.

Summum Mummies

The religious organization Summum also offers mummification, but without future reanimation in mind. First, the embalmers

immerse the body in a chemical solution for 30 to 60 days to dissolve the water in the body. Next, they wrap the body in gauze and apply a layer of polyurethane, followed by a layer of fiberglass and resin. The body is then sealed in a stainless-steel or bronze mummiform capsule.

Summum has a growing list of (still-living) human clients. The organization asks for a donation to cover its services, usually $67,000 for the process—not including the mummiform.

A Near-Perfect Mummy

The most impressive modern mummies come from a process called Plastination. First, embalmers pump the corpse full of a substance that halts decay. Then, they remove the skin and certain other surface tissues and immerse the body in an acetone solution, which dissolves the water and fats. Next, they immerse the body in liquid plastic inside a vacuum chamber and drop the pressure until the acetone boils and evaporates.

The resulting vacuum in the body sucks in the plastic so that it permeates every nook and cranny. Before the liquid solidifies into hard plastic, embalmers pose the body. The result is a clean, educational sculpture, which also happens to be an actual corpse.

German anatomist Gunther von Hagens invented Plastination in 1977, and he's signed up in the neighborhood of 8,000 body donors—many of whom are now mummies in the traveling Body Worlds exhibition. It's completely free to sign up, so if you're looking to stick around after you pass on and you don't mind posing with tourists for the next few thousand years, the value is hard to beat.

Chapter Eight

Bizzarre Truths About the Wild

Who Needs Hands to Open a Jar?

You've probably heard that an octopus is capable of unscrewing the lid of a jar with its tentacles. You've probably also wondered if it's just an urban legend. Well, rest assured—it's true.

✳ ✳ ✳ ✳

Proof Positive

THE EVIDENCE IS in a video on YouTube. As Strauss's "Thus Spake Zarathustra" swells in the background, Violet the octopus unfurls a snaky tentacle and grasps a closed jar that contains a crab. Then, much like a magician draping a scarf over a top hat, she covers the jar with her body. A few minutes later, the jar reemerges . . . without the lid. Or the crab.

Violet isn't the only octopus that can perform this nifty trick.

Octi, a resident of New Zealand's National Aquarium, regularly entertains visitors with its ability to extract food from a variety of sealed jars. According to the aquarium's staff, Octi is a friendly, gentle creature that enjoys playing with toys and often reaches out to touch the hands of its keepers—at least when there are no jars around to work on.

How It's Done

An octopus relies on suction to unscrew a lid. The underside of an octopus's arms and body are covered with highly sensitive suction cups that each contain up to 10,000 neurons. These cups convey a wealth of information to the brain, allowing the octopus to vary pressure on the lid and eventually twist it off.

In the wild, an octopus can pry open the most stubborn clam. But since potential meals don't come packed in jars at the bottom of the ocean, the question naturally arises: How does an octopus learn that these strange glass cylinders in the zoo are a source of snacks? The answer: It uses its natural curiosity and plenty of smarts.

Though they may not look very bright, octopuses, also known as cephalopods, are among the intellectual giants of the deep. They have the largest brains of all invertebrates relative to body weight. Their brains are divided into lobes and resemble those of birds or mammals more closely than they do those of fish. Jennifer Mather, a psychologist at Canada's University of Lethbridge, has conducted studies that suggest that octopuses can even be right-eyed or left-eyed, much like humans, who are neurologically wired to favor the right or left hand.

Other Tricks

Mather is a pioneer in the field of octopus intelligence. She believes that octopuses have distinct personalities and are adept at some relatively complex tasks. What's more, biologist Jean Boal of Millersville University in Pennsylvania has tested their navigational skills with underwater mazes and given them high marks for geographical memory.

And they're champs at camouflage. At the Woods Hole Marine Biological Laboratory in Massachusetts, an octopus has been observed quickly changing shape and color, transforming itself into an innocent-looking rock drifting along the ocean floor.

What's the I.Q. of an average octopus? That's still a mystery, but we do know that they can help you open a stubborn pickle jar.

Cockroaches: Nuke-Proof, to a Point

We've all heard that cockroaches would be the only creatures to survive a nuclear war. But unless being exceptionally gross is a prerequisite for withstanding such an event, are cockroaches really that resilient?

✳ ✳ ✳ ✳

COCKROACHES ARE INDEED that resilient. For one thing, they've spent millions of years surviving every calamity the earth could throw at them. Fossil records indicate that the cockroach is at least 300 million years old. That means cockroaches survived unscathed whatever event wiped out the dinosaurs, be it an ice age or a giant meteor's collision with Earth.

The cockroach's chief advantage—at least where nuclear annihilation is concerned—is the amount of radiation it can safely absorb. During the Cold War, a number of researchers performed tests on how much radiation various organisms could withstand before dying. Humans, as you might imagine, tapped out fairly early. Five hundred Radiation Absorbed Doses (or rads, the accepted measurement for radiation exposure) is the lethal amount for humans. Cockroaches, on the other hand, scored exceptionally well, withstanding up to 6,400 rads.

Such hardiness doesn't mean that cockroaches will be the sole rulers of the planet if nuclear war breaks out. The parasitoid wasp can take more than 100,000 rads and still sting the heck out of you. Some forms of bacteria can shrug off more than one million rads and keep doing whatever it is that bacteria do.

Not all cockroaches would survive, anyway—definitely not the ones that lived within two miles of the blast's ground zero. Regardless of the amount of radiation a creature could withstand, the intense heat from the detonation would liquefy it. Still, the entire cockroach race wouldn't be living at or near ground zero—so, yes, at least some would likely survive.

It's Better than a Sixth Sense: A Squish Sense

With some natural aptitude and years of training in an Eastern monastery, you may acquire certain fighting skills that let you drop a grown man to his knees in an instant—but even the most agile martial arts master struggles when it's time to swat a fly.

✳ ✳ ✳ ✳

A Bug's Life

INSECTS MAY BE tiny and seem relatively powerless, but they have adaptations that give them an edge against the many larger forms of life that want to do them in. For starters, the bugs that you most want to squish—flies, cockroaches, and the like—are equipped with compound eyes. A compound eye is a collection of structures called *ommatidia*. A fly, for example, has 4,000 ommatidia in each eye; each ommatidium has its own light-sensing cells and focusing lens that's positioned for a unique field of vision.

Collectively, the elements of its compound eyes produce a panoramic view of the bug's surroundings. The resolution of the resulting image isn't so hot, but it does the trick for detecting sudden movements from almost any direction.

Even when their supercharged vision fails them, insects have other ways to escape your wrath. Many bugs can actually feel the flyswatter approaching thanks to special sensory hairs called *setae*. When you start your bug-smashing motion, you push air between you and your target. This shift in air pressure stimulates the bug's setae, which signal its brain that something is coming. The movement of the setae gives the bug an idea of where the threat is coming from, and the bug reacts by scurrying in the opposite direction.

Planning Ahead

It also helps that some bugs are thinking about their getaways before it even seems necessary. In 2008, biologists at the California Institute of Technology used high-speed cameras to observe a group of flies. They found that it takes less than a tenth of a second for a fly to identify a potential threat, plan an escape route, and position its legs for optimal takeoff. In other words, when you're sneaking up on a fly and getting ready to strike, that fly has probably already spotted you and is prepared to zip away. This little bit of extra preparation helps pave the way for a Houdini-like escape.

Will the valuable information gleaned from this research enable us to finally gain the upper hand—quite literally—in our ongoing chess match against bugs? Don't count on it.

---

* The male Australian lyrebird is such a skilled mimic that he can reproduce mechanical sounds, such as automobile horns, and is famous for his 24-inch tail feathers that assume the shape of a lyre when fanned.

* Oysters must hitchhike on fish if they want to grow up. Oyster larvae catch a ride on a passing fin and hang on for several months, feeding on their benefactor's body until they grow large enough to let go and settle into a spot of their own in the oyster bed.

* The monkeylike common potto is the only mammal that keeps part of its backbone on the outside, with a row of bare bones protruding slightly from its back. The potto has a defensive pose where it clamps down its feet and hands and lowers its head to bring forth the exposed vertebrae.

* Africa's multimammate mouse might appropriately be called the "mother of all mice," although it's more closely related to the rat. Females boast 8 to 12 pairs of teats, many more than the average 5 pairs found on most rodents. This allows the multimammate mouse to breed at a furious rate, bearing litters of up to 20 pups at a time.

Famous Feral Children

If your mother annoys you or your dad says something embarrassing in public, cut them some slack. If they didn't abandon you to wolves, keep you locked in a room, or make you live in a chicken coop, they couldn't have been that bad. You could have had it a lot worse. Check out the following stories of feral, or "wild," children, kids who were raised with either very little human contact or none at all.

✳ ✳ ✳ ✳

Amala & Kamala

R EVEREND JOSEPH SINGH, in charge of an orphanage in the northern part of India in 1920, kept hearing villagers speak of ghostly girls who ran with wolves at night. Singh camped out one evening to watch for these alleged figures and discovered the myth was reality. Two seemingly unrelated girls were found in a wolf den. Their hair was matted, their eyes were bugged out, and they walked on all fours. Singh tried to rehabilitate the girls, but being raised by wolves for the first years of their lives had an indelible effect. The girls tore off their clothes and only ate raw meat. Neither Amala nor Kamala lived very long—Amala was 3 when she died, Kamala somewhere between 14 and 17. Both learned a few words of English, and Kamala was able to walk on her own, though with an odd stride.

Oxana Malaya, the "Ukrainian Dog Girl"

Between the ages of three and eight, Ukrainian-born Oxana Malaya either was forced by her parents to live in a dog kennel in the backyard or was neglected to the point that the doghouse became a better place for her to live. It's been reported that her alcoholic parents did allow her to come into the house occasionally, but Oxana spent most of her time with the dogs, learning to growl, bark, and sniff her food before she ate it. When she was rescued in 1991, Oxana was put into a home for the mentally disabled and has since regained many human abilities, including speech. Now in her twenties, Oxana still resides in a home for the mentally challenged.

Victor, the Wild Child of Aveyron

Victor's story is important because he was one of the first well-known cases of a feral child. In 1799, an 11-year-old boy was discovered digging for acorns in Aveyron, France. Victor couldn't speak and behaved like a wild animal. A doctor took him in and made rehabilitating Victor his life's work, though teaching the boy anything was reportedly rather difficult. Unlike many other feral kids before and after him, Victor lived a relatively long life, dying at age 40.

Sidi Mohamed

In 1935, when he was about five years old, Sidi Mohamed wandered away from his family in North Africa. After three days in the wild, he came upon an ostrich nest. Flash forward about ten years, when Sidi was found by hunters and relayed his story. He had been living with the birds all that time, running with them, eating grass and plants, and sleeping with them at night (two ostriches covered him with their wings while he slept.) Sidi was able to rejoin the human race with relative success.

Ivan Mishukov, "The Russian Dog Boy"

In the late 1990s, there were approximately two million kids living on the streets in Russia due to the country's collapsed economy. Four-year-old Ivan Mishukov befriended a pack of alley dogs, and in return for the scraps he could beg off passersby, the dogs provided him with protection and shelter from the frigid temperatures that could reach -25 degrees Fahrenheit at night. Ivan reportedly lived with the dogs for two years before the police were able to separate him from his new family. He could speak, since he'd been raised by his parents for the first few years of his life before being abandoned, and he eventually went to school and adapted to a typical Russian life.

They Don't Call It an Anteater for Nothing

An anteater eats a whopping 35,000 ants per day. And if its beloved ants aren't available, it will settle for an equal number of termites.

✳ ✳ ✳ ✳

Ants Aren't Exactly Filling

IT MIGHT SOUND as if an anteater consumes a belly-busting number of insects, but keep in mind that the average ant or termite weighs only three milligrams. So despite the large number of insects it eats, the voracious anteater commonly consumes less than an ounce of food at every meal. Fortunately, the anteater's metabolism is very slow. Anteaters typically maintain a body temperature of only 90.9 degrees Fahrenheit—one of the lowest temps in the animal kingdom—which enables them to thrive on this highly specialized diet.

How do they eat? After locating a large nest of ants or termites, an anteater gouges out a hole with its powerful front claws, pokes its nose in, and starts chowing down. Its long, snaky tongue is the ideal utensil for scooping up those tiny ants. Coated with sticky black hairs, the tongue extends more than two feet from the anteater's mouth and flicks in and out at the amazing rate of 150 times a minute. Because it lacks teeth, the anteater also uses its tongue to crush the ants against the roof of its mouth before swallowing.

Why Ants?

How come ants are an anteater's favorite meal? According to zoologists, anteaters cannot produce the gastric juices that other mammals use to digest food. Ants and termites are highly acidic and decompose easily in the anteater's stomach without additional acids.

Incidentally, anteaters in zoos enjoy a more varied diet, with occasional fruits, vegetables, and honey. But their keepers must make sure they receive the right balance of acid, or the anteaters will not survive.

A full-grown giant anteater is a hefty creature, measuring about five to seven feet long from the end of its nose to the tip of its tail. Adult males can weigh upwards of 100 pounds, females a little less than that. Anteaters are native to South America. Their primary habitat is east of the Andes Mountains in northwest Argentina and parts of Uruguay.

Though they rarely threaten humans, anteaters have often been hunted for sport and are presently considered endangered by the International Union for Conservation of Nature. Yet anteaters themselves are excellent conservationists. An anteater will never clean out an entire ant nest at a single sitting. It will always leave enough ants to allow the colony to regenerate, thus ensuring a future meal.

These are pretty smart tactics for a creature with a fairly small brain. Maybe some big-brained mammals should follow the anteater's example to conserve their own natural resources.

Say What?

Nobody will ever win the Battle of the Sexes. There's just too much fraternizing with the enemy.

—Henry Kissinger

I have bad reflexes. I was once run over by a car being pushed by two guys.

—Woody Allen

Steer Clear of This Diet

It's commonly thought that "eating like a bird" is a good thing. For the most part, however, this couldn't be further from the truth.

✳ ✳ ✳ ✳

The Benefits Are Minor

I F PHILOSOPHER THOMAS HOBBES had not used the phrase "nasty, brutish, and short" to describe the life of a human being, he could have used it for the bird—specifically, for its eating habits. The bird is not a critter we want to emulate when we're at the dinner table.

In fairness, the bird does possess some worthy culinary habits. Birds tend to eat in small installments—say, hundreds of tiny seeds over the course of a day. For many birds, diet varies with the season; nonmigrating songbirds, for example, eat insects during the bountiful days of summer but resort to seeds in cold weather. Analogous habits are encouraged in humans—nutritionists say that people should eat numerous small meals a day instead of ingesting all of our nutrition in two or three large doses, which can cause wild swings in blood sugar and mood and lead to even worse eating habits. Nutritionists also note that before the era of global commerce, we tended to eat what was in season, which gave us a wider and more complete range of the nutrients we need. But that's about it for the benefits of eating like a bird.

Would You Like Some Ketchup on Your Gravel?

Now, here are some avian eating habits—perhaps we should say hazards—that no human would want to emulate:

✳ Some birds can become drunk and die from eating fermented fruit.

✳ Some birds remove ticks from deer and moose. Sometimes the birds will eat the ticks right away; in other instances, they'll stash them away for later consumption.

* Some birds drop food onto the ground to crack it open, making it easier to eat.

* Certain lake birds ingest lead sinkers left behind by anglers. The small pebbles in a bird's gut grind up the sinker, which then poisons and kills the animal.

* About the aforementioned pebbles: Many birds eat them to provide a medium for breaking up food in their bellies, so that it can be digested. Birds don't have teeth.

* Many birds can't go more than a couple of days without food. They eat right up until bedtime, and they start eating the minute they get up, because their fast metabolisms and low levels of body fat mean they don't have much of a cushion of stored energy to live off between feedings.

Human life may be nasty, brutish, and short, but we were endowed with enough evolutionary advantages to have the leisure to do things besides eat—like invent fire and the tube-powered guitar amplifier. Birds are too focused on food to indulge in any of that good stuff.

---

* In an ironic twist, Mel Blanc, best known as the voice of Bugs Bunny, had an aversion to raw carrots.

* *Guinness World Records* holds a record of its own. The hefty book is considered the most commonly stolen volume from libraries around the world. When it comes to bookstores, however, the Bible is actually considered the most commonly shoplifted book in America.

* If you order "white tea" in China, you'll end up with a cup of plain boiling water.

* About 500 pounds of Silly Putty are produced every day.

* There are more horses than people in the country of Mongolia.

* In Hebrew, dogs are quoted as saying "hav hav" instead of "bow wow."

* November 19 is considered by many to be "Have a Bad Day Day."

The Busy Lives of Beavers and Bees

They're nature's overachievers, making everyone else in the animal kingdom appear lazy by comparison. But which is busier, the beaver or the bee?

✳ ✳ ✳ ✳

The Showdown

WATCH A NATURE program focused on any other animal, and you'll see big cats sunning themselves, bears swimming in rivers, and penguins sliding around on their stomachs. Most animals know how to kick back and relax. Not so with the beaver and the bee. It's all elbow grease and nose-to-the-grindstone with these two. Surely, however, one must have an edge over the other when it comes to business. Let's take a look:

In the course of its lifetime, a single worker bee will make $1/12$th of a teaspoon of honey. This does not seem like a lot, but each bee is contributing to a hive along with tens of thousands of other bees. Their combined effort piles up fast. That same bee will leave the hive ten times in a day; will travel up to a mile and a half from the hive on any one of these trips; and will carry about 113 percent of its own body weight in pollen and nectar every time it returns to the hive. At the end of the day, a worker bee will have transported 1,130 percent of its body weight. That's a busy bee.

Beavers live in colonies of six to eight and build dams and the lodges they live in. Unlike the bee, a beaver's productivity is dependent on its environment. The size of a dam depends on the width of the river, and the size of a lodge is contingent on the number of beavers it is intended to house. At night, the beavers leave the lodge and commence work on the dam, repairing any damages incurred during the daylight hours and increasing the height of the dam if the water level appears to have risen. A single beaver can fell a six-inch-diameter aspen tree in about 20 minutes. It then gnaws the tree into logs of a more manageable size and drags these logs back to the river. A beaver can transport a log weighing about 100 percent of its own body weight, but it often uses the river to aid in the wood-gathering process by floating logs downstream toward the dam.

And the Winner Is...

While beavers live longer (up to 15 years in the wild) and have a great effect on their environment (second only to humans), the winner by a proboscis in this productivity showdown seems to be the bee. A bee's every action has a profound place in nature's big picture. It's true that beavers work smart: They have the capacity to size up a river and design a dam according to depth, width, and even the speed of the current. When they're not working on the dam or the lodge, they are gathering food to store around the lodge for the winter. But in terms of sheer productivity, based on their brief time on the earth, bees take the prize. Over the course of 45 days—the summer life-span of a garden-variety honeybee—a worker will move about 50,000 percent of its own weight in nectar and pollen.

The worker bee spends its every waking moment dedicated to its job, all so that other animals can steal the honey it produces. Fortunately, bees don't seem to mind: They're up at the crack of dawn anyway, ready to punch the clock and begin again.

---

* Australian toilets are designed to flush counterclockwise.

* Barbie has a full name that many people don't know: Barbara Millicent Roberts. Not quite as catchy.

* It's often referenced, but not everyone knows that Timbuktu is in Mali, West Africa.

* Guinea pigs are born fully developed, with their fur and teeth in place and their eyes open.

* A third of people say they flush while still sitting on the john.

A Tall Tale from the Animal Kingdom

The notion that elephants are scared of mice has been especially persistent, reaching at least as far back as the first century A.D. It seems, however, that the elephant has gotten a bad rap.

✳   ✳   ✳   ✳

The Theory of Unreasonable Fear

NO, IT DOESN'T seem logical that such an impressive beast would cower before such a diminutive one, but that's the appeal of the myth. Unreasonable fear is a human trait, and applying human traits to animals is one way we form connections with them. After all, many humans fear harmless insects and, yes, mice: The image of a shrieking housewife standing on

a kitchen chair is as ubiquitous as that of an elephant rearing back on its hind legs at the sight of a rodent.

The difference is this: Many a housewife has indeed taken refuge on many a kitchen chair, yet few elephants have been spooked by mice. In fact, upon being presented with a mouse face to face, most elephants don't react at all. If they have a fear, it's of stepping on the little creature and getting creamed mouse all over the bottom of their feet.

We May Never Know How the Rumor Started

The origins of the myth are lost to history. Pliny the Elder, an ancient Roman writer and philosopher, mentioned the elephant's fear of mice about 2,000 years ago in his *Natural History*. There may have once been an elephant that had the misfortune of letting a mouse catch it off guard, and that elephant may have overreacted in front of the wrong crowd (elephants are skittish creatures and can be easily spooked).

Once it happened, there was no taking it back—an amused crowd never forgets.

One theory is that elephants are afraid of mice because they think the rodents might crawl up their trunks. It's more likely that the elephant smells or hears something unfamiliar and reacts as though it's in danger. The idea that a mouse might climb up an elephant's trunk, and that the elephant would be afraid of this happening, is another example of humans projecting human traits on animals. We imagine how we would feel with a mouse crawling around on us, trying to find a way inside us, and shudder with the unpleasantness of the scenario.

There may or may not have been an original incident with an elephant and a mouse. No one can say for sure. But we can say this with relative certainty: Outside of cartoons, elephants are not especially afraid of mice. The thought of public speaking, on the other hand, makes them break into a cold sweat.

* The world's largest bowling alley is the 156-lane Nagoya Grand Bowl in Japan.

* Legend has it the man who invented the lightbulb, Thomas Edison, was quite scared of the dark.

* Astronaut Buzz Aldrin, the second man to walk on the moon, has a second connection to the giant circle in the sky: His mother's maiden name was, fittingly, Moon.

* Bamboo is the world's tallest grass, growing as much as 90 centimeters, or a little more than 35 inches, in a single day.

* An airplane mechanic came up with the idea for the Slinky toy while working with engine springs.

* Mr. Potato Head holds the honor of being the first toy featured in a television commercial.

* In Tennessee, it's apparently okay to shoot whales from a moving car, but in landlocked Oklahoma, hunting whales is forbidden.

The Exact Pace of a Snail

The word "slow" hardly begins to cover it. These animals make all others look like Speedy Gonzales. Next to the snail, tortoises look like hares, and hares look like bolts of furry brown lightning.

✳ ✳ ✳ ✳

ALL OF THIS snail talk brings to mind a bad joke: What did the snail say when it was riding on the tortoise's back? *Whee!* But enough of the jokes—you want to know just how fast a snail travels.

Garden snails have a top speed of about 0.03 mile per hour, according to *The World Almanac and Book of Facts*. However, snails observed in a championship race in London took the 13-inch course at a much slower rate—presumably because snails lack ambition when it comes to competition. To really get a snail moving, one would have to make the snail think its life was in jeopardy. Maybe the racing snails' owners should be hovering behind the starting line wearing feathered wings and pointed beaks, cawing instead of cheering.

The current record holder of the London race, the Guinness Gastropod Championship, is a snail named Archie, who made the trek in two minutes and 20 seconds in 1995. This comes out to 0.0053 mile per hour. At that rate, a snail might cover a yard in 6.4 minutes. If he kept going, he might make a mile in a little less than eight days.

In the time it takes you to watch a movie, your pet snail might travel about 56 feet. You could watch a complete trilogy, and your snail might not even make it out of the house. Put your pet snail on the ground and forget about him, and there's a good chance he'll be right around where you left him when you return—as long as no one steps on him, that is.

The Weirdest Creature in the Sea

Once you hit a certain depth, every sea creature is weird—
but one stands out even amid such strangeness.

✳ ✳ ✳ ✳

Dracula of the Deep Sea

THERE'S THE TERRIFYING angler fish, famous for its appearance in the movie *Finding Nemo*; the purple jellyfish, which lights up the sea like a Chinese lantern; the horrid stonefish, with a face only a mother could love; and the straight-out-of-science-fiction chimaera, or ghost shark, with its long snout and venomous dorsal spine. Yes, there are a lot of "weirdest creature" candidates down there. For the winner, we're going with one of the ocean's lesser-known oddities: the ominous vampire squid.

The sole member of the order Vampyromorphida, the vampire squid's scientific name is *Vampyroteuthis infernalis*, which translates literally into "vampire squid from Hell." The squid is as black as night and has a pair of bloodshot eyes. Full-grown, it is no more than a foot long. For its size, it has the largest eyes of any animal in the world. Its ruby peepers are as large as a wolf's eyes, sometimes more than an inch in diameter.

All Lit Up

Like many deep-sea denizens, the vampire squid has bioluminescent photophores all over its body. The squid can apparently turn these lights on and off at will, and it uses this ability—combined with the blackness of its skin against the utter dark of the deep—to attract and disorient its prey.

The vampire squid is not a true squid—the order Vampyromorphida falls somewhere between the squid and the octopus—and does not possess an ink sac. In compensation, the vampire squid has the ability to expel a cloud of mucus when threatened; this mucus contains thousands of tiny bioluminescent orbs that serve to blind and confuse predators while the vampire squid escapes into the shadows. As a second deterrent to predators, the vampire squid can turn itself inside out, exposing its suckers and cirri (tiny hair-like growths that act as tactile sensors) and making the creature look as though it is covered with spines.

Despite its name, the vampire squid does not feed on blood; its diet consists mostly of prawns and other tiny, floating creatures. Other than that, all that's missing for this Béla Lugosi mimic are the fangs and the widow's peak. But before you reach for a wooden stake, you should know that the vampire squid poses absolutely no threat to humans. It's found mostly at 1,500 to 2,500 feet below the surface, so the odds of encountering one are pretty slim.

* A crafty insect called an ant lion digs a sand pit by scooting itself backward and using its head as a shovel. It then hides itself in the pit with only its giant mouth sticking out and waits for an ant to tumble down into the pit.

* Whirligig beetles, which live in ponds and streams, have eyes that are divided into two sections: One part is suitable for underwater viewing, and the other part is good for ogling the atmosphere on the water's surface.

* Froghoppers are small insects that look a bit like frogs. Young froghoppers clamp onto plant stems and drain them of juice while excreting a whitish foam from their abdomens until they are completely covered in a bubble-bath disguise of their own making—one that resembles a blob of spittle.

* Tree crickets sing in exact mathematic ratio to the temperature of the air. There's no need for a thermometer on a summer night—just count the number of chirps a cricket makes in 15 seconds, add 40, and the result will be the current air temperature in degrees Fahrenheit.

* The female praying mantis is a pitiless lover. Her mate is also her dinner, and she often eats his head as an appetizer while he is still in the act of fertilizing her eggs.

Fish out of Water

It's hard being a big fish in a small pond. When food gets scarce, there's no place to go—unless you are a Clarias batrachus, Anabas testudineus, *or* Periophthalmus modestus. *In that case, you just climb onto dry land and go looking for new digs.*

✳ ✳ ✳ ✳

All It Needs Is a Walking Stick

THE WALKING CATFISH, climbing gourami, and mudskipper (the respective common names for the aforementioned fish) are the three main species of ambulatory fish—fish that leave the water voluntarily rather than at the end of a line.

The walking catfish, which can grow to be nearly a foot long, has an omnivorous appetite and a nasty sting and is the most notorious of the bunch. Native to Southeast Asia, it is also found in Sri Lanka, eastern India, and the Philippines. It arrived in the United States in the early 1960s as an aquarium fish that was imported to southern Florida by exotic animal dealers. A few escaped into the wild, and by the 1970s they had spread to freshwater ponds throughout the state.

In reality, "walking" is not quite what these catfish do. The Thai call it the "dull-colored wriggling fish," a far more accurate description. On land, the catfish propels itself with a snakelike motion. It breathes through labyrinth organs, which are located above the gills and absorb oxygen from the air. How far can they wriggle? A few yards at most, according to observers.

This One Even Scales Trees

The climbing gourami, another freshwater denizen, does the walking catfish one better. Originally from Africa, these fish can now be found in India, Malaysia, Southeast Asia, and the Philippines. The gourami uses its gill plates, fins, and tail as primitive legs and has been reported to climb over small trees on its journeys from pond to pond. Like the walking catfish, the gourami breathes through labyrinth organs and can survive for several hours on land, as long as its skin remains moist.

And This One Breathes Air

The third member of this trio, the mudskipper, is the champ among walking fish. It is the most widespread, too, found on the coasts of West Africa, Australia, Madagascar, India, Japan, Indonesia, and the Philippines. Genuinely amphibious, the mudskipper seems just as comfortable on land as in the water. These fish venture ashore for extended periods of time, using their strong pectoral fins and tail for locomotion. They can even flip themselves like acrobats. Oxygen is absorbed directly through a mudskipper's skin by a process known as cutaneous air breathing. In fact, the mudskipper is so well adapted to land, it will drown if it spends too much time submerged in the water without a trip to the surface for a breath of fresh air.

So if you happen to see a fish walking along the beach when you're on your next tropical vacation, it's not because you had a few too many Mai Tais. That fish is probably out taking a stroll while the tide is low. Just like you.

Say What?

We have just enough religion to make us hate, but not enough to make us love one another.

—JONATHAN SWIFT

I've been on so many blind dates I should get a free dog.

—WENDY LIEBMAN

I can't reconcile my gross habits with my net income.

—ERROL FLYNN

Elephant Graveyard

Do dying elephants actually separate themselves from their herd to meet their maker among the bones of their predecessors?

✳ ✳ ✳ ✳

JUST AS SEARCHING for the Holy Grail was a popular pastime for crusading medieval knights, 19th-century adventurers felt the call to seek out a mythical elephant graveyard. According to legend, when an elephant senses its impending death, it leaves its herd and travels to a barren, bone-filled wasteland. Although explorers have spent centuries searching for proof of these elephant ossuaries, not one has ever been found, and the elephant graveyard has been relegated to the realm of metaphor and legend.

Elephants Never Forget

Unlike most mammals, elephants have a special relationship with their dead. Researchers have revealed that elephants show marked emotion—from actual crying to profound agitation—when they encounter the remains of other elephants, particularly the skulls and tusks. They treat the bones with unusual tenderness and will cradle and carry them for long periods of time and over great distances. When they come across the bones of other animals, they show no interest whatsoever. Not only can elephants distinguish the bones of other elephants from those of rhinoceroses or buffalo, but they appear to recognize the bones of elephants they were once familiar with. An elephant graveyard, though a good way to ensure that surviving elephants wouldn't become upset by walking among their dead every day, does not fit with the elephants' seeming sentiment toward their ancestors.

Honor Your Elders

The biggest argument against an elephant burial ground can be found in elephants' treatment of their elders. An elephant would not want to separate itself from the comfort and protection of its herd during illness or infirmity, nor would a herd allow such behavior. Elephants accord great respect to older members of their herd, turning to them as guiding leaders. They usually refuse to leave sick or dying older elephants alone, even if it means risking their own health and safety.

But What About the Bones?

Although there is no foundation for the idea of an elephant graveyard, the legend likely began as a way to explain the occasional discovery of large groupings of elephant carcasses. These have been found near water sources, where older and sickly elephants live and die in close proximity. Elephants are also quite susceptible to fatal malnutrition, which progresses quickly. When an entire herd is wiped out by drought or disease, the bones are often found en masse at the herd's final watering hole.

There are other explanations for large collections of elephant bones. Pits of quicksand or bogs can trap a number of elephants; flash floods often wash all debris (not just elephant bones) from the valley floor into a common area; and poachers have been known to slay entire herds of elephants for their ivory, leaving the carcasses behind.

In parts of East Africa, however, groups of elephant corpses are thought to be the work of the *mazuku*, the Swahili word for "evil wind." Scientists have found volcanic vents in the earth's crust that emit carbon monoxide and other toxic gases. The noxious air released from these vents is forceful enough to blow out a candle's flame, and the remains of small mammals and birds are frequently found nearby. Although these vents have not proved to be powerful enough to kill groups of elephants, tales of the *mazuku* persist.

The Term Trudges On

Although no longer considered a destination for elephants, the elephant graveyard still exists as a geologic term and as a figure of speech that refers to a repository of useless or outdated items. Given how prominent the legend remains in popular culture, it will be a long time before the elephant graveyard joins other such myths in a burial ground of its own.

It Doesn't Just Happen in *Jaws*

A shark really can swallow you whole, which is something to consider the next time you're about to take a dip in the ocean.

✳ ✳ ✳ ✳

Gone in an Instant

"THIS SHARK, SWALLOW you whole. Little shakin', little tenderizin', an' down you go." Anyone who's heard this line from the shark hunter Quint in *Jaws* knows the chill that it can deliver, even if you're in the safety of your theater seat.

The movie premiered in 1975, and for 30 years thereafter, marine experts thought that a shark capable of swallowing a human was merely a figment of Hollywood's imagination. Then on June 4, 2005, a great white shark that was some 20 feet long appeared off the coast of Cape Town, South Africa. Henri Murray, a 22-year-old medical student, was scuba diving with a friend, Piet van Niekerk, in shallow water near shore. When the shark began to threaten them, van Niekerk shot it with his spear gun. The next instant, Murray was gone.

"It was incredibly fast," recalled a witness who was sitting on a nearby jetty. "A huge shark surged from under the water, taking the one diver from his legs upwards to his arms in its jaws." Subsequent searches for Murray's body conducted by the National Sea Rescue Institute retrieved only a mask, a flipper, a spear gun, and a weight belt that looked as if it had been shredded by a knife.

He Lived to Tell About It

About a year and a half after the Murray incident, on January 23, 2007, Eric Nerhus, an Australian diver, was the victim of a similar attack near Cape Howe, off Australia's southeast coast. This time, though, a nine-foot shark tried to swallow the man headfirst, and that made all the difference. With his head, upper body, and right arm inside the shark's mouth, Nerhus knew that he had only one chance: Reaching up with his left hand, he poked the shark in the eye. Startled, the shark opened its mouth just enough to allow the diver to wrench himself free.

"I've never felt fear like it 'til I was inside those jaws, with those teeth being dragged across my body," Nerhus told reporters from his hospital bed. He lived to dive another day.

How common are shark attacks on humans? According to the International Shark Attack File, maintained by the Florida Museum of Natural History, there were 1,021 verifiable shark attacks worldwide between 1990 and 2007; of those, 99 were fatal. In U.S. coastal waters, there were 621 attacks and 12 fatalities during the same time period.

It doesn't hurt to use a little common sense at the beach. The Global Shark Attack File organization offers a list of safety tips on its Web site. Chief among them: Listen to what the locals say. If fishermen tell you that they have seen sharks lurking in the water, believe them.

The best place to see a shark swallowing a person is on the movie screen. That way, when that great white attacks, the only pain you'll feel will be in your eardrums, because everyone else will be screaming as loudly as you.

---

* Zebras are black with white stripes (not white with black stripes) and have black skin.

* Hummingbirds consume fewer than ten calories per day.

* Howler monkeys are the loudest land animals; their calls can be heard up to three miles away.

* The dark-purple color of a giraffe's tongue protects it from getting sunburned while the animal eats leaves from tall trees.

He's Not Chucking Wood

"How much wood would a woodchuck chuck, if a woodchuck could chuck wood?" This classic tongue twister has been part of the English lexicon for ages. But has anybody even seen a woodchuck chucking wood?

❋ ❋ ❋ ❋

PART OF THE confusion lies in the origin of the word "woodchuck." A woodchuck (*Marmota monax*) actually is a groundhog. In the Appalachians, it's known as a whistle pig. According to etymologists, the word *woodchuck* is probably derived from early colonial British settlers who bastardized *wuchak*, the local Native American word for groundhog. Many early Americans couldn't be bothered to learn languages other than English (sort of like Americans today), so they simply transformed the Algonquian word into an English word that sounded similar.

Still, the question remains. What if woodchucks could chuck wood? Not surprisingly, there is little research on the topic. Indeed, no studies as of yet have proved that woodchucks are even capable of chucking wood, though there is ample evidence that woodchucks enjoy gnawing through wood when they encounter it.

There is, however, one thing that woodchucks are adept at chucking: dirt. The average woodchuck is quite a burrower—their tunnels have been known to reach more than 45 feet in length, with depths of several feet. Based on these measurements, one woodchuck expert determined that if the displaced dirt in a typical burrow was replaced with wood, the average whistle pig might be able to chuck about 700 pounds of it.

In the end, the best answer is probably provided by the rhyme itself. "How much wood would a woodchuck chuck, if a woodchuck could chuck wood? A woodchuck would chuck all the wood he could, if a woodchuck could chuck wood." Which would probably be none.

Slithering Danger

The fear of snakes, ophidiophobia, is one of the most widespread phobias in the world. There are many types of harmless snakes, but the venom from some poisonous varieties can kill a person. The following snakes have the most potent venom.

✳ ✳ ✳ ✳

Hook-nosed Sea Snake: The worst of the worst is this four-foot-long waterborne menace that lives along the coastlines of South Asia. The hook-nosed sea snake doesn't attack humans often, but when it does, just 1.5 milligrams of its venom can cause death. Its preferred prey are fish, which the snake paralyzes with its venom.

Russell's Viper: This three- to five-foot-long yellowish brown snake is common in Pakistan, India, Southeast Asia, and China. The Russell's viper preys primarily on rodents but will also kill cats, squirrels, crabs, and even scorpions. In humans, its bite causes pain, swelling, and bleeding, as well as decreased blood pressure and heart rate.

Inland Taipan: Averaging nearly six feet in length, this snake lives in dry regions of Australia. The venom injected by an average bite from an inland taipan is estimated to contain at least 50 lethal human doses. Fortunately, this snake shies away from people and dines on rodents, which it subdues by striking quickly and hanging on until they die. In contrast, it releases larger prey after biting them to avoid getting hurt in a struggle, then it tracks them down after the venom kicks in.

Dubois's Sea Snake: This treacherous swimming snake is found from the coasts of western and northern Australia to the islands of New Guinea and New Caledonia. Although the Dubois's sea snake has one of the deadliest venoms known, its bite delivers less than one-tenth of a milligram—more than enough to kill a mouse but generally not enough to kill a person.

Eastern Brown Snake: Another species native to Australia, the Eastern brown snake averages three to four feet in length but has been known to grow longer than six feet. This aggressive land snake injects very little venom when it bites, but it's still enough to cause rapid death in its victims (including humans). It eats mostly small mammals, such as rats, mice, and reptiles, but will also eat eggs, birds, and frogs.

Black Mamba: This nasty serpent from southern and central Africa is actually greenish yellow or gray; its name comes from the color of its mouth. One of the quickest and largest deadly snakes, it averages 8 feet in length but can grow to more than 14 feet. The black mamba preys on small mammals and birds, delivering small, fast bites. If it attacks a person, as little as two drops of its venom can cause dizziness, rapid heart rate, and shallow breathing. Some of its human victims have fallen into a coma and died.

Boomslang: Africa's savannah grasslands are home to the deadly five-foot-long boomslang, which feasts on chameleons and other lizards, as well as birds and their eggs. Even small amounts of boomslang venom can kill a person; the victim experiences nausea, dizziness, and a deceptive recovery before dying suddenly from internal hemorrhaging.

Common Indian Krait: This deadly slitherer is found across India, Pakistan, and other parts of southern Asia. It is not aggressive, but if alarmed it will bite and inject its venom, which can cause sleepiness and respiratory failure and will kill most human bite victims who don't receive antivenom. Kraits, which average around four feet long, eat not only small lizards but also snakes—including other kraits.

✳ If you add up all the time you blink during a day, you'd have about half an hour of shut-eye.

✳ About a quarter cup of sweat comes out of your feet daily.

✳ When the first location opened in 1955, a McDonald's hamburger sold for 15 cents.

The Original Headbangers

With all the wood-pecking they do, woodpeckers would seem destined to wind up with scrambled brains. Fortunately, their tiny craniums are built to take a pounding.

✳ ✳ ✳ ✳

Why So Much Pecking, Anyway?

OH, THE LENGTHS the earth's inhabitants will go for a little love and affection. Manakin birds perform elaborate dance routines that resemble early Michael Jackson more than anything ornithological. Hippos attract their mates by defecating all over the place. Humans seek attention from the opposite sex by putting smelly chemicals on their skin and installing sweet neon lights around their license plates. But to the lovelorn of all species, the woodpecker's efforts may seem the most fitting: During mating season, male woodpeckers bang their heads against any available hard surface up to 12,000 times a day.

Though metaphorically apt, it seems that this head-banging ritual would be awfully painful. And it leads us to wonder whether woodpeckers get headaches. Fortunately, Philip May, a neuropsychiatrist at the University of California, spent a good deal of time studying this subject. And though he didn't definitively answer the question of whether woodpeckers get headaches—after all, it's impossible to ask a woodpecker how its head feels—he did figure out why woodpeckers are able to bash their faces against trees all day (with the equivalent force of running into a wall face-first at 16 miles per hour) without turning into pulp.

Its Skull Is a Fortress

According to a 2002 *British Journal of Ophthalmology* article summarizing May's findings, the woodpecker is blessed with an anatomy particularly well suited to head-banging. The woodpecker's skull, for example, is proportionally thicker than your average animal cranium. At the same time, its brain is housed in a skull that's virtually devoid of the cranial fluid that humans have. So while a few blows to the noggin will send the human brain swimming, the woodpecker's sits firmly in place.

In addition, the woodpecker has special musculature along its jaw and neck that act as shock absorbers. It also has a nictitating membrane—also known as a third eyelid—that closes every time the bird hammers against a tree, preventing eye injuries. Finally, the woodpecker's uncanny geometric ability to strike wood at a perfectly perpendicular angle helps disperse force equally throughout the head and body.

Of course, the woodpecker's anatomy is both a blessing and a curse. While its makeup may help it lure a mate, it may never be able to use the excuse that has helped countless males and females: "Not tonight, honey—I have a headache."

＊ An average McDonald's Big Mac bun has 178 sesame seeds.

＊ The word "spa" dates back almost 2,000 years to when Roman soldiers, marching home from battle, stopped overnight in a Belgian village that had hot mineral springs. The town, named "Spa," became a popular resting spot for Roman soldiers returning from battle.

＊ If Pablo Picasso had signed his full name on his paintings, he'd have had little room left for the painting itself. Picasso's full name was Pablo Diego José Francisco de Paula Juan Nepomuceno María de los Remedios Cipriano de la Santícima Trinidad Clito Ruiz y Picasso.

＊ John Lennon was the first person to be featured on the cover of *Rolling Stone* magazine.

＊ Manhattan is about half the size of Disney World.

＊ A caterpillar has nearly five to six times as many muscles in its body as a human.

For Raging Bulls, Any Color Will Do

Red has been the color of choice of bullfighters for centuries, which begs the question: Why red?

✳ ✳ ✳ ✳

THE BRIGHT-RED CAPES of bullfighters are used to incite their bovine opponents into spectacular rages. In fact, the phrase "seeing red" is believed to have originated from the fury that the color seems to provoke in the bull. What is it about red that ticks off bulls?

The truth is: nothing. Bulls are partially color-blind and don't respond to the color red at all. The red color of the cape is just eye candy for the audience, much like the bullfighter's *traje de luces* ("suit of lights").

Then is it the motion of the cape that infuriates the bull? The truth is: no. There's nothing that the matador does that makes the bull angry—it's in ill humor before it even enters the ring. These bulls aren't bred to take quiet walks in the park on Sunday afternoons. No, they are selected because they exhibit violent and aggressive behavior. By the time they hit the bull-fighting arena, just about anything will set them off.

We're talking about bulls that have personalities like John McEnroe. The color red doesn't make them angry—*everything* makes them angry. Then again, having a bullfighter trying to plunge his sword into the bull's neck might have something to do with the beast's nasty disposition, too.

* Bees have five eyes. There are three small eyes on the top of a bee's head and two larger eyes in front.

* A newborn turkey chick has to be taught to eat, or it will starve.

* The body of a typical spider has approximately 600 silk glands, which it uses to spin webs.

Undiscovered Animals

Since about 1.3 million animal species around the planet have been identified and named, you might think we're down to the last few unknown critters by now. But according to many biologists, we're probably not even 10 percent of the way there.

✳ ✳ ✳ ✳

The Mysteries of the Oceans and Rain Forests

EXPERTS ESTIMATE THAT the planet holds 10 million to 100 million undiscovered plant and animal species, excluding single-celled organisms like bacteria and algae. This estimate is based on the number of species found in examined environments and on the sizes of the areas we have yet to fully investigate.

The broad span of the estimate shows just how little we know about life on Earth. At the heart of the mystery are the oceans and tropical rain forests. More than 70 percent of the planet is underwater. We know that the oceans teem with life, but we've explored only a small portion of them. The watery realm is like an entire planet unto itself. Biologists haven't examined much of the tropical rain forests, either, but the regions that they have explored have turned up a dizzying variety of life. It's hard to say exactly how many life forms have yet to be discovered, but the majority are probably small invertebrates (animals without backbones).

It's All About Insects

Insects make up the vast majority of the animal kingdom. There are about 900,000 known varieties, and this number will probably increase significantly as we further explore the rain forests. Terry Erwin is an influential coleopterist—in other words, a beetle guy—who estimated that the tropics alone could contain 30 million separate insect and arthropod species. This number is based on his examination of forest canopies in South America and Central America, and it suggests that you're on the wrong planet if you hate bugs.

Cataloging all of these critters is slow going. It requires special knowledge to distinguish between similar insect species and to identify different ocean species. It also takes real expertise to know which animals are already on the books and which have never before been documented. Qualified experts are in short supply, and they have a lot on their plates.

In some respects, time is of the essence. Deforestation and climate change are killing off animal and plant species even before they've been discovered. You may not particularly care about wildlife, but these are big losses. The knowledge gained from some of these undiscovered creatures that are on death row could help to cure diseases and, thus, make the world a better place.

Say What?

Maturity is only a short break in adolescence.

—JULES FEIFFER

The only disability in life is a bad attitude.

—SCOTT HAMILTON

Experience is the name everyone gives to his mistakes.

—OSCAR WILDE

A wise man will make more opportunities than he finds.

—SIR FRANCIS BACON

If you want to know what God thinks of money, just look at the people he gave it to.

—DOROTHY PARKER

Good manners can replace morals. It may be years before anyone knows if what you are doing is right. But if what you are doing is nice, it will be immediately evident.

—P. J. O'ROURKE

There's a difference between a philosophy and a bumper sticker.

—CHARLES M. SCHULZ

Animal Crime and Punishment

Rats declared public enemies, pigs hung in the town square, wolves tried and executed... it's hard to imagine animals held criminally responsible for their actions, but it has happened!

✳ ✳ ✳ ✳

Ox Murderers

PERHAPS THE EARLIEST recorded mention of legal prosecution of an animal is an Old Testament verse in Exodus chapter 21, verse 28: "When an ox gores a man or a woman to death, the ox shall be stoned, and its flesh shall not be eaten; but the owner of the ox shall not be liable."

It's unknown how many Israelite oxen were actually stoned and left uneaten after jabbing unwary citizens, but it's clear that such responses were backed by ancient biblical edict.

The Case of the Reticent Rats

In medieval France, rats were legally charged with the crime of eating barley. But it was extremely difficult to get the rats to appear in court, as villagers of Autun discovered in 1522. The village judge appointed a defense lawyer for the rats and waited for them to show up. The lawyer argued that his clients inhabited many towns so one summons was insufficient to reach them all. The rats were given more time, and villagers were advised to keep their cats from eating any court-bound rats. Eventually, the case was dismissed.

Marauding Mice

Perhaps the people of Autun had heard about a similar action taken in 1519 in Glurns, Switzerland. A farmer asked the court to charge area field mice with damage to his hay. But he was careful to request counsel for the mice so they would receive a fair trial. The farmer claimed he had observed mice eating area hay fields for at least 18 years and found corroborating testimony from a field worker and another farmer.

The defense counsel asserted that the mice were also help-ful, assisting in insect control in the fields. He asked for a safe field for the mice to live in and for relocation assistance for any pregnant mice. The sentence allowed the mice two weeks to move out of the damaged fields and banned them for eternity. In a show of leniency, pregnant mice and infants were allowed an extra 14 days to relocate.

Insect Indictments

Rats were not the only creatures to prey upon barley and other staple crops. Weevils, locusts, and worms were regularly charged by formal courts during the Middle Ages. Because most courts were administered by the church, insect pests could even be excommunicated or formally barred from ser-vices and the Lord's Supper.

One famous case again occurred in France. In 1546, a mas-sive population of weevils that threatened the barley crop was miraculously decimated when the villagers practiced some extreme religion and performed many penitent acts. The wee-vils stayed away for four decades but returned with a vengeance in 1586. This time a full trial was held, defense counsel was hired for the weevils, and a settlement was attempted. The peasants offered the weevils their own tract of land if they would just stay there, but the defense persuaded the court that the land in question was not fertile enough to support his cli-ents. Ironically, insects ate the final record of judgments in the case, leaving the fate of the barley weevils unknown.

Prosecuting Porky

In ancient times, livestock were often left to roam village streets and squares, foraging for garbage and other "found" food. Accidents were bound to happen, and pigs attacked children and other vulnerable humans from time to time. Records of pig prosecution exist in a number of European countries and show that they were by far the most common species brought to trial for murder of humans. Suspected pigs were usually kept in the same jail as human criminals and were sometimes tortured for "evidence," their frantic grunts and screams accepted as confessions. Execution methods included hanging or live burial. In 1457, a sow and her six piglets were accused of killing a five-year-old boy and were sentenced to death. The sow was hung by her hind legs on a gallows, but the piglets were forgiven due to their youth and the fact that they were corrupted by their mother.

Kitty Kriminals

The old wives' tale that cats smother infants dates back at least to 1462, when a cat was tried for just such a crime. It was found guilty and hanged. During the great witch trials of the Middle Ages, cats were often thought to be spirit companions of accused witches and were often killed with their owners.

Beasts of the Burden of Proof

Bulls, horses, oxen, and goats were often tried as humans, especially in cases of bestiality. However, in 1750, a female donkey was found not guilty in a case in France because a group of respectable citizens all signed a document testifying that they had been acquainted with the animal for her entire life and she had never acted scandalously. The creature's human assaulter, however, was sentenced to death.

Beavers in Contempt

A resident of Pierson, Michigan, received a letter from the state government in December 1997 threatening to charge the "unauthorized" contractors building two wood dams in nearby Spring Pond $10,000 a day if they did not stop. The government was informed by the resident's landlord that the illegal builders were a couple of beavers and that if these two animals were forced to pay fines, beavers all over the state would have to be treated similarly. The state dropped its case.

Forget the Cheddar—the Mouse Wants Chocolate

Who moved your cheese? Chances are, if you are a mouse, you won't care all that much. But relocating your peanut butter, corn chips, or chocolate? That's another matter entirely.

✳ ✳ ✳ ✳

Earth-Shaking News

WE'VE ALL SEEN the cute cartoons of mice nibbling away on a big, luscious hunk of cheese. In 2006, however, Dr. David Holmes, an animal behaviorist at Britain's Manchester Metropolitan University, stunned the world when he announced: No, mice really don't like cheese.

"Mice Hate Cheese!" the venerable *Manchester Guardian* declared. Other news sources mourned the break-up of the old "mice-cheese love team." Not surprisingly, Holmes and his colleagues were bombarded with messages from irate cooks, telling them that mice certainly do eat cheese, along with fried chicken, salami sandwiches, and anything else they can get their thieving paws on, including the plastic coating that insulates copper wires. (Mice have been to blame for more than one short circuit in the kitchen.)

To defuse the tense situation, Holmes explained that his research was intended to identify those foods preferred by a wide range of animals under optimal conditions. Yes, mice eat many things, he stated, but they evolved as vegetarians. That means their ideal meal consists of grains, nuts, seeds, beans, fruits, and other substances high in carbohydrates and sugar— which explains the little rodents' predilection for chocolate.

The Origins of a Myth

Where did the myth that mice love cheese come from? No one knows, exactly. One thought is that mice were known to be stowaways on ships, hiding themselves in the holes of Swiss cheese. When sailors found mice in the cheese, they assumed it was because mice loved cheese.

Before refrigeration, cheese was stored in the pantry. Because making cheese is a labor-intensive process and uses a lot of precious milk, people were probably angrier than usual when they discovered that they were sharing their cheddar with furry invaders. Or perhaps the old folktale about the city mouse that impressed its country cousin with a gourmet spread of cosmopolitan treats created the impression that mice like rich, fatty foods.

In reality, researchers discovered that high concentrations of fat can give mice indigestion, which puts cheese fairly far down on their list of preferred snacks. So you can keep your Brie, Stilton, and Camembert. If you really want to catch a mouse, try a dab of peanut butter, a piece of potato, or a few raisins— the chocolate-covered kind should do nicely.

---

* The top-selling tie color is blue.
* Honey was used to pay tax in ancient Rome.
* Domino's has marketed a reindeer sausage pizza in Iceland.
* Apples are considered the most popular fruit in America.
* Blondes typically have more individual hairs on their heads than brunettes. Redheads have the fewest of the three.
* An average human beard has more than 15,000 hairs.
* The longest recorded underwater kiss is 2 minutes and 18 seconds.
* An average office chair moves a total of roughly eight miles over the course of a year.
* The chili and the frijole are the official vegetables of the state of New Mexico.
* The square dance is the official folk dance of Utah.
* Princess Diana appeared on the cover of *People* magazine more than 50 times.

Snakes in the Toilet

It's true—the yucky reptiles have been known to slither through pipes and right into the bowl while a person is conducting his or her business.

✳ ✳ ✳ ✳

Unwanted Visitors

WE HESITATE TO inform you of this, since it might lead to a lifetime of bathroom paranoia, but yes, snakes (and other nasty creatures) do indeed climb up through toilets now and again. And yes, some have bitten people who have been busy at work in the john.

There are two ways for an animal to make its way up into your toilet. First, if your house is connected to a municipal sewer system, the drain leading from your toilet connects to a large network of pipes that go all the way to a sewer treatment plant. This network has many small entry points, including manholes and other people's toilets.

Because of the food everyone washes down the sink, these pipes are popular hangouts for rats; because there are delicious rats everywhere, the pipes also are popular with snakes. Water rarely fills the pipes all the way and usually moves slowly, so snakes and rats can come and go as they please. Every once in a while, a snake or a rat will follow a pipe all the way to a toilet, swim through the little bit of water in the bowl, and pop out to see what's going on.

The second way in is much quicker. Most houses have a vent that runs from the sewage drainpipe to the roof. The vent allows noxious sewer gas to escape without stinking up the house. If the vent isn't covered, rats, snakes, frogs, and even squirrels can fall in and land unexpectedly in the main drain line. They scurry for the nearest exit—the toilet. (It's probably a good idea to cover that vent if you haven't already.)

Tales from the Bowl

There have been many reported cases of unexpected toilet visitors, including a venomous water moccasin that bit a Jacksonville, Florida, woman in 2005 and a baby brush-tailed possum that crawled out of a toilet in Brisbane, Australia, in 2008. If you have a snake phobia, the creepiest story might be that of Keith, a ten-foot-long boa constrictor that kept poking out of toilets in an apartment building in Manchester, England, in 2005. The snake, a pet that its owner had set free after being evicted, lived the high life, eating sewer rats and freaking people out for months before a building resident lured him into a bucket.

Take this as a warning not to dilly-dally for too long in the bathroom. There are safer places to catch up on your reading.

---

* In Blacksburg, Virginia, in 2003, a six-point buck ran into a supermarket. The deer leapt over soup cans and knocked over displays before escaping out a back door, where he was hit, but not killed, by a passing vehicle.

* The legend of a ghost deer echoes through the canyons of Mt. Eddy in northern California. Hunters describe a giant buck with 12 points on one antler and 10 on the other. Those who have shot at it say bullets pass right through, and its tracks are said to disappear at natural barriers such as great ridges or lakes.

* On August 1, 2003, Joshua Laprise spotted a pure white albino deer eating in a field in Rhode Island. The chances of seeing an adult albino white-tailed deer in the wild are about one in a million. Most albinos do not live more than a few years due to lack of protective coloration, but such deer are protected by law in Illinois, Iowa, Tennessee, and Wisconsin.

* Coffee is technically a fruit, as its beans are made from fruit pits.

* A hippopotamus can open its mouth wide enough to accommodate a four-foot-tall child.

* Egyptian artwork from 3,000 years ago reveals Bes, the god of birth and carnal pleasures, wearing a condom-type device. The Chinese were said to have worn a silk sheath as a prophylactic 2,000 years ago.

The World's Biggest Insects

Although most people consider insects to be one of life's little annoyances, the following species are more like something out of a science-fiction movie. It's not likely you'd try to swat one of these.

✳ ✳ ✳ ✳

South American male acteon beetle (*Megasoma acteon*): Not only is the acteon beetle regarded as the bulkiest insect on the planet, it also has an impressive frame. Males can grow to be three and a half inches long by two inches wide and an inch and a half thick, with three sets of menacing tarsal claws. Its thick, smooth armor and robust thoracic horns make it look like a miniature cross between a rhinoceros and an elephant. It's commonly found in the South American tropics, where it likes to consume tree sap and fruit.

Hercules beetle (*Dynastes hercules*): This beast can grow to be seven inches long. About half of that length is consumed by a threatening, sword-shape horn and a second smaller horn that curves back toward the head. The male Hercules is smooth and shiny with attractive green-and-black wing cases. This beetle feeds on tree sap and lives in North America.

Giant New Zealand weta (*Deinacrida heteracantha*): The Maori people of New Zealand call this insect "the God of the ugly things," an appropriate observation. It looks like a thwarted attempt to cross a cockroach with a cricket. The weta's body typically measures three inches in length, excluding its protruding legs and antennae, which can more than double its size. It eats leaves, other insects, fungi, dead animals, and fruit.

Borneo stick insect (*Pharnacia kirbyi*): At close to 13 inches in length (20 inches when it stretches its legs), this is the longest insect on the planet. It is also known as the bent twig insect for its amazing ability to bend its body at an acute angle and stay that way for hours. The female feeds primarily on bramble during the night, and during the day she keeps very still to avoid being spotted by predators. Males are not quite as big.

Giant Brazilian ant (*Dinoponera gigantea*): The heavyweight champ of ants measures in at more than one inch, and its ability to lift 20 times its body weight makes it one of the strongest creatures in the world. It also displays amazing memory and learning skills, as well as the ability to correct mistakes. It lives in the wetlands and woodlands of the Brazilian jungle and feeds primarily on lowland plants.

South American longhorn beetle (*Titanus giganteus*): This species, also known as the titan beetle, can grow to six inches in length and has extremely powerful legs. The beetle's most prominent—and most menacing—feature is its huge mandible, which can allegedly snap pencils in half. This bug's diet consists of plants, shrubbery, and decaying organic matter.

Giant Fijian longhorn beetle (*Xixuthrus heros*): This intimidating native of the Fijian island of Viti Levu has a body length of five and a half inches and emits a frightful hissing noise when challenged. Ounce for ounce, its jaws are as powerful as those of a killer shark. Luckily for humans, it prefers to snack on tropical plants.

South American giant cockroach (*Blaberus giganteus*): The baddest of the cockroach clan lives in dark caves and can reach lengths up to four inches. It discourages predators by mimicking the color of noxious beetles and emitting a foul odor. This cockroach will eat anything but prefers fruit and vegetation.

---

* The oldest known wheel—from roughly 3500 B.C.—was found in Mesopotamia. Archaeologists disagree as to how much earlier than that the wheel was invented.

* When his housekeeper asked him for his last words, Karl Marx stated: "Go on, get out—last words are for fools who haven't said enough."

The Balancing Act of Birds

Our avian friends possess the unique ability to sleep on tree limbs without falling off.

✳ ✳ ✳ ✳

N O MATTER WHERE you live, birds are likely to be a part of the landscape. But you probably aren't as likely to see birds in one of their most vulnerable states: sleeping.

Nest-building birds don't sleep in nests; they just use them to raise their families. Some birds crouch down in the grass or in bushes to get some shut-eye. However, there are many species of birds that sleep while perched on tree limbs. It seems impossible that they could stay up in a tree while asleep—after all, when people (as well as many other animals) fall asleep, they usually go limp. But perching birds, or passerines, are different, and it's all because of their feet.

Most birds have four toes on each foot, and these toes can be arranged in different configurations depending on the type of bird. A passerine typically has an anisodactyl foot, which consists of three toes that face forward and a "big toe," or hallux, that faces backward. This type of bird possesses an ingenious tendon-locking mechanism (TLM) that causes a special ligament in the back of the leg to tighten automatically when the bird sits on a limb.

This tendon locks the toes and secures the bird onto the perch. Because of the TLM, a bird doesn't have to keep its muscles actively engaged to maintain its grip. The bird stays on the limb until it retracts its toes. Other animals—bats, for example— have a similar mechanism to allow them to hang upside down without falling.

On a morbid note, the TLM doesn't disengage when a bird dies, either. Skeletons have been found still perched in trees.

Nature's Night Pilots

Fireflies dive and swoop through the darkness like tiny prop planes, communicating their location and intent with a series of flashing lights.

✳ ✳ ✳ ✳

Let There Be Light

WHAT'S UP WITH these firefly lights, anyway? To potential predators, these lights say, "Stay away." To potential mates, they say, "Come hither." To a child running around the yard with a Mason jar, they can mean a lamp that will grow brighter and more fascinating with each bug that is caught.

Like all animals possessing bioluminescent traits, fireflies produce their light by means of chemical reaction. The bugs manufacture a chemical known as luciferin. Through a reaction powered by adenosine triphosphate and an enzyme called luciferase, luciferin is transformed into oxyluciferin. In the firefly, this reaction takes place in the abdomen, an area perforated by tubes that allow oxygen to enter; the oxygen feeds the chemical reaction and bonds with the luciferin and luciferase produced by the insect. Oxyluciferin is a chemical that contains charged electrons; these electrons release their charge immediately, and the product of this release is light.

All fireflies emit light in the larval stage. This is thought to be a warning sign to animals looking for snacks: Chemicals in the firefly's (and the firefly larvae's) body have a bitter taste that is undesirable to predators. Studies have shown that laboratory mice quickly learn to associate the bioluminescent glow with a bad taste, and they avoid food that radiates this light.

Mating Games

In adult fireflies, bioluminescence has a second purpose: Some species of firefly use their glow—and distinctive patterns made by dipping and swooping, in which they draw simple patterns against the black of night—to attract a mate. Each firefly species, of which there are 1,900 worldwide, has its own pattern. Male fireflies flit about and show off, while the females sit in a tree or in the grass. The females will not give off light until they see a male displaying the wattage and sprightliness they're looking for in an attractive mate.

They must choose carefully, however, as there are certain adult firefly species that are unable to manufacture luciferin on their own. These species obtain the chemical by attracting unwitting members of other species and consuming them. They do this because without the chemical, they appear to predators much as any other night-flying insects; they need the chemical to advertise their bitter taste.

In the end, this effort might be for naught. The firefly's flavor has that special something that some frogs cannot get enough of. For these frogs, the blinking lights are not so much a warning as a sign reading, "Come and get it!"

Say What?

You can only be young once but you can be immature forever.

—DAVE BARRY

If you can count your money, you don't have a billion dollars.

—J. PAUL GETTY

People do not seem to realize that their opinion of the world is also a confession of character.

—RALPH WALDO EMERSON

I don't like nostalgia unless it's mine.

—LOU REED

What's money? A man is a success if he gets up in the morning and gets to bed at night and in between does what he wants to do.

—BOB DYLAN

The Air Down There

Ever wonder how worms get oxygen when they're buried in the soil? The answer has more to do with absorption than actual breathing.

✳ ✳ ✳ ✳

WORMS SPEND MOST of their lives underground, but they don't burrow in the traditional sense. Unlike most "underground" creatures, worms don't make tunnel systems and dens—instead, they squish, slide, and squirm through the soil, leaving nary a trace of their presence. Since they don't create any more room than they need for themselves in the earth, how is it possible for them to breathe? There can't be much air down there.

A worm lacks the accoutrements that are typically associated with breathing (i.e., a mouth, a nose, lungs). It breathes by taking in oxygen through the pores in its skin. To make this possible, the worm's skin must be moist. (This is why, after it rains, worms that are stranded on the sidewalk perish before they can get back into the soil—the sun dries them right out, suffocating them.) Oxygen is absorbed by the capillaries that line the surface of a worm's slimy skin; from there, it goes straight into the bloodstream. In mammals, this process is longer by one step: They take oxygen into their lungs, where it is then transferred to the bloodstream.

Worms can survive underwater for a sustained period of time, but their pores don't function the same way a fish's gills do, so a submerged worm will eventually drown. Some scientists believe that this is why worms come to the surface during a rainstorm: The soil becomes too wet and threatens to drown them. Of course, as we mentioned, this pilgrimage to the surface can lead to a different set of problems.

It seems that the key to a worm's longevity is to successfully squirm the fine line between too little and too much moisture—and to avoid the pinching fingers of anglers and curious kids.

The Secrets of Hibernation

They binge then go comatose. Does this sound like something that's happened to you after you polished off a quart of ice cream? Can you imagine your food coma lasting all winter?

✳ ✳ ✳ ✳

Preparation Is the Key

ANIMALS THAT HIBERNATE have triggers that warn them to gorge themselves for the winter ahead. As the days get shorter and colder, each critter's internal clock—which marks time through fluctuations in hormones, neurotransmitters, and amino acids—tells them to fill up and shut down. Bingeing is important; if these creatures don't build up enough fat, they won't survive. The fat that they store for hibernation is brown (rather than white, like human body fat) and collects near the brain, heart, and lungs.

Animals have a number of reasons for hibernating. Cold-blooded creatures such as snakes and turtles adjust their body temperatures according to the weather; in winter, their blood runs so cold that many of their bodily functions essentially stop. Warm-blooded critters can more easily survive the extreme chills of winter, but they have a different problem: finding food. They most likely developed their ability to hibernate as a way of surviving winter's dearth of munchies.

After an animal has heeded the biological call to pig out, its metabolism starts to slow down. As it hibernates, some bodily functions—digestion, the immune system—shut down altogether. Its heartbeat slows to ten or fewer beats per minute, and its senses stop registering sounds and smells. The animal's body consumes much less fuel than normal—its metabolism can be as low as 1 percent of its normal rate. The stored fat, then, is enough to satisfy the minimal demands of the animal's body, provided the creature found enough to eat in the fall and is otherwise healthy.

Waking Up

It can take hours or even days for the animal's body temperature to rise back to normal after it awakens from hibernation. But time is of the essence—the beast desperately needs water, and thirst drives it out of its nest. However, the animal is groggy and slow of foot—it walks like a drunk—so it can be easy prey if it doesn't hydrate quickly.

Which animals hibernate? Small ones, mostly—cold-blooded and warm-blooded critters alike. The first category includes snakes, lizards, frogs, and tortoises; the second includes dormice, hedgehogs, skunks, and bats.

But what about the bear, the animal that is most closely associated with hibernation? Here's a shocker: Bears don't hibernate. They slow down, sleep a lot, and lose weight during winter, but they don't truly hibernate. So if you're ever taking a peaceful nature walk on a sunny winter morn, beware. A bear might be awake out there.

---

* The fastest (nonstorm) wind ever recorded was 231 miles per hour at Mount Washington, New Hampshire, on April 12, 1934.

* The state of Louisiana loses 30 square miles of land each year to erosion and sinking.

* Mosquito Bay in Puerto Rico is filled with bioluminescent organisms (720,000 per gallon) that glow when the water is disturbed.

* Caddisfly larvae construct little houses in ponds to live in until they reach their winged stage. Some species build little structures from bits of leaves to achieve dome or turret shapes, some stack up small pebbles and shells, and one is able to exactly reproduce the shape of a snail shell by binding sand with a silky extrusion.

* Earwigs, once widely (and wrongly) reputed to crawl inside human ears to lay their eggs, actually feed mostly on caterpillars, slugs, and already dead flesh. They're still creepy, though, due to the large, pincerlike, prey-grabbing claws protruding from their rear ends.

Chapter Nine

Bizarre Truths About Love and Physical Attraction

Love at First Sight

It happens all the time in Hollywood, but in the real world, there are rarely instant fireworks between two people.

✳ ✳ ✳ ✳

Here Are the Facts, Romeo

YOUR EYES MEET from across a crowded room—*Shazam!* Sparks fly. Fireworks explode. In an instant, you both know that you have found the missing piece to your puzzle. You are the yin to his yang. She is the chocolate to your peanut butter.

At least that's usually how it goes in those corny chick flicks. What about in real life? Can two strangers simply lock looks and spontaneously combust into an epic romance, just like Romeo and Juliet, Scarlett and Rhett, and Dharma and Greg?

Sorry, but relationship researchers say that love at first sight is rare. Only 11 percent of couples in one research survey said they had fallen in love at first glance. The survey—conducted by social psychologist Ayala Malach Pines, author of *Falling in Love: Why We Choose the Lovers We Choose*—also revealed that more couples, one-third of them, said they fell in love gradually.

But who wants to watch a movie about a guy and a girl cautiously getting to know one another over a couple hundred soy lattes? It's much more exciting to see—and feel—a fiery spark of desire. Maybe that's why some people seem to stray into the trap of falling in love at first sight over and over again.

Love vs. Lust

Remember Pepé Le Pew from the Looney Tunes cartoons? In search of *l'amour*, he falls at the sight of Penelope in almost every episode. It goes to show that there's a difference between love at first sight and lust at first leer. Penelope isn't even the "petite femme skunk" Pepé thinks she is—she's a black cat with a white stripe painted down her back. In other words: not a suitable life partner.

Hey, sometimes the eyes see what they want to see (especially when they're wearing beer goggles). Interestingly, when this kind of instantaneous physical attraction strikes, it usually is the guys who fall prey to it. In their defense, evolutionary psychologist David Buss says that in a biological sense, this is perfectly logical. Buss's research suggests that a man is taken by the physical appearance of a woman because it gives him cues about her fertility and reproductive value. From an evolutionary standpoint, love at first sight enabled early men and women to spot each other and start breeding straight away.

From a more modern perspective, researchers in the Face Research Lab at the University of Aberdeen in Scotland say that love at first sight might exist, but it's more about ego and sex than love and romance. So forget what you saw in that Lifetime movie. To put it plainly: People are attracted to those who are attracted to them. Hey, baby—do you believe in love at first sight, or should I walk by again?

---

* **If you need something superfast, ask for it in a yoctosecond. That's the smallest unit of time.**

* **A female ferret can die from going into heat and not mating.**

* **For passengers who may not quite get it, American Airlines printed instructions on their peanut packages. "Open packet, eat nuts." Ever-helpful advice.**

The Appeal of Dear Old Dad

Scientists call it "sexual imprinting"—when a woman falls for a guy who is just like her father.

✳ ✳ ✳ ✳

ASK A WOMAN if she wants a man as dependable, kind, and quietly confident as dear old Dad, and the chances are good that she'll say yes. Ask if she wants a man who looks like dear old Dad, and she'll probably say, "Huh?" or "Eww!"

Nonetheless, dear old Dad may be a little hotter than some women are willing to admit. According to a couple of studies by European researchers, many women fall for men who look like their fathers, whether they intend to or not.

Researchers at Hungary's University of Pécs measured proportions of the facial features of members of 52 families. Based on this data, they found that the faces of young men and their fathers-in-law had some strong resemblances, most notably around the nose and eyes. Comparable results came out of a similar study conducted jointly by Durham University in England and the University of Wroclaw in Poland.

For the record, the Oedipal implications of the findings extend to men as well: Most guys go gaga for girls who resemble Mom. The studies found that resemblances between young women and their mothers-in-law occurred in the lips and jaw. (Insert mother-in-law-mouth joke here.)

Scientists offered no substantive explanations for why we choose mates who look like our parents. However, it seems that the likelihood of a woman choosing a man who looks like her father depends on her relationship with him—if the relationship tends to be negative, the woman might stray to other facial types.

Dad may scratch his behind and belch when he emerges from the bathroom, but to many women, he's still got it goin' on.

Oysters: Nature's Viagra

One of the most enduring food myths is that oysters have aphrodisiac properties. And the thing is, it's actually true.

✳   ✳   ✳   ✳

MANY PEOPLE SWEAR that a plate of raw oysters can put even the coldest fish in the mood for love. Rumor has it that Casanova would dine on oysters before an amorous encounter. Some nut-jobs have even gone so far as to feed Viagra to oysters to increase the sexual power of the shellfish.

For years, scientists attempted to show that oysters don't have any libido-increasing abilities. A simple chemical analysis of an oyster reveals that it is made of nothing more than water, carbohydrates, protein, and trace amounts of sugars, fats, and minerals. None of these elements, whether taken separately or together, have been shown to have any effect on sexual desire or prowess.

But in 2005, at a meeting of the American Chemical Society, the oyster's sexual secrets were finally revealed. A group of American and Italian researchers discovered that the oyster belongs to a family of shellfish that has been shown to increase the release of certain sexual hormones. Oysters apparently contain amino acids that, when injected into rats, increase the levels of testosterone in males and progesterone in females. Elevated levels of these hormones in their respective genders have been linked to an increase in sexual activity.

So this myth appears to be grounded in fact. If you want to keep your libido humming, it might not be a bad idea to chow down on a dozen or so oysters.

Loving Lolita: The Scandal of Naughty Nabokov

The name "Lolita" has become synonymous with any sexy, underage lass with a come-hither look. The story of Humbert Humbert, a grown man who develops lusty designs on a 12-year-old girl, raised eyebrows and concerns when it was published in 1955. Critics and the public alike wondered, "Where does literature end and pornography begin?"

✳   ✳   ✳   ✳

The Author

RUSSIAN-BORN VLADIMIR NABOKOV fled his homeland with his family after the 1917 Russian Revolution. He attended school in England and took up writing novels and poetry in Paris in the late 1930s. Nabokov and his family fled again in 1940, this time to the United States, as the Nazis began their assault on Europe. The author took up residence at Wellesley College near Boston, where he gained notoriety as a brilliant writer and lecturer, as well as an expert butterfly collector. Nabokov became a U.S. citizen in 1945 and continued as a college professor at Harvard and Cornell. While traveling in Oregon, he wrote his greatest, and most controversial, novel.

The Book

Lolita follows a college professor who has a perverse preoccupation with adolescent girls. Settling in New England, he is smitten with Dolores (whom Humbert calls "Lolita"), the 12-year-old daughter of his widowed landlord. He is so enamored of Lolita that he marries her mother just to be close to his "stepdaughter." But his wife dies, leaving Humbert to care for Lolita. She takes up with a potential rival, a man named Clare Quilty, and distances herself from Humbert. Some years pass before Humbert hears from Lolita, now married and pregnant at 17 years old. Humbert trades his fortune to Lolita for the name of her former paramour. He finds Quilty, shoots him dead, and winds up imprisoned for murder. While waiting for the trial, he writes a book called *Lolita* and then dies. At the close of the novel, Lolita dies in childbirth.

The Reaction

Despite Nabokov's literary reputation, no U.S. publisher would touch *Lolita*. A novel about pedophilia, no matter how well-written, was taboo in the United States in the mid-1950s. A publisher in Paris finally put out 5,000 copies in 1955; they quickly and quietly sold out. A London reviewer noted that it was one of the best books of the year, prompting a competitor to claim that *Lolita* was "the filthiest book I have ever read" and "sheer unrestrained pornography." These declarations led to the book being banned in England and France. When it was finally published in the United States in 1958, there was praise for the writing style but condemnation for the subject. Yet the controversy made it a best seller—the first novel since *Gone with the Wind* to sell more than 100,000 copies in its first three weeks.

Many public libraries banned the book from their shelves, and the *Chicago Tribune* refused even to review it. *The New York Times* called the book "highbrow pornography." Nabokov eventually wrote the screenplay for Stanley Kubrick's 1962 cinematic version of *Lolita*. Years before the establishment of the MPAA rating system, it was recommended for "persons over 18 years of age"; film posters asked, "How did they ever make a movie of *Lolita*?" (To start with, they made her 14 years old rather than 12.)

The Aftermath

Lolita is regarded as one of the greatest works in 20th-century American literature. Its eventual success allowed Nabokov to move with his family to Switzerland, where he continued to write and chase butterflies. Before his death in 1977, Nabokov said that he was most proud of writing *Lolita*. He once noted, "I am probably responsible for the odd fact that people don't seem to name their daughters *Lolita* any more. I have heard of young female poodles being given that name. . . . but of no human beings."

Why Spouses Start to Look Alike

Have you ever met a husband and wife who looked so alike you could have sworn they were brother and sister? Well, scientific research has come up with a few explanations as to why.

✳ ✳ ✳ ✳

Compatibility Counts

FOR STARTERS, IT seems that we seek out mates who have features that are similar to our own. Recent studies suggest that we're attracted to those who look like us because they tend to have comparable personalities.

It's often said that women "marry their fathers." Research at the University of Pécs in Hungary supports this notion. Women tend to choose husbands who resemble their natural fathers—even if they're adopted. Scientists characterize it as "sexual imprinting," and it's known to occur in many animal species. Glenn Weisfeld, a human ethologist at Wayne State University in Detroit, says that there seems to be an advantage to selecting mates who are similar to ourselves: "Fortuitous genetic combinations" are retained in our offspring.

This doesn't give you carte blanche to marry your cute first cousin Betty. When it comes to mating, it's best to avoid people who are members of your family tree. But it doesn't hurt to pick a guy or gal who shares your dark features or toothy smile. Studies show that partners who are genetically similar to each other tend to have happier marriages.

Togetherness

It seems the longer couples stay together, the more their likenesses grow. A study by Robert Zajonc, a psychologist at the University of Michigan, found this to be the case—even among couples who didn't particularly look alike when they first got hitched. In Zajonc's study, people were presented with random photographs of men's and women's faces and asked to match up couples according to resemblance. Half of the photos were individual shots of couples that were taken when they were first married; the other half were individual shots of the same couples after 25 years of wedlock.

What do you know? People were able to match up husbands and wives far more often when looking at photographs of the couples when they were older than when they were younger. It seems with time, the couples' similarities became much more discernible.

Why? Zajonc says husbands and wives start looking like each other because they spend decades sharing the same life experiences and emotions. Spouses often mimic the facial expressions of each other as a sign of empathy and closeness. Think of that the next time you and your spouse exchange smiles, sighs, or looks of contempt. Before you know it, you'll be sharing a life complete with matching facial sagging and wrinkle patterns! Hey, it's better than being told you look like your dog.

Say What?

It is sad to grow old but nice to ripen.

—BRIGITTE BARDOT

Heredity is a splendid phenomenon that relieves us of responsibility for our shortcomings.

—DOUG LARSON

Women who seek to be equal with men lack ambition.

—TIMOTHY LEARY

Beautiful young people are accidents of nature, but beautiful old people are works of art.

—ELEANOR ROOSEVELT

The Six Wives of Henry VIII

A lot of people think that England's King Henry VIII had a penchant for chopping off the heads of his wives. In truth, only two of his brides got the ax.

✳ ✳ ✳ ✳

ENGLAND's KING HENRY VIII (1491–1547) was certainly the marrying type—he had six wives—yet he held no qualms about ending a marriage that inconvenienced him. How he ended those marriages is where historical fact blurs into misconceptions. Many people believe that as Henry lost interest in his wives, they lost their heads on the executioner's block.

But Henry wasn't quite the lady killer he's perceived to be. In actuality, two of Henry's wives survived their marriage to him, and only two were beheaded. Here's a brief look at how things really ended between Henry and his brides.

Catherine of Aragon (1485–1536): married 1509, divorced 1533. Catherine of Aragon proved to be the most tormented of Henry's wives. It didn't help that she wasn't considered attractive, but she was doomed by her inability to provide Henry with a male heir (their only surviving child, Mary, would later establish her own blood-stained reign). Catherine suffered through Henry's scorn, neglect, and public infidelities, most notably with her eventual successor in the royal marital bed, Anne Boleyn.

By 1526, desperate for a son and smitten by Anne, Henry began his ultimately unsuccessful petitioning of Pope Clement VII for an annulment from Catherine. In 1533, he denounced Clement's authority and married the now-pregnant Anne. That same year, the Archbishop of Canterbury annulled Henry's marriage to Catherine, who died in prayer-filled exile in dark, damp Kimbolton Castle three years later.

Anne Boleyn (c. 1500–36): married 1533; executed 1536. Henry truly loved Anne—just not while they were married.

She, too, fell out of Henry's favor for not producing a son (their only child would later rule as Queen Elizabeth I). She also had a knack for making enemies among powerful members of Henry's court. Those same enemies, taking advantage of Henry's growing infatuation with Anne's lady-in-waiting, Jane Seymour, pinned trumped-up charges of adultery, witchcraft, and treason on Anne that cost her her head in 1536.

Jane Seymour (1509–37): married 1536, died 1537. Only days after Anne's head rolled, Henry rolled the matrimonial dice with Jane Seymour. Jane produced the male heir Henry longed for (the future Edward VI) in October 1537 but died of complications from childbirth two weeks later. Her reward was to be the only one of Henry's wives to be buried with him in his Windsor Castle tomb.

Anne of Cleves (1515–57): married January 1540, divorced July 1540. Henry agreed to marry Anne of Cleves in order to gain her brother, the Duke of Cleves, as an ally against France. Upon first glance of Anne, Henry called her a "Flanders mare" and declared his dislike. He married her anyway in January 1540, but his gaze quickly turned to the younger and prettier Catherine Howard. Anne, looking to save her neck, agreed to an annulment seven months later. The man who arranged the marriage, Henry's chief minister, Thomas Cromwell, was beheaded shortly after.

Catherine Howard (c. 1522–42): married 1540, executed 1542. Henry fell hard for Catherine Howard, whom he married 19 days after his annulment from Anne of Cleves. But the 49-year-old Henry lacked the sexual oomph to satisfy teenage Catherine, who began to seek satisfaction from men her age. The jilted Henry had her beheaded for adultery in February 1542.

Katherine Parr (1512–48): married 1543, widowed 1547. Henry took his final marital plunge with the twice-widowed Katherine Parr. Their marriage nearly ended over religious differences, but after patching things up they got along swimmingly— until Henry died in 1547, making Katherine a widow yet again.

The Ingredients of Love Potion No. 9

Love potions have long been credited with having major magical influences over the whims and woes of human attraction. And they just might work.

❋ ❋ ❋ ❋

I Put a Spell on You

IN THE SECOND century A.D., Roman writer and philosopher Apuleius allegedly concocted a potion that snagged him a rather wealthy widow. Relatives of the widow brought Apuleius to court, claiming the potion had subverted the woman's true wishes. Apuleius argued that the potion (supposedly made with shellfish, lobsters, spiced oysters, and cuttlefish) had restored his wife's vivacity and spirit—and the court ended up ruling in his favor.

Love potions have been the stuff of history and legend since ancient times. These alluring elixirs played a major role in both Greek and Egyptian mythology and even made an appearance in the 2004 fairy-tale flick *Shrek 2*. In the movie, the Fairy Godmother gives the King of Far Far Away a bottled potion that is intended to make Fiona fall in love with the first man she kisses.

Turpentine and Indian Ink?

The bottle in *Shrek 2* was marked with Roman numeral IX, a clear nod to the formula made famous in "Love Potion No. 9," which was recorded by The Clovers in 1959 and The Searchers in 1963. According to the song, penned by legendary songwriters Jerry Leiber and Mike Stoller, the ingredients for the concoction "smelled like turpentine, and looked like Indian ink."

Doesn't sound too appealing, huh? Well, it apparently did enough to help a guy who was "a flop with chicks." That is, until he "kissed a cop down on 34th and Vine."

At any rate, if you're a forlorn lover looking to make a little magic of your own, you just might be in luck. In the mid-1990s, Leiber and Stoller worked with former guitarist and part-time perfumer Mara Fox to develop a trademarked cologne spray bearing the name of their hit song.

According to the label, Love Potion #9 is made with water, SD40B alcohol, isopropyl myristate, isopropyl alcohol, and the fragrances of citrus and musk. Can this cool, clean scent really heighten your passion and arousal and make you attractive to the opposite sex?

Hey, if George Clooney or Angelina Jolie happens to be in the area, it certainly wouldn't hurt to dab a little on, just in case. However, the perfume does come with a disclaimer: "No guarantee of success is granted or implied."

---

* Insomnia is the top health complaint reported to American doctors. Lower back pain is the top physical problem.

* In 1900, the average white woman's life expectancy was only 48.7 years. For women of color, the life expectancy was 33.5 years.

* Brussels sprouts are ranked as the most hated vegetable in America.

* Your stomach creates a new mucous layer every two weeks.

* Your body produces 300 billion new cells every day.

* America goes through 12 billion bananas in a typical year.

* Humans are among only 3 percent of mammals that practice monogamy.

* Breast reduction is the fifth most popular plastic surgery procedure for men.

* Thomas Edison preferred to do his reading in Braille, and he proposed to his wife in Morse code.

Two Genders Are Quite Enough, Thank You

Aren't dating and marriage complicated enough as it is? Imagine having to contend with dozens of genders. We'd never stop yelling at each other. But if you put relationship difficulties aside, it seems like it would make better sense to have a plethora of sexes—or maybe even just one.

✳   ✳   ✳   ✳

We're Here to Reproduce

BIOLOGICALLY SPEAKING, THE main mission in life is reproduction. In a species with only two sexes, you can mate with only 50 percent of the population, assuming the sexes are distributed equally. If you added a third sex, you could mate with two-thirds of the population. And in a species with only one sex, you could mate with 100 percent of the population. From this point of view, two is actually the worst possible number of sexes for finding a mate. Why, then, do almost all animal species have only two sexes?

According to the leading scientific theories, human beings and other animals are divided into two sexes because of "mitochondria"—specialized microscopic power plants. Mitochondria exist inside all your cells, converting the chemical energy stored in the food that you eat into a form of energy that your body can use. Without mitochondria, life as we know it could not exist.

Mitochondria share many of their features with primitive bacteria—in fact, scientists now suggest that our mitochondria actually evolved *from* bacteria, millions and millions of years ago. The prevailing theory is that, in the far-off mists of time, a single-celled organism engulfed a bacterium, probably in an attempt to eat it.

But instead, the two worked out a symbiotic relationship—the organism gave food to the bacterium, which, in turn, produced a vast amount of energy that the organism could use to sustain a higher level of development.

Even though our mitochondria seem to have once been an independent form of life, they are now firmly integrated as components of our cells. But there's still a genetic holdover from their bacterial origin. Normally when we think of DNA, we picture the genetic information inscribed on the chromosomes inside the nuclei of our cells—the genetic material that determines our hair and skin and eye colors, helps shape our personalities, and controls the creation of almost every component of our cells. Every component, that is, except those mysterious mitochondria. That's because each mitochondrion has its own internal DNA (called mitochondrial DNA or mtDNA), stored on a simple loop. It's more like the primitive DNA of bacteria than the complex chromosomes in a cell nucleus.

Thanks, Mom

Another major difference between your mitochondrial DNA and your normal DNA is that you inherit your mtDNA entirely from your mother (and from her mother, and from her mother's mother, and so on). This has led scientists to theorize that there's a serious evolutionary advantage—although they don't agree on what exactly it is—if only one parent's mtDNA is passed on to the couple's offspring. According to this theory, the biological differences between the two sexes first emerged as a way to ensure that only one parent in a couple could give mtDNA to the next generation.

In early organisms, the differences between the two sexes—let's call them passers and nonpassers—were slight. But over millions of years of evolution, the organisms became more complex and each of the two sexes grew increasingly distinct. Eventually, the passers became female and the nonpassers were male.

There are a few species with multiple versions of males—almost like a third sex. Some harvester ant species have a type of male that produces worker ants and another type that makes queens.

Weird Ways to Attract True Love

It's likely that you or one of your single friends spends a good deal of time complaining about how difficult it is to meet people worth dating. Problem solved! These strange customs from all over the world give single people inventive ways to find true love. Go get an apple and we'll show you.

✳ ✳ ✳ ✳

An Apple a Day...

IN ELIZABETHAN TIMES, it was desirable for a girl to peel an apple and stick it under her armpit until it was saturated with sweat. The girl would then give it to her potential beau so that he could inhale her heavenly scent. We figure most men would prefer a hanky scented with Chanel N°5, but whatever works.

Eat Your Greens

Ladies, a few directions: Go to Ireland. Find a shamrock. Eat said shamrock while thinking of your true love. Wait for the gentleman to arrive, fully in love with you. In certain parts of Ireland, this custom is said to work like a (lucky) charm.

Backyard Safari

If you can spare the time on Valentine's Day, go on a little wild-life trek to help clarify your romantic future and streamline your selection process. According to old European folktales, the types of animals you see on February 14 foretell the person that you'll end up marrying. Squirrels mean you'll find a cheapskate; gold-finch sightings point to a millionaire; a robin means you'll marry a crime fighter. And if you should find a glove that day, the owner of the other glove is your true love.

Pillaging, Etc.

If you're a warrior or male tribal member who happens to be looking for love, why not try the ancient custom of a hostile takeover? They're always dramatic, and you don't have to worry about a curfew. But beware: If your new bride's family comes looking for her, you have to hide out with her for as long as it takes the moon to go through a full cycle.

Spooning

Dating back to 17th-century Wales, men carved spoons when they had a crush on a woman. Much like the secret codes in flower-giving (i.e., red roses=love, daisies=loyalty, etc.), the spoons were carved with various embellishments that let the girl know the man's intentions. Vines meant that feelings continued to grow, for example, and a circle inside a square signified a desire for children.

Victorian Dating Bureaucracy

If you think the politics of dating are weird today, you don't know how good we have it. In the Victorian age, dating among the elite was more complicated than filing taxes. First of all, nothing happened without a chaperone, and everything usually took place in full view of the entire family/town. Before a man could even speak to a woman, he had to be formally introduced. After that, he gave her his card. If the young lady was interested, he might be able to take her out for a stroll. Ironically, many "bodice-ripping" books and films are set in the Victorian era, which just goes to show that nothing makes for a good story like repressed erotic love.

Sniffin' for Love

A study at the University of New Mexico found that when some women are ovulating, their sense of smell is seriously elevated, allowing them to evaluate how attracted a man is to them just by sniffing his worn shirts.

Say What?

Love doesn't make the world go round. Love is what makes the ride worthwhile.

—FRANKLIN P. JONES

The Baddest of the Bad Boys

What is it about bad boys that women find so appealing? And what about those infamous guys who, despite their horrible deeds, still seem to attract the ladies? Maybe it's as poet Sylvia Plath once wrote, "Every woman adores a fascist."

❋ ❋ ❋ ❋

ADOLF HITLER REPORTEDLY had a relationship with his 20-year-old half-niece, Geli Raubal, who eventually shot herself. He had several more girlfriends: Fran Hoffman, Jenny Hang, and Helene Hanfstaengl (who prevented Hitler from killing himself). Teenager Eva Braun, whom Hitler met in 1929, became Frau Hitler on April 29, 1945—less than 24 hours before they killed themselves as the Allies closed in on them.

Hitler contemporary and cohort Joseph Stalin was married to Ekaterina Svanidze, who passed away. Nadezhda Alliluyeva was wife number two, but she later committed suicide (although some allege Stalin murdered her). It was speculated that Stalin was secretly married a third time to his mistress, Rosa Kaganovich.

Commune leader Charles Manson first moved in with UC Berkeley librarian Mary Brunner. Soon he convinced Brunner to allow more than a dozen women to move in with them. Later, Manson moved to Spahn Ranch with his infamous "Manson family," made up mostly of his female lovers. The infamous 1969 Tate-LaBianca murders were committed by some of these women, following Manson's instruction.

Brothers Lyle and Erik Menendez both married pen pals they met while serving life sentences for the 1989 murders of their parents. Erik and wife Tammi have been married since 1998, but their only contact is in the prison's public visiting area.

Some women waste no time: Scott Peterson, convicted in 2005 of murdering his wife and unborn child, had barely been on death row an hour when he got his first proposal!

Bizarre Truths About High (and Low) Technology

Ready, Set, Flush

Don't let this one keep you up at night. If everyone flushed the toilet at the same time, mayhem wouldn't ensue, and we wouldn't see our pipes burst or sewage flowing in the street.

✳ ✳ ✳ ✳

A Primer on Pipes

LET'S REVIEW SEWAGE 101. When you flush your toilet, the water and waste flow through a small pipe that leads to a wider pipe that runs out of your house. If you have a septic tank, your waste's fantastic voyage ends there—in a big concrete tub buried under your yard. But if your pipes are connected to a city sewer system, the waste still has a ways to go: The pipe from your house leads to a bigger pipe that drains the commodes of your entire neighborhood; that pipe, in turn, leads to a bigger pipe that connects a bunch of neighborhoods, which leads to a bigger pipe, and so on. It's a network that contains miles and miles of pipe.

Eventually, all the waste reaches a sewage treatment plant. The pipes slant steadily downward toward the plant so gravity can keep things moving. Where the terrain makes this impossible, pumps are used to move the sewage uphill. Fortunately for us, the pipes at each stage are large enough to accommodate the unpleasant ooze that results from all the flushing, bathing, and dishwashing that goes on in the connected households, even at peak usage times.

It's true that if an entire city got together and really tried, it could overwhelm its sewage system—pumping stations and treatment plants can only deal with so much water at a time, and pipes have a fixed capacity, too. Sewage would overflow from manholes and eventually come up through everyone's drains. But toilet flushes alone aren't enough to wreak such horrific havoc.

A flush typically uses between 1.5 and 3.5 gallons of water. (Federal law mandates that no new toilet can use more than 1.6 gallons of water per flush, but older toilets use more.) There's plenty of room for that amount of water in the pipes that lead out of your house—even if you flush all your toilets at once. Similarly, if an entire city were to flush as one, there would still be space to spare. To create a true river of slime, you and your neighbors would have to run your showers, dishwashers, and washing machines continuously; you could even add a flush or two for good measure. (Note that every area's sewer system is self-contained; flushing in unison all over the world wouldn't make things worse in any particular city.)

Frightening Flushes

Despite all of this, the fear that such a calamity could occur has inspired some persistent urban legends, like the so-called Super Bowl Flush. In 1984, a water main in Salt Lake City broke during halftime of the big game, and reporters initially said that it was the result of a mass rush to the can. In reality, it was just a coincidence—mains had been breaking regularly in Salt Lake City at the time. But the story stuck, so when the Super Bowl approaches, you're bound to hear that it's best to stagger your flushes at halftime—for the good of the city.

Odd Scientific Experiments

Popular culture often credits scientists with a sort of noble eccentricity. Sometimes, though, even a genuine experiment can seem less off the bell curve and more off the bell tower.

✳ ✳ ✳ ✳

Will Eat Vomit to Graduate

IN 1804, STUBBINS H. FFIRTH, a medical student at the University of Pennsylvania, set out to prove that yellow fever could not be transmitted from person to person. He smeared himself with blood, urine, sweat, saliva, and fresh black vomit from yellow fever patients. When this failed to make him ill, Ffirth heated more vomit in a sand bath and inhaled the fumes. Then he made the residue into pills, swallowed them, and chased them with more vomit. Having emerged from this crucible in glowing health, Ffirth wrote up the results of his work for his graduation thesis. (For the record: Yellow fever is highly contagious, but it is most effectively transmitted by mosquitoes directly into the bloodstream. Ffirth was incredibly lucky.)

Gua, the "Human" Ape

If a human child raised by wolves starts acting like a wolf, would a baby chimp adopted by humans begin to act human? This was the question Winthrop Kellogg sought to answer in 1931 when he adopted a 7½-month-old female chimp named Gua. For the next nine months, Kellogg's baby son, Donald, had a "sister." The two were treated exactly the same by adults, and soon Gua was playing with her "brother," kissing her "parents," opening and closing doors, wearing clothes and shoes, eating with a spoon, and even walking upright—all the same tasks that Donald learned. The only thing she could not master was speech. One can only imagine what she might have said.

Which Is Worse: Nail Biting or Sleep Deprivation?

In the summer of 1942, Lawrence LeShan of the College of William and Mary in Williamsburg, Virginia, tried to get a group of boys to stop biting their nails through subliminal messages. While the boys slept, LeShan played a record in their dormitory with one single phrase recorded on it: "My fingernails taste terribly bitter." When the record player broke down, LeShan took up the slack by repeating the phrase himself all night. By the end of the summer, 40 percent of the boys had kicked the habit, but LeShan was presumably ready for a long nap.

Bow-Wow Holy Cow

In 1954, Soviet surgeon Vladimir Demikhov presented a bizarre creature to the world: an adult German shepherd with the head, neck, and front legs of a puppy grafted onto its neck. The heads snarled at each other, nibbled each other's ears, and lapped milk in tandem. Demikhov created 20 such Frankenpups, but none lived for more than a month before tissue rejection set in. Demikhov's main research focus was cardiology and the development of surgical techniques for heart transplants. He even performed the first canine heart transplant in 1946, followed by a lung transplant on a dog the following year.

Remote-Control Bull

In 1965, Jose Delgado, a professor at the Yale School of Medicine, stepped into a bull-fighting ring in Spain. A bull was released and charged the matador's red cape, but moments before the beast's horns made contact, the professor pressed a button on a radio transmitter, and the bull braked to a halt. The professor then pressed another button, and the animal trotted away. The day before, Delgado had implanted several wires into the bull's brain, and he was now effectively remote-controlling—or at least remotely influencing—the bull's movements. He performed similar experiments on other animals and undoubtedly influenced countless science-fiction writers through his work.

Impending Doom

In the early 1960s, the U.S. Army loaded ten soldiers into an airplane for what was supposed to be a routine training mission. Mid-flight, one of the propellers failed, and the pilot announced over the intercom that the plane was about to crash into the ocean. A steward then began distributing insurance forms for the soldiers to fill out. After the last one was finished, the pilot suddenly revved the propeller back up and made a second announcement: The emergency had been a joke. The Army was simply conducting an experiment on whether people made more mistakes under the stress of imminent death. The soldiers must have gotten a kick out of that one.

Tripping Elephant

On August 3, 1962, psychiatrists from the University of Oklahoma injected 297 milligrams of LSD into the rump of a 14-year-old elephant named Tusko. They wanted to determine whether the acid—3,000 times the typical human dose—would plunge the animal into musth, which is a natural state of temporary madness and sexual aggression that bull elephants periodically experience, typically in association with the rutting season. Things didn't go quite as the researchers had planned: After stumbling and lurching around his pen, poor Tusko keeled over dead. Defending themselves later to the public, the researchers claimed that they hadn't expected such a severe reaction to the drug, since some of them used LSD themselves.

Brains vs. Body

What does it take to excite a turkey? This important question was investigated by Penn State University researchers Martin Schein and Edgar Hale in the 1960s. It turns out that a female turkey really doesn't need much to arouse a male turkey's interest—she doesn't even require a body. When researchers constructed a lifelike model of a female turkey and then dismantled it piece by piece, they observed that the males retained interest in the "female" even when nothing remained of the model except for a head on a stick. Oddly enough, the same males showed little interest in courting a female body that didn't have a head.

Life Before Alarm Clocks

Imagine how difficult it was to wake up before good old clock radios and other loud-sounding devices existed. Fortunately, there were some workarounds.

✳ ✳ ✳ ✳

The Knocker-Up

EVERYONE HAS A trick for waking up on time. Some people put the alarm clock across the room so that they have to get out of bed to turn it off; some set the clock ahead by ten or fifteen minutes to try to fool themselves into thinking that it's later than it is; some set multiple alarms; and some—those boring Goody Two-Shoes types—simply go to bed at a reasonable hour and get enough sleep.

We don't necessarily rely on it every day, and some of us definitely don't obey it very often, but just about everybody has an alarm clock. How did people ever wake up before these modern marvels existed?

Many of the tough problems in life have a common solution: Hire someone else to do it. Long ago in England, you could hire a guy to come by each morning and, using a long pole, knock on your bedroom window to wake you up so that you would get to work on time. This practice began during the Industrial Revolution of the late 18th century, when getting to work on time was a new and innovative idea. (In the grand tradition of British terminology that makes Americans snicker, the pole operator was known as a "knocker-up.") There's no word on how said pole operator managed to get himself up on time, but we can guess.

The Alarm Clock Within

The truth is, you don't need any type of alarm, and you never did. Or so science tells us. Your body's circadian rhythms give you a sort of natural wake-up call via your body temperature's daily fluctuation. It rises every morning regardless of when you went to bed. Studies conducted at Harvard University seem to indicate that this rising temperature wakes us up (if the alarm hasn't already gone off).

Another study, conducted at the University of Lubeck in Germany, found that people have an innate ability to wake themselves up very early if they anticipate it beforehand. One night, the researchers told 15 subjects that they would be awakened at 6:00 A.M.

Around 4:30 A.M., the researchers noticed that the subjects began to experience a rise in the stress hormone adrenocorticotropin. On the other two nights, the subjects were told that they would get a 9:00 A.M. wake-up call—but those diligent scientists shook them out of bed three hours early, at 6:00 A.M. And this time, the adrenocorticotropin levels of the subjects held steady in the early morning hours.

It seems, then, that humans relied on their bodies to rouse them from the dream world long before a knocker-up or an alarm clock ever existed.

✳ **"Texas" evolved from the Caddo Indian greeting** *te shas.* **Since there is no "sh" sound in Spanish, early explorers and missionaries writing about their travels replaced the unfamiliar syllable with an "x" to make "te xas."**

✳ **The longest overdue book in the United States is 145 years (in Ohio). The longest in the world is 288 years (in Germany). We can't even imagine the late fees.**

✳ **Roses are the symbol of the Virgin Mary. Catholic "rosaries" were originally made of 165 dried and rolled rose petals.**

✳ **Disney's Space Mountain roller coaster was the first thrill attraction to be operated by a computer.**

The Mushroom Cloud

It's one of the most menacing, awe-inspiring sights there is—the result of a nuclear explosion.

✳   ✳   ✳   ✳

ANYONE WHO GREW up during the Cold War remembers the old "duck and cover" school drill. The fire alarm would go off, and students would dive beneath their desks and curl into a fetal position. (Did anyone really believe those desks would provide protection during a nuclear attack?) In those days, the threat of nuclear war seemed very real, and nothing symbolized it more powerfully than the image of a mushroom cloud.

Of course, we could just as easily be calling it a cauliflower cloud; a raspberry cloud; or, in one of the least-catchy nick-names of the 20th century, a "convoluting brain cloud." Each of these terms was bandied about after the first nuclear tests in the 1940s. Regardless of what it is called, the cloud formed by a nuclear explosion remains unique.

When a nuclear device is detonated, an almost incomprehensible amount of thermal energy is released, which creates a massive fireball that incinerates everything below it (as was the case in Hiroshima and Nagasaki during World War II). As the fireball rises into the air, convection currents (the same physical principle that forces hot water through radiators) rush after it, sucking up debris into a column. Eventually, the fireball reaches the peak of its upward movement and expands outward, creating the mushroom-shape head.

This physical process occurs in other forms of explosions as well, including volcanic eruptions. It can even be mimicked by a certain type of cloud called the cumulonimbus, which is often a harbinger of a tornado.

Nowadays, the threat of a nuclear holocaust seems minimal. Still, it can't hurt to keep a school desk nearby, just in case.

A Shocking Invention: The Electric Chair

Electrocution was meant to be a more humane form of execution, but things didn't exactly work out that way.

✳   ✳   ✳   ✳

Alfred Southwick's Lightbulb Moment

DR. ALFRED SOUTHWICK was a dentist in Buffalo, New York, but he was no simple tooth-driller. Like many of his contemporaries in the Gilded Age of the 1870s and 1880s, he was a broad-minded man who kept abreast of the remarkable scientific developments of the day—like electricity. Though the phenomenon of electric current had been known about for some time, the technology of electricity was fresh—lightbulbs and other electric inventions had begun to be mass produced, and the infrastructure that brought electricity into the businesses and homes of the well-to-do was appearing in the largest cities.

So Southwick's ears perked up when he heard about a terrible accident involving this strange new technology. A man had walked up to one of Buffalo's recently installed generators and decided to see what all the fuss was about. Despite protests from the men working on the machinery, he touched something he shouldn't have and, to the shock of the onlookers, died instantly. Southwick pondered the situation with a cold, scientific intelligence and wondered if the instant and apparently painless high-voltage death could be put to good use.

Southwick's interest in electrocution wasn't entirely morbid. Execution was much on people's minds in those days. Popular movements advocated doing away with executions entirely, while more moderate reformers simply wanted a more humane method of putting criminals to death. Hangings had fallen out of favor due to the potential for gruesome accidents, often caused by the incompetence of hangmen. While the hangman's goal was to break the criminal's neck instantly, a loose knot could result in an agonizingly slow suffocation; a knot that was too tight had the potential to rip a criminal's head clean off.

To prove the worth of his idea, Southwick began experimenting on dogs (you don't want to know) and discussing the results with other scientists and inventors. He eventually published his work and attracted enough attention to earn himself an appointment on the Gerry Commission, which was created by the New York State Legislature in 1886 and tasked with finding the most humane method of execution.

The three-person commission investigated several alternatives, but eventually it settled on electrocution—in part because Southwick had won the support of the most influential inventor of the day, Thomas Alva Edison, who had developed the incandescent lightbulb and was trying to build an empire of generators and wires to supply (and profit from) the juice that made his lightbulbs glow. Edison provided influential confirmation that an electric current could produce instant death; the legislature was convinced, and a law that made electrocution the state's official method of execution was passed.

William Kemmler Gets Zapped

On August 6, 1890, after much technical debate and a few experiments on animals, axe murderer William Kemmler became the first convicted criminal to be electrocuted. Southwick declared it a success, but reporters who witnessed it felt otherwise. Kemmler had remained alive after the first jolt, foam oozing from the mask over his face as he struggled to breathe. A reporter fainted. A second jolt of several minutes was applied, and Kemmler's clothes and body caught fire. The stench of burned flesh was terrible.

Despite a public outcry, the state of New York remained committed to the electric method of execution. The technology and technique were improved, and eventually other states began to use electrocution as well. Today, nine states still allow use of the electric chair, though lethal injection is the preferred option.

Boats in Bottles

People have been putting stuff in empty bottles for centuries. But getting a model ship into one of those tiny glass tubes seems to be a particularly delicate trick.

✳   ✳   ✳   ✳

The Art of Bottling

BEFORE SHIPS CAUGHT on, "patience bottles" were filled with scenes of religious imagery (Jesus on the cross, for example), and aptly named "mining bottles" had multilevel scenes of ore mining. The earliest mining bottle, which dates to 1719, was created by Matthias Buchinger, a well-known entertainer of the time who had no arms or legs. Mining bottles originated in what is now Hungary.

People started shoving ships into bottles in the mid- to late 18th century. Most people did not write the dates on their creations, and since many were made with old bottles that had been sitting around, the date on the actual bottle doesn't necessarily mean that's when the ship was put in it. The earliest ship in a bottle that someone bothered to date (on the sails) was constructed in 1784. Bottling ships really caught on in the 1830s, when clear glass became more common. It is still a popular hobby these days, with clubs and associations around the world devoted to the skill.

Sleight of Hand

But how do you get that boat into the bottle? It's actually pretty simple (not easy, but simple). The hull (or bottom of the boat) is narrow enough to fit through the neck of the bottle. The masts are hinged so that they can be pushed flat against the hull. While the ship is outside the bottle, the sails are attached, and a string is tied to the mast. The masts and sails are bent so they lie flat on the deck, and then the whole thing is pushed through the bottleneck. Glue or putty on the bottom of the bottle keeps the ship anchored. Once the ship is in, a long tool, shaped like a rod or skewer, is used to position it. Finally, the string that is attached to the masts is pulled to bring up the sails and complete the illusion.

There are some types of boats—motorboats, for example— that are too wide to get into the bottle in one piece. These are assembled inside the bottle using rods, which takes a lot of patience and a steady hand.

Getting a ship out of a bottle? Easy—navigate it toward an iceberg or a jagged rock.

---

* In the 10th century, the Grand Vizier of Persia, Abdul Kassem Ismael, carried 117,000 books with him as he traveled. It took 400 camels to carry the volumes.

* The average human being sheds as many as 40,000 dead skin cells every minute.

* In 1966, radio pioneer Gordon McLendon bought KGLA-FM in Los Angeles, changed the call letters to KADS-FM, and aired only commercials. He returned the station to "regular programming" in 1967.

* The first time an instant replay was seen on TV was during an Army-Navy football game on December 7, 1963. CBS director Tony Verna masterminded the idea.

* Candy bars in the early part of the 20th century included Chicken Dinner and Chick-O-Stick (neither of which contained chicken) and Baby Lobster bar (which was seafood-free).

* More than 25 percent of all the gold in the world is held in a vault in New York City. It's owned by 122 countries and organizations that buy, sell, and trade it there.

* The launch of the shuttle *Discovery* was once delayed after woodpeckers pecked holes in the spacecraft's foam insulation. Decoy plastic owls, purchased at Wal-Mart, deterred the woodpeckers and solved the problem.

Sparks

*You've always been told never to put metal
in a microwave, right? Here's why.*

✳ ✳ ✳ ✳

MICROWAVE OVENS WORK by permeating your food with
microwave radiation. That sounds a little scary, but don't
worry: We're not talking about the kind of radiation that gave
us the giant lizard that stomped Tokyo. Instead, this radiation
excites the water molecules that make up a large portion of
every kind of food we eat. The vibrating water molecules start
to get hot, which in turn heats the food.

Simple so far, right? It gets a little trickier. Metal responds quite
differently to the electromagnetic field that a microwave oven
creates. Unlike water, which can absorb the microwave energy,
metal *reflects* the radiation. And the energy of the electromagnetic field can also cause a charge to build up in metal—
especially if the metal is thin and pointy, like the tines of a fork,
the handle of a Chinese take-out box, or the decorative rim on
your Young Elvis commemorative plate.

When enough of a charge builds up, all of that energy in the
metal can leap joyfully through the air. We see this leap as a
spark—like a small-scale bolt of lightning. These arcs of electricity are most likely to emanate from sharp edges, like the tines of a
fork or the ridges of crumpled aluminum foil. A solid object with
no sharp edges should be okay, because any electrical charge that
develops is more likely to spread itself around evenly.

But even then, there's a danger—the metal could reflect the
microwave radiation back at the magnetron tube that creates
the electromagnetic field. This could damage the magnetron
tube, and then you'd be stuck with a useless microwave.

So here's an equation for you: metal + microwave = really bad
idea. Stick to zapping only food.

Lights, Camera, Technicolor!

Moving pictures were astonishing to the audiences who first saw them. It wasn't too hard to get used to seeing them in black and white. But when movies went to color, all of a sudden, that was like real life.

✳ ✳ ✳ ✳

Tripping the Shutter

THE MARVEL OF moving pictures was first demonstrated by Californian Eadweard Muybridge, who set up a series of 24 still cameras at a racetrack in Palo Alto, California, in 1878. The shutter of each camera was connected to a string; as the horse galloped by, the strings were tripped, and each camera captured an image. Muybridge fashioned a crude process to project the images in sequence, demonstrating his process to an art society in San Francisco in 1880.

Inventor Thomas Edison set up a lab in West Orange, New Jersey, and patented a 35mm motion picture camera called the Kinetograph in 1891. The novelty of moving pictures quickly became big business in the entertainment world at the turn of the 20th century. Edison hired Edwin S. Porter, a camera technician, in 1900. Porter quickly realized that entire stories could be told with film, and he proceeded to do just that. Other major film studios opened in Chicago but, by the mid-teens, inclement weather and labor issues there drove filmmakers to sunny Southern California.

Problems Persist

As the film industry continued to grow, several issues remained. The cinema was silent and images were black-and-white— hardly realistic. During the 1920s, feature films were usually accompanied by live piano or organ music, improvised by the theater musician as action unfolded on the screen. Some studios tried to increase the visual experience by hand-tinting certain scenes in various washes of color.

Color movies had been tried with limited success in England. Known as Kinemacolor, the process involved special cameras and projectors that used black-and-white film with two colored filters. But the result was questionable, producing fringed and haloed effects that distracted from the projected image. Even so, more than 50 American films had been produced with the Kinemacolor process by the late teens.

The Color of Money

Technicolor picked up where Kinemacolor left off. Three chemical and mechanical experts named Kalmus, Comstock, and Wescott recognized the need for a realistic color film stock and created the Technicolor Company in 1915 (taking Tech from their alma mater, Massachusetts Institute of Technology). Their two-color dye process gained limited use for some sequences in epics from the 1920s, including *The Phantom of the Opera*, *The Ten Commandments*, *King of Kings*, and *Ben-Hur*. By 1933, the two-color process had reached talking pictures with *The Mystery of the Wax Museum*.

Still, Technicolor was garish and didn't look real. Kalmus convinced Walt Disney to try a new, refined three-color Technicolor process on his animated short *Flowers and Trees*. The result was a breathtaking success: an Academy Award for Disney and a contract to produce all future Disney films in Technicolor (which remained in force until the Hollywood Technicolor plant closed in 1975).

The new Technicolor process used a series of filters, prisms, and lenses to create three films: a red, blue, and green record. The three were then combined, and the result was a three-strip print. The success of this film stock was not lost on Hollywood, as budgets were increased to allow for color productions. While black-and-white features, such as *Citizen Kane*, *Casablanca*, and *Treasure of Sierra Madre*, became classics from the 1930s and '40s, Technicolor became part of the visual story for such '30s blockbuster films as *Robin Hood*, *The Wizard of Oz*, and *Gone with the Wind*.

Aging Somewhat Gracefully

By the 1950s, television had taken a large bite out of movie-going America. To fight back, Hollywood tried gimmicks such as wide screens (CinemaScope and VistaVision, for example) and three-dimensional projection (3-D). Technicolor continued to thrive and was used for 3-D features including *House of Wax* and *Dial M for Murder*. But by the 1970s, the costs for Technicolor prints had become very high, and the dye process was too slow to serve the country's theaters with enough prints. *The Godfather* and *The Godfather: Part II* were among the last films to use the Technicolor process.

---

* Both the Republican Party and the Democratic Party owe the popularization of their respective mascots—the elephant and the donkey—to a political cartoonist of the 1870s, Thomas Nast of *Harper's Weekly*.

* Founding Father George Washington was a distant relation of King Edward I, Queen Elizabeth II, Sir Winston Churchill, and General Robert E. Lee.

* One of the U.S. presidents was not a U.S. citizen at his time of death: John Tyler, a Virginia native, died on January 18, 1862, a citizen of the Southern Confederacy.

* West Virginia is the only state to have formed by seceding from a preexisting state.

* The original Library of Congress was burned down by the British in 1814 along with the Capitol. To replace it, the Congress bought Thomas Jefferson's personal book collection, which consisted of approximately 6,500 volumes.

* *Time* magazine rarely deviates from the familiar red band on its covers. A black band commemorated the terrorist attacks of September 11, 2001, and a green band celebrated the environment on April 28, 2008.

* The United States has more country-music–playing radio stations than any other music format.

The Smelliest Things on the Planet

A skunk is synonymous with stink—but there are worse odors out there, some of which have been concocted by humans.

❋　❋　❋　❋

Records Are Made to Be Broken

PERHAPS THE SKUNK gets a bad rap. When someone wants to describe an object—or perhaps an acquaintance—as stinking up the place, the poor skunk is invariably used as a reference point.

It's true that *Guinness World Records* lists butyl seleno-mercaptan, an ingredient in the skunk's defensive burst, among the worst-smelling chemicals in nature. According to scientists and laboratory tests in various parts of the world, however, there are far fouler odors than a skunk's spray. Some of the most offensive of them are made by humans. Dr. Anne Marie Helmenstine, writing in *Your Guide to Chemistry*, suggests that a couple of molecular compounds—which were invented specifically to be incredibly awful—could top the list.

Who-Me?

One such compound is named Who-Me? This sulfur-based chemical requires five ingredients to produce a stench comparable to that of a rotting carcass. Who-Me? was created during World War II so that French resistance fighters could humiliate German soldiers by making them stink to high heaven. The stuff proved almost as awful for its handlers, who found it difficult to apply so that they, too, didn't wind up smelling like dead flesh.

For commercial craziness, consider the second compound cited by Helmenstine. American chemists developed a combination of eight molecules in an effort to re-create the smell of human feces. Why? To test the effectiveness of commercially produced air fresheners and deodorizers. Ever imaginative, the chemists named their compound "U.S. Government Standard Bathroom Malodor."

Stinky Cheese

For many people, cheese comes to mind when thinking of awful smells that make the eyes water. There is, in fact, an official smelliest cheese—a French delight called Vieux Boulogne. Constructed from cow's milk by Philippe Olivier, Vieux Boulogne was judged the world's smelliest cheese by 19 members of a human olfactory panel, plus an electronic nose developed at Cranfield University in England. London's *Guardian* newspaper insisted that Vieux Boulogne gave off an aroma of "barnyard dung" from a distance of 50 meters.

The Dreaded Bombardier Beetle

A skunk would have a hard time matching that cheese, and Pepé Le Pew might even take a backseat to the Bombardier beetle. This insect is armed with two chemicals, hydroquinone and hydrogen peroxide. When it feels threatened, the chemicals combine with an enzyme that heats the mixture. The creature then shoots a boiling, stinky liquid and gas from its rear. Humans unfortunate enough to have endured the experience claim that there's nothing worse.

No less a luminary than 19th-century naturalist Charles Darwin allegedly suffered both the smell and sting of the Bombardier beetle's spray when, during a beetle-collecting expedition, he put one in his mouth to free up a hand. Consider Darwin a genius if you like, but his common sense left something to be desired.

✳ **The eagle on the Great Seal of the United States faces the olive branch in its right talon. However, until 1945, the eagle on the Presidential Seal faced the arrows gripped in its left talon.**

✳ **Sportscaster Foster Hewitt is credited with being the first person to say, "He shoots! He scores!" It happened at a hockey game between 1931 and 1935.**

The Face of Technology

Hedy Lamarr's beauty camouflaged the genius that dwelled within.

✳ ✳ ✳ ✳

Beauty and Brains

CELL PHONES ARE a marvel of today's high technology. But you may be surprised to learn that a progenitor of modern telecommunications is actually a famous actress from the past.

Hedy Lamarr had a classically beautiful face that instantly stole men's hearts. Throughout the 1930s and '40s she was MGM's "It" girl, starring in such movies as *Samson and Delilah* and *Algiers*. But to tell of Lamarr's film exploits is to reveal only half the picture—this beauty was as smart as she was seductive.

Ahead of Her Time

Born in 1913 as Hedwig Eva Maria Kiesler, the Austrian-born beauty swapped monikers when she hit Hollywood in 1937. Not only was she gorgeous, Lamarr was also mathematically gifted and had a head for scientific thinking. It was through her first husband, a munitions manufacturer, that she first became interested in weapons and how they work.

When America entered World War II, Lamarr learned that radio-controlled missiles were being blocked when the enemy discovered their operational frequencies. She reasoned that if frequencies could be switched simultaneously at the transmitting *and* receiving ends, then the enemy couldn't block the signal. Her hunch was ultimately correct but ahead of its time. Nevertheless, with the aid of composer and inventor George Antheil, Lamarr would patent their "Secret Communication System" in 1942.

Lamarr's idea was updated and adopted by the U.S. Navy for use in its telecommunications sector in 1962. Years later, it would be applied to cellular technology. When asked her preference, acting or inventing, Lamarr replied, "Films have a certain place in a certain time period. Technology is forever."

The Ups and Downs of the Vomit Comet

This aptly named airplane has been used by NASA for more than 50 years to train astronauts and conduct experiments in a zero-gravity environment.

✳   ✳   ✳   ✳

THE VOMIT COMET simulates the absence of gravity by flying in a series of parabolas—arcs that resemble the paths of especially gut-wrenching roller coasters. When the Vomit Comet descends toward the earth, its passengers experience weightlessness for the 20 to 25 seconds it takes to reach the bottom of the parabola. Then the plane flies back up to repeat the maneuver, beginning a new dive from an altitude of over 30,000 feet.

Being weightless and buoyant might bring on nausea all by itself, but when the plane arcs, dips, and ascends again, the occupants feel about twice as heavy as usual. The wild ride induces many of its otherwise steely stomached passengers to vomit—hence, the name. (The plane is also called, by those with a greater sense of propriety, the Weightless Wonder.)

NASA has used the Vomit Comet to train astronauts for the Mercury, Gemini, Apollo, Skylab, Space Shuttle, and Space Station programs. The first Vomit Comets, unveiled in 1959 as part of the Mercury program, were C-131 Samaritans. A series of KC-135A Stratotankers came next. The NASA 930 was the most famous of these; it was used to film the scenes of space weightlessness in the 1995 movie *Apollo 13*. It is now on public display at Ellington Field, near Johnson Space Center in Houston.

After the 930 was put out to pasture, another KC-135A—the NASA 931, which was retired in 2004—took over. The 931 flew 34,757 parabolas, generating some 285 gallons of vomit. Yes, the engineers at NASA measured the barf.

You Don't Want to Play Catch with This Football

Don't start practicing your Heisman moves just yet. The nuclear football is less like a traditional pigskin and more like—actually, exactly like—a 45-pound leather-clad metal briefcase that belongs to the president of the United States.

✳   ✳   ✳   ✳

THE NUCLEAR FOOTBALL contains crucial information and plans that the president would need in the event of a nuclear war. No matter where the president goes, the football is within easy reach.

The nuclear football first became a presidential accessory during John F. Kennedy's administration. Shortly after the Cuban Missile Crisis, it sadly became apparent that the president should always be prepared to respond to a nuclear attack. The president doesn't have to carry the football personally, of course; that job is handled by a rotating staff of five military aides.

Officially known as the president's emergency satchel, its nickname originated with one of the government's early nuclear war plans, which was code-named "Dropkick." It is said to carry a secure satellite phone that can connect the president to the Pentagon and two emergency command centers that are bunkered in the mountains of Colorado and Pennsylvania. Other goodies include war plans, activation codes for launching nuclear weapons, and guidelines for where in the country the president should go during an emergency.

If you really did manage to play catch with the nuclear football, you'd probably barely even notice the pain in your back. You'd likely be much more focused on the gang of angry Secret Service agents pummeling you into submission.

New Uses for Cold War Relics

In response to the Cold War, the U.S. government began constructing secret nuclear missile complexes throughout the country. Each one housed a fully operational, locked-and-loaded nuclear missile that could be fired at will once the launch sequence was activated. But as the Cold War ended, the complexes were no longer needed. And by 1965, most of them were abandoned, leading to an interesting question: Just what does one do with a multimillion-dollar abandoned missile silo? More than you might think!

✳ ✳ ✳ ✳

School's a Blast!

IN 1969, THE Holton, Kansas, school district paid $1 million to the federal government for land that had been used to house a nuclear missile base until 1964. As ground was broken for the new Jackson Heights High School, many wondered what would be done with the abandoned silo. The answer was simple: Incorporate it into the school. And that's exactly what they did. They turned the silo's command center into a classroom, then they sealed off the missile bay doors and turned the bay into a bus garage.

The Ultimate Bachelor (Launch) Pad

Late one night in 1985, Bruce Townsley was watching *The Tonight Show* as Johnny Carson talked about people who were turning old missile silos into homes. From that point on, Townsley was obsessed. His dream finally came true in 1997, when he moved from Chicago to Oplin, Texas, and bought his very own missile silo.

Townsley has spent years working on the silo, which was originally one of several missile bases operated by Dyess Air Force Base. However, he still hasn't figured out what to do with the 185-foot-deep chamber that used to house the missile.

Nuclear Scuba

Because the silos were made to launch missiles, you might assume that visitors to one would spend their time looking up into the sky. Not so in Midland, Texas, where a silo has been converted into the world's largest indoor deep-diving training facility. Dive Valhalla, now part of Family Scuba Center, is an old ICBM (intercontinental ballistic missile) silo filled with water up to ground level. Divers gear up in the silo's old control room before moving on to where the missile was housed. From there, divers enter the water, where they can descend to depths of more than 120 feet, exploring the old silo as they go.

Titan Missile Museum

Because old missile silos have quite an allure, you don't need to do much to attract people to them. Case in point: the Titan Missile Museum in Sahuarita, Arizona. Declared a national historic landmark in 1994, the museum represents the only Titan II missile site in the United States that is open to the general public. Most of the silo has been preserved just as it was when it was operational in the 1960s, from the three-ton blast doors to the 103-foot Titan II ICBM in the launch duct. (Don't worry—the active warhead has been removed!) If you're looking to get a taste of doomsday, tours offer visitors the chance to sit through a simulated missile-launch sequence.

A Safe Place to Park Your Plane

If you're looking for a spacious silo to call your own, head to the Adirondack State Park in upstate New York, where in 2007 "the world's most unique luxury home" went on the market. Above ground, you'll get 2,000 square feet of living space, complete with a master suite and fireplace. If you'd like to spread out, just follow the 125-foot stairwell down to the silo and the launch control center, which offers an additional 2,300 square feet of luxurious living space, including marble floors and a whirlpool. If all of that isn't enough of a selling point, consider this: The silo/house even comes with its own private FAA/DOT-approved runway!

So Which Way Is North?

If, like most people, you think the topmost symbol on a compass always points north, take care not to get lost in the Southern Hemisphere.

✳ ✳ ✳ ✳

The North Magnetic Pole

NORTH, SOUTH, EAST, and west: These directions are meant to be set in stone, the unchangeable points of reference that lead sailors through treacherous seas and intrepid adventurers through mysterious, unknown lands. Yet even these directions, such stalwarts of clarity and precision, come with a medley of misconceptions and unexpected truths.

One misconception is that a compass points to the North Pole. In reality, a compass points toward Earth's Magnetic Pole, which is different from the geographic pole that you'll find on a map. Earth has a magnetic field, which is created by the swirling motion of molten lava that resides in its core. This magnetic field makes an angle with Earth's spin axis. The geographic poles, in contrast, are the places that Earth's imaginary spin axis passes straight through. So while the geographic and magnetic poles are close to each other, they are never in the exact same place. If you're heading "due north" as the compass reads, you're heading to the North Magnetic Pole, not the North Pole. But compasses don't work close to a magnetic pole, so if you're going to the North Pole, a compass will take you only so far.

To complicate matters further, the North Magnetic Pole is always moving, because the motion of the swirling lava changes. In 2005, the North Magnetic Pole was 503 miles from the geographic North Pole, placing it firmly in the Arctic Ocean, north of Canada. Meanwhile, the South Magnetic Pole was 1,756 miles from the geographic South Pole, in Antarctica just south of Australia. The rates of change of the magnetic poles vary, but lately they've been moving at approximately 25 miles per year.

Scientists project that in 50 years, the North Magnetic Pole will actually be in Siberia.

The South Magnetic Pole

On to misconception two—that the "N" on a compass always points north. Assuming the designation "north" always coincides with the notion of "up," the runaway North Magnetic Pole reminds us that "up" is relative. Earth is a sphere, so any single point could be designated as the arbitrary top, making whatever lies opposite the arbitrary bottom. It made sense for early mapmakers to draw the North Pole at the top of the map, their approximation of where the compass pointed. But as the North Magnetic Pole wanders from the point cartographers deemed the "North Pole," the designation of this geographical location as due north may eventually become obsolete.

Meanwhile, in the Southern Hemisphere, a compass points toward the South Magnetic Pole and more or less toward the corresponding yet inevitably inaccurate location that is deemed the geographic South Pole. Early mapmakers hailed from the Northern Hemisphere, so the North Pole is logically represented as being at the top of the map and the top of the world. Yet in the Southern Hemisphere, it would be equally logical to place the South Pole at the top of the map.

Say What?

Marriage can be viewed as the waiting room for death.

—MIKE MYERS

The path of least resistance is the path of the loser.

—H. G. WELLS

He was a self-made man who owed his lack of success to nobody.

—JOSEPH HELLER

Women should be obscene and not heard.

—GROUCHO MARX

Closer than You Think: An Elevator to Outer Space

Rockets are for suckers. Looking for a cheaper way to build space stations and launch satellites, NASA scientists have an idea that sounds ludicrous but that they swear is feasible: an elevator that reaches from Earth's surface to outer space.

✳ ✳ ✳ ✳

"**H**OW COULD AN elevator to outer space be possible?" you ask. The answer is nanotubes. Discovered in 1991, nanotubes are cylindrical carbon molecules that make steel look like a 98-pound weakling. A space elevator's main component would be a 60,000-odd-mile nanotube ribbon, measuring about as thin as a sheet of paper and about three feet wide.

It gets weirder. That ribbon would require a counterweight up at the top to keep it in place. The counterweight, hooked to the nanotube ribbon, would either be an asteroid pulled into Earth's orbit or a satellite. Once secured, the ribbon would have moving platforms attached to it. Each platform would be powered by solar-energy-reflecting lasers and could carry several thousand tons of cargo up to the top. The trip would take about a week. Transporting materials to outer space in this fashion would supposedly reduce the cost of, say, putting a satellite into orbit from about $10,000 a pound to about $100 a pound.

The base of the elevator would be a platform situated in the eastern Pacific Ocean, near the equator, safe from hurricanes and many miles clear of commercial airline routes. The base would be mobile so that the whole thing could be moved out of the path of potentially damaging space junk orbiting Earth. Although there are a lot of theoretical kinks to work out, the more optimistic of the scientists who have hatched this scheme believe the whole thing could be a reality within a couple of decades.

All That and a Corkscrew, Too?

A nation known for its neutrality comes up with the most versatile piece of military technology ever known.

✳ ✳ ✳ ✳

SWITZERLAND STAYS OUT of international disputes, so it's hard to imagine how its army became associated with what may be the best known, most beloved, and most commonly used piece of military hardware in the world—the Swiss Army Knife.

The distinctive multitool pocketknife was the brainchild of Swiss cutlery manufacturer Karl Elsener. A true patriot, Elsener bristled at the fact that Swiss soldiers got their standard-issue knives from a German manufacturer, and he set out to win the contract from his government. In the 1890s, he designed a unique spring mechanism for pocketknives that allows the handle to hold several blades. That was clever, but Elsener's true moment of genius came when he decided that he would include several basic tools in his knife—a can opener, a hole punch, and a screwdriver. According to some sources, it was the screwdriver that won over the Swiss military brass; the nation's infantry had just begun using a new type of rifle, and soldiers needed screwdrivers to perform basic maintenance on the weapon.

Elsener dubbed his creation the "Soldier's Knife" and followed it up with a lightweight version with a few more tools called the "Officer's and Sports Knife." Before long, handymen around the world were carrying them in their pockets, but it wasn't until World War II—when American GIs dubbed it the Swiss Army Knife—that the tool got the name we use today.

Elsener's company, Victorinox, is still in business, producing 34,000 knives a day in some 300 configurations. Almost any tool can be found on one model or another: corkscrew, wire strippers, toothpick, fish scaler, ruler, nail file, saw, chisel, magnifying glass, flashlight—even a ballpoint pen or a tracheotomy knife!

Who Needs a Radio When You've Got Dental Fillings?

It's not beyond the realm of possibility that you can pick up radio stations on your dental work.

✳ ✳ ✳ ✳

Lucy's Strange Story

IF YOU'VE WATCHED enough *Gilligan's Island*, you know that it can happen on TV. And maybe you've heard that it happened in real life to Lucille Ball of *I Love Lucy* fame. According to Jim Brochu, author of *Lucy in the Afternoon*, the actress claimed that her dental fillings picked up radio signals as she drove to her home outside Los Angeles in 1942. She also claimed that the signals were later traced to a Japanese spy who was eventually taken into custody by law enforcement authorities, perhaps the FBI.

Who knows if Lucy's tale is true? Nobody's found documented evidence of a Japanese spy nest infiltrating California in 1942, and Lucy's FBI file contains no mention of such an event. (Yes, Lucy had an FBI file. At the urging of her grandfather, she had registered to vote as a Communist in the 1936 elections, so she had some 'splaining to do when she was investigated by the House Select Committee on Un-American Activities in 1953.) Not long ago, the Discovery Channel television show *MythBusters* devoted a segment to debunking Lucy's claims.

The Voices in His Head Were Real

Other people have claimed that they picked up radio signals via the metal in their heads, whether it was dental work or something else. The anecdotal accounts are easy to find but hard to verify. In 1981, however, a doctor in Miami wrote to *The American Journal of Psychiatry* to report that he had treated a patient who suffered from headaches and depression and complained of hearing music and voices. The patient was a veteran who had been wounded by shrapnel to the head during combat 12 years earlier. But after receiving successful treatment for the headaches and depression, the patient claimed that he still heard the mental music.

This led the doctor to sit down with the patient and a radio; the two of them listened to various stations, trying to find one that matched what the patient heard in his head. When they found what seemed to be the offending frequency, the doctor listened to the radio with an earphone while the patient described what he was hearing in his head. Although the patient couldn't hear the voices clearly, he passed the test convincingly; he was even able to tap out the rhythm and hum along with the songs that played. The doctor concluded that the shrapnel in this man's head was receiving radio signals and conducting the sound through bone to his ear.

So apparently, it is possible for the metal in your head to receive radio transmissions—but don't look for the American Dental Association to begin marketing the iTooth portable music player anytime soon.

✳ Tickets to the first Super Bowl went for $12—and that was for the most expensive seat.

✳ The exclamation point is short for the Latin word "io," which means "exclamation of joy." It used to be written with a lowercase "i" over a lowercase "o." That eventually gave way to the abbreviation (!) we use today.

✳ The dollar sign abbreviation started as a "P," to match the shorthand for the peso. It then morphed into a "P" with an "S" over it, which then gave way to the symbol ($) we use now.

✳ An average shower uses 30 gallons of water.

The Great Escape

Unlike outrunning an explosion, this action-hero plan actually works. If someone happens to be shooting at you, you can avert the gunfire by diving underwater.

❋   ❋   ❋   ❋

A Shield of Water

A 2005 EPISODE OF the Discovery Channel's *MythBusters* proved that bullets fired into the water at an angle will slow to a safe speed at fewer than four feet below the surface. In fact, bullets from some high-powered guns in this test basically disintegrated on the water's surface.

It might seem counterintuitive that speeding bullets don't penetrate water as easily as something slower, such as a diving human or a falling anchor. But it makes sense. Water has considerable mass, so when anything hits it, it pushes back. The force of the impact is equal to the change in momentum (momentum is velocity times mass) divided by the time taken to change the momentum.

In other words, the faster the object is going, the more its momentum will change when it hits, and the greater the force of impact will be. For the same reason that a car suffers more damage in a head-on collision with a wall at fifty miles per hour than at five miles per hour, a speeding bullet takes a bigger hit than something that is moving more slowly.

The initial impact slows the bullet considerably, and the drag that's created as it moves through water brings it to a stop. The impact on faster-moving bullets is even greater, so they are more likely to break apart or slow to a safe speed within the first few feet of water.

It's Not Foolproof

The worst-case scenario is if someone fires a low-powered gun at you straight down into the water. In the *MythBusters* episode, one of the tests involved firing a nine-millimeter pistol directly down into a block of underwater ballistics gel. Eight feet below the surface seemed to be the safe distance—the ballistics gel showed that the impact from the bullet wouldn't have been fatal at this depth. But if a shot from the same gun were fired at a 30-degree angle (which would be a lot more likely if you were fleeing from shooters on shore), you'd be safe at just four feet below the surface.

The problem with this escape plan is that you have to pop up sooner or later to breathe, and the shooter on shore will be ready. But if you are a proper action hero, you can hold your breath for at least ten minutes, which is plenty of time to swim to your top-secret submarine car.

---

* Argan oil, which is used for flavoring foods and in cosmetics, is made by grinding nuts from the argan tree. Sometimes, though, the nuts are first processed through a goat's digestive system. These are not the nuts recommended for eating.

* In 1985, 300 people who were alive in 1910 gathered to watch Halley's Comet make its first celestial return to Earth's realm in 75 years.

* Marijuana was used in the 19th century to relieve muscle spasms. The doctor of Britain's Queen Victoria prescribed marijuana to her for the relief of menstrual cramps.

* Isaac Newton's mother pulled him out of school to help run her farm. Newton's uncle, however, saw potential and insisted the boy receive further education.

* The Recording Industry Association of America tried to sue Gertrude Walton for illegally downloading files despite the fact that the woman had died nearly two months earlier.

* In 1967, the town of St. Paul, Alberta, built the world's first UFO landing pad as a project to mark Canada's 100th birthday.

* The striped barber pole apparently has a bloody past. Barbers were also surgeons in the old days, and according to legend, they would hang up blood-soaked towels to dry on poles outside their shops, thereby creating the red-and-white stripe design still replicated today.

Taser: From Children's Book Concept to Riot Policing Tool

Like a .357 Magnum, the Taser makes troublesome suspects less troublesome. Unlike the .357, the tased suspect generally survives to stand trial, and the police save a bundle on coroner costs.

✳ ✳ ✳ ✳

Tom Swift

YOU'VE PROBABLY HEARD of the Hardy Boys and Nancy Drew. But unless you're a baby boomer or older, you may never have heard of Tom Swift books, which belonged to the same "teen adventure" genre. Tom, the precocious protagonist, is a young inventor who resolves crises and foils wickedness. One book in the series, called *Tom Swift and His Electric Rifle* (1911), has quite a stimulating legacy.

In 1967, NASA researcher Jack Cover, who grew up on Tom Swift, realized that he could actually make some of the gee-whiz gadgetry from the series. In 1974, he finished designing an electricity weapon he named the "Thomas A. Swift Electric Rifle," or TASER. (In so doing, he departed from canon. Tom Swift never had a middle initial, but Cover inserted the "A" to make the acronym easier on the tongue.)

How It Worked

Cover's first "electric rifle," the Taser TF-76, used a small gunpowder charge to fire two barbed darts up to 15 feet. Thin wires conducted electricity from the weapon's battery to the target, causing great pain and brief paralysis with little risk of death—except in the young, elderly, or frail. That was okay, since the police rarely felt compelled to take down children or senior citizens.

The police saw potential in the Taser. The TF-76 showed great promise as a nonlethal takedown tool.

Federal Shocker

Never underestimate the creativity-squelching power of government. The Bureau of Alcohol, Tobacco, and Firearms (BATF) wondered: How do we classify this thing? It's not really a pistol or a rifle. It uses gunpowder... *Aha!* The BATF grouped the TF-76 with sawed-off shotguns: illegal for most to acquire or possess. A .44 Magnum? Carry it on your hip if you like. An electric stunner that takes neither blood nor life? A felony to possess, much less use. This BATF ruling zapped Taser Systems (Cover's new company) right out of business.

Second and Third Volleys

Taser Systems resurfaced as Tasertron, limping along on sales to police. In the 1990s, a creative idealist named Rick Smith wanted to popularize nonlethal weapons. He licensed the Taser technology from Cover, and together they began changing the weapon. To deal with the BATF's gunpowder buzzkill, Smith and Cover designed a Taser dart propelled by compressed air. They also loaded each cartridge with paper and Mylar confetti bearing a serial number. If the bad guys misused a Taser, they wouldn't be able to eradicate the evidence.

To Tase or Not to Tase: That Is the Question...

Modern Tasers reflect the benefits of experience. In 1991, an LAPD Taser failed to subdue a violent, defiant motorist named Rodney King. The events that followed (including the cops beating King with billy clubs) made the public think of the Taser as unreliable. This was compounded by occasional deaths from tasing. The public might justly ask: "Does this thing really work? Does it work too darn well?"

One fact isn't in question. A nightstick blow to the head or a 9mm police bullet are both deadlier than a Taser. As a result, the debate revolves more around police officers' overwillingness to use the Taser rather than whether or not they should carry one.

In 2007, the United Nations ruled that a Taser could be considered an instrument of torture.

Ben Franklin and Electricity

*It's not exactly accurate to say that the Founding
Father "discovered" electricity, but he certainly
expanded our knowledge of the energy force.*

❊   ❊   ❊   ❊

THE ANCIENT GREEKS knew about static electricity long
before Ben Franklin. They observed amber, which they called
elektron, drawing feathers and twigs to itself when rubbed with a
cloth. Static electricity remained an amusing trick until the 18th
century, when Englishman Stephen Gray found that electricity
could be "sent" hundreds of feet if the right material was used to
conduct it. Dutch professor Pieter van Musschenbroek of Leyden
accidentally electrocuted himself by touching a wire sticking out
of a jar, prompting him to figure out that electricity can be stored
in water-filled jars. Leyden jars became the rage among scientists.

News of Leyden jars and electrical displays eventually reached
the intellectual backwater of North America, where Franklin
saw a demonstration and became fascinated. He ordered jars and
scientific journals from London and set up his own experiments.

Technically, Franklin didn't discover electricity. But he did
discover a lot about it. Franklin was determined to find a real,
practical use for the strange energy. He vigorously pursued this
goal—and was even knocked senseless while arranging to use
electricity to kill and roast a turkey.

Like other scientists, Franklin suspected that lightning was
pure electricity. Two years after his accident, Franklin and his
son launched a specially built silk kite into a stormy sky. The
kite was not, in fact, struck by lightning. However, by simply
remaining airborne under storm clouds, the kite was electrified—and so was the metal key that was tied to its tail near
Franklin's hand. It seems simple now, but figuring out a way to
prove that lightning is electricity made Franklin famous.

Goofy Planes

In a little over a century, humans have taken powered flight from rattletrap lattices covered with canvas to spy planes that circumnavigate the globe. In the process, we have come up with some creative aviation concepts.

✳ ✳ ✳ ✳

Kalinin K-12 (first flew 1936): It was a big flying wing with no tail to speak of and vertical stabilizers at the wingtips. This twin-engine prototype was made of canvas over a steel frame!

Messerschmitt Me-163 (1941): This was the only rocket inter-ceptor ever sent to war. The "Komet" was a flying wing with a vertical stabilizer; it dropped disposable wheels after takeoff and landed on a ski. Its noxious fuel gave it eight minutes of powered flight: It climbed, made a pass, climbed again, made one more pass if feasible, and glided down to land once all fuel was exhausted.

Chance Vought XF5U-1 (1942): The comical Flying Pancake was aptly named: It was a big saucer with two large props in front and two vertical stabilizers in back. It might have been an outstanding naval aircraft, but by the time testing was done, the age of the jet fighter was here.

Fieseler Fi-103R (1944): We're so used to thinking of the pilot-less German World War II V-1 "buzz bomb," we don't realize it was technically the Fi-103 cruise missile. The R variant had a pilot. It was difficult to make a safe bailout (much less to land); the jet engine intake was directly above and behind the cockpit.

Yokosuka MXY7 (1944): The Ohka ("Cherry Blossom") was designed for suicide attacks. It could neither take off nor land; a medium bomber carried it into battle. United States warplanes tended to shoot down the bombers short of the target, forcing them to launch the Ohkas too soon. Few reached their targets and fewer still harmed them.

Bachem Ba-349 (1945): Many odd aircraft were born of German World War II desperation, such as this ungainly vertical-launch wooden rocket interceptor. It was armed only with two dozen 73mm unguided rockets, and once those were expended, the Ba-349 was to be disassembled in the air. The pilot and engine were to parachute down. Evidently, 36 were built for battle, and only two were crewed. Those both crashed, killing the pilots.

Taylor Aerocar (1949): After World War II, some people thought that private planes would become the new family cars. Moulton B. Taylor's Aerocar was a high-wing monoplane with an upside-down vertical stabilizer and a "pusher" (rear-mounted) propeller. The wings folded up for road travel. Clever idea, except that hardly anyone bought it.

Convair YF-7A (1953): You've likely noticed that there aren't very many jet-powered flying boats. Well, it has been tried. The YF-7A looked a lot like a Cold War delta-wing jet interceptor and could land on water. It had "hydro-skis" to help it get airborne. The skis caused a lot of vibration, however, and the Navy gave up on the aquatic jet fighter.

SNECMA C.450 (1959): Picture a fat aluminum barrel with four tail fins raised on casters. Now cut the beaky nose off an F-14 Tomcat, mount it vertically atop the barrel, and you have the Coléoptère ("Beetle"). It couldn't taxi—a launch trailer resembling a dump truck had to maneuver it into takeoff position. After the prototype went splat, so did the C.450 program.

Martin Marietta X-24B (1973): A rocket-powered research vehicle that looked like a big dart, the Martin was long and thin with wings swept so sharply it hardly had any. It didn't become the next dominant fighter, but it enabled some useful testing.

Antonov An-225 (1988): This gargantuan six-jet-engine Soviet design was created to haul their space shuttle into orbit. You could barely park it on two football fields side by side. It could lift more than 550,000 pounds of cargo and had 32 landing wheels.

Chapter 11

Bizarre Truths About Mother Nature

The Snowflake Man

His name was Wilson Bentley—and he was the person who assured us that no two snowflakes are alike.

✳ ✳ ✳ ✳

A Life Spent Studying Snowflakes

IN 1885, WILSON BENTLEY became the first person to photograph a single snow crystal. By cleverly adapting a microscope to a bellows camera, the 19-year-old perfected a process that allowed him to catch snowflakes on a black-painted wooden tray and then capture their images before they melted away.

A self-educated farmer from the rural town of Jericho, Vermont, Bentley would go on to attract worldwide attention for his pioneering work in the field of photomicrography. In 1920, the American Meteorological Society elected him as a fellow and later awarded him its very first research grant, a whopping $25.

His Famous Words

Over 47 years, Bentley captured 5,381 pictographs of individual snowflakes. Near the end of his life, the Snowflake Man said that he had never seen two snowflakes that were alike: "Under the microscope, I found that snowflakes were miracles of beauty. Every crystal was a masterpiece of design and no one design was ever repeated."

Since Bentley's original observation, physicists, snowologists, crystallographers, and meteorologists have continued to photograph and study the different patterns of ice-crystal growth and snowflake formation (with more technologically advanced equipment, of course). But guess what? Bentley's snow story sticks.

No Proof to the Contrary

Scientists still agree: It is extremely unlikely that two snowflakes can be identical. It's so unlikely, that Kenneth G. Libbrecht, a professor of physics at Caltech, says, "Even if you looked at every one ever made, you would not find any exact duplicates."

How so? Says Libbrecht, "The number of possible ways of making a complex snowflake is staggeringly large." A snowflake may start out as a speck of dust, but as it falls through the clouds, it gathers up more than 180 billion water molecules. These water molecules freeze, evaporate, and arrange themselves into endlessly inventive patterns under the influence of endless environmental conditions.

And that's just it—snow crystals are so sensitive to the tiniest fluctuations in temperature and atmosphere that they're constantly changing in shape and structure as they gently fall to the ground. Molecule for molecule, it's virtually impossible for two snow crystals to have the same pattern of development and design.

"It is probably safe to say that the possible number of snow crystal shapes exceeds the estimated number of atoms in the known universe," says Jon Nelson, a cloud physicist who has studied snowflakes for 15 years. Still, we can't be 100 percent sure that no two snowflakes are exactly alike—we're just going to have to take science's word for it. Each winter, trillions upon trillions of snow crystals drop from the sky. Are you going to check them all out?

Running Through the Rain vs. Walking Through the Rain

Which technique keeps you driest? Read on to learn the answer.

✳ ✳ ✳ ✳

IT MAKES INTUITIVE sense that running through the rain will keep you drier than walking. You will spend less time in the rain, after all. But there's a pervasive old wives' tale that says it won't do any good. So every time there's a downpour and you need to get to your car, you are faced with this confounding question: Should you walk or run?

The argument against running is that more drops hit your chest and legs when you move more quickly. If you're walking, the theory goes, the drops mainly hit your head. So the walking proponents say that running exposes you to more drops, not fewer.

Several scientists have pondered this possibility. In 1987, an Italian physicist determined that sprinting keeps you drier than walking, but only by about 10 percent, which might not be worth the effort and the risk of slipping. In 1995, a British researcher concluded that the increased front-drenching of running effectively cancels out the reduced rain exposure.

These findings didn't seem right to two climatologists at the National Climatic Data Center in Asheville, North Carolina, so they decided to put them to the test. In 1996, they put on identical outfits with plastic bags underneath to keep moisture from seeping out of the clothes and to keep their own sweat from adding to the rainwater. One ran through the rain for roughly 330 feet; the other walked the same distance in the rain. They weighed the wet clothes, compared the weights to those when the clothes were dry, and determined that the climatologist who walked got 40 percent wetter than the one who ran. In other words, if you want to get less wet when you're out in the rain, *run!*

Weird Weather

We've all heard that neither rain, snow, sleet, nor hail, will stop our determined mail carriers, but how about a few rounds of ball lightning or tiny frogs dropping from the sky? Apparently, Mother Nature has a sense of humor. Here are some of the weirdest weather phenomena encountered on planet Earth.

✳ ✳ ✳ ✳

Goodness, Gracious, Great Balls of Lightning!

PERHAPS IT WAS ball lightning, an unexplained spherical mass of electrical energy, that Jerry Lee Lewis was singing about in the tune "Great Balls of Fire." In 1976, the strange phenomenon supposedly attacked a woman in the United Kingdom as she ironed during an electrical storm. A ball of lightning emerged from her iron, spun around the room, then threw her across the room, ripping off half her clothes. In 1962, a Long Island couple was astounded to see a fiery basketball-size orb roll into their living room through an open window. The fireball passed between them, continued through the room, and disappeared down an adjacent hallway. Exactly how lightning or any other electrical anomaly can form itself into a ball and zigzag at different speeds is not well understood.

Otherworldly Lights: St. Elmo's Fire

A weird haze of light glimmering around a church steeple during a storm, a rosy halo over someone's head, or a ghostly light swirling around the mast of a wave-tossed ship—these are all possible manifestations of the strange, bluish-white light known as St. Elmo's Fire, which may be a signal that a lightning strike to the glowing area is imminent. The light is a visible, electric discharge produced by heavy storms. It was named after St. Erasmus, aka St. Elmo, the patron saint of sailors.

When the Moon Gets the Blues

Everyone understands that the phrase "once in a blue moon" refers to a very unusual occurrence, since blue moons are rare.

But a blue moon is not actually blue. In fact, a blue moon is determined by the calendar, not by its color. Typically, there is one full moon per month, but occasionally, a second full moon will sneak into a monthly cycle. When this happens, the second full moon is referred to as a "blue moon," which happens every two to three years. But at times, the moon has been known to appear blue, or even green, often after a volcanic eruption leaves tiny ash and dust particles in the earth's atmosphere.

Green Flash: When the Sun Goes Green

The term *green flash* may sound like a comic book superhero, but it is actually a strange flash of green light that appears just before the setting sun sinks into the horizon. Some have suggested that rare fluctuations in solar winds may be responsible for green glows and flashes that sometimes appear in the atmosphere just before sunset. Some believe it's just a mirage. But others contend that a green flash occurs when layers of the earth's atmosphere act like a prism. Whatever causes the emerald hue, seeing a flash of green light along the horizon can be an eerie and unsettling experience.

Double the Rainbows, Double the Gold?

Rainbow stories abound; ancient Irish lore promises a pot of leprechaun's gold at the end of a rainbow, and biblical tradition says God set a rainbow in the sky as a promise to Noah that Earth would never again be destroyed by water. Rainbows are formed when sunlight passes through water droplets, usually at the end of a rainstorm, and the droplets separate the light like tiny prisms into a spectrum from red to violet. A secondary rainbow, set outside the first one and in the reverse order of colors, is formed by a second set of light refractions to create the spectacular double rainbow. Conditions have to be just right to see the double rainbow because the secondary arch of colors is much paler than the primary rainbow and is not always visible.

Lava Lamps in the Sky: Aurora Borealis

Like a neon sign loosened from its tubing, the aurora borealis sends multicolored arches, bands, and streams of luminous beauty throughout the northern skies whenever solar flares are at their height. This occurs when electrons ejected from the sun's surface hit Earth's atmospheric particles and charge them until they glow. The electrons are attracted to Earth's magnetic poles, which is why they are seen mainly in the far northern or southern latitudes. In the Southern Hemisphere, they are called *aurora australis*. *Aurora polaris* refers to the lights of either pole.

It's Raining Frogs!

Startling as the thought of being pelted from above by buckets of hapless amphibians may be, reports of the sky raining frogs have occurred for so long that the problem was even addressed in the first century A.D., when a Roman scholar, Pliny the Elder, theorized that frog "seeds" were already present in the soil. But in 2005, residents of Serbia were shocked when masses of teensy toads tumbled out of a dark cloud that suddenly appeared in the clear blue sky. *Scientific American* reported a frog fall over Kansas City, Missouri, in July 1873, in numbers so thick they "darkened the air." And in Birmingham, England, the froglets that reportedly dropped from the heavens on June 30, 1892, were not green but a milky white. In 1987, pink frogs fell in Gloucestershire, England. No one knows for certain why this happens, but one theory is that the small animals—fish, birds, and lizards are also common—are carried from other locations by tornadoes or waterspouts.

Spouting Off

Ancient people feared waterspouts and understandably so. Waterspouts are actually tornadoes that form over a body of water, whirling at speeds as fast as 190 miles per hour. Waterspouts start with parent clouds that pull air near the surface into a vortex at an increasing rate, until water is pulled up toward the cloud. One of the world's top waterspout hot spots is the Florida Keys, which may see as many as 500 per year. They can also occur in relatively calm areas such as Lake Tahoe, on the California-Nevada border. There, a Native American legend said that waterspouts, which they called "waterbabies," appeared at the passing of great chiefs to take them to heaven.

Mirages: Optical Confusion

Mirages have been blamed for everything from imaginary waterholes in deserts to sightings of the Loch Ness Monster. They come in two forms: hallucinations or environmental illusions based on tricks of light, shadow, and atmosphere. In April 1977, residents of Grand Haven, Michigan, were able to plainly see the shimmering lights of Milwaukee, Wisconsin, some 75 miles across Lake Michigan. The sighting was confirmed by the flashing pattern of Milwaukee's red harbor beacon. Another rare type of water mirage is the *fata morgana*, which produces a double image that makes mundane objects look gigantic and may account for some reports of sea monsters.

Cobwebs from Heaven?

On their 40-year desert tour with Moses, the Israelites were blessed with a strange substance called manna that fell from the sky. People in other places have also witnessed falls of unknown material, often resembling cobwebs. In October 1881, great quantities of weblike material fell around the cities of Milwaukee, Green Bay, and Sheboygan, Wisconsin. Newspapers speculated that the strong, white strands had come from "gossamer spiders" due to their lightness. The same thing allegedly happened in 1898 in Montgomery, Alabama. Not all falls of unknown material have been so pleasant—a yellow, smelly substance fell on Kourianof, Russia, in 1832, and something similar was reported in Ireland around 1695.

---

* Rod Stewart once dug graves for a living.

* Sean Connery once polished coffins for cash.

* Danny DeVito almost became a professional hairdresser.

The Amount of Rain in a Rain Forest

Technically, in order to qualify as a rain forest, a heavily wooded area must get at least 80 inches of rain per year.

❋   ❋   ❋   ❋

THERE SHOULD BE no feelings of inadequacy among forests whose drops per annum don't quite make the 80-inch cut, however. If a forest has a rate of precipitation that comes close to that mark, scientists will most likely let it into the fold.

Rain falls about 90 days per year in a rain forest. As much as 50 percent of this precipitation evaporates, meaning that rain forests recycle their water supply. In non-rain forest areas, water evaporates and is transported (via clouds) to different regions. In a rain forest, however, the unique climate and weather patterns often cause the precipitation to fall over the same area from which it evaporated.

A rain forest is comprised of evergreen trees, either broadleaf or coniferous, and other types of intense vegetation. These regions collectively contain more than two-thirds of the plant species on the planet. There are two types of rain forests: tropical and temperate. Tropical rain forests are located near the equator; temperate rain forests crop up near oceanic coastlines, particularly where mountain ranges focus rainfall on a particular region.

Rain forests can be found on every continent except Antarctica. The largest tropical rain forest is the Amazon in South America; the largest temperate rain forest is in the Pacific Northwest, stretching from northern California all the way to Alaska.

At one time, rain forests covered as much as 14 percent of the earth, but that number is now down to about 6 percent. Scientists estimate that an acre and a half of rain forest—the equivalent of a little more than a football field—is lost every second. The trees are taken for lumber, and the land is tilled for farming.

Pangaea: Putting the Pieces Together

Pangaea was a giant supercontinent that existed on Earth some 270 million years ago. Unlike the smaller, broken pieces of contemporary continental plates, Pangaea had it all—literally.

✳ ✳ ✳ ✳

A History Lesson

THE ALL-ENCOMPASSING LANDMASS known as *Pangaea* straddled the equator in roughly the shape of a "C," surrounded by one of the largest (if not *the* largest) expanses of water ever to exist on planet Earth: the Panthalassa Ocean. Only a few chunks of land lay to the east, including bits of what we now call northern and eastern China, Indochina, and part of central Asia. A smaller "sea," called the Tethys Sea, was located within the "C" and is thought to have been the precursor to today's Mediterranean Sea.

The climate was warm at this time, with no true polar ice caps. Because of the high temperatures, life flourished during the Pangaea years. Early amphibians and reptiles roamed the giant continent; dinosaurs and archosaurs ran amok. When the supercontinent finally broke apart, other plant and animal species arose, each developing as a direct result of being cut off from their own species. In other words, thanks to the breakup of Pangaea, our planet's organisms became extremely diverse.

The Pangaea Puzzle

German meteorologist Alfred Wegener was the first to coin the term *Pangaea* (which means "all earth" in Greek) in the early 20th century. He was also the first to publicly propose and publish—to the dismay of the scientific community—the idea that Earth's continents once lay together in the huge landmass of Pangaea. Even more shocking was Wegener's theory that the supercontinent broke apart over millions of years, with the pieces ultimately reaching their current spots on Earth millions of years later. His beliefs were based on many scientific discoveries of his time, including identical fossils found in Africa and North America—and especially on the obvious giant jigsaw puzzle "fit" of the continents.

Now known as the "father of the continental drift theory," Wegener was a pariah in his own time. He was the victim of his own ideas, as he could not come up with a logical mechanism to explain the movement of the continents. Few of his contemporaries believed his idea, many of them citing the fact that Wegener was merely a meteorologist, not a geologist. But finally—almost three decades after his death in 1930—Wegener was vindicated, thanks to additional rock and fossil evidence and satellites that track the minute movements of the continents.

Getting the Drift of Continental Drift

Scientists now believe the shifting of the continental plates is caused by the moving mantle, the thick layer of viscous, liquid rock below Earth's crust. Based on fossil evidence, they believe two huge continents, Laurasia (north of the equator and made up of today's North America and Eurasia) and Gondwanaland (or Gondwana, south of the equator and made up of today's Africa, Antarctica, Australia, India, and South America) collided 270 million years ago during the Permian Period, forming Pangaea. Not long after (in terms of geologic time), around the Triassic Period 225 million years ago, the attraction waned.

This was the beginning of the end for the supercontinent, as a volcanic seam called a seafloor-spreading rift (similar to today's Mid-Atlantic Ridge) ripped the continent apart. A second pair of continents formed, also called Laurasia and Gondwanaland; over the next tens of millions of years, they eventually plowed across the earth, taking the positions we're so familiar with today. So far, there is no fossil or rock evidence that the supercontinent ever formed again. And although we will never know because our lifespans are so short, it's possible that as the continents move over the coming millions of years, another supercontinent may form.

Frying an Egg on the Sidewalk: Easier Said than Done

Claiming that "it's so hot outside that you can fry an egg on the sidewalk" is an exaggeration—unless you have the proper tools.

✳   ✳   ✳   ✳

EGGS MUST REACH 144 to 158 degrees Fahrenheit to change from liquid to solid and be considered cooked, according to the American Egg Board. Even on the most searing summer days, the typical sidewalk falls way short of the 144 degrees necessary to get eggs sizzling and coagulating.

Pavement of any kind is a poor conductor of heat, says Robert Wolke in his book *What Einstein Told His Cook: Kitchen Science Explained.* For starters, when you crack an egg onto pavement, the egg slightly cools the pavement's surface. In order to fry an egg, the temperature of a sidewalk has to climb enough to start and maintain the coagulating process. Lacking a constant flame or source of heat from below or from the sides, pavement can't maintain a temperature that's hot enough to cook eggs evenly. Forget sunny-side up—you're likely to end up with a runny mess.

But frying an egg on the sidewalk is not impossible. Just ask the contestants of the Solar Egg Frying Contest, held each Fourth of July in the little town of Oatman, Arizona. People come from far and wide in hope of winning a trophy for "the most edible" solar-cooked egg.

Technically, these people are cheating. Contestants in the Oatman egg fry are allowed the use of mirrors, magnifying glasses, aluminum reflectors, and any kind of homemade cooking surface or contraption they can devise to harness the power of the sun. It also seems that sidewalk cooking is a bit more plausible in Arizona in July: Heat is high, humidity is low, and the liquid in the cooking eggs dries out a little faster.

Noise Pollution: A "Deafenition"

It's a very real phenomenon, and one that forces us to understand the true meaning of the word "pollution."

❋　❋　❋　❋

Trash in the Air

MOST PEOPLE KNOW about pollution, thanks to the various crusades designed to make us more aware of it and because, well, it's everywhere—in our surroundings, in our eyes, and in our lungs. When we think of pollution, we tend to think of scattered trash, dirty air, or dangerous industrial chemicals that we don't see but learn about from news stories and political stumping. To understand noise pollution, we need to take a wider view of the word "pollution."

To define pollution as an "undesirable state of the natural environment being contaminated with harmful substances as a consequence of human activities," as *WordNet* does, doesn't quite get at noise pollution, because noise isn't a substance—it's simply the movement of air. But defining pollution as an "undesirable change in the physical, chemical or biological characteristics of the air, water or land that can harmfully affect the health, survival or activities of human or other living organisms," as the New Zealand government does, encompasses noise pollution handily.

The Damage Done

The ill effects of noise pollution are documented beyond any doubt. Coming largely from transportation systems—cars and trucks mostly, but trains and buses in urban areas as well—noise pollution is proved to cause annoyance, aggression, hypertension, high stress, ringing in the ears, hearing loss, and more. One study showed that being subjected to moderately high levels of noise for eight hours—as a carpenter or factory worker might be—can raise blood pressure from five to ten points and cause feelings of stress, both of which can contribute to heart disease.

Noise pollution also is thought to have serious effects on animals, which depend on hearing more acutely than humans and can find their vital hunting, self-protection, and communication abilities impaired by unnatural noise.

There is no doubt that the world is a far, far noisier place than it was before humans invented machines—especially machines with engines that propel them—and that noise has an unhealthy effect on people and animals. If loud noise doesn't seem like pollution, strictly speaking, it's probably because noise doesn't have a visible or permanent effect on our environment the way blowing trash, seeping chemicals, and oil spills do. It acts invisibly and temporarily on the air through which it moves so violently.

But that violence is felt by the ears of humans and other animals, and by our bodies in many powerful ways, most of them unhealthy. That sounds like pollution to us.

* Some fans swear that Shirley Temple had exactly 56 curls in her hair in every one of her movies.

* Women tend to shave about 412 square inches of their bodies, while men shave only 48.

* Grab your shades: Earth is closest to the sun at the beginning of the year, on January 3.

* Tap water in New York City is considered nonkosher, as it has been found to contain microorganisms that qualify as shellfish.

* The player silhouette in the NBA logo was created from the image of former Los Angeles Laker Jerry West.

* Using proper form, the word "stewardess" is typed using only the left hand.

* December is the most common month for children to be conceived.

* Scrabble was originally called Criss-Cross when an unemployed architect came up with the idea in 1931.

Beware of Killer Plants

The good news is, unless you're a character in Little Shop of Horrors, *no plant is going to kill you with malicious intent or for food. But that doesn't mean you shouldn't fear death by plant.*

❋　❋　❋　❋

Steer Clear of These Green Meanies

THERE ARE SOME obvious ways you could be killed by a plant: A tree could fall on you or twist your car into a pretzel if you veer off the road. But the more gruesome scenarios involve eating something you shouldn't. Here's a sampling from the menu of killer plants:

❋ Aconitum (aconite, monkshood, or wolfsbane) will start your mouth burning from the first nibble. Then you'll start vomiting, your lungs and heart will shut down, and you'll die of asphyxiation. As luck would have it, your mind will stay alert the entire time. And you don't even have to eat aconitum to enjoy its effects: Just brush up against it and the sap can get through your skin.

❋ Hemlock is another particularly nasty snack. In fact, the ancient Greeks gave it to prisoners who were condemned to die (including Socrates). Ingest some hemlock and it will eventually paralyze your nervous system, causing you to die from lack of oxygen to the brain and heart. Fortunately, if you happen to have an artificial ventilation system nearby, you can hook yourself up and wait about three days for the effects to wear off. But even if there is a ventilation system handy, it's best if you just don't eat hemlock.

* Oleander is chock full of poisony goodness, too. Every part of these lovely ornamental plants is deadly if ingested. Just one leaf can be fatal to a small child, while adults might get to enjoy up to ten leaves before venturing into the big sleep. Even its fumes are toxic—never use oleander branches as firewood. Oleander poisoning will affect most parts of your body: the central nervous system, the skin, the heart, and the brain. After the seizures and the tremors, you may welcome the sweet relief of the coma that might come next. Unfortunately, that can be followed by death.

So, while there is no need to worry about any plants sneaking up on you from behind with a baseball bat, there are plenty of reasons not to take a nibble out of every plant you see.

---

* The first chalkboard for classroom use was recorded in 1714.

* The first recorded e-mail was sent in 1972.

* Many doctors think babies dream in the womb.

* American presidents who were bald include John Quincy Adams, Martin Van Buren, and Dwight D. Eisenhower.

* Root beer used to be the most popular soda in the United States, but now it's only about 5 percent of the market.

* Americans drink 50 times more soda now than they did a century ago.

* It takes about 2,893 licks to get to the center of a typical Tootsie Pop.

* Parsley is the most popular herb worldwide.

* A pelican doesn't have nostrils.

* A Twinkie contains 68 percent air.

* In 1995, blue M&M's replaced tan M&M's.

* If you use lipstick, the odds are high that you've spread fish scales on your lips. A common makeup ingredient called "pearl essence" or "pearlescence" uses fish compounds to create a shimmer effect.

Hawaii's Upside-Down Waterfall

Hawaii's third largest island, Oahu, touts the state's most unusual waterfall—one that defies gravity.

✳ ✳ ✳ ✳

Tears in the Mist

THE LUSH NU'UANA VALLEY on the eastern coast of Oahu stretches from Honolulu to the Ko'olau Range and ends quite suddenly in steep cliffs called the Pali. Here, on only the rainiest and windiest days, visitors can see the famous Upside-Down Waterfall, where water cascading from the 3,150-foot summit of Mount Konahuanui falls only a few feet before being blown back up by strong trade winds. The water dissipates into mist, creating the illusion of water slowly falling upward.

Natives call the waterfall *Waipuhia*, or "blown water." Legend says it was named for a young local girl whose bright eyes pleased the gods. One day, the girl's true love was lost in a storm, and when she wept for him, her tears were caught halfway down the cliff by the god of wind and tossed into the spray by the god of mist.

Lookout Lore

Weather permitting, the best view of the waterfall is from the 1,186-foot Nu'uanu Pali Lookout, an infamous spot in Hawaiian lore. As legend goes, in 1795, King Kamehameha I drove the Oahu warriors up the Nu'uanu Valley to the Pali, where thousands of them were driven over the cliffs to their deaths.

While scholars pooh-pooh the story, natives say that at night the cries of long-dead warriors can be heard echoing through the valley. Others tell of seeing ghost warriors falling from the cliffs as well as a ghostly white figure—perhaps the king—on the paved road that today leads up to the Lookout. Now called the Pali Highway, that road was built in 1898. Apparently, workers encountered several bones during the project—and simply laid the road right over them.

The Last Days of Pompeii

In the early days of the new millennium, Pompeii was a popular, bustling city. In an instant, it was over.

✳ ✳ ✳ ✳

Calm and Quiet

IN AUGUST A.D. 79, Pompeii was a bustling Roman city of about 20,000 people. Located in a fertile agricultural region on the Bay of Naples, the city was the center of Rome's Mediterranean trade. Only a few days travel from Rome, Pompeii was a popular resort for wealthy Romans. It was also famous for the production and sale of *garum*, a spicy sauce made from fish entrails.

Mount Vesuvius had been quiet for 800 years; in fact, it had been such a long time that practically no one remembered that the volcano even existed. However, minor earthquakes were common, and there had been a major earthquake 17 years earlier. After that catastrophe, Pompeii had rebuilt and carried on. But in mid-August of 79, the earth began to rumble once more. Streams and wells dried up, and the sea became unusually turbulent. The townspeople murmured about portents and omens, but they were not alarmed enough to evacuate the city.

Buried in Ashes

Our only eyewitness accounts of the disaster come from two letters written by Pliny the Younger, who was a teenager when he watched the eruption from the town of Misenum, across the Bay of Naples. According to Pliny, Vesuvius erupted in the early afternoon of August 24, sending a cloud of smoke that billowed into the sky "like an umbrella pine." Modern scientists estimate that the eruption shot 12 miles into the air. By the time Pliny and his mother decided to evacuate, "a dense black cloud was coming up behind us, spreading over the earth like a flood." When the darkness finally thinned, "we were horrified to see everything changed, buried deep in ashes like snow drifts."

It looked bad from afar, but the situation was far worse in Pompeii. The disaster began with a light fall of ash, which accelerated into a hail of lava shards and pumice. At first, people retreated into their homes. Clouds of ash filled the air, making it hard to breathe and cloaking the city in darkness. As the falling stones grew larger and volcanic debris began to accumulate at the rate of five to six inches per hour, many people tried to leave the city. Those who fled inland, carrying a few possessions, had a chance for survival. Those who fled toward the sea found their escape blocked by violent waves made more dangerous by floating pumice.

Continuing Horror

By sunset, the volcano's activity seemed to slow. Some Pompeians who had survived the initial eruption dug their way out of their homes and tried to escape the city, scrambling over an accumulation of pumice and ash that was two feet deep. As the evening progressed, the rain of pumice turned from white to gray, and the size of the stones continued to increase. By midnight, first-floor doors and windows were completely blocked. The accumulated volcanic debris was now five feet deep.

Shortly after, the eruptions entered a second, more dangerous, phase. As the volcano's power waned, portions of the crust collapsed. As a result, avalanches of hot ash, pumice, rock fragments, and volcanic gases rushed toward the cities around the Bay of Naples at a speed scientists estimate was approximately 60 to 180 miles per hour. Surge and flow destroyed everything in their path with a deadly combination of heat and speed, and then covered the ruins with a flood of hot volcanic debris.

The first two surges did not get as far as Pompeii; the third surge reached the city in the early morning. Roofs collapsed under the weight of falling rock. Those who were not buried alive died from extreme heat or suffocated from breathing in the hot ash. Three more surges followed in quick succession. By 8 A.M., the city of Pompeii was obliterated, frozen in time by more than 12 feet of volcanic debris.

Slower than Even a Snail

Jet cars and supersonic airplanes get all the glory for their high-speed records, but there are some objects that are just as notable for their amazing slowness. In fact, they go so slowly that scientists need special equipment to detect their movement.

On Your Marks, Get Set, Go...

So, WHAT EXACTLY moves slowest of all? The answer just might be right under your feet.

The surface of the earth is covered by tectonic plates, rigid slabs made of the planet's crust and the brittle uppermost mantle below, called the lithosphere. Some of the plates are enormous, and each is in constant movement—shifting, sliding, or colliding with other plates or sliding underneath to be drawn back down into the deep mantle. The plates "float" on the lower mantle, or asthenosphere; the lower mantle is not liquid, but it is subjected to heat and pressure, which softens it so that it can flow very, very slowly.

When an earthquake occurs, parts of the plates can move very suddenly. Following the Great Alaska Earthquake in 1964, America's largest ever, the two plates involved shifted about 30 feet by the end of the event. However, most of the time, tectonic plates move relatively steadily and very slowly. Scientists use a technique called Satellite Laser Ranging (SLR) to detect their movement.

SLR relies on a group of stations spread around the world that use lasers to send extremely short pulses of light to satellites equipped with special reflective surfaces. The time it takes for the light to make the round-trip from the satellite's main reflector is measured. According to the U.S. Geological Survey, this collection of measurements "provides instantaneous range measurements of millimeter level precision" that can be used in numerous scientific applications. One of those applications is measuring the movement of the earth's tectonic plates over time.

Now *That's* Slow

How slowly do tectonic plates move? The exact speed varies: The slowest plates move at about the same rate of speed that your fingernails grow, and the fastest plates go at about the same rate that your hair grows. A rough range is 1 to 13 centimeters per year. The fastest plates are the oceanic plates, and the slowest are the continental plates. At the moment, the Slowest Object Award is a tie between the Indian and Arabian plates, which are moving only three millimeters per year.

If you're wondering who the runners-up are in the race to be slowest, it appears to be glaciers. The slowest glaciers creep a few inches each day, still faster than tectonic plates. However, some glaciers are so speedy they can cover nearly eight miles in a single year. And sometimes a glacier can surge—in 1936, the Black Rapids Glacier in Alaska galloped toward a nearby lodge and highway, averaging 53 meters a day over three months. That leaves tectonic plates in the dust.

Say What?

Never miss a good chance to shut up.

—WILL ROGERS

Never go to bed mad. Stay up and fight.

—PHYLLIS DILLER

It is amazing how much can be accomplished if no one cares who gets the credit.

—JOHN WOODEN

Those who do not feel pain seldom think that it is felt.

—DR. SAMUEL JOHNSON

A word to the wise ain't necessary—it's the stupid ones that need the advice.

—BILL COSBY

One Man's Weed Is Another Man's Salad

What's the difference between a weed and a plant? Nothing, really.

❋ ❋ ❋ ❋

THE SIMPLEST DEFINITION of a weed is a plant you don't like that's in the midst of plants you do like. Take good old ground ivy. In your yard's natural area, it's a lovely ground cover; in your garden, it's a strangling weed. Dandelions, meanwhile, can be used for medicinal purposes, and they're edible—a little bacon, sliced hardboiled egg, chopped onion, and a dash of vinegar, and, mmm, you have a salad. On American lawns, however, dandelions are almost universally considered hated weeds.

A weed is a nuisance in a lawn or garden because it competes for sun, water, and nutrients with the plants that you desire. Weeds are hardy and maddeningly adaptable. They can be annuals, like crabgrass, which produces seeds for one season; they'll drive you nuts and then die off. Or they can be biennials, which bloom and then go dormant for two years. The classy sounding Queen Anne's lace, also known as the wild carrot, is a biennial weed.

Perennial weeds are the guests that won't leave. They hunker down and mooch off the "good" plants, and are often buggers to get rid of. Dandelions are classic perennials and have a highly effective seed-spreading system—every time a breeze or a kid blows the white puffy seeds off a dandelion, hundreds of opportunities for new dandelion plants fly through the air.

If you've decided that the thing growing in your yard is a weed and not a plant, how do you kill it? You can douse it with herbicides (be careful not to hurt the "good plants") or smother it with newspaper, plastic, or landscaping cloth. Or you can yank it from the ground, but remember that many weeds are very resilient, and if a morsel of root is left behind, it'll return again and again, like *Rocky* movies.

Gone with the Wind: Myths About Tornadoes

It's a warm afternoon, and the skies have turned a greenish-gray color that can only mean trouble. Many misconceptions swirl around the subject of tornadoes. What many believe to be fact may actually be fiction.

✳   ✳   ✳   ✳

The southwest corner of your house is the safest place to be during a tornado. In fact, occupying the area that is closest to the approaching tornado—whether it's above ground or in the basement—results in the most fatalities. A prominent study in the 1960s showed that the north side of a house is the safest area, both on the ground floor and in the basement. Many homes shift from their foundations during a tornado, toppling walls in the same direction as the storm's path. If the storm approaches from the southwest, then the home's southwest walls will fall into the structure, while north and northeast walls will fall away from the interior as the tornado moves away.

During a tornado, you should open all windows to equalize air pressure and reduce damage. The question of air pressure differences is really no question at all. Engineers agree that a storm with 260-mile-per-hour winds—classified as an F4, or "devastating," tornado—creates a pressure drop of only 10 percent. Homes and buildings have enough vents and natural openings to easily accommodate that. In fact, running around opening windows can increase the possibility of interior damage and personal injury, and it can take valuable time away from finding a safe place to ride out the storm.

A highway overpass is a safe place to wait out a storm when you're on the road. A video clip of a TV news crew surviving a tornado by huddling under an overpass was seen around the world in the 1990s, leading many to believe this is a location out of harm's way. But most trained storm chasers consider highway overpasses extremely dangerous places to be when a tornado strikes. National Weather Service meteorologists judge overpasses to be poor shelters from severe weather because high winds essentially channel themselves under these structures, carrying with them flying debris.

Tornadoes never strike large cities. The following big cities (each having a population of at least 300,000) have witnessed tornadic activity:

On a single day in 1998, three major tornadoes struck Nashville, Tennessee. St. Louis, Missouri, witnessed ten tornadoes between 1871 and 2007, resulting in more than 370 deaths. An F3 tornado roared through Dallas in 1957. In 1997, tornadoes touched down in Miami and Cincinnati, and another tore through Fort Worth, Texas, in 2000.

Yet, this myth about large cities persists. The combination of traffic, dense activity, and considerable amounts of concrete and asphalt in large cities creates what is known as a "heat island." This rising warm air has the potential to disrupt minor tornadic activity, but it's no match for the fury of larger tornadoes. Cities occupy a much smaller geographic area than rural regions of the country, so the chance that a tornado will strike a city is relatively small.

You should use your vehicle to outrun a tornado. Experts say that you can try to drive away from a tornado—but only if it's a long way off. Tornadoes can travel as fast as 70 miles per hour and can easily overtake a vehicle. Even if a tornado is traveling at a much slower speed, the accompanying storm will likely produce strong winds, heavy rain, and hail that make driving difficult, if not impossible. What's more, tornadoes are dangerously erratic and can change direction without warning. If you're caught in a vehicle during a tornado, your best bet is to abandon it and seek shelter in a sturdy building or nearby ditch or culvert.

Rocks that Grow

It is indeed a strange phenomenon, though you'd have to stare at them an awfully long time to notice the difference.

✳ ✳ ✳ ✳

THE ROCKS THAT we're talking about here grow at a rate of about one millimeter every million years. Oh, and don't forget to hold your breath while you're watching and waiting, because they're under the ocean.

Known as iron-manganese crusts, these rocks grow on the surfaces of undersea mountains. But they aren't alive—they don't reproduce like we do. Instead, they slowly and steadily collect chemical elements from seawater. An estimated 200 billion tons of iron-manganese crusts sit on the floors of the world's oceans. Some of these rocks contain high concentrations of metals such as cobalt, nickel, and platinum, making them a potentially lucrative target for mining.

Scientists find iron-manganese crusts fascinating, in the way that only scientists can find something fascinating. Because these rocks have been growing slowly over millions of years, their chemical compositions hold some valuable secrets about changes in the chemistry and circulation of the oceans over time.

Examining the chemical makeup of these rocks helps scientists to understand how the planet's geologic processes work and gives them clues about what sort of impact humans have had on the planet. These clues aren't exactly the stuff of an Agatha Christie detective novel, but don't try telling that to the men and women in lab coats.

✳ **The last letter added to the English alphabet was "J."**

✳ **The first bubble gum was invented in 1906, but it failed miserably. It wasn't until 1928, when Dubble Bubble came out with its famous pink gum, that the stuff started to catch on.**

Yellowstone: A Ticking Time Bomb

This beloved national park is actually a giant volcano, which means that it's only a matter of time before the whole place blows sky-high.

✳ ✳ ✳ ✳

Not What It Appears

ABOUT THREE MILLION people visit Yellowstone National Park each year. They do a little hiking, maybe some fishing. They admire the majesty of the mountains and antagonize a few bears for the sake of an interesting picture. And, of course, they visit the geysers. Hordes of tourists sit and wait patiently for Old Faithful to do its thing every 90 minutes or so. When it finally blows, they break into applause as if they've just seen Carol Channing belt out "Hello, Dolly." And then they go home.

Few of these tourists give much thought to what is going on below their feet while they are at Yellowstone. Geologists, however, have known for years that some sort of volcanic activity is responsible for the park's strange, volatile, steamy landscape. Just one problem: They couldn't find evidence of an actual volcano, the familiar cone-shaped mountain that tells to us in no uncertain terms that a huge explosion once took place on that spot.

In the 1960s, NASA took pictures of Yellowstone from outer space. When geologists got their hands on these pictures, they understood why they couldn't spot the volcano: It was far too vast for them to see. The crater of the Yellowstone volcano includes practically the entire park, covering about 2.2 million acres. Obviously, we're not talking about your typical, garden-variety volcano. Yellowstone is what is known as a supervolcano.

It's Already Erupted a Bunch of Times

There is no recorded history of any supervolcano eruptions, so we can only use normal volcanic activity as a measuring stick. Geologists believe that Yellowstone has erupted about

140 times in the past 16 million years. The most recent blast was about 100,000 times more powerful than the 1980 eruption of Mount St. Helens in Washington, and it spread ash over almost the entire area of the United States west of the Mississippi River. Some of the previous Yellowstone eruptions were many times more destructive than that.

And here's some interesting news: In the past 20 years or so, geologists have detected significant activity in the molten rock and boiling water below Yellowstone. In other words, the surface is shifting.

Nearby, the Teton Range has gotten a little shorter. Scientists have calculated that Yellowstone erupts about every 600,000 years. And get this: The last Yellowstone eruption took place about 640,000 years ago.

There's No Need to Worry...Yet

Before you go scrambling for the Atlantic Ocean, screaming and waving your arms in the air, know that the friendly folks who run Yellowstone National Park assure us that an eruption is not likely to happen for at least another 1,000 years. And even then, any eruption would be preceded by weeks, months, or perhaps even years of telltale volcanic weirdness.

So don't worry. It's safe to go to Yellowstone. For now. But go easy on the bears, okay? Photography may be your favorite hobby, but theirs is mauling.

* The first bachelor to become president was James Buchanan. He had been engaged 37 years earlier but backed out of the wedding. His fiancée, Ann Coleman, overdosed on medication soon after.

* The Kentucky Derby is the oldest continually held sports event in the United States. The second oldest is the Westminster Kennel Club Dog Show.

* The only marsupial that is native to North America is the Virginia opossum.

The Year Without a Summer

"The Year Without a Summer" may sound like Armageddon, but it describes an actual year—1816, which Americans nicknamed "eighteen-hundred-and-froze-to-death." It was a year of floods, droughts, and unparalleled summertime frosts that destroyed crops, spread diseases, incited riots, and otherwise wrought havoc upon the world. The culprit of this global meteorological mayhem was the eruption of Tambora, a volcano on the Indonesian island of Sumbawa—the largest explosive eruption in recorded history.

✳ ✳ ✳ ✳

Monster Eruption

TAMBORA WAS CONSIDERED inactive until 1812, when a dense cloud of smoke was seen rising above its summit. But neither the smoke, which grew denser and denser over the next three years, nor the occasional rumbles heard from the mountain, could prepare the islanders for what was to come.

When Tambora exploded in April 1815, the blast was heard 1,700 miles away. So much ash was ejected that islands 250 miles away experienced complete darkness. Only 2,000 of the island's 12,000 inhabitants survived the fiery three-day cataclysm. Altogether, the eruption and its after-effects killed more than 90,000 people throughout Indonesia, mostly through disease, polluted drinking water, and famine. Ash rains destroyed crops on every island within hundreds of miles.

Global Cooling

Along with about 140 gigatons of magma, Tambora expelled hundreds of millions of tons of fine ash, which was spread worldwide through winds and weather systems. It is this ash that scientists now blame for the subsequent "Year Without a Summer." The sulfate aerosol particles contained in it remained in the atmosphere for years and reflected back solar radiation, cooling the globe. The effect was aggravated by the activity of other volcanoes: Soufrière St. Vincent in the West

Indies (1812), Mount Mayon in the Philippines (1814), and Suwanose-Jima in Japan, which erupted continuously from 1813 to 1814. To make matters worse, all this took place during an extended period of low solar energy output called the Dalton Minimum, which lasted from about 1795 to the 1820s.

Spring of 1816 in the New World

Although the last three months of 1815 and February 1816 were all warmer than usual, the mild winter hesitated to turn into spring. Under the influence of the hot ash winds from the equator, the low-pressure system usually sitting over Iceland at this time of year shifted south toward the British Isles, and America was penetrated by polar air masses. By March, weather was becoming erratic.

On Sunday, March 17, Richmond, Virginia, was treated to summerlike temperatures; however, the next day, there was hail and sleet, and on Tuesday morning, the flowers of apricot and peach trees were covered with icicles. At the end of May, there were still frosts and snowfall from Ohio to Connecticut.

June 1816

The first days of June were deceptively warm, with 70s, 80s, and even low 90s in the northeastern United States. But on June 6, temperatures suddenly dropped into the 40s and it began to rain. Within hours, rain turned to snow, birds dropped dead, and some trees began shedding their still unexpanded leaves. This distemper of nature continued through June 11, when the wind shifted. The cold spell was over... or so people thought.

But strange weather continued to vex the population. Gales and violent hailstorms pummeled crops. On June 27, West Chester, Pennsylvania, reportedly experienced a torrential storm during which hailstones the size of walnuts fell from the sky.

July 1816

Just as the farmers were beginning to think that the damage to their crops might be minimal, another cold spell checked their hopes. On July 6, a strong northwestern wind set in, and for the next four days, winter descended upon New England and the Mid-Atlantic states once more as temperatures again dropped to the 30s and 40s. The outlook for a successful harvest was looking bleaker day by freezing day; what vegetation remained intact in New England was flavorless and languid.

August 1816

On August 20, another wave of frost and snow finished off the fruit, vegetables, vines, and meager remains of the corn and bean crops. The fields were said to be "as empty and white as October." For many farmers, that spelled ruin. Even though wheat and rye yielded enough to carry the country through to the next season without mass starvation, panic and speculation drove the price of flour from $3 to nearly $20 per barrel. Animal feed became so expensive that cattle had to be slaughtered en masse. Many New England farmers, unable to cope, loaded up their belongings and headed west.

Summer Overseas

Meanwhile, Europe was faring no better. Snow fell in several countries in June. Alpine glaciers advanced, threatening to engulf villages and dam rivers. In France, grapes were not ripe enough to be harvested until November, and the wine made from them was undrinkable. Wheat yields in Europe reportedly fell by 20 to 40 percent, both because of cold and water damage and because rains delayed and hampered harvesting.

Famine hit Switzerland especially hard. People began eating moss, sorrel, and cats, and official assistance had to be given to the populace to help them distinguish poisonous and nonpoisonous plants. In Rhineland, people reportedly dug through the fields for rotten remains of the previous year's potato harvest. Wheat, oats, and potatoes failed in Britain and Ireland, and a typhus epidemic swept the British Isles, killing tens of thousands. Grain prices doubled on average; in west-central Europe, they rose between three and seven times their normal price. This was a disaster for the masses of poor people, whose average expenditures for bread totaled between one-quarter and one-half of their total income.

Dearth led to hunger, and high prices led to increased poverty, which led to mass vagrancy and begging. People looted grain storages and pillaged large farms. There was a wave of emigrations to America. The European economy was still unsteady from the aftermath of the Napoleonic wars, and the crisis of 1816 led to a massive retreat from liberal ideas. By 1820, Europe was in the grip of political and economic conservatism—thanks in no small part to a volcanic eruption in Indonesia.

Who's to Blame?

Theories for why summer failed to come in 1816 abound. Many lay the blame directly on the sun. Due to volcanic particles in the air, the solar disk had been dimmed all year, which made large sunspots visible to the naked eye. Others believed that the ice persisting in the Atlantic and the Great Lakes was absorbing great quantities of heat from the atmosphere.

Silver Lining

In 1816, Geneva, Switzerland, had experienced the coldest summer it would face between 1753 and 1960. It was this bad weather that kept Mary Wollstonecraft Godwin, Percy Shelley, and Lord Byron indoors at the Villa Diodati on the shores of Lake Geneva in June 1816. As they listened to the wind howl and watched the awesome thunderstorms rage over the lake, they recited poetry and told each other ghost stories, which they vowed to record on paper.

His mood very much under the weather, Byron penned his lengthy poem *Darkness*, a vivid imagination of the Apocalypse, which the weather made seem altogether at hand. ("Morn came and went, and came, and brought no day...") And Mary Wollstonecraft Godwin, who would later become Mary Shelley, Percy's wife, began work on a masterpiece that would eventually bear the title *Frankenstein or the Modern Prometheus*.

The "Lone Strike" Theory

The adage "lightning never strikes the same place twice" seems nearly as old as lightning itself, but it's about as accurate as your average weatherman's seven-day forecast. The truth is, lightning can—and often does—strike the same place twice.

✳ ✳ ✳ ✳

Debunking a Myth

To UNDERSTAND WHY this belief is an old wives' tale, we need a quick refresher course on how lightning works. As Ben Franklin taught us, lightning is pure electricity. (Electricity is a result of the interplay between positive and negative charges.) During a thunderstorm, powerful winds create massive collisions between particles of ice and water within a cloud; these encounters result in a negatively charged electrical field. When this field becomes strong enough—during a violent thunderstorm—another electrical field, this one positively charged, forms on the ground.

These negative and positive charges want to come together, but like lovers in a Shakespearean tragedy, they need to overcome the resistance of the parental atmosphere. Eventually, the attraction grows too strong and causes an invisible channel—known as a "stepped leader"—to form in the air. As the channel reaches toward the ground, the electrical field on the earth creates its own channels and attempts to connect with the stepped leader. Once these two channels connect, electricity flows from the cloud to the ground. That's lightning.

Lightning is an amazing phenomenon. The average bolt is about 50,000 degrees Fahrenheit, or about ten times the temperature of the sun's surface. During a typical thunderstorm, nearly 30,000 lightning bolts are created. The National Oceanic and Atmospheric Administration estimates that more than 25 million bolts of lightning strike the earth each year.

Given that huge number, it's hard to believe that lightning doesn't strike the same place twice. In fact, it does—especially when the places in question are tall buildings, which can be struck dozens of times a year. According to the National Lightning Safety Institute, the Empire State Building is hit an average of 23 times a year.

The Human Lightning Rod

But tall buildings aren't the only objects that have attracted multiple lightning strikes. Consider park ranger Roy Cleveland Sullivan. For most of his career, Sullivan patrolled the hills of Virginia's Shenandoah National Park, keeping an eye out for poachers, assisting hikers, checking on campers—and being struck by lightning.

From 1942 to 1977, Lightnin' Roy was struck by lightning seven times. His eyebrows were torched off, the nail on one of his big toes was blown off, his hair was set aflame, and he suffered various burns all over his body.

Sullivan is recognized by *Guinness World Records* as the individual struck by lightning more recorded times than any other human being. He died in 1983—but not, ironically, as the result of a lightning strike.

* Lightning can develop any time there is a major static charge in the atmosphere. Volcanic eruptions, snowstorms, and even large forest fires have been associated with lightning discharges.

* Mount Baker in Washington State is the world record holder for the most snowfall in one season. In the winter of 1998–99, the ski resort recorded 1,140 inches of snow.

* Divine wind? Japan was saved from invasion twice because of storms. Both times that the Mongolians tried to invade the island nation, typhoons destroyed most of their fleets.

* Corn has an even number of rows on each ear. The average ear has 800 kernels arranged in 16 rows.

Forever Slim: Finally, Something to Admire About Insects

It's not surprising that you don't see any obese insects ambling around your yard. If you existed on a diet of leaves, garbage, and rotting corpses, would you overeat? But as it turns out, insects can't get fat even if they want to—their bodies won't allow it.

✳ ✳ ✳ ✳

The Skinny on Exoskeletons

INSECTS (as well as other arthropods, such as spiders, scorpions, and crustaceans) have exoskeletons—rigid outer body parts that are made of chitin and other material—instead of internal skeletons like humans have. The hard stuff is all on the outside, while the fat and other squishy stuff is all on the inside. The only way for an insect to get bigger is to molt, which involves forming a new exoskeleton underneath the old one and casting off the old material.

Some species start off as smaller versions of full-grown adults and go through progressive molts until they reach their full sizes. Others start off in larval stages, grow steadily, and then enter pupal stages so that they can metamorphose into adults. (For example, a caterpillar forms a cocoon and turns into a butterfly or moth.) If an insect eats a lot while it's still growing, it will simply molt sooner rather than get chunky.

Were an insect to overeat after reaching full maturity, the fat wouldn't have anywhere to go because the exoskeleton is rigid. The results would be catastrophic. Researchers learned this by severing the stomach nerves of flies, so that the flies couldn't sense that they had had their fill. The flies kept feeding until they burst open.

The Perfect Metabolism

Bugs have an innate sense of exactly how much sustenance they need. There's evidence that insects adapt their metabolisms over multiple generations, depending on how much food is in their environments. A study published in 2006 showed that diamondback moth caterpillars that lived in carbohydrate-rich environments going back eight generations could load up on more carbs without adding fat than could caterpillars that had evolved in carbohydrate-poor environments over the same time period.

The study could be a sign that other animals, including human beings, will evolve metabolic adaptations based on the food in their environments. This doesn't help us much today, but if we start pounding Whoppers, nachos, and Big Macs now, perhaps our descendants will be able to scarf them down without gaining a single pound.

The Real Dirt on the Desert

Sand dunes, scorching heat, mirages. If this is your image of the desert, you're in for a surprise. There are many stories about the desert that have spawned numerous myths. Here are two favorites.

✳ ✳ ✳ ✳

Myth:

It never snows in the desert.

Fact:

Believe it or not, the largest desert on Earth is Antarctica, where it snows a lot—the mean annual precipitation ranges from 5.9 to 10.2 inches. So why is Antarctica considered a desert? The definition of a desert is a region that receives very little rain. To be precise, a desert landscape exists where rainfall is less than 10 inches per year. Rain, of course, is needed to sustain certain types of plants and animals, but snow doesn't count as rain. So Antarctica—with all its wet snow—is dry enough to be considered a desert and too dry for a person to survive without water.

Myth:

Most sandstorms occur in hot, dry deserts.

Fact:

It's true that dangerous sandstorms commonly occur in hot, dry deserts, including the Sahara and the Gobi. But they also occur frequently in a place you might never consider—North China, particularly around the area of Beijing. Since 2000, there have been 70 sandstorms—with an average of more than 13 per year.

A ten-year research project found that sandstorms affecting China were closely related to the cold front from Siberia, according to the Inner Mongolia Autonomous Regional Meteorological Station. As the cold front swirls through the Gobi and other large desert areas, it often combines with cyclones in Mongolia, consequently bringing sandstorms to China. So if you're planning a trip to the Great Wall of China, prepare to dust yourself off!

Temperature Extremes

In Montana, 100-degree temperature swings in one day aren't out of the question.

✳ ✳ ✳ ✳

Weird Happenings in the Treasure State

YES, MONTANA IS the place to go if you want to witness a 100-degree temperature swing within a 24-hour period. While a 100-degree rise or drop in temperature is extremely rare, it has happened at least twice since meteorologists started keeping records—and both times, it was in the Treasure State. When the weather turns on a dime, it's usually because of a collision of weather fronts—the boundaries between huge masses of air with different densities, temperatures, and humidity levels. And Montana happens to be ground zero in a perpetual weather-front war.

The biggest 24-hour temperature swing on record occurred in Loma, Montana, on January 14 and 15, 1972. The thermometer climbed from −54 degrees Fahrenheit up to 49 degrees, a change of 103 degrees. This barely beat the previous record, which had been set 190 miles away in Browning, Montana— on January 23, 1916, the temperature went from 44 degrees down to −56 degrees. Even though this is no longer the record for the biggest overall 24-hour temperature swing, it's still the mark for the most dramatic drop in such a time period.

Montana owns the 12-hour records, too. Temperatures in Fairfield, Montana, dropped 84 degrees between noon and midnight on December 14, 1924. And on January 11, 1980, the temperature in Great Falls, Montana, jumped 47 degrees in just seven minutes.

Why Montana?

What makes the weather in Montana so volatile? It's all because of chinook winds—warm, dry air masses caused by high mountain ranges. Chinooks form when moist, warm air from the Pacific Ocean encounters the Rocky Mountains along Montana's western border. As an air mass climbs the western slopes of the mountain range, its moisture condenses rapidly, creating rain and snow.

This rapid condensation sets the stage for the chinook effect by warming the rising air mass. Then, as the air mass descends the other side of the mountain range, the higher air pressure at the lower altitude compresses it, making it even warmer. The result is an extreme warm front that can raise temperatures drastically in a short period of time. But the effect is often short-lived: Montana also is in the path of bitter Arctic air masses, so cold fronts sweep into the state just as warm air masses leave.

This raises the question: How the heck do Montanans decide what to wear when they get up in the morning?

---

* Fingerprints are unique to each individual, of course. But the same goes for tongue prints and lip prints.

* Until 1862, currency from the U.S. Mint took the form of coins. During the Civil War, the Union Congress authorized the Treasury to print the first paper money, which became known as "legal tenders" or "greenbacks" because of the green ink used.

* While working as a cook in New York during the early 1900s, Mary Mallon, who became known as "Typhoid Mary," infected at least 53 people, 3 of whom died. She was quarantined for three years, released for a short time when she promised she would no longer work as a cook, then quarantined again after she broke her promise. She was never released from her second quarantine, which lasted 23 years until her death.

* Beginning with Super Bowl XXXIV in 2000, footballs used in the big game have been marked with synthetic DNA to prevent sports-memorabilia fraud. Souvenirs from the 2000 Summer Olympics were marked with human DNA in the ink.

* A raisin dropped into a glass of a carbonated drink will float up and down continually from the bottom of the glass to the top.

If Earth Stopped Spinning...

You know when you slam on the brakes in your car and the CDs and soda cans go flying? Now imagine slamming on the brakes when you're going 1,100 miles per hour, the planet's rotational speed at the equator.

* * * *

An Unrecognizable Planet

THE INSTANT THAT Earth stopped spinning, its atmosphere and inhabitants—along with soil, plants, buildings, oceans, and everything else that isn't firmly attached to the rocky foundation of the planet's crust—would keep on going at 1,100 miles per hour. The face of the planet would be wiped clean.

Let's say you were up in the Space Shuttle and missed all the planet-wiping excitement. What would life be like when you got back to now-still Earth? The good news is that there would be no change in gravity, which means that you wouldn't fall off the planet and the atmosphere wouldn't go away. But you would notice plenty of other differences. First of all, the cycles of day and night as we know them would no longer exist. Wherever you were, it would be light for about six months and then dark for about six months. As a result, one side of the planet would be icy cold and the other side would be extremely hot.

The planet's overall wind patterns would change significantly, too. Major wind patterns are caused by the sun heating the planet unevenly. The sun's rays hit the equator directly and the North and South Poles at an angle, which means the area around the equator gets much hotter than the mass around the poles. This heat gradient continually drives warmer air toward the poles and cooler air toward the equator, which establishes a basic global wind pattern.

But the spinning motion of the planet complicates this basic northerly and southerly airflow, creating smaller wind systems called convection cells in each hemisphere and leading to prevailing easterly and westerly winds. These systems interact to generate the weather that dictates the climates around the globe. If Earth didn't spin, we wouldn't see the same complex weather patterns. Warm air would simply rise at the equator and rush to the poles, and cold winds would move the opposite way.

Finally, a nonspinning Earth would not generate a magnetic field. Compasses would be useless, but there'd be a much bigger problem: Earth would no longer possess the magnetic field's protection against cosmic rays. The radiation from the sun and other stars would damage your DNA, leading to severe health problems. But the extreme heat or cold and total lack of animal and plant life would kill you well before the radiation did.

The Stuff of Fiction

Don't fret, though. There is virtually no chance that any of this could happen. For Earth's rotational speed to change radically, it would need to collide with an asteroid the likes of which humans have never seen. Even if that happened, it's extremely unlikely that the collision would stop the planet from spinning altogether—it would probably just slow it down. In any case, we would see something that big well in advance, which would give Bruce Willis enough time to go and blow it up.

Say What?

My advice to you is get married: if you find a good wife you'll be happy; if not, you'll become a philosopher.

—SOCRATES

I have never killed a man, but I have read many obituaries with great pleasure.

—CLARENCE DARROW

A hero is no braver than an ordinary man, but he is braver five minutes longer.

—RALPH WALDO EMERSON

Fresno's Underground Gardens

An ingenious immigrant named Baldassare Forestiere handcrafted a complex network of underground gardens when he realized his plot of land couldn't grow wine grapes.

✳ ✳ ✳ ✳

No Vino

IN 1905, Baldassare Forestiere and his brother arrived in California's San Joaquin Valley. They had come to "the land of opportunity" to seek their fortune by growing fruit trees. Unfortunately, the land they bought was a lemon—but not the kind you can harvest and sell. Instead of giving up after buying land that was totally unfit to grow much of anything, Forestiere combined his knowledge of farming and his fascination with Roman architecture and went underground.

Dig It, Baby!

The cool cellarlike tunnels Forestiere dug provided naturally air-conditioned rooms to beat the oppressive Fresno heat. And with access to groundwater and enough sunlight, he figured he might actually be able to grow something underground.

Forestiere first built a home that provided shelter from Fresno's hot summers, and for the next 40 years, he kept on digging. Shovel by shovel, he and his brother carved their worthless farmland into a maze of underground caverns where their dreams of plant cultivation were realized.

By 1923, they had carved out more than ten acres of tunnels, rooms, patios, and grottos in the rocky soil—all by hand. They dug bed niches, bath alcoves, peepholes, stairways, grape arboretums, gardens, and holes that reached up through the bedrock so that trees growing beneath could get sunlight. Forestiere's underground home even had a parlor with a fireplace.

Visitors can still tour Forestiere's underground digs, which are cared for by Forestiere's relatives.

Quicksand: Its Malevolent Powers Are Overrated

In a battle between you and quicksand, you definitely have the advantage—even if you happen to be the black-hatted villain from a classic Western who totally deserves that slow, sandy death.

✳ ✳ ✳ ✳

Really, It's Just Sand

QUICKSAND IS NOTHING more than ordinary sand that has been liquefied, usually by water that seeps up from underground. Why does a little water make such a difference? Normally, a sand dune can hold you on its surface because of the friction that the individual grains of sand exert on each other—when you step on the sand, the grains push on each other and, collectively, hold you up. But when the right amount of water seeps into a mass of sand, it lubricates each individual grain, greatly reducing the friction. If you agitate quicksand by walking through it, it acts like a thick liquid, and you sink.

This sandy sludge is denser than water, however—and much denser than your body. This means that you'll only sink waist-deep before you reach your natural buoyancy level; after that, you'll float. In other words, you won't gradually sink all the way to the bottom until only your hat remains, like that villain from the classic Western.

Still, it's fairly difficult to free yourself from quicksand. Once you're in, the quicksand settles into a thick muck around you. When you try to lift your foot, a partial vacuum forms underneath it, and the resulting suction exerts a strong downward pull. A 2005 study that was published in the journal *Nature* suggests that the force needed to pull a person's foot out of quicksand at one centimeter per second is equal to the force needed to lift a medium-size car. The best way to get free, according to this study, is to wriggle your arms and legs very slowly. This opens up space for water to flow down and loosen the sand around you, allowing you to gradually paddle to freedom.

Exceptions to the Rule

Does all of this mean that you don't need to fear death by quicksand? Not exactly. There are still a number of ways to die in the sandy goo. First, if you really freak out, you could thrash around enough to swallow huge quantities of sand. Second, if you're carrying a heavy backpack or are inside of a heavy car, you could sink below the surface of the quicksand. Third, if you get stuck in quicksand near the ocean, you might not be able to free yourself before the tide comes in and drowns you. Finally, if you don't know the wriggling trick, you might just give up and expire of dehydration and boredom.

---

* Draft dodging between the United States and Canada has a long tradition. So many U.S. draft dodgers went to Canada during the Civil War that locals began to worry about competition for jobs. During the Vietnam War, Canada was still the draft dodger's destination of choice when as many as 80,000 men crossed the border northward. But the practice was no one-way street. Canadian draft dodgers often headed south to escape entering WWI; that is, until the United States entered the conflict in 1917.

* There are 27 moons orbiting Uranus.

* Traces of peanuts can be found in dynamite.

* Jell-O once tried to market a celery flavor. It also tried coffee and cola with equally poor success.

* A watermelon contains 92 percent water.

* A pound of peanut butter is made up of 720 peanuts.

* A typical American family goes through 6,000 pounds of food in any given year.

Strange Catastrophes

Life is full of surprises, some less pleasant than others. From beer floods to raining frogs to exploding whales, headlines continually prove that truth is sometimes stranger than fiction.

✴ ✴ ✴ ✴

The London Beer Flood

IN 1814, A VAT OF BEER erupted in a London brewery. Within minutes, the explosion had split open several other vats, and more than 320,000 gallons of beer flooded the streets of a nearby slum. People rushed to save as much of the beer as they could, collecting it in pots, cans, and cups. Others scooped the beer up in their hands and drank it as quickly as they could. Nine people died in the flood—eight from drowning and one from alcohol poisoning.

The Great Siberian Explosion

Around 7:00 A.M. on June 30, 1908, 60 million trees in remote Siberia were flattened by a mysterious 15-megaton explosion. The huge blast, which occurred about five miles above the surface of the earth, traveled around the world twice and triggered a strong, four-hour magnetic storm. Magnetic storms occur about once every hundred years, and can create radiation similar to a nuclear explosion. These storms start in space and are typically accompanied by solar flares.

The 1908 explosion may have started with a comet of ice, which melted and exploded as it entered Earth's atmosphere. Or, it may have been an unusual airburst from an asteroid. Others believe that the source was a nuclear-powered spacecraft from another planet. However, no physical evidence of the cause has ever been found.

The Boston Molasses Disaster

On an unusually warm January day in 1919, a molasses tank burst near downtown Boston, sending more than two million gallons of the sticky sweetener flowing through the city's North End at an estimated 35 miles per hour. The force of the molasses wave was so intense that it lifted a train off its tracks and crushed several buildings in its path. When the flood finally came to a halt, molasses was two to three feet deep in the streets, 21 people and several horses had died, and more than 150 people were injured. More than 90 years later, people in Boston can still smell molasses on sultry summer days.

Oregon's Exploding Whale

When an eight-ton sperm whale beaches itself in your town, what do you do? That's a question residents of Florence, Oregon, faced in November 1970. After consulting with the U.S. Navy, town officials decided to blow up the carcass with a half ton of dynamite. Spectators and news crews gathered to watch but were horrified when they were engulfed in a sandy, reddish mist and slapped by flying pieces of whale blubber. A quarter mile away, a car was crushed when a gigantic chunk of whale flesh landed on it. No one was seriously hurt in the incident, but when the air cleared, most of the whale was still on the beach. The highway department hauled the rest of it away.

* The term "soap opera" comes from the fact that the shows used to work advertisements for soap powder into the plotlines.

* Stephen King's first story, "I Was a Teenage Grave Robber," was published in a fanzine when he was 18 years old.

* A hummingbird can dive at up to 60 miles per hour.

* A greyhound runs about 41 miles per hour.

* Before James Madison, U.S. presidents wore knee breeches instead of long pants.

* The soda 7-Up originally contained lithium.

* Muhammad is the most common name in the world.

* Johan Palmstruch of the Stockholm Banco introduced paper money to Europe in 1661. A better innovator than bookkeeper, he was imprisoned for life after the bank collapsed.

Ocean Currents

Why don't all the fish die when lightning strikes the ocean? For the same reason we don't all die when lightning strikes the ground: The ocean and the ground both conduct electricity relatively well, but the current from a lightning bolt dissipates quickly as it spreads through the earth or through a large body of water.

❋　❋　❋　❋

THANKS TO ALL of its dissolved salt and other impurities, seawater is a good conductor. The charge from a powerful lightning strike could spread out more than 100 feet, and any fish in the immediate area would probably get zapped—but only if they aren't swimming too deep. This is because electricity likes to flow along the surfaces of conductors rather than through their interiors, so when lightning strikes the ocean, most of its current spreads out over the water's surface. And even if some fish are near the surface, they won't necessarily take the full brunt of the charge. Electricity follows the path of least resistance, and seawater conducts currents much better than fish do—in other words, the electricity would want to flow around the fish rather than through them. Even so, if a fish happens to be swimming too close to the site of a powerful strike, the jolt will be deadly.

Fortunately for fish, lightning strikes the ocean far less frequently than it hits land. One of the conditions that makes thunderstorm formation possible is the rapid heating of low-lying air. But oceans don't reflect nearly as much heat as the ground does, so the atmospheric trends that exist over the ocean aren't particularly conducive to forming thunderstorms.

But don't take this information as clearance to run into the ocean when a storm is brewing. When there's lightning around, you want to be surrounded by insulators (like your house), not dog-paddling in a giant electricity conductor.

Man vs. Lava

You never know when you're going to get stuck in the middle of a volcanic eruption, so it's only appropriate to ask this all-important question: Can a person outrun lava? It would depend on how fast the human could run and how fast the lava flowed.

✳ ✳ ✳ ✳

Number Crunching

THE ABSOLUTE FASTEST humans in the world can run a little better than ten meters per second, but only for 100 meters. For a 5,000-meter Olympic race, peak human performance is just more than six meters per second. Assuming you'll have a major adrenaline boost due to the dire circumstances, we'll say that you can maintain a speed of three to five meters per second. This speed could vary greatly, however, depending on your physical condition and the distance you need to run, which might be several kilometers. (Note that women run a bit slower than men, on average.)

The speed of lava is affected by its temperature and viscosity (which are related), the angle of the slope it is flowing, and the expulsion rate of the volcano. There are different types of volcanoes and varieties of lava. Some, you could probably outwalk; other types of lava would swallow and incinerate an Olympic-class runner before he or she took a single step.

A Pyroclastic Flow: You're Toast

A pyroclastic flow isn't actually made of lava—it's a column of hot ash and gas that collapses under its own weight and roars down the side of the volcano like an avalanche. These flows can reach speeds of 40 meters per second—you have no chance of outrunning them.

A Basaltic Flow: You've Got a Chance

Basaltic lava has a high temperature and low viscosity, which means that it can move quickly, approaching speeds of 30 meters per second. However, many basaltic flows are much slower—two meters per second or less. You could outpace it for a while, but basaltic lava is relentless and often flows ten or more kilometers from the volcano before cooling and coming to a stop. You might outrun the slower flows, but it would be a challenge.

Mount Kilauea in Hawaii has been continuously issuing basaltic lava flows since 1983. Occasionally, the flows extend to nearby towns, most of which have been abandoned. When there are Hawaiians in the path of the lava, however, they are able to run away from the generally slow flows.

A Rhyolitic Flow: You'll Leave It in the Dust

Rhyolitic lava moves very slowly because it has a relatively low temperature and high viscosity. It may move only a few meters in an hour. It is still dangerously hot, however, so while you can easily outpace it with a brisk walk, you shouldn't dilly-dally.

---

* A typical child laughs 26.67 times more per day than a typical adult does.

* A champagne cork flying out of a bottle can travel as fast as 100 miles per hour.

* Mayonnaise used to be considered a delicacy and was used only for fine dining. It wasn't until 1912, when Richard Hellmann began selling it in jars in his New York deli, that the condiment became commonplace.

* The stuff in Play-Doh was first used for cleaning wallpaper.

* Vatican City claims the honor of having both the lowest divorce rate and the lowest birth rate of anywhere in the world.

* Peanut butter soup used to be popular in the 1920s.

* Graceland reports getting daily calls from people asking to speak with Elvis—still.

Chapter 12

Bizarre Truths About Places

Somewhere over the Rainbow

*We've put in some serious detective work to
try to discover the true location of Oz.*

✳   ✳   ✳   ✳

We Know It's Not in Kansas

IS THERE A soul in the civilized world who hasn't traveled
with Dorothy and Toto to the magical kingdom of Oz,
which was brought to life in the 1939 classic *The Wizard of
Oz?* The young Dorothy (Judy Garland) and her beloved dog
are whisked off their Kansas farm by
that tornado and ultimately follow the
Yellow Brick Road to Oz, where they
meet the mighty wizard.

Beyond the fantasy, though, why not
pin down the actual physical location of Oz? Impossible, you say? No,
indeed. First of all, we can rule out
one state because Dorothy utters the
famous line, "Toto, I've a feeling we're not in Kansas anymore."

So where could the tornado have tossed Dorothy and her
pooch? Well, even assuming this was one of the most dev-

astating twisters of all time—an F5 on the Fujita scale used by meteorologists—there's a limit to how far a human being can be carried by a tornado. According to researchers at the Tornado Project in St. Johnsbury, Vermont, small objects have whooshed great distances, but the farthest a human being has been thrown is about one mile.

How About Missouri?

So Dorothy couldn't have gone far—let's say a mile and a half because she was smaller than a full-grown adult. Therefore, Dorothy must have lived right on the Kansas border. And not out in the middle of nowhere, either, because at the start of the film, farm worker Hickory makes this statement: "But someday, they're going to erect a statue to me in this town."

So liftoff was near some kind of city or village right at the edge of Kansas. And you have to assume that Oz itself couldn't have been in an empty cornfield, either, because there would have needed to be some sort of population where Dorothy and Toto landed. Only the northern and eastern borders of Kansas provide search points, because most tornadoes move from southwest to northeast. A twister on either of the state's other two borders would have carried Dorothy and Toto farther into Kansas.

There is only one location that fits the description provided in the movie. Dorothy's Uncle Henry and Aunt Em must have lived just outside of Atchison, Kansas—east of Highway 7 near the Missouri River—and the infamous tornado carried girl and dog little more than a mile to the outskirts of Rushville, Missouri: Oz.

Before you scoff, consider some curious coincidences. Tornado activity in the Rushville area is 143 percent greater than the overall U.S. average. Oh, and Atchison is the birthplace of Amelia Earhart. The gallant aviatrix, Atchison's most famous daughter if you aren't counting Dorothy, vanished on her flight around the world in 1937 but was declared dead in 1939—the same year *The Wizard of Oz* was released. Perhaps Amelia can be found over the rainbow.

"Siberia" for Siberians

The frozen and desolate expanse of Siberia is infamous as a place of forced exile for Russian political dissidents. But if you already lived in Siberia and ran afoul of the authorities, where would you be sent?

✳   ✳   ✳   ✳

IF YOU LIVED in Siberia and were exiled, you'd probably wind up in a prison elsewhere in Russia—and anywhere would likely be better than Siberia.

Russia is the world's largest country by landmass, and Siberia accounts for more than 75 percent of it—it's about 5.2 million square miles. Until very recently, large areas of Siberia were difficult to get to . . . and, thus, difficult to escape from. This made it an ideal place to send those who questioned Russian authority. The Russian government started banishing people to distant parts of the country—not just Siberia—around the 17th century, and it continued to do so until after World War II.

Political and criminal exiles were sent to Siberian labor camps known as gulags. Many of these gulags were in remote areas in northeast Siberia. Sevvostlag, a system of labor camps, was set up in the Kolyma region within the Arctic Circle. Parts of the Kolyma mountain range weren't even discovered until 1926. It's a land of permafrost and tundra, with six-month-long winters during which the average temperature ranges from -2 degrees to -36 degrees Fahrenheit.

Siberia's first settlements were established relatively late in Russia's history, around the 17th century, but the region now supports several cities of more than half a million people. These are situated mostly in the south and have been accessible by rail since the early 20th century. The storied Trans-Siberian Railway runs from Moscow east to Vladivostok, a distance of about 5,800 miles. It was built by a workforce of soldiers and labor-camp inmates.

The Numbskull Who Named a Floating Block of Ice "Greenland"

Indeed, there might not be a place on the planet that has a more ill-suited name—and for that, we can thank the Vikings.

✳   ✳   ✳   ✳

White Is More Like It

LET'S FACE IT: Explorers weren't always the brightest bulbs. Brave? Yes. Self-reliant? Maybe. But intelligent? Not so much. To be fair, the great explorers of yore were working without reliable maps. Still, one has to admit that it was boneheaded for Christopher Columbus to think that an island in the Caribbean was India. And what about the guy who landed on an enormous iceberg and decided to call it Greenland? Talk about a moron.

Greenland, perhaps best known as the largest island that is not a continent, sits way up in the North Atlantic near the Arctic Circle. Ninety percent of the island is covered by an ice cap and smaller glaciers, which means that the place is mostly uninhabitable. Although the northern coasts of Greenland have been settled for thousands of years by the Inuit (the same folks who brought you the igloo), the island was largely unknown to Europeans until the late 10th century.

So how did a country that boasts almost no green land get the name Greenland? Theories abound, including the legend that Iceland switched names with Greenland to avoid being invaded by barbarians. (Barbarians were dumb, but not that dumb.) While this explanation borders on preposterous, it's not as far off the mark as you may think.

Erik the Red Goes Green

Many historians believe that Greenland's name may be a part of one of the biggest—and earliest—marketing scams of all time. In the 10th century, a Viking named Erik the Red fled his home of Iceland after committing murder. Erik took the opportunity to explore the islands and lands to the west of Iceland.

Drifting across the Atlantic, Erik eventually came to the rocky coast of an enormous island that was covered in ice. He had an idea: If he couldn't be with his people, then he'd bring his people to him. Though only a sliver of land was actually green, he promptly named the island Greenland, which, according to the Icelandic sagas, was because "men will desire much the more to go there if the land has a good name."

Icelanders, believing the marketing hype, came in droves, settling along the southern coast of Greenland, where they flourished for several hundred years. To be fair to Erik, archaeologists believe that the island's climate was a bit more temperate during the Vikings' heyday than it is now. Still, calling this arctic landmass Greenland is a bit like a modern-day housing developer grandly naming its cookie-cutter development Honey Creek, even though the only "creek" nearby is a sewage canal. At any rate, Erik the Red pulled off one heck of a real-estate swindle.

Interestingly, it is Erik the Red's son, Leif Eriksson, who is widely considered to be the first European to visit North America. In the early 11th century, Leif ventured with a band of explorers across the Atlantic Ocean, where he discovered the cold, wintry islands of what are now Newfoundland and Labrador, Canada. Leif named the region as only the son of Erik the Red could: Wine Land.

✳ **The original name of the game volleyball was "mintonette." It was created in 1895 when a YMCA gym teacher borrowed from basketball, tennis, and handball to create a new game.**

Luck of the Irish

There are no snakes in Ireland—and there never have been.

✻ ✻ ✻ ✻

SNAKES HAVE NEVER set foot, er, slithered into Ireland, so there's no validity to the rumor that Saint Patrick rid the country of the scaly reptiles by driving them into a sea of green beer. Just kidding...about the beer, not the snakes.

Initially, what is now known as Ireland lacked a climate that was warm enough to accommodate snakes. About 8,500 years ago, temperatures rose enough to make Ireland a nice home for slitherers, but it wasn't to be. The veritable heat wave melted the ice that connected Ireland to Europe, and it became the island that it is today. Talk about the luck of the Irish: Since it was surrounded by water, it was beyond the reach of those scary snakes.

So why does Great Britain, Ireland's closest neighbor and also an island, have snakes? Great Britain was connected to Europe until about 6,500 years ago. Three species of snakes made it to Great Britain before the melting glaciers created the English Channel and isolated it from the mainland. Great Britain is as far as the snakes got—by then, Ireland was an island.

Ireland also has only one species of lizard, frog, toad, and newt. In the 1960s, humans introduced the "slow worm," a legless lizard that some mistake for a snake, into the wild.

What about the legend of Saint Patrick driving the snakes from Ireland? Well, as anyone who majored in English in college knows, allegory is a powerful form of storytelling. In the case of Saint Patrick, snakes might have represented pagans as he worked tirelessly to convert people to Christianity.

If you really hate snakes, you'll be heartened to learn that Ireland isn't the only place on the planet without them. New Zealand, Iceland, Greenland, and Antarctica are also snake-free.

Geographic Oddities

The world's diverse landscapes, seascapes, and climates provide some interesting, and unusual, sightseeing opportunities.

✳ ✳ ✳ ✳

Atacama Desert (Chile): This 600-mile stretch of coastal desert is so lung-searingly dry that if you die there, your corpse will barely decay. In some parts, no rainfall has been recorded by humans, but a million people still live in the region.

Bay of Fundy's Tides (Nova Scotia/New Brunswick, Canada): As water moves in and out of this bay, the difference between high and low tide reaches 52 feet. Imagine a four-story building at water's edge, from which you could exit to dry land at low tide. Come high tide, the entire building would be submerged.

Black Canyon of the Gunnison (Colorado): When a river flows across hard volcanic rock for millions of years, it cuts a deep course, and its sides don't collapse much. This explains the formation of the Black Canyon, which at one point is a quarter mile across and a half mile deep. From the air it looks like a vast, dark crack in the earth.

Blue Hole of Belize (Lighthouse Reef off Belize, Central America): Sixty miles out from Belize City, there's a circular reef in the shallow water about a quarter mile across, encasing a perfectly round, 400-foot-deep pool of midnight blue.

Cliffs of Moher (County Clare, Ireland): Here you can be rained on from above and below. The sheer cliffs rise more than 600 feet above sea level, and the surf's force is violent enough to send spray all the way to the top. When it's raining, one gets the stereo effect of being thoroughly drenched from both ends.

Dead Sea (Israel/Jordan): The Dead Sea is eight times saltier than seawater. You can't sink unless you're weighted down (not encouraged). It's referred to as "dead" because no fish or plant life can tolerate the high salinity, though its rich mineral content draws health enthusiasts from around the world.

Devil's Bath (North Island, New Zealand): Near Rotorua is a collection of geothermal attractions. The Champagne Pool (a hot, steamy, bubbly lake) spills over to create a bright, sulfury, yellow-green pond called the Devil's Bath. It looks like a pool of molten sulfur and smells worse than one would expect.

Giant's Causeway (Antrim, Northern Ireland): There are some 40,000 brown basalt columns (most but not all of them hexagonal) packed together on and around a peninsula sticking out of Ireland. The result looks like stepping stones for a prehistoric titan and is one of the strangest and most popular sights in Ireland.

North Pacific Gyre Trash Vortex (Pacific Ocean): About a third of the way from California to Hawaii, a swirling ocean current collects garbage and doesn't easily let it go. This patch, now the size of Texas, consists mostly of floating plastic debris such as bottles and grocery bags. Unfortunately, as the pieces degrade, birds and fish eat them and die.

Punalu'u Black Sand Beach (Hawaii): Some places have beautiful beaches with sand that's white, tan, or even dark gray. Rarely, however, does one see sand that's as black as charcoal. The peculiar sand of Punalu'u is made of lava that exploded when it hit the water and has since been ground very fine. If that isn't strange enough, there are freshwater springs beneath the saltwater surf.

Uluru (Northern Territory, Australia): Once known as Ayers Rock, this enormous rusty sandstone monolith rises more than 1,100 feet from the desert floor and is about two miles wide. The rock is spiritually sacred to the Anangu (Australian Aborigines).

Uyuni Salt Flats (southern Bolivia): Roughly 25 times the size of the Bonneville Salt Flats in the United States, this saline landscape covers more than 4,000 square miles of Bolivia at an altitude of 12,500 feet. Because of brine just below the surface, any crack in the salt soon repairs itself.

The Fountain of Youth

It's been an obsession of explorers for centuries.

✳ ✳ ✳ ✳

SPANISH EXPLORER JUAN PONCE DE LEÓN was supposedly searching for the fabled fountain of youth when he discovered Florida. However, it wasn't until after his death in 1521 that he became linked with the fountain.

The first published reference associating Ponce de León with the fountain of youth was the *Historia General y Natural de las Indias*, by Gonzalo Fernandez de Oviedo in 1535. The author cited the explorer's search for a fountain of restorative water to cure his impotence, but the veracity of this account is questionable since Ponce de León had children at the time of his 1513 voyage and didn't even mention the fountain in his travel notes.

Moreover, the fountain of youth legend predates Ponce de León. In Arabic versions of the *Alexander Romance*, a collection of myths about Alexander the Great, the Macedonian king and his troops cross a desert and come to a fountain in which they bathe to regain strength and youth. This story was translated to French in the 13th century and was well-known among Europeans.

If a fountain of youth actually exists, no one has found it in any of its supposed locations, including Florida, the Bahamas, or the Bay of Honduras. A fountain of youth may actually exist in science, however. David Sinclair, a Harvard University professor and the founder of Sirtris Pharmaceuticals, discovered in 2003 that the molecule resveratrol could extend the lifespan of worms and fruit flies. In 2006, Italian researchers prolonged the life of the fish *Nothobranchius furzeri* with resveratrol.

Drugs that are based on this research could be on shelves soon, though initially they will be designed only to aid people with diabetes. It's not quite eternal life—it's basically just extended fitness. But that's more than Ponce de León found.

The Route to China via a Hole

What would you encounter if you tried to dig a hole to China? Hopefully a chiropractor, because severe back pain is about all that your journey would yield. It's obviously impossible to carve out such a tunnel, but for the sake of knowledge, we'll look into what would happen if you did.

✳ ✳ ✳ ✳

We'll Start in the United States

BEFORE BEGINNING OUR dig, let's establish that the starting point for our hole is in the United States, where this expression appears to have originated. Nineteenth-century writer/philosopher Henry David Thoreau told the story of a crazy acquaintance who attempted to dig his way to China, and the idea apparently stuck in the American popular mind.

We also need to clear up a common misconception. On a flat map, China appears to be exactly opposite the United States. However, roughly 500 years ago, humanity established that planet Earth is round, so we should know not to trust a flat representation. If you attempted to dig a hole straight down from the United States, your journey—  about 8,000 miles in all—would actually end somewhere in the Indian Ocean. Therefore, our hole will run diagonally; this will have the added benefit of sparing us from having to dig through some of the really nasty parts of the earth's interior.

Let's Dig

The hole starts with the crust, which is simply the planet's outer layer, the part we see every day. The earth's crust is anywhere from about 3 to 25 miles thick, depending on where you are. By the time we jackhammer through this layer, the temperature will be about 1,600 degrees Fahrenheit—hot enough to fry us in an instant. But we digress.

The second layer of the earth is the mantle. The rock here is believed to be slightly softer than that of the crust because of intense heat and pressure. The temperature in the mantle can exceed 4,000 degrees Fahrenheit, but who's counting?

Since our hole is diagonal, we'll probably miss the earth's core. At most, we'll only have to contend with the core's outermost layer. And it's a good thing, too: Whereas the outer core is thought to be liquid, the inner core, which is about 4,000 miles from the earth's surface, is believed to be made of iron and nickel. It is extremely difficult to pierce, particularly with a shovel. But either way, it would be hotter than hot; scientists think the outer core and inner core are 7,000 and 9,000 degrees Fahrenheit, respectively.

And you thought the hot wings night at your local bar took a toll on your body! No, unless fire and brimstone are your thing, the only journey you'll want to take through the center of the earth is a hypothetical one.

* **Thomas Morgan and Elizabeth Caerleon were married for 81 years. When she died on January 19, 1891, their aggregate age was 209 years, 262 days.**

* **Shredded pieces of aluminum dropped by American planes during World War II to baffle enemy radar were called** *chaff.*

* **English men were once legally barred from witnessing childbirth.**

* **In Chico, California, bowling on the sidewalk is not only illegal, it is punishable by a fine. If you're wearing one of those silly bowling shirts, there may be possible imprisonment.**

* **President Zachary Taylor died in office in 1850 from gastroenteritis. The mysterious circumstances of his sudden death caused his descendants to exhume his body in 1991. Nothing unusual was discovered.**

The World's Worst Places to Live

*Depending on your criteria, the candidates range from
Pittsburgh, Pennsylvania, to Port Moresby, Papua New Guinea.*

✳ ✳ ✳ ✳

A Matter of Opinion

MUCH LIKE BEAUTY, the worst place to live is in the eye of
the beholder (or the resident). If you enjoy long hikes in
untrammeled countryside, then the megalopolis Tokyo would
probably be a bad match for you. Similarly, if you enjoy the
rich culture of a big city, a life spent in Maza, North Dakota
(2007 population: four), might seem akin to burning in hell.
If you wake up each morning to find that your ex has again
slashed your car tires and left a flaming sack of solid waste on
your doorstep, then the town in which you reside is most likely
the worst place in the world to live.

When serious types sit down to make their worst-cities-in-
the-world lists, they usually look at quantifiable measures such
as pollution or infant mortality rate. *Popular Science* magazine,
for instance, placed Pittsburgh, Pennsylvania, on its list of the
world's ten worst cities because of its toxic air quality. Sure, the
'Burgh could stand to learn a thing or two about going green,
but take in a baseball game at beautiful PNC Park and head
over to Primanti Brothers for a pastrami and cheese, and then
try to say it's a terrible place to live.

Another factor that many "worst" lists point to is war. Makes
sense. The likelihood of getting killed simply by walking out
your front door is a flaw that most prospective homeowners
would be unable to overlook. Popular choices in this category
feature any number of cities in the war-torn Congo. But bad
wars can happen to good cities. There have been a number of
violent conflicts in Paris, but most people will agree that the
City of Lights has rebounded nicely.

There's Bad, and Then There's This Place

If only there was a city that could bring it all together—a city that could take the constant threat of violence, mix in government corruption, and top it off with squalid living conditions. Well, *The Economist* found just such a place. After reviewing 130 world capitals, the magazine declared that Port Moresby, the capital of Papua New Guinea, is the world's worst place to live. Port Moresby has exceptionally high rates of murder and rape, massive unemployment, and no welfare system.

This sounds horrendous, but remember, it was a survey of only world capitals. Surely there's some off-the-map sinkhole that makes Port Moresby look like Aspen. We'll keep looking, but in the meantime Port Moresby is the champ.

✳ Sea horses are the only animal species in which the males are capable of giving birth.

✳ The original source of the Hearst family fortune was gold, which was discovered by George Hearst in California. Late in his life, he also served as a Democratic senator from that state.

✳ There are 27 bones in that appendage at the end of your arm. Now give yourself a hand!

✳ During World War I, Hermann Göring took over as the commander of the "Flying Circus" after original commander Manfred von Richthofen—the Red Baron—and his replacement were killed. Göring later became commander of the German Luftwaffe during Word War II.

✳ Can you spell that for me, please? People who fear the number 666 suffer from hexakosioihexekontahexaphobia.

✳ Ramses II of Egypt had an impressive number of children. The latest studies suggest that the pharaoh had as many as 50 sons and 53 daughters.

✳ More than 29 years after the Japanese surrendered in World War II, Lieutenant Onoda Hiro was discovered in the Philippines. He refused to surrender until he was ordered to do so by his commanding officer.

Centralia, Pennsylvania: It's Hot, Hot, Hot

If dodging nasty potholes during your commute makes you a bit hot under the collar, just imagine what the few people who still live in this now-defunct mining town must go through.

* * * *

Whoops!

FOR MOST OF the first half of the 20th century, the northeastern Pennsylvania mining town of Centralia was a perfectly functional small town. The population hovered around 3,000, and there were shops and cafés, businesses and schools. Miners worked hard in the coal-rich region, and all was well.

Then in 1962, all that changed forever. Though the logic seems dubious now, it was common practice in those days to turn open mine pits into garbage dumps. After all, the mining holes were wide dips in the earth, which made for perfect fire pits—there was little risk of starting forest fires because the garbage would burn below ground level. No one thought about the possibility of the fire going underground. But that's exactly what happened.

The garbage dumpers picked a very, very bad place to set their trash alight. As it turns out, the pit, an abandoned mine in the southeastern part of town, was smack in the middle of a robust coal vein. And what does coal do best? Burn. The trash ignited the trail of coal, and the coal began to slowly burn underground, spidering out to other coal veins beneath the surface of Centralia. This was not good.

Everybody Out

The underground fire sizzled its way into coal veins under the businesses, schools, and homes of Centralia. Over time, the fire started causing health problems for residents. Carbon monoxide gases caused lightheadedness and hacking coughs as the smoke continued to curl up from the ground. Wildlife was making a mass exodus, and the air smelled bad. Pavement started to crack, building foundations were at risk, and it began to dawn on the people of Centralia that this underground fire wasn't going to fizzle out on its own.

The next two decades were spent trying to extinguish the fire, but to no avail. Firefighters, engineers, and concerned individuals came up with plan after failed plan. Some thought the best solution was to flush the mines with water; others tried to excavate the burning material. Some figured that drilling holes into the ground might help locate the boundaries of the fire, but that only fed the fire with more oxygen.

By the early 1980s, the fire was burning under a few hundred acres. After a young boy fell into a burning sinkhole in the sidewalk, the government stepped in to help Centralians relocate. Eventually, the few remaining buildings in town were condemned, and the government took ownership of the land.

Pennsylvania's government looked into putting the fires out for good, but ultimately, it seemed more reasonable to just move people out than to shell out $660 million to trench the entire area, with no guarantee of success. Several million dollars had already been spent on the fire, and apparently, that was enough.

Visit Scenic Centralia . . . or Not

An engineering study in 1983 concluded that the mine fires could burn for another couple of centuries or more, perhaps spreading over more than 3,500 acres before burning out.

That means that if you want to visit a slow-roasted town, you've got plenty of time. You'll have to look hard for Centralia, though—the town doesn't even exist on a lot of maps these days. Visitors will occasionally see smoke rising from cracks in the road or catch a whiff of sulfur here and there. Though tourism is obviously not encouraged—and we certainly don't advise it—it's not against the law to explore the town. Just keep an eye out for burning sinkholes, of course.

Road Trip: Pakistan's M2 Highway

On Pakistan's paradoxical M2 highway, law and order is exactly what you'll get when you get behind the wheel.

✳ ✳ ✳ ✳

Sharif's Dream

IN 1991, Pakistan's Prime Minister Nawaz Sharif decided that his country needed a new highway. It took him more than six years to get the job done, but in 1997, the M2 was officially open for business. The road begins in the city of Lahore and runs 367 miles through the hills and valleys and over the rivers of the Punjab province until it reaches Islamabad, the capital of Pakistan.

One of the most extraordinary characteristics of the M2 is its perfectly manicured appearance—it's probably the only road in the world that is swept by hand. Crews work diligently to keep the pride and joy of the Pakistani roadways neat and tidy, actually using brooms to brush away the grit.

The Changing Landscape

A trip that used to take six hours on the older roads now takes three hours on the M2. There are six lanes to choose from, but that doesn't mean it's an über-fast highway like Germany's Autobahn. The speed limits are strictly enforced, especially near the hairpin turns that occur in the northwest Salt Ranges. In that area, going over 20 miles per hour is extremely dangerous.

In some areas of Pakistan, police have been known to take a bribe from time to time, but that behavior won't fly on the M2. Impeccably dressed highway police watch the highway with radar guns at the ready and aren't shy about pulling over those with a lead foot.

For as proud as Pakistan is of its meticulously maintained highway, there aren't too many people using it. High fuel costs, civil unrest, a poor economy, and a relatively low number of drivers mean that the M2 is a pretty lonely, empty road.

The Mysterious Area 51

Who killed JFK? Did Americans really land on the moon? Conspiracy theorists have been debating these questions for years. But they all agree on one thing—these conspiracies pale in comparison to the mother of all conspiracies: Area 51.

✳ ✳ ✳ ✳

ALIEN AUTOPSIES. COVERT military operations. Tests on bizarre aircraft. These are all things rumored to be going on inside Area 51—a top secret location inside the Nevada Test and Training Range (NTTR) about an hour northwest of Las Vegas. Though shrouded in secrecy, some of the history of Area 51 is known. For instance, this desert area was used as a bombing test site during World War II, but no facility existed on the site until 1955. At that time, the area was chosen as the perfect location to develop and test the U-2 spy plane. Originally known as Watertown, it came to be called Area 51 in 1958 when 38,000 acres were designated for military use. The entire area was simply marked "Area 51" on military maps. Today, the facility is rumored to contain approximately 575 square miles. But you won't find it on a map because, officially, it doesn't exist.

An Impenetrable Fortress

Getting a clear idea of the size of Area 51, or even a glimpse of the place, is next to impossible. Years ago, curiosity seekers could get a good view by hiking to the top of two nearby mountain peaks, White Sides and Freedom Ridge. But government officials soon grew weary of people climbing up there and snapping pictures, so in 1995, they seized control of both. Currently, the only way to legally catch a glimpse of the base is to scale 7,913-foot-tall Tikaboo Peak. Even if you make it that far, you're still not guaranteed to see anything because the facility is more than 25 miles away and is only visible on clear days with no haze.

The main entrance to Area 51 is along Groom Lake Road. Those brave (or foolhardy) souls who have ventured down the road to investigate quickly realize they are being watched. Video cameras and motion sensors are hidden along the road, and signs alert the curious that if they continue any further, they will be entering a military installation, which is illegal "without the written permission of the installation commander." If that's not enough to get unwanted guests to turn around, one sign clearly states: "Use of deadly force authorized." Simply put, take one step over that imaginary line in the dirt, and they will get you.

Camo Dudes

And just exactly who are "they"? They are the "Camo Dudes," mysterious figures watching trespassers from nearby hillsides and jeeps. If they spot something suspicious, they might call for backup—Blackhawk helicopters that will come in for a closer look. All things considered, it would probably be best to just turn around and go back home. And lest you think about hiring someone to fly you over Area 51, the entire area is considered restricted air space, meaning that unauthorized aircraft are not permitted to fly over, or even near, the facility.

Who Works There?

Most employees are general contractors who work for companies in the area. But rather than allow these workers to commute individually, the facility has them ushered in secretly and en masse in one of two ways. The first is a mysterious white bus with tinted windows that picks up employees at several unmarked stops before whisking them through the front gates of the facility. Every evening, the bus leaves the facility and drops off the employees.

The second mode of commuter transport, one that is even more secretive, is JANET, the code name given to the secret planes that carry workers from Las Vegas McCarran Airport to Area 51 and back again. JANET aircraft come and go from their own terminal, which is located at the far end of the airport, behind fences outfitted with special security gates. JANET even has its own private parking lot. Several times a day, planes from the JANET fleet take off and land at the airport.

Bob Lazar

The most famous Area 51 employee is someone who may or may not have actually worked there. In the late 1980s, Bob Lazar claimed that he'd worked at the secret facility he referred to as S-4. In addition, Lazar said that he was assigned the task of reverse engineering a recovered spaceship in order to determine how it worked. Lazar had only been at the facility for a short time, but he and his team had progressed to the point where they were test-flying the alien spaceship. That's when Lazar made a big mistake. He decided to bring some friends out to Groom Lake Road when he knew the alien craft was being flown. He was caught and subsequently fired.

During his initial interviews with a local TV station, Lazar seemed credible and quite knowledgeable as to the inner workings of Area 51. But when people started trying to verify the information Lazar was giving, not only was it next to impossible to confirm most of his story, his education and employment history could not be verified either. Skeptics immediately proclaimed that Lazar was a fraud. To this day, Lazar contends that everything he said was factual and that the government deleted all his records in order to set him up and make him look like a fake. Whether or not he's telling the truth, Lazar will be remembered as the man who first brought up the idea that alien spaceships were being experimented on at Area 51.

What's Really Going On?

So what really goes on inside Area 51? One thing we do know is that they work on and test aircraft. Whether they are alien spacecraft or not is still open to debate. Some of the planes worked on and tested at Area 51 include the SR-71 Blackbird and the F-117 Nighthawk stealth fighter. Currently, there are rumors that a craft known only by the codename Aurora is being worked on at the facility.

If you want to try to catch a glimpse of some of these strange craft being tested, you'll need to hang out at the "Black Mailbox" along Highway 375, also known as the Extraterrestrial Highway. It's really nothing more than a mailbox along the side of the road. But as with most things associated with Area 51, nothing is as it sounds, and the "Black Mailbox" is actually white. It belongs to a rancher who owns the property nearby. Still, this spot is where people have been known to camp out all night for a chance to see something strange in the night sky.

The Lawsuit

In 1994, a landmark lawsuit was filed against the U.S. Air Force by five unnamed contractors and the widows of two others. The suit claimed that the contractors had been present at Area 51 when large quantities of "unknown chemicals" were burned in trenches and pits. The suit alleged that, as a result of contact with the chemical fumes, two of the contractors died and five survivors suffered respiratory problems and skin sores. Reporters worldwide jumped on the story, not only because it proved that Area 51 existed but because the suit was asking that many classified documents be entered as evidence. Would some of those documents refer to alien beings or spacecraft? The world would never know, because in September 1995, while petitions for the case were still going on, President Bill Clinton signed Presidential Determination No. 95–45, which basically stated that Area 51 was exempt from federal, state, local, and interstate hazardous and solid-waste laws. Shortly thereafter, the lawsuit was dismissed for lack of evidence, and all attempted appeals were rejected. In 2002, President George W. Bush renewed Area 51's exemptions, ensuring once and for all that what goes on inside Area 51 stays inside Area 51.

So at the end of the day, we're still left scratching our heads about Area 51. We know it exists, and we have some idea of what goes on there, but there is still so much more we don't know. More than likely, we never will know everything. But then again, what fun is a mystery if you know all the answers?

Still Sticky: The La Brea Tar Pits

The animals are much smaller than they used to be—no saber-toothed cats or woolly mammoths—but the famous pits continue to trap critters like lizards and birds.

✳ ✳ ✳ ✳

TAR PITS ARE created when crude oil seeps through a fissure in the earth's crust. When oil hits the surface, the less dense elements of the oil evaporate, leaving behind a gooey, sticky substance known as asphalt, or tar. *La Brea* is a Spanish name that translates literally to "the tar." These famed pits are located in Hancock Park in Los Angeles; they constitute the only active archeological excavation site to be situated in a

major metropolitan area. The pits are tended by staff members of the George C. Page Museum, which is nearby. It is at the museum that the fossils currently being excavated from the pits are cleaned and examined.

Not only do the staff members get to parse through the well-preserved remnants of prehistory, but they also sometimes witness the natural process by which these remnants are preserved. An average of ten animals every 30 years get trapped in the pits.

The tar pits, which are about 40,000 years old, work like a large-scale glue trap. If an animal lets just one paw hit the surface of the asphalt, it sticks (especially on warm days, when the asphalt is at its stickiest). In its frenzy to free itself, the animal gets more stuck. Eventually, its nose and mouth will be covered, and then it's all over—just one more carcass for scientists to excavate.

The Many Locations of No Man's Land

For a place so seemingly desolate, remote, and forlorn, this place sure pops up a lot.

✳ ✳ ✳ ✳

TAKE A LOOK at a map and you will find a No Man's Land in the Caradon district of southeast Cornwall, England; a No Man's Land on East Falkland Island; and a Nomans Land Island (also charted No Man's Land or No Man's Island) in Chilmark, Massachusetts. And that's just to name a few.

Some of these spots are indeed uninhabited—for good reason. The terrain of the Falkland Island No Man's Land is extremely rough due to mountains known as Wickham Heights. And No Man's Island, Massachusetts? Only three miles off the coast of Martha's Vineyard, it was once a bombing practice range.

In more general terms, No Man's Land is a phrase that has been around since at least the 14th century. It's often used to reference an unoccupied area between the front lines of opposing armies, or to designate land that is unowned, undesirable, or otherwise under dispute.

A good example: Following the Louisiana Purchase between the United States and Spain, an area called No Man's Land (aka the Neutral Strip or Sabine Free State) was designated neutral ground because the two governments could not agree on a boundary. From 1806 to 1819, both countries claimed ownership of this tract, but neither enforced any laws or control. No wonder it became a haven for outlaws and renegades.

In its earliest use, No Man's Land likely referred to a plot of land just outside the north walls of London. In the early 1300s, this No Man's Land was a place where criminals were executed and left out in the open for public view. There goes the neighborhood.

The Island that Isn't an Island

Rhode Island isn't surrounded by water, so how the heck did it get its name?

✳ ✳ ✳ ✳

Nobody's Perfect

THE HISTORY OF exploration is, in some ways, a history of mistakes. Ponce de León, the Spanish explorer who is credited with discovering and naming Florida, actually thought it was an island. Ferdinand Magellan believed that it would take only three days to sail from South America to Indonesia (try four months). And, of course, Christopher Columbus was so confused as to believe that a tiny island in the Caribbean was India.

To some extent, these mistakes are understandable—no European had been to the Caribbean previously—but others, not so much. For example, it would take a geographically challenged individual of the highest order to believe that a body of land bordered on only one side by water should be called an island. Yet that's precisely what the founders of Rhode Island seem to have done.

A quick glance at the map will tell you that islands do make up a chunk of Rhode Island's decidedly small landmass, though the vast majority of it lies on the continent, wedged between Massachusetts and Connecticut. And a quick glance at the Constitution will tell you that Rhode Island isn't the official name of the state at all. The official name is "The State of Rhode Island and Providence Plantations." How Rhode Island got that name is almost as confusing as how a body of land the size of a postage stamp can be legitimately termed a state in the first place.

A Comedy of Errors

This whole mess may be the result of a misunderstanding. Some historians argue that Rhode Island was named by confused settlers who believed that they were living on a body of land that the 16th-century explorer Giovanni da Verrazzano likened to the Mediterranean Greek island of Rhodes; hence, they began calling their home Rhode Island. The only problem is that the island about which Verrazzano had waxed classical was a different island—the one that is now called Block Island.

The official story, though, is that Rhode Island got its name from the Dutch explorer Adriaen Block—he whose namesake island should actually be called Block Island—who called the region *Roodt Eylandt* ("Red Island") after the color of the local clay. When British settlers moved in, they anglicized the name to Rhode Island.

In 1636, Roger Williams, after being kicked out of the Massachusetts Bay Colony, founded his own settlement on the mainland beside Narragansett Bay. He named it Providence in the belief that divine intervention had led him there. Williams, a theologian who advocated tolerance and free thinking (neither of which had any place in the Massachusetts Bay Colony), eventually convinced settlers of the bay's islands—which included Rhode—to join him. The eventual State of Rhode Island and Providence Plantations was born, later shortened to Rhode Island by lazy Americans.

A Good Little Place

Despite the series of blunders that led to its name, Rhode Island forged and maintains a reputation for culture and tolerance. The state was one of the first to pass laws banning slavery and one of only two that currently has laws allowing prostitution. Fourteen colleges and universities are crammed into its borders, and the Ivy League's Brown University is considered one of the finest educational institutions in the world. Its geography department, however, must be considered suspect.

✳ The last composition that Mozart wrote was meant for a funeral.

✳ A cow can drink more than 50 gallons of water every day— more than enough to fill a bathtub.

The Devil Is Alive and Well... and Living in New Jersey

The Pine Barrens consist of more than a million acres of forested land in central and southern New Jersey. So named because the area's sandy, acidic soil is bad for growing crops, it has proven a fertile home for an amazing collection of trees and plants. Of course, if the stories are true, the area is also home to a bizarre winged creature known as the Jersey Devil.

✳   ✳   ✳   ✳

Birth of the Devil

THERE ARE MANY legends concerning the origin of the Jersey Devil. The most popular involves the Leeds family, who came to America from Europe in the 1730s and settled in the southern area of the Pine Barrens. The Leeds family quickly grew by leaps and bounds, and before long, their house was filled with a dozen children. Needless to say, when Mother Leeds found out she was pregnant with child number 13, she was less than enthusiastic. In fact, she supposedly yelled out that she was done having children and that this child "could be the devil" for all she cared. Apparently someone was listening, for when the 13th child was born, it allegedly resembled a devil, complete with wings, a tail, and cloven hooves. Once born, the child devoured its 12 siblings and its parents, then promptly disappeared into the Pine Barrens, where it still lives to this day.

The First Sightings

One of the first, and most intriguing, sightings of the Jersey Devil took place in the early 1800s when Commodore Stephen Decatur saw an odd creature flying overhead as he was test-firing cannons at the Hanover Iron Works. Perhaps wishing to test the accuracy of the cannons, Decatur took aim and fired upon the creature overhead, striking one of its wings. To the amazement of Decatur and the other onlookers, the creature didn't seem to care that it had just been shot by a cannonball and casually flew away.

From the mid-1800s until the early 1900s, there were numerous sightings of the Jersey Devil throughout the Pine Barrens and beyond. Those who actually witnessed it described it as being everything from short and hairy to tall and cranelike. But there was one thing everyone agreed upon—whatever the creature was, it was not of this earth.

1909: The Year of the Devil

At the beginning of 1909, thousands of people encountered the beast in the span of a week. On Saturday, January 16, a winged creature believed to be the Jersey Devil was spotted flying over the town of Woodbury, New Jersey. The following day, residents of Bristol, Pennsylvania, also reported seeing something strange flying in the sky. Later the same day, bizarre tracks were discovered in the snow. Then on Monday, January 18, residents of Burlington, New Jersey, and neighboring towns were perplexed by the strange tracks in the snow on their rooftops. They had no clue as to who or what left them. All the while, reports kept coming in of something strange flying overhead with a head resembling a horse and hooves for feet.

In the early morning hours of January 19, Nelson Evans and his wife got up close and personal with the Jersey Devil outside their Gloucester, New Jersey, home. At approximately 2:30 A.M., a creature standing more than eight feet tall with a "head like a collie dog and a face like a horse" peered into the Evanses' window. Although they were petrified, Nelson mustered up the courage to open the window and yell at the creature. Startled, the creature turned, made a barking sound, and then flew off. Later that day, two Gloucester hunters claimed they had tracked strange footprints in the snow for nearly 20 miles. As they followed the tracks, they noticed that whatever this creature was, it not only had the ability to fly or leap over large areas, but it could also squeeze underneath fences and through small spaces.

By Wednesday, January 20, local towns were forming posses intent on tracking down the Jersey Devil. They were all unsuccessful, although they did have several sightings of the winged creature flying toward neighboring towns. Then on Thursday, things really got out of hand. The day began with the Devil reportedly attacking a trolley car in Haddon Heights. It was also during this time that local farmers reported finding some of their livestock missing or dead. And in Camden, New Jersey, a dog was attacked by the Jersey Devil and only managed to survive when its owner chased the beast away.

By Friday, the Devil had been spotted all over New Jersey and in parts of Pennsylvania. It had been shot at (and supposedly struck by several bullets) and was even hosed down by a local fire department, but this didn't seem to faze the beast at all.

Sightings Continue

As news of the Jersey Devil spread, it seemed the entire nation descended upon New Jersey to try to catch a glimpse of or, better yet, snare the creature. But despite all the searching and even a $10,000 reward for the beast's capture, it was never caught.

It appears that after its very busy week in 1909, the Jersey Devil decided to lay low. In fact, though sightings did continue through the years, they were few and far between. Because of this, people started to believe that the Jersey Devil was a harbinger of doom and would only be sighted when something bad was going to happen. Of course, this did not stop hundreds of people from wandering through the Pine Barrens in search of the beast. But no matter how hard people looked, not a single photograph or piece of video exists of the creature. Part of the reason certainly has to be that the Pine Barrens has remained virtually the same vast and undeveloped area, making it the perfect place for a devil to hide. So for now, the Pine Barrens is keeping its secret.

Tales from the Golden Gate Bridge

More than two dozen people have survived their falls from the iconic bridge. That sounds like a lot—until you learn that more than 1,300 have taken the leap since it opened in 1937.

✳ ✳ ✳ ✳

A Gruesome Way to Go

THE 21-STORY DROP from the Golden Gate Bridge, which spans the opening of the San Francisco Bay, is obviously one of the more effective suicide methods. It's also one of the nastiest. After four seconds of hurtling through the air (just enough time for a change of heart), the jumper hits the water at 75 miles per hour. In most cases, the force of the impact—15,000 pounds per square inch—will break the jumper's ribs and vertebrae. The broken ribs usually pierce the lungs, spleen, and heart, and cause massive internal bleeding. If a jumper somehow survives, he or she likely will drown.

A handful of jumpers lived to tell the tale because they hit the water feet first. Kevin Hines jumped and survived in 2000, when he was 19 years old. Immediately after taking the leap, he changed his mind and prayed to survive. In the rapid fall, he managed to turn himself so that he hit feet first. Hitting vertically helped Hines's body penetrate the water, reducing the force of impact. The force was great enough to break his back and shatter his vertebrae, but none of his organs were punctured. In 1979, a man survived in good enough shape—his worst injury was several cracked vertebrae—to swim ashore and drive to a hospital.

There is roughly one documented jump from the bridge every two weeks, making it the most popular suicide spot in the world. (There likely are other cases in which no one saw the jumper and the body washed out to sea.) The bridge is a jumping hotspot for two reasons: First, some people see it as romantic to leap from such a beautiful structure into the water; second, it's incredibly easy to do. The bridge has a pedestrian walkway, and all that stands between a suicidal person and the plunge is a four-foot railing. One possible explanation for this short railing is that the chief engineer of the bridge, Joseph Strauss, was only five feet tall and wanted to be able to enjoy the view.

Building a Safer Bridge

Over the years, calls to add a barrier to the Golden Gate Bridge have been met with resistance in San Francisco. Opponents declare that the money would be better spent elsewhere; they object to compromising the beauty of the bridge to stop people from attempting suicide, since these people would likely just resort to different methods.

In October 2008, the Golden Gate Board of Directors voted to build a net system 20 feet below the bridge's platform to catch and hold jumpers. The board then began working on raising the 40 to 50 million dollars needed to install the nets.

---

* Two men attempted to kill President Harry Truman at the Blair House in 1950. They failed, but one White House police officer and one of the assassins were killed. Two other White House police officers and the second assassin were wounded, but each recovered. Truman later commuted the death sentence of the second assassin.

* For about 1,500 years—from A.D. 393 until 1894—there were no Olympic Games. The games were reintroduced by Frenchman Pierre de Coubertin in an effort to encourage global peace.

* The remains of a giant ape, perhaps ten feet tall and weighing 1,000 pounds, were found in a cave in China. It's believed the beast lived 300,000 years ago.

* In Sri Lanka, nonverbal signals for agreement are reversed from those in Western countries: Nodding your head means "no" and shaking your head from side to side means "yes."

* About five years after his surrender at Appomattox Court House, Virginia, Confederate General Robert E. Lee died of pneumonia. His last words were reportedly, "Strike the tent."

The Most Crowded Place on Earth

We know what you're thinking: The most crowded place on earth must be Disneyland on the first day of summer vacation. Or perhaps the Mall of America on the morning after Thanksgiving. Right? Wrong.

✳ ✳ ✳ ✳

Packed In Like Sardines

WHILE PLACES SUCH as Disneyland and Mall of America are definitely hectic at certain times, there is a section of Hong Kong that has them both beat 365 days a year. It's called Mong Kok, which translates to "flourishing/busy corner." The name is apt because, according to *Guinness World Records*, Mong Kok is the most densely populated place on the planet.

About 200,000 people reside in Mong Kok, an area just slightly larger than half a square mile. That's about 70 square feet per person. Add in the buildings and you've got a district in which it is physically impossible for everyone to be outside at the same time.

Mong Kok's bustling Golden Mile—a popular stretch of shops, restaurants, and theaters—compounds the crowding issue: A half-million or so tourists routinely jostle for position in the streets. Residents told *The New York Times* that the streets are often completely full, with every inch of pavement covered.

Going Up, Up, Up

How is it possible to squeeze so many people into such a small area? You build up. Mong Kok is home to an array of high-rise apartment buildings. Families who live in these apartments sometimes rent out rooms to other families. There might be ten or more people in a single apartment—they sleep in two or three rooms and share a small kitchen and a single bathroom. The apartments are so small that people sleep in bunk beds that are three or four tiers high, and they keep their belongings in chests and baskets that are suspended from the ceiling.

Remember Mong Kok the next time you're elbowing your way through a crowded store on Black Friday, trying to secure the season's must-have toy. When you return home and sit at the table for dinner, at least there won't be two other families smiling back at you.

* A bolt of lightning is about as thick as your thumb. You can see it from so far away because of its luminescence.

* Warthogs can run fast—up to 35 mph. That's fast enough to whiz past a chicken, which can only run 9 mph.

* Sharks continually grow new teeth to replace those lost in their search for food. The average shark tooth lasts about ten days, which might be why you never see shark dentists.

* The only product Elvis Presley ever promoted was Southern Made Donuts. He made a radio commercial for the snack food that aired during *Louisiana Hayride* on November 6, 1954.

* The sole golf course on the island of Tonga has only 15 holes.

* Time to rethink that new career? A person can't be a sumo wrestler unless he weighs more than 154 pounds and is taller than five feet seven inches.

* The first snowboard was called a snurfer and was made with two skis attached together.

* Police started collecting and using fingerprints as evidence in the late 1800s.

* During his nine-year reign as pope (beginning in 955), John XII was charged with multiple sexual acts and toasting the devil with wine. He was allegedly killed by a jealous husband.

"England Yard" Is More Like It

British nomenclature is loaded with misleading terms. For example, plum pudding is not pudding, nor does it contain plums. Given this legacy of verbal imprecision, it's not surprising that the headquarters of the famous police force that patrols London is called Scotland Yard.

✳ ✳ ✳ ✳

IT STARTED IN 1829, when Charles Rowan and Richard Mayne were charged with organizing a citywide crime-fighting force in London. At the time the two men lived together in a house at 4 Whitehall Place, and they ran their fledgling outfit out of their garage, using the back courtyard as a makeshift police station. "Rowan and Mayne's Backyard" wasn't an appropriate name for the headquarters of a police force. Instead, it was called Scotland Yard.

Why? After years of research, word sleuths have narrowed the origin of the name to two likely possibilities. According to the first explanation, Scotland Yard sits on the location of what was once the property of Scottish royalty. The story goes that back before Scotland and England unified in 1707, the present-day Scotland Yard was a residence used by Scottish kings and ambassadors when they visited London on diplomatic sojourns. The other, less regal possibility is that 4 Whitehall Place backed onto a courtyard called Great Scotland Yard, named for the medieval landowner—Scott—who owned the property.

Regardless of the name's true origin, the metropolitan police moved on—sort of. In 1890, they decided that they needed new digs and moved to a larger building on the Victoria Embankment. Given a chance to redeem themselves and give their headquarters a name that actually made sense, what did the London police choose? New Scotland Yard.

It's Worse than First

Surely nobody wants his or her country to be identified as "Third World," yet some places are indeed categorized as such. Who makes the call?

✳ ✳ ✳ ✳

Not Even the Experts Are Sure

BEING A THIRD WORLD country is kind of like residing in a trailer park: You don't really want to admit where you live, you're poor, and every once in a while, a natural disaster that the rest of the world barely notices wipes you out. What exactly constitutes a Third World country? Strap in—the answer is a bit complicated.

Much like the political and economic situations in Third World countries themselves, the discourse surrounding the term "Third World" is incredibly muddled—academics and theorists rarely agree on much of anything, and this definition is no exception. Countless articles, essays, and books have been devoted to detailing not only which countries are in the "Third World," but also what the term itself means and where it originated.

Origins of a Phrase

Let's start with the term's origin. Most sources attribute "Third World" to a 1952 article by French economist and demographer Alfred Sauvy. His term, *tiers monde*, was meant to evoke another French term, "Third Estate," which referenced the commoners who rose to power during the French Revolution by taking advantage of the power struggle between the clergy and the nobility. In much the same way, Sauvy's "Third World" described the group of nations that existed ideologically and politically outside of the power struggle between the Western democratic powers (the "First World") and the Eastern-bloc Soviet countries (the "Second World"). In those days, it was pretty easy to place countries in one of the three "worlds."

The Third World Since the Cold War

In these post–Cold War days, it's a bit more complicated. In general usage, anyway, the terms "First World" and "Third World" have come to take on more economic and developmental—rather than ideological—connotations; the "Second World," meanwhile, has pretty much disappeared. And while there is no "official" body that decides which countries are in the "Third World," there are various organizations that make an effort. For example, the United Nations publishes an annual Human Developmental Index—a scale that takes into account factors such as average education levels, gross domestic product, and life expectancy. (The countries that dominate the bottom of this list are in Africa, the Middle East, and Southeast Asia.)

Some theorists argue that the end of the Cold War may have actually done the Third World a disservice. No longer concerned about whether nonaligned countries fall under capitalist or communist sway, First World nations pay less attention to Third World countries, which—much like trailer parks—wallow on, ignored, as everyone else worries about what iPhone apps to download.

---

* Revolutionary Fanya Kaplan attempted to kill Russian leader Vladimir Lenin in August 1918. Lenin survived, but Kaplan was executed the following month. A bronze monument to her was erected in Moscow in 2002.

* Although it has not been proved, there are reports of South American anaconda snakes measuring 120 feet in length. That's longer than two average ranch homes built end-to-end.

* The Library of Congress was started in 1815 when President James Madison bought almost 6,500 books from former President Thomas Jefferson's library.

* British Admiral Horatio Nelson did not escape injury in his illustrious career. He lost sight in his right eye in 1794, and his right arm was amputated in 1797. He was mortally wounded in the Battle of Trafalgar in 1805.

Share a Toast with a Ghost

Visitors to the Golden Fleece, a 16th-century pub and inn in York, England, can spend a few minutes or a full night with numerous ghosts at the city's most haunted site. Located at the end of one of Europe's best-preserved medieval streets known as "the Shambles," the Golden Fleece is a well-kept but ancient building surrounded by a mysterious atmosphere.

✳   ✳   ✳   ✳

Enjoy Some Spirits with Some Spirits

UPON ENTERING THE Golden Fleece, visitors sense spirits from the pub's past. Even when the front room is nearly empty, many visitors glance around nervously, expecting to see other guests standing in a dark corner. Unexplained shadows move and then vanish, and the sound of phantom glasses clinking can be heard. It's truly an eerie place.

Many guests will witness the Golden Fleece's ghosts if they go looking for them. For the best ghostly encounters, explore the pub's quirky corridors and cozy public rooms. Ghosts have been reported in every part of the pub and also in the haunted yard immediately behind it. Most people see the spirits as flickering figures, off to one side. Others see full apparitions, such as the colorful ghost of Lady Alice Peckett.

Lady Peckett Kept Her Head, but Thomas Percy Didn't

Lady Alice Peckett haunts both the Golden Fleece and Lady Peckett's Yard directly behind it. Her husband, John, who owned the building, was the Lord Mayor of the city of York in 1701. He left the pub when he died, but his wife decided to stay. No one is certain why she lingers, but some claim that she was too spirited and fun loving for her more serious politician husband. Perhaps she doesn't want to miss out on anything at the Golden Fleece.

Lady Alice generally manifests as an older woman wearing sweet perfume, but don't let her serene demeanor fool you. She's a mischievous ghost who likes to surprise people by walking through solid walls around the Function Room.

Another ghost to keep an eye out for is Thomas Percy, the Seventh Earl of Northumberland. Percy, a relatively harmless ghost who's also known as the Headless Earl, floats around the Shambles, near the entrance to the Golden Fleece, in search of his missing head.

During the reign of Queen Elizabeth I, when Catholics were burned at the stake, Percy held steadfast in his Catholic beliefs. Despite this, he was a favorite of the queen for many years. Unfortunately, Percy didn't realize his vulnerability. In 1569, he led a rebellion against Elizabeth and planned to replace her with her Catholic cousin, Mary, Queen of Scots. When the rebellion failed, Percy was beheaded in a public execution not far from the Golden Fleece. Though his body was buried, his head was left on public display as a warning to others. After some time, the head was simply thrown away.

A Fine "Cold Spot" in the Pub

If the weather is sultry or the pub is crowded, find a seat at the booth in the back corner of the pub. The spirits will oblige by keeping that corner cool and breezy. During a June 2007 visit, a group of American tourists complimented the staff on how well the booth was cooled. They were startled to learn that there is no air conditioning in the pub.

The chilling effect may be thanks to "One Eyed Jack," a 17th-century ghost dressed in a red coat, wig, and crisply pressed breeches. He's sometimes seen carrying a flintlock pistol and creates a refreshing breeze as he paces up and down the room, waiting to be served.

A Full Night of Good Spirits

Above the pub is an inn, and guests can spend the night encountering various spirits. Look for the gruesome, blue-tinted face of an inebriated World War II airman who fell to his death from a window.

Or listen for the confused whimpering of a little boy who appears in Victorian clothing. In the late 1800s, he was crushed to death as a cart backed up to the pub door to deliver ale. He's often seen around the front room of the pub and has even been known to pick pockets.

If you encounter a ghost wearing a noose, that spirit has escaped from the pub's basement. After being executed, corpses were sometimes stored in the cellar of the Golden Fleece, but in many cases, the bodies were never claimed and may be buried in the basement. Perhaps they're wandering the Golden Fleece hoping that someone will recognize them and give them a proper burial.

Most often, overnight guests at the Golden Fleece hear music and loud laughter coming from downstairs. When they investigate the noise, they discover that the pub is closed, the lights are off, and the downstairs rooms are empty...unless you count the ghosts, of course.

Just remember that if you see a Roman soldier who seems to be walking on his knees, nothing terrible happened to his legs. He's haunting from a time when the streets of York were several feet lower than they are now. That's the level where his ghostly feet are.

Say What?

I eat at this German-Chinese restaurant and the food is delicious. The only problem is that an hour later you're hungry for power.

—Dick Cavett

We rarely confide in those who are better than we are.

—Albert Camus

Chapter 13

Bizarre Truths About Outer Space

The "Moon Illusion"

The moon looks bigger when it's near the horizon, a phenomenon that has flummoxed brilliant minds for thousands of years. Aristotle attempted an explanation around 350 B.C., and today's scientists still don't know for sure what's going on.

✳   ✳   ✳   ✳

Here's What We Do Know...

W E MAY NOT know exactly why the moon looks bigger when it's near the horizon—something that's known as the "moon illusion"—but great thinkers have at least ruled out several possible explanations. Hey, that's progress.

First, the moon is not closer to Earth when it's at the horizon. In fact, it's closer when it's directly overhead.

Second, your eye does not physically detect that the moon is bigger when it's near the horizon. The moon creates a .15-millimeter image on the retina, no matter where it is. Test this yourself: Next time you see a big moon looming low behind the trees, hold a pencil at arm's length and note the relative size of the moon and the eraser. Then wait a few hours and try it again when the moon is higher in the sky. You'll see that the moon is exactly the same size relative to the eraser. The

.15-millimeter phenomenon rules out atmospheric distortion as an explanation for the moon's apparent change in size.

Third, a moon on the horizon doesn't look larger just because we're comparing it to trees, buildings, and the like. Airline pilots experience the same big-moon illusion when none of these visual cues are present. Also, consider the fact that when the moon is higher in the sky and we look at it through the same trees or with the same buildings in the foreground, it doesn't look as large as it does when it's on the horizon.

A Matter of Perception

What's going on? Scientists quibble over the details, but the common opinion is that the "moon illusion" must be the result of the brain automatically interpreting visual information based on its own unconscious expectations. We instinctively take distance information into account when deciding how large something is. When you see a faraway building, for example, you interpret it as big because you factor in the visual effect of distance.

But this phenomenon confuses us when we attempt to visually compute the size of the moon. According to the most popular theory, this is because we naturally perceive the sky as a flattened dome when, in reality, it's half of a sphere. This perception might be based on our understanding that the ground is relatively flat. As a result, we compute distance differently, depending on whether something is at the horizon or directly overhead.

According to this flattened-dome theory, when the moon is near the horizon, we have a fairly accurate sense of its distance and size. But when the moon is overhead, we unconsciously make an inaccurate estimate of its distance and so incorrectly estimate its size.

In other words, based on a faulty understanding of the shape of the sky, the brain perceives reality incorrectly and interprets the moon as being smaller when it's overhead than when it's on the horizon. That's right—your brain is tricking you. So what are you going to believe—science or your lying eyes?

Teleportation: Not Just the Stuff of Science Fiction

Scientists say that it's only a matter of time before we're teleporting just like everyone does on Star Trek.

✳ ✳ ✳ ✳

Beam Us Up

WE'RE CLOSER THAN you might think to being able to teleport, but don't squander those frequent-flyer miles just yet. There's a reason why Captain Kirk is on TV late at night shilling for a cheap-airfare Web site and not hawking

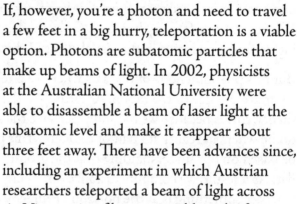

BeamMeToHawaiiScotty.com. For the foreseeable future, jet travel is still the way to go.

If, however, you're a photon and need to travel a few feet in a big hurry, teleportation is a viable option. Photons are subatomic particles that make up beams of light. In 2002, physicists at the Australian National University were able to disassemble a beam of laser light at the subatomic level and make it reappear about three feet away. There have been advances since, including an experiment in which Austrian researchers teleported a beam of light across the Danube River in Vienna via a fiber-optic cable—the first instance of teleportation taking place outside of a laboratory.

These experiments are a far cry from dematerializing on your spaceship and materializing on the surface of a strange planet to make out with an alien who, despite her blue skin, is still pretty hot. But this research demonstrates that it is possible to transport matter in a way that bypasses space—just don't expect teleportation of significant amounts of matter to happen until scientists clear a long list of hurdles, which will take many years.

Here, Gone, There

Teleportation essentially scans and dematerializes an object, turning its subatomic particles into data. The data is transferred to another location and used to recreate the object. This is not unlike the way a computer downloads a file from another computer miles away. But your body consists of many trillions of atoms, and no computer today could reliably crunch numbers powerfully enough to transport and precisely recreate you.

As is the case with many technological advances, the most vexing and long-lasting obstacle probably won't involve creation of the technology, but rather the moral and ethical issues surrounding its use. Teleportation destroys an object and recreates a facsimile somewhere else. If that object is a person, does the destruction constitute murder? And if you believe that a person has a soul, is teleportation capable of recreating a person's soul within the physical body it recreates? These are questions with no easy answers.

---

* **The stripes on a tiger's face are used for identification, since no two tigers sport the same stripe pattern.**

* **In 1939, a group of Soviet meteorologists who studied Arctic temperatures over a decade concluded that the world's temperature was slowly rising and predicted global warming.**

* **Temperature variations on Earth's moon can range from 280 degrees Fahrenheit during the daytime to −400 degrees Fahrenheit at night.**

* **English Queen Elizabeth I felt she had a homely face and had all mirrors removed from her palace and forbade any artist from drawing her likeness except "especial cunning painters."**

* **Erich Alfred Hartmann, "The Black Devil" of the German Luftwaffe during World War II, flew more than 1,400 combat missions and scored 352 aerial victories, the most of any German pilot.**

* **Only three men—Dan Reeves, Mike Ditka, and Tony Dungy— have appeared in the Super Bowl as a player, an assistant coach, and a head coach.**

The Cold Realities of a Sunless Earth

If that fiery ball in the sky went out, the future of our planet would not be bright. And that's putting it mildly.

✳ ✳ ✳ ✳

IF THE SUN suddenly stopped emitting light and warmth, Earth would get dark in about eight minutes—the length of time it takes for light to reach us once it escapes the sun—and would gradually become colder. It's been hypothesized that crops would freeze and die within days, rivers would freeze within weeks, and the warming Gulf Stream waters in the Atlantic would freeze within months.

None of us would live much longer than a few weeks, thanks to subtle factors including scarcity of food and water, more drastic factors such as severe weather, and absolutely nutso factors such as widespread panic. And the only reason anyone would last even a few weeks is that Earth and its atmosphere have some capacity to retain heat, which explains why it doesn't become frigid immediately every night.

Now, if the sun's core stopped undergoing fusion (which is possible but entirely unlikely), up to a million years would pass before we felt the full effect, as that's how long it takes light that's generated by fusion to escape from the plasmalike material that makes up the sun. But long before that, scientists would detect clues—such as the lack of neutrinos (tiny elementary particles) coming from the sun and pulsations on its surface owing to the imbalance between its weight (which produces gravitational force) and the heat-and-pressure force of the fusion, which counteracts the gravity and keeps everything in balance—that would tell us there's something wrong. Slowly the sun would start to shrink.

So you'd rather have the sun die than just suddenly stop emitting light and heat. But either way, the picture isn't pretty.

Taking Care of Business in Outer Space

Weightlessness sure seems fun. You see those astronauts effortlessly floating around, mugging for the camera, and magically spinning their pens in midair. But what you don't get to see is what happens when nature calls.

✳ ✳ ✳ ✳

The Final Frontier

Y OU CAN BE sure that as much as astronauts enjoy swimming through the air like waterless fish, there's one place on Earth where all astronauts thank their lucky stars for gravity: the bathroom.

On the Space Shuttle, the astronaut sits on a commode with a hole in it, not unlike a normal toilet—except for the restraints that fit over the feet and thighs to prevent his or her body from floating away. Suction takes the place of gravity, so the seat is cushioned, which allows the astronaut's posterior to form an airtight seal around the hole. If everything is situated properly, the solid waste goes down the main hole: A separate tube with a funnel on the end takes care of the liquids. Since there's so much going on, relaxing with a newspaper is not really an option.

Today's astronauts have it easy compared to their forebears on the Apollo missions (1961–75). When an Apollo astronaut had to go number two, he attached a specially designed plastic bag to his rear end. The bag had an adhesive flange at its opening to ensure a proper seal.

But if you think that this procedure couldn't have been any more undignified, consider this: There was no privacy. The astronauts would usually carry on with their duties while they were, you know, doing their duty. In the words of Apollo astronaut Rusty Schweickart, "You just float around for a while doing things with a bag on your butt." With no gravity and no suction, getting the feces to separate from the body was, generally, an hour-long process. It began with removing the bag—very carefully—and ended with lots and lots of wiping.

Waste Management

Where does all this stuff go? Fecal material is dried, compressed, and stored until the ship returns to Earth. (Some scientists believe that manned missions to Mars will require waste to be recycled and used for food. If you were hoping to sign up for one of those flights, you may want to think twice before dropping your application in the mail.) Urine, on the other hand, is expelled into space. The memory of this procedure caused Schweickart to wax darn-near poetic, calling a urine dump at sunset, "one of the most beautiful sights" he saw in space.

"As the stuff comes out and hits the exit nozzle," Schweickart went on, "it instantly flashes into ten million little ice crystals, which go out almost in a hemisphere. The stuff goes in every direction, all radially out from the spacecraft at relatively high velocity. It's surprising, and it's an incredible stream of . . . just a spray of sparklers almost. It's really a spectacular sight."

And you thought stars looked cool.

---

* *The Spirit of Ecstasy* is the name of the sculpture on the hood of a Rolls-Royce.

* In 1988, the U.S. Patent Office awarded a patent to Harvard University for developing a genetically engineered mouse, the first patent ever awarded for an animal.

* The Battle of Long Island was the largest battle fought during the American Revolution. In August and September 1776, British troops drove the Continental Army first from Long Island and then Manhattan.

* The official U.S. presidential theme song is "Hail to the Chief." The music was originally written for verses of Sir Walter Scott's poem "The Lady of the Lake" in 1810.

Watch Out for That Meteor!

NASA estimates that about once every 100 years, a meteorite substantial enough in size to cause tidal waves wallops Earth's surface. About once every few hundred thousand years, an object strikes that is large enough to cause a global catastrophe. So future hits—both larger and smaller—are inevitable.

✳ ✳ ✳ ✳

Scanning the Skies

NASA's NEAR EARTH OBJECT PROGRAM surveys the heavens and observes comets and asteroids that could potentially enter Earth's neighborhood. It has been keeping close tabs on an asteroid called Apophis, aka MN2004. According to NASA, on April 13, 2029, Apophis will be close enough to Earth that it will be visible to the naked eye. At one time, the odds were estimated to be as great as 1-in-300 that Apophis would hit Earth. However, NASA has now ruled out a collision, thank goodness, because the asteroid would have hit Earth with the force of an 880-megaton explosion (more than 50,000 times the power of the atomic bomb dropped on Hiroshima, Japan, in 1945).

Perhaps the best-known meteor hit occurred 50,000 years ago, when an iron meteorite collided with what is now northern Arizona with a force estimated to be two thousand times greater than the bomb dropped on Hiroshima. Now named the Meteor Crater, the 12,000-meters-wide crater is a popular tourist attraction.

What to Do?

A direct meteor hit isn't even necessary to cause significant damage. On June 30, 1908, what many believe was a small asteroid exploded high in the air near the Tunguska River in Russia. Taking into consideration the topography of the area, the health of the adjoining forest, and some new models concerning the dynamics of the explosion, scientists now believe that the force of the explosion was about three to five megatons. Trees were knocked down for hundreds of square miles.

NASA hopes to provide a few years' warning if there is a meteor approaching that could cause a global catastrophe. The organization anticipates that our existing technology would allow us to, among other things, set off nuclear fusion weapons near an object in order to deflect its trajectory. Or we can simply hope that Bruce Willis will save us, just like he did in the 1998 movie *Armageddon*.

---

* On November 21, 1980, 83 million Americans tuned in to watch the finale to the *Dallas* cliffhanger "Who Shot J. R.?" A few weeks earlier, 85.1 million Americans voted in the Reagan-Carter presidential election.

* In 1981, when Nabisco purchased the Standard Brands Company—the original maker of Baby Ruth and Butterfinger—the recipes for these popular candy bars were misplaced. So Nabisco had to come up with new recipes that tasted the same as the old ones.

* The ancient Maya believed that the gods had created them for the sole purpose of cooking delicious foods for the deities—whom they presumed were made of corn themselves. (*Mayan* actually means "men of corn.")

* The first fairy tale adapted into cartoon by Walt Disney was *Little Red Riding Hood,* released in 1922.

* Each of your nostrils registers smell differently. Your right nostril detects the more pleasant smells, but your left one is more accurate.

* The custom of men buttoning their clothes from the right and women from the left comes from the fact that men traditionally dressed themselves and were typically right-handed. Women were more often dressed by maids, who preferred to work from their right—the wearer's left.

Space Dog

The first occupied spacecraft did not carry a human being or even a monkey. Instead, scientists launched man's best friend.

✳ ✳ ✳ ✳

THE SPACE AGE officially began on October 4, 1957, when the Soviet Union launched humanity's first artificial satellite, *Sputnik I*. Even more astounding was the launch of *Sputnik II* on November 3. The spacecraft carried the first living creature into orbit, a mongrel dog from the streets of Moscow named Laika.

A 20th-Century Dog

A three-year-old stray that weighed just 13 pounds, Laika had a calm disposition and slight stature that made her a perfect fit for the cramped capsule of *Sputnik II*. In the weeks leading up to the launch, Laika was confined to increasingly smaller cages and fed a diet of a special nutritional gel to prepare her for the journey.

Sputnik II was a 250-pound satellite with a simple cabin, a crude life-support system, and instruments to measure Laika's vital signs. After the success of the *Sputnik I* launch, Soviet Premier Nikita Khrushchev urged scientists to launch another satellite on November 7, 1957, to mark the anniversary of the Bolshevik Revolution. Although work was in progress for the more sophisticated satellite eventually known as *Sputnik III*, it couldn't be completed in time. Sergei Korolev, head of the Soviet space program, ordered his team to design and construct *Sputnik II*. They had less than four weeks.

The First Creature in Space

The November launch astonished the world—and ignited a debate about the treatment of animals when the Soviets announced that Laika would not survive the journey. The hastily built craft's life-support system failed, and Laika perished from excess heat after only about five hours. Despite her tragic end, the heroic little dog paved the way for occupied spaceflight.

A Traffic Jam in Space

No one gives much thought to all the stuff we launch into space and don't bring back, but it creates a major hazard.

✳ ✳ ✳ ✳

Steer Clear of that Satellite

IF YOU THINK it's nerve-wracking when you have to swerve around a huge pothole as you cruise down the highway, just imagine how it would feel if you were hundreds of miles above the surface of the earth, where the stakes couldn't be higher. That's what the crew of the International Space Station (ISS) faced in 2008, when it had to perform evasive maneuvers to avoid debris from a Russian satellite.

And that was just one piece of orbital trash—all in all, there are tens of millions of junky objects that are larger than a millimeter and are in orbit. If you don't find this worrisome, imagine the little buggers zipping along at up to 17,000 miles per hour. Worse, these bits of flotsam and jetsam constantly crash into each other and shatter into even more pieces.

The junk largely comes from satellites that explode or disintegrate; it also includes the upper stages of launch vehicles, burnt-out rocket casings, old payloads and experiments, bolts, wire clusters, slag and dust from solid rocket motors, batteries, droplets of leftover fuel and high-pressure fluids, and even a space suit. (No, there wasn't an astronaut who came home naked—the suit was packed with batteries and sensors and was set adrift in 2006 so that scientists could find out how quickly a spacesuit deteriorates in the intense conditions of space.)

The U.S. and Russia: Space's Big Polluters

So who's responsible for all this orbiting garbage? The two biggest offenders are Russia—including the former Soviet Union—and the United States. Other litterers include China, France, Japan, India, Portugal, Egypt, and Chile. Each of the last three countries has launched one satellite during the past 20 years.

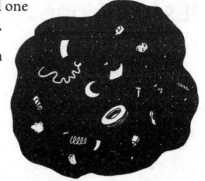

Most of the junk orbits the earth at between 525 and 930 miles from the surface. The space shuttle and the ISS operate a little closer to the earth—the shuttle flies at between 250 and 375 miles up, and the ISS maintains an altitude of about 250 miles—so they don't see the worst of it. Still, the ISS's emergency maneuver in 2008 was a sign that the situation is getting worse.

NASA and other agencies use radar to track the junk and are studying ways to get rid of it for good. Ideas such as shooting at objects with lasers or attaching tethers to some pieces to force them back to the earth have been discarded because of cost considerations and the potential danger to people on the ground. Until an answer is found, NASA practices constant vigilance, monitoring the junk and watching for collisions with working satellites and vehicles as they careen through space. Hazardous driving conditions, it seems, extend well beyond the earth's atmosphere.

✳ The most active hurricane season on record was in 2005. So many storms formed that year that the National Hurricane Center ran out of names on its list and had to use Greek letters for the last six storms. What's more, there were a record-breaking four category-five monsters, including the devastating Katrina.

✳ Low barometric pressure generally indicates stormy weather, and high pressure signals calm, sunny skies. The lowest pressure ever recorded was 25.69 inches during Typhoon Tip in 1979. The highest pressure, 32.01 inches, was measured in 1968 on a cold New Year's Eve in northern Siberia.

It's Not Alone

Contrary to popular belief, the Great Wall of China isn't the only manmade object that's visible from space.

✳ ✳ ✳ ✳

"**S**PACE" IS A tricky term to define—a lot of people swap "space" with "the moon." So, is the Great Wall of China the only manmade object that's visible with the naked eye from the moon? No manmade object is visible from the moon, which is 240,000 miles away. In fact, at an altitude of just a few thousand miles above Earth's surface, you can't see any of humankind's handiwork. (We say "a few thousand miles" because nobody's really put a finger on the magic point at which it all disappears—astronauts have far more important things to do.) From the moon, you can barely see the continents, let alone the Great Wall. And if you went out to Mars, Earth would appear to be just a fairly bright star in the sky.

"Space," on the other hand, is a lot closer than people might think—it begins about 60 miles above Earth's surface. Until you get somewhere between 150 and 300 miles above the surface (vague for the same reasons as before), the Great Wall is visible with the naked eye, provided the weather and lighting are exactly right. You'll still have to squint a bit, though, since it's a similar color to the landscape around it.

But before you start throwing this fact around trying to win bar bets, know this: From that height, lots of manmade objects are visible, including highways, railways, and sailing ships. Cities are, of course, quite easy to distinguish from the countryside, especially at night when there are millions of lights on. From the lowest areas of space, you can even see some individual buildings and airplane contrails.

Space Ghosts

Shortly after the Soviet Union successfully launched Sputnik 1 *on October 4, 1957, rumors swirled that several cosmonauts had died during missions gone horribly wrong, and their spacecraft had drifted out of Earth's orbit and into the vast reaches of the universe.*

✳ ✳ ✳ ✳

IT WAS EASY to believe such stories at the time. After all, the United States was facing off against the Soviet Union in the Cold War, and the thought that the ruthless Russians would do anything to win the space race—including sending cosmonauts to their doom—seemed plausible.

However, numerous researchers have investigated the stories and concluded that, though the Soviet space program was far from perfect and some cosmonauts had in fact died, there are no dead cosmonauts floating in space.

According to authors Hal Morgan and Kerry Tucker, the earliest rumors of deceased cosmonauts even mentioned their names and the dates of their doomed missions: Aleksei Ledovsky in 1957, Serenti Shiborin in 1958, and Mirya Gromova in 1959. In fact, by the time Yuri Gagarin became the first human in space in April 1961, the alleged body count exceeded a dozen.

Space Spies

So prevalent were these stories that no less an "authority" than *Reader's Digest* reported on them in its April 1965 issue. Key to the mystery were two brothers in Italy, Achille and Giovanni Battista Judica-Cordiglia, who operated a homemade listening post with a huge dish antenna. Over a seven-month period, the brothers claimed to have overheard radio signals from three troubled Soviet spacecraft:

✳ On November 28, 1960, a Soviet spacecraft supposedly radioed three times, in Morse code and in English, "SOS to the entire world."

* In early February 1961, the brothers allegedly picked up the sound of a rapidly beating heart and labored breathing, which they interpreted to be the final throes of a dying cosmonaut.

* On May 17, 1961, two men and a woman were allegedly overheard saying, in Russian, "Conditions growing worse. Why don't you answer? We are going slower...the world will never know about us."

The Black Hole of Soviet PR

Rumors of dead cosmonauts seemed plausible because the early Soviet space program was extremely secretive, revealing little about its program or the people involved. In contrast, the United States publicly touted its program as a major advance in science and its astronauts as heroes.

It's not surprising, then, that the Soviet Union did not reveal the death of Valentin Bondarenko, a cosmonaut who died tragically in a fire after he tossed an alcohol-soaked cotton ball on a hot plate and ignited the oxygen-rich chamber in which he was training. He died in 1961, but it wasn't reported publicly until 1986.

The rumors were further fueled by the fact that other cosmonauts had been mysteriously airbrushed out of official government photos. But most had been removed because they had been dropped from the space program for academic, disciplinary, or medical reasons—not because they had died during a mission. One cosmonaut, Grigoriy Nelyubov, was booted from the program in 1961 for a drunken brawl at a rail station (he died five years later when he stepped in front of a train). Nelyubov's story, like so many others, was not made public until the mid-1980s.

Only one Soviet cosmonaut is known to have died during an actual space mission. In 1967, Vladimir Komarov was killed when the parachute on his *Soyuz 1* spacecraft failed to open properly during reentry. A Russian engineer later acknowledged that Komarov's mission had been ordered before the spacecraft had been fully debugged, likely for political reasons.

Blinded by the Light?

In grade school, you were warned about looking at a solar eclipse, but if this danger were real, wouldn't there be blind people everywhere?

✳ ✳ ✳ ✳

CONSIDER: IT'S THE day of the eclipse, the sky starts to darken, you look up to see what's going on, and boom—you're poking your way around with a white cane for the rest of your life. Where's the logic? Well, amazingly, the concept actually isn't completely far-fetched.

First off, staring at the sun at any time isn't a good idea. Prolonged exposure to the ultraviolet radiation from the sun can damage the nerve endings in the eye, leading to vision problems such as spotting, blurriness, and in extreme cases, blindness. Exposing the retina to intense visible light causes damage to its light-sensitive rod and cone cells.

The light can trigger a series of complex chemical reactions within the cells that damages their ability to respond to a visual stimulus and, in extreme cases, can destroy them. There are many factors that affect how your eyes will respond to this kind of abuse, including the size and color of your eyes, preexisting eye problems, and the angle of the sun.

As a result, it is difficult to say exactly how long one can look at the sun without injury, but you should try to limit your exposure to less than a minute. That can be easier said than done. What makes solar eclipses so dangerous is that the stare-prohibiting glare of the sun is greatly diminished.

Just how dangerous are eclipses? Staring at one won't cause instant blindness. And the term "blindness" is a bit of an overstatement— eye impairments can be as minor as a slight discoloration in the visual field. This type of damage typically is temporary, and many people recover their normal vision within a few weeks.

Plan B for Imperiled Astronauts: Parachutes

It seems like parachutes wouldn't do much good, but they're part of an escape system devised by NASA for space shuttle missions after the 1986 Challenger *disaster, in which seven astronauts died when a rocket booster exploded shortly after liftoff.*

✳ ✳ ✳ ✳

Bailing Out

THE PARACHUTES THAT astronauts now wear are part of a coordinated plan that offers them a chance to bail out if problems arise during launch or landing. For obvious reasons, jumping from the shuttle is impossible while its rockets are firing. But there are scenarios in which escape would be an option. One would be after the rockets finish firing but before the shuttle reaches space. Another would be if the rockets fail after launch and the astronauts face a dangerous emergency landing in the ocean.

How would an escape work? First, the crew would guide the shuttle to an altitude of about 25,000 to 30,000 feet—just lower than the altitude reached by commercial airline flights—and jump from the shuttle through a side hatch.

To avoid hitting a wing or an engine pod during their escape, the astronauts would extend a 12-foot pole from the side of the shuttle, hook themselves to it, slide down, and jump from there. NASA's space suits are designed to work automatically during an escape. The parachute opens at 14,000 feet, and when the suit detects impact with water, the parachute detaches.

More Life-Saving Gadgets

The astronauts have other gizmos up their sleeves (and pant legs) that help in an emergency. When water is detected, the suit automatically deploys a life preserver. Also contained within the suit is a life raft, complete with a bailing cup to remove water that sloshes into it. Once safely afloat, the astronaut can pull a set of flares from one leg pocket and an emergency radio from the other. The suit, which is designed to keep the astronaut alive for 24 hours, is pressurized, thermal, and even comes equipped with a supply of drinking water.

The explosion that killed the *Challenger* crew was sudden and caused instant death, so this escape system would not have helped them. But because of that tragedy, today's space shuttle astronauts are better prepared if they need to make a daring escape.

---

* Francis Scott Key wrote the lyrics of "The Star-Spangled Banner" to the tune of the 18th-century British drinking song "To Anacreon in Heaven." The pub tune was the theme song of London's Anacreontic Club, which took its name from the ancient Greek poet known for his devotion to the god of wine.

* The maiden name of Blondie Bumstead in the comic strip *Blondie* is "Boopadoop."

* Newly hatched queen bees fight to the death to kill all other newly hatched—and unhatched—queens, until only one is left standing. There can only be one queen in a hive.

* Human beings are the only animals that cry emotional tears.

* The phrase "last laugh" is derived from the laughlike sound a bullet shot through the heart sometimes causes in its victim before death.

* Contrary to popular belief, the gladiators of ancient Rome did not kill each other. Because the government invested so much money in their training and preparation, they fought only to the "first blood," at which point the injured gladiator would raise his finger in surrender.

* More than 50 percent of people admit to checking their e-mail in the bathroom.

* The tradition of the white wedding dress dates back to Queen Victoria, who in 1840 chose white not as a display of purity but of wealth, since white fabric was an expensive luxury. (Not to mention impractical because of its difficulty to keep clean.)

Interesting Celestial Objects

*Some you can see with the naked eye; others we didn't
learn about until we sent exploratory probes. Here are
some of the most intriguing features of the heavens.*

✳ ✳ ✳ ✳

Within Our Solar System

Mercury: Eons ago, the planet nearest to the Sun experienced a
meteor strike that created an 800-mile-wide crater that we refer
to as Caloris Basin. The strike actually raised hills on the other
side of the planet.

Venus: Its buttery cloud cover is mostly carbon dioxide mixed
with sulfur dioxide. Atmospheric pressure at the surface is equal
to being half a mile below Earth's seas. The surface temperature
can reach 900 degrees Fahrenheit.

Mars: Mercury has the crater; Mars has the volcano. Olympus
Mons rises 16 miles above the planet's surface—three times the
height of Mount Everest—and is the size of Arizona. It's a shield
volcano (like the ones in Hawaii), the result of lava flowing out
over the ages. The caldera (central crater) alone is large enough to
swallow a medium-sized city.

Jupiter: The largest planet has a moon collection that thus far
exceeds 60, but one of the most interesting is Io. Astronomers
have watched some of Io's 400-plus active volcanoes erupt, and a
few of its mountains rise higher than Mount Everest.

Saturn: If you've never seen the rings, you can do so easily with
a basic telescope. Like Jupiter, Saturn has a big moon collection.
Its largest, Titan, has an atmosphere (mostly nitrogen with some
methane) and standing liquid on its surface. Titan is much bigger
than Earth's moon and close in size to Jupiter's largest moons.

Uranus: It's the farthest planet from Earth visible to the naked
eye, but you have to know exactly where to look. The odd thing

about Uranus is that it's oriented on its side. Earth is tilted 23.5 degrees out of the plane of the solar system (our local "up" reference point in space). Uranus is tilted 98 degrees, so its poles are in the middle and its equator runs from top to bottom.

Neptune: You can't see Neptune without a good telescope; it's dimmer than Jupiter's larger moons. Its main moon, Triton (a little smaller than our own), is doomed. In as little as ten million years, when Triton falls from the sky and spirals toward Neptune, the planet's gravity will crumble it into a huge ring.

Pluto: It got kicked out of the Planet Club but not out of orbit. Its orbit is off kilter—it's out of line with the solar system and elliptical enough that for periods of 20 Earth years at a time, Pluto is closer to the Sun than Neptune is.

Eris: It's the (non)planet that got Pluto kicked out of the Planet Club. Given the argument that ensued, how fitting that it was named for a goddess of strife. Officially a dwarf planet, Eris is a little bigger than Pluto and has one dinky moon that we know of. It's way out there, with a year more than twice as long (557 Earth years) as Pluto's (248 Earth years).

Beyond Our Solar System

Magellanic Clouds: Earth's nearest galaxies are visible only in the Southern Hemisphere. Both are irregular blobs that appear to the naked eye as fuzzy patches. If we ever go to other galaxies, these would surely be the first objects we'd visit.

Andromeda Galaxy: Visible to the naked eye and easily enjoyed with binoculars, Andromeda is the closest spiral galaxy (like our own Milky Way). Spot it on a night and in a place with little light pollution in the Northern Hemisphere, ideally in November.

Crab Nebula: We watched this one blow itself apart (or rather, we watched the light reach us). In A.D. 1054, Arab and Chinese astronomers noted a star visible during daytime—now it has puffed out a big gas cloud. It's in Taurus (winter, mainly in the Northern Hemisphere), just above the tip of the lower "horn."

You can get a reasonable view of the cloud surrounding the star's wreckage with a four-inch telescope, but binoculars will reveal something too.

Ring Nebula: Not visible to the naked eye but fascinating in pictures or through a big telescope, this looks like a smoke ring surrounding a small star. Just south of Vega in the constellation Lyra (summer, mainly in the Northern Hemisphere) is a little parallelogram of stars, and the Nebula is in the middle of its bottom short side. In 14,000 years, Vega will be our North Star again as Earth's axis cycles around.

Coalsack Nebula: It's smack in the middle of the Milky Way and big enough to block out most of the "milk." You have to get below the equator to see it, but its position just left of and below the Southern Cross makes it easy to spot all year round. This interstellar dust cloud obscures objects behind it.

Orion Nebula: Find it (winter, Northern Hemisphere; summer, Southern Hemisphere) in the dagger of Orion's three-star belt; it's easily to see the haze with binoculars.

Pleiades: Some say this star cluster is home of the aliens who will soon arrive. These are one of the highlights of binocular astronomy, easy to spot in Taurus (winter, Northern Hemisphere; summer, Southern Hemisphere). Look for a little coffee-cup shape of blue-white stars that show up sapphire in light magnification.

Algol: It's an eclipsing binary star (a bright star eclipsed at intervals by a dimmer nearby star). From Earth, the star seems to vary in brightness; visibility will go from easy to difficult. The eclipses last several hours and occur every three days.

Milky Way: Our own galaxy dazzles as it traces a broad path of light the full width of the sky. The Milky Way is a spiral galaxy that formed about 14 billion years ago; our solar system is just a small part of it. Most of the stars we can see are in our galaxy. The Sun, along with Earth, is around 26,000 light-years from the center, halfway to the edge of the galaxy along the Orion spiral arm.

Chapter 14

Bizarre Truths About History's Mysteries

Dunce Caps Weren't Always for Dunces

Those tall, conical paper hats shamed many a struggling student back when our classrooms were a little less enlightened than they are today. It would be a stretch to say that dunce caps represent a proud tradition, but they certainly are part of a long-standing one.

✳ ✳ ✳ ✳

The Story of John Duns Scotus

DUNCE CAPS DATE back hundreds of years, and surprisingly, they were named after a real guy. That unfortunate guy's name was John Duns Scotus. (Duns was his family name, while Scotus was a Latin nickname meaning, roughly, "You know, that guy from Scotland.") He was a philosopher, Franciscan friar, and teacher who lived during the late Middle Ages. He is still remembered as the founder of a dense and subtle school of philosophy called Scotism. He was influential during his lifetime, and today he is regarded as one of the most important philosophers of his era.

His arcane and convoluted logic seemed the height of sophistication at the time and inspired a school of followers—known as the Dunsmen or, more casually, Dunces—who emulated his academic style and dominated the universities of Europe. But by the 16th century, a new intellectual movement was attacking the old traditions. The Renaissance humanists hated the obscure and overly complicated method of reasoning that the Dunces employed. They labeled the Dunsmen as "old barking curs" who lacked the ability to reason, and they began using "dunce" as an insult to describe a thickheaded person.

This is where the headgear comes in. One of Scotus's stranger opinions was particularly easy for the humanists to ridicule: He had claimed that conical hats actually make you smarter by funneling knowledge down to your brain. (This also explains why cones were the hat of choice for wizards, by the way.) After the humanists succeeded in turning "dunce" into an insult, the cone hat became the official headwear of the stupid.

Dunce Caps in the Classroom

How these peculiar hats made it into schools isn't entirely clear, but by the 19th century, American and European teachers punished ignorance by making students wear paper dunce caps and sit in the corner of the classroom. The idea was to encourage kids to learn by shaming them when they didn't.

These days, dunce caps occasionally pop up in cartoons, but they're no longer standard classroom equipment. Dunce caps went out of vogue at around the same time as corporal punishment, and for the same basic reason. Beginning in the 1950s, B. F. Skinner and other behaviorist psychologists demonstrated that positive reinforcement—rewarding desired behavior—is a far more effective way to motivate students than punishment. According to Skinner, people "work harder and learn more quickly when rewarded for doing something right than when punished for doing something wrong," and he maintained that punishment should be a last resort in the classroom.

Skinner's beliefs slowly took hold. By the 1980s, spanking and shaming became rarities in public schools. While some still swear by the power of the paddle, nobody seems to feel strongly enough about the dunce cap to defend it as a learning tool.

Who Downed the Red Baron? The Mystery of Manfred von Richthofen

He was the most successful flying ace of World War I, the conflict that introduced the airplane as a weapon of war. And his demise has been credited to a number of likely opponents, both in the sky and on the ground.

✳ ✳ ✳ ✳

A Precious Little Prussian

MANFRED VON RICHTHOFEN was born in Silesia, Prussia (now part of Poland), in May 1892. Coming from a family steeped in nobility, the young von Richthofen decided he would follow in his father's footsteps and become a career soldier. At 11 years old, he enrolled in the cadet corps and, upon completion, became a member of a Prussian cavalry unit.

Up, Up, and Away

The Germans were at the forefront in using aircraft as offensive weapons during World War I. Von Richthofen was recruited into a flying unit as an "observer"—the second occupant of a two-seat plane who would direct the pilot over areas to gather intelligence. By 1915, von Richthofen decided to become a pilot himself, having already downed an enemy aircraft as an observer.

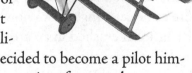

The young, green pilot joined one of the premier German *jagdstaffeln* ("hunting squadrons"). In late 1916, von Richthofen's aggressive style brought him face-to-face with Britain's greatest fighter pilot, Major Lanoe Hawker. After a spirited battle in the sky, the German brought Hawker down in a tailspin, killing him. Von Richthofen later mounted the machine gun from the British plane over the door of his family home as a tribute to Hawker. The bold flying ace often showed a great deal of respect and affinity for his foes. Yet, he remained ruthless, even carrying with him a photograph of an Allied pilot he had viciously blown apart.

Creating an Identity

Von Richthofen quickly became the most feared, and respected, pilot in the skies. He decided he needed to be instantly recognizable and had his plane painted bright red, with the German Iron Cross emblazoned on the fuselage. The "Red Baron" was born.

The End—but at Whose Hands?

By the spring of 1918, the Red Baron had shot down 80 Allied airplanes, earning him the distinguished "Blue Max" award. He assembled his own squadron of crack-shot pilots known as "the Flying Circus."

But von Richthofen also had failures. He suffered a head wound during an air battle in July 1917, which may have left an open wound exposing a small portion of his skull. Some theorize that this injury resulted in brain damage and may have caused serious errors in judgment that led to his death on April 21, 1918.

On that day, von Richthofen was embroiled in a deadly dogfight with British Royal Air Force Sopwith Camels. As the Red Baron trained his machine-gun sights on a young pilot, enemy fire came seemingly from nowhere, striking his red Fokker. Von Richthofen crashed in an area of France occupied by Australian and Canadian allies. He was buried with full military honors by a respectful British Royal Air Force (RAF).

Questions remain as to who exactly killed von Richthofen. He suffered a fatal bullet wound through his chest. The RAF credited one of their pilots, but another story says Canadian soldiers murdered the Red Baron at the crash site. Still other tales claim he was shot from the ground as he flew overhead.

The answer is lost, perhaps forever. But the greatest flying ace of the First World War remains the Red Baron.

How Did Houdini Die?

Ehrich Weiss, better remembered as Harry Houdini, was the master escape artist and illusionist of his time—perhaps of all time. Contrary to rumor, though, he did not die at the hands of angry spiritualists.

✳ ✳ ✳ ✳

SEVERAL OF HOUDINI'S stunts almost did him in, especially if sabotage or malfunction affected the gear. He finished numerous escapes bleeding, bruised, or otherwise broken. But he was always a "show must go on" performer, and that's ultimately what caused his death.

Houdini was a consummate showman, but he was also a trifle odd. He developed the macho habit of encouraging people to test his stony abs by slugging him in the gut. In 1926, while visiting Houdini backstage before a performance in Montreal, a college student asked to give the famous abs the punch test. The eager recruit hit him before the magician could brace himself for the repeated blows, and a terrible pain shot through Houdini's side. Despite his agony, that night's performance went on.

Later that evening, still in severe pain, Houdini was reading a newspaper while waiting for a train to his next gig, in Detroit. A burly "fan" approached him and drove a fist through the paper and into the performer's stomach, worsening matters considerably.

In Detroit, Houdini finished his show by sheer will before finally checking into a hospital. Doctors found that he had an abnormally long appendix that spanned his pelvis, and as a result of the blows, it had ruptured. Rumors began to swirl that the student who had punched Houdini was actually an offended member of a group of spiritualists whom Houdini often spoke against and attempted to expose. The truth isn't quite so sensational. Houdini died of peritonitis six days after he was hospitalized—quite fittingly, on Halloween.

Off with the Dresses...
On with the Pants

Women wearing pants doesn't seem like a big deal nowadays, but it caused quite a stir back in the mid-1800s.

✳   ✳   ✳   ✳

An Early Feminist Statement

THINK OF A political firebrand who encourages women everywhere to cast off the constricting bonds of man-pleasing fashion. If you're imagining a throwback to the 1960s, you're on the right track—but forget the bra-burning feminists of the hippie era and go back more than 100 years earlier. Sure, the garments were a little different—corsets were undoubtedly trickier to set aflame—but the sentiment was the same. And for these early feminists, there was a simple wardrobe solution: pants.

One of the leaders of this cause was Amelia Jenks Bloomer, a reformer who was present when the women's suffrage movement was born at the Seneca Falls Convention in 1848. The following year, Bloomer established a newspaper for women called *The Lily: A Monthly Journal, Devoted to Temperance and Literature*. Sometime around 1851, Bloomer began advocating dress reform from the pages of her influential journal. She encouraged women to eschew the whalebone corsets, petticoats, heavy skirts, and other cumbersome garments that were then in vogue. To show that she meant business, she began making public appearances in full-cut pantaloons, also known as Turkish trousers, which she wore under a shorter skirt.

The Birth of Bloomers

Bloomer wasn't the first woman to don this scandalous style. Others, including actress Fanny Kemble (the Lindsay Lohan of her day), had rocked Turkish trou even earlier. But because of Bloomer's high-profile promotion of the garments, they came to be known popularly as "bloomers."

The name caught on, but the look didn't. Bloomer was often ridiculed for wearing her bloomers, and even prominent members of the women's movement soon abandoned the style because they felt that it was doing their cause more harm than good.

Hollywood Makes Pants Fashionable

It wasn't until the 20th century that pants became a respectable fashion choice for women. Hollywood stars such as Marlene Dietrich and Katharine Hepburn began wearing pants in the 1930s, and by 1939, *Vogue* magazine was insisting that slacks were a fashion essential.

But back to Bloomer, the pioneer of women's pants. She wanted nothing more than to improve the United States—she boldly advocated temperance and equal rights for women. But unfortunately, her legacy resides in those preposterous pantaloons.

✳ The *Sabino*, a steamship in Mystic, Connecticut, and the San Francisco cable car are the only two moving National Historic Landmarks in the United States.

✳ The turkey is said to be the least intelligent of all farm animals.

✳ "Auld Lang Syne" translates to "times gone by."

✳ Contrary to popular belief, karate was actually invented in India.

✳ Pumpkin is the most favored holiday pie for American families.

✳ You can form the number 12,345,678,987,654,321 by multiplying 111,111,111 by 111,111,111.

✳ Chicago's O'Hare airport sells more hot dogs than any other airport in the world.

✳ The "WD" in WD-40 stands for Water Displacement. The "40" came about because it took the creators that many attempts to get the formula right.

✳ A U.S. Green Card is actually yellow.

✳ North Carolina has both a city named Republican and a city named Democrat.

Dread Pirates of History and Their Fates

When did piracy begin? Probably 15 minutes after the first ancient meeting of two river canoes. From the European perspective, the Golden Age of Piracy began around A.D. 1660; by 1730, the problem was largely under control. Here are some of the most notorious rascals of this era, plus noteworthy pirates from other times.

✳ ✳ ✳ ✳

John Taylor: English. Taylor earned his fame capturing the Portuguese carrack *Nossa Senhora do Cabo* in 1721. It was one of the richest prizes of its time, carrying diamonds and other portable loot. No idiot, Taylor then bought a pardon in Panama, where he likely retired wealthy.

"Blackbeard" Edward Teach: English. The infamous Blackbeard was a full-time drunkard who terrorized the Carolina coast, racking up captures and loot. But it wasn't all about money and rum: He once raided Charleston and took hostages until townsfolk gave him much-needed medicine for his venereal disease. In 1718, the Royal Navy ran down and killed Blackbeard just off Ocracoke Island.

Thomas Tew: English. His 1692–94 Indian Ocean rampage made Tew rich enough to retire in New York under the protection of his friend, Governor Benjamin Fletcher. In 1695, his former crew talked him into one more voyage to raid Moghul ships. Piracy was a little like gambling: Most people lose, and winners should probably quit. Tew didn't, and in 1695 he was disemboweled by cannon fire.

Jean-David Nau: French. Also known as François l'Olonnais, Nau was a psycho in a sick line of work. Nau whittled prisoners with his cutlass, once allegedly eating a beating heart. Let us all thank the Native Central Americans for tearing him apart alive in 1668.

"Calico" Jack Rackham, Anne Bonny, and Mary Read:
English, Irish, and English. The fancy-dressing Rackham got
his buccaneering start under the notorious Charles Vane, whom
he soon deposed in a mutiny. Rackham fell in love with Anne
Bonny, who was stuck in an unhappy marriage in the Bahamas.
They eloped and began a new piratical career aboard the sloop
Revenge, where Bonny's hard-living, hard-fighting style earned
her respect in a male-dominated business.

Anne soon discovered another incognita in men's clothing: Mary
Read, who became her close friend and peer in the arts of fighting, swearing, and drinking. When pirate hunter Jonathan Barnet
caught up with the *Revenge* in 1720, Read and Bonny were
among the few crewmembers sober and brave enough to fight.

As Rackham was marched off to hang, Bonny showed her contempt for him: "If ye'd fought like a man, ye needn't hang like a
dog." (One suspects that history has omitted a volley or two of
choice profanities.)

Both women escaped Calico Jack's fate by revealing their preg-
nancies to the court. In 1721, Read died amid disgusting jail
conditions, but Bonny was most likely ransomed by her father.

Charles Vane: English. When the reformer Woodes Rogers
showed up to clean out the Caribbean pirates' favorite lair (New
Providence, now Nassau), the wily Vane was the only captain to
reject the proffered amnesty. He kept marauding—losing ships
and gaining them—until his luck and cunning finally ran out. He
was captured and hanged in 1720.

Edward Low: English. Low was hideously scarred by a cutlass
slash to the jaw, but the tortures he inflicted upon others would
have nauseated a Stalin-era KGB interrogator. It's said that
he once forced a man to eat his own severed ears—with salt.
According to some sources, he was last seen running from a
Royal Navy warship; good thinking on his part, given his record.
It is believed he was hanged by the French after 1723.

Sir Henry Morgan: Welsh. Spain was the dominant colonial power in the Americas, shipping home gold and silver by the boatload. Morgan served English foreign interests by raising merry hell with Spanish shipping and colonial interests. He was rewarded with a knighthood and a governorship. He died a wealthy man, succumbing to dropsy or liver failure in 1688.

Olivier "la Buze" Levasseur: French. "The Buzzard" collaborated with John Taylor and actually wore an eye patch. Unlike Taylor, though, Levasseur didn't quit while he was ahead but kept up his piratical career until his capture by French authorities at Madagascar in 1730. He was hanged.

Gráinne ni Mháille: Irish, aka Grace O'Malley. Rebel, seagoing racketeer, admiral—she was all these and more, engaging in piracy to champion the Irish cause against England. Gráinne didn't even kowtow to Queen Elizabeth I, though she did visit for tea and chitchat. She died of old age in 1603.

Howell Davis: Welsh. This sneaky rogue once captured two ships in one encounter. After the first catch, he forced the captives to brandish weapons at the second, inflating his apparent numbers. Davis was planning to seize a Portuguese island governor when the local militia recognized him and shot him in an ambush in 1719.

Rachel (Schmidt) Wall: American. She turned pirate with her husband, George, luring likely prizes with convincing distress cries. After George drowned in a storm, Rachel forsook the sea for petty thieving along the Boston docks. In 1789, she was arrested for trying to steal a woman's bonnet and was then accused of murdering a sailor. She stood trial, confessed to piracy, and was hanged.

Zheng Yi Sao: Chinese, aka Ching Shih. Hundreds of pirate ships sailed the Chinese coast under her command. Although rare in piracy, she enforced strict rules—notably, a prohibition on rape. Her fleet so dominated the coasts that in some places it functioned as a government. Zheng quit while she was ahead, swapping her fleet for a pardon. She died of natural causes in 1844.

The Watseka Wonder

The story of the "Watseka Wonder," a phenomenon that occurred in a small town in Illinois in the late 1800s, still stands as one of the most authentic cases of spirit possession in history. It has been investigated, dissected, and ridiculed, but to this day, no clear explanation has ever been offered.

✳ ✳ ✳ ✳

An Otherworldly Connection

BEGINNING ON July 11, 1877, 13-year-old Watseka resident Lurancy Vennum started falling into strange trances that sometimes lasted for hours. During these trances, she claimed to speak with spirits and visit heaven. But when she awoke, she could not recall what had occurred during the spell.

Doctors diagnosed Lurancy as mentally ill and recommended that she be sent to the state insane asylum. But in January 1878, a man named Asa Roff, who also lived in Watseka, visited the Vennums. He told them that his daughter Mary had displayed the same behavior as Lurancy nearly 13 years before, and he advised the family to keep Lurancy out of the asylum.

Roff explained that his 19-year-old daughter Mary had died in the state insane asylum on July 5, 1865, a short time after her parents took her there. She had been hearing strange voices, would fall into long trances and speak as though possessed by the spirits of the dead. And she had developed an obsession with bloodletting, poking herself with pins, applying leeches to her body, and cutting herself with a razor.

The Strange Case of Lurancy Vennum

At the time of Mary's death, Lurancy was barely a year old. She moved with her family to Watseka a few years after Mary's death and knew nothing of the girl or her family. When Lurancy's attacks began, her family had no idea that she was suffering from the same type of illness that Mary had.

On the morning of her first trance, Lurancy collapsed and fell into a deep sleep that lasted more than five hours. When she awoke, she seemed fine. But the spell returned again the next day, and this time, while Lurancy was unconscious, she spoke of seeing angels and walking in heaven. She told her family that she had talked to her brother, who had died three years before.

As rumors about Lurancy spread, Asa Roff realized how similar her symptoms were to those of his daughter, and he was convinced that the illnesses were the same. When it was suggested that Lurancy be institutionalized, he knew he had to speak up.

When Roff contacted the Vennum family on January 31, 1878, they were skeptical, but they nonetheless allowed him to bring Dr. E. Winchester Stevens to meet with Lurancy. Like Roff, Dr. Stevens was a spiritualist. They felt that Lurancy was not insane but was possessed by spirits of the dead.

When Dr. Stevens arrived, Lurancy began speaking in another voice, claiming that she was a woman named Katrina Hogan. A few moments later, her voice changed again, and she said that she was Willie Canning, a boy who had killed himself many years before. Willie spoke for more than an hour. Then, just as Dr. Stevens and Asa Roff prepared to leave, Lurancy threw her arms into the air and fell on the floor stiff as a board. After Dr. Stevens calmed her down, Lurancy claimed she was in heaven and that spirits, some good and some bad, were controlling her body. She said the good spirit who most wanted to control her was a young woman named Mary Roff.

The Return of Mary Roff

After about a week of being possessed by the spirit of Mary Roff, Lurancy insisted on leaving her own house, which was unfamiliar to her, and going "home" to the Roff house. Mrs. Roff heard what was going on and rushed over to the Vennum house with her daughter Minerva. Watching the two women hurry up the sidewalk, she cried out, "There comes my ma and my sister Nervie!" "Nervie" had been Mary's pet name for her sister.

It seemed evident that Mary's spirit had taken over Lurancy's body. She looked the same, but she knew nothing of the Vennum family or her life with them. Instead, she had intimate knowledge of the Roffs and acted as though they were her family. Lurancy treated the Vennums politely, but they were strangers to her.

On February 11, realizing that it was best for their daughter, the Vennums allowed her to go stay with the Roffs. Lurancy told the Roffs that she would only be with them until "sometime in May."

On their way home, as the Roffs and Lurancy traveled past the house where they'd lived when Mary died, Lurancy wanted to know why they weren't stopping. The Roffs explained that they'd moved to a new home a few years back, which was something that Lurancy/Mary would not have known.

Within a short time, Lurancy began to exhibit signs that she knew more about the Roffs and their habits than she could have possibly known if she was only pretending to be Mary. She knew of incidents and experiences that were private and had taken place long before she was even born.

As promised, Lurancy stayed with the Roff family until May. When it was time for Mary to leave Lurancy's body, she was deeply saddened, but she seemed to understand that it was time to go. On May 21, Lurancy returned to the Vennums. She showed no signs of her earlier illness, and her parents and the Roffs believed that she had been cured of her affliction by the possession of Mary's spirit.

Lurancy grew into a happy young woman and exhibited no ill effects from the possession. She married and had 13 children.

An Unsolved Mystery

Lurancy had no memories of being possessed by Mary, but she felt a closeness to the Roffs she could never explain. She stayed in touch with them even after they moved away in 1879. Each year, when they returned, Lurancy would allow Mary's spirit to possess her, and things were just as they were for a time in 1878.

White House Ghosts

The colonial-style mansion at 1600 Pennsylvania Avenue may be America's most famous address, as well as one of the most haunted. Day and night, visitors have seen spirits that include presidents William Henry Harrison, Andrew Jackson, and Abraham Lincoln. The spirits of these men are almost as powerful today as when they ruled America.

✳ ✳ ✳ ✳

William Henry Harrison Feels a Little Blue

WILLIAM HENRY HARRISON was the first American president to die in office. While giving his inauguration speech on an icy, windy March 4, 1841, Harrison caught a cold that quickly turned to pneumonia.

There are stories about Harrison, half-conscious with fever, wandering the corridors of the White House, looking for a quiet room in which to rest. Unfortunately, there was no escape from the demands of his office . . . nor from the doctors whose treatments likely killed him. While Harrison's lungs filled with fluid and fever wracked his body, his doctors bled him, then treated him with mustard, laxatives, ipecac, rhubarb, and mercury. It is speculated that the president died not from the "ordinary winter cold" that he'd contracted, but from the care of his doctors. William Henry Harrison died April 4, 1841, just one month after taking office.

Harrison's translucent ghost is seen throughout the White House, especially in the residential areas. His skin is pale blue, and his breathing makes an ominous rattle. He appears to be looking for something and walks through closed doors. Some believe he's looking for rest or a cure for his illness. Others say he's searching for his office, so he can complete his term as president.

Andrew Jackson Likes the Ladies

If you'd prefer to see a happier ghost, look for Andrew Jackson. He's probably in the Queen's Bedroom where his bed is displayed. But Jackson may not necessarily be looking for his old bed—in life he was quite the ladies' man and, today, the Queen's Bedroom is reserved for female guests of honor.

Mary Todd Lincoln frequently complained about the ghost of Andrew Jackson cursing and stomping in the corridors of the White House. When she left the presidential estate, Jackson stopped complaining.

Visitors may simply sense Jackson's presence in the Queen's Bedroom or feel a bone-chilling breeze when they're around his bed. Others have reported that Jackson's ghost climbs under the covers, sending guests shrieking out of the room. But Jackson isn't the only president who haunts this room.

Two Wartime Leaders Meet

During World War II, the Queen's Bedroom was called the Rose Room, and it wasn't reserved for women. While visiting the White House during the war, Winston Churchill strolled into the Rose Room completely naked and smoking a cigar after taking a bath. It was then that he encountered the ghost of Abraham Lincoln standing in front of the fireplace with one hand on the mantle, staring down at the hearth. Always a quick wit, Churchill said, "Good evening, Mr. President. You seem to have me at a disadvantage."

According to Churchill, Lincoln smiled at him then vanished. Churchill refused to stay in that room again, but Lincoln wasn't finished surprising guests.

Lincoln Wakes Up the Queen

When Queen Wilhelmina of the Netherlands stayed in the Queen's Bedroom in 1945, she was hoping to get a good night's sleep. Instead, she was awakened by noisy footsteps in the corridor outside her room. Annoyed, she waited for the person to return to his room, but he stopped at her door and knocked loudly, several times. When the queen finally opened her door, she was face to face with the specter of Abraham Lincoln. She said that he looked a bit pale but very much alive and was dressed in travel clothes, including a top hat and coat. The queen gasped, and Lincoln vanished.

Lincoln's ghost may be the most solid-looking and "real" spirit at the White House, and hundreds of people have encountered it. Strangely enough, Lincoln, who seemed to be in touch with "the other side" even before he died, claimed he once saw his own apparition and talked about it often.

Abraham Lincoln Sees His Own Ghost

The morning after Abraham Lincoln was first elected president, he had a premonition about his death. He saw two reflections of himself in a mirror. One image was how he usually appeared, fit and healthy. In the other reflection, his face was pale and ghostly. Lincoln and his wife believed it predicted that he wouldn't complete his second term in office.

Later, Lincoln saw his own funeral in a dream. He said that he was in the White House, but it was strangely quiet and filled with mourners. Walking through the halls, he entered the East Room, where, to his horror, he saw a body wrapped in funeral vestments and surrounded by soldiers.

He said he approached one of the soldiers to find out what had happened. "Who is dead in the White House?" Lincoln demanded in his dream. "The president," the soldier replied. "He was killed by an assassin!"

A few days later, that fateful day when he attended Ford Theatre for the last time, President Lincoln called a meeting of his cabinet members. He told them that they would have important news the following morning. He also explained that he'd had a strange dream . . . one that he'd had twice before. He saw himself alone and adrift in a boat without oars. That was all he said, and the cabinet members left the president's office with a very uneasy feeling.

The following morning, they received news that the president had been assassinated.

Lincoln Never Leaves

Lincoln's apparition has been seen clearly by hundreds, including Eleanor Roosevelt's maid, who saw him sitting on a bed, removing his boots. Franklin Roosevelt's valet ran out of the White House after encountering Abe's spirit. Calvin Coolidge's wife saw Lincoln's face reflected in a window in the Yellow Oval Room.

President Lincoln has been seen in many places in the White House but most frequently in the Lincoln Bedroom. Although the late president's bed is now in this room, during his lifetime, it was the cabinet room in which he signed the Emancipation Proclamation.

Ghosts of Presidents' Families and Foes

Abigail Adams used to hang laundry on clotheslines in the White House's East Room. Her ghost appears there regularly in a cap and wrapped in a shawl. She's usually carrying laundry or checking to see if her laundry is dry.

Dorothea "Dolley" Madison defends the Rose Garden that she designed and planted. When Woodrow Wilson's second wife, Edith, ordered gardeners to dig up the garden for new plants, Dolley's apparition appeared and allegedly insisted that no one was going to touch her garden. The landscaping ceased, and Dolley's roses remain exactly as they were when the Madisons lived in the White House in the early 1800s.

Abraham Lincoln's son Willie died in February 1862 after a brief illness. Soon after, the First Lady began holding séances in the White House to communicate with him. The president was equally obsessed with his son's death and had his coffin reopened at least twice, just to look at him. Willie's apparition has been seen at the White House regularly since then, most often appearing in the second-floor bedrooms, where his presence was witnessed by Lyndon Johnson's daughter Lynda.

However, Lynda's bedroom may have been haunted by other spirits as well. Harry Truman's mother died in that room, and Lynda used to report unexplained footsteps in the bedroom. Sometimes, her phone would ring in the middle of the night and, when she answered, no one was on the line.

Also on the second floor, people have heard the ghost of Frances Cleveland crying, perhaps reliving a time when her husband, Grover, was diagnosed with cancer.

One very out-of-place spirit appears to be a British soldier from around 1814, when the White House was sieged and burned. The uniformed soldier looks lost and is holding a torch. When he realizes that he's been spotted, he looks alarmed and vanishes.

The White House's Oldest Ghost

David Burns may be the oldest ghost at the White House. He donated the land on which the house was built. One day, Franklin Roosevelt heard his name being called, and when he replied, the voice said that he was Mr. Burns.

FDR's valet, Cesar Carrera, told a similar story. Carrera was in the Yellow Oval Room when he heard a soft, distant voice say, "I'm Mr. Burns." When Carrera looked, no one was there.

Later, during the Truman years, a guard at the White House also heard a soft voice announce himself as Mr. Burns. The guard expected to see Truman's Secretary of State, James Byrnes, but no one appeared. What's more, the guard checked the roster and learned that Byrnes hadn't been in the building at all that day.

The White House may be America's most haunted public building. Ghosts are seen there, day and night. On the White House's Web site, staff members talk about their regular ghostly encounters. In the words of Harry Truman, the White House is haunted, "sure as shooting."

Murder by Rail: It Didn't Just Happen in Silent Movies

Indeed, there are recorded instances of people being tied to railroad tracks—although it wasn't exactly the most efficient way to kill someone.

✳ ✳ ✳ ✳

I've Been Working on the Railroads

EVERYBODY IS FAMILIAR with the scene: The hero, tied to the railroad tracks, struggles desperately as the locomotive charges onward and blows its horn loudly and futilely. Will the train stop in time? Will the hero free himself in time? He will, of course. (Sorry if we wrecked the suspense.)

More interesting, however, is the question of whether this was ever a common occurrence in real life. The scenario is perfect for a melodrama, but come on—aren't there more efficient ways to get rid of someone?

The whole tied-to-the-railroad-tracks cliché has been around for a long time—about as long as railroads themselves. The new means of transportation, coupled with the public's insatiable hunger for unlikely melodrama, prompted a number of playwrights and hack serial writers to use the scenario in their work in the latter half of the 19th century. By 1913, the set-up had become such a cliché that it was lampooned in one of the

first Hollywood parodies, the silent film *Barney Oldfield's Race for a Life.* Of course, for those of us who weren't alive in 1913, it was Snidely Whiplash of the *Dudley Do-Right* cartoons who ingrained in our prepubescent minds the idea that tying somebody to the railroad tracks was a preferred method of murder.

The Real-Life Story of August Gardner

As it turns out, tying folks to the railroad tracks didn't just happen in Hollywood or cartoons. There are some documented cases of this dastardly occurrence happening in real-life America. Way back in 1874, for example, a Frenchman named August Gardner was abducted and robbed by three men in Indiana who proceeded to tie him to the railroad tracks and leave him for dead. Gardner wrestled with his bonds as the train approached, freeing one hand and then another. As the train drew closer, he loosed one of his feet. It seemed, in classic melodramatic fashion, that our hero was going to escape with his life.

But alas, he fumbled untying the last knot—the train ran over his foot and cut it off. The plucky Gardner spent the night in a culvert, then hobbled on one foot into a nearby town, where he was able to relay his story before dying.

Of course, the number of documented cases of evil-doers tying people to railroad tracks is far smaller than silent films and *Dudley Do-Right* cartoons would have you believe. But that's okay—we can accept that the real world doesn't always mirror what happens in the movies or on television. Just don't try to tell us that bad guys don't really twirl their handlebar mustaches as they prepare to enact their devious plans.

---

* A shark's jaws are not attached to the rest of its skeleton; that great maw is held in place by muscles and ligaments.

* When the purportedly penny-pinching executives, or "Scotch bosses," at the Minnesota Mining and Manufacturing Company (3M) didn't put enough adhesive on their tape, people complained. They responded by putting better adhesive on their new product. The tape stuck—and so did the name.

* During his 16th-century reign, Süleyman the Magnificent extended the Ottoman Empire from Algiers all the way to the Austrian border.

The Great Famine

More than a million people starved to death in Ireland from 1845 to 1851, but only one crop failed: the potato. How could this have killed so many? Why didn't the Irish just eat other stuff?

❋ ❋ ❋ ❋

As Usual, the Poor Get the Shaft

THE REASON THE Great Famine, as it's called, took such a toll is simple: Those who starved were poor. For generations, the impoverished in Ireland survived by planting potatoes to feed their families. They had nothing else. Ireland's wealthy landowners grew all kinds of crops, but these were shipped off and sold for profit. Most rich folks didn't care that the poor starved.

How did things get so bad? Irish History 101: The Catholics and the Protestants didn't like each other, and neither did the English and the Irish. Back then, the wealthy landowners were mostly Protestants from England, while the poor were Catholic peasants. The Irish peasants grew their food on small parcels of land that were rented from the hated English.

In the 16th century, a hitherto unknown item, the potato, crossed the Atlantic from Peru, originally arriving in England and finally getting to Ireland in 1590. Spuds grew well in Ireland, even on the rocky, uneven plots that were often rented by peasants, and they quickly became the peasants' main food source. Potatoes required little labor to grow, and an acre could yield 12 tons of them—enough to feed a family of six for the entire year, with leftovers for the animals.

We think of potatoes as a fattening food, but they're loaded with vitamins, carbohydrates, and even some protein. Add a little fish and buttermilk to the diet, and a family could live quite happily on potatoes. Potatoes for breakfast, lunch, and dinner might sound monotonous, but it fueled a population boom in Ireland. By the 19th century, three million people were living on the potato diet.

Nature's Wrath

In 1845, though, the fungus *Phytophthora infestans*, or "late blight," turned Ireland's potatoes into black, smelly, inedible lumps. Impoverished families had no other options. Their pitiful savings were wiped out, and they fled to the workhouses—the only places where they could get food and shelter in return for their labor.

When the potato crop failed again the next year, and every year through 1849, people began dying in earnest—not just from starvation, but from scurvy and gangrene (caused by a lack of vitamin C), typhus, dysentery, typhoid fever, and heart failure. Overwhelmed and underfunded, the workhouses closed their doors. Many people who were weakened by hunger died of exposure after being evicted from their homes. To top the disaster off, a cholera epidemic spread during the last year of the blight, killing thousands more.

The exact number who perished is unknown, but it's believed to be between one and two million. In addition, at least a million people left the country, and many of these wayward souls died at sea. All during that terrible time, there was plenty of food in Ireland, but it was consumed by the wealthy. The poor, meanwhile, had nothing. They were left to starve.

Say What?

If I weren't earning $3 million a year to dunk a basketball, most people on the street would run in the other direction if they saw me coming.

—Charles Barkley

Doing nothing is better than being busy doing nothing.

—Lao Tzu

The best time to make friends is before you need them.

—Ethel Barrymore

Arf! Dog-Men in History

Dog may be man's best friend, but he's also been invoked to explain the unexplainable, and even to denigrate enemies—reasons why tales of men with the heads of dogs are not uncommon throughout the historical record.

✳ ✳ ✳ ✳

Dog-Headed Foreigners

ANCIENT STORIES ABOUT dog-headed men unwittingly reveal an apprehensiveness about the power of canines. We love our pooches, but let's face it: They have claws and sharp teeth, they run faster than we do, and they can eat our faces if they feel like it. Historically, this small bit of disquiet bubbling beneath our adoration has encouraged cultures to invoke dog-like creatures for diverse purposes, sometimes as gods, such as Egypt's Anubis, and frequently to belittle other cultures.

Whatever the motives, the eventual effect of these pervasive tales was to make fantastical dog-men seem very real. Most imaginative of all, though, were ancient writers from China, India, and Europe, who relayed purportedly true stories of human beings who literally had the heads of dogs.

Sit, Cynocephali!

Dog-headed peoples are often referred to as *Cynocephali*, Greek for "dog-head." In the 5th century B.C., Greek historian Herodotus described a distant country inhabited by "huge snakes and the lions, and the elephants and bears and asps, the Kunokephaloi (Dog-headed) and the Headless Men that have their eyes in their chests."

Herodotus was not alone in his testimony about dog-headed peoples. Fellow Greek historian Ctesias claimed that on the mountains in distant India, "there live men with the head of a dog, whose clothing is the skin of wild beasts."

In accounts of this nature, it's difficult to sort out myth from fact. Like many of today's bloggers, ancient historians made implausible claims based on hearsay rather than direct observation. Writers played so fast and loose with the available facts that many believed—and made their readers believe—that some foreign societies barked rather than spoke.

Some historians tried to legitimize their claims by skipping down the road of pseudo-science. The 2nd-century Greek historian Aelian included the Cynocephali in his book of animals. He declared that beyond Egypt one encounters the "human Kynoprosopoi (Dog faces) . . . they are black in appearance, and they have the head and teeth of a dog. And since they resemble this animal, it is very natural that I should mention them here [in a book about Animals]."

Racism Collides with Legend

Many present-day historians charge that these accounts of dog-headed tribes aren't simply reflections of a fear of foreigners, but racist ignorance. Repeated accounts of dog-headed groups in northern Africa suggest that race did indeed help encourage some dog-driven tales. These African groups were often referred to as the Marmaritae, who engaged in on-again off-again warfare with the Romans. Legend has it that St. Christopher was a captured dog-headed slave from a Marmaritae tribe—paintings that depict the saint with the head of a brown dog still exist. According to lore, Christopher's dog head was replaced with a normal human head after he was baptized.

Modern scholars believe that historical references to dog-headed tribes derived from the lore created by many tribes in Central Asia, who described their own origins as having roots in the progeny of a human female who mated with a male dog. Such startling biology certainly would have tickled the imaginations of outsiders and reinforced the notion that dog-headedness signified a profound and culturally expedient "otherness" of foreigners.

Long Live Lenin

Using a heady mixture of chemicals, the Russians have kept former Soviet leader Vladimir Lenin's body almost perfectly preserved for nearly a century.

✳ ✳ ✳ ✳

A Commission for Immortalization

ON JANUARY 21, 1924, Soviet leader Vladimir Lenin died after a series of strokes. Two days later, pathologist Alexei Abrikosov embalmed Lenin's body so it would be presentable for viewing. A makeshift wooden tomb was designed and built by architect Alexey Schusev on Red Square by the Kremlin Wall in Moscow. More than 100,000 people visited the tomb within a month and a half.

By August, people were still coming to pay their respects to the man who had spearheaded the Bolshevik Revolution in Russia and brought about Communist rule. Scientists Vladimir Vorbiov, Boris Zbarsky, and others routinely reintroduced the preservative chemicals into Lenin's body to keep it from putrefying.

Joseph Stalin, Lenin's successor, perhaps sensing that the fervor attached to Lenin could be harnessed for his own purposes, created the Commission for Immortalization, and the decision was made to preserve Lenin's body until the end of the Soviet state—presumably forever.

Lenin is kept in a glass coffin at Lenin's Mausoleum on Red Square. The only visible parts of his body are his head and his hands. (Stalin was placed in the same tomb upon his death in 1953, but was removed in 1961 by then-Soviet leader Nikita Khrushchev.) Lenin wears a plain suit, and the lower half of his body is covered with a blanket.

Strange Brew

Vorbiov and Zbarsky devised a permanent embalming technique: Every 18 months, Lenin's body is immersed in a glass tub of a solution of glycerol and potassium acetate. The chemicals penetrate his body, and he becomes like any living human insofar as 70 percent of his body is liquid. After he's taken out of the tub, Lenin is wrapped in rubber bandages to prevent leakage. He is then dressed and groomed. Occasionally, a bacterial growth will develop, but it is quickly scrubbed off.

Lenin has remained in his tomb since 1924, except for a brief evacuation to Siberia during World War II when it looked as if the Nazis might take over Moscow. Lenin's tomb is one of Moscow's main tourist attractions. The Soviet state is long gone, having collapsed in 1991, but its father lives on. Sort of.

---

* *Mariner 9* was the first successful Mars orbiter, transmitting more than 7,000 images of the Red Planet and providing exploratory information to lay the groundwork for later missions to find frozen water beneath the ice caps.

* The first radio commercial aired on WEAF in New York on August 28, 1922. It was a ten-minute advertisement for the Queensboro Real Estate Corporation.

* In the early- to mid-1800s, a trip by Conestoga wagon from Philadelphia to Pittsburgh—a distance of about 300 miles—took roughly three weeks.

* Following Walter Raleigh's beheading in 1618, his head was embalmed and given to his widow. She willed it to her son, Carew, who kept it until his death. It was buried with him.

* The world's smallest submarine was built by Pierre Poulin and made its dive to qualify for the record on June 26, 2005, in Memphremagog Lake, near Magog, Quebec, Canada. Submarines are measured by displacement, and its displacement was 1,367 pounds (620 kilograms).

* During a 60-year life span, an average tree will produce nearly two tons of leaves to be raked.

* Confederate volunteers in the Civil War were paid $11 per month in 1861. Their pay was increased to $18 per month by 1864, but by then the currency was almost worthless.

Nostradamus: Seer of Visions

Nostradamus was born in December 1503 in Saint-Rémy-de-Provence, a small town in southern France. Little is known about his childhood except that he came from a very large family and that he may have been educated by his maternal great-grandfather. In his teens, Nostradamus entered the University of Avignon but was only there for about a year before the school was forced to close its doors due to an outbreak of the plague. He later became a successful apothecary and even created a pill that could supposedly protect against the plague.

✳ ✳ ✳ ✳

Looking to the Future

IT IS BELIEVED that some time in the 1540s, Nostradamus began taking an interest in the occult, particularly in ways to predict the future. His preferred method was scrying: gazing into a bowl of water or a mirror and waiting for visions to appear.

Nostradamus published a highly successful almanac for the year 1550, which included some of his prophecies and predictions. This almanac was so successful that Nostradamus wrote more, perhaps even several a year, until his death in 1566. Even so, it was a single book that caused the most controversy, both when it was released and even today.

Les Prophéties

In addition to creating his almanacs, Nostradamus also began compiling his previously unpublished prophecies into one massive volume. Released in 1555, *Les Prophéties* (*The Prophecies*) contained hundreds of quatrains (four-line stanzas, or poems). It would become one of the most controversial and perplexing books ever written. Even as he put the collection together, however, Nostradamus worried that some might see his prophecies as demonic, so he encoded them to obscure their true meanings. To do this, Nostradamus did everything from playing with the syntax of the quatrains to switching between French, Greek, Latin, and other languages.

When the compilation was first released, some people did indeed think that Nostradamus was in league with the devil. Others simply thought that he was insane and that his quatrains were nothing more than the ramblings of a delusional man. As time went on, though, people started analyzing Nostradamus's prophecies to see if they were coming true. It became a common practice in the aftermath of a major historical event for people to pull out a copy of *Les Prophéties* to see if they could find a hidden reference to it buried in one of Nostradamus's quatrains. It is a practice that has continued to this day and only gets more and more common as the years go by.

Lost in Translation

One of the interesting and frustrating things about Nostradamus's *Les Prophéties* is that due to the printing procedures in his time, no two editions of his book were ever alike. Not only were there differences in spelling or punctuation, but entire words and phrases were often changed, especially when translated from French to English. Presently, there are more than 200 editions of *Les Prophéties* in print, all of which have subtle differences in the text. So it's not surprising that people from all over the world have looked into their version and found references to the French Revolution, Napoleon, the rise of Hitler, the JFK assassination, even the *Apollo* moon landing. But of all the messages reportedly hidden in Nostradamus's quatrains, the most talked about recently are those relating to the terrorist attacks on September 11, 2001.

Soon after the Twin Towers fell, an e-mail started making the rounds that claimed Nostradamus had predicted the events and quoted the following quatrain as proof:

In the City of God there will be a great thunder,
Two Brothers torn apart by Chaos,
While the fortress endures,
The great leader will succumb,
The third big war will begin when the big city is burning
　　　　　　　　　　　　　　　　　—Nostradamus, 1654

Anyone reading the above can clearly see that Nostradamus is describing September 11, the Twin Towers ("Two Brothers") falling, and the start of World War III. Pretty chilling, except Nostradamus never wrote it. It's nothing more than an Internet hoax that spread like wildfire. It's a pretty bad hoax, too. First, Nostradamus wrote quatrains, which have four lines. This one has five. Also, consider that the date Nostradamus supposedly penned this—1654—was almost 90 years after he died. Nostradamus might have been able to see the future, but there's no mention of him being able to write from beyond the grave.

However, others believe Nostradamus did indeed pen a quatrain that predicted September 11. It is quatrain I.87, which when translated reads:

Volcanic fire from the center of the earth
Will cause tremors around the new city;
Two great rocks will make war for a long time
Then Arethusa will redden a new river.

Those who believe this quatrain predicted September 11 believe that the "new city" is a thinly-veiled reference to New York City. They further state that Nostradamus would often use rocks to refer to religious beliefs and that the third line refers to the religious differences between the United States and the terrorists. Skeptic James Randi, however, believes that the "new city" referred to is Naples, not New York. So who's right? No one is really sure, so for now, the debate continues . . . at least until the next major catastrophe hits and people go scrambling to the bookshelves to see what Nostradamus had to say about it.

Punk Rock and the Mohawk

Blame it on Robert De Niro. Sources say that the legendary actor's portrayal of sociopath Travis Bickle in the 1976 film Taxi Driver *helped make the Mohawk hairstyle a symbol of the punk rock movement.*

✳ ✳ ✳ ✳

Angst = Mohawk

Yes, it all started with *Taxi Driver*'s Travis Bickle, whose chilling hair transformation signified his descent into insanity. Frustrated with unemployment and inflation, many young people in the 1970s related to the character's feelings of alienation, desperation, and angst, and they expressed themselves through punk rock's radical brand of music and fashion. The punks were anarchist, loud, and angry—it was an image that was diametrically opposed to that of the hippies of the 1960s, who wore long hair and love beads while preaching wishes for peace.

The Mohawk was an apt hairstyle for the punks. It has its origins in the Native American Mohawk tribe of the Northeast. Mohawk warriors would shave off the hair on their scalps, save for a strip running down the middle that was three-fingers wide, before going off to battle. During World War II, some U.S. paratroopers from the 101st Airborne Division wore Mohawk cuts and war paint for good luck before going on missions. What better hairstyle than a warrior's to symbolize the punk sentiment of charging into combat against everyday society?

Punks manipulated the remaining hair strip to stand vertically on end by using stiffening styling products such as gel or hairspray, or harder substances such as Elmer's glue, egg whites, or Knox gelatin. They could make the hairdo even more off-beat and dramatic by cutting it into varied shapes or patterns, grooming the ends into fierce spikes, or coloring the brush of hair in bright shades with food coloring.

Add some safety-pin body piercings, especially on the face, and the effect was even more threatening. The cringe-inducing fashion didn't stop there. Other accoutrements included theatrical makeup, studded jewelry or dog collars, ravaged clothing reconstructed with the beloved safety pins or tape, combat boots, and nearly anything else that appeared incongruous with mainstream culture.

Mohawk Lite

The punk movement faded into history following its heyday in the late 1970s, but the Mohawk lives on. However, today's softer facsimiles have more to do with studied fashion sense than listening to aggressive music and flouting authority. In short, there's less pouting and more posing. It is positively *de rigueur* on fashion models, professional athletes, rap musicians, business executives, teenybopper contestants on *American Idol,* and even celebrity tykes such as actress Angelina Jolie's son Maddox.

So don't be alarmed if someone sporting a Mohawk walks up to you and asks, "You talkin' to me? You talkin' to me?" Simply grin and say, "No doubt, dude! And have I got some cool styling tips for you!"

＊ The brass at Gillette thought they'd come up with a great idea. For the cost of only one million dollars, they were able to supply Mach3 razors for all welcome bags given out to delegates at the 2004 Democratic National Convention. Unfortunately, security officers worried that the razors presented a threat to attendees and promptly confiscated any that they tried to carry into the convention hall.

＊ As General George Patton crossed a bridge over the Rhine into Germany during World War II, he stopped in the middle and urinated into the river.

True Colors of the White House

Legend claims that the residence of the U.S. president acquired its name—and hue—after an arson attack by British soldiers during the War of 1812. Here's the real story.

✻　✻　✻　✻

THE "PRESIDENT'S HOUSE," as it was originally named, is situated at 1600 Pennsylvania Avenue NW in Washington, D.C. It was designed by Irish architect James Hoban under the direction of George Washington. The cornerstone was laid in the fall of 1792, but Washington left office before construction was completed. In 1800, the home's first occupants, President John Adams and his wife, Abigail, moved in. By that time, though, the gray quarried-sandstone exterior of the building had started to look weathered and was therefore given a coat of whitewash to protect it from harsh winter conditions. A year later, Thomas Jefferson moved into the residence as the third U.S. president, and from that point on, the famous home was given a fresh application of white paint whenever it was needed.

At the Battle of York during the War of 1812, Canadian Parliament buildings were felled as a result of arson. In a retaliatory act, British troops set fire to many structures in Washington, including the residence of President James Madison and his wife, Dolley. And while Madison ordered the charred and blackened limestone walls to be repainted in the familiar white, the designation of the building as "the White House" predates the attack. Sometime in 1811, a British ambassador referred to the residence as "the White House at Washington." In March 1812, a congressman by the name of Bigelow reported that "there is much trouble at the White House, as we call it—I mean the President's House." Yet the familiar nickname would not become official until September 1901, when President Theodore Roosevelt signed an executive order that designated the building "the White House."

Honest Abe's Air Corps

That's right—President Lincoln's troops took to the air during the Civil War, long before the airplane existed.

✻ ✻ ✻ ✻

Taking Flight

O N June 18, 1861, President Abraham Lincoln received an extraordinary message. "I have the pleasure of sending you this first telegram ever dispatched from an aerial station," his correspondent wrote, noting that from his vantage point, he could see the countryside surrounding Washington, D.C., for 50 miles in any direction. The "station" was an enormous hot-air balloon that was tethered across from the White House and hovering 500 feet in the air. Thaddeus Lowe, the balloon's operator, had run a telegraph line from the passenger basket down to a ground cable that was connected to both the president and the Union Army War Office.

A self-taught scientist, engineer, and aeronaut, Lowe had been piloting balloons for a decade. He was also an ardent supporter of the Union. He had mounted his balloon demonstration because he wanted to serve his country—not on the ground, like other soldiers, but in the air. One of the Union's greatest fears was that the Confederacy would launch a sneak attack on Washington, D.C., via northern Virginia. Who better to keep an eye on enemy maneuvers, Lowe asked, than a spy in the sky?

Lincoln agreed. A few days later, on June 21, the president created the Union Army Balloon Corps and appointed Lowe as its first chief. Over the next two years, Lowe made three thousand balloon ascents. His telegraph apparatus relayed crucial information to the ground troops. During the Peninsula Campaign of 1861–62, for example, Lowe alerted General George McClellan to the movements of rebel troops three miles away; it was the first time in history that a commander was able to use aerial intelligence to rout an enemy. At the Battle of Fair

Oaks (May 31–June 1, 1862), Lowe's messages guided an entrapped Union battalion to safety.

Ever alert for new possibilities, Lowe also commandeered a barge from which he could make balloon ascents over the Potomac River, thus creating the first "aircraft carrier." His constant presence in the sky was such an irritant to the South that he became, according to author Carl Sandburg, "the most shot-at man of the Civil War." Though his balloon sailed too high for Confederate artillery to reach—the craft could climb to five thousand feet—Lowe did have a few close calls. At one point, he actually caught a cannonball in his basket.

Ahead of His Time

Despite his daring, Lowe's balloon corps proved too controversial for the army. Rival balloonists, perhaps jealous of his success, accused him of mismanaging funds. Some generals found the balloons too cumbersome and expensive to transport. In addition, Lowe himself suffered ill health from a bout of malaria. The corps was officially disbanded in August 1863, and a disappointed Lowe returned to civilian life.

His exploits were not forgotten, however. He received the Franklin Institute's Grand Medal of Honor in 1886. A mountain near Pasadena, California, bears his name. And in 1988, he was posthumously inducted into the U.S. Military Intelligence Corps Hall of Fame, the sole balloonist among its honorees. It is a fitting tribute to the nation's original spy in the sky.

---

* The working title of the Beatles hit "With a Little Help from My Friends" was "Bad Finger Boogie."

* According to Hollywood lore, silent film actress Norma Talmadge started the tradition of stars putting their footprints in the cement at Grauman's Chinese Theatre when she accidentally stumbled onto the freshly laid sidewalk in front of it in 1927.

* Pepsi-Cola was the first foreign consumer product sold in the former Soviet Union.

A Strange—and Costly—Burial Tradition

As if death wasn't a big enough downer, it accounts for one of the biggest expenses the average person will ever incur. From caskets to flowers to embalming services, people pay through the nose for a decent burial. And until fairly recently, you could say that the dead also paid through the eyes.

✻　✻　✻　✻

Keeping the Soul Safe

THE MOST COMMON explanation for the tradition of putting coins on the eyes of the dead points to the mythical Greek figure of Charon, one of the Western world's first undertakers. Typically depicted as a morose, somewhat creepy old man (undertakers haven't changed much in 3,000 years, apparently), Charon was a ferryman who conveyed the souls of the dead to the land of the dead across the rivers Styx and Acheron.

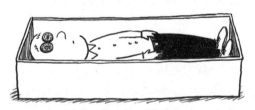

Much like today's undertakers, Charon's services came at a price. The cost of a ride to Hades was an *obol*, an ancient Greek coin valued at one-sixth of a drachma (the equivalent of $15 to $20 in today's world). Placing the coins on the corpse's eyes, the Charon theory holds, was to ensure that the soul would reach its final destination.

More Money Myths

Though this explanation seems convincing, a thorough review of Greek mythology identifies one major flaw in the argument: Charon, who was a picky sort, would only accept payment if the coin was placed in the mouth of the corpse. Hence, the tradition in ancient Greece was to put coins in dead people's mouths, not in their eye sockets.

However, the ancient Greeks were not the only people who believed that money was a necessity in the afterlife. Many civilizations, including the ancient Egyptians and the Incas, buried their beloved dead with money and other treasure to help ensure that the deceased were comfortable for eternity. So it is possible that the erroneous attribution to Greek mythology is actually rooted in fact.

Getting Some Shut-Eye

A more likely explanation, though, is a combination of this mythology and simple practicality. When a human body dies, rigor mortis sets in. One of the more troubling aspects of this condition is the tendency for the eyelids to pop open. Not only is it creepy to have a dead person staring at you, but in many ancient traditions, it was considered bad luck for the dead person to cross into the afterlife with his or her eyes open—the corpse, it was believed, would look for someone to take with it to the next world. Coins—which happen to fit nicely into the eye sockets, are weighty enough to counteract the effects of rigor mortis, and could be used as emergency funds at a postmortem tollbooth— were the ideal solution.

Among some people, the custom of putting coins in the eyes of the dead continued until at least the late 19th century, when mortuary scientists figured out how to deal with rigor mortis. Besides, undertakers no longer require payment from the orifices of the dead. Just those of the living.

❊ The Chicago Cubs sued newspaper carrier Mark Guthrie in 2004 to get back the $301,000 they mistakenly paid to him instead of to actual Cubs' pitcher Mark Guthrie.

❊ The first American president to be photographed was John Quincy Adams.

❊ In October 1916, Margaret Sanger opened the first birth-control clinic in the United States. Nine days later, it was raided, and Sanger was jailed for 30 days.

The Papacy and the Ex-Wives Club

Many believe that popes in the Catholic Church have never been allowed to marry. But celibacy has not always been Church doctrine, and past popes-to-be simply left their wives before ordination.

✳ ✳ ✳ ✳

Pope, Plus Wife and Child

THE FURTHEST THINGS from anyone's mind upon hearing the word *pope* are marriage and its close companion, sex. Yet there have been married popes, sexually active popes, and even popes with brothels. The relationship between popes and celibacy has changed drastically over time.

Records indicate that St. Peter, considered by some to be the first pope, was married. Christian communities at that time were small, scattered, and based largely on close familial relationships. Yet when Christianity became the official religion of the Roman Empire, the attitude toward betrothed clergy evolved from "the more, the merrier" to "one is the holiest number." As the Church became married to politics, the powers-that-be feared wedded clergy would leave money and land to their families rather than the Church. This became pressing in the Middle Ages, when bishops and priests received land and money in exchange for allegiance to the local lord. Various Church regulations discouraged the clergy from marrying, but marriage itself was still allowed.

Resisting Temptation

Despite regular resistance to the Church's antimarriage mandates, throughout the first millennium A.D., some clergy members embraced the doctrine of celibacy. Popular Christian philosophy saw the spiritual as pure and the material as fleeting and corruptive. Hence St. Augustine's 5th-century claim that "nothing is so powerful in drawing the spirit of a man downwards as the caresses of a woman." Carnal relations were considered incompatible with sacred ritual, and therefore clergy were not allowed to perform their duties within certain time periods of having sex. The ascetic monastic traditions that were imported from the Orient also emphasized the spiritual transcendence associated with celibacy.

Overall, then, it was considered a good thing to resist sexual temptation, and in many circles, celibate priests had a leg up on their married counterparts. Finally, there was good old-fashioned misogyny, illustrated by Pope Gregory VII's insight that "the Church cannot escape the clutches of the laity unless priests first escape from the clutches of their wives."

Pope, the Perpetual Bachelor

The higher-ups in the Church had a vested interest in encouraging celibacy among the priests, yet this meant the popes and bishops had to practice what they preached. This was a problem for those who were already married, and the solution was to declare a pope's marriage retroactively invalid on the day of his ordination. Pope Siricius of the 4th century A.D. left his wife and child when he was ordained. Other popes kept their families nearby, but their wives were technically demoted to concubine status. Thus, despite apparent efforts to shield the papacy from nepotism, between A.D. 400 and 1000, six popes were sons of popes and nine popes were sons of bishops or priests.

The issue came to a head in A.D. 1139, when the Second Lateran Council finally and officially outlawed marriage within the clergy. All existing marriages were declared null and void, and any new clergy hopefuls had to sever their matrimonial unions.

Many popes continued to nurture their own nests of illegitimate children, including Innocent VIII, Alexander VI, Pius IV, and Gregory VIII. It was in part the liaisons of Renaissance-era popes that prompted the Catholic Counterreformation of 1560. Since that time, no pope has been known to be sexually active during his papacy, and certainly none were married. The actual number of married popes in history is difficult to quantify, as the nuances of Catholic law in this area have fluctuated. Of history's 266 popes, approximately 35 were married at some point in their lives.

Bra Burning—from Media Myth to Revolutionary Reality

In the late 1960s, the media reported that feminists were burning their bras at organized protests. The initial reports weren't true, but the label "bra-burning feminists" stuck.

✻ ✻ ✻ ✻

Firey Feminists

IN 1968, ROBIN MORGAN and other influential feminist activists organized a protest of that year's Miss America beauty pageant. The demonstrators had considered burning bras and other symbols of the female beauty culture, but they decided this would be a fire hazard. Instead, they threw bras, girdles, handbags, and cosmetics into trash cans.

The mainstream media, however, got wind of the initial plan and inaccurately portrayed the hypothetical bra-burning incident as though it had actually happened. Doubtlessly titillated by the word *bra* and all it brings to mind, the male-dominated media began to report on bra burnings as though they were central to the feminist movement. Before long, "bra burners" became a catchphrase for radical feminists.

A Sterotype Goes Down in Flames

Historians and researchers have gone to great lengths to prove that there were no bra burnings at the famed protests. Many have interpreted the obsession with the idea as an attempt to reduce feminist politics into snide remarks about silly girls who torch their unmentionables. Although such bra-burning reductionism is sure to be found in many reports on the feminist movement, recent feminists have since taken up the media's reports and burned their own bras as the radical symbolic statement it was meant to be. Thus, though the famous bra burnings that the media reported never occurred, the spirit of creative destruction as a form of protest is not a myth.

Those Hairless Egyptians

Shaving away all body hair—most notably the eyebrows—was part of an elaborate daily purification ritual that was practiced by Pharaoh and his priests.

✳ ✳ ✳ ✳

THE ANCIENT EGYPTIANS believed that everything in their lives—health, good crops, victory, prosperity—depended on keeping their gods happy, so one of Pharaoh's duties was to enter a shrine and approach a special statue of a god three times a day, every day. Each time he visited the shrine, Pharaoh washed the statue, anointed it with oil, and dressed it in fresh linen.

Because Pharaoh was a busy guy, high-ranking priests often performed this duty for him. But whether it was Pharaoh or a priest doing it, the person had to bathe himself and shave his eyebrows beforehand.

Shaving the eyebrows was also a sign of mourning, even among commoners. The Greek historian Herodotus, who traveled and wrote in the 5th century B.C., said that everyone in an ancient Egyptian household would shave his or her eyebrows following the natural death of a pet cat. For dogs, he reported, the household members would shave their heads and all of their body hair as well.

Herodotus was known to repeat some wild stories in his books—for instance, he reported that serpents with batlike wings flew from Arabia into Egypt and were killed in large numbers by ibises. Herodotus claimed he actually saw heaps of these serpent skeletons. So you just might want to take his eyebrow-shaving claim with a grain of salt . . . and a pinch of catnip.

✳ The U.S. government owns about a third of all American land.

✳ Less than 1 percent of the poems written by Emily Dickinson were published during her lifetime.

✳ Your nose is capable of smelling 10,000 different distinct scents.

The Men in the Silly White Wigs

How in the world did it ever become fashionable for guys to don white headpieces? You can credit—or blame it on—Louis XIII of France and his premature baldness.

✳ ✳ ✳ ✳

We Have a Remedy

Louis XIII of France took to wearing a wig in 1624 at age 23 in order to cover up his dome, and it started a fashion craze. By mid-century, wigs were a staple of court fashion for the middle and upper classes in both France and England.

In the case of Louis—and his son Louis XIV, whose bald pate and taste in headwear mirrored those of his dear old dad—the wigs were long, flowing, and curly. (If you're turning up your nose at this, explain your affection for 1980s hair bands such as Mötley Crüe, Dokken, Poison, and Quiet Riot.)

Louis XIII Wasn't the First

Long, abundant hair on men has been considered manly since at least biblical times (see the story of Samson, for example), and the early white wigs were—in their own way—manly. What is harder to explain is the shorter and more oddly shaped wigs of the 18th century, which made their way to North America along with the settlers.

Part of the explanation is expediency. Today we take for granted what the average stylist can do for us at the drop of a hat for about 15 bucks. But 300 years ago, it wasn't that easy. In addition to the time and cost of hair care, there were scourges like lice to worry about. Tara Maginnis, a fashion expert for Costumes.org, says that men chose wigs for "ease of hairdressing (send your hair out to be done, and you don't have to sit for hours in curlers), ease of cleaning (if you got lice, you could boil your wig and shave your head and—voila—no lice), comfort while sleeping (short hair beneath), ability to change styles and/or color as quickly and easily as putting on a hat, and class considerations (wigs were expensive and looked it)."

Fashion Is Fickle

By the time men's wigs fell out of favor in the late 1800s, they had been through myriad changes in shape and size and often had been dyed various colors, not just white. Protestant and Catholic clergy preferred certain types of wigs, as did barristers (lawyers who handled matters in court) and others. Posh parties called for their own special wigs, which were usually more flowing, full, and curly.

Indeed, what appears sexy to one generation or culture can appear grotesque to another. Consider how off-putting the clothing that you wore a decade ago seems to you now.

---

* Most people take about 23,000 breaths a day.

* A skin cell doesn't live for more than a day.

* Air Canada banned smoking before any other North American airline did.

* Modern-day "tightie whities" derived from the European-style bathing suit.

* The first paper towel came from defective toilet paper. Someone at the Scott company saw a crumpled, seemingly ruined roll of TP and decided it should be sold as a kind of disposable hand towel.

* The first modern (and recorded) vending machine was used to sell tobacco in England during the 17th century.

* The yo-yo has been used as an actual weapon for hunting in the Philippines.

* Women's hearts beat faster than men's hearts.

* Men get hiccups more often than women.

* Tijuana, Mexico, is the foreign city that is most visited by Americans.

History's Maddest Rulers

We all complain about our nation's leadership from time to time, but check out these crazy rulers and their devilish deeds.

✳ ✳ ✳ ✳

Vlad the Impaler

EVERYONE HAS HEARD of the infamous Count Dracula. Half man, half bat, this beastly hybrid lived to drink human blood. But not everyone knows that novelist Bram Stoker's inspiration for the evil madman came from an actual person who was much worse than he's been portrayed. Vlad III Dracula (1431–76) governed Wallachia, a Hungarian principality that later merged with neighbors Transylvania and Moldavia to form Romania. To say that Dracula ruled with an iron fist barely scratches the surface—an "iron stake" is more accurate. During his six-year reign of terror, it is believed that Dracula murdered as many as 40,000 people whom he considered enemies. Most of these unfortunates met their end by impalement, hence Dracula's ominous moniker. With a sharpened stake as wide as a man's arm, his victims were often pierced from the anus to the mouth, not through the heart as Hollywood legend implies. The madman often blinded, strangled, decapitated, hanged, boiled, burned, or skinned his victims. Once, a concubine hoping to spare her life claimed that she was carrying Dracula's child. When he discovered she was lying, he had her womb cut open and remarked, "Let the world see where I have been."

Idi Amin Dada

To the eye, Ugandan president Idi Amin Dada (1925–2003) was a deceptive contradiction. Viewed as a cartoonlike character by the press (*Time* dubbed him a "killer and clown, big-hearted buffoon and strutting martinet"), the former major general nevertheless found a way to kill an estimated 300,000 people while in power. Many of his victims were killed to squelch the ruler's paranoid fears of being overthrown.

Others were eliminated simply for the president's own ghoulish pleasure. Known as the "butcher of Uganda," Amin reportedly kept severed heads in his refrigerator and may have eaten some of his victims. And allegedly, when Amin learned that his second wife was pregnant with another man's child, he had her dismembered. After this ghoulish command was carried out, he further ordered that her remains be stitched together so that he could show her corpse to their children.

Justin II

In the final days of his reign, Byzantine Emperor Justin II (ca. 520–78) descended into an overwhelming insanity that was only briefly punctuated by moments of lucidity. Accounts tell of a daft ruler who went mad after suffering a nervous breakdown. Monitored closely by attendants, the emperor sometimes needed to be physically restrained to keep him from commiting undue harm to himself or to others. The off-his-rocker ruler would often lunge at his attendants in an attempt to bite them, and reports suggest that he actually devoured a number of his faithful servants during his reign.

King George III

Great Britain's King George III (1738–1820) suffered recurring bouts of dementia while he was on the throne. Believed to have been suffering the ill effects of porphyria, a blood disorder that can produce psychotic symptoms, the king often acted in an outlandish manner. Fits of gloom and melancholy often alternated with excited periods during which the king would talk incessantly and behave strangely. During one such episode, George III reportedly spoke nonsense for a period lasting some 58 hours. But whether or not the king was insane, his "caregivers" were a bit on the shady side as well, at least by today's standards. Doctors often tried bleeding him to remove bad substances. When this failed, another doctor decided to draw the poison out of his brain by cutting small holes in his forehead. The king was also confined to a straightjacket, denied heat in the winter, and fed chemical agents that did nothing more than make him vomit.

King George III eventually went blind and died in a back room of Windsor Castle. Such a tale, however, begs the obvious question: Who was really mad here?

Vitellius

If an unquenchable bloodlust is the hallmark of a true madman, then Roman emperor Aulus Vitellius Germanicus Augustus (A.D. 15–69) ranks near the top. Simply known as Vitellius, he took perverse joy in watching his victims squirm. His actions sound like something lifted from a Stephen King novel, yet they are reportedly true. Consider this: On impulse, and purely for his own amusement, Vitellius would summon personal friends and acquaintances to his court, then order them killed, or do the deed himself. On one occasion, two sons begging for their father's life were executed beside him. At another time, Vitellius gave a glass of poisoned water to a thirsty man stricken with fever and watched in utter glee as it took effect. Psychological tortures also factored heavily into this madman's repertoire. The ruler once issued a reprieve to a subject who was to be executed. As the man praised the emperor for his mercy, Vitellius ordered him killed in his presence saying that he wished to "feast [on] his eyes." His motives for such loathing are shrouded in mystery, but in the end, Vitellius was tortured, killed, and thrown in the Tigris River by the leader of an opposing faction.

Caligula

The infamous Caligula (Gaius Caesar Augustus Germanicus) lived from A.D. 12 to A.D. 41 and served as emperor of Rome from A.D. 37 until his death. During that time, he reputedly engaged in long-term incestuous relationships with his sisters; forced losers of an oratory competition to erase their wax tablets with their tongues; ordered men's heads shaved (due to his own insecurity over his baldness); bestowed a consulship and priesthood upon his favorite horse; and ordered spectators to fight lions and tigers to the death during a shortage of criminals. In A.D. 41, Caligula was stabbed to death by his own Praetorian guards. Live by the sword; die by the sword.

Unidentified Submerged Objects

Much like their flying brethren, unidentified submerged objects captivate and mystify. But instead of vanishing into the skies, USOs, such as the following, plunge underwater.

✳ ✳ ✳ ✳

Sighting at Puerto Rico Trench

IN 1963, while conducting exercises off the coast of Puerto Rico, U.S. Navy submarines encountered something extraordinary. The incident began when a sonar operator aboard an accompanying destroyer reported a strange occurrence. According to the seaman, one of the subs traveling with the armada broke free from the pack to chase a USO. This quarry would be unlike anything the submariners had ever pursued.

Underwater technology in the early 1960s was advancing rapidly. Still, vessels had their limitations. The USS *Nautilus*, though faster than any submarine that preceded it, was still limited to about 20 knots (23 miles per hour). The bathyscaphe *Trieste*, a deep-sea submersible, could exceed 30,000 feet in depth, but the descent took as long as five hours. Once there, the vessel could not be maneuvered side to side.

Knowing this, the submariners were stunned by what they witnessed. The USO was moving at 150 knots (170 miles per hour) and hitting depths greater than 20,000 feet! No underwater vehicles on the planet were capable of such fantastic numbers. Even today, modern nuclear subs have top speeds of about 25 knots (29 miles per hour) and can operate at around 800-plus feet below the surface.

Thirteen separate crafts witnessed the USO as it crisscrossed the Atlantic Ocean over a four-day period. At its deepest, the mystery vehicle reached 27,000 feet. To this day, there's been no earthly explanation offered for the occurrence.

USO with a Bus Pass

In 1964, London bus driver Bob Fall witnessed one of the strangest USO sightings. While transporting a full contingent of passengers, the driver and his fares reported seeing a silver, cigar-shape object dive into the nearby waters of the River Lea. The police attributed the phenomenon to a flight of ducks, despite the obvious incongruence. Severed telephone lines and a large gouge on the river's embankment suggested something far different.

Shag Harbour Incident

The fishing village of Shag Harbour lies on Canada's east coast. This unassuming hamlet is to USOs what Roswell, New Mexico, is to UFOs. Simply put, it played host to the most famous occurrence of a USO ever recorded.

On the evening of October 4, 1967, the Royal Canadian Mounted Police (RCMP) were barraged by reports of a UFO that had crashed into the bay at Shag Harbour. Laurie Wickens and four friends witnessed a large object (approximately 60 feet in diameter) falling into the water just after 11:00 P.M. They could clearly detect a yellow light on top of the object, floating approximately 1,000 feet off the coast.

The RCMP promptly contacted the Rescue Coordination Center in Halifax to ask if any aircraft were missing. None were. Shortly thereafter, the object sank into the depths of the water and disappeared from view.

When local fishing boats went to the USO crash site, they encountered yellow foam on the water's surface and detected an odd sulfuric smell. No survivors or bodies were ever found. The Royal Canadian Air Force officially labeled the occurrence a UFO, but because the object was last seen under water, such events are now described as USOs.

Pascagoula Incident

On November 6, 1973, at approximately 8:00 P.M., a USO was sighted by at least nine fishermen anchored off the coast of

Pascagoula, Mississippi. They witnessed an underwater object an estimated five feet in diameter that emitted a strange amber light.

First to spot the USO was Rayme Ryan. He repeatedly poked at the light-emitting object with an oar. Each time he made contact with the strange object, its light would dim and it would move a few feet away, then brighten once again.

Fascinated by the ethereal quality of this submerged question mark, Ryan summoned the others. For the next half hour, the cat-and-mouse game played out in front of the fishermen until Ryan struck the object with a particularly forceful blow. With this action, the USO disappeared from view.

The anglers moved about a half mile away and continued fishing. After about 30 minutes, they returned to their earlier location and were astounded to find that the USO had returned. At this point, they decided to alert the Coast Guard.

After interviewing the witnesses, investigators from the Naval Ship Research and Development Laboratory in Panama City, Florida, submitted their findings: At least nine persons had witnessed an undetermined light source whose characteristics and actions were inconsistent with those of known marine organisms or with an uncontrolled human-made object. Their final report was inconclusive, stating that the object could not be positively identified.

✳ Residents of Andorra, a small country located in the mountains between France and Spain, have the highest life expectancy at birth, living 5.5 years longer than Americans, who rank 45th.

✳ The Panama Hat actually originated in Ecuador. In the 1880s, when Americans were building the Panama Canal, they erroneously named it, thinking it was a local creation.

✳ The human heart produces enough pressure to squirt blood more than 30 feet.

✳ The smallest frog hails from Cuba and measures less than a half inch when fully grown.

H. H. Holmes: Serial Killer at the World's Fair

H. H. Holmes was one of the cruelest, most horrifyingly prolific killers the world has ever seen. From his headquarters at a Chicago hotel, he slaughtered at least 27 people starting in the early 1890s. Many filmmakers, scholars, and authors have tried to understand the mind of the madman Holmes. Here is an overview of the twisted, convoluted details of the real-life "Doctor Death."

✳ ✳ ✳ ✳

Troubled Child

BORN IN MAY 1860, Herman Webster Mudgett was a highly intelligent child and did well in school, but he was constantly in trouble. As a teen, he became abusive to animals and small children—a classic characteristic of serial killers.

Fascinated with bones, skeletons, and the human body, Mudgett decided to pursue a degree in medicine. He changed his name to H. H. Holmes, married Clara Lovering, and with her inheritance, enrolled in medical school in Burlington, Vermont.

Swindler, Liar, Cheat

In medical school, Holmes was able to be around skeletons, cadavers, and fresh corpses all the time, which suited him just fine. Very soon, however, it was obvious that Holmes wasn't in the medical field for humanitarian reasons. Ever the swindler, Holmes came up with a scheme whereby he'd take insurance policies out on family members he didn't actually have. He would steal cadavers from the school, make them look as if they'd had an accident, then identify the bodies as those of his family members to collect the insurance money. Some of these frauds brought in $10,000 or more per body.

When authorities became suspicious of all these dead "family members," Holmes abandoned Clara and their newborn baby. Where he went after that is a little murky, as the next six or so years of Holmes's life are not well documented. But by the mid-1880s, Holmes was back on the radar as a charming, intelligent, bold-faced liar and thief with murderous intentions. This time, his mark was Chicago. The city would become the site of Holmes's biggest, deadliest swindle of all.

The Roots of a Murderous Plan

If you lived in Chicago in the late 1800s, you were likely consumed with thoughts of the World's Fair. Officially known as the World's Columbian Exposition of 1893, the colossal event had most of the Midwest working for its success. It would make America a superstar country and make Chicago one of the country's A-list cities. The Great Fire of 1871 had demolished the town; the World's Fair vowed to bring it back in a big way.

It was during the years of preparation for the big fair that Holmes began his path of murder. With so many people flooding the city every day looking to nab one of the thousands of new jobs in the area, Chicago was experiencing a population boom that made it very easy to lose track of people. Holmes recognized this as an opportunity to lure women into his clutches while most people had their focus elsewhere.

He married his second wife, Myrtle, in 1885, even though he had never actually divorced Clara. While Myrtle lived in suburban Wilmette, Holmes took a place in Chicago, and the couple lived apart for most of their marriage. Holmes needed to be in the city because he was working at a drugstore in Chicago's Englewood neighborhood. He worked for the elderly Mrs. Holdens, a kind woman who was happy to have such an attractive young doctor help out at her busy store. When Mrs. Holden disappeared without a trace in 1887 and Holmes purchased the store, no one suspected a thing.

Holmes (who now had full access to a well-stocked drugstore with countless medical tools, chemicals, and medicines) purchased a vacant lot across the street from the drugstore and began construction on a house with a strange floor plan he'd designed himself. The three-story house would have 60 rooms, more than 50 doors placed in an odd fashion throughout the structure, trapdoors, secret passageways, windowless rooms, and chutes that led down to a deep basement. Holmes hired and fired construction crews on a regular basis, and it was said that his swindler's streak got him out of paying for most (or perhaps all) of the materials and labor used to create what would later be known as the "Murder Castle."

Death: Up & Running

As construction of the "castle" wrapped up, Holmes made plans for several of his employees. The bookkeeper Holmes had at the store around 1890 was Ned Connor, a man who had come to Chicago with his lovely wife, Julia, and their baby daughter, Pearl. Holmes found Julia irresistible and quickly put the make on her, firing Ned so his wife could take his place. It is believed that as his new bookkeeper, Julia was possibly an accomplice in the fraudulent actions at the drugstore, which eased Holmes's mind and allowed him to concentrate on his new building.

Advertised as a lodging for World's Fair tourists, the building opened in 1892. Holmes placed ads in the newspaper to rent rooms, but also listed fake classifieds, calling for females interested in working for a start-up company. He also placed ads for marriage, posing as a successful businessman in need of a wife. Any woman who answered these fake ads was interviewed by Holmes, was told to keep everything a secret, and was instructed to withdraw all funds from her bank account in order to start a new life with him as his worker, wife, or whatever role he had offered. Holmes was a brilliant liar and quite the charmer, and naive 19th-century women fell for it. Once they passed Holmes's tests, these women became his prisoners, doomed to meet their grisly ends.

Gas pipes were secretly installed throughout the house with nozzles that piped noxious fumes into the rooms. Holmes would turn on the gas so that the victim du jour would drop to the floor unconscious. While she was out cold, Holmes would usually rape her, then send the girl down to the basement via the chute. Once there, he would perform experiments on her at his dissection table or torture her with various equipment. He reportedly listened to the screams of the victims from an adjacent room.

Once he had brutalized the poor soul, he would dump her body into a vat of lime acid to destroy the evidence. Other times, he sold bones and organs to contacts in the medical field. Holmes murdered at least 22 people in his home, mostly women, though every once in awhile a worried male neighbor or relative looking for a missing young woman would get too suspicious for Holmes's liking and go missing themselves.

While the "Murder Castle" was in operation, Holmes continued to marry various women and carry out insurance fraud and other deviant acts. After the World's Fair ended, creditors put pressure on him again, and Holmes knew it was time to flee. He traveled across the United States and Canada, scamming and murdering along the way. Strange as it seems, when Holmes was finally caught and brought to justice, it wasn't initially for homicide but for a horse-swindling scheme he attempted to pull off with longtime partner-in-fraud Ben Pietzel. When authorities searched Holmes's Chicago dwelling, their investigation turned up a lot more than they anticipated.

The End of "Doctor Death"

Over the years, one detective had been hot on Holmes's trail. Detective Frank Geyer, a veteran Pinkerton detective, had done his best to follow this creepy man whose identity changed with the weather. Geyer had traced many of the missing World's Fair women back to Holmes's lodging house and had discovered trails that pointed to his fraudulent activities. In 1895, Holmes entered a guilty plea for the horse-fraud case, and Geyer took that opportunity to expand the investigation. He was particularly interested in the whereabouts of three children—Howard, Nellie, and Alice Pietzel, children of Holmes's murdered accomplice, Ben Pietzel.

Geyer traced the children—and then Holmes—by following his mail. When his search took him to Canada, Geyer knocked on doors all over Toronto to track down Holmes. Finally, he found a house where Holmes had allegedly stayed with several children in tow. Buried in a shallow grave in the backyard were the bodies of the two Pietzel girls. The boy was found several months later in an oven in an Indianapolis home.

When the evidence was brought back to court, Geyer got full clearance to investigate every dark nook and cranny of Holmes's house and business. As detectives and police officers uncovered layer after layer of hideous evidence, the public became more and more frightened—and fascinated. The *Chicago Tribune* published the floor plan of the "Murder Castle," tourists flocked to ogle the building, and tabloids ran horrifying descriptions of what had happened to the victims inside, events both real and embellished. Then, in August 1895, Holmes's house of horrors burned to the ground.

While all that took place, inside his heavily guarded cell, Herman Webster Mudgett confessed to his crimes. He officially confessed to 27 murders, six attempted murders, and a whole lot of fraud. What he didn't confess to, however, were any feelings of remorse. Holmes claimed at times to be possessed by the devil, though depending on the day, he'd also claim to be innocent of any wrongdoing whatsoever. All told, estimates of his victims may have hit the 200 mark. Just because he confessed to 27 murders doesn't mean that's what his final tally was—indeed, with the kind of liar Holmes was, it's pretty certain that the number isn't accurate at all.

Holmes was executed by hanging in 1896. He was buried in a coffin lined with cement, topped with more cement, and buried in a double grave—instructions he gave in his last will and testament so that "no one could dig him back up." Was he ready to rest eternally or was he afraid that someone would conduct experiments on him as he had done to so many hapless victims?

Walking the Plank

No one said pirate justice was fair. The instigators of plank-walkings—the guys brandishing swords at your back to force you off the side of the ship—weren't exactly known for their commitment to justice.

✳   ✳   ✳   ✳

Plank-Walking: Myth or Reality?

ONE OF THE earliest definitions of the phrase "walking the plank" appears in the 1788 book *A Classical Dictionary of the Vulgar Tongue*, which explains it as "a mode of destroying devoted persons or officers in a mutiny on ship-board." The victim was bound and blindfolded and forced to walk on a board that was balanced on the ship's side until he fell into the water. This way, "as the mutineers suppose," they might avoid the penalty for murder. Since no record exists of charges being brought against anyone who forced their officers to walk the plank, maybe those old scalawags were right.

On the other hand, it's possible that plank-walking was an extremely rare occurrence—if it ever really happened at all. In fact, some experts scoff at the notion, saying that the practice existed only in fiction. But journalists wrote about it, too. In 1821, a Jamaican newspaper reported that pirates from a schooner had boarded the English ship *Blessing*. When the pirates were unable to get any money out of the *Blessing*'s captain, the lead marauder made him walk the plank. The buccaneers then shot the ousted captain three times as he struggled to stay above the water before musket-whipping the captain's teenage son, pitching him overboard, and setting the entire ship aflame. (Now that's a thorough job!) Another sailor, George Wood, confessed a similar crime to a chaplain just before being hanged for mutiny in 1769. No other documentation exists to validate either story.

A Wacky Idea

Where did the notion of walking the plank originate? It's possible that it was conjured by the pirates who plagued the Mediterranean Sea when it was dominated by the Roman Empire. Yes, there were pirates in those days, and when they captured Roman ships, they would mock the sailors by telling them that they were free to walk home. Of course, at sea, there's no place to walk without sinking like a stone.

But if walking the plank wasn't actually used as a form of maritime punishment, how were unwanted men dealt with at sea? Marooning—leaving a man on a desert island to die—was a popular practice among both pirates and mutineers. In addition, prisoners were tied up and tossed overboard to drown or be eaten by sharks. Eyewitness accounts of hanging, shooting, whipping, and torturing prisoners abound. Fun guys, those pirates.

* Dancing the tango was considered a sin in Paris during the early 1900s.

* Kissing was once a crime in England. In the mid-1400s, King Henry VI declared it to be a disease-spreader.

* The letters "SOS" don't actually stand for "Save Our Ship." In fact, they were only selected because they translate into a simple Morse code message of three dots, three dashes, and three dots. The letters never meant anything more.

* An average porcupine has 30,000 quills.

* Every male warthog has four warts, while every female has two.

* Television master chef Antony Thompson had to hastily rewrite his recipe for an organic salad after recommending a dash or two of henbane for flavor. Henbane is a toxic poison.

* A manhole cover weighs more than 80 pounds.

Mysterious Disappearances in the Bermuda Triangle

The Bermuda Triangle is an infamous stretch of the Atlantic Ocean bordered by Florida, Bermuda, and Puerto Rico where strange disappearances have occurred throughout history. The Coast Guard doesn't recognize the Triangle or the supernatural explanations for the mysterious disappearances. There are some probable causes for the missing vessels—hurricanes, undersea earthquakes, and magnetic fields that interfere with compasses and other positioning devices. But it's much more interesting to think they were sucked into another dimension, abducted by aliens, or simply vanished into thin air.

✳ ✳ ✳ ✳

Flight 19

ON THE AFTERNOON of December 5, 1945, five Avenger torpedo bombers left the Naval Air Station at Fort Lauderdale, Florida, with Lt. Charles Taylor in command of a crew of 13 student pilots. About 90 minutes into the flight, Taylor radioed the base to say that his compasses weren't working, but he figured he was somewhere over the Florida Keys. The lieutenant who received the signal told Taylor to fly north toward Miami, as long as he was sure he was actually over the Keys. Although he was an experienced pilot, Taylor got horribly turned around, and the more he tried to get out of the Keys, the further out to sea he and his crew traveled. As night fell, radio signals worsened, until, finally, there was nothing at all from Flight 19. A U.S. Navy investigation reported that Taylor's confusion caused the disaster, but his mother convinced them to change the official report to read that the planes went down for "causes unknown." The planes have never been recovered.

The *Spray*

Joshua Slocum, the first man to sail solo around the world, never should have been lost at sea, but it appears that's exactly what happened. In 1909, the *Spray* left the East Coast of the United States for Venezuela via the Caribbean Sea. Slocum was never heard from or seen again and was declared dead in 1924. The ship was solid, and Slocum was a pro, so nobody knows what happened. Perhaps he was felled by a larger ship or maybe he was taken down by pirates. No one knows for sure that Slocum disappeared within the Triangle's waters, but Bermuda buffs claim Slocum's story as part of the area's mysterious and supernatural legacy.

USS *Cyclops*

As World War I heated up, America went to battle. In 1918, the *Cyclops*, commanded by Lt. G. W. Worley, was sent to Brazil to refuel Allied ships. With 309 people onboard, the ship left Rio de Janeiro in February and reached Barbados in March. After that, the *Cyclops* was never seen or heard from again. The U.S. Navy says in its official statement, "The disappearance of this ship has been one of the most baffling mysteries in the annals of the navy, all attempts to locate her having proved unsuccessful. There were no enemy submarines in the western Atlantic at that time, and in December 1918, every effort was made to obtain from German sources information regarding the disappearance of the vessel."

Star Tiger

The *Star Tiger*, commanded by Capt. B. W. McMillan, was flying from England to Bermuda in early 1948. On January 30, McMillan said he expected to arrive in Bermuda at 5:00 A.M., but neither he nor any of the 31 people onboard the *Star Tiger* were ever heard from again. When the Civil Air Ministry launched an investigation, they learned that the SS *Troubadour* had reported seeing a low-flying aircraft halfway between Bermuda and the entrance to Delaware Bay. If that aircraft was the *Star Tiger*, it was drastically off course. According to the Civil Air Ministry, the fate of the *Star Tiger* remains unknown.

Star Ariel

On January 17, 1949, a Tudor IV aircraft like the *Star Tiger* left Bermuda with seven crew members and 13 passengers en route to Jamaica. That morning, Capt. J. C. McPhee reported that the flight was going smoothly. Shortly afterward, another more cryptic message came from the captain, when he reported that he was changing his frequency, and then nothing more was heard—ever. More than 60 aircraft and 13,000 people were deployed to look for the *Star Ariel*, but no hint of debris or wreckage was ever found. After the *Star Ariel* disappeared, production of Tudor IVs ceased.

Flight 201

This Cessna left Fort Lauderdale on March 31, 1984, en route to Bimini Island in the Bahamas, but it never made it. Not quite midway to its destination, the plane slowed its airspeed significantly, but no distress signals came from the plane. Suddenly, the plane dropped from the air into the water, completely vanishing from the radar. A woman on Bimini Island swore she saw a plane plunge into the sea about a mile offshore, but no wreckage has ever been found.

Teignmouth Electron

Who said that the Bermuda Triangle only swallows up ships and planes? Who's to say it can't also make a man go mad? Perhaps that's what happened on the *Teignmouth Electron* in 1969. The *Sunday Times* Golden Globe race of 1968 left England on October 31 and required each contestant to sail his ship solo. Donald Crowhurst was one of the entrants, but he never made it to the finish line. The *Electron* was found abandoned in the middle of the Bermuda Triangle in July 1969. Logbooks recovered from the ship reveal that Crowhurst was deceiving organizers about his position in the race and going a little bit nutty out there in the big blue ocean. The last entry of his log was dated June 29—it is believed that Crowhurst jumped overboard and drowned himself in the Triangle.

Unbelievable Beliefs

Faith is a very personal experience, and by definition, it is not based on fact. Over the centuries, people have expressed their faith in a variety of unique philosophies.

✳ ✳ ✳ ✳

The Hollow Earth Theory

IN THE EARLY 19th century, John Cleves Symmes promoted the Hollow Earth Theory, which stated that the planet was actually several populated worlds nesting inside one another. Symmes's ideas influenced Cyrus Teed, who developed Koreshan Unity, a religion based on the theory. For about 100 years, Koreshan Unity drew thousands of followers worldwide. The Hollow Earth Theory was revived during World War II, when some authors theorized that the Nazis actually came from an underground civilization. More recently, Kevin and Matthew Taylor spent 12 years investigating the idea; they wrote a book about their findings, *The Land of No Horizon.*

The Millerites

William Miller, a farmer in northern New York, founded a doomsday cult in the 1800s. Studying the Bible convinced Miller that humanity was due for damnation. He began preaching this message in the early 1830s. His first prediction was that Jesus Christ would "come again to the earth, cleanse, purify and take possession of the same" between March 1843 and March 1844. When a comet appeared early in 1843, a number of his followers killed themselves, believing the end was near. However, when his prophecy didn't come to pass and the world survived, Miller stood by his message but became reluctant to set actual dates. Some of his followers took it upon themselves to announce October 22, 1844, as the big day, and Miller reluctantly agreed. This date came to be known as The Great Disappointment. Regardless, Miller and his followers established a basis on which the Seventh-Day Adventist Church was later founded.

The Raelian Movement

Claude Vorilhon, a French race car driver and onetime musician, asserted that he was visited by an extraterrestrial in 1973. It was a life-altering experience for him that caused him to change his name to Rael and found the Raelian Church. Rael's religion proclaims that the Elohim ("those who came from the sky") created everything on Earth. Although many turn a skeptical eye toward Vorilhon, whose faith also preaches free love, the Raelian Movement is said to include as many as 65,000 members worldwide.

The Vampire Church

The Vampire church has offices throughout the United States, Canada, and Australia. However, don't expect to find much about the "undead," as vampires have been portrayed in stories since Bram Stoker wrote *Dracula* in 1897. Instead, the church offers insight into vampirism as a physical condition that sometimes requires unusual energy resources, such as blood. In addition, it explains the difference between psychic vampires and elemental vampires.

The Church of Euthanasia

"Save the Planet—Kill Yourself." These words are the battle cry of the Church of Euthanasia, which was established by Bostonian Chris Korda in 1992. Korda, a musician, had a dream one night about an alien who warned her that Earth was in serious danger. The extraterrestrial, which Korda dubbed "The Being," stressed the importance of protecting the planet's environment through population control. As a result of the encounter, Korda established the Church of Euthanasia, which supports suicide, abortion, and sodomy (defined as any sex act that is not intended for procreation). According to the church's Web site, members are vegetarian, but they "support cannibalism for those who insist on eating flesh." Although it reportedly has only about 100 members in the Boston area, the church claims that thousands worldwide have visited its Web site and been exposed to its message.

Bizarre Truths About Your Health

Got Allergies? If So, Eat a Worm

In the dark ages of medicine, the leech was used to fight illness. Of course, we know better now. Our high-tech remedies are created in sterile labs, not dredged up from muddy lakes. Right?

✳ ✳ ✳ ✳

Nature's Cure

ACTUALLY, SOME DISGUSTING parasites may be useful in treating certain conditions that have foiled modern medicine. In 2004, Dr. David Pritchard, an immunologist at Britain's University of Nottingham, deliberately infected himself with hookworms for an allergy experiment, and his gamble worked.

Hookworms are nasty buggers. An untreated infestation can lead to severe anemia and even death. Hookworms are common in undeveloped tropical countries, where it just so happens that allergies are relatively rare. In the developed world, the problems are just the opposite: Few people need to worry about parasitic worms, but allergies are more and more common, causing at least two million emergency room visits each year.

While conducting research in Papua New Guinea, Pritchard began to wonder if this was more than coincidence. Are worms a key to preventing allergies? To test his hypothesis, he gave a group of villagers pills to kill their worms and asked if, in return, they would give him what he politely termed their "fecal matter" to study. Since Pritchard and his assistants didn't speak the local language, they must have used some interesting gestures to get their point across. But it turned into a win-win situation for both parties—the New Guineans got health care and Pritchard got scientific evidence. By comparing the number of worms eliminated by each patient with the concentration of antibodies in the bloodstream, he could see how worms affected the immune system. Since an allergic reaction is basically the body's attempt to defend itself against a hostile invader, worms must be able to suppress this response in order to survive in the gut.

This ability intrigued Pritchard. People with a lot of allergies have hypersensitive immune systems, so perhaps a few worms might lower these from constant states of "red alert" to something more akin to "yellow" or even "green." Back home in Britain, Pritchard infected himself to prove that a small dose of worms was not dangerous to the average healthy Westerner. After that, he was able to obtain funding and 30 willing volunteers for a clinical trial. Within a week, the 15 subjects who had ingested a mere 10 worms each found their allergy symptoms disappearing. The others, who had received a placebo, showed little or no improvement. When word of these results hit online discussion boards, inveterate sneezers began demanding Pritchard's "helminthic therapy" to ease their symptoms.

Worm Pills

If you have hay fever but are not keen on ingesting hookworms for relief, wait a few years. Scientists are trying to isolate the specific substance that worms use to disarm allergic reactions and are aiming to produce it in pill form. Hopefully, someday soon, you'll be able to pop one of these pills, get a good night's rest, and be fresh as a pollen-proof daisy by morning.

Pop! Goes Your Stomach

Although eating the explosive candy Pop Rocks while drinking a soda isn't considered a healthful way to snack, it isn't fatal—despite what a persistent urban legend would have us believe.

✳ ✳ ✳ ✳

IN 1975, to the delight of bored kids across the country, General Foods unveiled Pop Rocks, aka Space Dust. These tiny pebbles of fruit-flavored candy release a bit of carbonation when held on the tongue, causing an "exploding" sensation.

Death by Pop Rocks?

Although the candy was invented in 1956 (thus allowing ample time for testing), its startling novelty caused the Food and Drug Administration to set up a Pop Rocks hotline to reassure parents who were concerned about product safety. Despite these efforts, it became widespread playground knowledge that consuming the candy along with a carbonated beverage would cause one's stomach to explode. By 1979, the rumor was so pervasive that General Foods put full-page ads in 45 major-market publications, wrote more than 50,000 letters to school principals, and sent the inventor on a "goodwill tour" to debunk the myths. When General Foods stopped marketing Pop Rocks in 1983, many took it as proof that the confection was too dangerous to sell.

Adding fuel to Pop Rocks's fire was the widely rumored death of a child star who supposedly died after consuming a combination of the candy and soda pop. The kid, known to most only as "Mikey" (his character in a long-lived Quaker Life cereal commercial), was actor John Gilchrist. Although rumormongers claimed that Gilchrist mysteriously "disappeared" from the public eye after the commercial's 1972 debut (proof, of course, of his death), he actually continued making commercials through 1988 before retiring from acting. He is alive and well today and works in radio advertising, although talk of his unfortunate demise persists.

After General Foods stopped marketing the candy, Kraft Foods purchased the rights to it in 1983 and sold it under the name Action Candy. Today, Pop Rocks are back on the market under their original name, available for purchase online and in stores—without so much as a warning label.

Rumors about the candy have died down, likely due to the high-profile debunking it has received on TV shows and Web sites. However, in 2001, a lawsuit revived some of the original concerns. The suit was filed on behalf of a California girl who was rushed to a hospital in considerable pain after swallowing Pop Rocks that were blended into a special Baskin-Robbins ice-cream flavor. Doctors had to insert a tube into the child's stomach to help relieve gas pressure, but the ice cream was never determined to be the cause.

As "Pop"ular as Ever

Despite that incident, Pop Rocks have enjoyed a revival, finding their way to the table as a mix-in for applesauce or yogurt and even as a garnish at retro-hip eateries (Pop Rocks-studded foie gras, anyone?). General Foods still holds U.S. patent number 4289794 for the "process of preparing gasified candy in which flavored sugar syrup—such as is used to make hard candy—is mixed with CO_2. The gas forms bubbles, each with an internal pressure of 600 pounds per square inch (PSI). As the candy melts on your tongue, the bubbles pop, releasing that pressure."

Although the thought of pressurized candy exploding into shards of crystallized sugar in your mouth or stomach sounds dangerous, it isn't. The amount of gas in a package of Pop Rocks is only one-tenth as much as there is in about an ounce of carbonated soda. Even if you combine Pop Rocks with a carbonated beverage, the pressure is not enough to make your stomach explode.

❋ **George Washington's Continental Army camped at Valley Forge, Pennsylvania, during the winter of 1777–78. More than two-thirds of the 2,000 people who perished in the camp were victims of disease.**

Who Are You?

*Some people never forget a face; others can't
seem to remember one. The latter group might be
suffering from a malady called face-blindness.*

✳ ✳ ✳ ✳

Faces: They're Everywhere

SOCIOLOGISTS ESTIMATE that an adult who lives in a busy
urban area encounters more than 1,000 different faces
every day. For most of us, picking our friends and loved ones
out of a crowd is a snap—homing in on the faces we know is
simply an instinct.

But what if you couldn't recognize faces? Not even the ones
that belong to the people you know best? If you seem to spend
a lot of time apologizing to your nearest and dearest—saying
things like, "Sorry, I didn't see you there yesterday. Did you get
a new haircut? Were you wearing a different shirt? A pair of
Groucho glasses?"—you might be face-blind.

No, you don't need a new pair of contact lenses. Face-blind
people can have 20/20 vision. And chances are, there's nothing
wrong with your memory either. You can be an absolute whiz
at trivia games—a veritable walking encyclopedia of arcane
information—and still not be able to recall the face you see
across the breakfast table every morning.

When Faces Blur Together

Many scientists believe facial recognition is a highly specialized
neurological task. It takes place in an area of the brain known
as the fusiform gyrus, which is located behind your right ear.
People who suffer an injury to this part of the brain are likely
to have *prosopagnosia*, a fancy medical term for face-blindness.
Others seem to be born that way.

Of course, everybody has occasional problems recognizing
faces. For the truly face-blind, however, faces may appear only

as a blur or a jumble of features that never quite coalesce into the whole that becomes Janice from accounting or Robert from your softball team.

How many people suffer from face-blindness? Statistics are rather difficult to come by, simply because many people are not even aware that the inability to recognize faces is a bona fide medical syndrome. However, recent research on random samples of college students indicates that prosopagnosia may affect as many as 1 out of every 50 people, or approximately 2 percent of the population.

The Work-Arounds

What can you do if you think that you are face-blind? Most people with prosopagnosia compensate without even knowing it. They unconsciously learn to distinguish people by the way they walk or talk or perhaps by distinctive hairdos or articles of dress. Many face-blind people write down the information to remind themselves later. Some people who suffer from this affliction compare it to being tone-deaf or colorblind—an inconvenience but hardly a life-threatening disability.

As with just about anything, a sense of humor helps, too. Ask your friend to warn you before she frosts her hair or he discards that Pearl Jam T-shirt he's proudly worn since you met in, oh, 1996. And if you really want to make sure that you see your friends and family in a crowd, tell them to wear something that you'll be sure to remember. Maybe the Groucho glasses. They work like a charm every time.

* The first speed limit in the United States was set in 1901 in Connecticut at 12 miles per hour.

* Oregon is the only state with an official state nut: the hazelnut, aka the filbert.

* Three U.S. states have a state muffin: Minnesota (blueberry), Massachusetts (corn), and New York (apple).

* Maryland is the only state with an official sport—jousting.

The Consequences of Sleep Deprivation

Dr. Nathaniel Kleitman, the father of modern sleep research, said: "No one ever died of insomnia." Still, what doesn't kill you can have some nasty side effects.

✳ ✳ ✳ ✳

VARIOUS STUDIES HAVE revealed that missing just one night of sleep can lead to memory loss and decreased activity in certain parts of the brain. So if you're planning an all-night cram session for the evening before the big midterm, you may be better off closing the book and getting a good night's sleep.

Then again, maybe not. Each person's body and brain handle sleep deprivation differently. Some folks are all but useless after one night without shut-eye, while others function normally. It's largely a matter of physiology.

Take Tony Wright. In May 2007, the 43-year-old British gardener kept himself awake for 226 hours. He said that he was aiming for the world's sleeplessness record and wanted to prove that sleep deprivation does not diminish a person's coherence. Wright admitted to some odd sensory effects during his marathon, but he insisted that his mental faculties were not compromised.

Wright's quest didn't amount to much more than a lot of lost sleep. *Guinness World Records* stopped acknowledging feats of insomnia in 1990 after consulting with experts at the British Association for Counseling and Psychotherapy. The experts believe that sleep deprivation threatens psychological and physical well-being. Muscle spasms, reduced reaction times, loss of motivation, hallucinations, and paranoia can all be triggered by sleep deprivation. That Wright apparently didn't suffer any of these ill effects doesn't mean you won't. Sometimes, it seems, you lose if you don't snooze.

Law and Disorder: The Finer Points of an Insanity Plea

No, judges don't keep a "You must be this nuts to get out of jail" sign hidden behind their benches. But you can be found not guilty by reason of insanity if you're cuckoo in just the right way.

✳ ✳ ✳ ✳

A Murky Defense

CRIMINAL INSANITY DOESN'T refer to any specific mental disorder, but it is related to mental illness. The reasoning behind the insanity defense is that some mental disorders may cause people to lose the ability to understand their actions or to differentiate between right and wrong, leaving them unable to truly have criminal intent. Intent is an important element of crime. If you intentionally burn down a house by dropping a lit cigarette in a trash can, we'd call you an arsonist. But if you do exactly the same thing accidentally, we'd probably just call you an inconsiderate (and perhaps a criminally negligent) jerk.

Similarly, the reasoning goes, you shouldn't be punished if a mental illness leads you to break the law without really comprehending your actions. Now, this doesn't apply to just any run-of-the-mill murderer with an antisocial personality disorder. A lack of empathy may lead someone to commit crimes, but if he understands what he's doing and he realizes that what he's doing is wrong, he's not insane.

How to Be Considered Legally Insane

You can only be found not guilty by reason of insanity in two cases: if mental illness keeps you from understanding your actions and deprives you of the ability to tell right from wrong, or if mental illness leaves you unable to control your actions and you experience an irresistible impulse to commit a crime. Details vary from state to state (and some states don't recognize the insanity defense at all), but these are the general criteria.

Some form of the insanity defense seems to date back to the 16th century, but early versions were awfully hazy. The 1843 trial of Daniel M'Naghten helped to clear things up. Thinking that the pope and English Prime Minister Robert Peel were out to get him, M'Naghten went to 10 Downing Street to kill Peel but ended up killing Peel's secretary. Witnesses claimed that M'Naghten was delusional, and the jury found him not guilty by reason of insanity. Queen Victoria was none too pleased, so a panel of judges was convened to clarify the rules governing the insanity defense as it involved the inability to distinguish right from wrong.

The definition has been controversial ever since, and every high-profile case in which it is invoked seems to throw the idea into question. Patty Hearst and Jeffrey Dahmer both tried to use the insanity defense unsuccessfully, while David Berkowitz (Son of Sam) and Ted Kaczynski (the Unabomber) seemed ready to pursue the defense but ultimately decided against it. But a jury did acquit John Hinckley Jr. of all charges related to his assassination attempt on President Reagan after it determined that he was insane.

It's No Sure Thing

A successful insanity plea is rare. In the 1990s, a study funded by the National Institute of Mental Health found that defendants pleaded insanity in less than 1 percent of cases, and that only a quarter of those pleas were successful. Those who are successful hardly ever get off scot-free—they're simply committed to mental institutions rather than sent to prisons. On average, those who are found insane end up spending more time confined to an institution than they would have in prison if they had been found guilty.

So unless you really love padded rooms, it's probably best to try another defense.

❋ **Golf balls were originally made of leather and stuffed with feathers. That didn't change until the mid-1800s.**

It's Okay to Awaken a Sleepwalker—Really

This is yet another old wives' tale that has been shredded by science. In fact, it's more dangerous not to awaken a sleepwalker.

✳ ✳ ✳ ✳

An Unsolved Puzzle

WE'VE ALL HAD the experience of waking up in the middle of the night to find ourselves drinking a Slurpee and singing Barry Manilow's "Copacabana" on the back porch of the neighbor's house. Wait, everybody has, right? Er, we meant that metaphorically.

Sleepwalking, or somnambulism, is one of the great medical mysteries. Anyone who has encountered a sleepwalker wandering around the house—or singing naked on the back porch—can attest that it is an eerie experience. Sleepwalking is listed in a group of sleep disorders known as parasomnia, and researchers aren't sure what causes it. They know that stress and irregular sleep patterns may contribute to episodes and that children are far more likely to suffer from the condition than adults. They also know that the old wives' tale warning that a person awakened from a somnambulist daze may die is just that—an old wives' tale.

Some experts trace this myth back to the beliefs of various indigenous cultures that thought when a person slept, his or her soul left the body, and if you woke up a sleepwalker, the soul would be lost forever. Others argue that the myth arose simply due to the distress and shock sleepwalkers sometimes experience when awakened.

Just Don't Use Cold Water

Though it is true that a sleepwalker may be distressed and disoriented upon being roused from a midnight stroll, there are no documented cases of sleepwalkers expiring from it. Indeed, sleep experts argue that not waking a sleepwalker can lead to more harm than waking one, especially if he or she is engaged in certain activities at the time (climbing, jumping, handling a knife, running the American government, etc.). In most cases, specialists suggest that it is best to gently guide the somnambulist back to bed.

There might be another reason to wake a sleepwalker. In 1982 an Arizona man named Steven Steinberg went on trial for killing his wife, who was stabbed 26 times with a kitchen knife. Despite overwhelming evidence and Steinberg's own admission that he had committed the crime, the defendant was unable to answer the simplest questions about the circumstances of his wife's death. Why? The man had killed his wife while sleepwalking. Steinberg was acquitted of the charges.

---

* The language of the Mazatecan Indians, natives of southern Mexico, is very tonal and harmonious. Conversations, therefore, can sound like whistling.

* Samuel Seymour was five years old when he was at Ford's Theater the night Abraham Lincoln was shot. He was the last survivor of that event. He died in 1956.

* Plateau Station, Antarctica, a scientific station that operated from 1965 to 1969, is on average the coldest place on Earth. The average annual temperature there is −70°F (−56°C).

* Hewlett-Packard, started in 1939 by Stanford University grads Bill Hewlett and Dave Packard, was the first company to move into what is now known as "Silicon Valley."

* The largest known meteorite to have landed on Earth was found at Grootfontein in Namibia, southwest Africa, in 1920. The space stone is nine feet long and eight feet wide.

* More men than women are left-handed. Some psychologists have noted that lefties are more often found in creative fields.

Steaks Are for Eating, Not Healing

Despite what you may have learned on TV as a kid, putting raw meat on a black eye will do absolutely no good.

✳ ✳ ✳ ✳

WE'VE LONG BELIEVED that everything you need to know in life can be learned from Saturday morning cartoons. Popeye teaches us that spinach makes you strong, Elmer Fudd shows us that it's fun to laugh at people with speech impediments, and Scooby Doo proves to us that meddling kids make the best detectives. And from Fred Flintstone we get this gem of a remedy: Nothing treats a black eye like applying a slab of meat to it.

Unfortunately, it turns out that obtaining medical advice from Saturday morning cartoons probably isn't a great idea. Despite the wonders that raw meat works for Fred and Barney, doctors agree that applying a T-bone to a black eye isn't going to help much.

In fact, putting raw meat anywhere near your eye probably isn't the best idea. Uncooked meat is not only laden with bacteria, it's a prime carrier of *E. coli*, a really gnarly bacterium that can cause bloody diarrhea and kidney failure. If you really feel the need to press meat against your eye, make sure it's wrapped and frozen. Applying an ice pack (in this case, one that is composed of meat) *can* help reduce swelling.

The next time you have a medical emergency, it might be wiser to visit a doctor than to consult Fred Flintstone. Just make sure that the doc's instruments aren't made by the Acme Corporation.

✳ Jim Clark, winner of 25 Grand Prix races, was the first driver to win the Indianapolis 500 driving a car with the engine in the rear.

✳ A group of iguanas is called a mess. A group of raccoons is a gaze. A group of hippos is called a bloat.

✳ Those roped-off areas where boxing matches take place actually used to be round, hence the term "boxing ring."

The Worst Ways to Die

Let's face it—there are no good ways to go. Some, however, are definitely less appealing than others.

✳ ✳ ✳ ✳

Just Be Glad You're Not a Thanatologist

THE PSYCHOLOGIST ERNEST BECKER posited that we're so preoccupied with cheating death that we don't actually live, in a meaningful sense anyway. His suggestion is that the worst type of death is one that follows an insignificant life. This sounds like a load of bull to us, and we'd rather live an insignificant life with a relatively painless death than, say, be consumed in a fire or devoured by hungry piranhas.

Speaking of wasting large amounts of time thinking about death, some people do it as a career—they're known as thanatologists. Some journalists also have spent a  lot of effort on the subject, including Anna Gosline, who wrote a long article for *The New Scientist* in 2007 in which she established two things: First, there are a lot of nasty ways to die; and second, she is a most curious person who would not be our first choice to take out to dinner but might be fun on Halloween.

The Gruesome List

Gosline's summary of a range of common painful deaths is magisterial. Here's a sampling of her findings:

Bleeding to death. This was the Roman aristocracy's favorite form of suicide. They would crawl into a warm tub, nick a vein, and slowly be carried off to the afterlife, full of self-righteous satisfaction at having thumbed their noses at the disagreeable emperors who were infringing on their wealthy prerogatives. Weakness, thirst, anxiety, dizziness, and confusion are common stages before unconsciousness from blood loss—but then, that sounds like a normal day for many of us.

Burning to death. As in frat houses and newsrooms, it's the toxic gases that get most victims. But those who die directly from a fire's flames suffer immensely, as the inflammatory response to burns only increases the pain.

Decapitation. Unless it's a botched job—as with Margaret Pole, the Countess of Salisbury, who fought her executioner in 1541 and was hit 11 times with the axe before succumbing—this seems relatively painless. Full-on death occurs in no more than seven seconds, when the brain's oxygen is used up. Of course, this means you would live for a few seconds after the blow, though that's only scientific speculation. Headless focus-group subjects are hard to rustle up.

Falling. To many people, this gravity-fueled gateway to the grave is, like drowning, one of the most frightening ways to go. Why? Because it can happen in the course of everyday life. Survivors have reported the sensation of time slowing down and feeling alert and focused on maintaining an upright position and landing feet-first—an instinct we share with cats and other animals.

Hanging. Apart from the awful dread that can only build from the moment you realize the jig is up, this is relatively quick and painless—unless the hangman's a hack and your fall is too short or the noose is poorly tied, in which case the struggle at the end of the rope is mighty uncomfortable.

Okay, we've had just about enough of this disconcerting topic, and we didn't even touch on crucifixion, lethal injection, the electric chair, and many other forms of death, natural and unnatural. Our personal un-favorite is an airplane crash, but frankly, we're too darned terrified of such a scenario to discuss it. Maybe Anna Gosline is free.

Common Germs on Your Telephone

We're not insinuating that you live in a dump, but there are an estimated 25,000 germs crawling over every part of your telephone receiver. The simple solution is to frequently wipe down your phone with an antibacterial solution. If you don't, say hello to some of these creatures.

✳   ✳   ✳   ✳

E. coli: *Escherichia coli* normally lives inside your intestine, where it assists in the breakdown of food. However, if *E. coli* gets into other parts of your body, it can cause major problems. Some types of *E. coli* are harmless; others can cause diarrhea, vomiting, cramps, stomach pain, and fever. How does *E. coli* get from your small intestine into other parts of the body? Well, if you don't wash your hands thoroughly after using the bathroom, there's a high likelihood that some *E. coli* will remain on your skin. From there, it's simply a matter of transferring it to the things you handle every day—such as the telephone. When the receiver touches your mouth, *E. coli* could be headed straight down your throat.

Klebsiella: *Klebsiella* is another bacteria that is abundant in the colon and helps keep everything functioning properly. Again, meticulous hygiene keeps it from thriving on your phone or anywhere else it shouldn't be. *Klebsiella* can cause real problems for a person with an already weakened immune system—including a rapid onset illness that leads to destruction of a part of the lung. *Klebsiella* infection can be fatal, so be sure to wipe down that receiver with an alcohol-based solution.

Group A *Streptococcus:* These bacteria are commonly found in the throat and on the skin and are transferred when an infected person coughs or sneezes. The bacterium simply needs to make contact with the eyes, nose, or mouth of other people to enter into their system. Infection can cause strep throat, which is characterized by painful, difficult swallowing. Strep bacteria can cause other serious infections, such as necrotizing fasciitis (flesh-eating disease) and streptococcal toxic shock syndrome (which causes a dangerous drop in blood pressure).

Salmonella: *Salmonella* live in the intestinal tract of humans and animals. People may become infected by eating foods that have not been properly prepared or by picking up bacterium in public washrooms or from public telephones. Salmonellosis (salmonella infection) can cause diarrhea, fever, and stomach cramps, symptoms that usually last four to seven days. In some cases, though, the infection may spread from the intestines to the bloodstream, which can be fatal if the person is not treated with antibiotics.

Staphylococcus aureus: Staph resides on the skin or inside the nose, placing it at prime proximity to your phone receiver. If it enters an open wound, the resulting infection can cause irritations ranging from rashes to cellulitis (inflamed tissue). If staph enters the body orally, it can cause pneumonia, meningitis, and septicemia (blood poisoning).

Campylobacter jejuni: These bacteria are commonly found in animal feces, so in homes with any type of pet, they can easily end up on the phone receiver. Infection with the bacterium can cause enteritis, a condition characterized by diarrhea, fever, stomach cramps, and a general feeling of lethargy. To avoid contamination, be sure household items are thoroughly cleaned, especially those to which Fido and Kitty have access.

Spirochetes: These distinctive bacteria are composed of long, spiraling cells that twist to facilitate motion, and they are easily distributed through the air. *Spirochetes* are responsible for, among other things, Lyme disease, syphilis, and leptosporosis. *Spirochetes* are widespread in the environment and can easily land on your phone.

Bacteroides: *Bacteroides* help break down food in the intestines and make up 30 to 50 percent of human feces. A contaminated phone is a conduit to oral contamination, which could result in periodontal disease, appendicitis, and gastrointestinal infection.

How to Treat a Hangover

The best way? Don't drink! But if it's too late for that, there are some remedies that just might do the trick.

✳   ✳   ✳   ✳

Preemptive Measures

L ET'S HOPE THAT you are not afflicted now, since reading—as well as moving, breathing, and maintaining consciousness—is too painful an activity to pursue while in the throes of *veisalgia*, the medical term for hangover. And frankly, the best time to treat a hangover is before it even starts, so if your pulse is already pounding in your temples and your stomach is doing back flips, you've missed your best chance to nip it in the bud. Still, feel

free to read on (if you can bear it) for some sage advice that can make the morning after that next Christmas party a little more pleasant.

A great deal of a hangover's agony is due to simple dehydration. Alcohol sucks the water out of you, so the smartest thing you can do while imbibing is to have one glass of water for each cocktail. Drink some more water before you stumble into bed and put a nice big bottle of H_2O on the nightstand to drink when you wake. Those frequent trips to the bathroom will totally pay off.

Another prehangover hint: Stick with clear liquor. Research shows that transparent tipples like vodka and gin are the best bets. Why? Darker liquors have more congeners in them. Congeners are by-products of fermentation; as your body processes them, it can produce formaldehyde, which (given formaldehyde's utility as an embalming fluid) helps to explain why you wake up the next morning feeling half dead.

When the Damage Is Already Done...

Sometimes all the foresight in the world won't prevent a hangover. So what can you do about it? We recommend a simple course of action:

Drink lots of fluids—water, fruit juice, or maybe even a bottle of your favorite sports drink. If you feel extremely dehydrated, avoid coffee and other caffeinated drinks because they'll only dry you out more. Down a pain reliever if you think your stomach can take it (and if your stomach isn't ready yet, you'll probably also want to avoid acidic drinks like orange, grapefruit, and tomato juices). Most importantly, crawl back into bed: More sleep will do wonders. If you can't sleep, take a warm shower to improve your circulation, and try some bland food like crackers, bananas, or toast. Once you're up, light exercise can help put the pain behind you.

One more thing—and repeat it over and over: "I promise never to drink this much again."

❋ A metal mechanical bank from the early 1900s dubbed Shoot the Chute and featuring the comic strip character Buster Brown—in working order without scratches and dents—is worth $30,000 or more to collectors.

❋ The Communist leader of Romania, Nicolae Ceauşescu—known as "the giant of the Carpathians"—banned the game Scrabble because he felt it was too intellectual. He also believed that baseball was subversive.

❋ President William Howard Taft was so obese that he used a reinforced steel chair while dining.

❋ The manner and site of execution of those imprisoned in the Tower of London was primarily dependent on the station of the condemned. For example, nobles such as Anne Boleyn were beheaded in private.

❋ The biggest type of spider in the world is the goliath bird-eating spider, a dinner-plate-size behemoth native to parts of South America.

The Black Death Lives On

It's still possible to contract the dreaded killer, but don't fret too much. As long as the human population continues to feel that it would rather not willingly share its space with thousands of rats, most people should remain refreshingly plague-free.

The Grim Reaper

THE PLAGUE, OR Black Death, killed 25 million Europeans—one-third of the continent's population— from 1347 to 1353. The plague is caused by the bacteria *Yersinia pestis*, which mainly spreads when a flea bites an infected rat (or other rodent) for breakfast and then bites a human for lunch or dinner, thus passing on the bacteria. The plague comes in three flavors: bubonic, pneumonic, and septicemic.

Bubonic is the cover girl of the bunch—the one most people associate with the term "plague." The telltale markers of bubonic plague are buboes, infected lymph notes on the neck, armpit, and groin. They turn black and ooze blood and pus.

Pneumonic plague occurs when a person inhales the bacteria from someone who is infected. "Cover your mouth when you sneeze," has never made more sense than with this little ditty.

Septicemic plague is when *Yersinia pestis* gets into your bloodstream. It can cause gangrene due to tissue death in extremities such as fingers and toes, turning them black. The gangrene and the black buboes and lesions all contributed to the term "Black Death."

Pneumonic and septicemic plague make bubonic plague look like a ray of hope: Untreated, they have close to a 100 percent mortality rate. Bubonic's death rate is a measly 60 to 75 percent if left untreated.

Times Have Changed

The fact that most people live in much more sanitary conditions these days means that the chances of getting the plague are low. However, it is still very much around. In India, between August and October 1994, 693 people contracted the plague, and 56 of them died. Ten to fifteen cases are reported every year in the United States, and there are 1,000 to 3,000 annual cases globally. Animals that carry the plague are found in Asia, Africa, and North and South America. Additionally, plague is a perfect candidate for biological warfare, particularly pneumonic plague since it can be airborne.

Treatment includes a very aggressive dose of antibiotics, which must begin early to improve the chance of survival. The Centers for Disease Control and Prevention recommends that people traveling in rural places that might harbor the disease take precautions against it. Those with the highest risk should start on preemptive antibiotics. Others should use insect repellent on their bodies and clothing.

So, if you're traveling in an area where you could be bitten by a plague-carrying flea, try to stick to bed-and-breakfasts run by human beings and skip the rodent-owned ones. Nothing ruins a vacation like the Black Death.

---

* In the National Basketball Association's first season, 1946–47, the top-paid player was Detroit's Tom King, who made $16,500. He also acted as the team's publicity manager and business director.

* It has been reported in *Ripley's Believe It or Not* that the toe tag from the corpse of Lee Harvey Oswald, President Kennedy's alleged assassin, sold at auction for $9,500.

* Michelangelo started his sculpture *Pietà* at age 22.

* The San Andreas Fault is slipping about two inches per year, which means that Los Angeles will be a suburb of San Francisco in 15 million years.

* Bibliophobia is the fear of books.

* In 2005, three and a half years after the company filed for bankruptcy, Polaroid chairman Jacques Nasser received $12.8 million for selling shares of the company. Meanwhile, 6,000 former employees each got $47 and lost their benefits.

The Medical Uses of Bee Venom

Believe it or not, a bee could one day save your life.

✳ ✳ ✳ ✳

All-Natural Apitherapy

AFRAID OF BEES? You might want to get over it, since bees make good medicine. For more than 4,000 years, the common honeybee has been used to treat everything from multiple sclerosis to rheumatoid arthritis, gout, asthma, impotence, epilepsy, depression, bursitis, shingles, tendinitis, and even some types of cancer. As part of a unique alternative-medical approach called *apitherapy*, practitioners use natural bee by-products such as raw honey, beeswax, pollen, royal jelly, and even bee venom to treat medical conditions that don't always respond to traditional medicine.

Facing the Stinger

Bee venom is currently being used to reduce inflammation and pain and to treat resistant skin diseases such as psoriasis. Although researchers have already identified more than 40 pharmacologically active substances in bee venom, very little is known about them or what they can do. One protein that is understood is *melittin*, which has been shown to stimulate the adrenal glands, which produce *cortisol*. Cortisol is a naturally occurring anti-inflammatory that promotes healing in the body. In multiple sclerosis patients, bee venom is thought to dissolve scar tissue on myelin sheaths, improving nerve transmissions.

Bee venom can be administered directly from the bee's stinger or via injection by a trained health-care professional. After identifying the affected area, the venom is injected, often at key acupuncture points, hence the term, "bee acupuncture."

While few published studies exist supporting the use of bee venom, hundreds of stories attest to its effectiveness. So at your next picnic, you may just want to let that annoying bee be.

Drink Up!

The practice of urine consumption, or urophagia, *dates back to the ancient Egyptians, Chinese, Indians, and Aztecs, who imbibed this very personal nectar for health purposes.*

✳   ✳   ✳   ✳

It Quenches Your Thirst in a Pinch

OF COURSE, "HEALTH PURPOSES" is a relative term. In dire circumstances in which no fresh water is available, drinking urine can supposedly help prevent dehydration. Given that urine is composed mostly of water, the first golden drink may be fairly harmless. If you were to go back to the urine well repeatedly, however, you'd run into the law of diminishing returns—the percentage of usable water in your pee would decrease and harmful flushed waste products would increase. These harmful substances could include drugs or other chemicals from the environment that exit the body in a hurry via the kidneys, which would take a beating as they continuously tried to recycle compounded toxins. In addition, the high salt content in urine would eventually lead to, not stave off, dehydration.

Urine as a Hallucinogen

If it's psychotropic trips you're after, perhaps scoring the Koryak tribe of Siberia as your new drinking buddies would be the thing. Koryak tribesmen swig each other's urine to prolong highs after consuming mind-altering mushrooms during rituals.

Medicinal Urine

Some cultures believe that supplemental consumption of urine keeps illnesses at bay. The holistic approach of Indian Ayurvedic medicine known as Amaroli uses urine to treat asthma, arthritis, allergies, acne, cancer, heart disease, indigestion, migraines, wrinkles, and other afflictions. There is no proof that these treatments work, but urine is sterile (as long as it isn't contaminated with the Koryak's psychedelic mushrooms), and it does have antibacterial, antifungal, and antiviral qualities.

Too Much of a Good Thing

Ever felt overwhelmed while on vacation? Join the club. But if it's an extreme case, perhaps it's Stendhal syndrome.

✳ ✳ ✳ ✳

Vacation Interrupted

SUPPOSE YOU'VE SPENT the day traipsing around the city of Florence, taking in the artwork and scenery. You end the day hiking up to the Piazzale Michelangelo to gaze over the city, but when you arrive at the summit, you're struck by delirium. You're out of breath, panicked, and a bit dizzy. In Italy, this affliction, suffered when one becomes overwhelmed by works of art or scenes in nature, is called Stendhal syndrome.

Sketchy Syndrome?

The syndrome was brought to the medical community's attention in the 1970s by Italian psychiatrist Graziella Magherini. The doctor named it after Marie-Henri Beyle, a renowned 19th-century French writer who wrote (under the pseudonym Stendhal) about the disorientation visitors feel when viewing the artifacts of the Italian Renaissance. Also known as the "tourist's disease," Stendhal syndrome affects a few hundred people per year in Italy. Symptoms usually subside in a few days after the person leaves the area.

Although Italy is known for cities that are brimming with beauty and culture, it's not the only place you can fall ill with awe. In Jerusalem, a similar sickness is called Jerusalem syndrome. There, the afflicted experience Stendhal symptoms, but they're caused by the weight of the city's religious importance. Doctors debate whether patients develop a psychosis as a result of their visit or if the visit is simply a trigger for a preexisting medical condition.

Real or imagined, the condition makes for a good story. It's even been a plot point in books, including Chuck Palahniuk's *Diary*, and in the horror movie *The Stendhal Syndrome*.

The Lobotomy: A Sordid History

The justifications put forth for performing these infamously life-altering procedures were shoddy at best.

✳ ✳ ✳ ✳

Beyond Hollywood

FEW PEOPLE HAVE firsthand experience with lobotomized patients. For many of us, any contact with these convalescents comes via Hollywood—that searing image at the end of *One Flew Over the Cuckoo's Nest* of Jack Nicholson, as Randle Patrick McMurphy, lying comatose. Hopefully, we've all experienced enough to know that Hollywood doesn't always tell it like it is. What would be the point of a medical procedure that turns the patient into a vegetable? Then again, even if Hollywood is prone to exaggeration, the fact is that a lobotomy is a pretty terrible thing.

Dissecting the Lobotomy

What exactly is a lobotomy? Simply put, it's a surgical procedure that severs the paths of communication between the prefrontal lobe and the rest of the brain. This prefrontal lobe—the part of the brain closest to the forehead—is a structure that appears to have great influence on personality and initiative. So the obvious question is: Who the heck thought it would be a good idea to disconnect it?

It started in 1890, when German researcher Friederich Golz removed portions of his dog's brain. He noticed afterward that the dog was slightly more mellow. The first lobotomies performed on humans took place in Switzerland two years later.

Those first six patients all had schizophrenia, and while some did show post-op improvement, two others died. Despite being an experimental procedure that killed 33 percent of its very first human subjects, the lobotomy was considered a success and became more commonplace. One early proponent of the surgery even received a Nobel Prize.

The most notorious practitioner of the lobotomy was American physician Walter Freeman, who performed the procedure on more than 3,000 patients—including Rosemary Kennedy, the sister of President John F. Kennedy—from the 1930s to the 1960s. Freeman pioneered a surgical method in which a metal rod (known colloquially as an "ice pick") was inserted into the eye socket, driven up into the brain, and hammered home. This is known as a transorbital lobotomy.

Freeman and other doctors in the United States lobotomized an estimated 40,000 patients before an ethical outcry over the procedure prevailed in the 1950s. Although the mortality rate had improved since the early trials, it turned out that the ratio of success to failure was not much higher: A third of the patients got better, a third stayed the same, and a third became much worse. The practice had generally ceased in the United States by the early 1970s, and it is now illegal in some states.

Who Got Them?

Lobotomies were performed only on patients with extreme psychological impairments, after no other treatment proved to be successful. The frontal lobe of the brain is involved in reasoning, emotion, and personality, and disconnecting it can have a powerful effect on a person's behavior. Unfortunately, the changes that a lobotomy causes are unpredictable and often negative. Today, there are far more precise and far less destructive ways of affecting the brain through antipsychotic drugs and other pharmaceuticals.

So it's not beyond the realm of possibility that Nicholson's character in *Cuckoo's Nest* could become zombielike. If the movie gets anything wrong, it's that a person as highly functioning as McMurphy probably wouldn't have been recommended for a lobotomy.

The vindictive Nurse Ratched is the one who makes the call, which raises a fundamental moral question: Who is qualified to decide whether someone should have a lobotomy?

The Buzzing in Your Head

It's gross, but true: That maddening noise might just be from an insect that crawled into your ear and can't get out.

✳ ✳ ✳ ✳

The Horror, the Horror

It's a popular urban legend that was even the subject of an episode of Rod Serling's *Night Gallery*: An earwig enters a man's ear, bores through his brain, and emerges from the other ear. The victim survives, but the earwig laid eggs, and its babies will feast on the man's delicious brain, growing big and strong.

Fortunately, earwigs do not enjoy the taste of brain. The half-inch-long insects use their sharp pincers to eat through leaves, fruits, vegetables, and, occasionally, other insects. They sometimes wind up in human ears—hence, their name—but only by accident.

It's Not Like the Bug Wants to Be There

Ear, nose, and throat doctors often see patients who have insects—cockroaches, spiders, beetles, and so forth—trapped in their ears, lost and confused in a maze of earwax. The easiest way to get an unwelcome visitor out of the ear is to drown it and then carefully extract it. Doctors use water, mineral oil, and  lidocaine (a local anesthetic) to drown bugs. Lidocaine immobilizes the insect the quickest, but if the intruder punctures the eardrum, you risk having the substance seep into the inner ear, which can cause dizziness and nausea for hours.

Typically, bug-in-the-ear syndrome is annoying but harmless. But a *Night Gallery*–worthy outcome is a possibility, however remote. In 1856, English explorer John Hanning Speke was camping in a tent in Africa when a beetle slithered into his ear. The bug panicked and started scratching Speke's ear to find a way out. Speke stabbed the beetle several times with a penknife, killing it. Unfortunately, he split the beetle into lots of pieces and couldn't get them all out of his ear. This led to a nasty infection that created a hole from his ear canal to his nasal cavity, as well as lesions and boils on his face and neck.

Speke survived, but not before enduring a great deal of pain. The takeaway message? Don't stab at the little bugger that's crawled into your ear—drown it.

---

* **Wine bottles are tinted to keep the liquid from being exposed to light. Even small amounts of exposure to light can cause the stuff to spoil.**

* **Airlines in America buy 20 million barf bags a year.**

* **More car crashes happen on Saturday than on any other day of the week.**

* **Lettuce is named for milk. The word is derived from the Latin word *lactuca,* which means milk. It's believed the term was used because of a white liquid that can come out of a lettuce stalk when it's snapped in two.**

* **The same person who came up with the comic book character Wonder Woman also came up with the polygraph.**

* **"Heroin" was once trademarked as a brand name. Bayer bought the rights to the word in 1898.**

* **Ever wonder what NERF actually stands for? Although some people have claimed it stands for "Non-Expanding Recreational Foam," NERF is not an acronym for anything, and it actually means absolutely nothing.**

* **An American baseball uses 108 stitches.**

* **An American football has only four seams.**

Top Reasons for Emergency Room Visits

As you might expect, the maladies run the gamut.

✳ ✳ ✳ ✳

1. **Injury and poisoning**—Injuries include burns, foreign bodies in tissue or cavities, fractures, intracranial injuries, open wounds, sprains and strains, surgical and medical complications, and unspecified injuries.

2. **Symptoms and signs of ill-defined conditions**

3. **Diseases of the respiratory system**—These include asthma, bronchitis, emphysema, and pneumonia.

4. **Diseases of the digestive system**—Such problems include appendicitis, food poisoning, and ulcers.

5. **Diseases of the musculoskeletal and connective-tissue systems**—These include osteomyelitis (bone infection), septic arthritis, and Lyme disease.

6. **Diseases of the nervous system and sense organs**—These include bacterial or viral meningitis, encephalitis (inflammation of the brain), and detachment of the retina.

7. **Diseases of the genitourinary system**—These include bladder infection, kidney infection, and kidney failure.

8. **Diseases of the circulatory system**—These include heart attacks, hypertension/high blood pressure, and pulmonary embolisms (blockage of arteries in the lungs).

9. **Diseases of the skin and subcutaneous tissue**—These include cellulitis and severe sunburn.

10. **Mental disorders**—These include bipolar disorder, dementia, and schizophrenia.

Don't Underestimate Leeches and Maggots

These disgusting creatures have pretty much been relegated to the "quack" chapter of medical history, but amazingly, they can be valuable in treating patients today.

✳ ✳ ✳ ✳

They're Even Recognized by the FDA

BEFORE THE ADVENT of modern medicine, there were some pretty wild treatments for bodily injury, disease, and dysfunction. If you had, say, persistent migraines, you might've tried to get rid of them by having a small hole drilled into your skull. Makes sense, right? And of course, there was the leech—the wormlike parasite that was thought to alleviate a vast number of ailments as it grew fat on a sick person's blood.

The medical community has come a long way since then, but there's still a place for the leech, along with a creature that's arguably even more disgusting, the maggot. In 2004, these two unsavory critters became the first living animals recognized by the U.S. Food and Drug Administration as medical devices.

Leech Therapy

Thankfully, contemporary doctors don't use leeches as a cure-all blood-drainer like the ancient Greeks and Egyptians and the medieval Europeans did. Today they're used primarily to help patients recover from major reconstructive surgery. As tissue re-forms following a skin graft, blood often drains abnormally, which can lead to swelling. The blood vessels in the ears and other delicate body parts are especially prone to clots that can kill the recovering tissue.

Leeches are a viable solution to these problems because they can drain blood, and their saliva contains more than 30 different proteins that keep blood flowing, numb pain, and reduce swelling. The amazing truth is, they are more effective at these treatments than any alternative that has been tried by modern medical practitioners.

Calling All Maggots

Meanwhile, the maggot—the larval form of the blowfly—is used to treat serious wounds that are infected or gangrenous. Maggots feed on the dead tissue; this effectively cleans the wound and arrests infection, allowing the damaged tissue beneath to heal. The maggots' secret weapon—a secretion of enzymes that turn dead tissue into a digestible mush—is known to help wounds that have resisted all other treatments.

The maggot procedure is an ordeal—and not just for squeamish types. Hundreds of the wriggling insects are applied to the wound and covered with a bandage. After a couple of days, the well-fed maggots are removed and replaced with a hungry group, and the process is repeated until the wound is healed. Sounds gross, huh? Luckily, good old Bactine and Band-Aids get the job done for more minor scrapes and cuts.

---

* The actor Paul Newman attempted to enlist in the Naval Air Corps during World War II, but he was discovered to be color-blind. He instead served in the U.S. Navy in the South Pacific.

* Of all the planets in the Sun's solar system, Venus is the only one that rotates clockwise.

* Radio station WLTO in Lexington, Kentucky, ran a contest to "win 100 grand." When the winner went to claim her prize, she received a Nestlé's 100 Grand candy bar. She sued for $100,000.

* Pope John XXI (1276–77) had been in office less than a year before the ceiling on a new wing of his palace collapsed on him while he slept. He died six days later.

* Stella Walsh, who won the women's 100-meter dash at the 1932 Olympics, was killed in 1980. During her autopsy, doctors discovered that she was really a he.

* First Lady Eleanor Roosevelt was forced to carry a pistol in her purse after receiving a number of threatening letters during the Great Depression.

Wacky Weight-Loss Fads

The U.S. weight-loss industry brings in more than $50 billion a year as people try new ways to slim down. We've all heard that the key to losing weight is to burn more calories than you consume, but most people don't want to work that hard to lose weight. Instead, they'll try some pretty odd diets and contraptions in the hopes of shedding unwanted pounds.

❋ ❋ ❋ ❋

Electric Ab Exercisers

COUNTLESS VERSIONS OF the same machine have been unleashed on the flabby public with the same results: none whatsoever. These machines claim to send an electric current to abdominal muscles via plates, electrodes, or bands, causing the muscles to contract and release and therefore burn belly fat. All the machines actually do is leave red marks on the stomach and a dent in the wallet.

The "7–7–7 Diet"

On this diet, which circulated online a few years ago, dieters get to eat seven eggs throughout the day. Seven eggs only. On day two, it's seven oranges; on day three, seven bananas. According to believers, on the fourth day you'll wake up seven pounds lighter. And very, very hungry.

The Breathing Diet

Overweight? Just breathe! For the low, low price of around $19.95, this diet claims to teach overeaters how to lose weight simply by learning how to breathe correctly.

The JumpSnap

It's a jump rope...without the rope! This invention gets people jumping as if they were using a jump rope but eliminates the pesky rope that usually trips them up. A snapping sound emanates from two battery-powered handles, and a voice tells you how and when to jump. Of course, there's another option: Save the cash, and just jump up and down.

The Vacunaut

The Vacunaut exercise system involves donning a rubbery neoprene suit attached to some vacuum hoses. As you run, the vacuum pressure is said to increase blood flow in the fatty tissue around the stomach and waist, whittling you down to that svelte god/goddess you've always wanted to be.

HandyTrim Light Pocket Gym

Step one: Take string out of pocket. Step two: Twirl. Step three: Watch those pounds melt off! The makers of this weight-loss gadget don't promise to turn you into a strapping hunk overnight, but they swear that with continuous use, the Pocket Gym will make a difference in your upper body. And since it's small and portable, you can exercise anywhere. Finally, a way to make those boring meetings productive!

The Cabbage Soup Diet

The supporters of this diet claim you can lose up to ten pounds in one week by eating little more than a super-green soup made largely from cabbage. Those who promote the diet claim that it's not a long-term thing—it just provides a kick-start when embarking on a more moderate diet. We imagine that anyone who actually likes cabbage at the beginning of the week will probably hate it by week's end.

The Dumbbell Phone

The Japanese have a word for the art of "unuseless" inventions: *chindogu*. What better problem than weight loss to inspire a thousand unuseless inventions? The dumbbell phone is a free-weight attachment for the telephone that purportedly helps build muscle every time you pick up the handset. This works best if you have a lot of short conversations and, thus, are lifting the phone and setting it down every minute or so. (Perfect for telemarketers, perhaps?)

Unusual Medical Maladies

The human body is able to play some nasty tricks on its owner. The six conditions described below are documented examples of some of the more unusual ones in its repertoire.

✳ ✳ ✳ ✳

Who Is That?

TAKE THE INTERESTING and perplexing diagnosis of *Capgras syndrome*, a rare psychological disorder that makes sufferers suspicious of their loved ones or even their own reflections. For a number of reasons, including schizophrenia, epilepsy, and malformations of the brain's temporal lobes, Capgras victims have difficulty making physical and emotional connections with the people, places, and things they see, even ones that have been a part of their lives for years. Sufferers see themselves in a mirror or other shiny surfaces and wonder who the stranger is that's peering back at them. According to Dr. V. S. Ramachandran, director of the Center for Brain and Cognition at the University of California, San Diego, people diagnosed with this disorder can also find themselves suspicious of animals or other objects, such as a pair of running shoes. In such cases, they convince themselves that someone has broken into their home and replaced familiar objects with imposters.

Can You Direct Me to the Loo?

Foreign accent syndrome is even more rare. It's a disorder that causes the afflicted to suddenly and inexplicably speak in an unfamiliar dialect. One of the first cases of FAS was discovered in 1941 after a young Norwegian woman sustained a shrapnel injury to her head during a wartime air raid. Although she had never been out of her home country, she suddenly began speaking with a German accent, which resulted in her being shunned by her family and friends. In Indiana, a 57-year-old woman suffered a stroke in 1999 and began speaking with a British accent, including colloquialisms like "bloody" and "loo."

Get Your Hand Off of Me!

If there was ever a malady that a high-school boy might envy, it's *alien hand syndrome*, also known as *Dr. Strangelove syndrome*. Alien hand syndrome is caused by damage to either the parietal or the occipital lobe of the brain. Those afflicted with the syndrome often find one of their hands operating independently from the rest of their body and sometimes completely against their conscious will. AHS sufferers often report incidences of a "rogue hand" getting involved in disobedient behavior such as undoing buttons or removing clothing. One patient reported a bizarre incident in which her right hand put a cigarette into her mouth. Before she could light it, her left hand yanked the cigarette out and crushed it in an ashtray.

Please Pass the Dirt

At one time or another, all children will experiment by eating an occasional handful of dirt. The good news is that it's a passing phase, at least for the majority of youngsters. The bad news is that if this fascination with eating nonfood items persists longer than a month, your child could be suffering from a condition called *pica*. Associated with developmental disabilities such as autism or mental retardation, pica typically affects children younger than 24 months. It can also appear in people with epilepsy and in pregnant women.

Pica sufferers find themselves craving and consuming a wide variety of nonfood items such as dirt, sand, hair, glue, buttons, paint chips, plaster, laundry starch, cigarette butts, paper, soap, and even feces. There was even one documented case of "cutlery craving," in which a 47-year-old Englishman underwent more than 30 operations to remove various items—including eight dinner forks—from his stomach.

Another form of pica, called geophagia, is practiced by cultures that purposely eat earth substances such as dirt and clay in order to relieve nausea, morning sickness, and diarrhea and to remove toxins from their bodies.

Something Smells Fishy Around Here

Bad breath, body odor, and the occasional flatulence—we've all had to deal with them in one way or another. But how would you like to live with someone who constantly smelled of pungent fish? A rare metabolic disorder called *fish odor syndrome* (also known as *trimethylaminuria,* or TMAU) results in the afflicted releasing an enzyme called trimethylamine through their sweat, urine, and breath. This enzyme also happens to give off a strong "fishy" odor. The condition appears to be more common in women than men, and researchers suspect that female sex hormones such as estrogen or progesterone may be at fault.

While there is no cure for fish odor syndrome, people afflicted can control the disease by avoiding eggs, certain meats, fish, legumes, and foods that contain choline, nitrogen, and sulfur. And, of course, showering regularly.

A Permanent Bad Hair Day

If you've suffered from the occasional bad hair day, consider yourself lucky—you could be afflicted with *uncombable hair syndrome.* UHS is a rare disease that affects boys and girls before puberty. In fact, it's so rare that there were only 60 cases reported in medical literature between 1973 and 1998.

UHS is an inherited disease with subtle hair changes noted in several preceding generations. It begins with a hair follicle that produces triangular hair shafts that have several longitudinal grooves and very little pigment and are exceptionally dry and brittle. Because the hair is so dry, it rarely lies down; instead, the hair grows straight out from the scalp.

So what should you do if you are diagnosed with UHS? First, cancel your appointment with your hairdresser. People afflicted with UHS typically experience alopecia, or periodic baldness. The hair that does grow frequently breaks off before it has time to mature. But there is hope: There has been some success with medication, and some cases have resolved spontaneously several years after the first outbreak.

The Mystery of the Ear Candle

It's not a candle that is shaped like an ear, nor is it a candle that is made from earwax. What the heck is this thing?

✳ ✳ ✳ ✳

A Dubious Device

AN EAR CANDLE (also called an ear cone) is an outdated and discredited remedy for earwax buildup. The candle is made from cotton muslin soaked in beeswax and rolled to form a candle that's hollow in the middle. To use the candle, you tilt your head sideways, put it in your ear, and light it at the top. Proponents of ear candles maintain that this creates a vacuum that softens the old earwax and pulls it—along with other toxins and debris from your ear canal—up into the hollow candle.

According to some fanciful claims, the candle even dredges up debris from the connected lymph nodes and the other facial orifices. After the flame comes within about two inches of your ear, you snuff it out and remove the candle. When you cut it in half, there's wax and other crud inside, so the obvious response is, "Yuck, look at all that mess that came out of my ear!"

But a 1996 study conducted by the Spokane Ear, Nose, and Throat Clinic showed that the wax is wax from the ear candle itself, and that the crud is just soot from the candle. In September 1998, the U.S. Food and Drug Administration issued a warning about the safety of ear candles, stating that they can damage both the ears and the face. Indeed, some doctors have treated patients with dried ear candle wax on their eardrums, which is an extremely painful problem. In the United States and Canada, it is illegal to make statements about the medicinal uses or benefits of ear candles.

It Didn't Work Then, It Doesn't Work Now

Some ear candle manufacturers claim that ear candling is an ancient tradition of the Native American Hopi tribe. However, the Hopi disavow any connection to ear candling. The actual origin of the ear candle is unknown. The ancient civilizations of Egypt and China, the monks of Tibet, and the pre-Columbian tribesmen of South America have all been mentioned as pioneers of ear candling. Regardless of who actually "invented" the ear candle, however, it was every bit as ineffective in those days as it is today.

* Not only was President Richard Nixon the first American president to visit both China and the Soviet Union, he was also the first to visit all 50 states while in office.

* Can you find the islet of Langerhans on a map of the world? Not even if you did well in geography. It's actually the name of a part of the pancreas that produces hormones.

* President James Garfield was shot by an assassin in 1881. Six doctors attempted to treat the wounded president, but several probed the wound with their bare fingers, introducing fatal infection into his body.

* In 1997, University of Nebraska sophomore Jeremy Sonnenfeld became the first bowler to "knock 900" by rolling three perfect 300 games in a row in an official tournament.

* During the 76 years of his life, French King Louis XIV took only three baths, each of them reluctantly. He masked his odor with large amounts of perfume.

* The average person is 33 percent more likely to be killed by a collapsing sand structure than by a shark attack.

* Male mites mate with their sisters before they are born. After birth, the females rush off in search of food and their brothers are left to die.

* Milk is the official beverage of 19 states: Wisconsin, North Dakota, South Dakota, Maryland, Pennsylvania, Oregon, Oklahoma, Vermont, New York, North Carolina, South Carolina, Mississippi, Louisiana, Kentucky, Delaware, Minnesota, Arkansas, Virginia, and Nebraska. (Nebraska actually has two state beverages—the second one is Kool-Aid.)

Chapter 16

Bizarre Truths About the Origins of Things

How Friday the 13th Came to Be So Unlucky

It's perhaps the most pervasive superstition in North America, Western Europe, and Australia. In fact, if you're like lots of other fearful folks, you won't take a flight, get married, sign a contract, or even leave your house on this most doomed of days.

✳　✳　✳　✳

It Started with the Ancients

WHAT EXACTLY MAKES Friday the 13th more luckless than, say, Tuesday the 5th? The answer is deeply rooted in biblical, mythological, and historical events.

Friday and the number 13 have been independently sinister since ancient times—maybe since the dawn of humans. Many biblical scholars say that Eve tempted Adam with the forbidden apple on a Friday. Traditional teachings also tell us that the Great Flood began on a Friday, the Temple of Solomon was destroyed on a Friday, and Abel was slain by Cain on a Friday.

For Christians, Friday and the number 13 are of the utmost significance. Christ was crucified on Friday, and 13 is the number of people who were present at the Last Supper. Judas, the disciple who betrayed Jesus, was the 13th member of the party to arrive.

Groups of 13 may be one of the earliest and most concrete taboos associated with the number. It's believed that both the ancient Vikings and Hindus thought it unpropitious to have 13 people gather together in one place. Up until recently, French socialites known as *quatorziens* (fourteeners) made themselves available as 14th guests to spare dinner parties from ominous ends.

Some trace the infamy of the number 13 back to ancient Norse culture. According to mythology, 12 gods had arrived to a banquet, when in walked an uninvited 13th guest—Loki, the god of mischief. Loki tricked the blind god Hother into throwing a spear of mistletoe at Balder, the beloved god of light. Balder fell dead, and the whole earth turned dark.

Today, 13 is still a number to avoid. About 80 percent of high-rises don't have a 13th floor, many airports skip gate number 13, and you won't find a room 13 in some hospitals and hotels.

An Infamous Combination

How did Friday and 13 become forever linked as the most disquieting day on the calendar? It just may be that Friday was unlucky and 13 was unlucky, so the two together was simply a double jinx. However, one theory holds that all this superstition came not as a result of convergent taboos, but of a single historical event.

On Friday, October 13, 1307, King Philip IV of France ordered the arrest of the revered Knights Templar. Tortured and forced to confess to false charges of heresy, blasphemy, and other wrongdoing, hundreds of knights were burned at the stake. It's said that sympathizers of the Templars then condemned Friday the 13th as the most evil of days.

No one has been able to document whether this eerie tale is indeed the origin of this superstition. And some scholars are convinced that it's nothing more than a phenomenon created by 20th-century media. So sufferers of paraskevidekatriaphobia (a pathological fear of Friday the 13th), take some comfort—or at least throw some salt over your shoulder.

Shop 'Til You Drop

*An Oklahoma entrepreneur used a simple folding
chair to change the way the world shopped.*

✳ ✳ ✳ ✳

IN THE LATE 1930s, Sylvan Goldman, like any good businessman, was trying to find a way to increase sales. At his two
grocery store chains in the Oklahoma City area, Standard and
Humpty Dumpty, he noticed that when the wire hand baskets
his stores provided became full or heavy, most customers headed
for the checkout. He imagined this problem could be remedied if
shoppers had a way to conveniently carry more items through the
aisles. Puzzling over the problem in his office one evening, he was
struck by inspiration when a simple wooden folding chair caught
his eye. What if that chair had wheels on the bottom and a basket
attached to the seat? Or better, why not *two* baskets?

Goldman explained his idea to Fred Young, a carpenter and
handyman who worked at the store, and Young began tinkering. After many months and many prototypes, the two men
hit on a design they thought would work. Goldman's first carts
used metal frames that each held two enormous baskets—
19 inches long, 13 inches wide, and 9 inches deep. When not in
use, the baskets could be removed and stacked together, and the
frames folded up to a depth of only five inches, thus preserving
the most precious commodity of any retail store: floor space.

Today, most of us couldn't imagine a grocery store without
shopping carts, but Goldman's customers were reluctant to
use the new contraptions at first. Ever the salesman, he hired
models of various ages to shop with his "folding carrier baskets."
Eventually, the carts caught on, not only at Goldman's stores
but also at retail outlets across the country. In 1937, Goldman
founded the Folding Carrier Basket Company to manufacture his carts for other stores. They became so popular that by
1940 he was faced with a seven-year backlog of new orders.

A Flight of Fancy:
The Peace Symbol

It's like a dove's foot, man. Far out. Actually, the bird footprint that many people see in the peace symbol is merely a coincidence.

✳ ✳ ✳ ✳

Give Peace a Chance

ENGLISH DESIGNER GERALD HOLTOM created the symbol in 1958 for the Campaign for Nuclear Disarmament (CND), a British antinuclear movement. Holtom based his design on signs from semaphore, a code that involves a signaler positioning two flags to represent letters. Semaphore was originally used in the British navy to communicate over long distances.

To represent nuclear disarmament, the designer combined the semaphore characters for *N* (two flags held in an upside-down *V*) and *D* (one flag held straight up and one held straight down). Holtom said that the symbol also represented despair with its suggestion of a figure kneeling with outstretched arms; he later regretted this dour interpretation.

The CND first used the symbol during a march to protest the Atomic Weapons Research Establishment in Aldermaston, England. In the 1960s, activists in Europe and the United States picked it up. It was often used in protests against the Vietnam War, and it came to represent peace in general rather than just nuclear disarmament. The symbol's popularity had a lot to do with its simplicity: It's easier to draw three lines in a circle than to draw a flying dove, which was the most common peace symbol before Holtom's. By the end of the 1960s, his peace symbol was entrenched.

Evil Origins?

But the story doesn't end there. As the symbol gained popularity, critics of the antiwar movement said it was actually an old anti-Christian sign called Nero's Cross. According to this explanation, Roman Emperor Nero crucified Saint Peter upside down in A.D. 67 and popularized the symbol—a representation of an inverted, broken cross—to mock Christianity. Critics also claimed that Satanists used the symbol in the Middle Ages and that Nazis adopted it in the 1930s. Some people still see it primarily as an anti-Christian symbol.

Historical details are murky, but it's clear that variations on the design appeared long before 1958. For example, in Germanic and Scandinavian runic alphabets that date back to A.D 150, it can be seen without the circle and with the fork facing both down and up. The Nazis were big fans of runic symbols, so this could have influenced the signs that they employed.

There's no evidence that Holtom had anti-Christian or Nazi connotations in mind when he created the symbol. If he was guilty of anything, it was shoddy research. Nazi connotations always result in bad press, especially when you're in the peace business.

---

* Nicholas Sparks, author of *The Notebook, Message in a Bottle*, and other novels, was a successful track-and-field athlete at the University of Notre Dame.

* Thomas Selfridge was the first person killed in a powered, fixed-wing aircraft. On September 17, 1908, his plane, piloted by Orville Wright, crashed after takeoff. Wright survived.

* In ancient Egypt, the tombs of pharaohs were believed to hold a curse that would befall anyone who entered them. In fact, it was said that death would come on wings to he who entered the tomb of a pharaoh.

* Julie Krone, one of the most successful female jockeys of all time, was the first woman to win a Triple Crown race, capturing the 1993 Belmont Stakes aboard Colonial Affair.

* The reproductive organs of the male spider are located on its legs.

Poor John

Of all the names in the English language, "John" might be applied in the most unflattering ways. What do we call the note that's left by a woman who's jilting her lover? A "Dear John" letter. Even worse, we call a bathroom the "john." What did John do to deserve so much disrespect?

✳ ✳ ✳ ✳

Tracking Down John

THE MOST COMMON explanation for why we call the bathroom the john is that it retained an association with the first name of British nobleman Sir John Harington, who invented the flush toilet in 1596. While this may be a good enough answer for Internet trivia sites, it is not good enough for our dear readers, who deserve the truth. And the truth is this: Although Harington is, in fact, commonly credited with devising a prototype of the flush toilet (it was not conceived by Thomas Crapper, as another popular myth would have it), the "john" moniker for the bathroom is almost certainly not related to his achievement.

The evidence for this is legion. First, when Harington invented the toilet, he termed it the "ajax,"—a pun on the term "jakes," which was slang for toilet at the time. Second, the newfangled toilet idea never really caught on during Harington's lifetime—the device didn't come into widespread use until after 1775, when another British inventor, Alexander Cummings, received a patent for it. It seems unlikely that Harington's name would have been attached to the toilet nearly two centuries after the fact. Also, consider that "john" as a term for the bathroom isn't recorded in print until the mid-18th century, nearly 150 years after Harington's moment of glory. But what really throws the whole theory into the, um, toilet, is that "john" is a distinctly *American* term—you won't hear people in Britain call the bathroom the "john" any more than you'll hear folks in the United States call it the "W.C." (Brit shorthand for "water closet").

Cousin John

So where does the term come from? Like many slang phrases, its origins aren't entirely clear. The tradition of calling an unknown or metaphorical person "John"—think John Doe, John Barleycorn, or even Johnny-on-the-spot—has been around for centuries.

The first recorded use of the term "john" to refer to the bathroom dates back to 1738 and is found in the rules that governed the actions of incoming Harvard freshmen: "No freshman," the rules say, "shall mingo against the College wall or go into the fellows' cuz john." Etymologists claim that "cuz john" was short for "cousin John," an 18th-century American slang term for the bathroom.

Cousin John's actual identity is a mystery, although he probably wasn't anybody in particular. Indeed, "going to visit cousin John" may have been little more than a euphemism for using the bathroom, in much the same way as "I'll be in my office" and "I'm going to see a man about a horse" have been used in more recent times. The word "mingo," incidentally, was slang for urinating, and it's rather amusing to note that the college elders at Harvard found it necessary to enact a rule that prohibited students from peeing on the sides of college buildings. On the other hand, it goes to show that the behavior of college students hasn't changed much in almost three centuries.

---

* Nearly 4 percent of American women claim that they never wear underwear.

* Rembrandt produced about 70 portraits of himself.

* The Pentagon goes through more than 600 rolls of toilet paper every day.

* The term "pumpkin head" comes from the pumpkin halves that were used as guides for haircuts in colonial Connecticut.

* Elvis Presley was a twin: His brother, Jesse Garon, died at birth. Elvis was born 35 minutes later and given the middle name "Aron" in honor of his father's friend, Aaron Kennedy.

Pardon My English

Indeed, is that what the French say when they swear? Not exactly.

✳ ✳ ✳ ✳

THEY PROBABLY SHOULD, but they don't. The phrase "Pardon my French" has an elusive origin, but it likely grew out of the long-standing rivalry between England and France. As a result of their history of mutual contempt, each country's everyday language contains many stock phrases and terms that denigrate the other.

The English have long thought of the French as champions of indecency and lewdness. As a result, the English used the terms "French pox" and "French disease" for syphilis and other venereal diseases as early as the 16th century. But the French weren't about to take this lying down. One of their more inventive phrases was *les Anglais ont débarqué*, which translates to "the English have landed." No big deal—until you learn that they used it to describe menstruation. This phrase probably stemmed from the bright red uniforms of the English soldiers who flooded into France to fight against Napoleon. The English were thus associated with an unwelcome crimson arrival.

In the 19th century, both countries came up with similar terms for things but swapped "French" and "English" as appropriate. A "French letter," for example, was an English euphemism for a condom, while a Frenchman would have preferred a *capote anglaise* (an "English hood"). "To take French leave" means "to leave without saying goodbye"; *filer à l'anglais* means "to flee like the English."

There isn't a similar symmetry with the phrase "Pardon my French." When the French swear and decide to apologize— after all, many people swear constantly without feeling sorry about it—they generally say, *Excusez moi* ("excuse me"), or they use another faintly regretful phrase. Such a response is logical, but hardly insulting. And what fun is that?

The Sign of the Devil

*The connection between the number 666 and evil has
its roots in the Bible's spooky Book of Revelation.*

✳ ✳ ✳ ✳

No, It Didn't Come from an Iron Maiden Song

LIKE MOST RELIABLE information on the subject, the link
between the Devil and the number 666 comes from the
Bible. And if you were a regular at Sunday school, you might
rightfully suspect that the explanation originates from the most
bizarre book of the Bible, the Book of Revelation.

The New Testament saved most of its creepy stuff for its final
act, in which we see Satan rise to power and destroy the world,
only to have Christ come back and pulverize him at the last
second. In Chapter 13 (how's that for spooky?) of the book, we
learn that an integral part of Satan's power-grab is sending an
emissary to Earth who will force its inhabitants to worship the
Devil. The chapter goes on to say that all who pledge allegiance
to this emissary must wear his mark on their hands or fore-
heads or else risk getting shut out of the new evil-topia.

Finally, at verse 18, we get this tidbit (depending on your
translation): "Wisdom is needed here; one who understands
can calculate the number of the beast, for it is a number that
stands for a person. His number is six hundred and sixty-six."
Thus, the number of both the Devil and the Antichrist is
revealed to be 666.

Why 666?

Many people have noted that this fact is unusually specific for
a book that otherwise deals with what are presumably symbols,
such as dragons coming out of the earth and fire shooting from
the sky. As with the interpretation of the Book of Revelation in
general, there has been a lot of debate about the precise meaning of this number.

On one side, there is the lunatic fringe, which ascribes the sign of the beast to whichever public figure has raised its ire. In the 1980s, for example, some malcontents pointed out that President Reagan's full name—Ronald Wilson Reagan—is composed of three six-letter groupings.

A more sane theory attributes the number 666 to the Roman emperor Nero. Nero blamed the Christians for the infamous burning of Rome in the first century A.D. and consequently started a brutal campaign of persecution against the fledgling religion. It is believed that the author of the Book of Revelation, John the Apostle, was attempting to send a coded message to his fellow Christians to give them hope that Nero's tyranny would soon come to an end.

To ensure that only other Christians would understand his message, John used Hebrew numerology. John chose Hebrew because it is the language of Judaism, the religion that Christianity grew out of after the arrival of Christ. In Hebrew, each letter corresponds to a number. The letters/numbers from Nero's full name in Hebrew, Neron Qeisar, add up to—you guessed it—666.

Essentially, John was telling his readers that Nero would be deposed, the persecution of the Christians would end, and Christ would return to start the Rapture. We're still waiting on John's third prediction to come true, but as a lesser prophet, Meatloaf, once said, "Two out of three ain't bad."

Say What?

A book is a version of the world. If you do not like it, ignore it; or offer your own version in return.

—SALMAN RUSHDIE

A business that makes nothing but money is a poor business.

—HENRY FORD

It's Definitely Not as Fun as Kick the Can

Some sociologists believe that we create so many euphemisms for death because we'd rather avoid the subject entirely, and the substitute labels help mask our discomfort. Apparently, we're more comfortable "kicking the bucket" than just dying.

✳ ✳ ✳ ✳

THERE ARE TWO possible origins of "kick the bucket," both appropriately morbid. The first involves the slaughter of pigs. In days of yore, a pig was hung up by its heels from a wooden beam after its throat was slit, allowing the blood to drain out. This beam was traditionally called a "bucket," possibly because the pigs were hoisted by means of a pulley system similar to that of an old-fashioned well. In the throes of death, the pig's heels would sometimes knock against the wood. Many a butcher heard the sound of a hog kicking the "bucket."

The second possibility comes from the act of suicide by hanging. In order to do this, a person must stand upon something, secure the noose around his or her neck, and either step down or kick the support away. In need of something small and easy to stand on, the theory goes, the person might choose a bucket. This explanation is compelling, except "kicking the bucket" doesn't refer exclusively to intentional death—the phrase is used to describe any kind of death.

Either way—whether the origin of "kicking the bucket" relates to slaughtered pigs or hangings—it isn't pretty. Of course, death is a dirty business, as evidenced by some other famous euphemisms that have been attached to it: buying the farm, pushing up daisies, taking a dirt nap, and going into the fertilizer business.

Grandpa, Stick Around a While: The Origins of Mummification

Turns out that the Egyptians—history's most famous embalmers—weren't the first. By the time Egyptians were fumbling with the art, Saharans and Andeans were veterans at mortuary science.

❋ ❋ ❋ ❋

Andes

IN NORTHERN CHILE and southern Peru, modern researchers have found hundreds of pre-Inca mummies (roughly 5000–2000 B.C.) from the Chinchorro culture. Evidently, the Chinchorros mummified all walks of life: rich, poor, young, old. We still don't know exactly why, but a simple, plausible explanation is that they wanted to honor and respect their dead.

The work shows the evolution of sophisticated, artistic techniques not much different from later African methods: Take out the wet stuff before it gets too gross, pack the body carefully, dry it out. The process occurred near the open-air oven we call the Atacama Desert, which may hold a clue in itself.

Uan Muhuggiag

The oldest known instance of deliberate mummification in Africa comes from ancient Saharan cattle ranchers. In southern Libya, at a rock shelter now called Uan Muhuggiag, archaeologists found evidence of basic seminomadic civilization, including animal domestication, pottery, and ceremonial burial.

We don't know why these people mummified a young boy, but they did a good job. Some date the remains to the 7400s B.C., others to the 3400s B.C. But even the most recent dating puts it before large-scale Egyptian practices. The remains demonstrate refinement and specialized knowledge that likely took centuries to develop. Quite possibly some of this knowledge filtered into Egyptian understanding, given that some of the other cultural finds at Uan Muhuggiag look pre-Egyptian as well.

Egypt

Some 7,000 to 12,000 years ago, Egyptians buried their dead in hot sand without wrapping. Given Egypt's naturally arid climate, the corpse sometimes dehydrated so quickly that decay was minimal. Sands shift, of course, which would sometimes lead to passersby finding an exposed body in surprisingly good shape. Perhaps this inspired early Egyptian mummification efforts.

As Egyptian civilization advanced, mummification interwove with their view of the afterlife. Professionals formalized and refined the process. A whole industry arose, offering funerary options from deluxe (special spices, carved wood case) to budget (dry 'em out and hand 'em back). *Natron,* a mixture of sodium salts abundant along the Nile, made a big difference. If you extracted the guts and brains from a corpse, then dried it in natron for a couple of months, the remains would keep for a long time. The earliest known Egyptian mummy dates to around 3300 B.C.

Desert Origins

It's hard to ignore a common factor among these cultures: proximity to deserts. It seems likely that ancient civilizations got the idea from seeing natural mummies.

Ice and bogs can also preserve a body by accident, of course, but they don't necessarily mummify it. Once exposed, the preservation of the remains depends on swift discovery and professional handling. If ancient Africans and South Americans developed mummification based on desert-dried bodies, it would explain why bogs and glaciers didn't lead to similar mortuary science. The ancients couldn't really keep a body frozen year-round, nor could they create a controlled minibog environment. But people could/did replicate the desert's action on human remains.

Today

We make mummies today, believe it or not. An embalmed corpse is a mummy—it's just a question of how far the embalmers go in their preservation efforts. To put it indelicately: If you've attended an open-casket funeral, you've seen a mummy.

Getting in Touch with Your Inner Dyngus

When was the last time you were awoken by the icy-cold sensation of a bucket of water being poured over your head? If you're among the thousands of folks who celebrate Dyngus Day, the answer is the day after Easter.

✳ ✳ ✳ ✳

DYNGUS DAY (also called Dingus Day, Easter Monday, Wet Monday, or *Smigus Dyngus*) is a Polish holiday that originated around A.D. 966, when Poland's Prince Mieszko I accepted Christianity and was baptized with his entire court. Since then, the celebration has evolved from an annual mock-baptism to a sort of courting ritual, during which a young man douses his dream girl in the hope that she'll be flattered.

Yes, you read that last sentence correctly. It seems like a strange tradition, but it's one still practiced today, especially in the communities of Buffalo, New York, and South Bend, Indiana. In those cities, everyone is packing at least a water pistol on Dyngus Day, and some more enterprising soakers make use of garden or even fire hoses.

Traditionally, however, Dyngus Day has meant more than just a water fight. In addition to the wet wake-up call, boys would fashion small whips out of pussy willow or birch branches and use them to strike their paramours on the shins. In Poland, where matchmaking is a big deal, a young girl who didn't receive these attentions was considered hopeless, romantically speaking.

Mercifully, the shin-swatting tradition has largely fallen by the wayside, and participants in Dyngus Day now focus almost exclusively on the irreverent fun that goes along with a citywide water war. Visitors to Poland, Buffalo, or South Bend on the day after Easter are advised to bring a few changes of clothes—and perhaps a bandolier of water balloons.

The Amount of Space Needed to Swing a Cat

If you were to put this well-worn phrase to the test—theoretically, of course—exactly how much room would be required?

✳ ✳ ✳ ✳

The Murky Origins of an Odd Phrase

QUARTERS ARE TIGHT here in the *Bizarre Truths* war room. Towers of folders that are overflowing with archival research teeter dangerously over our postage-stamp-size desks, where we slave away amongst a heady blend of ink, paper, and each other. It's not pleasant. Anyway, in our cramped office, the following phrase is frequently muttered with dismay: "There's not enough room in here to swing a cat." And that got us wondering: Just how much room might one need to accomplish the task?

To answer this question, we need to trace the phrase's origin. There are multiple theories, and no, they have nothing to do with the Jazz Age and all of its swingin' cats. Furthermore, according to the first explanation, the phrase might not even have anything to do with felines. It seems that back in the 17th and 18th centuries, any sailor in the British navy who misbehaved was rewarded with a flogging with a whip that featured nine knotted lashes. This menacing little device was known as a "cat o' nine tails." Because a great deal of open space was required for the whip to be used effectively—and because floggings were frequently done in view of other sailors as a lesson—the old cat o' nine tails was only broken out in a spacious area, such as the poop deck.

A second camp argues that the phrase originated with a medieval archery game in which a cat was put into a leather bag and swung from the nearest tree or rafter and used for target practice. This theory has some weaknesses, not the least of which is determining a conceivable reason for archers to practice so cruelly. There is also little historical evidence to back up this claim, though in Shakespeare's *Much Ado About Nothing*, the cantankerous Benedick says, "If I do, hang me in a bottle like a cat and shoot at me; and he that hits me, let him be clapped on the shoulder, and called Adam."

The Measurements

Neither of these theories seems to indicate that there was ever a time when people were swinging actual felines by the tail. But what if you wanted to? It seems clear that swinging a cat requires space, but just how much? Fortunately, we remember our geometry. Let's say that the average cat is about 24 inches long and that its tail is about 12 inches long. We also need space for our arms, and the average human male's arms are 28 inches long.

This means we'll need 64 inches, or more than five feet of swinging radius. Recalling our handy little formula for the area of a circle, we know that the total area required is 12,867 inches. Of course, most rooms aren't circular. The area of a square room with sides of 128 inches (the diameter of our circle) is about 114 square feet. In other words, a space far, far larger than our office.

Say What?

Where lipstick is concerned, the important thing is not color, but to accept God's final word on where your lips end.

—JERRY SEINFELD

Sometimes I wonder if men and women really suit each other. Perhaps they should live next door and just visit now and then.

—KATHARINE HEPBURN

The Original Bean Counters

The term "bean counters" evokes an unflattering image of an army of grim-faced, calculator-holding, briefcase-toting accountants. In the days of yore, accountants didn't really count beans, did they?

✳ ✳ ✳ ✳

BEANS HAVE LONG had negative connotations—and not just because they're the fruit that makes you toot. Think about it: The phrase "He doesn't know beans" suggests that someone is clueless, and "It doesn't amount to a hill of beans" means that something is meaningless or worthless. You would be hard-pressed, then, to find anything more boring or joyless than counting beans, which is partially why accountants are associated with this label.

One anecdotal explanation posits that the derogatory nickname originated in the 1920s, when the marketing and sales-analysis firm the Nielsen Company (now better known for its television ratings system) was just a fledgling operation. The story goes that founder A. C. Nielsen was so diligent in his analysis that his employees counted the beans one by one at grocery stores they were auditing.

This would have been an unimaginably excruciating exercise. And while this explanation certainly seems apt, it's probably not true, especially because the preferred unit of a crop economy is the bushel, not individual grains, seeds, ears, or legumes.

The term "bean counter" first surfaced in a 1975 *Forbes* article, in reference to a particularly careful accountant. It expanded to mean any accountant and then took on a negative implication, suggesting that accountants overlook value for numbers.

Today the term is used to describe any soulless individual who cares more about the bottom line than quality. In other words: "The bean counters in the corner offices have decided that you're expendable." It's little wonder that no one likes the bean counters.

The Wrong Side of the Bed: Left vs. Right

This is truly a matter of critical importance, lest you spend every minute of every day in a funk. Those who get up on the wrong side of the bed, as we all know, are a blight on society, casting a pall on everyone who comes into their presence.

✳   ✳   ✳   ✳

The Right Side Is the Right Side

To HELP YOU avoid being the one under the rain cloud, we'll let you in on the secret: It's the left side. Do whatever you have to do in order to get up on the right side—pushing your bed against the wall works nicely—and you should be fine.

But what's wrong with the left side? If you were a Roman living around the time of Julius Caesar, you might ask, "What *isn't* wrong with the left side?"

The ancient Romans distrusted everything having to do with the left: left-handedness, entering a house with the left foot forward, even setting the left foot down first when getting out of bed. If it could be done on the right side, with the right hand, or with the right foot, then that was the way it should be done.

Are Left-Handers Sinister?

There is an entire history of myths that associate evil with left-handedness. For instance, the devil is reputed to be left-handed, and it is with his left hand that he baptizes those who follow him. Or so they say. Also, according to the Satanic Bible, Satanists follow the "Left-Hand Path," which is the path opposite that of the Christian faith.

From the very beginning of recorded time, the left side has been viewed with suspicion. In fact, the Latin word for "left" (*sinistro*) is the root of the English word "sinister." In almost all cultures, there has been such a distrust of the left.

Left-handed people are no longer treated as devil worshippers, as they once were by practitioners of the Catholic faith. Sure, biases continue to exist—scissors, notebooks, and guitars all spring to mind—but lefties are treated as average human beings in most respects.

Still, just to be safe, remember to get up on the right side of the bed. That is to say, the correct side, which is also the right side. And just for good measure, you should probably let your right foot hit the floor first. Your day might be better for it.

---

* The Chinese are credited with inventing paper. The earliest form, made from hemp, was created in Shaanxi between 206 B.C. and A.D. 24. Cai Lun improved the paper-making process in A.D. 105.

* Lloyds of London paid out $3,019,400 in insurance claims to the families of the victims who perished in the *Titanic* disaster.

* One eyebrow can include as many as 550 hairs.

* Keelhauling was a punishment inflicted on sailors up until the middle of the 19th century. The victim would be pulled under the bow of a ship, which often resulted in drowning.

* The Sony Corporation was originally known as Totsuken, but the company changed its name because, rightly so, it was felt that Sony would be easier to pronounce.

* Bill Gates's first business was Traff-O-Data, a company that developed machines to record the number of vehicles passing selected road points.

* Brain surgery is often performed with the patient awake. Since the brain has no nerves, the patient doesn't feel any pain.

* In the last month of his life, Vincent van Gogh completed a painting a day.

* George Washington had only one tooth left by the time he was elected president. It is believed his loss of teeth was due to a mercury oxide treatment for malaria and smallpox.

* Over an entire lifetime, the average person sheds more than 40 pounds of skin.

Sloshy Slumber

Nothing says the 1980s like a waterbed. But is it possible the concept is much, much older than one would think?

✳ ✳ ✳ ✳

ALTHOUGH WATERBEDS WERE fixtures in university dorm rooms in the 1970s and 1980s, there is evidence to suggest that the Persians slept on goat skins filled with water more than 3,600 years ago. However, it's generally acknowledged that acclaimed Scottish physician Neil Arnott invented the first official waterbed in the early 1800s. The Hydrostatic Bed for Invalids—basically a trough of water covered with a rubber cloth—was designed to prevent bedsores. Its therapeutic value was noted by author Elizabeth Gaskell, who references a waterbed as a possible remedy for the character Mrs. Hale in her 1855 novel *North and South*. Mark Twain also mentions the waterbed in an 1871 article he wrote for *The New York Times*.

Curiously, Dr. Arnott did not patent his device, which allowed other inventors to create their own versions. Dr. William Hooper of Portsmouth, England, obtained the first waterbed patent in 1883. Resembling a giant hot-water bottle, Hooper's invention was cold and leaky, and thus it was a commercial flop, as were all the other waterbeds that followed it for decades to come. It wasn't until the invention of durable, waterproof fibers such as vinyl that the idea of a workable waterbed managed to stay afloat. In 1968, three students at San Francisco State University attempted to make a new and innovative chair by filling a large vinyl bag with cornstarch. Not surprisingly, these experiments failed. When they decided to switch their focus from sitting to sleeping and substituted fluid for cornstarch, the modern waterbed was born.

How Murphy Got His Own Law

Murphy's Law holds that if anything can go wrong, it will. Not surprisingly, the most widely circulated story about the origin of Murphy's Law involves a guy named Murphy.

✳ ✳ ✳ ✳

Project M3981

IN 1949, Captain Edward A. Murphy, an engineer at Edwards Air Force Base in California, was working on Project M3981. The objective was to determine the level of sudden deceleration a pilot could withstand in the event of a crash. It involved sending a dummy or a human subject (possibly also a dummy) on a high-speed sled ride that came to a sudden stop and then measuring the effects.

George E. Nichols, a civilian engineer with Northrop Aircraft, was the manager of the project. Nichols compiled a list of "laws" that presented themselves during the course of the team's work. For example, Nichols's Fourth Law is, "Avoid any action with an unacceptable outcome."

"If There Is Any Way to Do It Wrong..."

These sled runs were repeated at ever-increasing speeds, often with Dr. John Paul Stapp, an Air Force officer, in the passenger seat. After one otherwise-flawless run, Murphy discovered that one of his technicians had miswired the sled's transducer, so no data had been recorded. Cursing his subordinate, Murphy remarked, "If there is any way to do it wrong, he'll find it." Nichols added this little gem to his list, dubbing it Murphy's Law.

Not long after, Stapp endured a run that subjected him to 40 Gs of force during deceleration without substantive injury. Prior to Project M3981, the established acceptable standard had been 18 Gs, so the achievement merited a news conference. Asked how the project had maintained such an impeccable safety record, Stapp cited the team's belief in Murphy's Law and its efforts to circumvent it. The law, which had been revised to its current language before the news conference, was quoted in a variety of aerospace articles and advertisements and gradually found its way into the lexicon of the military and of pop culture.

Beyond Murphy

It's important to note that "laws" that are remarkably similar to Murphy's—buttered bread always lands face down; anything that can go wrong at sea will go wrong, sooner or later—had been in circulation for at least a hundred years prior to Project M3981. But even if Edward Murphy didn't break new ground when he cursed a technician in 1949, it's his "law" we quote when things go wrong, and that's all right.

---

* It's been rumored that SPAM stands for "SPiced hAM." Not so, says Hormel, the company that makes the canned meat. Their official stance on the topic: "In the end, SPAM means SPAM."

* An umpire at the first professional baseball game was given a six-cent fine for using profanity.

* Vincent van Gogh didn't die until two days after he shot himself.

* An average human eats about 60,000 pounds of food in his or her lifetime.

* Ketchup was first created in China.

* The world's largest Kentucky Fried Chicken is located in the Chinese city of Beijing.

* Americans spend more cash on cat food than on baby food each year.

* Croissants are a bit of a mystery. No one is sure when they were invented or where. One story goes that croissants were invented in 1680, after the people of Vienna defeated the invading Turks. A local baker made pastries in the shape of the crescent moon on the Turkish flag as a reminder that the Viennese had "devoured" the Turks.

* Israel's postage stamps use kosher adhesive.

* Passing gas in a NASA spacesuit can damage it.

The World in Wax

Madame Tussaud's waxworks might seem like a fun place for a "celebrity" encounter, but there is a little-known dark side to the origins of wax portraiture.

✳ ✳ ✳ ✳

MADAME TUSSAUD'S OF London exhibits wax portraits of historical persons and contemporary celebrities, tableaux of significant events, and a Chamber of Horrors. It remains the most well-known collection of wax figures in the world.

Born Marie Grosholtz in 1761 in Strasbourg, France, Madame Tussaud learned her craft from an uncle, Dr. Philippe Curtius of Bern, Switzerland. Dr. Curtius made wax models of human limbs and organs as medical teaching tools because cadavers were so difficult to obtain. A talented modeler, Dr. Curtius extended his business to include miniature portraits in wax.

Around 1770, Dr. Curtius moved to Paris to open a wax studio and an exhibition of life-size figures of prominent people. A few years later, Marie became his apprentice at the studio. At age 17, she made a portrait of Voltaire, which still survives.

Madame Tussaud's Exhibitions

Marie inherited her uncle's talent for wax portraiture, and she began teaching wax modeling to the royal court at Versailles. Soon the young artist was caught up in the winds of political change as the French Revolution swept the country with a fury. Marie was arrested for having royalist sympathies, but the revolutionaries spared her life in order to put her skills to use. She produced death masks of some of the most famous royal heads ever to be severed by the bloody guillotine, including Louis XVI and Marie Antoinette. She also modeled the head and body of revolutionary Marat, who was stabbed to death in his bath by Charlotte Corday.

Marie married engineer Francois Tussaud in 1795, and the couple had two sons. Unfortunately, the marriage failed, and in

1802, Madame Tussaud and her children moved to London, taking 70 wax exhibits with them. For 33 years, Marie toured the United Kingdom with her wax figures and tableaux, generating a loyal following for her exhibition of history come to life.

At age 74, she acquired a permanent home for her waxworks on Baker Square in London. Among Marie's most famous wax figures was a self-portrait modeled by her own hand when she was 81. Marie died on April 6, 1850, but her waxworks continued to expand. In 1884, the museum and studio were moved to their present site on Marylebone Road, and descendants of Madame Tussaud continued her craft until great-great-grandson Bernard Tussaud died in 1967. Wax figures are still produced by Madame Tussaud's for their museums.

The Legacy of Madame Tussaud

A living witness to some of the most important events in history, Madame Tussaud excelled at re-creating important historical figures and events. Though waxworks today tend to focus on movie stars and celebrities, many of them are still dedicated to re-creating history—offering children a chance to experience that history in a colorful, unpretentious venue.

Marie was also party to another side of history—a darker, more notorious side not found in schoolbooks. Who can say what effect making death masks of guillotine victims had on the young woman caught in the middle of a revolution? One of the most famous rooms in Madame Tussaud's is the Chamber of Horrors, where murderers and tyrants executing their brutal, bloody deeds are captured for all eternity. Also featured are instruments of torture and tools of murder. Later wax museums followed Madame Tussaud's lead and included their own chambers of horrors, making this type of exhibit standard. Yet, few had first-hand knowledge of the dark side of history like Marie Grosholtz Tussaud. For decades, the centerpiece of Madame Tussaud's Chamber of Horrors was a working model of a guillotine, which she displayed in the "Separate Room."

Dead Flowers

Nothing brightens a grave site quite like a bouquet
or two, but how did this tradition get started?

✳ ✳ ✳ ✳

A Path to the Next World

THIS TRADITION CAN be traced to the ancient Greeks, who performed rites over graves that were called *Zoai*. Flowers were placed on the resting places of Greek warriors; it was believed that if the flowers took root and blossomed, the souls of the warriors were declaring that they had found happiness in the next world.

The ancient Romans also used flowers to honor soldiers who died in battle. The Romans held an elaborate eight-day festival during February called *Parentalia* ("Day of the Fathers"), during which roses and violets were placed on the graves of fallen soldiers by friends and family members.

Coming to America

According to historian Jay Winik, the tradition took root in America at the end of the Civil War, after a train had delivered Abraham Lincoln to his final resting place in Springfield, Illinois. In his Civil War book *April 1865*, Winik writes: "Searching for some way to express their grief, countless Americans gravitated to bouquets of flowers: lilies, lilacs, roses, and orange blossoms, anything which was in bloom across the land. Thus was born a new American tradition: laying flowers at a funeral."

Following Lincoln's burial, people all over the country began decorating the graves of the more than 600,000 soldiers who had been killed—especially in the South, where women's groups also placed banners on the graves of soldiers. The practice became so widespread that in 1868, General John Alexander Logan—the leader of the Grand Army of the Republic, a Union veterans' group—issued an order designating May 30 as a day for "strewing with flowers or otherwise decorating the graves of comrades who died in defense of their country." The day was originally called Decoration Day, but it later became known as Memorial Day. On May 30, 1868, thousands gathered at Arlington National Cemetery in Virginia to decorate more than 20,000 graves of Civil War soldiers. In 1873, New York became the first state to declare Decoration Day a legal holiday.

A Boon to the Flower Industry

Today, the tradition is stronger than ever. In addition to being placed on graves, flowers are often displayed in funeral homes and churches for burial services. The most elaborate arrangements are positioned around the casket, perhaps a hopeful hearkening back to the belief of the ancient Greeks that a flower in bloom signifies happiness in the afterlife.

---

* Three Musketeers candy bars got their name because they used to have three layers: vanilla, chocolate, and strawberry. Now, the bars only have chocolate.

* A cat sweats through its paws.

* A cell phone in 1984 would have cost you just under $4,000.

* The screwdriver was somehow invented before the screw.

* Belgium once experimented with using cats to deliver mail.

* The human ear has nine muscles, though they are mostly nonfunctional.

* Reading about yawning is enough to make many people yawn.

* An average male beard would grow 13 feet long over a lifetime if never shaved.

* Female turkeys don't gobble.

* The "dog days of summer" refers to the ancient Roman belief that Sirius, the Dog Star, was closer to Earth from July 3 to August 11, causing unusually high temperatures.

* Dominoes were developed as a game by French monks and named after the first lines of Psalm 110, which in Latin reads *Dixit Dominus meo* ("said my Lord").

Chapter 17

Bizarre Truths About This and That

Just Don't Stick Those Dollar Bills in the Washing Machine

If only the black art of money laundering were as simple as putting your cash through a spin cycle or two.

✳ ✳ ✳ ✳

Hiding the Loot

You KNOCK OVER an armored car and suddenly your mattress is overflowing with cash. But if you enjoy your ill-gotten gains by treating yourself to something big—a mega-yacht, say—the Feds will want to know where the money came from. And if you can't point to a legitimate source, it's off to the big house with you.

When faced with this dilemma, criminals turn to money laundering, the process of making "dirty" money look "clean"—in other words, making it appear that the money is legitimate income. For relatively small amounts of dirty cash, the go-to trick is to set up a front: a business that can record the cash as profit. For example, Al Capone owned laundromats all over Chicago so that he could disguise the income from his illegal liquor business as laundry profits (how appropriate). There wasn't any way to know how much money people really spent at the laundromat, so all the profit appeared to be legitimate.

On a larger scale—when drug traffickers take in millions, say—the laundromat doesn't really work; a more complex ruse is needed. But no matter how elaborate the scheme, it usually has three basic steps: placement, layering, and integration.

Step One: Placement

In this stage, the goal is to get the cash into the financial system, which usually means depositing it into some kind of accounts. In the United States, banks report transactions above $10,000 to authorities, so one placement strategy is to make small cash deposits into multiple bank accounts over time. Another is to deposit the money in a bank in a country with lax oversight.

Step Two: Layering

The goal in layering is to shift the money through the financial system in such a complicated way that nobody can trace it back to the crime. The criminals try to disguise the fact that they put the money into the financial system in the first place. Every time launderers move money between accounts, convert it into different currency, or buy or sell anything—particularly in a country with lax laws—it adds a layer of confusion to the trail.

Step Three: Integration

Finally, in the integration stage, the criminals get the money back by some means that looks legitimate. For example, they might arrange to have an offshore company hire them as generously paid consultants, so the money looks like personal income.

Money laundering is big business and key to drug trafficking, embezzling, even terrorism. Many nations have beefed up laws and boosted enforcement to crack down on money laundering, but it won't stop unless everyone is vigilant. As long as there are countries with lax financial regulations that trade in the world economy, criminals will have a way to launder their funds.

So, if you've been scrubbing your ill-gotten cash in the kitchen sink and hanging it on the line to dry, don't waste your time. You're doing it wrong.

Who's Rushing?

The term "rush hour" was coined in New York around 1890, presumably to describe the frantic pace of life in the city. In today's world, it refers to peak times for traffic. But really, could there be a more blatant misnomer?

✳ ✳ ✳ ✳

THE TERM "RUSH HOUR" makes no sense. First the "rush" part—no one can rush because there are too many cars on the road. Oh, sure, there's the occasional bonehead who's weaving back and forth, changing lanes, and tailgating every car he gets behind, as if his manic behavior is going to somehow make everyone else suddenly, magically speed up. "Rush" in this sense refers not to speed, but to the rush of commuters flooding the transportation system—not just the roads, but also public transportation, where finding a seat can be nearly impossible.

Then you've got the "hour" part. The "hour" in rush hour may be even more misleading than the "rush" part. If you live in anything resembling a large city, you know that this "hour" lasts a heck of a lot longer than 60 minutes. In the morning, the roads can start to get hopelessly clogged by 7:00 A.M., and they stay that way until past 9:00 A.M. In the evening, you're talking 4:00 P.M. to 7:00 P.M.

No, this is not your traditional chronological hour. This definition of "hour" is one of those secondary classifications—a vague, unmeasured block of time. Not unlike the way it's used in "happy hour," which, come to think of it, is not a bad way to bypass rush-hour frustration altogether.

Not All Graves Are Created Equal

Today, going out in style is retiring to a house with a fishing boat docked out front. Centuries ago, people looked at things a bit differently. Forget cozy cottages and rainbow trout—we're talking gold-plated resting places for your bones in the afterlife.

✳ ✳ ✳ ✳

So Many Choices

PEOPLE ONCE HAD to tackle decisions on tombs, sarcophagi, crypts, and sepulchers that make today's debates over whether to splurge on the cherry casket for Grandma seem pretty straightforward. What are the differences between these burial places?

The Good Old Tomb

Let's start with the easy one. A tomb can be something as simple as a hole in the ground, but it typically refers to a structure or vault for interment below or above ground. It can also mean a memorial shrine above a grave—a tradition that may have humbly started in prehistoric times, when families buried their dead underneath their dwellings. In the Middle Ages, Christian tombs became breathtaking structures that sometimes saw entire churches built over the graves of departed dignitaries. In 1066, for example, King Edward the Confessor was entombed in front of the high altar at Westminster Abbey in Great Britain.

Tales from the Crypt

A crypt is a specific type of tomb, usually a vault or chamber built beneath a church. Outstanding servants of a particular church—bishops, for example, or extremely loyal parishioners—are often buried in the crypt underneath. Centuries ago in Europe, these vast burial chambers also served as meeting places. We suspect, however, that no one held Christmas parties in them.

Between a Rock and a Hard Place: The Sepulcher

A sepulcher is another old-timey word for a tomb or place of burial. It often describes tombs carved out of rock or built from stone. Usually when the word "sepulcher" is thrown around, it's in reference to the tomb in which Jesus was laid to rest, a sepulcher near Calvary. The reputed site is commemorated by the Church of the Holy Sepulchre, which was dedicated in the 4th century, destroyed and rebuilt several times, and is now visited by thousands of tourists every year.

The Sarcophagus Was Good Enough for Tut

Finally, a sarcophagus is a bit different from the other three burial places we've described in that the term generally refers to an elaborate casket that isn't sunk into the ground. The oldest are from Egypt, box-shaped with separate lids; later Egyptian sarcophagi were often shaped like the body. The most famous sarcophagus holds Egypt's Tutankhamun, better known as King Tut. Discovered in 1922, Tut's sarcophagus is made of quartzite, has reliefs of goddesses carved into the sides, and sports a heavy granite lid.

In today's world, the good ol' hole in the ground is the most popular choice for burial. After that retirement house on the lake has been paid off, there usually isn't enough money left to do up death in King Tut style.

---

* Ancient Romans believed the walnut was a physical model of the brain: The hard shell was the skull, the papery partition was the membrane, and the two pieces of nut were the two hemispheres of the brain.

* The most frequently performed school plays are *Seussical* and *A Midsummer Night's Dream,* followed by *Grease* and *The Crucible.*

* The most often portrayed characters in literature are Sherlock Holmes and Dracula.

* Silly Putty was the result of a failed attempt by General Electric to create a synthetic rubber for use in World War II. Seeing that it had no industrial uses, the sticky substance was marketed as a toy instead.

* Most American car horns honk in the key of F.

High Tide: Tales of Survival

When it comes to staring down death, very little beats grueling tales of survival for days, weeks—even months—lost at sea.

✳ ✳ ✳ ✳

Hold On Tight

Ocean-going tales of survival have a certain mythic status. They bring to mind epic travels and age-old yarns of sea monsters and mermaids. Yet legend aside, even factually verified survival stories seem implausible. To be stranded on the sea (and live to tell the tale) seems, well, unreal.

A hierarchy applies when gauging the relative extremity of a sea survival story. Those in cold water are worst off, since hypothermia sets in within minutes. Survival time also depends on whether the person is holding onto something or treading water. Survival time is also cut short by solitude—humans have a tough time being alone for extended periods. The best-case scenario, if one exists, is to be stranded on a boat, in warm water, with some comrades. What follows are some recent record breakers that run the gamut of these hapless scenarios:

Juan Jesus Caamano: Survived 13 hours with no boat in cold waters

In 2001, a fishing boat capsized off the coast of Spain. Nine of the 16 men made it into a lifeboat; another two jumped into the frigid waters without bodysuits (and died immediately), while five more got their suits on before the boat sank.

Two of those five were 36-year-old Juan Jesus Caamano and his brother-in-law. Their boat had sent out a mayday signal before sinking, so planes, helicopters, and ships from several countries were sent to look for the victims. After only four hours, the nine men in the lifeboat were saved. Experts, who estimated a man in Caamano's circumstances could survive a maximum of 3¹/₂ hours, were surprised when, after 13 hours, Caamano was found alive, afloat in the stormy waters, tied to his dead brother-in-law. In all, six men died.

Laura Isabel Arriola de Guity: Survived six days; found clinging to driftwood in warm waters

In 1998, Hurricane Mitch ravished Central and Latin America, killing more than 7,000 people in Honduras alone. Isabella Arriola, 32, lived in a small coastal Honduran village that was literally swept away by the ocean. She survived for six days with no life jacket, drifting in and out of consciousness, while clinging to driftwood. She survived high waves and winds of 185 mph. Arriola was eventually spotted by a coastguard aircraft and was rescued by helicopter. Unfortunately, her husband, children, and half her village had perished in the storm.

Steven Callahan: Survived 76 days on a small raft

In 1982, Steven Callahan, a naval architect, was participating in a sailing race when his boat was damaged during a storm and sank in the Atlantic Ocean. Callahan managed to salvage a tiny amount of food before setting off in an inflatable rubber raft. He survived for 76 days on rainwater, fish, and seabirds before being rescued by a fishing boat. Callahan's extensive background and experience with the high seas helped him survive the ordeal. He holds the longest known record for surviving alone on a raft.

Maralyn and Maurice Bailey: Survived 117 days on a small raft

In 1973, Britons Maralyn and Maurice Bailey set out on a voyage from England to New Zealand on their yacht, which was struck by a large whale and capsized off the coast of Guatemala. Maurice was an expert on maritime survival skills; before they boarded their rubber raft, they collected a small amount of food, a compass, a map, an oil burner, water containers, and glue. When they ran out of food, they caught sea animals with safety pins fashioned into hooks. After two months, the raft started to disintegrate and needed constant care. Finally, 117 days later, a Korean fishing boat rescued them.

When One Life Sentence Isn't Enough

There are good reasons for multiple life sentences, and they don't have anything to do with reincarnation.

✳ ✳ ✳ ✳

JUDGES HAND DOWN multiple sentences to punish multiple criminal offenses. Multiple charges may be decided in the same trial, but they are still considered separate crimes and often yield separate punishments. Even in cases of life imprisonment, multiple sentences can be very important in the rare instances in which convictions are overturned on appeal.

Say a jury finds a man guilty of killing five people. The judge might sentence him to five life sentences. Even if any one of the convictions is overturned (or even if four of them are overturned), the murderer still has to serve a life sentence. To walk free, he would have to be exonerated of all five murders.

Furthermore, "life" doesn't always mean an entire lifetime. Depending on the sentencing guidelines of the state, the judge may sentence a man to life imprisonment with the possibility of parole. In this instance, life is the maximum length of the sentence, meaning that the defendant could conceivably go free if a parole board releases him after he's served the minimum time (30 years, for example).

If, however, a defendant is convicted on multiple charges, the judge may hand down multiple life sentences with the possibility of parole—but the judge can also specify that those sentences are to be served consecutively rather than concurrently. This way, the prisoner will not get a parole hearing until the minimum time for all the sentences put together has been served.

Consider multiple life sentences to be a safeguard, a way to ensure that the bad guys never see the light of day.

Are You Going to Eat That Jesus?

Images of religious icons sometimes show up in the oddest places. Some people believe they are divine. What's the story?

✳ ✳ ✳ ✳

SIGHTINGS OF RELIGIOUS symbols or images, called religious simulacra, in unexpected places are now part of pop culture. Many people consider them miraculous events. Some also claim that the objects have special beneficial properties.

Jesus and Mary

For Christians, Jesus and the Virgin Mary are among the most significant religious figures, and not coincidentally, they also seem to make the most common appearances—often in food. Perhaps the quintessential sighting of a Christian religious symbol in food occurred in 1978, when a New Mexico woman named Maria Rubio was making a burrito. She noticed that a burn on the tortilla appeared to be in the shape of Jesus' head. After receiving the blessing of a priest, she built a shrine to house the tortilla and even quit her job to tend to the shrine full-time.

Islamic Words

Religious sightings do not always involve Christian figures or symbols. In the Islamic world, the perception of the Arabic word for Allah roughly parallels the sighting of Jesus and other religious figures by Christians. Similarly, the objects involved sometimes have mystical properties ascribed to them. In 2006, a Kazakh farmer discovered an egg that villagers claimed had the name of *Allah* on its shell. After the sighting was verified by the local mosque, the farmer who discovered the egg decided to keep it, saying, "We don't think it'll go bad." The name of *Allah* has also been sighted on fish scales, beans, and tomato slices.

Selling Simulacra

Sightings of religious images can have commercial as well as spiritual implications. In 1996, someone at a coffee shop in

Nashville, Tennessee, discovered a cinnamon bun that bore a striking resemblance to Mother Teresa. The coffee shop parlayed the discovery into a line of merchandise, including coffee mugs and T-shirts. The merchandise was marketed with a NunBun trademark after Mother Teresa asked the shop to stop using the phrase "Immaculate Confection."

The proliferation of Internet auction sites such as eBay has created a market for such objects. One of the best-known auctions occurred in 2004, when a woman named Diane Duyser used eBay to auction part of a grilled cheese sandwich she claimed bore the image of the Virgin Mary. Duyser asserted that the sandwich, which she had been storing since it was made in 1994, had never grown moldy and had brought her good luck, allowing her to win $70,000 at a casino. The sandwich was purchased by another casino for $28,000.

Religious sightings are not always viewed positively. In 1997, Nike produced several models of basketball shoes that unintentionally featured a logo that, when viewed from right to left, resembled the Arabic word for Allah. The Council on American-Islamic Relations (CAIR) quickly demanded an apology, and Nike recalled the shoes. The settlement between Nike and CAIR also included Arabic training for Nike graphic designers and Nike-built playgrounds in Muslim communities.

A Scientific Explanation?

While the parties involved in sightings of religious symbols often consider them to be miraculous in nature, the prevailing scientific view is that, rather than miraculous, they are occurrences of pareidolia, a psychological phenomenon in which random stimuli are interpreted as being meaningful in some way. As part of its intellectual process, the mind tries to make sense of what may be unrelated images. This is the same phenomenon that psychologists credit with forming the likeness of a man in the moon or shapes in clouds. It's also what's involved when the brain creates pictures from the famous Rorschach inkblots.

Air Sickness: True Stories of People Being Sucked Out of Planes

All sorts of objects—including human beings—can be hurled out of shattered windows, broken doors, and other holes in the skin of an aircraft in flight. The problem in any case like this is explosive decompression, a situation in which the keys to survival include the height at which the plane is flying and the size of the aircraft cabin itself.

✳ ✳ ✳ ✳

Pressure Drop

MOST PASSENGER PLANES are pressurized to approximate an altitude of 8,000 feet or less. If there is a break in the skin of the plane at an altitude considerably higher than that—commercial jets normally fly at 30,000 feet or more—all sorts of bad things can happen. And quickly. For one thing, a lack of oxygen will render most people unconscious in little more than a minute at 35,000 feet.

As for being sucked out of the plane, this sort of tragedy generally occurs when the decompression is very sudden. The difference in pressure between the inside and outside of the plane causes objects to be pulled toward the opening. Whether or not someone survives sudden decompression depends on several things, including luck.

Fogg Nearly Disappears into the Fog

Critical care nurse Chris Fogg was almost sucked out of a medical evacuation plane on a flight from Twin Falls, Idaho, to

Seattle in 2007. Fogg had not yet buckled his seat belt when a window exploded while the plane was flying at approximately 20,000 feet. His head and right arm were pulled out of the window, but Fogg held himself inside the aircraft with his left hand on the ceiling and his knees jammed against a wall.

Fogg, who weighed 220 pounds, summoned enough strength to push himself backward, which allowed air to flow between his chest and the window. This broke the seal that had wedged him in the opening. The pilot managed to get the plane to a lower altitude, and everyone aboard—including a patient who had been hooked to an oxygen device—survived the ordeal.

Tales of Terror

Not everyone has been so fortunate in cases of explosive decompression. In 1989, a lower cargo door on a United Airlines flight came loose at 23,000 feet, and the loss of pressure tore a hole in the cabin. Nine passengers were sucked out of the plane, along with their seats and the carpeting around them. A year earlier, an 18-foot portion of roof tore off an Aloha Airlines flight at 24,000 feet, hurling a flight attendant out into the sky.

Although scenes of people and debris whistling all over the place in adventure movies have been exaggerated, the threat of explosive decompression is real—even if it is rare. It's a good idea to take the crew's advice about wearing your seat belt at all times, and if there is a sudden loss of oxygen, put on that mask in a hurry. They're not kidding about the possible consequences.

* President Gerald Ford was a male model in his youth.

* The rubber band was patented in 1845, a year after Charles Goodrich discovered vulcanization.

* Liberty Island, the location of the Statue of Liberty, was called Bedloe's Island until President Eisenhower approved the name change in 1956.

* People share their mattress and pillow with up to ten million dust mites, each of which is about a hundredth of an inch long.

Nauseating Info About "New-Car Smell"

Actually, the scent we all know and love should be called "volatile organic chemical off-gassed vapor." That's a far more accurate—and unsettling—description.

✳ ✳ ✳ ✳

It's Not What You Think

YOU MAY THINK of "new-car smell" as the aroma of cleanliness, but chemically speaking, it's quite the opposite. The distinctive odor is a heady mix of potentially toxic chemicals from the plastics, sealants, adhesives, upholstery, paint, and foam that make up car interiors. Many of the chemicals in these materials are volatile organic compounds. The key word here is "volatile"—these compounds can evaporate at normal temperatures in a process known as "off-gassing." In other words, when the material is new, some of it turns from a solid to a gaseous vapor, and you breathe it all in while you cruise around showing off your new wheels. Heat things up by parking your car in the sun and you get an especially rich chemical cloud.

I Love the Smell of Formaldehyde in the Morning

Don't think the term "organic" means that the chemicals are good for you—it merely signifies that they are carbon-based. In 2006, the nonprofit group the Ecology Center released a report showing that new cars emit potentially dangerous chemicals from manufacturing, and at much higher concentrations than in a new home or building. The study identified phthalates—a class of chemicals used to make PVC plastic more flexible—as one of the biggest problems. Some varieties of phthalates cause liver, reproductive, and learning issues in lab animals, and they may be carcinogenic.

The study also cited polybrominated diphenyl ethers (PBDEs), which are commonly used as fire retardants in cars, as a major concern. Research shows that PDBEs can cause neurodevelopment and liver problems. Other nasty new-car chemicals include formaldehyde (also used as an embalming fluid) and toluene (a noxious chemical that is also found in gasoline and paint thinner). Wonderful, huh?

Car manufacturers (and crafty salesmen) may also spray interiors with a "new-car smell" perfume in order to add more zest to their products. This fragrance may not be as bad for you as the phthalates and PBDEs, but it contains questionable chemicals, too.

The good news is that the Ecology Center report and other studies have spurred carmakers to reduce the use of potentially dangerous materials in new cars. For example, Toyota has developed an alternative car plastic made from sugar cane and corn, while Ford has come up with a soy-based foam for its seats. Don't you just love soy-based smell?

---

* **A bank in Vernal, Utah, was built from bricks delivered by the U.S. Postal Service in 1916. The builders discovered that it was cheaper to mail them than to ship them from Salt Lake City.**

* **The Museum of the Royal College of Surgeons of England acquired two sections of Napoleon's intestine in 1841. The specimens were destroyed during the Battle of Britain in World War II.**

* **Sports you don't see at the Olympics anymore: golf, lacrosse, croquet, waterskiing, powerboating, and rugby. Each of these were official events at one time or another.**

* **Prince Albert, who would later become King George VI of England, played doubles at Wimbledon with partner Louis Grieg. His parents, King George V and Queen Mary, were there to watch the match.**

* **Empress Elizabeth of Austria was assassinated in Geneva by Italian anarchist Luigi Lucheni in 1898. When asked why he committed the act, Lucheni stated, "I wanted to kill a royal. It did not matter which one."**

* **Cal Hubbard is the only person inducted into three different sports halls of fame: baseball, college football, and pro football.**

Curious World Currencies

Paper, coins, and plastic are what we use as money today, but that wasn't always the case. Throughout history, people have used various animals, vegetables, and minerals to conduct business.

✳   ✳   ✳   ✳

COWS REPRESENT THE oldest of all forms of money, dating from as early as 9000 B.C. The words "capital," "chattels," and "cattle" have a common root, and the word "pecuniary" (meaning "financial") comes from pecus, the Latin word for cattle. But cattle weren't the only livestock used as legal tender: Until well into the 20th century, the Kirghiz (a Turkic ethnic group found primarily in Kyrgyzstan) used horses for large exchanges, sheep for lesser trades, and lambskins for barters that required only small change.

Cowry shells—marine snails found chiefly in tropical regions—were the medium of exchange used in China around 1200 B.C. These shells were so widely traded that their pictograph became the symbol for money in the written language. The earliest metallic money in China were cowries made of bronze or copper.

Throughout history, salt and pepper have been used as money, owing to their value as seasonings and preservatives and for their importance in religious ceremonies. In ancient Rome, salt was used as money. (*Sal*, the Latin word for salt, is the root of the English word "salary.") Roman workers were paid with salt, hence the expression "worth one's salt." And in England in the Middle Ages, rent could be paid in peppercorns.

The largest form of money are 12-foot limestone coins from the Micronesian island of Yap. A coin's value was determined by its size. Displaying a large one outside your home was a sign of status and prestige. Because of the coins' size and immobility, islanders would often trade only promises of ownership instead of the actual coins. Approximately 6,800 coins still exist around the island, though the U.S. dollar is now the official currency.

The Dirtiest Place in the House

Believe it or not, there's a place in the house that's even grosser than the toilet or the trash can. We're talking about the kitchen sink.

✳ ✳ ✳ ✳

A Sea of Scuzz

How can the place where you wash things get so icky? Well, most people use the kitchen sink to rinse and prepare items such as chicken carcasses and store-bought produce. According to Dr. Philip Tierno, director of New York University's microbiology department and the author of *The Secret Life of Germs*, these raw foods carry tons of potential pathogens, including salmonella, campylobacter, and *E. coli.* And you're just splashing and spreading them around.

Right now, your kitchen sink's faucet handles and basin are probably teeming with microscopic creepy-crawlies. In fact, there are typically more than 500,000 bacteria per square inch in the sink drain alone! The average garbage bin has only about 411 bacteria per square inch. Grossed out yet? Well, there's more.

What about those damp dishrags and sponges that you toss into the sink, the ones you use to wipe the kitchen counter? Tierno says they can hold "literally billions of bacteria." Dr. Charles Gerba (aka Dr. Germ), an environmental microbiology professor at the University of Arizona, suggests that it might be better for you to live like a slob than to meticulously clean kitchen surfaces with a salmonella-laden sponge. According to Gerba's findings, your kitchen sink is dirtier than a post-flush toilet bowl.

Cleaning 101

Done gagging? Alright, then grab your trusty scrub brush. You can have a much cleaner kitchen sink in a jiffy. Just mix one tablespoon of chlorine bleach with one quart of water, and use this solution to scrub your sink basin clean. Tierno recommends you do this twice a week.

Weird Fetishes

Although most people give the word fetish a sexual connotation, the dictionary also describes a fetish as "any object or idea eliciting unquestioning reverence, respect, or devotion." Since that covers a wide range of territory, here are just a few of the more interesting fetishes reported of late.

✳ ✳ ✳ ✳

✳ A Tennessee man complained that his home had been burgled; among other things stolen were more than 300 tongue rings.

✳ A British machinist with bad earaches was found to have a pregnant spider living in his ear. He told a reporter that he had grown fond of the spider and intended to keep it as a pet.

✳ A 12-year-old Michigan boy has had an obsession with vacuum cleaners since infancy, when according to his mother, he was mesmerized by the whirring noise. The boy enjoys vacuuming so much that he does the house up to five times a day with one of the 165 vacuum cleaners in his collection. Said a teacher, "It's not that he doesn't like recess, it's just that he prefers to stay in and clean."

✳ A Canadian woman really likes her daily newspaper. She not only reads it, but she eats it in strips and has done so for the past seven years—because it tastes good. Her only problem occurred when she developed a blockage of her esophagus, whereupon doctors found a ball of paper. After removing it, her doctors said that aside from the obstruction, eating newspaper is not bad for your health.

✳ In Detroit, a man was arrested for the seventh time—this time for stealing a mannequin outfitted in a French maid's uniform. The arrest came days after he was released for his sixth offense: stealing a mannequin with bobbed hair displaying a pink dress.

Pet-Rock Peculiarities

How many gullible people became the proud owners of a Pet Rock by Christmas morning of 1975? At least 1.3 million.

✳ ✳ ✳ ✳

The Perfect Alternative to Messy Pets

REMARKABLY, THAT FIGURE of 1.3 million counts only the original Pet Rocks. In the months before Christmas, thousands of cheaper imitations were also sold, and no one can guess how many of those changed hands.

Gary Dahl, the marketing genius who thought up the Pet Rock, got the idea from listening to his friends complain about their troublesome pets. He persuaded a former boss to back him financially and arranged to haul two and a half tons of pebbles from Rosarita Beach in Mexico to his Northern California headquarters. After packaging them in carrying crates filled with nesting straw and cut with air holes, he introduced the Pet Rock at gift shows that autumn.

An Instant Millionaire

Soon Dahl was shipping thousands of rocks per day to stores such as Neiman-Marcus and Macy's. Dahl earned 95 cents for every authentic Pet Rock sold at $3.95. He became a millionaire three weeks before Christmas, appeared on TV talk shows, and was written up in *Newsweek, People,* and many major newspapers.

What sparked such an insane fad? Dahl took a stab at explaining it, saying, "I think the country was depressed and needed a giggle." He was probably right, because for most people, the real fun of having a Pet Rock was reading the manual. Written by Dahl and titled *The Care and Training of Your PET ROCK*, the 32-page booklet described how to teach your new pet basic commands such as "Stay," "Sit," and "Play dead." Although rocks learned these tricks quickly, more complicated commands such as "Come" required "extraordinary patience" from the trainer.

A Footnote in History

Nostalgic attempts to recreate the magic, or take it a step further with Rock Concerts or Rock Families (often with googly eyes glued onto the rocks), fell flat. In 2000, Pet Rocks were packaged and sold with minimal changes to the original design. One noticeable omission in the 2000 version of the manual was the "Attack" command. In 1975, owners were told that when confronted by a mugger, they should, "Reach into your pocket or purse [and] extract your pet rock. Shout the command, ATTACK. And bash the mugger's head in." Presumably, the 21st century is too litigious to give this advice to rock owners.

None of the redux sales strategies worked. Pet Rocks enjoyed their 15 minutes of fame in 1975, but since that initial—and legendary—success, all attempts to remarket Pet Rocks have dropped like a stone.

---

* The final resting place of Dr. Eugene Shoemaker, a geologist, is the moon. He arranged to have his ashes placed on board the Lunar Prospector spacecraft that was launched on January 6, 1998.

* A shrieking baby's cry can reach 113 decibels. A shrieking car alarm can reach 120 decibels. Being exposed to either for half an hour per day will damage your hearing.

* James Brudenell, the seventh Earl of Cardigan, is known for leading what came to be called "The Charge of the Light Brigade" during the Crimean War in 1854. But he also popularized the cardigan, a knitted jacket worn by his troops.

* Eddie Arcaro, one of the greatest jockeys in horse-racing history, lost 250 races before he won his first. Ultimately, in a career spanning 1931 to 1961, Arcaro rode 4,779 winners.

Top Ten Crime-Scene Traces

Have people learned nothing from TV crime shows? Here's a hint: Just walk through a room, let alone commit a crime, and you'll leave a trace that will detail your every action.

✳ ✳ ✳ ✳

1. **Tool marks:** If you use any sort of object to commit your crime—a pickax on a door lock, a ladder to reach a window, a knife or a rag (for any purpose)—it will be traceable. Tools used in any capacity create tiny nicks that can be detected, identified, and tracked by a crime-scene investigator.

2. **Paint:** A paint chip left at a crime scene reveals volumes. If it's from the vehicle you used in committing the crime, it indicates the make and model. If paint is found on the tool you used to break into a house, it could place you at the scene. Think it's too hard to distinguish specific paint colors? There are 40,000 types of paint classified in police databases.

3. **Broken glass:** Microscopic glass fragments cling to your clothes and can't be laundered out easily. Crime labs examine tint, thickness, density, and refractive index of the fragments to determine their origins.

4. **Dust and dirt:** Even if you're a neat-and-tidy sort of criminal, dust and dirt are often missed by the most discerning eye. These particles can reveal where you live and work and if you have a pet (and what kind). If you've trudged through fields or someone's backyard, researchers can use palynology—the science that studies plant spores, insects, seeds, and other microorganisms—to track you down.

5. **Fibers:** The sources include clothing, drapes, wigs, carpets, furniture, blankets, pets, and plants. Using a compound microscope, an analyst can determine if the fibers are manufactured or natural, which often indicates their value as evidence. The more specific the fiber, the easier it will be to identify (consider

the differences between fibers from a white cotton T-shirt and those from a multicolored wool sweater). There are more than a thousand known fibers, as well as several thousand dyes, so if an exact match is found, you will be too.

6. **Blood:** A victim's blood tells investigators a lot, but they're also looking for different kinds of blood—including yours if you were injured at the scene—and the patterns of blood distribution. Detectives are well trained in collecting blood evidence to estimate when the crime occurred and who was involved. By the way, don't bother to clean up any blood, because investigators use special lights that reveal your efforts.

7. **Bodily fluids:** Saliva, urine, vomit, and semen are a crime-scene investigator's dream, providing DNA evidence that will implicate even the most savvy criminal. Saliva is commonly found left behind by a criminal who took time out for a beverage, a snack, or a cigarette.

8. **Fingerprints:** One of the best ways to identify a criminal is through fingerprints left at the scene. But you kept track of what you touched and then wiped everything down, right? It doesn't matter: You still left smeared prints that can be lifted and analyzed. Investigators enter fingerprint evidence into national databases that can point directly to you.

9. **Shoe prints:** If you wore shoes, you left behind shoe prints. They could be in soil or snow or perhaps on a carpet or bare floor. The particular treads on the soles of shoes make them easy to trace, and the bottoms of most shoes have nicks or scratches that make them easy to identify.

10. **Hair:** Humans shed a lot of hair from all parts of their bodies. Hairs as tiny as eyelashes and eyebrows have unique characteristics that reveal a lot about a person, including race, dietary habits, and overall health. And don't forget: While your hair is dropping all over the crime scene, the victim's hair is clinging to your clothing.

Weird Web Buys

Today's consumers have no qualms about purchasing goods online. But, as it turns out, there are some truly bizarre cyber-bargains to be had at the touch of a keypad.

✳ ✳ ✳ ✳

The Anti-ticket Donut

CATERING TO THE stereotype of the donut-loving police officer, this product (a fake donut available in chocolate or "sprinkle") retails for $9.95, fits easily into a glove compartment, and is designed to dissuade hungry police officers from issuing traffic tickets.

Bacon Strips Adhesive Bandages

Who needs plain old pink bandages when you can dress your wounds in simulated bacon? This novelty item (you get 15 strips for about five bucks) could be seen as a key argument against unchecked capitalism, but apparently the market is there for this meat/medical supply hybrid.

Fish 'n' Flush

The family john can be an ugly piece of porcelain. So why not arrange to have a fully functioning tropical fish tank built into the back of it? As an added benefit, goldfish funerals will be remarkably convenient.

Flatulence Filters

The "TooT TrappeR" is a charcoal filter shaped like a seat cushion that's designed to silence and deodorize any unwanted outbursts. It comes in gray or black and makes a rather awkward Christmas gift.

Garden Gnomes in Compromising Positions

Not the normal garden variety of gnome, these lewd lawn statues depict one gnome burying another, a gnome "dropping a moon," and other assorted indecencies—and you thought all they did was hold shovels and wheelbarrows!

Ghost in a Jar

One of eBay's zaniest offerings was an alleged spirit trapped inside a glass jar. Fourteen bids were registered by people hoping to have their very own pet poltergeist.

Gourmet Oxygen

Although it's likely intended to be a novelty item, "Big Ox" brand oxygen, which comes in flavors such as Tropical Breeze, Mountain Mint, Citrus Blast, and Polar Rush, may provide a sinister glimpse of future consumer goods in a world with depleted natural resources.

Mint-Flavored Golf Tees

It's important to have fresh breath when you're out on the links, and these tees will help—as long as you don't mind sucking on sharpened sticks of wood. A word of caution, however: Only use these tees once, otherwise the dirt tends to get in the way of the mint flavor.

Shoot the Poop

Sick of carrying around a plastic bag when you walk your pooch? Try shooting your dog's poop with Poop-Freeze, which forms a "white crusty film" over the droppings and solidifies them for easy pickup for proper disposal or safekeeping in your prized pet's baby book.

Stainless-Steel Lollipops

The Zilopop is a German product that promotes fresh breath through the frequent licking of a cold steel circle. After a two- to four-minute suck on this lollipop look-alike, mouth odors are neutralized. And it's reusable! Unlike the Tootsie Pop, no amount of licking will ever get you to the center of a Zilopop.

Virgin Mary Grilled Cheese Sandwich

This lunchtime miracle sold for $28,000 on eBay. In 1994, Diane Duyser of Florida was one bite into her sandwich when she noticed a radiant face staring out at her from the top slice of toast. Grace is indeed everywhere!

Very Odd Jobs

From weed farmers to barnyard masturbators, our world is teeming with offbeat jobs that rarely, if ever, find ink in newspaper classifieds. Here are a few that might make you look at your job title in an entirely different way.

✳ ✳ ✳ ✳

Ant Catcher

REMEMBER WHEN YOU were a kid and got down on your hands and knees to search for ants? Well, imagine being a grown-up that gets paid to do so. Ant catchers collect the little critters to populate colonies in toy ant farms.

Barnyard Masturbator

The job of the barnyard masturbator, or BM, is to collect sperm from a bull for fertility studies or artificial insemination. To do this, the BM must step in at the most intense moment of bovine arousal; replace the living, breathing female with an artificial one; and grab the bull by the "horns," so to speak. A thankless job, but someone has to do it.

Boner

In days past, the term boner meant a blunder or an error. Today, although it could mean an activity not remotely fit for this book, a boner is also a textile worker who inserts stays into women's corsets and brassieres.

Brain Picker

Here's another job that is not as it seems. A brain picker does not extract information from geniuses in a think tank. He or she splits the skulls of slaughterhouse animals for the sole purpose of picking out their brains.

Chicken Sexers

A person with this job gets to distinguish between male and female chicks. This is necessary in the poultry industry so that egg-laying females are separated from their male counterparts.

In some cases, the gender of specially bred hatchlings can be determined by their feathers. But in most cases, poultry sleuthing requires that feces be squeezed from the chick in order to obtain an inside view of its reproductive organs. If a small bump (not unlike that found on a "Ken" doll) is discovered, the chick is deemed male.

Circus Elephant Tender

Visitors to a circus have seen these workers and likely sympathized with their plight. Their job is to follow elephants around and pick up after them. With a gritty air of determination and an ever-present shovel, these unsung heroes unceremoniously perform their duties. The downside includes poop inhalation and the risk of being trampled to death should Dumbo get rambunctious.

Citrus-Fruit Colorer

The next time you marvel at the vibrant color of an orange or tangerine, you should know that a citrus-fruit colorer probably had as much to do with this agreeable veneer as Mother Nature did—maybe more. Because citrus fruit is generally picked before it is fully ripe, a squad of "artists," aided by steam and chemicals, steps in to help things along.

Furniture Tester

When and where is the statement: "Get off your lazy butt and get back to work!" almost never heard? At a facility that employs furniture testers, of course! Part of the tester's job requires sitting and/or lying down on the pieces being tested, so it's probably the furniture tester's favorite part of the day.

Hooker Inspector

If this misleading job were advertised in the classifieds, perhaps a thousand men would apply. Despite its suggestive name, however, the men would not be checking out painted ladies at a bordello. Instead, they'd find themselves in a drab textile mill twisting skeins—yarn or thread wound around reels—on a hooking machine. The device is so named because it "hooks" each end of the skein to clasps on the machine. Get your mind out of the gutter!

Hot Walker

Though the term hot walker conjures up images of a super-model sashaying seductively along a beach, its real meaning is a bit more mundane. In reality, a hot walker walks racehorses just after a competition or workout to aid the four-leggers in the cooling-down process. As off the mark as its name sounds, it's a highly necessary duty. If this task is not performed, the horse could suffer kidney damage.

Weed Farmer

The trend of misleading job titles continues with weed farmer, a job that sounds like something straight out of a Cheech & Chong movie. Its true meaning, of course, is far less intoxicating and far more legal. A weed farmer merely grows weeds that will later be sold to chemical companies and universities for herbicide research, not for turning on, tuning in, and dropping out.

Wrinkle Chaser

Unfortunately, a wrinkle chaser does not provide transportation to the fountain of youth. Nor does he or she perform at-home facials. This worker simply irons away wrinkles in footwear that have emerged during the production process so that shoes are smooth as silk when they arrive at stores for sale.

---

* Deke Slayton, the only astronaut of the Mercury Seven not to fly in the Mercury program, finally escaped Earth's gravitational pull as a member of the Apollo-Soyuz project.

* In 1964, archaeologists discovered one of the earliest known battle sites near the northern border of Sudan. The skeletons of 59 people—dating from 13,000 years ago and pierced by numerous arrowheads—were found.

* The female boomslang, a type of African tree snake, looks so much like a tree branch that birds—its main prey—will land right on it.

No Laughing Matter: Coulrophobia

It's a malady in which the sufferer has an abnormal or exaggerated fear of clowns, and experts estimate that it afflicts as many as one in seven people.

✳   ✳   ✳   ✳

Beware of the Man with the Red Nose

THE SYMPTOMS OF this strangely common affliction range from nausea and sweating to irregular heartbeat, shortness of breath, and an overall feeling of impending doom. Is the sight of Ronald McDonald more chilling than your Chocolate Triple Thick Shake? There could be a few reasons why.

The most common explanation for coulrophobia is that the sufferer had a bad experience with a clown at a young and impressionable age. Maybe the clown at Billy Schuster's fifth birthday party shot you in the eye with a squirting flower, doused your head with confetti, or accidentally popped the balloon animal he was making for you. Some of the most silly or mundane things can be petrifying when you are young. And though the incident may be long forgotten, a bright orange wig or bulbous red nose might be enough to throw you back into the irrational fears that plagued your younger days.

When Good Clowns Turn Bad

Who could blame you? If television and movies have taught us anything, it's that clowns often are creatures of pure evil. There's the Joker, Batman's murderously insane archenemy; the shape-shifting Pennywise from Stephen King's *It*; the human-eating alien clowns in *Killer Klowns from Outer Space*; and a possessed toy clown that comes to life and beats the bejesus out of a young Robbie Freeling in Steven Spielberg's *Poltergeist*.

Real-life serial killer John Wayne Gacy didn't do much for the clown cause, either. Before authorities found the bodies of 27 boys and young men in his basement crawl space, Gacy was known as a charming, sociable guy who enjoyed performing at children's parties dressed up as Pogo the Clown or Patches the Clown. That ended when his crimes were discovered, but even on death row, he still had an unwholesome interest in clowning—he took up oil painting, and clowns were his favorite subjects.

Be Afraid—Be Very Afraid

It's enough to give anyone the heebie-jeebies. But some experts say there's more to coulrophobia than traumatic childhood events or pop-culture portrayals. Scholar Joseph Durwin points out that since ancient times, clowns, fools, and jesters have been given permission to mock, criticize, or act deviantly and unexpectedly. This freedom to behave outside of normal social boundaries is exactly what makes clowns so threatening.

A *Nursing Standard* magazine interview of 250 people ages 4 to 16 revealed that clowns are indeed "universally scary." Researcher Penny Curtis reported some kids found clowns to be "quite frightening and unknowable." Seems it has a lot to do with that permanent grease-painted grin. Because the face of a clown never changes, you don't know if he's relentlessly gleeful or about to bite your face off. In the words of Bart Simpson: "Can't sleep; clown will eat me."

---

* A sloth is sometimes so slow that moss grows on its back. Still, slow is one thing, stationary is another—snails can sleep for three years straight.

* In Paraguay, only registered blood donors may legally duel.

* The shotguns used by American forces during World War I proved to be so effective that the Germans cried, "Foul!" and tried to have them banned.

* In some countries, guinea pigs aren't cute, cuddly, children's pets—they're a diet staple. Peruvians, for example, annually eat 63 million guinea pigs. In a church in the town of Cusco, a guinea pig is on the table in a painting of the Last Supper.

Nine Odd Things Insured by Lloyd's of London

Average people insure average things like cars, houses, and maybe even a boat. Celebrities insure legs, voices, and some things you might not want to examine if you're a claims adjuster. Here are a few unusual things insured by the famous Lloyd's of London over the years.

✳ ✳ ✳ ✳

1. In 1957, world-famous food critic Egon Ronay wrote and published the first edition of the *Egon Ronay Guide to British Eateries.* Because his endorsement could make or break a restaurant, Ronay insured his taste buds for $400,000.

2. In the 1940s, executives at 20th Century Fox had the legs of actress Betty Grable insured for $1 million each. After taking out the policies, Grable probably wished she had added a rider to protect her from injury while the insurance agents fought over who would inspect her when making a claim.

3. While playing on Australia's national cricket team from 1985 to 1994, Merv Hughes took out an estimated $370,000 policy on his trademark walrus mustache, which, combined with his 6′4″ physique and outstanding playing ability, made him one of the most recognized cricketers in the world.

4. Representing the Cheerio Yo-Yo Company of Canada, 13-year-old Harvey Lowe won the 1932 World Yo-Yo championships in London and toured Europe from 1932 to 1935. He even taught Edward VIII, the Prince of Wales, how to yo-yo. Lowe was so valuable to Cheerio that the company insured his hands for $150,000!

5. From 1967 to 1992, British comedian and singer Ken Dodd was in *The Guinness Book of Records* for the world's longest joke-telling session—1,500 jokes in three and a half hours.

Dodd has sold more than 100 million comedy records and is famous for his frizzy hair, ever-present feather duster, and extremely large buckteeth. His teeth are so important to his act that Dodd had them insured for $7.4 million.

6. During the height of his career, Michael Flatley—star of Riverdance and Lord of the Dance—insured his legs for an unbelievable $47 million. Before becoming the world's most famous Irish step dancer, the Chicago native trained as a boxer and won the Golden Gloves Championship in 1975, no doubt dazzling opponents with his fancy footwork.

7. The famous comedy team of Bud Abbott and Lou Costello seemed to work extremely well together, especially in their famous "Who's on First?" routine. But to protect against a career-ending argument, they took out a $250,000 insurance policy over a five-year period. After more than 20 years together, the team split up in 1957—not due to a disagreement, but because the Internal Revenue Service got them for back taxes, which forced them to sell many of their assets, including the rights to their many films.

8. Rock and Roll Hall of Famer Bruce Springsteen is known to his fans as *The Boss*, but Springsteen knows that he could be demoted to part-time status with one case of laryngitis. That's why in the 1980s he insured his famous gravelly voice for $6 million. Rod Stewart has also insured his throat and Bob Dylan his vocal cords to protect themselves from that inevitable day when they stop blowin' in the wind.

9. Before rock 'n' roll, a popular type of music in England in the 1950s was skiffle, a type of folk music with a jazz and blues influence played on washboards, jugs, kazoos, and cigar-box fiddles. It was so big at the time that a washboard player named Chas McDevitt tried to protect his career by insuring his fingers for $9,300. It didn't do him much good because skiffle was replaced by rock 'n' roll, washboards by washing machines, and McDevitt by McCartney.

No Free Snacks . . . and No Parachutes

Airline spokespeople and former pilots will tell you that parachutes are not used on commercial flights. It seems illogical, but there are good reasons why.

✳ ✳ ✳ ✳

A Parachute Would Be Pointless

ONE KEY REASON why you won't find a parachute under your seat, in the carry-on compartment, or anywhere else is that commercial planes fly too high. Parachute jumps are made from between 10,000 and 14,000 feet above Earth's surface; commercial airplanes fly between 30,000 and 40,000 feet up. At that height, a parachutist could freeze, suffer hypoxia (lack of oxygen), and lose consciousness—or be sent into free-fall by air currents that are too strong for the chute to tame.

And even if you waited until the falling plane was within parachuting distance of the ground, you could be injured by falling debris or get caught in some part of the plane. Furthermore, the cabin is pressurized—once the door was opened, you could be sucked out so quickly that you wouldn't have time to get your chute on. On top of all that, most airplane accidents occur on or near the ground, during takeoff or landing; so again, a parachute would prove useless.

Nevertheless, the parachute idea had proponents. In 2003, inventor Pete Hilsenbeck patented a parachute that could be attached to the back of a passenger seat and be used for bailing out of a disabled plane. But his invention got a swift thumbs-down from aviation ace Guy Norris, then an editor for the respected aerospace weekly publication *Flight International*. "It's got sheer terror written all over it," he told *The New York Times*.

What About One Giant Parachute?

In the 1990s, Robert Nelson, chairman of Ballistic Recovery Systems (BRS), developed a super-size parachute that is strong enough to hold aloft some 4,000 pounds—or the weight of a small airplane. The parachute is stored in the rear of the plane and is attached to the plane's wings, nose, and tail with ultrathin, high-strength wire. In an emergency, it can be fired through the rear window by a miniature rocket. Once outside, it deploys like a huge umbrella and brings the craft to a safe landing. How well does it work? In 2004, Albert Kolk lost control of his small plane while flying over British Columbia. He fired off his BRS parachute, and seconds later, he was gliding, uninjured, to Earth.

NASA officials were so impressed with Nelson's chute that they awarded him a grant to develop one for commercial jets. "Weight and speed are always the challenge," Nelson says. Commercial jets weigh tens of thousands of pounds and travel at speeds of more than 600 miles per hour.

At some point, maybe there will be one aboard every aircraft, enabling pilots to land a disabled plane not just on a wing and a prayer, but with a parachute, too.

---

* The chapel where Joan of Arc worshipped was the Chapelle de St. Martin de Sayssuel in Chasse, France. The chapel was moved to Marquette University in 1964. Within the chapel is the Joan of Arc Stone, on which Joan is said to have prayed, kissing the stone when she was finished. To this day, that stone feels colder to the touch than the surrounding stones.

* In 1985, Wilbur Snapp, the organist for minor league baseball's Clearwater Phillies in Florida, played "Three Blind Mice" to protest a call made by umpire Keith O'Connor. The ump tossed him from the game.

Some Coffins Are 18 Inches Under

It's widely believed that the standard graveyard procedure is to put a coffin six feet under. But the truth is, burial depths vary considerably.

✳ ✳ ✳ ✳

Different Feet for Different Folks

WE'VE ALL HEARD the line in a cheesy movie that, against our better judgment, has sucked us in and stuck us to the couch: "One more move, and I'll put you six feet under." Whether the words are growled by a cowboy in a black hat or a mobster in pinstripes, everyone knows what those six feet represent: the depth where coffins reside after burial.

Or do they? The bad guy may well mean what he says, but the final resting place for someone unfortunate enough to be in a coffin varies depending on the site of the burial. These depths can range from 18 inches to 12 feet. There's no world council that has decreed that a person must be put to rest exactly six feet under. Think about it. Digging a six-foot grave in a region below sea level, such as New Orleans, would get pretty soggy. (Of course, a corpse floating up from the grave might add some flair to that cheesy movie.)

Who Makes the Call?

Most grave depths are determined by local, state, or national governments. New Orleans has dealt with its topographical issues by placing most of its dead above ground in crypts. The area's gravesites in the ground are almost always less than two feet deep—and even that doesn't prevent the occasional floater.

The California requirement is a mere 18 inches. In Quebec, Canada, the law states that coffins "shall be deposited in a grave and covered with at least one meter of earth" (a little more than three feet). This is similar to New South Wales in Australia, which calls for 900 millimeters (slightly less than three feet).

And the Institute of Cemetery and Crematorium Management in London says that "no body shall be buried in such a manner that any part of the coffin is less than three feet below the level of any ground adjoining the grave."

The Turn of a Phrase

If burial depths vary from place to place, how did the phrase "six feet under" come to life? (Sorry, couldn't resist.) Historians believe it originated in England. London's Great Plague of 1665 killed 75,000 to 100,000 people. In Daniel Defoe's book *A Journal of the Plague Year*, he writes that the city's lord mayor issued an edict that all graves had to be dug six feet deep to limit the spread of the plague outbreak. Other sources confirm Defoe's claim.

Of course, the plague is a scourge of the past, and today's world has no uniform burial depth. But who really cares? It still makes for a winning line in an otherwise schlocky movie.

---

* On August 21, 1975, Rick and Paul Reuschel of the 1975 Chicago Cubs combined to pitch a shutout, becoming the first brotherly duo to pull off such a feat.

* The first FAX machine was patented in 1843 by a Scottish inventor named Alexander Bain, 33 years before Alexander Graham Bell demonstrated the telephone.

* Objects weigh slightly less at the equator than at the poles.

* In 1963, the first artificial heart was patented by Paul Winchell, better known as the Grammy-winning voice of Tigger from Disney's *Winnie the Pooh* cartoons.

* The Seven Years' War, which began in 1756, pitted Great Britain, Prussia, and Hanover against Sweden, Russia, Austria, France, and Saxony. It's referred to as the French and Indian War in the United States. Winston Churchill called it the First World War.

* Thomas Eagleton, George McGovern's first Democratic running mate in the 1972 presidential election, resigned from the ticket when it was learned he had previously received electroshock therapy for depression.

Who Ya Gonna Call?

Your house is oozing with ectoplasm. Strange moaning and wailing keep you up at night. If you're a fan of old movies, you'll dial up the ghostbusters—except that the kind we're talking about are real.

✳ ✳ ✳ ✳

The Ghost Whisperer

BONNIE VENT, the founder of the San Diego Paranormal Research Project, is actually more of a ghost whisperer than a ghostbuster. In fact, Vent prefers the term "spirit advocate." According to a 2008 article in *The New York Times*, she can cleanse your home of spooky visitors with a little friendly coaxing.

Vent doesn't believe in rituals—instead, she engages the ghost in conversation to find out why it's there. "Spirit people are people," she says. "You have to get to the root cause." Vent's spirit advocacy is not cheap: She charges $125 an hour for her services. And sometimes the ghost decides to stick around anyway, in which case she recommends that you "try to work out a livable situation." Conveniently, Vent doubles as a real estate agent and invites potential buyers and sellers of haunted houses to advertise on her Web site.

The Paranormal Investigator

If your definition of a "livable situation" includes only the living, call Fiona Broome, who bills herself as a "paranormal investigator." Broome, like Vent, recommends talking to the ghost. If that doesn't work, she resorts to an arsenal of traditional remedies, including garlic, sea salt, holy water, and hex signs. Or she offers this tip: Place your shoes at the foot of the bed pointed in opposite directions. This apparently causes the ghost to become so confused that it will depart to seek more orderly digs.

Smudge Sticks Work, Too

Mary Ann Winkowski, another buster of ghosts, suggests burning bundles of white sage, known as smudge sticks, to banish ghosts from the premises. Smudge sticks are used in many Native American cleansing ceremonies, and Winkowski claims that they have helped her to rout ghosts from homes, offices, schools, and even cars. Winkowski serves as a consultant for the popular CBS television drama *Ghost Whisperer*, as does her fellow psychic, James Van Praagh.

Van Praagh describes himself as a "clairesentient"—that is, one who is able to receive information from spirits through his emotions. Unlike other ghost whisperers, Van Praagh doesn't seek to get rid of ghosts. Rather, he specializes in locating spirits for those who want to connect with dead loved ones.

Patty A. Wilson of the Ghost Research Foundation spends more time looking for ghosts than getting rid of them. The author of a series of books on ghost hunting in Pennsylvania, she acknowledges that "ghost stories are not neat and clean. They're real stories about real people." And they don't always end with the ghost drifting off into the great beyond.

---

* Approximately one out of a thousand baby sea turtles survives after hatching.

* Sea turtles absorb a lot of salt from the seawater in which they live. They excrete excess salt from their eyes, so it often looks as though they are crying.

* In Paris, France, there are more dogs than people.

* The large cats of the world are divided into two groups—those that roar, such as tigers and African lions, and those that purr. Mountain lions purr, hiss, scream, and snarl, but they cannot roar.

* Giraffes not only have long necks—they also have very long tongues. A giraffe can clean its ears with its 21-inch tongue.

* Most elephants weigh less than the tongue of a blue whale.

* Crocodiles and alligators are surprisingly fast on land, but they lack agility. If you're being chased by one, run in a zigzag line.

* The surface gravity of Jupiter is more than two-and-a-half times greater than that of Earth.

The Rise and Fall of the Pink Lawn Flamingo

It stands on thin metal legs, an icon of mid-20th-century booms: the baby boom, the suburbia boom, and the home-ownership boom.

✳ ✳ ✳ ✳

AS UPWARDLY MOBILE working-class families left crowded cities following World War II to become landed gentry on tidy plots in the suburbs, American popular culture adopted a whimsical new aesthetic. Automobiles sprouted useless fins, and garish vinyl and Formica dinette sets replaced sturdy kitchen tables. Forward-looking young homeowners embraced modernity, adorning their groomed green yards with splashes of color, including the fiery pink plastic flamingo.

Conceived in 1957 by Don Featherstone—a designer at the Union Products lawn-ornament company in Leominster, Massachusetts—plastic flamingos were an instant hit. Millions roosted on front lawns from coast to coast.

But by the 1970s, a backlash began. Some housing developments banned them. Pranksters kidnapped them and sent the owners pictures of their purloined birds perched in exotic locales around the globe. Sales were slow into the early 1980s.

Then, like bowling shirts and the Village People, fake flamingos returned as hip kitsch. Union Products was selling as many as 250,000 annually into the 1990s. The company had to halt production in 2006, however, due to financial problems and rising production costs. But in April 2007, another company bought the copyright and molds, intending to resume production.

Featherstone once offered to *The New York Times* a reason for the pink flamingo's initial popularity. "We tried to design things for people of taste," he said, "but we found out there were not too many of them. So we went for the flamingos."

A New Twist on Turning Yourself In

It's highly unlikely that a criminal could collect a reward on himself, but it's not entirely outside the realm of possibility.

✳ ✳ ✳ ✳

He Who Offers the Reward Doles It Out

A NYONE CAN OFFER a reward: the family of a crime victim, a concerned citizens' group, a corporation, and a nonprofit organization such as Crime Stoppers, which pays for anonymous tips. And some local government bodies even offer rewards in certain criminal investigations. But there are no uniform laws or regulations regarding how these rewards are disbursed.

In point of fact, whoever offers the reward gets to determine who can collect the money. Nonetheless, it's difficult to imagine a provision that would allow the perpetrator of the crime to pocket the dough.

The business of rewards can be tricky. A well-publicized, big-money offer sometimes works against an investigation by attracting greedy tipsters who provide useless leads to overworked detectives. Law enforcement agencies generally don't discourage reward offers, but they do try to use them strategically. Often, they won't publicize a reward until an investigation nears a dead end, the hope being that it'll renew interest in the crime and jog the memories of legitimate tipsters.

Money's Not Always the Issue

Many police officials concede that offers of rewards rarely lead to successful investigations. Most useful tips, they say, come from honest citizens with good intentions that go beyond recompense.

And the existence of a reward doesn't necessarily mean the tipsters will know how to collect it. In July 2008, the FBI offered a $25,000 reward in its search for Nicholas Sheley, a suspect in a series of killings. Sheley, it seems, walked into a bar in Granite City, Illinois, to get a drink of water. The bar's patrons had seen his face on the TV news. One called the police; another ran outside and flagged down a squad car. Sheley was quickly taken into custody. Four months later, an FBI spokesman said that nobody had stepped forward to collect the 25 grand.

So never mind the bad guys. Apparently, sometimes even the good guys don't get the money.

---

* A mother kangaroo can have two babies of different ages in her pouch at the same time. She produces different milk for each of them, depending on their age and nutritional needs.

* George Welch, a flying ace and Medal of Honor recipient, claimed to have broken the sound barrier on October 1, 1947, two weeks before Chuck Yeager.

* Only one person has played both Major League baseball and NHL hockey. Jim Riley played baseball for St. Louis and Washington and hockey with Chicago and Detroit.

* The Nike swoosh was designed by Carolyn Davidson, a graphic design student at Portland State University. She was paid $35 for the famous trademark.

* In 1960, the USS *Triton*, a nuclear submarine, was the first vessel to circumnavigate the planet while submerged. It only surfaced once during its journey, to remove a sick crew member.

* Harlequin bass and hamlet fish take turns being male and female, including releasing sperm and eggs during the mating process.

* The Great Fire of London started in a bakery in 1666 and lasted three days. It consumed the older section of the city and destroyed 13,200 homes. Some reports state that only 16 people died.

* An official balance beam in women's gymnastics is just four inches wide, less than the length of a ballpoint pen.

Anarchy and Peace: The Dutch Provo Movement

In the summer of 1965, Holland's media were preoccupied with the activities of the Provos, a self-described anarchist group whose witty pranklike "happenings" appealed to the country's politically minded youth—and bothered the hell out of the Dutch police, who often were the unwitting victims of Provo mischief.

✳ ✳ ✳ ✳

Where Ideals Converge

PROVO PRANKSTERISM TRACES back to the late 1950s, beginning with Robert Jasper Grootveld, a young performance artist seemingly impervious to embarrassment. In one prank, Grootveld wrote "cancer" across cigarette billboards. It wasn't subtle, but it did have an impact.

Grootveld's early activities coincided with those of the Nozems, a group of disaffected, unemployed Dutch teens who got a kick out of mild, aimless troublemaking. By 1965, an intellectual named Roel Van Duyn realized that the Nozems' aggression could be channeled into "revolutionary consciousness." Together, Van Duyn and Grootveld became the nexus of a new, performance-oriented sort of social protest: The Provos.

The Provo agenda was rife with fascinating contradictions: Laziness and action. Protest and peace. Intellect and ignorance. The Provos were fueled by the power of those contradictions and embraced the opposite pillars of protest movements: the educated intellectuals who criticize society from behind ivory towers, and the uneducated punk riffraff who protest society by refusing to participate in it.

Provo political activities played like cleverly planned comedic farces that were almost too absurd to be true. One plot was designed to reveal the police force's ineptitude when it came to marijuana laws. To do so, the Provos continuously called the police on themselves and got arrested for possession, though the *faux* pot would prove to be tea and legal herbs. With this Trojan horse, the police were made to appear foolish time and time again; eventually they became afraid to arrest anyone for cannabis for fear they would be victim of another Provo plot.

Outing the Inept

The Provos also enacted their "White Plans," which were political plans to improve society. The White Bicycle Plan called for the use of communal bikes and the outlawing of cars in Amsterdam. The Provos dispersed 50 white bikes throughout the city, which were immediately impounded by the police. Others included the White Chimney Plan (the chimneys of serious polluters were painted white), the White Wives Plan (promoting free women's clinics), and the White Kids Plan (promoting free child care).

The cleverest Provo plot involved White Rumors, in which the group terrorized the police force simply by spreading rumors. For example, to protest the wedding of Holland's Princess Beatrix to a former member of the Hitler Youth, Provos spread wild rumors about themselves: The Provos would dump LSD into the public water supply; the Provos would build a giant paint gun to attack wedding guests; the royal horses were to be drugged. Paranoid authorities requested 25,000 troops to protect the wedding from the Provos, who were actually planning on doing very little. Mayhem ensued, and the police ended up beating unarmed citizens and foreign journalists.

Power to the Provos

Eventually, the police and government were so afraid of the Provo movement that by mid-1966, arrests and riots spread throughout the Netherlands. The public sympathized with the Provos, who were never violent themselves. Due to Provo activism, private citizens, academics, and politicians called for investigations into police behavior. By 1967, the mayor of Amsterdam and the police commissioner had been fired. Provo was accepted into the mainstream, and some Provos members even took political office. In May 1967, the Provos disbanded.

The Provos succeeded in revealing police violence, and many scholars credit the Provos for Amsterdam's famously lax cannabis laws and innovations in public transportation—their White Bicycle Plan was the progenitor to similar plans that are in effect today throughout Europe. As the Provo magazine explained, "Provo has to choose between desperate resistance and submissive extinction. Provo calls for resistance wherever possible. Provo realizes that it will lose in the end, but it cannot pass up the chance to make at least one more heartfelt attempt to provoke society."

Say What?

We all have ability. The difference is how we use it.

—STEVIE WONDER

The most savage controversies are those about matters as to which there is no good evidence either way.

—BERTRAND RUSSELL

Patriotism means to stand by the country. It does not mean to stand by the president.

—THEODORE ROOSEVELT

Remind people that profit is the difference between revenue and expense. This makes you look smart.

—SCOTT ADAMS

Cross-country skiing is great if you live in a small country.

—STEVEN WRIGHT

Nothing is work unless you'd rather be doing something else.

—GEORGE HALAS

A hospital bed is a parked taxi with the meter running.

—GROUCHO MARX

Lingering Spirits of the *Eastland* Disaster

Chicago has a dark and deadly history of disasters. One of the most tragic took place July 24, 1915. On that cool, cloudy summer day, hundreds died in the Chicago River when the Eastland *capsized a few feet from the dock. The calamity left an ongoing ghostly impression on the city.*

✳   ✳   ✳   ✳

Company Picnic Turns Tragic

JULY 24 WAS going to be special for thousands of Chicagoans. It was reserved for the annual summer picnic for employees of the Western Electric Company, which was to be held across Lake Michigan in Michigan City, Indiana. And although officials at the utility company had encouraged workers to bring along friends and relatives, they were surprised when more than 7,000 people arrived to be ferried across the lake on the five excursion boats chartered for the day. Three of the steamers— the *Theodore Roosevelt*, the *Petoskey*, and the *Eastland*—were docked on the Chicago River near Clark Street.

The *Eastland*, a steamer that was owned by the St. Joseph– Chicago Steamship Company, had already developed a reputation for top-heaviness and instability. On this fateful morning, however, it was filled to its limit with passengers. In addition, the new federal Seaman's Act, passed as a result of the 1912 *Titanic* disaster, required more lifeboats than the previous regulations had. These two factors only served to make the ship even more unstable than it already was. It was truly a recipe for disaster.

Death and the *Eastland*

As passengers boarded the *Eastland*, she began listing back and forth. This had happened before, so the crew began filling and emptying ballast compartments to help level her out. As the boat was preparing to depart, some passengers went below

deck, hoping to warm up on the overcast morning, but many on the overcrowded steamer crammed onto the deck to wave to onlookers on shore. The *Eastland* tilted once again, but this time more severely, and passengers began to panic. Moments later, the *Eastland* rolled onto her port (left) side and came to rest on the river bottom, only 18 feet below the surface. A portion of the hull's right (starboard) side was actually above the water's surface.

Passengers on deck were tossed into the river, where they flailed about in a mass of bodies. The overturning of the ship created a current that pulled some of the floundering swimmers to their doom, while many of the women were dragged under by their long dresses, which had become snagged on the ship.

Passengers inside were thrown to the port side of the ship when it capsized. The heavy furniture on board crushed some of them, and those who were not killed instantly drowned a few moments later when water rushed inside. A few managed to escape, but most didn't. Their bodies were later found trapped in a tangled heap on the port side of the *Eastland*.

Firefighters, rescue workers, and volunteers soon arrived and tried to help people escape through portholes. They also cut holes in the portion of the ship's hull that was above the water line. Approximately 1,660 passengers survived the disaster, but they still ended up in the river, and many courageous people from the wharf jumped in or threw life preservers, lines, boxes, and anything that floated into the water to help the panicked and drowning passengers.

In the end, 844 people died, many of them young women and children. Officially, no clear explanation was given for why the vessel capsized, and the St. Joseph–Chicago Steamship Company was not held accountable for the disaster.

The bodies of those who perished in the tragedy were wrapped in sheets and placed on the *Theodore Roosevelt* or lined up along the docks. Marshall Field's and other large stores sent wagons to carry the dead to hospitals, funeral homes, and makeshift morgues, such as the Second Regiment Armory, where more than 200 bodies were sent.

After the ship was removed from the river, it was sold and later became the gunboat USS *Wilmette*. It never saw action but was used as a training ship during World War II. After the war, it was decommissioned and eventually scrapped in 1947.

The *Eastland* may be gone, but her story and her ghosts continue to linger nearly a century later.

Hauntings at Harpo Studios

At the time of the *Eastland* disaster, the only public building large enough to be used as a temporary morgue was the Second Regiment Armory, located on Chicago's near west side. The dead were laid out on the floor of the armory and assigned identification numbers. Chicagoans whose loved ones had perished in the disaster filed through the rows of bodies, searching for familiar faces, but in 22 cases, there was no one left to identify them. Those families were completely wiped out. The names of these victims were learned from neighbors who came searching for their friends. The weeping, crying, and moaning of the bereaved echoed off the walls of the armory for days.

The last body to be identified was Willie Novotny, a seven-year-old boy whose parents and older sister had also perished on the *Eastland*. When extended family members identified the boy nearly a week after the disaster took place, a chapter was closed on one of Chicago's most horrific events.

As years passed, the armory building went through several incarnations, including a stable and a bowling alley, before Harpo

Studios, the production company owned by talk-show maven Oprah Winfrey, purchased it. A number of *The Oprah Show*'s staff members, security guards, and maintenance workers claim that the studio is haunted by the spirits of those who tragically lost their lives on the *Eastland*. Many employees have experienced unexplained phenomena, including the sighting of a woman in a long gray dress who walks the corridors and then mysteriously vanishes into the wall. Some believe she is the spirit of a mourner who came to the armory looking for her family and left a bit of herself behind at a place where she felt her greatest sense of loss.

The woman in gray may not be alone in her spectral travels through the old armory. Staff members have also witnessed doors opening and closing on their own and heard people sobbing, whispering, and moaning, as well as phantom footsteps on the lobby's staircase. Those who have experienced these strange events believe that the tragedy of yesterday is still manifesting itself in the old armory building today.

Chicago River Ghosts

In the same way that the former armory seems to have been impressed with a ghostly recording of past events, the Chicago River seems haunted, too. For years, people walking on the Clark Street bridge have heard crying, moaning, and pleas for help coming from the river. Some have even witnessed the apparitions of victims helplessly splashing in the water. On several occasions, some witnesses have called the police for help. One man even jumped into the river to save what he thought was an actual person drowning. When he returned to the surface, he discovered that he was in the water alone. He had no explanation for what he'd seen, other than to admit that it might have been a ghost.

So it seems that the horror of the *Eastland* disaster has left an imprint on this spot and continues to replay itself over and over again, ensuring that the unfortunate victims from the *Eastland* will never truly be forgotten.

Which President's Day?

*Making big plans to celebrate Presidents' Day? Be careful—
the U.S. government says there's no such holiday.*

✳ ✳ ✳ ✳

IT ALL BEGAN in 1885, when the federal government made
George Washington's birthday, February 22, a national
holiday—thus making Washington the first person to have
a federal holiday named after him. This was fine until 1968,
when Congress passed the Uniform Monday Holidays Act,
which moved Washington's birthday to the third Monday in
February. Several other holidays were also moved, supposedly
so that families could spend more recreational time together.
Cynics have long suspected that the real reason had to do with
boosting both tourism and holiday retail sales.

During discussions of the Monday holiday law, some members of Congress lobbied to change "Washington's Birthday"
to "Presidents' Day," thereby including Abraham Lincoln in
the honors. They figured Lincoln deserved equal billing, and
besides, the third Monday in February always falls between
Washington's birthday and Lincoln's birthday. But the effort
failed and the federal holiday remained Washington's Birthday.

At least, officially. After all, there is no law declaring that states
have to play by the federal government's holiday rules. So while
some states went along, a few decided to rename the holiday Presidents' Day. Other states celebrate Washington's and
Lincoln's birthdays separately, and some even moved the dates
to completely different months.

If that weren't bad enough, there's apparently no agreement on
the spelling of the day, which can be Presidents' Day, Presidents
Day, or President's Day, depending on where you live. The official name of the holiday is Washington's Birthday, regardless of
what all the retail ads that weekend say.

The Death of John Dillinger... or Someone Who Looked Like Him

On July 22, 1934, outside the Biograph Theater on Chicago's north side, John Dillinger, America's first Public Enemy Number One, passed from this world into the next in a hail of bullets. Or did he? Conspiracy theorists believe that FBI agents shot and killed the wrong man and covered it all up when they realized their mistake. So what really happened that night? Let's first take a look at the main players in this gangland soap opera.

✳   ✳   ✳   ✳

Hoover Wants His Man

BORN JUNE 22, 1903, John Dillinger was in his early thirties when he first caught the FBI's eye. They thought they were through with him in January 1934, when he was arrested after shooting a police officer during a bank robbery in East Chicago, Indiana. However, Dillinger managed to stage a daring escape from his Indiana jail cell using a wooden gun painted with black shoe polish.

Once Dillinger left Indiana in a stolen vehicle and crossed into Illinois, he was officially a federal fugitive. J. Edgar Hoover, then director of the FBI, promised a quick apprehension, but Dillinger had other plans. He seemed to enjoy the fact that the FBI was tracking him—rather than go into hiding, he continued robbing banks. Annoyed, Hoover assigned FBI Agent Melvin Purvis to ambush Dillinger. Purvis's plan backfired, though, and Dillinger escaped, shooting and killing two innocent men in the process. After the botched trap, the public was in an uproar and the FBI was under close scrutiny. To everyone at the FBI, the message was clear: Hoover wanted Dillinger, and he wanted him ASAP.

The Woman in Red

The FBI's big break came in July 1934 with a phone call from a woman named Anna Sage. Sage was a Romanian immigrant who ran a Chicago-area brothel. Fearing that she might be deported, Sage wanted to strike a bargain with the feds. Her proposal was simple: In exchange for not being deported, Sage was willing to give the FBI John Dillinger. According to Sage, Dillinger was dating Polly Hamilton, one of her former employees. Melvin Purvis personally met with Sage and told her he couldn't make any promises but he would do what he could about her pending deportation.

Several days later, on July 22, Sage called the FBI office in Chicago and said she was going to the movies that night with Dillinger and Hamilton. Sage quickly hung up but not before saying she would wear something bright so agents could pick out the threesome. Not knowing which movie theater they were planning to go to, Purvis dispatched several agents to the Marbro Theater, while he and other agents went to the Biograph. At approximately 8:30 P.M., Purvis believed he saw Dillinger, Sage, and Hamilton enter the Biograph. As she had promised, Sage wore a bright orange blouse. However, under the marquee lights, the blouse's color appeared to be red, which is why Sage was forever dubbed "The Woman in Red."

Purvis tried to apprehend Dillinger right after he purchased tickets, but he slipped past Purvis and into the darkened theater. Purvis went into the theater but was unable to locate Dillinger in the dark. At that point, Purvis left the theater, gathered his men, and made the decision to apprehend Dillinger as he was exiting the theater. Purvis positioned himself in the theater's vestibule, instructed his men to hide outside, and told them that he would signal them by lighting a cigar when he spotted Dillinger. That was their cue to move in and arrest Dillinger.

"Stick 'em up, Johnny!"

At approximately 10:30 P.M., the doors to the Biograph opened and people started to exit. All of the agents' eyes were on Purvis. When a man wearing a straw hat, accompanied by two women, walked past Purvis, the agent quickly placed a cigar in his mouth and lit a match. Perhaps sensing something was wrong, the man turned and looked at Purvis, at which point Purvis drew his pistol and said, "Stick 'em up, Johnny!" In response, the man turned as if he was going to run away, while at the same time reaching for what appeared to be a gun. Seeing the movement, the other agents opened fire. As the man ran away, attempting to flee down the alleyway alongside the theater, he was shot four times on his left side and once in the back of the neck before crumpling on the pavement. When Purvis reached him and checked for vitals, there were none. Minutes later, after being driven to a local hospital, John Dillinger was pronounced DOA. But as soon as it was announced that Dillinger was dead, the controversy began.

Dillinger Disputed

Much of the basis for the conspiracy stems from the fact that Hoover, both publicly and privately, made it clear that no matter what, he wanted Dillinger caught. On top of that, Agent Purvis was under a lot of pressure to capture Dillinger, especially since he'd failed with a previous attempt. Keeping that in mind, it would be easy to conclude that Purvis, in his haste to capture Dillinger, might have overlooked a few things. First, it was Purvis alone who pointed out the man he thought to be Dillinger to the waiting agents. Conspiracy theorists contend that Purvis fingered the wrong man that night, and an innocent man ended up getting killed as a result. As evidence, they point to Purvis's own statement: While they were standing at close range, the man tried to pull a gun, which is why the agents had to open fire. But even though agents stated they recovered a .38-caliber Colt automatic from the victim's body, author Jay Robert Nash discovered that that model was not even available until a good five months after Dillinger's alleged death! Theorists believe that when agents realized they had not only shot the wrong man, but an unarmed one at that, they planted the gun as part of a cover-up.

Another interesting fact that could have resulted in Purvis's misidentification was that Dillinger had recently undergone plastic surgery in an attempt to disguise himself. In addition to work on his face, Dillinger had attempted to obliterate his fingerprints by dipping his fingers into an acid solution. On top of that, the man who Purvis said was Dillinger was wearing a straw hat the entire time Purvis saw him. It is certainly possible that Purvis did not actually recognize Dillinger but instead picked out someone who merely looked like him. If you remember, the only tip Purvis had was Sage telling him that she was going to the movies with Dillinger and his girlfriend. Did Purvis see Sage leaving the theater in her orange blouse and finger the wrong man simply because he was standing next to Sage and resembled Dillinger? Or was the whole thing a setup orchestrated by Sage and Dillinger to trick the FBI into executing an innocent man?

So Who Was It?

If the man shot and killed outside the theater wasn't John Dillinger, who was it? There are conflicting accounts, but one speculation is that it was a man named Jimmy Lawrence, who was dating Polly Hamilton. If you believe in the conspiracy, Lawrence was simply in the wrong place at the wrong time. Or possibly, Dillinger purposely sent Lawrence to the theater hoping FBI agents would shoot him, allowing Dillinger to fade into obscurity. Of course, those who don't believe in the conspiracy say the reason Lawrence looked so much like Dillinger is because he was Dillinger using an alias. Further, Dillinger's sister, Audrey Hancock, identified his body. Finally, they say it all boils down to the FBI losing or misplacing the gun Dillinger had the night he was killed and inadvertently replacing it with the wrong one. Case closed.

Not really, though. It seems that whenever someone comes up with a piece of evidence to fuel the conspiracy theory, someone else has something to refute it. Some have asked that Dillinger's body be exhumed and DNA tests be performed, but nothing has come of it yet. Until that happens, we'll probably never know for sure what really happened on that hot July night back in 1934. But that's okay, because real or imagined, everyone loves a good mystery.

Index

✳ ✳ ✳ ✳

Elephant tender, 654
Elevators, 287, 391
Elizabeth, Empress, 643
Elizabeth I (queen), 484, 489, 516
"El Paso," 211
Elsener, Karl, 392
E-mail, 416, 503
Emergency room visits, 594
Emerson, Ralph Waldo, 345, 440
Empire State Building, 103
Ends of the earth, 32
England and France, mutual contempt,
    611
English language, 97
E pluribus unum, 83
Ergonomics, 260–61
Ergot, 198–99
Ericksson, Leif, 453
Erik the Red, 452–53
Eris, 505
Escamoles, 91
Escherichia coli (E. coli), 581
Essex, Linda, 61
Estrogen, 282
Euthanasia, 566
Everest, Mount, 216
Exclamation point, 394
Exoskeletons, 434–35
Eye blinks, 69, 305–6, 328
Eyebrows, 622
Eye patches, 170–71
Eyes, compound, 305–6

F

Face-blindness (prosopagnosia),
    571–72
Falling in Love (Pines), 349
Falls/falling, 580
Family Feud, 39–40
Family Scuba Center, 388
Farouk, King, 106–7
Fathers and daughters, 351
FAX machines, 663
FBI, 677–80

Fear, 315–16
Featherstone, Don, 666
Feiffer, Jules, 333
Feminism, 545
Feral children, 307–8
Ferrets, 350
Fetishes, 646
Feuds, 39–40
Ffirth, Stubbins H., 368
Fiber-Optic Link Around the Globe
    (FLAG), 31
Fibers, 649–50
Fields, W. C., 160
Fieseler Fi-103R, 400
Fingernails. *See* Nails.
Fingerprints, 438, 479, 650
Finland, 293
Firecrackers, 103
Fireflies, 344–45
Fire hydrants, 129
Fish, 99, 122, 125, 296, 298, 320–21,
    668
Fish, Albert, 97
Fish odor syndrome, 601
Fish-tank toilets, 651
Five for Fighting, 212
Flatley, Michael, 659
Flies, 305–6
Flight 19, 562
Flight 201, 564
Flowers and death, 628–29
Flynn, Errol, 321
Flynt, Larry, 435
Fogg, Chris, 640–41
Food
    average consumption, 625
    eating contests, 231–32
    gluttons, 106–8
Football, 223–24, 249, 377, 394, 438,
    593, 643
Ford, Gerald, 44, 641
Ford, Henry, 613
Fordyce, George, 107–8
Foreign accent syndrome, 599
Forensic pathology, 45–46, 268–69

Hippos, 279, 340, 578
Hiro, Onoda, 461
Hitler, Adolf, 186, 365
Hockey, 383, 668
Holliday, Doc, 58–59
Hollow Earth Theory, 565
Holly, Buddy, 264
Holmes, David, 337
Holmes, H. H., 555–59
Holmes, Oliver Wendell, Jr., 261
Holmes, Sherlock, 45–46, 634
Holtom, Gerald, 607
Holzer, Hans, 133
Honeybees, 293
Hong Kong, 478–79
Hooker inspectors, 654–55
Hookworms, 567–68
Hooper, William, 623
Hoover, Herbert, 181
Hoover, J. Edgar, 677–80
Horse racing, 427, 608, 648, 655
Horses, 312
Horsley, John Calcott, 88
Hot-air balloons, 539–40
Hotel del Coronado, 141–43
Hot walkers, 655
Houdini, Harry, 511
House of Windsor, 57
Howard, Catherine, 358
Howler monkeys, 325
Hubbard, Cal, 643
Hughes, Howard, 10–13
Hughes, Irene, 26–27
Hughes, Merv, 658
Human tower building, 252
Hummingbirds, 325, 445
Hunter cocktail, 100
Hunza people, 242
Hurkos, Peter, 25
Hurricanes, 497

I

Ice climbing, 234
Ice cream, 87

Iceland, 452–53
Iceman, 8
Icke, David, 187
If I Ran the Zoo (Seuss), 88
Iguanas, 578
Illuminati, 187
Immune system, 568
Impotence, 287
Ince, Thomas, 144
Indigestion, 86–88
Insanity pleas, 574–75
Insects
    biggest, 341–42
    bioluminescence, 344–45
    crime and punishment, 335
    exoskeletons, 434–35
    eyes, 305–6
    undiscovered species, 332–33
Insomnia, 360
Instant replay, 377
Intelligence and brain size, 273–74
International Banana Club Museum,
    196
International Space Station (ISS),
    496
Interstate highway system, 48, 242
Ireland, 454, 527–28
Iron-manganese crusts, 425
Islam, 638
Islet of Langerhans, 603
Ismael, Abdul Kassem, 377
Israel's postage stamps, 625
Issei, Sagawa, 97
Iwo Jima photograph, 168–69

J

Jackson, Andrew, 521
Jackson, J. Nickie, 152
Jack the Ripper, 24
"Jack the Stripper," 211
James Bond, 102–3
JANET, 466–67
Japan, typhoons, 433
Jaws, 324

THE WINES OF CALIFORNIA
THE PACIFIC NORTHWEST
AND NEW YORK

*Including the First Classification
of the Best Vineyards and Wineries*

ROY ANDRIES DE GROOT

Maps by Cal Sacks

Summit Books **S** *New York*

10   9   8   7   6   5   4   3   2   1
First Edition

Library of Congress Cataloging in Publication Data

De Groot, Roy Andries, 1912–
  The wines of California, the Pacific Northwest,
and New York.

  Includes index.
  1. Wine and wine making—United
States. I. Title.
TP557.D4 1982   641.2'22'0979   82-10638
ISBN 0-671-40049-5

ACKNOWLEDGMENTS

It has taken almost twenty years to assemble all the tasting notes for this book and to get to know the winemakers well enough to understand the fullest implications of their philosophies and techniques. Then, it has taken five years to assemble the material into a logical plan and to write the narrative text. It would be quite impossible to find the space to thank every single person, in every corner of this vast land, who gave me a helping hand. But I remember every one of them, every incident, with warm gratitude.

The center and heart of all factual and statistical information about the California wine industry since 1934 has been The Wine Institute in San Francisco. I shall always remember with grateful thanks its former president, Harry Serlis, for so much sound advice and such strong support during his entire ten-year association with the Institute, from 1965 to 1975. My thanks, also, to his executive assistant, Harvey Posert, for fifteen years of friendship and practical help; to Bill Houlton; and to other members of the original staff at the time that this book was conceived. Today, I feel an equal degree of approval and practical assistance from the brilliant, new Wine Institute president, John De Luca, from his executive assistant, Brian St. Pierre, from Jean Valentine, and from other current members of the institute's staff.

At the University of California's Department of Viticulture and Enology at Davis, I remember with warm admiration Dr. Harold "Hod" Berg, the then-director of the department who, in a lengthy series of brilliant tape-recorded interviews, gave me an in-depth survey of the American wine industry and its future prospects.

In New York State, I am grateful for informational services to Jim Trezises, the executive director of the New York State Winegrowers Association at Penn Yan and to Mary Plane of Ovid.

In Oregon, I received most useful technical advice and help from

7

Dr. Barney Watson of the Department of Wine Technology at the University of Oregon in Corvallis, and from Diana Lett, a member of the board of directors of the Winegrowers Council of Oregon, who supplied information on Oregon laws governing the production and labeling of state wines.

In Washington State, my thanks for much help to Dr. Gerry Warren, the president of the Enological Society of the Pacific Northwest, and to a number of the society's members, including especially Dorothea Checkley, also, for technical information, to Dr. Charles Nagel of the Department of Wine Technology at the University of Washington in Pullman, also to Dr. Mohammed Amadullah, the director of the university's Agricultural Experimental Station at Prosser in the Yakima Valley.

A very special note of thanks to Charles Olken and Earl Singer, the editors, publishers, and writers of the excellent newsletter "The Connoisseurs' Guide to California Wines." They often acted as my "ears and eyes" on the West Coast, while I was at work on the East Coast—leading me to interesting and sometimes outstanding new wines, often from promising new vineyards. They invariably gave me permission to make use of their research and technical material, and, while I sometimes differed with their subjective judgments, I never failed to admire the accuracy, detail, and diligence of their enological and viticultural investigations.

My special thanks to Jim Nassikas, the president of the Stanford Court Hotel in San Francisco, who maintains one of the finest and largest cellars of California wine in the country and has always allowed me to browse freely among its bins, choosing any bottle, however old and valuable, for tasting and appraisal. This "freedom of opportunity" at every visit to San Francisco—especially when combined with Jim's advice based on his vast experience and knowledge —was a contribution to this book of inestimable value.

I am especially grateful to so many of my colleagues among the wine journalists and writers, who have never failed to help with advice, to give frank answers to difficult questions, to supply often exclusive information, or to send me copies of their own private documents. I am particularly grateful to Jeffrey Alan Fiskin, the wine editor of *California Magazine* of Los Angeles, who was the first "technical expert" asked by the publisher to read and appraise my finished manuscript. He helped to find a substantial number of errors. He made invaluable suggestions for stylistic improvements. And he made important proposals toward a clearer organization of the book. I consider his contributions to be of major importance. Others, among my literary colleagues, to whom I feel a sense of gratitude are Gerald Asher of *Gourmet*, Robert Lawrence Balzer of the *Los Angeles Times*, the late Stan Reed of the *Seattle Post-Intelligencer*, Harvey Steiman of the *San Francisco Examiner*, Tom Stockley of the *Seattle Times*, and Bob Thompson, the author of a number of wine books.

This book, which was, to say the least, an extremely complicated structure during its building, would never have been possible without the devoted, efficient, and loyal work of my associates, professional specialists, and staff, especially Elizabeth Tihany, who did the historical research; my wife, Katherine, who was the primary editor; also, Sophie Clarke, Christina Dieckman, Dona de Sanctis, Pamela Tait, and Diane Van Doren.

I am grateful for the professional services of the publisher, Summit Books, especially its president, Jim Silberman, who was my revered and valued editor on this book; the copy editor, Jay Hyams; Kate Edgar; and other members of the publishing staff.

I owe, as always, a debt of gratitude to my literary agent, Bob Cornfield, for smoothing ruffled feathers and always remaining calm and charming, even under impossible extremes of tension.

Finally, a pat on the head for my dog, Ateña, for her willingness to sleep quietly for hours under my desk while I was writing, but for always being ready to dash off to any vineyard anywhere to chase rabbits among the vines. She was sometimes willing to sniff wine— never to taste it. I think she misses one of the joys of living.

Roy Andries de Groot

June 1, 1982
New York City

To Joe Heitz and Fred McCrea
two great winemakers
who gave me a sense of the art and balance
in the creation of wine
and led me to the
disciplined exhilaration of tasting

CONTENTS

*"O, for a draught of vintage! that hath been
Cool'd a long age in the deep-delved earth,
Tasting of Flora and the country green,
Dance, and Provençal song, and sunburnt mirth!"*

—*John Keats*
1819

*"The Art of Good Living frowns on the habit of
scrambling with nondescript drink and mediocre
food as though one is racing to catch a plane. Time
means so much in the life of a fine wine, that Time
should not be stinted in its appreciation. The wine of
pedigreed lineage is poured to be courted and played
with—not instantly tossed down the throat. It is a
delicate pleasure to sense its bouquet expanding
under the warmth of the hand. Knowledge and
patience are among the essential virtues of the
connoisseur."*

—*H. Warner Allen*
London, 1961

PREAMBLE ONE:

The Mechanics of Tasting

This book cannot possibly hope to classify every vineyard and winery in the United States. Even the great French Classification of 1855 ranked only the sixty-two best vineyards out of about three thousand at that time in Bordeaux alone. Some sort of wine is made in every one of our fifty states, in more than six hundred vineyards of every conceivable size and type, hidden away in every corner of our land. Clearly, I have not been able to visit them all, much less taste all their wines. As a first, practical limitation, we must say that this is a classification of the best of America—the FINE, NOBLE, SUPERB, and truly GREAT wines of the United States.

This book might have been produced, as a team responsibility, by a hundred tasters and writers, dividing the territory up among themselves and fanning out in all directions. But I think that the enjoyment and judgment of wine is a very personal pleasure—not readily adaptable to a team operation. I have participated in hundreds of tasting panels. Sometimes, rarely—when all the members are completely professional, when each of them tastes by classical rules, judging without emotion, eliminating all complications of sensuous pleasure—it can happen that there is a final unanimity and a single result. But with the majority of wine-tasting panels, there is such a wide divergence of personal opinion, so many sensuous judgments in direct conflict with each other, cancelling each other out, that the final result throws little light on anything. From the very beginning of this project, I have discarded that kind of tasting. I have sought to make this a book in which each wine was appraised within exactly the same frame of human and technical reference.

To this end, I have tasted every wine against a professional wine rating chart (see page 37) which allocates scoring points to each of

17

the special characteristics of each wine, including its aroma and bouquet, its taste, its acid-alcohol-sugar balance, its body texture, and its
degree of maturity. If the wine is terrible, it scores under 10 points
and is marked UNDRINKABLE. A final score of 10 to 22 points
means that the wine is of EVERYDAY DRINKING quality. A final
score of from 23 to 26 points means that the wine is marked GOOD.
A final score of 27 to 30 points means SUPERIOR, the top of the
range for sound, family table wines.

Above a final score of 30 points comes the range of the outstanding wines. From 31 to 36, the wine is marked as FINE, from 37 to 42,
a NOBLE wine; from 43 to 46, a SUPERB wine; and, at the very top
of the tree, from 47 to 50, a rare wine that is truly GREAT. Obviously,
the rating of a single vintage wine can hardly provide an accurate
classification of a vineyard or of a winemaking performance. Just as
in 1855, it is still the average success and popularity of the wine, year
after year, with the repeated demonstrations of the skill of the winemaker in good years and bad, that ultimately sets the ranking of the
vineyard or winery. For each wine that I have tasted during the
almost twenty years of research for this book—an approximate total
of 128,500 bottles—a note card was made and filed under the name
of the vineyard or winery. Gradually, over the years, as each group
of cards expanded and the information could be averaged, a clearer
and clearer pattern emerged for that vineyard, and its classification
became less and less a question of emotional judgment, more and
more a matter of mathematical configuration.

This book, then, will be successful to the extent that it strikes the
right balance between art and mathematics. You can measure the
popularity of a wine by recording the number of bottles sold. You
can rate its prestige by charting the prices that buyers were willing to
pay for it. But the joy of judging wine is an art, and the pleasure of
drinking it is one of the deep satisfactions of the Good Life. Sensuous
delight must also be a factor in the process of classification.

PREAMBLE TWO:

Why Do You Like This Wine
Better Than the Others?

When an experienced connoisseur tastes a wine, in the very first instant, many qualities of that wine are simultaneously, unemotionally appraised and noted. But with a drinker of limited experience, with less knife-edge sharpness of judgment, with sensuous feelings less coldly under control, the instantaneous first impression of a new wine is not so clearly focused. I have shared thousands of bottles with such average drinkers, carefully observing their reactions. I am convinced that there is one single factor, above all others, that makes the taster of limited experience say, "Oh! I *like* this wine."

It is the presence in the wine of a very small quantity of unabsorbed grape sugar. In other words, the first thing you notice at the first sip is a very slight sweetness—or the absence of it. This is what professional tasters define as "dryness," or "softness," or "richness." These definitions do not mean that the wine has full sweetness. A sweet wine—often called a dessert wine—is in a different category. We are dealing with minuscule levels of sugar that still allow the wines to be "table wines," suitable for drinking with various kinds of foods. Since this book is organized, at least in part, according to the dryness, softness, richness, or sweetness of the wines, it is important to understand, from the beginning, the part played by the sugar during the harvesting, fermentation, and vinification of the wines.

In the final weeks of the growing and ripening of the bunches of grapes on the vines, the farmer-vintner has sugar on his mind almost all the time. As the bright sun warms the bunches of grapes, the acid in each berry falls, and the amount of sugar rises. On sunny days, several times each week during the final month, the farmer-vintner walks among his vines, picking grapes here and there so that he can measure the sugar and assess the acid-sugar balance by means of a small scientific instrument he carries, the refractometer. He puts the crushed grapes into the instrument, then holds it up to the light, looks through the eyepiece, and takes the readings. As the grapes approach perfect ripeness, the falling percentage of acid is translated into a descending curve on the chart on the clipboard hanging at the farmer's belt. At the same time, the increasing percentage of sugar becomes a rising curve on the chart. When these two curves are approaching the right balance with each other, the farmer can predict, at least ten days in advance, the exact time when the sugar balance will be dead-right—the precise day to start the harvest.

When the sweet grapes are picked and piled into the crusher, so that the juice flows into the fermentation vat, everything soon begins to boil, bubble, and heave. Romantic writers used to call this "the mystery of the living wine." In these scientific days, there is no mystery anymore. The fermentation is rather like a ballet performance in which one group of dancers must appear on stage on a precise cue, must complete its assigned part exactly, then disappear, making way for the next group, which, in turn, gives way to the next, and so on. When the fermentation begins, the first dancers are the millions of benevolent bacteria, the microscopic mushroom-type yeasts that are as essential to the wine as the grape itself. Their assignment is to gobble up the sugar in the mash, digest it quickly, and break it up into its elements as liquid alcohol and carbon-dioxide gas—hence the violent bubbling. But the dance is not quite as simple as that.

When each yeast cell has done its work, converting sugar into alcohol, it dies a noble death. When so much sugar has been converted that the alcohol content of the fermented juice rises to about 14 or 15 percent, the yeast cell simply suffocates from the results of its own work and dies. If there is a surplus of yeast cells, all the sugar will have been consumed before the yeasts die, and the fermented wine will be, as the winemakers say, "completely dry." But suppose there are not enough yeast cells to complete the job before they all die—then there will be in the fermented wine, to use the technical term, a certain amount of "residual sugar," measured as a percentage of the volume of the whole. This is what makes a "soft," or "rich," or "sweet" wine. There is, also, a perfectly natural way in which the winemaker can create this effect. He can, moment by moment, all through the fermentation, measure the remaining sugar. If he wants to hold some of it, he can, at any time, stop the fermentation. These days, virtually every winery includes equipment for "cold fermentation"—that is, fermentation in refrigerated vats, so that the precise temperature of the bubbling, heaving, fermenting juice can be strictly controlled. This means that, at any moment, the winemaker can lower the temperature and stop the fermentation by putting the yeast cells to sleep, so to speak. Then the remaining yeast cells can be filtered out of the wine, and the rest of the sugar will remain unconsumed as "residual sugar."

If you can find out what the residual sugar percentage is in any particular wine—either from the label or by asking questions—you will know in advance whether you will find that wine dry, or soft, or rich, or sweet. Very few wines have absolutely zero residual sugar. The usual figure for a completely "dry" wine is a sugar percentage of between 0.05 and 0.15 percent. But, with normal tastebuds, it is virtually impossible to begin to taste any sugar, to feel that the wine is anything but dry, until the residual sugar percentage reaches 1.2 to 1.5 percent. At those figures, or below them, you are likely to feel, provided the wine is cold, that it is dry.

Above these minimum figures, the question of human tastebud sensitivity becomes more complicated and more variable. Above 1.5 percent and on up to 2.5 percent, your tastebuds are certainly going to tell you that it is a soft wine—though different tasters, of different degrees of experience, will disagree strongly as to how soft.

Above this, the borderlines become quite blurred. Certainly at 3.75 percent or 4 percent, or 4.5 percent, you are likely to call the wine "rich." When it reaches 5, or 6, or 7 percent, the verdict will be increasingly unanimous that it is a sweet dessert wine. When the residual sugar reaches percentages around 12, then the wine is so honey sweet that, in reality, sweetness virtually ceases to be a factor in judging the wine. Our tastebuds can no longer differentiate between, say, 12 percent and 14 percent. When tasting the great, old vintages of the honey-sweet Sauternes of Bordeaux, one tends to think of the extraordinarily refreshing balance of the lemony acid and the marvelous range of the aromatic flavors—while the sweetness becomes entirely secondary.

In the low-sugar ranges, however, the taster's perception of dryness or softness or richness is, in my experience, the all-important factor in deciding which wine you like best and in finding other wines of the same acceptable character. So three of the following chapters divide the white wines of America into the three groups which, with their dominant grapes, are controlled by the absence or presence of sugar. From each chapter, you should be able to find the wines you like best in that group, with alternatives for the expansion of your tasting experience and, within each separate category, a classification of the best wines made by the most consistently successful vineyards and wineries. Then, after the central chapters have separately surveyed the various groups of white, red, rosé, sweet, and sparkling wines, a Classification of the Top 200 American Vineyards and Wineries appears on page 225. Finally, the classified vineyards, listed alphabetically, are discussed in the last section of the book, beginning on page 295.

PART ONE

HISTORY REPEATS ITSELF

CHAPTER I

A Time to Take
the Measure of American Wines

The extraordinary thing about the making of wine is the way history repeats itself. At least twice, in modern times, huge segments of the world's wine industry have been killed off completely. In Europe, during the 40-odd years between 1860 and around 1900, the terrible vine-root disease, phylloxera, killed the plants in virtually every wine district and brought winemaking to an almost total standstill. (This is discussed in greater detail in Chapter VI.) In the United States during the fourteen years between 1919 and 1933, the political disease of Prohibition achieved the same result for the American industry. Yet in spite of businesses bankrupted, families at the point of starvation, homes and lands lost, and lives having to be started over, the short-term agony did bring some good long-term results—a cleansing and purification of the quality of the wine for its eternal future.

The purification came through the people who make the wine. They were divided by the immediate disaster into the "professionals" and the "amateurs," those who were wholly committed and those whose commitment was less deep. In Europe, thousands of winemaking families were convinced that there would never again be a wine industry. They sold their homes and their lands and moved away. In California, too, thousands of families gave up and left the state or pulled up their wine vines and planted table grapes instead. It has taken almost fifty years to bring these "lost lands" back into wine growing. Indeed, some of the less-good lands and the less-dedicated families have never come back.

Yet the owners of the great Château Latour in France were so sure that the phylloxera disease would be overcome that they spent their time and much capital, while there were no vines on their land, improving the arrangement and construction of the subsoil and the

25

drainage. In the same way, in California, the great Martini family, never doubting for a moment that Prohibition was a mistake that would sooner or later be corrected, spent their time improving their lands and preparing for a better future. These two examples—chosen from among hundreds—dramatize the most basic principle in the making of noble and great wine. It can never be a completely mechanized, mass-produced, factory process. It always involves human struggle—hard choices between quality and quantity, difficult decisions between prestige and profit. The ruling factor is always the winemaker's degree of dedication.

So the first thing to be known about a wine—if it is to be "classified," so that its character and quality may be judged from the label before the bottle is opened—is the name of the maker. The second vital piece of information—the other essential factor controlling the character and quality of the wine—is the precise piece of earth where the particular variety of grape was grown. But, of course, these are modern considerations. For thousands of years of wine history, they were not taken into any account.

Drinking Wine Without the Faintest Idea
What Is in the Glass

For centuries, through the Middle Ages, by far the most experienced of wine importers and drinkers were the British, and that was the result of a political accident. The movie *The Lion in Winter* reminded us that when King Henry II of England married France's Queen Eleanor of Aquitaine in the year 1152, she brought with her, as part of her dowry, all the great vineyard lands of Bordeaux. These vineyards were the source of what the British certainly thought were the best—light, clear, and joyous—red wines in the world. In a short time, hundreds of British ships appeared in the great estuary of the Gironde off the Bordeaux docks, to sail away with barrels of wine. Not one of the barrels was labeled. Not one British drinker would ever know from which vineyard it came or who had made it.

This British concentration on Bordeaux wine began in the middle of the 12th century, but not until five hundred years later, toward the end of the 17th century, was there the first written mention in English of the name of a French château: Samuel Pepys wrote in his diary on April 10, 1663, that his favorite French wine was "Hobryan" (Haut-Brion).

Many British families in those medieval times left diaries and letters describing exactly how they bought their wines, how they stored them, and how they drank them. The wine was shipped in rough wooden casks, often with badly fitting steel hoops, so that there was steady leakage, and casks were topped up with any kind of ordinary wine that happened to be available. When you wanted something to drink with your dinner, you sent your servant to the local wine merchant with a kind of bottle-jug, a long-necked potbellied flagon, in which the wine was brought home. It was paid for by the pint. Corks were unknown. The neck might be stoppered with a twist of straw to keep dirt out; some Italian wines were sealed with a slug of olive oil in the neck.

Once the wine was out of the cask and exposed to the air, it wasn't expected to last for more than a couple of days. It would then go sour and was either used as vinegar or thrown out. No one understood why it soured. Several hundred years would pass before the great French chemist Louis Pasteur would explain, with the help of his microscopes, the actions of the vinegar bacteria in the air. Meanwhile, English drinkers continued to buy fresh wine every day—something expendable, something generic, something a bit mysterious, since it was never known who had made it, or where, precisely, it had come from. One hoped that one vintage would last until the next, but often it did not.

The Drinking Habits of
Henry Purefoy and His Mother

A vivid picture has been left to us in the diaries and letters of Henry Purefoy, who was the squire of a smallish village about sixty miles outside London in the 18th century. Although the Purefoys had a fair amount of money to spend and were determined to drink "only the very best wine," they knew virtually nothing about what they bought and what went into their cups. The only aspect over which they had any control—and not much, even over that—was the price. Mrs. Purefoy preferred white wine and bought it by the jug at about a shilling a pint. If it were "strong mountain wine," she would dilute it with water. She insisted, again and again, that, wherever the wine came from, "it must be dry." Henry preferred red and bought it by the cask, but was always concerned with how long it would last after it was drawn out of the barrel—whether two days, or three—because "if a large quantity of it goes sour, then it becomes an expensive matter." Sometimes, when all his red went sour, he was forced temporarily to fall back on his mother's white. They found some of it "so raw and rough" as to be undrinkable, and they proposed to return it to the wine merchant. But instead they sold it to some neighbors who were even less knowledgeable about wine than they were. After this experience, the Purefoys began looking at the wine advertising in the newspapers in the hope of finding a new wine merchant who might be able to supply them with "brisker wine."

A New Queen—A New Wine

This chaotic wine situation might have gone on forever had it not been for another political accident. In 1662, King Charles II of England married Portugal's Queen Catherine of Braganza, who brought with her, as part of her dowry, some of the Portuguese wines of the Douro Valley. By this time, the wine relationship with France had almost completely changed. Two hundred years earlier, in 1453, the French counterrevolution that had been started by Joan of Arc had finally thrown the British out of Bordeaux, and since that time trade with France had steadily deteriorated. Now, with the arrival of a Portuguese queen, the British thought it was a good time to switch to Portuguese wine. In 1703, the Methuen Treaty was signed in order to encourage the importation of Portuguese wines into Britain.

These Douro wines were exceedingly sour—almost undrinkable —unless you could keep some sweetness in them during the fermentation by adding a small dosage of grape brandy. But brandy with the new wine was awful. What was needed—as the producers put it —was for the brandy lion to be given time to lie down with the sweet lamb. The wine needed to be aged. How could that be done while protecting it from attack by the vinegar bacteria?

Someone working in the cool, dark depths of one of the lodges, the cellar warehouses at the docks of the city of Oporto, had a stroke of genius. Why couldn't the wine be stored in bottles? Why couldn't the bottles be sealed with the newly discovered, flexible bark of the cork oak tree which grows so profusely in Portugal? Why couldn't the shape of the potbellied bottle-flagon be changed to a straight-sided cylinder that could be tightly stacked, making the most efficient use of storage space?

Then, in quick succession, there came a series of revolutionary discoveries. If the bottle were left standing up, the cork would quickly dry out, and there would be a leakage of air, forming a bubble just beneath the cork, the ideal place for vinegar bacteria to congregate and breed, attacking the wine and souring it. But if the bottle were laid on its side, the wine would bathe the cork, and it would not shrink. At the same time, any air bubble would be up against the impermeable glass, safely sealed off from any contact with the outside air. No bacteria could enter. The wine could age safely. It was the birth of modern "vintage wine."

Almost certainly, the first vintage port to be matured in a bottle was in 1775, but we have no record as to how long it was allowed to develop. The experiment must have seemed exceedingly risky, and we do not know when this bottle was opened and the wine drunk. There are really no documented records of port vintages until the year of Waterloo, 1815.

And on Each Bottle
a Label with a Name and a Place

When vintage wine began to be shipped and sold in bottles—first from Portugal, but, very soon afterward, also from Bordeaux—not only was the wine better, it also lost its anonymity. For the first time in the wine business, every bottle could have a label, a direct communication from the producer of the wine to the consumer. From now on, every arrogantly proud French owner of even the smallest Bordeaux vineyard gave his house (even if it were only a cottage) and his property some fancy château name, until soon there were more castles in Bordeaux than in Spain! Equally important, many of the labels named the precise geographical place where the grapes were grown and harvested and the wine made and put into the bottle. This was the beginning of the rise to international fame of the château, commune, village, and district names that today are associated with some of the world's greatest wines.

The First Vintage Bottling of Château Lafite

During the summer of 1797, the great cellar beneath Château Lafite in Bordeaux was partially reconstructed so that it could be used for the storage of bottles as well as casks. In due course, a substantial part of that 1797 vintage, after it had had its proper time in the wooden *barriques*, the specially shaped Bordeaux barrels of 225 liters, was bottled, tightly corked, and stored in glass to see what would happen to it. The vintage was not good, but in spite of that disadvantage the wine in the bottles developed better than the wine that had remained in the wooden *barriques*. Lafite had proved its point. Before long, every other Bordeaux château that could afford to do so was imitating Lafite. They were rewarded by a series of magnificent vintages—1798, 1811, and 1815—which established beyond any shadow of doubt the value of bottle aging.

In the United States, Different Wines but the Same Mistakes and Problems

It can be argued that the beginning of serious winemaking in North America was the summer day in 1769 when a Franciscan friar, Padre Junipero Serra, rode on his white horse from the border of the Mexican district of Baja California into the Spanish province of Alta California, along the coastal road that would soon be called El Camino Real. That night, the padre stayed at the newly dedicated Mission San Diego, and in the morning he planted in the gardens the root cuttings that he had brought with him, in his saddlebag, of the Spanish Criolla grape, now called the Mission grape in California. Before long, they were making wine at almost all of the twenty-one missions along El Camino Real as far north as Mission Dolores in San Francisco.

Admittedly, there had been some earlier, less successful experiments. Two hundred years before, French Huguenot settlers under Spanish rule in Florida had made wine from local native Scuppernong grapes, but they were very soon forbidden from doing so by King Phillip II of Spain, who wanted to suppress competition with wines from Spain. In the 17th century, Mexican Franciscans brought their Spanish Mission grapes to New Mexico and pressed them there into sacramental wines. In 1732, James Alexander developed the native *Vitis labrusca* "Alexander" grape in Pennsylvania, and it was transplanted to various eastern states, but the wine made from it was virtually undrinkable. It was the same story with the wine made in the Susquehanna Valley near Philadelphia, in the Chautauqua grape country of New York, in the first vineyards of the Ohio Valley in Cincinnati, the first Croton Point wines of the Hudson River Valley, and the first wines from Hammondsport on the Finger Lakes. In 1833, the first French vines were imported into California and planted within the city limits of Los Angeles.

All these New World winemakers—even the earliest—had behind them hundreds of years of European winemaking experience from which to draw their lessons. Yet they repeated the same basic mistakes made for centuries past by the French and the Portuguese. These American wines were generally vinified crudely and harshly. They were blended carelessly. Worst of all, they were not precisely labeled, so that no one could tell who made them or where they came from.

Nothing dramatizes these faults and problems better, at the end of the first one hundred years of American wines, than the story of the man who came to be called "the father of modern Californian viticulture." He was the Hungarian adventurer, entrepreneur, exploiter, promoter, "Colonel" or "Count" (in fact, he was neither) Agoston Haraszthy, who came to California for the Gold Rush in 1848 but made his fortune out of the developing wine industry. He speculated in converting farmlands into vineyards and in importing European vine-root cuttings, which he sold all over the state to farmers who wanted to get into the business of growing wine grapes. In 1861, Haraszthy got himself appointed by the governor of California to make an official visit to Europe to study wine-growing methods and to bring back a huge selection of European grape varieties. After six months of travel, he brought back one hundred thousand root cuttings of about three hundred varieties of grapes.

These cuttings were sold off virtually without identification, and the chaos that resulted in the California wine industry took almost a hundred years to clear up. All across the state, the wrong vines were planted in the wrong places, and the wrong grapes were harvested at the wrong times. Only the most detailed and patient "microclimatic research" by the Department of Viticulture and Enology of the University of California at Davis—research which was begun in 1861 and which continued well into the 1960s—finally got the wrong vines uprooted and the right vines planted on the right plots of earth. Meanwhile, millions of gallons of California wine were sold without the consumers knowing what types of wine they were drinking.

Even in the 1960s, when I began interviewing the executives of the largest companies for my magazine articles, I found these marketing men still obsessed by the idea of mass production in the making and selling of wine. They had heard of the great châteaux of Bordeaux—of Haut-Brion, Lafite, Latour, Margaux—but they did not want to emulate them. They wanted to go on selling vast quantities of blended "Mountain Red," or "Mountain White," or "Country Rustic," or "Happy Chablis," or "Hill Country Red." These powerful companies, with profits running into millions of dollars, were afraid of their customers. They feared that if people got to know a particular wine made in a particular vineyard from a particular grape in a particular place they might begin to demand that wine at the store. Then, it was argued, the mass sales of nondescript mass-production blended wines might be jeopardized. Even twenty-five or thirty years ago, some American mass-marketing men still thought of wine as a kind of alcoholic cola drink—a habit-forming thirst quencher with no variation to it, absolutely uniform from year to year, that would be sold under a national trade name. The last thing they wanted to encourage would be quality judgments and deliberate choices on the part of the drinkers.

The French Solution:
The Classification of 1855

About 150 years earlier, France had been in almost the same position as the United States. Nondescript wines were made and blended and sold in barrels without anyone knowing precisely who had made the wine and where it came from. A few famous vineyards had become well known all over Europe and even across the Atlantic. To such connoisseurs as Thomas Jefferson, the names of Haut-Brion, Lafite, Latour, and Margaux were familiar. Most other proud French vineyard owners were struggling to make the finest wines to get their vineyards known and to gain for them popularity and prestige. But in general the great mass of wine was still anonymous.

One of the most devoted and farsighted aficionados of French wines was Prince Napoleon (later the Emperor Napoleon III). He was convinced that the future of French wine lay not in the anonymous barrel wines but in those of the individual vineyards producing the vintages of top quality. In 1853, within a few weeks of being crowned as emperor, Napoleon took charge of the planning for a grand exhibition to be held in Paris in 1855 to project to the world the glory of France. Napoleon wanted particularly to display the great wines and to publish an officially sponsored list of the finest vineyards. It was an ambitious project. Who would dare to decide which were the top names?

Since Bordeaux was the leading wine region, the job of preparing the list was finally given to a "Tasting Commission" chosen from among "the most eminent and best qualified" Bordeaux wine brokers, the men who tasted and sold the wines every day of their lives. There were three Frenchmen on the commission and one British merchant, the famous Nathaniel Johnston. They set out to produce a list of vineyard wines in the order of their average continuing excellence, popularity, and value. They could use as guides quite a number of previous lists, some private and secret, some actually published.

A hundred years earlier, in 1755, a first attempt had been made to rank the wines of Bordeaux. When you read this ancient and tattered list, the amazing thing about it is that it entirely ignores any concept of a vineyard as a separate entity, or the name of any person who put the wine into the barrels, or even the name of any particular place where the grapes were grown and the wine was made. Those concepts had simply not occurred to anyone at that time. Instead, the wines were divided and grouped within the parishes of the local country churches. It was said that the wines around such-and-such a church were the best—that those close to that other church were the second best—and so on. Yet, today, if you trace out those ancient parish boundaries on the old maps, you will discover that the old parish rankings match almost exactly the legal "controlled appellations" of today. After all, 250 years is only a moment of time to nature —neither the growing conditions nor the qualities of the earth have changed.

Then came the French Revolution, with its major battles between Church and State, battles reflected in Bordeaux by the complete elimination of the church parish as the dividing principle for wines. In a ranking list published in 1833, all mention of churches has disappeared, and we have the modern concept of château vineyard names, grouped by communes, villages, and districts, exactly as they are today.

Armed with these and their own secret lists, the members of the Tasting Commission began their work in November 1854, and, often meeting every day, continued into the spring of 1855. They did not restrict their judgments entirely to the geographic location, the soil, and the tasting quality of the wine. They also considered the efficiency of the agricultural management of the vineyard and the technical skill of the vinification. They said that they tried to think of each vineyard and each wine as it was at that moment, but they thought also of its long-term possibilities for future development and improvement. They gave some of the credit for the excellence of a wine to the human factor, but most of the credit went to nature's gift of the earth and the location. (Incidentally, almost all of these considerations, more than fifty years later, were written into the French *Appellation Contrôlée* wine law. Under the various ministerial decrees, the geographic location of a vineyard became the main criterion for its legal right to an appellation ranking, with, as subsidiary factors, the grape varieties used in the wine, the degree of alcohol, and the typical regional character of the finished wine.)

Each member of the 1854 Tasting Commission, obviously, had his own ideas as to the order of importance of the vineyards. No one questioned "the four greats," which consistently brought the highest prices: châteaux Lafite, Latour, Margaux, and Haut-Brion. Below them came the second, third, fourth, and fifth rankings, with, down at the bottom, the least important vineyards divided between Superior, Ordinary, and Peasant. Finally, they produced the most famous wine list in the world, still in valid use today as "the Classification of 1855." From the first moment of its creation, it was deadly controversial. Every owner of every château not on the list loudly claimed that it was totally inaccurate and incomplete. It has been consistently attacked for 125 years. But it has remained the most important and influential ranking list of all time. It has been imitated in many other wine districts and regions. It has—perhaps more than any other single document—projected the fame and prestige of French wines.

There is absolutely no doubt that the French Classification of 1855—and the other classification lists that followed for other wine districts and regions—changed the course of European wine history. Suddenly, serious wine consumers knew what they were drinking. They were able to select the qualities of the wines from the labels and to form their personal preferences. For the first time, wine drinking could become an exciting hobby—a conscious act instead of a thoughtless habit. A knowledge of wine could be one of the arts of good living—worthy of serious concentration. All this because the names of the most important vineyards were now known, listed, and ranked.

The Time for
a Classification of American Wines

These historical thoughts were strongly in my mind when I arrived in California in the spring of 1969 on a special assignment. *Esquire* magazine had sent me to write a report on the 200th anniversary of wine in California—the 200th year since the Franciscan Padre Junipero Serra had crossed the Mexican border and had planted his first wine grapes at the Mission San Diego. My task was to review 200 years of wine progress, but my editor had challenged me to find the answer to the double-barreled question: "Is there truly great wine in California?—is there balm in Gilead?"

This meant, of course, that I would spend a minimum of time with the very large mass-producers and would make a maximum effort to search out the growing number of smaller vineyards and wineries producing the top-quality wines. Some people thought I was wasting my time. The president of one of the largest companies, in the course of a stormy discussion in his office, told me that California was and always would be "the Big State," and that its future in wine (as in everything else) lay in "big-scale production." That conversation took place a decade ago, and I wonder if he realizes today—looking back over the progress of the last ten years from his retirement ranch in the mountains—how wrong that prophecy was. The dazzling upsurge of California prestige and quality has come from the breakup into smaller vineyard units; from the acceptance of the basic principle of the "microclimate"—the inexorable viticultural fact, known for centuries in France, that a particular variety of grape will make a beautiful wine on one particular tiny patch of earth, but will make mediocre wine on another patch perhaps less than a hundred yards away. The key to progress has been the proliferation of the small vineyard making a particular wine from a particular grape grown on a particular piece of earth.

In that summer of 1969, the owners of some of the top small vineyards of California offered me for tasting a few of the oldest bottles in their cellars—sometimes the very last bottle of a magnificent vintage that had aged to its peak of perfection. I still remember a 1941 vintage of the Italian Charbono grape offered me by John Daniel, a descendant of the pioneer founder of the once-great Inglenook Vineyard, the Finnish sea captain Gustave Niebaum. That ancient Charbono from those grapes planted at Inglenook in the 1930s was a supreme wine—the noblest American I had ever tasted up to that time. It was followed by a superb white Pinot Chardonnay made by Fred McCrea at his minuscule Stony Hill Vineyard on a mountaintop above the Napa Valley. There were also a 1940 Cabernet Sauvignon from the Beaulieu Vineyard and, as some sort of unbelievable peak, a 1929 "sacramental wine" from the depths of Prohibition, a Muscatel from the Louis M. Martini Vineyard—a honeyed white wine that had been in the bottle for at least thirty-five years!

As I tasted these and dozens of other outstanding American wines, the idea became rooted in my mind that there should be a classification of American vineyards and wineries.

To appraise all the major vineyards of the United States would be an immense project. But I regarded it as so important that, as a serious wine taster and as a writer on wine technology, I was prepared to tackle the huge job myself.

I began—using as reference a copy of the federal register of bonded wineries—by typing a complete card file of every vineyard and winery in every state of the United States. There were, in those days in the late 1960s, close to five hundred wineries across the entire United States, just about half of them concentrated in California and the rest located—sometimes surprisingly, in terms of climatic areas —in a wide sweep covering Alabama, Arkansas, Colorado, Connecticut, Delaware, Florida, Georgia, Hawaii, Idaho, Illinois, Indiana, Iowa, Kentucky, Louisiana, Maryland, Massachusetts, Michigan, Minnesota, Mississippi, Missouri, New Hampshire, New Jersey, New Mexico, New York, North Carolina, Ohio, Oklahoma, Oregon,

Pennsylvania, Rhode Island, South Carolina, Texas, Vermont, Virginia, Washington State, and Wisconsin. When I started looking into the individual names and activities of the wineries—and began talking to their owners and winemakers by telephone—the list was fairly rapidly reduced. Some wineries made only raspberry or strawberry wine—not exactly the perfect examples for my book. Others were minuscule family operations, making only a few bottles at a time, for sale over the counter to a limited group of local customers or simply to passing motorists. To count all of these, I felt, would thoroughly unbalance my survey. Thus, by a process of careful, slow attrition, I arrived at a practical, national list of important and serious vineyards and wineries—each card showing the varieties of grapes being grown and the types of wines being made.

I began devoting a part of each year to traveling to various wine areas, spending substantial time in the more important regions, tasting whole ranges of wines, and talking at length to the winemakers. From the first, however, I had always to keep in mind that I was not planning to write an "encyclopedia of American wines," but a book of limited scope and size, devoted to the best wines, the top third of the quality spectrum, the supreme winemakers of this country. Right away, I had to set a lower limit, a minimum standard, below which a wine would not be acceptable. Each was tasted "blind," with no advance knowledge of the name of the wine or of the label information. To make sure that each wine would be appraised against a fixed standard of comparison, I have consistently used a wine-rating chart first shown me by a group of German professionals at tastings in Wiesbaden, where it is customary to taste continuously for four hours at a steady rate of thirty wines per hour—120 wines at each session. During such an intense tasting, if you fail to enter immediate notes on a chart, you will become hopelessly confused. The form of my chart was later adapted and revised (to make it more widely useful in other countries) by Jean-Paul Gardrère, the winemaker of Château Latour. (For more detailed discussion of the technical features of this chart, see Preamble One.)

During my complete survey of U.S. vineyards and wineries, each wine has been tasted and scored on this chart. All wines within the range of EVERYDAY DRINKING were eliminated—as were all wines within the average GOOD to SUPERIOR range. In order to qualify for inclusion in the charts in this book, a wine had to come just within the FINE range—with a score of at least 31 points out of a possible total of 50.

For almost twenty years of searching, this has been the cold hard test for every wine and its maker. I have the most enjoyable and vivid memories of my travels in search of the wines and winemakers that can pass the test. While crisscrossing northern Illinois, I found, in the village of Monee, an interesting and refreshing Champagne-type sparkling wine and another memorable sparkler made in Indianapolis. In Maryland, one cannot fail to admire deeply the pioneering work done by Philip Wagner, both at his original Boordy Vineyards and through his brilliant books. Off the coast of Massachusetts, there is a beautiful small winery, called Martha's Vineyard, on the island of Martha's Vineyard. I have tasted and traveled all over the wine areas of Michigan and visited lovely hillside vineyards in Missouri, along the Missouri River. The wines of Connecticut, New Jersey, and New York are, of course, delivered to my door in Manhattan. In northern Ohio, I have taken a boat across Lake Erie to the sheltered vineyards on Isle St. George, and in the South, around Cincinnati, I have visited lovely vineyards in the deep Ohio Valley and drunk gorgeously refreshing, beautifully pure, wonderfully fruity, nonalcoholic juices of Catawba and de Chaunac grapes handsomely bottled in magnums. I almost wished, at that moment, that nonalcoholic grape juice could qualify as wine. When I delivered a lecture at Rhode Island University, the professor who was my host afterward took me to visit the tiny winery he was developing, Wickford Vineyard, offering me a taste of his Pinot Chardonnay. While staying in Washington, D.C., I have wandered thirstily around Virginia, and while in Wisconsin, I have repeatedly enjoyed the dry cherry wine distilled from the wonderful Door County cherries by the small winery of Dr. Charles von Stiehl at Algoma. From other places, too far away—and where the average weather made the finding of an outstanding wine too small a chance—bottles were delivered to me in New York, and I talked to winemakers by telephone. Friends in all parts of the country collected information and wines for me and passed them along.

Wherever I went, I was offered the most delightful and sincere hospitality. Whenever I called for a favor, I was given complete and immediate cooperation. From almost every source, the wines were excellent as everyday, simple, eminently drinkable, family beverages —to be drunk down to quench a thirst, rather than slowly sipped for the sensuous pleasure of tasting—to quaff in a hammock under the shade of a tree on a hot afternoon, or to accompany a simple family supper. The hard fact is that the great majority of these American wines do not rise above the average, everyday ratings and, therefore, do not qualify for inclusion in this book. At the end of my long search, lasting almost twenty years, I am able to confirm that the ideal soil and weather conditions for outstanding, magnificent, supreme wines exist, so far, only in California, Idaho, New York, Oregon, and Washington State. After this book has been published (and, I hope, widely read), perhaps some distant and so far unknown winemaker—possibly even in South Dakota—may send me a bottle of wine so excellent that it passes all the tasting tests with colors flying. I certainly promise that that wine, with its maker and its vineyard, will be honored and named in our next edition.

Meanwhile, within the present outstanding wine areas, the fixed factors controlling the quality and taste of the wines are the earth and the grapevine varieties. The variable factors are always those of the weather and human judgment. It is the human factor that I have found to be enormously important in the United States—more so than in any other part of the world. The making of the best wine in the United States seems to be inextricably intertwined with the basic concept of American individualism.

In Europe, the winemaker is substantially a slave of the land of his district and his region. If you are, let us say, a grower of grapes and maker of wine in the Chablis district of northern Burgundy, you are tightly bound, by every aspect of law and by centuries of tradition, to a clear concept of precisely what a Chablis wine should be like. Every judgment you make, every step you take, is directed toward making wine in that traditional mold. You may try to make your particular Chablis better than that of your neighbors, but first of all you have to make a legally definable, traditionally recognizable Chablis. Your success depends, ultimately, on the degree to which you can achieve that. If you were suddenly to show an almighty independence of spirit—if you suddenly came up with a Chablis that was different from all the others but unique to you—you would be regarded as a failure by your neighbors, and, if you went too far, you might be legally barred from even using the name "Chablis" on the labels of your bottles. There is no such thing in the district of Chablis as "freedom of winemaking."

But "winemaking freedom" is the very essence of the life of the

American vintner. There is just no such thing as a "traditional wine" of the Napa Valley of California, or of the Yakima Valley of Washington State, or of the Willamette Valley of Oregon, or of the Finger Lakes of New York State. Each American winemaker—in all the thousand-and-one decisions and judgments, from the care of the vines to the picking of the grapes, from the fermenting of the newly pressed juice to its aging and bottling—makes and finishes the wine to an individual standard of personal satisfaction. Oh, yes, most of them do think, have to think, of the selling of the wine, but the enormous variety of American wines proves beyond question that the winemakers do not think of a standardized type of wine destined for a standardized drinking public.

So I have found it essential, when classifying a vineyard, to classify the winemaker as well. Whenever I visit a vineyard and taste the wine, I interview the winemaker and assess, in my own mind, the relationship of human judgment and philosophy with the wine. There are many winemakers who go far beyond the normal requirements of engineering efficiency and technical skill. They are creators with a continuing vision of what they want to achieve. They impose, so to speak, their personal signature on every wine they make. Generally, they have the authority to experiment because they are owners, or partners, of the vineyard. When I meet one of these inventive, forward-pushing winemakers, I add the name of the person to the name of the vineyard in the classification lists of this book.

During my interview with each winemaker, I ask, directly or indirectly, the most basic of questions: How good is the management and how high the technical skill in this vineyard? How much dedication to the ideal of perfection? Will the vines be pruned properly so that there will be not too many bunches of grapes and those that remain will be well nourished from the roots? At the harvest of the grapes, will the quality of the wine be stressed above the quantity? In the winery, is there the best possible vinification equipment? Is the winery adequately capitalized, so that it can be kept modernized? Will the earth from which the grapes grow be kept in perfect repair, properly analyzed, adequately drained from the rainfall, its chemical and mineral composition intact? Will there be continuing experimentation and research on the vine types that will grow best on this particular piece of earth? The answers to these questions (and a good many more) are a measure of the winemaker's dedication to the maintenance and raising of future quality. They add up to a key factor in the classification of the vineyard and the excellence of its wine.

Thus, after more than twenty years of exploration of the interplay of the immutable forces of nature and the brilliant creativity and flexibility of human skill, this book is a judgment and a report.

PART TWO

THE BEST WINES
OF THE
BEST VINEYARDS
AND WINERIES

CHAPTER II

The Dry White Wines

Perfectionist winemakers say that it is very difficult to make an extremely good dry white wine. A small amount of residual sugar—a tiny taste of softness on the tongue—can cover a multitude of minor sins. When the wine is absolutely dry, it must also be virtually perfect in its balance and cleanness. There can be no mistakes in the vinification. There is nothing to cover up even the slightest off-flavor. There can be nothing in it that should not be there. This is why, in almost twenty years of tasting for this book, I have found so few SUPERB dry white wines—and never a supremely GREAT one.

Yet the dry whites, in the everyday to middle ranges of quality, are the most universal and useful of wines—made in every wine district and region of the United States and in virtually every vineyard where wines are produced. They glint in the glass with bright shades of gold, green, and yellow. They release the aromatic perfumes of flowers and fruit. They are joyous, light, refreshing, thirst quenching. The dry whites have been called "the workhorses of the wine world" because they do so many useful things in so many efficient ways. A glass of iced dry white wine is for gulping down to slake a summer thirst on a broiling day while you lounge in a hammock under a shade tree. It is for sipping as a tastebud-clearing aperitif before lunch or dinner. Or it is the perfect accompaniment to all the simple, basic family foods. The average dry white wine does not call much attention to itself. It plays a secure second fiddle— going down easily, gently, smoothly. This is why, even if you keep only a very few bottles in your wine library at home, a good number of them should be dry whites.

As always with wine, you have the widest possible choice from among the products of some of the most famous of the world's white-wine grapes—each variety with its strongly individual character and personality. There are wines so dry they almost bite your tongue; others so tart they might have been spritzed with lemon. Some dry whites are bland and gentle, with a quality of velvet. Some are as light as a spring zephyr; others as bold and domineering as fall thunder. It is up to each serious wine taster to learn, first, which grapes produce his favorite wines; second, which style of wine is preferred within that grape; and, third, who are the winemakers consistently, year after year, making the best examples of that style of wine. For these practical reasons, each principal grape variety and its wines will be analyzed and discussed separately.

CHENIN BLANC (dry) *Also called Pineau de la Loire, or Pinot d'Anjou, or, quite wrongly, White Pinot or White Zinfandel, and, in South Africa, Steen*

In an ideal wine world, it would be possible for the taster to choose the particular wine he wanted for a particular occasion by looking for a particular grape name on the label. Nature has not made it that simple. The problem is dramatized by the Chenin Blanc grape, which is one of the most successful vine varieties transplanted from Europe to the United States. It came, originally, from that demiparadise of soft breezes, easy living, and warm sun, the valley of the river Loire, where the grape was already being grown in the 9th century by the monks of the Abbey of Glenfeuilles on the slopes of Mont Chenin. If you could go with me tomorrow to the Loire and its capital city of Tours, I would take you across the river and up the steep hill to the world-famous wine village of Vouvray, where Saint Martin first planted the Chenin Blanc under its Loire name of Pineau de la Loire and where it remains the unchallenged monarch of every one of those brilliant vineyards bearing the appellation Vouvray.

We could taste the wines for two or three days, and you would be confused, muddled, and, finally, appalled. You would find no uniformity whatsoever from the Chenin Blanc grape. Some of the wines would be bone dry, and others would cover the entire range from slightly soft to richly heavy; some would be honey-sweet dessert wines; and, just to give your survey a dramatic finish, there would be a range of Chenin Blanc sparkling wines, also covering the full range from *brut,* dry, to *demi-sec,* sugary sweet. If that is the way it is at the heart of the Chenin Blanc's homeland, you certainly have to watch your Chenin Blanc labels in the United States.

From its beginning in the 9th century along the Loire, this grape, which was a favorite of Rabelais, has made attractive, bright, delicate, fruity, light, refreshing wines that reflected the life along the valley that is "Le Jardin de France." Through the centuries, the Chenin Blanc remained almost exclusively a Loire Valley grape, its plantings in other parts of France and in other countries around the world remained minuscule—until it was transplanted to California. Here, beginning seriously in 1955, it virtually exploded, both as a vine in the earth and as a wine in the thirsty throats of immediately enthusiastic aficionados. Beginning with a few hundred acres of vines in the Napa Valley and Sonoma County, the vine acreage has expanded, within not much more than twenty-five years, to more than 20,000 acres. It is now also expanding into other states of the United States.

The story of Chenin Blanc on our side of the Atlantic has been a very much foreshortened reflection of its long history in the Loire Valley. Our vintners have made wines ranging from the bone dry to the honey sweet—from the superb to the mediocre. In this chapter, we concentrate on the dry Chenin Blanc.

Right after the repeal of Prohibition in 1933, there were some very small California plantings of Chenin Blanc, and a few dry wines were made and labeled, not as Chenin Blanc, but as White Pinot, botanically an entirely inaccurate name. The correct name, Chenin Blanc, was not used on a California label until 1955, when the famous winery of Charles Krug offered a medium-soft version. This label received large praise and publicity at the California State Fair of that year, and at once Chenin Blanc took off in market popularity, but always in soft, rich, and sweet versions. No serious drinkers remembered that Chenin Blanc could also be a dry wine of fine character and personality.

Then, finally, came the tremendous experimental upsurge of California wines in the late sixties. New small vineyards managed by new young idealistic winemakers dedicated to perfectionist production and, above all, the development of the "cold fermentation technique," combined to prove that the Chenin Blanc grape, when its marvelous fruitiness was protected by slow fermentation at low temperatures, could produce a truly noble dry white wine. The experiments started slowly, but they were so quickly successful that the growth of dry Chenin Blanc boomed early in the 1970s. Several small vineyards that are now famous—such as Dry Creek, Lyncrest, Stag's Leap, and Stonegate—first became known for their stunning, experimental dry Chenin Blancs.

The combined result of the prestige created by these extraordinary experimental wines (and others that have followed from other vineyards), the easy growth of the Chenin Blanc vine and the high production of its grapes, and the national "white-wine boom" which has gripped the country since the mid-1970s have made Chenin Blanc the biggest-selling white varietal wine in the United States. In fact, Chenin Blanc almost certainly outsells even the red Cabernet Sauvignon, Gamay Beaujolais, Grenache, and Zinfandel. The Chenin Blanc name on a label seems to have an almost magical attraction for wine buyers. Certainly, Chenin Blanc is the clear popular leader among all dry white wines in the United States.

One only wishes that its quality could be at as high a level as the quantity of its distribution. The hard, sad fact is that the majority of dry Chenin Blancs are drab in flavor, lackluster in fruity refreshment, with an underlying bitterness and a vague vegetable earthiness. It is clear that, since the great expansion of quantity began in 1955, the average quality has noticeably fallen. There is an easy economic explanation of this phenomenon. As the Chenin Blanc grape became fantastically popular, two facts were discovered about this famous vine. The first was that, in California, it could be efficiently grown in the hot climate of the Central Valley—a far hotter climate than it has ever known along the Loire Valley. The second was that, in that hot climate, the vine could be, in agricultural terms, "pushed" to yield as much as twelve tons of grapes per acre—an extraordinary production, three or four times greater than the average for all other grapes. These discoveries have quickly brought about an enormous change in the way that most of the Chenin Blanc is now grown in California, a change that largely explains the degradation of the quality of the average wine.

When Chenin Blanc began to be grown in California, it was planted in the best locations of the best northern districts around San Francisco, what are known technically as the Northern Coastal Counties, where the weather is relatively cool, the earth is superb, and the growing conditions are almost ideal. The Chenin Blanc vines shared space with their noble counterparts: Pinot Chardonnay, Sauvignon Blanc, and White Riesling. More than 90 percent of those early Chenin Blanc grapes came from the very best growing areas of the state. By 1978, the Chenin Blanc growing picture was almost completely reversed. Now, 85 percent of all Chenin Blancs came from the hot Central Valley. The grapes were grown in enormous vineyard operations by mass-production growers who would not make the wine but would be anonymous middlemen, involved in bulk sales of the grapes to wineries all over the state. From the point of view of pure quality, everything was wrong with this operation. The hot climate was not good for the optimum development of the grapes. The harvesting and handling were on a mass scale. The grapes had to be trucked over long distances before they reached the wineries where the wine would be made. A long time before the vinification began, the grapes were no longer in prime condition. No wonder that the high number of average Chenin Blanc wines on the market shelves are unrelenting examples of coarse mediocrity.

But there is still a fair proportion of good news for serious Chenin Blanc drinkers. There are still many competent, fine, idealistic, perfectionist vineyards and wineries where noble examples of Chenin Blanc wines continue to be made year after year.

I confess that I have never found, either in France or in the United States, a dry Chenin Blanc that rated, mathematically, on my tasting charts, as a truly GREAT wine. Perhaps this grape cannot quite reach the highest peak. But consistently the American best, always towering above all the others—achieving an average rating of SUPERB quality—is the dry Chenin Blanc from:

- Chalone Vineyard on Mount Chalone in the Gavilan Range of the Santa Lucia Mountains in Monterey, with its winemaker, Peter Graff

It is always an extraordinary wine—huge in body and flavor, strong with the "smoke of oak" from the French barrels in which it was aged, mouth-filling with luscious power, bright and clear with fruity refreshment—a wine that stands alone.

The consistent second on the average rating of my charts—my second-best Chenin Blanc—is from:

- Ste. Chapelle Vineyards at Sunny Slope near Caldwell in the Snake River Valley of Idaho

The winemaker, Bill Broich, while his vines are growing and maturing, has been using grapes from the Sagemoor Farms of Washington State to produce wines that are elegant and light, yet with intense fruit, consistently achieving a NOBLE quality rating.

Third place on the average of my charts—my third American Chenin Blanc—is from:

- Chateau Ste. Michelle Vintners at Woodinville near Seattle in Washington State, using grapes grown in the Yakima Valley of Washington State

The wine can be dramatically dry, an icily aggressive refreshment, steadily rating a NOBLE quality.

I have also tasted Chenin Blancs of NOBLE quality from these vineyards and wineries:

- Burgess Cellars near St. Helena in the Napa Valley, with owner-winemaker Tom Burgess—grapes from the Steltzner Vineyard
- Dry Creek Vineyard at Healdsburg in the Dry Creek Valley of Sonoma, with owner-winemaker David Stare
- Mirassou Vineyards at San Jose in Santa Clara
- Mount Veeder Winery on the Mayacamas Range above the Napa Valley, with its owner-winemaker, Mike Bernstein
- Stevenot Vineyards at Murphys in Calaveras in the foothills of the High Sierras

And I have tasted dry Chenin Blancs of FINE quality from these vineyards and wineries:

- Alexander Valley Vineyards east of Healdsburg in northern Sonoma
- Callaway Vineyard at Temecula in the Riverside district of southern California
- Cassayre-Forni Cellars at Rutherford in the Napa Valley
- Chappellet Vineyard on Pritchard Hill east of Rutherford above the Napa Valley
- Kenwood Vineyards at Kenwood in the Valley of the Moon in Sonoma
- Landmark Vineyards at Windsor in the Dry Creek Valley of Sonoma
- Mont Elise Vineyards at Bingen in the south Columbia Basin of Washington State, with owner-winemaker Chuck Henderson

- Preston Vineyards near Healdsburg in the Dry Creek Valley of Sonoma
- San Martin Winery at San Martin in the Santa Cruz Mountains of Santa Clara
- Sierra Vista Winery at Placerville in El Dorado in the foothills of the High Sierras
- Simi Winery at Healdsburg in the Alexander Valley of Sonoma, with its winemaker, Zelma Long
- Sonoma Vineyards at Windsor in Sonoma, with its winemaker, Rod Strong
- Stag's Leap Wine Cellars on the Silverado Trail near Yountville in the Napa Valley, with its winemaker, Warren Winiarski
- Stonegate Winery at Calistoga in the Napa Valley

PINOT BLANC *Also called, in Alsace, Klevner; in Italy, Pinot Bianco; in Germany, Weissburgunder*

Although the Pinot Blanc is a nobler grape—it belongs, after all, to the great international Pinot family, and its homeland is Burgundy— it is far less successful in life than its extroverted and popular rival, the Chenin Blanc. In recent years, while the statisticians have been telling us that there are more than 20,000 acres of Chenin Blanc growing in California alone, they also say that there are fewer than 1,500 acres of Pinot Blanc. This is obviously because the Pinot Blanc is a much less profitable partner for the farmer-grower and the winemaker. The most basic of facts are, first, that the Pinot Blanc yields about half as many of its pale greenish yellow grapes per acre as other varieties of vines, and, second, they sell for about half the price. Pinot Blanc grows best, all over the world, in the coolest, most ideal wine-growing regions. That means, in the United States, the cool Northern Coastal Counties of California, around San Francisco, where there is the greatest competition for vineyard space, and where the growers, for obvious reasons, choose the more profitable grapes.

The Pinot Blanc might not be worth defending were it not for the fact that it can make a lovely, light, dry white wine of unique character and personality.

The original vine roots were brought here from Burgundy,

where the Pinot Blanc has for centuries been interplanted and blended with the Chardonnay, so as to give a special softness to the resulting wine. Pinot Blanc was known and recognized for its contributions to the wines of Burgundy as far back as the 16th century, when it was already firmly entrenched in the vineyards of the Côte d'Or and of Chablis. But it was left to California to be the first wine region in the world to print the name of Pinot Blanc on the label of a bottle of wine, after the repeal of Prohibition in 1933. Since then, the Pinot Blanc has proved itself to be a difficult and expensive grape to grow and a difficult wine to make—a wine demanding, during its production, a great deal of watching and a high degree of technical skill.

But all the effort and expense are well worthwhile. A noble, dry Pinot Blanc has a beautiful aroma, a purity of flavor that often, to me, speaks of the windswept exhilaration of a mountain peak, the crisp refreshment of fruit with a kind of monastic sparseness, yet all balanced and delicate and smooth, with the touch of a body of velvet. To achieve all these effects, of course, the grapes have to be crushed very quickly after the picking, and the juice has to be "cold fermented" in temperature-controlled vats. In short, the grapes demand constant and devoted service from the farmer while they are growing, and the wine, even from near-perfect grapes, demands brilliant judgment and skill during its production and refinement.

As to the best Pinot Blancs of the United States, three brilliant California winemen have, to my mind, proved themselves to be the masters of the specialized techniques of growing these difficult grapes and making this challenging wine. Dick Graff, the owner with his brother, Peter, the winemaker, of Chalone Vineyard on Mount Chalone in the Gavilan Range of the Santa Lucia Mountains in Monterey, grows his own grapes on his rocky plateau and makes wines that are immense in every way and that have consistently rated on my charts as being of SUPERB quality—the best Pinot Blanc now available in America.

Joe Heitz, owner and winemaker of Heitz Wine Cellars near St. Helena in the Napa Valley, was, from 1964 to 1971, the most dazzling maker of SUPERB Pinot Blancs. The late Fred McCrea, the founder, owner, and winemaker of the great Stony Hill Vineyard above the Napa Valley (now owned and run by Fred's widow, Eleanor), was, in my opinion, the most expert grower of the Pinot Blanc grape, although he did not choose to make the wine. He sold his grapes to Heitz, who produced wine that I consistently rated as of SUPERB quality. After the harvest of 1971, McCrea decided that he wanted to expand his Chardonnay plantings on his very limited estate, and he uprooted his Pinot Blanc vines. Heitz continued for one more year trying to make wine with grapes from another source, but his perfectionist spirit could not be satisfied with grapes of lesser quality, and, in 1972, he made the decision, tragic for all lovers of SUPERB Pinot Blanc, to discontinue his production. This has left Chalone, since 1973, alone at the top of the SUPERB quality peak.

At the next level on the rating charts, my second-best Pinot Blanc of the United States is from:

- Chateau St. Jean at Kenwood in Sonoma, with its winemaker, Richard Arrowood

The wine is light and lovely, clear and pure in taste, suffused with fruity refreshment, rating a NOBLE quality.

My third-best Pinot Blanc among the American dry white wines is from:

- Wente Brothers at Livermore in the Livermore Valley of Alameda, with the owner-winemaker, Eric Wente

They make a classic wine of high elegance and outstanding clarity of aroma and flavor, rating a NOBLE quality.

Finally, wines that are consistently in the FINE quality classification are the Pinot Blancs made by these vineyards and wineries:

- Almadén Vineyards at San Jose in Santa Clara, with its winemaster, Klaus Mathes, using grapes from the Paicines Vineyards in San Benito
- Charles Krug Winery at St. Helena in the Napa Valley
- Mirassou Vineyards at San Jose in Santa Clara

SAUVIGNON BLANC (dry) *Also called Blanc Fumé, or Fumé Blanc, Fié, Fleur de Sauvignon, or Surin*

This classic and famous vine—which grows grapes that are most often golden, greenish yellow, but also sometimes pink—helps to produce some of the world's greatest wines. It is a partner with other grapes in the production of the noble whites of the Graves district of Bordeaux, of the supreme sweet wines of Sauternes, and, on its own, in the famous Loire wines of the appellations of Pouilly-Fumé and Sancerre. The name Sauvignon is said to have come from the original birthplace of the grape in the ancient district of Savignin in the French Jura mountains on the border of Switzerland. In California, the Sauvignon Blanc is less important in terms of acres of vines than the Chenin Blanc and more important than the Pinot Blanc. At present, there are more than 5,000 acres devoted to Sauvignon vines—as against Chenin Blanc at four times that acreage and Pinot Blanc at only 1,500—with quite small additional plantings in other states.

So it is obvious that, in the United States, the highest possibilities of the Sauvignon Blanc have not yet been fully realized. Making a wine from it involves walking a tightrope of difficulties and delicate judgments. When you taste the ripe grape on the vine, you find it has a quite powerful character of Muscat, and this is its most dangerous flaw. That power can easily become an aggressive, hard, pungent, rough flavor in the wine. The danger can first be countered by growing the grapes in the lightest possible, gravelly, part-sandy soil. The second defense must come from the skill of the winemaker, who controls his vinification so as to hold on to the fruity, tangy, thirst-quenching quality of the grapes.

The first root cuttings of the Sauvignon Blanc were brought to California from Bordeaux in the early 1880s, but the name was never printed on labels, and the grape was ignored by early wine drinkers. The first idea was to convert the grape into a sweet wine—to make, so to speak, an American Château d'Yquem—but that high-falutin' project was doomed to failure. Some of the new vines were planted in the gravelly, sandy soil of the Livermore Valley, on land that would soon become the vineyard of that old pioneering master, Herman Wente. He saw that, in the loamy soil, with good sun and the cooling breezes from San Francisco Bay, his Sauvignon Blanc vines were thriving. So he proceeded to make the finest dry Sauvignon Blanc that had been achieved in the United States up to that time. In fact, it turned out to be better than many Sauvignon Blancs made in France. But Americans were not interested in buying it, and it languished until Prohibition ended.

After Repeal in 1933, Wente dreamed up the idea that has revolutionized American wine labeling. Absolutely for the first time, he labeled a bottle of wine with the varietal name of the grape that had made it—in this instance, "1932 Dry Sauvignon Blanc." The wine was so outstanding that the entire production was immediately sold in toto to the fashionable Palace Hotel in San Francisco. There, in the magnificent Garden Court Restaurant, the nabobs of San Francisco drank the Wente wine with their sumptuous dinners, loved it, and made it, overnight, California's most prestigious white. Then, Frank Schoonmaker arrived from New York, all aglow from the success of his wine articles in *The New Yorker* magazine, and used his fame to develop a wholesale wine business. He stayed at the Palace, tasted the Sauvignon Blanc, and loved it. He also loved the idea of naming wines by their grapes. He proceeded to take over a whole group of California wines, including the Wente, relabeled them with varietal names as "Schoonmaker Selections," and put them into distribution all over the United States. Thus, largely through Sauvignon Blanc, America became aware for the first time of serious American wines.

Sauvignon Blanc expanded slowly, but there was no explosion. Then, in the 1960s, with the coming into fashion of Chardonnay, Johannisberg Riesling, and others, the Sauvignon began to decline. As old vineyards were replanted or wiped out by "urban sprawl," growers turned to these other grapes. Then came the one-man revolution!

As often happens, the great leap forward was the result of the accidental juxtaposition of several apparently unconnected events. By the mid-1960s, the new technology of "cold fermentation" had swept like a prairie fire across the California wine industry.

At about the same time, Robert Mondavi, one of the important California wine pioneers, had broken away from his family's wine business and was building his own ultramodern Robert Mondavi Winery at Oakville in the Napa Valley. Naturally, among all the most advanced equipment, he installed cold fermentation. While he was waiting for the winery to be completed, Mondavi made several study trips to France. On the Loire, he tasted the Sauvignon Blanc made into the famous Pouilly-Fumé, with its dry, flinty, fruity, racy, slightly smoky ambience and character. Mondavi became convinced that, if American Sauvignon Blanc were gently treated, were slowly fermented at low temperatures, thus holding all the fruit, a Fumé-type wine might be made in the United States. After experimenting through 1965 and 1966, Mondavi was successful beyond his wildest dreams. In 1967, he launched his wine, which, in deference to its French counterpart, he labeled "Fumé Blanc," literally, "smoky white."

It was a light and lovely, brilliantly refreshing, easy-to-drink

young wine, and such a popular success that, within a couple of
years, almost every major California vineyard had jumped on the
bandwagon—from Almadén with its "Blanc Fumé" to the Christian
Brothers with their "Napa Fumé," to Charles Krug's "Pouilly-
Fumé," as well as various proprietary names. It was a complete turn-
around for the Sauvignon Blanc grape. Plantings of the vine rapidly
increased, from a low at the end of the 1960s of around 800 acres to
a peak toward the end of the 1970s of almost 5,500 acres. This has
meant, from the taster's point of view, that there has been a continually new parade of vineyards and wineries, each offering its first
effort in making a dry Sauvignon Blanc wine. A winemaker's first
experience with this difficult grape does not always produce the happiest result. This is why I firmly believe that the greatest days of the
Sauvignon Blanc in America are still in the future—with magnificent
Sauvignon Blanc tasting experiences to come for all of us.

The best Sauvignon Blanc I have ever tasted in the United States
—a wine I have consistently rated near the top of the NOBLE quality
range—is from:

- Chateau Ste. Michelle Vintners at Woodinville near Seattle in
    Washington State, using grapes from the Yakima Valley of
    Washington State

The wine is almost always memorably elegant, fresh, and fruity.

An average of a few points below this peak, but still clearly
within the NOBLE quality range, my second-best American Sauvignon Blanc is the brilliant "Fumé Blanc" from:

- Iron Horse Vineyards at Sebastopol in the Russian River Valley
    of Sonoma, with its winemaker, Forrest Tancer, the wine
    beautifully light, delicately and refreshingly tart, perfectly
    clean and dry in the mouth, with a distinct aftertaste of fresh
    ripe fruit

My third-best American Sauvignon Blanc, still in the NOBLE
quality range, is from the place where it all began:

- Wente Brothers at Livermore in the Livermore Valley of Ala-
    meda, with its owner-winemaker, Eric Wente

I have tasted other Sauvignon Blancs of NOBLE quality from
these vineyards and wineries:

- Richard Carey Winery at San Leandro in Alameda on San Fran-
    cisco Bay—Richard makes the wine and labels it "Fumé
    Blanc"

- Dry Creek Vineyard at Healdsburg in the Dry Creek Valley of Sonoma, with winemaker David Stare also using the "Fumé Blanc" label
- Firestone Vineyard at Los Olivos in the Santa Ynez Valley of Santa Barbara, with its winemaker, Alison Green
- Robert Mondavi Winery at Oakville in the Napa Valley, with its winemaker, Tim Mondavi
- Spring Mountain Vineyards near St. Helena in the Napa Valley
- Vōse Vineyards on Mount Veeder east of Oakville in the Napa Valley, for its "Fumé Blanc"

At the next lower range of quality—Sauvignon Blancs that have come out on my charts with consistent FINE ratings—are these vineyards and wineries:

- Almadén Vineyards at San Jose in Santa Clara, with its winemaster, Klaus Mathes, using grapes from the Paicines Vineyards of San Benito and labeling the wine "Fumé Blanc"
- Beaulieu Vineyard at Rutherford in the Napa Valley, with its winemaker, André Tchelistcheff, until his retirement, making a series of outstanding wines all labeled "Sauvignon Blanc"
- Davis Bynum Winery at Healdsburg in Sonoma, with the wine labeled "Fumé Blanc"
- Cakebread Cellars at Rutherford in the Napa Valley
- Concannon Vineyard at Livermore in the Livermore Valley of Alameda
- Congress Springs Vineyards above Saratoga in the Santa Cruz Mountains of Santa Clara, with the wine labeled "Fumé"
- Hargrave Vineyard at Cutchogue on the North Fork of Long Island, with its winemaker-owner, Alec Hargrave
- Charles Krug Winery at St. Helena in the Napa Valley, with the wine labeled "Pouilly Fumé"
- Mirassou Vineyards at San Jose in Santa Clara
- Monterey Vineyard at Gonzales in the Salinas Valley of Monterey
- Monteviña Wines at Plymouth in the Shenandoah Valley of Amador in the foothills of the High Sierras, with owner-winemaker Cary Gott producing wines with an extraordinary intensity of flavor
- Joseph Phelps Vineyards near St. Helena in the Napa Valley,

with its winemaker, Walter Schug, producing wines of rare delicacy, lightness, and freshness of fruit

- Preston Wine Cellars at Pasco in the Columbia Basin of Washington State, where its winemaker, Robert Griffin, produces a "Fumé Blanc" of the extraordinary intensity that is possible in this region of irrigated vineyards under a fierce sun
- San Pasqual Vineyards at Escondido in the San Pasqual Valley east of San Diego, with the wine labeled "Fumé Blanc"
- Sokol Blosser Winery at Dundee in the Willamette Valley of Oregon
- Robert Stemmler Winery west of Healdsburg in the Dry Creek Valley of Sonoma
- Ventana Vineyards along the Arroyo Seco River southwest of Soledad in the Salinas Valley of Monterey

FOLLE BLANCHE *Also called, around Nantes in France, Gros Plant; and in the Armagnac region, Picpoule; also Enrageat Blanc*

Just as some ancient races of humans and some breeds of animals have become extinct, so, perhaps, some varieties of vines may someday disappear from the world. The light green grapes of the Folle Blanche may be among these. For centuries, it was the principal grape in the Charente region of western France for making the light white wine that was distilled into the great Cognacs. But it has been almost completely replaced by "more modern" grapes. In the same way, it grew in southwestern France, and its wine was distilled into the great Armagnac brandies, but there, too, since the beginning of the 20th century, it has been largely replaced. When root cuttings were brought to the United States, they were first planted in California, where the wine has been blended into jug wines and used for making brandy. But the latest statistics now show only about 350 acres of Folle Blanche vines in California in the late 1970s.

Apart from its anonymous role in blends for jugs, I know of only one American wine in which the Folle Blanche plays the principal role and where its name appears in the position of honor on the label of the bottle. This wine is, year after year, so charming, so delightful to drink, so refreshing and fruity on the tongue, so well balanced and light in the throat, that, on its own merits, it demands a proper classification of the Folle Blanche grape. This dry white consistently rates on my charts a FINE quality—bringing that rating to the maker:

- Louis M. Martini Winery in St. Helena in the Napa Valley, with its owner-winemaker, Louis P. Martini

FRENCH COLOMBARD *Also called Colombier, Pied Tendre, Queue Tendre, Queue Verte*

This is in some ways an amazing grape. Enormous quantities of it are grown all over the world—and especially in California—but, until the last four or five years, it was almost completely anonymous. Millions of gallons of light wine have been made from its light golden grapes, but they were blended into this, that, or the other, and the name was never given any honorable space on any label. Like the Folle Blanche, the French Colombard was first grown in the Charente region of western France, where some of its wine was distilled into Cognac, but a large part was exported by boat from the port of La Rochelle to Amsterdam. Dutch wine drinkers took a great liking to the dryness, fruitiness, lightness, and firm character of the wine.

When it was brought to the United States, it was first planted in California, where it was soon found to add so much flavor and personality to a jug-wine blend that its growing was expanded at a riotous rate. It was found to be profitable to grow, since each vine provided an exceptional number of bunches of grapes. It was also easy to grow in almost all the climatic regions of the state. So, by the late 1970s, there were almost 30,000 acres of French Colombard in California alone!

Then, of course, came the "wine boom," coupled with the veritable explosion of varietal labeling. The wine-drinking public—according to the new theories of the marketing men—would not buy a serious wine unless it had the name of a grape on its label. So it was inevitable that, by the mid-1970s, we would all be tasting the first French Colombard wines. One must say, frankly, that it has not yet produced (and is unlikely to produce) any GREAT, SUPERB, or

NOBLE wines. But I have consistently rated dry French Colombard as of FINE quality.

The best version I have ever tasted—my top French Colombard of the United States—was made by:

- Chalone Vineyard on Mount Chalone in the Gavilan Range of the Santa Lucia Mountains in Monterey, with its wine-maker, Peter Graff, using grapes from the Cyril Saviez Vine-yard in the Napa Valley

I have also consistently tasted and rated a FINE quality French Colombard from:

- Bargetto Winery at Soquel in the Santa Cruz Mountains south of San Francisco Bay, with its winemaker, Lawrence Bar-getto

GREY RIESLING *Also called Grey Duchess; also, in France, Chauché Gris*

These oval, reddish brown grapes have suffered through a series of identity crises, have been accused of being complete phonies, and have had some terrible ups and downs. This vine came to the United States in the 1860s and was planted, among many places, in the Livermore Valley of California by the great pioneer winemaker Herman Wente. In the gravelly, light Livermore soil of the Wente Brothers family vineyard, Grey Riesling vines did especially well, producing wines of a remarkable clarity and bright fruitiness. But, of course, they remained anonymous until after the repeal of Prohibition, when Herman Wente launched the policy of putting the name of the grape on the label.

At that time, the Grey Riesling was the one grape that a small, steady coterie seemed to appreciate and want. In his fine book on grapes, Bern Ramey wrote of that time that it was, perhaps, the "Golden Age" of the Grey Riesling. It made the bottle of dry, light American white wine that was most often poured at banquet dinners, at Christmas or Thanksgiving feasts, at any time when it seemed the right thing to do to show off a U.S. wine.

But then came the national upsurge of interest in wine, with a lot of serious study, a great deal of tasting, and a small flood of articles and books of increasing sophistication. There followed a kind of exposé of the Grey Riesling. The first terrible discovery was that it is not a Riesling at all—not in any way a member of the great, international, noble Riesling family. It had no connection whatsoever with the world-famous Johannisberg Riesling, or White Riesling of Germany. Instead, it was a French grape called Chauché Gris, which came originally from the Charente region of western France and (just like the Folle Blanche and French Colombard) had been partially used for making light white wines to be distilled into Cognac. The next horrible discovery was that French wine laws denigrated the grape to more-or-less a second-class position among the wine grapes of France. At this point, many American drinkers started saying that the Grey Riesling was a phony and began refusing to drink its wine —turning, instead, to the newer and more fashionable grapes. The production of Grey Riesling declined sharply.

But in the early 1970s, the scandal subsided—as all scandals eventually do—and the acceptance of Grey Riesling came full circle. As grape prices took off into the stratosphere—and as "cold fermentation" brought new qualities of lovely fruitiness to the lighter wines —serious drinkers and growers rediscovered the virtues of the Grey Riesling: its easy growing and excellent production of grapes on each vine, the clean and simple refreshment of its wine. In the last few years, its national popularity has risen far above the previous peak of its original "Golden Age." Today, Wente Brothers, the originators, sell more of this wine than any other in their repertoire. It is made, also, by virtually every major California winery; most restaurant wine lists across the entire country include it.

In my tasting experience, I have consistently rated some Grey Rieslings that gave the numbers on my charts for a FINE quality classification. My best American label is from:
- Amity Vineyards in the village of Amity in the Yamhill district of the Willamette Valley of Oregon, with its winemaker, Myron Redford

My second rating of Grey Riesling—also of FINE quality—comes from:
- Wente Brothers at Livermore in the Livermore Valley of Alameda, with their owner-winemaker, Eric Wente

My third FINE Grey Riesling is from:
- The Christian Brothers on Mont La Salle above the Napa Valley, with its winemaker, Brother Timothy

SYLVANER *Also called Sylvaner Riesling; in Luxemburg, Feuille Ronde; in Germany, Franken Riesling; in Switzerland, Gros Riesling; in Austria, Schwabler, or Gruber; in Hungary, Szilvani Zolz and Selenzhiz*

These famous greenish yellow grapes grew originally in Austria, then spread all across Central Europe, into Bulgaria and Russia, Germany, Italy, and Switzerland, then across the Rhine into the Alsace wine region of France. They seem to make lovely, bone-dry crackly crisp, irresistibly perfumed, airily light white wines everywhere, and, particularly in Alsace, they can be of superb quality. I have often wondered why this apparently magnificent grape has never caught on in the United States and why our winemakers do not seem to have mastered the techniques of converting it into anything more than an average, middle-of-the-road wine. While there are almost 7,000 acres of this famous vine in France alone, we Americans have hardly more than 1,000 acres.

To deepen the mystery, let us note that this vine is wildly fertile and could, therefore, be a very profitable partner to the farmer-grower. It is also tough and vigorous. It can stand off a late spring frost and, because each vine produces such a very large number of buds, can go on beyond a freeze to a lavish harvest of fine, ripe grapes. Its roots are so efficient at drawing nourishment from poor soil, that it can produce good wine even from mediocre locations. The grapes do, though, have thick skins, and when they are crushed, they mash down into a rather mushy and pulpy "jam," which requires expert handling by the winemaker. His objectives must always be, for the finished wine, freshness, lightness, and a sense of youth. The answer to the Sylvaner in America is, I suppose, that it has just never become fashionable. It needs an aggressive, hard-driving, publicity-conscious impresario to fall in love with it and, then, put it on the map.

The best American Sylvaner I have tasted is the FINE quality made by:

- Reuter's Hill Vineyards at Forest Grove in the Willamette Valley of Oregon, under the control of its winemaker, David Wirtz

My second-best American Sylvaner, also rating a FINE quality, is from:

- Bargetto Winery at Soquel in the Santa Cruz Mountains south of San Francisco Bay, with its owner-winemaker, Lawrence Bargetto, using grapes from the Vine Hill Vineyard

My third-best American Sylvaner, also of FINE quality, is from:

- Monterey Vineyard at Gonzales in the Salinas Valley of Monterey, with its winemaker, Dick Peterson

Other Sylvaners I have tasted achieve the FINE quality classification for these vineyards and wineries:

- Charles Krug Winery at St. Helena in the Napa Valley, where the wine is labeled "Riesling"
- Paul Masson Vineyards at Saratoga and in the Pinnacles district of the Santa Cruz Mountains in Santa Clara
- Robert Mondavi Winery at Oakville in the Napa Valley, with its winemaker, Tim Mondavi, who labels his wine "Riesling"

CHAPTER III

The Medium-Soft
White Wines

The title of this chapter raises a first and difficult question. What is a medium-soft wine? In technical terms—as explained in Preamble Two—the word "soft" refers to the amount of natural sugar in the wine and can be mathematically and precisely defined. A medium-soft wine has a residual sugar content of somewhere between 1.5 and 2.5 percent. But what does this mean in tasting on the tongue?

A dry wine, which has almost no residual sugar, is always lemony and sharp on the tongue—mouth clearing, refreshing, sometimes so dry as to be slightly acetic and harsh, but, if beautifully made, always a cleansing and lovely experience to those who, like myself, are devoted to the best of the dry wines. "Soft" means, at once, a gentler wine, with just enough extra sugar to make it feel silky on the tongue but, if it is "medium-soft," certainly not enough extra sugar to make it taste in any way sweet. If it is well made, it is never bitter, or harsh, or sharp. It is still suitable with many foods. It has long been argued that the medium-soft wines are those that are most popular among average American drinkers who "like a glass of wine" but have never taken the time or given the thought to becoming connoisseurs or experts. Let us say that the medium-soft wines are those to which amateurs first turn for their wine experience. These are the wines that require the least explanation—the least serious thought while drinking them. With wider experience, the serious wine taster will inevitably come to an appreciation of the dry wines.

But when we take a few steps forward from this definition and try to find the best medium-soft white wines by reading their labels, we run at once into difficulties. Which are the dominant grapes that produce the finest medium-soft wines? I firmly believe that the White

64

Riesling, growing in the best soil and vinified by the best winemakers, produces the finest and largest number of medium-soft wines.
But you cannot be guaranteed this by the words on a label. So much
depends on the philosophy of the winemaker. A few of them produce White Riesling wines that are virtually dry. At the other end of
the scale, there are many White Rieslings that are deliberately left
with so much residual sugar that they are sweet far beyond the
medium-soft definition. In recent years, a few White Rieslings have
been deliberately made as honey-sweet dessert wines (see Chapter
VIII). So the following discussion of the world-famous White Riesling
grape and the often great wines it produces should be accepted as
representing the majority point of view among the great winemakers,
while recognizing that there are exceptions. I shall point them out
along the way.

WHITE RIESLING *Also called, in Germany, Rheingauer, or Grauer Ries-*
ling; in Hungary, Rizling Rajnai; in Italy, Petracine

The Riesling is one of the most famous of the international noble
families of the vine. It grows virtually everywhere on earth, and there
are so many branches of the family that each of them demands a first
name. The correct botanical name of the main variety is the White
Riesling, but, for almost a hundred years in the United States, we
have given it the popular name of Johannisberg Riesling in the hope
of making its wines more saleable. Many of us have considered this
a ridiculous custom, and, for at least ten years, the more modern
thinkers have favored stopping the foolish pretense that our Riesling
wines are imitations of those of Germany. As my contribution to the
discussion—even at the risk of repetition—I propose to retell the
probably apocryphal story of how the Emperor Charlemagne invented the word "Johannisberg."

At the end of the 8th century, Charlemagne was "Master of
Europe." From his palace, Ingelheim, on a hill overlooking the valley
of the Rhine, he ruled from Spain to what is now Poland—from
Saxony in the north to Lombardy in the south. One spring day,
standing on the watchtower, the emperor looked out on the incomparable view of the great river and the towering slopes on the far

side. He noticed that the snow on one of them was melting in a curious way—softening at the top while still ice-hard at the base. Charlemagne, who was famous both for his knowledge and love of wine, said to one of his nobles, "The sun strikes that slope from a very high angle. It would be an excellent place to plant vines. See that it's done." When the hill began to be cleared, it was found to be covered by wild black-currant bushes, called *Johannisbeeren*, "St. John's berries," in German, so the hill was named *Johannisberg*, "St. John's mountain." Charlemagne was right. The grapes grew excellently.

In the year 1100, the hill was given to the Benedictine monks, who worked patiently for seven hundred years to improve the grapes and make better wines. By selecting and grafting, they gradually developed a special strain of vine with tight little bunches of small greenish yellow grapes that ripened to deep gold. At maturity, they offered an incomparable aroma, an entrancing taste, which seemed to be compounded of the essences of all the other fruits of the immense Rhine Valley—of black currants, peaches, blackberries, even of pineapples and walnuts. The monks named their vine the Riesling. It remains supreme in Germany. It has also successfully traveled to all the other major wine areas of the world.

But, of course, its product is different everywhere—in different climates, in varying soils, the Riesling produces different wines under different methods of vinification. So it seems ridiculous to call it Johannisberg when it is growing in the Napa Valley of California, or the Yakima Valley of Washington State! In fact, some of the very best of our Riesling wines now challenge the best of Germany. How foolish, then, to continue to pretend that we are imitating them!

Root cuttings of the famous vines from the Rhine were first carried across the Atlantic to the vineyards of Chile, and, from there, in the 1850s, they traveled north to California. In the cool Northern Coastal Counties, on fairly steep slopes with good water drainage in slaty schist and clay soil, the White Riesling has proved itself to be more happily at home than anywhere else on earth except along its native Rhine. By the end of the 1970s, there were almost 9,000 acres planted in California—more than four times as much as in all of France. There is now, also, an area of almost 200 acres growing in New York State, with substantial acreage in the Pacific Northwest (under difficult winter conditions), and many small experimental plantings in all the temperate parts of the United States. One of the newest áreas for growing White Riesling in the far-northern Lake County district of California, roughly northeast of the Napa Valley, where the vine seems to be growing superbly, producing wines of a complex aroma and taste, subtly reminiscent of a multitude of flowers, fruits, and spices.

Whenever it is grown under good conditions—whenever it is carefully harvested and vinified by an experienced and skilled winemaker—White Riesling regularly produces one of the greatest of all white wines—with exquisite bouquet and flavor, a caressing, silky feel in the mouth, an opulent richness of taste, and a cleanness of aftertaste that always leaves behind a magnificent memory of the wine, a memory of simple pleasure for the beginner, a memory of subtle complications for the connoisseur.

As I steadily tasted these wines over a period of almost twenty years, keeping precise records for each vineyard (by the system explained in Preamble One), the average rankings gradually became established. The classifications that follow are not the result of any single vintage, but represent the continuing performance of each vineyard, its owner, its winemaker, as demonstrated by bottle after bottle, year after year.

The best White Riesling I have tasted and rated in the United States, the wine that steadily earns the scores on the charts for GREAT quality—the only GREAT White Riesling I have found in America—is the annual production by Eleanor and the late Fred McCrea at:

• Stony Hill Vineyard on the mountain above the Napa Valley. Here the grapes are grown under near-perfect conditions, weather exposure, and quick drainage of the soil. The grapes are ripened slowly, with time to develop their best acid-sugar balance and fullest fruit flavor. They are carefully harvested and, with minimum delay, vinified slowly at low temperature, toward a delicate floweriness, a subtle flavor complexity. The completed wine is luscious and soft, crisp and light, without ever being obviously sweet. Stony Hill White Riesling is a wine that has steadily rated near the top of my quality scale.

The second-ranking White Riesling I have found in the United States—repeatedly rated as of SUPERB quality—are the vintages of:

- Joseph Phelps Vineyards near St. Helena in the Napa Valley, with its winemaker, Walter Schug

This is the only White Riesling in the SUPERB range—a few points below the GREAT classification.

The third place in the United States—rating consistently on my charts as of NOBLE quality—have been the vintages of White Riesling produced by:

- Chateau Montelena at Calistoga in the Napa Valley

This is the vineyard that has built an international reputation by winning a number of blind tastings in France, with French experts cross-tasting between French and U.S. wines. Several times, these French panels have given the highest scores to Chateau Montelena, thinking that the wine was a great French label!

There are other White Rieslings that I have rated in the NOBLE classification, from the following vineyards and wineries:

- Amity Vineyards in the village of Amity in the Yamhill district of the Willamette Valley of Oregon, with its winemaker, Myron Redford
- Beringer Vineyards near St. Helena in the Napa Valley, with its winemaker, Myron Nightingale
- Chappellet Vineyard on Pritchard Hill east of Rutherford above the Napa Valley
- Chateau St. Jean at Kenwood in Sonoma, with its winemaker, Richard Arrowood, using grapes from the Robert Young Vineyard
- Elk Cove Vineyards at Gaston in the Willamette Valley of Oregon
- Freemark Abbey Winery near St. Helena in the Napa Valley
- Grgich Hills Cellar at Rutherford in the Napa Valley, with its partner-winemaker, Mike Grgich
- Gundlach-Bundschu Vineyard at Vineburg in the Valley of the Moon in Sonoma, with its winemaker, John Merritt
- Heitz Wine Cellars near St. Helena in the Napa Valley, with its owner-winemaker, Joe Heitz
- Knudsen-Erath Winery at Dundee in the Willamette Valley of Oregon, with its winemaker-partner, Dick Erath
- Mirassou Vineyards at San Jose in Santa Clara, with grapes from Monterey
- Robert Mondavi Winery at Oakville in the Napa Valley, with its winemaker, Tim Mondavi

- Ponzi Vineyards at Beaverton in the Willamette Valley of Oregon
- Ste. Chapelle Vineyards at Sunny Slope near Caldwell in the Snake River Valley of Idaho, with its winemaker, Bill Broich
- Simi Winery at Healdsburg in the Alexander Valley of Sonoma, with its winemaker, Zelma Long
- Stag's Leap Wine Cellars on the Silverado Trail near Yountville in the Napa Valley, with its winemaker, Warren Winiarski, using grapes from the Birkmyer Vineyard
- Trefethen Vineyards near the town of Napa in the Napa Valley
- Tualatin Vineyards at Forest Grove in the Willamette Valley of Oregon

The White Rieslings that I have consistently rated as of FINE quality have come, year after year, from these vineyards and wineries, from both the West Coast and New York State:

- Alexander Valley Vineyards east of Healdsburg in northern Sonoma
- Almadén Vineyards at San Jose in Santa Clara with its winemaker, Klaus Mathes, using grapes from their Paicines Vineyards in San Benito
- Associated Vintners at Bellevue near Seattle in Washington State, with its winemaker, Dr. Lloyd Woodburne, using grapes from the Yakima Valley of Washington State
- Bargetto Winery at Soquel in the Santa Cruz Mountains south of San Francisco Bay, with its owner-winemaker, Lawrence Bargetto, using grapes from the Cypress Vineyard in Monterey
- Burgess Cellars near St. Helena in the Napa Valley, with its owner-winemaker, Tom Burgess, using grapes from the Winery Lake Vineyard
- Callaway Vineyard at Temecula in the Riverside district of southern California
- Chateau Ste. Michelle Vintners at Woodinville near Seattle in Washington State, using grapes from the Yakima Valley of Washington State
- Concannon Vineyard at Livermore in the Livermore Valley of Alameda
- Conn Creek Vineyard on the Silverado Trail near Rutherford in the Napa Valley

- Franciscan Vineyards at Rutherford in the Napa Valley, with its winemaker, Tom Ferrell
- Hacienda Wine Cellars in the Valley of the Moon in Sonoma
- Heron Hill Vineyard at Hammondsport on Lake Keuka in the Finger Lakes district of New York State
- Hillcrest Vineyards at Roseberg in the Umpqua Valley of Oregon
- Jekel Vineyard at Greenfield in the Salinas Valley of Monterey
- Konocti Cellars at Kelseyville in the Northern Lake County, with grapes from the Lake County district in northern California
- Charles Krug Winery at St. Helena in the Napa Valley
- Leonetti Cellars at Walla Walla in the south Columbia Basin of Washington State
- Louis M. Martini in St. Helena in the Napa Valley
- Mont Elise Vineyards at Bingen in the south Columbia Basin of Washington State, with its owner-winemaker, Chuck Henderson
- Monterey Vineyard at Gonzales in the Salinas Valley of Monterey, with its winemaker, Dick Peterson
- Novitiate Wines above Los Gatos in the Santa Cruz Mountains of Santa Clara, producing one of the few American wines still made by Jesuit monks
- Oak Knoll Winery at Hillsboro in the north Willamette Valley of Oregon
- Pedroncelli Winery northeast of Geyserville on a ridge above the Dry Creek Valley of Sonoma
- Pendleton Winery at San Jose in Santa Clara
- Preston Wine Cellars at Pasco in the Columbia Basin of Washington State, with its winemaker, Robert Griffin
- Raymond Vineyard at Calistoga in the Napa Valley
- Reuter's Hill Vineyards at Forest Grove in the Willamette Valley of Oregon, with its winemaker, David Wirtz, using grapes from Washington State
- Rutherford Hill Winery east of Rutherford near St. Helena in the Napa Valley
- San Martin Winery at San Martin in the Santa Cruz Mountains of Santa Clara
- Sebastiani Vineyards in the Valley of the Moon in Sonoma

- Sherrill Cellars at Woodside in the Santa Cruz Mountains of San Mateo
- Shown & Sons Vineyards on the Silverado Trail above Rutherford in the Napa Valley
- Smith-Madrone Vineyard high on Spring Mountain above the Napa Valley
- Sonoma Vineyards at Windsor in Sonoma, with its winemaker, Rod Strong
- Souverain Cellars near Geyserville in the Dry Creek Valley of Sonoma
- Turgeon & Lohr Winery at San Jose in Santa Clara
- Manfred J. Vierthaler Winery at Sumner in the Puyallup Valley of Washington State
- Wente Brothers at Livermore in the Livermore Valley of Alameda
- Hermann J. Wiemer Vineyard at Dundee in the Finger Lakes district of New York State, with its winemaker-owner, Hermann Wiemer
- Yverdon Vineyards on Spring Mountain west of St. Helena in the Napa Valley

CHENIN BLANC (medium-soft)

The character and history of the Chenin Blanc vine were discussed earlier (beginning on page 46) in terms of its vinification into dry wines. But many American winemakers—especially now that they have available to them the advanced technology of low-temperature, slow fermentation—are leaving higher percentages of residual sugar in their Chenin Blanc wines, making them gentle and soft on the tongue, often with a quite wonderful intensity of fruity refreshment. Among those wines that I have tasted and rated over the years, none has scored as high as GREAT or SUPERB, but I consistently found wines of a NOBLE quality from these vineyards and wineries:

- Charles Krug Winery at St. Helena in the Napa Valley
- Robert Mondavi Winery at Oakville in the Napa Valley
- Yakima River Winery at Prosser in the Yakima Valley of Washington State

At the next lower scoring level, I have consistently tasted and rated wines of FINE quality from these vineyards and wineries:

- The Christian Brothers on Mont La Salle above the Napa Valley
- Monterey Vineyard at Gonzales in the Salinas Valley of Monterey
- Parducci Wine Cellars at Ukiah in Mendocino
- Pope Valley Winery in the Pope Valley—a small cut between the hills on the east side of the Napa Valley
- Preston Wine Cellars at Pasco in the Columbia Basin of Washington State
- Ste. Chapelle Vineyards at Sunny Slope near Caldwell in the Snake River Valley of Idaho, with its winemaker, Bill Broich
- San Martin Winery at San Martin in the Santa Cruz Mountains of Santa Clara
- Sterling Vineyards at Calistoga in the Napa Valley
- Wente Brothers at Livermore in the Livermore Valley of Alameda
- Yverdon Vineyards on Spring Mountain west of St. Helena in the Napa Valley

EMERALD RIESLING

The Emerald Riesling is one of that small group of vines that were "invented" in and remain unique to the United States. Its original birth, in 1935, was an accident. One of the main centers of wine research in America is on the campus of the University of California in the town of Davis, near the state capital of Sacramento, in the foothills of the High Sierra mountains. Around the university buildings are experimental vineyards growing virtually every strain of grape known in the world at every stage of development. In 1935, there were rows of vines, fairly close to each other, of the German White Riesling and of the French Muscadelle du Bordelais—the latter a soft, slightly sweetish grape, strongly associated with Bordeaux, but also used for making sweet Champagnes. The two rows of vines flowered at the same time, so that the spring breezes and the insects carried the pollen from one row to the other. Nature took its inevitable course, and eventually the Davis researchers had in their hands, ready to plant, the seeds of a new vine that was a perfect marriage between the Muscadelle and the Riesling.

Two years earlier, a brilliant young botanical geneticist, Dr. Harold Olmo, had joined the staff at Davis. He supervised the development and testing of the new vine. After several years of work, it was chosen for commercial development because it gave a very high yield of grapes (about eight to twelve tons per acre) and because it had large leaves that could be trained to shade the grape bunches from the hot sun. This was exactly what Dr. Olmo was looking for—vines that could grow satisfactorily in the hot central valleys of California and thus open up new lands to wine production.

The berries of the new vine matured to a deep bluish green, producing, with skilled winemaking, a brilliantly clear, light green juice that ferments into pale green wine. For these reasons, Dr. Olmo named his new vine the Emerald Riesling. It seemed at first to combine some of the good points of both of its noble European parents. It holds the subtle Muscat aroma and taste of the Muscadelle and some of the fragrant delicacy of the German Riesling. To this extent, Dr. Olmo has proved that genetic science can be applied to plant breeding.

It took four years, until 1939, before there were twenty-two vines growing in the vineyards at Davis and the first Emerald Riesling wine could be made in sufficient quantity for proper tasting and testing. Then, ten experimental vines were planted and raised in the cooler climate of the Napa Valley. It took another seven years, until 1946, before the commercial producers began their development toward national sales. Finally, in 1955, this totally new wine grape was launched in a blaze of publicity. Twenty years had passed since the spring breeze had blown the pollen across the two rows of vines for that strange intercourse of nature. From this early success, Dr. Olmo has gone on to "invent" other new cross-grafted varieties of vines and to give them romantic names: Carmine, Carnelian, Centurion, Flora, and Ruby Cabernet, among others.

I feel I must be allowed a frank comment. The subject of genetic experimentation is highly controversial these days. It is also controversial, I believe, in terms of grapes and vines. Stated simply, I have never tasted a truly memorable or outstanding wine made from a cross-grafted vine variety. It is, to me, almost as if nature resents and rebels against this human interference with the most basic of all botanical life processes. But we should briefly discuss the Emerald Riesling.

If you walk among the rows of ripe Emerald Riesling close to harvest time, pick a few entirely mature berries, and bite into them, you will not find them to be the normal, crisp, fruitily refreshing, juicily exploding grapes. The flesh of the Emerald Riesling is distinctly gelatinous, definitely pulpy, quite soft, even at times a little bit slimy. The skin was deliberately developed to be thick and tough to make it easy for the grapes to be picked by mechanical harvesters. But these heavy skins are a considerable disadvantage during the crushing, for they release strong tannic flavors and have to be removed from the juice as quickly as possible. When the grapes are crushed, the must, or mash, is gelatinous and thick, with a most unfortunate tendency to turn brown upon being exposed to the air. So the whole organization of the harvesting and the crushing has to be extremely fast. Then, the skins and the gelatinous must have to be quickly separated from the clear juice. Even the tiny bits of must floating around in the juice have to be removed at once, either by filtering or, preferably, by a centrifuge, which whirls the liquid around at high speed and throws the solids outward. But a wine centrifuge is a very expensive piece of machinery—beyond the means of small wineries. Even after all these skilled manipulations, the free juice often becomes murky, leading to difficult, slow fermentation and vinification.

Although, between the end of the sixties and the end of the seventies, the California plantings of Emerald Riesling vines have increased from about 400 acres to slightly more than 3,000 acres, the grape is still not seriously accepted by the expert critics. The California wine writer Bob Thompson places it among the varieties that "cling to frail existences." He finds it "not intensely aromatic," often "fresh and pleasant, well suited for homely chicken dinners . . . wine that is soft and flaccid." I agree. Not one of the large-scale wines I have tasted and rated has scored enough points for even minimum classification for its maker in this book.

But there is one shining exception—an Emerald Riesling that scores in the NOBLE range. In 1948, Walter Ficklin, a wealthy farmer and wine aficionado in the hot, central San Joaquin Valley, decided to set up a vineyard about seven miles south of the town of Madera, about sixteen miles from the city of Fresno. His two sons, Walter and David, were trained in viticulture at the University at Davis, and one of their professors, of course, was Dr. Olmo. The young men decided that the climate on their home vineyard in the Central Valley was far too hot for any but the semitropical port and Madeira grapes of the Douro Valley of Portugal and the Portuguese island of Madeira. From these vines, the Ficklin family has consistently made, with supreme skill, over more than thirty years, absolutely the finest port-type wines of the United States. Since Walter, Sr.'s death, his two grandsons, young Walter and Pete, have, in their turn, been trained at Davis and are taking over the work with their fathers and with equal idealism and skill.

When Dr. Olmo developed his Emerald Riesling, the Ficklins decided that it would be nice to have a table wine for their family and their local friends. In one corner of their hot land, they planted an acre of Emerald Riesling vines. The Ficklins never let the grapes get fully ripe under the hot sun. They pick them in August, while the berries still have plenty of acid, to make sure that the wine will be crisp and fresh. In very hot summers, the sugar develops so rapidly that it simply overrides the acid. In those years, the Ficklins make no Emerald Riesling. They sell off the grapes in bulk to one of the local mass producers of blended jug wines.

But in 1965, the Ficklins felt that their vintage Emerald Riesling was good enough to present to San Francisco connoisseurs for a blind tasting. Some of these experts decided that the Ficklin pale green was better than some of the noble whites of Bordeaux. On the average, there have been vintages of this NOBLE Ficklin wine about once every three years. They made it in 1975, then again in '78, but there has been no other up to this writing. It is never distributed through commercial channels. When it is available, you have to go to the winery to get it. It is a rare and outstanding American wine:

- Ficklin Vineyards at Madera near Fresno in the San Joaquin Valley, with the owner-winemaker, David Ficklin

SAUVIGNON BLANC (medium-soft)

The character, history, personality, and taste of the Sauvignon Blanc vine (with its wines often also called Fumé Blanc, Blanc Fumé, etc.) have already been discussed (beginning on page 53) in terms of its dry wines. But many American winemakers—especially since the advent of the new technology of low-temperature controlled refrigeration, slow fermentation, which guards the fruity qualities of the grape—have deliberately decided to leave more residual sugar in the wine and have produced medium-soft Sauvignon Blancs of extraordinary charm, delicacy, and lovely balance of flavor. As they have been released, I have consistently tasted and rated them.

The Sauvignon Blanc that I have found to be of NOBLE quality —my best in the United States—is from:

- Chateau St. Jean at Kenwood in Sonoma, with its winemaker, Richard Arrowood, using their own estate grapes to produce an elegant and light, intensely fruity wine that he labels "Fumé Blanc"

At the next lower ranking, I have consistently rated as FINE the Sauvignon Blancs from these vineyards and wineries:

- The Christian Brothers on Mont La Salle above the Napa Valley, producing a delicate and gentle wine labeled "Napa Fumé"
- DeLoach Vineyards at Santa Rosa in the Russian River Valley of Sonoma, with its "Fumé Blanc"
- Parducci Cellars near Ukiah in Mendocino
- Santa Ynez Valley Winery east of Solvang in the Santa Ynez Valley of Santa Barbara
- Sonoma Vineyards at Windsor in Sonoma

SEMILLON *Also called in France Chevrier, Colombier, or Blanc Doux; in Spain, Malaga*

The Semillon vine has been a noble prince in Europe for 1,800 years —a prince who has not yet found his worthy estate on our side of the Atlantic. I am one of those who believe that its important American future is still to come. It is certainly a lovely and luscious wine. Its grapes, at maturity, are a beautiful pinkish white, and if you bite into one of them in the vineyard, you will find a delicate Muscat, almost figlike flavor. It is this aromatic quality that makes the Semillon such an important partner in many of the greatest wines in Bordeaux—the magnificent sweet Sauternes and the dry and medium-soft whites of Graves. Many of the supreme white wines of France are based on the Semillon, usually in partnership with the Sauvignon Blanc and the Muscadelle du Bordelais. So important is the French Semillon that, at the beginning of the 1970s, there were almost 100,000 acres of it in full growth and production.

Against this huge spread, there were, in the United States, at the latest count, only about 3,000 acres planted in California and a few additional small areas in other states. On our side, the vine seems to thrive in soil that is a mixture of clay and gravel, and, provided it has enough water from irrigation, it can stand high summer temperatures. One great difference between the Semillon in America and in France is that it is always used in partnership with other grapes in France, while here we generally insist on its performing a solo act.

When it first arrived on our shores, before Prohibition, the winemakers tried to use the Semillon to make a "California Sauterne" (leaving off the final "s" to prove that we were, somehow, different from the Sauternes of France). Amazingly, some of these "imitation sweet wines" turned out to be completely dry. Not until 1964 did the winemaker Myron Nightingale, then working with the Cresta Blanca Winery in the Livermore Valley, succeed in producing a magnificently aromatic, truly sweet Semillon—a wine that reasonably challenged the Sauternes of Bordeaux. It was a huge prestige success, but it was so expensive to produce that this memorable experiment has never been repeated. It certainly placed Nightingale among the top technicians of the American wine industry—a position he continues to hold.

Today, there are still many signs that American winemakers don't quite know what to do with the dominant character and strong personality of the Semillon. When the grape grows in the hot central California valleys, the fierce sun seems to cook out some of its stronger flavors, turning it toward a gentler, more widely acceptable wine. So more and more Semillon is being planted, for example, in the San Joaquin Valley. Wherever it is grown, the Semillon, of course, needs to be handled by an imaginative winemaker. In the right hands, it can be marvelously delicate and fresh, both in medium-soft and sweet types. Fred McCrea, at his great Stony Hill Vineyard in the Napa Valley, developed a memorable, aromatic, clean, elegant, refreshing, and rich "Semillon de Soleil," which continues to be produced every year by his wife, Eleanor (for a detailed discussion of the techniques with Semillon at Stony Hill, see page 286). Stony Hill provides the ultimate proof of what can be done— what could and should be done—with the American Semillon grape if only more winemakers would learn to understand its special characteristics. Meanwhile, I have tasted and rated very few Semillon wines that consistently scored sufficient points for my classification list.

The only Semillon wines I have found within classifiable range are those in the medium-soft group (below) and among the sweet wines (see Chapter VIII). I have found no GREAT or SUPERB medium-soft Semillons, but I have rated one of NOBLE quality from:

- Chateau Ste. Michelle Vintners at Woodinville near Seattle in Washington State, using grapes from the Yakima Valley of Washington State

At the next slightly lower level of rating scores, I found the following wines consistently of FINE quality from these vineyards and wineries:

- Concannon Vineyard at Livermore in the Livermore Valley of Alameda
- Wente Brothers at Livermore in the Livermore Valley of Alameda

CHAPTER IV

The Powerful Rich
White Wines

If you ask a connoisseur of French wines which is the greatest white in the world, the answer will almost always be one of the supreme whites from the Côtes d'Or, the "golden slopes" of southern Burgundy—most probably from the great hill of Le Montrachet, "the bald mountain," above the villages of Chassagne and Puligny. What makes these golden wines so great (at least those that are brilliantly made from fully ripe grapes in their finest vintage years) is, above all, their power and richness. Long before the edge of the glass reaches your lips, your entire face, all your senses, are enveloped by the dominance and concentration of the aroma and bouquet. The instant the golden liquid enters your mouth, it gives the feeling of being brushed by silk and velvet. An instant later, the complex array of flavors expands in your mouth to fill it entirely with the dominance of aromatic, fruity, perfumed, spicy sensations of taste. It begins in the mouth, then moves to the back of the nose and down into the throat. This is what is meant by the phrase "a big wine."

Many of the great Montrachets are so big that they overpower gentle foods—so big and powerful that they can often replace red wines as accompaniments to meats, strong cheeses, even some game. Today, in the United States, our winemakers have learned how to produce big white wines that compete in power and richness with the major wines of Europe. This chapter discusses and classifies those white wines. We begin with the grape that produces the greatest white wines both in France and in the United States.

PINOT CHARDONNAY *Also called Chardonnay, Pinot Blanc Chardonnay, Aubaine, Melon Blanc, Beaunois, Epinette Blanche, Petite Sainte-Marie; in Germany, Weisser Clevner*

The Pinot Chardonnay is not the most widely distributed of the world's great grapevines. That honor belongs to the White Johannisberg Riesling. These little amber yellow Pinot Chardonnay grapes are certainly difficult to grow. They are prone to virtually all the vinous diseases. They are often sickly and temperamental. They are the favorite midnight feast of many wild animals and innumerable birds. Even if, finally, the grape gets harvested and crushed without frost damage, to which it is very susceptible, the making of a great Pinot Chardonnay wine is a matter of brilliant technical skills and a most delicate sense of balance.

And yet no other grape that has immigrated to our shores has had the dazzling success of Pinot Chardonnay. It has taken to our climate, our soil, our water, our total ecology, like the mallard duck to the waters of Chesapeake Bay. Within a relatively few years, Pinot Chardonnay has become the number-one white wine for American connoisseurs. Its marketing success—the range of prices paid for it —is an extraordinary story of the creation of a huge nationwide thirst for a wine that has built for itself a high quality reputation.

The arrival of Pinot Chardonnay in the United States has even involved—in the pattern of many thousands of previous immigrants —a change of name. Within a few years of the first plantings in California, Dr. Harold Olmo published a learned and logical scientific paper arguing that Pinot Chardonnay was the wrong name. This grape was not, he alleged, a botanical member of the international Pinot family and was not, as had been previously thought, the white version of the Burgundian red Pinot Noir. The conclusion of the good doctor's thesis was that the grape should simply be called "Chardonnay." A majority of American winemakers have jumped onto this bandwagon because, I suspect, of a subconscious desire to "Americanize" this precious grape and to give its wines on our side of the Atlantic a different label from those of Europe. On the other hand, some of the greatest of California winemakers, including Joe Heitz of Heitz Cellars and the late Fred McCrea of Stony Hill, have firmly continued to label their top wines "Pinot Chardonnay." The other day, when I asked a Napa Valley winemaker why he did not go along with Dr. Olmo's theory, the smiling reply was "Harold Olmo doesn't even know how to make wine!" The debate continues, but somehow it seems slightly irrelevant. I can't help feeling that a rose or a Pinot Chardonnay, by any other name, smells and tastes just as lovely and sweet.

What is loveliest about it is its extraordinary diversity. In France, it can be an immensely powerful Montrachet, an elegantly crisp Chablis, a superb Blanc de Blancs Champagne, a rich Meursault, a simple Mâconnais, a laughingly light Pouilly-Fuissé or Saint-Véran. In the United States, it produces just as much variety. Grown and vinified in California, it makes an almost entirely different wine— but no less attractive—than when it is grown in New York State or the Pacific Northwest. It makes, at Schramsberg, the best American sparkling wine; at Chalone, the biggest and most powerful "smoky" wines; at Stony Hill, the most delicate and sophisticated of American dinner wines. It is certainly the greatest American white wine. It may very well be the greatest American wine of any color.

The serious production of Chardonnay is relatively recent in our viticultural history. It did not begin until about 1957. A full understanding of the extraordinary developments since then involves some personal reminiscences. Quite a few years ago, I lunched in Beaune at the home of one of the great Burgundian *vignerons*, André Gagey, and his wife, Marie-Hélène. She, as usual, had organized a memorable meal precisely planned to magnify the best qualities of the great wines he had searched out in the cellars of the Louis Jadot firm, which he serves and helps to direct. After the inevitable Champagne in the *salle de réception*, the first course at table was a *tarte de fromage au pot-de-crème*, with the pastry made from cream that had been skimmed off the milk used for the *collage*, the clearing and fining of the white wines—cream left standing in a *pot de lait* for several days until it had just started to turn sour. The filling was dominated by the flowery, nutty richness of the Beaufort *artisanal*, handmade cheese of the high Alps. To match this balance of flavors the accompanying wine was a white from a Côtes-d'Or vineyard owned by Jadot and planted, of course, in Pinot Chardonnay, a Chevalier-Montrachet "Les Demoiselles." Apart from all its supreme Burgundian and Chardonnay qualities, the wine had a quite exceptional twist to its balance of flavors, a distant, subtle, almost vague smokiness.

Monsieur Gagey explained that this was generally known in the professional talk of Burgundian *vignerons* as "the little smoke of new oak." He said, "There has been the tradition in Burgundy for centuries, and I follow it exactly, of always putting the great white wines into new Limousin oak barrels until you get on the nose and on the tongue that delicate smokiness." After that first experience at lunch, I continued tasting with André Gagey, over the next couple of days, perhaps a hundred white wines, and he taught me how to recognize and appreciate the subtlety of the true Burgundian flavoring of the Pinot Chardonnay with that "little smoke of oak."

When the Pinot Chardonnay came to the United States, Fred McCrea of Stony Hill was among the first to study it seriously. He had done a lot of tasting in Burgundy and knew all about the delicate and subtle injection of oak flavor into the wine by aging and storing in Limousin oak barrels. But the "big push" for Chardonnay came about ten years after the start at Stony Hill. James D. Zellerbach, the San Francisco paper manufacturer who had been ambassador to Italy, had loved Burgundies all his life. He planned as his retirement hobby to build and run a small showplace vineyard in the Sonoma Valley called Hanzell in honor of his wife, Hannah. No expense was spared to model this tiny vineyard after the famous Burgundian domaine of the Clos Vougeot—in order to produce Burgundian-style wines of a quality, if possible, as great as any in France. Burgundian barrels, Burgundian equipment, and Burgundian experts were imported. The best and ripest Pinot Chardonnay grapes were vinified in the Burgundian manner and aged in Limousin oak. The result was wine of an intense flavor and stronger "smoke of oak" than was traditional in Burgundy. To many American winemakers without much experience of tasting in Burgundy, these Hanzell wines came as a revelation of what could be done to make a plain old Pinot Chardonnay more exciting.

During the 1960s and 1970s more and more wineries began making big, heavily oaky Chardonnays. A very smoky wine is exciting at the first sip, especially to an inexperienced taster. The effects in the nose and on the tongue are so powerful that they fairly knock you over. Some of the extremely smoky wines began to win prizes at tastings. The competition between wineries became so fierce that all restraint was thrown overboard. Some of the wines should have been labeled "essence of ripe fruit and smoke of oak."

Against this wild exaggeration, Fred McCrea put up a powerful one-man opposition. He posed the question, "Is more really always better?" While some of the wilder winemakers were pushing up the alcohol in their Chardonnays as high as 14 percent, with big brassy body and overpowering oaky-smoky flavor, Fred's philosophy was to stand for his own principles. The powerhouse wines are almost impossible to drink with dinner since they tend to overrule all foods. Fred continued to make his wines as graceful accompaniments to the finest and subtlest of foods. One evening after dinner up at Stony Hill, Fred argued his point of view: "When you accent the fruit in Pinot Chardonnay, it develops that marvelous honey-apple flavor. What more do you want? Why all this excitement about heavy oak? To me, oak is like garlic. You need some. But if that's all you taste, it's too much."

If Fred McCrea were alive today, he would not have to fight his battle alone. Although some of those immense, dominant, dramatic, powerful, smoky, solid Chardonnays continue to be produced at some of the most famous California mountaintop vineyards (David Bruce, Chalone, Mount Eden, Mayacamas, among others), an increasing number of equally prestigious vineyards have turned away from the extremes to produce Chardonnays of a more reasonable balance, more restrained and subtle—wines that can always be counted on to frame and magnify an excellent dinner menu (Chateau Montelena, Freemark Abbey, Heitz, Long, Preston of Yakima, Spring Mountain, always Stony Hill). These vineyards prove that our American winemakers are now also masters of the true Burgundian technique, in which the lovely apple-honey of the fruit dominates, while the smoke is a distant, light, sophisticated and subtle, aromatic accent.

As to the heavy, oaky wines, I have come to the conclusion, finally, that these power Chardonnays should not be associated with any meal. They cannot be aperitifs, because they overpower the canapés and hors d'oeuvres; they cannot be dessert wines, because they are too dry, and their "tannic bitterness" clashes with sugar. They should be sipped at some restful hour in between meals, as "exotic liqueurs," essences of fruit and smoke, to be drunk ice-cold in tiny liqueur glasses that have come straight from the freezer and are slightly ice coated.

The Problems of Finding
Good-Value Chardonnays

It would be very far from the truth to assume that every American Chardonnay is either a powerhouse liqueur or a magnificent Burgundian-type masterpiece. For every one of these, there are many average, middle-of-the-road labels and quite a few that are distinctly mediocre. This is not entirely bad. One does not always want a big and expensive wine for a festive occasion. My experience in exploring the wide world of the less-expensive Chardonnays is that it is usually possible to find fair value at almost every price level.

To be successful in finding your way among the 200-odd American Chardonnay labels, you have to be aware of at least a few facts about the agriculture and economics of this temperamental grape. A basic fact is that it does not develop its intense varietal flavor unless, before it is picked, it achieves a high degree of ripeness, with a strong balance of sugar against its natural acid. Without that intense varietal flavor, even the most skilled winemaker cannot make a distinguished wine. Yet, in some years, in some vineyards, the Chardonnay never reaches the perfect ripeness. It has simply been planted in some places in the United States where it should never have been expected to grow. With experience in tasting, you will soon learn the names of some of those vineyards and will avoid wines grown there. Then, in poor vintage years, when there are just not enough hours of warm sunshine during the growing season, there are dull and lifeless Chardonnay wines made from grapes that were not ripe enough when they were picked.

Another factor that shows up strongly in the finished wine is the native and universal inability of the Chardonnay vine to feed and support a large number of bunches of grapes. Even at its best, in ideal climate and soil, the harvest of fruit of a Chardonnay vine is relatively small. In order to get grapes of supreme quality, the farmer-grower must, in the spring, deliberately prune back his vines to reduce the number of bunches of grapes. Even for the most idealistic grower, this is a very hard decision, since it directly reduces the income from each acre of vines. Grown men have been known to cry as they stand in front of the vine, pruning shears in hand, deciding which tiny bunches of undeveloped grapes they will destroy. In recent years in California, as the price of Chardonnay grapes has risen to astronomical heights, the problem of pruning has grown tougher and tougher. Sometimes grapes have been harvested from vines that have not been sufficiently cut back. These grapes are below the highest average of quality, and their inadequacy is reflected in their wines.

During the 1970s, the demand for Chardonnay was so overwhelming that new vineyards were planted at a speed that increased the supply of grapes by almost 1,000 percent, and acreage was multiplied more than ten times. But a Chardonnay vine takes six years before it gives an adequate harvest of grapes, and, even then, these young grapes do not have the flavor and quality that comes from mature vines. Often the quality of a finished wine depends strongly on the proportion it contains of grapes from new and old vines.

Then there is the inescapable law of supply and demand. So irresistible was the demand for Chardonnay in the early 1970s, that the price of harvested grapes sold by the growers to the wineries "broke the sound barrier," rose above $1,000 per ton and continued upward to the unheard-of price of $1,800 per ton. (In the middle 1960s, the price had hovered around $350 per ton.) Yet the winemakers did not hesitate to buy the grapes even at these astronomical prices, because they knew that they could sell every bottle of Chardonnay they could make at virtually any price they cared to ask for it. The fashionable demand for Chardonnay in the early 1970s merged smoothly into "the white-wine explosion" of the late 1970s, and the national market pressure for Chardonnay has never really stopped increasing.

Then, in 1976 and 1977, the severe drought in California brought a general decrease in wine production. Some vineyards reported that their grapes were so dry and small that, at the pressing, the gallonage of liquid juice was down by as much as 75 percent. More and more wineries had to go into the open market to buy grapes. If they insisted on very high quality and perfect ripeness, they would have to pay very high prices. On the other hand, if they wanted to hold down the prices of their finished wines, they would have to buy grapes of less than perfect quality and ripeness, and this would be reflected in the lowering of the quality of their wines. Any compromise on grape quality leads inevitably to the difficult question of blending. The federal law has recently been considerably tightened, but it does still allow a winemaker to label his wine "Chardonnay," for example, even if he blends into it up to 25 percent of some other grape. I hasten to add that all the greatest Chardonnays are 100 percent. A 75 percent wine may be a very good thirst quencher for a hot summer afternoon, but it is never going to be an intense varietal Chardonnay.

These are the principal factors that have to be taken into account when exploring the lesser and less-expensive Chardonnays. Some of this information is sometimes on the label. If your wineshop's staff is well informed, they may be able to answer some of the important questions. As a last resort, you can always call or write the winery. Above all, it is most important that you keep your own wine-tasting notes—that you set down the basic information on the wines you like and dislike—so that, quite quickly, you will build your own indispensable reference list.

The problems are quite different when you move up to the much smaller range of the supreme Chardonnays, where you are searching for perfection, regardless of the cost. In this area, you can be strongly guided by the names of the most prestigious producers (see the classification lists below), but an all-important factor is, also, the sensitivity of the Chardonnay vine to geographic location—the degree to which the quality of the wine depends on the precise place, the makeup of the soil, the slope of the land, the direction of the prevailing winds, the runoff of the rains, the angle of the sun, all the natural factors at the spot where the grapes were grown.

I have found Chardonnays of extraordinary interest, for example, from the vineyards on the hills between the Napa Valley and Sonoma. These hills form a huge, curving amphitheater, stretching from San Pablo Bay northward to join with the Mayacamas Mountains. This area of not-too-high, rolling hills is called the Rincón de los Carneros, "the lonely place of the sheep." In the last forty years, since Louis M. Martini began buying land there and planting vines, the sheep have been largely expelled by the grapes. Twenty years after Martini, another winemaker, André Tchelistcheff, persuaded his then employers, Beaulieu Vineyard, to expand beyond their Rutherford estates on the floor of the Napa Valley up into the Carneros Hills. Tchelistcheff was convinced that the average year-round climate was so close to that of the upper slopes of Burgundy that this would be an ideal place to grow a typical Burgundian grape such as

Pinot Chardonnay. But the man who really brought Carneros and Chardonnay together with more conviction and determination than anyone else—and who put the Carneros name on the wine map— was a dedicated farmer and grape grower, René Di Rosa, who planted mainly Chardonnay in a vineyard that he named Winery Lake, Carneros. He audaciously insisted that the name be printed on the labels of bottles of wine made by any producer from Di Rosa grapes. Soon it was on the labels first of Z D, then Burgess and Veedercrest—all three producing outstanding wines from the Carneros grapes.

Many professional tasters now share the view that in important ways the Carneros Chardonnays are similar in quality to those of Burgundy. This may be due to the Carneros soil, mainly sandy loam, very rough and rocky in places, with a clay topsoil that causes the water to run off extremely quickly, thus, according to the classical wisdom, "making the grapes suffer, as all good wine grapes must." Also, the temperature on the slopes of the hills almost never gets as high as it does down on the valley floor, so the hill grapes ripen slowly, developing intensity of flavor and, in satisfactory vintage years, a good sugar balance.

As the fine qualities of the Carneros grapes are being more widely recognized, new vineyards are being established up in the hills. One of these is Carneros Creek, where Francis Mahoney has planted 10 acres of Chardonnay, with high hopes for future wines that may combine delicacy of flavor with superb balance, austerity with great longevity. At his Veedercrest Winery, Alfred Baxter is using more and more Carneros grapes and producing, in his Chardonnays, a family quality of refreshing crispness, a lovely sense of the fruit, a subtle Burgundian distant feel of smoke and a wake-up tartness.

But the Rincón de los Carneros is only one example of an area that is rapidly developing its own geographic appellation and its own recognizable character for its own wines. Virtually all the other famous California districts are now engaged in lobbying, with the federal authorities in Washington and the state authorities in Sacramento, to have the right to their own appellations on their wine labels—"Napa Valley," "Sonoma," "Monterey," "Central Coast," "Alexander Valley," "Mendocino," "Livermore Valley," and so on. From all of them the flow of Chardonnay wines during the 1980s promises to rise to a flood, a veritable tidal wave.

There are now more than 14,000 acres of Chardonnay in California alone. The newest development—worth careful watching in the immediate future—is that the second place among Chardonnay-growing states has now been taken by New York—with just about 200 acres planted and coming into production. New York State's wine regions sometimes have winters (especially in the Finger Lakes) that can be devastatingly cold, while the summers can alternate rapidly between scorching heat and inhibiting coolness. So the Chardonnay vine is difficult to grow, but, if the special techniques of protecting the roots are properly mastered, the wine can be of extraordinary interest, showing unusual character, striking intensity of fruit flavors, and a solidity of body construction that gives a feel almost of satin on the tongue. This exciting effect is the direct result of the slow ripening of the grapes in a generally cool climate and, clearly, will be the unique contribution of New York to the sweep of Chardonnay qualities.

Much of the early wine development in New York was undertaken by big wineries owned by large corporations for whom mass production was a primary goal. Now the state authorities (seeing the explosion of quality from the small vineyards in California) are strongly encouraging the planting of small vineyards, with family ownership and management. A state winery license used to cost many thousands of dollars (and still does for large corporate developers), but a bona fide family applicant can now get a license for under $200. This has opened the way for such potentially excellent small wineries as Glenora (page 338), Heron Hill (page 345), and Plane's Cayuga (page 381). The first Chardonnay released by the latter—the grapes grown and the wine made by Mary and Robert Plane—is a NOBLE experimental success, a promise of an important future for New York State wines.

Chardonnay is also developing rapidly and substantially in the South Columbia Basin and the Yakima Valley of Washington State, as well as in small areas in Idaho and a number of other states. So we can certainly expect a substantial increase in the total American production and a steady improvement in quality throughout the decade of the 1980s. I have already said that there are now more than 200 different Chardonnay labels, and this number will also increase steadily. In some ways, the expansion has been (and is still) too fast. New and relatively inexperienced winemakers are not being entirely successful with their first tries at making Chardonnay. Almost every month, new wineries are adding to the list of labels without adding to the list of drinkable, fine, sound wines. For every exciting new discovery—every Jekel, every Keenan, every magnificent Chardonnay from Zelma Long, every Ventana—I have opened a dozen bottles that have been disappointments.

Yet, in spite of all the difficulties and setbacks, the Pinot Chardonnay grape remains one of America's greatest success stories. It will be even greater in the future, when nature gives us better vintages, when the vines have grown to greater maturity in the vineyards, when we develop more experienced winemakers, and when we learn how to handle and age our wines with a more secure discipline. Until then, I must classify the American Pinot Chardonnay as my ratings show it at its present stage of development.

During my years of appraising and keeping formal records on American wines, I have found only one Pinot Chardonnay that has consistently rated on my tasting charts as truly GREAT quality. It is, without question, the greatest white wine of the United States. Beginning in 1948, it was made by Fred McCrea and is now being continued by his wife, Eleanor, at their estate:

- Stony Hill Vineyard on the mountain above the Napa Valley

The wine is made entirely from the grapes grown and vinified on the estate. (For a detailed discussion of this magnificent wine and the extraordinary family that created it, see page 273.)

Within the range of 2 to 5 points below this highest level, I have found eight Chardonnays consistently rating at a SUPERB quality from these vineyards and wineries:

- Chalone Vineyard on Mount Chalone in the Gavilan Range of the Santa Lucia Mountains in Monterey, with its winemaker, Peter Graff
- Chateau Montelena at Calistoga in the Napa Valley, with winemakers Mike Grgich (up to 1977) and Jerry Luper (up to 1982) who made the sequence of wines that won the sensational tasting victory in Paris in 1976, when French experts, tasting blind, picked this American wine over some of the best whites of France
- Freemark Abbey Winery near St. Helena in the Napa Valley
- Heitz Wine Cellars near St. Helena in the Napa Valley, with its owner-winemaker, Joe Heitz

- Long Vineyard on Pritchard Hill above the Napa Valley, with its owner-winemaker, Zelma Long
- Mayacamas Vineyards on the Mayacamas Range above the Napa Valley, with its owner-winemaker, Bob Travers
- Preston Wine Cellars at Pasco in the Columbia Basin of Washington State, with its winemaker, Robert Griffin
- Spring Mountain Vineyards near St. Helena in the Napa Valley, with its owner-winemaker, Mike Robbins, using grapes from the Winery Lake Vineyard on the Carneros Hills

Within the next lower tasting range, the following Chardonnays have consistently rated on my charts as NOBLE in quality from these vineyards and wineries:

- Acacia Winery in the Carneros Hills above the Napa Valley
- Ahlgren Vineyards at Boulder Creek in the Santa Cruz Mountains south of San Francisco Bay, with grapes from Monterey
- David Bruce Winery above Los Gatos in the Santa Cruz Mountains south of San Francisco Bay
- Davis Bynum Winery at Healdsburg in Sonoma
- Chateau St. Jean at Kenwood in Sonoma, with its winemaker, Richard Arrowood, vinifying grapes from the Belle Terre Vineyard and the Robert Young Vineyards in the Alexander Valley
- The Christian Brothers on Mont La Salle above the Napa Valley, with its winemaker, Brother Timothy
- Edna Valley Vineyard in the San Luis Obispo district of the Central Coast region, with its winemaker, Gary Mosby
- Fisher Vineyards in the Mayacamas Mountains of Sonoma, with its winemaker-owner, Fred Fisher, using grapes from the Whitney Vineyard on the estate
- Grgich Hills Cellar at Rutherford in the Napa Valley, with its winemaker-partner, Mike Grgich
- Hinzerling Vineyards at Prosser at the base of the Rattlesnake Hills in the Yakima Valley of Washington State, with its winemaker-partner, Mike Wallace
- Iron Horse Vineyard at Sebastopol in the Russian River Valley of Sonoma, with its winemaker, Forrest Tancer
- Keenan Winery on Spring Mountain above the Napa Valley
- Kistler Vineyard above Glen Ellen and the Valley of the Moon in Sonoma, with its winemaker-owner, Steve Kistler

- Knudsen-Erath Winery at Dundee in the Willamette Valley of Oregon, with its winemaker-partner, Dick Erath, using grapes from the Salmon River Valley in Idaho
- Louis M. Martini Winery in St. Helena in the Napa Valley, with its winemaker-owner, Louis P. Martini
- Mount Veeder Winery on the Mayacamas Range above the Napa Valley, with its winemaker-owner, Mike Bernstein, using grapes from the Carneros Hills
- Joseph Phelps Vineyards near St. Helena in the Napa Valley, with its winemaker, Walter Schug
- Plane's Cayuga Vineyard on Cayuga Lake in the Finger Lakes region of New York State, with its winemaker-owner, Robert Plane
- Martin Ray Vineyards above Saratoga in the Santa Cruz Mountains of Santa Clara, with its winemaker-owner, Peter Martin Ray
- Ste. Chapelle Vineyards at Sunny Slope near Caldwell in the Snake River Valley of Idaho, with its winemaker, Bill Broich
- St. Clement Vineyards near St. Helena in the Napa Valley
- Shafer Vineyards on the Stag's Leap Slope east of Yountville in the Napa Valley, with its winemaker, Nikko Schoch
- Stag's Leap Wine Cellars on the Silverado Trail near Yountville in the Napa Valley, with its winemaker-partner, Warren Winiarski
- Sterling Vineyards at Calistoga in the Napa Valley
- Turgeon & Lohr Winery at San Jose in Santa Clara, with grapes from the Arroyo Seco in Monterey
- Veedercrest Vineyard high on Mount Veeder in the Mayacamas Range above the Napa Valley, with its winemaker-owner, Al Baxter
- Wente Brothers at Livermore in the Livermore Valley of Alameda, with its winemaker-partner, Eric Wente

Finally, at the next ranking, my rating charts have classified as FINE the Chardonnays from these vineyards and wineries:

- Alexander Valley Vineyards east of Healdsburg in northern Sonoma
- Almadén Vineyards at San Jose in Santa Clara, with its winemaster, Klaus Mathes, using grapes from their Paicines Vineyard in San Benito
- Alta Vineyard at Calistoga in the Napa Valley

- Associated Vintners at Bellevue near Seattle in Washington State, with its winemaker, Dr. Lloyd Woodburne, using grapes from the Yakima Valley of Washington State
- Bargetto Winery at Soquel in the Santa Cruz Mountains south of San Francisco Bay, with its owner-winemaker, Lawrence Bargetto, using grapes from the Vine Hill Vineyard
- Beaulieu Vineyard at Rutherford in the Napa Valley
- Beringer Vineyards near St. Helena in the Napa Valley, with its winemaker, Myron Nightingale
- Burgess Cellars near St. Helena in the Napa Valley, with its owner-winemaker, Tom Burgess
- Cakebread Cellars at Rutherford in the Napa Valley, with its owner-winemaker, Jack Cakebread
- Carneros Creek Winery in the Carneros Hills above the Napa Valley, with its owner-winemaker, Francis Mahoney
- Chappellet Vineyard on Pritchard Hill east of Rutherford above the Napa Valley
- Chateau Ste. Michelle Vintners at Woodinville near Seattle in Washington State, using grapes from their vineyards in the Yakima Valley of Washington State
- Clos du Val on the Silverado Trail near Yountville in the Napa Valley, with its owner-winemaker, Bernard Portet
- Conn Creek Vineyard on the Silverado Trail near Rutherford in the Napa Valley
- Cotes des Colombe Vineyard at Banks in the North Willamette Valley of Oregon
- Dehlinger Winery at Sebastopol in the Russian River Valley of Sonoma
- Devlin Wine Cellars near Soquel in the Santa Cruz Mountains south of San Francisco Bay
- Dry Creek Vineyard at Healdsburg in the Dry Creek Valley of Sonoma
- Elk Cove Vineyards at Gaston in the Willamette Valley of Oregon
- Eyrie Vineyards at McMinnville near Dundee in the Willamette Valley of Oregon, with its owner-winemaker, David Lett
- Far Niente Winery at Oakville in the Napa Valley
- Firestone Vineyard at Los Olivos in the Santa Ynez Valley of Santa Barbara, with its winemaker, Alison Green

- E. B. Foote Winery at South Park near Seattle in Washington State
- Franciscan Vineyards at Rutherford in the Napa Valley, with its winemaker, Tom Ferrell
- Glenora Wine Cellars on Seneca Lake in the Finger Lakes district of New York State, with its winemaker, Mike Elliott, vinifying grapes from the McGregor Vineyard at Dundee
- Gundlach-Bundschu Vineyard at Vineburg in the Valley of the Moon in Sonoma, with its winemaker, John Merritt
- Hacienda Wine Cellars in the Valley of the Moon in Sonoma
- Hanzell Vineyards in the Valley of the Moon in Sonoma
- Harbor Winery near Sacramento on the Sacramento River, vinified by its owner-winemaker, Charles Myers with grapes from the Napa Valley
- Hargrave Vineyard at Cutchogue on the North Fork of Long Island, with its winemaker-owner, Alec Hargrave
- Heron Hill Vineyard on Lake Keuka in the Finger Lakes district of New York State
- Hoffman Mountain Ranch above Paso Robles in the Santa Lucia Mountains of San Luis Obispo, with its winemaker, Michael Hoffman
- Husch Vineyards at Philo in the Anderson Valley of Mendocino
- Jekel Vineyard at Greenfield in the Salinas Valley of Monterey
- Charles Krug Winery at St. Helena in the Napa Valley
- Thomas Kruse Winery at Gilroy in the Santa Cruz Mountains of Santa Clara
- Lambert Bridge Winery west of Healdsburg in the Dry Creek Valley of Sonoma
- Matanzas Creek Winery in the Bennett Valley southwest of Santa Rosa in Sonoma, with its winemaker, Merry Edwards
- Milano Winery south of Hopland in the Redwood Valley of Mendocino, with grapes from the Lolonis Vineyard
- Mill Creek Vineyards southwest of Healdsburg in the Russian River Valley of Sonoma
- Mirassou Vineyards at San Jose in Santa Clara, with grapes from their vineyards in Monterey
- Robert Mondavi Winery at Oakville in the Napa Valley, with its winemaker, Tim Mondavi

- Monterey Peninsula Winery on the Monterey-Salinas Highway in Monterey
- Mount Eden Vineyards near the peak of Mount Eden in the Santa Cruz Range above Saratoga in Santa Clara
- Napa Wine Cellars north of Yountville in the Napa Valley
- Navarro Vineyards at Philo in the Anderson Valley of Mendocino
- Parducci Wine Cellars near Ukiah in Mendocino
- Pedroncelli Winery northeast of Geyserville on a ridge above the Dry Creek Valley of Sonoma
- Pendleton Winery at San Jose in Santa Clara
- Ponzi Vineyards at Beaverton in the Willamette Valley of Oregon
- Quail Ridge Vineyards on Mount Veeder above the Napa Valley, with its owner-winemaker, Elaine Wellesley
- Raymond Winery at Calistoga in the Napa Valley
- Ridge Vineyards above Cupertino on Black Mountain in the Santa Cruz Range, with its winemaker-partner, Paul Draper, using grapes from the Monte Bello vineyards on the winery estate
- Roudon-Smith Vineyards at Scott's Valley in the Santa Cruz Mountains south of San Francisco Bay
- Round Hill Cellars north of St. Helena in the Napa Valley
- Russian River Vineyards south of Forestville in the Russian River Valley of Sonoma, with its owner-winemaker, Michael Topolos
- Sanford & Benedict Vineyards at Lompoc in the Santa Ynez Valley of the Santa Barbara district
- Sausal Winery east of Healdsburg in the Alexander Valley of Sonoma
- Simi Winery at Healdsburg in the Alexander Valley of Sonoma, with its winemaker, Zelma Long
- Smith-Madrone Vineyard high on Spring Mountain in the Napa Valley
- Smothers Winery east of the town of Santa Cruz in the Santa Cruz Mountains south of San Francisco Bay
- Sonoma Vineyards at Windsor in Sonoma, with its winemaker, Rod Strong, using grapes from the River West Vineyard
- Souverain Cellars near Geyserville in the Dry Creek Valley of Sonoma

- Trefethen Vineyards near the town of Napa in the Napa Valley
- Ventana Vineyards along the Arroyo Seco River southwest of Soledad in the Salinas Valley of Monterey
- Villa Mt. Eden Winery at Oakville in the Napa Valley.
- Mark West Vineyards north of Forestville in the Russian River Valley of Sonoma
- Hermann J. Wiemer Vineyard at Dundee in the Finger Lakes district of New York State, with its winemaker-owner, Hermann Wiemer
- Willowside Vineyards northwest of Santa Rosa in the Russian River Valley of Sonoma
- Zaca Mesa Vineyard at Los Olivos in the Santa Ynez Valley of Santa Barbara
- Z D Wines on the Silverado Trail east of Rutherford in the Napa Valley

GEWÜRZTRAMINER *Also called, in France, Traminer Musque, Gentil Rose Aromatique; in Hungary, Furmint; in Yugoslavia, quite rarely, Formentin; in California, Red Traminer*

Many serious wine tasters have asked why this exotic, unique grape continues to be known by its German name. After all, the German word *gewürz* simply means "spicy," and since there already exists an established grape family named Traminer, why not just call this clonal variation the Spicy Traminer? The answer to the question is buried somewhere in the strange history and worldwide pilgrimage of this extraordinary vine.

The fact that the perfume and taste of its grapes, when they are fully ripe, are so strongly identifiable as "musky," inescapably links the Gewürztraminer with what is probably the oldest of all grape families, the Muscats of Arabia and Persia. Some grape historians believe that every modern variety of noble wine grape is a variation of a descendant from one or another of the branches of the Muscat family. The ancient grape was given its English name in honor of the fact that it smells and tastes of musk—originally, the naturally secreted oil released by the deer to attract the doe, an ingredient much used in the making of many perfumes. Natural musk oil is also present in many fruits and is, for example, a part of the attractive aroma and taste of a ripe apple, many types of melons, pears, peaches, and in the perfume of roses.

From the Middle East this grape was carried westward—perhaps by Phoenician traders or Roman soldiers—until it reached Hungary, where it grew and prospered mightily and developed into the famous Furmint of Tokay. Next, it moved into Rumania and Yugoslavia where it became known as the Formentin. Then it crossed the Adriatic Sea to the mountainous district of northeastern Italy known as the South Tyrol. This land was once owned by Austria, so the people speak both German and Italian dialects. The village where the Yugoslav Formentin vine was planted and where it grew most prolifically is called, in Italian, Termeno, and, in German, Tramin. Before long, both the grape that grew so well here and the wine that was made here were called Traminer. With its new name, the vine continued its travels westward into Germany and was heavily planted in the sheltered, sunny, warm district of the Palatinate on the Rhine. Here, the German vintners achieved the great transformation.

They began noticing that some vines, growing in certain favored corners of the vineyards, produced grapes of a much more pronounced spiciness of aroma and taste than others. They began isolating these special vines and crosscutting them with others of the same type in order to intensify the spiciness. The blander vines were uprooted, and eventually whole vineyards were filled with the spicy vines, which were then named Gewürztraminer to differentiate them from the bland Traminer. In fact, an entirely new clonal strain of the Traminer grape was being developed. Its wine was so exciting, so unique, that the blander Traminer was virtually eliminated by the German vintners, and, in honor of their creative work, the new grape has held its German name ever since.

After the Franco-Prussian War of 1870, when Germany took Alsace from France, the Gewürztraminer vine crossed the Rhine and reached its absolute peak of viticultural production on the lower slopes of the Vosges mountains. Not only were the climate and soil absolutely right for a superbly heady and racy version of Gewürztraminer, but the Alsatian vintners developed the special techniques of precisely timed harvesting and slow fermentation for Gewürztraminer wines of a quality seldom equaled elsewhere. The Alsatians have set the standard by which all other Gewürztraminers must be judged.

The vine came to the United States early in our wine history. At least 125 years ago, the California pioneer Agoston Haraszthy planted the German Gewürztraminer. Though our early growers admired the handsome look of the oval, russet pink berries, their perfume and flavor were considered much too exotic for the American taste. So nothing much was done with the Gewürztraminer until after Prohibition had passed and the major wine developments of the 1950s, sixties, and seventies had begun.

In the 1950s, there was a revival of interest in the Gewürztraminer vine in America. In the 1960s, small, experimental plantings were started in some of the cooler regions of the Salinas Valley of Monterey, in Sonoma and Mendocino, in the Willamette Valley of Oregon, and in the Yakima Valley of Washington State. By 1965, in the three states, total plantings were no more than 100 acres. At the latest count, in the 1970s, the acreage has increased to 3,000. In 1970, only seven California, Oregon, and Washington State wineries were making Gewürztraminer wines. By 1975, the number had expanded to twenty-three.

But—let us face the fact frankly—the American Gewürztraminer has not so far become anything like the exotic, intense, perfumed, spicy wine of Alsace. When the grapes are ideally grown and harvested with skill and speed so that the wine can be perfectly made, the final result can be the most distinctive and spiciest of all white wines. With its aromatic qualities, it is perfumed, mellow, and soft, but not necessarily subtle. Of all the famous white wines, this is surely the most exciting, exotic, fascinating, powerful, and, as the French say, *bien charpenté*, "sturdily constructed." In Alsace, when I attend the great banquets of La Confrérie de Saint Etienne, the wine society of the region, at which they serve no red wines with their menus, because none is produced in Alsace, a superb Gewürztraminer is considered strong enough to accompany a roast rack of lamb and, toward the end of the meal, to be the partner of the monstrously aggressive Münster cheese.

Producing the perfect Gewürztraminer, however, presents some of the most difficult problems in all of winemaking. The first is to pick the grapes at their absolutely ideal moment of ripeness. There is a saying in Alsace that, if you want to pick your Gewürztraminer grapes at the dead right moment, you had better move your bed out to the vineyard and sleep there. Pick the grapes a couple of days too early, and your wine will be bland and dull. Then, quite suddenly, one morning, as the sun begins to warm the vines, the grapes will signal their perfect ripeness by releasing a magnificent and penetrating musky perfume. At once, it alerts and attracts the birds and bees, other insects, raccoons, and small marauders, and, if you don't move very fast, few of the grapes will be left for making wine—and those that are left will, within a day or two, have deteriorated so rapidly that wines made from them will be sharply acid, unpleasant, even undrinkable. For the winemaker, the Gewürztraminer is a very tough customer indeed, and this inescapable fact must be central to any discussion of the success or failure of the grape in the United States.

I believe that, so far, most American winemakers have been afraid of the Gewürztraminer—on two counts. They fear its problems in the vineyard, when it suddenly releases its magnetic perfume and invites the bees and birds to a delectable feast. So the growers have been picking the grapes a few days before they become fully ripe— before the "day of the perfume"—before the picking problems arise. But—in exacting Gewürztraminer terms—these early picked grapes have a low sugar balance and no winemaker, however brilliant his technique, can make a great Gewürztraminer wine without a proper acid-sugar balance. What comes out, under the label of "American Gewürztraminer," may be an attractive, light, refreshing little summer sipping wine, but it has nothing about it of the great tradition of this magnificent grape. No great wine will ever come from this frightened point of view.

The second fear of many American winemakers is that, if they were to go all out to make the big, intense Gewürztraminers, the majority of American wine drinkers would not like them and would not buy them. I think that these winemakers secretly believe, deep in their hearts—although they would never say so publicly—that America is "not yet ready for a great Gewürztraminer."

I am thankful to be able to report that, as the number of winemakers turning their attention to Gewürztraminer grows, there are a few happy exceptions to this general rule. By 1978, the number of wineries producing Gewürztraminer had grown to thirty-four, and among them there have been some brave new spicy wines of hauntingly memorable quality from the wineries of Grand Cru, Hacienda, Louis M. Martini, and Wente Brothers. As we enter the decade of the 1980s, Gewürztraminer, at least on the West Coast, is booming— with new plantings of the vines in the cool areas of the California Central Coast region, in the Carneros Hills above the Napa Valley, in Oregon, and in Washington State. It has become one of the four highest-priced grapes in California—in some years, second in value only to Pinot Chardonnay—and seems to be on its way to becoming another American wine success story.

At my tastings, I have never found a truly GREAT American Gewürztraminer. That supreme honor remains with Alsace. The single U.S. Gewürztraminer that regularly achieves a SUPERB rating is from:

- Simi Winery at Healdsburg in the Alexander Valley of Sonoma, with its winemaker, Zelma Long, using grapes grown along the foggy banks of the Russian River

Three other vineyards and wineries are consistently within a point or two in the same SUPERB classification:

- Grand Cru Vineyards at Glen Ellen in the Sonoma Valley, with its partner-winemaker, Bob Magnani, using grapes from the Alexander Garden Creek Vineyard
- Hillcrest Vineyards near Roseburg in the Umpqua Valley of Oregon
- Stony Hill Vineyard on the mountain above the Napa Valley, with its owner-winemaker, Eleanor McCrea

In the next group a few points below I have consistently found wines rating at a NOBLE quality from these vineyards and wineries:

- Almadén Vineyards of San Jose in Santa Clara, with its winemaster, Klaus Mathes, using grapes from the small estate vineyard at La Cienega in San Benito
- Firestone Vineyard at Los Olivos in the Santa Ynez Valley of Santa Barbara, with its winemaker, Alison Green
- Hacienda Wine Cellars in the Valley of the Moon in Sonoma
- Hinzerling Vineyards at Prosser at the base of the Rattlesnake Hills in the Yakima Valley of Washington State, with its partner-winemaker, Mike Wallace
- Louis M. Martini Winery at St. Helena in the Napa Valley with its owner-winemaker, Louis P. Martini, using grapes from his Monte Rosso Vineyard in Sonoma
- Joseph Phelps Vineyards near St. Helena in the Napa Valley, with its winemaker, Walter Schug
- Ste. Chapelle Vineyards at Sunny Slope near Caldwell in the Snake River Valley of Idaho, with its winemaker, Bill Broich

In the next classification, I have consistently found wines that rated a FINE quality from these vineyards and wineries:

- Associated Vintners at Bellevue near Seattle in Washington State, with its partner-winemaker, Dr. Lloyd Woodburne, using grapes from the Yakima Valley of Washington State
- Buena Vista Vineyard in the Valley of the Moon in Sonoma
- Chateau St. Jean at Kenwood in Sonoma, with its winemaker, Richard Arrowood
- The Christian Brothers on Mont La Salle above the Napa Valley, with its winemaker, Brother Timothy
- Clos du Bois at Healdsburg in the Alexander Valley of Sonoma
- Evensen Vineyards between Oakville and Rutherford in the Napa Valley
- Fetzer Vineyards near Ukiah in the Redwood Valley of Mendocino, with its owner-winemaker, John Fetzer, using a blend of local grapes with others from San Luis Obispo
- Heitz Wine Cellars near St. Helena in the Napa Valley, with its owner-winemaker, Joe Heitz
- Paul Masson Vineyards at Saratoga and in the Pinnacles district of the Santa Cruz Mountains in Santa Clara, with grapes from their Pinnacles Vineyard in Monterey
- Matanzas Creek Winery in the Bennett Valley southwest of Santa Rosa in Sonoma, with its winemaker, Merry Edwards
- Mirassou Vineyards at San Jose in Santa Clara
- Mont Elise Vineyards at Bingen in the South Columbia Basin of Washington State, with its owner-winemaker, Chuck Henderson
- Monterey Vineyard at Gonzales in Monterey, with its winemaker, Dick Peterson
- Navarro Vineyards at Philo in the Anderson Valley of Mendocino
- Parson's Creek Winery south of Ukiah in the Ukiah Valley of Mendocino
- Pedroncelli Winery northeast of Geyserville on a ridge above the Dry Creek Valley of Sonoma
- Preston Wine Cellars at Pasco in the Columbia Basin of Washington State, with its winemaker, Robert Griffin
- Sterling Vineyards at Calistoga in the Napa Valley
- Wente Brothers at Livermore in the Livermore Valley of Alameda, with its owner-winemaker, Eric Wente, using grapes from their Arroyo Seco Vineyard in the Salinas Valley of Monterey

- Yakima River Winery at Prosser in the Yakima Valley of Washington State, with its owner-winemaker, John Rauner
- Z D Wines on the Silverado Trail east of Rutherford in the Napa Valley

MUSCAT *Also called, in France, Muscat de Frontignan, Muscat de Hambourg, Muscat Romain, Panse Musquée; in California, Flame Muscat; in England, White Frontignan; in Germany, Weisse Muskateller; in Greece, Muskuti; in Italy, Moscata Bianca, Moscato Canelli, Zibibbo; in Portugal, Muscatel Branco; in South Africa, White Hanepoot; in Spain, Moscatel Romano; in Turkey, Iskendiriye Misketi*

I have already referred briefly to the huge, worldwide grape family of the Muscats, which, in the most ancient of times, grew and thrived in the hot climates of Arabia and Persia—and from which all other varieties of noble wine grapes may have descended. Meanwhile, the original Muscats themselves have proliferated and traveled to virtually all wine regions. Today, there must still be at least a hundred clonal variations of this immense and versatile family—all substantially different from one another. The grapes range in color from blue black to the palest yellow. Their wines range from excellent to absolutely horrible. Most of them are sweet, and these are discussed in detail in Chapter VIII. But there are a few Muscat wines in which the sugar has been fermented out to a reasonable, though still rich, dryness—so that the wine can be served as an accompaniment to lunch or dinner. They are, of course, big, powerful wines—all with that musky aroma and flavor that is also the attractive characteristic of the Gewürztraminer. The Muscat grape thrives all over the world under a hot sun, and whether you eat it at your table as a grape or a raisin or drink it as a wine, it seems to give back to you the lovely strength and warmth of brilliant sunlight. As a wine, made with imagination and skill, it can be irresistibly attractive.

Each branch of the family is usually named for some place where that particular strain of the grape was developed, or where it grows at its best. The Muscat has been quite extensively planted in California, but seldom to any good vinous purpose. One variety is the Muscat Blanc, also often called the Moscato Canelli (the name of the Italian village near Asti in the Piedmont), but the worst offender, on the grand scale of almost 12,000 acres planted, is the Muscat of Alexandria (after the Egyptian city), which has been used to make the fortified Muscatels—the cheap substitutes for spirits usually associated with bums drinking from bottles as they lie prone in the gutters of the skid rows of city slums.

The best of all the Muscat varieties is the Golden Muscat of Frontignan (the famous wine village on the Mediterranean coast of the south of France), which makes the best of all beautiful, golden Muscat wines. It does almost as well when it is planted in the warmer regions of California.

The best American Muscat I have tasted—of SUPERB quality, a Muscat of Alexandria strain—is produced by:

- Tualatin Vineyards at Forest Grove in the Willamette Valley of Oregon, with its owner-winemaker, Bill Fuller, using grapes grown at Grand View in the Yakima Valley of Washington State

His wines are very dry, with a lovely perfume of strong Muscat character.

My second-ranking dry Muscat—a perfumed, rich wine, made from the Italian Moscato Canelli strain—rated of NOBLE quality, comes from:

- Simi Winery at Healdsburg in the Alexander Valley of Sonoma, with its winemaker, Zelma Long, and André Tchelistcheff as consultant on this particular wine

Finally, a point or two below, I have found a Muscat that consistently rates at a FINE quality, a "Dry Malvasia," produced from a different clonal strain of the Muscat grape by the:

- Novitiate Wines above Los Gatos in the Santa Cruz Mountains of Santa Clara—the wine is dry enough to go with food, but with the softness of the Muscat perfume to add a sensuous excitement

CHAPTER V

The Dry Light Red Wines

No expert has ever been able to reveal to me the secret of why so many millions of wine drinkers all over the world have been so irresistibly attracted by the name Beaujolais. Certainly, the word itself has a lovely lilt. Surely, the sound of it is partly made up of *beau*, "beautiful," *jolie*, "pretty," and *lait*, "milk," which has always been an attractive drink to a lot of people. But, above all, I think, Beaujolais represents a dream—a dream, by millions of people who have never been there, of a lovely, easy-to-understand, miniparadise in France, where there gushes naturally from the earth a beautiful, joyous, light, supremely refreshing wine of the color of ripe strawberries—a kind of gently alcoholic soft drink with which you can quench your thirst in unlimited quantities with never a headache or twinge of pain.

So powerful and vivid is this dream, that millions of people around the world buy millions of bottles of alleged Beaujolais imported from France and more-or-less "illegal" Beaujolais made thousands of miles away from France, simply on the strength of the name and, perhaps, a certain distant connection in the color, but certainly a minimum connection in the taste. Yet the dream continues from generation to generation.

When the great French writer Colette was nearing the end of her life, one of her last requests was to be driven south from Paris to visit "my beloved Beaujolais." They parked her car in the huge doorway of one of the wineries, and she was able to watch the Gamay grapes being crushed. She returned home to Paris and wrote of the experience with the emotion of a love affair. The love is delightful, and it is real—if you live in the region of Beaujolais. In the rest of the world, it is largely unreal. Nowhere has this unreality been more evident than in the introduction of Beaujolais and its grapes into the United States. For many years, before the start of the mass love affair between American wine drinkers and American Beaujolais, I visited the French Beaujolais region late each November to taste and judge the new wines. I always stayed in the tiny village of Vonnas, at the charming little auberge Chez La Mère Blanc, which has been in the Blanc family for three generations and is now run by Jacqueline and Georges Blanc. While I reveled in the brilliant food—the menu an extraordinary mixture of the creamy-rich traditional specialties of the Bresse region handed down from Georges's mother, with the lightest of *nouvelle cuisine libre* dishes invented by the modernistic young Georges (who recently won three stars in the Michelin Guide)—I was able to taste from his cellar and discuss with Georges his virtually unlimited supply of *Beaujolais Nouveau*.

This "new Beaujolais" is a legally defined label, under French federal law, for a wine harvested, say, at the end of September, or the beginning of October, and permitted to be fermented and stabilized so quickly that it may be bottled and sold starting at midnight on November 15 of the same year. When Georges and I drink one of these wines, the bouquet, color, fruitiness, lightness, perfume, taste, and texture are so exquisite—combining into such a perfect blend of joyous delicacy—that I say to myself, every time, that I will never again want to taste Beaujolais except in the Beaujolais region.

The sheer beauty of this young wine, with the feel on the tongue of strawberry-pink lace, is achieved with impossibly severe difficulties. Nothing so good can come easily. The wine is so young, so minimally refined and stabilized, that it cannot travel and will not last. It goes on sale, legally, on November 15, but its life span is legally ended with the stroke of midnight on New Year's Eve, when French law requires that a new label and a new Beaujolais come into existence. It is called *Beaujolais de l'Année*, "Beaujolais of the year," a wine much more carefully made, more solidly balanced and stabilized, so that, while it is still a very young wine, it will remain in current consumption until the next harvest.

All this may be fine in Beaujolais, but when the new, unstable wine, for the sake of quick profit and big publicity, is shipped to New York and San Francisco, with the loud claim that here is the fresh, young, *nouveau* wine, the whole affair becomes ridiculous nonsense. The wine, of course, is ruined. It often starts refermenting in the bottle, throwing a deposit, perhaps blowing its cork, frothing and spritzing. Peter Alan Sichel, an English expert on French wines, once wrote that to drink a so-called *Beaujolais Nouveau* in New York in December was just about as incongruous as a lovely Hawaiian girl, dressed only in a lei and a grass skirt, dancing the hula at an icy-snowy New Year's Eve celebration in Times Square.

The only place in the world where you can taste the young French Beaujolais in the full, joyous bloom of its youth is among the green, rolling hills of the Beaujolais region. After a few days of steady tasting with Georges Blanc at his auberge, he and I would drive into the heart of the peaceful, smiling vineyard country, uncrowded, the life uncomplicated and unhurried, the roads shaded by tall trees, the rising slopes of the hills bright green with the large leaves of the Gamay vines, our progress punctuated by memorable meals in the handsome villages with the famous wine names—all the delights that are added to the wine of the Beaujolais. One learns quite soon that there are many more types of wine than the fluffy *nouveau*. There are château and domain bottlings, slowly aged and matured over years, worthy to take their places with the important wines of France. You learn that, although the Gamay grape is the king of Beaujolais, there are quite a number of different strains and varieties of the vine, and they produce different qualities of wine. The young *nouveau* wines are almost all made from a grape called Gamay Noir à Jus Blanc, "black Gamay with white juice." But the more mature château wines are mostly made from a grape called Gamay de Beaujolais. These two, entirely distinct vines are indiscriminately intermixed in Beaujolais vineyard estates, but, of course, they are harvested separately, and their different functions are clearly understood in France.

Since all of these facts about Beaujolais have been known by scientists and viticulturalists for almost a hundred years, it seems extraordinary that the transfer of the Gamay vine to the United States, the proper legal use of the Beaujolais name, the marketing of Beaujolais-type wines in the United States, and the intelligent guidance of the "mass love affair" that has predictably developed between American wine lovers and the name Beaujolais have all involved so much miscommunication, misconception, misinformation, mislabeling, and misunderstanding—even to the extent of an international incident, with a formal complaint by the French government to the United States. Let us review the embarrassing story from its beginning.

NAPA GAMAY AND GAMAY BEAUJOLAIS *Also called, in France, Gamay Noir à Jus Blanc, Gamay de Beaujolais, Petit Gamai, Gamay Rond, and Bourguignon Noir*

There might be no Gamay vine in existence today if Philip the Bold, Duke of Burgundy, had had his way in 1395. In that year, he banned the growing of the Gamay grape in his domain. His "royal decree" accused the vine of being "very bad and most disloyal" in trying to outshine the Pinot Noir. One French historian has written, "Fortunately for us, Philip's subjects were not entirely obedient. They continued to grow the Gamay in Burgundy for their everyday wine. But, to guard against the danger of the Duke enforcing his ban, the Burgundians also developed and rapidly expanded Gamay vineyards further South in Beaujolais—on lands that were not under the control of the Duke. This was the start of the Beaujolais as an independent and separate wine region."

Around 1900, Gamay root cuttings began to be sent from France, often in small quantities, to private buyers in California. The shipments came quite irregularly and with no sort of properly organized scientific system of indexing or labeling. When these early root cuttings arrived, many of them were planted in vineyards south of San Francisco Bay, in Santa Clara and Monterey. The French boxes of cuttings were marked "Gamay Beaujolais," and, as the vines thrived, that was what the grapes were called.

The Napa growers, of course, very soon heard of the experimental plantings south of the Bay and began ordering their own Gamay root cuttings from other producers in France. In good time, boxes began arriving in Napa marked "Gamay Noir." The name was slightly different, but, even so, the young vines that grew were considered by the Napa growers to be exactly the same as the vines of Monterey. As the vines matured, however, there were visible differences between the Monterey and Napa grapes. In Napa, they ripened earlier and produced more fruit per vine. But it was assumed that these variations were due to differences in soil and weather. All the same, the Napa growers decided they would like to have a different name, and so, remembering the original markings on the French boxes, they called their vines "Napa Gamay Noir," or, for short, "Napa Gamay." It was the start of "the great confusion."

Meanwhile, the growers south of the Bay, in Monterey and Santa Clara, were discovering that their vineyards were producing liquid gold. By labeling their wines "Gamay Beaujolais," they had the magic word that guaranteed a mass demand for every bottle they released. As they planted more vines, by the hundreds of acres, as quickly as possible, they realized with increasing certainty that this Gamay Beaujolais vine was an entirely different strain from the Napa Gamay. When you looked at the Gamay Beaujolais vine closely, judging the color and construction of its leaves, the shape and size of its berry bunches, the aroma and taste of its ripe grapes, you could hardly tell the difference between this vine and the Pinot Noir. When the Monterey growers held the Gamay Beaujolais clusters in their hands, they became convinced that these little black grapes must belong to the same family as the Burgundian Pinot Noir. The question was there, but no one raised it publicly. They were all too busy selling "American Beaujolais."

This happy state of viticultural innocence continued until after the end of World War II. Then, in 1946, France dropped the bombshell. The French Foreign Ministry sent a formal note to our Department of State asking that the American wine industry "shall cease and desist" from using the phrase "Gamay Beaujolais" on the labels of bottles of American red wine on the grounds that Beaujolais is a geographical region of France. Our industry was able to show that, in fact, the phrase "Gamay Beaujolais" was not a geographical designation, but was the generic name of a variety of grape—a name that the French themselves had created and had been using in their enology textbooks for more than fifty years. The French government admitted the validity of this argument and withdrew its complaint.

But the American wine industry was now convinced that the massive confusion about the Gamay in California must be cleared up once and for all time. The industry turned to the University of California and Dr. Harold Olmo, inviting him to go to Beaujolais and conclusively identify the clones of the vines on their home earth. After what must have been a delightful working trip—coupled with essential working wine-tasting—Dr. Olmo returned to announce that the grape called in California the "Napa Gamay" was, in fact, the universal Beaujolais grape called, over there, Gamay Noir à Jus Blanc. However, what the Californians called the "Gamay Beaujolais," while it was also grown in Beaujolais, was not a Gamay at all, but was a clonal variation of the Pinot Noir. Olmo also reported that the original mistakes in naming the vines was understandable because the various strains of the Gamay and the Pinot Noir are grown side-by-side all over Beaujolais. Dr. Olmo certainly achieved scientific clarity; marketing clarity is a tougher problem.

As soon as the Napa growers heard from Dr. Olmo that their grape was the universal Gamay of Beaujolais, they began using the name "Napa Gamay of Beaujolais." Almost immediately the price of the Napa grape began to climb, until it commanded the highest prices of any of the grape varieties from Beaujolais or Burgundy. Vineyard acreage of Napa Gamay more than quadrupled during the 1970s. A fairly recent survey reported that there are now over 6,000 acres planted in "Napa Gamay of Beaujolais" against almost 4,500 of Gamay Beaujolais. The statistician who provided these figures added a wistful note. He said that the significance of these two names for what he thought was the same grape was not clearly understood! Finally, in 1971, the U.S. federal government stepped into the mess with a gentle nudge to the wine industry toward integrity and truth. The business of wine in America, including the vital matter of "truth in labeling," is legally controlled by a Washington agency known to every winemaker as the "BATF," the Bureau of Alcohol, Tobacco and Firearms of the Treasury Department. (Every wine label, for example, before it is printed and used on bottles, must be approved by the BATF.) As to the misnaming of Gamay, the BATF—presumably remembering the French government's complaint and Dr. Olmo's report from Beaujolais—began to approach a solution by issuing a formal statement of policy that California Gamay Beaujolais should now be recognized not as Gamay but as Pinot Noir. Also, Napa Gamay, or Gamay, should now be recognized as the true Gamay. The BATF then proposed a solution to the confusion based on a policy of, shall we call it, gracious gradualism. The BATF stated: "Wine made from grapes identified as Napa Gamay may be labeled either as 'Napa Gamay,' or as 'Gamay,' and a wine made from grapes identified as Gamay Beaujolais may be labeled as 'Gamay Beaujolais,' or as 'Pinot Noir.' " So far so good. But then came the hint of enforcement. The BATF went on to state: "The vines which are currently erroneously named Gamay Beaujolais will be replaced, over the years, by new plantings of either Napa Gamay or Pinot Noir. All such new plantings will not be permitted to be titled Gamay Beaujolais and, accordingly, the use of the term Gamay Beaujolais will be entirely terminated with the life of the present plantings." Nothing could be clearer than that. It is, plainly, the intention of the U.S. government that the word "Beaujolais," so jealously guarded by the French government, shall in time totally disappear from the labels of American wine bottles.

Obviously, this is not exactly the happiest of prospects for the people who market and promote the wines. On the lists of some of the largest U.S. producers, the biggest-selling item is "American Beaujolais." Obviously, as long as they can find a single Gamay Beaujolais grape to crush, they will continue, legally, to print the magic phrase on their labels. Obviously, every grower of Gamay Beaujolais vines will hold on to them, pamper them, and keep them going for as many years as possible. But a grapevine does not live forever. Depending on climate and soil, after twenty, thirty, or forty years, it grows old and dies. During the 1980s and 1990s, more and more of these old vines will have to be replaced, according to the law, by Napa Gamay or Pinot Noir, but not by anything with the word "Beaujolais" attached to it. As each vineyard or winery runs completely out of Gamay Beaujolais, that fact will be certified by the BATF in Washington, and, from that moment onward, no more labels with the word "Beaujolais" will be approved for that producer. As we approach the year 2000, there will be fewer and fewer bottles of American wine carrying the magic word. As we go into the 21st century, "Beaujolais" as an American word will have disappeared. The taste of our light red Gamay wine will not have changed one iota. What's in a name, anyway?

For my own drinking and tasting, I have always taken a nonpartisan point of view between the two competing grape varieties. Both grapes, when skillfully handled by the winemakers, can produce delicate, delightful, light red wines. Therefore, in the classification lists that follow, I have not separated the wines by grape types—I have simply pulled them all together as light red wines with the general character of the Gamay grape and with the techniques of vinification that can be distantly associated with memories of Beaujolais.

During the almost twenty years of searching out and tasting for this book American light red wines of the Gamay and Beaujolais types, I have not found any that rated on my charts as high as GREAT or even SUPERB in quality, but I have found several of NOBLE quality. Of these, the best I have ever tasted is the big bold Napa Gamay of:

- Joseph Swan Vineyards at Forestville in the Russian River Valley in Sonoma, with its winemaker-owner, Joe Swan

My second ranking among these light reds—still within the NOBLE range—has been consistently reached by the Napa Gamay produced by:

- Robert Mondavi Winery at Oakville in the Napa Valley, with its winemaker, Tim Mondavi

Third place has been consistently held within the NOBLE range by the Gamay Beaujolais of:

- Stag's Leap Wine Cellars on the Silverado Trail near Yountville in the Napa Valley, with its winemaker-owner, Warren Winiarski

A few points below, in the FINE quality range, I have consistently tasted Gamays from these vineyards and wineries:

- Beaulieu Vineyard at Rutherford in the Napa Valley
- The Christian Brothers on Mont La Salle above the Napa Valley, with its winemaker, Brother Timothy
- Dry Creek Vineyard at Healdsburg in the Dry Creek Valley of Sonoma, with its owner-winemaker, David Stare
- Fetzer Vineyards near Ukiah in the Redwood Valley of Mendocino, with its owner-winemaker, John Fetzer, using Napa Gamay grapes from the Bartolucci Vineyards in Lake County
- Gemello Winery at Mountain View in the Santa Cruz Mountains in Santa Clara, with its owner-winemaker, Mario Gemello, using Gamay Beaujolais grapes from the Durney Vineyard in the Carmel Valley of Monterey
- Monterey Vineyard at Gonzales in the Salinas Valley, with its winemaker, Dick Peterson
- Pedroncelli Winery northeast of Geyserville on a ridge above the Dry Creek Valley of Sonoma
- Roudon-Smith Vineyards at Scott's Valley in the Santa Cruz Mountains south of San Francisco Bay

- Sebastiani Vineyards in the Valley of the Moon in Sonoma
- Simi Winery at Healdsburg in the Alexander Valley of Sonoma, with its winemaker, Zelma Long, using Gamay Beaujolais grapes
- Trentadue Winery south of Geyserville in the Alexander Valley of Sonoma
- Wente Brothers at Livermore in the Livermore Valley of Alameda, with its owner-winemaker, Eric Wente

MERLOT *Also called, in France, Petit Merle, Vitraille, Crabutet Noir, and Bigney*

The Merlot grape, with its oval, smallish, blue-black berries, is, according to grape historians, one of the four or five most ancient and honorable of the noble *Vitis vinifera* vines of the Old World. It has been associated for centuries with Bordeaux and, long before the great châteaux vineyards of the Médoc district were established, long before Châteaux Lafite, Latour, and Mouton were world famous, there were many vineyards in all parts of Bordeaux that were wholly planted in Merlot. During the great expansion of the Bordeaux region in the 19th century, Merlot might easily have become the principal grape of the entire vast wine district had it not been for the fact that the Cabernet Sauvignon turned out to be tougher, more capable of standing up to adverse weather conditions, more resistant to the rainstorms, hailstorms, and unexpected frosts that are so much a part of the Bordeaux climate. So, in some of the most famous vineyards of the region, Merlot, by an accident of fate, became the junior partner of the Cabernet. In almost all the greatest vintages, about one-third of the wine, on the average, is Merlot.

But, in many vineyards, Merlot remains what it once was, the king in its own right. One of the very greatest of all vineyards in Bordeaux—one that is considered by experts to be more representative of the greatness of the region even than Château Lafite—the magnificent "First Growth" Château Pétrus on top of the hill of Pomerol, is planted more than 90 percent with Merlot. Also, the superb "First Growth" Château Cheval Blanc, the top-rated vineyard of the Graves district of St. Emilion, has no Cabernet Sauvignon in its makeup, and its principal ingredient is Merlot. This vine is also grown on its own in many other parts of France, especially in the south, where it ripens quickly under the hot sun and gives a wine of fruity softness and remarkable quality. In France, in the early seventies, there were almost 65,000 acres of Merlot vines. By that time, in the United States, there were already almost 5,000 acres.

American producers of some of our finest wines soon discovered that, although the Cabernet Sauvignon grows differently in our soil and gives a wine of a different taste from that of Bordeaux, the addition of controlled amounts of Merlot is valuable. In most years, the Merlot can contribute a roundness of balance, a softness of body, to the finished wine. It can sometimes offset an over-high acidity, or a too-harsh tannin in the Cabernet. Merlot can add a charming aromatic bouquet. It can strengthen the sense of fruit. It can contribute the almost indefinable qualities of a sophisticated finesse and grace to a wine that would otherwise be peasanty and rough. Today, a large number of American Cabernet Sauvignon reds contain balanced proportions of Merlot.

But the winemakers of the U.S. West Coast have gone much further in recognizing the high qualities of Merlot. They have been experimenting with it as a wine grape in its own right—either with light red wines made 100 percent from the Merlot grape, or by turning the tables and using the Cabernet Sauvignon as the junior partner to improve, say, an 80 or 90 percent Merlot. The first experiments failed because the Merlot seemed to lack a fresh bouquet and a refreshing acid tang. These faults, it was soon discovered, were the result of the first Merlot vines being planted in the wrong places and inefficiently tended during their growth. At the end of the fifties and the beginning of the sixties, Merlot vines began to be planted in the cool coastal valleys of California, where they thrived. In 1968, the first 100 percent Merlot wine was released by Louis P. Martini, always an aggressive experimenter and courageous pioneer in every new wine development. Then the Merlot moved southward to the newly opening, cool wine-growing regions in Monterey and around Santa Barbara. In time, Merlot vineyards also expanded northward into Idaho, Oregon, and Washington State.

Unquestionably, Merlot has won its battle on the West Coast as a blending wine with Cabernet Sauvignon. What I am concerned with here is Merlot as a wine on its own. In this direction, it has not yet quite fully established itself. Frank Schoonmaker, who all his life managed successfully to juggle the competing roles of wine critic, wine expert, wine merchant, wine taster, and wine writer (and who did so much to promote American wines), once said that Merlot by itself could only rarely rise above "a soft, round, eminently agreeable red wine, without much distinction, or depth." I suspect that if Frank were alive today and could taste some of the Merlots currently on the market, he would be a good deal more enthusiastic. Certainly, there is no slackening in the continually expanding demand for Merlot grapes. Their price has always been within about 10 percent of Cabernet Sauvignon. Actually, after many of the harvests of the seventies, Merlot achieved a higher price than Cabernet. The demand by the wineries remains fierce, and this is clearly because more and more winemakers are experimenting with Merlot as a varietal wine on its own.

I have tasted, I believe, virtually every serious varietal Merlot currently on the market. I have enjoyed many of them. Certainly, there is no Château Pétrus or Château Cheval Blanc among them. In general, they are dry, easy-to-drink, light, soft, summery, thirst-quenching red wines. They are for drinking down—not for serious and thoughtful sipping. One does not assess the firmness of their construction, or judge the degree of their elegance, or measure the depth of their complexity. But none of this prevents them from being delightful, fruity refreshers. And they are improving all the time, as the grape growers and winemakers continue to experiment. This is a new wine for the United States that every serious American wine drinker should at least get to know.

I have not found, among American Merlot reds, any that rated on my tasting charts at the highest level of GREAT quality or even in the SUPERB range, but I have discovered some examples scoring consistently at a NOBLE quality. Among these, the best American Merlot I have tasted was from Preston in Washington State, vinified by winemaker Robert Griffin, using a balanced assemblage of grapes harvested from the Preston estate, from the Kiona Vineyard, and from Sagemoor Farms—all these famous vine growths being irrigated from the Columbia River. The resulting magnificent wine gives the NOBLE classification to:

- Preston Wine Cellars at Pasco in the South Columbia Basin of Washington State

My second ranking of American Merlot is from the Santa Ynez

Valley of the California Central Coast region, where the Merlot vines seem to grow consistently with extraordinary power and rich concentration of flavors. The grapes here were grown in the vineyards of the Leonard Firestone estate and vinified by winemakers Tony Austin and Alison Green. The resulting wine—my second best of all Merlots of the United States—gives the NOBLE classification to:

- Firestone Vineyard at Los Olivos in the Santa Ynez Valley of Santa Barbara

My third American Merlot was produced in the Napa Valley, the estate-grown grapes vinified by the French-born owner-winemaker from Bordeaux, Bernard Portet; the resulting magnificently smooth and velvety wine—my third best of all Merlots in the United States—brings the NOBLE classification to:

- Clos du Val on the Silverado Trail near Yountville in the Napa Valley

There is one other American Merlot that has consistently rated at a NOBLE quality, and this, therefore, becomes my fourth best of the United States. It is produced in the wine region of western Oregon—the grapes vinified by the husband and wife owner-winemakers of the estate, Susan Sokol and William Blosser—the resulting most excellent wine brings the NOBLE classification to:

- Sokol Blosser Winery at Dundee in the Willamette Valley of Oregon

I have also consistently tasted Merlots with ratings that bring the FINE classification to these vineyards and wineries:

- Burgess Cellars near St. Helena in the Napa Valley, with its owner-winemaker, Tom Burgess, using Merlot grapes from the Winery Lake Vineyard in the Carneros Hills
- Richard Carey Winery at San Leandro in Alameda on San Francisco Bay, with its owner-winemaker, Dick Carey
- Chappellet Vineyard on Pritchard Hill east of Rutherford above the Napa Valley
- Chateau St. Jean at Kenwood in Sonoma, with its winemaker, Richard Arrowood
- Chateau Ste. Michelle Vintners at Woodinville near Seattle in Washington State, using grapes from their vineyards in the Yakima Valley of Washington State
- Duckhorn Vineyards on the Silverado Trail near St. Helena in the Napa Valley

- Gundlach-Bundschu Vineyard at Vineburg in the Valley of the Moon in Sonoma, with its winemaker, John Merritt
- Markham Winery north of St. Helena in the Napa Valley
- Louis M. Martini Winery at St. Helena in the Napa Valley, with its owner-winemaker, Louis P. Martini
- Joseph Phelps Vineyards near St. Helena in the Napa Valley, with winemaker Walter Schug's Insignia wine of 86 percent Merlot and 14 percent Cabernet Sauvignon
- Ste. Chapelle Vineyards at Sunny Slope near Caldwell in the Snake River Valley of Idaho, with winemaker Bill Broich
- Souverain Cellars near Geyserville in the Dry Creek Valley of Sonoma
- Sterling Vineyards at Calistoga in the Napa Valley

GRIGNOLINO

Italy's Grignolino is not one of the noble wine grapes of ancient lineage and high prestige. In fact, it is not even included in some of the more serious wine grape reference books. It might not have been included here but for the intervention of an accident of fate.

When, in 1961, Joe Heitz bought his first tiny vineyard in the Napa Valley (see page 251), it consisted of 8½ acres of thriving Grignolino vines. The Grignolino family is large, and in Italy there are quite a number of different clonal strains, each with recognizable variations, for better or for worse, in the finished wines. The previous owner of that first little Heitz vineyard, a man called Leon Brendel, liked to claim that his Grignolino was the only one of its kind in the United States. To prove it, he labeled his wine "Only One." Joe didn't go along with that little piece of nonsense, but he did like the quality of the grapes, and when he expanded his property, making more of the right soil available, he increased his Grignolino plantings until he had about 15 acres—all of that same original clone.

But what is most important is that Joe, always the brilliant experimental winemaker, has learned to extract the best from those Grignolino grapes as if he were a musician drawing the sweetest sound from his instrument. Year after year, under widely differing weather conditions, he varies his techniques to produce two always memorable wines: a unique "Estate Bottled" Grignolino red and a beautiful, orangy pink Grignolino rosé. The latter is, by the ratings of my tastings, the best rosé of the United States (see Chapter VII).

Joe might make even more of these wines were it not for the intervention of his wife, Alice, a devoted and skilled cook. When Joe harvests his Grignolino grapes, which more or less surround the family home, he brings a portable crusher out into the vineyard. As the bunches of grapes are tipped in, the dark juice runs from the spout in a steady stream. Alice watches from the kitchen window and, at the crucial moment, saunters out carrying two enormous jugs. She proceeds to fill them with the basic raw material of her famous (and marvelous!) Grignolino jelly. Joe, who is picking among the vines, calls out, "Hey, Alice, take it easy—that stuff is worth money." Alice smiles sweetly as she brings out more empty jugs.

Much as I love Alice's food, it is Joe's wine that compels me to include the Grignolino grape in this chapter. The red wine (as distinct from the rosé) is not and never will be popular in a mass way. It is a wine to which a small coterie of drinkers is deeply attached because it is "very Italian" in its character—at the same time light, lean, strongly tart, and, shall we say, bursting with acid refreshment—a kind of alcoholic lemonade. If all that sounds faintly unpleasant, it is not; certainly not in terms of the Grignolino grown and vinified by Joe Heitz. Underlying the tartness is a delicate, distant, citrous touch of orange Curaçao liqueur. This seems to be unique to the Grignolino strain used by Heitz. I cannot find it even in other Grignolino reds made from grapes grown in other parts of the Napa Valley no more than a few miles from the Heitz vineyard. Joe keeps his version lively and young. To preserve the touch of orange, he does not age the wine in wood barrels. He does not vintage date his labels, because he likes to control the tartness by sometimes adding a small balanced quantity of an older wine, but, of course, he always keeps it 100 percent Grignolino and gives it the "Napa Valley" appellation.

I have tasted a substantial number of other Grignolinos in other parts of California, but, I must confess, without much personal pleasure and without seeing any significant ratings on my charts. There are a number of old-time Italian vineyards still active around the town of Gilroy in Santa Clara, but in that more southerly climate and earth, the tartness seems to be overwhelming, coupled with pale color, a tannic bitterness, and, sometimes, an unpleasantly earthy aroma. Finally, I found a Grignolino in the far-northern district of Mendocino, but I could taste not a trace of orange in it.

Thus, after long years of searching and tasting, the ratings on my charts force me to report that I have found only one Grignolino red in the United States consistently worthy of placing its producer in the NOBLE quality classification:

• Heitz Wine Cellars near St. Helena in the Napa Valley, with its owner-winemaker, Joe Heitz

CHAPTER VI

The Powerful Rich
Red Wines

The one grape that dominates the world of red wine—the "Grand Potentate of the Reds," as it is often called—is the Cabernet Sauvignon. If this book were being written about French wines rather than American, the Cabernet Sauvignon would probably have been included in the chapter on "light wines" rather than among those that are "powerful and rich." For centuries, in Bordeaux, the natural and principal home of the Cabernet Sauvignon, its function was to make the delicate, light, and joyful clarets, so called because they were *clairets*—"clear," light-colored red wines that you could easily see through, wines that were so much loved by the British and so popular everywhere. Through all those early centuries, it was left to the Pinot Noir grape of Burgundy to provide the powerful, dominant, sensuous, strong, and solid wines. It was always said, in those days, that a Bordeaux claret was like a charming, half-innocent, wide-eyed young wife—while a Burgundy was like a dark-eyed, demanding, forceful, insatiable, full-of-intrigue mistress.

But when the Cabernet Sauvignon came to the United States, the climate and soil of its new home and the new treatment it received from its new agricultural and vinous masters brought about extraordinary changes in the character and personality of its wines. We shall see how the Cabernet Sauvignon became the most dominant, prestigious, and richest of all the noble red wines of the New World. But not only here. The Cabernet Sauvignon has also become the "Lord of the Reds" in Australia, New Zealand, South Africa, Bulgaria, Hungary, Italy, Rumania, Spain, Yugoslavia, Argentina, Chile, and virtually every other wine region.

Yet the extraordinary success of the Cabernet Sauvignon is, in part, an accident. The modern history of this noble vine is inextricably intertwined with the dreadful vine disease which, during the forty years from 1860 to about 1900, virtually wiped out the wine industry of the entire world—the disease that is centered in a small insect known as *Phylloxera vastatrix*. To understand fully the success of the Cabernet Sauvignon, you must know a little of its history and something of its relationship to the fearful phylloxera.

There is no doubt about Cabernet Sauvignon being one of the most ancient, if not *the* most ancient, of the noble vines. In Roman times during the 1st century A.D., Pliny the Elder described a vine, generally known as *Vitis dura*, which was clearly a forerunner of the Cabernet. Very soon after that, it was firmly established as one of the vines in the region at the mouth of the Gironde that would become Bordeaux. But, through the centuries, during the three hundred years of British rule, the Cabernet Sauvignon was never "top dog." It shared the acreage, the honors, and the work with other such vines as Cabernet Franc, Malbec, Merlot, Petit Verdot, among others. When the "Golden Age" of vintage Bordeaux began toward the end of the 1700s and into the early 1800s, there was a distinct possibility that Merlot might become the most important of the Bordeaux blending grapes. But then came the great disaster.

In 1860, a ship from the United States tied up in the port of Marseilles and discharged her cargo, which included a number of cases of American vine-root cuttings that had been ordered by various French growers for experimental purposes. One case was sent to a botanical laboratory in London. There, a young botanist discovered that some of the roots were infested with a small louselike insect that, as part of its life cycle, bored holes into the roots and sucked out, for its own nutrition, some of the "lifeblood" sap of the vine. The amount of sap that the louse consumed—and, of course, there were many lice on each root—was not the most dangerous thing. The deadly part of it, the part that very soon killed the entire vine, was that once the holes were opened, the root continued to "bleed," so that the vine lost all its strength and died as it stood there, from the roots upward.

When the louse completed its deadly work, it climbed to the surface of the earth, spread a pair of wings that had up to this point remained safely enclosed within niches in its body, and flew off to the next vineyard to deposit its eggs around the roots of other vines. Since the insect could fly as many as ten miles in one season, and since it deposited thousands of eggs, it is easy to understand how quickly the phylloxera spread from vineyard to vineyard, from district to district, from region to region, from country to country, and how devastating was its cumulative destruction. The primitive chemical insecticides of the time simply could not reach the underground nests of the insects. Some vineyards, on lowlands near water, were flooded, but even when a current attack was overcome, new infestations arrived every day from the surrounding vineyards on higher ground. Within a few years, in France alone, 2.5 million acres of vines were utterly destroyed. Many wine people were sure that there would never again be a wine industry. They sold their vineyard lands and went away to earn their livings in other fields. Many thousands of workers from Bordeaux packed up all their belongings and fled, in a great trek, across the mountains into Spain, hoping that the wine industry there would somehow escape and survive. Of course, it did not. All of Europe was ravaged. Then the phylloxera louse traveled on to the ends of the earth—South Africa, Australia, New Zealand, Latin America, then northward, full circle, to California, in the United States, from where it had originally come.

It was at about this point that the extraordinary discovery was made that the United States, which had originally exported the terrible disease, could now provide the cure. Though phylloxera existed in the northeastern United States among the native *labrusca* vine roots (grapes such as Catawba, Concord, Delaware, Elvira), the botanists found that the roots of these strong native vines were immune to the attacks of the phylloxera louse—not because the louse could not bore a small hole as it wanted to, but because the vine had the power to reseal the hole and avoid "bleeding to death." In other words, the native vine had the same power as do we humans to seal the cut and grow new skin. All American native vines were found to have this characteristic and to be, therefore, immune from death by phylloxera.

The saving news spread to every grower of grapes in every part of the world. The rebirth of the wine industry would depend on replanting American native roots and then grafting on to them the local grapevine. But which local type should be selected for grafting? Imagine, for example, the appalling fears of the desperate Bordeaux vineyard owners. Their land lay wasted before them. They were not sure it could ever be revived. As they agonized over which variety of vine should be chosen—as they worried through sleepless nights—

they leaned increasingly toward a vine that would be botanically strong, able to withstand physical difficulties, able to overcome the vicissitudes that clearly lay ahead. These considerations were far more important in their minds than questions of beautiful and delicate wines. If these vines did not survive on their new American roots, there would be no wines at all.

In Bordeaux the more they thought of the Cabernet Sauvignon, the more it seemed to be the right choice. It flowered late, so there would be less danger of its being damaged by late spring frosts. Its tough-skinned berries resisted spoilage and all kinds of bad weather. The vine itself stood up to hail and rainstorms. It could even handle reasonable drought and flooding. It resisted many of the vine diseases. In short, it was a strong, tough vine.

So in Bordeaux and in virtually every wine region of the world, after the nightmare of the phylloxera, the "chosen instrument" for the rebirth of the red-wine industry was the Cabernet Sauvignon. It has repaid the trust placed in it by producing many of the world's greatest wines—wines with a majestic life span, slowly developing a soft velvet, coupled with pungent power, richness, and warmth, full of an aromatic complexity of flavors, yet rounded and subtle, with a superb bouquet touched with wild forest violets; a total wine of charm, intense pleasure, and supreme richness of style.

AMERICAN CABERNET SAUVIGNON *Also called, in France, Petit-Cabernet, Vidure, Petite-Vidure, and Bouchet*

The Cabernet Sauvignon vine was probably brought to the United States around the middle of the 1800s, but it was no more a "kingpin" on this side of the Atlantic than it had been in Bordeaux. It was just one among equals of the blending grapes. In those days, in Bordeaux, there was a traditional system for blending the various grape types into the wine of each château. One did not blend the wine in liquid form, in carefully balanced, measured amounts during the vinification, as we do today. If you wanted, say, 30 percent of Merlot in your wine, you simply planted 30 percent of Merlot vines on each acre of your vineyard, perhaps in single rows, possibly even in single vines, interspersed here and there among the others. If you wanted, say, 25 percent of Cabernet Sauvignon plus 15 percent of Malbec plus

15 percent of Petit Verdot, you interspersed those in the proper proportions in your vineyard. This technique was known as field blending. The childishly simple theory was that when you harvested your
grapes you would automatically have exactly the right balance of
each variety in your wine. It didn't work out that way at all. First,
the different grape varieties didn't ripen at the same time. The harvest was a sad mixture of ripe, unripe, and overripe grapes—hardly
conducive to the best possible quality of wine. Second, the volume
of grapes on each vine varied from year to year, according to the
weather, some varieties being more affected than others, so there
was never any fine control of the balance of the blend of the grapes.
Field blending has now been completely eliminated. The different
vine varieties are grown in separate patches, harvested separately,
vinified separately, and the final blending is a matter of scientific
judgment and measurement inside the winery.

But in the 1850s in California, the winemakers were so determined to imitate Bordeaux that they interplanted their vineyards for
field blending between the four principal Bordeaux vine types. They
produced red wines—quite famous at the time—which they called
California Médoc. They even won a gold medal with it at a Paris Fair.
But, in the 1870s, when the deadly phylloxera reached California, all
these mixed vineyards were wiped out, and Cabernet Sauvignon
virtually disappeared. It did not begin to reappear—grafted onto
eastern American native roots—until after the end of Prohibition in
1933. At that time, the total acreage of Cabernet Sauvignon in the
entire United States was a mere 200 acres.

In 1938, I have been told by wine people speaking from memory,
Cabernet Sauvignon vines were being grown and its wine was being
made only at Beaulieu, Beringer, Inglenook, and Simi. In 1947, when
the trade journal *Wines and Vines* published the names of vine types
recommended for planting in California, Cabernet Sauvignon was
not even on the list. It was not until the mid-1960s that the dramatic
explosion began. At that time, the total plantings of Cabernet Sauvignon were just over 1,500 acres. The next ten years, up to the mid-
1970s, saw an amazing increase to almost 27,000 acres—with expansion into Idaho, Oregon, and Washington State, into the Midwest
and some eastern states—a total acreage not very far behind France.

This sudden, tremendous American drive toward Cabernet Sauvignon did not proceed in an orderly, organized, smoothly efficient

way. It lacked even the rudiments of proper planning. Hundreds of winemakers suddenly became aware—almost, it seems, by process of osmosis—that Cabernet Sauvignon was the top prestige red wine and that, if you wanted to be a top prestige winery, you had to have some of it at the top of your list. This irresistible desire preceded any serious technical knowledge about the best places to plant Cabernet Sauvignon, about the requirements of the vine in terms of American climate and earth—and, once you had an American planting, the special techniques for vinifying it under American conditions. No serious winemaker was fool enough to think he could simply imitate Bordeaux. Obviously, there would be large and important differences.

The result of this wild haste, during the late 1970s, was a higgledy-piggledy flood of new American Cabernet Sauvignon labels— some brilliant, but most of extremely doubtful, at times even undrinkable, quality. Soon more different Cabernet Sauvignon labels were available in California than for any other red varietal wine.

Sorting Out the Chaos

The great "gold rush" of the 1970s to plant Cabernet Sauvignon was not led and managed by the conservative, established, experienced leaders (or even by the accepted top winemakers) of the California industry—such men as Tom Burgess, Mike Grgich, Joe Heitz, Louis Martini, Robert Mondavi, Myron Nightingale, André Tchelistcheff, Warren Winiarski—men who would have based their decisions on calculations of climate and soil, on scientific estimating and planning. The Cabernet Sauvignon boom was financed by the capital and created by the energy of young people who have become captivated by the romance of winemaking. To say that what they have produced so far is a glorious kind of chaos is, I am convinced, not too harsh or inaccurate a comment.

As we enter the 1980s, we are overwhelmed by wave upon wave of new wineries. Almost twenty years of wine boom has more than quadrupled the number of new wineries—virtually every single one of them producing one or more blends of Cabernet Sauvignon.

This state of affairs means chaos for the wine drinker, who wants easy rules as to which wines to buy for maximum pleasure, and who is now quickly discovering that, although there are many Cabernet Sauvignons from which to choose, there are still relatively few worth drinking at a fair price. It means double chaos for serious wine collectors, who want to know the keeping qualities of the wines for laying down in their home cellars. It means confusion and disorder for the wine retailer, who simply does not have the time to keep up with the background study on all the hundreds of new bottles he is being asked to stock on his shelves and explain to his customers. The American wine business is becoming exceedingly complicated. Now that the standard Bordeaux blending grapes—the Merlot, Cabernet Franc, Malbec, Petit Verdot—are also being grown in California, many wineries are putting out several different blends of Cabernet Sauvignon, under different labels. My guess is that there is no single owner of a vineyard or winery anywhere in the United States who does not dream of one day producing a great Cabernet Sauvignon. I certainly predict that, within a year or two, there may be as many as 250 wineries producing at least 350 different labels of Cabernet Sauvignon.

If only we could hope that they would all bring us deep drinking pleasure. The hope is obviously farfetched because only a relatively small percentage of the California Cabernet Sauvignon is planted in places where it has any real hope of producing outstandingly good grapes—the grapes from which the great wines can be made.

Soon after the first plantings in California, two vital discoveries were made about the growing of Cabernet Sauvignon. First, it was a total failure in the hot Central Valley, where the fierce sun "burned off" or "cooked out" virtually all the basic Cabernet character and personality. In the desert, it became a totally uninteresting grape. Second, in the very cool far northern districts, there was not enough sunny warmth during its slow growing season to ripen the grapes fully, and when you make wine from unripe Cabernet, you get an acid, green, raw flavor that no amount of later aging can eliminate. Cabernet Sauvignon has to be planted in the most favorable coastal districts and regions, but, as it turned out, some were a good deal more favorable than others. Weather in a particular vineyard, from year to year, is a matter of luck. Tending the vines and protecting the growing grapes is always a matter of human judgment and skill. But, over the long term, the original choice of the location is the most important of all the factors. The structure of the soil around and beneath the roots, the chemical composition of the earth, the flow of water above and below ground, the angle of the earth to the sun, the normal fall of rain, the circulation of the air and blowing of the winds, the settling of the morning and evening mists—all these ultimately control the excellence of the grapes on the vines. Every grower with whom I have ever discussed the subject in Bordeaux has always told me that, for Cabernet Sauvignon, vineyard location is the absolutely critical factor.

Of all grapes grown in California, Cabernet Sauvignon is the most difficult to locate perfectly, because it must be given the chance to develop high sugar over a long, slow growing and ripening season. During the wild boom years, many thousands of acres of Cabernet Sauvignon were planted in extremely doubtful locations, under exceedingly speculative conditions, at costs running as high as (or even above) $15,000 per acre. Since it takes about ten years to develop significant wines from a newly planted vineyard, we still do not have definitive results from many of these new acres. It will also take several more years for the winemakers to develop the new techniques for dealing with these new wines and an equal number of years for wine drinkers seriously to explore the new labels and to decide which new variations of Cabernet Sauvignon, from which new districts, they like best.

Apart from gambling with untested locations in questionable new districts, certain wine areas of California are already well established as supremely successful for the cultivation of the Cabernet Sauvignon and for its vinification into GREAT and SUPERB wines, wines that have placed California on an equal footing with Bordeaux as one of the major red-wine regions of the world (see the discussion of Heitz Cellars on page 253). These proven, supreme districts for growing Cabernet Sauvignon are, however, relatively small compared to the general wine areas of California and the rest of the United States. Since it is usually possible to identify these districts on the labels of bottles, it may be of practical value to the serious wine taster to review them briefly here.

If it is argued (as I certainly argue, on the basis of my tasting charts) that the greatest single Cabernet Sauvignon planting in America is the 15 acres of Martha's Vineyard, which appears on the labels of the great Cabernet Sauvignon wines of Heitz Cellars, then we should also argue that this famous vineyard is at the center of the most prestigious section of red-wine land in the United States. It is known as the Rutherford Bench in the Napa Valley, a gravelly area of about 2,500 acres, largely between the villages of Yountville and Rutherford, around St. Helena and on up to the Silverado Trail. Not only does the great Heitz wine come from here, but also splendid Cabernets from Beaulieu, Freemark Abbey, Robert Mondavi, Spring Mountain, and others.

Another small area of about 300 acres has also proved to be outstanding—the land around Stag's Leap Rock a mile or two east of Yountville, on the floor of the Napa Valley, being brilliantly developed by Warren Winiarski at his Stag's Leap Wine Cellars, and by Bernard Portet at Clos du Val, Francis Mahoney at Carneros Creek, Bill Collins at Conn Creek and John Shafer at Shafer Vineyard. Most of this land was covered by prune orchards until it was discovered that it was an ideal location for Cabernet Sauvignon.

Farther up the Napa Valley, especially around the village of Calistoga, there are some very small but extremely promising gravelly pieces of land, especially around the Eisele and Raymond vineyards.

Another comparatively new development (of the past ten to fifteen years, which means "very new" in wine-growing terms)—a development also of proven perfection—is the planting of various, isolated, fairly small "mountain vineyards" of Cabernet Sauvignon at several carefully chosen locations in the Mayacamas range along the western border of the Napa Valley. In sum, they total only a few hundred acres, but they are producing extraordinary grapes, vinified by such wineries as Burgess, Chappellet, Diamond Creek, Fisher, Kistler, Louis M. Martini, Mayacamas, Mount Eden, and Mount Veeder.

In the Sonoma Valley, there are some excellent plantings of Cabernet Sauvignon on the land around the village of Glen Ellen, as has been conclusively proved by some of the wines from Glen Ellen Vineyard, Kenwood and Chateau St. Jean. I believe there is the potential for greatness in certain very small sections of the Alexander Valley and the Dry Creek Valley, and I think I have found indications of this, though the vines are still very young, in some of the red wines from the Sonoma Vineyards. Even from farther north, I have sensed a coming nobility, with the increasing maturity of the vines, in Cabernet reds from Edmeades at Philo, Fetzer in the Redwood Valley, Parducci at Ukiah, all in the Mendocino district. In these wines I find high promise, if not yet greatness.

Farther south, there are hopeful signs in the Cabernet reds of the Monterey Peninsula Winery. Still deeper in the south, in the wine regions around San Luis Obispo and Santa Barbara, the Cabernet Sauvignon vines are still too young for any accurate judgment as to the future quality of the wines. Those most worth watching, according to the slowly rising ratings on my tasting charts, are from vineyards in the Paso Robles district and in the Santa Ynez Valley.

There is also—in a setting that is the most beautiful, dramatic, and unusual of all—the newest California wine region, beyond Sacramento, in the narrow, steep foothill valleys of the High Sierras, mainly in Amador and El Dorado. Here, of course, everything will be sharply different—the high mountain growing conditions, the lay of the land, the composition of the earth, the weather and winemaking techniques—but already there are some signs of dramatic progress, with these mountain Cabernet Sauvignon grapes being delivered to such wineries as Carneros Creek, Harbor, and Monteviña.

Beyond California, in the Pacific Northwest, there are pockets of extraordinary Cabernet Sauvignon. I have very recently tasted wine from the Ste. Chapelle Vineyard in the Snake River Valley of Idaho of such exciting quality that it proves that the grapes grown on the Sunny Slope side of the valley must be of supreme quality. In the ancient, volcanic soil of the Yakima Valley of Washington State, in vineyards irrigated from the Columbia River, there are some outstanding plantings of Cabernet Sauvignon, reflected in the wines of Preston Cellars of Pasco.

And yet, if I now carefully calculate the acreage of all these much-favored pieces of earth that are actually planted in Cabernet Sauvignon vines and are currently bearing fruit (because you must remember that some of the already proven locations are still covered by prune orchards or lesser grape varieties)—and if I then include in my list all acreage where there is good hope for the future, the hard, sad fact is that only about 12 percent of the Cabernet Sauvignon vines in the United States have any chance of eventually producing magnificent red wines. We may have a flood of grapes, of wines, of new wineries, and of new labels, but there is (and will continue to be in the foreseeable future) a severe shortage of magnificent wines. The remaining 88 percent of American Cabernet Sauvignon is a matter of romantic dreams and eternal hope. Let us face it: very many vineyards are so badly located that they will never produce quality above pleasant, everyday, inexpensive family table wines.

Some wine writers have already loudly stated that we now have enough Cabernet Sauvignon of our own and that we no longer need to import any from abroad. This is arrant nonsense. Our truly great Cabernets are absolutely magnificent, the equals in every way of the best from Bordeaux, and that means, of course, the best in the world. But we do not yet have the volume of the great wines, nor enough great labels, to be independent of Bordeaux—and, in any case, what serious wine taster would ever want to eliminate Bordeaux from his life? The supreme joy of wine is the infinity of its variety.

At the levels of quality of Cabernet below the greatest, we do not yet have the clear and sharply defined differences between the various blends and types they have in Bordeaux. We know almost exactly what to expect from a Médoc, a Graves, a St. Émilion, a Pomerol, or one of the smaller districts. In Bordeaux, there are strongly traditional, unifying characteristics among various districts and regions. The Bordeaux vintners have been experimenting with soils and techniques for hundreds of years. Our American winemakers, after a modern experience of hardly more than two decades, are still too busy experimenting in every direction to have any set traditions. All honor to them for their courageous flexibility. In Cabernet Sauvignon, as in other noble grape varieties, California, combined with the Pacific Northwest, is now established as one of the great wine regions of the world.

After almost twenty years of meticulous tasting of our American Cabernet Sauvignons, the ratings on my tasting charts show that, consistently, year after year, the greatest wines have been made from the grapes grown on Martha's Vineyard in the Napa Valley, the grapes vinified by the winemaker Joe Heitz at his own winery. This Heitz Cabernet Sauvignon, according to my ratings, is both the greatest Cabernet Sauvignon and the greatest of all red wines made in the United States. (For a detailed discussion of the work of Joe Heitz and the making of this truly GREAT wine, see the vineyard profile on page 251.) These wines thus give the GREAT classification to:

- Heitz Wine Cellars near St. Helena in the Napa Valley, with its owner-winemaker, Joe Heitz, using Cabernet Sauvignon grapes from Martha's Vineyard

I have tasted several other magnificent American Cabernet Sauvignons, my charts showing them to be only a few points below the first position. My ratings indicate that the second-best American Cabernet Sauvignon I have ever tasted has been, consistently, the Beaulieu Vineyard "Georges de Latour Private Reserve," the Cabernet Sauvignon grapes grown on the Beaulieu estate vineyard at Rutherford and vinified by André Tchelistcheff. This gives the SUPERB classification to:

- Beaulieu Vineyard at Rutherford in the Napa Valley

The third-greatest American Cabernet Sauvignon, consistently, according to the ratings on my charts, is from Stag's Leap Wine Cellars, the Cabernet Sauvignon grapes grown on the estate, vinified by its owner-winemaker, Warren Winiarski, giving the SUPERB classification to:

- Stag's Leap Wine Cellars on the Silverado Trail near Yountville in the Napa Valley

I have also tasted Cabernet Sauvignons consistently of SUPERB quality from these vineyards and wineries:

- Burgess Cellars near St. Helena in the Napa Valley, with its owner-winemaker, Tom Burgess
- Caymus Vineyards at Rutherford in the Napa Valley
- Chateau St. Jean at Kenwood in Sonoma, with grapes from the Glen Ellen Vineyard, vinified by winemaker Richard Arrowood
- Glen Ellen Vineyards in the Mayacamas Mountains above the Valley of the Moon in Sonoma, with its winemaker, Jeff Baker
- Louis M. Martini Winery at St. Helena in the Napa Valley, under its "Reserve" label, with its owner-winemaker, Louis P. Martini
- Mount Eden Vineyards near the peak of Mount Eden in the Santa Cruz Range above Saratoga in Santa Clara
- Ridge Vineyards above Cupertino on Black Mountain in the Santa Cruz Range, with its winemaker-partner, Paul Draper, making two separate wines, one using grapes from the Monte Bello estate vineyards, the other with grapes from York Creek on Spring Mountain in the Napa Valley
- Ste. Chapelle Vineyards at Sunny Slope near Caldwell in the Snake River Valley of Idaho, with its winemaker, Bill Broich
- Shafer Vineyard on the Stag's Leap slope east of Yountville in the Napa Valley, with its winemaker, Nikko Schoch
- Sonoma Vineyards at Windsor in Sonoma, under the label "Alexander's Crown," vinified by its winemaker, Rod Strong

- Spring Mountain Vineyards near St. Helena in the Napa Valley

At a point or two below this range, I have consistently tasted Cabernet Sauvignons showing ratings that bring the NOBLE classification to these vineyards and wineries:

- Almadén Vineyards at San Jose in Santa Clara, with its winemaster, Klaus Mathes, using grapes from their Paicines Vineyards in San Benito
- Associated Vintners at Bellevue near Seattle in Washington State, with its winemaker, Dr. Lloyd Woodburne, using grapes from the Yakima Valley and the Columbia Basin of Washington State
- Beringer Vineyards near St. Helena in the Napa Valley, with its winemaker, Myron Nightingale
- David Bruce Winery above Los Gatos in the Santa Cruz Mountains south of San Francisco Bay, with its owner-winemaker, David Bruce
- Carneros Creek Winery in the Carneros Hills above the Napa Valley, with its owner-winemaker, Francis Mahoney, using grapes from the Steltzner Vineyard near Yountville
- Chateau Montelena at Calistoga in the Napa Valley
- Chateau Ste. Michelle Vintners at Woodinville near Seattle in Washington State, using grapes from the Yakima Valley of Washington State
- The Christian Brothers on Mont La Salle above the Napa Valley, with its winemaker, Brother Timothy
- Clos du Val on the Silverado Trail near Yountville in the Napa Valley, with its owner-winemaker, Bernard Portet
- Conn Creek Vineyard on the Silverado Trail near Rutherford in the Napa Valley, with its owner-winemaker, Bill Collins
- Dehlinger Winery at Sebastopol in the Russian River Valley of Sonoma
- Diamond Creek Vineyards in the hills above Calistoga in the Napa Valley, with grapes from the Volcanic Hill Vineyard on the estate
- Firestone Vineyard at Los Olivos in the Santa Ynez Valley of Santa Barbara, with its winemaker, Alison Green
- Fisher Vineyards in the Mayacamas Mountains of Sonoma, with its owner-winemakers, Fred and Juelle Fisher, using grapes from the Wedding Vineyard on the estate

- Freemark Abbey Winery near St. Helena in the Napa Valley
- Gemello Winery at Mountain View in the Santa Cruz Mountains in Santa Clara
- Gundlach-Bundschu Vineyard at Vineburg in the Valley of the Moon in Sonoma, with its winemaker, John Merritt
- Hoffman Mountain Ranch above Paso Robles in the Santa Lucia Mountains of San Luis Obispo
- Iron Horse Vineyards at Sebastopol in the Russian River Valley of Sonoma, with its winemaker, Forrest Tancer
- Kenwood Vineyards at Kenwood in the Valley of the Moon in Sonoma, with its winemaker, Bob Kozlowski
- Kistler Vineyards on the western slopes of the Mayacamas Mountains above the Valley of the Moon in Sonoma, with its owner-winemaker, Steve Kistler
- Matanzas Creek Winery in the Bennett Valley southwest of Santa Rosa in Sonoma, with its winemaker, Merry Edwards
- Mayacamas Vineyards on the Mayacamas Range above the Napa Valley, with its owner-winemaker, Bob Travers
- Robert Mondavi Winery at Oakville in the Napa Valley, with its winemaker, Tim Mondavi
- Monterey Peninsula Winery on the Monterey-Salinas Highway in Monterey
- Mount Veeder Winery on the Mayacamas Range above the Napa Valley, with its owner-winemaker, Mike Bernstein
- Parducci Wine Cellars near Ukiah in Mendocino
- Joseph Phelps Vineyards near St. Helena in the Napa Valley, with its Insignia blend by winemaker Walter Schug
- Preston Wine Cellars at Pasco in the Columbia Basin of Washington State, with its winemaker, Robert Griffin
- Ravenswood Winery at Forestville in the Russian River Valley of Sonoma
- St. Clement Vineyards near St. Helena in the Napa Valley
- Sebastiani Vineyards in the Valley of the Moon in Sonoma
- Simi Winery at Healdsburg in the Alexander Valley of Sonoma, with its winemaker, Zelma Long
- Sterling Vineyards at Calistoga in the Napa Valley, for the estate-bottled "Reserve"
- Turgeon & Lohr Winery at San Jose in Santa Clara
- Villa Mt. Eden Winery at Oakville in the Napa Valley

Finally, my rating charts have consistently shown Cabernet Sauvignons that bring the FINE classification to these vineyards and wineries:

- Alatera Vineyards near the town of Napa in the Napa Valley
- Boeger Winery near Placerville in the Apple Hill district of El Dorado in the foothills of the High Sierras
- Buena Vista Vineyard in the Valley of the Moon in Sonoma
- Cakebread Cellars at Rutherford in the Napa Valley
- Richard Carey Winery at San Leandro in Alameda, with its owner-winemaker, Dick Carey, using grapes from Lake County
- Chappellet Vineyard on Pritchard Hill east of Rutherford above the Napa Valley
- Clos du Bois at Healdsburg in the Alexander Valley of Sonoma
- Cotes des Colombe Vineyard at Banks in the North Willamette Valley of Oregon, with its owner-winemaker, Joe Colombe, aging his wines with Oregon oak
- Cuvaison Vineyard on the Silverado Trail above Calistoga in the Napa Valley
- Dry Creek Vineyard at Healdsburg in the Dry Creek Valley of Sonoma, with its owner-winemaker, David Stare
- Durney Vineyard in the Carmel Valley of the Santa Lucia Mountains in Monterey
- Edmeades Vineyards at Philo in the Anderson Valley of Mendocino
- Fenestra Winery at Pleasanton in Livermore Valley of Alameda
- Fetzer Vineyards near Ukiah in the Redwood Valley of Mendocino, with its owner-winemaker, John Fetzer
- Foppiano Vineyards at Healdsburg in the Russian River Valley of Sonoma
- Hacienda Wine Cellars in the Valley of the Moon in Sonoma
- Harbor Winery near Sacramento on the Sacramento River, with its owner-winemaker, Charles Myers, using grapes from both the Napa Valley and the High Sierra foothills of the Amador district
- Hinzerling Vineyard at Prosser at the base of the Rattlesnake Hills in the Yakima Valley of Washington State, with its partner-winemaker, Mike Wallace
- Inglenook Vineyards at Rutherford in the Napa Valley

- Charles Krug Winery at St. Helena in the Napa Valley
- Mill Creek Vineyards southwest of Healdsburg in the Russian River Valley of Sonoma
- Mirassou Vineyards at San Jose in Santa Clara, with grapes from their vineyards in Monterey
- Monteviña Wines at Plymouth in the Shenandoah Valley of Amador in the foothills of the High Sierras, with its owner-winemaker, Cary Gott
- Martin Ray Vineyards above Saratoga in the Santa Cruz Mountains of Santa Clara, with its winemaker, Peter Martin Ray
- Raymond Winery at Calistoga in the Napa Valley
- Roudon-Smith Vineyards at Scott's Valley in the Santa Cruz Mountains south of San Francisco Bay
- Rutherford Vintners north of Rutherford in the Napa Valley
- San Martin Winery in San Martin in the Santa Cruz Mountains of Santa Clara
- Santa Ynez Valley Winery east of Solvang in the Santa Ynez Valley of Santa Barbara
- Sotoyome Winery south of Healdsburg in the Russian River Valley of Sonoma
- Souverain Cellars near Geyserville in the Dry Creek Valley of Sonoma
- Stony Ridge Winery at Pleasanton in the Livermore Valley of Alameda
- Sunrise Winery west of Felton in the Santa Cruz Mountains south of San Francisco Bay
- Tulocay Winery east of the town of Napa in the Napa Valley
- Veedercrest Vineyard high on Mount Veeder in the Mayacamas Range above the Napa Valley, with its owner-winemaker, Al Baxter, using grapes from the Gamay Acres Vineyard
- Yverdon Vineyards on Spring Mountain west of St. Helena in the Napa Valley
- Zaca Mesa Winery at Los Olivos in the Santa Ynez Valley of Santa Barbara

PINOT NOIR *Also, in France, called Noirien, Auvernat Noir, Vert Doré; in Alsace and Germany, de Burgunder, de Blauer, Blauer Klevner, and Schwartz Klevner; in Switzerland, Savagnin Noir Cortaillod*

The ancient and noble Pinot Noir vine—already known to Julius Caesar and his Roman legions when they invaded Gaul 2,000 years ago—is generally regarded in the modern era as the second-greatest red grape of the world, the prince behind the Cabernet Sauvignon king. But this judgment is not so much a matter of hard assessment of the relative qualities of the wines, for some of the greatest Pinot Noir reds have been among the most magnificent wines ever made —the secondary position of the Pinot Noir seems to be a question of such intangible qualities as breeding, character, reputation, and, above all, universality. In only one region of the world—along a single narrow strip of French earth, consisting of low, rolling hills, no more than forty miles long and hardly five miles wide, known for a thousand years as the Dukedom of Burgundy—have the small, oval, blue black Pinot Noir grapes made some of the most powerfully perfect of all red wines. While the Cabernet Sauvignon can achieve greatness under the right conditions wherever it is grown, the Pinot Noir has never succeeded in approaching its supreme Burgundian greatness anywhere away from Burgundy.

In one way, Pinot Noir is equal to the Cabernet Sauvignon. Each, in France, is "Lord of its own Domain." Under current French federal wine law, if you are a vineyard owner in Bordeaux and you plant so much as a single Pinot Noir vine on your property, you have committed a criminal breach of the regulations. When one of the constantly roving *inspecteurs* of the INAO (the National Institute for Controlled Appellations of Origin, the federal agency in Paris that polices the French wine industry) finds the evidence of your crime, you will be charged, tried, fined, and, probably, imprisoned. The Pinot Noir vine is banned by law from any part of the legally delimited area of Bordeaux. Conversely, if you are a vineyard owner in Burgundy, you would be equally punished if you planted a single Cabernet Sauvignon vine there, where the Cabernet is banned. Thus, the French government tries to maintain and protect the ethnic and racial purity of the wines of Bordeaux and Burgundy on which the fame of these regions has been built for thousands of years.

Some of my own memories of the Pinot Noir in Burgundy are suffused with a brightness and glory that could easily be confused with illicit, advance visits to paradise. I remember a day of tasting with Madame Lalou Bize, one of the most important and influential of Burgundian wine women, *directrice* of the famous shipping firm of Maison Leroy and a half-owner of what is, almost certainly, the greatest group of red-wine vineyards in the world, the Domaine de la Romanée-Conti. We spent all of one day in her huge storage cellars in the village of Meursault, opening some of the supreme bottles her father had bought for his stocks over the past fifty years. Finally, toward the end of the afternoon, we drove to the village of Vosne-Romanée and descended into the almost cathedral-like cellars of the Domaine de la Romanée-Conti.

We were received by the extraordinarily dignified, enormously respected, technically perfectionist *maître de chais*, "the cellarmaster," responsible for all the vineyards of the domain, André Noblet. Madame Bize said, "André, why don't you let Monsieur de Groot walk with you along the racks of our most ancient bottles and allow him to choose a few that might interest him to taste, so that we can open them here immediately and, perhaps, compare them, one against the other." When the thought flashed through my mind of the tens of thousands of bottles stored here—bottles no longer in circulation anywhere in the world, vintages going back to the 1840s and 1850s —I felt I might quite easily sink through the earthen floor. My second thought was that this was also a typically Burgundian test of my discipline and good wine judgment. My crystal-clear memory of that fantastic afternoon is of an old La Romanée of which Madame Bize (who is one of France's top mountain climbers) said, "It is so big, it could jostle Mont Blanc." It rated 49 out of a possible 50 points on my tasting chart.

What one remembers, above all, of these supreme Pinot Noirs is a touch on the tongue of satin, silk, and velvet. But, within the velvet glove, there is the smoothly irresistible power of a penetrating aroma and of a distinctive, dominant taste. All these controlled appellation Burgundian wines—ever since Duke Philip the Bold of Burgundy, in 1395, banned all other grapes from his domains—are required by French wine law to be made 100 percent from the Pinot Noir grape.

On the basis of its extraordinary reputation in Burgundy, the Pinot Noir vine has been planted in a large number of other places:

Germany, Switzerland, Austria, Hungary, Italy, Rumania, South Africa, Australia, New Zealand, Chile, as well as in California, Idaho, Oregon, and Washington State. Everywhere, the Pinot Noir has proved itself to be one of the most (if not *the* most) demanding, difficult, recalcitrant, and temperamental of all grapevines. For even reasonable success, it requires near perfection of growing conditions. Even at its very best, away from Burgundy one seldom finds the joyous feel on the tongue of satin, silk, and velvet.

In the first place, the Pinot Noir vine is genetically delicate, sensitive, unstable, and weak. During each growing season, it demands a complicated agricultural technique. If the weather is dry and hot, the grapes suffer from sunburn, become slightly "raisined," and the resulting flavor in the wine overrides virtually all the basic Pinot Noir character. The vine flowers early, so it is always in danger of being severely damaged by late spring frosts. It is easily subject to what the French call *coulure*, the "running out," the falling of the tiny berries that later normally form the bunches of grapes. A bad case of *coulure* in a vineyard can easily cut its grape production by half. During the winter, the roots of the Pinot Noir vine can be severely damaged by frost. All kinds of molds, viruses, and other diseases can attack the grape clusters and the leaves.

Even the healthiest of Pinot Noir vines is an extremely low producer of grapes—on the best possible earth, with ideal weather, seldom more than four tons per acre, but, often, for the best maturity and quality of fruit, the vine has to be pruned back to an average of one ton per acre. At that level, it is hard for a grower of Pinot Noir to make a profit. The grapes ripen extremely early, at the end of summer, when the sun is still generally very hot, and unless the grapes are harvested very quickly, they rapidly tend to become overripe. This is because the Pinot Noir vine does not produce sufficient leaves to shade the grape clusters properly—a particularly dangerous failing in California, where overripe grapes lead to wines too light in color and too low in flavor intensity. But even when the grapes are of first-rate quality when they are harvested, the rich color, aromas, and flavors that develop during fermentation all seem mysteriously to fade away when the wine is aged and bottled. Once in the bottle, the wine seems to have a most unfortunate tendency to become acid on the tongue.

In the light of Pinot Noir's impossible temperament and its virtual failure all around the world, a haunting question rises again and again: Why do American vintners continue to struggle with Pinot Noir? Perhaps this is one grapevine that simply cannot be successfully grown in the United States. I put this most basic of questions to the dean of California winemakers, André Tchelistcheff, who was on one of his rare visits to New York and with whom I had a date for lunch. His immediate response was that there was no doubt whatsoever in his mind that we, in the United States, could eventually "break through" all the immense problems and "win with Pinot Noir," and he added he was sure it could be done within, say, ten years. No wine practitioner in the United States is better qualified than André to make such a firm prediction on this particular problem.

I still remember how, in 1946, when he was dazzling the wine connoisseurs of California as the brilliant, new young winemaker at Beaulieu, he made a Pinot Noir of such supreme grandeur that it has remained as the standard by which all others have since been judged. But, when he tried again in 1947, he achieved (as he puts it) only "half a success." When I retasted the 1946 with André in 1975, after almost thirty years, it was still a beautiful wine. But the 1947 had faded and died within ten years. Every outstanding American Pinot Noir seems to have been a one-time accident. Neither André nor anyone else has ever discovered the secret for making a continuing series of successful American Pinot Noirs. André said, "In my more than forty years of winemaking in the Napa Valley, I consider that I have made only one and one-half top Pinot Noirs."

So why does he—and so many others—go on trying? As far back as 1896, at the University of California, in the annual report to the Board of Regents by the Dean of the School of Agriculture, Dr. Eugene W. Hilgard, reviewing the work of the Department of Viticulture, said, "I doubt that Pinot Noir has any potential for producing fine wine in California."

Today, as we approach the 100th anniversary of that Cassandra warning, there are quite a few wine people who agree with Dr. Hilgard—but André Tchelistcheff is not among them. There are now substantial numbers of "American Burgundians," for whom the challenge of the Pinot Noir has become nothing less than the obsessive interest of their lives, the challenge to find the technical "breakthrough" that will enable them to achieve in America what all the world has failed to do: to produce the first supreme Pinot Noir wines outside Burgundy. Almost all of these deeply determined, starry-eyed enthusiasts began as devoted lovers of the great wines of Burgundy.

Ken Burnap, for example, is a Los Angeles businessman who has built his own winery, the Santa Cruz Mountain Vineyard, with an accent on planting Pinot Noir, so that, over the next twenty years or more, he can experiment in every possible direction. He will try to find out why our Pinot Noirs are often so light in color, why it seems so hard to achieve, in our New World, the satin, the silk, and the velvet of the wine on the tongue that exists in the Old World. Why do our Pinot Noirs not grow old gracefully? What is the ultimate effect in the glass of the various clones of the vines, of the pruning back for small yields of fruit, of the effect of climate and soil? And what about the yeasts we use and the temperatures we allow for the fermentation of the crushed grapes at the harvest? And what is the effect of the kind of oak that is used (whether it is French Limousin, or Navarre, or Nevers, or American Tennessee) to make the barrels in which the wine will be aged? These are some of the questions that must be definitively answered if our winemakers are to hope for a consistent performance with the temperamental Pinot Noir grape. The amount of research to be done—the challenge to be faced—is immense.

Yet André Tchelistcheff thinks that the job will certainly be done: "Many of these people think that great French Burgundy is the most magnificent wine in the world. To try to equal that is an American pioneering challenge they simply can't resist. After all, the main features of great French Burgundies are bigness and richness—two of the principal goals of America since the beginning of its history!"

These great expectations have produced some strange side effects in California. American Pinot Noir wine, usually clean and fruity but a bit colorless and thin, often somewhat acid on the tongue, has never been a best-seller in the retail shops across the nation. Yet, the momentum of the enthusiasm behind its production has meant continuing substantial expansion of plantings of the vine.

In the ten years from 1969 to 1979, the acreage of Pinot Noir bearing fruit in California alone has been multiplied six times—from about 2,500 to more than 15,000—and, in 1978, 24,000 tons of grapes were crushed and converted into wine, while, in 1979, this figure rose to 33,000 tons—enough wine to fill 24 million bottles. What is going to be done with all that wine toward the "breakthrough" into the dream of a magnificent American Pinot Noir?

I doubt that any winemaker has completed more serious experiments with Pinot Noir than André Tchelistcheff. I asked him how he thought he had achieved his brilliant 1946 Beaulieu. He said that the vines had been planted in 1902 by the late Georges de Latour, the French-born founder and owner of Beaulieu, who had the root cuttings sent from Burgundy. They were planted in gravelly soil on the floor of the Napa Valley in the home vineyards surrounding the Beaulieu Winery at Rutherford. The particular clone, or subvariety, was called Petit Pinot Noirien, and when they were harvested in 1946, the vines were already forty-four years old and yielded hardly more than one ton of grapes per acre. This clone no longer exists anywhere in the United States. Both the viticultural experts at the University of California at Davis and other growers were so horrified by the economic impossibility of such a low yield of fruit that the university research botanists at once began developing new Pinot Noir clones that would produce up to six tons of grapes per acre. Increasingly, over the years, these newly developed, high-yield vines have replaced the older stock because of the larger profit possibilities. André does not believe that supreme Pinot Noir wine can be made from high-yield harvesting. He stresses that, in 1946, the vines were old, they were planted in ideal soil, they were ungrafted Burgundian vines not "mucked about" by botanical experimentation, the yield of fruit was extremely low, and, therefore, the concentration of flavor oils within each grape was exceptionally high. Above all, they were the right clone.

This question of Pinot Noir clones is one more of the severe problems of this most difficult of grapes, but it may be one of the main keys toward that future "breakthrough." Perhaps one can explain clones by thinking of dogs. All dogs are descended from an original source, a wild, roaming breed of jackal. But, across the centuries, different dogs have been used for different functions, and certain genetic changes have taken place. As these changes have been repeated, over and over again millions of times, different breeds and subbreeds and sub-subbreeds of dogs have developed. It is exactly the same with grapevines. Originally, almost certainly, they all came from the same source. But widely different varieties have developed, and, within each variety, there are small subvarieties, and these, in general, are the clones of the botanists.

Ampelography is the science of studying grapevines, and, if you look at the major reference books on ampelography, you will find beautiful color pictures of grapes and leaves, with detailed descriptions of the features of every vine. This is not just a matter of theoretical interest. It is of supreme importance to the farmer who is growing grapes that he be able to recognize the precise clones that are growing in his vineyard. He may have ordered certain root cuttings, but the wrong ones may have been sent him. He must know, as soon as the vine begins to grow, what he has under his hand. The grapes, the bunch clusters, the leaves, the stems, will all be slightly different in color, construction, shape, size, etc. Above all, the taste of the ripe grapes will be slightly different, and they will make slightly different wines.

For the Cabernet Sauvignon vine, there are about twenty known different clones. For the Pinot Noir, the estimated total number of clones may be almost a thousand. This is just one more way in which the Pinot Noir is impossibly difficult to grow. André Tchelistcheff is sure that he had the right clone in 1946. He wonders whether California has ever had the right one since then.

We know that, in the 1850s, before the phylloxera disease struck in Europe, many other California vineyard owners besides Georges de Latour at Beaulieu had Pinot Noir root cuttings sent to them from the greatest vineyards of Burgundy. Captain Gustave Niebaum had them sent to his Inglenook Vineyard. Charles Krug received them. So did Paul Masson. So did Carl Wente in the Livermore Valley. So did quite a few other of those original pioneers. Then, in the 1870s, when the phylloxera vine disease reached California, we have to assume that all these promising, low-yield Pinot Noir vineyards were simply wiped out. Then, before the growers could recover, they were again destroyed—this time economically—by the devastation of Prohibition.

When that agony was over, in 1933, the slow return of Pinot Noir and its propagation in the vineyards by budding, crosscutting, and grafting was not always done with the sole objective of attaining maximum quality. On the contrary, the average grower would look first for the most vigorous vines that would give the largest volume of grapes and make the largest profits for the vineyard. Even in the research laboratories and on the experimental vineyards at the University of California at Davis, the principal interests of the research botanists seemed to be centered, first, on the maximum production of fruit and, second, on developing vines with good immunity to virus diseases. Both very praiseworthy objectives from the point of view of the California industry, but not from the point of view of the great wine in the glass. What is really needed is research in the relationships between the various current Pinot Noir clones and the quality of the wines produced by their grapes. Perhaps the whole future of Pinot Noir wine in America will depend on finding and planting the right clones of the vines.

When it comes to deep discussion and long-range thinking about Pinot Noir, there are two Andrés in my vinous life. The second is André Gagey, a Burgundian who speaks only French—in deep, relaxed, rolling, sonorous basso-profundo tones that, I am convinced, come from the constant lubrication of the throat with the hour-by-hour tasting of the silken wines. He is the director general of the domains of the great Burgundian growing and producing family of Louis Jadot in Beaune. This André knows virtually all there is to know about the tending of Burgundian Pinot Noir vineyards and the making of the great wines. He is the first to admit that he knows no more about Pinot Noir in the United States than has been told him by visiting American professionals and from what he has seen on several brief vacation visits to California with his wife, Marie-Hélène, who is also a Burgundian vineyard owner.

André has said to me for years that he is convinced that one of the main creative differences between Burgundian and Californian Pinot Noir is the winemaker's approach to the temperature of the fermenting wine in the tank. He said, "You Americans are marvelous mechanical and technical inventors. You developed—for your hot California climate—the system of refrigerated tanks for so-called cold fermentation, which is such a wonderful advance in the fruitiness of white wines that we and all the rest of the entire world have adopted it. You are now so 'sold on it' that you also use it—I think, to the point of excess—for your red wines and, especially, for your Pinot Noir. When the grapes are crushed and go into the fermentation vat, we all know that they tend to 'boil' extremely hard. Your vintners seem to be afraid of this, and so they cool the tank down by refrigeration to, perhaps, sixty degrees Fahrenheit or seventy degrees

Fahrenheit, where our fermentation is around ninety degrees Fahrenheit. At that higher temperature—to put the whole thing as simply as possible—more of the essential and vital glycerines and oils are extracted from the grapes, and these are the necessary ingredients of the great, velvety wines. I do believe that this is one change that might be tried in the U.S.A. toward the improvement of your Pinot Noirs."

Another point on which André Gagey feels strongly is the inclusion of at least some of the stems of the grapes in the fermentation of the wine. He thinks that there are certain flavor oils, aromatic ingredients, and tannin compounds in the tiny stems that add to the quality of the wine, especially in terms of its silkiness and velvet. Marvelously efficient new destemming machines have now been developed that can remove every last stem from a load of grapes as it comes in from the vineyard—or the same machine can be adjusted to allow a certain proportion of the stems to pass through into the crusher and so get into the fermentation vat. Where it all used to be a matter of hard hand labor, the job is now smoothly automated and completely under the control of the winemaker. André says that, in some years, depending on the ripeness and sugar levels of his Burgundian grapes, he uses about 20 percent of the stems. In other years, he may use 50 percent or 75 percent, or even 100 percent. In certain years, he may use no stems at all. Here is another area where American experimentation is now beginning.

There is one other big (and quite complete) difference in the way the Pinot Noir grapes are vinified in Burgundy and in California. As I have explained (in Preamble Two), the fermentation of the crushed grapes is started by the action of the yeasts, a group of benign bacteria that converts the sugar in the grape into alcohol. The vast majority of the bacteria are friendly and positive in their actions. A few are deadly enemies. (We all know, for example, of the vinegar bacteria, which, if it manages to gain control, turns the wine sour.) Every vineyard is full of natural wild yeasts. They settle on the skins of the grapes, and when the fruit is harvested and crushed, these wild yeasts get into the fermentation vat and start the boiling and bubbling going. This is how they let it work in Burgundy. They are not afraid of the few bad bacteria, because they feel that these will be overpowered and destroyed by the huge majority of good bacteria. When the fermentation has been finally completed, and the wine has been racked off into aging barrels, the remaining mash of skins, pits, stalks, etc., all still infested with the good bacteria, is spread back onto the earth of the vineyards, partly to rot as fertilizer, partly to encourage the continuation of the breeding of the good yeasts for future harvests. After hundreds of years of this annual cycle, the Burgundian vineyards are chock-full of all the best yeasts for the Pinot Noir vines. The Burgundian growers argue that having this complicated breeding ground for, literally, thousands of different strains of yeasts helps to make the complexity of flavors of Burgundian wines.

In California, the point of view of the bacteriological and viticultural scientists at the university is quite different. They argue that our American earth is still much too young as wine land—that it has not been planted to vines for a thousand years or more, as has the earth of Burgundy—and that our natural wild yeasts might still be quite dangerous and might harm the wine. So every California winemaker who strictly follows the rules laid down by the university adds a strong dose of sulphur dioxide to the crush to kill off all the natural yeasts after the grapes have been crushed and transferred into the fermentation vats. After the crushed fruit has thus been "purified," a measured dose is added of a laboratory cultured yeast —that is, a strain of a particular yeast, suitable for the job but grown in isolation under completely sanitary conditions in a chemical-botanical laboratory. The performance of this yeast is exactly traditional. It will act as a well-behaved, perfectly mannered member of the winery team. It is all tightly controlled, and it makes for complete consistency in the quality of the wine. But does it make for greatness in Pinot Noir?

The California wine writer Gerald Asher raised this question in a recent article. He pointed out that when you use a single strain of laboratory yeast, you may get conformity, but you don't get complexity or variety. When you have hundreds of different wild yeasts, you may have hundreds of different little threads, all woven into a rich tapestry of multiplicity of flavors. The University of California has taken a stand against this. They opt for a policy of meticulous control. They believe that predictable reliability is far better than an unpredictable shot at greatness. Surely, one of the important aspects of the greatness of Burgundian Pinot Noir is the subtle sweep of the many shadings of its flavors, which are so fleeting, so immeasurable, so indefinable, so unexpected. How can we possibly hope ever to reproduce such qualities in our wines through deliberate laboratory control? We shall see, a little bit later in this discussion, that the young, revolutionary winemakers who are breaking through to success with their Pinot Noirs are also breaking through the orthodox, straitjacket, traditional, technical rules.

Many other questions remain to be answered. All the best California Pinot Noirs, virtually without exception, have been made—as was André Tchelistcheff's famous 1946 Beaulieu—from vines that produced no more than about one ton of grapes per acre. This is about one-tenth of the normal average production from other varieties of grapevines. Will it ever be possible, economically, to produce a viable California Pinot Noir? Will it be economically possible to uproot all the thousands of acres of vines of the wrong strains that have been planted in bad locations and replace them with vines of the right strains in good locations as these are discovered and tested over the years to come? In the wineries, what kind of oak barrels should be used for aging the wine? How long should the wine stay in the barrels before it is bottled?

Then—all of a sudden—an extraordinary new development made many of these questions seem virtually academic.

The Magnificent Explosion in Oregon

About twenty years ago, I became interested in the so-called Pacific Northwest wine area, a definition that seems to include, legally and technically, the states of Idaho, Oregon, and Washington, as well as British Columbia, just across the Canadian border. My interest was first sparked by my friend the late Stan Reed, who was, for more than twenty years, the wine editor of the *Seattle Post-Intelligencer* and had urged me to come to Washington to visit the vineyards and taste the wines. When I finally accepted his invitation, I was sharply impressed, not so much by the immediate magnificence of the then-current wines, but by the clearly superb prospects of the land, the grapes, and the exploratory attitude of the winemakers. My interest was so much aroused that it has drawn me back to the region several times each year.

One of the newest and fastest-growing wine districts of this Pacific region is the northwestern coastal area of Oregon. At the beginning of the 1970s, there were only three wineries in the valleys of the Umpqua and Willamette rivers. Now, in the decade of the 1980s, there are almost thirty wineries. There is a fascinating connection between the French hills of Burgundy and the small, hilly, rough, seemingly inhospitable wine districts of Oregon. Because Burgundy, on the map of France, appears to be halfway down toward the Mediterranean and the south, one tends to think of the wine region as being southerly. Few of us seem to realize, at least in wine terms, how far Burgundy is to the north. If you look on a world map and read the north-south latitudes of Burgundy—and especially if you have a map showing the world's isothermal lines of average temperatures—you may be surprised to find that Burgundy is not level with New York or Boston, but with the most northerly parts of Maine, where it touches the Canadian border. The Burgundian city of Beaune is about level with Mount Katahdin in northern Maine. If you follow the lines across the United States, you find that they stay pretty close to the Canadian border all the way to the West Coast, where they come out nowhere near California, but about at the mouth of the Columbia River on the border of Oregon and Washington. So it is with some element of truth that the Oregon winemakers claim that they are the real equivalents of Burgundians in the United States.

There are other strange similarities. The French soil of Burgundy is cleared ancient forestland, and the earth, deep down, is rich with the organic remains of rotted old roots and disintegrated forest fungus. The Oregon vineyards, too, are cleared from the primeval forest. The weather in Burgundy is generally cool and damp, with relatively short days in terms of sunshine. This is the sort of climate that suits the Pinot Noir vine. Conditions are much the same in the wine valleys of Oregon, which are a good deal nearer to the North Pole than they are to the Equator. Certainly, in Oregon, there is never the problem of the grapes getting burned by too much of a too-fierce sunshine. On the contrary, the grapes ripen more slowly than the average, and instead of being harvested in early September, they often continue to hang on the vines until mid or late October. This enriches the grapes with color and tannin.

I turned these thoughts over and over in my mind and wondered, more and more, about Pinot Noir in Oregon. I decided to go to Portland and talk to a leading young wine writer there, Matt Kramer. He set up for me a memorable tasting of then-current Oregon vintages. The one that almost knocked me out of my chair was a 1975 Pinot Noir made by the quite-small Eyrie Vineyard in the Willamette Valley. Here, like a sudden burst of light, for the first time on our side of the Atlantic, was at least a sense on my tongue of the satin, the silk, and the velvet. The owner-winemaker of Eyrie is a young pioneer, David Lett, born in Salt Lake City, trained in viticulture at the University of California, who wanted to try new things in a new region and had started out, on a shoestring, in Oregon. He converted an old turkey-processing plant into a winery, and his only stainless-steel tanks are old drums originally used for Coca-Cola syrup. Five minutes after tasting his wine, I was on the phone to him. The first question I asked was, "How high did you let the temperature go when you fermented your Pinot Noir grapes?" David's answer had the impact of a clap of thunder, "Oh, I don't have any refrigerated fermentation vats, so I guess it boiled up to a little above ninety degrees Fahrenheit."

The following year, I was invited to be one of the judges at the annual Pacific Northwest Wine Festival in Seattle. David Lett's 1975 Pinot Noir was entered and seemed to me to have substantially improved with another year of bottle age. I fought hard to award it a gold medal, but my colleagues, with, I suppose, palates more conservative than mine, outvoted me and settled for a silver medal.

The next year, a French food-and-wine magazine in Paris organized what it chose to call an International Olympiade of wines from all over the world. David Lett's 1975 Eyrie Pinot Noir was chosen as one of the reds to represent the United States. The panel of French judges—all, of course, tasting blind—picked the Eyrie as the winner in its class over a number of prestigious Burgundies. When the labels were uncovered and the results were known, there was consternation among the commercial French winemen, who had come to Paris expecting a glorious victory. One of them, a leading producer in Burgundy, Robert Drouhin of the famous firm of Joseph Drouhin, complained that the organization and rules of the Paris tasting had been unfair to his wines, and he suggested that he would like to set up a second tasting, to be restricted to "wines made from Burgundy-type grapes," to be held, under his auspices, in Burgundy. David Lett, by telephone from Oregon, at once gave his approval.

A few weeks later, the Burgundian tasting was organized in Beaune by Robert Drouhin. Considerable controversy surrounded the arrangements. Since Monsieur Drouhin was the "principal adversary," in terms of the wines on the tasting table, it was considered somewhat questionable that he should have been the organizer and should have a large say in picking the judges. Also, against the young American and other foreign wines, all from vintages of the 1970s, Monsieur Drouhin insisted on entering, from the French side, some of his finest older bottles—a 1961 Chambertin-Clos de Bèze, a 1959 Chambolle-Musigny, a 1964 Aloxe-Corton, and so on. The judges tasted blind and handed in their scores. The labels of the bottles were uncovered, and the results were not only the equivalent of an earthquake in Burgundy, but front-page wine news around the world. First place had gone to the Drouhin 1959 Chambolle-Musigny. But second place—above five of the most prestigious wines of Burgundy—went to David Lett's 1975 Eyrie Pinot Noir. A group of highly skilled Burgundian tasters had preferred, above some of their own best wines, an unknown wine from a region of the United States that no one had ever heard of! Monsieur Drouhin was not available for comment. *The New York Times* headlined its story: "An Oregon Pinot Noir That Measures Up to the Noble Reds of Burgundy." The wine editor commented: "So unlikely was the quality of the Eyrie, that a bottle lay in my cellar for several months, untried, until I heard the latest results from France. Upon tasting it, I found it to be far more elegant and subtle than other American Pinot Noirs, with a lingering bouquet."

Now, of course, the wine writers of the entire country converged upon Oregon. I was invited to be a judge at the Tri-Cities Wine Festival in the Yakima Valley of Washington State, where we would taste not only the best of Washington, but, also, most of the very good wines from Oregon. And I would be able to meet many of the important young owners and winemakers. One of the very top wines of the judging—to which we all unanimously awarded highest honors and a gold medal—was the 1977 Pinot Noir of the Amity Vineyard in the Willamette Valley of Oregon, vinified by the owner-winemaker brothers, Myron and Steve Redford. Other labels of Oregon Pinot Noir which we tasted showed a relentless consistency of impressively high quality, proving that there is a rightness in the climate and soil that transcends even the skills of the individual winemakers.

You can tell an Oregon wine by its finesse, its delicate subtlety, by the way it complements and frames food without ever overriding it. The Oregon vines are still comparatively young, so the wines will increase in complexity and depth every year, with every new vintage. But already they have a dramatic elegance, a lingering and memorable, faintly peppery aroma and a lovely, deep color. They are not imitations of Burgundy. They are certainly not competitors of California. They are Oregonians.

But the secret source of the extraordinary explosion of quality in Oregon lies not only in the land. A good part of the credit belongs to the winemakers—a new, young breed of passionately idealistic "pioneers in the wilderness," still with such small production, still so free of marketing pressures, that they can experiment to the outer limits of their imaginations. Almost all of them were trained in California, and some worked there for a while, but none wanted to stay. They preferred the challenge of the wild, untamed land. As David Lett said to me, "I didn't want to settle down and become one more winery on 'Winery Row.' It would have been easy—a comfortable and financially successful life—just falling into the traditions of everything that had been done before. Here, a few days ahead of the harvest, you look out of your window and see a big black bear and a couple of deer gorging themselves on your grapes. And the birds— oh, my God, those birds! A flock of blackbirds, or starlings, can come down on to your ripe grapes like a black hailstorm, and if you don't do something about it fast, you can lose half your production in a few hours. This is a difficult life—but it's a challenge—and that's all that matters."

Naturally, the news of the Oregon success flashed around California as if it were the discovery of a new gold strike at Sutter's Mill. One wonderful thing you can say about all winemakers, everywhere in the world, is that they have no professional secrets from one another. They pick up the telephone and call, if necessary, halfway around the world, at the drop of an idea or the hint of a rumor. The Oregon technical successes (which, of course, were already showing their signs several years before David Lett's blaze of publicity) set off a chain reaction of new experimentation in California. The results there, too, are beginning to show in the increasing excellence of the wine in the glass.

One of these new, young California winemakers, Josh Jensen,

after training and working for two years in Burgundy, has found a piece of chalky land with limestone outcroppings (the ideal soil balance for Pinot Noir) in the Cienega Valley of the Gavilan Mountains of Monterey. He established his Calera Winery (*calera* is Spanish for "lime pit") and, in 1976, planted about 24 acres of Pinot Noir. In 1981, he harvested less than one ton of grapes per acre of vines. When the fruit crush went into the fermentation vat, about half the stalks went in too, and Josh allowed the natural wild yeasts on the skins of the grapes to get the fermentation started. It went so well that no artificial yeasts needed to be added, and the fermentation temperature was allowed to rise to 92 degrees Fahrenheit. (As I have said, all these techniques are normal practice in Burgundy, but are considered as "rank heresy" in the classical terms of orthodox winemaking in California.) It is, of course, much too early for a definitive judgment of the Calera Pinot Noirs, but the young wines are certainly dark in color, with a spicy aroma, strong and vigorous in taste, hard and hopeful, with tannin for the future.

Farther south, at the Firestone Vineyard in the Santa Ynez Valley of the Santa Barbara district, its first winemaker, Tony Austin, also experimented with Pinot Noir techniques that were quite a ways off the beaten track of California traditionalism. He made some wines from slightly overripe grapes deliberately held on the vines until the end of October. The vines had also deliberately been pruned back so that, when the grapes were picked, there was no more than one and one-quarter tons of fruit to the acre—thus concentrating the flavor oils, the thickening glycerides, and the sugar. When the crush went into the fermentation vat, about 25 percent of the stalks went in too —for extra side components of flavors and tannins. The fermentation temperature had been allowed to go above 92 degrees Fahrenheit. It had all been worked by the natural wild yeasts on the skins of the grapes—no artificial yeasts had been added. Here, again, was the completely unorthodox Pinot Noir pattern—small yield of grapes at the harvest, stalks added to the crush, fermentation by natural wild yeasts, high fermentation temperature, aging in French Limousin oak barrels. The wine was still too young to be released, but it showed high promise.

Another of the experimentally oriented wineries in the Santa Ynez Valley is that of the Sanford & Benedict Vineyards, where the partner-winemaker, Michael Benedict, has about 40 acres of Pinot

Noir under his control. Each spring, he carefully prunes back the bunches of grapes so that, at the harvest, he will get no more than one and one-quarter tons of fruit per acre of vines. (Remember that some growers—particularly those who do not make wine but are concerned only with selling their grapes for cash—often manage to grow as much as five or six tons per acre.) After crushing the grapes, Michael adds some of the stalks to the fermentation vats. He lets the natural wild yeasts start the fermentation but then, later, may add some artificial yeasts for flavor control. He is convinced that the wild yeasts give a complexity and subtlety to the wine. He allows the fermentation temperature to rise above 92 degrees Fahrenheit. The result of these unorthodox techniques is that the wine is aromatic in bouquet, dark in color, strong in tannin, with an excellent future ahead of it.

Any discussion of the new breed of Pinot Noir revolutionaries in California would hardly be complete without mention of Merry Edwards, who, in the 1970s, while she was still winemaker at the Mount Eden Vineyards in the Santa Cruz Mountains, produced several vintages of Pinot Noir that brought her considerable acclaim, admiration, and professional prestige. Now that she has moved to the Matanzas Creek Winery in Sonoma (where it seems she has more freedom to develop her own ideas), one hears rumors that her first Pinot Noir vintages show future prospects nothing short of splendid. I asked Merry what she thought were the most essential requirements for such excellence. She said that first and most important of all is planting the right clone of the Pinot Noir vine; second, pruning back the fruit for low and concentrated yield; third, adding some of the stems to the fermentation and aging the wine in French Limousin oak barrels.

However, let no reader misunderstand me. The average, inexpensive Pinot Noir remains a thin, slightly acid, undistinguished, merely thirst-quenching drink. The enormously improved wines discussed above are all made from grapes harvested at the low yield of around one to one and one-half tons of fruit per acre, and, at that level of relatively uneconomic production, the wine has to be a good deal more expensive. In other words, these wines are made for quality, regardless of every other consideration. So far, there are relatively few of these important new wines, and the big question is whether serious wine drinkers are going to be willing to pay the price for them. If they will, then the present trickle of very high quality labels may soon become a reasonable flow—never, I think, a flood, but a regular, small supply.

Looking over my charts, both for California and for Oregon, as well as for the most promising wines in Idaho and Washington State, I believe I can end this discussion of Pinot Noir with two firm statements. First, we in America have not yet produced a Pinot Noir red wine to equal the ancient greatest of Burgundy. And second, of all the wine regions of the world outside Burgundy where the Pinot Noir vine is grown, we are doing the best work and producing the best results. After all, to be second to thousand-year-old Burgundy, after fewer than a hundred years of serious trying, is not too bad a record.

My steady tasting of American Pinot Noir reds, over the years, has been particularly difficult. There has never been, at least to my knowledge, a continuous line of vintages, from a single producer under a single label, for which one could assess steady progress and make comparative judgments, year by year. Instead, newly experimental wines have appeared and disappeared at every turn in the long road. Of the wines listed in the following tabulations of classifications, I can only say, in many cases, that the labels are so new that I have only been able to taste a few fairly recent vintages. All of them will, I am convinced, improve steadily over the next five to ten years, as the Pinot Noir vines age and mature in their vineyards. Analyzing my tasting charts, the rating figures show that I have not yet been able to find an American Pinot Noir of truly GREAT quality, but that I have found several that rate a few points below, at the SUPERB classification. Of these, the best I have discovered is from:

- Eyrie Vineyards at McMinnville near Dundee in the Willamette Valley of Oregon, with its owner-winemaker, David Lett

My second ranking of American Pinot Noirs is almost level with the first and also rates at a SUPERB quality, from:

- Amity Vineyards in the village of Amity in the Yamhill district of the Willamette Valley of Oregon, with its owner-winemaker, Myron Redford

My third American Pinot Noir, also within the SUPERB range, is from:

- Ponzi Vineyards at Beaverton in the Willamette Valley of Oregon, with its owner-winemaker, Dick Ponzi

In the next lower range, I have tasted Pinot Noirs that bring the NOBLE classification to these vineyards and wineries:

- Beaulieu Vineyard at Rutherford in the Napa Valley
- Calera Wines at Hollister in the Cienega Valley of the Gavilan Mountains in San Benito, with its owner-winemaker, Josh Jensen
- Carneros Creek Winery in the Carneros Hills above the Napa Valley, with its owner-winemaker, Francis Mahoney
- Caymus Vineyards at Rutherford in the Napa Valley
- Chalone Vineyard on Mount Chalone in the Gavilan Range of the Santa Lucia Mountains in Monterey, with its winemaker, Peter Graff
- Edna Valley Vineyard in the San Luis Obispo district of the Central Coast region, with its winemaker, Gary Mosby
- Elk Cove Vineyards at Gaston in the Willamette Valley of Oregon
- Firestone Vineyard at Los Olivos in the Santa Ynez Valley of Santa Barbara, with its winemaker, Alison Green
- Heitz Wine Cellars near St. Helena in the Napa Valley, with its owner-winemaker, Joe Heitz
- Iron Horse Vineyards at Sebastopol in the Russian River Valley of Sonoma, with its winemaker, Forrest Tancer
- Knudsen-Erath Winery at Dundee in the Willamette Valley of Oregon, with its partner-winemaker, Richard Erath
- Louis M. Martini Winery at St. Helena in the Napa Valley, with its owner-winemaker, Louis P. Martini
- Matanzas Creek Winery in the Bennett Valley southwest of Santa Rosa in Sonoma, with its winemaker, Merry Edwards
- Robert Mondavi Winery at Oakville in the Napa Valley, with its winemaker, Tim Mondavi
- Mount Eden Vineyards near the peak of Mount Eden in the Santa Cruz Range above Saratoga in Santa Clara
- Oak Knoll Winery at Hillsboro in the North Willamette Valley of Oregon
- Preston Vineyards near Healdsburg in the Dry Creek Valley of Sonoma
- Preston Wine Cellars at Pasco in the Columbia Basin of Washington State, with its winemaker, Robert Griffin
- Joseph Swan Vineyards at Forestville in the Russian River Valley of Sonoma, with its owner-winemaker, Joe Swan

- Wente Brothers at Livermore in the Livermore Valley of Alameda, with its owner-winemaker, Eric Wente

And, in the next lower classification, my charts have rated Pinot Noirs to bring the FINE classification to these vineyards and wineries:

- Almadén Vineyards at San Jose in Santa Clara, with its winemaster, Klaus Mathes, using grapes from their Paicines Vineyards in San Benito
- Associated Vintners at Bellevue near Seattle in Washington State, with its winemaker, Dr. Lloyd Woodburne, using grapes from the Yakima Valley of Washington State
- Burgess Cellars near St. Helena in the Napa Valley, with its owner-winemaker, Tom Burgess
- Davis Bynum Winery at Healdsburg in Sonoma
- The Christian Brothers on Mont La Salle above the Napa Valley, with its winemaker, Brother Timothy
- Fetzer Vineyards near Ukiah in the Redwood Valley of Mendocino
- Freemark Abbey Winery near St. Helena in the Napa Valley
- Gundlach-Bundschu Vineyard at Vineburg in the Valley of the Moon in Sonoma, with its winemaker, John Merritt
- Hoffman Mountain Ranch above Paso Robles in the Santa Lucia Mountains of San Luis Obispo
- Inglenook Vineyards at Rutherford in the Napa Valley
- Johnson's Alexander Valley Wines at Healdsburg in the Alexander Valley of Sonoma
- Keenan Winery on Spring Mountain above the Napa Valley
- Kenwood Vineyards at Kenwood in the Valley of the Moon in Sonoma, with its winemaker, Bob Kozlowski, using grapes from the Jack London Vineyard
- Charles Krug Winery near St. Helena in the Napa Valley
- Thomas Kruse Winery at Gilroy in the Santa Cruz Mountains of Santa Clara
- Pedroncelli Winery northeast of Geyserville on a ridge above the Dry Creek Valley of Sonoma
- Joseph Phelps Vineyard near St. Helena in the Napa Valley, with its winemaker, Walter Schug, using grapes from the Heinemann Mountain Vineyard
- Sanford & Benedict Vineyards at Lompac in the Santa Ynez Valley of the Santa Barbara district, with its partner-winemaker, Michael Benedict

- Santa Cruz Mountain Vineyard above the town of Santa Cruz south of San Francisco Bay, with its owner-winemaker, Ken Burnap
- Zaca Mesa Vineyard at Los Olivos in the Santa Ynez Valley of Santa Barbara
- Z D Wines on the Silverado Trail east of Rutherford in the Napa Valley, with Pinot Noir grapes from the Winery Lake Vineyard in the Carneros Hills above the valley

PETITE SIRAH *The French ancestor of this American grape, the Syrah, is also called, along the Rhône and in other parts of France, Schiras, Sirac, Syrac, Hignin Noir, Entournerien, Serine, Serenne*

As for the other French ancestor of the American grape, the Durif, the alternative names are Dure, Duret, Plant Durif, Pinot de Romans, Pinot de l'Ermitage, Nerin, Bas Plant, Plant Fourchu, Sirane Fourchue

In the 12th century, the wars of the Crusades had reached a peak of violence, with the armies of the Christians and Muslims swirling around Jerusalem and Damascus. Steel swords flashed in the sunlight. Blood spurted from falling bodies. One French knight, Gaspard de Stiremberg, was so repulsed by the savagery, that he left the fighting, returned to France, and decided to spend the rest of his life in solitary contemplation. The world-weary knight built his tiny hermitage on a mountain on the left bank of the River Rhône and occupied a part of his lonely time in cultivating a vineyard. He planted vine-root cuttings he had brought back from the Middle East (which, as we all now know, is the original heartland of all grapes), and since his cuttings had come from lands variously called Persia, Shiraz, and Syria, Gaspard de Stiremberg called his vines Syrah. Over the centuries, these magnificent grapes, the hill on which they are still grown, and the wine which they still produce—hill and wine both called Hermitage—have become world famous.

In the 19th century, the vine was brought to the United States, but, as with the Gamay Beaujolais, the planting and development have been burdened by mistakes and misunderstandings caused by inefficient labeling and record keeping. The Syrah has become mixed up with a second vine type from the Rhône—a variety that began to be planted in the valley of the great river around 1880—a common grape with none of the superb qualities of the Syrah. This lesser grape was developed by a French amateur botanist, Dr. François Durif, so the vine was given his name. (Incidentally, in almost all American reference books, the name is wrongly spelled as Duriff.) Today, under current French federal wine law, the Durif vine is forbidden to be grown in any vineyard that claims on its bottle labels the controlled appellation "Vin du Rhône." This means that the Durif is gradually being eliminated from the Rhône Valley. But, long before this death sentence was passed, huge quantities of Durif root cuttings were imported into California.

From the point of view of pioneer growers in the 1800s, who did not know much about French wine history, the argument seemed logical enough. This new variety was also a Rhône grape. It was cheaper to buy than the prestigious Syrah. Perhaps in California soil the new grape would perform just as well. When it didn't, the pioneer growers tried to improve it by cross-grafting it with some original Syrah. But they kept no records of what they did. Before very long, they had a new vine with substantially smaller, round, black grapes. They decided to give it a new name, including a French word for prestige, and something a bit easier to spell than Syrah. Both requirements were met by calling the new American vine Petite Sirah. To this day, no one really knows its precise parentage—what percentage is the noble Syrah and how much the ordinary Durif?

It was easy to find a new name; it was not so easy to put quality into the wine. It was always powerful and strong, with a deep, almost black color, but its taste was ordinary and rough, with virtually no interest of bouquet or varietal character. It was an ironic twist that millions of gallons of wine from this Rhône-based grape became the foundation blend for jug wines labeled "California Burgundy."

Petite Sirah might have remained in that inferior position forever had not the more imaginative of the California winemakers begun experimenting, on the off chance that they might, with careful use of the new techniques of cold fermentation, even bring some character and smoothness to the dark, powerhouse red of Petite Sirah. Almost immediately, the winemakers came up against severe problems. Among the roughly 5,000 acres of Petite Sirah planted in various parts of California, there were many different types of vines—different varieties within the same family. The early pioneers had cross-grafted in different proportions between the French Syrah and the

Durif, and each grower had then propagated (and, possibly, sold to other growers) his own variation.

Because of these difficulties, even the most brilliant of California winemakers, while producing a few interesting varietal wines made 100 percent from the Petite Sirah grape, have not been able to give us a wine to compete with the powerful Hermitage or the Château-neuf-du-Pape of the Rhône. But for drinkers and tasters who like strong wine—what George Saintsbury, the famous English wine writer, called "manly wine"—there are deep-red Petite Sirahs that are hefty, mouth filling, chewy, providing the satisfaction of an un-complicated, fruity grapiness, with dominant power and tannin. This is, clearly, not a wine of mass appeal. It is a wine for a limited group of "fanciers" of the particular type—people who don't even mind if the deep-red wine stains their teeth. It is true, of course, that almost every well-made Petite Sirah will improve with reasonable aging; the sharp edge of its tannin will be dulled by a few years in the bottle at a cool cellar temperature of, say, 55 degrees Fahrenheit.

But, in spite of steady and substantial improvements in the mak-ing of Petite Sirah since the first varietal experiments of the mid-1960s, there are many signs that the number of its devoted and loyal fans is growing smaller. My wine friends in the retail business tell me, more or less unanimously, that they are selling and stocking less of it. Wine drinkers no longer seem to be buying it in dozens to lay down in their cellars, but only one or two bottles at a time, generally, it seems, as an accompaniment to powerful game meats or very strong cheeses. Two wineries that made excellent versions of Petite Sirah—Burgess in the Napa Valley and Kenwood in the Sonoma Valley—have simply stopped making it altogether. From these and other signs, one simply has to draw the conclusion that Petite Sirah is slowly sliding out of fashion. It has been, for the last few years, perhaps the biggest, brashest, brawniest wine ever made in the United States. Perhaps it is the proof of our new wine sophistication that brawn without complexity and depth—shall we say, brawn without brain—can no longer command success within the world of wine. The truth of this is being confirmed by one of the best of the new California vineyard owners, Joseph Phelps, who has recently begun to bring over from France and to plant in the Napa Valley the original Syrah vine from the Hermitage hill where Gaspard de Sti-remberg first grew it 800 years ago.

Perhaps it will seem strange to some readers that I now propose to award some fairly high marks to certain vineyards and wineries for their production of Petite Sirah reds. Let me explain my position. I do not believe that Petite Sirah is a wine for connoisseurs—to be sipped slowly, to be tasted and judged in a formal setting, by experts sitting in silence around a big table, with lines of crystal glasses. For one thing, if you taste a lot of Petite Sirah in a short time, your mouth soon becomes coated and overwhelmed by an excess of tannin, and you lose all pleasure in the tasting. For another, there is not enough complexity in Petite Sirah to make it fair game for serious, analytical comparisons between one version and another.

But if, instead, you drink a well-made, nicely balanced, smoothly aged Petite Sirah, not as the centerpiece of attention, but in its secondary role as an accompaniment to the right food at the dining table —drinking it comfortably, easily, and simply, preferably with powerful meats or strong cheeses—then some of the excellent California Petite Sirahs can be very enjoyable and pleasant wines. They are not "stars"; they are "supporting players," and it is on their excellent performances in these lesser roles that I have rated them, with the vineyards and wineries that have produced the best versions over the years.

There is one exception, with which we must begin our classification, since it is of deep importance and great interest to the serious student of wine. Unquestionably the best American Syrah-type red I have tasted during the years of research for this book was not made from the American Petite Sirah grape, but from the authentic, original French Syrah of the Rhône Valley, which, as I have said, is now being imported by the Joseph Phelps Vineyard in the Napa Valley.

In 1975, although his vines were not yet fully mature, Joe Phelps was able to buy some French Syrah grapes, and from them he made an American Hermitage Syrah, which he began aging in oak barrels. Then, in 1976, Phelps made the first vintage of his own Hermitage Syrah. One Sunday morning early in 1978, in the Napa Valley, he invited me to taste these two wines, side by side. They were extraordinarily different, mainly, perhaps, because of the difference in the ages of the vines. The grapes from the twenty-year-old vines gave a bigger bouquet, a greater aromatic complexity of flavors. The grapes from the five-year-old vines produced a fruitier wine, with more vigor and youth. Both wines rated, on my tasting charts, as being of SUPERB quality, giving this classification to their producer:

- Joseph Phelps Vineyards near St. Helena in the Napa Valley, with its winemaker, Walter Schug

My second-best of this type—the best of the American Petite Sirah grape—a wine of exquisitely skillful construction and aged to a remarkable smoothness, brings the NOBLE classification to its maker:

- Stonegate Winery at Calistoga in the Napa Valley, with its winemaker, David Spaulding, using grapes from the Maryroy Vineyard

Other Petite Sirahs bring the NOBLE classification to these vineyards and wineries:

- Carneros Creek Winery in the Carneros Hills above the Napa Valley, with its owner-winemaker, Francis Mahoney
- Concannon Vineyard at Livermore in the Livermore Valley of Alameda
- Cuvaison Vineyard on the Silverado Trail above Calistoga in the Napa Valley
- Fetzer Vineyards near Ukiah in the Redwood Valley of Mendocino, with its owner-winemaker, John Fetzer
- Freemark Abbey Winery near St. Helena in the Napa Valley, with grapes from the York Creek Vineyards on Spring Mountain
- Robert Mondavi Winery at Oakville in the Napa Valley, with its winemaker, Tim Mondavi
- Ridge Vineyards above Cupertino on Black Mountain in the Santa Cruz range, with its winemaker-partner, Paul Draper, using grapes from York Creek on Spring Mountain in the Napa Valley
- Stag's Leap Wine Cellars near Yountville in the Napa Valley, with its winemaker, Warren Winiarski

And in the next ranking, I have rated Petite Sirahs that bring the FINE classification to these vineyards and wineries:

- Ahlgren Vineyard at Boulder Creek in the Santa Cruz Mountains south of San Francisco Bay, with its owner-winemaker, Dexter Ahlgren, using grapes from the Ventana Vineyards in the Arroyo Seco of Monterey
- Davis Bynum Winery at Healdsburg in Sonoma

- Callaway Vineyard at Temecula in the Riverside district of southern California
- Caymus Vineyards at Rutherford in the Napa Valley
- Dry Creek Vineyard at Healdsburg in the Dry Creek Valley of Sonoma, with its owner-winemaker, David Stare, using grapes from the Shell Creek Vineyards near San Luis Obispo
- Field Stone Winery at Healdsburg in the Alexander Valley of Sonoma
- Foppiano Vineyards at Healdsburg in the Russian River Valley of Sonoma
- Gemello Winery at Mountain View in the Santa Cruz Mountains in Santa Clara
- Monterey Peninsula Winery on the Monterey-Salinas Highway in Monterey, with Petite Sirah grapes from the Arroyo Seco vineyards in Monterey
- J. W. Morris Wineries at Concord in Contra Costa
- Mount Veeder Winery on the mountain above the Napa Valley, with its owner-winemaker, Mike Bernstein
- Parducci Wine Cellars near Ukiah in Mendocino
- Santa Cruz Mountain Vineyard above the town of Santa Cruz in Santa Clara
- Sherrill Cellars at Woodside in the Santa Cruz Mountains of San Mateo
- Sycamore Creek Vineyards southwest of Morgan Hill in the Santa Cruz Mountains of Santa Clara

ZINFANDEL *Also called, in southern Italy, Primitivo di Gioia; in Hungary, Plavac; in Yugoslavia, Plavina*

The Zinfandel vine is the unique grape of California that is said to grow nowhere else and that has had built up around it a complete romantic history. It is generally called "the mystery vine of California." It grows, easily and lavishly, virtually all over the state. Yet botanists tell us that it is not a native vine. At some point in time, it was imported. But no one has ever been able to find out when, or from where. The botanists—presumably by observing its growth behavior—are sure that it belongs to one of the noble grape families of Europe. But they have never been able to discover—after 150 years of searching—its European ancestors. Nor have they ever been able to trace the origin of the name Zinfandel. The widely circulated and popularly accepted explanation is that this mystery vine was one of the 100,000 root cuttings brought over from Europe by the California pioneer Agoston Haraszthy in 1852 (see page 31). The story goes that the label attached to this particular cutting was partially washed out by rain, and that "Zinfandel" was the half-guessed-at, half-made-up word put together from the still-visible bits of ink on the label. So the root was sold to some grower as Zinfandel. He propagated it, found that it flourished mightily in the California climate and soil, sold his cuttings to other growers, and, within a hundred years or so, Zinfandel was one of the most prolific of California vines.

A nice story—very much in tune with the characteristic California love of adventure, mystery, and romantic pioneering—but quite out of tune with cold reality and hard truth. I have never found any mystery surrounding the Zinfandel vine. The only problems have been the usual quota of mislabelings, mistakes in record keeping, and misunderstandings. Apart from these usual human errors, every step of Zinfandel's progress can be explained in completely logical, scientific terms.

In the first place, it could not possibly have been brought from Europe by Agoston Haraszthy in 1852 because it was already growing in the United States, under the name Zinfindal in 1830. There are in existence unquestionable documentary records of a Black Zinfindal Vineyard on Long Island, New York, in 1830, and another, in the 1840s, at Salem, Massachusetts. As to the name, it seems perfectly clear that on the original root cuttings brought from Europe the label was either destroyed or lost. The importer, whoever he was, feeling that he could get a better price for his cuttings if they had a known pedigree, simply picked out of the European book the name of the Austrian red grapevine known as the Zierfandler. No plant pathologist has ever suggested that there is the slightest botanical connection between the American and Austrian grapes. But the name has a nice ring to it, and, once the spelling had been deliberately simplified (just as the spelling of the French Syrah was simplified to Sirah), the name stuck.

As to the positive botanical identification of the wine and the delineation of the connecting links with its European ancestry, here, too, there are no more question marks. Twenty or thirty years ago, botanists had to depend largely on visual signs—leaf color, shape, and structure; form, size, and tightness of the berry clusters; structure of the individual grapes—for the positive identification of vine varieties, and they often ran into virtually insoluble problems. But, in this electronic age, the botanists have automated probing tools, based on ultra-high-frequency beam systems called electrophoresis, which can actually analyze the enzymes within the plant and provide a form of botanical fingerprinting. By this method, the American Zinfandel has been clearly linked to a vine of southern Italy called Primitivo di Gioia. It also grows in Hungary, under the name Plavac, and in Yugoslavia as Plavina. American professional winemakers who have visited these areas and tasted the best wines made from these grapes have recognized the similarities of character and personality with the Zinfandels from home.

During the first century and a half of its American life, the Zinfandel played a supporting role in our slowly developing wine industry. Its name never appeared on labels. It provided, efficiently and steadily, body and color in an infinite number of "California blends." Frank Schoonmaker once described it to me as "about as nice and useful a *vin ordinaire* as you could hope to find."

Then came the quality explosion of the 1960s and 1970s, and Zinfandel began to show that it had far greater possibilities. It began to be treated as a "noble vine"—planted on cool hillsides, in the best wine districts, pampered in its growth, harvested and vinified with care, imagination, and skill—and it showed at once that it was much more than just a mass-production grape. It developed its own recognizable character and personality, its own range of bouquets and flavors, its brilliant ruby color, its fresh fruitiness that reminded the drinker of Beaujolais with an added touch of wild woodland blackberries. In other words, Zinfandel has shown that it can be a wine of fine style.

But the rarest quality of Zinfandel is its extraordinary and unique flexibility. In its earliest days in California, when it was considered to be a sort of illegitimate orphan, thoroughly misunderstood and underrated, the growers thought it would flourish anywhere, so they planted it everywhere—often in dreadful places. But the vine—which, under good conditions, could produce the fantastic yield of up to ten tons of grapes per acre—even under the worst conditions never gave up completely. In poor soil, it would give very light, yet fruity, ordinary wines. Under better conditions, the wines would be medium bodied, well balanced, demanding to be taken much more seriously. In other locations, the wines were dark and strong, intense and tannic—and so on, up to the top of the quality scale. It always seemed as if the grape would give back, with interest, whatever good things were put into it by the climate, the soil, and the skills of the grower and the winemaker. In short, if you treated it as a classic grape, it would be most likely to give you a classic wine.

It is this exciting promise of Zinfandel that has intrigued almost all the best California winemakers—so that the price range of Zinfandel red wines runs from the least-expensive varietal bottles up to a few of the most expensive of California labels. So wide is the range of wines possible from this grape that some wineries regularly produce as many as six competing labels each year from Zinfandel grapes grown in different vineyards.

At the beginning of the 1970s, there were about fifty wineries in California producing Zinfandel reds—mostly fairly light, simple, everyday wines. But as the new experimentally minded winemakers began developing their ideas, more and more of them became aware of the flexibility and potential of the Zinfandel grape. New Zinfandel labels began popping up as fast as spring mushrooms in a mountain meadow. I have never subscribed to the theory that the Zinfandel is as great a grape as the Cabernet Sauvignon or the Pinot Noir. But, if the winemaker pampers the Zinfandel, treating it in every way as if it were the greatest of wine grapes, it will respond by producing wines that are big, deep, solid, tannic—wines to be laid down for slow maturing over decades of time. These may not be supremely great wines, but they are big and important American wines.

When the young Frenchman Bernard Portet moved from his home in Bordeaux to the Napa Valley and bought the vineyard property that he has since named Clos du Val, there was a good deal of excitement, because Bernard's father was the director general of Château Lafite. We all naturally assumed that Bernard's main interest would be in growing Cabernet Sauvignon and making red wines in the Bordeaux style. We were wrong. He did, indeed, cover a large part of his estate with plantings of Cabernet but, while waiting for the five years that it takes for new vines to produce their first adequate harvest, Bernard became fascinated by California's unique Zinfandel. By focusing all his imagination and his Bordeaux point of view and training on this American grape, he has already produced some Zinfandel reds of quite extraordinary quality—reds that are different from anything previously produced in California.

But young Portet is not alone. Memorable Zinfandels have also been produced, within the last few years, by Paul Draper at the Ridge Vineyards, by Joseph Swan at his own winery, by the late Bernard Fetzer at his winery in Mendocino, by Bob Trinchero at his Sutter Home Winery in the Napa Valley, by Francis Mahoney at his Carneros Creek Winery, and by Mike Bernstein at his Mount Veeder Winery above the Napa Valley—and there are others.

All these "Special Selection" Zinfandels—which have always been made in quite small quantities and have always been fairly expensive—share certain memorable characteristics. Though they do not, in my view, achieve greatness, they have a range of irresistible flavors, a depth of complexity, a fine balance of taste and texture, a feel on the tongue of fruity refreshment, a distant memory of wild woodland blackberries, and, finally, the potential for continuing improvement in the bottle. Clearly, Zinfandel, in terms of prestige and quality, has moved from being an everyday working wine to becoming one of the expensive and major labels of California.

An Entirely New Wine
from a Very Old Source

One afternoon, early in 1974, I climbed the steep hill to visit Nonie and Bob Travers at their Mayacamas mountaintop vineyard high above the Napa Valley. Bob is an experimental winemaker, and, when I visit him, he often has something interesting and new for tasting. On this occasion, it was a new Zinfandel that, one might say, he had "invented" by accident.

In 1968, he had contracted with the owners of a neighboring vineyard to buy their entire harvest of Zinfandel grapes. Such contracts are usually signed many months before the grapes are ripe. The purchaser then has to accept and pay for the grapes regardless of their condition at the time they are picked. When the 1968 harvest time came, Mayacamas found itself up against a problem that is common among small vineyards where the winemaking equipment is limited. Bob ran into a severe "traffic jam." Large quantities of grapes—both those of his own vineyards and those he was buying from others—were all becoming ripe for harvesting at the same time. The Mayacamas crusher couldn't handle such a huge flow of fruit all at once. Part of the harvest would have to be delayed. Bob decided that the Zinfandel grapes—although they were now at a perfect degree of ripeness for picking—must remain on their vines for a few days longer. He was taking an appalling risk. Had the weather broken—had there been a fierce hailstorm—he might have lost his entire crop, which was, of course, already his property. He was lucky. The weather held. The Zinfandel vines, once again, demonstrated their extraordinary flexibility. The grapes had to be left hanging for nine days beyond the optimum point for harvesting. Every day, as the hot sun shone down, the vines continued to convert the solar energy into more sugar, until the grapes contained almost double the amount needed for winemaking.

When the grapes were finally brought in, they were magnificently sweet to eat, but Bob wondered about the conversion of all that extra sugar into alcohol during the fermentation. As soon as the crush went into the fermentation vats, it immediately began to boil and bubble furiously—a fermentation that was virtually uncontrollable in its violence, as the yeast cells consumed the sugar and converted it into alcohol. The readings shot up, they soon passed the standard 11.5 percent of alcohol, and, by the time the fermentation was completed, had reached the fantastic figure of 17.3 percent of alcohol. This is a level that technicians consider impossible to reach by natural fermentation. Bob aged the wine in oak casks until he felt that its sharp corners had been rounded off, and then he aged it further in bottles until, finally, he felt it was ready for tasting. To say that this dominant, powerful, unique wine—without question the most dramatic Zinfandel I have ever tasted—was simply a "Late Harvest" style would be a total understatement. It was so enormously big, with such fantastic intensity of flavor, such a magnification of fruit, of richness, of spice—that I could only describe it in the words of a famous French winemaker when he referred to one of his great vintages as "a concentrated essence of wine." If we were in the kitchen, rather than the winery, dealing with, say, a Zinfandel sauce, one might describe the Mayacamas vintage as "a reduction of the sauce to its essence." In sensual terms, the wine was so luscious that it filled my mouth, and I almost felt that I could chew it.

I do not know whether Bob Travers actually "invented" this "Late Harvest" style of Zinfandel red wine. For all I know, some other winemaker, in some other part of California, may have been first with this new technique. But my discovery of it was in Bob's tasting glass at Mayacamas. Clearly, this dark, intense wine opened up a whole new world for the amazing Zinfandel.

The news, naturally, got around very quickly, and other winemakers were eager to try out the new style. Where could they find ultraripe, high-sugar Zinfandel grapes? The search led toward the towering Sierra Nevada Mountains a hundred miles inland from the cool coastal vineyards—across the hot Sacramento Valley—to one of the almost-forgotten historic wine districts of California's early history.

One night, in San Francisco, I dined with Paul Draper, the winemaker-partner and Zinfandel specialist of the Ridge Vineyards, who gave me a basic lesson in California wine history. "Those venerable mountain Zinfandel vineyards," Paul told me, "are California's greatest winemaking legacy." It is a legacy that comes down to us from the days of the Gold Rush, and it seems to prove that the Zinfandel is one of the oldest grapes to be cultivated in California— older than any of the vines being grown by the almost 450 vineyards and wineries now making California wines.

If you drive east from San Francisco to California's capital at Sacramento and then continue eastward for about another thirty-five miles in the general direction of the snow-capped High Sierras, you reach two of the most historic counties, Amador and El Dorado. Here, in 1848 and 1849, in these sharply rising foothill valleys, the rumors about the Mother Lode of "layers of solid gold" brought in thousands of prospectors.

By 1856, the gold fever was already abating, and some of the miners, having put together a small amount of capital, decided to settle down in these beautiful valleys, building homes for themselves and planting acres of Zinfandel vines. The wine they made was not for commercial distribution but for the use of the family and for occasional sale to neighbors. The grapes flourished in this bracing, dry, alternately hot and cold climate. When the dreaded phylloxera disease devastated the wine industry of the entire world and destroyed the California coastal and Central Valley vineyards at the end of the 1800s, the deadly insect was never able to reach the high valleys of Amador and El Dorado. When Prohibition put a stop to the wine industry, the home winemakers were entirely unaffected. In fact, the Amador and El Dorado growers found a new market for themselves—shipping their grapes, neatly packed in boxes, to thousands of home winemakers from Los Angeles to Minneapolis.

All this, however, was one of the best-kept secrets in California. Even the California Wine Institute, with its 430-odd members, had never heard of the century-old Zinfandel vineyards in Amador or El Dorado. Every vineyard or winery making commercial wines has to be bonded by the federal government in Washington—but not vineyards that make wine for home use. The ancient mountain vineyards were simply not on anyone's list until the end of the 1960s, when the big search began for new sources for "Late Harvest" grapes.

One man who has always known about Amador and El Dorado is Darrell Corti, a wine connoisseur and a member of a family that owns and runs a number of luxury wineshops in Sacramento. Amador and El Dorado are virtually on Darrell's doorstep. At the end of the 1960s, at just about the time when Bob Travers at Mayacamas was completing his first "Late Harvest" Zinfandel, another Napa Valley producer, Bob Trinchero, the owner-winemaker of the Sutter Home Winery, wanted to try his hand at the new style of Zinfandel but could find no suitable grapes anywhere. Then Darrell Corti and Charles Myers (who now owns Harbor Winery) visited Trinchero with a bottle of homemade Zinfandel from one of the growers in Amador. Trinchero, who considered himself a master specialist on Zinfandel, was virtually bowled over by the fantastic intensity, power, and quality of the Amador wine. Within a matter of hours, Darrell and Bob were touring the Amador and El Dorado valleys and talking to the growers at those ancient Zinfandel vineyards.

The extraordinary feature of the vinous life in these high mountain valleys is the massive daily swing of the weather. During the spring and summer growing seasons, the vital period while the grapes are developing, all through the middle part of each day, the wind blows almost continuously up the valley, dry and hot from the desert of the Sacramento Valley far down below—and the temperature, day after day, goes up over 100 degrees Fahrenheit. But every day, in the early evening, the wind reverses itself and blows down the valley, down from the snow-capped peaks of the Sierra Nevada—so that the evenings and the nights are cool—and, as the sun rises, there is heavy morning dew. When these temperature variations are combined with the dryness of the soil, which stresses and concentrates the grapes, they become, year after year, more than fully ripe, with considerably above-average percentages of sugar, and without ever losing the taste of their acid tang, or becoming moldy or mushy. In short, these are ideal grapes for the production of the intense "Late Harvest" Zinfandels.

Bob Trinchero, who was always a bit chauvinistic about the supreme quality of the grapes from the Napa Valley, found it hard to believe that his Sutter Home Winery could make top-quality wine from grapes that would have to be trucked a hundred miles from Amador to Napa, but he gave his first order for a meager twenty tons of Amador grapes. They arrived, beautifully and neatly packed in boxes as if they were being shipped to a home winemaker, in perfect condition, gloriously ripe, sweet with sugar. The wine was so good and sold so well that within three years Sutter Home was fermenting 200 tons of Amador grapes. It did not take long for other wineries to join the movement. The price of Amador grapes went up from about $70 a ton to around $500 a ton.

With so many new Zinfandel reds appearing—in the dramatic "intense" style of the mountain grapes, in the more conservative "noble" style of the cool coastal vineyards, and in the simple "Beaujolais" style of the everyday wines—it is easy either to underrate or overrate these wines. You have to stop and clarify your impressions. It is easy to remember it in the days before it became so fashionable: Zinfandel was the all-purpose, everyday family table wine produced in huge quantities and available everywhere. It was, indeed, the American answer to Beaujolais. That type is still available, relatively as inexpensive as it was, and these clean, fresh, fruity, light, simple wines—at least those that are well made—continue to represent very good value for thirst-quenching drinking, the wine drunk without pompous snobbery, consumed young, never laid down for aging.

At the opposite end of the scale, it is easy to allow oneself to be persuaded that the noble forms of Zinfandel, in its most pampered productions and most elevated prices, leave even the greatest of Cabernet Sauvignons in a shadow. This is, of course, very sweet talk to American chauvinists, who long to believe that a unique American grape might be the top of the heap. It is equally sweet talk to the accountants, who would like to see stratospheric prices obtained for wines from an American grape that grows easily everywhere and can produce ten tons of fruit to the acre where the noble Pinot Noir produces only a single ton. The sweet talk is to be taken with several grains of salt.

Without in the slightest denigrating the technical achievements of our American winemakers with Zinfandel, I feel bound to say that, in its high-cost, high-prestige versions, where it begins to lay claim to high nobility, it shows limitations. When we think of wine as one of the deep pleasures of civilized living, we think of it in partnership with food. Apart from formal wine tasting, which is a hobby, most of us expect wine to be the equal partner of food—neither its dominating master nor its self-effacing servant. We all remember some of the wonderful marriages of food and wine we have experienced— when each magnified the other. One evening, when I was dining at Château Latour, the director general said grace, beginning it, "We thank Thee, O Lord, for providing us with the Hollandais cheese with which to taste our Bordeaux wine." It is in this basic area where Zinfandel seems to me to fail.

In the first place, it always has the very direct and strong flavor of ripe, tangy fruit. Many of my serious Californian tasting friends say that they somehow associate it with wild blackberries, or cherries, or even crushed cranberries. Although these fruity wines are not sweet, in terms of measured sugar percentages, they still give an impression of sweetness on the tongue. At the same time, their fruit projects a certain acid sharpness, or tartness. So there is an overall sweet-sour effect, which can make Zinfandel an extremely difficult companion to food. I have tried Zinfandel with a number of main dishes, and I find that the wine often seems to have sharp edges, a kind of piercing quality that tends to clash with virtually all complex and subtle foods. It does best with country fare—with pasta and pizza—with farm and peasant dishes. But it simply does not have the ability to accommodate all kinds of foods, the universal social graces of the red wines that have earned their greatness over 2,000 years.

When it comes to the powerful "Late Harvest" wines—most of them made from high-sugar mountain grapes from Amador or El Dorado—the problem with food becomes virtually insuperable. These wines are so dominant that they instantly kill any food. Their flavors have been variously described as "melted chocolate," or "crushed fresh mint," or "wild mountain raspberries." Some of them have so much residual sugar that they qualify for appearance after dinner in place of port. None of them, to my mind, should be served with a savory main entrée. They are dramatic and exciting wines, but they cannot be compared with the great red wines of the world. Perhaps the best thing to serve with a robust Amador Zinfandel is a dish of walnuts and raisins.

In summary, I believe the record of my tasting charts provides an accurate definition of American Zinfandel red wine. It has provided no wines of truly GREAT quality, but a substantial number of wines of SUPERB quality. In its slightly lesser versions, it rates as NOBLE, and even in its simpler forms it can be a wine of FINE quality.

Through my years of continuous tastings of all the many styles of Zinfandel reds, the single label that has won the highest ratings on my charts—the wine that has always seemed to me to combine the maximum of dramatic excitement with a balance of supreme excellence—is the series of "Late Harvest" vintages made from Napa Valley grapes by owner-winemaker Bob Travers, giving the SUPERB classification to:

- Mayacamas Vineyards on the Mayacamas Range above the Napa Valley

My second ranking on the rating charts—very close to the first in terms of elegance and excitement—is the "Late Harvest" vinified from Napa Valley Zinfandel grapes, bringing the SUPERB classification to:

- Chateau Montelena at Calistoga in the Napa Valley

My third Zinfandel was made from ancient mountain vines of Amador, the wine vinified with restraint and sophistication by the owner-winemaker, Francis Mahoney, with grapes grown on the Ernest Esola Vineyards in the Shenandoah Valley, bringing the SUPERB classification to:

- Carneros Creek Winery in the Carneros Hills above the Napa Valley

Other Zinfandels I have tasted have brought the SUPERB classification to these vineyards and wineries:

- Clos du Val Wines on the Silverado Trail near Yountville in the Napa Valley, with its French owner-winemaker, Bernard Portet

- Mount Veeder Winery on the Mayacamas Range above the Napa Valley, with its owner-winemaker, Mike Bernstein, using some of the old Zinfandel vines on the Simmons Ranch
- Ridge Vineyards above Cupertino on Black Mountain in the Santa Cruz Range, with its winemaker-partner, Paul Draper, making three separate wines: the first using grapes from Fiddletown at the Eschen Ranch in Amador in the foothills of the High Sierras; the second with grapes from Geyserville in Sonoma; and the third using grapes from York Creek on Spring Mountain in the Napa Valley
- Sutter Home Winery near St. Helena in the Napa Valley, with its owner-winemaker, Bob Trinchero, vinifying Zinfandel mountain grapes from the Ken Deaver Ranch and the John Ferrero Vineyard, both in Amador
- Joseph Swan Vineyards at Forestville in the Russian River Valley of Sonoma, with its owner-winemaker, Joe Swan, using grapes from the Teldeschi Vineyard in the Dry Creek Valley

At a point or two below this top range, I have tasted Zinfandels that have consistently brought the NOBLE classification to these vineyards and wineries:

- Almadén Vineyards at San Jose in Santa Clara, with its winemaster, Klaus Mathes, using "Late Selection" grapes from the small estate vineyard at La Cienega in San Benito
- Burgess Cellars near St. Helena in the Napa Valley, with its owner-winemaker, Tom Burgess, using grapes from Sonoma
- Richard Carey Winery at San Leandro in Alameda on San Francisco Bay, with its owner-winemaker, Dick Carey
- Caymus Vineyards at Rutherford in the Napa Valley
- Cuvaison Vineyard on the Silverado Trail above Calistoga in the Napa Valley
- Dehlinger Winery at Sebastopol in the Russian River Valley of Sonoma
- Dry Creek Vineyard at Healdsburg in the Dry Creek Valley of Sonoma, with its owner-winemaker, David Stare
- Edmeades Vineyards at Philo in the Anderson Valley of Mendocino

- Fetzer Vineyards near Ukiah in the Redwood Valley of Mendocino, with its owner-winemaker, John Fetzer
- Grand Cru Vineyards at Glen Ellen in the Sonoma Valley, with its owner-winemaker, Bob Magnani, making a wine from a blend of 75 percent Zinfandel with 25 percent Petite Sirah and a few other grapes from the 19th-century vineyard surrounding the winery
- Grgich Hills Cellar at Rutherford in the Napa Valley, with its partner-winemaker, Mike Grgich
- Kenwood Vineyards at Kenwood in the Valley of the Moon in Sonoma, with its winemaker-partner, Bob Kozlowski
- Lytton Springs Winery north of Healdsburg in Sonoma, with grapes from the Valley Vista Vineyard
- Mastantuono Winery west of Templeton near Paso Robles in the Santa Lucia Mountains of San Luis Obispo
- Mirassou Vineyards at San Jose in Santa Clara, with grapes from their vineyards in the Salinas Valley of Monterey
- Monterey Vineyard at Gonzales in the Salinas Valley of Monterey, with the "Late Harvest" by its winemaker, Dick Peterson
- Monteviña Wines at Plymouth in the Shenandoah Valley of Amador, with owner-winemaker Cary Gott using grapes from some ancient vines among the foothills of the High Sierras east of Sacramento
- Ridge Vineyards above Cupertino on Black Mountain in the Santa Cruz Range, with its winemaker-partner, Paul Draper, making two separate wines, one using grapes from Paso Robles at the Dusi Ranch in San Luis Obispo, the other from Shenandoah at the Esola Vineyard in Amador in the foothills of the High Sierras
- Santino Wines east of Plymouth in the Shenandoah Valley of Amador in the foothills of the High Sierras, with its winemaker, Scott Harvey
- Shafer Vineyard on the Stag's Leap slope east of Yountville in the Napa Valley, with its winemaker, Nikko Schoch
- Sonoma Vineyards at Windsor in Sonoma, with winemaker Rod Strong vinifying grapes from their River West Vineyard

At the next ranking level, I have tasted Zinfandels that have consistently scored to bring the FINE classification to these vineyards and wineries:

- Bargetto Winery at Soquel in the Santa Cruz Mountains south of San Francisco Bay, with its owner-winemaker, Lawrence Bargetto
- Boeger Winery near Placerville in the Apple Hill district of El Dorado in the foothills of the High Sierras
- Buena Vista Vineyard in the Valley of the Moon in Sonoma
- Davis Bynum Winery at Healdsburg in Sonoma
- Cakebread Cellars at Rutherford in the Napa Valley
- Calera Wines at Hollister in the Cienega Valley of the Gavilan Mountains in San Benito, with its owner-winemaker, Josh Jensen
- Chateau St. Jean at Kenwood in Sonoma, with its winemaker, Richard Arrowood
- The Christian Brothers on Mont La Salle above the Napa Valley, with its winemaker, Brother Timothy
- Cresta Blanca Winery at Ukiah in Mendocino
- Cygnet Cellars at Hollister in the Cienega Valley of the Gavilan Mountains of San Benito
- Diablo Vista Winery at Benicia on the Sacramento River in Solano
- Enz Vineyards at Hollister in the Cienega Valley of the Gavilan Mountains in San Benito
- Fortino Winery near Gilroy in the Santa Cruz Mountains of Santa Clara
- Gemello Winery at Mountain View in the Santa Cruz Mountains in Santa Clara
- Gundlach-Bundschu Vineyard at Vineburg in the Valley of the Moon in Sonoma, with its winemaker, John Merritt
- Hacienda Wine Cellars in the Valley of the Moon in Sonoma
- Harbor Winery near Sacramento on the Sacramento River, with owner-winemaker Charles Myers vinifying Zinfandel mountain grapes from the Ken Deaver Ranch in the Shenandoah Valley of Amador
- Hop Kiln Winery at Healdsburg in the Alexander Valley of Sonoma
- Kalin Cellars at Novato near San Rafael on San Pablo Bay north of San Francisco

- Charles Krug Winery at St. Helena in the Napa Valley
- Louis M. Martini Winery at St. Helena in the Napa Valley, with its owner-winemaker, Louis P. Martini
- Robert Mondavi Winery at Oakville in the Napa Valley, with its winemaker, Tim Mondavi
- Monterey Peninsula Winery on the Monterey-Salinas Highway in Monterey
- Parducci Wine Cellars near Ukiah in Mendocino
- Joseph Phelps Vineyards near St. Helena in the Napa Valley, with its winemaker, Walter Schug
- Rafanelli Winery at Healdsburg in the Dry Creek Valley of Sonoma
- Simi Winery at Healdsburg in the Alexander Valley of Sonoma, with its winemaker, Zelma Long
- P. & M. Staiger Winery above Boulder Creek in the Santa Cruz Mountains south of San Francisco Bay
- Stonegate Winery at Calistoga in the Napa Valley
- Stony Ridge Winery at Pleasanton in the Livermore Valley of Alameda
- Ventana Vineyards along the Arroyo Seco River southwest of Soledad in the Salinas Valley of Monterey
- Wente Brothers from its winery at Pleasanton in the Livermore Valley of Alameda, with its owner-winemaker, Eric Wente
- Yverdon Vineyards on Spring Mountain west of St. Helena in the Napa Valley
- Z D Wines on the Silverado Trail east of Rutherford in the Napa Valley, with Zinfandel mountain grapes, 71 percent from the Gott's Vineyard in the Shenandoah Valley of Amador and 29 percent from the Clements Vineyard in El Dorado

CHAPTER VII

The True Rosé Wines

When the popularity of rosé wines seemed suddenly to explode across the United States toward the end of the 1940s, soon after World War II, the force behind the explosion appeared to be the promise that, if you chose rosé with your dinner, you avoided the appallingly difficult decision as to whether the food on the table required the accompaniment of red or white wine. Millions of American men and women, believe it or not, simply could not face this terrible question of red or white. So they escaped by making what came to be known as "the choice of the coward." This problem was satirically discussed by the French food and wine critics Henri Gault and Christian Millau, in their Paris magazine, *The New Guide*, under the headline, "Rosé: Good with Everything, or Good for Nothing?" The question is still with us today—more than thirty years later.

To understand whether any rosé wine is any good at all in any direction whatsoever, you have to know a little bit of why and how it is made. It was invented and developed in France several hundred years ago, not as a compromise over a marriage with food, but as a wine with a definite character, to play a precise part in the vinous spectrum. It was planned, not for its color, nor for its easy virtues of adaptability, but for a personality about halfway between the dominant tannin of an average red wine and the delicate subtlety of the average white. It was supposed to have much less tannin than a red —much more than a white. It was to be a third type, midway between the others.

There are at least two brilliant rosés in France that meet the specifications. One is the Château de Tigné of the Loire; the other is the Pinot Rosé d'Alsace made by the Lorentz family of the village of Bergheim in Alsace. The latter is the only rosé on the wine list of the

174

Ritz Hotel in Paris. Why? Because there are certain foods on the menu of the Ritz—for example, a delicately light Terrine of Duck—against which even the lightest of red wines would be too strong, while no white wine would have exactly the right character. Only the Pinot Rosé is quite perfect. The only considerations are character and taste. Color has nothing to do with it.

The secret lies in the skill with which the wine is made. A red wine (or a rosé) draws much of its tannic character (and all of its red or rosé color) from the skins of black or red grapes. The red pigment is entirely in the skin. No power on earth can make a red wine from green or white grapes. During the fermentation of the crushed grapes after the harvest—including their juice, their pulp, their pits, their little stalks, and their skins—the winemaker draws out more (or less) red color directly in proportion to the length of time the skins remain in the fermentation vat. If he wants a deep red wine, with heavy tannin, he may leave the skins in the fermentation vat for anything from one week to several weeks. But if he wants a true rosé, with only a very light tannic character and a beautiful light pink color, he will remove the skins from the juice by filtering them out within, perhaps, three or four hours, or after an overnight soaking, or, at the very most, within twenty-four hours. Then the pink juice continues to ferment on its own, without its skins, exactly as if it were a white wine. This is why a true rosé has some of the character of both a red and a white.

As with any wine, the best rosé is made from a single variety of grape. If you drink your way—as I have done—among the hundreds of rosés along the River Loire, you will find a majority of deadly dull wines with labels marked "Rosé d'Anjou" or "Rosé de Touraine." The moment you find one marked "Rosé de Cabernet" of Anjou or Touraine, you have in your glass a charming, interesting wine of character and personality. So the first simple rule for choosing a rosé, in the United States as in France, is to look for the varietal name of a grape.

So much for the "true rosé"—the wine made in the traditional way by the control of the skins during fermentation. There is another method for making rosé, which I propose to call the "fast mix" method. The American market, whenever it sets up a huge demand for a product, becomes a force of irresistible power. At the end of the 1940s, America wanted rosé wine—and more rosé and still more rosé. So, of course, the producers in France (and all over the world) simply could not resist. It was impossible to make rosé fast enough by the traditional techniques. But you could make enormous quantities of it almost instantaneously—you could control your inventory and meet the demand virtually minute by minute—by the simple process of mixing together already made white wine with already made red wine. Just take the biggest vat you have, fill it about 80 percent full of any old white wine you happen to have in stock, then stir in about 20 percent of any old red wine. If you are lucky, you may get a rather nice color. If you are the greedy type—greedy for faster and bigger profits—you can use this method to get rid of any old junk wines you haven't been able to sell in other ways. Mix well. Design a pretty label marked "Vin Rosé," and you're in business! So the second basic rule for buying rosé is to be very wary of any label simply marked "Vin Rosé," with no indication as to the varieties of the grapes or the sources of the wines.

I am compelled, by years of tasting experience, to say that I have never found a "Vin Rosé," with no further definition on the label, regardless of its price, that has been worth drinking. I have not been able to find one "Vin Rosé" with a tasting score high enough to be included in this book. If we eliminate all the nondescript, poor-quality rosés—generally too sweet, often dull and flat, lacking in vivacity—we are still left with a substantial number of excellent American varietal labels from which to choose. More and more imaginative winemakers are turning their skills toward rosés as one way of meeting the double problem of a glut of red grapes and the continuing preference of many American drinkers for wines to be served ice cold. The best of the American varietal rosés can have a distinctive style reflecting the ideas and personality of its maker, with a perfumed varietal bouquet, a sense of fruity refreshment, and a good balance of tastes and textures. Naturally, the rosés vary considerably in character and personality according to the variety of the grapes used.

ROSÉ OF CABERNET SAUVIGNON

The Cabernet Sauvignon is a difficult grape from which to make rosé. The tannic character is so strong that, even when the skins are left in the juice for only the minimum number of hours to get a fine pink color, there is, usually, already in the wine a slight underlying flavor of Chinese jasmine tea—sometimes just strong enough to pucker one's mouth with tannin—plus a delicate touch of fresh mint. These are not unpleasant flavors, but they make difficulties for the marriages with foods. In spite of this basic problem, André Tchelistcheff, through all the years that he was in charge at Beaulieu Vineyard, held on to the idea that a Rosé of Cabernet might be a very useful stepping-stone for wine beginners to move from an appreciation of white wine (where they all start) to an entry into the world of red wine. André did not have the opportunity or the time to try out his dream until he retired from Beaulieu and became a consultant to the Simi Winery in Sonoma, where he worked with the young winemaker Mary Ann Graf.

I remember being driven to the Alexander Valley for an across-the-board tasting at Simi of the newly developing Graf-Tchelistcheff wines from the barrels. Simi was owned at that time by Russell Green, who invited us all to have lunch in the charming new winery dining room. The kitchen was not yet completed, so a delightful menu of picnic food was brought in by Russ's wife, Betty Jean, while Tchelistcheff opened one of the earliest vintages of his dream wine, the Rosé de Cabernet Sauvignon. Perhaps because of the lovely food —perhaps because of the charm and warm hospitality of the occasion —I found the wine to be near-perfect, with none of the expected faults. Consistently, since that day, I have found the Simi—at first vinified by Mary Ann Graf, and in more recent years by Zelma Long —to be among the best of American rosés.

Others have followed where Simi and André Tchelistcheff led. Bob Kozlowski, at his Kenwood Winery in Sonoma, has produced a very good Cabernet Rosé. Also, since André Tchelistcheff shares his consultation time with Brooks Firestone at his ranch vineyard in the hills above Santa Barbara, André's Cabernet Rosé techniques have been worked out here too by the winemaker, Tony Austin, who has released an outstanding wine under the Firestone label—the wine made from Cabernet Sauvignon vines grown in the Santa Ynez Valley of the Central Coast region.

ROSÉ OF GAMAY

Since the Gamay makes the wonderfully light Beaujolais of France and its equally delicate versions in the United States, it ought, at a first guess, to be an ideal production base for rosé. The grape, by its very nature, is refreshingly fruity, but although it gives excellent color to the wine, it does not seem to have quite a strong enough character. It requires, apparently, a certain degree of concentration of flavor during its vinification. The winemaker who consistently solves this problem with the greatest success is Louis P. Martini, who ages his Gamay Rosé in redwood tanks, giving the faintest (and most welcome) touch of wood to the taste of the wine. In good vintage years, his rosé has a certain dominance and strength, placing it among the very best American Gamay Rosés.

Also, Robert Mondavi, at his family winery in the Napa Valley, makes a rosé that is excellent in good years, using the appellation "Napa Gamay" to indicate that all the grapes that went into the wine were actually grown in the now legally delimited area of the Napa Valley.

ROSÉ OF GRENACHE

The Grenache is the only grape used in the United States almost exclusively for rosé wines. A few halfhearted attempts have been made to produce a red wine from it, but none has been successful. The Grenache has one serious physical fault—the dark skin of the grape is very short of pigment. So if you want to make a deep red wine from it, you certainly have to blend it with a more colorful grape, such as the Carignane or Syrah. The Grenache on its own, or in combination with other grapes, is ideal for rosé and has a brilliant European record in that field.

The Grenache vine comes from Spain, where it is known mainly as the Alicante, but, also, in some districts, as the Granacha. In France, it is the main ingredient of the world-famous Tavel of the Rhône Valley, one of the most brilliant of all rosés. In the south of France, in Provence, along the Mediterranean coast, the Grenache grows well under the hot sun and produces various, excellent dry, slightly sweet, and very sweet wines.

So it was hardly surprising that, when the big upsurge of rosés began in the United States in the 1940s, the wine writer Frank Schoonmaker should have suggested to Louis Benoist, then the president of Almadén Vineyards, that they might try making an American Grenache rosé. There were plenty of Grenache vines growing happily under the hot sun of the California Central Valley, but, until that moment, the grapes had always been used for blending into so-called California Burgundy, and the name of the grape had never appeared on a label. Almadén launched into the project with an enormous national publicity campaign to make the name of Grenache known to every American wine drinker. No grape could ever hope for a better send-off. The wine was nice, clean, dry, refreshing. The entire project was a great success. It was the first American varietal wine to achieve mass distribution. Millions of bottles have been sold. At least twenty other wineries have followed Almadén's lead, but the originator still seems to set the standard. Today, more than thirty years later, Grenache remains California's biggest-selling rosé.

But, although Grenache rosé is a delightful, delicious, perfumed picnic wine, ideal to accompany a roast-beef sandwich beside a waterfall, in terms of pure quality, it has now been overtaken by other, nobler grapes. In the 1950s and 1960s, those "nobler grapes" were in such short supply that they were not available for what was still considered a lesser project, the making of rosé. Today, for the first time in California wine history, there is a glut of red grapes, and some of the best can be turned toward the improvement of the rosé breed.

Beaulieu Vineyard—quite properly, in view of its fame and prestige—is one producer of Grenache rosé that does not follow in the Almadén footsteps. The Beaulieu version is noticeably darker and drier than the others—a beautiful and delightful wine well worth tasting.

ROSÉ OF GRIGNOLINO

There seems to be only one winemaker brash enough to produce a commercial rosé from his particular clone of the Italian Grignolino vine. But, since that winemaker happens to be Joe Heitz, the result consistently turns out to be, to my taste, the best rosé made in the United States. I have already explained (see page 251) how Joe, entirely by accident, found this unusual strain of Grignolino on his land when he bought it, how he has developed and expanded the vineyard, and now makes an interesting red Grignolino wine. At each harvest, he sets aside a certain portion of the crush to make his rosé, which he vinifies, ages, bottles, and releases more quickly than any of his other wines, so that his rosé from last year's harvest is available early in July, for hot-weather drinking—and what delightful, interesting, and solid drinking it is. The wine demands our attention. It is bright cherry and orange in color, richly fruity, dry and tart, with not a perceptible trace of sugar. Each ice-cold mouthful wakes you up and sets you going. This wine has so much character that it can replace a red at a backyard barbecue of red meats.

Joe Heitz has no quality competition for his extraordinary rosé—except for very small amounts, made excellently, but only occasionally and in such minuscule quantities as to be noncommercial, by Tom Kruse at his small winery at Gilroy in Santa Clara.

ROSÉ OF PETITE SIRAH

Although the Petite Sirah vine has had a California career of doubtful virtue (see page 154) as a red wine, it can make an excellently dry and nicely fruity rosé if it is handled with imagination and skill. The best version, by my tasting, is produced by the winemaker Al Baxter, at his Veedercrest Winery near the top of Mount Veeder above the Napa Valley. Al makes some of the most beautiful and serious wines in California, but he seems to expend as much effort and take as much interest in producing the best possible Petite Sirah rosé. He gets his Petite Sirah grapes from the Teldeschi Vineyard in Sonoma and gives the wine a slight and most unusual taste of wood by aging it, for a short time, in small French Limousin oak barrels.

Another excellent Petite Sirah rosé is made by the Mirassou family at their winery in San Jose, with grapes from their own vineyards in Monterey.

ROSÉ OF PINOT NOIR

The Pinot Noir has been in such short supply for so many years and so much in demand for experiments with red wines that it has given us virtually no rosés. Now, at last, the pressure is beginning to ease. The first Pinot Noir rosé came, in minuscule quantities, from Tony Husch at his small winery in the Anderson Valley of the Mendocino district. His wine offered an exciting promise of what an outstanding Pinot Noir rosé could be. Its color was a true, light red. It gave a beautiful sense of fruit, both in the bouquet and in the taste, a feel on the tongue of dry refreshment. It was, obviously, a wine for ideal marriages with many informal and serious foods. Yet it had a character strong enough that it could be iced for thirst-quenching on a hot day. One hoped, at once, for much more of this most excellent wine.

More did follow from Tony and, now, from others. Tom Kruse has produced a small amount of a memorable Pinot Noir rosé at his winery at Gilroy in Santa Clara. David Bruce has paused in his endless struggle toward the production of great red and white wines, at his winery in the Santa Cruz Mountains above Los Gatos, to make a very good Pinot Noir rosé. Brooks Firestone, at his ranch-vineyard in the hills above Santa Barbara, has launched a fine version.

Other winemakers showing proud production include Bob Kozlowski at Kenwood and Zelma Long at Simi in the Alexander Valley, both in Sonoma.

But the dramatic surprise has been a wine made from Pinot Noir grapes grown in the Snake River Valley of Idaho then shipped to Oregon and vinified there by Bill Fuller, at his Tualatin Vineyards at Forest Grove in the Willamette Valley, into a wine of extraordinary quality.

ROSÉ OF ZINFANDEL

Since this uniquely American grape is supremely fruity, often with a distant sense of wild woodland blackberries, it is a tangy-tart berry flavor that comes out strongly in its rosé. This flavor is superimposed onto a wine full of character, generally quite dry with perhaps a more complex balance of tastes and textures than any other type of rosé.

The best version, by my tastings, has been consistently made by the Concannon Vineyard in the Livermore Valley of Alameda in California. The wine is light, fruity, with an interesting and strong character and a beautiful color.

Also (though it is only made in some years) I have tasted an outstanding Zinfandel rosé made by Bob Travers at his Mayacamas mountain vineyard above the Napa Valley. Another memorable rosé comes from the Pedroncelli family winery at Geyserville in Sonoma. They vinify the Sonoma Zinfandel grapes almost completely dry and then give the wine a short period of aging in wood casks, for extra complexity of taste.

Against all these admirable rosés, I am unstinting in my harsh criticism of badly made, untruthfully labeled cheap-jack and run-of-the-mill rosés. They represent poor wine value at any price. But well-made, honestly labeled rosé can offer a great deal of delightfully fruity refreshment, more often than not at a very fair price.

Let me stress again that the rosés with the varietal names on the labels make by far the best drinking, and it is hardly surprising that the grapes that make the best red wines also make the best rosés.

On that historic day in the 1940s, when, so the story goes, Frank Schoonmaker and Louis Benoist were inspecting a Grenache vine-yard at Almadén, they were accompanied by Oliver Goulet, who was then winemaker of the company. When Frank suggested that they should use some of the Grenache grapes to make rosé, it is said that Oliver asked, "What's rosé?" Since that fateful moment, more and more imaginative and skilled winemakers have turned toward rosé as a demanding and interesting challenge. In the most recent years, they have not only been making more and more of it—they have been making it better and better.

I have often been asked by beginning wine drinkers the half-satiric question, "Is there a great rosé?" The answer is, emphatically, that there is not. Nor have I ever found, in my almost twenty years of tasting, a SUPERB or a NOBLE American rosé. All the names that now follow are rated in the FINE classification. But, even within this range, covering a spread of six rating points on my tasting charts, some rosés are distinctly finer than others.

The rosé that consistently rates highest on my tasting charts is the Grignolino that is grown, vinified, and estate bottled by the prestigious Napa winemaker Joe Heitz at his:

• Heitz Wine Cellars near St. Helena in the Napa Valley

My second rosé in the FINE classification is a relatively new entry on the California wine scene—the "Pinot Noir Blanc de Noirs," grown, vinified to a beautiful blush pink, aged, and estate bottled under the supervision of winemaker Forrest Tancer in the dry, rocky hill country of northwestern Sonoma between Santa Rosa and the Pacific Ocean at:

- Iron Horse Vineyards at Sebastopol in the Russian River Valley of Sonoma

My third ranking is a wine outside the traditional pattern of California production from estate-grown grapes. These Pinot Noir vines were grown by Dick Symms on his family fruit ranch in the Snake River Valley of Idaho. After the grapes were harvested, they were shipped to Oregon, where they were crushed, vinified, aged, and bottled under the supervision of the owner-winemaker Bill Fuller, bringing the FINE classification to his winery:

- Tualatin Vineyards at Forest Grove in the Willamette Valley of Oregon

Beyond these three rosés at the top of my list, I have tasted many others also scoring on my charts to bring the FINE classification to these vineyards and wineries. (Since they are all varietal rosés with the character of the wine varying substantially according to the presiding grape, I have thought it useful to divide the following tabulation according to the grape varieties):

ROSÉ OF CABERNET SAUVIGNON

- Dry Creek Vineyard at Healdsburg in the Dry Creek Valley of Sonoma, with its owner-winemaker, David Stare
- Firestone Vineyard at Los Olivos in the Santa Ynez Valley of Santa Barbara, with its winemaker, Alison Green
- Kenwood Vineyards at Kenwood in the Valley of the Moon in Sonoma, with its winemaker-partner, Bob Kozlowski
- Mill Creek Vineyards southwest of Healdsburg in the Russian River Valley of Sonoma
- Monterey Vineyard at Gonzales in the Salinas Valley of Monterey, with its winemaker, Dick Peterson
- Simi Winery at Healdsburg in the Alexander Valley of Sonoma, with its winemaker, Zelma Long

ROSÉ OF GAMAY

- Louis M. Martini Winery at St. Helena in the Napa Valley, with its owner-winemaker, Louis P. Martini

- Robert Mondavi Winery at Oakville in the Napa Valley, with its winemaker, Tim Mondavi

ROSÉ OF GRENACHE

- Almadén Vineyards at San Jose in Santa Clara, with its winemaster, Klaus Mathes
- Beaulieu Vineyard at Rutherford in the Napa Valley
- Burgess Cellars near St. Helena in the Napa Valley, with its owner-winemaker, Tom Burgess
- Chateau Ste. Michelle Vintners at Woodinville near Seattle in Washington State, using grapes from their vineyards in the Yakima Valley of Washington State

ROSÉ OF GRIGNOLINO

- Thomas Kruse Winery at Gilroy in the Santa Cruz Mountains of Santa Clara

ROSÉ OF PETITE SIRAH

- Mirassou Vineyards at San Jose in Santa Clara
- Veedercrest Vineyard high on Mount Veeder in the Mayacamas Range above the Napa Valley, with its owner-winemaker, Al Baxter

ROSÉ OF PINOT NOIR

- David Bruce Winery above Los Gatos in the Santa Cruz Mountains of Santa Clara, with its owner-winemaker, David Bruce
- Chalone Vineyard on Mount Chalone in the Gavilan Range of the Santa Lucia Mountains in Monterey, with its winemaker, Peter Graff, giving his rosé the evocative French name "Vin Gris de Pinot Noir"
- Firestone Vineyard at Los Olivos in the Santa Ynez Valley of Santa Barbara, with its winemaker, Alison Green

- Husch Vineyards at Philo in the Anderson Valley of Mendocino
- Johnson's Alexander Valley Wines at Healdsburg in the Alexander Valley of Sonoma
- Kenwood Vineyards at Kenwood in the Valley of the Moon in Sonoma, with its winemaker-partner, Bob Kozlowski
- Thomas Kruse Winery at Gilroy in the Santa Cruz Mountains of Santa Clara
- Monterey Vineyard at Gonzales in the Salinas Valley of Monterey, with its winemaker, Dick Peterson
- Souverain Cellars near Geyserville in the Dry Creek Valley of Sonoma

ROSÉ OF ZINFANDEL

- David Bruce Winery above Los Gatos in the Santa Cruz Mountains south of San Francisco Bay, with its owner-winemaker, David Bruce
- Concannon Vineyard at Livermore in the Livermore Valley of Alameda
- Pedroncelli Winery northeast of Geyserville on a ridge above the Dry Creek Valley of Sonoma
- Pope Valley Winery in the Pope Valley—a small cut between the hills on the east side of the Napa Valley

CHAPTER VIII

The Golden
Natural Sweet Wines

Some "amateurs of wines" have strange ideas about the sweet wines, or, as they are often inaccurately called, the "dessert wines." These people believe that either you are a sophisticated wine drinker—in which case you must admire and enjoy only dry wines—or you are uneducated and unsophisticated—in which case you enjoy only sweet wines. There is no room, within this theory, for the idea that there is a place and time for dry, another place and time for sweet. Let me say at once that I regard this "either-or" theory as the purest nonsense.

It was on my sixth birthday that my father dribbled a few drops of a gorgeously golden Château d'Yquem into the glass of plain water on my supper table and, in this practical way, began my training in the theory and practice of sweet wines. My father was passionate about them. He was deeply interested in all the fine shadings of the white wines that went with the early courses of dinner—the hors d'oeuvres, soups, eggs, pastas, and fish. He was equally knowledge-able about the strengths and tastes of all the red wines that made perfect marriages with the birds and meats of the main courses. But his interest extended to the moment when the sweet wines came on stage to play their many parts—to cut the richness of the foie gras that was often served after the main dish, to balance certain desserts, to magnify and uplift some very important cheeses, and, finally, to assume a dominant and serious role after the coffee.

My father then had the choice of serving several different kinds of sweet wines. It might be a vintage port, or perhaps a sweet grape liqueur, or an Alsatian Gewürztraminer. In the multiple after-dinner choices, there may be some confusion about the fine shadings be-tween fortified sweet wines, natural sweet wines, and the dozens of sweet liqueurs. What, exactly, do I mean by "a sweet wine"? There are so many kinds. A Spanish Oloroso sherry is, obviously, a sweet wine. So is a Malmsey Madeira. There are some very sweet French Champagnes. There are hundreds of different labels around the world of sugar-sweet, distilled, or fortified—meaning, of course, man-made, not naturally made—drinks that started out as grape wines. Since this chapter is going to concentrate on "natural sweet wines," perhaps we had better begin by defining our terms according to the various ways sweet wines are made.

The simplest way is to make a grape wine and then add sugar to it. I have stood outside the winery of a certain French producer and observed sacks of raw granulated sugar being unloaded from a ten-wheel trailer truck. Sweetness can also be added, in a slightly more sophisticated way, with natural grape sugar syrup. In either case, the resulting sweet wine is not by legal definition a "natural wine" and is not, therefore, included in this book.

As I have already explained (in Preamble Two), a winemaker can, within certain broad limits, make his own decisions as to the final sweetness of the wine he is fermenting. During the fermentation, the yeast cells consume the sugar in the grape juice and convert it into alcohol. Once enough sugar has been converted to provide the percentage of alcohol the winemaker wants, all the remaining sugar can be retained by eliminating the activity of the remaining yeast cells. The traditional way of achieving this result—still practiced in the port vineyards of the Douro Valley of Portugal—is to add a measured amount of high-proof grape brandy. When the alcohol content rises so sharply and suddenly, all the yeast cells are suffocated to death. What is left is not a natural wine, but a sweet, fortified wine. For this reason, neither port, Madeira, nor sherry is included in this book.

The most modern wine technology offers other, more natural ways of inhibiting the yeast cells than killing them off with brandy. If the winemaker begins with one of the varieties of grapes that normally run up to a high content of sugar—such as the Malvasia, the Italian Moscato Canelli, the Muscat of Alexandria, the Muscat de Frontignan—all grapes held on the vine until they are overripe with extremely high sugar—then the winemaker can get all the alcohol he wants and still have enough sugar left over for a strongly sweet wine. This can be achieved at the precisely right moment during the fermentation by chilling the wine by refrigeration to such a low temperature that the yeast cells simply go to sleep and remain dormant. Later, by means of superfine filters, the inert yeast cells can be removed from the liquid, thus stabilizing the sweet wine by an entirely natural process. Some extraordinary sweet wines, classified in this chapter, have been made in this natural way.

From the earliest days of California winemaking in the 1870s, the most famous of all sweet wines, as it still is today, the one that every California producer longed to imitate, was the French Sauternes of Château d'Yquem. One of the wine pioneers, Charles Wetmore, who founded the original Cresta Blanca Winery in the Livermore Valley, was so determined to link his wines to this world-famous château that he traveled to France and visited Yquem. At that hallowed vineyard, Wetmore was given permission to collect root cuttings of the three vine varieties that go into the Yquem wine: the Muscadelle du Bordelais, the Sauvignon Blanc, and the Semillon. They were carried back home and planted in the Livermore Valley. In 1883, these vineyards were sold to Carl Wente, head of Wente Brothers winery. Later, Carl's son, Herman, knowing about the noble ancestry of the vines on his new land, decided to use the three grape types to make a "sweet Sauterne" (in California they always leave off the final French "s"), and he chose to label it—why not!— "Wente Brothers' Château d'Yquem." After all, Herman argued, they are the same grapes, in the same mix, in the same shape of bottle. Why be modest about it? Who would know the difference?

Hardly unexpectedly, the French government lodged a complaint with the U.S. Department of State, and the Bureau of Alcohol moved quickly to let Herman Wente know that his label was neither the perfect tactful ideal in terms of international diplomacy nor the master example of absolutely precise truth in packaging. Washington politely asked Herman, either to withdraw his label voluntarily or to face legal action to compel its elimination—the first time in American wine history that the federal government had intervened in the matter of a bottle label.

The entire wine industry rushed to Herman's defense with the claim that, under the free-enterprise system, Herman had the undoubted right to call any of his wines anything he liked and with the countercharge that Washington's demand was a most unreasonable intrusion into the private affairs of a private industry. But Herman was a very reasonable man. He withdrew his "Château d'Yquem" label. Instead, he named his wine "Château Wente." It was an outstanding sweet wine and a huge success in its time. It was served at the Palace Hotel in San Francisco during the days of that great establishment's dazzling revival after Prohibition.

The Strange Plant Disease with the Midas Touch

American winemakers were imitating the great sweet wines of Europe. But those—the most expensive and most magnificent of the sweet wines of the world—were not produced by filters, or refrigerators, or scientific technique, but by the haphazard, mysterious, almost temperamental workings of a grape disease—a disease so beneficent that it is known in English as "the noble mold," in French as *la pourriture noble*, in German as *das Edelfäule*, both of these translatable as "the noble rot." Its scientific name is *Botrytis cinerea*, and it was discovered, entirely by accident, in the Rhine Valley of Germany in the 1780s—many years before the discovery of that other beneficent mold, Penicillin.

At the time, most of the greatest vineyards of the Rhine were still owned by the Church and worked by monks. It was the rule that, each year before the grapes could be harvested, the bishop of the region had to give his official permission. This particular year, the bishop had gone on a pilgrimage to Rome, but he had promised to be back in time for the start of the grape picking.

During his return journey, on horseback, he and his party were attacked by robbers. The bishop was slightly hurt and had to rest for three weeks before he could continue his journey. He remembered the grapes and sent a messenger ahead with a document properly signed and sealed with the impression of his ring. The messenger was also attacked by highwaymen and never reached his destination.

Meanwhile, back at the vineyard, the abbot who was responsible for the vines was desperate. Something had gone wrong with the grapes still hanging on the vines. Almost all the bunches were covered with a downy, gray, lacelike fuzz. Under it, large numbers of the grapes had become half-dry and shrunken—their skins almost transparent. As day after day of hot sunshine continued, the gossamer of the mold became thicker. More and more of the grapes became discolored, shriveled, withered, and unpleasant. The abbot was in total despair.

At last, a month late, the bishop returned, sick and weak. The abbot was convinced that his entire crop was lost. But he prayed in church and felt inspired to try to salvage what he could. He sent his pickers into the vines. A few weeks later, he discovered to his utter amazement (and that of all his neighbors along the valley) that the developing young wine was the best, the most beautiful golden color, the richest and spiciest, the sweetest they had ever made.

For more than a hundred years, the winemakers of Germany looked for the strange mold, studied it, and worked with it, without really understanding anything about it. It came only in certain districts, to certain vineyards. It was quite temperamental. It did not come every year. In some years, it developed only partially and then stopped. Clearly, it was closely connected to the weather. It seemed to need cool nights, foggy mornings with heavy dew, and hot, dry, sunny days. Without these conditions, it did not appear at all. Without their continuation, it did not develop. The story of this extraordinary mold traveled around the world, and winemakers everywhere began to be on the lookout for it. Soon it was discovered in the Sauternes district of Bordeaux, where it has developed to an extraordinary degree and is uniquely responsible for the marvelous sweet Sauternes wines, including the great Château d'Yquem.

We now know a good deal about how *Botrytis cinerea* works. Part of its natural operation was explained by the bacteriological discoveries of Louis Pasteur. Much more recently, there have been discoveries about *Botrytis,* based on new research at the University of Bordeaux. Some of the bacteriologists there speak of *Botrytis* as "the bugs in the walls."

How do they work to make such magnificent sweet wines? If we regard the microscopic *Botrytis* cells, which fly through the air, as spores, so tiny as to be entirely invisible except under a microscope, then we can say that they grow from and are released by patches of spawn that are hidden in the cracks of the walls of old buildings and in the crevices of the bark of old trees and in little safe pockets among rocks—in thousands of tiny places in and around the old vineyards. By the magic of nature, when the grapes are ripe, the cells are released, each attached to a tiny, invisible feather, so that it can float on the breeze until it lands on a grape. Then it needs a cool, damp, foggy atmosphere, so that it can stick itself to the grape skin and begin its life cycle of boring through the skin to draw nourishment from the grape.

Many cells simultaneously attack the skin of each grape. The skin becomes porous, thin, almost transparent, and tiny little droplets of water from inside the grape appear on the outer surface of the skin. Now the hot sun must come up and evaporate all those little droplets of water, leaving the skin dry again, ready for the next series of droplets to be squeezed out in the cool of the evening. Every night must be cool, to bring out the water. Every day must be dry and hot, to evaporate the water. In this way, day after day, the water in the grape is gradually reduced—like the reduction of a fine sauce in cooking—so that the glycerides, the flavor oils, and the sugar syrup at the heart of each grape become more and more concentrated. Thus the wine that is eventually made from these "practically waterless" grapes is a kind of "concentrated essence" of wine. When the grapes are fully shriveled by the *Botrytis*, there is so little juice in them that it takes one picker an entire day to collect enough grapes for one bottle of wine!

Because *Botrytis* depends on exactly the right weather and, therefore, does not appear every year, the German winemakers have developed precise terms to indicate the degree of sweetness of each wine from the various pickings of each harvest—according to the degree of overripeness of the grapes and the extent of the development of *Botrytis* on them. If, after the general harvest is completed, some sections of the vineyard are left unpicked, so that these grapes will get more sunshine, with a better chance for the development of *Botrytis*, the wine eventually made from these grapes will be labeled, under German law, *spätlese*, "late picked," with the expectation that it will be richer and sweeter, and fetch a higher price on the market.

After this late picking, the grower may decide that some bunches of grapes are worth leaving even longer, to absorb more sunshine, develop even more ripeness, and, hopefully, more *Botrytis*. When these individual bunches are harvested, the wine made from them is labeled, under German law, *auslese*, "selected picking," producing a wine almost always much richer and sweeter, and fetching a substantially higher price.

In one of those years of "perfect weather" (rare in Germany, perhaps once every five years or so), when the sun continues to shine warmly down to the end of November and well into December, some bunches of grapes may still be left on the vines for more development, and, when the pickers go back into the vineyard to comb through it once more, these highly trained experts with their small clippers may actually select individual overripe single grapes! Then the wine made from these will be labeled, under German law, *beerenauslese*, "selected berry picking." Finally (perhaps, on the average, once every ten years), the last individual grapes to be brought in are the dried, shriveled ones, and the wine made from them is labeled, under German law, *trockenbeerenauslese*, "selected dry berry picking." This most aromatic, golden rich, intense, spicy wine, with a perfect balance of sweetness against acid tang, is the highest expression of the beneficent working of *Botrytis cinerea*—the perfection of the art form of the sweet wine. Every drop of it should, quite properly I believe, be worth its weight in gold.

Botrytis cinerea
as an American Citizen

In the early days of American winemaking—even as recently as the post-Prohibition period, and on to the early 1960s—although we all knew about the natural operation of *Botrytis* in Europe, none of us seemed to feel there could be *Botrytized* wines in the United States. I clearly remember one sunny morning in the early 1960s, when, on the campus of the University of California at Davis, I talked to Dr. Harold Berg, who was then chief of the Department of Viticulture and Enology. In his office overlooking his acres of experimental vines and next to his various chemical laboratories and testing workshops, we discussed the question of *Botrytis cinerea*. Harold said that there was plenty of proof that it did exist in the United States. He doubted, though, that the average weather in California would make it easy for the *Botrytis* to develop, to spread, and to blanket our huge, rolling, hillside vineyards. Our weather, on the average, was too extreme in dryness and heat. We did not have enough clammy fogs. Our strong winds would simply blow the *Botrytis* away. It might come, but it would have to be in small, sheltered pockets, here and there. In this prophecy, Harold Berg has been absolutely right.

Then he made a second statement about *Botrytis* in the United States—a deeply significant observation that I have played back to myself many times from the tape on which I recorded it. In his deep, broadly Western voice, Harold Berg said, "Somehow, I don't think that our American vineyard earth is as yet old enough for massive infestation by *Botrytis cinerea*. In Europe, they've been growing vines for thousands of years. We've only been operating, off and on, for a couple of hundred years. It takes time—a long slow time—for *Botrytis* to lay down and gradually expand its spawn in the deep cracks of the walls of very old buildings, in rocks, and old forests near the vineyards, perhaps even in the earth itself around the vines. We don't have thousand-year-old buildings with deeply cracked walls. Everything, with us, is still too new, too clean and sanitary. But the *Botrytis* spores are out there, and, given time, they will develop." Said more than twenty years ago, it was a moment of extraordinary vision.

At just about the same time, another American wine technician was thinking deeply about *Botrytis cinerea*. Myron Nightingale was then in charge of all technical operations at the Cresta Blanca Winery, then a subsidiary of the Schenley whiskey distillers and still operating in the Livermore Valley. Myron had fallen in love with the magnificent *Botrytized* wines of France and Germany. He conceived a massive experiment to discover whether such a wine could be made in the United States. He was sure that *Botrytis* could not yet be developed in an open vineyard. But, if he could set up an indoor space with a completely controlled atmosphere and then infest his grapes with live *Botrytis* spores, the question could be answered as to whether the "noble mold" would develop and whether a superlative sweet wine could be made here.

Myron talked persuasively to the people who held the money-bags at Schenley. In the hope of making wine history, they gave him a massive budget. He built an enormous shed, completely equipped with air-conditioning, humidity, and temperature controls. He arranged for shipments, from France and Germany, of huge quantities of live *Botrytis* spores suspended in a spray solution. He left his Semillon grapes on the vines as long as possible to get them as overripe as they could be under California weather conditions. He harvested the bunches, carefully laid them out in single layers on trays in his huge shed, sprayed them with *Botrytis*, and gave them exactly the "weather conditions" they needed—cool nights, damp foggy mornings, dry hot days—each at the push of the proper button. Everything went according to plan, and, in time, Myron Nightingale and Cresta Blanca released the 1962 "Premier Sweet Semillon," a distinguished wine—not quite as complex as a great French Sauternes, or a magnificent German *trockenbeerenauslese*—but a huge victory for Myron Nightingale.

It seemed somewhat less of a victory to the Schenley accounting people when they saw how much it had all cost against how much they would get back. Myron was not given the opportunity to repeat the experiment. But it was done again, under different circumstances and on a smaller scale, by owner-winemaker Bob Travers, at his Mayacamas mountain winery. His "controlled atmosphere" *Botrytized* sweet Sauvignon Blanc was also excellent and brought the final proof that *Botrytis cinerea* was a practical hope for the U.S. wine industry.

These heavily publicized experiments with natural sweet wines served to alert grape growers everywhere to the possibilities of *Botrytis cinerea*. If the owner of a vineyard is entirely unaware of the "noble mold," he may never notice it at its beginning stage. He may harvest his grapes in the normal way, and those patches of mold, here and there, go out with the bathwater. But, if he is aware of the economics of *Botrytis*—of the increased value of the "nobly rotted" grapes, based on the future high price of the sweet wine that will be made from them—then he will be watching continually for the signs, and, presto, *Botrytis* will suddenly be visible. This is exactly what happened during the middle 1960s. But then a fascinating administrative and bureaucratic legal confrontation developed.

In 1967, Louis P. Martini discovered that some Semillon grapes in one of his vineyards were nicely infected by the *Botrytis* "noble rot." Louis, naturally, was delighted. He watched the grapes for a few more days, then harvested them and brought them, in an open gondola truck, to his winery for some serious experimentation. Now —as I have explained—the U.S. wine industry is closely regulated by both federal and state governmental agencies. The federal bureau responsible for watching the public-health aspects of winemaking is the Food and Drug Administration. It happened that, when Louis P. Martini's truckload of *Botrytized* Semillon arrived at the winery, a federal inspector was on the premises, and he took a cursory look at those moldy grapes. He was absolutely horrified by what he saw. One section of the U.S. federal wine law stipulates that "wine for commercial distribution shall be produced only from clean, healthy and sanitary grapes." When Louis started explaining to the federal inspector, who had never heard of *Botrytis cinerea*, the latter said that as far as he was concerned, it was gray rot, and that under federal law they should be destroyed. Otherwise, the Martini winery would be prosecuted and, if found guilty of manufacturing a tainted food-stuff, would be fined and closed.

Louis P. Martini is not exactly a "li'l ole winemaker." His family firm is one of the most influential and prestigious in the United States. In the next few hours, Louis burned up the telephone wires —to Washington, to the various federal offices in California, to the governor of California in Sacramento. He gave quite a few administrative people a short course on the history of sweet wines in Europe over the past 200 years. The Food and Drug Administration decided to investigate immediately. One of its representatives appeared at a well-known San Francisco retail wineshop in order to requisition some bottles of French Sauternes and German *trockenbeerenauslese* because they had all been made with "unclean, spoiled and rotten grapes" and should be analyzed forthwith to make sure that the wine did not contain any dangerous bacteria or poisonous substances that could be harmful to the American public. Perhaps these wines ought to be banned from importation! The FDA representative chose a number of European labels, but when he was shown a Château d'Yquem and told that it cost $200 the bottle, he said, "I don't think we'll need that one. No wine at *that* price could possibly be poisonous."

The threat of prosecution under the U.S. wine laws, or the pure food laws, continued to hang over Louis P. Martini—and soon, also, over Karl Wente, who had followed his uncle Herman as head of Wente Brothers in the Livermore Valley and who was now also becoming quite deeply involved with *Botrytis cinerea*. Karl wanted to enlarge his vineyards, but this was impossible in the Livermore Valley because of the expansion of the city of Oakland. So he took the "great leap forward" and went south to buy vineyard land in the Salinas Valley of Monterey—in a narrow canyonlike area, near the town of Greenfield, called the Arroyo Seco. Very soon it was discovered that this was one of the rare pockets for the natural development of *Botrytis*. In 1969, the weather was right for the "noble mold" to envelop the Wente White Riesling grapes, and Karl was able, for the first time in the United States, to release a naturally developed, noble sweet wine, the equivalent of a German *spätlese*. He was able to do it again in 1972—with improvements resulting from greater experience with the *spätlese* techniques. Then, in 1973, with the weather cooperating to the point of perfection, Wente was able to produce a magnificent, extra-rich *auslese* that astonished even experienced German tasters, who found in it the complexity of a true *auslese*.

Then *Botrytis* came to the Napa Valley. There had been small signs of it, here and there, for several years, but the weather had not been right. However, in 1973, there was the proper succession of coolness and heat, of dews and fogs, of alternating dampness and dryness in the air, of fierce midday sunshine. With surprising speed, one of the main White Riesling vineyards at Rutherford of the Freemark Abbey Winery became heavily infested with the gossamer lace of the "noble rot." The young winemaker of Freemark Abbey, Jerry Luper, guided it through with extraordinary devotion and skill. The final result was something quite new in American wine, the Freemark Abbey White Riesling "Edelwein" (the German word for "noble wine")—marvelously rich, a fantastic balance between sweetness and lemony tang, the refreshment of the fruit coming through, yet with a touch of herbs and spices—clearly and strongly an American equivalent of a German *beerenauslese*.

This "landmark wine" proved, once and for all time, that there were no limitations on the future possibilities for magnificent golden sweet nectars in the United States. With my first sip of this glorious "Edelwein," I realized, instantly, that our winemakers were not going to suffer under any permanent disability from what Dr. Harold Berg had called the youth of our vineyard earth. Although Europe had a 200-year head start, we, after our first ten years of trying, were already catching up and moving into a challenging position.

In 1974, the federal authorities in Washington—finally freeing themselves from the concept that *Botrytized* grapes were "unclean, spoiled and rotten"—promulgated new regulations defining more sharply the various types of sweet wine and separating the new American tradition from the old German one. Up to this time, since most of the techniques with *Botrytized* grapes were German, it had been fashionable to use German words on American labels. For example, Miljenko "Mike" Grgich, when he was in charge of technical operations at Chateau Montelena, in the Napa Valley, made two golden sweet White Rieslings, both of which he labeled as *auslese*. When this word is used on a label in Germany, the law requires that the wine shall achieve certain legally defined levels of alcohol and residual sugar. Mike's wines, although he called them *auslese,* did not reach the German legal standards and, thus, appeared as unfair competition to the German wine industry. So Washington ruled that German words should no longer be used on American labels— henceforward *spätlese* would be translated as "Late Harvest" and *auslese* would be "Selected Clusters."

The Iceman Cometh
and Maketh Lovely Wine

There is one other way of making natural golden sweet nectar wines, the result of a freak of nature that happens, perhaps, only once every ten years. So far, it has been an exclusive German technique. If you look at a world map of wine regions, you will see that the German vineyards of the Moselle and the Rhine are among the most northerly. This is why they suffer, occasionally, from very rough weather. One of their fiercest dangers is a sudden ice storm at the precise moment when the ripe grapes are still hanging on the vines, a few days before the harvest. Fortunately, such a disaster is usually local —involving, perhaps, one wine village and its surrounding vineyards. Let us imagine, for our descriptive purposes, that it happens (as it often has) in the village of Bernkastel on the Moselle, with its steep, cliff-hanging vineyards above the river.

Suddenly, around midnight, the temperature drops dramatically to about 20 degrees Fahrenheit. Warning thermometers, fixed outside bedroom windows, turn on wake-up alarm bells. Sleepy fingers switch on the radios announcing the fact that an ice storm is rolling down toward Bernkastel from the high mountains. All the church bells start tolling the alarm. Management people from the vineyards run from house to house waking up the regular pickers, but the whole village is aware of the emergency, and hundreds of volunteers —fathers, mothers, young people, and teenagers—rush to get dressed in their warmest clothes and, carrying flashlights, hurry toward the vineyards. Arrived there, they are given heavy clippers and thick, insulated gloves.

Meanwhile, the ice hail has fallen, and each single grape is frozen solid into a rock-hard, round pebble, covered with a coating of ice. Just as home pipes will burst when the water inside them freezes, so the skin of each grape has split inside the ice shell. If these grapes were to be left hanging until the morning thaw, all their juice and pulp would simply fall to the ground, and the entire crop would be a total loss. What follows now is the desperate method for saving at least part of the value of the crop.

At breakneck speed, the solidly frozen bunches of grapes are cut off, loaded into the baskets, and lowered down the terraced cliff face to waiting trucks on the road below, for the five-minute trip across the bridge to the winery on the other side of the river. It is all icy, back-breaking work. A basket of frozen grapes, encased in the ice that fell from the sky, weighs about three times as much as the grapes alone.

In the winery, which is kept as cold as possible by opening all the windows, the frozen bunches are at once loaded into the press. The solid ice will not go through. What does trickle down into the fermentation vat is the heart of each grape—those thicker, higher-density, more-syrupy liquids, which did not freeze; the glycerides that give body to the wine, the flavor oils and acids, the natural sugar syrup, and certain other chemical components. The total amount of liquid that flows from each ton of grapes is, of course, less than half the normal average. The rest of the grape juice remains behind as solid ice. As this mass of crushed ice builds up in the top of the crusher, it is shoveled out and thrown away. Load after load of frozen grapes give up their heart juices in this unnatural way.

As the dawn comes up over the hills, the job is done. The crop has been rescued. The fermentation of the heart juices begins. The final result is very much the same as if the grapes had been "evaporated and reduced" by *Botrytis cinerea*. What eventually goes into the bottle is the very essence of a golden, honey-sweet nectar of the wine. It may be labeled, under German wine law, as an *Eiswein*. A great *Eiswein* from a famous vineyard may fetch a starting price of, say, $500 per bottle. After all, think of the hand labor that went into it during the night of frozen disaster.

There has never been, so far as I know, an ice storm over the vineyards of California, which are located a great deal farther south than those on the Moselle or the Rhine. But it has happened 600-odd miles to the north of the upper California border, in the Yakima Valley, the central fruit and wine region of Washington State, where the summer temperatures may go up over 110 degrees Fahrenheit, but the falls and winters are cold. During the night of November 8, 1978, the temperature suddenly plummeted to below 20 degrees Fahrenheit, and, although there was apparently no precipitation of ice hail, all the White Riesling grapes hanging on the vines in two vineyards were frozen.

You may well ask what these or any grapes were doing still hanging on the vines at that late date. A good question. All the normal harvesting of the dozens of vineyards in the district had long since been completed. These two remaining vineyards were partially infested with *Botrytis cinerea*, and, solely for that reason, the growers were "hanging on" and taking a fairly large risk in the hope of catching more sunshine and developing more of the "noble mold." Then, with no warning, the ice ax fell.

The first victim was the Sagemoor Farms on the Columbia River at North Richland, which does not make its own wines but sells its expertly grown grapes to many of the producers of the region. Those White Riesling grapes still on the vines were already the property of Bill Preston, owner of the Preston Wine Cellars, a few miles away at Pasco. The vines had been netted over to encourage the development of the *Botrytis*. Soon after midnight, a call came to the Preston wine-maker, Robert Griffin—the voice in the night from Sagemoor said, "My God! the grapes are frozen solid. What do we do?" Bob had only read about German *Eiswein*. He had never actually faced the problem. This was, almost certainly, the first time that an *Eiswein* might be made in the United States. He said, "Obviously, we'll have to pick and crush them tonight. Can you get hold of your pickers? We'll be right over."

The scene developed exactly as in Bernkastel. Bill, Bob, their families and friends, the entire staff of the Preston winery, plus as many helpers as could be corralled by telephone, drove hell-for-leather the five miles or so to the Sagemoor vineyard. The frozen grapes were cut down, loaded, trucked over to Preston, and crushed by dawn. Bill later told me, "By God, Roy, when those hard-ball grapes went into my crusher, it sounded as if we were trying to grind up solid gravel. The noise was so awful I thought every one of my machines would be wrecked. We finally gave up crushing and just put the frozen mash straight into the press." Bob added, "We normally expect to extract about one hundred seventy gallons of juice from every ton of grapes. This time, we got only about seventy gallons of syrupy liquid from each ton of ice mash."

The Preston "essence of wine" fermented very slowly, through the rest of November, all of December, and to the end of January. Then it was aged for more than a year and, finally, bottled for the start of distribution during 1980. It turned out to be a lovely, golden nectar. The Bureau of Alcohol in Washington, D.C., insisted that it be labeled, not as *Eiswein*, but as "Ice Wine."

The second vineyard to be frozen solid by the November 1978 ice front is known as Yakima Rattlesnake #3 and is owned by the largest producer in Washington State, Chateau Ste. Michelle, with its huge winery in the suburb of Woodinville, just outside Seattle. This means normally that grapes harvested in the various vineyards in the Yakima Valley have to be carried in refrigerated trucks for 200-odd miles over one of the high passes of the Cascade Mountains and down to the north side of Seattle. When the emergency after-midnight call came through to Ste. Michelle's winemaker, Joel Klein, he realized at once that the frozen grapes would thaw out and be ruined if they were trucked for so many hours. Fortunately, there was a small subsidiary winery at Grand View in the Yakima Valley, and, by urgent telephoning from Seattle, Joel was able to get it opened up and staffed within two or three hours. Pickers were also alerted by telephone, and the Bernkastel scenario was repeated. Joel headed his car up over the mountains toward Yakima.

Incidentally, the reason these White Riesling grapes were still on the vines was again a partial infestation with *Botrytis*. Joel was so keen to make golden nectar wines that he had been spraying certain Riesling vineyards with imported *Botrytis* spores, hoping that the weather would cooperate and that the "noble mold" would develop. There had been signs of it in the Yakima Rattlesnake #3 vineyard, so the grapes had been left "hanging on," in the hope of more sunshine and mold development. Then the ice attacked.

Joel's night operations were highly successful. Chateau Ste. Michelle has fermented, vinified, aged, and bottled a beautiful "Ice Wine," with the extraordinary sweetness of 18 percent of residual sugar, but balanced by an excellent tang of lemony refreshment. Both the Chateau Ste. Michelle and the Preston are American golden nectar wines to remember for a long time to come.

Beyond these freaks of nature, the newest developments in our golden sweet wines are dramatic, even explosive, in terms of qualitative and quantitative progress. We have all discovered that there is a strong demand for these beautiful wines, these smooth essences of nectar, even at the highest prices ever commanded by American wines. The law of supply and demand is in full operation. The growers are going to use every scientific stimulant toward the production of the grapes. The winemakers will devote more and more of their energies toward the making of all the different types of sweet wines —as fast and as often as nature allows.

When I began doing formal tastings and chartings of the early examples of the golden sweet wines, in the late 1960s and early 1970s, they were being produced by fewer than a dozen California wineries. Now, as we progress through the decade of the 1980s, my estimate is that more than fifty additional producers, including some of the very top winemakers, are vinifying the golden sweet wines. It is now estimated that approximately 25 percent of all White Riesling wines are sweet types.

Naturally, you cannot produce them without the overripe, *Botrytized* grapes, and there is always some risk involved for the grower who tries to develop the perfect fruit for the perfect golden wine. Each year, he must gamble on the weather, letting his grapes hang there on the vines, hoping for extra sunshine. If the weather goes wrong, nothing is left at the end but a vineyard of really rotten, entirely useless, totally lost grapes. His gross income for the year will have vanished. Yet more and more growers, working from more and more experience, with better and better weather forecasting services available to them, have been extremely lucky and have been rapidly increasing the production of perfect fruit available to the California winemakers.

So the decade of the 1980s will be a time of exciting expansion, with one new and magnificent golden wine after another coming on to the market. A few of them—after only about twenty years of California production—may succeed in achieving true greatness even when judged by the highest standards of 200 years of European experience.

A Note on the Classifications
of the Sweet Wine Vineyards and Wineries

The following classifications of the top vineyards and wineries that produce the best of the American golden sweet wines will have to be interpreted slightly differently from the classification lists for other types of wine in the other chapters of this book. So far, we have been dealing with the "standard" production processes of fermenting and vinifying normally ripe grapes and painstakingly and slowly converting the fruit into drinkable wine with maximum care, imagination, and technical skill. Thus, with each vineyard and winery, there can be a certain continuity, from year to year, in the character and recognizable family traits of the wine, reflecting the personality and philosophy of the winemaker. If a great winemaker has produced great red wines regularly over the years, you can be sure that, even though in certain years the weather prevents the making of the very greatest wines, the products will always be in the top group, always worth searching out and tasting.

No such continuing guarantee is possible with the wines described in this chapter. The golden sweet wines are dependent on the evanescent factors of the growth (or nongrowth) of a natural mold that responds to narrow and precise weather conditions. We are dealing with a temperamental continuity. The winemaker who produced a superb golden nectar last year because nature's bounty provided overripe *Botrytized* grapes may not be able to make any kind of sweet wine this year, or next year, or the year after that.

What the following lists tell us is that these vineyards and wineries have, in past years, produced golden sweet nectar wines that have been rated at SUPERB, NOBLE, or FINE quality and that these technicians have the experience, the know-how, the scientific skill to take immediate advantage of all current and future opportunities as the grapes grow in the vineyards. My own feeling, then, is that if we all want to continue to explore the world of the American natural sweet wines, with its convolutions of aromatic balances and combinations, of tastes and of textures, we can reasonably expect to find many of the most dramatic new golden sweet wines under the label names listed below. Where there is a current wine available and the percentage of residual sugar is known, I give that figure as an indication of the sweetness of the wine—as explained in Preamble Two.

The best golden sweet wine I have ever tasted up to the moment of this writing was made in 1977 from "Late Harvest—Selected Clusters" of heavily *Botrytized* Gewürztraminer grapes grown in the Yakima Valley of Washington State, fermented and vinified by owner-winemaker Mike Wallace, who shares control of the family vineyard with his father, producing a magnificent wine named "Die Sonne," "the sun." I was one of the judges, in 1978, at the Pacific Northwest Wine Festival when we awarded a gold medal to this aromatic, beautiful, and luscious wine. It brings the SUPERB classification to its makers:

- Hinzerling Vineyards at Prosser at the base of the Rattlesnake Hills in the Yakima Valley of Washington State, a golden nectar with 15.6 percent residual sugar

My second choice among the golden sweet wines of the United States was made by Zelma Long in 1978 in the classic California "Johannisberg Riesling" style from "Late Harvest" *Botrytized* White Riesling grapes grown on the Long family vineyard, fermented and vinified by her at the winery which she still runs with her former husband, Bob. This beautifully aromatic wine—the first released by Zelma and Bob from their newly constructed winery—was deliberately held low in alcohol in order to stress the tang of the fruit against the golden richness of the sugar, giving it a perfection of balance and bringing the SUPERB classification to its makers:

- Long Vineyard on Pritchard Hill above the Napa Valley, with the golden nectar containing 8.5 percent residual sugar

My third golden sweet nectar wine, by the scores on my rating chart, is the 1978 "Ice Wine" described earlier in this chapter, harvested under storm conditions and vinified by winemaker Robert Griffin to a magnificent wine, bringing the SUPERB classification to:

- Preston Wine Cellars at Pasco in the Columbia Basin of Washington State, the golden wine with 10 percent residual sugar

I have also tasted and rated other golden sweet wines bringing the SUPERB classification to these vineyards and wineries:

- Alatera Vineyards near the town of Napa in the Napa Valley, with "Late Harvest—Bunch Selected" White Riesling, vinified to a golden nectar of quite extraordinary balance and complexity

- Burgess Cellars near St. Helena in the Napa Valley, with its owner-winemaker, Tom Burgess, using "Late Harvest" *Botrytized* White Riesling grapes from the Winery Lake Vineyards in the Carneros Hills above the valley, the golden wine with 5.2 percent sugar
- Richard Carey Winery at San Leandro in Alameda on San Francisco Bay, with its owner-winemaker, Dick Carey, using "Late Harvest" *Botrytized* Gewürztraminer grapes from the Bien Nacido Vineyards above Santa Barbara, the golden wine having 6 percent sugar
- Chateau St. Jean at Kenwood in Sonoma, with its winemaker, Richard Arrowood, with "Individual Dried Bunch Selected —Late Harvest" White Riesling from the Robert Young Vineyard in the Alexander Valley, the golden honeyed nectar with a fantastic 37.5 percent residual sugar
- Chateau Ste. Michelle Vintners at Woodinville near Seattle in Washington State, with its former winemaker, Joel Klein, vinifying their "Ice Wine" (discussed on page 200) from *Botrytized*, frozen White Riesling grapes to a golden nectar of regal luxury at 17 percent residual sugar
- The Christian Brothers on Mont La Salle above the Napa Valley, with its winemaker, Brother Timothy, using grapes from "Late Harvest" heavily *Botrytized* White Riesling from their own vineyard at 10 percent residual sugar
- Freemark Abbey Winery near St. Helena in the Napa Valley, with its former winemaker, Jerry Luper, making their "Edelwein" from "Late Harvest" heavily *Botrytized* White Riesling from their vineyard at Rutherford, with a residual sugar of 15.5 percent
- Jekel Vineyard at Greenfield in the Salinas Valley of Monterey, from "Late Harvest" *Botrytized* White Riesling, with 10 percent residual sugar
- Louis M. Martini Winery at St. Helena in the Napa Valley, with its owner-winemaker, Louis P. Martini, vinifying a superb series of classic golden Muscatels
- Joseph Phelps Vineyards near St. Helena in the Napa Valley, with winemaker Walter Schug vinifying "Late Harvest—Se-

lected Bunches" of White Riesling golden nectar of extraordinary richness with 30 percent residual sugar

- Wente Brothers at Livermore in the Livermore Valley of Alameda, with its owner-winemaker, Eric Wente, with "Late Harvest—Selected Bunches" of White Riesling from their vineyards in the Arroyo Seco Canyon of Monterey

At the next scoring level I have tasted golden sweet wines that have brought the NOBLE classification to these vineyards and wineries:

- Almadén Vineyards at San Jose in Santa Clara, with its winemaster, Klaus Mathes, vinifying "Late Harvest" *Botrytized* White Riesling to a golden nectar up to 11.7 percent residual sugar
- Bargetto Winery at Soquel in the Santa Cruz Mountains south of San Francisco Bay, with its owner-winemaker, Lawrence Bargetto, using "hand selected *Botrytized* bunches" of White Riesling from the Tepusquet Vineyard for a golden wine with 10 percent sugar
- Beringer Vineyards near St. Helena in the Napa Valley, with its winemaker, Myron Nightingale, vinifying "Late Harvest—Selected Bunches" of White Riesling from Sonoma
- Caymus Vineyards at Rutherford in the Napa Valley, with "Late Harvest—Selected Bunches" of White Riesling
- Firestone Vineyard at Los Olivos in the Santa Ynez Valley of Santa Barbara, with its winemaker, Alison Green, using "Selected Harvest" grapes
- Grgich Hills Cellar at Rutherford in the Napa Valley, with its winemaker, Miljenko "Mike" Grgich, with "Late Harvest" White Riesling with 6.7 percent residual sugar
- Gundlach-Bundschu Vineyard at Vineburg in the Valley of the Moon in Sonoma, with its winemaker, John Merritt, vinifying *Botrytized* grapes from the McFadden Ranch to a golden nectar with 11.6 percent residual sugar
- Mayacamas Vineyards on the Mayacamas Range above the Napa Valley, with its owner-winemaker, Bob Travers, pioneering the spray-*Botrytized* Sauvignon Blanc
- Robert Mondavi Winery at Oakville in the Napa Valley, with its winemaker, Tim Mondavi, using their own heavily *Botry-*

tized White Riesling grapes to make a golden nectar with the extraordinary residual sugar of 21 percent

- Raymond Winery at Calistoga in the Napa Valley, using "Late Harvest—Selected Clusters" of White Riesling
- Sterling Vineyards at Calistoga in the Napa Valley, with "Late Harvest" *Botrytized* Chenin Blanc
- Stony Hill Vineyard on the mountain above the Napa Valley, with its winemaker, Mike Chelini, vinifying the estate's "Late Harvest—Selected Bunches" heavily *Botrytized* Semillon grapes into their elegant, golden, light "Semillon de Soleil," with 10 percent residual sugar
- Turgeon & Lohr Winery at San Jose in Santa Clara, vinifying "Late Harvest—Selected Clusters" of heavily *Botrytized* Pinot Chardonnay from the Tanoak Vineyard in the Arroyo Seco Canyon
- Veedercrest Vineyard high on Mount Veeder in the Mayacamas Range above the Napa Valley, with its owner-winemaker, Al Baxter, vinifying an unusual blend of "Late Harvest—Selected Clusters" of heavily *Botrytized* White Riesling with an added 8 percent of Gewürztraminer and 5 percent Muscat of Alexandria into a golden nectar of rare delicacy with 7.5 percent residual sugar

At the next ranking, I have tasted and scored golden sweet wines that have brought the FINE classification to these vineyards and wineries:

- Callaway Vineyard at Temecula in the Riverside district of southern California, with its own "Late Harvest" Chenin Blanc, vinified into a golden sweet wine named "Sweet Nancy" with 7 percent residual sugar
- Chateau Montelena at Calistoga in the Napa Valley, using "Late Harvest" *Botrytized* grapes
- Heitz Wine Cellars near St. Helena in the Napa Valley, with its owner-winemaker Joe Heitz vinifying "Late Harvest" *Botrytized* Semillon into a golden wine named "Alicia"
- Sonoma Vineyards at Windsor in Sonoma, with winemaker Rod Strong vinifying "Late Harvest" *Botrytized* White Riesling, from the LeBaron Vineyard, the golden wine having 7 percent residual sugar
- Yakima River Winery at Prosser in the Yakima Valley of Wash-

ington State, with its owner-winemaker, John Rauner, vinifying "Late Harvest" *Botrytized* White Riesling as the impressive first release from his small winery, a golden wine with 5 percent residual sugar

CHAPTER IX

The American
Native Sparkling Wines

There is always, first, the crucial question: Are they Champagnes, or champagnes? The French point of view is that Champagne is a place —a historic region (north of Burgundy, east of Paris, with the glorious city of Reims as its showplace) and that only sparkling wines made within the legal limits of the region should be labeled Champagne. That is the law, wherever the French government has jurisdiction.

In 1976, when the giant French conglomerate firm of Moët-Hennessy started producing sparkling wines in the Napa Valley—although their American operation is, of course, technically owned and run by a subsidiary American corporation under American law— they stayed within French law, never even whispered the word "Champagne," and have firmly called their product "Napa Valley Sparkling Wine."

There have been major court battles in Britain, Canada, and Germany, among other places, instigated by the French producers, seeking to prevent the use of the word "Champagne" on the labels of non-French sparkling wines. Most of the courts have accepted the French point of view.

On the other hand, the U.S. legal position is that "champagne" is a generic word describing a type of sparkling wine and that we have every right to use it, provided that we print in front of it some qualifying word such as "California champagne," or "New York State champagne," or "American champagne." We also feel that we have the right, according to the same legal argument, to use the words "cognac," "port," "sherry," "burgundy," "chablis," or even "bordeaux." We also make cheese with holes and call it "American

Swiss." We are the only country in the world that gets away with all this.

Apart from the legal and political maneuvering, the scientific way of deciding whether an American champagne is the same as a French Champagne is to compare them as sparkling wines. What are the differences and similarities between a sparkling wine made in the Napa Valley of California and one made in Epernay in the Champagne region of France? A great many facts are known about both places and both wines.

First, there are the comparative climates. If you check the general latitude of Epernay and Reims (about 49 degrees north), then trace it across the Atlantic and on across the United States, you won't hit northern California, but about 800 miles to the north, roughly at the border where Washington State meets British Columbia. And if you start with the latitude of the Napa Valley (about 36 degrees north), and trace your way back toward Europe, you will find yourself among the desert sands of Morocco in North Africa. This large difference in latitude between Epernay and Napa makes for quite a difference in the weather. Napa days are that much hotter and the sunshine is a great deal brighter, which means, in terms of plant photosynthesis of sunlight energy, that the California grapes ripen much faster and become much sweeter, with considerably less acid than the French grapes.

This climate requires different growing and production techniques on the American side. Too much sugar in the grapes leads to a sparkling wine with too much alcohol dominating a taste that is not dry enough. Too little acid means that the sugar is not balanced by a lemony tang, so that the finished wine can easily become cloyingly sweet. If the fruity refreshment is lacking, there is no counterbalance to any remaining natural sweetness. The wine tastes bland and uninteresting. Without being guilty of the dreadful sin of using an acid additive (a not entirely unknown procedure), a winemaker cannot increase the acid originally provided for him by the grapes. But he can easily lose some of the acid through inefficient techniques during the fermentation and vinification. So there are special, uniquely American methods for producing our top sparkling wines.

Virtually every region in the United States where sparkling wines are made is very hot in summer and has a dangerously low average rainfall during the summer months when the grapes are developing and ripening. The result is that the grapes grow too ripe and too sweet too soon and have to be harvested, for sparkling wines, while still unripe, usually toward the end of August. If this is not done with extreme accuracy of timing, in addition to the greatest of care and skill, the resulting wine can have a background character of earthiness, of slightly bitter sourness, of basic unripeness, of heaviness and herbaceous weediness. These are the unpleasant characteristics of a poorly made sparkling wine, which almost always will lack complexity, depth, and fruity richness.

The second major difference between the New World and the Old is in the earth. In the Champagne region of France, the vines are grown in almost pure limestone, an extremely poor soil that gives the grapes intense flavors because (according to the old proverb) they "suffer." In fact, the soil and temperature conditions in the French Champagne region are so bad that the growers are always running dangerously near to the impossibility of growing grapes at all. This is why, centuries ago, they put in the bubbles—a brilliant marketing device—to enable them to sell their, until then, sour and undrinkable wines from their almost always unripe grapes. No such problems plague our North American grape growers. We make our sparkling wines from fat, pampered, rich grapes, which we have to harvest before they are fully ripe so that they won't get too sweet. It's all completely different from France, and it makes a very different wine.

Third, there is the blend of the grape varieties. On both sides of the Atlantic, the sparkling winemakers use the Pinot Chardonnay and the Pinot Noir. Our Pinot Chardonnay is a good deal more aromatic, more solid, stronger than the French. That alone makes for a substantial difference. But, then, the remainder of the traditional blend is entirely different. In France, they add the Pinot Meunier. We do not grow it, so we use the Pinot Blanc, the Folle Blanche, and, in small quantities for certain sparkling wines, a new grape, crossbred at the University of California at Davis by Dr. Harold Olmo, between the Gewürztraminer and Semillon—a California variety named Flora.

How can anyone seriously argue that two sparkling wines, made on two different continents, from two different blends of grapes, can be the same wine, both to be labeled and marketed as "Champagne"? Why do American sparkling-wine producers still feel that they must imitate the French? Our American native sparkling wines are now so outstandingly good that they do not have to be copies of something else from some other part of the world. Surely now we are mature enough, self-assured enough, and sophisticated enough to cut our umbilical cord to Europe.

Every American sparkling wine has to meet certain special conditions during its production—and remember that "production," in terms of a top sparkling wine, will be somewhere between two and five years. They are extremely expensive to produce, involving much time and hand labor, many delicate operations, much complicated and high-capital equipment in the winery. So the sparkling wines now share with the sweet wines the highest prices among all American labels.

An Intelligent Reading of the Label
Shows the Top Quality and the Best Value

There are certain legal requirements for basic information on the label of a sparkling wine, and, if you can understand the formal words, you will begin to know how good the wine in the bottle is and whether it is worth the asking price. There are three general methods for making sparkling wine, and the label must tell you which method was used—so you know, at first glance, whether you are facing a mass-produced product, or one of the hand-crafted wines, or something in between.

The cheapest way of putting bubbles into wine is by forcing carbon-dioxide gas into the liquid by the process of carbonation. This is equivalent to making alcoholic club soda. Under international law, the product may not be called "sparkling wine," but must be labeled as "aerated wine." It hardly needs to be said that no wine of this type is listed in this chapter.

The mass-produced true sparkling wines are almost all made by the so-called bulk process invented by the Frenchman Eugéne Charmat. After the grapes have been fermented and vinified into a basic still wine—or, perhaps, several different still wines blended together —it is run into a large tank, which can be sealed off so that pressure can be developed within it. Then a second fermentation is initiated within the wine by the addition of more yeast, but the released carbon-dioxide gas is imprisoned within the liquid by the pressure in the tank. Finally, this "wine under pressure" is filtered and bottled (still under pressure), so that the bubbles will not escape until the bottle is eventually uncorked and the wine poured. This manufacturing process is easy, efficient, and fast, but it is difficult to develop delicacy of flavor in the finished sparkling wine. All labels must be marked "bulk process" or "Charmat process." Any sparkling wines made by this process are indicated as such in the lists at the end of this chapter.

The second principal method of production, which can achieve a considerably higher level of quality—although it still allows manufacturing speed and substantial automation—is known as the "transfer process." The basic blend of the new still wine is run into the bottles and then measured amounts of yeast are added just before the bottles are tightly corked. The secondary fermentation then takes place inside the sealed bottle, under pressure, so that the bubbles of carbon-dioxide gas are, again, imprisoned in the liquid.

Eventually, of course, after the proper time for aging and development, the wine has to be cleared by the removal of the yeast. This is done by opening the bottle under pressure, emptying its contents into a big tank, still under pressure, thousands of bottles at a time, removing the dead yeasts by filtering them out, and, finally, filling the now perfectly clear sparkling wine back into clean bottles, each with a suitable small dosage of sugar. Sparkling wine made in this way must legally be labeled "naturally fermented in the bottle." Some very good American sparkling wines are made in this way, but none of the absolute best. These "transfer process" wines are indicated in the lists at the end of this chapter.

The third and most prestigious process of production—the one involving the greatest expense, the largest amount of skilled hand labor, the longest time for aging and gradual development—is always known by its French name, *la méthode champenoise,* the only method legally permitted in the Champagne region. It is, in fact, used for the top sparkling wines of every region all over the world. The basic blend of still wine is filled into the bottle in which it will remain until it is consumed. A precisely controlled amount of yeast is added to each bottle, which, then, is tightly corked. The secondary fermentation develops inside the bottle, producing about eighty to ninety pounds of carbon-dioxide-gas pressure. The yeast remains in the bottle for a period of from two to five years, depending on the prestige, the projected price, and the planned quality of the product.

Here, again, the wine must be cleared by the removal of the yeast. Gradually, over a period of several weeks, the bottle is turned upside down and shaken so that the yeast solids slide down and settle in the neck, just behind the cork. The neck is then frozen solid in a special machine, and the plug of ice, including all the yeast, is instantly removed, and the bottle is topped off with a measured dosage of natural grape sugar dissolved in a tiny measure of brandy, plus extra wine of the same vintage to fill up the space. This operation, which is completed in a second or two, for minimum loss of internal gas, is called "disgorgement." The permanent cork is then put in, and the bottle is ready for slight extra aging and, finally, distribution and sale. American sparkling wines made in this finest way must always be legally labeled "naturally fermented in this bottle." The *méthode champenoise* labels are indicated in the lists at the end of this chapter.

In discussing the different ways of making sparkling wines I am not trying to suggest that overall quality is entirely linked to the method of manufacture. That would be a snobbish point of view, and it is simply not true. The Christian Brothers, for example, consistently show us, year after year, with their California champagne, that the Charmat bulk process, when it is efficiently and honorably used, can produce a very good sparkling wine indeed. The fact that all the most outstanding labels come under the *méthode champenoise* system is not only due to the system but also to the general principle that these top producers, who command the highest prices, use the best grapes to make the finest base wines, employ the most highly skilled winemakers, have installed the most modern equipment, and have the capital resources for the slow aging of the wines on the best strains of yeasts, for many years if necessary.

In all of the United States, there is only a handful of these top-quality producers, but their number is slowly and steadily increasing. An industry survey in 1974 showed twenty-eight sparkling-wine producers, of which nine were using the *méthode champenoise*. A similar survey in 1979 showed thirty-nine producers, with nineteen using the *méthode champenoise*. Among these, I find, again and again, six names competing fiercely for the highest quality honors: Domaine Chandon (the American offshoot of France's Moët-Hennessy),

Hanns Kornell, and Schramsberg (all three in the Napa Valley), Korbel in Sonoma, Mirassou in Monterey and Santa Clara, and Chateau Ste. Michelle in Washington State.

Each of these wineries releases a range of labels covering different prices, varying styles, alternative degrees of sweetness—running from bone dry to very sweet. In my experience, the precise degree of sweetness is one of the principal factors in making the average drinker either like or dislike a wine. Since sparkling wine is almost completely a man-made product, and the sweetness is totally under the control of the winemaker, there ought to be a simple and universally understandable way of defining the sweetness on the label. It does seem a pity that virtually all producers continue to use the traditional Anglo-French words, which have almost no meaning because they are always differently interpreted.

The label word "natural," often printed in French as *nature* or *au naturel,* is supposed to mean that no dosage of sugar was added at the moment when the yeast was disgorged (see above), that the wine is in its natural state and is, therefore, very dry. But each winemaker has his own personal taste as to what "very dry" is, and the label does not tell you how sweet the original grapes were and, therefore, how sweet the basic wine was before the sparkle was put into it. I submit that the word "natural" is pretty well meaningless. Up the sweetness scale comes the word "brut," a stretchable definition that can be made to cover many deadly sins. In France, it is supposed to be a teensy-weensy bit sweeter than the driest. Everything depends on how much is teensy-weensy! Next in the nonsense department comes "extra dry," or *extra sec* in French or *sehr trocken* in German. All of which, believe it or not, are supposed to be sweeter than brut. Next comes *demi-sec,* or "half-dry," which is a virtual guarantee that the wine is very sweet. If all this seems total gobbledegook—it is. It is all part of the ancient French mystique to which American producers still cling as if their lives depended on it.

Against all this, there is one perfectly simple and totally accurate way of defining the degree of sweetness of the sparkling wine in the bottle. It is to print on the label the percentage figure of residual sugar measured in the wine after the disgorgement and dosage. Meanwhile, I suggest that you should demand, either from the retailer who sold you the bottle or from the producer, to know the residual sugar figure. Then—with adjustments, of course, for your own personal taste—you should apply the figure to the following scale:

- It is rarely possible to remove absolutely all sugar from a wine, but if the residual is substantially less than 1 percent, I believe you will find the sparkling wine tasting ascetically dry on your tongue.
- If the residual sugar is between 1 and 1.5 percent, I believe you will find the sparkling wine tasting very delicately sweet on your tongue.
- If the residual sugar is above 1.5 percent but not quite up to 3 percent, I believe you will find the sparkling wine tasting medium sweet to pretty sweet, according to the sensitivity of your tongue.
- If the residual sugar is at 3 percent or more, I think you will find the sparkling wine tasting very sweet and on up to an increasing degree of a sense of honey on your tongue.

These percentage figures simply cannot lie. Once you have established, to your own taste satisfaction, what percentage of sugar you enjoy, you can go on forever getting it at precisely that amount. Nothing could be fairer than that. Finding exactly the right sparkling wines, then, for the particular purposes of your dining and entertaining, is a matter of knowing your favorite producers, recognizing the differences between the various labels of each one, and being aware of the current price being charged against the quality being offered.

I cannot resist mentioning two oddities before closing this report. Neither is a commercial sparkling wine, but each is a delightful experience in the drinking, and each represents the independently minded perfectionism of a serious and successful winemaker. The great California producer Louis P. Martini has not shown any interest in commercial sparkling wines and has never released one. But he does make—now and then, when it pleases him and for his own amusement—a lovely, little, delicately sweet, gently sparkling wine that he calls "Moscato Amabile," literally "Amiable Muscat." He makes it only when he can get exactly the right clone or type of Muscat of Alexandria grapes at exactly the right degree of overripeness—a juxtaposition of events that comes only every three or four years. Even then, his production is minuscule.

He puts none of it into commercial distribution, but holds most of it for his friends and sells a few final bottles to visitors at the winery. The demand for it among his admirers (myself always near the head of the line) is immense, and each vintage of "Moscato Amabile" disappears as if it were a flash of summer lightning. It is not made by any process as fancy as *la méthode champenoise*. Louis simply ferments and vinifies the wine under very cold refrigeration —so cold, in fact, that the fermentation continues sometimes for as long as three years. It stops automatically when there is a certain degree of alcohol, but still with a good deal of residual sugar and a certain amount of carbon-dioxide gas that cannot get out because of the low temperature. Louis then bottles the half-finished wine under tightly wired corks. The fermentation continues inside the bottle, and a small amount of carbon-dioxide-gas pressure develops. Because the wine is never completely stabilized, it is always stored under refrigeration. An ice-cold, gently bubbling glass of it, sipped while swinging in a hammock under a shade tree on a day when the sun is broiling down, is one of the purest of summer joys.

In the mid-1800s, the German immigrants to the Midwest planted their vineyards along the Ohio River and thought it would become "the American Rhine." As we all know, the dream failed— major reasons being Prohibition and the deep-rooted Midwestern antipathy to Demon Alcohol. One of the major wine producers of the Ohio Valley and the Great Lakes is still in business in Cincinnati, Meier's Wine Cellars, under the direction, until his recent death, of its winemaker, Henry Sonneman. Now, in the decade of the 1980s, a product that Henry once described to me as "my proud invention" is still being very widely distributed.

It is a beautiful champagne bottle, complete with handsome black-and-silver label, a wired champagne cork, and lots of shiny silver foil. The cork comes out with the pop of a cannon shot. I couldn't wish for a handsomer bottle for my daughter's wedding party, for the most important celebration dinner, for the most hopeful bon voyage or the most triumphant homecoming. But when you pour it into the glass, you find that it is perfectly clear, beautifully bubbling, entirely nonalcoholic juice of the Catawba grape. The first time, with slight shock, I went back to the label and found that it precisely and truthfully described exactly what it is, "Meier's Sparkling Catawba Grape Juice." I tasted it again. It was an excellent product—clean, refreshing, not at all too sweet, rich with the taste of the fruit. Demon Alcohol, who needs you?

Tasting and rating the best American sparkling wines over the years has been a difficult project, at times uncomfortably frustrating, quite often distinctly embarrassing. When one tries to judge and write as a completely unbiased critic, one certainly hopes to be able to distribute one's praise with reasonable equality between the various top competing producers. If I were a critic of automobiles, I would hardly expect (or want to be forced to say) that the best car every season, year after year, came from General Motors. If I were a fashion writer, I would not want to be forced to admit that the best designs came exclusively from Christian Dior. If I were a TV critic, I would be disturbed about being forced to write that all the best shows were always on CBS. Yet this is exactly what has happened with American sparkling wines.

Consistently the best, year after year, has come from the historic Schramsberg Vineyards in the Napa Valley, founded in the 1860s, abandoned and falling into decay for almost fifty years, then taken over in the 1960s and brilliantly revived by its new owners, the husband and wife winemaking team, Jack and Jamie Davies (see the vineyard profile on page 263). Year after year, we have lined up a dozen or so of the top American sparkling wines (with all identifying labels carefully covered) and have poured them into numbered flute glasses, so that there was absolutely no way of my knowing which wine I was tasting. After going back and forth along the line at least a dozen times—after comparing them in pairs in every conceivable combination—when the covers were removed from the labels and the numbers of the glasses identified, not only the highest score on the rating charts, but, also, the second and third positions, were found to be held by the different grades and types of Schramsberg. This seemed to me, quite frankly, a difficult result to have to report in my book. It might inadvertently seem to imply favoritism. So I began tasting and rating all over again. New bottles were assembled and arranged in different order—poured into glasses with different numbers. Again, after every possible twist of juggling the glasses, after a total concentration on every single factor and point of quality, when the labels were uncovered, my rating charts showed the same results. Finally, I asked for the help of six friends who are all aficionados of American sparkling wines. I offered them the same blind tastings and asked them to give me their votes. They were not entirely unanimous, but a substantial majority gave, as I have done, the first three places to Schramsberg.

Perhaps, after all, this result is not so surprising. From the moment they assumed ownership of the old Schramsberg estate in 1965, Jack and Jamie Davies have worked with the absolute determination that the quality of their sparkling wines shall be the paramount objective, above every other consideration. Where other producers measure their output in hundreds of thousands of cases, Schramsberg has restricted itself to a fixed maximum of 25,000 cases. Where other producers age their wines on the yeasts for two or three years, Schramsberg has gradually increased the aging of its top wines to four or five years. And these are only the first factors of what is, deliberately, a very limited, prestige operation.

The best American sparkling wine I have ever tasted is the Schramsberg "Crémant," the French generic definition of a rather rare, unique, sweet, sparkling dessert wine, with only about half the normal internal gas pressure. This means that when it is poured, it foams and froths, forming a creamy head. As you take your first sip, your lips are, so to speak, "kissed" by the velvet touch of the delicately creamy foam. That is the meaning of the name *crémant,* "creaming." But this magnificent wine cannot live by froth alone. Its *demi-sec* dessert sweetness (with about 4.5 percent of residual sugar) is balanced against a lemony tang, so that it is never cloying or honeyed. Although it is a classic French title, this version is peculiarly American, made almost entirely from the newly cross-grafted Flora. The color of this lovely wine is a combination of light gold and opal. It is classically made by the *méthode champenoise,* and the final result is richly elegant and excitingly spicy, with the perfume of wild flowers. My tasting charts have consistently scored it with a GREAT quality rating.

My second sparkling wine—almost exactly level with the first— is the Schramsberg "Reserve," the outstanding dry *cuvée* (or "blend") of the best available wine of the estate each year, assembled with no other consideration than that of pure quality. I find in it an extraordinary richness, coupled with the excitement of a delicate tannic character. The sparkle is put in by the *méthode champenoise,* and the wine is finished virtually with no residual sugar. Yet the taste is intensely fruity, luxurious, yeasty, with small elegant bubbles in the glass. The remarkable complexity of flavors comes from five years of aging on the yeast in the bottle. This "Reserve" also rates on my charts as of GREAT quality and, with the "Crémant," brings the GREAT classification to the makers:

- Schramsberg Vineyards at Calistoga in the Napa Valley, with its owner-winemakers, Jack and Jamie Davies

My third ranking in American sparkling wines is the Schramsberg "Blanc de Noirs" ("white from black") made primarily from Pinot Noir grapes with the dark skins held away from the juice so that the wine will not absorb any red coloring. Yet the flavor of this grape of strong character is clearly in the wine, even after some Pinot Chardonnay has been added for lightness. The sparkle is developed by the *méthode champenoise,* and the wine is finished with virtually no residual sugar. Yet it has an extraordinary complexity of personality, an intense aromatic flavor, a dryness and richness that give it a SUPERB quality rating.

There is one other American sparkling wine that I have consistently rated on my tasting charts and that has shown scores to bring the SUPERB classification to its maker:

- Domaine Chandon at Yountville in the Napa Valley, also with a "Blanc de Noirs," delicately sweet, 100 percent from Pinot Noir grapes, with some color absorbed from the skins, giving the wine a lovely pinky-salmon cast, the wine aged for two years in the bottle on the yeast under the supervision of the prestigious French cellarmaster Edmond Maudière

I have also tasted a number of sparkling wines consistently of a NOBLE quality rating from others of the top producers. (Incidentally, in the following list, the names of some of the producers may be repeated several times, under the various labels that they release.) These sparkling wines bring the NOBLE classification to their makers, the following vineyards and wineries:

- Beaulieu Vineyard at Rutherford in the Napa Valley, "Cuvée de Chardonnay Brut," delicately sweet, *méthode champenoise*
- Domaine Chandon at Yountville in the Napa Valley, "Napa Valley Brut," delicately sweet, *méthode champenoise*
- Louis M. Martini Winery at St. Helena in the Napa Valley, "Moscato Amabile," sweet, transfer process
- Mirassou Vineyards at San Jose in Santa Clara, "Late Disgorged," lightly sweet, *méthode champenoise*, Monterey grapes, four years' bottle aging on the yeasts
- Schramsberg Vineyards at Calistoga in the Napa Valley, "Blanc de Blancs," *méthode champenoise*, Pinot Chardonnay and Pinot Blanc

- Schramsberg Vineyards at Calistoga in the Napa Valley, "Cuvée de Pinot," dry, *méthode champenoise*, pinky-salmon color, two-thirds Pinot Noir and one-third Napa Gamay

At the next tasting level, a point or two lower, I have tasted a number of sparkling wines that have consistently rated as being of FINE quality. (Again, some of the producers' names are repeated, with the several different labels they release.) These wines bring the FINE classification to their makers, the following vineyards and wineries:

- Almadén Vineyards at San Jose in Santa Clara, "Blanc de Blancs," dry, transfer process, mostly Pinot Chardonnay, with some Pinot Blanc, less than 1 percent residual sugar
- Almadén Vineyards at San Jose in Santa Clara, "Chardonnay Nature," dry, transfer process, 85 percent Pinot Chardonnay, remainder Folle Blanche and Pinot Blanc, no sugar dosage
- Almadén Vineyards at San Jose in Santa Clara, "Oeil de Perdrix," dry, transfer process, Pinot Noir grapes give light bronze color like the eye of a partridge, from which this wine takes its name, about 1 percent residual sugar
- Chateau Ste. Michelle at Woodinville near Seattle in Washington State, "Blanc de Noirs," dry, *méthode champenoise*
- The Christian Brothers on Mont La Salle above the Napa Valley, "California Champagne Brut," slightly sweet, Charmat bulk process
- Korbel Winery at Guerneville in the Russian River Valley of Sonoma, "Blanc de Noirs," dry, *méthode champenoise*, made from 100 percent estate-grown Pinot Noir grapes
- Korbel Winery at Guerneville in the Russian River Valley of Sonoma, "Brut," slightly sweet, *méthode champenoise*
- Hanns Kornell Cellars north of St. Helena in the Napa Valley, "Muscadelle du Bordelais," medium sweet, *méthode champenoise*
- Hanns Kornell Cellars north of St. Helena in the Napa Valley, "Sehr Trocken," extra dry, *méthode champenoise*, heavy reliance on Riesling grapes in the German style
- Paul Masson Vineyards at Saratoga and in the Pinnacles district of the Santa Cruz Mountains in Santa Clara, "Brut," dry, transfer process

- Mirassou Vineyards at San Jose in Santa Clara, "Au Naturel," dry, no dosage, *méthode champenoise*, thirty-two months of aging in the bottle on the yeasts, Monterey grapes
- Sonoma Vineyards at Windsor in Sonoma, "Brut," delicately sweet, *méthode champenoise*, the base wine aged in oak casks for a year before the sparkle was added, giving to the finished sparkling wine an unusual and attractive flavor

PART THREE

A FIRST CLASSIFICATION OF THE TOP 200 AMERICAN VINEYARDS AND WINERIES

	VINEYARD / WINERY	COMMUNITY	DISTRICT / REGION	STATE
GREAT	Heitz Wine Cellars	St. Helena	Napa Valley	California
	Schramsberg Vineyards	Calistoga	Napa Valley	California
	Stony Hill Vineyard	Stony Hill	Napa Valley	California
SUPERB	Alatera Vineyards	Napa	Napa Valley	California
	Amity Vineyards	Amity	Willamette Valley	Oregon
	Beaulieu Vineyard	Rutherford	Napa Valley	California
	Burgess Cellars	St. Helena	Napa Valley	California
	Richard Carey Winery	San Leandro	Alameda	California
	Carneros Creek Winery	Carneros Hills	Napa Valley	California
	Caymus Vineyards	Rutherford	Napa Valley	California
	Chalone Vineyard	Mount Chalone	Monterey	California
	Chateau Bouchaine	Carneros Hills	Napa Valley	California
	Chateau Montelena	Calistoga	Napa Valley	California
	Chateau St. Jean	Kenwood	Sonoma	California
	Chateau Ste. Michelle	Woodinville	Seattle	Washington
	Christian Brothers	Mont La Salle	Napa Valley	California
	Clos du Val	Yountville	Napa Valley	California
	Domaine Chandon	Yountville	Napa Valley	California
	Edna Valley Vineyard	Edna Valley	San Luis Obispo	California
	Eyrie Vineyards	McMinnville	Willamette Valley	Oregon
	Forman Winery	Spring Mountain	Napa Valley	California
	Freemark Abbey Winery	St. Helena	Napa Valley	California
	Glen Ellen Vineyards	Glen Ellen	Sonoma	California
	Grand Cru Vineyards	Glen Ellen	Sonoma	California
	Grgich Hills Cellars	Rutherford	Napa Valley	California
	Hacienda Wine Cellers	Sonoma	Sonoma	California
	Hillcrest Vineyards	Roseburg	Umpqua Valley	Oregon
	Hinzerling Vineyards	Prosser	Yakima Valley	Washington

225

	VINEYARD / WINERY	COMMUNITY	DISTRICT / REGION	STATE
SUPERB				
	Jekel Vineyard	Greenfield	Salinas Valley	California
	Kistler Vineyard	Glen Ellen	Mayacamas Mountains	California
	Long Vineyards	Pritchard Hill	Napa Valley	California
	Louis M. Martini Winery	St. Helena	Napa Valley	California
	Mayacamas Vineyards	Mount Veeder	Napa Valley	California
	Mount Eden Vineyards	Saratoga	Santa Cruz Mountains	California
	Mount Veeder Winery	Mount Veeder	Napa Valley	California
	Joseph Phelps Vineyards	St. Helena	Napa Valley	California
	Piper. Sonoma Winery	Windsor	Sonoma	California
	Ponzi Vineyards	Beaverton	Willamette Valley	Oregon
	Preston Wine Cellars	Pasco	Columbia Basin	Washington
	Ridge Vineyards	Cupertino	Santa Cruz Mountains	California
	Ste. Chapelle Vineyards	Sunny Slope	Snake River Valley	Idaho
	Shafer Vineyards	Stag's Leap, Yountville	Napa Valley	California
	Simi Winery	Healdsburg	Sonoma	California
	Sonoma Vineyards	Windsor	Sonoma	California
	Spring Mountain Vineyards	St. Helena	Napa Valley	California
	Stag's Leap Wine Cellars	Yountville	Napa Valley	California
	Sutter Home Winery	St. Helena	Napa Valley	California
	Joseph Swan Vineyards	Forestville	Sonoma	California
	Tualatin Vineyards	Forest Grove	Willamette Valley	Oregon
	Wente Brothers	Livermore	Livermore Valley	California
NOBLE				
	Acacia Winery	Carneros Hills	Napa Valley	California
	Ahlgren Vineyard	Boulder Creek	Santa Cruz Mountains	California
	Almadén Vineyards	San Jose	Santa Clara	California
	Associated Vintners	Bellevue	Seattle	Washington
	Bargetto Winery	Soquel	Santa Cruz Mountains	California

Beringer Vineyards	St. Helena	California
David Bruce Winery	Los Gatos	California
Davis Bynum Winery	Healdsburg	California
Calera Wines	Hollister	California
Chappellet Vineyard	Pritchard Hill	California
Concannon Vineyard	Livermore	California
Conn Creek Winery	Rutherford	California
Cuvaison Vineyard	Calistoga	California
Dehlinger Winery	Sebastopol	California
Diamond Creek Vineyards	Calistoga	California
Dry Creek Vineyard	Healdsburg	California
Edmeades Vineyards	Philo	California
Elk Cove Vineyards	Gaston	Oregon
Fetzer Vineyards	Ukiah	California
Ficklin Vineyards	Madera	California
Firestone Vineyard	Los Olivos	California
Fisher Vineyards	Mayacamas Mountains	California
Gundlach-Bundschu Vineyard	Vineburg	California
Hoffman Mountain Ranch	Paso Robles	San Luis Obispo
Iron Horse Vineyards	Sebastopol	Sonoma
Robert Keenan Winery	Spring Mountain	Napa Valley
Kenwood Vineyards	Kenwood	Sonoma
Knudsen-Erath Winery	Dundee	Willamette Valley
Charles Krug Winery	St. Helena	Napa Valley
Lytton Springs Winery	Healdsburg	Sonoma
Mastantuono Winery	Paso Robles	Santa Lucia Mountains of San Luis Obispo
Matanzas Creek Winery	Santa Rosa	Sonoma
Mirassou Vineyards	San Jose	Santa Clara
Robert Mondavi Winery	Oakville	Napa Valley

	VINEYARD / WINERY	COMMUNITY	DISTRICT / REGION	STATE
NOBLE	Monterey Peninsula Winery	Monterey	Monterey	California
	Monterey Vineyard	Gonzales	Monterey	California
	Monteviña Wines	Plymouth	Amador	California
	Oak Knoll Winery	Hillsboro	Willamette Valley	Oregon
	Parducci Wine Cellars	Ukiah	Mendocino	California
	Plane's Cayuga Vineyard	Lake Cayuga	Finger Lakes	New York
	Preston Vineyards	Healdsburg	Sonoma	California
	Ravenswood Winery	Forestville	Sonoma	California
	Martin Ray Vineyards	Saratoga	Santa Cruz Mountains	California
	Raymond Winery	Calistoga	Napa Valley	California
	St. Clement Vineyards	St. Helena	Napa Valley	California
	Santino Wines	Plymouth	Amador	California
	Sebastiani Vineyards	Sonoma	Sonoma	California
	Sokol Blosser Winery	Dundee	Willamette Valley	Oregon
	Sterling Vineyards	Calistoga	Napa Valley	California
	Stevenot Vineyards	Murphys	Calaveras	California
	Stonegate Winery	Calistoga	Napa Valley	California
	Trefethen Vineyards	Napa	Napa Valley	California
	Turgeon & Lohr Winery	San Jose	Santa Clara	California
	Veedercrest Vineyard	Mount Veeder	Napa Valley	California
	Villa Mt. Eden Winery	Oakville	Napa Valley	California
	Vöse Vineyards	Oakville	Napa Valley	California
	Yakima River Winery	Prosser	Yakima Valley	Washington
FINE	Alexander Valley Vineyards	Healdsburg	Sonoma	California
	Alta Vineyard	Calistoga	Napa Valley	California
	Boeger Winery	Placerville	El Dorado	California
	Buena Vista Vineyards	Sonoma	Sonoma	California
	Cakebread Cellars	Rutherford	Napa Valley	California
	Callaway Vineyard	Temecula	Riverside	California

Cassayre-Forni Cellars	Rutherford	California
Clos du Bois	Healdsburg	California
Congress Springs Vineyards	Saratoga	California
Cotes des Colombe Vineyard	Banks	Oregon
Cresta Blanca Winery	Ukiah	California
Cygnet Cellars	Hollister	California
DeLoach Vineyards	Santa Rosa	California
Devlin Wine Cellars	Soquel	California
Diablo Vista Winery	Benicia	California
Duckhorn Vineyards	St. Helena	California
Durney Vineyard	Carmel Valley	California
Enz Vineyards	Hollister	California
Evensen Vineyards	Oakville	California
Far Niente Winery	Oakville	California
Fenestra Winery	Pleasanton	California
Field Stone Winery	Healdsburg	California
E. B. Foote Winery	South Park	Washington
Foppiano Vineyards	Healdsburg	California
Fortino Winery	Gilroy	California
Franciscan Vineyards	Rutherford	California
Gemello Winery	Mountain View	California
Glenora Wine Cellars	Seneca Lake	New York
Hanzell Vineyards	Sonoma	California
Harbor Winery	Sacramento	California
Hargrave Vineyard	Cutchogue	New York
Heron Hill Vineyard	Hammondsport	New York
Hop Kiln Winery and Griffin Vineyard	Healdsburg	California
Husch Vineyards	Philo	California
Inglenook Vineyards	Rutherford	California

| Napa Valley |
| Sonoma |
| Santa Cruz Mountains |
| Willamette Valley |
| Mendocino |
| San Benito |
| Sonoma |
| Santa Cruz Mountains |
| Solano |
| Napa Valley |
| Monterey |
| San Benito |
| Napa Valley |
| Napa Valley |
| Alameda |
| Sonoma |
| Seattle |
| Sonoma |
| Santa Cruz Mountains |
| Napa Valley |
| Santa Cruz Mountains |
| Finger Lakes |
| Sonoma |
| Yolo |
| Long Island |
| Lake Keuka in the Finger Lakes |
| Sonoma |
| Mendocino |
| Napa Valley |

229

VINEYARD / WINERY	COMMUNITY	DISTRICT / REGION	STATE
FINE			
Johnson's Alexander Valley Wines	Healdsburg	Sonoma	California
Kalin Cellars	Novato	San Pablo Bay	California
Konocti Cellars	Kelseyville	Lake	California
Korbel Winery	Guerneville	Sonoma	California
Hanns Kornell Cellars	St. Helena	Napa Valley	California
Thomas Kruse Winery	Gilroy	Santa Cruz Mountains	California
Lambert Bridge Winery	Healdsburg	Sonoma	California
Landmark Vineyards	Windsor	Sonoma	California
Leonetti Cellars	Walla Walla	Columbia Basin	Washington
Mark West Vineyards	Forestville	Sonoma	California
Markham Winery	St. Helena	Napa Valley	California
Paul Masson Vineyards	Saratoga	Santa Cruz Mountains	California
Milano Winery	Hopland	Mendocino	California
Mill Creek Vineyards	Healdsburg	Sonoma	California
Mont Elise Vineyards	Bingen	South Columbia Basin	Washington
J. W. Morris Wineries	Concord	Contra Costa	California
Napa Wine Cellars	Yountville	Napa Valley	California
Navarro Vineyards	Philo	Mendocino	California
Novitiate Wines	Los Gatos	Santa Cruz Mountains	California
Parson's Creek Winery	Ukiah	Mendocino	California
Pedroncelli Winery	Geyserville	Sonoma	California
Pendleton Winery	San Jose	Santa Clara	California
Pope Valley Winery	Pope Valley	Napa Valley	California
Quail Ridge Vineyards	Mount Veeder	Napa Valley	California
Rafanelli Winery	Healdsburg	Sonoma	California
Reuter's Hill Vineyards	Forest Grove	Willamette Valley	Oregon
Roudon-Smith Vineyards	Scott's Valley	Santa Cruz Mountains	California
Round Hill Cellars	St. Helena	Napa Valley	California
Russian River Vineyards	Forestville	Sonoma	California

Rutherford Hill Winery	St. Helena	Napa Valley	California
Rutherford Vintners	Rutherford	Napa Valley	California
San Martin Winery	San Martin	Santa Cruz Mountains	California
San Pasqual Vineyards	Escondido	San Diego	California
Sanford & Benedict Vineyards	Lompoc	Santa Ynez Valley	California
Santa Cruz Mountain Vineyard	Santa Cruz	Santa Cruz Mountains	California
Santa Ynez Valley Winery	Solvang	Santa Ynez Valley	California
Santino	Plymouth	Amador	California
Sausal Winery	Healdsburg	Sonoma	California
Sherrill Cellars	Woodside	Santa Cruz Mountains	California
Shown & Sons Vineyards	Rutherford	Napa Valley	California
Sierra Vista Winery	Placerville	El Dorado	California
Smith-Madrone Vineyard	Spring Mountain	Napa Valley	California
Smothers Winery	Santa Cruz	Santa Cruz Mountains	California
Sotoyome Winery	Healdsburg	Sonoma	California
Souverain Cellars	Geyserville	Sonoma	California
P. & M. Staiger Winery	Boulder Creek	Santa Cruz Mountains	California
Robert Stemmler Winery	Healdsburg	Sonoma	California
Stony Ridge Winery	Pleasanton	Livermore Valley	California
Sunrise Winery	Felton	Santa Cruz Mountains	California
Sycamore Creek Vineyards	Morgan Hill	Santa Cruz Mountains	California
Trentadue Winery	Geyserville	Sonoma	California
Tulocay Winery	Napa	Napa Valley	California
Ventana Vineyards	Soledad	Monterey	California
Manfred J. Vierthaler Winery	Sumner	Puyallup Valley	Washington
Hermann J. Wiemer Vineyard	Lake Seneca	Finger Lakes	New York
Willowside Vineyards	Santa Rosa	Sonoma	California
Yverdon Vineyards	St. Helena	Napa Valley	California
Zaca Mesa Winery	Los Olivos	Santa Ynez Valley	California
Z D Wines	Rutherford	Napa Valley	California

231

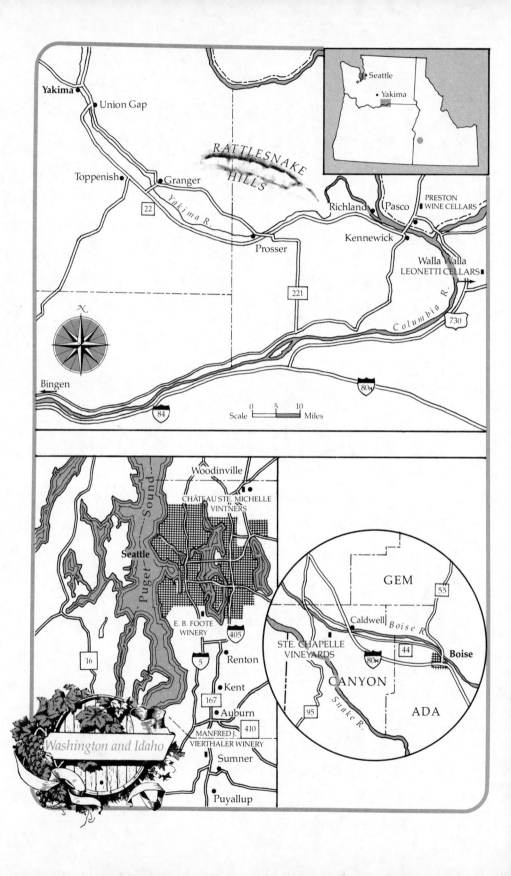

Seattle
Yakima

Yakima • Union Gap
Toppenish • • Granger
22
Yakima R.
RATTLESNAKE HILLS
Richland • Pasco
PRESTON WINE CELLARS
Kennewick
Prosser
221
Walla Walla
LEONETTI CELLARS
Columbia R.
730
Bingen
84
80N
Scale 0 5 10 Miles

Woodinville
CHÂTEAU STE. MICHELLE VINTNERS
Seattle
Puget Sound
E. B. FOOTE WINERY
16
405
5
Renton
Kent
167
Auburn
410
MANFRED J. VIERTHALER WINERY
Sumner
Puyallup
Washington and Idaho

GEM
55
Caldwell Boise R.
STE. CHAPELLE VINEYARDS
80N 44 **Boise**
CANYON
95 Snake R.
ADA

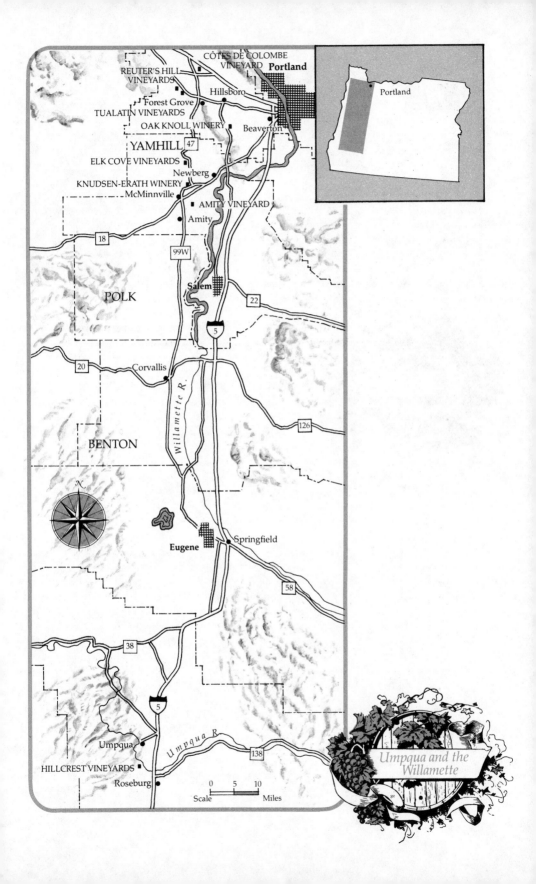

CÔTES DE COLOMBE
VINEYARD
Portland

REUTER'S HILL
VINEYARDS

Hillsboro

Forest Grove
TUALATIN VINEYARDS

OAK KNOLL WINERY

Beaverton

YAMHILL 47

ELK COVE VINEYARDS

Newberg

KNUDSEN-ERATH WINERY
McMinnville

AMITY VINEYARD

Amity

18

99W

POLK

Salem

22

5

20 Corvallis

Willamette R.

BENTON

126

N

Eugene Springfield

58

38

5

Umpqua R.

Umpqua 138

HILLCREST VINEYARDS

Roseburg

0 5 10

Scale Miles

Portland

*Umpqua and the
Willamette*

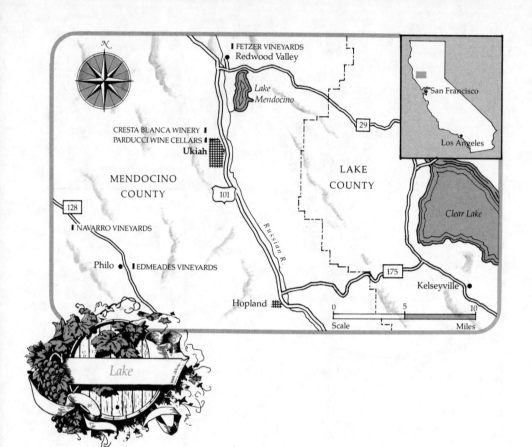

FETZER VINEYARDS
Redwood Valley

Lake Mendocino

CRESTA BLANCA WINERY
PARDUCCI WINE CELLARS
Ukiah

MENDOCINO
COUNTY

LAKE
COUNTY

San Francisco

Los Angeles

Clear Lake

128

NAVARRO VINEYARDS

Philo   EDMEADES VINEYARDS

Hopland

Kelseyville

0   5   10

Scale   Miles

29

101

Russian R.

175

Lake

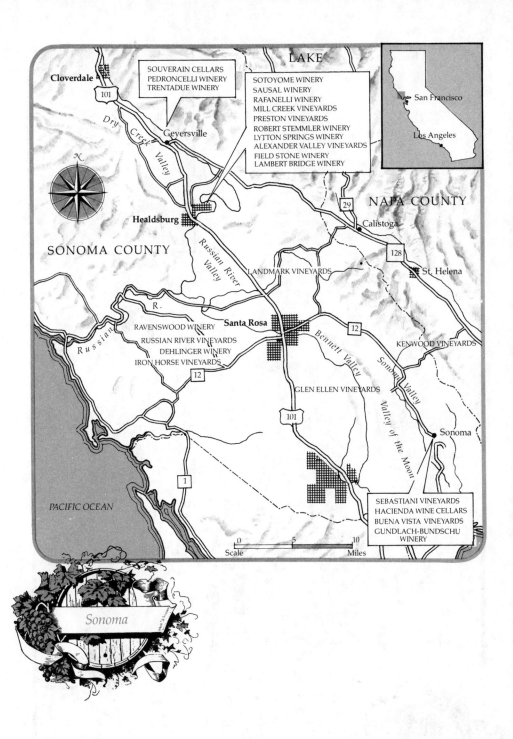

SOUVERAIN CELLARS
PEDRONCELLI WINERY
TRENTADUE WINERY

SOTOYOME WINERY
SAUSAL WINERY
RAFANELLI WINERY
MILL CREEK VINEYARDS
PRESTON VINEYARDS
ROBERT STEMMLER WINERY
LYTTON SPRINGS WINERY
ALEXANDER VALLEY VINEYARDS
FIELD STONE WINERY
LAMBERT BRIDGE WINERY

Cloverdale

101

Dry Creek Valley

Geyserville

LAKE

San Francisco

Los Angeles

NAPA COUNTY

29

Calistoga

128

St. Helena

Healdsburg

SONOMA COUNTY

Russian River Valley

LANDMARK VINEYARDS

Russian R.

RAVENSWOOD WINERY

RUSSIAN RIVER VINEYARDS
DEHLINGER WINERY
IRON HORSE VINEYARDS

12

Santa Rosa

Bennett Valley

12

KENWOOD VINEYARDS

Sonoma Valley

Valley of the Moon

GLEN ELLEN VINEYARDS

101

Sonoma

1

PACIFIC OCEAN

SEBASTIANI VINEYARDS
HACIENDA WINE CELLARS
BUENA VISTA VINEYARDS
GUNDLACH-BUNDSCHU
WINERY

0   5   10
Scale   Miles

Sonoma

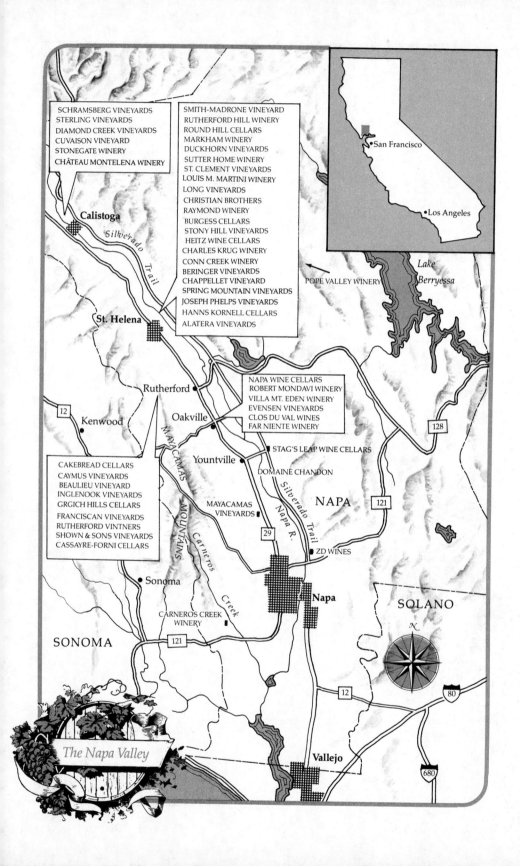

SCHRAMSBERG VINEYARDS
STERLING VINEYARDS
DIAMOND CREEK VINEYARDS
CUVAISON VINEYARD
STONEGATE WINERY
CHÂTEAU MONTELENA WINERY

SMITH-MADRONE VINEYARD
RUTHERFORD HILL WINERY
ROUND HILL CELLARS
MARKHAM WINERY
DUCKHORN VINEYARDS
SUTTER HOME WINERY
ST. CLEMENT VINEYARDS
LOUIS M. MARTINI WINERY
LONG VINEYARDS
CHRISTIAN BROTHERS
RAYMOND WINERY
BURGESS CELLARS
STONY HILL VINEYARDS
HEITZ WINE CELLARS
CHARLES KRUG WINERY
CONN CREEK WINERY
BERINGER VINEYARDS
CHAPPELLET VINEYARD
SPRING MOUNTAIN VINEYARDS
JOSEPH PHELPS VINEYARDS
HANNS KORNELL CELLARS
ALATERA VINEYARDS

San Francisco

Los Angeles

Calistoga

Silverado Trail

Lake Berryessa

POPE VALLEY WINERY

St. Helena

Rutherford

NAPA WINE CELLARS
ROBERT MONDAVI WINERY
VILLA MT. EDEN WINERY
EVENSEN VINEYARDS
CLOS DU VAL WINES
FAR NIENTE WINERY

12   Kenwood

Oakville

STAG'S LEAP WINE CELLARS

128

Yountville

DOMAINE CHANDON

CAKEBREAD CELLARS
CAYMUS VINEYARDS
BEAULIEU VINEYARD
INGLENOOK VINEYARDS
GRGICH HILLS CELLARS
FRANCISCAN VINEYARDS
RUTHERFORD VINTNERS
SHOWN & SONS VINEYARDS
CASSAYRE-FORNI CELLARS

MAYACAMAS
VINEYARDS

NAPA

121

29

ZD WINES

Sonoma

SOLANO

CARNEROS CREEK
WINERY

Napa

SONOMA

121

N

12

80

The Napa Valley

Vallejo

680

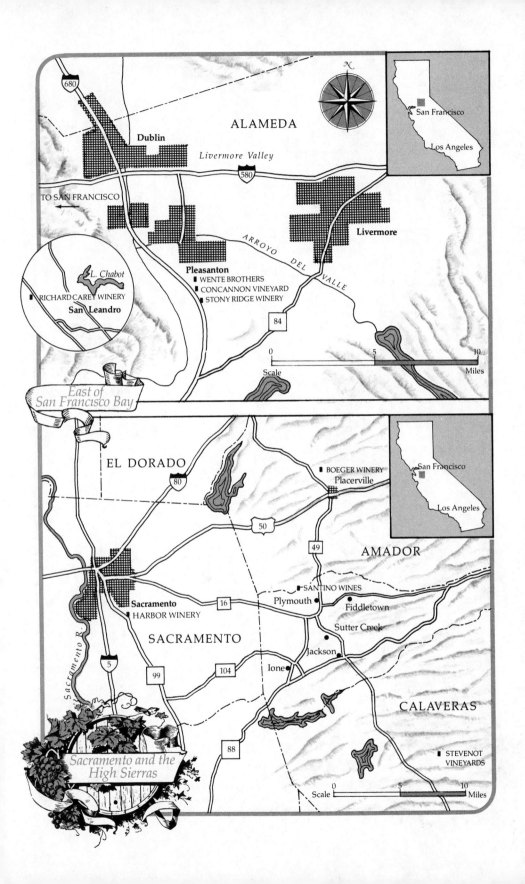

N

ALAMEDA

Dublin

Livermore Valley

680

580

TO SAN FRANCISCO

Livermore

ARROYO DEL VALLE

Pleasanton
■ WENTE BROTHERS
■ CONCANNON VINEYARD
■ STONY RIDGE WINERY

84

L. Chabot
■ RICHARD CAREY WINERY
San Leandro

San Francisco

Los Angeles

0   5   10
Scale   Miles

East of
San Francisco Bay

EL DORADO

80

■ BOEGER WINERY
Placerville

San Francisco

Los Angeles

50

49

AMADOR

Sacramento
■ HARBOR WINERY

16

● SANTINO WINES
Plymouth ●   ● Fiddletown

Sutter Creek
●

Sacramento R.

5

99

104

Jackson ●

Ione ●

SACRAMENTO

CALAVERAS

88

■ STEVENOT
VINEYARDS

Sacramento and the
High Sierras

0   5   10
Scale   Miles

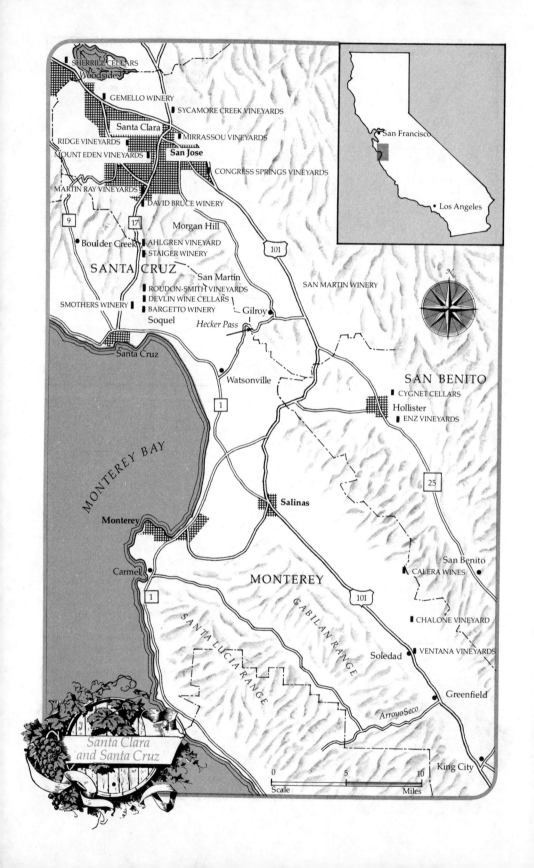

SHERRILL CELLARS
Woodside

GEMELLO WINERY

SYCAMORE CREEK VINEYARDS

Santa Clara

RIDGE VINEYARDS
MOUNT EDEN VINEYARDS

MIRRASSOU VINEYARDS

San Jose

CONGRESS SPRINGS VINEYARDS

MARTIN RAY VINEYARDS

DAVID BRUCE WINERY

9

17

Morgan Hill

Boulder Creek

AHLGREN VINEYARD

STAIGER WINERY

101

SANTA CRUZ

San Martin

SAN MARTIN WINERY

ROUDON-SMITH VINEYARDS

SMOTHERS WINERY

DEVLIN WINE CELLARS

BARGETTO WINERY

Soquel

Gilroy

Hecker Pass

Santa Cruz

Watsonville

1

MONTEREY BAY

SAN BENITO

CYGNET CELLARS

Hollister

ENZ VINEYARDS

25

Salinas

Monterey

MONTEREY

San Benito

Carmel

CALERA WINES

1

101

SANTA LUCIA RANGE

GABILAN RANGE

CHALONE VINEYARD

VENTANA VINEYARDS

Soledad

Greenfield

Arroyo Seco

0   5   10

Scale   Miles

King City

San Francisco

Los Angeles

N

*Santa Clara
and Santa Cruz*

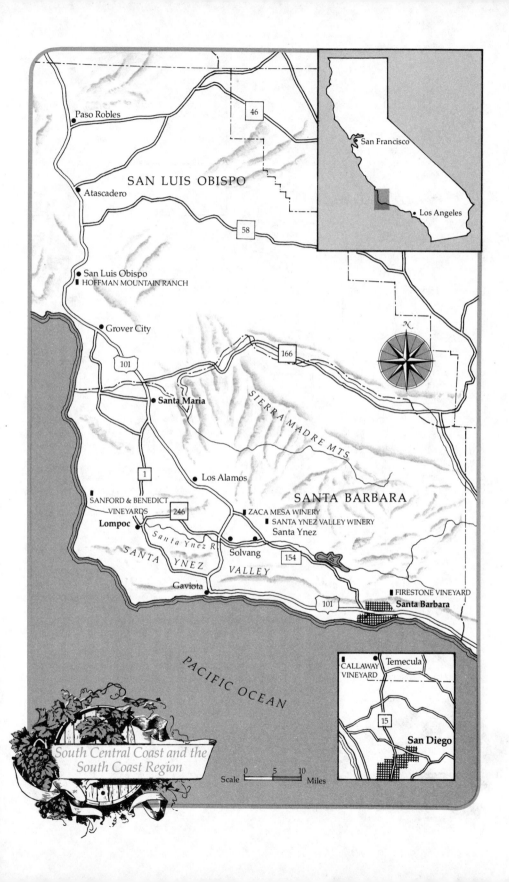

PACIFIC OCEAN

South Central Coast and the
South Coast Region

Scale 0   5   10 Miles

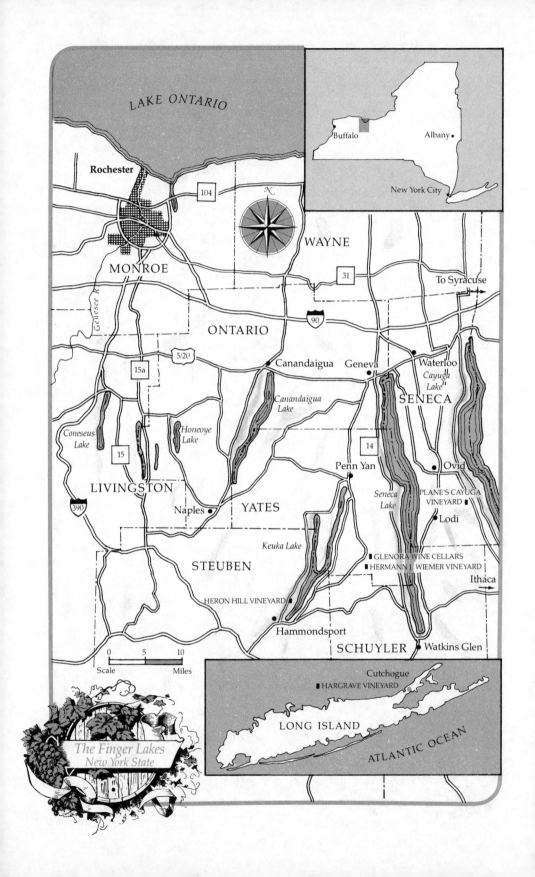

LAKE ONTARIO

Buffalo   Albany •

New York City

Rochester

104

N

WAYNE

To Syracuse

31

ONTARIO

90

Genesee R.

5/20

15a

Canandaigua   Geneva   Waterloo

Cayuga Lake"

SENECA

Canandaigua Lake

Coneseus Lake

Honeoye Lake

15

14

Penn Yan   Ovid •

Seneca Lake   PLANE'S CAYUGA VINEYARD ■

LIVINGSTON

390

Naples •   YATES   Lodi •

Keuka Lake

STEUBEN   ■ GLENORA WINE CELLARS
■ HERMANN J. WIEMER VINEYARD

Ithaca

HERON HILL VINEYARD ■

Hammondsport   SCHUYLER   Watkins Glen •

0   5   10
Scale   Miles

The Finger Lakes
New York State

Cutchogue
■ HARGRAVE VINEYARD

LONG ISLAND

ATLANTIC OCEAN

PART FOUR

PROFILES OF THE CLASSIFIED VINEYARDS, WINERIES, AND WINEMAKERS

The People
Behind the Wines

So far, we have dealt with the vineyards and wineries as if they were impersonal agricultural and mechanical organisms for the production of wine. We have awarded higher or lower marks as if by some mysterious process of natural selection, of good or less good earth, of better or worse exposure to essential sun and rain, of more or less efficient machinery, of cool or less cool cellars, of oak aging barrels with major or minor degrees of magical properties. All these factors are immensely important. Yet, perhaps above all, a wine is a reflection of a human personality.

Every vineyard and winery is directed by owners and winemakers who, first of all, set a policy for their operations based on a master philosophy. Their objective may be, for example, to make the greatest possible wine regardless of any other consideration. Or, they may be working toward the greatest possible financial profit from their venture as the primary motivation for everything they do. Between these two extremes, there are a thousand human decisions and judgments to be made within the complex technology of wine—several decisions and judgments, virtually every day, that may have profound effects on the wine for years into the future. So, when you read the label of a bottle of wine before buying it, and when you taste the wine in order to judge it, one of the factors you must take into account is the person who made that wine, or whose philosophy controlled its making. This second half of the book deals with these people.

From a practical point of view, then, the first half of this book is planned to help you find the type of wine you like or the quality you need to accompany a particular menu—whether it be a dry or soft, a rich white, a light or powerful red, a rosé, a golden sweet, or a sparkling wine—with clear indications as to the varying qualities of the best and best-known labels. Then, if you follow my advice and keep notes on the wines you taste, you will soon find that you are again and again delighted, impressed, pleased, and satisfied by the wines of a particular producer. You will become interested in knowing more about the people who run that vineyard and winery. You may want to visit them or write to them. The requisite information, about every vineyard and winery mentioned in this book, now follows. At the end of each "profile," you will also find suggestions as to other wines of that label worth trying. You will not, however, find information as to vintage years, nor any vintage charts. Perhaps this deliberate omission requires a few words of explanation.

First, as to current vintage information, I am convinced that the sales of popular and publicized wines move so quickly these days and that the news about them is changing so continuously, that a book is not the most efficient vehicle for communicating current vintage buying advice. Frankly, if you want the very latest news about the best current vintages, you should subscribe to one of the well-informed monthly wine newsletters, or turn to a well-written wine column in the daily newspaper. All kinds of little, pocket-size books have recently been published, claiming more or less to make you an "instant expert" in finding superb current vintage wines. Since it takes several months from the time the manuscript is finished to the time the book appears in the shops, most of them are already out-of-date on the day of publication. Certainly, after it has been out for three months, one of these little books is totally useless as a current vintage buying guide. It would be easy for me to say, for example, that the 1974 Heitz "Martha's Vineyard" Cabernet Sauvignon is a GREAT wine. You would be surprised to find how little of it there is around—even if you are willing to pay the price (to which it has been lifted by the demand) of between $75 and $100 a bottle. This is the basic and incontrovertible reason why I do not give current vintage information on wines in this book. You may ask why I do not give vintage charts for older wines?

The Vintage Chart as Conventional Wisdom

After using the classic vintage charts of the principal European wine regions for many years for comparative tastings, for buying wines, and for ordering them in restaurants, I have come to the conclusion that those plastic cards with the numbers on them are an anachronism, a piece of "conventional wisdom" held over from the 19th century. I firmly believe that they serve no other purpose today than to mislead the unskilled and unwary wine buyer into paying too high a price for a wine that is often not as good as it is cracked up to be. I realize that this may sound like an extreme point of view, and, before defending it in print, I decided to discuss the subject with an expert on the business side of the buying and selling of wine. I was on a visit to San Francisco and spent some time with my old friend Gerald Asher, who is not only a philosopher of wine and a fine writer on the subject, but actually earns his living on the staff of one of the large distributing firms involved both with European and American wines.

We agreed at once that the vintage chart is a holdover from the 19th century, when almost all wine was bought by a relatively few wealthy people, who lived in large stone houses with deep, cool wine cellars. They never bought their wines for immediate drinking, always expecting to age them in their own cellars for at least ten, or twenty, or even thirty years. It was a normal tradition, when a son was born, to lay down a case of wine for him to be opened at his twenty-first birthday party. The making of wine, in those days, was dangerously haphazard—dependent on nature and good luck. Many wines went sour long before they achieved a drinkable maturity. The customer had to have enormous faith in the honesty and good judgment of his wine merchant. So, when the merchant offered a list of wines for sale, he usually included a chart measuring his expectations of the future of each wine. That was the origin of the modern vintage chart. Note at once the most basic of all points about vintage charts—as valid today as it was 150 years ago—that the chart is *not* a measure of the quality of the wine as it is now, but as it may be expected to be when it achieves full maturity, perhaps ten or twenty years from now.

Gerald remembered a striking example, from his days in Europe in the early 1960s, of how large numbers of people were fooled by misreading the vintage charts. The 1961 Bordeaux red wines had just come onto the market with ratings on the vintage charts implying that they would one day be truly GREAT. At the same time, the 1959s were available, also with exceedingly high figures on the charts. In between these two enormously publicized vintages, there

was the quiet little 1960, which had been marked low on the vintage
charts and, for that reason, was selling at bargain prices. But the eyes
of the inexperienced "stargazers" at vintage charts were fixed on the
"super" wines, and nobody bothered with the 1960s. In fact, the big
wines were still hard and tannic, virtually impossible to drink, while
their prices had taken off into the stratosphere. Against these, the
little 1960 was absolutely delicious to drink immediately—the perfect
wine of the moment. But the misleading and misread vintage charts
had ruined its chances. Gerald said, "It was as if expensive, unripe
peaches were being eaten in preference to inexpensive, superbly ripe
apples." Foolish people simply did not understand that the wine
with the high vintage chart rating is potentially GREAT but not automatically GREAT from the day it is bottled.

Another grave fault of the vintage chart system—even when a
single chart covers only a very small area, such as, for example,
Pomerol in Bordeaux, or Chablis in Burgundy, or the Napa Valley in
California—is that the vintage chart gives a single numerical quality
rating to the whole area, while, in fact, there may be quite large
variations between one vineyard and another within that area. Frost
can settle and strike the grapes in a vineyard at the bottom of the
valley while leaving entirely unscathed the vines at the top of the
slope. (This well-known effect is caused by the simple fact that ice-
cold air is heavy and tends to roll downhill.) One grape grower may
have harvested his fruit at the beginning of the week, while his next-
door neighbor waited a few days longer and was struck by a heat
spell that scorched his grapes or by a hailstorm that destroyed them.
One vineyard is invaded by grape rot, while another goes scot-free.
A damaging rainstorm may strike down one vineyard, while at another, a mile away, it isn't even raining. No vintage chart can ever
reflect these variations within even a small area.

All these faults of the vintage chart system apply equally in
Europe and in the United States, but then there is the special American "experimental problem." Gerald is strongly of the opinion—and
I fully agree with him—that weather is only one of the variable factors that make vintage charts (even those confined to small areas)
impossibly inaccurate. American winemakers are so innovative, so
experimental in their attitudes, so much dedicated to "trying something new" every time they make a fresh batch of wine, that the
variations from winery to winery, even within a few square miles,

can be immense—far beyond the possibility of being measured by a single number on a vintage chart. From vineyard to next-door vineyard, the timing of the harvesting of the grapes will be different, the method of the picking (by hand, or by machine) will be different, so will the crushing and the force used in the pressing, so will the technique of fermentation and the number of hours that the skins are left in contact with the juice and the temperature of the fermentation, the strains of yeast used will be different, so will the methods of fining, so will the types of wood and the sizes of the aging barrels be different. Two vineyards, actually side by side, may both be growing exactly the same variety of Cabernet Sauvignon in virtually the same earth, yet the two finished wines they produce will be substantially different. Multiply such differences a hundred times within the same area, and you can see at once the utter impossibility of an accurate American vintage chart.

If, however, you are a vintage chart "addict" and feel you cannot "kick the habit," my advice is that you read the American charts with intelligent understanding and a strong dose of self-discipline. Remember that a really big, beautifully made, American classic red wine, heavy with tannin in its youth so that it will live long, may take at least ten years to mature and smooth out into a magnificent drinking experience. If you allow yourself to be dazzled and fooled by the high rating on the vintage chart, so that you open a bottle at home or allow yourself to be pushed by the wine waiter into ordering it at a restaurant, before it is ready, all you will get for your exaggerated price will be such a degree of bitterness and harshness that all the wonderful aromatic and fruity qualities waiting to open up in that wine will be completely obscured. What a waste of money. Baron Elie de Rothschild once called it "infanticide." What a tragic misuse of the vintage chart! If you are looking for a red wine to drink tonight—and you insist on using your vintage chart—you would do far better to look for the low numbers of lesser wines that do not have the strong tannin of the big ones and are, therefore, at their peak and ready to drink within three or four years. It is always a far better experience to pour a humbler vintage at its peak of delicious drinking than a huge, prestigious vintage that is still completely underdeveloped, unready, and unresponsive. If you must lean on the crutch of a vintage chart, at least don't allow yourself to be misled by it.

The Great Vineyards
and Wineries

Heitz Wine Cellars near St. Helena in the Napa Valley

I first met Joe Heitz on the porch of his old farmhouse home facing his small 1898 stone winery at the dead end of Taplin Road in a tiny cut between the hills on the eastern side of the Napa Valley one sunny March afternoon in 1969. I remember every detail, and I have a recorded tape with the voices of Joe, his wife, Alice, his daughter, Kathleen, then fourteen, his sons, David, eighteen, and Rollie, who was having his eleventh birthday on that day, and my own fairly amazed comments on the wines I tasted. One has to mention the entire Heitz family because they are all participants in the making of the wines. That meeting became a significant incident in my enological evolution. Of the many factors which that year contributed to my determination to classify the American wines and write this book, perhaps the most persuasive was the absolute magnificence of one of the wines which, on that day, Joe Heitz piped out of one of his aging barrels and siphoned into a glass for me to taste. It was the final proof that, indeed, "great wine" was a fact in California.

In the exciting years since that day, my records show that I have opened slightly more than 2,200 bottles of Heitz wines and have tasted virtually every one of his varieties, vintages, and blends. The rating figures on my tasting charts confirm my own personal judgment that the Heitz winery is, in terms of consistent success year after year, the greatest producer of red wines in the United States. This hard appraisal at once dramatizes the very substantial differences between a "great winery" of the United States and a *premier grand cru* of France. In Bordeaux, for example, Château Lafite and Château Latour are neatly boundaried pieces of vineyard land, growing legally delimited varieties of grapes, converting them into a single wine, in a single building, on a single estate. It is all relatively simple.

Joe Heitz's operation—although it is minuscule in California production terms—is a good deal more complicated. He does own some vineyard land and grows some grapes, but they make up a very small percentage of his total production of wine. He said to me, "I'm not really interested in growing grapes. I guess I don't like mud on my boots. My training is as a winemaker, and I'm interested, above all, in the chemistry of wine—in the work in the laboratory and, perhaps more than anything else, in the 'perfecting' of the wine among the barrels in the cellar." If Joe were working in France, he would be called an *éleveur négociant*.

He buys his grapes from farmer-growers—virtually the same people every year—whom he knows intimately and trusts completely. It could hardly be different if he owned the land. If he thinks highly enough of these growers, he puts their names on his labels. He also buys wines made by other people—wines usually at a beginning stage of development—which he "perfects" by his skilled technical methods and which he may then use for blending into his nonvintage, less-expensive wines. Finally, Joe is up against the ridiculous American tradition, still obstinately maintained by the marketing people, that every winemaking firm must put out a whole range of vinous products, from an aperitif appetizer, through Champagne and sherry types, to varieties of vermouth. To meet this puerile problem, Heitz, for example, buys sparkling wine already bottled from a Napa Valley neighbor and merely puts a Heitz label on it. I feel reasonably sure that Joe will approve of my decision to restrict my discussion of his work to those important wines in the production of which he has been a creative participant.

Joe Heitz belongs to that small band of winemakers with such powerful enological personalities that they impose their individual stamp on every wine they make. Joe has a personal style that I believe I can often recognize in blind tastings. You can line up a dozen glasses of wine—all of roughly the same type—of which one is made by Heitz, and I believe I will be able (more than 50 percent of the time) to find it. Heitz's wines strongly reflect, in my view, the personality of the man. All his life, he has made bold decisions, and he always tries to make bold wines—as big and bold as the strength of the grapes of that vintage will allow. He likes to smell and taste in his wines—in varying degrees—the "smoke of oak," and, therefore, he virtually always matures them for a planned period in oak barrels. The Heitz home is comfortable, large, and warmly hospitable. The wines too, I find comfortable, large, and warm. As Joe's prestige and success have grown, he has become self-assured, with a certain attractive and charming arrogance. His wines, also, have attained an elegant assurance, a certain bravura, often with aspects of charm and delicacy, sometimes with an irresistible swagger. Alice Heitz once told me that if ever they made their first million, she would like to throw out all their present table settings of china, cutlery, and glass and replace them with beautiful, hand-painted dishes and plates, hand-blown wineglasses of superb balance, and hand-hammered, richly polished solid-silver forks and spoons. Joe's wines are like that. They have the balance and beauty of fine china, the clarity and purity of crystal glass, the richness and warmth of silver. How did such winemaking skill develop?

Joe Heitz was born on a farm near the small town of Princeton, Illinois. "I was introduced to wine early," Joe told me, "by my German grandfather, who made it from the Concord grapes in our small vineyard. He also fermented wild fruit, and, as a child, I was sent out to gather blackberries, wild grapes off the fence rows and creek banks, the chokecherries, elderberries. . . . To us, in the Midwest, it was our only source of comforting, warming alcohol. I didn't drink the stuff. It was just one of my chores."

During World War II, he joined the U.S. Air Corps and was stationed in California—the first time he had been to the West Coast —as a Night Fighter Crew Chief at an air base near Fresno in the Central Valley. In need of a little extra money, he looked for an off-base, part-time job for evenings and weekends. He found work as a nightman at a local winery, running the juice-concentrating evaporator, maintaining the temperature control, and monitoring the liquid flow through the filtering system. The winery manager seemed to sense some special qualities in the young man and invited him home to Sunday dinners with some comparative tastings of wines. The talk was all of the ultrabright future of the wine business in California. He urged Joe to come into it after the war, but (since he had already had a couple of years of college horticulture at the University of Illinois) he should get his degree by specializing in winemaking chemistry, enology, and viticulture—looking toward top management jobs. The manager praised the Department of Viticulture and Enology of the University of California in the small town of Davis just outside Sacramento. All this sparked a small fire inside Joe.

As soon as he could, he married Alice, the South Dakota girl he had met in Fresno, and they moved to Davis, where he enrolled at the university in the Department of Viticulture and Enology. Two years later, there followed a number of jobs in the quality-control laboratories of important wineries, starting at Gallo and, after several exploratory moves, settling down, in 1951, at Beaulieu Vineyard in the Napa Valley, as assistant to the legendary winemaker of California, André Tchelistcheff. No ambitious young man in winemaking could have a better teacher. After seven years with Tchelistcheff, Joe went back to Fresno, to the state college there, to set up and launch an academic program in enology and viticulture. He directed the program and taught the students for almost four years, but the longing was growing, deep within him, to own his own vineyard and make his own wine. He was sure that for his own happiness and satisfaction it must be the Napa Valley.

Finally, after desperate months of searching, they found the minuscule 8½-acre Leon Brendel Vineyard, planted with an Italian Piedmontese strain of red Grignolino grapes, on the main Napa Valley highway a mile or two outside the town of St. Helena. Since this was the only planting of this particular clone of Grignolino in the valley, the former owner, as a spare-time hobby, made a light red wine labeled "Only One." For this allegedly unique little vineyard, the asking down payment was $5,000. (Just think what it would be today!) In 1961, Joe borrowed the down payment from a friend and put up his first sign on the highway: "Heitz Wine Cellars."

The winery was about the size of a three-car garage, and there was only a very small house where Joe, Alice, and the three children could squeeze in to live. Joe knew at once, naturally, that they could not possibly survive on the profits from that tiny vineyard. If he were to achieve any kind of viable volume of distribution and profitable sales of his bottles, he would have to buy grapes grown by other people and make them into his own wines. He might even have to buy first-stage wines made by other people and use his own skilled techniques to "complete" them, to "perfect" them, to "refine" them —as the *éleveurs* do in France. But the problems immediately ahead of him seemed almost insuperable. He had no spare room for a single extra machine of any kind in his tiny winery. Even worse, he had no storage space anywhere—for barrels in which to age substantial quantities of wine—no walls with racks to hold bottles, no warehousing for cases of wine. The future looked distinctly bleak.

Within a few hundred yards of the small Heitz building on the main highway, there was a side turning, a country road called Zinfandel Lane merging into Taplin Road that rose gently, twisting between farm properties, through a cut into the hills on the eastern side of the valley. Joe had heard that, up at the dead end of Taplin Road, there was a lovely, old, historic stone winery that had been built in the late 1800s. One Sunday, he and Alice decided to drive up to see it. They found it—half dug into the hillside for coolness, its front right in the yard of an old, rambling, white clapboard farmhouse. While they were looking around, the owners, Alice and Fred Holt, came out and invited Alice and Joe to sit down at the picnic table on the lawn for a drink of cold lemonade. Short life stories were exchanged, and then, quite suddenly, Fred said, "Alice and I have been thinking a lot about retiring and going south. We have been discussing selling this place. Would you like to buy it? There's one hundred and sixty acres here, and part of it was a working vineyard in the eighteen-eighties."

It was on the porch of that house, facing the old stone winery, five years later, that I first met Joe Heitz. He told me, "By the time I needed to borrow more money to buy the old Taplin Road farm, I guess the local bank presidents had been drinking my wines for three or four years and liking them. Loans were available, and in nineteen sixty-four, I took over this Taplin Road place and converted the building down on the main highway into the Heitz Tasting Room and Retail Shop for the tourist trade. But I still had my basic distribution problem. At about the same time we moved up here, the great California wine pioneer James D. Zellerbach died and his Hanzell Vineyard was sold, and I was lucky enough to be able to buy all the very fine red and white wines he had in barrel storage. That gave us a very good quality boost and pretty well completely filled all the new extra space in the old stone winery here. So now we are working at full capacity, and, before long, let's face it, we will need even more space. Already, I find no difficulty in selling my top-quality fine wines, but no one can ever make a large quantity of the best wine. The grapes are simply not available—neither here, nor in any part of the world. Fine wines are always made, always will be made, in small quantities. For the volume business, I have to make more modest wines, such as, for example, my generic California Burgundy and Chablis. . . . My main problem, from now on, is to get my volume up. Naturally, I shall concentrate first on the fine wines, and, as they develop, I will devote less and less time to the more modest types."

The Wine in the Icebox
That Led to the Golden Opportunity

Within a few months of moving up to his new place, there came the extraordinary "accident of history" that offered Joe his golden opportunity and, in time, gave him the shining victory that has put him in the top ranking among the greatest winemakers of the United States. Two young people from the East, Martha and Tom May, were married, decided to live in California, and bought themselves a 15-acre vineyard just south of the village of Oakville, against the western foothills at the heart of the Napa Valley. They had had no experience of viticulture, but they planned to hire professionals to run the vineyard. Since Tom had once had a summer cottage on the island of Martha's Vineyard off Cape Cod, he thought it would be amusing and romantic to call their new Napa estate "Martha's Vineyard." When they took over, in 1965, it had already been planted with Cabernet Sauvignon vines, and the first crop of grapes was beginning to grow.

As they settled into the old house on the vineyard which was to be their new home, Martha found a charming bottle of wine left in the icebox by the previous owners—a bottle labeled "Heitz." They had just arrived in the valley and knew no one. Where and who was this Heitz? After a couple of telephone calls, they got out the car and drove over to buy more of the same wine. A few hours later, Joe was at Martha's Vineyard looking over the grapes growing on this extraordinary piece of earth. His expert eye thought so highly of the potential quality of the grapes that, then and there, he made an offer to buy the entire crop—provided that the grapes would be picked on a date of his choice so that they would be precisely at his required degree of ripeness. Martha and Tom accepted. It was the fantastic start of the relationship that has now continued for nearly twenty years and has dazzled the world of American wine.

In 1965, Martha's vines were still very young, and their first harvest of grapes was relatively small. So Joe simply blended them into his regular Cabernet Sauvignon of that year, and the wine contained about one-third of Martha's grapes, with two-thirds from other Napa vineyards. When the wine had been aged and developed, it was found that Martha's grapes had made a considerable contribution in terms of character, flavor, floweriness, a certain delicate softness that came from the sweetness of the fruit, yet with a firm texture. There could be no doubt about the rightness of Joe's decision that, the following year, when he would have the first full crop of Martha's grapes, he would make a 100 percent "Martha's Vineyard" wine.

So, beginning in 1966, there were two versions of Heitz Cabernet Sauvignon: his "Napa Valley," with grapes from his regular sources, and his "Martha's Vineyard," with that name printed on the Heitz label. Joe once told me, "I put the name of a vineyard on my label not for publicity or salesmanship, but only when I believe that the grapes are decidedly and substantially better in quality than the run-of-the-mill average which, in the Napa Valley, is pretty high. When you see the name of a vineyard on one of my labels, you know that I think extremely highly of the care that was taken in growing those grapes."

The 1966 and 1967 "Martha's Vineyard" wines were, in my opinion, still experimental. Joe was trying out various techniques, and most of his new variations on the classic methods were extremely successful. Both of these vintages were important prestige successes among the professionals in the Napa Valley and the amateur connoisseurs in San Francisco. The 1966 grew up to be considered a gutsy, hearty wine, strong with tannin, full of the promise of a long life. The vintage of 1967 was much lighter—the wine complex and delicate, but with Joe already achieving the beautiful balance that would become his signature on so many future wines.

Then came the extraordinary year of 1968—a year of weather that produced exceptional wines in almost all parts of California, but nowhere quite so extraordinary as within the charmed partnership of Joe Heitz and Martha's Vineyard. The weather through the spring, summer, and fall was near to perfection. The ripeness and sugar balance of Martha's grapes were near to perfection. Joe was as ready as a coiled spring for his greatest adventure and opportunity. The result was (and still is) the greatest red wine ever produced in America up to that time. It is the wine that has raised the question as to whether Martha's Vineyard is possibly (or certainly) the greatest growth of the Cabernet Sauvignon vine in the United States—the question "Is it the Château Lafite of America?" These judgments are not mine alone. They have been confirmed and reconfirmed by connoisseurs and critics in virtually unanimous agreement, with hard rating figures at innumerable blind tastings, in the United States, in France, and in every other corner of the world where the drinking and appraisal of wine is a joyous and serious business.

I must explain at once that none of this was immediately apparent in 1968. Heitz is extremely conservative as to the aging and slow development of his Cabernet Sauvignon. After the vinification of the wine had been completed by the end of November, he pumped it from the fermentation vats into a series of 1,000-gallon aging tanks of American white oak and left the wine quietly to settle down and find itself, until August 1970. At that time, the wine was pumped into small 60-gallon barrels of French Limousin oak, where, again, the wine was left strictly alone to "make the classic exchange with the wood" of flavors and oils for another two years, until about July 1972. Only then was the great 1968 Cabernet Sauvignon fined, filtered, and bottled. By then, of course, Joe already knew that he had a supremely great wine under his belt. After swearing me to secrecy, he allowed me a small tasting. Although the wine was now three and one-half years old, he still felt that he wanted to keep it almost another year in the bottle before releasing it. Finally, the famous 1968 came onto the market in March 1973.

Within a few months, Joe could have sold every one of the 8,980 bottles he had available. But he was convinced that the wine was as yet nowhere near its peak, and he wanted to know how it would develop. He made the flat rule that, during 1973, he would not sell one bottle more than half his inventory, 4,490 bottles. The following year, 1974, he refused to sell more than 40 percent of the stocks he had left, a release of a further 1,796 bottles. The price was rising sharply. In a shop in San Francisco, I saw a bottle tagged at $30. In 1975, Joe sold another 50 percent of what he had left, 1,347 more bottles—for 1976, two-thirds of what he had left, 898 bottles—and, in 1977, the last 449 bottles. The collectors' price for a single bottle is now anywhere between $100 and $200.

A Tasting of Cabernet Sauvignon
to Shock the International Wine World

Fairly recently, I was able to join an extraordinary "straight-line vertical tasting" of Heitz Cabernet Sauvignon wines, beginning with his first experiments with the Martha's Vineyard grapes in 1965, down to the almost-current wines of today, still aging and developing in the French Limousin oak barrels in his cellars. I have to say "almost-current" because Joe, even in his most cooperative moods, draws the line at allowing "outsiders" to taste the raw wines, more or less fresh from the upheavals of the fermentation, still struggling to find themselves and settle down. The complete sweep of this tasting was made possible by the generosity of a small group of wine-lover members of a California tasting society, who are aficionados and amateur collectors of Heitz vintages. Joe no longer has, even in his private library cellar, any more of the oldest bottles, but some of these collectors did.

By circulating a list of what was needed and inviting everyone to come, with their bottles, to the Heitz Cellars on a certain date, we were able to put all the bottles into a "straight line," and Joe promised to fill in with the latest vintages from his bottle storage racks and even from some of his aging barrels. I can only describe the experience as an inspiring sensuous exercise and—if any such proof is still needed—it laid to rest forever in my mind any idea that the United States is a second-class wine-producing country. Two other powerful points were firmly established by this memorable tasting: first, the wonderful way in which the older wines had developed with time, proving how soundly they had been "constructed" by their maker; second, the extraordinary variety of the different vintages, proving the overriding influence of the natural forces of wind and weather. These impressions were strongly reflected in my recorded notes:

- The 1965, tasted almost fifteen years later, remains well balanced, aromatic, and firm, still with a sense of fruit. The 1966 and 1967, after the passage of the years, still have a deep color and the bouquet of a delicate sweetness of grapes.
- The great 1968 may now be approaching the fullness of its maturity. I rate it once again. It scores 49 out of a possible 50 points. Its aroma is superb. The feel of the wine expands as if

it were liquid velvet on the tongue. The complexity of its va-
nilla-touched flavors is immense. I hear the voices of other
tasters around me commenting on its beautiful aromatic balance, its dazzling depth, its richness.

- In 1969, Joe had another extraordinary year, with both his
  wines—just about level in quality with 1968. This time, his
  "Napa Valley" (Lot C–91) scores in quality ratings just a few
  points ahead of his "Martha's Vineyard." The blended
  "Napa" has a deep color, extraordinary strength, a striking
  raspberry fruitiness, a powerful texture of tannin, giving the
  wine a solid body, an almost meaty chewiness in the mouth,
  yet with a graceful balance. This is nothing short of another
  great wine. It rates 48 points out of a possible 50.

- In 1970, Martha's grapes, slowly ripened through a warm,
  languorous summer, again gave Joe (for the third year) another superb wine—complex and intense in character, austere
  and subtly delicate, with a long and noble future. In 1971, after
  three magnificent years, the honeymoon with the weather is
  over. It is an impossible year for great wine—the summer
  terrible, the vintage extremely poor. Joe and everyone else in
  the valley do the best they can. No "Martha's Vineyard" wine
  is held for separate bottling in this vintage.

- In 1972, good grape times show some promise of returning,
  but it is still a below-average vintage year, with small yield of
  fruit and uneven ripeness. Joe makes a mellow, warm wine
  from Martha's grapes—a lovely aroma, with a flowery, fruity
  intensity, soft and velvety on the tongue, clean and very dry,
  but obviously still developing and not yet at its peak—unlikely
  ever to be one of the supreme wines.

- The 1973 harvest of Cabernet Sauvignon in the central Napa
  Valley will be remembered as one of the proudest of local
  vintages. Everything—from the spring rains to the sunshine
  at the picking—was near to perfection. Martha's grapes were
  of supreme quality with high sugar. Joe's wine went into the
  barrels with levels of alcohol and tannin that promised a very
  long life. The wine has a perfection of balance, a supreme
  complexity of flavor interest, a fullness and roundness in the
  mouth. It is developing slowly and will take years to reach its
  top performance.

- Then came the extraordinary 1974. No sooner had Joe completed his work on his magnificent 1973, when he had to turn at once to the exciting possibility that the 1974 vintage would out-perfect even the perfection of the previous year. It was a fantastic turn of events. The grape growers realized, quite early in the season, that all the cellars were jammed full of last year's enormously abundant harvest and that, therefore, they would meet strong sales resistance in offering this year's grapes. The winemakers—their storage facilities already full —would be very snooty about the quality of the grapes they would buy in 1974.

- So the growers began very strongly pruning back their vines to reduce the quantity of grapes and increase the quality. This move was supported ideally by the weather. It was a long, cool summer that encouraged the grapes to develop and concentrate above-average amounts of aroma and flavor oils. Then, in October, came an "Indian Summer" of hot sunshine to boost the sugar in the berries, and that, of course, led to a superb fermentation.

- Joe's 1974 is unquestionably the most magnificent Cabernet Sauvignon of "Martha's Vineyard" that he has produced since his GREAT wine of 1968. This 1974, still in its youth, has already the feel of satin and velvet on the tongue. The complexity of the aromas and flavors is entirely extraordinary. Already—at the very beginning of its career, which will clearly run well into the 21st century—it achieves a rating of 48 out of 50 on my tasting charts—a firm indication that it will develop into a more important and significant wine even than the 1968. Joe says of his 1974 (with his usual slight touch of irrepressible self-assurance and immodesty!) that "it is the best Cabernet Sauvignon or Bordeaux available."

- When we come to the 1975, we are in the area of such relatively young wines that, at the time of this writing, definitive judgments are still difficult. The 1975 has good color, a developing fruity aroma and flavor, with a somewhat austere character, but a substantial, mouth-filling body texture. Although it was a difficult year for Cabernet, this wine already rates on my charts as of NOBLE quality.

- The first tasting of the 1976 was a few days after it had been bottled, and the young wine was still suffering from what Joe calls "bottle fatigue." It already has a good deep color, a developing fruity aroma, complexity of flavors, and a certain richness on the tongue. It has plenty of tannin, so it will continue to develop for several years—a child worth watching for its maturing and progress. As the great wine writer André Simon once said, "With wine, you can do nothing without time."

As I listened to Joe, standing in the middle of his cellar surrounded by his wines, discussing his techniques and answering the questions from the tasting group, I could not help again being aware of the international significance of the wine experience in which we had all just been involved. There could no longer be a shadow of a doubt that these American wines were of "world class"—competing on equal terms with any wine (however ancient its label, or famous its name, or high its prestige) from any other vineyard area in Europe, or from any other place on earth.

Opportunities for Tasting Heitz Wines Across the United States

Joe Heitz is a rigid, unorthodox disciplinarian—with himself, with his wines, and in the way he runs his business. He could easily sell all his fine wines (as against his inexpensive, nonvintage, lesser wines) to a relatively small number of wealthy California collectors. But he now feels, since he is nationally known, he should be nationally available through at least a limited network of fine wineshops in the major cities. So he deliberately limits his California sales to about 50 percent of each release of each of his wines. The remainder goes into the normal national distribution channels, and this gives us a fair chance of finding a bottle of Heitz wine if we make the effort to learn who is the local representative.

The trouble is that, in comparison to the huge national brands, there is very little Heitz wine available, and since it has a lot of aficionados, the supply of each wine very soon runs out. For this reason, I find it useful to know the pattern of Joe's fixed rules for aging, bottling, and releasing each of his wines. It is a rigidly disciplined system, and the same wine is always released into the market during the same month every year. So, if I know when the wine is expected, I can watch for it and be among the first to select my bottles for tasting.

I have already explained, above, his schedule for his Cabernet Sauvignon, which he releases into the market at the end of February or the beginning of March each year, about four and one-half years after the wine was made. (As a simple rule, add five to the vintage year to get the release year.) But since he continues, as explained above, to release the same wine in further batches over the next four additional years, his system gives me an exceptional freedom of choice. It means that, if I search in a well-stocked wineshop, there might be, at any one time, at least five vintages of Cabernet Sauvignon from which to choose. This means, in fact, five vintages of the "Martha's Vineyard" label, plus more vintages from the other vineyards from which Heitz buys grapes and which he names on his labels, including the "Nathan Fay Vineyard" and the "Bella Oaks Vineyard." Naturally, some of the older wines may make much better drinking than the current young vintage and may be a good deal more expensive, but that "ain't necessarily so." Some of the older vintages may have been less good and cost less. The important thing is that I can pick up a few odd single bottles, can take them home, taste them, and compare them.

Joe Heitz's second most important wine is his big, elegant, rich, white Pinot Chardonnay, which he ages and releases on an equally disciplined schedule, but to a two-year, instead of a five-year, cycle. He told me, "After we make it, usually in October, it is aged in one-thousand-gallon American white oak tanks for just about three months, up to January or February of the following year. Then it is transferred to sixty-gallon French Limousin oak barrels and continues the aging process for one more full year. Then it is bottled and held in the glass a few more months." This means that he releases a new vintage of his Chardonnay each October, exactly two years after the vintage date. But he releases only 80 percent of his total production. The remaining bottles—just as with the Cabernet Sauvignon—are held in his aging cellars untouched for another twelve months. Then, the following October, he releases three-quarters of the remaining bottles, and in October a year later, the final bottles are let go to close out that vintage. So—at any one time—if I am looking for Heitz vintage Chardonnay in a well-stocked store, I should be able to find three vintages available, of three different ages, at three different prices.

As to his white Johannisberg Riesling, Joe told me, "We make it, of course, in September and October, then hold it in one-thousand-gallon American white oak tanks for about seven months. We bottle it in June or July and begin releasing it in September or October for Christmas, when it is just about a year old." Here there is no complication of "holdback"—the entire production is continuously distributed until it is all gone. The same applies to his other red wines, including his Pinot Noir, Barbera, and the Grignolino which he grows himself.

Finally, there is his Grignolino rosé, classified as the best rosé of the United States, bright, fruity, beautifully orangy pink, refreshing, silky, and tangy, which he makes as the youngest wine in his repertoire. He says, "The wine I sell in its youngest state is my Grignolino rosé. You might call it the equivalent of a *Beaujolais de l'Année*. It is made in September and October, then bottled as soon as it is perfectly clear and stable, usually within three to five months, from December to March. So we can release it for hot-weather drinking, from May, June, and July onward."

Questions on Secrets of Quality

Now that Joe Heitz is basking in the warmth of his international success, now that his son David has come into the winery as an ambitious, serious, and increasingly skilled working partner; now that his daughter, Kathleen, is helping with the business administration; now that some of the weight is being taken off his shoulders, Joe is becoming almost mellow, and I have been trying to draw from him some of the deeper reasons for the memorable qualities that seem to pervade all his wines. Joe remains—quite deliberately, I am sure—fairly hard to pin down.

I have, again and again, returned to the question of the relationship between him and the people who grow his grapes. How does it work, fundamentally, for a finicky, fussy, perfectionist winemaker not to have complete control over the growing of his grapes? Does he ever do battle with his growers? "You bet I do," he replied. "There is always a basic conflict of interest between the growers and the winemakers—just as there is, shall we say, between landlords and tenants. Once Labor Day is past, the grower begins to worry about the imaginary danger of a terrible rainstorm coming and destroying all his grape crop. It has happened, and the grower then can lose his entire viticultural income for that whole year! So every grower wants to have his grapes picked and safely transferred out of his hands certainly no later than Halloween, regardless of the ripeness of the berries. Against that point of view, my interest is to get every last hour of sunshine onto those grapes, to inject every last bit of ripeness and sugar into them. So I am always quite sure that the weather is going to be perfect this year right up to Thanksgiving, and I want those grapes to hang in there on those vines as long as possible. Neither side can ever win the argument. So, each year, we listen to the long-range weather forecasts and compromise."

I have asked him many times about the actual picking of the grapes. Does he demand some control as to how it is done? Again, "You can bet your life I do," he told me. "If they send me a load of grapes with lots of leaves and stalks and cola bottles and milk cartons —I'll send them back! But I've only had to do that a very few times."

I have asked him whether he does not agree that the very modern methods of mechanical crushing of grapes are not a bit too harsh —bring out too much of the bitter tannic elements into the wine? Joe said, "Once upon a time, they used to believe that good wine could only be made when the grapes were crushed by the bare feet of virgins. The trouble was that they ran out of virgins. I wouldn't exchange my mechanical crusher for a hundred virgins any day."

What does he think of the new movement for so-called natural wines, wines made with as little "processing" as possible, with minimum filtering and fining, with, in short, the making of the wine left largely to the natural sequence of fermentation and aging? Joe's answer: "I basically believe that Mother Nature is a mean old gal who certainly doesn't know how to make wine—only vinegar—and we scientists have to help her all we can!"

I have often tried throwing him that most-curving of all dangerous spitballs, the question as to whether it is a fundamental fact that a small winery will always produce better wines than a large winery. Joe fairly snorted at me: "I know several small wineries whose production is pure crap. But those wines still sell, because people say, 'Oh, this was made by little so-and-so, and he does it all himself.' That's ridiculous. These days, a bunch of rank amateurs is coming into the wine business, because it's a romantic thing to do. That won't necessarily make good wine. These people may have been

great attorneys, great doctors, great stockbrokers, great shoe salesmen, great atomic scientists. . . . When they were on the outside,
looking in, they thought there was nothing to winemaking. Now,
many of them are finding out. A small winery, *per se,* does not guarantee good wine. On the other hand, big wineries, with lots of
money, can buy the best of equipment and hire the most skilled of
help. But—with absentee ownership, with relatively disinterested
workers—the big winery often lacks one absolutely essential ingredient: intense desire for perfection. Not that perfectionism by itself
can make good wine. But, on the whole, a dedicated small winery
has a better chance of reaching the peak, provided it is run by skilled
professionals, all suffering from that incurable fever known as 'intense desire.' "

A couple of summers ago, Alice and Joe spent their vacation
touring the vineyards and tasting the best wines of France. When he
got back home, I asked Joe whether he was prepared to say if the
best of France was as good as, or better than, the best of the United
States. "Is the best blonde as much fun as the best brunette?"

Schramsberg Vineyards at Calistoga in the Napa Valley

People who live and work in the Napa Valley, taking an interest in
its history, are pretty well agreed that the valley's most famous resident of all time was the great Scottish writer Robert Louis Stevenson,
the author of such famous and great works as *The Strange Case of Dr.
Jekyll and Mr. Hyde, Treasure Island,* and *A Child's Garden of Verses.*
Stevenson's entire life was shaped by the terrible scourge of incurable
tuberculosis. In search of the warmth of the sun, he went to the south
of France and there fell deeply in love with an American woman,
Fanny Osbourne. When she returned to San Francisco to end an
unhappy marriage, Stevenson followed her, and in due time they
were married. Since they were as poor as church mice (as the Scottish
saying goes), they decided to spend a camping and hiking honeymoon in the one place around the Bay that had the highest reputation
for romantic beauty, concentration of sunshine, and sheltered
warmth—the Napa Valley.

It took them two days to reach the "villages" of Napa and St.
Helena, both farm market centers. They were virtually unaware of

the half-dozen or so small vineyards in the valley. Fanny and Robert laboriously struggled up the trail on a spur of Mount St. Helena, and, high among the madrones and pines, they found the historic old Silverado Trail and an abandoned and crumbling silver mining camp. One of the log cabins that still had its walls and roof intact was the old bunkhouse and, delighted to find a place where they could stay without having to pay rent, the honeymoon couple moved in, cleaned it up, and called themselves "The Silverado Squatters." Of this strangest-of-all-places for a lovers' honeymoon, Stevenson wrote some of his most romantic lines:

> I will make you brooches and toys for your delight
> Of bird-song at morning and star-shine at night.
> I will make a palace fit for you and me,
> Of green days in forests and blue days at sea.

> I will make my kitchen, and you shall keep your room. . .
> And you shall wash your linen and keep your body white
> In rainfall at morning and dewfall at night.

Every day, through that idyllic spring and summer, Stevenson and his bride explored a different corner of the Napa Valley. The most famous of the earliest wineries—the first hillside vineyard, as against those on the valley floor—was owned by Jacob Schram and was called Schramsberg. Situated above the village of Calistoga, it had deep rock cellars cut into the mountainside, a huge house built in the style of a château, and steeply sloping vineyards. Naturally, Stevenson and Fanny arranged a visit, and, of course, the writer later described that memorable day:

> Some way down the valley below Calistoga, we turned sharply to the south and plunged into the thick of the wood. A rude trail rapidly mounting, a little stream tinkling by on the one hand . . . overhead and on all sides a bower of green and tangled thicket, still fragrant and still flower-be-spangled by the early season, where thimble-berry played the part of our English hawthorn and the buckeyes were putting forth their twisted horns of blossom. . . . The houses, with their vineyards, stood each in a green niche. . . . in this deep and narrow forest dell . . . no more had been cleared than was necessary for cultivation; close

around . . . ran the tangled wood—the glen . . . basking in sun and silence, concealed from all but the clouds and the mountain birds.

Mr. Schram's . . . is the oldest vineyard in the valley, eighteen years old, I think, yet he began a penniless barber and even after he had broken ground up here . . . he continued to tramp the valley with his razor. Now, his place is the picture of prosperity, stuffed birds in the verandah, cellars far dug into the hillside . . . all trimness, varnish, flowers and sunshine among the tangled wildwood.

Stout, smiling Mrs. Schram . . . entertained Fanny in the verandah, while I was tasting wines in the cellar. To Mr. Schram this was a solemn office. His serious gusto warmed my heart; prosperity had not yet wholly banished a certain neophyte . . . a trepidation, and he followed every sip and read my face with proud anxiety. I tasted all. I tasted every variety and shade of Schramsberger red and white . . . the latter with a notable bouquet . . . I fear to think how many. The stirring sunlight and the growing vines and the vats and bottles in the cavern made a pleasant music for the mind. Here, also, earth's cream was being skimmed and garnered and the . . . customers can taste . . . the tang of the earth in this green valley. . . . The smile of jolly Mr. Schram might mantle in the glass.

Who was this "jolly Mr. Schram" whose name is still on every label of some of the GREAT American sparkling wines? He was born and raised along the river Rhine in Germany, near the wine city of Worms. All around was magnificent grape-growing country, and although the Schram family was not involved in winemaking, it was, apparently, a dream in the heart of young Jacob from his earliest years. At the age of fourteen, he emigrated to New York, where he began at once to earn a living by becoming an apprentice barber. He heard that good wine was being made in California, and he was determined to get there as soon as possible. He signed on as the barber on a ship bound for the Golden Gate—not through the Panama Canal, which had not yet been opened, but sailing around Cape Horn, at the iceberg-ridden, storm-tossed antarctic tip of South America, a very long and difficult voyage in those days.

At the age of twenty-six, Jacob Schram opened his own barber-shop on Montgomery Street in the booming financial district of San Francisco. He saved his money and, probably, picked up some good investment tips from the bankers and stockbrokers who were his regular customers. He was building his capital to bring him nearer to his dream of wine.

In 1857, after only five years in San Francisco, he moved his barbershop to the town of Napa in the valley and began looking for vineyard land. Five years later, in 1862, he found what he wanted at a price he could afford to pay—about 300 acres of steep hill slope of "tangled woods" that, somehow, reminded him of certain parts of the banks of the Rhine. He gave his still totally untamed "estate" a typically German name, "Schramsberg," "Schram's Mountain."

Over the next ten years, Jacob Schram was enormously helped by an accident of American history. The transcontinental railroad was being built, linking the east and west coasts, and thousands of Chinese laborers had been brought, shipload by shipload, from Canton to work all across western America in the railroad gangs. Just when Jacob was beginning to develop his land, the railroad work was coming to an end—the final "golden spike" was driven in at Promontory Point, Utah, in 1869—and thousands of strong Chinese laborers drifted back to San Francisco looking for work. There was a huge oversupply of low-cost labor. Hundreds of Chinese came into the Napa Valley as cooks, gardeners, agricultural workers, builders, carpenters, and general laborers. It is safe to say that Jacob Schram could never have planned his Schramsberg project on such a large scale had it not been for the unlimited supply of cheap Chinese labor.

The wine came first; comfortable living was a secondary priority. Jacob and his wife built a small cabin in the woods and lived there for more than ten years before they started on the building of the big house. A hundred acres of the hillside were cleared and planted in vines. The winery was built, and the simple hand presses and other machinery installed. But his biggest and most dramatic project was to set his Chinese laborers to cutting deep cellar tunnels into the hard rock of the mountain, to give him naturally cool storage for his wines. These rock tunnels—perhaps fifty feet in diameter and boring half a mile into the mountain—are still in use today and are, unquestionably, one of the primary secrets of the extraordinary quality of the modern Schramsberg sparkling wines. There were five tunnels, at different levels, joined by cross-tunnels, so that the winds would blow into them and through them, providing the most natural form of air conditioning for the barrels and racks of bottles. Finally, when all this work was pretty well completed, they began to build "the big house"—in a château style, with a huge verandah, a dining room to seat fifty people, four stories, and about twenty-five rooms.

All Jacob Schram's work on his estate was just about finished and everything was in perfect order when Robert Louis Stevenson and Fanny came to call in the spring of 1880. It must have been one of Jacob's happiest and most memorable days—to be visited by one of the most famous writers of the time—a climax to Jacob's success. Quite soon afterward, he was overtaken by disaster and tragedy. The dreaded phylloxera vine disease reached the Napa Valley, and all his vines were destroyed. Prohibition was already on the horizon. Jacob had extended himself to the absolute limit of his finances to buy the land and develop the estate. He simply had no backlog of capital to restart his wine business. In 1905, he died—perhaps of a broken heart. His wife and son were then forced to sell the Schramsberg estate to that inevitable, indefinable entity, "a group of Eastern investors."

Over the following fifty years, Schramsberg must have had at least a dozen different owners. Two or three seriously tried to replant the vines and revive its winemaking capacity. None succeeded. It was as if Stevenson's "tangled woods" wanted to take back what belonged rightfully to them. Some of the owners tried to make of the big house a grand weekend "pleasuredome," with huge parties and gaudy show. The house responded by falling slowly into ruinous disrepair. In modern inflationary times, it was too big to keep up just as a country house. Finally, in the 1950s, it was virtually abandoned. The moss grew green and thick on the walls of the rock tunnels, water dripped from the roofs, the machinery lay rusted and broken, the air smelled damp and musty, field mice nested in the house, windows were broken, walls were crumbling . . . Schramsberg seemed to have no part to play in the booming wine industry of the Napa Valley. Clearly, it needed a new, modern, 20th-century Jacob Schram—a man, a woman, or both, with the strength and the vision to accept the old challenge, to embrace the old dream, to be caught by the perfectionist ideal of trying to make supreme wine. The rebirth of Schramsberg has been the extraordinary personal success story of

Jack and Jamie Davies, its present owners and the makers of the extraordinary sparkling wines that have now carried the Schramsberg name to greatness. One might almost say that the earlier life experience of this closely knit husband and wife team was a preparation for the high adventure into which the two of them are now launched in the Napa Valley.

New Young Perfectionists on Their Way to Schramsberg

Jack Davies was born in 1923 in Cincinnati, the son of a businessman whose work required him and his family to move, first, for a few years, to Chicago and then to Beverly Hills in California. Jack returned to Chicago to attend Northwestern University, and after army service in World War II, he completed his education at Stanford and the Harvard Business School. He joined an international management consulting firm in San Francisco and was launched into the world of big business administration and marketing. He played his cards toward steady promotion with finesse and success—moving from one company to another, as planning staff, as division chief, as general manager, as vice president, as president, as chairman. Had Jack Davies been an "ordinary businessman," he would have been perfectly satisfied with his position, his progress, and his future prospects. He was on the way up. There was no need for any change in direction, probably for the rest of his life.

But Jack had, subconsciously, deep within him, a desire to be creative in the direction of a perfectionist ideal. Coupled with this was a secondary desire—growing stronger as he grew older—to be his own man, his own master, to strive and struggle for himself in a situation where he was not the servant of a large organization. All these still-indistinct, half-hidden urges would be made clear and sharp through the developing relationship with the young woman who would become his wife.

Jamie Peterman was born in Pasadena, California, the daughter of an attorney. She was, from her teen years onward, a modern young woman who wanted to follow her own career. After studying the fine arts at the University of California, at Boston University, and at the Otis Art Institute in Los Angeles, she came to San Francisco and, with a friend, opened the Hansen-Peterman Gallery of Modern

Art, which helped to introduce many of the modernistic movements to San Francisco and became a prestige success. (Although Jamie is no longer connected with it, the gallery still exists.) She met Jack, and they dined together. They found at once that their first strong mutual bond was food and wine. Both were excellent cooks and aficionados of wine. As their mutual attraction developed, as they talked deeply and at length about a future together, Jamie, with her training in art, her understanding of the creative processes, at once brought a sensitive understanding to Jack's secret longings for a change in his life. Perhaps it was Jamie who first caught the idea that they might, together, develop and manage an outstanding vineyard and make magnificent wine.

After they were married, they tried to gain some experience in the business of wine by investing in one of the famous California wineries. They found it a frustrating disappointment. Investors were pampered and spoiled but were firmly kept as outsiders—not allowed to learn any of the inner secrets. Jack and Jamie withdrew their investment and began looking around for a winery they might buy for themselves. At the same time, they threw themselves into university courses and special studies in winemaking. One day, they were at a party in the Napa Valley at the Stony Hill Vineyard of Eleanor and Fred McCrea. Fred spoke of the old Schramsberg estate, which had not grown grapes or made wine for about fifty years and had fallen badly into disrepair. Then he added, almost as a casual afterthought, "I know the present owner wants to sell the place. Would you like to drive over to see it?" About fifteen minutes later, Jack and Jamie were going up the same path through the tangled woods that Robert Louis Stevenson had described eighty-five years earlier.

Jack and Jamie, naturally, had read Stevenson's little book of essays on his honeymoon in the Napa Valley, *Silverado Squatters.* Although they had never visited Schramsberg, it was almost like coming to a place they already knew intimately. Perhaps, in the wild abandon of the tangled wood reclaiming this place, they sensed, in a flash, the dream of perfection that old Jacob Schram had planted here. Certainly, they felt the challenge and instantly grasped it. In short, they fell in love with Schramsberg and, then and there, were both determined to own it.

Back home in San Francisco, Jack was appalled by the problems that would have to be solved. He had planned to buy a fairly small vineyard—where the capital costs of purchase and development would be possible as a relatively simple family matter, involving no large-scale financial operations. But Schramsberg was a huge project —huge in capital cost, huge in demands for enormous rehabilitation. Jack would have to go to his banking and business friends, would have to set up a powerful and wealthy board of directors, would have to undertake and sustain major financing. The famous tunnels into the mountainside were running with water, overgrown with mosses, infested with rats and snakes, and all the massive doors had rotted off their hinges. The hundred acres of cleared vineyards had all disappeared under the expanding greenery of the wild forest growth. All the old machinery had rusted. Parts of the old winery buildings had fallen down and would have to be rebuilt. Even the great house, which had been lived in by later owners, would now need major repairs.

The High Cost
of Striving for Perfection

But perhaps the largest financial problem (and the one that would cause difficulty for the longest time) was based on Jack's dream of perfection. He was absolutely determined that he wanted to make just one kind of wine—entirely the best "American Champagne," the finest sparkling wine produced anywhere in this country. The production problems for the very best sparkling wines, whether in the Champagne country of France or anywhere else in the world, are no mystery. After you have gathered the best possible grapes and made from them the best possible wine, you must let it age in its bottle "on the yeast" for several years—the longer the better. Most of the famous labels are aged somewhere between twelve and twenty-four months. To achieve the degree of perfection that he would demand, Jack would insist on aging his Schramsberg wines not for two years, but for three, or four, or even five. Think of the financial stress involved in that plan. He would have to operate the vineyard on his capital for the first year, pay for the harvesting and purchase of grapes, pay for the making of the wine and its bottling. Then, when he had these few thousand bottles, he would not sell them for an immediate income but would stash them away in his cellar tunnels as "liquid assets" of no value for immediate cash flow. He would have to work on his capital in the same way for the second year, with no income return. And for the third year, with no income. And for the fourth year, and possibly even a fifth. Only then would he be free to sell the bottles from the first year. For a specialist in business administration, it was a terrifying prospect.

But the force of Jack's dream was so strong that he put together all the plans, and, in 1965, he and Jamie and their children moved out to live and work on the Schramsberg vineyard. Some of Jack's business colleagues in the big cities told him he was out of his mind. Some of the country people in the Napa Valley were quick to suggest that Jack and Jamie were big-city sophisticates looking for "instant rural life" who would never face the hard work and would meet with disaster. It was the hardest work—both of brain and of hand—they had ever known, but they took each small step together, and that was the deep joy of it for both of them.

The first year, they cleared and replanted only 5 acres of the original Jacob Schram hillside vineyard. After the harvest, they were able to make only 500 gallons of wine, about 2,400 bottles to be stacked on racks in the cool cellar tunnels. The second year, 15 more acres were cleared and replanted—about 5,000 more bottles stacked away.

Every day, the installation of new machinery, the restoration of the working buildings and the big house went forward, step by small step. Every decision was made jointly by Jack and Jamie—especially the blending of each *cuvée* of the wine. The *cuvée* is the delicate combination of flavors achieved by mixing together the various wines that are available after the harvest and the vinification. The gradual blending of the *cuvée*—the adding of a little bit more of this or that to achieve the perfection of taste or texture—is the heart and soul of the making of the supreme Champagne in France, or sparkling wine anywhere. Jack and Jamie have always, since their very first day at Schramsberg, been their own winemakers—sitting together at the tasting tables, assembling their own *cuvées*—so that their personal tastes have always been directly reflected in the magnificent wines of Schramsberg.

An Experimental Approach Toward Greatness

The Davies never stop experimenting toward improving the wine. At the same time, they continue the daily work of rebuilding and modernizing the Schramsberg estate, rehabilitating and reconstructing the cellar tunnels in the mountainside. Jack has been installing new machinery in the winery, clearing 40 acres of the old vineyards and replanting them in Chardonnay and Pinot Noir vines. Jamie has been increasing the comforts of the big house, the beauty of its flower gardens, and the gastronomic values of its herb and vegetable patches. Some of the large steps they have taken—some of the new types they have launched—have given American sparkling wine a more prominent place in the world family of the grape and the vine.

In 1967, they produced their classic "Blanc de Blancs," meaning that it was a white wine made entirely from white grapes, not, as is the tradition in France, including some red grapes from the Pinot Noir. The Schramsberg is a white wine of extraordinary clarity and lightness, made entirely from Pinot Chardonnay and Pinot Blanc. Today, virtually every producer has a sparkling wine of this type, but Schramsberg was the first in the United States. It is very dry, with a balance of complex flavors giving it a NOBLE quality rating.

In 1971, they released their "Blanc de Noirs," meaning a white sparkling wine made basically from red Pinot Noir grapes, but with the skins removed immediately after the grapes were crushed so that almost none of the red color gets into the juice. Schramsberg was the first to make this SUPERB quality wine in the United States, but now, of course, the name and style are copied everywhere.

In 1972, they produced their first wine that has consistently rated on the tasting charts at the highest level of truly GREAT quality, their sweet dessert sparkling wine, "Crémant," the French generic word meaning "creaming" or "frothing." The wine in the bottle is pressured to only half the normal effervescence, so that it forms a foamy head in the glass, with the sweetness of 4.5 percent residual sugar. This extraordinary dessert wine remains unique to Schramsberg.

Beginning in 1968 and culminating in 1979, Jack and Jamie began experimenting toward a "pink champagne" that would not be as bland and dull as the stuff which, in the Victorian era, was supposed to have been poured into ladies' slippers. At Schramsberg, they began with the Napa Gamay grape, allowing only a very small amount of color to come out of the skins into the juice, but drawing considerable aromatic character from the flavor oils of the red grape. A sparkling wine from the Gamay had never before been made in the United States. Gradually, step by step, they added more and more Pinot Noir with the Gamay, finding that they could achieve more delicacy, finesse, and lightness. At last, the Pinot Noir predominated, and they named the wine "Cuvée de Pinot." It has an attractive, golden, salmon pink color, a strong sense of fruit, yet is quite dry, with a rating of a NOBLE quality.

In 1980, Jack and Jamie took perhaps their largest single step toward their perfectionist ideal. Each year, after the grapes have been picked and crushed, there are always some lots of wine, some barrels, or tanks, or vats, that have come out particularly well—noticeably above the average. It might be some Pinot Chardonnay, or Pinot Blanc, or even white juice from Pinot Noir. In a normal winery operation, these "better lots" are generally just mixed in with the others and immediately forgotten. There is neither administrative nor technical machinery for dealing separately with unforeseen "special qualities." At Schramsberg, they decided to change all this. Every year, the special lots of the very best wines are set aside and then combined into a very special *cuvée,* which is called "The Schramsberg Reserve," implying the finest Schramsberg of all. This reserve has exceptional treatment. It is aged, on the average, a year longer than the other wines. This program began "in secret" in 1974. The first Schramsberg "Reserve" was released in 1980—six years after the harvest. It rates on the tasting charts at the highest level as a truly GREAT wine.

Stony Hill Vineyard
on the Mountain Above the Napa Valley

Stony Hill is a "domain estate" in the purest sense of that European phrase. If it were in Bordeaux, it would certainly be called a château. It is a single unit of vineyard land, immediately surrounding the house and the winery, where grapes are grown and wine is made and bottled, with never a single added grape coming in from outside. It is the classic practice of making "estate-bottled wine," and it is permitted, by the tight, tough federal wine-labeling law, to print on its label the magic phrase "Grown, produced and bottled by Stony Hill Vineyard." Between Stony Hill and the two other great vineyards already discussed, there is one unifying and significant factor: Each of these extraordinary wineries was founded and is owned and managed by an independent and perfectionist family dedicated to the simple principle: "Let's see how good we can make the wine if we try hard enough."

Stony Hill Vineyard was founded and built by a husband and wife, Eleanor and Fred McCrea, with, almost from birth, their children, Mary and Peter.

The first time I heard from Fred McCrea was in a letter from him in 1966, when he sent me two bottles of the Stony Hill Pinot Chardonnay. At that time, production was still so small that none of the wine was available through stores in New York. I rated that 1962 Chardonnay the best American white wine I had ever tasted. Since then, my note cards show that I have opened 466 bottles of Stony Hill wine. The numbers on my rating charts prove that Stony Hill is the greatest white wine of the United States.

I had first heard about Stony Hill from the president of the British Wine and Food Society, André L. Simon, who had flown from London to Chicago to attend the international meeting of the society. Naturally, the local Chicago members wanted to show Monsieur Simon the best of everything they knew, and, when he reached his room at the Drake Hotel, he found an ice bucket with some bottles of an American wine that was entirely unknown to him. He reported to a few of us, some hours later, that the wine was of extraordinary quality, reminding him distinctly of the texture of a French Burgundian Corton-Charlemagne. He found the Stony Hill, certainly, the finest American white wine he had ever tasted. So little of it was made, apparently, that none was ever shipped out of California.

This challenge of rarity led me, inevitably, to my first letter to Fred McCrea and my first tasting of his 1962 Chardonnay. It was a beautiful wine, of matchless clarity and purity, with a quite superb sense of the character of the fruit. It had much less of the "smoke of oak" than is usual even in Burgundy. It was solidly constructed (what the French call *bien charpenté*) for a body texture that promised a long life of increasing development. This was the product, obviously, of a winemaker with a sharply defined philosophy, supported by the determination, the personal force, and the technical skill to shape the wine to his own preconceived plan. I wrote to McCrea saying how highly I thought of his wine.

McCrea wrote in answer, "You call Stony Hill 'the best U.S. white wine.' These are pretty strong words. Wines vary from year to year, as you know. Wouldn't it be better for you and, also, my relations with my peers, if you toned down your opinion to 'one of the best'? You don't want to alienate anyone, and, also, when one gets too much praise, the competitors jump on one. I do hope that when next you get to California, you will let us know. Our winery is pretty small, but this vineyard is quite beautiful. I would like to take you around it."

It was several years before I was able to accept the invitation. Meanwhile, Fred McCrea sent me for tasting single bottles of each of his succeeding vintages of his Pinot Chardonnay. Each taste increased my eagerness to experience the vineyard. Finally, I took the road from San Francisco around the Bay and into the Napa Valley. Near the base of Spring Mountain, we turned into a narrow, sharply steep, unpaved driveway-*cum*-path-*cum*-tiny road, with rocky rubble crackling under the tires. Almost immediately, we crossed a small brook over a rather sturdy wooden bridge. Nevertheless, there was a printed notice on a board attached to a post: "This bridge is considered to be unsafe for automobiles. You cross it at your own risk. Frederick H. McCrea." He told me, later, that this notice was the most efficient method he had yet discovered for discouraging haphazard tourists from driving up the hill to the house, ringing the front door bell, and asking for a tour of the vineyards with a tasting of the wines. McCrea said he had no interest in either of those activities since he had nothing to sell.

I always find considerable joy in at last visiting a vineyard which for many previous years, in glass after glass of its wine, has brought me an admirable satisfaction. At Stony Hill, the joy was magnified by the beauty and wildness of the setting. It is uncleared, forested mountain slopes of oak, pine, madrone, and manzanita now preserved, in an area that entirely surrounds the Stony Hill Vineyard, as the Bothe Napa Valley State Park. It has the ambience of some closed-in corners of the Highlands of Scotland. The wind shooshing (as the Scots say) through the trees sounded the same. The rain-washed earth smelled the same. My dog had pushed her head as far out as she could through the open window of the car, and her nostrils were pumping at high speed. Her body, under my arm, was wriggling with excitement. I believe, as did Cesare Pavese, that to be anywhere near forests or woods without a dog is to miss most of the awareness of hidden existences. My dog multiplies for me the pleasures of discovery in wild places. Only when we were very near to the top were we aware of the military rows of the vines. Then there was a wide flat graveled area in front of a graceful one-story ranch house with an enormous, brass-trimmed oak door.

We talked and tasted in the very large living room, sitting in front of a big open fireplace, also reminiscent of Scotland, with crack-ling, snapping, and spitting logs. The east end of the room was a picture window with an immense view across the Napa Valley, to the farther and higher peaks of the Mayacamas Range. The path that has led Eleanor and Fred McCrea to this lovely place is neither very long, nor exceptionally complicated. The complexities of their lives have been involved with the dream and the creation of the wine. Fred was born in Minnesota, and, when he got out of college (in 1919, the year when good wine was legally removed from the Amer-ican scene), he came to San Francisco. His first job was in advertising with the McCann-Erickson agency, where he rose to be a vice presi-dent and stayed for the rest of his working life. Eleanor was born in Buffalo, New York, the daughter of a family in the lumber business. "We followed timber right across the country," she told me, "and eventually reached the West Coast. When my father died, I went to San Francisco and got a job."

She met Fred, they courted and became engaged, all during Prohibition. Their knowledge of wine remained minimal. Fred told me that on the night of Repeal in 1933, "I took my future bride to dinner at the Garden Court of the Palace Hotel and tried to show off to her by more or less blindly picking out some wines from the newly printed, enormous list. We were social dabblers, not serious connois-seurs. On weekends, we would drive to different places around the Bay, and we very soon discovered that the Napa Valley was the most beautiful, and it was always known as 'the Wine Country.' So when the children started to arrive, and we felt we needed a summer place, it was natural that we thought first of looking around Napa. One day, we were visiting friends who had a house at two thousand feet on Spring Mountain, and I said, 'Well, isn't there any place around here that you could buy?' and they said, 'Well, there's that old goat ranch down there below us. It's so steep it makes you feel as if you're just going to fall right off the edge, but if you like it . . . ' So, that same afternoon, we walked down and over to it, and, boy, we were crazy about it."

There was no house at the top. It was all completely wild. But there were a couple of cottages at the bottom of the hill that had been used by the foreman when the place was still being farmed. "From our first view of it," Fred told me, "we thought the place was simply beautiful. That, I think, influenced us more than anything else.

Growing grapes was no part of any plan in our minds. But, you know, I always believe that, at heart, I'm a 'canny Scot,' and, just before buying the place, I had one of the local farmers whom I knew, a German who was highly skilled, come up and check the soil. We were just being careful."

They bought the place in 1943, right in the middle of World War II, when they could get neither equipment nor help. They called it, simply, what it was, Stony Hill. They spent weekends and summer vacations with their children in the foreman's cottage, without electricity, a septic tank, or telephone. "As we got to know people in the valley," Fred said to me, "especially Alice and Joe Heitz, almost all the dinner-table talk was about grapes and wine. People seemed to think it was a pity that a potentially good mountain vineyard such as mine should not be planted in vines as soon as possible. It seemed to them a waste, and, as you know, a Scot doesn't like waste. So Eleanor and I began driving over to the University of California Department of Viticulture and Enology at Davis and talking to the various experts there. Some of them came and looked Stony Hill over and gave it as their opinion that the possibilities were pretty good.

"Now, you'll probably ask whether our preliminary planning was completely scientific, whether we studied the angle of the land to the sun, whether we observed the movements of the prevailing fogs and winds around the outcroppings of rock, whether we analyzed the mineral content of the soil, whether we traced the flow of the water during rainfall, and all that. Nothing of the kind. This is a very rocky, steep place. You can't just bring in a bulldozer. There are certain plateaus and terraces that are just level enough to be workable, and almost all of them had been cleared by the previous farmer. They make up about thirty-five acres out of the one hundred sixty that we own here. So we simply planned to plant those cleared fields one by one. Eleanor and I intended to do pretty well all the work ourselves. It took us a couple of years of study before we thought we were ready to go. I had heard a lot about the relatively new Pinot Chardonnay grape of which very little was as yet being grown, and I wanted to plant that. But the experts at Davis warned me that it was a very difficult and temperamental vine. It was easily subject to all kinds of diseases and was a most uneven producer in terms of weather conditions. One year you could get a magnificent crop and make superb wine. The next year might be a total failure. The Davis people advised us to 'split our risk' by planting some Chardonnay, but also some of the more dependable varieties such as Pinot Blanc and White Riesling. So we did. We calculated, though, that if we were going to do a near-perfect job of planting, we couldn't do more than about two to four acres a year."

The Planting of a Great Vineyard

One morning in 1946, there was delivered by truck a load of wire-bound bundles, each containing one hundred rootstocks, packed under six inches of sand. Each stock was about sixteen inches long, with a developed root at one end. Fred told me, "You dig a straight row of holes, put in as good soil as you have available, and plant the root cuttings with their tops showing four inches above ground. Then you cover those tops with little mounds of earth. You do all this generally in April, and then nothing happens until you see a green shoot growing up out of the mound, usually by July or August."

So far what is growing is only the rootstock. The decision must now be made as to which variety of grapevine is to be "budded" onto it. That first year of 1946, Eleanor and Fred received as gifts from their neighbors a supply of buds, or scions, cut from mature Pinot Chardonnay vines growing in the Napa Valley. These were cut into the roots and grew up as the first Pinot Chardonnay vines of Stony Hill.

"We rather enjoyed the game of planting," Eleanor told me, "and, as soon as they were old enough, so did our children. We came every weekend and, during the summer, from the day after school was out until the day after Labor Day. I think the reason why Mary and Peter so love this place and will take it over after we are gone is that they helped to build it. How hard they worked! We kept planting at least two new acres every year, of Chardonnay, of Pinot Blanc, and of White Riesling. Later, we also put in some Gewürztraminer, Semillon, and Pinot Noir. Every year there was more and more work because the vines that were already in and in various stages of development had to be looked after and watched over."

There is no really useful harvest of grapes from a newly planted vine for the first three or four years. The McCreas still had no thought of making any wine. They intended to sell the grapes to their wine-making neighbors. When they gathered their first small harvest in 1950, Fred wrote in the vineyard daybook on Sunday, September 3: "Picked our first grapes, a little over three boxes, crushed them into the first eight gallons of Stony Hill juice. The whole family—Eleanor, her sister, and Mary and Peter—tasted it." As she closed the faded daybook, Eleanor said, "But, really, nothing was planned. We made decisions on the spur of the moment. We had some grapes left over that first year, so we got a householder's permit that allowed us to make wine at home for our own use. In the old barn, we fermented the juice in a good clean secondhand barrel and made some wine. It tasted so good to us and our friends that we decided to make some more and store it in a couple of extra secondhand barrels for our future use."

The wine was not noticeably above average at first. They made more of it, a bit better each time, fruitier in taste. They enjoyed their own wines more and more (and were encouraged by their friends among the other winemakers), so they decided in 1951 to become a small commercial operation. They were federally bonded in 1952. Fred's retirement was still ten years away, but they were already agreed that they would eventually live full-time at Stony Hill and hope to be fully professional winemakers. They began thinking about the building of their ranch house on a small plateau at the top of the hill facing the magnificent view. As the first step in the planning of this area, they built their beautiful, almost-miniature stone winery. It has never been (and can never be) expanded because, at its back, the cliff falls straight down, and at its sides the rocks rise sharply. As Fred put it, "It has no place to go. You couldn't even add on one more aging room. The only way to expand would be to put up an entirely new building on some other part of the estate." But Fred always wanted the winery near the house, so that at any time of the day or night he could drop in to listen to how hard the wine was fermenting or to taste a sample to check how the wine was aging and developing in an experimental barrel.

Of their first "commercial vintage" of 1952 Fred said, "That year I think we threw away half of our wine. For the rest, we had a few friends who thought that it was all a crazy experiment but who bought it anyway. We still have our first sales book. But our production was infinitesimal. Within a couple of years, we wanted to enter our wine in the State Fair, but you have to certify that your wine was actually on the market and that you were producing a minimum of one hundred and twenty gallons, that's fifty cases, or six hundred bottles. It took us quite a while before we could meet that requirement."

A Philosophy of Winemaking
for a Mountain Vineyard

The next vintages were the formative years of Stony Hill wines. They were not destined automatically by nature to be great. We know now, with the advantages of hindsight, that they had greatness thrust upon them by a certain Mozartian quality in the character of Fred McCrea. By devouring every book on wine technology, by talking wine talk incessantly to his winemaking neighbors, by driving out again and again to the University at Davis and questioning Dr. Maynard Amerine and the other specialists of the Department of Viticulture and Enology, Fred had reached the outer limits of the classical knowledge. Then Fred took off into the unknown, along paths and into regions of experimentation previously uncharted and unexplored. Fred began thinking about the particular problems of grapes grown in a very small vineyard. He started analyzing the peculiar conditions of soil and weather on an exposed mountaintop. He went to France and drank Pinot Chardonnay in Burgundy from Chablis, Corton-Charlemagne, Beaune, and Meursault to Montrachet.

He developed certain philosophical ideas about winemaking that were to be uniquely his own. He said, "The point I feel very strongly is that the wines from a small winery are bound to be quite noticeably different from year to year. This is one of the problems and possibly one of the pleasures of Stony Hill. This may be unfortunate for some consumers, but in other ways it's good. It avoids too much uniformity and adds interest to the sequence of vintages. Since we have no long-term storage arrangements, we have to clear out each vintage to make room for the new one being harvested. You get the crop as it comes in each year and do the best you can with it. There seems to be too much variation in temperatures, amount of winter rains, dates of picking the grapes, methods of handling them, and so forth. This simply eliminates the kind of uniformity that a big winery can count on. So I decided early on to play my wines for their differences instead of their uniformity."

Yet almost all the Stony Hill wines have had a recognizable family thread running through them and linking them. Whether they have been big in rich years or relatively light in lean years, they have always had a delicate balance, a flavor of subtle rather than aggressive intensity, slightly withdrawn sophistication rather than flamboyant elegance—these are qualities that come most often from mountain grapes. Comparing Fred McCrea's wines, in a general way, to those of Burgundy, his Stony Hill is nearer in character to the hilltop wines of Corton-Charlemagne than it is to the valley wines of Meursault or Montrachet.

French *vignerons* often say, *"Pour faire le bon vin les raisins doivent souffrir"* ("To make good wine, the grapes must suffer"). Fred McCrea developed into a fine art the *élevage*, the bringing out of the best qualities of the "suffering" grapes on his Stony Hill. He said, "Our Stony Hill vines are wide open at all times to all kinds of extremes of weather. Since there is no protection from wild rainstorms, the earth gets soaked. In the wettest years, the earth can absorb no more, and the water simply races off and down. One winter we had fifty-four inches of rainfall, and I seem to remember other winters with even more. We don't have much protection either from those two other severe California hazards: sudden spring frosts, when the grapes first appear; and bursts of advance winter cold in the fall, when the grapes are ripening. Our mountaintop is always fully exposed to the fairly regular danger of too much heat in the summer, when the grapes can begin to dry out and shrivel.

"These and other special factors here at Stony Hill—the lightness of the stony soil, for instance—give our grapes a delicacy, you might almost call it a shyness, of flavor compared to the big aggressive fruit that grows down in the valley. With our grapes, the most important work toward quality comes after they are picked, the way they are handled by the winemaker. He must make difficult decisions about how to crush them, how much sulphur to add to the juice, what kind of oak to use to store the new wine, and all these choices are different each year for each variety of grape." The problems were continually different. Yet, as time passed and his experience widened, there was an increasing uniformity about Fred's decisions, based on a philosophy he was developing, a personal theory on the making of wine in a mountain vineyard.

The 1953 vintage of Stony Hill Pinot Chardonnay was the first to start a buzz of excitement among the professionals in the Napa Valley. Several winemakers have told me that they remember being surprised by it and finding it "amazingly good." The 1955 was of such quality, defined by many professionals as "absolutely extraordinary," that it burst upon the valley with an explosive impact. Eleanor and Fred were still doing almost all the work themselves, the new plantings, the care of the growing vines, the picking of the grapes, the making and the aging and bottling of the wines, with some help from their own two children and now and then a few high school students hired by the hour. Production of Stony Hill wine remained extremely low, around two hundred cases, 2,400 bottles a year. Fred was so interested in his experiments with the Chardonnay, that, as the Pinot Blanc and White Riesling vines came into bearing, he simply sold those grapes to other vintners in the valley. For seven years, Joe Heitz made from McCrea grapes what several of my colleagues and I think was the best Pinot Blanc ever produced in the United States (see page 52). Heitz thought so highly of the quality of the grapes that he printed the McCrea name with his own on the bottle labels. Production at Stony Hill rose gradually to three hundred, then four hundred, then six hundred cases of Chardonnay per year, but it was still not an efficient or profitable way of running a small vineyard.

Eleanor and Fred had now reached the point in time for several major decisions. They wanted to start building the house at the top of the hill, where they would live as full-time vintners. The planning and supervision of this project would absorb a good block of their time. They were already realizing that they couldn't go on doing all the work themselves in this mountain vineyard that was so difficult to cultivate. They would have to find some full-time professional help, at least a vineyard foreman who would look after the growing of the vines and the harvesting of the grapes, with a trained winemaker to work as cellarmaster under Fred's direction. Nor could they go on making do with homemade equipment. If they wanted to hire good people and buy modern machinery, they would have to produce a lot more wine. They would have to take the big step from being a family hobby to the organization of a cost-efficient small business.

On Fred's sixtieth birthday, they slept for the first time in the house on top of the hill, and the two small houses at the bottom were available for the new vineyard foreman and cellarmaster. Fred wanted to expand his Pinot Chardonnay plantings. Since the space at the top of the mountain was entirely limited by the surrounding outcroppings of rock, he decided to uproot his oldest Pinot Blanc vines and replace them with bud cuttings from his best Chardonnay vines already at maturity. Some of these produced much better grapes than others. Fred marked the better vines and took cuttings for replanting only from these. In this way, he steadily upgraded every one of his fields. Each vine is sharply pruned back at the start of the growing season. "If you leave too much wood," Fred told me, "too many canes to produce new shoots, the vine root can't support so many bunches of grapes, and they ripen too slowly and do not develop enough sugar. But if you prune the vines back, the bunches of grapes will be perfectly ripe when they are picked, and you will get the best possible wine. This is why it takes many years to grow a strong vineyard and to learn how to handle the vines. You have to get to know these vines in relation to this land almost as if they were your own children. You watch them flower and pray that rain- or windstorms will not come at that moment to shatter the tiny forming grapes.

"As the bunches grow, you are always on the lookout for mildew, and you run the jeep along the rows about every ten days with the sprayer. Remember that every field is not at the same stage of development at the same time. We have some Chardonnay at about eight-hundred-feet elevation and some at about twelve hundred, and they ripen almost always about three weeks apart. Beginning roughly in August, you walk out at least once a week into the middle of each field with your refractometer and crush an odd berry here and there and read off its sugar content and enter the figure on your chart. Every day of sunshine, the sugar is going up and the acid is going down. When they are at the right balance, you set the date for the picking."

"I don't even need a refractometer," Eleanor added, "to sense the ripeness of the grapes. You can judge by just looking at them. Instead of being hard little green marbles, all of a sudden they begin to get translucent. Then you pick one and taste it. You just slightly lift a bunch in your hand, and it feels flexible and soft and kind of heavy. Then you know you had better keep watching very carefully every day."

The Search for Perfection
in the Making of the Wine

At the picking, the baskets of grapes are tipped into the crusher in the yard outside the winery door. The crushing at Stony Hill is deliberately extremely light, just enough to break the skins. Then the mash slides down a stainless-steel chute into an old-fashioned basket press with wooden staves, all sitting in a large stainless-steel pan. The basket acts as a sieve, allowing only the juice to run through the staves into the pan. Then this juice is pumped through a hose into the barrels in the winery. "We don't want any of the pumice," Fred told me, "the skins, pits, little bits of stalks. We simply want the free-run juice. With the best modern equipment, say a Willmes press or one of the very new designs, you can get from a ton of grapes easily one hundred fifty to one hundred sixty gallons of juice. Against that, we average, we deliberately want to average, no more than about one hundred ten to one hundred fifteen gallons per ton. To all intents and purposes, ours is free-run juice, just with a little nudge from the press."

The McCreas believe in cold fermentation to guard and hold the fullest possible fruit flavor of the grapes. They use the modern stainless-steel refrigerated fermenters only in a very limited way, preferring to ferment in the old Burgundian way in oak barrels of various sizes from 50 to 200 gallons. Since the winery is so small, they cool the entire space to any temperature they want, most of the time to 55 degrees Fahrenheit. "I am not one of those 'nature boys,' " Fred said, "who believe that the wild yeasts which are on the grapes when they are picked should be left alone to ferment the juice and make the wine. Wild yeasts can have a lot of dangerous bacteria mixed in with them. I prefer to stun them into helpless inactivity with a dose into the juice of one hundred parts per million of sulphur dioxide. Then, when the juice is 'yeast sterile,' we put in a pure cultured French yeast from Champagne or Montrachet at four ounces per thousand gallons. The yeast is dissolved in wine, heated precisely to one hundred ten degrees Fahrenheit, then measured amounts are added to each barrel.

"We try to keep the fermentation as gentle and slow as possible to hold on to every bit of the flavor of the fruit. Sometimes the bubbling continues from October into January." When the residual sugar falls to somewhere between 0.1 percent and 0.2 percent, the wine is considered to be completely dry and is ready for its year of slow maturing in the barrel. Up to this point each barrel is only about three-quarters full to allow for the upheavals of the fermentation. Now wine is transferred from one to the other until each barrel is completely filled and all air is excluded. Then the bungholes are sealed with wooden plugs—but, of course, the wine is checked and topped up each week. Eleanor, Fred, and their cellarmaster, Mike Chelini, taste from each barrel at least once a week, watching for any adverse developments and generally checking progress. Fred is always on the lookout for over-accentuation of the oak flavor.

The Space Problem
Controls the Release of the Wine

The following August, as harvest time approaches, the barrels have to be emptied, as the cooperage is needed for the new crush. So the year-old wine is fined, filtered, and bottled, and the aging of the Chardonnay continues in the bottles for another full year. Each Chardonnay vintage is finally released to its small national distribution in a September "offering list" just two years after the harvest. All wine on that list is usually gone within thirty days. The selling of their wines takes up extraordinarily little of the McCreas' time.

As soon as Fred had established a reasonably efficient production cycle for his Chardonnay, he moved to begin making wines from his other grape varieties. He had developed mature plantings of Gewürztraminer and White Riesling. They are somewhat less demanding than the Chardonnay, although Fred set almost impossibly high standards for the wines he wanted to make from them. "We have a long way to go, here in California," he said, "to match the dry, perfumed, light floweriness of the best Gewürztraminer of Alsace." As to his Riesling, he thought of it as being in the same family as the scented, soft, subtle "Johannisberg" of the Rhine of Germany. The Stony Hill Gewürztraminers and Rieslings remain in the barrels for only about six or seven months, are bottled in June, and released to the market in September, when they are just one year old. Production of Gewürztraminer began slowly in 1966 with about 150 cases, 1,800 bottles. By 1969, newly planted vines on the highest part of the mountain were coming into production in spite of a heavy late frost in May, and the September-October harvest and crush showed an all-round substantial increase in production. There were 1,000 cases, 12,000 bottles, of Chardonnay; 400 cases, 4,800 bottles, of Gewürztraminer; and 200 cases, 2,400 bottles, of White Riesling.

The same year, Fred began a new small experimental project. He was anxious to know whether, at his mountain elevation, he could make a natural simple sweet wine. In one of the sunniest corners of a field with a southern exposure and a rock wall behind it that might reflect the sun's heat downward, he had planted a few dozen vines of Semillon, one of the component grapes of the Sauternes of Bordeaux. With fine hot weather through August and September, these grapes were picked with an exceptionally high sugar content. To build up even more sugar, the bunches were then set out in single layers on prune-drying trays and left to catch the maximum sun in one of the few available level spaces, the parking area in front of the house. That night, the raccoons had a glorious feast. Almost a third of the grapes were lost. In the morning, Eleanor had to dash down to the supermarket in St. Helena and buy every available roll of clear plastic wrap. After seven or eight days of steady exposure to the hot sun, the sugar content had increased by another 50 percent. The grapes were then crushed, and the eventual result was about twenty gallons, just over eight cases, 100 bottles of a fine little sweet dessert wine which the McCreas christened "Semillon de Soleil" and have been offering in gradually increasing numbers of half-bottles ever since.

Another small Stony Hill experimental project was started mainly to please the young cellarmaster, Mike Chelini, who is of Italian ancestry and perhaps for that reason thinks that no vineyard, however famous for its whites, can be spiritually complete without any red wine in its repertoire. Again and again he begged the McCreas to let him plant some red grapes and make some "house wine," if only for the use of their family and his. "Well, Mike," said

Fred, "I can't guarantee that we can make a Domaine de la Romanée-Conti." Mike's eager voice was unaffected by this sobering thought as he replied, "You know, we just might!" So a corner of the vineyard was chosen with the right exposure for Pinot Noir and about two hundred vines were planted. Mike now vinifies the annual crush of these grapes in two classical ways. He ferments half the juice without the skins and produces a light pink wine that can be bottled within three or four months and drunk ice cold without aging, somewhat in the style of a *Beaujolais de l'Année*. This is labeled Stony Hill "Blanc de Noirs," with about 60 cases, 720 bottles, a year, and it is pretty well the favorite summer drink of both the McCrea and the Chelini families and their guests. Mike converts the other half of the crush into a nice, full, dark red Pinot Noir, also about 60 cases, usually served with summer lunches on the terrace. Neither of these has yet been offered on a Stony Hill public list. Nor have I succeeded in acquiring any for my own use. "We like them so much," Eleanor told me, "there's never enough to go around."

The summer of 1972 was extraordinarily dry and hot on the mountain, and the grapes were approaching full ripeness exceptionally early. Then, all of a sudden, there were cold nights and clammy early morning fogs, slowing down the final development of the sugar in the berries. That year about 20 percent of the crop was lost, but the remaining grapes, having suffered more than usual, made wine of an extraordinary intensity of flavor—almost a kind of concentrate of Stony Hill wine. In contrast, the grapes seemed hardly to suffer at all the following year, 1973. The weather in the Napa Valley, during the entire growing season, was close to perfection, and there were all the early signs at Stony Hill that Eleanor and Fred had probably made the greatest wines since they began the vineyard. The balance was superb, the aromatic complexity showed great promise for development, the body structure of the wine guaranteed long years in the bottle of fresh and probably dazzling life. After these wonderful wines had been safely made and put away, there arrived the unique experience of "the great snowstorm" on the mountaintop. Fred described it in one of his letters to me.

"Our vineyard was covered," Fred wrote, "by at least six or eight inches for five days, and the road up the hill to our house was completely blocked. The heat was off for twenty-five hours. The phone was out. Our wonderful young cellarmaster, Mike Chelini, who as you know lives in the house at the bottom of the hill, managed finally to climb his way up on foot on the second day. Then he backpacked groceries to us several times. All we had was one can of Sterno to cook on. I think you would have approved of our reactions. The first night, with no communications with the outside world, Eleanor began the preparations for dinner by boiling one egg on the Sterno. Our daughter, Mary, had sent us a jar of caviar for Christmas, and we sat in the living room before a huge log fire in our open hearth (our only heat) and toasted a slice of bread and had a bottle of Schramsberg 'Blanc de Noirs' and caviar for supper. Pretty high class, I'd say."

I had my first chance to judge the development of the amazing 1973 Stony Hill wines at midsummer in 1974, when I visited Eleanor and Fred and tasted from the barrels in the winery. The Gewürztraminer already had a lovely flowery bouquet, a fresh and fruity taste, an early developing sense of spice. The White Riesling was showing a softness of distant sugar—it was obviously going to be rich on the tongue, a wine that would eventually be all silk and velvet. As to the Pinot Chardonnay, it would clearly be the greatest wine that Fred had ever made—already, considering that it had only just completed its fermentation, it had an amazingly rich bouquet, the aggressive drive of youth, the faint aroma and taste of apples and honey, the potential of a very long life and considerable power.

I continued to taste the 1973 wines regularly and steadily to chart their development through 1974, 1975, and into 1976. They were improving so dramatically, each time I came back to them after a few months, that I found it hard to believe that they could go on rising to such stratospheric peaks of balanced quality.

Then, I spent the Bicentennial weekend in 1976 in the Napa Valley. It was a deliberate decision on my part. I feel strongly that one of the major achievements of the first two hundred years of U.S. history is our success in the art and technique of making fine, noble, and great wines. There were many big parties that weekend in the valley. We celebrated with Elizabeth and Louis Martini. There was a monster picnic in the garden of Joe Heitz. But perhaps the most memorable event, for me, was a small dinner party given at Stony Hill by Eleanor and Fred McCrea. Eleanor's food was delicate and simple, of rare excellence to match the entirely extraordinary sequence of wines poured by Fred. It was, I believe, somehow the peak of his career as the great vintner of Stony Hill.

While we were sitting out on the terrace before dinner, facing the magnificent mountain view, nibbling small boiled Bay shrimp, the cellarmaster brought up from the winery the 1975 Gewürztraminer, taken from the barrel, which we cross-tasted against the 1973. The barrel sample was already of utterly SUPERB quality. The 1973 was still NOBLE, light and lovely, fruity and refreshing, now gently sweet, magnificent. But, at that moment of tasting the two glasses, I realized, with amazement, that in the two years between these two wines, Fred had already moved onward and upward in his art. Great as was the 1973, Fred had substantially improved on it in creative technique by 1975.

Next, still on the terrace, the cellarmaster brought from the winery the 1974 Pinot Chardonnay, and we cross-tasted it against the very GREAT 1973. Again, there was the shock of realizing that Fred had surpassed himself. The 1974, not yet released, hardly with any age upon it, already rated as a GREAT wine. The 1973 was also still GREAT, now luxurious and rich with its years, rising toward its peak, unquestionably more sharply defined in its personality than the younger wine, but it was certainly being challenged by the 1974.

At table, we drank the 1975 White Riesling, also brought up from the cellar, not yet released, already SUPERB. Then, to show us the qualities of a truly aged Stony Hill Chardonnay, Fred poured the 1971 vintage, now with an almost unbelievable degree of aromatic complexity—a wine that I rated as superbly GREAT, the supreme wine of the evening. When I congratulated Fred on the night's extraordinary display of excellence, he said, "It isn't so much that we're better, but that we started earlier and perhaps are a little bit farther along the road. We were very lucky. We started with Chardonnay almost right at the beginning, before anyone really knew how great and how popular it was going to be. We got into it just as it was coming up. Now we have been lucky again with Gewürztraminer. We got into it just as that was beginning to come up. These days virtually everyone is making it. But we're just a shade ahead. We have had that little bit of extra experience in how to handle it and work with it. We've just been lucky."

This magnificent evening was, as I have said, some kind of climax to his career as a vintner. It was also the culmination of our friendship. It would be the last time that I would ever be with him— the last meal we would ever share. There would still be many letters and telephone calls. He would still have one more vintage at Stony Hill—one more set of wines to lay down.

Farewell to the "King of the Hill"

On January 1, 1977, quite suddenly and unexpectedly, at the age of eighty, Fred McCrea died on his mountaintop. It can be said without stretching any point that the manner of his departure was as graceful, as gracious, as sensitive as his Stony Hill wines. All the years he was up there at the vineyard, one of his greatest pleasures was to gather his entire family (increasingly spread out to far places) around him for a joyous home festival that would last, if possible, for several days. His son, Peter, was an oil engineer working for Aramco in Saudi Arabia. His daughter, Mary, was married to a television sports-caster in Schenectady, New York. But they and their children were by no means the only guests Fred wanted to have around him. He often described these parties in his letters to me.

"We flew all of our family," he wrote, "three boys and one girl, their spouses and eight grandchildren, out here for my birthday. The other two boys are my nephews, Don and Al, whom I more or less adopted years ago, when they were in their teens, at the time of their father's sudden death. Don and his family now live in southern California, Al and Joel and their four children near Philadelphia. There were also Eleanor's two sisters. The celebration lasted for al-most ten days. So you can imagine what a grand commotion that was. I'm such a tight Scot that I bought some gallon jug wines from a neighboring vineyard in the valley for everyday occasions, but we drank a whole case of our own Chardonnay for the birthday feast itself. We got to know our children all over again. They got to know each other a little better, and altogether we had a delightful time. By the end, however, we were tired enough to collapse."

There was another monster family party for Christmas and New Year's Eve in 1976. Now there were nine grandchildren. The follow-ing morning, New Year's Day, the guests were beginning to think about packing up and going off their several ways. It was the birth-day of Eleanor's older sister, so there was a final merry celebration lunch. Fred was the merriest of them all. After his coffee and a small glass of "Semillon de Soleil," he said, "Well, that was a lovely lunch.

But I've had it. I think I'll go and lie down for a few minutes." He walked quickly the length of the living room to their bedroom, which is on the same level. Ten minutes later, Peter went to ask him a question. He was lying on Eleanor's bed. He was gone.

It almost seemed as if he arranged it so that Eleanor would not be alone at that feared moment but would be surrounded by all the people best able to comfort and support her. Mary and the baby stayed on for two weeks. Peter began at once to help with the business direction of the Stony Hill Vineyard. The vintners of the Napa Valley showed the depths of their admiration and affection for Fred McCrea. Eleanor wrote me, "Mike and Peter and I will plan to keep Stony Hill up to the standards Fred set for us."

The *Los Angeles Times* headed its eulogy: "King of the Hill." The text, in part, continued, "Fred McCrea was the uncrowned king of California Chardonnay. . . . He left a legacy of matchless wines. . . . His Chardonnays (and often his White Rieslings) were the best of the State. . . . He was the proud owner of America's greatest white wine estate. . . . Stony Hill Chardonnays have been glorious. . . . In a straight line of superb vintages. . . . Long-lived wines with extraordinary vigor and concentration of flavor. . . . Fred McCrea was an inspiration to tiny, idealistic winery owners. The feeling was that if he could do it, they could too. . . . Stony Hill's are, literally, handmade Chardonnays on a tiny estate that today is probably worth millions."

A New Team Makes New Wines

Eleanor McCrea is keeping Stony Hill on a steady course. After the 1977 harvest, the first that she had supervised alone, Eleanor wrote, "The harvest was just perfect except that there wasn't enough of it. But we did ten tons better than last year, which is really a miracle considering the drought. I thank Heaven that we made it through this year one way or another. I have saved a few bottles for you, but don't feel obligated to take them. I have several hundred unfilled orders and a lot of mad people who would be happy to get even a single bottle. As you know, once upon a time we thought the pressure would be off if we could reach one thousand cases per year. Now we are up to two thousand cases, but more and more people seem to want the wine, and the pressure is hard as ever."

All of Eleanor's decisions, ideas, plans are discussed with two men on a day-to-day, week-to-week rhythm. The Stony Hill cellar-master, Mike Chelini, lives with his family in the house at the bottom of the hill and is available day or night for any vinous or viticultural emergency. He is both the vineyard foreman, responsible for the health and harvesting of the vines, and the winery manager, watch-ing over the fermentation of the juice and the slow aging of the wines in wood and glass.

The other man is Eleanor's son, Peter McCrea, in his early for-ties, who will eventually take charge of Stony Hill, sharing the own-ership with his sister, Mary. His work as an engineer has brought him back from the Middle East, via a tour of duty in Holland, to his company's main office in San Francisco. Peter and his family have a weekend house on the Stony Hill estate, and he is helping his mother with the burdens and pressures of even a small wine business.

My own deep interest in the Stony Hill wines is, of course, stronger than ever. One is now involved in the fascinating opportu-nity of judging, first, how the truly magnificent wines of Fred's final peak period will develop over the years and, second, what subtle changes may (or may not) come from the judgments and decisions of "the new management." I attended an important dinner given by Eleanor in 1978, when one of the guests was Joe Heitz, whom I consider to be—in addition to his recognized brilliance with red wines—one of the major experts on Pinot Chardonnay in the Napa Valley. We tasted, again, the great Stony Hill 1973 Chardonnay, at what would be, for any normal white wine, the ripe middle age of five years. Raising the glass high, Joe said, "Look at that magnificent deep gold color. That means that this wine is now approaching its proper maturity. Historically, as we all know, the Stony Hill Char-donnays don't truly begin to come into their own until they are at least five years old, or even older. Only then do they begin to develop their maximum aromatic complexity. This wine is now approaching that point." I found no decline whatsoever in the quality rating of the wine—it was still very GREAT. We also retasted the 1973 Gewürztraminer, still flowery and light, still full in fruit and spice, with no diminution of its rating, still of NOBLE quality. The dinner ended with the 1975 "Semillon de Soleil," this one with almost 8 percent sugar, but beautifully balanced by a refreshing lemony tang, a wine with a gorgeously rich personality. All these wines still tasted equally good when I returned to Stony Hill in 1979. They seem almost to be indestructible!

Eleanor talks of the present and future, only rarely of the past. One evening, over coffee and a glass of "Semillon de Soleil," she said, "The lovely thing to remember from the first thirty years of Stony Hill is that being a 'wine wife' is one of the few careers where the woman is so nearly on an equal footing with her husband. (I am sure that all the other 'partners' of the Napa Valley would confirm this: Alice and Joe Heitz, Jamie and Jack Davies at Schramsberg, Nonie and Bob Travers at Mayacamas, and dozens more.) In a tiny operation like this, the wife has to do a little bit of everything, which certainly adds to the charms of making it a way of life.

"If one is extrovert and social, as I am, there is another delightful advantage to this way of life. Now that our wine has made the Stony Hill name well known, you never know who is going to be on the other side of that front door when the bell rings. The people who want to come here because they like our wine all seem to be interesting and unusual, and meeting them provides me with continuous pleasure. The other day there was a call from the Opera House in San Francisco, where Joan Sutherland was singing in a new opera. Miss Sutherland, apparently, knew and liked Stony Hill wine. Could she come out and visit us? Naturally, I invited her to lunch. She stayed about four hours. There was a letter from a young man in Baltimore who also liked our wine and said he played for the Baltimore Colts. Could he visit Stony Hill while he was on the West Coast? He was a charming young man. When visitors come, you don't have to hassle around to make sandwiches and prepare canapés. All they want is to drink a glass of Stony Hill right here on the spot where it is made.

"Another fascinating thing about the business of making wine is that you never get to the point of thinking that you have made your best, that you can't improve a little bit more. You never get to the end of the learning. Never a week passes, at least for me, that I don't feel that I have learned some new important or unimportant little twist. Then think of all the viticultural problems, of all the possible diseases of the vines, of mildews and leaf molds, of marauding birds and insects, think of all the bacteriological and biochemical problems inside the wine. . . . There's really no end to it. It's almost like being at battle stations during a war." The technique of making wine is essentially very simple, yet there are all these side factors and problems that interlock in a most complex way. There are so many variables, so many different things you could try at every point in the cycle. But you might not know the result of the experiment until years later.

The Napa Valley is still full of memories of Fred, and of anecdotes about him. Perhaps, as the years pass, the stories may become ever so slightly exaggerated. Who knows? But they remain significant.

There was said to be the visit to Stony Hill by a Texas millionaire who, suddenly, right out of the blue, said, "Mr. McCrea, how much would you take to sell this place?" They say that Fred didn't even bat an eyelid as, very quietly, he answered, "Mr. Conoly, you don't buy a vineyard like this. You build it yourself."

The Superb, Noble, and
Fine Vineyards and Wineries

ACACIA WINERY *in the Carneros Hills above the Napa Valley*

A quite small vineyard, still so new (since 1979) that it has hardly
yet had time to settle down and show the best of which it is capable.
It has 50 acres, up in the Carneros Hills, of Pinot Chardonnay vines
that are still far from mature. So grapes have been bought from the
famous Carneros Winery Lake Vineyard. The Acacia owners are aficionados of Burgundy, and what they want to make, above all else,
is big, Montrachet-style Chardonnay and Beaune-style Pinot Noir. At
first, they were somewhat handcuffed by having no winery of their
own. The first bottle I tasted had been made in Kenwood in Sonoma,
while their winery was being planned for the Carneros Hills next to
the vineyard. Up there, they hope eventually to produce about
200,000 bottles a year—concentrating entirely on Carneros grapes.
Acacia's owners are ambitious and dedicated.
> ** (NOBLE rating) The beautifully perfumed, luxuriously rich,
> velvety, clean, and dry Chardonnay, with grapes from the
> Winery Lake Vineyard in the Carneros Hills—a memorable
> wine that promises an exciting future for this new winery.

AHLGREN VINEYARD *at Boulder Creek in the Santa Cruz Mountains
south of San Francisco Bay*

A family-owned-and-run vineyard, founded in 1976, with an
estimated production of about 14,500 bottles a year. It is a "mountain
vineyard" at about 1,000 feet, growing, mainly, Pinot Chardonnay,
but with additional grapes bought from Monterey, San Luis Obispo,
Santa Clara, and Sonoma. Valerie and Dexter Ahlgren run, virtually,

a "home operation." The winery is in the basement of their house, and the 2½-acre vineyard is more or less in the back garden. They make tiny lots of wine—seldom more than fifty bottles at a time—doing everything by hand, with extreme dedication to quality. But smallness does not guarantee greatness, and they are not always entirely successful with every wine.

    ** (NOBLE rating) The "estate-bottled" Chardonnay.

    * (FINE rating) The dark, fruity Petite Sirah.

ALATERA VINEYARDS *near the town of Napa in the Napa Valley*

This is a fairly new winery (first release in 1979), owned by a partnership of growers with about 70 acres of important vineyard land around Yountville (see page 126). They seem to be dedicated to maintaining small quantity at high quality. They are distributing under the Alatera label about 36,000 bottles a year—but this will gradually be increased toward at least minimum national distribution.

    *** The "Late Harvest—Bunch Selected" Johannisberg Riesling (White Riesling), a golden sweet, honeyed wine of intense fruit, rates as SUPERB.

    * Also some FINE ratings of Cabernet Sauvignon.

ALEXANDER VALLEY VINEYARDS *east of Healdsburg in northern Sonoma*

This winery (and the entire Alexander Valley district) took its name from Captain Cyrus Alexander, the fur trapper who, in the 1840s, homesteaded the famous 48,000-acre land grant given by General Mariano Vallejo, one of the last Mexican military governors of Alta California. Captain Alexander's adobe house is still used for storage by this winery. The present owners began planting their 120 acres of vines in 1970, made their first wine in 1975, and are now steadily climbing toward their production objective of about 250,000 bottles a year. Their quality achievements are variable, but a few of their wines are well worth tasting, at very fair prices.

    * Try the dry, refreshing Chenin Blanc; also, the medium-soft, aromatic White "Johannisberg" Riesling; and the very dry, luscious Chardonnay, all of FINE quality.

ALMADÉN VINEYARDS *at San Jose in Santa Clara*

One of the oldest of California wineries, founded in 1852 by the Frenchman Charles Lefranc, who brought his vine-root cuttings from Burgundy to join his Burgundian friend, Etien Thée, to plant a vineyard at Los Gatos in Santa Clara—almost at the exact spot where the giant Almadén headquarters are today. The name eventually chosen for those original vineyards came from the fact that there was, in the same valley where the vines were planted, an old quicksilver mine. The Spanish people of the valley called it by the Moorish phrase, *Al Madén*, "the silver mine." The lovely, sonorous name, with its implication of beauty and wealth from the earth, was given to the entire valley and all its vineyards. In the 1950s, when the Santa Clara Valley became industrialized, Almadén moved its vineyard operations southward and bought many thousands of acres in Monterey and San Benito to become one of the largest vineyard owners in the country. Today, it is a colossus of American winemaking. Since 1967, it has been owned by the huge National Distillers conglomerate, with almost 7,000 acres of vineyards from which are made more than sixty different kinds of still, sparkling, and fortified wines at the current estimated rate of about 150 million bottles a year. Yet, with all this immense "flow-through" of millions of gallons, its highly imaginative executive winemaster, Klaus Mathes, still finds time to make some small lots of "Special Selection" wines of quite exceptional quality and of strong experimental interest—generally released with regional appellations and often with actual vineyard names on the labels. The standard wines are distributed under the Almadén name —some special wines, at higher prices, under the subsidiary Charles Lefranc label. The wide range of Almadén production is always impressive, from good value, quite inexpensive mass wines, up to medium-priced sparkling wines of above-average quality and the special labels, including "Late Harvest," of more than slight interest to the connoisseur.

      ** (NOBLE ratings) The velvety smooth Charles Lefranc Monterey appellation Cabernet Sauvignon; the extraordinary, dry "Late Selection" Zinfandel from old vines in the La Cienega Valley; the exceptionally aromatic and fruity Gewürztraminer, also from old vines in La Cienega; the golden sweet "Late Harvest" White "Johannisberg" Riesling, with a remarkable 11.7 percent residual sugar; and the three top sparkling wines: the Chardonnay "Blanc de Blancs," the "Chardonnay Nature," and the "Oeil de Perdrix," using Pinot Noir grapes.

* (FINE ratings) The dry Pinot Blanc and Blanc Fumé (Sauvignon Blanc), the rich Chardonnay, the light Pinot Noir, and the famous Grenache Rosé.

ALTA VINEYARD *at Calistoga in the Napa Valley*

This hillside vineyard was originally founded in 1878, but its new ownership, with complete modernization of its winery and re-planting of its 10 acres (now all in Chardonnay), began in 1970. The first wines were released in 1979, and production is now estimated at about 25,000 bottles a year, with a gradual expansion to 40,000 bottles.

* Try the Chardonnay, light, dry, attractively aromatic—at a FINE rating.

AMITY VINEYARDS *in the village of Amity in the Yamhill district of the Willamette Valley of Oregon*

As a judge at the Pacific Northwest Wine Festival, I was repeatedly surprised, in blind tastings, by the extraordinary quality of the Amity Pinot Noir. In 1980, it was unanimously awarded the gold medal as the best wine of the festival. When I finally met Amity's partner-winemaker, Myron Redford, I found him an idealistic perfectionist. He was born in Seattle, developed a taste for wine while vacationing along the Moselle in Germany, and began to learn about winemaking at the State University of Washington. He joined with his mother, his brother, and a partner, in 1974, in buying 72 acres of largely undeveloped forestland around Amity in Oregon. They have cleared 11 acres and planted them with vines, principally Burgundian clones of Pinot Noir, which grows superbly in this shallow loam soil and cool climate. With some extra grapes bought, they have been producing, since 1976, an average of about 55,000 bottles a year. Continuing competitive success and gradually increasing production will bring them limited national distribution.

*** Each of the three Pinot Noir clones (identified on the label) rates as SUPERB—the "Burgundian Gamay," the "Burgundian Pommard," and the "Oregon Wadensville," the latter developed from original Wädenswil cuttings in the experimental vineyards of the state university. Tasting these three side by side is an absorbing vinous experience.

** There is also a fruity, refreshing White Riesling that generally achieves a NOBLE rating.

* Also FINE ratings of Cabernet Sauvignon and Merlot released under a subsidiary label, Redford Cellars.

ASSOCIATED VINTNERS *at Bellevue, near Seattle in Washington State*

One of the first and still among the most important and influential of the high-prestige wineries of the Pacific Northwest. Its executive winemaker, Dr. Lloyd Woodburne, was a professor of psychology at the University of Washington and began making wine at home in 1951. He was joined at weekends by some of his academic colleagues—a meteorologist, a law professor, a teacher of English, among others. Soon they had outgrown their home facilities and decided to build their own winery. At the same time, they developed their exclusive sources of grapes in the Yakima Valley. The resulting wines were so good and the demand for them so strong, that the next step was the launching of a small commercial operation. Dr. Woodburne resigned from the university and became a full-time winemaker. Although they have steadily grown and have twice rebuilt their winery on a larger scale, they remain, at core, a partnership of dedicated wine enthusiasts. The production is now expected to rise steadily toward an eventual maximum of about 375,000 bottles a year, with substantial national distribution on the way.

** (NOBLE rating) The Cabernet Sauvignon with grapes from the cooler sections of the Yakima Valley from vineyards around Sunnyside and Grand View.

* (FINE ratings) The medium-soft White Riesling, the rich Chardonnay from the hotter parts of the Columbia Basin, a remarkably spicy Gewürztraminer, and the Pinot Noir.

BARGETTO WINERY *at Soquel in the Santa Cruz Mountains south of San Francisco Bay*

A family-owned-and-run operation producing about 400,000 bottles a year. They distribute their wines under two labels, Bargetto and Santa Cruz Cellars. After being known only locally, in the coastal town of Soquel, since 1933, they are now moving toward national distribution. The quality of the wines is variable.

   ** (NOBLE rating) The golden sweet "Late Harvest" White "Johannisberg" Riesling.

   * (FINE ratings) A dry French Colombard, a fruity-dry Sylvaner, a crisp Chardonnay with grapes from the Santa Barbara district, a dry White Riesling, and a Zinfandel.

BEAULIEU VINEYARD *at Rutherford in the Napa Valley*

Perhaps the first truly great vineyard in the United States. Certainly among the most influential and one of the major success stories in our wine history. The success rests on two men: Georges de Latour, the French immigrant who founded the vineyard in 1900 and set it up as a family-owned-and-directed enterprise that would last for almost seventy years; and André Tchelistcheff, the Russian immigrant, brought to Beaulieu by Georges de Latour in 1938, to stay for thirty-five years as a supremely imaginative and innovative winemaker and teacher of most of the important technicians of our time. During the era of de Latour and Tchelistcheff, Beaulieu became informally known as the "Chateau Latour of Napa Valley." The dream of perfection ended in 1969, when Georges de Latour was dead, André Tchelistcheff was close to retirement, and Beaulieu was sold to a huge, corporate, absentee owner, interested primarily in marketing the prestige of the Beaulieu name. During the first ten years of corporate operation, from 1970 to 1980, the production of Beaulieu wines was pushed up by 500 percent, from around half a million bottles up to 2.5 million. Inevitably, the complexity and richness of the wines have declined. However, even a lesser Beaulieu can sometimes still be head-and-shoulders above some others.

   *** The SUPERB rating is almost always the "Georges de Latour Private Reserve" Cabernet Sauvignon.

   ** The Pinot Noir regularly rates as NOBLE.

   * Also, FINE ratings of white Pinot Chardonnay and Sauvignon Blanc, red Gamay, and a Rosé de Grenache.

BERINGER VINEYARDS *near St. Helena in the Napa Valley*

This is another of the historic old California wineries. It was founded by German-born Jacob Beringer and his brother in 1876. Since 1970, it has been expanded and modernized to an immense size under the ownership of the vast International Nestlé conglomerate and its various subsidiaries. In spite of the mass-production drive of recent years, the quality of the wines has also been substantially modernized and upgraded by the admirable skills of the veteran California winemaker Myron Nightingale. The wines are released under two labels: the more serious vintaged varietals, at higher prices, as Beringer; the large-scale, less-expensive jug wines and similar types as Los Hermanos ("the brothers"). Total estimated production, from the almost 3,000 acres of vineyards plus large additional purchases of grapes, is estimated at about 17 million bottles a year.

    ** (NOBLE ratings) The delicate, light Cabernet Sauvignon and the golden sweet "Late Harvest—Selected Bunches" White "Johannisberg" Riesling with grapes from the Knights Valley.

    * (FINE rating) The fruity, light Chardonnay.

BOEGER WINERY *near Placerville in the Apple Hill district of El Dorado in the foothills of the High Sierras*

A small vineyard of absorbing interest in the extraordinary country that was at the heart of the Gold Rush and where some of the oldest vines date back to the prospectors of that time. Greg Boeger runs the 20-acre vineyard and makes the wine, with his wife, Susan, and their partners, on the actual site of an 1860 winery and distillery. They began replanting parts of the vineyard in 1972 and built their winery in 1973. Production is now gradually reaching toward their objective of about 125,000 bottles a year. In the "old days," the town of Placerville used to be called Old Hangtown, so the Boegers label their inexpensive blended wine as "Hangtown Red"—a name that seems to express the dash and daring of these wines of the mountain valleys.

    * Try the aromatic, luscious, strong Cabernet Sauvignon; also the powerful, raisiny Zinfandel, both rating as FINE.

DAVID BRUCE WINERY *above Los Gatos in the Santa Cruz Mountains south of San Francisco Bay*

The small vineyard in the lovely setting at 2,000 feet began as the summer weekend hideaway and later became the consuming hobby of Dr. Bruce, a medical specialist in practice in Los Gatos and the surrounding cities. The hobby became a passion, and when there was too much wine for himself and his friends, a small commercial operation was started in 1964, with about 25 acres of mountain vineyards. Production is now estimated at about 100,000 bottles a year. Dr. Bruce has a dominant, iconoclastic personality, and he makes dominant, unorthodox wines—big, mouth-filling, powerful. They can hardly be taken lightly. Connoisseurs either hate them or love them.

** (NOBLE ratings) The huge, luscious, Burgundian-style Chardonnay; the dark, intense Cabernet Sauvignon; and the brawny, exotic Zinfandel, with grapes from Amador in the High Sierras.

* (FINE ratings) The elegant, dominant Rosé of Zinfandel and the less formal and serious Rosé of Pinot Noir.

BUENA VISTA VINEYARDS *in the Valley of the Moon of Sonoma*

One of the most historic of all California vineyards—its story runs back into the time when Alta California was still part of the Mexican empire. Buena Vista was originally part of the 8,000-acre wine estate of one of the most popular of the military governors, General Mariano Vallejo. Soon after California joined the United States, part of the Vallejo family property was sold to the flamboyant pioneer of American wine, the Hungarian "Count" Agoston Haraszthy, who, in the 1850s, built magnificent stone wineries and tunneled deep into the limestone hillsides for cool cellar storage. The vines were destroyed by the phylloxera disease in the 1890s, and the buildings and tunnels collapsed during the 1906 San Francisco fire and earthquake. Haraszthy had given up and gone to Nicaragua, where, trying to cross a jungle river, he was eaten by crocodiles. Buena Vista was abandoned and neglected until the 1940s, when the San Francisco journalist Frank Bartholomew, bidding at an auction in Sacramento for some Sonoma land on which to build a summer home, found himself the owner of a piece of property without really knowing what it was. When he explored the land, at the back of the town of Sonoma, tramping through its forested and tangled undergrowth, he found the ruins of ancient stone buildings and the entrances to collapsed tunnels and realized that he had rediscovered Buena Vista. He decided, as an aficionado of wine, to make it his life's work to bring back the ancient vineyard to a modern success. Over the following twenty-five years, he achieved fame for himself, for Buena Vista, and for its new wines. In 1968, he sold the vineyard to a Los Angeles chain of supermarkets—a group with big ideas for expansion. They have developed 700 acres of vines in the Carneros Hills (see page 86) with a large, ultramodern winery. Finally, what is now claimed to be "the oldest winery in California" was sold, in 1979, to a German corporate group, which seems determined to maintain the expansion program and the high reputation of the Buena Vista name. Production is now estimated at about 1¼ million bottles a year. The ancient stone winery buildings and tunneled cellars are kept going as a showplace for tourists.

    * Try the delicately sweet, flowery, refreshingly tart Gewürztraminer; also the gentle Cabernet Sauvignon; and the fruity, soft Zinfandel, all scoring FINE ratings.

BURGESS CELLARS *near St. Helena in the Napa Valley*

Tom Burgess, in 1972, was an amateur who came into the business of making wine for the love of it. He was a pilot for the private planes of an international corporation. He saved his money and bought a winery on the eastern hill slopes above the Napa Valley. When I first met him, in 1974, I found him troubled by the immense problems of capitalization, of bank financing, of loans and mortgages, required by even a small winery operation. When I talk to him now, I find him self-assured, on the high road of success, producing about 250,000 bottles a year of wine of admirable quality. Tom tells me that he is now concentrating entirely on Cabernet Sauvignon, Chardonnay, and Zinfandel—all vintaged, all 100 percent from Napa grapes.

    *** The Cabernet Sauvignon "vintage selection" rates as SUPERB and so does the golden sweet "Late Harvest" Johannisberg Riesling (White Riesling).

** The dark, powerful red Zinfandel rates as NOBLE, so does the fruity, refreshing Chenin Blanc.
* The crisp dry Chardonnay rates as FINE; so does the light, nicely aromatic Rosé of Grenache.

DAVIS BYNUM WINERY *at Healdsburg in Sonoma*

Bynum and his son, Hampton, are "amateurs of wine" who have become professionals. They began in Berkeley as home wine-makers. Next, they sold their wines, from a Berkeley shopfront winery, mainly to professors and students of the university. Then, in 1973, they bought an ultramodern hop kiln near Healdsburg at the entrance to the Alexander Valley. Doing most of the conversion work on the kiln themselves, they had no time to think about growing vines, so they made partnership arrangements with local growers in the Alexander Valley, the Dry Creek district, and the Russian River Valley, for an estimated production of almost 300,000 bottles a year. General quality is somewhat variable, but a few of the wines are excellent.

** (NOBLE rating) The fruity, luscious Chardonnay.
* (FINE ratings) The refreshing "Fumé Blanc" (Sauvignon Blanc), the solid Petite Sirah, the bold Pinot Noir, and the mouth-filling Zinfandel.

CAKEBREAD CELLARS *at Rutherford in the Napa Valley*

Yes, there actually is a family called Cakebread in charge around here—Dolores and Jack as principal partners and their son, Bruce, as winemaker. They began planting their 22 acres of vines in 1973, and their production is now estimated to have reached about 125,000 bottles a year, just achieving limited national distribution for a group of wines still somewhat variable in quality.

* Try the dry, frugal, tense Sauvignon Blanc, with grapes from the home vineyard; also the earthy, simple Chardonnay; also the fruity, luscious, powerful Cabernet Sauvignon, with grapes from the famous Steltzner Vineyard in one of the best microclimates on the floor of the Napa Valley; and the dominant, intense, alcoholically "hot" Zinfandel, with grapes from the Hills Vineyard—all, in good years, of FINE quality.

CALERA WINES *at Hollister in the Cienega Valley of the Gavilan Mountains in San Benito*

This relatively new small vineyard, family owned and run by Josh Jensen and his wife, Jeanne, was begun in 1975 and now has an estimated production of about 500,000 bottles a year. Josh served his apprenticeship for two years in Burgundy and seems to want, more than anything, to produce Burgundian-style Pinot Noir. Searching for his own vineyard, he looked especially for chalky, limestone soil, and, having found it, has planted 24 acres of Pinot Noir. *Calera* means "lime kiln," and the winery, built at several levels in an old lime-crushing plant, has vague aspects of an Inca temple. While waiting for the Pinot Noir to mature, other grapes are being bought and other wines made.

   ** (NOBLE rating) One of the first Pinot Noirs to be released.
    * (FINE rating) A rich, soft Zinfandel, with grapes from the Butte district toward the foothills of the High Sierras.

CALLAWAY VINEYARD *at Temecula in the Riverside district of southern California*

This "vineyard in the desert" has been called "the Miracle at Temecula." The statement is somewhat of a promotional exaggeration. Yet there is something extraordinary about this Callaway project —almost certainly the most southerly serious vineyard in California. It produces drinkable wines under climatic conditions of such extreme adversity that, even a few years ago, they would have been considered impossible to overcome. Ely Callaway is a brilliant Southerner from Georgia who first made his success in the Northeast in the textile business, finally achieving the presidency of the huge Burlington Mills. During vacations, he and his wife, Nancy, became enamored of the dry, hot desert country of southern California and maintained a house at Palm Desert. When he retired, they decided they would live in that part of the country and, as an interesting hobby, would grow grapes and make wine. The fact that the climate they preferred was more or less incompatible with the healthy growth of fine wine grapes became just one more challenge for Ely to meet and overcome. Near the village of Temecula, he found a site behind a gap in the Coast Range where he was sure that the Pacific Ocean breezes would blow through and the mists would roll in. Beginning in 1969, as he planted and developed his 150 acres of vines, every square yard, of course, had to be irrigated. During each harvest, the bunches of grapes are not left, even for five minutes, in the searing sun, but are at once piled into refrigerated cabs that move among the vines. Every last operation in the winery is air conditioned and temperature controlled. More capital has probably been poured into this production operation than any other in the history of California wine. Also, in the style of the textile business, Callaway was prepared to spend huge sums on "product promotion." As his first wines were released, in 1974, a massive publicity campaign promised extraordinary results. Perhaps, if the advance buildup had not been so big, there would have been less disappointment about the wines. Some of them are quite reasonably good, but the inexorable forces of nature have provided no miracles. Current production is estimated at about 850,000 bottles a year. This may now expand considerably as a result of Callaway's decision to sell his vineyards and winery to the Canadian distillery conglomerate Hiram Walker—but Callaway will continue as president and public figurehead for several years into the future.

> * Try the fruity, simple, slightly sweet Chenin Blanc; the medium-soft White Riesling; the gentle, smooth Petite Sirah; and the golden sweet "Late Harvest" Chenin Blanc, which Ely names, in honor of his wife, "Sweet Nancy," usually with about 7 percent residual sugar and a vaguely earthy, aromatic flavor, different from any other sweet wine of California—all attaining FINE ratings.

RICHARD CAREY WINERY *at San Leandro in Alameda on San Francisco Bay*

A young winery owned and run by a young and charming husband-and-wife team with forceful energy and considerable combined skills. Richard started his career as a professor of biology, but soon saw nothing ahead but boredom and switched with minimum specialized training to the excitements of winemaking. His wife, June, has a degree in biochemical research—which she is now focusing onto the problems of winemaking. When I met them at lunch, they told me they had not the patience to start by presiding over the slow, five-year development of vines. Instead, in 1977, they converted an old waterfront warehouse a few miles south of Berkeley into a winery and began buying grapes virtually from all over California. In this way, they have pushed up their production, with fantastic acceleration, to almost 150,000 bottles a year. They hope, eventually, to double this and, also, to move from their present city location to one of the wine-growing regions, where they will buy land for their own vineyards. While some of the wines are excellent and others show Richard's somewhat self-taught status, he is to be praised for trying to maintain reasonable prices on all Carey wines.

> *** The golden sweet "Late Harvest" Gewürztraminer, with grapes from the Bien Nacido Vineyard near Santa Barbara, has 6 percent residual sugar and rates as SUPERB.
> ** Two wines rated as NOBLE: a dry Blanc Fumé (Sauvignon Blanc) and a red Zinfandel.

CARNEROS CREEK WINERY *in the Carneros Hills above the Napa Valley*

Since its start in 1971, this has become one of the most excellent, small estate vineyards in the United States. It has a magnificent microclimate for growing Pinot Chardonnay and Pinot Noir in the Carneros Hills, facing toward San Pablo Bay and getting all the benefits of the cooling ocean breezes. Beyond these local gifts, its partner-winemaker, Francis Mahoney, has gained a high reputation for the aromatic red Zinfandels he has been making since 1973 from the old vine grapes trucked to him in refrigerated gondolas the hundred miles or so from the foothill valleys of the High Sierras in Amador. From all these sources, including, also, some vineyards down on the floor of the Napa Valley and others in Sonoma, the production averages about 145,000 bottles a year. Some of these bottles may be a good deal more interesting than others, but it is fair to say that all of them are distributed at reasonable prices.

> *** A powerful Zinfandel, with grapes from Amador, rates as SUPERB.
> ** Three wines rate as NOBLE: a Cabernet Sauvignon with grapes from the Fay Vineyard near Yountville, a Pinot Noir with grapes from the Carneros Hills, and a Petite Sirah.
> * And a FINE rating for a Chardonnay with grapes from the Carneros Hills.

CASSAYRE-FORNI CELLARS *at Rutherford in the Napa Valley*

As its name implies, this winery (which has no vineyards) has been owned and run, since its start in 1977, by two families. The current estimated production, all from purchased grapes, is about 50,000 bottles a year and will continue rising gradually to about 120,000 bottles. They buy grapes in the Napa Valley from the Dry Creek Valley of Sonoma and from the High Sierras foothills.

   * (FINE rating) TRY the dry, nicely tart Napa Chenin Blanc.

CAYMUS VINEYARDS *at Rutherford in the Napa Valley*

For a good many years, Charles Wagner has been a well-known grape grower, owning about 60 acres in one of the best vineyard areas. In the early seventies, he decided that, instead of selling all his grapes to other producers, he would make his own wines under his own labels. Caymus, where operations began in 1972, is the result of this decision, with an annual production approaching 140,000 bottles of top-quality varietal wines. In addition, from purchased grapes, there are about another 100,000 bottles of relatively less expensive, often extremely good value wines under a subsidiary Liberty School label.

   *** Hardly surprising, the Cabernet Sauvignon "Reserve," made with grapes from the famous Rutherford growing district, is of SUPERB quality.

   ** Three wines generally rate as NOBLE: the red Pinot Noir and Zinfandel, with, also, a golden sweet "Late Harvest—Selected Bunches" White Riesling.

CHALONE VINEYARD *on Mount Chalone in the Gavilan Range of the Santa Lucia Mountains above the Salinas Valley in Monterey*

One of the most famous, influential, and prestigious vineyards in the United States. Everything about it is dramatic and exotic, with a certain cultist offbeat magnificence. On my first visit for lunch "on the mountaintop" with the partner-winemaker brothers, Dick and Peter Graff, we drove up from the Salinas Valley into the wilderness of semidesert chaparral, along a road that was hardly more than a cart track. We felt hopelessly lost, then, suddenly, at the top, we found the rows of vines in the glaring sun. If grapes must suffer to make great wine, they seemed to have a plenitude of adversity here in the arid, sparse soil and the unshaded heat.

The winery had the look almost of a temporary encampment on the mountain. The living quarters, where we lunched, were lean-to, prefabricated cabins. Dick Graff said, "We like this life, first because it is in a remote and wild place, but also because it is so varied. We are not only winemakers, but barrel repairers, builders, cement mixers, machinists, mechanics, plumbers, pump men, hewers of wood, and drawers of water." It all might have seemed an evasion of reality were it not for the fact that the wines made at Chalone are among the most magnificent of the United States.

This extraordinary mountain "bench," or shelf, of about 125 acres of grape-growing earth, was discovered, almost a hundred years ago, by a Frenchman who found here outcroppings of calcite and calcium in almost exactly the same proportions as in Burgundy. It took many years to develop the place, to bring over and plant the right Burgundian root cuttings, to do the experimental work and develop the special techniques for this dry clearing on the mountain. For many years, the grapes were simply picked and trucked down the hill to be sold to other wine producers. Finally, in 1965, Chalone was bought by Dick Graff (with a small investing group), and he dreamed, at last, of making supreme wines on the mountaintop. He had studied winemaking in California and in Burgundy. Peter had his degree in viticulture from the University of California. In 1969, they released their first vintage under the Chalone label. Since then, their success has been immense—with big, bold wines of enormous power, dramatic and exciting with the "smoke of oak," intense with the fruit of the mountain grapes. To tens of thousands of wine aficionados able to afford the relatively high Chalone prices for their 140,000 bottles a year, they have become virtually a cult. Chalone wines launched a new fashion in California winemaking, and their style has been imitated by many other producers.

   *** Three wines are consistently (at every good vintage) of SUPERB quality: the highest in prestige is the Chardonnay, which regularly rates (with Stony Hill) as one of the two greatest white wines of the United States, while the dry

Chenin Blanc and the dry Pinot Blanc are absolutely the best American versions of these wonderful varieties.

** With a fairly consistent rating as NOBLE, there is the red Pinot Noir.

* And with a FINE rating, a dry white French Colombard.

CHAPPELLET VINEYARD *on Pritchard Hill east of Rutherford above the Napa Valley*

In 1967, Los Angeles industrialist Donn Chappellet planted 100 acres of vines high on this eastern boundary hill of the valley and, in the forest near the top, hidden by the trees, built an ultramodern winery in the form of a fifty-foot pyramid. To complete this "miniempire of wine," he added a luxurious home for his family with gorgeous views from the mountaintop. The wines are released under two labels: the more expensive estate bottlings as Chappellet; the less prestigious, less costly as Pritchard Hill. Since this mountain vineyard is partially faced toward the north, the relatively cool microclimate gives intense flavors to the wines. Production is now estimated at about 250,000 bottles a year.

** (NOBLE rating) The delicately flowery and slightly sweet White "Johannisberg" Riesling.

* (FINE ratings) The dry Chenin Blanc; the intensely fruity Chardonnay; the complex, dark Cabernet Sauvignon; and a 100 percent Merlot.

CHATEAU BOUCHAINE *in the Carneros Hills above the Napa Valley*

This is an extremely new estate vineyard and winery which, at the moment of this writing, has not yet released any of its wines. But there are already two harvests of grapes vinified into new wine resting in Limousin oak barrels in its aging cellars, and I have been allowed to taste them. I find all the signs and signals that, in the not very distant future, Chateau Bouchaine will be in the front rank of Napa vineyards and wineries—partly because of the excellence of its Carneros earth; partly because of its exceptional climatic position on the hills almost exactly halfway between the Napa and Sonoma valleys, facing the cooling breezes of San Pablo Bay; and, not least, because of the experience and technical skills of its staff. Chateau

Bouchaine—the name is that of a branch of one of the owning families—comes within a relatively new format of vineyard organization —an extremely well-financed corporation with absentee owners who expect to play no part in the day-to-day management of the operation. The main financing comes from Delaware, from various sections and subsections of the du Pont family and some high executives of the du Pont de Nemours corporation. The second financing source comes from Washington, from certain successful and well-known journalists. A third source is the family in Cincinnati that owns the Cincinnati Reds. But perhaps the most important fact about Chateau Bouchaine is that its on-the-spot management—from the growing of the grapes to the making and aging of the wines—will be totally under the command of one of the most prestigious and successful of Napa Valley winemakers, Jerry Luper. He has been made a "limited partner" in the operation, and although one knows that he will never be able to force the grapes to grow exactly right or to guarantee good weather at the proper time, one is sure that all the technical operations will be as near to perfection as human skill can make them. There are 30 acres of Chardonnay already planted, but the vines are still so young that it will be a year or two before there is a workable harvest. Meanwhile, Jerry is buying grapes from his neighbors, concentrating entirely on Chardonnay and Pinot Noir, which will be the only two varieties released by Bouchaine. This part of the Carneros Hills is an ideal location for growing Pinot Noir, and Jerry will be able to choose the finest grapes available in the district. Total production of Chateau Bouchaine is projected at, within a few years, 300,000 bottles per annum.

   *** No wine has as yet been released but on the basis of a careful tasting of the Pinot Noir now aging in the barrels in the cellars, I conservatively predict that the Pinot Noir will eventually achieve a SUPERB quality rating. I am not now prepared to say that the first release will reach that level of quality, but I do believe that later harvests—as the experimental methods of making and developing the wine are perfected—will eventually reach a very high quality.

CHATEAU MONTELENA *at Calistoga in the Napa Valley*

There is a sense of shock at the first visit when one finds, not a classic château, but a typically American mansion with, alongside it, an ornamental lake with an island supporting a wildly colored, full-sized Chinese pagoda approached by stylized Chinese footbridges. It is all reasonably explained by the history of this excellent and famous vineyard.

It was founded and named in the 1880s by a New Englander who made millions in shipping in San Francisco but was in love with France. For his Napa Valley estate, he imported French vine-root cuttings, a French winemaker, a French architect, and French stone with which to build a French château surrounded by its vineyards. Later all was destroyed by fire. The estate was then taken over by a wealthy Chinese gentleman, who built a new house and, when he looked out his window in the early morning and saw the mists swirling around the hills, wanted to imagine that he was back home in China. So he perfected his view with the lake and the pagoda. There was still a winery, but it was abandoned for twenty years.

The modern winemaking revival of Chateau Montelena began with the coming of the present owners in 1972 and the replanting of the 100 acres of vines, with annual production gradually rising to about 250,000 bottles. For the first four years, the new Chateau Montelena moved forward slowly. Then, quite suddenly, in 1976, it was catapulted into worldwide fame. An Englishman living in Paris organized an "international tasting" between the six best American Pinot Chardonnays he could find and six famous Burgundian Pinot Chardonnays. They were "tasted blind" in Paris by a group of top French wine experts. When the tasting was finished, the scores handed in, and the labels uncovered, it was found that the "winner of the tasting" was the Chateau Montelena Chardonnay. The shock waves rocked France and made sensational headlines around the world. It was the first international recognition of the new supremacy of American wine.

Naturally, the immense publicity has brought Chateau Montelena a large popular success. It has been built up by concentration on the production of big, bold wines from Cabernet Sauvignon, Chardonnay, Zinfandel, and limited production of dry White Riesling.

> *** The Chardonnay continues to rate consistently as SUPERB —and so does the Zinfandel.
> ** Two other wines regularly rate as NOBLE: the "estate-bottled" Cabernet Sauvignon and the dry White Riesling.

CHATEAU ST. JEAN *at Kenwood in Sonoma*

A fairly large, relatively new winery—its main building, vaguely in the design of a European country château, completed in 1976—with an estimated production of about 1,200,000 bottles a year. I am told that the "Saint Jean" of the title (spelled in the French masculine form) is actually in honor of the wife of one of the owning partners, all of whom are convinced of the heavenly qualities of her character. I am convinced of the exceptional qualities of the many types of dry white and golden sweet wines for which Chateau St. Jean's wine-master, Dick Arrowood, has gained high prestige. He controls about 75 acres of owned vines, but also buys grapes from many of the top vineyards of Sonoma, Napa, and Mendocino. The policy is to vinify separately the output of each vineyard, putting its name on the label. Thus, in one year, they made seven different Chardonnays, all quite different in character. Under Arrowood, this is one of the most experimental of all wineries in northern California.

    *** A dramatic wine of incredible balance and SUPERB quality has been the honey sweet "Individual Dry Bunch Selected —Late Harvest" White Riesling with grapes from the Robert Young Vineyard in the Alexander Valley, and an extraordinary 37.5 percent residual sugar.

    ** Four wines at a NOBLE rating: an "estate-bottled" medium-soft "Fumé Blanc" (Sauvignon Blanc) was the best American wine of this type I have ever tasted—the others include a dry Pinot Blanc with grapes from the Forrest Crimmins Ranch; and two dry Chardonnays, with grapes, respectively, from the Belle Terre and Robert Young vineyards.

CHATEAU STE. MICHELLE VINTNERS *at Woodinville near Seattle in Washington State*

This is probably the oldest and certainly the largest winemaking operation of the Pacific Northwest. The huge winery, in a still-countrified suburb of Seattle, has, indeed, much of the magnificence of a château in a beautifully landscaped 800-acre private park, originally the showplace home of a wealthy pioneering family in the lumber business. In the 1930s, immediately after Prohibition, there was a "wine boom" around Puget Sound. Over the years, several small companies merged into a single unit, which then invited the great California winemaker André Tchelistcheff to be its consultant. Under his direction, in 1967, they produced their first serious wine from noble grapes and called it "Ste. Michelle." So great was the promise of this and other wines that followed, that, in 1974, the Ste. Michelle group was bought by the giant U.S. Tobacco conglomerate. At the same time, large vineyard holdings have been developed about one hundred miles from the winery, across the Cascade Mountains in the irrigated Yakima Valley and Columbia Basin. There are now eight "vineyard ranches" with about 750 acres. The early technical direction of this huge operation was set by a California-trained winemaker of considerable imagination and skill, Joel Klein, who recently resigned to develop his own vineyard operation, but remains as a consultant to Chateau Ste. Michelle. The current production is estimated at 3.5 million bottles a year—with an ultimate goal, five years or so ahead, of 12 million bottles. It is a tribute to Klein's dedication that, in spite of mass-production pressure, he still found the time to make some small lots of outstanding wines.

   *** The extraordinary and unique "Ice Wine," made from frozen White Riesling grapes in the Yakima Valley (see page 200) achieved a SUPERB rating.

    ** At a point or two below, there have been NOBLE ratings for the crisply dry Sauvignon Blanc, the delicate medium-soft Semillon, and the complex, intense Cabernet Sauvignon.

     * And FINE ratings for the softly flowery White Riesling; the crisply dry Chardonnay; the lightly refreshing 100 percent Merlot; the bright, fruity, delicately sweet Rosé of Grenache; and an excellent new sparkling wine, a beautifully dry "Blanc de Noirs" made by the *méthode champenoise*, the first in commercial distribution in the northwest.

THE CHRISTIAN BROTHERS *on Mont La Salle above the Napa Valley*

This is not—as some people have suggested to me—a commercial winery headed by two brothers named Christian. It is a Catholic Order of Lay Brothers who have taken vows of celibacy and poverty and make wine on a large scale in order to finance (with many millions of dollars) a network of schools for underprivileged children. The brothers are currently celebrating the 300th anniversary of their founding by Saint Jean Baptiste de La Salle in Rheims, France, the 100th anniversary of the beginning of their winemaking in the U.S., and the 50th anniversary of the building of their huge Mont La Salle Winery on the mountain above the Napa Valley, where, today, they are the largest single owners of prime vineyard land (about 1,600 acres) and by far the largest producers of wine (about 50 million bottles a year).

Clearly, then, the brothers are engaged in the mass production of good quality wines at fair prices for the everyday use of the average drinker. Occasionally, when nature offers the opportunity, they seize it to make wines of quite exceptional quality. The cellarmaster who has wrestled with the technical problems of this "empire" for almost fifty years and has become, by his charm, his conservative judgment, his devotion to quality, his wisdom and wit, a legendary figure in the American wine industry, is Brother Timothy, born Anthony Diener, originally a teacher in one of the schools. He says that he draws his philosophy from the Bible's First Book of Timothy, 5:23 —"Take a little wine for thy stomach's sake and thy frequent infirmities."

*** A recent example of a SUPERB wine was the "100th Anniversary—Late Harvest" White Riesling made with *Botrytized* Napa Valley grapes, a golden sweet wine with 10 percent residual sugar.

** Two NOBLE wines are the red Cabernet Sauvignon "Tricentennial" and the dry white Chardonnay.

* Among the FINE wines are the Grey Riesling, the Pineau de la Loire (Chenin Blanc), the medium-soft "Napa Fumé" (Sauvignon Blanc), the spicy white Gewürztraminer, the Napa Gamay, the Pinot Noir, and a strong Zinfandel.

CLOS DU BOIS *at Healdsburg in the Alexander Valley of Sonoma*

The owners, Frank Woods and his partners, began, in 1964, planting about 1,000 acres of vines in the Alexander and Dry Creek valleys. At the beginning, the business was entirely the selling of grapes to other producers. Then, inevitably, there followed the desire to develop their own label and distribute their own wines. This began in 1976 and is now approaching an estimated production of about half a million bottles a year. They have no winery of their own—they use the plant of a neighboring producer but age the wines in their own cellars.

　　* Try the intensely fruity, delicately sweet Gewürztraminer; also the aromatic, earthy Cabernet Sauvignon, with Russian River grapes, each achieving a FINE rating.

CLOS DU VAL *on the Silverado Trail near Yountville in the Napa Valley*

When, in 1970, the young Frenchman Bernard Portet bought 120 acres of some of the best heartland of the valley, there was considerable professional and social excitement. Bernard was, after all, the son of the director general of Château Lafite-Rothschild. It was reasonable to assume that he would be trained in the techniques of Bordeaux-style Cabernet Sauvignon and, in fact, his Napa land was soon planted mainly with the classic vine types. But, while waiting for his own grapes to develop, Portet seems to have fallen in love with the unique American grape, the Zinfandel. Applying to it some of his Bordeaux techniques, he has produced some extraordinary wines. He has also experimented with American-style Chardonnay, and now that his Cabernet is coming to maturity, his production is rising to about 300,000 bottles a year. Some of the lesser wines, at slightly lower prices, are released under the subsidiary Grand Val label.

　*** The Zinfandel is of SUPERB quality, and one can only hope that there will be more and more of it in the future.
　** Still a few points below, the Cabernet Sauvignon achieves a NOBLE rating with enormous improvement to come as the vines mature. There is also a 100 percent estate-grown Merlot of NOBLE quality, one of the two or three best wines of this variety made in California.
　* The Pinot Chardonnay seems, so far, to be less developed at a FINE rating.

CONCANNON VINEYARD *at Livermore in the Livermore Valley of Alameda*

A venerable and admirable winery that has been in the same family since the first James Concannon came from Ireland around 1883. For almost a hundred years, there has virtually always been an eldest son named James running the production of wine—currently at an estimated 1 million bottles a year. They have about 250 acres of vines in the gravelly, sparse Livermore soil (ideal for intense whites) immediately around the winery. After the first Concannon century, the family cycle has been broken by the sale of the company to Agustin "Cucho" Huneeus, a wealthy member of the famous Chilean wine family, now in exile from his homeland, who is building a small vineyard empire in California. But Jim Concannon is staying on as president of the company, to continue, it is to be hoped, his dedication to experimentation, innovation, and the further improvement of the quality of all Concannon wines.

 ** (NOBLE rating) The complex, fruity, rich, velvety Petite Sirah, one of the best of California.
 * (FINE ratings) The delicate, gentle "Blanc Fumé" (Sauvignon Blanc); the medium-soft White Riesling; the delicately sweet Semillon; and the extraordinary, fruity and rich, virtually unique Rosé of Zinfandel.

CONGRESS SPRINGS VINEYARDS *above Saratoga in the Santa Cruz Mountains of Santa Clara*

Vines were planted by a French immigrant on this steep mountain slope as far back as 1890, but the present name and winery operation date only from 1976. It has about 70 acres of vines, and its production is moving up gradually to a projected average of about 100,000 bottles a year. The partner-winemaker, Dan Gehrs, and his associates are devotedly dedicated to the preservation and development of the special character of the Santa Cruz Mountains wines. They use only the local grapes and stress the Santa Cruz district appellation on their labels, covering minuscule lots of Cabernet Sauvignon, Chenin Blanc, Pinot Blanc, Pinot Noir, Semillon, and Zinfandel. Some of these show considerable promise for the future.

 * Try the dry, aromatic and lemony "Fumé Blanc" (Sauvignon Blanc), of FINE quality.

CONN CREEK WINERY *on the Silverado Trail near Rutherford in the Napa Valley*

A new vineyard, planted in 1970, the modern winery completed in 1979, has a beginning production objective of about 250,000 bottles a year. Their first wines, released in 1974, brought them immediate substantial prestige. Most of their wines are "estate bottled" with their own grapes from about 100 acres of vineyards on some of the best Napa land just east of Yountville. The latest feather in Conn Creek's cap is that they have entered into a partnership with the French owners of the great Château La Mission Haut-Brion in Bordeaux. The French owners, Françoise and Francis Woltner, have bought 180 acres of prime Napa Valley vineyard land, and after the several years it will take to develop it, the wine will be made at Conn Creek by American and French technicians working together. The results should be of great interest to all serious wine drinkers.

* ** (NOBLE rating) The complex, fruity, rich, tannic Cabernet Sauvignon.
* * (FINE ratings) The medium-soft White Riesling and the crisp, fruity, rich, solid Chardonnay.

COTES DES COLOMBE VINEYARD *at Banks in the north Willamette Valley of Oregon*

A miniature and brand-new winery, owned and run by a Frenchman, Joe Colombe, who has started off by planting 3½ acres but hopes to expand fairly quickly (by buying grapes) up to the full capacity of his present winery, about 55,000 bottles a year. At the same time, the vineyard will expand, first to 10 acres, then to 20 acres. Distribution is still strictly limited to central Oregon, central Washington State, Portland, and Seattle.

* * Try the clean, luscious Chardonnay; also the fairly light, soft, uncomplicated Cabernet Sauvignon, both rating at FINE.

CRESTA BLANCA WINERY *at Ukiah in Mendocino*

This is one of the historic old vineyards of California, which has, today, to a certain extent lost its identity by being a "division" of one of the American giants, Guild Wineries, the conglomerate owner of six major winemaking corporations and the overall producer of about 300 million bottles a year. The high-prestige, high-quality bottles among this mass total are almost all made by Cresta Blanca—at a rumored rate of about 1¼ million bottles a year. It was originally founded as an independent small vineyard in the Livermore Valley in 1882 by the California wine pioneer Charles Wetmore, who bought 480 acres for $200. From the winery there was a distant view across the valley of chalky white cliffs, which the Mexican vineyard workers called *Cresta Blanca*. Wetmore scored a considerable coup when he visited Château d'Yquem in France, bringing back and planting in the Livermore Valley root cuttings of the Yquem vine varieties. From these, years later, Cresta Blanca's famous winemaker, Myron Nightingale, made the first *Botrytized* golden sweet wine, the "Cresta Blanca Premier Semillon," to be produced in the United States (see page 193). In 1941, Cresta Blanca was sold to the Schenley Corporation, and within a few years the winery went into a slow decline. In 1965, the Livermore operation was closed, and, in 1971, there was the sale to Guild, with the move to a new winery in the far northern district of Mendocino.

    * (FINE rating) Try the fruity, strong Zinfandel.

CUVAISON VINEYARD *on the Silverado Trail above Calistoga in the Napa Valley*

    This fairly small winemaking operation had a shaky start after its founding in 1970, with a series of owners who didn't seem to be sure what kind of wine they wanted to make. There are 17 acres of vineyards, with substantial extra buying of grapes to achieve a projected production of about 250,000 bottles a year. The operation now seems to be gaining momentum and achieving higher quality under the efficient management of its newest owner, a Swiss banker from Zurich. He has now purchased about 400 acres of new land, to be planted in Pinot Chardonnay, in the Carneros Hills above the valley (see page 87). Eventually, Cuvaison will make only Cabernet Sauvignon and Chardonnay.

    ** (NOBLE ratings) Two excellent wines being made while waiting for the development of the new vineyards are the strong Petite Sirah and the dominant, rich Zinfandel—it seems a pity that they may be discontinued.
    * (FINE rating) The complex, dark, intense mouth-puckering Cabernet Sauvignon "Reserve."

CYGNET CELLARS *at Hollister in the Cienega Valley of the Gavilan Mountains of San Benito*

A small winery, with no vineyards of its own, concentrating almost entirely, since 1977, on buying mountain grapes locally grown around the Paso Robles area in the San Luis Obispo district, which produces wines of a strong local appellation character. Production of these quite special bottles is climbing toward a projected total of about 60,000 a year. Distribution is limited to California.

> * (FINE rating) Try the dominant, heady, spicy "Late Harvest" Zinfandel, about 17 percent in alcohol.

DEHLINGER WINERY *at Sebastopol in the Russian River Valley of Sonoma*

A small vineyard of 14 acres, its winery produces only about 36,000 bottles a year. Everything in this charmingly modest place, founded in 1976, belongs to the Dehlinger family, who, however, have no need for modesty about the quality of the wines they make. They have placed themselves among the top prestige wineries of Sonoma. Too bad that, for the moment, their wines are available only in California. They are under such pressure of demand that they talk vaguely about increasing the production.

> ** (NOBLE ratings) The beautifully balanced Cabernet Sauvignon and the fruity, intense, powerful Zinfandel.
> * (FINE rating) The delicately light Chardonnay.

DeLOACH VINEYARDS *at Santa Rosa in the Russian River Valley of Sonoma*

A new winery, owned and run by the DeLoach family since 1979, with about 123 acres of vines produces an estimated average of 140,000 bottles a year. Within the next three or four years, they hope to double this production and move toward at least limited national distribution.

> * (FINE rating) Try the dry, clean, fruity, tartly refreshing "Fumé Blanc" (Sauvignon Blanc).

DEVLIN WINE CELLARS *near Soquel in the Santa Cruz Mountains south of San Francisco Bay*

A small winery, owned and run by the Devlin family since it was started in 1978, now has an estimated production climbing toward their objective of 60,000 bottles a year. They have no vineyards, but buy their grapes, with some exceptions, in the San Luis Obispo district. Most of their wines, therefore, maintain the character of the Santa Cruz Mountains appellation.

    * (FINE rating) Try the dry, aromatic, delicate Chardonnay.

DIABLO VISTA WINERY *at Benicia on the Sacramento River in Solano*

A tiny production unit with no vineyards of its own, is located far from any of the established wine regions. It demonstrates the modern theory that, with the benefits and flexibility of refrigerated transportation for grapes plus precisely controlled temperatures for winery work, you can, in fact, make wine anywhere. Two partners, both part-time wine aficionados, in 1977, leased an old industrial building and converted it into a winery and storage cellar. To this unlikely and unromantic spot, they bring Chardonnay grapes from the foothills of the High Sierras, Cabernet Sauvignon grapes from the Napa Valley, Zinfandel grapes from Sonoma. From these (and others) they make, with great care, minuscule lots of high-quality varietal wines of considerable interest to connoisseurs. For the moment, of course, production is still so small (about 5,000 bottles a year) that none of it reaches beyond the best wineshops of Sacramento and San Francisco. But, this experimental work is so good that it will, obviously, quickly expand.

    * Try (when you are in northern California) the aromatic, fruity, solid Sonoma Zinfandel, the best wine they have made so far, attaining a FINE rating.

DIAMOND CREEK VINEYARDS *in the hills above Calistoga in the Napa Valley*

Only one wine is made here—a Cabernet Sauvignon in the classic "Bordeaux-blend" of supporting grapes, Merlot, Cabernet Franc, and Malbec. The 20-acre vineyard was planted in 1968, and the first wine made in 1972, with a projected production of about 50,000 bottles a year. The vineyard is divided into three parts, according to differences in the soils and in the exposure angles of the slopes, so that a different wine is made from each part. They are labeled Gravelly Meadow, Red Rock Terrace, and Volcanic Hill. The wines seem to be made with the objective of austerely intensifying the differences among them.

> ** (NOBLE ratings) A side-by-side tasting comparison between these three Cabernet Sauvignons is a fascinating experience —they are all significantly different, yet they share a family resemblance, an austere complexity, a fruity tartness, a feeling of rough power.

DOMAINE CHANDON *at Yountville in the Napa Valley*

In 1976, when I first met John Wright in a Napa Valley restaurant and he opened for me two bottles of unlabeled sparkling wine, he was a man without an office or a winery, the president of a company that did not yet exist. It was, in fact, the beginning of "the great European invasion" of the Napa Valley. Wright's company, at that time, was called M.H. Vineyards, and the initials stood for the giant French conglomerate Moët-Hennessy—one of the most efficient, richest, and most successful corporations in the world, makers of Dom Perignon Champagne and Hennessy Cognac, owners of Christian Dior and other French luxury companies. Having conquered most of the world with these products, they decided to make sparkling wine in the Napa Valley.

So they created Domaine Chandon and launched onto the U.S. market the two sparkling wines I first tasted with John Wright. So great has been their success with American drinkers—partly, perhaps, because of their prestigious French name, certainly because of their excellent quality and fair prices—that John has been authorized to spend an estimated $20 million of French money on his viticultural developments in the Napa Valley. He has built—and twice rebuilt to double its size—a beautifully designed and landscaped winery, with luxurious public tasting rooms in a French decor, with a handsome *haute cuisine* French restaurant, all crowded with visitors every day during the tourist season. He has bought, for his French owners, more than 1,300 acres of the best Napa Valley and Carneros Hills grape-growing land toward his currently projected production of about 3 million bottles a year. Under French law, none of it will ever be labeled "Champagne."

    *** The "Blanc de Noirs" made with red Pinot Noir grapes, but with the skins removed at once so that no red color is absorbed, rates as SUPERB.

    ** The "Napa Valley Brut," made mainly with Pinot Chardonnay and Pinot Blanc, rates a point or two lower as NOBLE.

DRY CREEK VINEYARD *near Healdsburg in the Dry Creek Valley of Sonoma*

This winery has become well known, in part for the excellence of some of its wines, in part because of the iconoclastic personality of its owner, David Stare. The son of a Harvard University professor, he studied civil engineering, then came to California and fell in love with winemaking. He studied at the University of California, then, in 1972, launched his 50-acre vineyard in the Dry Creek Valley, where his estimated production is now about 400,000 bottles a year.

    ** (NOBLE ratings) The dry, light Chenin Blanc; the soft "Fumé Blanc" (Sauvignon Blanc); and the aromatic, strong Zinfandel.

    * (FINE ratings) The clean, crisp Chardonnay; the refreshing Gamay Beaujolais; the fruity, gentle Cabernet Sauvignon; the tough Petite Sirah; and the elegant Rosé of Cabernet Sauvignon.

DUCKHORN VINEYARDS *on the Silverado Trail near St. Helena in the Napa Valley*

This quite new, small winery, starting in 1978, is owned and run by the Duckhorn family. They are concentrating for the moment on buying Cabernet Sauvignon, Merlot, and Sauvignon Blanc, with a beginning production objective of about 45,000 bottles a year.

    * Try the light, refreshing 100 percent Merlot, with grapes from the Three Palms Vineyard, Duckhorn's first vintage of this varietal, earning a FINE rating.

DURNEY VINEYARD *in the Carmel Valley of the Santa Lucia Mountains in Monterey*

The Durney family started this vineyard in 1968 and concentrated, for almost ten years, on simply selling the grapes from their 80 steeply sloping acres facing the Pacific. Then they decided they wanted to become known for their own labels on their own bottles of wine. They use two labels, Durney Vineyard and Carmel Valley Winery. Their estimated production is now gradually approaching an average of about 180,000 bottles a year.

    * (FINE rating) Try the dry, aromatic, fruity, solid Cabernet Sauvignon.

EDMEADES VINEYARDS *at Philo in the Anderson Valley of Mendocino*

The unusual name belongs to the owning family, which planted the 35-acre vineyard in 1964 and built the winery in 1972. Estimated production is now gradually rising to about 150,000 bottles a year. Quality can be up and down, with some excellent wines in good years.

    ** (NOBLE rating) The powerful, spicy Zinfandel.
    * (FINE rating) The earthy, fruity, relatively simple Cabernet Sauvignon.

EDNA VALLEY VINEYARD *near San Luis Obispo in the Central Coast region of California*

This is a new label based on a working partnership between Paragon Vineyards in the Edna Valley just south of San Luis Obispo and Chalone Vineyard (see page 308) on Mount Chalone above the Salinas Valley. Paragon has 565 acres of vines and, since 1976, has been selling grapes to other producers. Now Chalone and its executive winemaker, Dick Graff, provide the technical know-how and staff to operate this new winery at Edna Valley and make Chardonnay and Pinot Noir from selected Paragon grapes. Chalone advises on all the quality aspects of growing these grapes, of vinifying them, and of aging them. The Chalone connection and my first tastings of the new wines vinified by the staff winemaker, Gary Mosby, promise exceptional quality for this new California label, which aims at an eventual production of about 300,000 bottles a year.

    ** (NOBLE ratings) The fruity, elegant Chardonnay and the rich, velvety Pinot Noir.

ELK COVE VINEYARDS *at Gaston in the Willamette Valley of Oregon*

I met the owners of this small winery, Dr. Joe Campbell and his wife, Pat, at the Tri-Cities Wine Festival in eastern Washington State and was much impressed by their dedication to the highest quality and their determination to expand slowly so that they could hold on to the "hand-crafted" techniques in the production of their wines. Pat and Joe are equal partners in everything, from the culture of the vines in their 22-acre vineyard to all the decisions in the vinification and aging processes. Pat's daily participation is a practical necessity, because "Dr. Joe" is still in practice as a country doctor in the area around the vineyard. They started planting their vines in 1972, and, beyond what they already have, they will gradually develop another 40 acres. They are projecting an estimated production of about 100,000 bottles a year.

    ** (NOBLE ratings) A beautifully flowery and delicately sweet White Riesling and an impressive, solid, velvety Oregon-style Pinot Noir.
    * (FINE rating) A big, crisp, fruity, rich Chardonnay.

ENZ VINEYARDS *at Hollister in the Cienega Valley of the Gavilan Mountains in San Benito*

The Enz family owns and runs this relatively small winery, which produces an estimated average of about 75,000 bottles a year. This is a historic vineyard, first planted in 1895, in the chalky, limy soil that is very close to the composition of the earth in Burgundy. The present owners modernized it and replanted 35 acres of vines in 1973. The wines they make now can hardly be called "Burgundian" —they are a good deal nearer to "country wines."

    * (FINE rating) Try the spicy, light "estate-bottled" Zinfandel.

EVENSEN VINEYARDS *between Oakville and Rutherford in the Napa Valley*

In 1979, the Evensen family started this minuscule winemaking operation, which, on a 20-acre vineyard, concentrates entirely on the Gewürztraminer grape and now has an estimated production of this one wine averaging about 25,000 bottles a year.

   * (FINE rating) Try the nicely aromatic, fruity Gewürztraminer.

EYRIE VINEYARDS *at McMinnville near Dundee in the Willamette Valley of Oregon*

A minuscule vineyard in the forested, iron-rich "red earth" of Oregon, producing, among several wines, an extraordinary Pinot Noir that gained international fame for Eyrie by sensationally outscoring, in several blind tastings in France, some of the greatest red wines of Burgundy. (These events are reported on page 146.) The vineyard, of about 20 acres, and the winery (converted from a turkey-processing plant) are managed and operated almost single-handedly by the young owners, Diana and David Lett. He came from Utah to California, was touched by the excitement of winemaking, took the university's master's program in viticulture at the University of California at Davis, extended his studies for a year in Europe, and then decided that he wanted to be a pioneer in the undeveloped new wine country of Oregon. They released their first bottling in 1966 and have gradually increased their production to an average of about 50,000 bottles a year. In the long, cool Oregon summers, David has experimented with small quantities of interesting wines from many rare grape varieties. But his outstanding success has been with Pinot Noir, which, with the slowed growth of the grapes in this climate, develops an intensity of flavor to make the best (and most Burgundian) Pinot Noir I have tasted in the United States.

   *** In good years, the Pinot Noir rates as SUPERB.

   * Generally, the Chardonnay rates in a lower range at a FINE quality.

FAR NIENTE WINERY *at Oakville in the Napa Valley*

The name, in Italian, means "without a care in the world," and it was given, in 1885, to the beautifully designed and planned stately stone winery just south of Oakville in the Napa Valley. It produced fine wines until it was closed by Prohibition, then abandoned and neglected for more than sixty years. In the late 1970s, the still-imposing old building was bought by its present owners, who began modernizing its interior to 20th-century efficiency and restoring its exterior to its 19th-century glory. Production for the new beginning —from, for the moment, about 80 acres of vines—is at an estimated average of about 50,000 bottles a year. They hope, eventually, for about 350,000 bottles—representing a rebirth of one of the great ancient labels of the Napa Valley.

> * Try their first vintage of a light, delicate, earthy Chardonnay, made from Napa grapes, having a FINE rating.

FENESTRA WINERY *at Pleasanton in the Livermore Valley of Alameda*

A small vineyard, starting in 1976, under the name Ventana. Then they discovered that there already was a vineyard of that name in Monterey, and they changed to their present label. Production is estimated at about 50,000 bottles a year. They have no vineyards of their own but buy grapes from Monterey, the Napa Valley, Santa Clara, Santa Cruz, and San Luis Obispo. A few wines have been very good, but in general quality has been quite insecure.

> * (FINE rating) Try the simple, soft Cabernet Sauvignon, with Napa grapes.

FETZER VINEYARDS *near Ukiah in the Redwood Valley of Mendocino*

This is very much an old, conservative, family winery. The Fetzers—originally lumbermen in Nebraska—are now headed by executive winemaker John, surrounded by enough other Fetzers virtually to organize a baseball team. They bought this 200-acre fruit ranch in 1958 but had to do a good deal of reorganizing and replanting before they could release their first wines in 1968. They have now built a modern winery, and their production is estimated at about 3 million bottles a year. They also use a subsidiary label, Bel Arbres. In spite of mass production of some undistinguished, inexpensive jug wines, John Fetzer finds the time for some interesting experiments with small lots of quite exceptional wines. In one recent year, for example, he made six different experimental Zinfandels from six different Mendocino vineyards, keeping each separate, under a designated vineyard label. In good years, his Petite Sirah can be quite memorable.

  ** (NOBLE ratings) The fruity, robust Petite Sirah; plus the brawny, raisiny, rich Zinfandel, with grapes from the local Ricetti Vineyard.

  * (FINE ratings) The aromatic, soft Gewürztraminer; the refreshing Gamay Beaujolais; the fruity, intense Cabernet Sauvignon; and the gently robust Pinot Noir.

FICKLIN VINEYARDS *at Madera near Fresno in the San Joaquin Valley*

This is one of the most extraordinary and idealistic of American winemaking families. (Their story is told in some detail beginning on page 74.) Their principal production, for three generations of the family, since 1946, has been magnificent ports from the classic varieties of Portuguese grapes that they grow in their vineyards under the hot desert sun. If they were being rated here for these fortified wines, they would certainly be among the GREAT wineries. But we are concerned with the fact that they also grow small quantities of California grapes and make some natural wine, proving that, by sheer technical skill, it is possible to produce memorable results even in this relatively incompatible, almost-tropical climate. The "secret trick" the Ficklins use is to pick the grapes substantially before they are fully ripe, before the sunshine has driven up the sugar content so high that it overwhelms the balancing acid tartness. The result is a wonderfully crisp and refreshing, beautifully balanced kind of "sun-kissed" wine with none of the blandness or thinness usually associated with "hot sun wines." The Ficklins manage this trick about once every three or four years. At the vintages in between, the sun is too hot—the sugar rises too fast before the acid balance is achieved. Then the Ficklins simply pick the grapes and sell them as fruit to one of the nearby bulk wineries. When they make their wine, it is for their own interest and pleasure—their "house wine," to be served at their own table. They never put it into commercial distribution. If you want a few bottles, you have to come to the winery to get them. The Ficklins are like that. They have something of the self-assurance of Rolls-Royce.

> ** (NOBLE rating) If ever you are in the neighborhood of Fresno, call the Ficklin Winery and ask if there is any available supply of their Emerald Riesling—it is the best wine of this type made in the United States—a crisp, tart drink of rare excellence and refreshment.

FIELD STONE WINERY *at Healdsburg in the Alexander Valley of Sonoma*

A substantial, corporate winemaking operation, started in 1976, owned by the Redwood Ranches group, this unit has an estimated average production of about 300,000 bottles a year. They have 140 acres of vines, including at least one stand of ancient Petite Sirah that was probably planted around 1895. Many of the white grapes are machine harvested, then field crushed and pressed in the vineyards immediately after picking to "preserve the flavor and freshness of the wines." One must add that this is both an unconventional and highly controversial method of processing. It is not applied to any of the red wines. These wines are hard to get—they are sold mainly to a regular group of steady customers on a California mailing list.

> * If you can get to the winery, try a few bottles of the Petite Sirah from those ancient vines, aromatic almost to the point of a peppery flavor, mouth filling, strong, a degree of tannin that demands for it to be aged for a few years in the bottle. It earns a FINE rating.

FIRESTONE VINEYARD *at Los Olivos in the Santa Ynez Valley of Santa Barbara*

Since Harvey Firestone made the millions and founded the dynasty with rubber tires in Akron, the family has shown an admirable sense of discipline and responsibility. Harvey's son, Leonard, served his country as diplomat, eventually as ambassador to Belgium, where he developed a serious interest in great food and wine. He was among the first to recognize the approaching wine boom in California and bought land in the Central Coast region, hardly more than 100 miles north of Los Angeles, among the rolling hills and flat-topped mesas behind Santa Barbara. Most of this area is hot, cattle-ranching, cactus, and sagebrush country. But there were sections of microclimate—particularly in the Santa Ynez Valley—where ecological tests showed that the European noble *vinifera* grapes might be expected to grow well. The valley is like a huge funnel, facing the ocean, drawing in the cooling breezes and the coastal fogs to bring dampness to the land and to shield the fierce rays of the sun. There were about 300 acres within this hopeful valley microclimate, a relatively new grape-growing area in California.

At just about the time these theoretical researches were completed, Brooks Firestone, Leonard's son, Harvey's grandson, reached a crisis in his life. He had been prepared and trained toward eventual leadership of the giant Akron operation. He had graduated in business economics from Columbia University. He had worked in the management group of Firestone for twelve years. He married Catherine, a lovely ballerina of the famous British Royal Ballet. She, unquestionably, added her artistic-idealistic philosophy to his growing doubts about his future in big business. They decided, together, that he should resign from Firestone, that they should move to California and throw themselves completely into the opportunity for the perfectionist pursuit of excellence in making wine.

In 1973, the planting of the 300 acres began with the best varieties of the noblest European vines. Everything was done on the finest and grandest scale. The most brilliant available architects were retained to design beautiful, low winery buildings that would merge into the lovely mesa and mountain landscape, green with eucalyptus trees under the cobalt blue sky. A major California artist was commissioned to paint pictures of the building of the winery, and when the first wines were released, these color impressions of the creation of the winery were used as the decorations on the labels.

The first winemaker was twenty-two-year-old Tony Austin, a protégé of the dean of American winemakers, André Tchelistcheff, and Tchelistcheff himself was retained as a regular consultant to the Firestone Vineyard. Although, obviously, the best possible physical and technical conditions have been created around him in every direction, much personal credit must go to Tony for the dramatic excellence of the first wines. He has achieved these results by courageous experimentation, by a willingness to throw fossilized traditions out the window, and by the application of an imaginative mind and considerable technical skill. Having established the wine-making policy at Firestone, Tony is moving on to found his own winery and is handing over his Firestone technical responsibilities to the assistant who has worked with him for the past six years, Alison Green. Current production of Firestone wines is now moving toward the projected goal of about 850,000 bottles a year.

** (NOBLE ratings) The reds are currently the most impressive, the Cabernet Sauvignon being developed in several different styles: 1. the lightest, labeled as Arroyo Perdido Vineyard 2. the more powerful, marked as "Vintage Reserve" 3. a new vineyard division of the estate (for Cabernet, Merlot, and Riesling) with labels marked The Ambassador's Vineyard 4. the regular run of estate-bottled Cabernet with no special designations on the labels—all these are well worth comparative side-by-side tastings to establish personal preferences among these Cabernets, which share a family resemblance in having a self-assured bouquet, a complexity of flavors, a rounded sense of velvet in the mouth. The Pinot Noir is rapidly improving every year and the wines made from selected estate grapes (the labels marked "Vintage Reserve") are among the top labels of California, made in the Burgundian style, aromatic and earthy, fat in the mouth, tannic for long life. The Merlot, as it grows here in the Santa Ynez Valley, makes a red wine of most unusual power and richness. Among the dry whites, there is the aromatic, elegant, fruity Gewürztraminer and the intense, refreshing, exquisitely clean Sauvignon Blanc. And, whenever nature allows, the magnificent, golden sweet "Late Harvest" White "Johannisberg" Riesling, widely praised, beautifully balanced, a sense of luxurious richness.

* (FINE ratings) At a few points lower, another white well worth tasting is the refreshingly ripe, mouth-filling, nicely fruity Pinot Chardonnay and the light, aromatic, interesting Rosé of Cabernet and Rosé of Pinot Noir.

FISHER VINEYARDS *in the Mayacamas Mountains of Sonoma*

When I was offered the glass with my first taste of Fisher Chardonnay, my host said, "You'll like this wine—it has 'body by Fisher!' " It was an unworthy crack, but, in fact, the founder-owner of this important new small vineyard, Fred Fisher, is a distant member of the famous Detroit family that built its worldwide reputation first on beautiful horse-drawn carriages, then on superb handmade bodies for early automobiles, before being absorbed into a division of General Motors. After graduating from Princeton and Harvard Business School, Fred began working for Cadillac in Detroit, but he soon realized that there were certain desires and urges deep within him that were not going to be satisfied by the life of big business in a big city. For one thing, he wanted to live in a lonely place, close to the earth, in pure air under an open sky. For another, he wanted to work with the skill of his hands. He was interested in wine, but still had no thought of ever running a vineyard. Nor did he have any idea of getting married. He saw himself, vaguely, as some sort of bachelor farmer.

He went to live in San Francisco, and, after a good deal of searching around in the Napa and Sonoma valleys, he bought a piece of mountain land at 1,200 feet in the Mayacamas Range, between the two valleys, on the Sonoma side. It was the first time in his life he had ever owned a section of earth. He was excited, but it was still no more in his mind than a work project for a weekend log cabin. He did all the woodworking and loved every minute of it. The cabin grew into a full-size house. He made many friends among the winemakers of Napa and Sonoma. They told him, virtually unanimously, that his land was ideal for the growing of noble vines. He began taking academic courses in viticulture. He apprenticed himself to a Napa winery. He consulted with more and more of his expert friends. In the spring of 1974, he bought a tractor, drove it himself (even though he had almost no previous experience), and planted a 9-acre Cabernet Sauvignon vineyard in front of the house. The next spring, he planted another 9 acres in Chardonnay at the back of the house, and this is designated on bottle labels as Whitney's Vineyard. At about this time, in San Francisco, Fred met a young woman, Juelle Lamb, from an agricultural family background in Alabama, South Dakota, and Utah, who fully shared his love of country living and his interest in the perfectionist challenge of winemaking. They were married in 1975 at the house behind the Cabernet Sauvignon vineyard, which is now named on bottle labels Wedding Vineyard. Together, they planned and put through the construction and equipment of Fisher Vineyards. It is all now in smooth operation, and Juelle and Fred do virtually all the work themselves. Since their own vines are not yet in full and mature production, they are buying grapes, for the time being, from the Dry Creek Valley and from the Napa Valley in the excellent Stag's Leap area near Yountville. This gives Fisher a total current production of about 50,000 bottles a year. Fred hopes to expand slightly and slowly, with about 50 more acres available for planting, but he does not want to go beyond the maximum that he can handle himself as winemaker—a projected total of 75,000 bottles a year.

    ** (NOBLE ratings) If Fred Fisher seems to have had a somewhat haphazard entry into the wine business, there is nothing amateur or casual about the first wines—they prove that the vineyards are on magnificent growing earth and that the winemaker has a natural gift of skill. The aromatic, fruity, intense, luxuriously rich, chewy, mountain-style Cabernet Sauvignon is currently a blend of estate grapes with others from the hills around the Dry Creek area and the Napa Valley. Soon there will also be a Cabernet Sauvignon 100 percent from the estate grapes of the Wedding Vineyard, and this (which I have recently tasted) will be of even higher excellence. There is also the beautifully balanced, complex, flowery, velvety Chardonnay, blended from the estate grapes of their Whitney's Vineyard and other grapes from the Dry Creek Valley. This will also be improved when they have enough of their own grapes to make a 100 percent estate wine.

E. B. FOOTE WINERY *at South Park near Seattle in Washington State*

Gene Foote demonstrates the truth of the total flexibility of the American wine industry. Gene is a full-time research engineer at Boeing, who, with his wife, Jeannie, operates a small commercial winery evenings and weekends a few blocks from his home in a residential suburb of Seattle. They buy their grapes from Jeannie's father, who owns and runs a small vineyard in the Yakima Valley, plus additional grapes from other Yakima growers at Grand View and Prosser, all in central Washington State. After each harvest, the grapes are shipped in refrigerated trucks about one hundred miles, over the Cascade Mountains, then they go into Gene's crusher hardly more than four hours after the picking. Gene, of course, always takes his annual vacation from Boeing at harvest time. Current production is running at an estimated average of about 15,000 bottles a year—all in vintage-dated varietals of such high quality that the bottles are all snatched up in and around Seattle, and few of them get any farther afield.

    * (FINE rating) In Seattle, try the bone-dry, austere, intense, refreshing, tangy Chardonnay.

FOPPIANO VINEYARDS *at Healdsburg in the Russian River Valley of Sonoma*

This is another of the famous Italian immigrant families that in the second half of the 1800s "headed north" from San Francisco into the wide-open country that looked to them like the hills and valleys of Tuscany. Louis John led the clan originally to the planting of their first vineyard—today, his great-grandson, Rod, makes the wine, with an estimated production at an average of about 2.5 million bottles a year. The best vintage-dated varietals are released under the Louis J. Foppiano label; the more general, less expensive, and jug-type wines are simply labeled Foppiano. The remarkable aspect of this family has been the way it has continually upgraded the quality of its products at every new step in its development. At first, for quite a few years, they sold grapes, then they sold bulk wines in barrels, then, Italian-style jug wines of more and more impressive quality with better and better values. Only in 1970 did they begin to think about bottling and labeling their own premium, vintage-dated varietals, and here, too, they have gradually solved the problems, producing year after year increasingly impressive wines. They have 200 acres of their own vines, but, of course, buy grapes from all around. Wines made from their own grapes are usually labeled with the designated appellation "Russian River Valley."

    * (FINE rating) Try the gentle, uncomplicated Cabernet Sauvignon; also the fruity, tannic Petite Sirah.

FORMAN WINERY *on the slopes of Spring Mountain above the Napa Valley*

This is a new winery, founded, with partners, by the well-known winemaker Ric Forman, previously in technical charge for almost ten years of the large Sterling Vineyards. As his responsibilities continually expanded, there came the moment, perhaps suddenly, when Forman longed to try to make "the perfect wine" on a small scale for himself. He developed his own 50-acre vineyard on impeccable grape-growing land on the upper slopes of Spring Mountain. On the basis of Forman's reputation and advance tastings, it is reasonably expected that his wines will be of SUPERB quality—with an eventual production of about 100,000 bottles a year of Bordeaux-style reds and whites, mainly from Cabernet Sauvignon, Sauvignon Blanc, and Semillon.

FORTINO WINERY *near Gilroy in the Santa Cruz Mountains of Santa Clara*

This is one of the historic "wine valleys" where, during the time long before Prohibition, many Italian families planted vineyards and made peasanty, rough, strong red wines. The Fortino family, originally from Calabria, remains in the same tradition—still making powerful reds (and some whites), but now, of course, with a good deal more advanced technique. In 1970, they took over the old Cassa Vineyard and bulk winery, which had been continuously in operation at this spot since immediately after Prohibition in 1935. The estimated Fortino production averages about 150,000 bottles a year, most of them sold at the winery to motorists driving over the Hecker Pass. Beyond this, there is limited distribution in San Francisco and around the Bay for these wines, which always seem to be in strong demand because of their excellent value.

    * (FINE rating) In the neighborhood, try the fruity, rustic Zinfandel.

FRANCISCAN VINEYARDS *at Rutherford in the Napa Valley*

This winery started in 1971, but soon ran into difficulties. In fairly quick succession, it failed twice, had five owners in eight years—the latest being a West German group, which, since 1979, seems to be willing to expend the capital, effort, and time to convert the

Franciscan operation into a long-term success. The experienced and skilled Napa Valley winemaker Tom Ferrell has been given total command, not only of the winery but also over the viticultural decisions in the 225 acres of vines in the Napa Valley and the 225 acres in the Alexander Valley of Sonoma. Tom will concentrate on Cabernet Sauvignon, Chardonnay, Merlot, White Riesling, Sauvignon Blanc, and Zinfandel—all strongly cut back for reduced quantity per acre at maximum quality. Estimated production is now rising toward a projected average of about 4 million bottles a year.

* (FINE ratings) Try the fruity, mouth-filling, delicately sweet White "Johannisberg" Riesling; also the aromatic, strong Chardonnay.

FREEMARK ABBEY WINERY *near St. Helena in the Napa Valley*

Since 1967, when the newly revived winery was "assembled" from a group of old stone buildings and pieces of land used off and on for wine since 1895, Freemark Abbey has become one of the major high-quality producers of California. Its name is not connected with any church. One of the founding owners was called Freeman; another Mark; and a third was Albert, but always known by his mother's pet name for him, Abbey. The smart new name covered the historic winery buildings, with about 150 acres of Napa Valley grape-growing land plus another 600 acres of vineyards individually owned by the partners. Almost immediately, then, it became a fairly large operation, and, in 1969, they released a Pinot Chardonnay of such dazzling quality that critics wrote about "a new winery of world class." This was confirmed by their 1973 "Edelwein," a dramatic breakthrough in a golden sweet wine from *Botrytized* grapes (see page 196). Freemark Abbey has slowly increased its production to about 300,000 bottles a year.

*** Two wines, whenever they are available in good years, consistently rate at a SUPERB quality: the Chardonnay and the famous, unique, golden sweet "Edelwein."

** Rated a point or two lower, three wines are of NOBLE quality: a medium-soft White Riesling, a Cabernet Sauvignon, and a Petite Sirah.

* On the next rung just below, the Pinot Noir generally earns a FINE rating.

GEMELLO WINERY *at Mountain View in the Santa Cruz Mountains in Santa Clara*

A family wine operation, started in 1934, is now approaching an estimated 150,000 bottles a year. They also use a subsidiary label, Mount View. This is an extraordinary place. First, you discover that Mountain View is not a tiny village community in a high valley of the wild mountains, but a bedroom suburb of "rabbit hutch" row houses on a traffic-jammed, gas-fumed highway. You find that the Gemello address is a bowling alley. The "wine cellar" is at the back, where, for many years, local Italian-American families used to come to the door to buy bargain bottles of rough-and-ready, almost home-made "Chianti-style" reds. Today the quality has improved enormously, the distribution is through more orthodox commercial channels, but the accent is still on the strong reds. It owns no vineyards but buys its grapes from regional growers, vinifying them excellently and aging some of them for above-average quality.

> * Try the top-quality Cabernet Sauvignon; the best Gamay Beaujolais; the most expensive Petite Sirah; and the top Zinfandel, the latter with grapes from Amador in the High Sierras, each scoring a FINE rating.

GLEN ELLEN VINEYARDS *above the Valley of the Moon in Sonoma*

An extraordinary small vineyard on the Glen Ellen bench (or shelf) at about 1,500 feet on the western slopes of the Mayacamas Mountains that border one side of the Sonoma Valley—the Valley of the Moon of Jack London's novels. The 75-acre vineyard has been planted since 1970, but it had no winery, and all its grapes were sold to other producers. Recently, Glen Ellen has been taken over by new owners who are building their own winery on the estate and plan to release their own wines under the Glen Ellen label. They have made the remarkable discovery that this vineyard has a near-perfect microclimate (the combination of natural conditions of soil and average weather) for the Cabernet Sauvignon vine, and the wines tasted from the barrels in which they are aging seem to promise that Glen Ellen will produce Cabernet reds in the SUPERB quality range. The technical direction for the development of this new wine has been taken over by Dick Graff of Chalone Vineyard (see page 308) as consultant, and staff winemaker is Jeff Baker, who has already had solid experience of mountain viticulture in the Mayacamas. There is also some Merlot and Zinfandel growing at Glen Ellen, but on the basis of the Cabernet Sauvignon excitement, other vines are likely to be uprooted and replaced by more Cabernet. It is hoped, eventually, to reach a production of about 120,000 bottles a year.

  *** Up to the moment of this writing, no Glen Ellen label has yet been released, but Glen Ellen Cabernet Sauvignon grapes have been regularly sold to some of the top winemakers of California and vinified by them into 100 percent Glen Ellen wines, generally rating a SUPERB quality—the 1978 Chateau St. Jean-Glen Ellen by winemaker Richard Arrowood—the 1979 Kistler-Glen Ellen by winemaker-owner Steve Kistler—the 1980 Mount Eden Vineyard (M.E.V.)-Glen Ellen made by Richard Graff—the 1981 Edna Valley Vineyard-Glen Ellen made by Graff and Jeff Baker. After 1983, when its own winery will be completed on the mountain, Glen Ellen labels will begin to appear.

GLENORA WINE CELLARS *on Seneca Lake in the Finger Lakes district of New York State*

This is one of the recently founded, small, highly innovative, top-quality wineries that make up the "new wave" in the historic wine country of New York. The planting and building began in 1977 by the Beers family in partnership with two local grape growers around the village of Dundee, where they have 250 acres of vines. They are gradually expanding their production toward a projected average of about 250,000 bottles a year. Considering the recurring difficulties for all producers in these far northern parts of New York State—where, in some winters, near-arctic cold spells can freeze the vine roots to death—Glenora is being extraordinarily successful, both with the noble *vinifera* vine varieties of Europe and with the more robust French hybrid types. They are also developing some extremely interesting and unique wines never before tried in the Finger Lakes. As of August 1981, Mike Elliott became head winemaker for Glenora. He was formerly with Spring Mountain Winery in California, working with John Williams.

  * Try the crisp, dry, intense, mouth-filling Chardonnay, with grapes from the McGregor Vineyard; also the fruity, refresh-

ing "Cayuga White"; and the interesting, delicately spicy "Foch Nouveau," all earning FINE ratings.

GRAND CRU VINEYARDS *at Glen Ellen in the Sonoma Valley*

One of the many small vineyards—this one founded in 1971—that started among a group of friends as a weekend hobby but ended up as a demanding day-to-day business operation. The Grand Cru partners were agreed, originally, that the red wine they enjoyed most was Zinfandel and the white, Gewürztraminer. So they bought this small old winery intending to use nothing but these grapes for a series of experiments in different winemaking styles. The costs, as always, were far greater than expected, and this forced the conversion of the winery to commercial operation, with the buying of all kinds of grapes from all parts of Sonoma. The winery has been expanded with a 30-acre surrounding vineyard, and production is gradually expanding to about 250,000 bottles a year.

   *** Their first love is still Gewürztraminer, which they make in a fragrant, light, intensely fruity style, at a SUPERB quality.

    ** At a point or two less, on the average, the Zinfandel rates a NOBLE quality.

GRGICH HILLS CELLARS *at Rutherford in the Napa Valley*

The man with the unpronounceable name, Miljenko "Mike" Grgich, is unquestionably now one of the major winemakers of America, a member of the small group of highly skilled men and women who, by some almost magical touch, brand their own personalities onto every wine they produce. Mike was born in Yugoslavia. ("But, never mind what the government calls me, I am a Croatian!") His father owned a vineyard. Since he had eleven sons and daughters, they never needed to buy a grape crusher. Mike was trained for a life with wine at the University of Zagreb. He arrived in California in 1958 and has made wine for most of the top producers. In 1973, at Chateau Montelena, he made the magnificent Napa Pinot Chardonnay that won the famous "Paris Tasting" over some of the supreme white wines of France (see Chateau Montelena). But always, of course, Mike secretly longed to be his own man in his own place.

The opportunity came in 1977, when he met Austin Hills, of the successful and wealthy coffee-importing family. Austin had become an aficionado of wine, had bought 140 acres of vineyards in the Napa Valley, and needed, as a partner, a top technician to control the final ripening of the grapes and to make the wine. Obviously, in vinous terms, where ultimate results are measured in decades, the partnership is still very new—but, already, some of the tastings have been magnificent, and the promise of the future is immensely exciting. So far, production has risen deliberately slowly toward its goal of 175,000 bottles a year. The Grgich name alone will ensure national distribution as soon as the volume makes it possible. They are using two labels: the top-quality estate wines under Grgich Hills, some less expensive types under Hills Cellars.

> *** The dynamic, powerful, raisiny Zinfandel, in good years, consistently achieves a SUPERB rating—so does the golden sweet "Late Harvest" White "Johannisberg" Riesling, with a delicate touch of peaches, the sugar deliberately kept down to 6 percent so as to magnify the fruit.
> ** At a point or two below, two wines regularly achieve a NOBLE rating: the brilliant, crisp, fruity, subtly rich Chardonnay and the medium-soft, clean, refreshing White Riesling.

GUNDLACH-BUNDSCHU VINEYARD *at Vineburg in the Valley of the Moon in Sonoma*

This may well be the oldest vineyard in California (or even, perhaps, in the entire United States) to remain in the hands of a single family—now for more than 125 years. In 1855, Jacob Gundlach came from Bavaria and planted vines on precisely the same 400 acres in the Sonoma Valley that the family owns today. After the first four years, Jacob needed help and was joined by his friend, Charles Bundschu, who sealed the partnership by marrying Jacob's daughter. Their lives were hardly easy. In the 1870s, their vineyards were wiped out by the terrible phylloxera vine disease. In 1906, their storage cellars and every drop of their large stocks of wines disappeared in the San Francisco earthquake and fire. Even their winery in Sonoma cracked and partially collapsed under the earth tremors. Before they could recover from these disasters, they were knocked out again by Prohibition. They gave up on wine, but they held on to their land. After Prohibition, in the 1930s, a certain bitterness and fear remained in their hearts. They again grew grapes and sold them to local producers, but they did not return to making their own wine. Then, in 1970, Jim Bundschu, the great-great-grandson of the founder, decided he wanted to put the family name back on the labels of bottles of wine. He joined with his brother-in-law, John Merritt, a skilled chemist, in rebuilding and re-equipping the old collapsed winery and in signing a national distribution contract with the Château and Estate Division of Seagrams for the new Gundlach-Bundschu wines. Current production is estimated at about half a million bottles a year, but, as grape delivery contracts with other producers expire so that more and more of their own grapes can be channeled into their own wines, total production is expected to increase fairly rapidly. The grapes, of course, are from mature vines, so the wines are exceptionally good.

> ** (NOBLE ratings) A refreshingly dry White Riesling; a complex, intensely fruity Cabernet Sauvignon, with grapes from the Batto Vineyard; a bold, robust Pinot Noir; and a golden sweet "Late Harvest" White "Johannisberg" Riesling, with 11.6 percent residual sugar.

> * (FINE ratings) The richly balanced Chardonnay "Special Selection"; the delicately fruity, yet firm, 100 percent Merlot; and the smoothly robust Zinfandel.

HACIENDA WINE CELLARS *in the Valley of the Moon in Sonoma*

Since 1973, this has been the latest adventure of the famous San Francisco "winemaking newsman," Frank Bartholomew, who achieved national publicity in 1941 by buying and reviving the legendary 1857 Buena Vista Wine Estate of the colorful California pioneer "Count" Agoston Haraszthy (see Buena Vista). In 1968, when Bartholomew sold Buena Vista, he held back for his own use about 50 acres of vineyards surrounding his private country house, with the understanding that he would make no separate commercial wine for at least five years. When that period was over, he formed his own Hacienda Wine Cellars and has operated them since with substantial success. In 1977, he began doubling the size of the winery and started a large-scale program of long-term contracts for buying grapes from other vineyards—gradually increasing his production to about 150,000 bottles a year.

    *** Consistently the best wine is the Gewürztraminer at a SU-PERB rating.

    * On a lower rung, four wines generally at a FINE rating: a dry white Chardonnay and a medium-soft White Riesling, a Cabernet Sauvignon and a Zinfandel.

HANZELL VINEYARDS *in the Valley of the Moon in Sonoma*

One of the most famous and important of American wineries, one which can truly be said to have changed the course of American wine history. (Its story is told in some detail, beginning on page 82.) The name comes from its founder, the San Francisco millionaire industrialist-turned-diplomat, Ambassador James D. Zellerbach, who, in 1957, dedicated his superb new winery to his wife, Hannah. As a devoted lover of Burgundy and its wines, Ambassador Zellerbach spent millions on building this winery as an exact small model of the glorious Bungundian Clos Vougeot, millions more on importing Burgundian Pinot Chardonnay and Pinot Noir root cuttings, Burgundian machinery, the first-ever Burgundian barrels, Burgundian technicians. Finally, Hanzell achieved the historic breakthrough of the American wine story—when the Pinot Chardonnays and Pinot Noirs had been made and aged, even professional Burgundian tasters could not tell that they had been produced in the New World. The immense project was cut short after only six years by the sudden death of Zellerbach, in 1963, followed very quickly by the sale of the property by Hannah, the purchase of all the magnificent wines in storage by Joe Heitz (see page 252), and a ten-year period of slow decline for Hanzell. In 1976, the property was bought by an Australian, Barbara de Brye, who, with her winemaker, Robert Sessions, is battling to return Hanzell to at least a reasonable reflection of its early glory. Current estimates of production from the 34 acres of Chardonnay and Pinot Noir, originally Burgundian vines, average about 35,000 "estate" bottles a year. Hanzell is on a northeast slope of the hills above the Sonoma Valley, and this is the appellation designated on the labels of these historic wines, always in short supply.

    * Try the FINE Burgundian-style, fruity, slightly "smoky with oak" Chardonnay, the original model of oak-aged wine, now copied by virtually every American producer.

HARBOR WINERY *near Sacramento on the Sacramento River in Sacramento County*

This is another small winery, without vineyards, in an unlikely and unromantic setting in a leased industrial building on the bank of the Sacramento River, in a district well away from any of the regular California wine regions (see also Diablo Vista). Harbor's owner and winemaker, Charles Myers, teaches English at Sacramento City College and runs his commercial winery in the evenings and on weekends. Since it is just as easy for him, in his central location, to look to the east toward the High Sierras, or to look west toward Napa, Sonoma, and the Pacific, he collects his grapes from both directions. He buys the magnificent Cabernet Sauvignon and Zinfandel grapes from the Ken Deaver Ranch in the Shenandoah Valley of Amador, also Chardonnay from some of the best microclimates in the Napa Valley. He started Harbor in 1972, and his current estimated production is about 20,000 bottles a year. His wines are so good and there is such a strong demand for them that there is virtually no distribution beyond the best wineshops of Sacramento and San Francisco.

* Try the beautifully balanced, complicated, intensely fruity Napa Chardonnay; also the smooth, strong Amador Cabernet Sauvignon; also the brawny, raisiny, lusciously rich Amador Zinfandel. All are of FINE quality.

HARGRAVE VINEYARD *at Cutchogue on the North Fork of Long Island*

Very few residents of New York City know that they, in fact, have their own *vin du pays*—a local wine of substantial stature grown and made almost (but not quite) within sight of the towers of Manhattan. At its far end, about seventy miles from the New York City line, Long Island divides into two prongs of a fork—each prong no wider than ten miles—with the Great Peconic Bay between them. The forks were formed, billions of years ago, by the forward edges of immense glaciers pushing rich alluvial soil in front of them as they slid down into the sea. The soil has become lightened by being mixed with sand, so that rain never makes it soggy, and the climate is always temperate, even in the depths of winter, because the land is surrounded on three sides by water. It seems surprising that no one has thought of growing anything around here except potatoes. Well, at least with one exception. On the North Fork, in the late 17th century, a Frenchman named Moses Fournier (no relation, apparently, to Charles Fournier, the famous winemaker of the Finger Lakes) planted European vine cuttings on some of these acres, probably employing local Indians as vineyard workers. In 1834, there is some evidence that Zinfandel vines were grown—well before they reached California—in Flushing. Into this setting and this tradition came, in the early 1970s, two young people with determination, imagination, considerable intellectual ability, a certain revolutionary spirit, and sufficient financing that they could control their future to an important and substantial degree. Alec Hargrave grew up in Rochester, New York, where his grandfather was the chief executive of Kodak. Alec's father was an attorney and banker, who insisted that his son go to Princeton and Harvard, where he finished with a degree in Chinese artistic culture. At a Harvard party, he met Louisa Thomas, who was studying American government at Smith College. They were married almost immediately. Both of them were deeply affected by the antiestablishment, antiwar worldwide emotions of the 1960s. They wanted to find some sort of work they could do together, as small entrepreneurs, outside the great circles of big business and high finance. After an injury to his back, Alec was immobilized for a year, and during this period of talking and thinking, they conceived the idea of together running a vineyard and making wine. When Alec could move again, they visited California and the Pacific Northwest, but decided, at last, that they would gain most satisfaction from the challenge of New York State. They came right home to Long Island (where Louisa had been born) and, on the North Fork, bought a 55-acre potato farm. They had their vines planted by 1973—all *Vitis vinifera*, the noble varieties of Europe. They converted one of the large, half-underground potato storage cellars into a winery. They live in the 17th-century farmhouse. Before they started making their own wines, Alec took courses at Cornell and Louisa went back to school to study wine chemistry, so that she could do the analytical work in their small laboratory. They hope, eventually, for a production (from their present 84 acres of vines) of about 100,000 bottles a year.

    * (FINE ratings) The aromatic and tangy, richly refreshing, almost austerely elegant Chardonnay is an excellent wine to counterbalance rich food; the sharply refreshing, chewy and mouth-filling, well-constructed Sauvignon Blanc is also a lunch or dinner wine *par excellence*.

HERON HILL VINEYARD *at Hammondsport on Lake Keuka in the Finger Lakes district of New York State*

Another of the "new wave" of outstanding, small wineries springing up in the historic wine region of northern New York. The planting of Heron Hill began in 1970 (and the winery was built in 1977) as a partnership between a New York City wine aficionado and an established grape grower near the famous wine town of Naples in the Finger Lakes. They began with 30 acres of the noble *vinifera* European vine varieties, which are sometimes difficult to keep alive during the ice-cold freezes of some northern New York winters. But on their parcel of somewhat-protected land on Bully Hill above Lake Keuka, they have so far been extremely lucky and successful. Their estimated production is gradually moving up toward the objective of about 100,000 bottles a year—of some of the best wines to come from New York State.

* Try the medium-soft, intensely flowery, refreshing "estate-bottled" White "Johannisberg" Riesling; also the fairly dry, quite spicy, strong Chardonnay—both usually FINE.

HILLCREST VINEYARDS *near Roseburg in the Umpqua Valley of Oregon*

This is one of the pioneer vineyards of Oregon. In 1969, Richard Sommer, trained in viticulture at the University of California, bought this 20-acre farm in one of the small side valleys that run down to the Umpqua River. Here he planted the first vines to prove that Oregon was top growing country for noble grapes, the White Riesling, Gewürztraminer, Cabernet Sauvignon, Merlot, and Malbec. In this microclimate of cool, long summers, the grapes develop an intensity of flavors. Richard makes his Gewürztraminer aromatic and bone dry, with a touch of smoke. Hillcrest has become a kind of community project. Sommer is a bachelor and works alone most of the time, but local housewives help with the pruning and picking, and local teenagers handle some of the mechanical operations in the winery. Current production averages about 75,000 bottles a year.

   *** The Gewürztraminer has a unique quality and consistently achieves a SUPERB rating.

    * Generally at a slightly lower range, the medium-soft White Riesling is usually at a FINE rating.

HINZERLING VINEYARDS *at Prosser at the base of the Rattlesnake Hills in the Yakima Valley of Washington State*

One of the most successful (both in terms of quality and distribution) of the small, family-owned vineyards of the Pacific Northwest. Jerry Wallace was Chief of Detectives of the City of Seattle. He grew weary of the endless and ferocious battle against crime and longed for the peace of tending a vineyard in the beauty and immensity of the Yakima Valley. His son, Mike, had the same dream. He trained in viticulture at the University of California, and the Wallaces, *père et fils,* became partners in the 55-acre Hinzerling Vineyards. The winery is a converted garage, where they built and installed much of the equipment themselves. They began planting their vines in 1971, and by 1976 made their first wine. Since then, Mike has been making wines of exceptional quality (including some highly experimental types) and has been winning gold medals at the annual festivals. Hinzerling's production is rising gradually to about 150,000 bottles a year.

   *** At the Pacific Northwest Wine Festival, this writer was one of the judges voting to award a top gold medal to the Hinzerling "Late Harvest—Selected Clusters" Gewürztraminer golden sweet wine, with 15.6 percent residual sugar, which to me was the most excitingly aromatic, most perfectly balanced, *Botrytized* American wine I had ever tasted, at a SUPERB rating.

   ** Two wines consistently at a NOBLE rating: the Chardonnay and the dry Gewürztraminer.

    * The Cabernet Sauvignon consistently at a FINE rating.

HOFFMAN MOUNTAIN RANCH *above Paso Robles in the Santa Lucia Mountains of San Luis Obispo*

This is one more story of a weekend amateur hobby that became a dominant full-time commercial enterprise. Dr. Stanley Hoffman was a well-known, extremely successful heart specialist in Beverly Hills who could afford one of those large mansions with big cellars, where, in the 1950s, he and his wife, Teressa, with their sons, David and Michael, enjoyed themselves as home winemakers. From there, it was a natural step to try to find a weekend ranch in the Santa Lucia Hills, where the exposure, the soil, and the angle of the slope would be right for planting vines. Stanley Hoffman doesn't believe in doing anything by halves. If he was going to make wine seriously, he might as well try for the best in the business. He persuaded the supreme winemaker, André Tchelistcheff, to become his consultant. In 1965, they found a mountain ranch at about 1,800 feet where the soil was chalky and limy (as it is in Burgundy) and began planting 120 acres of Hoffman's favorite Burgundian Pinot Noirs and Chardonnays. In 1972, the wines began to flow, and they were, hardly unexpectedly, exceedingly good. So good, in fact, that the doctor gave up his Beverly Hills practice and moved permanently out to the ranch, hoping to become a full-time winemaker. Not quite. Several of his mountain neighbors began bringing their heart problems to the good doctor, and he has had to open an office in Paso Robles. But his sons are both now fully trained, and production is approaching 400,000 bottles a year.

      ** (NOBLE rating) Although they claim to be specialists in Burgundian styles, I currently find the Cabernet Sauvignon to be the best—this may change as the other vines mature.
     * (FINE ratings) The delicately fruity "estate" Chardonnay and the bold, elegant, robust Pinot Noir.

HOP KILN WINERY AND GRIFFIN VINEYARD *at Healdsburg in the Russian River Valley of Sonoma*

A vineyard was planted on this site in 1880, but not much seems to be remembered of it. Probably its vines were wiped out by the deadly phylloxera disease around 1890, and then, apparently, with the succeeding disaster of Prohibition, winemaking here was completely forgotten. After a break of fifty years, in the mid-1970s, it was all brought back to vinous life by a new owner, Dr. Martin Griffin, a psychiatrist and amateur winemaker. He converted a hop kiln drying barn into a winery in 1975, and since then his estimated production —mostly from his own 60 acres of vines—has been gradually rising toward a projected average of about 75,000 bottles a year. They are released under three labels: the best vintage-dated varietals as Hop Kiln Winery, a Colombard-White Riesling blend as "One Thousand Flowers," and a strong, Italian type from some wines of dubious ancestry as "Marty Griffin's Big Red." These are sold mainly at the winery, locally around northern Sonoma, and in San Francisco.

> * (FINE rating) In the neighborhood, try the peasanty-rough, ripe, strong Zinfandel.

HUSCH VINEYARDS *at Philo in the Anderson Valley of Mendocino*

This vineyard was founded in 1968 by a most excellent wine-making family, Tony and Gretchen Husch, who introduced a number of early interesting wines (see page 180). In 1979, however, they sold out (but permitted the continuing use of their name) to a local fruit-growing family named Oswald. Parts of their three large ranches around the Ukiah Valley are now being replanted in noble *vinifera* vine varieties to supply the winery. There is also a "home vineyard" of 23 acres at the winery, planted mainly in Chardonnay, Gewürztraminer, and Pinot Noir. Current production is estimated at about 65,000 bottles a year. It may take the new owners a period of practice before they can match the extremely high standards set by the previous owners.

> * Try the intensely fruity, delicately spicy "estate-bottled" Chardonnay; also the aromatic, elegant, refreshing Rosé of Pinot Noir, one of the very best of all California rosés (see page 180). The new owners tell me that they have temporarily discontinued the rosé, in order to put all their Pinot Noir into red production, but they promise to bring back the rosé as quickly as possible. FINE ratings for both.

INGLENOOK VINEYARDS *at Rutherford in the Napa Valley*

This is, by a strange juxtaposition of historical events, at the same time one of the greatest names and greatest tragedies of American wine history. In 1879, the Finnish sea captain Gustave Nybom, having "made his pile" in the Alaskan seal-catching trade, decided to retire at the age of thirty-five. He chose winemaking as his hobby and bought a vineyard called Inglenook just north of Rutherford.

Nybom (the name, later, changed to Niebaum) was an absolute perfectionist. His objective was nothing less than to make the finest
wines in the world. He imported the best root cuttings from all the
greatest wine regions of Europe, built a Gothic-style winery and a
magnificent mansion. The captain operated without regard for primary expense, or ultimate gain. He once said, "The only wines on
which I make a profit are those I give to my friends." A journalist of
the time wrote that Inglenook was a California combination of the
ambience and mystique of Château Lafite, Château Yquem, and
Schloss Johannisberg. At the pinnacle of his success, in 1908, Niebaum died, at the age of sixty-six. Prohibition followed, and Inglenook was closed.

At Repeal, in 1933, Niebaum's widow, Suzanne, took charge and
entrusted the rebirth of Inglenook to two men—Carl Bundschu of
the famous Sonoma winemaking family, and her grand-nephew,
John Daniel. Her primary rule, on which she insisted absolutely, was
that no wine of less than top quality should ever carry the Inglenook
label. Suzanne died, and Daniel became the owner and master of
Inglenook for twenty-five more years. I shall always remember meeting him shortly before he died and tasting some of his extraordinary
old Inglenook vintages—the first truly great wines of America. Then,
wanting to retire and having no son to carry on, he shocked us all,
in 1964, by selling Inglenook to the giant United Vintners Cooperative, which itself, four years later, was swallowed up by the enormous Heublein conglomerate. Soon the entire accent of winemaking
at Inglenook changed completely. The search for peak quality was
converted to a drive toward peak profits. The objective became the
maximum mass marketing of the glamor and prestige of the great
Inglenook name. In achieving this objective, the Inglenook standard
of quality has been totally debased. Instead of the few thousand
bottles of supreme Inglenook wines that came, originally, from the
family vineyards, the current production of bottles bearing the Inglenook label—most of them having no connection whatsoever with the
Inglenook vineyards and containing wines that are average to mediocre—is running at about 18 million a year. Inglenook, in fact, has
been converted into a commercial "brand name." The wines are released under three significantly different labels. First, there are Inglenook Estate wines. These, at least in legal theory, ought to be made
in the original Niebaum winery, from grapes grown exclusively on

the original family vineyards. They are not. They are made in a huge, concrete, boxlike, industrial, factory-style winery, built at Oakville specifically to automate and expand enormously the Inglenook production. Then, to expand equally the grape supply, the harvests are brought in from 1,500 additional acres of vineyards belonging to members of the giant cooperative, and these are, so to speak, all thrown into the Inglenook pot, without any real consistency of quality. But they are all finally labeled Inglenook Estate. The second label is Inglenook North Coast Counties (at a lower price), and these wines have even less connection with the great name. They are made from grapes bought all over northern California and taken straight to the factory winery "near" Inglenook. The third label is Inglenook Navalle—this latter word being the name of a small creek that meanders through the Inglenook property. These wines are low-priced blends, generics, and jug-type wines, made from grapes gathered from all over California, including the semidesert San Joaquin Valley. They are brought, not to Inglenook, but to the huge United Vintners wine factory at Asti. These Navalle wines never get nearer than about fifty miles to Inglenook. They have as much right to that prestigious name as a VW Rabbit would have the right to call itself a Mercedes!

    * Try the wine that remains one of the most carefully made of the Inglenook "estate" bottlings, the full, fairly fleshy, tannic "Cask Selection" Cabernet Sauvignon; also the smooth, strong Pinot Noir. Each scores a FINE rating.

IRON HORSE VINEYARDS *at Sebastopol in the Russian River Valley of Sonoma*

In the early 1970s, when Sonoma Vineyards was at the peak of its expansion, with more than 5,000 acres of vines, one of its most attractive and subtle Chardonnays was, year after year, the one labeled Iron Horse Ranch, a magnificent vineyard in northern Sonoma, first planted in 1876. When financial storms forced a contraction of the Sonoma "empire," the 120 acres of Iron Horse vines (plus an additional 130 acres of land for future expansion) were sold, in 1976, to Audrey Sterling, who made it her home and family vineyard for the development of supreme wines. The possibilities remain good. The climate is cool, the soil rocky and rough, the exposure is rolling hills, the Pacific Ocean fogs swirl in through the Petaluma Gap in the

Coast Range—conditions combining to slow the ripening of the grapes and to stress the berries for concentrated and intense flavors. By 1979, a modern winery had been built and its direction taken over by winemaker Forrest Tancer. He and his wife, Kate, became partners in the Iron Horse management, bringing into it the harvests from 30 more acres of vines planted on their 450 acres of new land in the Alexander Valley, east of Healdsburg. Current production is about 120,000 bottles a year; but, with 550 acres possibly available for expansion, production could gradually rise to 350,000 bottles a year, and the present limited national distribution could be substantially extended.

    ** (NOBLE ratings) The brilliant, crisp, delicately dry, intensely fruity Chardonnay; the complex, deep, dominant, tannic Cabernet Sauvignon from the Alexander Valley; the magnificent, powerful estate-grown Pinot Noir; and the delicately soft, elegant "Fumé Blanc" (Sauvignon Blanc).

    * (FINE rating) The fruity, light, refreshing Rosé of Pinot Noir.

JEKEL VINEYARD *at Greenfield in the Salinas Valley of Monterey*

A family-owned vineyard planted in 1972 on 140 acres in the excellent grape-growing microclimate of the Arroyo Seco Canyon. After developing their vineyards and selling their early harvests to other producers, they built their own winery and started releasing wines under their own label in 1978, with a projected production of about 350,000 bottles a year.

    *** The Arroyo Seco is famous for local development (see page 195) of the noble *Botrytis* mold, and one of the first Jekel wines to be released was a "Late Harvest" White Riesling with 10 percent residual sugar and a SUPERB rating.

    * In the lower range, there is an unusually well balanced Chardonnay and a medium-dry White Riesling, both at a FINE rating.

JOHNSON'S ALEXANDER VALLEY WINES *at Healdsburg in the Alexander Valley of Sonoma*

A fairly small vineyard, owned and run by the Johnson family, first planting their 45-acre vineyard in 1952 and selling their grapes to other producers. Then, beginning in 1975, they built a winery to make and bottle their own wines. Since then, their estimated production has risen gradually to an average of about 90,000 bottles a year. Although they have now had considerable experience in wine-making, they seem, somehow, to keep an amateur feeling about their wines, with disturbing variations in quality between different batches and various varieties. Yet the wines are popular and they are all sold fairly quickly at the winery, around northern Sonoma, and in San Francisco.

　　* In the neighborhood, try the smooth, spicy Pinot Noir; also the consistently good, dry, full-of-character Rosé of Pinot Noir, probably the best thing they do—both usually FINE.

KALIN CELLARS *at Novato near San Rafael on San Pablo Bay north of San Francisco*

This is a small, highly experimental winery in leased space in a waterfront industrial building on the northern sweep of San Francisco Bay. Grapes are trucked here from nearby Sonoma but are also brought the three hundred miles or so from the Santa Barbara district as well as from the foothill valleys of the High Sierras about one hundred miles to the east. The main interest here is always in the direction of making unusual, unique, experimental wines, rather than stressing commercially saleable products. But the wines turn out to be so good and so interesting that connoisseurs snap them up anyway—and at above-average prices. For example, there have been nine separate versions of Pinot Noir, each from a different designated vineyard, as well as various comparative versions of golden sweet "Late Harvest" White Riesling. Since the start of all this, in 1976, production has been rising gradually toward the objective of an average of about 35,000 bottles a year. Distribution is pretty well instantly absorbed by the always-thirsty market of connoisseurs in San Francisco.

　　* In San Francisco, try the extraordinary, luscious, raisiny, smooth, yet heady-with-alcohol Zinfandel, rated FINE.

ROBERT KEENAN WINERY *on Spring Mountain above the Napa Valley*

A very old vineyard on a very steep slope near the top of Napa's famous "wine mountain" is being revived after many years of abandonment and neglect. It was first planted in 1891, and an old stone winery was built in 1904. Then, apparently, after a brief period of winemaking, it was all forgotten for about fifty years. In 1977, the 17-acre vineyard was bought and revived by Robert Keenan, who decided to replant and produce only Chardonnay, Cabernet Sauvignon, and Pinot Noir. While he is waiting for his own vines to mature, he is buying grapes and producing an average of about 100,000 bottles a year. Eventually, all the wines will be made from grapes grown on the estate. Quality is high—so are the prices.

    ** (NOBLE rating) The fruity, luscious first vintage of Chardonnay.

    * (FINE rating) The still-young Pinot Noir, which should greatly improve with bottle aging.

KENWOOD VINEYARDS *at Kenwood in the Valley of the Moon in Sonoma*

This relatively small winery has been made famous by the highly experimental policies of its technical direction, under Bob Kozlowski, the research-chemist-turned-winemaker who is also one of the owners of the old vineyard, originally founded in 1906 by an Italian family forced to flee from San Francisco after the earthquake and fire. The 20-acre vineyard on Sugar Loaf Ridge at the northern end of the Sonoma Valley was bought by the present owners in 1970. Current production is estimated at about half a million bottles a year.

    ** (NOBLE ratings) The all-round outstanding Cabernet Sauvignon, with grapes from the Jack London Vineyard; and the powerful, smooth Zinfandel.

    * (FINE ratings) The dry, fruity Chenin Blanc; the most unusual Pinot Noir (fermented in stainless steel); the elegant Rosé of Cabernet Sauvignon; and the aromatic Rosé of Pinot Noir.

KISTLER VINEYARD *on the western slopes of the Mayacamas Mountains above Glen Ellen and the Valley of the Moon in Sonoma*

This brand-new 35-acre mountain vineyard, planted about half in Cabernet Sauvignon and half in Chardonnay, is still waiting for its own vines to mature—but its young winemaker-owner (in partnership with his family), Steve Kistler, is already building a considerable reputation for himself with the wines he is making from purchased grapes. He told me, "Although I graduated in Liberal Arts from Stanford University and tried, at first, to earn my living as a writer, it was always somehow at the back of my mind that I would some day want to make wine. This was the influence of my grandfather who was a great collector and connoisseur of French wines. So, before long, I went to Fresno State College to learn about grape growing and viticulture and then to the University of California at Davis to take a degree in enology." He was very lucky with his first job—as an assistant winemaker to the brilliant Paul Draper at Ridge, where he stayed for three years and learned the extreme disciplines and perfectionisms required for the making of supreme wines. Then, naturally, he wanted to be the master of his own winery. He told me, "This little place we have here represents the extraordinary faith and trust in me of my family. My father and my two brothers have put virtually all their savings behind this vineyard. My brother John and I have done all the building, the clearing, and the planting ourselves up here on the top of the mountain." They hope to have their first wines from their estate in two years, but they will continue to buy the impeccable grapes that are now their main sources. Their projected maximum production is expected, eventually, to be about 72,000 bottles a year of wines carefully crafted by hand, according to the old-fashioned traditions.

  *** (SUPERB ratings) The various magnificently fruity, rich, and velvety Cabernet Sauvignons made with grapes from the Glen Ellen Vineyards.
  ** (NOBLE ratings) The aromatic, elegant, fruity Chardonnays, especially those made with grapes from the Winery Lake Vineyard in the Carneros Hills or with grapes from the Dutton Vineyard near Sebastopol.

KNUDSEN-ERATH WINERY *at Dundee in the Willamette Valley of Oregon*

One of the important vineyards of Oregon with about 90 acres of vines and an estimated production of about 180,000 bottles a year. Dick Erath was an electronics engineer in California, became interested in home winemaking, and took an enological course at the university, where one of his classmates was Richard Sommer, owner of the famous Hillcrest Vineyard in Oregon. Later, when Dick visited Hillcrest, he was completely sold on the challenge and excitement of making wine in the Northwest. In 1968, he found a potential vineyard in the Chehalem foothills of the Willamette Valley. Meanwhile, Cal Knudsen, a wealthy lumberman from Seattle, had adopted wine as a hobby and was developing a vineyard in the Red Hills of Dundee. Since he had to spend most of his time in Seattle, he needed a technician to manage his property, and Erath was just the man for the job. They formed a loose relationship, which has now grown into a full and complete partnership. Beyond the present vineyards, they have another 170 acres to be gradually developed. Eventually, they hope to be able to produce about 400,000 bottles a year. They use the standard Oregon system of "milk carton irrigation," and they claim to have a "special permit" allowing them to harass the robins that perform fantastic feats of mass-banqueting on the ripe grapes hanging on the vines just before the harvest.

    ** (NOBLE ratings) The medium-soft White Riesling; the crisp, fruity, subtle, tart Chardonnay; and an Oregon-style, bold, smooth, velvety Pinot Noir, which has won gold medals at various festivals.

KONOCTI CELLARS *at Kelseyville in the northern Lake County*

This area is a kind of "new frontier" of California wine. It is the inland wine district to the "far north" of the regular wine regions—north of the Napa Valley, east of Mendocino—where the grapes ripen slowly in a cool climate and develop often-startling intensities of fruit flavors. So far, a majority of the growers here have been shipping their grapes to many of the famous producers farther south. But, in 1975, Konocti was formed as a cooperative of thirty-eight growers, and, in 1979, their winery was completed, so that the making and aging of the wines could begin. The members have, between them, 510 acres of vines, and their estimated production is rising to their first objective of an average of about 275,000 bottles a year. Later, they hope to reach and surpass 1 million bottles a year. Their future, of course, will depend on the national acceptance of the special and unusual qualities of these far-northern wines—qualities which I, for one, find extremely attractive.

> * Try the medium-soft, wonderfully flowery, intensely fruity White Riesling—a FINE rating.

KORBEL WINERY *at Guerneville in the Russian River Valley of Sonoma*

One of the oldest and certainly the largest company concentrating, now entirely, on sparkling wines and brandies. It was founded in 1862, and a part of the group of big winery buildings still in use was constructed in the late 1870s, with the Brandy Tower dating back to 1889. Today, their estimated production of what they like to call "California Champagne," all made by the prestigious French *méthode champenoise*, is running at an average of about 4½ million bottles a year. They have 600 acres of their own vines, but, of course, they have to buy enormous quantities of the slightly acid grapes that are needed for sparkling wine, and these come, usually, from the cool-climate districts in all parts of the northern half of California. When one realizes that, adding together the sparkling-wine operation and the brandy distilling, Korbel is turning out almost 11 million bottles a year, it becomes obvious that this is an immense mass-production organization. So it seems all the more praiseworthy that their best sparkling wines have been, for many years, of such very good quality at such very fair prices.

> * Try the faintly sweet, delicately fruity, crisp "Brut," with copious small bubbles, made mainly from Chardonnay grapes; also the relatively new, almost bone-dry, velvety "Blanc de Noirs," with tiny bubbles, made 100 percent with Pinot Noir grapes. Both with FINE ratings.

HANNS KORNELL CELLARS *north of St. Helena in the Napa Valley*

Another "famous name" maker, exclusively, of sparkling wines, but with a slightly different accent from most of the others. This is no smoothly automated, mass-production organization, but strictly the "one-man show" of a determined, dogged, perfectionist, self-assured winemaker from Germany, Hanns Kornell, who remembers his former homeland and likes to give his wine at least a touch of the Germanic style of sparkling *sekt*. Where other producers print French phrases on their "champagne" labels, Hanns translates "very dry" into *sehr trocken*. Where other producers use the French Pinot Chardonnay grape, Hanns uses the German Riesling. He started in the Napa Valley in 1952, and, today, his estimated production of top-quality, bottle-fermented sparkling wines is at an average of about 1½ million bottles a year. They are divided into seven types, with the "Sehr Trocken" as the driest, top-quality, most-expensive label. The others seem to go down in price as they go up in sweetness, and this is very much in the German tradition. But, with all of them, the Kornell skill seems always to achieve a dancing lightness on the tongue and a velvety softness in the throat.

> * Try the "Sehr Trocken," made mostly with Riesling grapes, aged on the yeast in the bottle for about five years instead of the usual two; also the Bordeaux-style, sweet dessert sparkler, the "Muscadelle du Bordelais," aromatic, very fruity, delicately complex; also, in the years when he makes it, try his interesting sparkler from the Muscat of Alexandria grape. All score a FINE rating.

CHARLES KRUG WINERY *at St. Helena in the Napa Valley*

This is certainly the oldest vineyard in the Napa Valley, among the oldest in California, and one of the largest of the group just below the giants. It harvests about 1,200 acres of vines from one end of the valley to the other and produces an estimated average of about 24 million bottles a year—an important part as inexpensive, good-value jug wines under the C.K.–Mondavi label. The better wines, the vintaged varietals, are labeled as Charles Krug. The firm was founded in 1861 by an immigrant Frenchman, Charles Krug, who was at once so successful that, by the time all his vineyards were killed off by the inexorable phylloxera vine disease in the late 1880s, his wines were known all over America. After about fifty years of eclipse, the company was sold, in 1943, to Cesare Mondavi, who soon brought in to help him his wife, Rosa, and his two sons, Peter and Robert. During the next twenty years, their main interest was in building a vast business in jug wines. Today, they still sell about 10 million half-gallon jugs a year. After the father's death, a fierce family feud developed between Robert, on one side, and Rosa and Peter on the other. In 1965, Robert walked out and founded his own now-famous Robert Mondavi Winery at Oakville, launching a huge lawsuit for damages against his brother and mother. It became one of the largest legal actions in the history of American wine, continued in the courts for more than ten years, and was finally won by Robert with a settlement running into many millions of dollars. The effect on Krug seems to have been minimal, and Peter remains in complete charge. During the modern boom in premium wines, he has shown more and more interest in upgrading the quality of the better and more expensive Charles Krug labels. The results are generally safely good, sometimes excellent.

> ** (NOBLE rating) The medium-soft, fruity, refreshing Charles Krug Chenin Blanc.
> * (FINE ratings) The "Riesling" Pinot Blanc; the Riesling made from Sylvaner grapes; the brisk, fruity Chardonnay; the light, fairly simple Cabernet Sauvignon "Cesare Mondavi Selection"; and the easy-to-drink Zinfandel—all under the Charles Krug label.

THOMAS KRUSE WINERY *at Gilroy in the Santa Cruz Mountains of Santa Clara*

A relatively minuscule, one-man vineyard, owned and run by a winemaker who has many times been called, with deep affection, a "crazy perfectionist." Certainly, there can be no question but that he places the quality of the wine, or the interest of the experiment, far above all commercial considerations. He started in 1971, selling most of his bottles directly from his winery, and his current production is estimated at an average of about 30,000 bottles a year. He puts his own names on the labels of wines that he thinks have turned out well. Others, where he feels that the experiment has not been a complete success, are labeled as Aptos Vineyards, but I have often found these "rejects of the builder" to be of fascinating interest and of outstanding value. Tom has a strong sense of the regional character of the wines of this historic old vineyard district around the Hecker Pass, and he uses mostly the local grapes that grow on these steep hillsides.

> * In the neighborhood, try the clean, luscious, spicy Chardonnay; also the smooth, strong Pinot Noir; the lean, refresh-

ing, tangy Grignolino Rosé; and the full-of-character Rosé of Pinot Noir. Each achieves a FINE rating.

LAMBERT BRIDGE WINERY *west of Healdsburg in the Dry Creek Valley of Sonoma*

A moderately small vineyard involved in the confusion of being near a bridge and being owned by a family—both called Lambert. The bridge was here long before the family arrived. They named the winery in 1975, and, today, their estimated production is at an average of about 100,000 bottles a year. They have about 80 acres, planted only in Cabernet Sauvignon and Chardonnay.

* Try the interestingly ascetic and austere, lean, tense Chardonnay, rating at FINE.

LANDMARK VINEYARDS *at Windsor in the Dry Creek Valley of Sonoma*

A medium-size winery, owned and run by the Mabry family, the architect father and winemaker son. They have 90 acres of vines, soon to be expanded to 150 acres. They began planting in 1972, completed their winery in 1974, and are now building up toward a projected average production of about 300,000 bottles a year.

* Try what is unquestionably their most successful wine so far, the fruity, lively Chenin Blanc typically with the Dry Creek regional, slightly earthy character, scoring a FINE rating.

LEONETTI CELLARS *at Walla Walla in the south Columbia Basin of central Washington State*

This minuscule vineyard (smallest in the state) of 2½ acres was planted in Cabernet Sauvignon, Merlot, and White Riesling by local businessman and wine aficionado George Leonetti. He has now passed the property on to his nephew and niece, Gary and Nancy Figgins. I met them at the Tri-Cities Wine Festival in central Washington and was impressed by their dedication to high quality and their determination to expand the tiny operation by buying grapes from some of the best growers in the Columbia Basin and the Yakima Valley. The winery was completed in 1977, and production is now averaging about 5,000 bottles a year. Distribution does not go much beyond Walla Walla, Spokane, and the central Washington towns.

> * In the neighborhood, try the medium-soft, delicately flowery, intensely fruity White Riesling, with grapes from the famous Sagemoor Farms on the hills above the Columbia River and of FINE quality.

LONG VINEYARDS *on Pritchard Hill above the Napa Valley*

Zelma Long has been in the top circle of California winemakers for more than ten years. She is an Oregonian, trained at Oregon State. At that time, the center of the U.S. wine world was the Napa Valley, so she and her former husband, Bob, moved there, and she took a temporary job "just to help out during the harvest" at the Mondavi winery. She stayed on and within two years was chief winemaker. Recently, she has gone on to become executive winemaker at Simi Winery, now owned by the giant French conglomerate Moët-Hennessy (see Domaine Chandon).

Meanwhile, behind the large-scale corporate success, Zelma and Bob have been working out their small-scale private dream. With the financial help of his family, they have bought and planted their own 15-acre mountain vineyard in the excellent grape-growing microclimate of Pritchard Hill, high above the Napa Valley. Bob has designed and built—doing much of the work himself—an almost miniature, ultramodern winery in which they hope eventually to produce about 25,000 bottles a year. Shortly before their general release, Zelma brought a few bottles of their first two wines to a professional viticultural meeting for some of us to taste. Their excellence was dazzling. Within a few months, the Long name had become virtually a "cult label" in California—wanted by every connoisseur—and the minuscule available quantity disappeared entirely from the open market. Now the only way you can hope to get a few bottles of Long wines is to write to the vineyard and have your name put on the waiting list for the next harvest.

> *** There are only two wines, both at a SUPERB rating: a buttery, fruity, rich Chardonnay and a golden sweet, fruity

tangy "Late Harvest" White Riesling, with a residual sugar of 8.5 percent—one of the two or three best American *Botrytized* sweet wines I have ever tasted.

LYTTON SPRINGS WINERY *north of Healdsburg in Sonoma*

The name covers a legendary group of old Zinfandel vineyards on the hills above the Russian River. The grapes from the 50 acres of eighty-year-old vines are of magnificent quality and, for years, were sold to Ridge (see page 389), where the name Lytton Springs appeared on many of the most-honored Ridge Zinfandel labels. Then, in 1975, the owners of these vineyards decided to make their own wines, built a winery, and started releasing bottles under the Lytton Springs label. They also bought grapes of equal quality from the neighboring Valley Vista Vineyard. Total production of the high-quality Zinfandels remains at about 60,000 bottles a year. If you like the character and personality of Sonoma Zinfandel, this is about the best you can get—if you try hard enough and are lucky enough to find it!

   ** (NOBLE rating) The Valley Vista Zinfandel is aromatic, big, chewy in the mouth, dominant, seeming to radiate a sunny warmth, mouth puckering with tannin, demanding to be aged for at least another ten years.

MARKHAM WINERY *north of St. Helena in the Napa Valley*

This is a fairly substantial winemaking operation, owned and run by the Markham family, with the development of their vineyards beginning in the early 1970s and the modernization of their one-hundred-year-old winery building completed in 1978. Since then, their estimated production has risen gradually to a current average of about 200,000 bottles a year. They release these bottles under two labels: their highest-quality, vintage-dated varietals as Markham; the less expensive types, made mainly from purchased grapes, as Vin Mark. They have three separate vineyards, which total about 300 acres in some of the best microclimate districts of the valley—one near Calistoga, the second just south of Yountville, and the third north of the town of Napa. These grapes produce such excellent wines—with the purchased grapes not far behind—and the whole operation is so well financed and efficiently organized that one has the feeling that it will expand fairly quickly to a substantial size.

　　* (FINE rating) Try the intense, smooth 100 percent Merlot Vin Mark.

MARK WEST VINEYARDS *north of Forestville in the Russian River Valley of Sonoma*

This medium-size winery, named for the nearby Mark West Creek, is family owned and run by Robert and Joan Ellis. They began planting in 1974, completed the building of their winery in 1976, and, today, are reaching toward an estimated production objective of about 175,000 bottles a year. They have 60 acres of vines for which Bob is responsible as the viticultural specialist, while Joan concentrates on the work in the winery. They seem to want to make Burgundian-style reds and Moselle-style whites in their excellent location on the hillside above the valley, with a cool microclimate and regular morning and evening mists—but they are not always successful in their objectives.

　　* (FINE rating) Try the delicately soft, easy, gentle Chardonnay.

LOUIS M. MARTINI WINERY *in St. Helena in the Napa Valley*

One of the best-known and most popular names on medium-priced American wine labels belongs to one of the great Italian-Californian wine families—admired and honored as statesmen of the wine business, as defenders of the beauty and ecology of the California land, and as a continuing progressive force in the technology of winemaking. The Martini production today is not large enough to put them among the giants, but it is in the upper-middle range among major U.S. producers—with between 5 and 6 million bottles a year. The founder of the dynasty was Louis M. (whose name still appears on every bottle), who came from Italy in the 1880s and was soon joined by his father, August. They ran a thriving fish business in San Francisco, but, like all Italians, wine was in their blood, and soon they were buying grapes, making strong young red, and selling it to their customers and to many of the hundreds of "boarding-houses" that dotted every neighborhood of the city. The wine was never bottled. The larger establishments bought barrels of it; the smaller places brought out jugs and filled them at the spigot of the barrel at the back of the Martini cart. It was very quickly obvious that there would be a larger profit if they grew their own grapes. So they started buying bits of land here and there, and some of these vine-yards are still a part of the Martini "empire." In 1906, they were wiped out by the San Francisco earthquake and fire. Prohibition was less of a problem. The Martinis were all devout members of the church, and they got the contracts to make the altar wines. When Prohibition ended, Louis M. moved to the Napa Valley, and within a few years his wines were a top-selling label all over the country. Joined by his son, Louis P. (who now heads the company), they developed more than 800 acres of magnificent vineyards above the Napa Valley, in the Carneros Hills, and in Sonoma. The Martini labels are always clearly and consistently informative. When, for ex-ample, a particular tank of Cabernet Sauvignon develops exception-ally well, that bottling will be labeled "Special Selection" and always represents an extremely good value.

    *** The "Special Selection" Cabernet Sauvignon, whenever it is available, consistently rates as SUPERB—so did an amazing series of golden sweet Muscatels, some of them made dur-ing Prohibition in 1929, yet still with a strong sense of fruit and SUPERB to drink after more than fifty years in the bot-tle.

    ** Scoring a few points lower, these wines regularly achieve a NOBLE rating: the Chardonnay, Gewürztraminer, the red 100 percent Merlot, and the Pinot Noir.

    * Just below in the ratings, regularly achieving a FINE quality, are the unique Folle Blanche, the grape used only by Martini for a charming, dry, lightly refreshing summer white (see page 58), the Zinfandel, and the Rosé de Gamay.

PAUL MASSON VINEYARDS *at Saratoga and in the Pinnacles district of the Santa Cruz Mountains in Santa Clara*

This is another of the most historic and old wine operations of California. It has grown into one of the "second-rung giants"—not as overwhelmingly immense as Gallo, nor as enormous as Guild, but in the next-size group, with such producers as Christian Brothers and Almadén. Indeed, Masson shares the same roots as Almadén and has always maintained a strong rivalry. In the 1960s, when I was interviewing successive Masson managements, they put their faith in nonvintaged, nonvarietal, blended wines with overdramatic proprietary names, such as "Baroque," or "Emerald Dry," or "Rubion," etc., with no indication as to which grapes were in the wine. The widely held theory of those times was that wine would develop as a kind of cola drink and that the consumers, by clever marketing, could become attached to a particular brand name. Then came the wine revolution, and it is to Masson's credit that they quickly changed their point of view. They began turning out millions of gallons of nonvintaged, nonappellation varietals, easy to drink, pleasant, simple, smooth, always with a tiny touch of sweetness, aimed at the broadest mass appeal. Finally, today, from their relatively new Pinnacles Vineyards, they are producing vintage-dated varietals of quite fair quality, with a Monterey appellation, reasonably priced, designated on each label as a Pinnacles Selection. Total production of all the wines—more than thirty different types—averages about 150 million bottles a year.

Paul Masson was a French immigrant, and the original vineyard was planted in 1852—the vineyard that later became the founding property of Almadén. Meanwhile, Masson had expanded into a small empire of other vineyards, and all of these, in 1942, were sold to the giant Seagrams Distilling Company. There followed an enormous expansion: 4,500 acres of vines planted in Monterey, including the mountain vineyards around the Pinnacles; an enormous, ultramodern winery at Soledad in the Salinas Valley; a big winery for sweet wines, ports, sherries, and vermouths in the San Joaquin Valley; and sparkling-wine cellars with bottling plants in Saratoga, south of San Francisco.

> * (FINE rating) Try the unusual, fruity, spicy Sylvaner, an Alsatian grape not sufficiently known in the United States (see page 64); also the aromatic, intense, delicately sweet Gewürztraminer Pinnacles Selection, one of the best wines they make; and the crisp, dry, fruity, sparkling "Brut," made by the transfer process (see page 212), good value at a very reasonable price.

MASTANTUONO WINERY *west of Templeton near Paso Robles in the Santa Lucia Mountains of San Luis Obispo*

The Mastantuono family has been running this winery since 1977. Their current estimated production is approaching the objective of about 25,000 bottles a year. They have 16 acres of vines, but, of course, are supplementing these by buying additional grapes. They concentrate, for the moment, entirely on one variety, Zinfandel—a grape for which this historic winemaking district is famous—and each bottle is labeled with a designated specific vineyard. This perfectionist policy is providing wines which, obviously, need aging, but show a bright promise for the future.

    ** (NOBLE rating) In northern California, try the dark, intensely fruity, spicy, strongly tannic Zinfandel, an extraordinary wine, in its natural state, unfiltered and unfined, made from the magnificent grapes of the ancient vines of the Dusi Vineyard.

MATANZAS CREEK WINERY *in the Bennett Valley southwest of Santa Rosa in Sonoma*

The wines of this fairly small vineyard have gained a reputation considerably above the average that might be expected from its geographical location and the volume of its production. The reason is, almost certainly, the creative dynamism of two highly imaginative young women, both extremely efficient, both with perfectionist idealism, both with strong personalities. The founder, proprietor, and administrator is Sandra MacIver, a daughter of wealthy parents who is deliberately turning away from the gilded life toward the simplicity of growing grapes in a quite remote agricultural community. The technical director and winemaker is Merry Edwards, who, during the first few years of her professional career, has already gained extraordinary prestige from her ability to make outstanding wines, strongly stamped with the mark of her personal creative philosophy and unique sense of style.

    Matanzas Creek was founded in 1977, and its current production is now running at about 50,000 bottles a year. In the Bennett Valley, in the area surrounding the winery, there are about 70 acres of estate vines solidly planted in Cabernet Sauvignon, Chardonnay, Gewürztraminer, Pinot Noir, and Merlot, but also with many small plots of experimental varieties (including six rare clones of Chardonnay) to feed into Merry's continuing program of making and tasting new types of wines. These include an estate-bottled sparkling Chardonnay. In addition, she buys grapes with particular qualities from special sources in various parts of northern California, including Pinot Blanc picked from ancient vines as far south as Los Gatos.

   *** (NOBLE ratings) For a clear sense of the special Matanzas Creek style, taste the Pinot Noir, the label marked Val Vista, made partly from estate grapes and partly with fruit from the Valley Vista Vineyard in the Sonoma Valley—a deep red with an intense bouquet, an aromatic earthiness, a complexity of flavors, a softness of velvet on the tongue; also the estate-grown Cabernet Sauvignon.

   * (FINE ratings) One of the most interesting, stylistically, of the whites is the dry Gewürztraminer, made with grapes from the St. Francis Vineyard, the wine then finished in the gentle, soft, understated, true Alsatian style—a modest wine, but beautifully refreshing and satisfying—as is, also, the dry, refreshing Pinot Chardonnay.

MAYACAMAS VINEYARDS *on the Mayacamas Range above the Napa Valley*

An outstanding mountaintop vineyard of 50 acres of vines, with the stone winery built in 1889 in an old volcanic crater 2,000 feet above the valley floor. It is family owned and run by Bob Travers, his wife, Nonie, and their three sons, producing—in this lonely, rocky, wild place—about 75,000 bottles a year. Bob was an investment banker in San Francisco. He and Nonie, both amateurs of wine, "dreamed the dream" of the challenge, the peace, and the satisfactions of owning a vineyard. Bob took viticultural courses at the University of California and then worked for Joe Heitz (see page 248). In 1968, the Travers bought 400 acres on top of the Mayacamas Mountains. Bob's progress as a winemaker has been punctuated by dramatic experiments. He was the first to make a "Late Harvest" Zinfandel—a technique now almost universally copied (see page 163). He developed a golden sweet Sauvignon Blanc with artificially induced *Botrytis* (see page 194). Above all, he is a classic vintner, producing wines to magnify the intense flavors of his mountain grapes.

  *** The "Late Harvest" Zinfandel, whenever it is available, rates a SUPERB quality; so does the aromatic, elegant, rich Chardonnay.

  ** At a few points below, two wines at a NOBLE rating: the big dominant Cabernet Sauvignon and the golden sweet Sauvignon Blanc.

MILANO WINERY *south of Hopland in the Redwood Valley of Mendocino*

A relatively small, Italian-American-style vineyard, taken over by its present owners in 1977, now approaching a production objective of about 75,000 bottles a year. The vineyards date back to the early 1900s but have been replanted, and an old hop kiln has been converted into a modern winery. While waiting for their own vines to mature, the owner-winemakers have been exploring the character possibilities of the grapes from many of the old Italian hillside vineyards of this region, using them to produce interesting wines (mainly strong reds) with a specific vineyard designation on each label. With these purchased grapes, plus, eventually, their own, the Milano owners hope gradually to double or treble their production.

  * Instead of one of the standard Italian reds, try the intensely fruity, rich, strong Chardonnay, with grapes from the Lolonis Vineyard, at a FINE rating.

MILL CREEK VINEYARDS *southwest of Healdsburg in the Russian River Valley of Sonoma*

A medium-size winery, owned and run by Charles Kreck and his family, who started planting in 1965 and released their first wines in 1976, with estimated production climbing toward a projected average of about 150,000 bottles a year. The wines are released under three labels: the best vintage-dated varietals as Mill Creek; the less-expensive varietals, made from purchased grapes, as Claus Vineyards; and the blended generic types as Felta Springs. They have 75 acres of their own vines in one of the very good microclimate districts of the Russian River Valley.

   * (FINE ratings) Try the delicate Chardonnay; also the fruity, gentle, light Cabernet Sauvignon; or the elegant, beautifully colored, refreshing Rosé of Cabernet Sauvignon, which they foolishly label as Cabernet Blush.

MIRASSOU VINEYARDS *at San Jose in Santa Clara*

Another of the old, large, and famous California wineries. It was founded in 1854 by an immigrant Frenchman, Pierre Pellier, whose daughter married a French neighbor, Pierre Mirassou—a fact that allows them, today, to describe themselves as "the fifth generation of America's oldest winemaking family." They own about 1,500 acres of vines in the Salinas Valley of Monterey and in Santa Clara, and their estimated average production is about 3½ million bottles of still and sparkling wines a year. For the first one hundred years of their existence, they made only bulk wines, selling them in barrels to be bottled and labeled by others. Then, in the early 1960s when the wine boom began, they decided to launch their own label. They now make about thirty different kinds and types. The best wines are usually designated on the label as "Harvest Selection." Most of the wines are designed for mass sales and easy immediate drinking—the reds a bit simple, the whites a bit too sweet. There are some excellent exceptions.

   ** (NOBLE ratings) The dry Chenin Blanc; the medium-soft flowery White Riesling; the smooth Zinfandel; and the nicely dry sparkling wine "Late Disgorged," made by the *méthode champenoise* from Monterey grapes.
   * (FINE ratings) The crisp, fruity Chardonnay; the light, smooth Cabernet Sauvignon "Harvest Selection"; and the refreshing Rosé of Petite Sirah.

ROBERT MONDAVI WINERY *at Oakville in the Napa Valley*

This is the ultramodern winemaking plant—housed, by a strangely contrasting twist, in a new building designed to be a kind of Hollywood set of a 17th-century Spanish mission—which Robert Mondavi built for himself and his children when, in 1965, he broke away from his mother and brother at the Charles Krug family firm (see page 357). Bob's eldest son, Michael, is now president, with the second son, Timothy, as winemaker, and the daughter, Marcia, helping with the administration. These are the only people who represent the firm in public, and, thus, the idea of a "family winery" is nationally projected. Behind this idealistic picture, of course, is a large and efficient corporation, with an estimated production (although the actual figures are kept secret) of about 15 million bottles a year. They own about 1,100 acres of vineyards and have long-term contracts with other Napa growers for large extra supplies of grapes. Far from the winery operation being "family style," much of it is automated, computerized, and mechanized—all performed in a running blaze of national publicity. It must be said, however, that Robert Mondavi is always dedicated to making his best wines with a brilliant, supremely elegant, racy finesse that is quite dazzling when, now and then, he brings it off. He now, also, makes about 6 million bottles a year of jug-type wines at a separate winery at Lodi in the Central Valley. They also use a subsidiary label, Oakville Vineyards. Another huge wave of international publicity broke recently when it was announced that Robert Mondavi had entered into a partnership agreement with Baron Philippe de Rothschild, the owner of the great "First Growth" of Bordeaux, Château Mouton, for the joint production from Napa grapes at the Mondavi Winery of a Bordeaux-style red wine, which is planned to be "the greatest and most expensive red wine the world has ever known." Of this modest little wine, 24,000 bottles were made in 1979 by Timothy Mondavi, working in double harness with the *maître de chais* ("cellarmaster") of Château Mouton, Lucien Sianneau, who commuted weekly from Bordeaux. The wine will be released simultaneously in the United States and France in 1983—under a "proprietary name." Perhaps it should be called "Monschild"?

** (NOBLE ratings) The famous, full "Fumé Blanc" (Sauvignon Blanc and Semillon) more or less invented by Robert Mondavi; the medium-soft Chenin Blanc; the Napa Gamay; the elegant, fruity, smooth Cabernet Sauvignon "Reserve"; the Pinot Noir; the Petite Sirah; and the golden sweet "Special Bunch Selection" White "Johannisberg" Riesling, with a residual sugar of 11 percent.

* (FINE ratings) The medium-dry "Riesling" from Sylvaner grapes; the austere, fruity Chardonnay; the brawny Zinfan-

del; and the fruity, refreshing, slightly sweet Rosé of Gamay, exceptionally good.

MONT ELISE VINEYARDS *at Bingen in the south Columbia Basin of Washington State*

The quiet, shy man who dominates Mont Elise by his perfectionist spirit is Chuck Henderson, the owner and winemaker. He ran a grain and cattle ranch in North Dakota, but his wife couldn't stand the cold winters and longed to come to the gentler climate of the Pacific Northwest. So Chuck exchanged his Dakota land, sight unseen, for 500 acres, partly in cherry orchards, at a place he had never heard of called Bingen-White Salmon at the Great Gorge of the Columbia River. He became fascinated by the connection between Bingen, United States, and Bingen-am-Rhein in Germany. A German friend gave him some Bingen wines to taste, and the idea of winemaking took hold of him. Vine-root cuttings were sent to him from Bingen, and with them, in 1965, he and his son began planting a 40-acre vineyard on a steep slope looking down on the Columbia. Meanwhile, Chuck found an industrial building in the prosaic little "Main Street" American town of Bingen, which he converted to a winery. The first wines were released in 1974. They were most unusual— fermented out bone dry, ascetic, austere, lean, and tense—just about as far from a German style as anything could be. Production is now running at about 75,000 bottles a year. More than 80 percent of these are sold to people who come to the winery for them—the remainder are distributed in the central Washington towns and in Seattle.

     * (FINE ratings) In the Pacific Northwest, try the dry, fruity, shockingly refreshing Chenin Blanc; also the flowery "Washington Johannisberg" White Riesling; or the delicately aromatic, faintly apricoty, smoothly dry Gewürztraminer.

MONTEREY PENINSULA WINERY *on the Monterey-Salinas Highway in Monterey*

This is another of those typical rags-to-riches, amateur-to-professional, weekend-hobby-to-commercial-enterprise wine stories. In

1974, two Monterey dentists, both originally good home winemakers, decided to set themselves up with professional equipment in a modern winery of their own design. They did not want to grow grapes—"We prefer not to have mud on our boots"—but wanted to buy the best they could find for their special purposes anywhere in California. Experimenting in every possible direction, they soon had the usual excess of wine on their hands and decided to "go commercial." They are now heading toward a projected production of about 300,000 bottles a year. This includes the wines they make to please themselves and some fairly inexpensive, blended generic wines, which they release under their subsidiary label, Monterey Cellars. For their best wines, the grapes from each vineyard are vinified separately (with the names on the labels), and this offers tasting opportunities of extraordinary interest. One year, for example, they made eighteen different Zinfandels. Such a wide range of experimentation cannot possibly always be successful. Some of their wines have been terrible—others quite wonderful.

   ** (NOBLE rating) The complex, intense, outstanding Cabernet Sauvignon, with grapes from Monterey.
   * (FINE ratings) The luscious, rich Chardonnay, with grapes from Monterey; the dark, handsome Petite Sirah from the Arroyo Seco; and the overwhelmingly rich Zinfandel, with grapes from the Ferrero Vineyard in Amador in the High Sierras.

MONTEREY VINEYARD *at Gonzales in the Salinas Valley of Monterey*

This will go down in our American wine history as the noble experiment that was transformed into a huge commercial success. In 1973, with about $10 million of "seed money" supplied by the huge McKesson's conglomerate, the Monterey Bay Company was formed to "put Monterey wines on the national map." About 9,600 acres of independently owned vineyards were loosely welded into a cooperative, and, more or less at its center, a huge ultramodern, automated stainless-steel winery was built. The man chosen to design and run that winery in 1974, and who is still running it today, is the highly experienced winemaker, from Gallo and Beaulieu, Dick Peterson. I shall always remember the shock of the tasting of the new wines in 1975. The problems of the Monterey microclimate had not yet been solved, and the wines were strangely unattractive. In the tight market of that time, they did not sell, and within two years the whole project collapsed. All that was left of it was this shining winery and a sadly discouraged Peterson. In 1977, both were taken over by the Coca-Cola people, and it has been dramatic to watch what a bit of Atlanta soft-drink capitalization can do to give Dick the time to turn around and work out his viticultural problems. He has been able to pick and choose his grapes instead of being forced to buy them on a fixed cooperative program. He has been able to slow down his production rate and improve the quality of many of the Monterey Vineyard wines. Only a relatively small part of the huge capacity of the winery is now used for the Monterey Vineyard label. It gets a lot of its income from contract vinification work. For example, it makes all those wines so brashly advertised by Coca-Cola as Taylor California Cellars. Adding together the totals of all these different operations, Peterson is now pushing through his huge winery a production of about 10 million bottles a year—of which, very soon, 1¼ million bottles will carry the M.V. label. Although the quality is improving, all the problems have not yet been solved.

  ** (NOBLE rating) Whenever it is available, the "Late Harvest" Monterey Zinfandel, memorably fruity and luscious, raisiny and rich, yet light on the tongue.
  * (FINE ratings) The light, slightly minty, refreshing Monterey Gamay Beaujolais, with a lovely wild raspberry color; also the elegant, full-of-character Rosé of Pinot Noir.

MONTEVIÑA WINES *at Plymouth in the Shenandoah Valley of Amador in the foothills of the High Sierras*

This is the largest, the most experimental, and the most influential modern vineyard in these extraordinary, high mountain valleys. Here, the damp mists roll down from the snow-capped peaks for the morning and evening dews, and during the day the hot winds blow up from the Sacramento Valley far below. Here, the first Zinfandel vines were planted by the miners in the 1850s after they had finished digging for gold in El Dorado and the Mother Lode. Almost none of the grape-growing ranchers of the district make commercial wine, but they sell their grapes—now at very high prices—to producers all over California (see page 167). But when Vickie and Cary Gott came here, in 1972, they wanted to grow grapes, make wine, and not be limited only to the classic Zinfandel. As a foundation, they first bought 80 acres of ancient, magnificently mature Zinfandel vines. Then they added 75 more acres for their experimental cultivation. Next, they built the first commercial winery in Amador. They now also grow Barbera, Cabernet Sauvignon, Primitivo di Gioia (see page 161), Nebbiolo, Ruby Cabernet, and Sauvignon Blanc. They made their first wines in 1973, and now they are approaching their production goals of about 450,000 bottles a year. This represents only about half of their output of grapes—the balance of their supremely rich fruit is sold to other producers. Apart from the classic Amador style of Zinfandel, all the other grape varieties, white as well as red, show that, in this fantastic climate, they become fat, luscious, raisiny ripe, rich, dominant, and powerful—sometimes so heady and "hot" with alcohol that they are awkward and difficult to drink. This ultimate fault of the Amador microclimate, though, happens only rarely at Monteviña. Most of the time, the Gotts maintain near-perfect control over their wines and the results are amazing, dramatic, often a memorable experience.

    ** (NOBLE ratings) The extraordinary, super-intense Zinfandel comes in various forms—the one designated on its label as "Montino" is fruity, relatively light, ready to drink now —the "Regular" is huge, rich, solid, a typically tannic Amador which will be lovely to drink if you hold the bottle for about ten years—the "Reserve" is even bigger and bolder and should be kept for twenty years!

    * (FINE ratings) The dry Sauvignon Blanc is like no white wine you have ever tasted—a fantastic intensity of the fruit, mouth filling, dominantly strong. There is also the Cabernet Sauvignon, a kind of Bordeaux-style equivalent of an Amador Zinfandel, with the intense flavor of the ripe fruit, a sense of tannic power—it will improve enormously with long aging.

J. W. MORRIS WINERIES *at Concord in Contra Costa*

The owner is, indeed, J. W. Morris, backed up by his partners and with Jim Olsen in technical charge of the winery. They began by producing only fortified port but have now expanded also into making natural wines. They started in 1975, and their current estimated production is now approaching their objective of about 150,000 bottles a year. They operate in an industrial building on a back street of the manufacturing district of the city of Oakland. They own no vineyards but have their grapes shipped in, mainly from Sonoma. The vineyard where the grapes were grown is almost always designated on the label. Port is now only about 20 percent of the production; the remaining 80 percent is red and white wine in a consistently luscious and strong style.

     * (FINE rating) Try the dark, aggressive, pushy, tannic Petite Sirah.

MOUNT EDEN VINEYARDS *near the peak of Mount Eden in the Santa Cruz Range above Saratoga in Santa Clara*

The original 23-acre mountaintop vineyard, 2,000 feet above the Santa Clara Valley at the southern end of San Francisco Bay, was originally known as the Martin Ray Vineyard and was owned by that "Peck's Bad Boy" of the California pioneers. Ray made magnificent wines, but was so difficult and temperamental that he feuded with everyone in sight and, in the early 1970s, was so deeply embroiled in epic legal battles with his investors that he lost control of the vineyard. Shortly afterward, he died, and the request of his will, that his ashes should be sprinkled among the vines, was carried out. The new owners changed the name to Mount Eden and elected Dick Graff of Chalone Vineyard (see page 308) as president of the group and executive winemaker. The quality of the wines has remained high and the prices are never modest—a single bottle can be $35 at the winery. The Mount Eden "estate wines" are made with grapes grown on the vineyard—additional purchased grapes, mostly from Monterey, are vinified and bottled under the subsidiary MEV label. These often represent interesting values. Production of the estate wines is running at about 25,000 bottles a year, with about another 15,000 bottles of the MEV wines.

     *** The Estate Cabernet Sauvignon at a SUPERB rating.
     ** At a point or two below, the Estate Pinot Noir at a NOBLE rating.
     * At a FINE rating, the Estate Chardonnay.

MOUNT VEEDER WINERY *on the Mayacamas Range above the Napa Valley*

Small, prestigious mountain vineyard of 20 acres 1,000 feet above the valley floor, with a potential production of about 60,000 bottles a year. It grows only Cabernet Sauvignon and Chenin Blanc in its own vineyard, from which the first grapes were harvested in 1972 and the first wine released in 1976. It also buys Zinfandel grapes from Amador in the High Sierras (see page 165) and makes one of the lightest and most sophisticated of this ubiquitous style of rich red wine. It also buys Chardonnay grapes for classic dry whites. Mount Veeder is family owned and operated by Mike Bernstein and his wife, Arlene, both dedicated to the pursuit of the highest quality. They spent seven years—from 1965 to 1972—carving out, planting, and developing the vineyard.

   *** The delicately rich Amador Zinfandel consistently at a SUPERB rating.
   ** A point or two lower, three wines at a NOBLE rating are the Estate Cabernet Sauvignon, the dry Estate Chenin Blanc, and the Chardonnay.

NAPA WINE CELLARS *north of Yountville in the Napa Valley*

There are 30 acres of vines attached to this small winery, but grapes are bought to increase the estimated production toward its objective of about 120,000 bottles a year. The concentration here since the start in 1975 has been almost entirely on Cabernet Sauvignon, Chardonnay, and Zinfandel.

   * Try the delicately balanced, nicely fruity, strong-personality Chardonnay rating at FINE.

NAVARRO VINEYARDS *at Philo in the Anderson Valley of Mendocino*

A medium-size winery, owned and run by its winemaker, Ted Bennett, who started it in 1975 and is now moving up toward a projected production of about 100,000 bottles a year. He has 33 acres of vines but buys additional grapes from growers in the Anderson

Valley and the Ukiah Valley. Bennett seems to find his main wine-making interest (and, perhaps, his greatest challenge) in trying to make Alsatian-style, very spicy Gewürztraminers. In some years, he is surprisingly successful at this almost impossibly difficult game. His other wines are simpler but often less interesting.

* In northern California, try the attractive, powerful, intensely spicy Gewürztraminer and the aromatic, refreshing Chardonnay, both of FINE quality.

NOVITIATE WINES *above Los Gatos in the Santa Cruz Mountains of Santa Clara*

One of the last U.S. wineries still run by a Jesuit brotherhood. It was started in 1888, mainly to make altar wines, but, since 1975, there has also been a substantial release of wines for commercial distribution. They control 600 acres of vines, and from these, with added grapes bought from other growers, their estimated production is moving toward a projected average of about half a million bottles a year. They are now taking the commercial side very seriously and are aware that, in the past, their quality has not been good enough to meet present-day competition. The ancient and historic winery on the steep hill is being modernized, with special stress on new equipment (including centrifuges and stainless-steel tanks) for dry white wines. Their sweet dessert wines have always been (and still remain) excellent.

* Try their new medium-soft, delicately flowery White "Johannisberg" Riesling; or the unusual, relatively dry, dominantly fruity, perfumed and rich Malvasia, both of FINE quality.

OAK KNOLL WINERY *at Hillsboro in the North Willamette Valley of Oregon*

Right after the end of Prohibition, in the 1930s, there was a "wine boom" in the Pacific Northwest, but it was long before the noble *vinifera* grapes arrived from Europe. The wines were made from fruit berries and Concord grapes, and, because virtually no sugar was added to the natural sweetness of the very ripe fruit, many of these products were quite excellent. Over the years, a number of European fruit specialists came into the field, among them a Belgian, Ronault Vuylsteke, who, with his American wife, Marjorie, began with one gallon of blackberry wine from an excess harvest in their back garden. Soon they were making almost twenty kinds of fruit wine—including just about the best dry raspberry I have ever tasted —and their production was heading up toward half a million bottles a year. When the noble grape varieties came to Oregon and the Yakima Valley of Washington State, it was not a very large step for Ron to move into vintaged varietal wines by buying grapes from neighboring vineyards. He started with Cabernet Sauvignon and then went on to Pinot Noir and Sauvignon Blanc. These wines are being released under the Château de Chêne label, and the production is now about 75,000 bottles a year. With a few exceptions, I still like the raspberry wine the best.

** (NOBLE rating) The Oregon-style, firm, smooth, solid Pinot Noir, with grapes from the Sweet Home Vineyard, a wine that has won silver medals at northwestern festivals.

* (FINE rating) The medium-soft, flowery, refreshing White Riesling, with grapes from the Shafer Vineyards near Forest Grove in Oregon.

PARDUCCI WINE CELLARS *near Ukiah in Mendocino*

In the early days of wine in California, the still fairly wild region directly north of San Francisco from upper Sonoma on into Mendocino was where hundreds of Italian families came to plant small vineyards, just because the rolling hills and the shapes of the forested slopes and the tumbling of the streams reminded them of Tuscany. They were sure, deep in their hearts, that grapes would grow here as well as they did in the region of Chianti! Not very many of these devoted Italian families have survived. The Parduccis have come through with fame and success. Their production is now estimated at somewhat above 3 million bottles a year. Adolfo Parducci came as a winemaker from Tuscany with his wife and his four sons soon after the San Francisco earthquake and fire. He was at once determined to make wine among the Mendocino hills. But Prohibition came first. Many of the small Italian vineyards gave up and closed. Adolfo bought their equipment and their land for hardly more than a song.

Then he waited, patiently, for almost fifteen years. The day Prohibition was repealed, Adolfo began making wine. Today, three generations later, the Parduccis own three vineyards totaling 400 acres and are making their popular, inexpensive, fairly simple wines better than ever. Wines that they consider to be of exceptional quality are designated on the label as "Cellarmaster's Selection."

   ** (NOBLE rating) The fruity, smooth, solid Cabernet Sauvignon "Cellarmaster's Selection."

   * (FINE ratings) The medium-soft Chenin Blanc; the light, refreshing "Fumé Blanc" (Sauvignon Blanc); the fruity, lemony, slightly tart Chardonnay; the dark, strong, tannic Petite Sirah; and the Zinfandel.

PARSON'S CREEK WINERY *south of Ukiah in the Ukiah Valley of Mendocino*

A fairly small, far-northern winery owned by its winemakers, Jess Tidwell and Hal Boran. They started in 1979 and are now gradually approaching a production objective of about 120,000 bottles a year—composed entirely of white wines. They have no vineyards of their own but buy grapes from various growers in the Anderson Valley and the Ukiah Valley of Mendocino, as well as the Alexander Valley of Sonoma. Distribution of these wines is, so far, limited to northern California.

   * In northern California, try the fairly sweet, fruity, spicy Mendocino Gewürztraminer with 3 percent residual sugar balancing a lemony tang, at a FINE quality.

PEDRONCELLI WINERY *northeast of Geyserville on a ridge above the Dry Creek Valley of Sonoma*

Another of those old-line Italian families that went north from San Francisco and, over many years, has continually upgraded its standards to win very substantial success. The vineyards and winery were founded in 1904 by the grandfather, Giovanni, who took advantage of the "pause" of Prohibition to improve the 135 acres of vines and modernize all the winemaking equipment. Today, their estimated production is running at an average of about 1.25 million bottles a year. For roughly the first fifty years of their existence, they produced and sold only bulk wines in barrels. Then, in the early 1960s, they began wanting to see their own name on their own labels. Section by section, they replanted the vineyards with the noble *vinifera* varieties of European vines. Step by step, in the winery, they felt their way and solved their problems, first with jug wines, then with blended generics, finally with excellent vintage-dated varietals, always at wonderfully reasonable prices.

* Try the medium-soft, flowery White Riesling; also the clean, crisp, faintly apricoty Chardonnay; also the rich, simple, slightly sweet Gewürztraminer; or the light, summery Rosé of Zinfandel, all at FINE ratings.

PENDLETON WINERY *at San Jose in Santa Clara*

This small winemaking unit, owned and run by the Pendleton family, was started in 1976 and, today, is moving up toward a planned objective of about 75,000 bottles a year. They have no vineyards but buy their grapes from various growers in Mendocino, Monterey, the Napa Valley, and in the San Luis Obispo district. The fruit is trucked to the winery in a city building in downtown San Jose. Usually, the vineyard where the grapes were grown is designated on each label. Quality is often good. Prices are always reasonable. Distribution is limited to northern California.

* In the neighborhood, try the medium-soft, delicately fruity White Riesling; also the light, intense Chardonnay, with grapes from Monterey; both at a FINE rating.

JOSEPH PHELPS VINEYARDS *near St. Helena in the Napa Valley*

In the late 1960s, a regular visitor to the Napa Valley was a modest, quiet man called Joe Phelps, who was head of his own construction company in Colorado. Although he was still comparatively young, he had already achieved substantial business and financial success. He wanted to change his life to something that he was quite sure would give him more pleasure and satisfaction for the remainder of his years. He wanted to be a grower of magnificent wines. He hired as winemaker a man with an established reputation in Europe, the German-trained Walter Schug. Starting in 1969, Phelps bought 700 acres of Napa Valley ranchland and began developing vineyards that would eventually total 230 acres. He and Schug planned and built a winery of the most beautiful possible design with the most advanced available technical equipment, capable of an eventual production of about half a million bottles a year. It was not surprising that winemaker Schug should turn first to the styles of wine he knew best, the golden sweet German-type *Botrytized* "Late Harvest." Among the first to be released, in 1976, was one described as "a miracle of winemaking"—a White Riesling in the *trockenbeeren-auslese* class, lifting the Phelps vineyard at once virtually to the peak of prestigious California producers. There followed a series of extraordinary wines: powerfully rich Zinfandels, intense Cabernet Sauvignons, experimental French-style Hermitage Syrahs, and others. The best "estate wines" are bottled under the Joseph Phelps label, some exceptional Cabernet blends are designated as Insignia, and some less-expensive wines are released under the subsidiary Le Fleuron label.

   *** The now-famous "Late Harvest—Selected Bunches" Johannisberg Riesling at a SUPERB rating, with extraordinary richness and 30 percent residual sugar—also SUPERB is the French-style Hermitage Syrah, the best red of this type I have ever tasted in the United States.

   ** A point or two below, three wines at a NOBLE rating are the Chardonnay, the Gewürztraminer, and the Cabernet Sauvignon Insignia.

PIPER.SONOMA WINERY *at Windsor in Sonoma*

This is the second major "invasion" of the American sparkling-wine market by one of the famous French Champagne houses. It is a joint venture between Sonoma Vineyards (see page 405) and Piper-Heidsieck of Rheims. The plan brings French technicians to California to make—using Chardonnay and Pinot Noir grapes provided by Sonoma Vineyards—sparkling wine by the French *méthode champenoise* which, after proper aging, will be distributed in the United States under the Piper.Sonoma label. The first bottles should be available for Christmas popping in 1982.

   ** No Piper.Sonoma sparkling wine has yet been released, but all the indications are—including advanced barrel and vat tastings—that it will eventually be of NOBLE quality.

PLANE'S CAYUGA VINEYARD *on Lake Cayuga in the Finger Lakes district of New York State*

Mary and Robert Plane represent a new type of small vineyard operation, a new attitude toward winemaking, a new vision of perfectionism in the widening range of New York State wines. The Planes work their vineyard themselves and give it fierce devotion. Mary has spent hundreds of hours down on her knees in the muddy earth, budding and grafting almost two thousand vines. Although Bob still has a full-time academic job, he has made every liter of wine that has come so far from their relatively new winery. After they took a year's Sabbatical to study winemaking in California, I asked them whether they did not secretly regret not having bought their vineyard out West, far from these arctic New York winters. They answered in unison: "No! It's too easy to make wine in California. Here, in New York, you have to accept a challenge—you have to learn your job— you have to become a true expert. We, our vines, and our wines, are the better for the struggle and the test of our strength." When I tasted their first Chardonnay, overwhelming in its intensity of fruit flavor, soft as satin on my tongue, I knew they had proved their point.

In the early 1960s, they were both on the staff of Cornell University, which is at one end of Lake Cayuga—he as chairman of the Chemistry Department and provost, she in the administration services. Looking forward to their retirement, they bought a handsome farm on the west bank of Lake Cayuga, hardly more than twenty-five miles from the university. Bob, as a chemist, was involved in the hobby of home winemaking, which was almost universal among the faculty at Cornell. They also attended tastings of commercial New York wines, including some Chardonnays that greatly impressed them. Bob told me, "I thought, if New York Chardonnay could be that good, I would like to make it myself." In 1972, they began planting 50 acres of their own vines—half in Chardonnay. Then came a severe problem. Bob was offered a job he could hardly refuse —the presidency of a college that would be not twenty-five miles, but 200 miles from their vineyard. For at least the next few years, he could only be a weekend winemaker. Mary, determined that they should go forward, took on the entire management of the viticulture and the administration of the vineyard. Their own winery was finally completed in 1980, and that year they made their first Chardonnay, which has been such a critical success. They hope, eventually, to plant a total of 65 acres of vines and to achieve a production of about 120,000 bottles a year.

> ** (NOBLE rating) The Chardonnay is the dazzler here, with a concentration of aromatic bouquet, a rich sense of fruit, a buttery softness in the mouth, among the best wines ever produced in New York—it will be followed soon by a White Riesling.

PONZI VINEYARDS *at Beaverton in the Willamette Valley of Oregon*

A small, family-owned 10-acre vineyard, founded and operated by Richard Ponzi and his wife, Nancy, on the lower slopes of the Cooper Hills about fifteen miles south of Portland. Dick originally lived in Detroit and learned to become a home winemaker there, first with Michigan grapes, then with fruit shipped in from California. Dick and Nancy longed to track these luscious grapes back to their source. They came to live in the Santa Clara Valley, picked their own grapes, and were determined to become professional winemakers. On a visit to Oregon, they met Dick Sommer at his Hillcrest Vineyards (see page 345), and the Ponzis were then sure they wanted to join the pioneers in the Pacific Northwest. In 1970, they bought their vineyard, planted it, and made their first wine in 1974. They have built their winery and done most of the mechanical work themselves. They irrigate their vines by what they call "a half-gallon milk carton system," whatever that may mean. Their current production is about 50,000 bottles a year. They supplement their income by raising beef cattle, goats for cheese and milk, plus a special breed of chickens that lays multicolored eggs.

> *** As usual in Oregon, the Pinot Noir (see page 144) is generally of SUPERB quality.
> ** A point or two below, the medium-soft White Riesling is consistently at a NOBLE rating.
> * A FINE rating for the Chardonnay.

POPE VALLEY WINERY *in the Pope Valley—a small cut between the hills on the east side of the Napa Valley*

Wine has been made here since 1909, and, since 1972, the winemaker has been Steve Devitt, backed up by his family, with an estimated production rising gradually toward the objective of about 175,000 bottles a year. They have no vineyards of their own but buy grapes from various growers, mainly, of course, in the Napa Valley, but also from the far-northern Lake County district and from Sonoma.

      * In northern California, try the medium-soft, fresh, light Chenin Blanc; also the very light, delicately fruity Rosé of Zinfandel; both at a FINE rating.

PRESTON VINEYARDS *near Healdsburg in the Dry Creek Valley of Sonoma*

High-quality 80-acre vineyard, family owned and run since its foundation in 1975 in the excellent grape-growing district on the west side of the valley. Average production is about 50,000 bottles a year, but after a much larger winery is built, the output is expected to rise gradually to about 150,000 bottles a year, and distribution will be extended outside California.

    ** (NOBLE rating) The dark, firm Pinot Noir.
    * (FINE rating) The dry Chenin Blanc.

PRESTON WINE CELLARS *at Pasco in the Columbia Basin of Washington State*

This is the second-largest grape grower and wine producer in the Pacific Northwest (for the largest, see Chateau Ste. Michelle), with 200 acres of vines in the immense, once semiarid, irrigated central basin of the Columbia River—now one of the finest fruit-growing regions of the nation. The owner, Bill Preston, head of an old established family business in farm and irrigation machinery, became interested in wine and, beginning in 1972, planted 50 acres of vines on his ranch. He hired California-trained Robert Griffin as winemaker and built a large winery. With his specialized experience in agricultural and irrigational engineering, Preston has developed unorthodox methods for the "care and feeding" of his vines during the extremes of summer heat and winter cold and for the vinification of his grapes. The results have been so good, both in terms of quality and demand, that the acreage of vines has gradually been increased to 200, and production is approaching 1 million bottles a year. Some of the Chardonnays have been quite extraordinary, and Bill Preston firmly believes that at some point in the future this region may become "one of the greatest white-wine areas of the world." His hope is based on the hothouse conditions of powerful sunshine coupled with the absolute control of the water, so that the vines can be deliberately rested by being "put to sleep," or can be "stressed" to any degree to develop the intensity of the flavor of the fruit. Preston wines have been awarded gold medals at various festivals and are now moving toward national distribution, at least in major cities.

 *** The Chardonnay consistently rates as SUPERB, as does the extraordinary golden sweet White Riesling "Ice Wine" (see page 197), with a residual sugar of 10 percent, one of the best American sweet wines I have ever tasted.

 ** A few points below, three wines regularly at a NOBLE rating are Cabernet Sauvignon, Merlot, and Pinot Noir.

QUAIL RIDGE VINEYARDS *on Mount Veeder above the Napa Valley*

This is a fairly new, small vineyard, founded in 1978, with a current production of just under 15,000 bottles a year and hopes of expanding, eventually, up to about 60,000 bottles. The start of this project has been marked by high success and deep tragedy. It began in the mid-1970s, when Elaine Wellesley, a young professional winemaker trained at the University of California, discovered that her husband, Jesse Corallo, an Italian wine aficionado without technical training, had a tasting palate of extraordinary sensitivity. Working together as partners in their home, they produced a small quantity of a Chardonnay from purchased grapes, and, when it came to the point of labeling it, they chose the romantic name of Quail Ridge. When this wine was tasted by some of the professional critics, they were virtually unanimous in acclaiming it as a stunning success. Elaine and Jesse decided to launch a small commercial vineyard. They bought 20 acres on one of the highest, steepest slopes of Mount Veeder (which dominates the Napa Valley), a slope so steep that they would have to clear the loose rocks by hand, burn off the weedy undergrowth, and terrace the mountainside. It would, obviously, be several years before any harvest came from this source.

Meanwhile, they organized a winery and, for some immediate cash flow, bought grapes from various sources in the Napa Valley. Their first commercial release of a Chardonnay, in 1980, was again hailed as a brilliant victory. Then one bright sunny morning the following spring, Jesse was up on the mountain burning off undergrowth to clear more of the vineyard for planting. He was alone. Suddenly, the wind changed. He was overcome by smoke asphyxiation and collapsed. The flames surrounded him. He was burned to death. Elaine, with extraordinary courage, has pressed forward with their project without a pause. Her latest wines—almost as if in tribute —have been made with even more care, imagination, and skill. Quail Ridge is still concentrating mainly on Chardonnay but will soon be adding French Colombard, with grapes from the old vines at the Cyril Saviez Vineyard in Napa. Eventually—perhaps two or three years into the future—there will also be a small production of Cabernet Sauvignon. One can be quite sure that Quail Ridge has not the slightest intention of ever becoming large enough for wide distribution beyond the major national cities—or of ever relaxing its almost impossibly high quality standards. This type of handmade connoisseurs' wine can never be inexpensive but may represent excellent value in terms of its peak performance.

> * The Chardonnay has a FINE quality, an attractive fruitiness, a sense of refreshment, a good balance between a lemony tang and a light sweetness, a sense of warmth and weight on the tongue.

RAFANELLI WINERY *at Healdsburg in the Dry Creek Valley of Sonoma*

The Rafanelli family owns and runs this winery, with Amerigo as the winemaker. It was started in 1974, and today its estimated production averages about 35,000 bottles a year, concentrating entirely on Gamay Beaujolais and Zinfandel. They have 25 acres of vines in a particularly good microclimate district, so that, in the best years, with strong pruning back, the grapes are wonderfully rich and ripe. The final result is wine of exceptional interest, and it is a great pity that it has such limited distribution—in California.

> * In the neighborhood, try the fruity, harmonious, spicy Zinfandel, the wine in its natural state, unfiltered, achieving a FINE rating.

RAVENSWOOD WINERY *at Forestville in the Russian River Valley of Sonoma*

This minuscule, new wine operation shows all the signs of being the start of a brilliant and rapidly expanding viticultural adventure. Of the three owning partners, Joel Peterson, the winemaker, has a long background of education and experience in enology. The second partner, Reed Foster, is a young San Francisco businessman who has worked in wine management and sales. The third member of the group is the well-known Berkeley artist David Lance Goines, who has designed a striking label for the Ravenswood bottles. They started in 1976, making only Cabernet Sauvignon and Zinfandel, mainly from grapes bought in the Amador and El Dorado districts of the High Sierras with some from the Dry Creek Valley of Sonoma. The resulting wines are of impressive complexity, firmly constructed, fleshy and rich, with intensely ripe flavors. Almost all of the very limited production—about 15,000 bottles—is being snapped up by connoisseurs in San Francisco.

> ** (NOBLE rating) The memorably aromatic, raisiny rich, powerful, smooth Cabernet Sauvignon, with grapes from the Madrona Vineyards in El Dorado.

MARTIN RAY VINEYARDS *above Saratoga in the Santa Cruz Mountains of Santa Clara*

Every serious student of California wine knows that Martin Ray was, for many years until his death in 1976, the *enfant terrible* of the West Coast. He did, admittedly, make some magnificent wines, but his iconoclasm, his wild accusations against everyone in authority, his public bad temper, his curmudgeonesque character, made him an impossible person. At the end of his life, he was involved in such monstrous litigation with his creditors, investors, and partners that his main vine plantings were removed from his control and became Mount Eden Vineyards (see page 374). What was left to Ray were his mountain house, with a small winery in the basement, and 5 acres of vines immediately surrounding it. When he died, a year later, these were taken over by his adopted stepson, Peter Martin Ray, who is a young professor of plant physiology at Stanford University. Peter seems to have learned all the best qualities of his stepfather and none of the bad. Efficiently and quietly—with no temperamental fireworks —he is buying magnificent grapes from Napa and Sonoma to supplement his own estate harvest and is now making about 60,000 bottles of big, dominant, intensely fruity, mouth-filling, powerful and solid wines that have, at once, drawn high attention to themselves in the top sector of the wine spectrum. Prices, also, are at the highest level.

    ** (NOBLE rating) The big, bold, bone-dry Chardonnay "Saratoga," which means from "estate grapes" of the vineyard around the house.

    * (FINE rating) The expansive, intense, tannic Cabernet Sauvignon, the best usually with designations of specific vineyards on the labels—lesser wines may have only regional appellations and are then usually designated on the label as "La Montana," generally a good deal less definite in character.

RAYMOND WINERY *at Calistoga in the Napa Valley*

A family vineyard with 90 acres of vines planted in 1971 so that the first wines could be released in 1974. Production is now approaching 250,000 bottles a year. The Raymond family has been involved with vines and wine since the 1870s. Their grapes are growing in some of the best Napa microclimates. They now have an ultramodern winery, completed in 1978.

    ** (NOBLE rating) The golden sweet "Late Harvest—Selected Clusters" White "Johannisberg" Riesling, beautifully aromatic.

    * (FINE ratings) The delicate, fruity, rich Chardonnay and the dark, deep, dominant, intense Cabernet Sauvignon.

REUTER'S HILL VINEYARDS *at Forest Grove in the Willamette Valley of Oregon*

This may be the oldest vineyard in Oregon—in the forested hill country about twenty-five miles southwest of Portland. In 1883, a German immigrant from Westphalia, Fred Reuter, bought the wooded slopes, cleared them, and began planting vines on what became known as Wine Hill. He built a farmhouse with an attached winery surrounded by 10 acres of farmland for his beef cattle, chickens, cows, ducks, geese, pigs, and sheep. He also grew his own fruit and vegetables. Finally, when his vines were mature, he was quite successful with his wines, even winning a medal for his Riesling at the 1904 St. Louis World's Fair. I heard the Reuter story, some years ago, from his two daughters, both in their nineties, both teetotalers who had never allowed a single drop of wine to pass their lips! With the coming of Prohibition, the Reuter's Hill vineyards were closed, and, after old Reuter died, they were abandoned for about fifty years. In 1966, the "wine boom" brought new young owners, the replanting of 33 acres of the vines, the rebuilding and re-equipping of the winery, and the reappearance on the bottle labels of the name Reuter's Hill. But—as often happens with lonely vineyards in fairly wild places—finding the precisely right owner to fall in love with this particular place has not been easy. Owners have followed each other in relatively quick succession. Slowly, the estimated production has grown to an average of about 150,000 bottles a year. As I write this, the vineyard is again having ownership problems, and the operation has been temporarily closed down. Nature, however, disregards human foibles. The grapes are growing and ripening beautifully on the vines. Someone, I am sure, will soon be found to convert this magnificent fruit into wine.

> * Quite a lot of Reuter's Hill wine is still in the Portland retail stores, where you should try the dry, intensely fruity, spicy, refreshingly tangy Sylvaner, the best U.S. version of this famous Alsatian grape I have ever tasted; also try the medium-soft, light, refreshing White Riesling. Both at FINE ratings.

RIDGE VINEYARDS *above Cupertino on Black Mountain in the Santa Cruz Range*

In terms of the grandeur of its bold, dominant, powerful red wines (often the equals of some of the most famous *grands crus* of Europe)—also in terms of the pioneering experimentation by its prestigious winemaker-partner, Paul Draper—this is one of the most important vineyards in the United States. The winery and its satellite group of about 50 acres of "home vineyards" are at almost 3,000 feet above the Pacific Ocean, on the wild and rocky Monte Bello Ridge of the Coast Range. There have been vines on these mountain terraces, off and on, since the 1870s, and the Ridge owners hope gradually to replant more of them until they have more than 100 acres of Monte Bello vines. Meanwhile, to increase their production, they have gone out all over northern and central California to buy the particular grapes they want from mature vines, and this practice has led to one of the most complicated labeling systems of any American winery. First, all wines from the "home vineyards" are labeled as Ridge Monte Bello. But as to "imported grapes," the name of the source vineyard is always printed next to the name of Ridge on the label. The grapes of each "foreign" vineyard are kept separate from those of every other, and the bottles are labeled separately. Thus, in one year, Ridge has been known to produce as many as six different Cabernet Sauvignons and nine different Zinfandels, each with remarkable variations in character and personality. But Ridge does put a certain "family stamp" on its wines. All are rich in complex nuances, intense and subtle, some of them needing years of aging before they give their fullest pleasure to the drinker. The owners of Ridge (including Paul Draper), who instituted this perfectionist winemaking policy, bought and reactivated the old winery in 1959. Since then, the founding partners—all of them scientists at the Stanford Research Institute, joined later by Paul—have brought a highly experimental and intellectual approach to the making of wine. Their production is now approaching about 500,000 bottles a year, with reasonable national distribution, but almost always in short supply because it is so much in demand by connoisseurs.

   *** Ridge is most famous for its SUPERB Zinfandels, especially the complex version labeled Geyserville in Sonoma, the spicy type from York Creek in the Napa Valley, and the brawny one marked Shenandoah from Amador in the High Sierras (see page 165); also SUPERB Cabernet Sauvignons, especially the versions from some of the vineyards immediately surrounding the winery and labeled Monte Bello. Also the beautifully aromatic version labeled York Creek with grapes from Spring Mountain in the Napa Valley.

   ** A few points below, a wine that generally rates at a NOBLE quality is the dominant and rich Petite Sirah, also from York Creek.

   * About 98 percent of Ridge's production is red wine, but there is a small Chardonnay vineyard on the mountain, and

from this comes regularly a FINE dry, elegant white, labeled Monte Bello, but normally produced in such small quantities that it is available only at the winery.

ROUDON-SMITH VINEYARDS *at Scott's Valley in the Santa Cruz Mountains south of San Francisco Bay*

This winery is owned and run by two families in partnership, and we hardly need to tell you their last names! The winemaker is Bob Roudon, who started in 1972 and who, today, has achieved an estimated production averaging about 120,000 bottles a year. They completed a new winery in 1979, which will allow them, eventually, to expand to about 200,000 bottles. They have 12 acres of their own vines, so they have to buy substantial quantities of grapes from various growers in Monterey, San Luis Obispo, and Sonoma. They generally designate the particular vineyard on each label. A few of their wines are reasonably successful in good years, but in general there seems to be an "amateur" quality—as if the wine didn't quite turn out as expected—about quite a number of their bottlings.

* Try the generally excellent, well-balanced, fruity, refreshingly tangy Chardonnay, with grapes from the Edna Valley of San Luis Obispo; also the regularly good, light, refreshing Gamay Beaujolais; also, in warm years, the complex, chewy, fleshy Cabernet Sauvignon, with grapes from Edna Valley of San Luis Obispo, all at a FINE rating.

ROUND HILL CELLARS *north of St. Helena in the Napa Valley*

A fairly large winery, started in 1975, with a current estimated production approaching the objective of about 1 million bottles a year. They have no vineyards of their own, but they buy grapes and young wines in barrels from growers and producers at various locations in the Napa Valley, Sonoma, and other North Coast districts. Their plan is to make relatively uncomplicated wines from these raw materials—both vintage-dated varietals and blends of wide appeal in the lower price range. A few of them represent very good values.

* Try the always reliable, nicely fruity, solidly constructed Napa Chardonnay, at a FINE rating.

RUSSIAN RIVER VINEYARDS *south of Forestville in the Russian River Valley of Sonoma*

This dramatic, rather famous, and certainly handsome showplace winery has recently been taken over by a somewhat dramatic, fairly famous, and distinctly handsome new owner—the winemaker and wine writer Michael Topolos. Quite a number of wineries in this region have been made from converted hop kilns, but this Russian River building was designed and constructed from the ground up as an architect's dream of what the perfect winery would be like if it were made to look like the perfect hop kiln—complete with two towers, public tasting rooms, and an attached restaurant for visiting tourists. In fact, the previous winemaker was also the chef of the restaurant, and there was some debate as to whether he was better at preparing food or making wine. When I talked to Michael the other day, I somehow felt that he had not quite made up his mind as to whether cooking should be part of the range of abilities of a "Renaissance man." The vineyard was started in 1964, and Topolos took control in 1978, reaching an estimated current production average of about 60,000 bottles a year, including a pleasant "Gravenstein Blanc" apple wine, sold to the tourists to slake their thirst as they walk around the winery. There are 25 acres of vines, but, also, additional grapes, including Cabernet Sauvignon, Chardonnay, and Petite Sirah, are bought from various local growers.

* Try the aromatic, fruity, intense Chardonnay, with grapes from the Dutton Vineyard, achieving a FINE quality.

RUTHERFORD HILL WINERY *east of Rutherford near St. Helena in the Napa Valley*

This story is convoluted enough and sufficiently full of high intrigue to make the plot of a Shakespearean drama. In the 1880s, vineyards were planted north of the village of Rutherford on the steep slopes of Howell Mountain and Rutherford Hill. In 1943, these ancient vineyards were derelict and were bought by one of the great wine pioneers of the Napa Valley, Lee Stewart, for the founding of his famous Souverain Winery, where some of the supreme early wines were made. In 1970, when Lee retired, his property was sold (for an enormous sum) to the giant Minneapolis flour milling conglomerate, Pillsbury. They were developing huge wine operations in Sonoma and wanted to concentrate everything there. So they sold the Rutherford Hill mountain vineyards to Tom Burgess for his new winery (see Burgess). But they held on to the winery, moved it down toward Rutherford, renamed it Souverain of Rutherford and teamed it, in double harness, with their new, large Souverain of Alexander Valley (see Souverain). Within six years, Pillsbury was totally disappointed, frustrated, and impatient with its huge incursion into the wine business—with its inability to reap fast, "industrial-size" profits on its investment. In a rare moment of corporate petulance, Pillsbury suddenly "got out from under" its irritating burden by disposing of everything at whatever price an instantaneous sale would bring.

At this precise moment, the new Freemark Abbey Winery (see page 336) was reaching its first peak of success in the Napa Valley. Its owner-partners were primarily grape growers, each individually owning quite large tracts of vineyard lands. Freemark wines were selling so well that its winery was no longer large enough to handle all the available grapes. Just when the partners were thinking about enlarging, the Souverain of Rutherford winery was put up for sale. It was the ready-made solution to the Freemark problem. They bought it and gave it back its original name from the 1800s, Rutherford Hill. I talked to the partners a few days after the sale had been completed. They stressed that it would be wrong to think of Rutherford Hill as a subsidiary label of Freemark Abbey. Rutherford Hill is a different winery, with a different winemaker, a different technical staff, and a different policy. It makes varietal wines that do not compete with Freemark Abbey and that are sold at slightly lower prices. From the start in 1976, Rutherford Hill has now reached an estimated production averaging about 600,000 bottles a year—but will continue to expand up to about 1¼ million bottles.

  * Try the medium-soft, delicately fruity, lightly refreshing White "Johannisberg" Riesling at a FINE rating.

RUTHERFORD VINTNERS *north of Rutherford in the Napa Valley*

A medium-size winery, owned and run by Bernard and Evelyn Skoda (with Bernard as the winemaker), that was started in 1976 and is now approaching a production objective of about 180,000 bottles a year. They have 30 acres of their own vines and buy additional Napa grapes. Bernard was, for quite a few years, on the staff of the Louis M. Martini winery, so he comes to the running of his own operation with substantial previous experience. Some of his early wines show considerable promise.

> * Try the nicely fruity, harmonious, spicy "estate-bottled" Cabernet Sauvignon—usually achieving a FINE quality.

ST. CLEMENT VINEYARDS *near St. Helena in the Napa Valley*

This family winery, in the cellar of a renovated, historic old mansion from 1876, is owned and run by a local medical practitioner, Dr. William J. Casey, and his wife, Alexandra. The house is where Mike Robbins started his Spring Mountain Vineyards before he moved up the hill to the Miravalle estate (see page 407). Dr. Casey bought the house in 1975 with its surrounding vineyard and now produces about 75,000 bottles a year, concentrating largely, for the moment, on Cabernet Sauvignon and Pinot Chardonnay, and just beginning with some small quantities of Sauvignon Blanc.

> ** (NOBLE rating) The lovely, very dry, balanced, complicated rounded Chardonnay; also the complex, fruity, intense, velvety soft yet powerfully tannic Cabernet Sauvignon.

STE. CHAPELLE VINEYARDS *at Sunny Slope near Caldwell in the Snake River Valley of Idaho*

Even a very few years ago almost no one would have believed that the noble vines of Europe could be commercially grown and vinified into magnificent wines within the climatic extremes of Idaho. The winemaker who has proved that it can be done is Bill Broich, first with his own fairly small vineyard in 1976 and now, on a much larger scale, in partnership with Dick Symms, who owns and runs the family fruit ranch first planted by his grandfather in the Snake River Valley. Symms is devoting a substantial part of his large acreage to the planting and maturing of all the important varieties of the noble vines. This means that Broich is now getting all the grapes he needs of the right maturity, quality, and ripeness for a range of top-caliber wines, aiming at a maximum production of 600,000 bottles a year. The winery—named Ste. Chapelle by Bill's wife, Penny, because she loves the church of La Sainte Chapelle in Paris—has been moved to the community of Sunny Slope so as to be near to the Symms vineyards, of which about 90 acres are now planted in noble grapes. The wines released so far have a memorable intensity of flavors and fruits—almost at once making Ste. Chapelle one of the important names in the U.S. wine world.

   *** The Cabernet Sauvignon consistently at SUPERB rating.
    ** A point or two lower, three wines generally at a NOBLE rating are the austerely dry Chenin Blanc, the flowery, medium-soft Johannisberg Riesling, and the Gewürztraminer.
   * A FINE rating for the Merlot and the Chenin Blanc.

SAN MARTIN WINERY *at San Martin in the Santa Cruz Mountains of Santa Clara*

An ancient and historic winemaking operation with some strange twists to its story. It is in the general location of Gilroy and the Hecker Pass, the famous mountain and valley area where, in the 1800s, a group of Italian immigrant families made some of the early important wines of California. Here, in 1892, the company that would later become San Martin was formed to make, believe it or not, berry and fruit wines, from apple to pear and raspberry. Not until 1908 did it get into grape wines, as a cooperative within a group of mountain growers. For a while, the main business was selling bottles at the winery to passing tourists from a roadside gift shop. The next phase was heavy involvement in jug wines. After several ownership changes, San Martin is controlled today by the giant Norton Simon conglomerate, and the estimated current production is running at about 10 million bottles a year. Among these, there are still some berry and fruit wines. Since the company has only 10 acres of its own vines, it obviously has to buy enormous quantities of grapes from all parts of the Central Coast region. The list of wines now includes many vintage-dated varietals, all of them fresh, fruity, simple, usually with a delicate touch of sweetness, designed for mass appeal on the broadest possible base and for immediate drinking. There are a few interesting exceptions, including, occasionally, golden sweet "Late Harvest" White Rieslings and Amador Zinfandels. The wines are always inexpensive, and many of them represent good values.

> * Try the dry, light, refreshing Chenin Blanc; also the medium-soft, fruity, joyous White "Johannisberg" Riesling, deliberately low in alcohol to stress the fruitiness; also the easy-to-drink, soft Cabernet Sauvignon. All at FINE ratings.

SAN PASQUAL VINEYARDS *at Escondido in the San Pasqual Valley east of San Diego*

Escondido is virtually a suburb of the city of San Diego, and the only wines that have previously been made on these low, rolling hills, under the hot sun, have been sold in jugs. Now comes San Pasqual and its owners to prove that, by imaginative and skillful techniques, quite excellent white wines can be locally produced. Planting of the 100-acre irrigated vineyard began in 1972, and the first wines were released in 1976. Since then, estimated production has gradually risen to a current average of about 350,000 bottles a year. In order to develop some complexity in their whites, they age some of them for short periods in French Nevers oak barrels. The outstanding quality is bringing rapid expansion, and there may soon be limited national distribution.

> * Try their first (and quite memorable) varietal, the almost dry, aromatic, fruity, rich "Fumé Blanc" (Sauvignon Blanc), part of it oak-aged for spice, the other part kept fresh and fruity in stainless steel, the two parts finally blended, achieving a FINE rating.

SANFORD & BENEDICT VINEYARDS *at Lompoc in the Santa Ynez Valley of the Santa Barbara district*

Dick Sanford and Michael Benedict are the owners, with Michael as the winemaker, of this Pacific Coast winery. Since it is so close to the ocean, it has an unusually cool microclimate. There are about 110 acres of vines, with the stress on the Pinot Noir grape, which is the principal interest of the owners. Trying to achieve high Pinot Noir quality, they prune back their vines for a fruit yield of only about one and one-quarter tons per acre—where the more standard expectation, in both Burgundy and the United States, is about two or three tons per acre. Their unorthodox winemaking methods include crushing some of the grape stems, using some wild yeasts, fermenting at relatively high temperatures, and fining the wines in the traditional French way with egg whites. They started planting in 1972, completed their winery in 1976, and since then have been rising toward a production objective of about 120,000 bottles a year. The finished and aged wines are certainly among the outstanding examples of the production of this region.

> * Try the aromatic, fruity, powerful, slightly smoky, richly tangy Chardonnay; also the distinctly Burgundian, well-constructed, chewy, complicated, smooth, strong Pinot Noir, all attaining FINE ratings.

SANTA CRUZ MOUNTAIN VINEYARD *above the town of Santa Cruz south of San Francisco Bay*

The owner, Ken Burnap, is a Los Angeles businessman who is an aficionado of French Burgundian wines and wants to try to make them for himself in California (see page 138). He searched around until he found what he thought was the right piece of earth—with the right chemical, mineral, and organic content of the soil—for the planting of the right Burgundian varieties of vines. Then he built a winery and filled it with precisely the right equipment, including barrels of exactly the right kinds of wood. At the very start, he swore that he would make no other kind of wine than Pinot Noir. But, during the years of maturing of his vines, he became bored and started exploring the Cabernet Sauvignon and the Zinfandel. Today, he seems to be much less of a "Burgundian specialist" than he once was. He started his Santa Cruz operations in 1975, and since then his estimated production has risen slowly toward a planned objective of about 350,000 bottles a year. He has 12 acres of Pinot Noir vines, but he has been impatiently buying substantial amounts of Cabernet Sauvignon, Petite Sirah, and Zinfandel grapes. Now only one bottle out of three is Pinot Noir.

> * There is considerable interest in tasting one of his first vintages of Pinot Noir and recognizing its positive factors without being over-dazzled by it, turned off by its acidity, its

un-Burgundian 15 percent alcohol, or its lack of balance. One can still be impressed by its complexity, fleshiness, power, and spice to give it a FINE rating.

SANTA YNEZ VALLEY WINERY *east of Solvang in the Santa Ynez Valley of Santa Barbara*

This medium-size winemaking operation is owned by three families—the Bettencourts, the Davidges, and the Branders—each bringing a vineyard property to the formation of the group in 1976. The Bettencourt and Davidge vineyards were planted in 1969 and were joined together as La Viña de Santa Ynez. The Brander land is called Los Olivos Vineyard. After these 140 acres were united, the owners converted a dairy farm into a winery (where Fred Brander became the winemaker) and released their first commercial wines in 1977. Since then, their estimated production has risen gradually to an average of about 125,000 bottles a year. The quality of some of these wines has been dramatically good.

* Try their best wine to date, the medium-soft, aromatic, complex, luscious, refreshing Sauvignon Blanc; also the fruity, smooth, spicy, strong Cabernet Sauvignon, at a FINE rating.

SANTINO WINES *east of Plymouth in the Shenandoah Valley of Amador in the foothills of the High Sierras*

A very new, very small, family operation in one of those fabulous high valleys about thirty-five miles southeast of Sacramento (see page 165). Matthew and Nancy Santino built their winery in 1979 and, having no vineyard of their own, are buying the magnificently rich and ripe grapes from their farmer-grower-rancher neighbors in the Shenandoah Valley. They are experimenting with different technical treatments of the mature Zinfandels, as well as Cabernet Sauvignons and some whites. The wines—hardly unexpectedly in this extraordinary climate—come out in chewy, fleshy, luscious, powerful, robust, rustic styles. They usually designate the name of the vineyard on the label.

** (NOBLE ratings) A fascinating and instructive experience is to taste, side by side, two of their sharply contrasting styles of Zinfandel: the first, their regular "Shenandoah," has enormous power, tremendous intensity of fruit, huge solidity in the mouth; the second, labeled "Early Release," is obviously the same wine from the same grapes but deliberately arrested in its development so that all the impressive and lovely qualities are there but in a much lighter degree, delicately skipping on the tongue rather than weighing on it—this is brilliant work by winemaker Scott Harvey.

* (FINE rating) In northern California, try the much simpler, but nonetheless impressive Zinfandel labeled as "Corti Reserve," with grapes from the Downing Vineyard.

SAUSAL WINERY *east of Healdsburg in the Alexander Valley of Sonoma*

A fair-size winemaking operation, owned and run by the Demostene family, started in 1973 and, since then, with estimated production gradually rising toward the equivalent of about 450,000 bottles a year. During the first phase of their history, they concentrated on selling grapes and bulk wines in barrels. Then—as always, with every proud wine family—the desire developed to put their own name on their own labels. The first wines from their 150 acres of vineyards, produced by winemaker David Demostene in 1974, were of memorably high quality, and the sense of "reaching for excellence" has continued with several later releases.

* (FINE rating) Try the warmly fruity, luscious, arrogantly spicy, tense Chardonnay.

SEBASTIANI VINEYARDS *in the Valley of the Moon in Sonoma*

This is the classic success story—of the little Italian wine family that went north of San Francisco to plant vines and grow grapes and stayed on to become one of the near-giants. They started in 1825, which certainly makes them the oldest vineyard in northern California. For more than a hundred years, of course, they made and sold bulk wine in the barrel, and the various varieties of grapes were interplanted for the system that was known, all over the world at that time, as "field blending." The theory was that, when you harvested the grapes, you automatically got the right blend for your wine between the various varieties of grapes. The theory never took into account the fact that different grapes ripen at different times, so, naturally, field blending has been eliminated everywhere. After Prohibition, Samuele Sebastiani decided to put the family name on the labels of bottles. Today, they produce about 50 million of those bottles every year—almost half still as inexpensive, good-value Italian-style jug wines. Their better-quality vintaged varietals are usually designated on the label as "Proprietor's Reserve." They own 400 acres of vines in Sonoma, but, of course, they buy grapes (and even ready-made wines in barrels and bottles) from every part of California.

> ** (NOBLE rating) Hardly unexpectedly, most of the average Sebastianis, sold when they are still very young, do not achieve high ratings at tastings—but, in fairness, I feel bound to report that I recently tasted a 1962 Cabernet Sauvignon "Proprietor's Reserve," and it certainly rated as a NOBLE wine—the lesson to be learned is that the best Sebastiani reds need to be aged for a good number of years.
>
> * (FINE ratings) The light, refreshing Gamay Beaujolais and the White Riesling.

SHAFER VINEYARDS *on the Stag's Leap slope east of Yountville in the Napa Valley*

Very few new vineyards have had such a sensational "opening success" as has Shafer with its first Cabernet Sauvignon—almost immediately hailed as a magnificent Napa Valley wine with prospects for development toward a peak of perfection in the future. This one wine at once puts the quiet, modest Shafer family—John, his wife, Elizabeth (Bett), and their four children, all partners in ownership of the vineyard—in the top group of Napa Valley vintners. Nor is there any question that the first wine was just a lucky meteoric flash. I have tasted the succeeding Cabernets, as well as the Zinfandels and the Chardonnays still resting in the aging barrels, and there can be no doubt as to the supreme quality of the wines that are on the way. The Shafer vineyard earth, obviously, has all the extraordinary and right qualities for growing perfect grapes, and Shafer's winemaker, Nikko Schoch, who comes from a family long connected with wine in the Napa Valley, clearly has all the requisite skills for converting exceptional grapes into memorable wines.

John Shafer has spent most of his working life in Chicago as an executive of a publishing house. Toward the end of the 1960s, he and Bett began to feel a frustration about their lives. Year after year, they seemed to be endlessly repeating the same pattern, with little challenge for the future. While they were still young enough to "start over," why couldn't they find a new career, one that would enable them to live in the country and that would give them a creative adventure and have reasonable prospects for future growth. John, as a conservative businessman, was skilled in the techniques of investigating the possibilities of new ventures. The more he looked (and calculated), the more he was drawn toward the business of wine. When, at last, they saw the beauty of the Napa Valley, they were completely sold. They bought about 226 acres, including some of the best vine-growing land in the valley, in the eastern foothills around the famous Stag's Leap rock in a microclimate that has already made several vineyards famous. In 1973, they began their program of planting Cabernet Sauvignon, Chardonnay, Merlot, and Zinfandel. At first, John had no thought of making wine. He told me, "I felt it was altogether too complex a venture for me to assimilate." He would grow the best possible grapes and sell them. But when he began tasting the wines made by his neighbors, he was "caught" by the challenge and plunged in completely. He took on Nikko Schoch as winemaker and completed the building of his own winery in time for the harvest of 1980. Even before that crucial date, John had some wines made for him under contract, in the wineries of his neighbors, and these, all made 100 percent with Shafer grapes, have also turned out extremely well. The planting program continues, now including small acreage of Cabernet Franc and, possibly, Petit Verdot, the classic varietals for blending into Bordeaux-style red Cabernet Sauvignon, and the projected production may eventually be about 120,000 bottles per year. They already have a limited national distribution in major cities across the country.

*** A generally SUPERB quality rating for the complex, rich, velvety Cabernet Sauvignon.
** The tasting charts usually show NOBLE quality ratings for the medium-light, well-constructed, fruity, refreshing Zinfandel and the big, aromatic, elegant, mouth-filling Chardonnay—the latter still made largely from purchased Chardonnay grapes but with the Shafer-grown percentage increasing every year.

SHERRILL CELLARS *at Woodside in the Santa Cruz Mountains of San Mateo*

This fairly small winery is owned and run by the Sherrill family, starting in 1973 with the planting of their vineyard, completing the building of their winery in 1979, and since then gradually achieving an estimated production averaging about 50,000 bottles a year. They use a subsidiary label for their lower-priced blended and generic wines, released as Skyline. Until their own vines are fully matured, they are buying grapes from various mountain growers and designating these vineyards on their labels.

* Try the medium-soft, delicate, gently refreshing White Riesling; also the dark, spicy, strong Petite Sirah, with grapes from the Shell Creek Vineyard, both of FINE quality.

SHOWN & SONS VINEYARDS *on the Silverado Trail above Rutherford in the Napa Valley*

There is an owner called Richard Shown, but he does not list any sons to justify the unorthodox name of this vineyard. They started in 1979, and since then their estimated production has been rising gradually to a projected average of about 180,000 bottles a year. They have 75 acres of vines and buy additional grapes.

* Try the unusually dry, delicately flowery, lightly refreshing White "Johannisberg" Riesling, of FINE quality.

SIERRA VISTA WINERY *at Placerville in El Dorado in the foothills of the High Sierras*

This is another of those small, experimental, romantic family wineries—with an almost pioneering atmosphere about them—started in the extraordinary "Gold Rush foothill valleys" of the Sierra Nevada, valleys where the climate and the soil combine to grow and ripen magnificent grapes. Here, near the town of Placerville (once known as Hangtown to the gold miners who came in the evenings to crawl from one bar to another), John and Barbara MacCready completed the construction of their winery in 1977 and, since then, have gradually built up an estimated production of about 40,000 bottles a year. They have 12 acres of their own vines and buy additional grapes from other El Dorado, Amador, Butte, and Calaveras farmer-grower-ranchers. In their own vineyard, they have a few acres planted in true French Syrah from the Hermitage hill of the Rhône Valley. It will be fascinating to see how this develops in the fantastic El Dorado climate.

    * Try the intensely fruity, dominantly powerful, amazingly aromatic Chenin Blanc, at a FINE rating.

SIMI WINERY *at Healdsburg in the Alexander Valley of Sonoma*

One of the historic vineyards of northern California, it was founded in 1867 by two Italian brothers, Giuseppe and Pietro Simi. They built an inexpensive, practical, small stone warehouse right on the railroad tracks that would carry the barrels of wine to San Francisco. Although it has all been dolled up and enlarged, the old buildings are still there. The long-unused rails have almost rusted away, and the tracks are covered by grass and greenery. Today's production, of about 1¼ million bottles a year, travels by road. Since the Simis, there have been several owners. In 1970, when Russ Green, a wealthy oil man, took it over and began redeveloping it, he discovered, in a bricked-up part of the cellar, some ancient bottles of Cabernet Sauvignon, Pinot Noir, and Zinfandel that had been laid down by the Simi family and then forgotten, leaving the bottles cool and undisturbed for almost forty years. The wine was found to be magnificent, and when it began to be sold at peak prices previously unheard of for American wines, it made the name of Simi famous among connoisseurs from coast to coast. New owners of the winery followed in fairly quick succession: a British beer company, then an American wine importing firm, and now, as part of its U.S. "empire," Simi has been taken over by the huge French Champagne-Cognac conglomerate Moët-Hennessy. The new winemaker, under the French regime, is the dedicated and widely experienced Zelma Long (see Long Vineyards). Under her direction, the expectation is that the Simi wines, which have been steadily improving over the last ten years, will continue to achieve increasing success.

    *** The Gewürztraminer, with grapes from the Russian River Valley, regularly at a SUPERB rating, is the best wine of this variety I have tasted in the United States.

** At a point or two lower, three wines consistently at a
NOBLE rating are the medium-soft White Riesling, the dry
Muscat Canelli, and the Cabernet Sauvignon.

* Among the wines with FINE ratings, there is the Gamay
Beaujolais, with grapes from the Alexander Valley; also one
of the best of all American pink wines for light summer
drinking, the Rosé de Cabernet; and the Chardonnay.

SMITH-MADRONE VINEYARD *high on Spring Mountain in the Napa Valley*

This fairly small vineyard—located on what has become known
as the Napa Valley's historic "Wine Mountain"—was originally
planted with vines as far back as 1880, but, with the double scourges
of the phylloxera vine disease and Prohibition, it was abandoned and
forgotten for more than fifty years. The land was bought, in 1971, by
its two present winemakers, Charles and Stuart Smith. They replanted 39 acres of vines, built a winery, made the first wine in 1977,
and since then have developed an estimated production averaging
about 30,000 bottles a year. The early wines have shown in their
construction considerable imagination and technical skill. They have
been quickly and completely snapped up by the connoisseurs of San
Francisco.

* Try the medium-soft, wonderfully fruity, aromatic and flowery, delicately refreshing White Riesling; also the dramatic,
harmonious, powerful, rich Chardonnay, both achieving a
FINE rating.

SMOTHERS WINERY *east of the town of Santa Cruz in the Santa Cruz Mountains south of San Francisco Bay*

When the Smothers Brothers ended their careers as television
entertainers, they both wanted to get into winemaking. Dick was the
first to jump in, but Tom has now followed at a different location.
There are rumors that, quite soon, the two operations will be consol-
idated into The Smothers Brothers Winery. Meanwhile, Dick got
started in 1977, and since then has gradually boosted his estimated
production to an average of about 25,000 bottles a year. Dick has
never been immodest enough to pretend that he knows the technol-

ogy of wine—from the first, he hired an experienced winemaker, William Arnold, who launched the winery with a memorable golden sweet "Late Harvest" Gewürztraminer. There was no need to plant vines, because the winery is on the ancient, superlative Vine Hill Vineyard, which grows, among other things, magnificently aromatic and ripe Chardonnay grapes. Dick, however, is planting vines on the new wine estate of his brother, Tom, at Glen Ellen in the Sonoma Valley, and Dick is expected, eventually, to move his winery there.

* If ever you find one of the now-rare bottles, try the wonderfully aromatic and sweet "Late Harvest" Gewürztraminer; alternatively try the austere, complex, elegant, slightly smoky, tangy Chardonnay, with grapes from the Vine Hill Vineyard, the wine aged in French Nevers oak barrels. Both are of FINE quality.

SOKOL BLOSSER WINERY *at Dundee in the Willamette Valley of Oregon*

William Roy Blosser was an urban-planning specialist working in a city office in Portland. His wife, Susan Sokol, was a university professor of world history. They decided to "get away from it all" and, romantically, make lovely wine together in the comparative peace of the Oregon hills. When I asked Bill why they decided to put the name of his wife first in the title of the vineyard, he said, "We were keen to use initials on some of our labels and letterheads, and we thought that 'S.B.' would look better than 'B.S.' " They have planted 45 acres of their own vines and have experimented with various varieties bought from other Oregon and Washington State growers. In 1977, they designed and built their own very modern winery. Their production has reached about 240,000 bottles a year, and they are planning to level off at about 300,000 bottles. To reach that figure, they will plant another 30 acres.

** (NOBLE rating) The lovely, light, intensely fruity, balanced and rounded 100 percent Merlot.
* (FINE rating) The very dry, almost austere, and wonderfully refreshing and fruity Sauvignon Blanc.

SONOMA VINEYARDS *at Windsor in Sonoma*

The Sonoma winery operation has grown in about twenty years from a minuscule husband-and-wife storefront business to one of the major wine producers of the nation, with an estimated output of almost 8 million bottles a year and complete national distribution. The moving spirit behind it is Rod Strong, who spent the first half of his life as a dancer in classical ballet. But he had come from a wine-making family on the German Rhine and the wine grape had always been a strong interest. At thirty-three, he and his wife started buying and selling wine in the small town of Tiburon in Sonoma, a few miles north of the Golden Gate, under the name Tiburon Vintners. Rod wanted to make his own wines, and, in 1962, he took over the small Windsor Winery nearby and renamed it Sonoma Vineyards. Almost at once, he was immensely successful, and the profits came rolling in. Not being an experienced businessman, Rod saved nothing for a rainy day, but plowed everything back into expansion and improvement of the wines. He built an enormous, fantastic winery that looks like a cross between the Great Pyramid of Gizeh and an Aztec temple. He bought vineyards all over Sonoma, until he owned about 5,000 acres. He could manage the production, but did not have the experience or manpower to organize national distribution, and when the inevitable recession came, so did the financial crisis at Sonoma. It was solved by Rod Strong giving up his personal control, sharing it with partners, including the Renfield Corporation as national distributors. Some vineyards were sold, and Rod now concentrates on his winemaking, with increasing improvement in quality. The latest feather in the Sonoma cap is an agreement with the famous French Champagne house Piper-Heidsieck to produce French *méthode champenoise* sparkling wines on the Sonoma estate from Sonoma grapes to be distributed throughout the United States (see Piper.Sonoma).

   *** The best Cabernet Sauvignon is usually designated "Alexander's Crown" and generally achieves a SUPERB rating.

    ** At a point or two below, a NOBLE rating is usually achieved by the Zinfandel, labeled from River West Vineyard.

     * Among the wines achieving a FINE rating are the Chardonnay from River West and a golden sweet "Late Harvest" Johannisberg Riesling with 7 percent residual sugar.

SOTOYOME WINERY *south of Healdsburg in the Russian River Valley of Sonoma*

During the final years of Mexican control of Alta California, there was a continuous and powerful drive to persuade competent settlers to "go north" to settle and begin usefully developing the vast uninhabited lands above the Russian River. The Mexican military governor, General Mariano Vallejo, was empowered to make huge land grants to the "right people." He gave one of the largest of these grants to his brother-in-law, Henry Fitch, who became the owner of a vast domain of 48,000 acres named Rancho Sotoyome after a band of Indians that hunted in the area. The modern Sotoyome Winery occupies a minuscule part of the ancient rancho, but it remembers its historic roots by printing an old map of the Sotoyome lands as the background for its wine label. All this stress on past events becomes understandable when one learns that the owner-winemaker, William Chaikin, was a professor of history at the University of California. The winery was completed in 1974, and since then the estimated production has risen gradually to an average of about 75,000 bottles a year—with almost complete concentration on red wines. They own or control 17 acres of vines and buy additional red grapes—mainly Cabernet Sauvignon, Petite Sirah, and Zinfandel—all strictly in the Russian River Valley, deliberately to maintain a local appellation and character to the wines.

    * Try the FINE aromatic, harmoniously fruity, mouth-filling, mellow, and smooth Cabernet Sauvignon.

SOUVERAIN CELLARS *near Geyserville in the Dry Creek Valley of Sonoma*

This handsome, large, very modern showplace winery—surrounded by fountains and gardens, with every comfort for the tourist visitor, including public tasting rooms and its own restaurant—was built in the early 1970s by the huge Pillsbury flour milling conglomerate of Minneapolis as part of its experimental entry into the wine business. (The story is told in some detail in connection with the Rutherford Hill Winery on page 391.) When, quite suddenly in 1976, the Pillsbury people decided to get out of the wine business and sell all their property, this Souverain winery was bought by the California North Coast Grape Growers Association, a cooperative partnership of 246 grape growers in Mendocino, the Napa Valley, and Sonoma. Naturally, they provide the fruit which the excellent winemaker, Bob Mueller, converts into an estimated production averaging about 6¼ million bottles a year. They are still expanding, and this winery could eventually produce up to 12½ million bottles.

> * Try the medium-soft, joyously light White Riesling; also the delicate, fruity "Vintage Select" Chardonnay; also the light, delicately spicy 100 percent Merlot; also the smooth, uncomplicated Cabernet Sauvignon; or the delightfully refreshing Rosé of Pinot Noir, all usually at FINE ratings.

SPRING MOUNTAIN VINEYARDS *near St. Helena in the Napa Valley*

This is a high-prestige, still steadily growing winery in one of the best grape-growing microclimates in the valley. It was started in 1968 and is family owned and run by Mike Robbins and his wife, Shirley, with their winemaker, John Williams, now reaching an estimated production of about 250,000 bottles a year. For a good part of his life Mike seemed to be unable to make up his mind what to do with it. He graduated from Annapolis and spent the period of two wars in the Navy—then real estate in San Francisco, then law school. He had been to Europe, had learned to know wine, and had been "irresistibly attracted by the life-style of the château owners of France." Then, when he discovered the Napa Valley, he was "mesmerized by it." In 1968, he bought an old Victorian-style house and a minuscule plot of possible vineyard land at the base of Spring Mountain. From this tiny start, he gradually expanded his land up the mountain to about 500 acres—with roughly 150 acres planted. During this expansion, Mike bought one of the historic, abandoned, private mansions on the upper mountain slope, the century-old, steepled, elegantly Victorian Miravalle. Mike has restored it in the setting of a Bordeaux château surrounded by its wine estate. All this accent on show does not prevent Spring Mountain from producing highly complex wines of outstanding quality, now virtually in national distribution.

> *** In good years, the Chardonnay almost always reaches a SUPERB rating; so does the intense Cabernet Sauvignon.

** At a point or two below, a NOBLE rating is regularly
achieved by the extremely dry Sauvignon Blanc, wonderfully complex, a model of what this variety should be.

STAG'S LEAP WINE CELLARS *on the Silverado Trail near Yountville in
the Napa Valley*

This name is not to be confused with that of another producer,
almost next door, called Stag's Leap Winery. They are often in the
courts trying to sort out their respective claims, but whatever may be
the rights or wrongs in the matter, the hard fact is that they are both
near a huge rock that for a century or more has been called on local
maps Stag's Leap, useful information, no doubt, for stags, but not
very helpful to wine drinkers trying to interpret labels.

This brilliant, small, 45-acre vineyard is a one-man tour de force
since 1972 by owner-winemaker, Warren Winiarski, whose production is now reaching about 180,000 bottles a year. His Stag's Leap
label suddenly rocketed to international fame in 1975 at the now-
fabled Paris blind tasting (see Chateau Montelena), when a group of
prestigious French professional experts placed this entirely unknown
American Cabernet Sauvignon in first place, assuming it to be a
Bordeaux and giving it more points than Château Mouton-Roth-
schild, Château Haut-Brion, as well as two other magnificent Bordeaux and five other established California reds. Most critics now
seem to feel that Warren's immediate success was well merited. His
dedication to perfectionism amounts almost to a fetish, both among
the vines and in the winery. He harvests by "selective picking," so
that virtually every bunch of grapes is at ideal ripeness. Warren says
he wants to practice only "the noblest kind of winemaking." Any
wine that does not entirely meet his highest standards is bottled
under the subsidiary label Hawk Crest.

*** The principal output is the "estate-bottled" Cabernet Sauvignon almost always at a SUPERB rating.
** At a point or two below, three wines generally achieve a
NOBLE rating: the luxuriously rich Chardonnay, the medium-soft Johannisberg Riesling with grapes from the Birkmyer Vineyard, and a dark red Petite Sirah.

P. & M. STAIGER WINERY *above Boulder Creek in the Santa Cruz Mountains south of San Francisco Bay*

A fairly small vineyard, owned and run by the Staiger family starting in 1973, and since then working up to an estimated production of about 6,000 bottles a year. They are in a magnificent location, above 1,000 feet, almost at the peak of the mountain, with about 12 acres of vineyards on steep slopes, originally planted in 1900 but now replanted with Cabernet Sauvignon and Chardonnay. From these vines, when they mature, the Staigers will make very small, "handcrafted" lots of "estate-bottled" wines. Meanwhile, they have been buying Pinot Noir and Zinfandel grapes, but these will be phased out. To avoid the danger of any diminution of the intense mountain flavors, they bottle their wines in the natural state, unfiltered and unfined.

> * In northern California, try the luscious, raisiny rich, spicy "Late Harvest" Zinfandel, at a FINE rating.

ROBERT STEMMLER WINERY *west of Healdsburg in the Dry Creek Valley of Sonoma*

Bob Stemmler learned about winemaking in Germany in the famous wine city of Bad Kreuznach at the heart of the Rhine region of the Nahe. After making wine there for three years, he came to California in 1961 and has worked for some of the major producers. He started this winery for himself in 1977 but is by no means concentrating only on German-style white wines. Estimated production is now gradually rising toward the objective of about 60,000 bottles a year. He has 4 acres of his own Chardonnay vines and buys additional grapes in Sonoma, Lake, Mendocino, and the Napa Valley. His early wines clearly show Bob's experience and skill. Also, he has one of the most beautiful of wine labels—an attractive, colorful, small reproduction of a medieval German tapestry showing wine workers at an ancient press, crushing the grapes and collecting the precious juice.

> * Try the dry, gently fruity, mellow-yet-tangy, elegant "Fumé Blanc" (Sauvignon Blanc), with grapes from the far-northern Lake district, at a FINE rating.

STERLING VINEYARDS *at Calistoga in the Napa Valley*

This has become, so to speak, the "Disney World" for weekend tourists in the Napa Valley. It looks like a Hollywood stage set of a kind of Moroccan fortress-palace rising sheer out of the top of a hill. There are arches, battlements, bell towers, stained-glass windows, and terraces. The tourists are taken up to it in a cable car and then propelled, by a "mass-movement circulation plan," this way and that along certain passageways, where they are shown, through picture windows, the normal features of a winery, while soothing voices from hidden loudspeakers tell them about the making of "supreme wine." The fact is that not much supreme wine has been made at Sterling since it was founded, in 1972, by a group of profit-and-publicity-oriented San Francisco industrialists. Within less than ten years they sold out to the Coca-Cola Company of Atlanta, the present owners. The results of this change have not been entirely heartening. The excellent former winemaker, Ric Forman, has resigned to found his own winery (see page 334). The number of wines produced from the 350 acres of vineyards has been sharply cut back to only four varieties, and production has been reduced by about 20 percent to an estimated current average of 700,000 bottles a year. The quality has fallen off significantly. Their best wines are labeled "Sterling Reserve."

    ** (NOBLE ratings) The fruity, rich Chardonnay; the complex, intense, subtle Cabernet Sauvignon "Sterling Reserve," with about 12 percent Merlot; and the golden sweet "Late Harvest" Chenin Blanc (which is being discontinued).

    * (FINE ratings) The fruity, lively 100 percent Merlot. There are also FINE Chenin Blanc and Gewürztraminer.

STEVENOT VINEYARDS *at Murphys in Calaveras in the foothills of the High Sierras*

Another of the new, small wineries in the high mountain valleys leading up toward the eternal snows of the Sierra Nevada. This one is owned by Barden Stevenot, who shares the winemaking responsibilities with Julia Iantosca. Wine began to be made here in 1978, and since then the estimated production has gradually increased to the equivalent of about 120,000 bottles a year. Of the four counties where grapes are grown and wine is now made in what might be called the "High Sierras Wine Region," Amador and El Dorado are by far the best known, while Butte and Calaveras are virtually unknown. Stevenot is a big booster of the special qualities of the grapes and wines of the Calaveras district—a particular microclimate that provides an identifiable regional appellation. They have 15 acres of their own vines, and, of course, they are virtually surrounded by ranchers growing grapes for other wine producers.

    ** (NOBLE rating) Their remarkable, almost completely dry, luscious, sensuous, velvety Chenin Blanc, a kind of white equivalent of the Sierras Zinfandels.

STONEGATE WINERY *at Calistoga in the Napa Valley*

Small family winery started in 1973 by James Spaulding, who is on the academic staff of the University of California at Berkeley. He is helped by his wife, Barbara, and their winemaking son, David. The project started as a weekend hobby, but now David and a small staff work full time toward a maximum production of about 180,000 bottles a year. They have about 30 acres of vines around the winery on the valley floor, with a second, mountain vineyard about 800 feet up the slope. They also buy grapes from other producers. Although some of the wines are extremely good and the general level of quality is slowly improving, there is still, about some of the wines, an amateur, unfinished character.

    ** (NOBLE rating) Whenever they choose to make it, their best wine is a dark, deep, strong Petite Sirah.
    * (FINE ratings) The dry Chenin Blanc and the fruity Zinfandel.

STONY RIDGE WINERY *at Pleasanton in the Livermore Valley of Alameda*

This medium-size vineyard was first planted in 1880, and some parts of the original stone building are still being used for the modern winery, which was restarted in 1975. Since then, estimated production has gradually built up toward an objective of about 250,000 bottles a year. So far, the wines give the impression that they are "safe and sound," but they seem to have no spark of excitement about them to lift them above the "average and ordinary." Their prices are very fair.

> * Try the easy, smooth Cabernet Sauvignon; also the dark, strong, tannic Zinfandel, both of FINE quality.

SUNRISE WINERY *west of Felton in the Santa Cruz Mountains south of San Francisco Bay*

A small mountain winery, owned and run by the Stortz family, starting in 1976 and since then slowly developing an estimated production averaging about 35,000 bottles a year. They are on a high mountain peak where it is virtually impossible to have their own vineyards, but they are associated with the Arrata's Vineyard at the Montalvo estate at Saratoga in the Santa Clara Valley. For the rest of their wines, they buy grapes from Mendocino, the Edna Valley in San Luis Obispo, and from Sonoma. It seems a pity that this vineyard, which claims on its labels to be dedicated to making small quantities of the highest-quality wines, should not be more devoted, more loyal to the mountain grapes of the Santa Cruz region.

> * Try the nicely aromatic, chewy, fleshy, tannic Cabernet Sauvignon, with local grapes from the Arrata's Vineyard, at a FINE rating.

SUTTER HOME WINERY *near St. Helena in the Napa Valley*

The original, historic winery was built here in 1874, and the handsome mansion, known at the time as The Sutter Home, was added in 1890. It was all closed down and abandoned when the phylloxera disease struck the vines and, again, through the years of Prohibition. Then, in 1946, it was bought and revived by the Italian-American Trinchero family, with so many members, of several branches and generations, that they could probably run half a dozen wineries. At first, they operated very much as a normal Napa Valley producer, making about forty different types and varieties of wines. Then, in the 1960s, they discovered, half-accidentally (as described on page 166), the extraordinary possibilities of the richly ripe Zinfandel grapes from the foothill valley of the High Sierras in Amador and

El Dorado. They were so impressed that, very soon, they were making virtually nothing else but Zinfandel—today at a rate approaching 1 million bottles a year. The wines are big, powerful, alcoholic, and they need a lot of aging, but the final reward, whenever the vintage is good, is magnificently luxurious and rich drinking.

> *** The Amador Zinfandel, with grapes from the Ken Deaver Ranch in the Shenandoah Valley, usually at a SUPERB rating; also the Amador Zinfandel, with grapes from the John Ferrero Vineyard, also in the High Sierra foothills.

JOSEPH SWAN VINEYARDS *at Forestville in the Russian River Valley of Sonoma*

A minuscule family winery started in 1969 by a former airline pilot with a very personal taste in wine, Joe Swan, making an estimated 22,000 bottles a year. Because of this tiny production and the highly specialized character of the wines, very few bottles are sold through normal commercial channels. They are picked up at the winery or sent to devoted regular customers on a mailing list, who send in their special subscriptions. Swan is a fierce perfectionist, who makes magnificently intense, big, deep, full-bodied, powerful, solid wines—strictly for his personal pleasure and to his own taste—from his own grapes on his 10 acres of vines and from some Zinfandel grown to his specifications in the Dry Creek Valley. He directs every detail of everything himself—from the spring pruning of each vine to the final stages of aging in the barrels.

> *** The extraordinary Zinfandel, part austerely repellent, part irresistibly attractive, grapes from the Teldeschi Vineyard, almost invariably at a SUPERB rating.
>
> ** At a point or two below, two wines generally achieve a NOBLE rating: the Napa Gamay is the best American version of this variety I have ever tasted; also usually a NOBLE rating to the big, bold Pinot Noir.

SYCAMORE CREEK VINEYARDS *southwest of Morgan Hill in the Santa Cruz Mountains of Santa Clara*

A medium-small winery, owned and run by Walter and Mary Parks (with Walter as winemaker), starting in 1976 and gradually building up toward a production objective of about 60,000 bottles a year. They have 14 acres of mountain vineyards with some ancient vines that were first planted by an Italian immigrant family in 1906. This is, in fact, the famous district of early Italian-American vineyards —on the hills and in the valleys around the Hecker Pass, where the Santa Cruz Mountains join the Santa Lucia Range and where many of the most successful early California wines were produced. When Walter and Mary took over, they found more or less a jug winery and rebuilt it for the production of vintage-dated varietals of generally above-average quality.

> * Try the fairly gentle, light, luscious, smooth Petite Sirah, with grapes from the old mountain vineyard, of FINE quality.

TREFETHEN VINEYARDS *near the town of Napa in the Napa Valley*

A family vineyard devotedly dedicated to the pursuit of the highest quality. It was founded in 1886 as the Eshcol Vineyard with an eighty-year record of selling almost all bulk wines and grapes. In 1968, when the Trefethens bought it, they dreamed of putting their name on the labels of their own wines. Toward this end, they built a modern winery in 1973. The changeover was a serious financial struggle. When you sell bulk wine, you receive a cash flow every year. But when you start laying down wines to age in bottles, you lose a substantial part of your annual income for several years. The Trefethens were determined to accept every sacrifice in order to make top-quality wines. Their current estimated production is about 360,000 bottles a year—including some lesser blends under their Eshcol subsidiary label—but they still have to sell about two-thirds of the grapes from their 600 acres of vines for essential, immediate working cash. They hope, gradually, to reduce the grape sales to below 50 percent and increase the wine production to about 750,000 bottles. Recently, their Chardonnays and Cabernet Sauvignons have gained sensational successes in blind tastings by professional experts in Europe, who placed the Trefethen wines first—the white Chardonnay above some of the greatest names of white Burgundy and the red Cabernet Sauvignon above some of the major châteaux of Bordeaux.

> ** (NOBLE ratings) The big, aromatic, fruity, luscious Chardonnay; and the medium-soft, mouth-filling, robust, rounded, strong White "Johannisberg" Riesling.

TRENTADUE WINERY *south of Geyserville in the Alexander Valley of Sonoma*

This fair-size vineyard, owned and run by the Trentadue family (with Leo Trentadue as winemaker), was started in 1969 and since then has developed an estimated production averaging the equivalent of about 250,000 bottles a year. They have about 200 acres of their own vines in some of the best microclimates of the Alexander Valley. Leo has had long and wide experience, first, as a grower of magnificent Zinfandel grapes, which he sold for years to Ridge (see page 388) and which were designated on their labels as Geyserville Zinfandel. Only in recent years has Leo tried his hand at making and bottling his own wines. He has been successful, in general, with his reds—a good deal less so with his whites.

* Apart from the Cabernet Sauvignon and Zinfandel, usually reliable in good years, try something unexpected, the delightfully flowery, lightly elegant, fruity, spicy, most refreshing Gamay Beaujolais, all, generally, at FINE ratings.

TUALATIN VINEYARDS *at Forest Grove in the Willamette Valley of Oregon*

One of the larger, better financed, and more ambitious vineyards of Oregon. The name is Indian—after the Tualatin River that turns and twists through the small valley between the hills about thirty miles west of Portland—and means "gently flowing." The managing partner and winemaker, Bill Fuller, gained most of his training and experience in California—degrees in chemistry and viticulture from the University at Davis; nine years with Louis Martini in the Napa Valley; then a partnership with a "financing and marketing expert" in San Francisco and the search began for their own winery, preferably not "among the crowds" but in some new pioneering region. At last, in 1973, they found this 160-acre orchard in the Tualatin Valley. They began by planting 60 acres of vines and made their first "estate-bottled" wine in 1976. The planting of new vines continues, and the projected production will eventually reach about 300,000 bottles a year. The accent, so far, has been on white wines, and although a few of them have been extremely good, the general quality has been somewhat unpredictable.

> *** A remarkable dry Muscat, made from the Muscat of Alexandria grape, achieved a SUPERB rating.
> ** A point or two below, a NOBLE rating for a medium-soft White Riesling.
> * A FINE rating for an intensely fruity Rosé of Pinot Noir.

TULOCAY WINERY *east of the town of Napa in the Napa Valley*

This small winemaking operation, launched in 1975, has developed since then an estimated production averaging about 12,000 bottles a year. It has no vineyards of its own. In spite of the miniature scale, the owners, Bill and Barbara Cadman, have admirably ambitious ideas. They want to concentrate entirely on making only vintage-dated varietal reds—from the finest qualities of grapes they can find—producing each wine in a kind of "hand-crafted" way in small lots of, generally, no more than 1,000 bottles of each wine. Such ideas are worthy of applause and support. One must also warn that Lilliputian winemaking can pose very severe problems. These wines will only be available in northern California.

> * In the neighborhood, try the intensely fruity, slightly smoky, well-constructed, tannic Cabernet Sauvignon, which offers a good promise but needs several years of aging in the bottle to achieve a FINE quality.

TURGEON & LOHR WINERY *at San Jose in Santa Clara*

In 1972, Jerry Lohr began planting his 280 acres of vines along the Arroyo Seco River near Greenfield in the Salinas Valley of Monterey. This is still known as the Lohr Vineyards. In 1974, Bernie Turgeon joined as a partner for the building of the winery in San Jose, which is now called the Turgeon & Lohr Winery. The first wines were released in 1975, and current production is estimated at about 1 million bottles a year. They also make jug wines under their subsidiary Jade label. Their partner-winemaker, Peter Stern, has recently released some interesting, experimental wines, including an extremely light *nouveau*-style Gamay Beaujolais and a quite sweet, *Botrytized* Pinot Chardonnay.

** (NOBLE ratings) The dry, aromatic, slightly austere, fruity, intense Chardonnay; the complex, dark, deep, solid, fairly tannic Cabernet Sauvignon; and a unique *Botrytized*, aromatically sweet "Late Harvest—Selected Clusters" Chardonnay, with grapes from the Tanoak Vineyard in the Arroyo Seco Canyon—a most unusual wine that continued fermenting steadily for eight months, finally giving a residual sugar of 7.2 percent, with bouquet overtones of peaches, honey, lemon verbena, raisins, and oak.

VEEDERCREST VINEYARD *high on Mount Veeder in the Mayacamas Range above the Napa Valley*

This is a most unusual, high mountain vineyard, at almost 2,000 feet above the valley floor, with a group of owners fiercely dedicated to the highest quality. The managing partner and winemaker is Alfred Baxter, who formerly taught philosophy at the University of California. Out of 300 rocky and wild acres owned at the crest of Mount Veeder, almost 100 will soon be planted in vines, and more grapes are being bought from such outstanding microclimate areas as those around the Stag's Leap rock near Yountville, the Carneros Hills facing San Pablo Bay, and in the Dry Creek Valley of Sonoma. Estimated production is about 170,000 bottles a year. Planting of the Mount Veeder vineyard began in 1972, but although there will eventually be a winery near the vineyard, Baxter has not yet been able to build it. Meanwhile, the wines are made in leased space in an industrial suburb of Oakland on San Francisco Bay. When there is a new and larger winery, production will rise to about 250,000 bottles. Many of the wines are outstanding in quality.

** (NOBLE ratings) The magnificent, powerful, rich Chardonnay, with grapes from the Winery Lake Vineyard in the Carneros Hills; and the golden sweet "Late Harvest—Selected Clusters" heavily *Botrytized*, extraordinary and unique blend of White Riesling, with some Gewürztraminer and Muscat of Alexandria, one of the most excitingly aromatic wines I have ever tasted, with 7.5 percent residual sugar.

* (FINE ratings) The broad, intensely fruity, strong Cabernet Sauvignon; and an elegantly refreshing, full-of-character Rosé of Petite Sirah.

VENTANA VINEYARDS *along the Arroyo Seco River southwest of Soledad in the Salinas Valley of Monterey*

With the enormous and explosive growth of grape growing and winemaking in Monterey in the last ten years, there has been fierce competition between the newer vineyards. Ventana, launched in 1978, has rapidly risen to the top level of importance and influence, under the management of its family owners, Doug and Shirley Meador, backed up by the imagination and skill of its young winemaker, Ken Wright. Production has risen rapidly to a currently estimated equivalent of about 300,000 bottles a year. They have 310 acres of their new vines, and this comparatively large supply of their own Salinas Valley grapes has enabled them to make some interesting wines with strong Monterey regional characteristics.

> * Try the dry, beautifully fruity, elegantly refreshing, tangy Sauvignon Blanc; also the elegantly rich, well-constructed, slightly smoky, delicately spicy Chardonnay; also the smoothly robust, chewy, fleshy, tannic Zinfandel; all generally achieving a FINE quality.

MANFRED J. VIERTHALER WINERY *at Sumner in the Puyallup Valley of Washington State*

In the early, pre-Prohibition days of "wine" in the Pacific Northwest—when "wine" meant apples, or berries, or, at best, Concord grapes—there were dozens of small, family wineries all around Puget Sound on the "wet west side" of the Cascade Mountains. Then, after Repeal and into the 1960s, when the noble *vinifera* vine arrived from Europe, demanding ideal growing conditions of soil, sunshine, and reasonable rainfall, all vineyards moved from the western to the eastern side of the huge Cascade mountain barrier, which holds back the Pacific rain and keeps the central irrigated valleys hot, hopeful, and happy for the vine. But there is one vineyard that has stayed on the west side, between the Cascades and the Pacific Ocean, where the grass is always wonderfully green because the air is always cool and humid, where the piled-up storm clouds roll in from the ocean and, breaking themselves on the crest of Mount Rainier, drop their rain in solid sheets. In this hardly propitious microclimate, a German winemaker, Manfred Vierthaler, grows his noble grapes and makes his remarkably successful German-style wines. He has 20 acres of vines, which he planted in 1977. During the next three years, he hopes to plant an additional 100 acres, including Gewürztraminer, Black Riesling, White Riesling, and Müller-Thurgau. Current production is running at an estimated average of about 50,000 bottles a year. Manfred came to the Pacific Northwest from Germany in 1953, and since the "wine boom" had not yet started up there (so that he could see no way of supporting himself by viticulture), he opened a German restaurant called The Bavarian in Tacoma and amused himself by testing the acceptance of German wines by his customers. He was soon convinced that the slight "touch of sweetness" that is in many German wines would be very acceptable to northwestern wine drinkers. So Manfred saved his money and, when the time came, bought his vineyard.

* In Seattle and the Pacific Northwest, try the delicately sweet, beautifully flowery, fruity, and lively White "Johannisberg" Riesling, at a FINE rating.

VILLA MT. EDEN WINERY *at Oakville in the Napa Valley*

An historic old winery, first built in the early 1880s, with vineyards planted around it. It was then abandoned and neglected for many years, until it was taken over and revived, beginning in 1970, as a well-financed family project by Anne and Jim McWilliams. The completely renovated winery is now surrounded by about 80 acres of vines. Since the first wines were made in 1974, production has steadily increased to about 150,000 bottles a year. The main interest of the owners is in making "hand-crafted" wines, all from their own estate, mainly Cabernet Sauvignon, Chardonnay, Chenin Blanc, Napa Gamay, and Pinot Noir. All the hand work, including "field crushing" at the harvest to protect flavor and almost everything in the winery being done by hand, compels high prices for the finished wines.

** (NOBLE rating) The memorable, complex, intensely fruity, powerfully tannic Cabernet Sauvignon.
* (FINE rating) The big, aromatic, austerely dry Chardonnay.

VŌSE VINEYARDS *on Mount Veeder east of Oakville in the Napa Valley*

The "quiet volcano," Mount Veeder, stands guard over the Napa Valley, and from the steep slopes of the massive mountain come some of the best grapes for a few of the most famous vineyards— Mayacamas, Mount Veeder, and Veedercrest among them. In 1970, an ambitious new wine initiate bought 463 undeveloped acres of the rough, rocky, forested side of the mountain. The new owner, with the fierce determination to undertake the heavy work of literally hacking out new vineyards, Hamilton Vōse, was described in a commercial text as a "demolition bomb-squad expert, a race-car driver, and a corporate executive." He has, to date, cleared 100 acres and planted them with Cabernet Sauvignon, Chardonnay, and Zinfandel. By 1977, he had built his winery near the town of Napa and was beginning to release small quantities of his wines. Since then, the estimated production has been slowly stepped up to an average of about 50,000 bottles a year. Vōse hopes, eventually, to double this production and, also, to double the acreage of vineyards on Mount Veeder. It is doubtful whether he will ever be able to use all his 400-odd acres for vines—parts of the mountain slope are just too rocky and steep to be workable—unless, of course, Vōse blasts the rocks away by bomb-squad demolition.

    ** (NOBLE rating) Apart from the generally impressive Cabernet Sauvignon and Chardonnay, there is something quite unusual about the arrogantly fruity, nose-enveloping, elegantly powerful, almost perfectly balanced, solidly textured "Fumé Blanc" (100 percent Sauvignon Blanc), with grapes brought from Sonoma.

WENTE BROTHERS *at Livermore in the Livermore Valley of Alameda*

This is another of the famous wine families of California—families that, generation after generation, have influenced and shaped the wine industry of the West. In many ways the history of the Wentes parallels that of the Martinis (see page 362). Both have been devoted to the progress of the industry toward higher standards of quality. The Martinis, coming from Italy, concentrated on red wines and set down their roots in the rich earth of the Napa Valley, best for the red grapes. The Wentes, coming from Germany, have always favored the white wines and planted their roots in the sparse gravel of the Livermore Valley, best for the whites. "Old Carl" Wente came first, in 1883, to found the firm at Livermore on 40 acres and soon handed it over to his two sons, Herman and Ernest. Herman had the driving force to become one of the greatest of all winemakers. Ernest had the charm—and still has, today, at the age of 96. After Prohibition, Wente were the first American producers to print grape names on their labels, thus leading the California industry toward the enormous success of varietal labeling. Today, Wente's estimated production is slightly above 10 million bottles a year. Herman retired and died. Ernest's son, "Young Karl," took over—faced by the immense problem that their 850 acres of vineyards in the Livermore Valley could not be expanded any further. Karl took the "giant step" of being the first major producer to "go south" and open up 550 acres of new vineyards in Monterey. Some brilliant Wente wines have come from the new region (see page 195). In 1977, Karl suddenly and tragically died, and the direction of the firm had to be taken over by his widow, Jean, and her three children—Eric as executive winemaker, Philip in charge of the vineyards, and Carolyn in administration. Wente Brothers remains a family operation. With such large production and distribution, there is greater stress on inexpensive and simple wines for mass sales. The big question for the newest, youngest generation is whether the future emphasis will be mainly on growth, or whether Wente's leadership will continue, also, in terms of the greatness of the wine.

 *** The top wines from the Monterey vineyards in the Arroyo Seco Canyon have been the vintages of golden sweet "Late Harvest—Selected Bunches" Johannisberg Riesling, usually about 5 percent sugar, all of them at a SUPERB rating.

 ** At a point or two below, four wines consistently at a NOBLE rating are the austere, fruity Chardonnay, the dry Pinot Blanc, the marvelously clean and clear Sauvignon Blanc, and the delicately light Pinot Noir.

 * Among the wines with a FINE rating, there are the famous, popular Grey Riesling and the medium-soft Semillon.

HERMANN J. WIEMER VINEYARD *on the west shore of Lake Seneca in the Finger Lakes district of New York State*

Hermann Wiemer's family, in the beautiful, narrow, twisting valley of the Moselle River in Germany, where some of the greatest wines in the world are made, has been involved—both on his father's and his mother's sides—in the growing of grapes and the making of wine for more than 400 years. His mother owned an estate in the wine village of Traben-Trarbach. His father was a well-known technical expert on grape grafting in the wine town of Bernkastel. Young Hermann was trained in enology, first at the District Wine School in Neustadt in the Palatinate of the Rhine and then at the National State College at Geisenheim—the top wine-training program in Germany. After working briefly at vineyards on the Moselle, Hermann decided that he wanted to try for the opportunities that seemed to him to be offered by life and work in the United States. He came across the Atlantic in 1968, when he was twenty-six years old, landed in New York, and gravitated at once toward the nearest wine area, the upstate Finger Lakes region. All doors were open to a young man with the solid background and training of Hermann Wiemer. He acclimatized himself to American conditions and techniques at the New York State Wine Experimental Station at Geneva and then got his first job as a winemaker. Since then, he has never been a day out of work. He has visited California, the Pacific Northwest, and other U.S. wine regions, but feels, somehow, deep in his bones, that the extremes of heat and cold he finds in New York give him a certain link with his home on the Moselle, where the winters are also harsh and the summers sometimes fierce. But what was always in his dreams was the hope of one day owning his own vineyard where he could grow his beloved Riesling grapes. The opportunity came, at last, in 1979, when he was able to buy about 90 acres on the slopes above the west shore of Lake Seneca. So far, he has planted about 50 acres in White Riesling and Chardonnay—he intends to concentrate entirely on these two noble varieties from Europe. He hopes, eventually, for a maximum production of about 175,000 bottles a year.

      * (FINE ratings) The sharply refreshing, fruity, beautifully clear and clean White Riesling ("Johannisberg Riesling") and the aromatic, elegant, well-constructed Chardonnay.

WILLOWSIDE VINEYARDS *northwest of Santa Rosa in the Russian River Valley of Sonoma*

This fairly small vineyard is owned and run by its winemaker, Berle Beliz, and his family. They started, in 1975, in an unromantic industrial building in the heart of the busy town of Santa Rosa and since then have achieved an estimated production averaging about 60,000 bottles a year. Just outside the town, they have their own 24-acre Mount Olivet Vineyard, and they buy additional grapes from other growers in the valley. The vineyard source of the grapes is almost always designated on each label. These wines are carefully made and properly aged.

> * Try the attractive, fruity, strong Chardonnay, with grapes from Furth's Chalk Hill Vineyard, at a FINE rating.

YAKIMA RIVER WINERY *at Prosser in the Yakima Valley of Washington State*

This is an extremely new, extremely small vineyard, family owned and run by John Rauner and his wife, Louise, who started their planting in 1976. John is a maintenance engineer in the giant Hanford atomic-energy complex, but he hopes soon to be a full-time winemaker, and after talking to him and tasting his wines, I think his imagination and his viticultural skills will bring him substantial success. This dedicated young couple has, so far, done all the work themselves—from the care of the vines to the building of the winery. They are starting with 5 acres on a southern slope, descending to the bank of the Yakima River—land planted in Chardonnay. But John's main long-range program is carefully planned on the basis of buying grapes; as he told me, "I want to get each variety from the vineyard that is known for the microclimate that grows it best." He is already receiving deliveries from such famous Washington State growers as Ciel du Cheval, Kiona, and the Mercer Ranches. John released his first three wines in 1980, and his production is now fairly quickly increasing to an average of about 15,000 bottles a year. He hopes and plans to be up, by 1985, to about 150,000 bottles a year. Until then, obviously, these excellent wines will have very limited circulation, in central Washington State and, perhaps, in Seattle. But I think this is a winery name to watch in the future.

> ** (NOBLE rating) The delicately sweet, very slightly *Botrytized* Chenin Blanc, with 2.2 percent of residual sugar, irresistibly aromatic but balanced by a refreshing lemony tang.
> * (FINE ratings) The full golden sweet "Late Harvest" White Riesling, with a 5 percent residual sugar; and the very dry,

strongly aromatic, almost austere Gewürztraminer, with the complex flavors developed by extra fermentation of the wine on the grape skins.

YVERDON VINEYARDS *on Spring Mountain west of St. Helena in the Napa Valley*

A fairly small winery, owned and run by the Aves family, with the father, Fred, and the son, Russell, starting in 1970 and doing almost all the work themselves. They have replanted about 50 acres of vines, in three separate parcels at different levels on the mountain. They have built, literally, stone upon stone, a fine modern winery, but in the old Napa Valley architectural style. Their estimated production is now running at about 60,000 bottles a year—from the vineyards on Spring Mountain and from another Aves vineyard on the floor of the valley at an excellent location just north of Calistoga. All these wines are so-to-speak hand-crafted, and the best of the early releases show considerable promise. Distribution, naturally, is quite local in northern California.

> * In the neighborhood, try the medium-soft, beautifully flowery, refreshing White Riesling; also the aromatic, intense, strong Cabernet Sauvignon; also the chewy, well-constructed, smooth, tannic Zinfandel, all usually at FINE ratings.

ZACA MESA WINERY *at Los Olivos in the Santa Ynez Valley of Santa Barbara*

The famous Zaca Mesa Ranch was originally 1,500 acres of open cattle country, most of it at least 1,500 feet above the Pacific Ocean. Those parts of it that were suitable for vines began to be planted in 1973. The first, experimental wines were good enough to persuade the owners to build a large and very modern winery, rising above the highest cliff at the top of the mesa. When it was finished, in 1978, Ken Brown took charge of it as winemaker. Today, about 220 acres have been planted in vines, and the estimated production has gradually risen to an average of about 200,000 bottles a year. Ken is still experimenting in the wide range of opportunities for variations of regional character among the wines from this multifaceted microclimate.

> * An interesting wine experience is to taste the three different styles of Cabernet Sauvignon experimentally made and released by winemaker Ken Brown; also try the dry, almost austere, earthy, slightly sharp, tense Chardonnay; and the aromatic, fruity Pinot Noir, all of FINE quality in good years.

Z D WINES *on the Silverado Trail east of Rutherford in the Napa Valley*

About six years ago, when, at a large and festive winemakers' lunch in my honor in Sonoma, I met for the first time the two men whose names give their initials the title of this minuscule winery, I was quite sure that this had to be the smallest commercial wine operation in the United States. As Gino Zepponi and Norman de Leuze told it to me, they had no vineyards, no storage cellars, virtually no winemaking equipment, only a wooden shed about the size of a postage stamp. They were the sole owners, with minimum capital, and, as to the winemaking, they said they worked by "arguing out" every technical decision between themselves. But the wines they gave me to taste at that lunch were so much above the average that I still remember every detail of my impressions. They were good enough, we all now know, to go forward steadily. They began working together in Sonoma in 1969, buying grapes wherever they could find the best possible fruit not already tied up by long-term contracts with much larger producers. More and more, they found that their best grapes were coming from the Napa Valley and the Carneros Hills. So, in 1979, they took the giant step and moved their winery operation to the Napa Valley. They have slowly and arduously pulled their production up by its bootstraps and are now approaching a projected average of about 90,000 bottles a year. Vineyard sources of the grapes are often designated on each label. The latest forward step by these two men who never stop battling for improvement is the acquisition of 4 acres of their own vines up in the Carneros Hills. Theirs is an admirable performance, which has produced many admirable wines.

> * Try the fruity, intense, rich Napa Chardonnay "La Casa Zepponi," with grapes from the Winery Lake Vineyard in

the Carneros Hills; also the delicately sweet, aromatic, powerful Gewürztraminer, with grapes from the Tepusquet Vineyards in the Santa Barbara district; also the chewy, complicated, smooth Pinot Noir; and the brawny, fleshy, smooth Zinfandel, all usually at FINE ratings.

NAMES AND ADDRESSES
OF VINEYARDS AND WINERIES

CALIFORNIA

ACACIA WINERY
Jerry Goldstein, President
Larry Brooks, Winemaker
2636 Las Amigas Road
Napa

AHLGREN VINEYARD
Dexter Ahlgren, Winemaker/Co-owner
P.O. Box 931
Boulder Creek, Santa Cruz

ALATERA VINEYARDS
Anthony Mitchell, President
Holbrook Mitchell, Winemaker
5225 St. Helena Highway
Napa Valley

ALEXANDER VALLEY
VINEYARDS
Hank Wetzel, Winemaker/Co-owner
8644 Highway 128
Healdsburg, Sonoma

ALMADÉN VINEYARDS
John McClelland, President
Klaus Mathes, Winemaster
1530 Blossom Hill Road
San Jose, Santa Clara

ALTA VINEYARD CELLAR
Benjamin and Rose Falk, Owners
Jon Axhelm, Winemaker
1311 Schramsberg Road
Calistoga, Napa Valley

BARGETTO WINERY
Lawrence Bargetto, Winemaker/
President
3535 Main Street
Soquel, Santa Clara

BEAULIEU VINEYARD
L. F. Knowles, Jr., President
T. B. Selfridge, Winemaker
1960 St. Helena Highway
Rutherford, Napa Valley

BERINGER VINEYARDS
LaBruyere Family, Owners
Myron Nightingale, Sr., Winemaker
2000 Main Street
St. Helena, Napa Valley

BOEGER WINERY
Greg Boeger, Winemaker/Partner
1709 Carson Road
Placerville, El Dorado

DAVID BRUCE WINERY
Dr. David Bruce, President
Steve Millier, Winemaker
21439 Bear Creek Road
Los Gatos, Santa Clara

BUENA VISTA VINEYARDS
Hubertus von Wulffen, President
Don Harrison, Winemaker
27000 Ramal Road
Sonoma

BURGESS CELLARS
Tom Burgess, Owner
Bill Sorenson, Winemaker
1108 Deer Park Road
St. Helena, Napa Valley

DAVIS BYNUM WINERY
Davis Bynum, Winemaker/President
8075 Westside Road
Healdsburg, Sonoma

CAKEBREAD CELLARS
Jack Cakebread, Owner
Bruce Cakebread, Winemaker
8300 St. Helena Highway
Rutherford, Napa Valley

CALERA WINES
Josh and Jeanne Jensen, Owners
Steve Doerner, Winemaker
11300 Cienega Road
Hollister, San Benito

CALLAWAY VINEYARD
Ely Callaway, President
Steve O'Donnell, Winemaker
32720 Rancho California Road
Temecula, Riverside

RICHARD CAREY WINERY
Richard Carey, Winemaker/
    President
1695 Martinez Street
San Leandro, Alameda

CARNEROS CREEK WINERY
Balfour Gibson, President
Francis Mahoney, Winemaker
1285 Dealy Lane
Napa

CASSAYRE-FORNI CELLARS
James Cassayre, President
Michael Forni, Winemaker
1271 Manley Lane
Rutherford, Napa Valley

CAYMUS VINEYARDS
Charles Wagner, Winemaker/
    President
P.O. Box 268
Rutherford, Napa Valley

CHALONE VINEYARD
Richard Graff, President
Peter Graff, Winemaker
P.O. Box 855
Soledad, Monterey

CHAPPELLET VINEYARD
Donn Chappellet, Owner
Cathy Cotizon, Winemaker
1581 Sage Canyon Road
St. Helena, Napa Valley

CHATEAU BOUCHAINE WINERY
David Pollak, President
Jerry Luper, Winemaker/Partner
1075 Buchli Station Road
Napa Valley

CHATEAU MONTELENA WINERY
Jim Barrett, President
Bo Barrett, Winemaker
1429 Tubbs Lane
Calistoga, Napa Valley

CHATEAU ST. JEAN
Allan Hemphill, President
Richard Arrowood, Winemaker
8555 Sonoma Highway
Kenwood, Sonoma

CHRISTIAN BROTHERS
Brother Cassian, President
Brother Timothy, Winemaker
Mont La Salle
Napa Valley

CLOS DU BOIS
Frank Woods, Proprietor
Tom Hobart, Winemaker
5 Fitch Street
Healdsburg, Sonoma

CLOS DU VAL
Bernard Portet, Winemaker/Owner
5330 Silverado Trail
Yountville, Napa Valley

CONCANNON VINEYARD
James Concannon, President
Sergio Traveras, Winemaker
4590 Tesla Road
Livermore, Alameda

CONGRESS SPRINGS VINEYARDS
Vic Erickson, Partner
Daniel Gehrs, Winemaker/Partner
23600 Congress Springs Road
Saratoga, Santa Clara

CONN CREEK WINERY
William Collins, Jr., Partner
Daryl Eklund, Winemaker
8711 Silverado Trail
St. Helena, Napa Valley

CRESTA BLANCA WINERY
Bob Ivie, President
Al Cribari, Winemaker
2399 North State Street
Ukiah, Mendocino

CUVAISON VINEYARD
Philip Togni, Winemaker/President
4550 Silverado Trail
Calistoga, Napa Valley

CYGNET CELLARS
Jim Johnson and Bob Lane, Partners
Frank DiMascio, Winemaker
11736 Cienega Road
Hollister, San Benito

DEHLINGER WINERY
Tom Dehlinger, Winemaker/
    Proprietor
6300 Guerneville Road
Sebastopol, Sonoma

DeLOACH VINEYARDS
Cecil DeLoach, Jr., Winemaker/Co-
    owner
1791 Olivet Road
Santa Rosa, Sonoma

DEVLIN WINE CELLARS
Charles Devlin, Winemaker/Owner
P.O. Box 723
Soquel, Santa Cruz

DIABLO VISTA WINERY
Leon Borowski, Winemaker/Partner
674 East H Street
Benicia, Solano

DIAMOND CREEK VINEYARDS
Al Brounstein, Owner
Rex Geitner, Winemaker
1500 Diamond Mountain Road
Calistoga, Napa Valley

DOMAINE CHANDON
John Wright, President
Dawnine Sample, Winemaker
P.O. Box 2470, California Drive
Yountville, Napa Valley

DRY CREEK VINEYARD
David Stare, Winemaker/Owner
3770 Lambert Bridge Road
Healdsburg, Sonoma

DUCKHORN VINEYARDS
Daniel Duckhorn, President
Thomas Rinaldi, Winemaker
3027 Silverado Trail
St. Helena, Napa Valley

DURNEY VINEYARD
W. W. Durney, President
John Estell, Winemaker
Box 222016
Carmel, Monterey

EDMEADES VINEYARDS
Deron Edmeades, President
Jed Steele, Winemaker
5500 California State Hwy. 128
Philo, Mendocino

EDNA VALLEY VINEYARD
Jack Niven, President
Gary Mosby, Winemaker
Biddle Ranch Road
San Luis Obispo

ENZ VINEYARDS
Robert Enz, Winemaker/Co-owner
1781 Lime Kiln Road
Hollister, San Benito

EVENSEN VINEYARDS
Richard Evensen, Winemaker/Co-
    owner
8254 St. Helena Highway
Oakville, Napa Valley

FAR NIENTE WINERY
Gil Nickel, Winemaker/Owner
Far Niente House
Oakville, Napa Valley

FENESTRA WINERY
Larry Replogle, Winemaker/Co-
  owner
83 East Vallecitos Road
Livermore, Alameda

FETZER VINEYARDS
John Fetzer, President
Paul Dolan, Winemaker
1150 Bel Arbres Road
Redwood Valley, Mendocino

FICKLIN VINEYARDS
David Ficklin, President
Peter Ficklin, Winemaker
30246 Avenue 7½
Madera, San Joaquin Valley

FIELD STONE WINERY
Marion Johnson, Owner
Deborah Anne Cutter, Winemaker
10075 Highway 128
Healdsburg, Sonoma

FIRESTONE VINEYARD
Brooks Firestone, President
Alison Green, Winemaker
P.O. Box 244
Los Olivos, Santa Barbara

FISHER VINEYARDS
Fred Fisher, Winemaker/Co-owner
6200 St. Helena Road
Santa Rosa, Sonoma

FOPPIANO VINEYARDS
Louis Foppiano, President
Rod Foppiano, Winemaker
12707 Old Redwood Highway
Healdsburg, Sonoma

FORMAN WINERY
Peter Newton, Co-owner
Ric Forman, Winemaker/Co-owner
2555 Madrona Avenue
St. Helena, Spring Mountain
Napa Valley

FORTINO WINERY
Ernest Fortino, Winemaker/Owner
4525 Hecker Pass Highway
Gilroy, Santa Clara

FRANCISCAN VINEYARDS
Peter Eckes, Owner
Tom Ferrell, Winemaker/Vice-
  President
P.O. Box 407
Rutherford, Napa Valley

FREEMARK ABBEY WINERY
Chuck Carpy, Partner
Larry Langbehn, Winemaker
3022 St. Helena Highway North
St. Helena, Napa Valley

GEMELLO WINERY
Louis Sarto, President
Mario Gemello, Winemaker
2003 El Camino
Mountain View, Santa Clara

GLEN ELLEN VINEYARDS
Ted Elliott, President
Jeff Baker, Winemaker
1700 Moon Mountain Drive
Glen Ellen, Sonoma

GRAND CRU VINEYARDS
Allen Ferrera, President
Robert Magnani, Winemaker
One Vintage Lane
Glen Ellen, Sonoma

GRGICH HILLS CELLARS
Austin Hills, Co-owner
Mike Grgich, Winemaker/Co-owner
1829 St. Helena Highway
Rutherford, Napa Valley

GUNDLACH-BUNDSCHU
VINEYARD
James Bundschu, President
John Merritt, Jr., Winemaker
P.O. Box 1
Vineburg, Sonoma

HACIENDA WINE CELLARS
Crawford Cooley, President
Steven MacRostie, Winemaker
1000 Vineyard Lane
Sonoma

HANZELL VINEYARDS
Barbara de Brye, Owner
Robert Sessions, Winemaker
18596 Lomita Avenue
Sonoma

HARBOR WINERY
Charles Myers, Winemaker/Owner
7576 Pocket Road
Sacramento

HEITZ WINE CELLARS
Joe Heitz, Owner
David Heitz, Winemaker
500 Taplin Road
St. Helena, Napa Valley

HOFFMAN MOUNTAIN RANCH
Dr. & Mrs. Stanley Hoffman,
    Owners
Michael Hoffman, Winemaker
Adelaida Road, Star Route
Paso Robles, San Luis Obispo

HOP KILN WINERY AND GRIFFIN
VINEYARD
Martin Griffin, Jr., Owner
Jack Fitzgerald, Winemaker
6050 Westside Road
Healdsburg, Sonoma

HUSCH VINEYARDS
Hugo Oswald, Winemaker/Co-
    owner
4900 Highway 128
Philo, Mendocino

INGLENOOK VINEYARDS
Robert Furek, President
John Richburg, Winemaker
1991 St. Helena Highway South
Rutherford, Napa Valley

IRON HORSE VINEYARDS
Audrey Sterling, Co-owner
Forrest Tancer, Winemaker/Co-
    owner
9786 Ross Station Road
Sebastopol, Sonoma

JEKEL VINEYARD
Bill and Gus Jekel, Owners
Dan Lee, Winemaker
40155 Walnut Avenue
Greenfield, Monterey

JOHNSON'S ALEXANDER
VALLEY WINES
James Johnson, President
Thomas Johnson, Winemaker
8333 Highway 128
Healdsburg, Sonoma

KALIN CELLARS
Terrance Leighton, Winemaker/
    Partner
61 Galli Drive
Novato, San Pablo Bay

ROBERT KEENAN WINERY
Robert Keenan, Owner
Joe Cafaro, Winemaker
3660 Spring Mountain Road
St. Helena, Napa Valley

KENWOOD VINEYARDS
John Sheela, President
Bob Kozlowski, Winemaker
9592 Sonoma Highway
Kenwood, Sonoma

KISTLER VINEYARD
Steve Kistler, Winemaker/Owner
2995 Nelligan Road
Glen Ellen, Sonoma

KONOCTI CELLARS
Walter Lyon, President
William Pease, Winemaker
4350 Thomas Drive
Kelseyville, Lake County

KORBEL WINERY
Adolf Heck, President
Jim Huntsinger, Winemaker
13250 River Road
Guerneville, Sonoma

HANNS KORNELL CELLARS
Hanns Kornell, Winemaker/Owner
Larkmead Lane
St. Helena, Napa Valley

CHARLES KRUG WINERY
Peter Mondavi, President
Donald Frazer, Winemaker
2800 Main Street
St. Helena, Napa Valley

THOMAS KRUSE WINERY
Thomas Kruse, Winemaker/Owner
4390 Hecker Pass Road
Gilroy, Santa Clara

LAMBERT BRIDGE WINERY
Margaret and Gerard Lambert,
    Owners
Dominic Martin, Winemaker
4085 West Dry Creek Road
Healdsburg, Sonoma

LANDMARK VINEYARDS
William Mabry III, Winemaker/
    Owner
9150 Los Amigos Road
Windsor, Sonoma

LONG VINEYARDS
Robert Long, Jr., Owner
Zelma Long, Winemaker
P.O. Box 50
St. Helena, Napa Valley

LYTTON SPRINGS WINERY
Bura Walters, Winemaker/President
650 Lytton Springs Road
Healdsburg, Sonoma

MARKHAM WINERY
Bruce Markham, President
Robert Foley, Winemaker
2812 St. Helena Highway North
St. Helena, Napa Valley

MARK WEST VINEYARDS
Robert Ellis, Co-owner
Joan Ellis, Winemaker/Co-owner
7000 Trenton-Healdsburg Road
Forestville, Sonoma

LOUIS M. MARTINI WINERY
Louis P. Martini, President
Michael Martini, Winemaker
P.O. Box 112
St. Helena, Napa Valley

PAUL MASSON VINEYARDS
Elliott Fine, President
Joe Stillman, Winemaker
13150 Saratoga Avenue
Saratoga, Santa Clara

MASTANTUONO WINERY
Pasquale Mastan, Winemaker/
    Partner
101-¾ Willow Creek Road
Paso Robles, San Luis Obispo

MATANZAS CREEK WINERY
Sandra MacIver, Owner
Merry Edwards, Winemaker
6097 Bennett Valley Road
Santa Rosa, Sonoma

MAYACAMAS VINEYARDS
Nonie and Bob Travers,
    Winemakers/Owners
1155 Lokoya Road
Napa Valley

MILANO WINERY
Jim Milone, Winemaker/Owner
14594 South Highway 101
Hopland, Mendocino

MILL CREEK VINEYARDS
Charles Kreck, President
Bob Kreck, Winemaker
1401 Westside Road
Healdsburg, Sonoma

MIRASSOU VINEYARDS
James Mirassou, President
Don Alexander, Winemaker
3000 Aborn Road
San Jose, Santa Clara

ROBERT MONDAVI WINERY
Robert Mondavi, Chairman
Tim Mondavi, Winemaker
P.O. Box 106
Oakville, Napa Valley

MONTEREY PENINSULA WINERY
Dr. Roy Thomas, Winemaker/
    President
2999 Monterey-Salinas Highway
Monterey

MONTEREY VINEYARD
Dr. Richard Peterson, Winemaker/
    President
800 South Alta Street
Gonzales, Monterey

MONTEVIÑA WINES
Walter Field, President
Thomas Gott and Jeff Runquist,
    Winemakers
Route 2
Plymouth, Amador

J. W. MORRIS WINERIES
J. W. Morris, President
Jim Olsen, Winemaker
4060 Pike Lane
Concord, Contra Costa

MOUNT EDEN VINEYARDS
Richard Graff, President
Fred Peterson, Winemaker
22020 Mount Eden Road
Saratoga, Santa Clara

MOUNT VEEDER WINERY
Mike Bernstein, Winemaker/Owner
1999 Mount Veeder Road
Napa Valley

NAPA WINE CELLARS
Charles Woods, Owner
7481 St. Helena Highway
Oakville, Napa Valley

NAVARRO VINEYARDS
Edward Bennett, Winemaker/Co-
    owner
5601 Highway 128
Philo, Mendocino

NOVITIATE WINES
Rev. Thomas Terry, President
Phillip Loechler, Winemaker
300 College Avenue
Los Gatos, Santa Clara

PARDUCCI WINE CELLARS
John Parducci, Winemaster
501 Parducci Road
Ukiah, Mendocino

PARSON'S CREEK WINERY
Jess Tidwell, Winemaker/Partner
3001 South State Street, #4
Ukiah, Mendocino

PEDRONCELLI WINERY
John Pedroncelli, Winemaker/Co-
    owner
1220 Canyon Road
Geyserville, Sonoma

PENDLETON WINERY
Brian Pendleton, Winemaker/Co-
    owner
2156 G O'Toole Avenue
San Jose, Santa Clara

JOSEPH PHELPS VINEYARDS
Joseph Phelps, President
Walter Schug, Winemaker
200 Taplin Road
St. Helena, Napa Valley

PIPER.SONOMA WINERY
Rodney Strong, Winemaker/
    Chairman
P.O. Box 368
Windsor, Sonoma

POPE VALLEY WINERY
James Devitt, Owner
Steve Devitt, Winemaker
6613 Pope Valley Road
Pope Valley

PRESTON VINEYARDS
Louis Preston, Winemaker/Owner
9282 West Dry Creek Road
Healdsburg, Sonoma

QUAIL RIDGE VINEYARDS
Elaine Wellesley, Winemaker/
  Owner
3230 Mount Veeder Road
Napa Valley

RAFANELLI WINERY
Amerigo Rafanelli, Winemaker/Co-
  owner
4685 West Dry Creek Road
Healdsburg, Sonoma

RAVENSWOOD WINERY
Joel Peterson, Winemaker/Partner
5700 Gravenstein Highway
Forestville, Sonoma

MARTIN RAY VINEYARDS
Peter Martin Ray, Winemaker/
  President
22000 Mount Eden Road
Saratoga, Santa Clara

RAYMOND WINERY
Walter Raymond, Winemaker/
  Owner
849 Zinfandel Lane
St. Helena, Napa Valley

RIDGE VINEYARDS
David Bennion, President
Paul Draper, Winemaker
17100 Monte Bello Road
Cupertino, Santa Cruz Mountains

ROUDON-SMITH VINEYARDS
James Smith, Co-owner
Bob Roudon, Winemaker/Co-owner
2364 Bean Creek Road
Scott's Valley, Santa Cruz Mountains

ROUND HILL CELLARS
Charles Abela, President
Doug Manning, Winemaker
1097 Lodi Lane
St. Helena, Napa Valley

RUSSIAN RIVER VINEYARDS
Michael Topolos, Winemaker/
  Owner
Gravenstein Highway
Forestville, Sonoma

RUTHERFORD HILL WINERY
William Jaeger and Chuck Carpy,
  Partners
Phillip Baxter, Winemaker
3022 St. Helena Highway
St. Helena, Napa Valley

RUTHERFORD VINTNERS
Bernard Skoda, Winemaker/
  President
1673 St. Helena Highway
Rutherford, Napa Valley

ST. CLEMENT VINEYARDS
Dr. William Casey, Owner
Dennis Johns, Winemaker
2867 St. Helena Highway North
St. Helena, Napa Valley

SAN MARTIN WINERY
Ed Friedrich, Winemaker
13000 Depot Street
San Martin, Santa Clara

SAN PASQUAL VINEYARDS
Milton Fredman, President
Kerry Damskey, Winemaker
13455 San Pasqual Road
Escondido, San Diego

SANFORD & BENEDICT
VINEYARDS
Michael Benedict, Winemaker/
  Partner
Santa Rosa Road
Lompoc, Santa Barbara

SANTA CRUZ MOUNTAIN
VINEYARD
Ken Burnap, Winemaker/Owner
2300 Jarvis Road
Santa Cruz

SANTA YNEZ VALLEY WINERY
Boyd Bettencourt, President
Fred Brander, Winemaker
365 North Refugio Road
Santa Ynez Valley, Santa Barbara

SANTINO WINES
Nancy Santino, President
Scott Harvey, Winemaker
Route 2, Steiner Road
Plymouth, Amador

SAUSAL WINERY
David Demostene, Winemaker/
   Manager
7370 Highway 128
Healdsburg, Sonoma

SCHRAMSBERG VINEYARDS
Jamie and Jack Davies, Owners
Gregory Fowler, Winemaker
Schramsberg Road
Calistoga, Napa Valley

SEBASTIANI VINEYARDS
Sebastiani Family, Owners
Doug Davis, Winemaster
389 Fourth Street
Sonoma

SHAFER VINEYARDS
John Shafer, President
Nikko Schoch, Winemaker
6154 Silverado Trail
Napa Valley

SHERRILL CELLARS
Nat Sherrill, Winemaker/Partner
1185 Skyline Boulevard
Woodside, Santa Clara

SHOWN & SONS VINEYARDS
Richard Shown, Partner
Tom Cottrell, Winemaker
8643 Silverado Trail
Rutherford, Napa Valley

SIERRA VISTA WINERY
John MacCready, Winemaker/
   Partner
4560 Cabernet Way
Placerville, El Dorado

SIMI WINERY
Michael Dixon, President
Zelma Long, Winemaker
16275 Healdsburg Avenue
Healdsburg, Sonoma

SMITH-MADRONE VINEYARD
Stuart Smith, Winemaker/Owner
4022 Spring Mountain Road
St. Helena, Napa Valley

SMOTHERS WINERY
Dick Smothers, President
William Arnold, Winemaker
2317 Vine Hill Road
Santa Cruz

SONOMA VINEYARDS
Kenneth Toth, President
Rodney Strong, Winemaster
P.O. Box 368
Windsor, Sonoma

SOTOYOME WINERY
William Chaikin, Winemaker/
   President
641 Limerick Lane
Healdsburg, Sonoma

SOUVERAIN CELLARS
Lee Chandler, President
Bob Mueller, Winemaker
P.O. Box 528
Geyserville, Sonoma

SPRING MOUNTAIN VINEYARDS
Michael Robbins, President
John Williams, Winemaker
2805 Spring Mountain Road
St. Helena, Napa Valley

STAG'S LEAP WINE CELLARS
Warren Winiarski, Winemaker/
   Partner
5766 Silverado Trail
Napa Valley

P.&M. STAIGER WINERY
Marjorie and Paul Staiger, Owners
1300 Hopkins Gulch Road
Boulder Creek, Santa Cruz

ROBERT STEMMLER WINERY
Trumbull Kelley, Partner
Robert Stemmler, Winemaker/
Partner
3805 Lambert Bridge Road
Healdsburg, Sonoma

STERLING VINEYARDS
Michael Stone, President
Theo Rosenbrand, Winemaker
1111 Dunaweal Lane
Calistoga, Napa Valley

STEVENOT VINEYARDS
Barden Stevenot, Owner
Julia Iantosca, Winemaker
San Domingo Road
Murphys, Calaveras

STONEGATE WINERY
Barbara and James Spaulding,
Owners
David Spaulding and Michael
Fallow, Co-winemakers
1183 Dunaweal Lane
Calistoga, Napa Valley

STONY HILL VINEYARD
Eleanor McCrea, President
Mike Chelini, Winemaker
P.O. Box 308
St. Helena, Napa Valley

STONY RIDGE WINERY
Harry Rosingana, President
Bruce Rector, Winemaker
1188 Vineyard Avenue
Pleasanton, Alameda

SUNRISE WINERY
Keith Hohlfeldt, Winemaker/Partner
1601 Empire Grade Road
Felton, Santa Cruz

SUTTER HOME WINERY
Bob Trinchero, Winemaker/
President
277 St. Helena Highway South
St. Helena, Napa Valley

JOSEPH SWAN VINEYARDS
Joe Swan, Winemaker/Owner
2916 Laguna Road
Forestville, Sonoma

SYCAMORE CREEK VINEYARDS
Terry Parks, Winemaker/Partner
12775 Uvas Road
Morgan Hill, Santa Clara

TREFETHEN VINEYARDS
John Trefethen, President
David Whitehouse, Jr., Winemaker
1160 Oak Knoll Avenue
Napa Valley

TRENTADUE WINERY
Leo Trentadue, Winemaker/Partner
19170 Redwood Highway
Geyserville, Sonoma

TULOCAY WINERY
William Cadman, Winemaker/
Partner
1426 Coombsville Road
Napa Valley

TURGEON & LOHR WINERY
Bernie Turgeon, President
Peter Stern, Winemaker
1000 Lenzen Avenue
San Jose, Santa Clara

VEEDERCREST VINEYARD
Ronald Fenolio, Partner
Al Baxter, Winemaker/Partner
1401 Stanford Avenue
Emeryville, Alameda

VENTANA VINEYARDS
Shirley and Douglas Meador,
Owners
Ken Wright, Winemaker
Los Coches Road
Soledad, Monterey

VILLA MT. EDEN WINERY
Anne and James McWilliams,
Partners
Nils Venge, Winemaker
600 Oakville Crossroads
Oakville, Napa Valley

VŌSE VINEYARDS
Hamilton Vōse III, Winemaker/
   President
4035 Mount Veeder Road
Napa Valley

WENTE BROTHERS
Eric Wente, Winemaker/President
5565 Tesla Road
Livermore, Alameda

WILLOWSIDE VINEYARDS
Berle Beliz, Owner
1672 Willowside Road
Santa Rosa, Sonoma

YVERDON VINEYARDS
Fred Aves, Owner
3787 Spring Mountain Road
St. Helena, Napa Valley

ZACA MESA WINERY
Louis Marshall Ream, President
Ken Brown, Winemaker
Foxen Canyon Road
Los Olivos, Santa Barbara

Z D WINES
Norman de Leuze & Gino Zepponi,
   Winemakers/Partners
8383 Silverado Trail
Napa Valley

IDAHO

STE. CHAPELLE VINEYARDS
Dick Symms, President
Bill Broich, Winemaker
Route #4
Caldwell
Snake River Valley

NEW YORK

GLENORA WINE CELLARS
Eastman Beers, President
Mike Elliott, Winemaker
Glenora-on-Seneca
Dundee

HARGRAVE VINEYARD
Alec Hargrave, Winemaker/
   President
Route 27
Cutchogue, Long Island

HERON HILL VINEYARD
Peter Johnstone, Winemaker/
   President
Hammondsport, Lake Keuka

PLANE'S CAYUGA VINEYARD
Mary and Robert Plane,
   Winemakers/Owners
6799 Cayuga Lake Road
Ovid, Finger Lakes

HERMANN J. WIEMER VINEYARD
Hermann Wiemer, Winemaker/
   Owner
Box #4
Dundee, Lake Seneca

OREGON

AMITY VINEYARDS
Myron Redford, Winemaker/
   President
Route #1, Box 348B
Amity, Willamette Valley

COTES DES COLOMBE
VINEYARD
Joseph Colombe, Winemaker/
   President
P.O. Box 266
Banks, Willamette Valley

ELK COVE VINEYARDS
Patricia and Joe Campbell,
   Winemakers/Owners
Route #3, Box 23
Gaston, Willamette Valley

EYRIE VINEYARDS
David Lett, Winemaker/President
935 East 10th Street
McMinnville, Willamette Valley

HILLCREST VINEYARDS
Richard Sommer, Winemaker/
  Owner
240 Vineyard Lane
Roseburg, Umpqua Valley

KNUDSEN-ERATH WINERY
Calvert Knudsen, Partner
Dick Erath, Winemaker/Partner
Worden Hill Road
Dundee, Willamette Valley

OAK KNOLL WINERY
Ron Vuylsteke, Winemaker/Partner
Route #4, Box 185B
Hillsboro, Willamette Valley

PONZI VINEYARDS
Richard Ponzi, Winemaker/Partner
Route #1, Box 842
Beaverton, Willamette Valley

REUTER'S HILL VINEYARDS
David Wirtz, Winemaker
P.O. Box 883
Forest Grove, Willamette Valley

SOKOL BLOSSER WINERY
Susan and William Blosser, Partners
Robert McRitchie, Winemaker
Blanchard Lane, Box 199
Dundee, Willamette Valley

TUALATIN VINEYARDS
William Malkmus, President
William Fuller, Winemaker
Route #1, Box 339
Forest Grove, Willamette Valley

WASHINGTON

ASSOCIATED VINTNERS
Lloyd Woodburne, Chairman
David Lake, Winemaker
Bellevue

CHATEAU STE. MICHELLE
Wallace Opdycke, President
Peter Bachman, Manager of
  Winemaking Operations
14111 N.E. 145th Street
Woodinville

E. B. FOOTE WINERY
Eugene Foote, Winemaker/Owner
3836 34th Avenue, S.W.
South Park, Seattle

HINZERLING VINEYARDS
Mike Wallace, Winemaker/President
1520 Sheridan Avenue
Prosser, Yakima Valley

LEONETTI CELLARS
Gary Figgins, Winemaker/Partner
1321 School Avenue
Walla Walla, Columbia Basin

MONT ELISE VINEYARDS
Chuck Henderson, Winemaker/
  President
315 West Steuben
Bingen, South Columbia Basin

PRESTON WINE CELLARS
Bill Preston, Owner
Robert Griffin, Winemaker
Star Route #1
Pasco, Columbia Basin

MANFRED J. VIERTHALER
WINERY
Manfred Vierthaler, Winemaker/Co-
  owner
17136 Highway 410 East
Sumner, Puyallup Valley

YAKIMA RIVER WINERY
John Rauner, Winemaker/President
Route #1, North River Road
Prosser, Yakima Valley

INDICES

GENERAL INDEX

See also Index of Grape Varieties on page 452, Index of Vineyards & Wineries on page 455 and Index of Winemakers on page 460.

Acid–sugar balance in grapes 20
Alcohol in fermentation 20
Alexander, Captain Cyrus, gives his name to Alexander Valley 296
Alexander, James, brings wine to Pennsylvania 31
Alexander Valley appellation 87
Alexander Valley of Sonoma 51, 69, 94, 99, 100, 102, 111, 131, 132, 153, 159, 172, 173, 177, 181, 183, 185, 296, 304, 313, 315, 329, 336, 351, 378, 398, 402, 403, 415
Al Madén, Moorish name for "silver mine" 297
Alsace 62; Confrérie de St. Etienne 97, develops perfect Gewürztraminer 95
Alta California 30, 302
Amador 57, 127, 132, 133, 165, 166, 170, 171, 302, 307, 337, 343, 371, 372, 375, 386, 389, 397, 412
American: Burgundians 137; Pinot Noirs now world's best outside Burgundy 151; winemakers afraid of Gewürztraminer 98; winemaking freedom 39
Amerine, Maynard 280
Ampelography, definition of 140
Amsterdam 59
Anderson Valley of Mendocino 93, 94, 100, 132, 170, 180, 185, 324, 348, 375, 378
Appellation contrôlée, French wine law 34, 134, 155
Appellations developing in California 87
Argentina, wine in 188

Armagnac 58
Arroyo Seco of Monterey 58, 91, 95, 158, 159, 173, 195, 205, 206, 351, 371, 416, 418, 421
Asher, Gerald 143, 245
Asti wine factory 350
Australia, wine in 118, 136
Austria, wine in 136

Baja California 30
Balance & cleanness in white wine 45
Bartholomew, Frank 302, 341
BATF: *see* Bureau of Alcohol
Beaujolais: American types 104; French château & domain types 105; French official complaint to U.S. 107; irresistible attraction of name 103; legal definitions of *de l'Année & Nouveau* 104; reasons for separation from Burgundy 106
Beers family 338
Benedictines first develop Riesling at Johannisberg 66
Bennett Valley of Sonoma 93, 100, 131, 365
Benoist, Louis 178, 182
Berg, Dr. Harold 192, 193, 196
Best Wines Rated: *see* Top Rated Wines
Birth of modern vintage wine 29
Bize, Madame Lalou 135
Blanc, Georges & Jacqueline, collect finest *Beaujolais Nouveau* 104, 105
Blending, legal limitations for quality control 86
Blind tasting of extraordinary Ficklin Emerald Riesling 75

442

INDEX OF GRAPE VARIETIES

*Page numbers in **bold** type indicate principal discussions of particular subjects.*

INDEX OF VINEYARDS
& WINERIES

*"C." indicates page number where vineyard or winery is
classified & ranked.
Page numbers in **bold** type indicate principal references.*

INDEX OF WINEMAKERS

*Page numbers in **bold** type indicate principal references.*